# THE
# CONTINUATION

Alexander
Shulgin

Ann
Shulgin

TRANSFORM
PRESS

For information, contact:
TRANSFORM PRESS
P.O. BOX 11552
BERKELEY, CA 94712
VM: (925)-934-2675
FAX: (925)-934-5999

www.transformpress.com

Additional copies may be purchased on our website.

Orders from Europe: Please contact Turnaround Ltd. at www.turnaround-uk.com

Edited by Dan Joy
Cover by Pamela Engebretson
Typeset by Wendy Perry Tucker

First Edition, Eighth Printing
ISBN: 0-9630096-9-9
ISBN 13: 978-0-9630096-9-2

**trypt-amine** \ 'trip-ta-,mēn \ n. [tryptophan fr. tryptic, fr. trypsin, fr. Gk. tryein, to wear down (from its occurrence in pancreatic juice as a proteolytic enzyme) + amine fr. NL ammonia] 1: A naturally occurring compound found in both the animal and plant kingdoms. It is an endogenous component of the human brain. 2: Any of a series of compounds containing the tryptamine skeleton, and modified by chemical constituents at appropriate positions in the molecule.

# TABLE OF CONTENTS

# FOREWORD

In 1991 an unusual book with an unusual title first began to circulate among an unusual set of people: those convinced that there were significant psychological and spiritual benefits to be derived from the use of psychedelic drugs. *PIHKAL: A Chemical Love Story*, consisted of two parts: Book I included a number of first-hand accounts of the use of a dozen or so psychedelics with enough detail for the reader to get a good feeling for the set and setting. Woven in with this was the story of how the authors, Ann and Alexander (Sasha) Shulgin (under the pseudonymous cloak of Alice and Shura) met, loved, and eventually married. Like all good love stories, a triangular suspense resolves when a German woman, with whom Shura was initially involved, eventually fades into the permanent past tense. In Book II of *PIHKAL*, the structures and syntheses of nearly 200 chemical compounds were given in "recipe" form followed in most cases by brief evaluations of their psychic or physical effects by self-experimentation on the part of various anonymous volunteers. The compounds of *PIHKAL*'s Book II are all in the class known as phenethylamines, which explains the acronym in the title: *Phenethylamines I Have Known And Loved*.

The present book is based on the same format, but the compounds of its Part II now fall into that other structural class to which almost all the remaining psychedelics belong, the tryptamines. *TIHKAL* stands for *Tryptamines I Have Known And Loved*. In *TIHKAL*, the human love triangle is no longer present, and so the first half of the book consists rather of a rich smorgasbord of narratives and essays concerning the origins and uses of psychedelics. Here the natural products chemist can enjoy a delightful ramble through the astonishing diversity of creatures — from fungi and frogs to flowers — which contain DMT or its chemical near cousins. The psychopharmacologist can wonder if a clue to the auditory hallucinations so typical of schizophrenia can be found in the unique activity of DIPT. A Jungian psychotherapist will be challenged by Alice's stories of the gentle synergism exercised by a skilled therapist and the entactogen MDMA. And, sadly, the civil libertarian may find reason to fear that something much like state-sanctioned religious persecution has found a foothold in this free country whose charter was penned by those who swore, "upon the altar of God, eternal hostility against every form of tyranny over the mind of man."

And yet the chemical love story continues for, throughout, Shura is a chemist of the old school, one who has a parent's — even a lover's — tenderness and affection for the structures he dreams of and creates. (Those familiar with the story of Albert Hofmann's discovery of LSD will be reminded of his feeling that "from the very beginning" he had "thought this substance was something special. It was just a feeling I had, when I was working and preparing substances.") Yet it is a scene of domestic contentment, a tranquil *ménage à trois* — for Alice developed her own chemical love affair, blossoming as she did into a sensitive and effective psychedelic psychotherapist.

But I have been preaching to the choir — musing with those who have known of the long gestation period of *TIHKAL* and who are now finally able to satisfy their curiosity. Most readers of this book will likely belong to that unusual set mentioned above who need no convincing of the value of psychedelic drugs. There will be others — not in the choir, not even in the congregation of true believers — who will greet this book's birthing with bafflement, shock, or even anger. As one who not long ago was himself among the doubters, let me try to speak to them. (The choir will not object, for they love hearing again and again the familiar story of repentance and conversion.)

First let me say that from my 18th year to my 50th, some four years ago, I was a member of the Jesuits, a Roman Catholic religious order of brothers and priests (I was ordained in 1974). I led a fairly sheltered life during the revolutionary days of the 60's and 70's, and knew nothing about psychedelic drugs except what the media told me: that they induced a bizarre state of mind much like madness, with lurid hallucinations; that people foolish enough to toy with these drugs would find themselves tormented by unpredictable and incapacitating episodes of recurrent flashbacks for the rest of their lives.

A decade ago, I earned my doctorate in synthetic organic chemistry from the University of Illinois at Chicago, and came to Loyola College in Maryland. After a few years there, I thought I would try to work up some more interesting topics for the "baby chem" course our non-science majors are required to take at Loyola College. "Drugs and Drug Dependency" seemed a course title sexy enough to keep them awake for a few hours a week. Soon I had some rough class notes, and before long I had a contract from the American Chemical Society to write a book stressing the history and human context of these fascinating chemicals. The book appeared in 1996 under the title *The Chemistry of Mind-Altering Drugs: History, Pharmacology, and Cultural Context*. But the process of seriously researching the actual scientific and literary record of these substances had greatly changed my opinions about many things. For example, as with many of those who have studied drug policy, I became convinced that the War on Drugs was at best as counterproductive as Prohibition had been, and at worst it was the first step on the path towards a police state.

But it was in the area of the psychedelics where my existing opinions were most challenged. I think that I can justly say that I have a fairly deep acquaintance with the Western tradition in meditation and mysticism, not only as a subject of academic inquiry but in particular as a lifetime practice: Jesuits in my generation were required to spend an hour daily in meditation which was expected to lead, in souls suitably disposed, to such higher states as the "prayer of silence." We made two or more 30-day retreats during the course of our formation, and yearly 8-day retreats; and we were expected to discuss our developing prayer life regularly with a "spiritual father." We also had a reasonably extensive training in pastoral counseling and psychotherapy.

And thus it was that when I read the accounts of the psychedelic experiences of Aldous Huxley, Bill Wilson, Alan Watts, Henry Osmond, Gordon Wasson, Walter Houston Clark, Huston Smith — (the list seemed endless) — the tales were all quite familiar. Skeptics might doubt the validity or significance of religious experience in general, but no one could doubt that these people were encountering the classic phenomenon itself — powerfully catalyzed, to my astonishment, by the ingestion of mescaline, psilocybin, or LSD. And I was the more astonished when I found the equally extensive and equally credible account of the use of these substances as adjuvants to psychotherapy. Providentially, I was in the very city, Baltimore, where one of the largest psychedelic treatment centers had been located — at Spring Grove Psychiatric Center, headed by Dr. Albert Kurland. After many a revelatory conversation here in Baltimore with Drs. Kurland, Richards, Yensen, and Dryer, my conversion was complete.

And so I return to the comforting faces of the choir. (I see they are singing Hallelujah! Another soul come Home!) *They* need no persuading that this class of drugs — nay, sacraments — needs to be researched with all the energy and intelligence that mankind has ever devoted to any pursuit, scientific or religious. *They* need no persuading that an animal model cannot ever determine whether a subtle yet profound alteration of consciousness has taken place; only courageous and experienced shamans and seekers like those in Shura's group will be able to tell the true from the counterfeit gold. And *they* need no persuading that much of the depression, despair, and hopelessness of our world — a world which foolishly fancies itself so advanced, but is in so many ways cut off from the human depths which were the everyday richness of "primitive" societies; a world which wearily turns to a new millennium after completing the most murderous and barbarous century of its history — might find solace and peace through the wise and compassionate use of these entheogens.

We are a small congregation, Sasha and Ann, but in our hearts there echoes a warm service of praise and thanksgiving to you for all you have done. You will never be forgotten!

Daniel M. Perrine, M.A., M.Div., Ph.D.
Associate Professor of Chemistry
Loyola College, Baltimore, Maryland

# NOTE TO THE READER

With this book, *TIHKAL*, we are making available a body of information concerning the conception, synthesis, definition, and appropriate use of certain consciousness-changing chemical compounds which we are convinced are valuable tools for the study of the human mind and psyche.

At the present time, restrictive laws are in force in the United States and it is very difficult for researchers to abide by the regulations which govern efforts to obtain legal approval to do work with these compounds in human beings. Consequently there has been almost no clinical research conducted in this area for about thirty years. However, animal studies can be done by the approved and qualified scientist who finds sources of research funding and who appeals to and obtains his supplies of drugs from an appropriate government agency, such as the National Institute for Drug Abuse.

Some of the stories in Book I are fiction.

Over half of the recipes in Book II of *TIHKAL* have been taken from the chemical literature. Some of these have been published with Shulgin as an author. The remaining recipes appear here for the first time in print.

No one who is lacking legal authorization should attempt the synthesis of any of the compounds described in the second half of this book, with intent to give them to man. To do so is to risk legal action which might lead to the tragic ruination of a life. It should also be noted that any person anywhere who experiments on himself, or on another human being, with any one of the drugs described herein, without being familiar with that drug's action and aware of the physical and/or mental disturbance or harm it might cause, is acting irresponsibly and immorally, whether or not he is doing so within the bounds of the law.

We strongly urge that a continuing effort be made by those who care about freedom of inquiry and the search for knowledge to work toward changes in the present drug laws, particularly in the United States. Open inquiry and creative exploration of this important area of research must be not only allowed but encouraged. It is essential that our present negative propaganda regarding psychedelic drugs be replaced with honesty and truthfulness about their effects, both good and bad.

There is much that we need to understand about the human psyche, and this book is dedicated to the pursuit of that understanding.

## COMMENTS ON THE TITLE

The first offering of this two-volume combination was called *PIHKAL*, which was constructed as an acronym for the true title, Phenethylamines I Have Known and Loved. From this we should have learned a lesson. Other than comments and discussions concerning how it should be pronounced (we like pee-cal but pickle is sometimes heard) the most frequent question that Ann and I were asked was a painfully obvious one, "What is a phenethylamine?" The answer was written out as a dictionary-like definition but, as far as I know, no one except a chemist ever truly understood that title. And here is *TIHKAL* (pronounced tee-cal) representing Tryptamines I Have Known and Loved. We can anticipate the question now, "What is a tryptamine?" Or a yet more difficult problem intrinsic to the use of the plural, "What are tryptamines?"

Let me start with the term expressed in the singular. How does one define a tryptamine to a non-chemist? Probably in exactly the same way you would define it for a chemist, except that you wouldn't use the technical jargon words that only a chemist would understand. Let's try it in everyday English words.

Tryptamine is a chemical. What is a chemical? It can be a solid thing such as crystal, a powder or a chunk of stuff which can be hard or soft or brittle. It can be any color from white to black, and anything in-between. Or it can be a liquid or something wet, maybe a wax or soap, or maybe fluid and runny. It may even be volatile. Or it can be gas which will tend to fill the space around you. These gases are usually without color, but there are exceptions which are brown or green or yellow. Some gases have no smell; others can be pretty rich. A chemical can display any of these forms. In short, a chemical is something tangible, and can be a solid or a liquid or a gas.

Most important, it is a single and homogeneous thing. Salt, for example, is something pure because no matter how you divide it, grind it up, pick it apart, sift or size it, the resulting solids are always exactly the same. It happens to be a white crystalline material in the form of cubes with a very high melting point and very water soluble. Tryptamine is a white crystal that is in the form of needles with a rather low melting point and is not soluble in water. These are two of the over ten million compounds that are known today. Tryptamines is a collective term that includes many compounds, not only tryptamine itself but any of the many derivatives of it that can be formed by putting some atoms, or a group of atoms, somewhere on the structural skeleton.

A few score of the more interesting ones are the stuff of the second part of *TIHKAL* and are individually described as to both chemistry and pharmacology. A great many more are gathered in the Appendix E. These are known compounds and all are potentially active CNS agents. Within the last year I saw two T-shirts bearing messages, clearly directed to these areas of interest. One: "Reality is for those who can't handle drugs;" the other: "So many drugs, so little time." Either one could be worn with pleasure. I wonder if I am now old enough to put them on?

# PREFACE

Returning from a conference on ecstasy, I sat next to a respected toxicologist who works for the British government. Eventually our conversation came round to the impending publication of this book. "It would be a complete disaster," he said. "A whole lot of new drugs would be released for which no tests exist and hundreds of new precursors would have to be controlled... The situation would become completely out of control. Publication must be prevented." But how? "I know the Americans have their First Amendment and all that, but when it comes to something important like this there are always ways." With that he ended the conversation and I was left haunted with images of government men setting up "accidents" for Sasha and Ann.

Completely out of control! Yes, this book not only reveals how psychoactives can be synthesized, but also how they can be extracted from so many ordinary plants that the means for psychedelic exploration can never be controlled again. The genie is out of the bottle and all the king's horses and all the king's men cannot put it back again.

What is the need for control? My traveling companion was concerned about the waste of public money on law enforcement, the hampering of industry through restrictions on precursors and the overloading of medical services with extra problems. But perhaps there is a more fundamental reason for the establishment to discourage the use of psychedelics.

A recent article by an Oxford professor of pharmacology refers to psychedelic experiences as "distorted sensations" and suggests that the real danger of psychoactive drugs is that they may profoundly and permanently alter the brain, ending with the warning: "Blowing one's mind may be literally just that."

To call psychedelic experiences "distorted" is the judgment of a sober, logical and materialistic thinker. However, a person under the influence of a psychedelic drug may well regard ordinary perception as severely limited, and therefore a distortion of the truth. I believe that the problem is one of language: words belong to our normal consciousness and are inadequate to describe another.

Conventional scientists cannot afford to accept the existence of other realities without undermining their own premises. In spite of having achieved so much, science has failed to explain consciousness, and cannot even accept the validity of many important aspects of human existence, such as religion, 'life force' or love. Only by keeping "the doors of perception" safely closed can accepted science be kept intact. Yet science is the exploration of nature, and should not be restricted just to avoid upsetting the status quo.

What this book achieves is profound. The information contained here provides a stepping stone for explorers of the spiritual side of our existence. A time will come when the legal and social taboos against psychedelic research will dissolve, and scientists will use this pioneering book to help them explore the uncharted territories of existence and the presently forbidden zones of the mind and life itself.

Nicholas Saunders
14 Neal's Yard, London

Nicholas Saunders writes books on ecstasy and the spiritual use of psychoactive drugs.

# INTRODUCTION

## WHY I DO WHAT I DO

Somewhere back in the early 1980's I was asked to come down to the University of California campus at Santa Barbara and give an address to a conference that was being put together by a small group of students. My attention was caught by the unusual fact that the whole meeting was to be devoted to the topic of psychedelic drugs. How does a student group at a major campus of the University of California manage to sponsor and widely advertise a symposium in a politically dicey area such as this?

I remembered a parallel occasion a number of years before this, when arrangements were made for a conference to be held on the Berkeley campus of the University of California, on the subject of LSD. As the date came closer and closer, apparently the tension felt by some of the faculty sponsors became intolerable. Pressure was being brought upon the organizers to cancel the meeting, to move it somewhere else, to make sure that So-and-so did not show up, to limit the advertising, and to separate the University name from it. A marvelous show of shared paranoia. Small events, such as the scribbling of the words Jew! Jew! Jew! on one of the announcement placards on the Berkeley campus (reputedly by a faculty member in the department of Psychology who had gone over the edge) encouraged the search for some alternate location. This was found in the University Extension Building, on Laguna Street in San Francisco.

Oh my, that was a memorable event. There were some dozen speakers and luminaries on the stage, several hundred very hip student and Haight Ashbury types in the audience, and five or six "suits" with white shirts and ties, walking back and forth in the outer aisles, continuously taking pictures of everything and everybody, presumably with high-speed film.

I can't find my notes from this LSD conference, so I can only comment on a scene or two taken from memory. One of the original invitees was Allen Ginsberg, but part of the compromise that had been struck to allow the show to proceed (besides moving it to San Francisco) was to dis-invite Ginsberg, and to invite the State Attorney General (I believe his name was Younger) to speak to the group, presumably about the legal aspects of drug use. By luck I caught a fascinating scene on the East porch of the auditorium. Ginsberg was jumping up and down, fists clenched in front of him, shouting directly at the AG who was facing him, "Eichmann, Eichmann, Eichmann!" And the look on the face of the Attorney General said quite clearly that he did not understand. In the opening address, an announcement was made to the congregation that Ginsberg had originally been invited (applause) but that orders had come down that he was not to appear on the stage as a participant (booing), but that now he could be on the stage as an observer and any comments he chose to make would be in this new role (wild applause). This gives the flavor of the meeting. In my memory the AG did not give a talk.

The evening sound show had the oil and colored filter light projections that were popular at the time, and the smell of pot was everywhere. Tim Leary was everybody's hero, and where he went, there followed a dedicated band of groupies. Needless to say, this was the last of any such conferences to be associated with the Berkeley campus.

But here was an invitation to something similar, at the somewhat more laid-back Santa Barbara campus of U.C. I was intrigued and curious, so I accepted.

My host was Robert Gordon-McCutcheon, an honor student in the area of religious philosophy. He had indicated that there would be a large audience of interested students and that I would be welcome with whatever I chose to say. Which is, after all, a very seductive invitation. But then, I also remembered the disastrous LSD meeting in San Francisco, where the invited speakers were not particularly welcomed by their academic hosts, and went back home with a few psychic scars. So I figured, a bit of an academically kosher image would be a superb defense against such a challenge! I'd play it with that thought in mind.

I have a few vivid memories of some of the preliminaries to this conference.

There was a meeting of many of the invited dignitaries at a private home up in the hills behind Santa Barbara. Alice and I went by car and found ourselves walking through a broad patio and into an equally broad living room, with maybe forty people sitting around in a three-deep circle. We were the unknowns, so we snuggled against a wall, behind a forward barricade of eager souls. First this, and then that, well-known person was introduced. Some names we recognized, but there was no opportunity to meet and talk with any of them. There was some hope expressed that this conference might serve as the launching pad for a revival of the psychedelic movement. This gentleman over here would write the definitive essay. That lady over there would contact her publishing agent to assure that this meeting would be recorded in history. Yet another person, over yonder, would serve as the press agent to document — through a radio interview tomorrow — the earth-shaking impact of this gathering of the elite. Alice and I left after a little while.

There was, indeed, a radio interview the next day. I sat in a small office with some half dozen notables of whom I can recall only Tim Leary. He was really all that was needed for bringing public attention to the meeting, and I was freed of having to answer anything, or even to speak to anyone. I left quietly, as I had agreed to a separate public encounter, a seminar at the U.C.S.B. Chemistry Department. This was one of the academic glue pieces that allowed the organizers to lend the term "scientific" to the conference. The University Administration could call upon the fact that there had been a Research Seminar in the Graduate School of Chemistry as a corollary to this "Psychedelic Meeting." See! It all was really proper and legitimate!

But things were not that smooth within the Chemistry Department itself. The inviting professor did not know me, or of me, and assumed that he would have to be host to some loose cannon who would be espousing drug use and drug abuse. With some misgivings he allowed the posting of the seminar, and was relieved to discover that there was to be an unprecedented turnout of graduates and undergraduates at the lecture. I was on my very best behavior, and gave a manic but scientifically impeccable presentation of the origins, syntheses, and possible mechanisms of action of compounds in the area of neurotransmitter agonists. It was one hundred percent kosher, filled with SN-2 reaction mechanisms and accurately drawn chemical structures, which I call "dirty pictures." It was a resounding success, and perhaps lent a bit of support to the organizers of the actual conference itself.

All I can remember concerning the putting together of this talk for the conference was sitting in the lab in the Life Science Building on the U.C. Campus, in the Department of Criminology, typing away on an old typewriter as my way of organizing the flow of what I wished to say. It was single spaced on yellow paper. I remember that I was not completely sure myself just why I did what I did, but that's what I wanted to express. Maybe if I were left alone for a couple of hours I might find the answer. Although I really didn't know ahead of time what I wanted to say, it came together as I wrote, and I ended up with an outline which I was sure would be okay. The talk would be a bit revealing for a person who had, up to then, kept a pretty low profile, but I was ready to catch a few people's attention. This is what I said almost twenty years ago, and it still speaks for me now.

## DRUGS OF PERCEPTION

When I was first asked by Robert Gordon-McCutcheon to come here tonight and talk about whatever I wished in the area of the psychedelic drugs, my first inclination was to decline.

After all, I am a student of chemistry and pharmacology, not of philosophy or religion, and I felt that I had contributed as much as I could at last year's meeting, with a review of the correlation between chemical structure and psychological activity.

But my wife intervened: "Why not tell them just *why* you do the work you do?"

This launched me onto an interesting question. Just why have I, for the last twenty-five years or so, conducted a persistent search into the design, the preparation, and the evaluation of new and different psychotropic drugs, be they hallucinogenic, psychedelic, dissociative, or merely intoxicating?

The flippant answer was right there at hand: one does it because it is there to be done. Like the answer to the question, "Why do you climb Mt. Everest?" "Because it's there." But that is not the reason that I conduct the research I do.

Whenever this question would come up during a seminar or panel appearance within the academic environment, I would place special emphasis on the word, "psychotomimetic," a term often applied by the scientific community to refer to the psychedelic drugs. In its origin, it is a blend of the prefix, "psychoto," from psychosis, and "mimesis," meaning to imitate. Thus, the term described one of the earliest properties assigned to these materials — that they could, to some measure, duplicate the symptoms of mental illness and, as such, might serve as exploratory tools in the study of some forms of psychosis and sensory disorder.

As an explanation of why I do what I do, this was both systematic and safe.

The explanation is systematic in that most of the many psychedelics that are known, currently about two hundred, can be classified by their structural backbone into two groups, one of them called the phenethylamines, and the other called the tryptamines. In the phenethylamine group, there are fifty or so relatives of mescaline, and an equal number of methyl homologues with the chemical chain of amphetamine. In the tryptamine group there is yet an equal number again, some of them quite simple with varying ring, chain, or nitrogen substitution patterns; some of them are condensed into yet more complex structures such as the $\beta$-carbolines (for example, harmaline) and the ergolines (for example, LSD).

The two principal neurotransmitters in the brain just happen to be a phenethylamine (dopamine) and a tryptamine (serotonin). Thus, there is encouragement to the neuroscientists to search for some neurotransmitter mismanagement, using the psychedelic drugs as chemically related probes.

This explanation is safe, because it is unthreatening and easily accepted by the academic community as well as by those who must decide who will receive government grants.

But it's not the truth. My work is indeed dedicated to the development of tools, but tools for quite a different purpose.

Let me lay a little background to establish a framework for these tools, in part to define them, and in part to give emphasis to the urgency that I feel is associated with them.

I firmly believe that there is a most remarkable balance being maintained between all aspects of the human theater. When there seems to be the development of a move that-a-way, there springs forth a compensatory and balancing development that effects a move this-a-way. If there must be a dichotomization of concepts into "good" and "evil," then the balance is maintained by the good containing a small but real quantity of unexpressed evil, and the evil containing a corresponding amount of unexpressed good. Within the human mind there must co-exist the Eros, the life-loving and self-perpetuating force, with the Thanatos, which is defined as "the death instinct, especially as expressed in violent aggression." Both are present in each of us, but they are usually separated from our awareness by the difficult-to-penetrate wall of the unconscious.

One definition of the tools I seek is that they should be words in a vocabulary, a vocabulary that might allow each human being to more consciously — and more clearly — communicate with the interior of his own mind and psyche. This might be called a vocabulary of awareness. A person who becomes increasingly aware of, and so begins to acknowledge, the existence of the two opposite contributors to his motives and decisions, may begin to make choices that are knowledgeable. And the learning path that follows such choices is the path to wisdom.

Just as there is a need for balance within the individual mind, there is an interesting parallel in society. Look for a few minutes at the record, the coincidences in history that have kept our human race in precarious balance.

Throughout the early centuries of this current millennium, there were carried out some of the most viciously inhumane wars known to man, all in the name of religion. The horrors of the Inquisition, with its lethal intolerance of dissent (called heresy) are well documented. And yet, it was during those dark years that the structure of alchemy was established, to acquire knowledge through the study of matter. The oft-quoted goal of the transmutation of lead into gold was not what was being sought. The value of the quest was in the doing and re-doing, and yet again re-doing, the processes of distillation and sublimation and a more exact understanding of these processes that there might emerge a synthesis, a union between the physical and spiritual worlds.

It was the doing and the re-doing that was its own reward. It was the learning of the discipline that established the vital balance in each individual alchemist.

In the last 100 years or so, this learning process has evolved into what we now call "science." But with this evolution there has been a gradual shift from the process itself to the results of the process. In this current age of science, it is only the end-result, the "gold" that really matters. It is no longer the search itself or the learning, but the final achievement that brings one the acknowledgment of one's peers, and with that, the recognition by the outside world, together with the wealth, influence, and power that comes with that recognition. But these achievements, these end-results, all show that same yin-yang structure of good and evil, with each containing a bit of the other. This has been our history for the past centuries. We have been taught to say that the fruits of science are devoid of ethics or morality, and that there is no intrinsic good or evil in the objective world of academic scientific inquiry. And of course that there is no meaning to the idea of a need for maintaining some sort of balance. But, still, I would like to illustrate some rather incredible coincidences of timing.

For example, in 1895, Wilheim von Roentgen observed that, when electricity was applied to an evacuated tube that contained certain gases, a nearby plate covered with an unusual inorganic film emitted a visible glow. And the next year, in 1896, Antoine Henri Becqueril found that these same metal-penetrating emanations, producing areas of light and color on the platinocyanide-covered plate, were being emitted from uranium.

Radioactivity had been discovered.

But it was just the following year in Leipzig, Germany, at 11:45 AM on the 23rd of November, 1897, that Arthur Heffter consumed an alkaloid that he had isolated from the "dumpling cactus," brought to the western world by the irrepressible pharmacologist, Louis Lewin. As Heffter wrote in his notes, following the ingestion of 150 milligrams:

"From time to time, dots with the most brilliant colors floated across the field of vision. Later on, landscapes, halls, architectural scenes also appeared ..."

Mescaline had been discovered.

During the 1920's and 1930's, both worlds — that of the physical sciences, involving radiation, and that of the psychopharmacological, involving psychotropic materials — continued to develop without any clear sense of polarity, without the "mine is good, and yours is evil" duality that was soon to come.

Radioactivity and radiation were becoming mainstays in medicine.

X-ray photography was invaluable in diagnosis, and radium therapy was broadly used in treatment. Controlled and localized radiation could destroy malignant tissue, while sparing the host.

And in the area of psychology, there were parallel developments. The theories of Freud and Jung were being developed into increasingly useful clinical approaches to mental illness, and the basis of experimental psychology was laid down in the pioneering studies of Pavlov.

There was another coincidence of timing, which in retrospect was the beginning of the division of science onto two diverging pathways, that occurred during World War II. In late 1942, Enrico Fermi and several other scientists at the University of Chicago demonstrated, for the first time ever, that nuclear fission could be achieved and controlled by man. The age of "unlimited power, and freedom from dependency on our dwindling fossil reserves" had begun.

The next year, on April 16, Dr. Albert Hofmann at the Sandoz Research Laboratory in Switzerland somehow absorbed an unknown amount of a chemical that he had made some five years earlier, and had just resynthesized. There was a disturbing awareness of restlessness and dizziness that lasted a couple of hours. Three days later, at 4:20 PM on the 19th of April, he took a measured dose, 250 micrograms, and subsequently reported:

"... (after the crisis of confusion and despair) ... I began to enjoy the unprecedented colors and plays of shapes that persisted. Kaleidoscopic, fantastic images surged in on me, alternating, variegated, opening and closing themselves in circles and spirals ..."

LSD had also been discovered.

But still, then, and up until the last decade, it was the rich promise of the nuclear age, first with the power of fission and later, with the virtually limitless potential of fusion energy, that carried the banner of the hopes of mankind. The area of the hallucinogens was categorized as being psychotomimetic (psychosis-imitating), and generally negative. It was not until sometime in the 1960's that a strange and fascinating reversal of roles took place.

The knowledge of nuclear fission and fusion took on a death-loving aspect in the minds of the public, with country after country joining the fraternity of those skilled in the capacity for eradicating the human species. But, as I said earlier, when an imbalance develops, there seems to spring forth a compensatory counterpart. In this case, the counterpart evolved on many fronts, in many forms, but its general character can be summarized as an increase of interest in the spiritual aspect of man and a desire for greater understanding of the human psyche. What had been seen as tools for the study of psychosis (at best) or escapist self-gratification (at worst) — the psychedelic drugs — were increasingly viewed, by large numbers of young adults in the western world, as tools of enlightenment and spiritual transformation.

Now that mankind's Thanatos has been entrusted with the *in perpetuo* knowledge of how we can completely destroy ourselves and this extraordinary experiment in life and love, some development must occur at the Eros side of our psyche which will afford the learning of how to live with that perpetual knowledge. It is the communication between these two sides of the human mind that requires a new vocabulary, a vocabulary of insight and awareness.

We need a way to communicate experiences of the deeper parts of ourselves, a way to share knowledge which has traditionally been called "occult," or "hidden." Until our time, this level of knowledge was considered the private preserve of those shamans, teachers or spiritual guides who had earned their way to it. In their hands was the responsibility of choosing the gifted, intuitive people who would become students or disciples. Those special individuals were taken into temples of learning, into the pyramids, the secret lodges, the monasteries or sacred kivas, to be gradually led into explorations of the spiritual world and an increased understanding of their own unconscious landscapes. This kind of learning was expected, in time, to produce healers and community leaders of uncommon wisdom.

If we had the time that our ancestors had, we could expect to see a gradual increase in the number of people aware of the inner workings, the energies, the complex balancing of drives, fears, instincts and learned patterns which make up the interior universe of the human being. We would have reason to anticipate an eventual growth in understanding of the nature of consciousness and the unconscious. However, in the last few decades, developments in physics, chemistry, biology, electronics, mathematics and information distribution have occurred at a speed never before seen in human history. These explosions of knowledge about the nature of the physical world have not had their necessary and vital counterpart in an increased understanding of the human psyche. Much has been discovered about the brain, but not about the mind. There has been no leap forward in our comprehension of those unconscious archetypes, emotions and energies which will determine how we eventually use our new scientific knowledge. Since almost all discoveries about the physical world can be used for both benign and lethal purposes, it is essential that we begin to develop a way of exploring and understanding those forces within our unconscious selves which will inevitably make those decisions.

What we do not allow ourselves to confront and acknowledge consciously may kill, not just one race or culture, but ALL of us.

Keep in mind that psychedelic drugs are not the only keys to our unconscious minds; they cannot be used for learning and growth by everyone.  There is no single drug or dosage level that will benefit all explorers equally.  And it cannot be said too often that what is being experienced in the use of a psychedelic drug or visionary plant does not come from the ingested chemical components, but from the mind and psyche of the person using the compound.  Every such drug opens a door within the user, and different drugs open different doors, which means that an explorer must learn how to most safely and successfully make his way through each new inner landscape. This takes time and should be done with the guidance of a veteran explorer, as is the case, ideally, with all deep emotional and spiritual explorations.

All of the above cautions aside, these tools — the psychedelic drugs and plants — offer a much faster method than most of the classic alternatives for the accomplishment of the goals we seek: conscious awareness of our interior workings and greater clarity as to our responsibilities towards our own species and all others with whom we share this planet.

It is in the crafting of these essential tools that I feel my skills lie, and this is exactly why I do the work I do.

—————————

Since my talk at Santa Barbara, we have not blown ourselves into oblivion or destroyed our species with biological warfare, but the potential is still there. We have not established an open, mutually respectful communication between the leaders of the world's countries, but the potential is still there.

As in the past, the people who lead us are fueled by the archetype of power, that aspect of the human psyche which drives to structure, control, and formulate rules and systems. The power drive shapes our world, and without it, mankind would have perished long ago.  When it is kept in balance with its several complementary energies, it gives us form; it builds civilizations.  But when the precarious balance is shifted, and too much energy flows from this archetype, structure becomes constriction, control becomes dictatorship, teaching degenerates into admonition and threat, vision and intuition create dogma, and caution evolves into paranoia. Communication with the loving and nurturing energy within us is lost, and with it the ability to choose wisely, either for ourselves individually or for our species.

Priests and kings, emperors and presidents, and all those who find comfort and safety within the structures maintained by the powerful, tend to be disturbed and angered by individuals who insist on striking off in new directions, ignoring the guidance of appointed leaders. To those in authority, there is the unconscious threat of chaos, the shattering of what is known, familiar and safe. The response to this threat can take many forms, from killing the offender (witch-burning) to — at the very least — warning him to keep his knowledge and opinions to himself (as with Galileo), lest they provoke the self-protective anger of the established order and of those who maintain power through it.

This has been the history of human development on this earth, a balance maintained — usually with great difficulty and often with violence — between the urge to control and the need to change and grow. And this is the way it should have been able to continue, but the technological growth-spurt of the past fifty years has put into mankind's hands a body of knowledge that changes the equation. However, just as the nuclear and chemical warfare genies are out of the bottle, never to be put back in again, so also will the psychedelic genie be forever amongst us.

Being human means being a soul that chooses — consciously or unconsciously — what it will do and what it will become. For my part, I prefer as much awareness as I can achieve in this lifetime, in order to make my choices wisely.

I am reminded of a dark and humorous quotation, from a hero of mine, Woody Allen. He was addressing a graduating class at a university, and these were his opening remarks:

> "More than any other time in history, mankind faces a crossroads. One path leads to despair and utter hopelessness. The other, to total extinction. Let us pray we have the wisdom to choose correctly."

I am more optimistic. We have survived for some decades with technological threats which have remained unexpressed. Maybe the "counterpoise" half of the human animal is making itself felt with reason and love. I hope so. I rather suspect that it is.

In the meantime, I continue to devote myself to the work of discovering new keys to an understanding of the human mind, and to the widest possible dissemination of whatever knowledge and information I have been able to gather. Whatever I cannot accomplish will be done by the many others throughout the world who share these goals.

Alexander T. Shulgin, Ph.D.

"The voters in this country should not be expected to decide which medicines are safe and effective."

Gen. Barry McCaffrey, Drug Czar, 1996.

"If people let the government decide what foods they eat and what medicines they take, their bodies will soon be a sorry state as are the souls of those who live under tyranny."

Thomas Jefferson, 3rd President of the U.S.

# BOOK I

## THE STORY CONTINUES

# Part One:

# Adventures
# and Misadventures

# CHAPTER 1. INVASION

(Alice's voice)

For over 20 years Shura has had a Drug Enforcement Administration analytical license which allows him to possess, identify, and analyze drugs in each of the five Schedules. He has to expect occasional (every few years) inspections of his laboratory by agents who are experts in detecting signs of illegal activity and/or non-adherence to regulations. Over the 15 years I've known him, he has been inspected twice — on each occasion by different DEA agents, two at a time — and the inspections had resulted in no complaints, no suggestions for changes to be made, and no difficulty in renewing his license annually.

Shura made one mistake. When he was originally granted the license, there was a handbook of regulations, and over the years he continued to do his work without inquiring as to whether new regulations might have been written. He assumed that, since his license had to be renewed every year, the DEA would notify him if there were any recent developments that he ought to be aware of. In retrospect, this was naive. As we learned later, the DEA expects the head of any licensed lab to ask them, to actively inquire, as to whether new rules might have been put into effect.

But, again, you'd think that the previous inspecting agents would certainly have been aware of new rules and regulations, and would have alerted Shura to their existence, as well as insisting that he conform to them. They never did.

There was another reason for Shura's lack of curiosity about possible new regulations applying to his license. For thirty years, one of his best and dearest friends was the administrator for the DEA western laboratories, Paul Freye. Paul liked to come out on an occasional Sunday and fool around in Shura's lab. He was fascinated by the chemistry of the psychedelics; he was also, as he put it, "Chickenshit about ever putting one of those things into myself; I just don't have that kind of courage." We never suggested that he might do so, because all of us knew that Paul's position in the DEA made it impossible for him to nibble anything that even came close to being a psychedelic drug, however legal.

During the years of friendship with Shura, Paul was in our house countless times, as well as in the lab. He saw the anonymous drug samples sent through the mail for analysis, most of which Shura had never touched, since he didn't want to do such work for people he didn't know. The little sample envelopes were piled up, gathering dust, here and there in two rooms, one of them Shura's office, the other a former bedroom, now a semi-lab containing his IR (infra-red) and NMR (nuclear magnetic resonance) machines, and shelves of records, both the business and music kind.

Among the samples sent to him for analysis, to give one example, might be a small amount of a drug found at a rave party by a researcher doing a government-funded study on rave dances. Such a researcher might have been told that the sample was XTC or some other scheduled drug, and knew he could send it to Shura for analysis, to find out exactly what the material was. By doing his research this way, he could accumulate his data and write his paper without running into such problems as having to report to the DEA on the names of young people at the raves who had given him samples (which would — needless to say — stop his research dead in its tracks, not to speak of the damage it would do to the young rave dancers involved). Shura would probably consider the analysis of such a sample to be worth doing just for the information to be obtained about what was happening on the rave scene.

Shura had always believed that his analytical license allowed him to do analysis, and that included analysis of anonymous samples and research samples. Our DEA friend Paul may have believed it did, too. But once, as he passed by the dusty little mound of samples in the former-bedroom-semi-lab, Paul remarked to Shura, "You know, these babies could be more trouble than they're worth: it wouldn't hurt to just toss 'em all out." Shura barely heard the words, his mind being focused on an exciting development in the lab which he wanted to show his friend, and Paul's gentle warning was forgotten.

Shura is a great research scientist, not a great housekeeper. A few small vials of questionable material — waiting for analysis or to be put away — might be found hiding behind stacked reprints on the top of his office filing cabinets, or tucked into a shoe box in the room with the infra-red, nicknamed Basement Four. There were no young children in our house, and the study and Basement Four were closed and off-limits during any party which might include children. The only people besides ourselves who might be in our home were friends and trusted acquaintances, none of whom would go to Shura's lab without his knowledge, or pick up dusty little envelopes with question-marks on them in his study, or touch a vial bearing chemical symbols in any room. Our friends are not sneaks, nor are they idiots.

When, long before I knew him, Shura received a box containing three peyote cacti from a priest of the Native American Church (a sort of shaman-to-shaman gift), Paul expressed his delight. He knew that Shura's analytical license allowed him to have the Divine Cactus in his possession. He also knew that Shura had a dream of someday taking apart the peyote, in order to finally pin down the numerous unknown trace alkaloids present in the plant, which have not — to this day — been analyzed. Shura put it this way in a letter to a friend:

"The bulk of the minor alkaloids have indeed been analyzed quite thoroughly. Actually my hope was to see if a synthetic mescaline analogue that I had made, a methoxymethylenedioxyphenethylamine and a most logical bio-synthetic precursor to peyote components such as anhalonine, lophophorine and peyophorine, was itself a natural component of this cactus. In fact I have, rather presumptively, named it lophophine, assuming that it would be a trace component. With the reference sample in hand, and a valid extract of the cactus, the 'discovery' of it as being there would be a piece of cake."

In the meantime, the beautiful, soft green cacti stood in their red clay pots against a wall of the patio, getting water and occasional loving words over the years.

Paul invited Shura several times to talk about psychedelic drugs to the chemists in the San Francisco DEA lab. On Shura's study wall was a photograph of himself shaking hands with Paul, while holding a plaque awarded to "Dr. Alexander Borodin, in Recognition of Your Significant Personal Efforts to Help Eliminate Drug Abuse," dated 1973; the bronze medallion was engraved at the top, "Department of Justice," and at the bottom, "Bureau of Narcotics and Dangerous Drugs," the forerunner of the present DEA. In the photograph, both Paul and Shura had full beards, wore dark suits and ties and looked appropriately stern.

Next to this plaque was a second award, given almost a decade later, this time from the Drug Enforcement Administration, "With Appreciation for the Valuable Contribution of Dr. Alexander Borodin, in Support of The Western Laboratory," signed by Paul, just before he retired. Shura admitted to me that he wasn't quite sure why he'd been awarded these plaques, but I think they were acknowledgments of his scientific integrity and his insistence on making available information about psychedelic drugs, their chemistry and their effects to anyone who wanted to know, including the government.

Paul officiated, as a minister of the Universal Life Church, at our wedding on the lawn behind our house. A year later, when he married a little blonde DEA intelligence agent, a sweet, tough and compulsively honest lady named Elena, the ceremony was performed on that same lawn. The Farm, as we call it, swarmed with DEA chemists and agents, and Shura took them all on a guided tour of our old farmhouse and the fabled lab, with its delicate, long-legged spiders and dried leaves blown in through the door by many gusts of wind over many winters. Among other sights shown to the visitors, a few yards from the lab, was the sump; this was a hole, dug deep by Shura, decades earlier, and lined with bricks, now filled almost to the top with earth. Into it, Shura poured the occasional pot residues, as he called them, and waste solvents — things that couldn't be safely thrown into a fire in the lab fireplace.

About two years after Paul retired, our book, *PIHKAL*, was published. The first half of the book told the stories of Shura and myself, our early lives and our difficult love affair, each one of us writing separately, in our individual voices, to create the totality of the adventure. Much of the story, which dealt with psychedelic experiences, was fiction, but it was based on the explorations that we each had made during the 60's, and the research we had done before the passage of the Analogue Drug Bill in 1986, which effectively brought all such exploration to a stop in this country.

That part of the book was controversial enough, because it also spoke out about the damage being done to our basic freedoms by the so-called War on Drugs, and it argued vehemently for the individual adult citizen's right to explore his own mind and soul in any way he chooses, provided that he takes care not to intrude on the rights of any other human being.

It was the second half of the book that caused shock waves in certain places. It was written for such time in the future when rationality would (we sincerely hope) replace the ugly police state mentality rapidly growing in this country. This second half consisted of 179 recipes, procedures for making psychedelic drugs. It was written in the style of the respected Journal of Medicinal Chemistry, and would be understood largely by professional chemists. There were also pages of commentary from anonymous contributors detailing the effects of each of these drugs at various dosage levels.

As soon as we had the completed, published book in hand, Shura proceeded to distribute free copies to all the chemists he knew in the DEA labs across the country, explaining that it should be a valuable reference work for them. It was immediately put to use as exactly that, and it is probable that many of those chemists never got around to reading the first half of the book, finding all the excitement they could possibly hope for in the second, the technical half.

Right after *PIHKAL* came out, we would lie in bed at night, imagining out loud to each other the various possible scenarios involving angry government officials, but as time went on, we relaxed and told ourselves that, after all, we live in a country that gives protection to free speech, and Shura had maintained an excellent relationship, over the years, with the people he knew in the DEA.

We had been aware for a long time that there were a few powerful men in the Washington, D.C. headquarters of the DEA whose feelings toward Shura were deeply hostile. There was one in particular who had the reputation of being a truly malignant person, determined to rise through the ranks of the agency. He was vehement in his hostility towards all uses of visionary plants or drugs, even by Native Americans; we could only hope that he would either ignore our book or dismiss it, after considering the fact that it had proven useful to many of the DEA chemists. This, too, might be seen in retrospect as naiveté on our part.

The general state of things in our house and in the lab was the same when Paul had been around (and when the two earlier inspections had taken place) as they were years later, in 1994, when our world was turned upside down.

Two years after *PIHKAL*'s publication, on a Tuesday in late September of 1994, a red car drove up our road and into the parking area above our old farmhouse. Three men got out and introduced themselves as agents of the DEA. We expressed, gently, our surprise that they had not phoned before coming, because during Paul's administration, he had insisted that agents who came to inspect the Borodin lab phone Shura in advance, to make an appointment.

The head agent, Mr. Fosca, a neatly dressed man of medium height, was polite and smiling; he ignored our reproachful comments as he shook our hands. The other two were dressed quite casually in sports clothes, which was most unusual for DEA people on duty. I offered coffee and tea, but the three men declined. I remembered then that DEA agents don't usually accept food or drink in a place they are inspecting, at least not until their work is finished and they have found nothing out of order.

The agents had brought a warrant with them. This was startling; no previous inspection had ever involved a warrant, and both Shura and I were taken aback and rather bewildered. Why did they need such a thing?

My daughter, Wendy, was working in Shura's office, doing the Transform Press business — processing orders for *PIHKAL* — as she did every week. She glanced up as Shura brought Mr. Fosca through the door, and smiled as he introduced her as the manager of the press. Then she went on with her work.

Shura and I were surprised by the unexpected visit, but not worried. After all, two previous inspections had turned up nothing considered a problem, and we assumed that this one would have the same outcome.

We were, at that moment, packing for a trip to Spain, where Shura was due to present several talks at a conference not far from Barcelona. Our plan was to leave the following day, and this official visit would mean taking several hours out of our scheduled preparations. Aside from that one concern, we had no reason to be apprehensive.

The agents went to the lab with Shura. It was just a few minutes later, around 2:00 p.m., when Wendy knocked on my bedroom door, where I was busy folding and squeezing things into suitcases, and told me that Michael Sun had arrived. I clapped my forehead, having forgotten completely that we'd made an appointment to meet with him for about an hour, that afternoon, just to catch up on recent events. Michael was (and is) one of my favorite people in the world, a gentle, soft-spoken, quietly brilliant young man who was engaged in pulling together a coalition of religious and spiritual practitioners and teachers throughout the country who believe that psychedelic plants and drugs have an immense potential as tools for exploring the human soul and spirit. He believes (as do we) that the best way to encourage changes in bad drug law is to work with people in the government, to explain and persuade, and to open their understanding of the ancient religious and spiritual traditions in most cultures which have used such materials.

I met Michael at the sliding glass doors between the dining room and the small outside patio. He handed me a tall glass bud vase which carried one single glowing red rose. I thanked him and gave him a hug, then said in a low voice, "We have some unexpected visitors, inspectors from the DEA; they came without phoning first — we didn't expect them at all — and I imagine you probably don't want to stick around to be introduced."

He grinned and agreed that he didn't think it would benefit anybody for him to remain. He said, "I'll phone you tomorrow and we can set up another time — " but I interrupted to remind him that tomorrow we would be on our way to Spain.

"Call us in three weeks, honey," I urged him, and after another hug and his wishes for a good and happy trip, he left. I put the rose in its shining vase on the tiled counter under one of the kitchen windows, where it would catch the sunlight.

I returned to the bedroom and continued packing until, about an hour later, I heard voices in the hallway. Shura was telling the agents that, yes, there were two other rooms in the house where some samples of drugs might be found, "There's stuff in my office and in the room we call Basement Four, which isn't a basement at all, by the way, but it's where I keep my IR — my infra-red equipment — and other instruments that might be corroded in the real lab."

I thought to myself, he sounds pretty cheerful; guess the inspection went all right.

During the next thirty minutes or so, my casual attitude underwent a change, as I heard Mr. Fosca say over and over again, "That is a violation of the regulations," always in a pleasant voice, sometimes with what I heard as a faint overtone of regret, especially when adding, as I heard him do once, "These violations can be worth a fine of up to twenty-five thousand dollars each, you know."

"Which regulations?" asked Shura, insistently, before retreating into a resigned silence.

There was supposed to be a safe in the lab, Agent Fosca continued, into which all scheduled drugs were placed under lock; there should be a system by which the local police station could be alerted by an alarm if unauthorized persons tried to gain access to the contents of that safe. He added, "After all, you don't want to be responsible for a tragedy, if some visiting child happens to discover one of those vials, do you?"

*That certainly sounds reasonable. But why didn't the earlier inspectors say anything about safes? They must have written an awful lot of new rules in the past few years. And nobody told Shura.*

I ventured out into the hallway, closing the bedroom door behind me, and watched from the doorway of Basement Four as Agent Fosca, moving from one cluttered surface to another, told Shura that, not only were the anonymous drug samples stacked up somewhere other than in the lab — where they belonged — but Shura's license did not authorize him to analyze anonymous drug samples anyway. "That kind of activity requires a separate license, which you don't have," he said, his voice fractionally more disapproving than before.

Shura replied, "Nobody ever told me that; after all, my license allows me to do analysis, doesn't it?" After a small silence, he shrugged, "But if I have to give up doing an occasional analysis, that'll be fine with me, because I don't like dealing with the damned things; I don't get paid for doing it, and most of the time, I don't learn anything interesting enough to justify the time and energy it takes."

During the next hour, Mr. Fosca sat at our dining room table, examining all of Shura's records, including receipts for chemical purchases going back several years. He asked for and got photo copies of purchase orders. All these were reasonable requests, and Shura complied without hesitation. But he was aware — more than I was, at that point — that the questioning had already gone well beyond that involved in any previous inspection.

By now, Shura's attitude had become one of innocent surprise (which was certainly genuine), combined with an apparently good-natured desire to cooperate, all of which he hoped would hide his growing anxiety. He went very slightly manic, asking several times, "Where can I get a copy of the new book of regulations?" and, "Why hasn't anyone told me about these new regulations?" There might have been a hint of disbelief to be detected underneath these questions, but all he got from Mr. Fosca was a promise that a copy would be mailed to our address, as soon as the agents got back to the office.

During the fourth hour of questioning about what this or that chemical was intended for, and why this or that scheduled drug was present in such quantity, and Shura's apparently cheerful explanations, I went and sat outside the dining room, where all this was going on, making myself comfortable in one of our molded plastic patio chairs, underneath the big canvas umbrella, with my eternal glass of iced tea. I got into conversation with the oldest of the three agents, about children and high schools — he was planning to attend a parents' night at his son's school, that evening — and now, when I offered him some plain iced water, he told me he would appreciate that, yes; it was pretty hot and he could use a drink. I was pleased that he was accepting my offer; I felt it was a generally good sign, although of what I couldn't be sure.

At the end of the fourth hour, Agent Fosca closed his notepad, stood up and said that he was going to need at least three — maybe four — more days to complete his inspection, and he was very sorry we were leaving for Spain, but he would be in touch as soon as we had returned, to set up the next session. Shura said "Yes, of course," and accompanied the three men out to the car to say good-bye.

As soon as the agents had left, he came back into the dining room and we stood and looked at each other, smiles gone, then we sat down at the table, in silence, to let it all sink in. Wendy came out of the office, saying, "Okay, I've finished," then sat down with us. I leaned back in my chair and said, "Jeeezus!"

"Bummer, huh?" Wendy looked from me to Shura and nodded to herself.

Shura muttered, "I wonder if there really are so many new regulations!"

I said, "Oh, there probably are, honey. Remember, Mister Fosca pointed out that the DEA can't be expected to notify every head of every lab in the country whenever there's a new regulation passed, so the lab heads have to keep track themselves. It just didn't occur to us that the rules might have been changed."

"So if there were new regs, how come the last two inspections came up with no complaints, not a single one!" Shura asked.

"Yeah," I said, "That doesn't make sense."

After a moment's silence, Shura said, "There was one reference to *PIHKAL*. I mean, he must have read it — or maybe he was talking about things we've said in interviews — because he asked me, when we were looking at stuff in Basement Four, 'Does your research group still meet these days?' and I said that we didn't meet any more for research, just socially, because you have to remember, the average age of the people is around seventy, and that kind of exploration is a young person's game. Besides, the Analogue Drug Bill pretty much put an end to all research in that area."

"What did he say?" Wendy asked.

"Nothing; just went on to other things."

"So after you get back from Spain," said Wendy, "They're doing some more inspecting?"

"He said three, maybe four more days," answered Shura, shoving his hair back with both hands, "What more can he do here that'd take three or four more days, for Pete's sake!"

"Twenty-five thousand dollars per violation," I said to Wendy, but Shura made a correction, "Up to, he said; up to twenty-five thousand dollars."

"Oh, okay. Depending on how benign they decide to be," I said.

"And you can just guess how benign the DEA is going to feel toward the author of *PIHKAL*, can't you?" Shura bared his teeth in a grimace.

For the first time that day, all three of us actually broke into laughter.

During the next two weeks we attended a conference on Consciousness Change in the ancient little town of Lerida, in the part of Spain known as Catalonia, and when the conference was over, we spent a few days in Barcelona, one of the loveliest cities in the world. During that time, Shura wrote his own notes on what had happened and how he felt about it.

He entitled it:

VISITORS FROM ANOTHER PLANET

(Shura's voice)

Act I:

Within a week I have had two most extraordinary encounters. Both seemed at first fundamentally benign and unthreatening, but both developed in ways that could not have been predicted, and which I am still trying to understand. In fact, both involved such complexities, I have lost most of the minute-to-minute detail, and will try here to give the music, accompanied by what little I can remember. In a figurative sense, both were visits from another planet.

The first of these occurred earlier this week, on Tuesday at the Farm, the day before we were booked for a flight to Spain, where I was to give an address to an international Change of States of Consciousness conference. Alice and I were in the final stages of preparation, she with the last odds and ends of packing and I with the making of the arrangements to have our mail picked up by the neighbors, and getting an itinerary made out for my son Theo and Wendy. Wendy, Alice's younger daughter, was doing the weekly books for Transform Press. We were expecting a drop-in visitor at about 2:00 PM, so we had opened the big wooden gate at the bottom of the driveway, but it was just a bit after noon when I heard a car drive up, above the house.

I went out to meet it, and watched three men, one relatively young and dressed in suit and tie, the other two older and more casually dressed, get out of the car. They came down the stairs from the parking area, shook my hand, and introduced themselves. I didn't recognize any of their names, but I did know the organization they worked for. It was the Drug Enforcement Administration, the DEA. I invited them into the house (they accepted), offered them coffee or tea, or something else to drink (they declined) and asked how I might help them. They mentioned that they were on an official visit (was it the office for compliance? the office for diversion?) and wanted to look at everything that might bear on my handling of scheduled drugs.

They handed me a few pages of something with a business card attached (I thought it might be a listing of what they were looking for) but I found out later on reading it that it was a search warrant allowing them pretty much free reign to look for, and to take, whatever they felt might be of interest to them. Alice came in from the packing tasks about then, and I introduced her. Once she realized that I was not making a joke as to the identity of our visitors, she played the role of the gracious hostess, and introduced them to Wendy who had come into the kitchen for a coffee refill.

The principal investigator was a young man of perhaps 35, carrying a clipboard with a yellow lined pad for taking notes, and a camera to photograph everything of interest. He was the asker of most questions, and he introduced himself as Agent Fosca. The other two were just sort of there, perhaps to be of help if help was called for, or to be witnesses of things said and done.

Our first major rallying point was over in the lab.

The exchange pretty much went according to the following routine: Mr. Fosca asks, "Where in this area (wherever we happened to be at the moment, with vials and petri dishes and small bottles and dirty beakers in front of us) are materials that are scheduled drugs?"

I reply, "Well, this is a sample from England, from a rave scene; it might be Ecstasy. Is it? I haven't analyzed it yet, so I don't know."

Fosca: "Who sent it to you?"

"I don't remember."

"Where is the record of it having been received?"

"I don't have any."

"Why don't you keep notes?"

"Why should I?"

"It is required by regulations."

"I never heard of any such regulation."

"There is a fine of up to $25,000 for every infraction of regulations."

"Which regulations?"

There were many variations on this theme, but each of them reflected the same basic content.

The two subordinate agents seemed to become more and more at ease as the day progressed, asking occasional questions apparently out of curiosity, rather than from any official need, and clearly disliking the smells of the lab. So they stayed outside, talking to each other, while Fosca and I continued as a twosome inside for an hour or so.

He inspected the licenses on the wall. There was one from the DEA for Schedule I-V drugs, for analytical purposes. There was one from the State Department of Radiology that allowed me some comfort in purchasing radioisotopes for my research work, and there was a Clinical Chemist toxicology registration.

Fosca picked up a Hamilton 100 microliter fixed needle syringe and asked what it was for. I told him, "For injecting small, known volume samples into the GC for chromatographic separations."

He picked up a packet of #18 1-inch hypodermic needles in sterile sleeves, and asked what they were for.

"For venting the positive argon gas pressure out through rubber grommets in sealed systems that have to stay dry," I said.

"They appear to be the size usually used for human injections."

"That's because I get them from the San Francisco General Hospital, where they are used with patients."

Everything that might be seen as having a drug orientation of course had a legitimate lab use as well, and he seemed to accept this; at least, he didn't argue with my explanations. Still, he continuously took notes and photographs. Scribble, scribble, click, click.

But the repeated emphasis was on scheduled drugs. Do you have scheduled drugs here?

"Well, yes."

"Here is a bottle that contains a few grams of 2C-B. How much does it weigh?"

"I don't know — a couple of grams."

"Could you weigh it?" Sure. Onto a sheet of paper on the top-loader scales. It was 3.4 grams.

"Why so much?"

"I use it as a chemical precursor for the synthetic exploration of new compounds carrying the 2,5-dimethoxyphenethylamine orientation, but with unusual substituents in the four position."

Scribble, click.

"Other scheduled drugs?"

"Well, here is a petri dish with some methcathinone in it."

"Why do you have that?"

"I made it," I said.

"Why did you make it?"

"To see if, from an analysis of trace impurities, I could tell which method was used. What are the methods that could be used? The major two are the oxidation of ephedrine with either permanganate or dichromate."

"Which did you use?"

"Let me look it up in my notes," I said, and looked it up. "It was dichromate."

"You keep notes on your research work?"

"Yes, in great detail."

"Why?"

"Because I work towards publication in the scientific literature or towards patents, and in either case things must be written up."

"But you don't take notes when you receive samples of what might be scheduled drugs, from different sources?"

"No."

"Why not?"

"Why should I?"

My mind wandered a bit as I remembered a somewhat parallel visit that had occurred at Solano Laboratories, many years ago, when I worked there, an inspection visit from a representative of the DEA forerunner which was called the Bureau of Narcotics and Dangerous Drugs. There was a gentleman named Special Agent Somebody, who sat in a small office with the head of the lab and me, and most aggressively cross-examined the two of us as to the security of our storage methods for poisons and drugs. As he talked, he carefully adjusted himself so that the gun that was tucked in behind the belt over his tummy was clearly visible.

I glanced at my DEA guest and saw no tell-tale bulge. There was a beeper evident; that was all. Maybe a concealed tape recorder? I wished I had one tucked away in my own pocket. But I didn't, and would have to depend on my faulted memory. I suspect he had no tape, but rather depended on scribble and click.

Another petri dish came to his attention, on the bench in the lab, possibly because of the first three letters of the name written on it: MDMone. "What is this?" he asked, tapping it a little. I explained that the story behind this was the search for an antidepressant akin to my Dimoxamine invention of some years ago, but cautioned him that this sort of information had to be kept confidential as I had not yet filed for a patent, and all this was privileged information. We weighed it as well (why, I am not sure) and everything was duly written down. Eventually I went outside to talk to the other two, and my questioner stayed in the lab for a few more minutes alone. Maybe he was taking pictures, maybe taking samples, maybe just tallying what he saw. In any case, I had little choice in the matter.

Up to the Quonset hut at the top of the stairs behind the lab, which I call my magic stock room. "Are there any scheduled drugs here?" asks Mr. Fosca, looking around at the shelves of glassware and chemical supplies. I remembered a large bottle of chloral hydrate and managed to find it amongst a large collection of dusty bottles on a shelf over at the far wall.

"Where did this come from?" asked Agent Fosca. I shrugged, "I don't remember — perhaps I was cleaning out some stock room somewhere and it was there as a chemical. It has the big C with the superimposed IV on the label, so it's probably kosher."

"Any record?" Fosca wanted to know. I said no. I decided to add an explanation.

"You see, there were a lot of research groups that were being harassed by environmental this and safety standards that, who simply chose not to fight the bureaucracy. They found it less stressful to abandon their store-rooms of occasionally used chemicals, and offered them to me for my eventual needs."

Outside, the other two agents were grooving on the view, and we joined them.

"How long have you lived here?" asks Fosca.

"Off and on, since my parents bought it in 1936 or 1937."

"Did you build the house yourself?"

"Not really — I helped my parents do it, but I was away in the Navy during World War II." To myself, I thought: maybe that will help him see this as a house-not-built-with-drug-money, as well as giving him a bit of good ole United States patriotism. But then, I must remember that I am dealing with a soldier and do not know his commanding officer, and this soldier is here for cause, and I do not know the cause, although I do have some suspicions. It occurred to me that, since he had said, at some point, "I don't make the final decisions, Doctor; I'm just a soldier," I should ask the identity of that un-named commanding officer, if only to be able to relish his attempts at evading the question. Sadly, I never got up the courage to say the words, and of course he did not volunteer any name.

Back we went to the house, to rallying point number two, which was the dining room. Here, Agent Fosca sat down at the oval table, put his clipboard flat in front of him, and asked to see my records for purchases of drugs — which is standard practice for any lab inspection — and asked a few questions about my storage of reference samples. Rather than take him to them, I brought them to him, which seemed to be okay.

I brought out my two vial boxes, with their indices. "May I have copies?" asks Fosca. Sure. Wendy made copies. Also out came my chemical purchase records. Copies of all of this? No problem.

Next we went into my office. Wendy was there at her desk and smiling, bless her.

"What do you call this room?"

"My office."

I hoped silently that Fosca would see and read the plaques on the wall, given to me several years apart by the DEA for services rendered or something of that sort. They were acknowledgments of my having given freely of my knowledge of psychedelic drugs over the years, having answered many questions from agents and chemists, and having given talks to the staff of the San Francisco DEA lab.

Fosca saw the plaques and read them in silence, before resuming the questioning.

"Are there any scheduled drugs in here?"

"I don't really know," I answered, truthfully. There were many things piled on top of my filing cabinets — journals, letters, card files, anonymous samples — all bearing an accumulation of dust, and I hadn't sorted any of it out for at least six months.

"Maybe here in this bowl?" Fosca was poking around. We came up with several things, all of them interesting. A set of small MDMA vials, with my writing on them, saying something like 10 mgs. MDMA.

"Is this your writing?"

"Looks like it," I say.

"And this vial (pointing to a vial of fluid, almost full, of something called LAD) what is this?"

"I don't recall."

"Is it LSD?"

"I doubt it, or I would have called it LSD."

There was a small pile of Marinol capsules (Marinol is the government approved form of THC, the active component of marijuana, given to selected patients suffering from certain medical problems) and I explained that I had probably been asked to do an analysis for someone who thought that his capsules did not contain the right ingredients.

"Who?"

"I can't remember."

"And, this vial with something called N-hydroxy-MDMA from someone called Charles; who is Charles?"

"I can't remember."

All of these samples (taken, and completely receipted) were placed on the top of my Xerox machine, and I was asked to write my thoughts and recollections about each one, and I did my best, suffering as I did from a very poor memory. Everything was photographed.

(In case anyone fails to understand why I would not choose to identify the senders of anonymous samples, I'll just say that these samples were sent to me on the assumption — which I shared — that I had the legal right to analyze them, without having to identify the sources to any authorities. This kind of work had been done, in the past, by at least one good laboratory which considered it a public service, but they had been forced to shut it down on order of the DEA, who insisted that this kind of quality control was an aid to illegal activity. In summary, my identification of a sender of an anonymous sample — if I knew who it was or might be — would be considered by me as a complete betrayal of a trust, and an unforgivable act of cowardice. I suspect that Agent Fosca understood this, although he continued to press me for the information.)

Somewhere about this time, I asked Fosca, "If the name of a sender of an anonymous sample had been kept, as a matter of record, and if the sample proved to be a scheduled drug, and if the DEA ever chose to collect this information, might not it be used as evidence in a criminal charge against the sender?"

His answer was, "I really couldn't say."

Into Basement Four.

"What do you call this room?"

"Basement Four." I didn't tell him that the room had been my son's bedroom and that, since there were three basement rooms below the house, it had seemed logical to rename the room Basement Four when I turned it into a semi-lab and library. I had the feeling that Agent Fosca might not have quite enough whimsical humor in him to appreciate the story.

"Are there any scheduled drugs in here?"

"I have no idea."

"What is this?" He had picked up a vial labeled with black pen, "Rosa."

"Obviously a sample from someone called Rosa."

"Who is she?"

"I don't know."

"What does it contain?"

"I haven't looked at it yet."

"Are all these other samples from people, and are they scheduled drugs?"

"I don't know. I haven't analyzed them yet."

I am exhausted. They know, because I had told them when they first arrived, that my wife and I have a 5:30 date for the Berkeley Repertory Theater and that we are expected in town soon. They seem to be prepared to accommodate me. Agent Number Two writes out a longish receipt for samples taken, and then Agent Fosca tells me that he will need three or four more days to complete his inspection. He says he'll phone to make arrangements after I return from Spain. The three men leave. It has been quite a day.

Off to the conference in Spain, and let's see what's what when we return.

Act II:

The second visitation was from an equally strange place, equally beyond my control, and it occurred on Friday the 30th, in Spain, just three days later. This was an interaction with my own unconscious. I had a most vivid dream involving a large house that was constructed on four levels which, Alice assured me, took no expertise to determine that it represented a laboratory, clearly my laboratory and the several stages of visiting that I had shared with the drug authorities. It was with fine humor that Alice shared her interpretations of the three remembered aspects of this bit of symbolism.

The earliest part of the dream that I recall was of a broom sweeping up leaves. The broom was something like the bundle of twigs tied to a handle that I had seen used in France by the street sweepers who collect debris in the gutters and push it all towards the sewer drain at the end of the block.

I had a real life memory of a flower stand on a sidewalk curb, in Paris, after a day's business, with the seller cleaning up for the night. All the leaves and blossoms and wrappings were cleared off the walkway into the gutter, then pushed with the help of some water source down into the drain hole under the sidewalk. All the unsold bunches of flowers were then shoved and jammed into that same drain hole, and I had the problem of imagining the status of the Parisian sewer system that evening, with the added burden of thousands of bouquets of roses from the many flower stands throughout the city, all being pushed into sewer drains at the same time. But then, simply trying to imagine the Parisian sewer system, even without these flowers, is completely beyond me.

In my dream, I was sweeping up leaves with a Parisian street-sweeper's broom, and the leaves were all sticky and tended to clump together. It was a Sysiphean task in that all I got for my efforts were the same leaves in a somewhat different arrangement. No piles, no constructive rearrangements, simply pointless redistribution. I cannot locate the scene in relationship to the four story house; maybe it was on the roof or maybe it was in front of it. I'm pretty sure it was an outdoors location as there was some air movement, which neither helped nor hurt my futile efforts.

Another remembered detail was a milk canister, the kind that one sees alongside the mail boxes on the rural roads in farming country, where the day's production is put out to be picked up by the tanker truck from the creamery. This canister was on its side, but I did not make any connection between the stickiness of the leaves and the possible presence of milk. They were sort of separate events, unconnected at the time. I ignored the canister and stayed with the task of rearranging the leaves. I told Alice that I felt it took no remarkable insight to construct some interpretation involving spilt milk. She laughed and said she had to agree.

Efforts to tidy up were being made as the house was apparently on the market, to be sold. The basement was a very poorly constructed place, due to the fact that it had been dug out after the rest of the house was completed. There were sections of brick walls that were not quite level, and the floor was concrete and sloped in some obscure direction, and there had once been a plan of having something heavy down there, but it had been an afterthought. At the time of the dream, I had wondered about a cyclotron, but it has just occurred to me that this heavy thing concept might represent the permanent magnet of an NMR, which is what I have in Basement Four, toward the back of the room.

And the sloppiness, the not quite levelness in the dream, was detectable in much of the rest of the construction of the house. Nothing quite fit. Doors didn't close well, drawers stuck, rain leaked in on occasion, and somewhere there was a desk or counter top that was clearly not level. But on it was something, maybe a balance, or computer, that was indeed level. I tried to bring into accord the non-levelness and the levelness, and it never quite came together. I can hear the interpretation now from my dear spouse, involving stuck drawers, not-quite closed doors, cyclotrons or NMR magnets in the basement, spectrophotometers that have functions that may be seen by visitors as being not quite on the level, spilt milk and all that.

I wonder if, with a little practice, I might be able some day to interpret my own dreams, without having to call on Alice for help. Are they all this obvious? That dream, at least, was pretty blatant.

I am writing this in Spain, during the almost three weeks that immediately followed the surprise visit. This is a marvelous time for reflection but it has the added twist that if there is a paranoid fantasy or pessimistic scenario available, my mind will act it out. There are obviously more acts of this play, but they cannot yet be written as the script is not under my control.

Just what is the problem? Who has been offended that is of sufficient clout to justify this kind of inspection? What is the "for cause" that convinced the judge to issue the search warrant that permitted this kind of fishing expedition to take place?

To bed, and sweeter dreams which I will not have cause to remember.

(Alice's voice)

A couple of days after our return from Spain, Agent Fosca phoned, as he had promised, to make an appointment for a continuation of the inspection. Shura agreed to keep Thursday open, even though he usually goes to the Owl Club on Thursdays around 3:30 p.m. to play his viola in the orchestra. He told me it was worth losing one evening of rehearsal to get this DEA thing over and done with, and I agreed.

I have to admit that, up to this point, my attitude toward the intense inspection of three weeks before was one of uneasy guilt, mixed with real bewilderment. Guilt, because I had been forced to see our neglected little vials and sample envelopes through the eyes of what I still believed was a very, maybe over-conscientious, dedicated agent, who was not enchanted by our magical, artistic mess, and saw only a lack of good housekeeping and basic inattention to the need for reasonable precautions.

The bewilderment was still there because of the unanswered question: why had the previous inspection teams found nothing amiss under exactly the same circumstances? I had certainly a strong suspicion, as did Shura, that official anger about our book PIHKAL, back in Washington, had fueled the intensity of the inspection, but I felt that it must still have been our fault; Shura's failure to stay abreast of the regulation changes, and my failure to insist on taking everything to do with drugs out of the house and into the lab. Of course, Shura and I considered the office and Basement Four as extensions of the lab, but I could understand that official outsiders might well see it differently.

Our friend, Paul, had phoned several times from his new home in Oregon, and told us he couldn't imagine what Agent Fosca was talking about, with all this violations of regulations stuff, which cheered us both somewhat, but only momentarily. Perhaps Agent Fosca was new on the job, and a stickler for rules, and we would just have to deal with it as best we could.

So, on Thursday morning, when Shura returned from the mailbox with the Chronicle tucked under his arm, he left the big farm gate unlocked. We managed to finish reading the paper with our morning coffee before 9:00 a.m., when we expected Agent Fosca and his two sidekicks to return.

At three minutes after nine, we heard the sound of engines and went outside to stand together in the little patio, smiles ready.

The first thing to appear up on the paved parking area was a small, square grey truck with the word, "Decontamination," stenciled on its side. It pulled up to the left of the garage. Behind it came Agent Fosca's red car; behind that, a huge yellow fire truck, which parked right above us, facing the house. Then, as we watched in mouth-open astonishment, a brown sedan found a space to the right of the grey truck. People were getting out of the first cars as yet another one, blue this time, drove up and parked. The rest of them we couldn't see from the patio, but the total for the day — I discovered later from Shura — was eight vehicles.

We stood there, Shura and I, while people of both sexes, in all sizes, wearing dark pants and jackets, bustled here and there, some of them calling out to each other, sounding cheerful. I could see white letters stenciled on the backs of the jackets. Some said, "DEA," others said, "Sheriff's Department," and one said, "State Narcotics." People were walking down the brick steps dressed in silvery moon suits with helmets. A portable shower was sticking out of the top of the decontamination truck, and the whole thing — funny little square vehicle with a dinky little shower head on a pole — looked as if it had materialized out of a cartoon by Gary Larsen.

Jaws dropped, mouths gaping, we stood there, watching this flood of cars and people as if it were a movie. Then Agent Fosca and a short, round-faced man in his forties came down the small stairway to the patio. The strange man held up a piece of paper about three feet from Shura's face and intoned, "Doctor Borodin, I have here a warrant to search these premises," and Agent Fosca, somewhat more diffidently, held out his own piece of paper and explained, "This is a renewal of the warrant we showed you last time."

For a small, endless moment, my one concern was that either Shura or I might have a heart attack, or a stroke. I'm sure we were white with shock. Our house, our sacred space, our beloved home, was about to be clawed at, taken apart, dismantled. The image that most horrified me was of strangers carrying out our files of correspondence, letters written over the years by people who felt they could tell us things they couldn't share with anyone else; people who might have signed names and addresses to long, moving accounts of life-changing LSD trips, or sessions with depressed, anxious friends, using that greatest of all therapy drugs, MDMA; people who could now be watched, followed, challenged and harassed, all because they had trusted us, not only to read and appreciate their stories — and perhaps answer their questions — but to make sure that their letters didn't fall into the wrong hands.

Shura, as he told me later, thought they were also going to take his computers and his reference files.

The stocky man was saying something. I caught the word, "Sump," and tried to focus on what was happening in front of me.

"This warrant entitles us to inspect the grounds around your laboratory and the location known as the sump for hazardous wastes," I heard, and suddenly relief poured through me like cool water. The man, probably aware of our state of shock — or at least seeing the blank incomprehension in our faces — was repeating what he'd just said, something about being from the County Environmental Protection Agency or some such, and the warrant was to enable him to —

"Sump," I said, turning to Shura; "Sump," he breathed back to me.

He managed a slight smile as he turned to the older official, "Sure, I understand. You have to do your job."

"Thank you," said that gentleman, heartily, "If we can have your cooperation, it'll all go faster, and we can get out of here that much sooner."

"Yes, yes," said I, suddenly able to move again, "Would you like some tea or coffee or mineral water?" I paused on my way back into the house.

"No, thank you, Ma'am, we've brought our own stuff. We'll be just fine."

Another middle-aged officer, his blue jacket declaring, in white letters, SHERIFF'S DEPARTMENT, asked me, "Is there anybody else besides you and the Doctor — here in the house, Ma'am?"

I said no, there was nobody else here.

*Big uncle type, comfy paunch, business-like, but seems sort of benign.*

I walked, arms folded, into the kitchen, wondered for a moment why I was there, and decided it was to pour myself another cup of coffee. Shura walked in behind me and muttered something about where did he put his coffee mug, then found it on the dining room table, and held it out to me for a refill.

We looked at each other, just for an instant, just long enough to see what we were feeling reflected in the other's eyes. We both knew what we had to do: be friendly, as casual as possible, hang slightly loose; innocent people with nothing to hide who were understandably upset by this invasion, but eager to cooperate. Et cetera, et cetera. The anger could wait until we were alone.

Shura went back outside, and I heard a loud voice from the hallway, "There's a locked door here; what do I do?"

I peered into the shadows of the hall and saw the officer who had asked me about other people in the house. He was twisting the knob of our bedroom door, and I called out to him, "It isn't locked. It just sticks a bit."

He turned his large, friendly face to me and said, "Thank you," and pushed the door open.

*Oh, shit! I haven't made the bed yet and everything's a shambles.*

Our bedroom was always off limits to anyone else. It was our private place, and it was always messy, due to my habit of piling clean clothes which I was too lazy to hang up on top of boxes of unsorted photographs, on top of backpacks I hadn't unpacked from the last trip, and so on and so on. Shura never complained, which always amazed me and made me deeply grateful, although no less guilty. He knew I'd eventually sort the whole mountain of stuff out, and the room would be neat and tidy, the tiled floors mopped, nothing out of place, for about 48 hours, before the accumulation began again.

I stood behind the officer, squinting past him at the familiar mess, and said some apologetic things about the unmade bed, while he looked behind the door and quickly scanned the room. He said, "Don't worry about that, Ma'am; I just have to make sure there's nobody else here." He closed the door behind him and continued down the hall, presumably to check the other rooms.

*So my word isn't enough; he still has to check it out. Okay.*

A second thought occurred to me: whom was he addressing, when he called out, "What do I do?" Was it Agent Fosca? If so, did that mean Fosca was the Big Honcho in this whole Super Inspection, or whatever you'd call it? Did the DEA always outrank everybody else in this sort of undertaking?

I went back to the kitchen and poured myself a glass of water and opened the freezer to get ice cubes. I heard Fosca's voice outside on the patio, raised slightly to carry over the noise of the small crowd around him, "Would you accompany us to the lab, Doctor Borodin, if you please?"

Shura's voice replied, "Certainly. Glad to."

My tall white-maned magician led Fosca through the dining room, down the hallway and through the back door — as he had done the last time — probably only vaguely aware of the number of people following him. There was a tall, heavy man in a light grey suit and red tie, with a tight, hard face; following him, a short, dark-haired woman who gave me a quick smile; she was wearing a jacket that said DEA, and carried a camera case; after her came a young, open-faced Japanese gentleman, whose jacket proclaimed

STATE NARCOTICS, and finally, a slender man in his 40's with curly hair and a pleasant, intelligent face, dressed in slacks and tweed jacket, who inclined his head briefly in greeting as he passed by me.

I stood, ice water in hand, as the crowd made their way outside, and saw my old friend, Officer Uncle, returning from his room check. He came up to me and asked, "Ma'am, do you have any guns in the house?"

Oh, God, I thought and said, "Yes, I have one."

"Where is it, Ma'am?"

I whispered, "Under my bed."

*That's funny. Why did I have to whisper? Probably because there's an instinct to be secretive about having a gun and about where you keep it. Jesus, I hope he's not going to go back into the bedroom and look under the bed; he'll see all the dust, and I'll die of embarrassment forever.*

But all he said was, "Okay. Just don't go into the bedroom, Ma'am, until we're all through, if you don't mind."

I actually smiled with relief. "Oh, I won't, sir. I promise you I won't."

*I guess I don't look the dangerous type. That's good.*

Suddenly, it occurred to me that this whole extraordinary event, this — what would you call it? — polite invasion, vehicles, people, moon suits, everything, should be photographed for posterity. Or at least for us to enjoy, maybe on cold winter evenings in front of a fire. I could imagine us leafing through the album and saying to each other, "Remember this? All those people with guns in their belts, the cute little decontamination truck, the warrants, the guys in moon suits, ah, what an amazing day that was!"

I went and got the camera.

Just as I was aiming it at the cars and trucks and the uniformed people lounging against their bumpers, above the house in the parking area, a male voice behind me said, "Ah, please don't do that, Ma'am," and I turned to see another member of the Sheriff's Department, a younger man this time, who was looking anxious and apologetic.

"What's the matter?" I asked, although I already knew the answer.

"We'd rather you didn't take pictures, Ma'am, if you don't mind," he said, "Because, you know, some of the officers are undercover, and it wouldn't — ah —,"

"Oh, of course," I said, locking the camera and putting it down on the dining room table, "I didn't think about that."

*Dammit. I'd give anything to have photos. Maybe I can put on my tape recorder without anyone knowing. What if they find out? Could get angry. Don't want anyone angry. Keep it peaceful and friendly, and we may survive all this — whatever it is.*

I went into the living room and sat down on my old blue couch, and thought to myself, how strange it was that the police, the authorities, could use cameras and tape recorders all over the place (although I hadn't actually seen tape recorders yet) but when I wanted to take photographs and tape conversations to document what was happening during this invasion of strangers, I not only wasn't allowed to, I actually felt like a criminal for wanting to do such a thing.

*That's very interesting. Why do I feel a faint sense of criminality when I think of getting things these people say on tape? Why should anyone feel they're doing something wrong if they try to record what authorities do and say? Am I identifying with the police's view of what's going on? Am I being sucked into their reality? What is their reality, then? That they are the Right people, doing the Right things, and that the rest of us are Wrong, or at least less Right than they are? And taping the police, or photographing them, is a sign of disrespect. Why? Because — because it implies that we Wrongies may be trying to catch the Righties in a mistake, maybe an important mistake. And that's disrespectful. And only the criminally inclined are disrespectful towards authorities. THAT'S IT! THAT'S IT! What brilliant thinking, by George! Brilliant!*

It might have been a rather elaborate way of getting some slight satisfaction out of this appalling day, but it felt good, and I realized I was grinning broadly, for a small, bright and pleasantly criminal moment.

I turned on the television, but couldn't concentrate on anything, even CNN. All I got out of watching the news was a nasty reminder of an old realization that the world outside, for the most part anyway, hadn't the slightest understanding of what Shura and I did, what we believed in or what we were willing to fight for. And if they did know, they would be shocked and outraged. Psychedelic drugs as research tools to understand the human mind, the human unconscious? Psychedelic drugs as tools of spiritual searching? Psychedelic drugs as ways of touching the spiritual dimension, and whatever it is we tentatively call God, The Great Spirit, the Ground of Being, and a thousand other names? Never heard of such rubbish, most of them would say.

I turned off the television and walked back toward the kitchen. As I came through the door, I could hear a male voice on the patio saying, "And he describes what it's like, you know, what you feel if you take them at different dosages, what happens if you —" but the speaking stopped as someone in his audience apparently caught sight of me. The voice had been enthusiastic and admiring, not antagonistic. I glanced outside, casually, wearing my usual friendly half-smile, as I passed by the glass doors and headed down the hall. What I saw was the young Japanese man from State Narcotics, perched on a brick ledge, facing a group of five officers seated around the patio table, under the big canvas umbrella, some of them eating lunch. There were shiny red and green soft drink cans on the white metal surface.

*Oh, that's right; these people bring their own food and drink so they don't have to risk being poisoned or something in a suspect's house.*

So he's read *PIHKAL* and he liked it, I thought, with a rush of affection for the one person in this whole pile of law enforcement who might have some positive feelings towards us.

I had nowhere to go in the hallway, so I went out the back door and stood there for a few moments, wondering what to do next. Then I heard voices, far down the dirt path that led to the lab.

*They're coming back. Wonder what happened this time.*

Up the hallway again. I was wearing only socks on my feet, so nobody could hear me coming. Which is why I was able to catch the tail end of a sentence spoken by the same big, grey-suited, unfriendly looking man I'd seen following Shura to the lab, earlier. He was standing with his back to me and I heard him clearly say, "— up to me, they'd demolish this whole damned place, just bring in a fucking bulldozer and plow it under," and his right hand made a wide, all-inclusive sweep in the air.

*Who the hell is THAT? He dresses civilian, I've never seen him before today, and he obviously hates us. Who is he and what's he doing here?*

There was an uncomfortable silence as I came into view, moving purposefully toward the kitchen, again. I thought once more of trying to sneak a tape recorder into some corner of the dining room, near enough to the sliding glass doors to perhaps catch conversation on the patio, but I couldn't think of any way to do it without being seen.

*Aha! Maybe if I take a drinking glass into the storage room, I can put it against the outer wall and hear what's being said outside on the patio. Won't hurt to try.*

I stepped down into the little room with its shelves and shelves of everything from instant rice to light bulbs, carrying with me a clean glass which I put, for the moment, next to a batch of evaporated milk cans. The corner of the room next to the wall was piled high with cardboard flats of cat food cans, and I began, in the almost-dark (I hadn't turned on the light), to lift the cardboard flats out of my way, stacking them in the middle of the floor. Suddenly, I was startled by a loud knock, and came around the edge of the open door to see who it was, a flat of small cans still in my hands.

A young female officer, rather short and chunky in her blue jacket, but with a round, pretty face, peered in at me and asked, "Would it be all right if I used your bathroom, Ma'am?"

"Yes, of course. It's the door next to this, to your right. You don't have to ask my permission; use it any time you want!"

*Well, she's seen me here, in the shadows, holding a flat of cans, apparently busy. There's no way I can stand in the corner, holding a glass to the wall, now. I could only have done that if nobody knew I was in here. I'll just have to leave and take the flat into the kitchen, and look as if I'm busy doing something that makes sense. Too bad. I would have enjoyed at least TRYING to overhear them.*

By the time the lady had come out of the bathroom, I had opened two of the little cans and was obviously carrying them somewhere, presumably to feed cats. She smiled at me and said, "Thank you; that feels better!" and we both laughed.

*I guess there's nothing like the joy of relieving a full bladder to forge a bond between strangers.*

When I returned from the cat porch (actually, considering the cast of characters who scrambled up there every night to feed on the cats' leftovers, it should have been called the "cat-raccoon-'possum porch"), three people were seated at the dining table. Agent Fosca had his back to me, Shura was opposite him and at the head of the table was the slender man with the tweed jacket and intelligent face who had nodded to me earlier as he followed the group going to the lab.

Fosca had his big yellow legal pad in front of him again. Shura was leaning an elbow on a stack of record books, engaged in conversation with Tweed Jacket. As I came into the kitchen, a few feet away from them, Shura looked up and made a grand gesture toward the stranger, telling me, "Alice, this is Mr. Joseph Goode from Washington. He's a chemist!"

Mr. Goode rose halfway from his chair, smiling; I nodded to him and sat down in my usual place, a carved captain's chair on the border between dining room and kitchen, where the smoke from my cigarette wouldn't intrude on people at the table.

For the next couple of hours, I sat and watched a three part drama, starring an increasingly frustrated DEA agent who kept trying to get answers to detailed questions from a slightly manic chemical genius, who was finding it easier to make himself understood to an obviously interested and even enthusiastic chief DEA chemist. The possibility that I might be watching the game called, "Good cop, bad cop," never entered my mind.

(Mr. Goode turned out, as we discovered later, to be the most highly-placed administrator in the DEA's headquarters, who had once been a chemist and knew the jargon; he'd been flown out from Washington, D.C., where he headed up the main DEA testing lab, just to join this investigation and act as interpreter of Shura's sophisticated chemistry-language to Agent Fosca.)

I watched Mr. Goode doing his best to translate the chemical concepts and ideas to the agent, while occasionally being distracted by the fun of the chemistry that was pouring out of Shura. At times, Fosca would draw a deep breath and complain, politely, that he wasn't getting the specific answers he needed for his report, at which both Shura and Goode would calm down and turn their heads towards the agent, and Mr. Goode would translate and explain, slowly and carefully, while Shura's eyes lost their twinkle briefly, and I could see in his face that he had remembered, yet again, where he was and what was going on at this table.

What I heard, generally speaking, were exchanges like this:

"This item here, do you have a record of that purchase?"

"Yes, of course, let me get it for you."

"I would like to take this with me, if you don't mind."

"Certainly, feel free!"

"Why do you have this amount of 2C-B in a bottle in your lab?"

"As I told you earlier, I use it for —" and he repeated what he had said in the lab.

(Followed by translation by Mr. Goode.)

"What do you use (this or that material or solvent) for?"

"Well, mostly I use it for —," then a rapid-fire list of chemical compounds, or intermediate steps to them.

(Translation by Mr. Goode.)

By this time, it was obvious even to me that this was not the kind of inspection we'd had before, and that Mr. Agent Fosca was doing more than just being over-conscientious. And Fosca didn't seem to have any satisfactory answer to the question that both Shura and I had asked three weeks earlier, and were asking again today. At one point, when Shura had gone to the office to get something, I asked it once more, "Why didn't our good friend, Paul, and all the previous inspectors who saw exactly the same conditions, tell us that something was out of order?"

Fosca shifted his chair so that he could glance in my direction, while still making notes on his pad. He said, "Well, sometimes friends don't like to say things; you know how it is. And it's also possible that your friend Paul didn't know all the regulations that applied to your license. He was an administrator, after all, not a lab specialist."

I persisted, "But the DEA inspectors should have known the regulations. Why didn't they say anything?"

Mr. Fosca looked at me and replied, a faint touch of impatience in his voice, "They were probably incompetent inspectors, Ma'am. Unfortunately, not all our inspectors are as good as they should be."

I still didn't get the message; I leaned forward, "Both teams of inspectors, Mr. Fosca? All four of them incompetent?"

This time, his impatience was obvious. He looked down at his papers and back up at me, and said abruptly, "It happens, Ma'am; sad to say, it happens."

*Incompetent. He can't possibly mean that. Is he making a joke? No, this man isn't joking. He's telling me — us — that this is his answer, and this is the way the story is going to be told. He's saying, Give It Up, Drop It.*

I was finally beginning to understand.

It had certainly taken me long enough.

Shortly after Shura returned to the table, the young Japanese State agent came in and made a remark to him, in a distinctly friendly voice, that no signs of criminal activity had been found, anywhere, and that the Good Doctor should keep in mind that this was merely a regulatory inspection. He was obviously trying to be reassuring; he also sounded relieved.

*Well at least they've played it straight; they didn't plant anything on us, thank God.*

The next act of the play took place in mid-afternoon, when Mr. Goode and Shura had left the table for the moment, to hunt down some reference in the office. Agent Fosca had changed his seat to the side of the table opposite me, and he drew out of his briefcase a large file of papers. Even from where I sat, across the room, I recognized a blurred photocopy of an interview with Shura and myself, which had been published by the interviewer, several months earlier, in a well-known counterculture magazine, (although we had given the interview for a book that was being written, not for publication in any magazine). It had amused and slightly annoyed us, when we saw the article in print, but we'd forgotten about it, until now. I said, brightly, "I see you've got a copy of the Flying High article!"

Fosca looked up at me and replied, in absolute seriousness, "Yes. You're famous," he said, "And your fame has saved you."

"What?" I was dumbfounded. What did he mean, our fame had saved us? From what?

*Besides, we don't have fame. Fame is the cover of Newsweek or Time. We're just well-known in a very small, specialized world.*

"Did you ever give scheduled drugs to the people in your research group?" asked Fosca, changing the subject.

My stomach twisted. What an idiotic question, I thought.

"No, Mr. Fosca," I said, "Please keep in mind that the book is fiction. The story part of it, I mean. Fiction."

"Yes, well," said Fosca, "A lot of people don't think it's fiction."

"Well, it is, Mr. Fosca. No matter what people may think."

"If I ever hear from any of your research group," continued Mr. Fosca of the DEA, "If any one of them ever comes to me and tells me that you gave them scheduled drugs —"

"Well, that's not likely, Mr. Fosca, because it never happened."

*Fosca has goofed. He shouldn't have let himself get into any kind of discussion about PIHKAL. This whole nasty business is not supposed to have anything to do with a book. It's purely a matter of regulations and making sure*

*Shura is doing things safely and legally. Nothing to do with a book. But at least I know for sure, now, what this is all about. It's called headquarters being mad as hell about PIHKAL. It's called letting us know who has the power, who has the clout, and who has to be feared.*

When Shura and Mr. Goode returned and took their seats at the table, the questioning continued, most of it around specific amounts of certain precursors which had been ordered from this or that chemical supply company. Then, finally, Mister Fosca was finished.

At this point, the strangest — and certainly the most schizophrenic — of all the events of the day took place. Agent Fosca was standing, packing up his notes, pads and various pieces of paper he had taken from Shura, when two jacketed men made their way into the dining room. Each of them held a copy of *PIHKAL*, and they asked Shura if he would autograph their rather worn books. He said he'd be delighted, and asked me to add my signature. Sure, said I, and obliged. Then a third agent (whose identifying back I couldn't see) asked if he might buy a copy. Of course, we said, and Shura brought out two books, and stripped the shrink-wrap off one of them, to allow for autographing. Another agent picked it up and began leafing through the pages, muttering, "Interesting, interesting," so we urged him to accept the second book as a gift, neither of us being sure that he could do so, under these rather peculiar circumstances. After a moment's hesitation, he thanked us and requested that we autograph the copy, which we did with genuine pleasure.

Mr. Fosca, having tucked his papers inside a briefcase, left the table and headed down the hallway in the direction of Basement Four. I watched him go, wondering if he was embarrassed, angry, or completely indifferent to the book-signing.

*Did they ask Fosca ahead of time if they could do this, or is it all a surprise to him, too? Wonder how he feels about it. He can't be too pleased. How nice a thing to have happened! How totally crazy and nice!*

Shura's facade of pleasantness cracked only once, when — toward the end of the visit — the big Uncle-policeman who had asked me, hours before, whether I had a gun, poked his head around the sliding glass door and asked, "Do you have any peyote cactus here, Ma'am?"

I answered, "Yes, of course, right behind you, against the wall."

There were several people on the patio, and every one of them froze, as if I had pointed out a boa constrictor in a corner. Then Uncle chuckled, "I *thought* so! I just had a feeling...."

Suddenly, there was a lot of activity around our little cactus friends. Somebody asked Shura why he had peyote cactus growing in pots, and Shura, seated at the dining table, talked through the open glass doors to the men outside, telling them about the completely unknown and un-named trace alkaloids which no one had yet analyzed. He spoke enthusiastically, comfortable in the knowledge that his license covered his possession of the cacti.

A short, heavy Asian man in his forties, with a large, tight face, pushed his way forward and leaned against the edge of the sliding door. He looked at Shura and spoke very clearly, emphasizing every word, "Doctor Borodin, we are going to have to take your peyote cactuses away. They are going to have to be destroyed. Do you understand?"

Shura rose, his face showing disbelief. "But I have a legal right to possess them, sir," he said, "My DEA license covers them; please check the regulations, and you'll find that I'm right."

Someone else spoke up, "Go get Fosca."

While Fosca was being summoned, the group of agents moved this way and that, looking down at the cacti, stooping down to examine them more closely, pointing out various interesting details to their companions. I leaned forward in my captain's chair, watching them.

*Well, well, so these DEA agents don't recognize peyote when it's right under their noses! Weird. When I pointed them out, they acted as if the poor little things might fly up and bite them. They're actually frightened of them, or is it that they're scared of what they think some of that cactus can do inside their heads or their souls? That's more like it. They've heard words like "crazy," and "psychotic," and they imagine all sorts of terrible amorphous horrors, because everyone's told them that's what you get when you eat a piece of one of these little soft green things.*

Agent Fosca came on the scene, and the stocky Asian man with the angry face took his arm and pointed at the cacti. Then he pulled Fosca off to the side of the patio and spoke urgently into his ear. Shura waited by the glass doors, eyes riveted on the two men. After a moment, Fosca walked over to where Shura stood and said, almost apologetically, "I'm afraid the cacti will have to go, Doctor Borodin."

"But I've been keeping them for years to do analytical work on them. Where in the regulations does it say I can't keep a peyote to do analysis for the alkaloids?"

"Show me," replied Fosca, "Where there's a cut, or where you've taken a slice; there isn't any sign of work being done on any of them, is there?"

"Not yet," said Shura, desperately, "I haven't had time yet. But that's what they're here for —"

He was interrupted by the Asian gentleman, who brought his face within a foot of Shura's and spat out, "We are taking the cactuses, Doctor, and if you keep on arguing about it, I'm going to have to read you your rights and put on the handcuffs. Am I making myself clear?"

He squinted at Shura long enough to see that he had made his point, then turned and gestured to the other men. They stooped and got to work.

Shura sat down again, slowly, like an old man with painful joints. There was no way to help it; all the people in that patio could tell they'd wounded him. I swore to myself that they would not read hurt in my face, but it didn't matter; Shura was the target, and they'd gotten to him. He was the one they wanted to punish, and Mr. Fosca and his hostile friend had the satisfaction, finally, of tearing the mask of cheerful pleasantness off Shura and exposing the helpless anger and sorrow underneath it.

The peyote were his darlings, his treasures, his honored and respected friends, full of mysteries called alkaloids, mysteries called Time and Space and Pattern and Meaning; it had taken ten years for the baby peyotes to grow to the modest size they now were, and before our eyes they were being ripped out of their pots and trampled under boots. We both turned our heads away.

*It's done. Even if they apologize later, it's done. If I were not on another path, I would be tremendously tempted to shape a curse on these people. But it would be wrong; it would poison me to carry that kind of hate inside. They even believe it's all right to enjoy a moment of triumph over a person like Shura, to enjoy his pain, because he's the Bad Man, the enemy, and they are the Good and Righteous. And it's okay. They'll die, some day, then they'll understand what they've done. They'll feel exactly what we're feeling right now, and they'll see what the Divine Cactus really is.*

By 5:00 p.m. it was all over. They were gone, leaving behind a promise by Mr. Fosca to return the next day for more questions and answers.

Late that night, curled up together in our bed, we summarized and speculated and reassured each other, and Shura said, "After all, keep in mind that, if this were Guatemala or Bolivia, they would simply have stood us up against the patio wall and executed us, right?"

"You have a point. And they didn't plant anything, either."

"So it isn't all bad."

"And they didn't take the house apart and they didn't remove our letters and computers."

"They still could, you know; they still might."

"No, honey," I said, "Tomorrow, we get in touch with that lawyer you liked when you talked with him over the phone, remember? You said he sounded intelligent and to the point and if you ever needed a lawyer ..."

"Yes, yes. Good idea. Cassman. First thing tomorrow, I'll give him a call."

"And we'll take every damned piece of correspondence out of here and — well, we'll put them somewhere safe."

"Let's wait and see what the lawyer advises."

"And we can back up all our writing and put the floppies in the care of friends, just in case they do take the computers," I added, not really believing that was going to happen, at this point.

"Remember," said Shura, "Tomorrow, the bastards are coming back for the last mop-up."

"You know, they were really amazingly polite, all in all. They even asked permission to use the bathroom. Wonder why they were so polite?"

"Stomping little peyote cacti under foot is not what I call good manners," he said, and the hurt was back again. I hugged him and kept quiet.

Fosca did return on Friday, this time with one fellow agent. The questioning took only a couple of hours, and was mostly a review of what had been asked and answered the previous day. The one important — and new — statement from Mr. Fosca was as follows:

"Washington wants your license, Dr. Borodin. That's the bottom line."

Shura, calm and quiet and not smiling today, said, "I assumed as much."

There was a discussion about whether, by offering to relinquish the license without a battle, Shura might guarantee that he would not be fined or further attacked by County, State or Federal authorities. And Agent Fosca repeated what he had said the day before, "It's not up to me, Doctor; I'm just a soldier, doing my job."

*And although we're sure we know who the General is, we'll never prove it. And what good would it do if we could? He gave the order, and it must have gone like this: "Get the bastard. Close him down. He's an embarrassment to us, with this book, and I want our license off his wall. Anyway you can manage it. Keep it legal, but get that license from him." Yes, something like that. But one thing they can't do; they can't stop us from writing. They can't stop the information from going out. There's the First Amendment to the Constitution, and it's still alive and well. Maybe not forever, the way things are going, but long enough.*

Finally, the Great Inspection was over. Or appeared to be.

A few days later, we went to the law offices of Mr. Ted Cassman, who turned out to be sharply intelligent, with a marvelously wry smile and a gently sardonic sense of humor, and told him our story.

The day after that, Shura and I brought carton after carton of letters — correspondence going back more than a decade — to the law offices, and left them there, as we'd been given permission to do by our new attorney.

What did we learn from all this? For one thing, that what one DEA inspector, years before, had referred to in his reports as a "quaint" laboratory, could be described by a later one in *his* report, as a "pigsty;" that just because you have absolute certainty as to your own rightness and the value and merit of what you do, you are not immune — nobody is immune — to attack by others who believe equally strongly that you are mistaken, wrong, and perhaps even truly "bad." For the most part, however, if the people you have annoyed are part of the government, their actions against you will be motivated less by beliefs or philosophies which run counter to your own, than by the simple desire to remind you that they have far more power than you do, and that, even if you don't fear that power, you should at least have a healthy respect for it.

(If you don't want, or can't afford, to take the risk of bringing down on your head some of the weight of the Great Grey Battleship of Government Authority, get out of the game and keep quiet.)

We also learned that, despite hostility and desire to punish, in this case at least, one government agency played it straight and did not do anything illegal. They did pull a few dirty tricks, as explained below, and lies were told, but nothing was planted on us, and soil samples were not doctored.

Finally, there was one lesson learned which was quite unexpected, and perhaps among the most valuable, since it had to do with human behavior. It was an insight into what I call the prosecutorial mind-set, and I had never understood this aspect of it before we saw it in action. I can put it this way: when people who are in law enforcement go into a place (in our case, a home) where there is a possibility of finding something amiss, they do not think, "I wonder if this person (suspect) is guilty of wrongdoing or not?" They do seem to go in thinking, "What can we find here which will help us make a case against this individual?"

The mind-set is one of assumption that something wrong has been done, whether it is a civil or criminal matter. The truth is, anyone who has spent time in law-enforcement of any kind, at any level — from beat cop to district attorney — gets used to people being found guilty of breaking regulations or laws. After a certain time, an unconscious assumption takes root, "If he weren't guilty, he wouldn't be under suspicion." Considering their day-to-day experiences, it is understandable that they should develop this perspective, but it is not good, either for them as individuals, or for the community which they serve.

Aftermath:

As I've explained earlier, the men in moon suits had been called in by the DEA to take samples of soil, both from the sump outside the lab, and from portions of the hill in that same area. It wasn't hard to guess that the DEA hoped to have the State Environmental Protection people do what the DEA wanted done: find severe pollution and order Shura's lab destroyed as a hazard to the community.

All the moon suits found, however, was a fraction too much mercury in one soil sample, and Shura followed up with the right sequence of actions, involving expensive soil-removal companies with steel drums and special trucks, who hauled away the offending yards of dirt. There were no other complaints.

Some months later, the DEA, obviously frustrated, brought in the Federal Environmental Protection Agency, hoping that *they* would do a better job. Their representatives were friendly, and made some suggestions, such as a fan to be set in the wall, to better ventilate the lab (Shura complied immediately), and a few other, very reasonable precautions against glass test tubes falling off shelves in an earthquake (Shura got to work on the problem), and these inspectors, too, declined to report the laboratory as a threat to humanity.

The magical laboratory still stands. In their official paper detailing their reasons for wanting Shura to relinquish his license, Agent Fosca reported that he felt extremely ill the day following the Thursday inspection, which he attributed to unknown hazardous influences in the lab air. Shura and I remember him clearly, that very same day-after, sitting with the single fellow agent, telling us about two *other* agents from the Thursday event who had fallen ill and couldn't come to work, after having breathed the air of the Dangerous Lab. Fosca, himself, was obviously fit and healthy, and did not claim to have felt any noxious, toxic effects.

We were told, later, that much of the film shot within the lab that Thursday, when developed, was unaccountably flawed and browned. Unusable. (When we heard that, we laughed and laughed, and I whistled the Twilight Zone theme.)

Not long after that Thursday, Mr. Fosca (with one fellow agent in tow) paid a visit to our friend Peter's laboratory in a San Francisco hospital, where Shura works once a week, doing research on nicotine. Mr. Fosca was more of a bully with the young Dr. Seltzer. He was, in fact, quite aggressive, mistaking Peter's quiet gentleness for weakness. Peter is, indeed, a very polite person, but his tolerance for rudeness is extremely limited, and he reached a boiling point within minutes; he gritted his teeth and continued answering questions, but an anger began to burn which was still throwing off sparks six months later.

Among other things, Mr. Fosca, it turned out, insisted on seeing "All your phenethylamines," which was a foolish request, since the only phenethylamines present in the lab (as Peter told him) were reference samples, of no use to anyone except as analytical standards in various chromatographic assays. However, the demand made glaringly clear that Mr. Fosca was focused on the main subject of *PIHKAL* — phenethylamines

— not on scheduled drugs in particular (the laboratory has its own DEA license) or on safety conditions or correct lab procedures. He didn't ask to be shown tryptamines; he didn't make a request for opiates; he didn't show any interest in stimulants; Mr. Fosca's insistence on seeing specifically any and all phenethylamines was tantamount to an admission that this lab inspection, too, was in reprisal for the publication of a book that had "Phenethylamines" in its title.

It was also a not very subtle attempt to poison the working conditions for one employee, Dr. Alexander Borodin.

A couple of mean-spirited actions (in the time of Watergate, this kind of thing was known as Dirty Tricks) were taken by person or persons unknown, after the Great Invasion. One day, a man representing the DEA, but otherwise not identified to Shura, made a phone call to an administrator at the Langley Porter Psychiatric Institute, with which Shura was linked by his job at the research lab.

To the administrator, the un-named man said, in effect, "Why do you employ a man like Doctor Borodin? Don't you realize he's one of the worst environmental polluters in the county?" The bewildered administrator mentioned the call to Peter, who told him what was going on, and informed him what the EPA inspectors had really found: of several samples taken and analyzed, one contained an amount of mercury just above the acceptable limit. It was easily cleaned up, and there were no other problems.

Second of the dirty tricks: two large chemical supply companies, with whom Shura had maintained a good business relationship for over 25 years, suddenly informed him that their rules of doing business had changed and that they, regretfully, had found it necessary to close his accounts with them. It was not, of course, possible to prove pressure by the authorities, and there would have been nothing gained by doing so.

The seemingly nice, sympathetic DEA chemist, Mr. Goode, upon meeting a friend of ours at a Washington, D.C. social function, was asked, "I hear you met the famous Doctor Borodin out West; what was your impression of him?" To which Mr. Goode replied, stiffly, "I haven't the slightest idea what you're talking about; I've never met the man," then turned and walked away.

Shura's possession of the peyote cacti was confirmed as being perfectly legal under his license. There was only one reason to destroy them, which was to cause pain.

A year later, having faced the fact that a court battle to retain his license would cost more than we could possibly afford, and realizing that in the end, he would undoubtedly be found guilty of having broken DEA lab rules (ignorance of the law is no excuse), Shura relinquished his analytical license and submitted to a heavy fine of $25,000, levied by a local deputy District Attorney who dismissed out of hand the suggestion that what was being attacked was, in truth, not broken rules, but a book.

Never again will Shura work with a sense of absolute freedom; he's had a taste of that particular form of power-flexing peculiar to people who are employed by government agencies. The authorities intended to frighten him and perhaps they even hoped to silence him, but that is not and will not be possible, while we are alive and able to speak and write. We felt, and still feel, that drug use is the right of a free adult citizen, as long as there is information supplied as to proper and safe use of each drug. Drug abuse, we believe, should be the concern of the medical community, not the police. We are far from alone in this point of view, but it runs counter to the presently accepted official policy in this country.

Education and legal access would, almost overnight, eliminate the drug cartels, the street wars and inner city killings associated with the drug/money/power circuit. But the education would have to be just that: education, *not* propaganda. (Several generations of high school and college students have grown up ignoring and disbelieving everything they've heard from officials and police about drugs, including information that was factual and valid, because they had discovered for themselves that most of what had been taught them was simply not true.)

Nobody in a position of real power and influence in government has the courage to say, publicly:

> "We made a mistake. Certain drugs which are now illegal can be used by healthy adults with relative safety and no threat of addiction, but you have to know what their effects are and how to use them properly. These include most psychedelics. Other drugs can be used safely by most people, but could be habituating to a few. Those few must have access to good medical care if they get into trouble. Some drugs seem to be either harmful or addicting to most users, and we will do our best to inform you fully regarding their effects and track records, as we now do with prescription drugs. Drug education will be provided across the country and the teachers will no longer be police or politicians, but physicians, chemists and pharmacologists who specialize in this field."

Most of those who believe that the War on Drugs is destructive, unwinnable and morally wrong, tend to blame an almost universal ignorance on the part of lawmakers, as well as most of the general public, about drugs in general and most particularly about the psychedelics and their appropriate uses in psychotherapy and spiritual exploration. It is also possible to blame the extraordinarily lucrative industries that have grown in response to the needs of the drug-war: urine testing, prison-building and maintenance and expansion of military power, among others, as explained later in Shura's chapter, "Cui Bono."

I blame something else. I believe that there is an intense, unconscious fear of the hidden depths of the human psyche, and an unacknowledged certainty that the Shadow, the dark side, is indeed the final, terrible, rockbottom truth about the nature of mankind. This fear, in most of us, has been nurtured in a thousand ways by family and culture, and too often by religion. Until there is a growth of understanding of the Shadow side of us, and realization that it is possible for that dark aspect to undergo transformation, this fear and hostility towards anything that opens up the human unconscious will continue. The present beginnings of a police state will flower into something still called the United States, but unrecognizable as a democracy and a land of freedom.

As far as the human species is concerned, if it is to survive much longer on earth, it will have to urge its best minds and most moral souls to devote their time and energy to further and deeper study of the human psyche and its dark side, using all the tools available, including psychedelic drugs and plants. Otherwise, between nuclear power, bacteriological mutations, ecological devastation and the rising anger of hungry, deprived people all across the world, our civilizations and our very species may have a short future indeed.

# CHAPTER 2. LOURDES

(Alice's voice)

One evening, I brought home a video tape of a movie. I told Shura, "This one's pure action, and it's famous for the special effects. It's called 'Terminator 2' and I thought we might give it a try."

He said, "Sure, why not," and then I filled him in on the gossip part of things — who the Great Arnold was, whom he had married, and the fact that his greatest virtue, I gathered, was that he didn't take himself too seriously. I said that the plot might or might not be terrific, but that in a movie like this, you don't pay attention to plot, just to the action and special effects.

I should add, parenthetically, that the only time Shura will sit still to watch a movie, or anything else on television, is when we've set aside an evening to spend with each other, usually once or twice a week. We call it "closing off," and we do just that; phone calls go on the answering machine, we warm up the bedroom with the little floor heater if it's winter, or turn on the big portable fan if it's the middle of summer, and we find music on the radio, and we make love and talk. By the time we're ready to leave the bed and heat up some good soup on the stove, we will have discussed everything that has happened during the past few days: phone calls we forgot to share, our worries and delights, and everything else we could think of.

When the soup is hot, we go into the living room and watch something on television. We both love "Northern Exposure," even in reruns, and perhaps I will have taped a few really interesting things, like an archeological dig in ancient Mayan ruins, or a documentary on the gangsters of the '30's, which I urge him to watch in the interests of his general education. (I sincerely believe that anyone raised in the United States who doesn't know anything about the St. Valentine's Day Massacre is suffering from severe cultural deprivation.)

Or I will have rented a movie, as was the case last night.

In the beginning of Terminator 2, there is a scene where the first

Terminator — the "good" one — is about to be delivered onto the floor of a wide, dimly-lit alley, in the middle of the night, his naked body spilling out of a patch of darkness. He has been sent there from the future. Before he appears, there is a lot of fancy crackling and zapping of electricity. I explained to Shura that all the lightning effects were — in case he was wondering — "A rent in the space-time continuum, of course," to which he grunted, as I continued, "There are always lots of electromagnetic disturbances when you tear a hole in the space-time continuum." Shura replied with a barely detectable nod of the head, knowing full well how much I know about electromagnetism and/or space-time continuums.

The movie was tremendous fun, as I'd hoped it would be. And today, in an idle moment, thinking about rents in time and space with or without lightning bolts, I remembered the closest I ever came — at least consciously and knowingly — to a real place where such a rent, such a tear, had actually happened.

The place is a very famous grotto in a town called Lourdes, in the south of France, and Shura and I stopped there — at my urging — during a trip to Europe in the early '80's.

We had attended a conference in northern Germany, at which Shura had given a talk. Now, we had embarked on the rest of our adventure, which included a stop in Lourdes, to be followed by a train trip along the French and Italian Rivieras, just to see what it all looked like.

After a stay overnight in a delightful little town we'd never heard of, called Libourne, (just in time for the weekly street market), we took our next train and settled down for a long stretch through beautiful wine-growing countryside around the Bordeaux area. As we watched through the train windows, the rolling hills and fields, the miles of grapevines and fruit trees, richly green against red-brown earth were — very gradually — replaced by a flatter, increasingly drier landscape. The earlier large, neatly tended cottages with their pretty gardens slowly gave way to little houses with bare, untended yards, unmistakable evidence of the depression of spirit and loss of energy that seeps in with poverty.

Most people of my children's generation have never heard of Lourdes and don't have the slightest idea who Saint Bernadette was. People of my age, in the United States at least, had some exposure to the story of the miracle of Lourdes when the movie, "The Song of Bernadette," came out — I think it was in the '40's — making a young actress, Jennifer Jones, famous and sending people like me to the libraries and bookstores to find out more.

I've always had a strong interest in so-called miracles, and I read everything available about Bernadette Soubirous. She was a not-very-bright 14 year-old who, in 1878, happened on a cave in the side of a hill near her village, where she was greeted by a Being she called "The Lady," and found herself in trouble when she told other people about it. Ever since I'd seen the movie and read those books, I had wanted to visit the actual place, to see and feel it for myself.

The grotto had become a Catholic shrine, famous for healings that had reputedly taken place (for a few lucky people), when water from the "miraculous" spring had been drunk, bathed in, or poured onto a sick limb or troubled head. The spring had come into being when the Lady told young Bernadette to scratch in the earth just inside the shallow cave; when water bubbled up, she informed the child that the water was holy and had the power to heal.

I knew that the shrine at Lourdes had become big business, and I was prepared for the inevitable commercialization and cheapening of it. I didn't care about any of that, and since I'm not a Catholic I wasn't coming to see the grotto with expectations of a cure or any kinds of answers to deep questions. I just wanted to see the actual rock, or cave, or tunnel, or whatever the grotto turned out to be, where the original miracle had taken place.

When I first proposed that we visit Lourdes, Shura had been his usual accommodating self, and said he thought it might be an interesting experience to actually see the site of a long-past miraculous event. He would roll up his scientific skepticism with the extra socks in his backpack, and enjoy the adventure with me. He had only one reservation, "You realize, don't you, there'll probably be a lot of crutches hanging around and tourist junk all over the place; are you ready for that?"

"Sure, I'm expecting junk and crutches; no sweat. It doesn't make me want to see the grotto less. It's just that I've never had a chance to see a miracle site, if that's what you call it ... "

"Well, it's all right with me," said Shura, "Just don't want you to be disappointed."

The dry foothills had grown into tree-covered mountains, the Pyrenees. We took our places near the open metal gate in the foyer of the train car and stood watching the dramatic peaks and chasms flashing by, taking in lungfuls of the sharp, piney air.

The first thing visible of Lourdes was a wide river flowing clean and ice-blue far below us. Then, as the train rounded a curve, there appeared on the bank of the river — completely unexpected and somehow shocking — an immense cathedral, white and blue and gold, shining against the deep green of the hills.

*Good ole Catholic Church, they sure know how to catch your attention!*

Finally, we pulled into the Lourdes station. Shouldering our backpacks, we stepped down from the train, somewhat surprised at the number of variously capped and cloaked nurses gathered on the platform, waiting for disabled and ill pilgrims who would need their help. There were numerous large black wheelchairs with hoods, lined up against the station wall. We didn't stay around to watch the stretchers coming off the train, but proceeded into the town to find a place to stay the night. Tired from the long ride, we registered at a modest little hotel on what appeared to be the main street, and went to bed early. Exploration would wait until morning.

The town of Lourdes, as we discovered after breakfast, is built on sloping hills which eventually take all feet down to the river which rushes, spitting and foaming under a wide, grey stone bridge.

As we made our way from our hotel along the gradually descending main street, we saw shop after shop, many with fronts open to the street, selling plastic water bottles (for the holy water from the spring) with Madonnas on them, Madonna spoons, hats, scarves, and even ashtrays. There were also little statues of Bernadette, of course, but it was obviously the Madonna who kept the tourist trade bustling.

We crossed over the river and walked into a lovely park which stretched far ahead of us to where we could see the spires of the cathedral. There were carefully tended lawns and beds of bright flowers. On the winding path we passed monks dressed in long, brown robes, sashed at the waist, walking at varying speeds. Some strolled meditatively, hands clasped behind them, while a few hurried, rosaries swinging and bouncing from their woven belts. I nudged Shura and whispered, "Looks like something out of the Middle Ages, doesn't it?" He grinned and focused his camera on a venerable patriarch in a long black robe, complete with bushy white beard and a somewhat incongruous black beret perched at a jaunty angle over his springing white eyebrows.

We came to a large oval of grass, and paused to appreciate and photograph. In the center of the oval was a stone pillar, supporting a life-sized statue of the Madonna, all of it surrounded by a bed of marigolds, petunias and tiny blue flowers I couldn't name.

We walked on until we came upon a modest statue of Bernadette Soubirous under a branching tree at the side of the path. She was kneeling over her own little garden of marigolds and pansies growing in the shade. I paused to look at the figure and Shura asked, "Is that the kid who started it all?" I said "Yes, indeed it is, bless her heart."

When we finally reached the plaza in front of the cathedral, my legs were beginning to tire. We paused to read the signs which indicated that the Grotto was somewhere to the right of the elaborate edifice towering above us. Strolling in that general direction, we soon found ourselves on a long, very wide boulevard, planted down the middle with carefully spaced trees. The river flowed to our right. To our left, as we began moving down the grey paving stones of the boulevard, was the side of the cathedral, built on top of a cliff which continued straight ahead for what might have been a quarter of a mile before it vanished into a hillside full of trees. Against the face of the cliff there were open bins of pale blue candles, priced according to length. We exchanged amused looks.

We moved on, and after a few minutes Shura turned to me and made a suggestion, "Well, now, why don't I leave you to wander at your own pace for a while, and I'm going to get brisk and follow the pavement to where it ends, just to get a general view — okay?"

"Sure, honey," I said, "Go ahead. I'll be somewhere around here. I've just got to track down the cave, and I'll be satisfied. See ya later."

He gave me a fast kiss on the cheek, wheeled around and took off.

There were people everywhere, nurses pushing what appeared to be mostly bent-over, elderly patients in the big, black-hooded wheelchairs, but I caught sight of one young invalid with a pale face, his thin body sprawled awkwardly in the seat, going past me. There were long benches and plain wooden chairs scattered across the promenade, facing in all directions. I passed some large, dark grey, room-sized enclosures, set against the cliff, which I decided must be the baths I'd read about, where sick people were immersed in the holy water.

I still couldn't see anything ahead of me to indicate the presence of a special place, a holy cave in the cliff side. So I went up to a French gendarme who was standing near one of the planted trees, hands clasped behind him, looking very bored.

"Oú est la Grotto?" I asked in my best French, feeling rather stupid.

"C'est lá, Madame," he snapped, gesturing toward the cliff face ahead of me in a way that implied I had to be blind not to see it. I thanked him profusely and continued walking.

As I approached the next tree, still scanning what I could see of the cliff face beyond where I was walking, I tried to guess from the placement of benches whether I was getting nearer. Suddenly, I felt wetness on my cheeks. I stopped, completely astonished. Tears were actually flowing from my eyes, for no discernible reason. I wasn't feeling sad; in fact, I was feeling very cheerful, even a bit excited by the search. I would have described myself as actually quite happy, at that moment. Tears made no sense. I decided to ignore them, and resumed walking.

*Maybe there's more emotion in my unconscious about this whole thing than I've realized. Maybe the tears are a sign of that. Maybe maybe.*

I had gone only a little way when it occurred to me that the benches immediately ahead were placed somewhat more purposefully than most of the others on the boulevard. Two rows of them were lined up at right-angles to the rock face, separated by several yards, and four or five benches faced the cliff, connecting the ends of the rows, forming three sides of a square.

And suddenly, I saw it. The place. Not a deep tunnel into the cliff, as I had imagined, but a shallow little cave, only a few feet deep.

I breathed deeply, and stopped to look. Halfway up the curve of the cave wall, on the right, was a ledge, and on it was standing a statue — perhaps four feet high — of the Madonna. My gaze followed the back of the cave around to the left, where bunches of flowers were gathered in ceramic vases on the ground, presumably surrounding the miracle spring.

Then, as I stood there, just taking everything in, I felt it: a sense of singing, almost but not quite audible, and an intense joy that beamed out directly to me from the cave. My breath caught, and I let it out very slowly, while my body resonated with the euphoria.

*My God! It's still here! Whatever happened to Bernadette Soubirous is still going on, still alive!*

I looked at the people sitting here and there on the benches, searching for a face among them which would reflect what I was sensing from the cave; someone else who was tuned in. I couldn't spot any face which conveyed a response to that unheard singing, but there were some still figures whose heads were bent to their chests; perhaps they were feeling it, I thought, maybe they were sitting so quietly, so unmoving, not looking around, because they were bathing in that energy.

*I can't ask them, so I'll never be sure.*

I walked slowly over to where worn velvet ropes indicated the proper place to stand in line. There were only a couple of people ahead of me, and I could move at my own pace. As I went past the statue, with its white robe and blue cape, I saw on the feet, which were at my eye-level, the gold-painted roses placed next to each big toe, and my mind sang a silly phrase, "She has rosies on her toesies," as I turned away, remembering that Saint Bernadette had described The Lady as having bare feet, with a golden rose on each.

I bent down to see the bubbling water of the sacred stream, under a thick oval of glass set in the floor of the cave, then straightened up and walked out. The sense of piercing joy was still there, singing through my body.

When Shura came up to me, a few minutes later, I was sitting on a bench, facing the cave, floating in what was coming from it. I turned at the feel of his hand on my shoulder and said, "Wow, honey, what an experience!"

He said, "Tell me about it."

"Stand here for a minute. Can you feel what's coming from the cave?"

Shura looked where I was pointing, and stood very still, then shrugged, "I guess I can't, sweet potatuh. What are you feeling?"

I stood and took his hand, "Well," I began, then realized that my throat was closing on tears. I coughed and continued, "It's like a singing without any sound. And there's an intense feeling of happiness, joy; it's just beaming out from that cave as if no time has passed since the whole thing first happened."

"Wow," said Shura, adding regretfully, "Wish I could tune into it. I'm picking up something, but it's probably from you."

"That's all right," I reassured him, feeling rather selfish, wishing he could share it. "Okay, let's go," I said, pulling him by the hand, heading back the way we'd come, "Want to take a look at the cathedral?"

"Sure," said my lovely, patient man, "May as well see all the highlights, while we're here!"

I paused and opened my purse, to search for the small plastic envelope containing 120 milligrams of MDMA that I'd brought with me from home. I told Shura, "I thought I'd take this now, so that maybe I can sharpen my ability to see whatever's in the cathedral. Do you mind?"

"Go ahead," said Shura, "Whatever turns you on!"

I went over to one of the taps built into the side of the rock face, near the bins of candles, and swallowed the white powder with water held in my cupped hands. Then I rejoined Shura, who was standing where I'd left him, hands in his pockets, rocking slightly on his heels. We resumed our slow walk toward the cathedral stairs which were visible at the end of the cliff face.

I told Shura about the strange tears which had run down my face, for no apparent reason, just before I'd reached the grotto, and described all over again the radiance which had pushed into me.

We reached the bottom of the broad stairway which led up to the cathedral, and I realized that my usually tired legs not only felt strong; they were actually tingling with energy, and before I could think about it, I found myself running up the stairs, shouting something like "Yah, yah, yah!"

At the top, there was a marble apron, ringed by a balustrade, where I panted for a while until I'd caught my breath. While I waited for Shura, who was climbing the stairs in the normal way, I gave myself a chance to look inward, to see if the MDMA had perhaps taken effect much faster than usual. I could feel nothing familiar. My energy level was more than high; I felt like a teenager, but I could detect nothing yet of the expected MDMA effect.

*There hasn't been enough time to feel effects since I took it. Needs ten more minutes, maybe.*

We went into the cathedral, but after only a few moments, we turned around and made our way back out, because there was nothing important inside to be experienced, for us, and we both knew it. The mystery was outside, in the little grotto, and all the rest was the Catholic church.

When we were walking in the park again, the cathedral behind us, I told Shura, "You know what, babe? The MDMA never took effect! I've been trying to figure out why, and I think I've got the answer. My energy level is so high — it's been extraordinary ever since I was at the grotto — I think the MDMA simply couldn't take me anywhere. I was already there! I still am, as a matter of fact," I added, laughing.

In the town, we stopped at a bookstore and when we went in, I asked for any book they might have about Bernadette Soubirous, and a young woman handed me what she explained was the only one available, a short, somewhat cheaply produced paperback in French; she apologized for not having anything in English.

Back at our hotel, I began to read, stopping occasionally to ask Shura to translate a word I didn't know, and what the little book told me was not only surprising, it was deeply satisfying. The only obvious question, I said to Shura, was why the church hadn't gotten rid of this publication, considering the holes it punched in their official story.

"It says that when the local priests told Bernadette to ask 'The Lady' what her name was, she did as she was ordered, kneeling as always at the entrance of the cave. The Lady answered, 'My name is Aquero,' which is a word used in this region to mean something like 'That's the way it is,' or 'So be it,' which made no sense to Bernadette, but she obediently carried the message back to the village authorities, who passed it on to the Vatican. After that, the Catholic church pronounced officially that the being known as The Lady was, indeed, the Madonna, mother of Christ, and would be venerated as such from then on. How do you like them apples?"

"And you're excited because the Lady didn't say she was the Madonna, is that it?"

"Yeah! She never said anything of the sort! She said, 'My name is Aquero,' which is a wonderful, in-your-face, zen kind of name, calculated to bewilder everyone, especially the church people. It's a totally new piece of information that nobody ever talks about. The church just took her over, and declared her the Madonna, and that was that. They weren't about to have some over-imaginative young girl's fantasy leaving the impression that there might be another explanation of who and what The Lady was!"

"Pretty good, I'd say," chuckled Shura, "And no one's questioned it since then, huh?"

"Of course not," I grinned, putting the book down and clasping my hands behind my neck, "And probably nobody bothers reading a little book like this, when they've come for a healing, and most of the tourists are probably Catholic anyway, and this whole Aquero thing wouldn't seem important to them."

"Makes sense," agreed Shura.

"And the more miraculous healings there were at the spring, the more it had to be the Madonna, of course."

We were both silent, thinking to ourselves, until I got up and said I thought it was a good time for me to start packing if we were leaving on the train early in the morning.

*There's still the great question remaining: how can that blast of joyous, heart-piercing singing still be going on, so many years afterwards? Does it mean that, once a tear is made in the fabric of our reality, it stays open? Does it mean that whatever came through in Bernadette's time will continue to come through, to be caught by the occasional visitor like me? What is its message?*

I folded shirts and socks into our backpacks, trying to sort out the sensations that had pushed into and around me.

*It was a kind of love — a form of love — which simply says Yes to everything. Love as energy, love as joy, love as the only reason there is, the only meaning. Which, of course, makes no sense, considering. But there it was. There it is. All you have to do is stand in front of that place, where the original opening was made, and it's all there. Time has nothing to do with it. It's outside of time. Whatever space it exists in, it can make a bridge to where we are, and the bridge remains.*

After I'd finished repacking, we went to bed. Curled to Shura's back, I murmured, "Thank you so, so, so much, honey, for coming here for me. It was much more than I'd expected. It turns out it's a real miracle place, and I never thought I'd actually experience one. I'm very grateful, and I love you to bits."

He yawned, then said, "Love you, too, little one. See you in the morning."

I kissed his spine, said goodnight, and, with the friendly sounds of people talking and laughing as they passed in the lamplit street below, we slept.

# CHAPTER 3.  THE DRED AND OTHER
# LEARNING EXPERIENCES

(Alice's voice)

Shura and I are very different people; in body chemistry, in the ways our minds work, in dozens of small yea's and nay's. We have different abilities and gifts, and sometimes dissimilar reactions to experimental drugs. But we are alike in a lot of ways, and one of the many things we share is an inability to enjoy marijuana. (We also share a dislike of Wagner's music, but that's another story.) We agree with the proponents of the plant about its incredible virtues, its general usefulness as a source of fabric and paper, and its well-established medical value.  For millions of people around the world, it is the preferred drug for relaxation and de-stressing. We also know that it can be habituating to some. Not physically addicting, but strongly habituating, which is certainly not in its favor. But when I say we dislike it, I mean something entirely personal; we feel uncomfortable with its effects, and as Shura says, neither of us seems to be able to learn anything worthwhile from taking it.

Ah, yes.  There's one exception to that non-learning statement: marijuana can be used, like no other drug I know, to slow down one's sense of time, and that can be a fascinating experience.

My first experiment with marijuana was when I was in my twenties, and it was a disastrous one. I found my awareness chopped into ten-second segments, separated by a wall of amnesia that clanged down, just as I had managed to remember who I was, where I was, and what was happening. After the wall had cut me off, I would begin the entire process of identifying myself and my reality all over again.

CLANG:

"Who am I?"
"I'm Alice."
"Oh, yes, that's right.  Well, where am I?"

"Sitting on my couch, in my home."
"What am I doing?"
"I've taken marijuana, and I'm trying to make sense out of all this."

CLANG:

"Who am I?"
"My name is Alice."

And so on and so on, for hours. When I finally came out of it, I resolved never to touch the stuff again.

But, of course, people are resilient and forgetful. In my thirties, for a while, I had a boyfriend called Steven who was brilliant, arrogant and extremely controlling, and he decided that the circumstances of my first experiment with pot — mind-set perhaps — must have been wrong in some way, and he insisted that I should take it once more, with him. "I promise you," he said firmly, "This time it will be a wonderful experience. Just leave it to me!"

He took me outside, had me sit down under the trees at the back of the house, gave me a marijuana cigarette and watched while I went through the usual coughing and recovery. He kept telling me to inhale, and inhale again, "Come on, come on! I want you to give this stuff a real try, this time. Trust me, Alice. Just breathe it in, that's my girl!"

So I kept inhaling until I began to feel very dizzy. When I said I'd had enough, that's it, he let me stop. He patted my head approvingly, took the cigarette out of my fingers and finished it himself, while I sat and saw the world split into one, two, three, four levels of vision, four levels of reality, four versions of Alice watching sunlight flowing over branches and twigs, wild plants and brown-edged leaves in the dry riverbed below.

I sat cross-legged, feeling the intense push of wave after wave of sensation, wondering if it would ever mellow out, slow down, stop coming at me. It was impossible to relax, because I had to stay braced against the next surge. I didn't enjoy the feeling. I knew it wasn't dangerous or hostile, just very strong, and it made me uncomfortable.

Suddenly there was a fifth and a sixth level, and I turned to Steven and said, "I want to go in, please. Things are getting complicated."

Inside the house, seated on my couch, I counted a final total of eight levels, and wondered which was the real one, the one I had been living in before smoking the marijuana.

Looking at the eight levels or tracks from the outside, which I could occasionally do, was like seeing an eight-story apartment building with the outer wall removed. I hoped that one of the apartments was my normal world. The other apartments looked similar, but here and there a piece of furniture — so to speak — was out of place, or a door didn't have the right shape, and everything kept shifting into something else. So I had to look carefully, to feel out every thought-form and all the not-quite-right versions of myself, if I was to sort it all out and bring an end to the loud confusion.

I glanced at my friend, seated across from me in an armchair, eyes closed, smiling, and became aware of a growing suspicion that he had known all this would happen — the fracturing, splitting —

*Wonder if this is how paranoia feels. I've got a sense that there's a secret agenda somewhere, that I'm being set up, betrayed, by somebody or something. I've got to get out. Got to find my way out.*

And on several of the eight levels or tracks, some versions of me decided, quite coldly and finally, that I'd had enough of this relationship with Steven, that it was time to stop being the classic approval-seeking victim; time to grow up and move on.

By the time the defensive mental scrambling had begun to clear, hours had gone by. The reality track that I belonged to had settled in, friendly and familiar, while the others slowly faded and thinned until finally, I was myself, I was where I belonged, and anxiety had been replaced by a lovely, simmering anger.

The next experiment with marijuana was many years later, and I shared it with Shura Borodin.

At the time, I hadn't known Shura for long — six or seven months, perhaps — and one day he invited me to go with him to a party. He phoned me on a Thursday evening and, after we'd caught up on general news, he said, "By the way, a couple of good friends of mine are having some kind of get-together on Saturday; they have a house in the woods near Santa Cruz, and I think you'd really enjoy them. Want to give it a try?"

"I'd love to, Shura. But aren't we going to the Gilbert and Sullivan thing on Saturday, with Ruth and George?"

"That's not 'til much later. The party in the woods is between noon and five-ish, so that gives us plenty of time to get back to San Francisco for Iolanthe."

"Oh, great! That'll work out nicely, then. Thank you — it sounds wonderful."

"I'll pick you up Saturday at eleven, all right?"

"I'll be ready."

It was a long drive, and the coast highway was unusually sunny; the fog hadn't yet resumed its summer habit of moving in from the ocean onto the coastal hills in the afternoon. The little car rounded a curve and we caught our breath at the sight of a particularly dramatic rock formation rising from the cobalt and silver sea. When we had passed it, Shura asked,

"Have I told you anything about Aaron and Grace, our hosts? I don't think I have."

"No, I don't remember hearing those names."

"Well, I've known them both for years; they're two of my favorite people; intelligent, funny, good friends. They co-authored a superb book on psychoactive mushrooms in ancient Scandinavia, including the use of the Amanita muscaria by a tribe known as the Berserkers — which you may have heard of — "

"I've heard of the Berserkers, but I didn't know about the Amanita part of it. That's the famous magic mushroom with the red cap and white spots, right?"

"You've got it. The one they put on the pretty Christmas cards."

We left the highway and drove uphill. Through the windows of the little green car, I caught glimpses of houses built on the slopes above and below us, snug redwood nests looking out over the blue-misted valley. Finally, Shura swung off the road, into a space between two parked cars, and announced, "Here's where we disembark. The house is about a block down from here."

Aaron met us at his gate, which was made out of raw redwood planks, and when Shura put his hand on my shoulder and introduced me, the stocky, curly-haired man smiled with real warmth, "Glad to meet you, Alice. Grace is in the kitchen, directing the food traffic." He led us down a short stairway between immense fern plants, to the front door. Inside, there was a living room with large windows, a long, worn leather couch and a couple of padded armchairs. Several oversized floor pillows were occupied (like the rest of the furniture) by a variety of sprawling people, some waving celery sticks and pretzels as they talked.

Aaron led us to the kitchen, where I was introduced to a slim woman, a few inches taller than I, who wore her long, red-brown hair in a thick braid down her back. She had a handsome, alive face, and when I said hello she leaned close to me, trying to be heard above the noise, "Hi, Alice! Make yourself at home. There's food everywhere. What would you like to drink?"

*Beautiful eyes that really see you, and the face says she laughs a lot. Lovely lady, with a figure to die for.*

Equipped with a glass of chilled apple juice, I left Shura talking animatedly with Aaron and another man he apparently knew, and made my way through sliding glass doors onto a wide deck running the length of the house. A few feet away, the trunk of an immense live-oak thrust upward through a circle cut in the weathered redwood floor, its branches and leaves shading almost the entire deck. People were everywhere, sitting and standing, talking and laughing, and I sat down on a bench, next to a long wooden table covered with a red and white checked tablecloth. I helped myself to some potato chips and salsa from earthenware bowls, and turned around on the bench so I could watch the other guests and see Shura when he came outside.

When Shura emerged onto the deck, he spotted me immediately and waved, smiling the smile I was already in love with. He joined me on the bench, holding a glass of red wine, as usual, and asked, "How ya doin', kid?"

I said I was doing fine, and that, from what I'd seen of them, Aaron and Grace seemed like the kind of people I would enjoy knowing. He said, cheerfully, "Believe me, they are and you will!"

A little over an hour later, Shura and I and one of the guests — a tall, lanky blond man who had happily identified himself as the best unrecognized artistic genius in Northern California — were engaged in an enthusiastic discussion of an exhibit at the Oakland Museum to which Shura had taken me the previous weekend. We found ourselves competing to deliver the most devastating description of the work of the featured artist, who — we all agreed — was an absolute con-man. His name was easy for me to remember, because there was a famous classical pianist I admired who had the same name.

Suddenly, a deep voice called out, "Hey, anybody who wants to share this with me is welcome." We turned and saw, at the far end of the deck, a rather stout man with thinning hair, dressed in old jeans and a bulky, blue jacket, waving what looked like a very large, fat, black cigar. Somebody called out, "What the hell is it, Chuck?"

"It's from Africa, it's marijuana, and it's called The Dred. Don't ask me why, man, that's its name. Real good stuff, powerful. It's like nothing you ever tried before, take my word!"

Shura said to me, "Some kind of African pot, looks like. Want to try it?"

"Maybe, just a bit." I shrugged, "I haven't had much luck with marijuana, so far, sorry to say."

"It's not my particular ally, either," said Shura, "But I guess a quick toke or two isn't going to do any harm."

"Probably not."

"I usually have a rule for myself." said Shura, "Don't take anybody else's drug, especially at somebody else's house."

"Well, if you think we shouldn't —" I began, hesitantly.

"No, no," he interrupted, "I confess I'm curious about that weird looking cigar. I'm not going to take more than a couple of drags, though, just in case that name constitutes a warning to the consumer. I wonder how 'Dred' is spelled?"

I laughed and we both joined the line of guests waiting to sample the cigar. When it was in front of me, I drew in the smoke carefully, not wanting to have a coughing fit in front of everyone. Despite the fact that I smoked cigarettes and should have been able to handle it smoothly, drawing in pot smoke always made me cough violently.

This time was no exception. I was surrounded by understanding smiles as I made my way, stopping every few steps for a coughing fit, to the opposite end of the deck, Shura just behind me. When we reached the railing, I turned to him and said, my voice rasping, "I'm sorry; that always happens to me."

"Don't apologize." he grinned, patting me on the back, "You okay now?"

I drew a shaky breath, and told him I was fine.

We stood together, sharing impressions about the house and its surrounding trees. Our young artist friend had gone elsewhere and, looking around for him, I noticed that the owner of the cigar was walking around the deck, apparently offering second draws to those who wanted them. When he came abreast of us, Shura accepted the cigar and took a deep lungful of the smoke, then I did the same, concentrating on inhaling smoothly, this time, not hurrying it. Only one cough followed, and I recovered immediately.

Shura said to the man called Chuck, "I think we'll stop there, thanks very much."

The blue jacket moved away, and Shura looked down at me, "Would you mind if I left you on your own, for a couple of minutes? I just spotted an old friend," he gestured, "And I'd like to say hello." He hesitated, looked closely at my face, and added, grinning, "I would introduce you, but this may not be quite the moment, am I right?"

I giggled, "Yeah, I can just see me in the middle of shaking hands when the effects hit!"

Shura pressed my arm, "That's what I was thinking, too."

"Go ahead," I said, "I'll be over at the food table, in case I get the munchies."

This time, I sat on the bench facing the plates of celery stalks and carrot sticks, potato chips, and pretty painted bowls of olives and salsa. I folded my hands on the checkered cloth in front of me, waiting — a bit nervously — for something to happen. I remembered that it usually took ten to fifteen minutes between inhaling and becoming aware of the first changes, at least with ordinary marijuana.

I was still sitting there, when, a moment later, something came down fast, from over my head. It felt like a narrow tent, or cone, and it enveloped me. There was no sound within the cone. I couldn't hear the voices of others on the deck; I couldn't hear anything. The Cone of Silence is not unknown among people who take psychedelic drugs, and it is usually associated with a feeling of peacefulness and interior quiet. But this was different. I was imprisoned, cut off. Then I realized that I was being poisoned. It was as if, from head to toe, I had been cored like an apple, and something toxic and acid-green was being poured into the hole.

I couldn't move. I sat frozen, helpless, wondering if I was going to pass out, or die. Strangely enough, there was a feeling of concern, perhaps even worry, but no real fear; my emotions, like my body, were in a state of suspension. But I could think.

*If I topple over sideways, it's going to scare everybody. Shura will be horrified, not knowing what's wrong, and I'll be dreadfully embarrassed in front of all these people. Maybe I won't fall over, if I just sit here, if I keep leaning forward onto the table until it passes. If I don't die, I'm sure it will pass.*

A hand cupped my shoulder, and Shura's voice came through the walls of the cone, sounding far away, "Are you all right, Alice?"

I couldn't manage speech. I could only sit there and hope I stayed upright.

I could see Shura's face in the periphery of my vision. He spoke again, the words echoing slightly inside the greenish cone that surrounded me, "Can you talk?"

I managed to move my head slowly from side to side.

"All right, then, my dear, listen to me carefully. I'm going to help you up and take you to where you can lie down, and then I'm going to bring you out of this, okay?"

I nodded, very slowly, my eyes fixed on the fingers tightly locked on the table before me.

I felt Shura's big hands in my armpits, and observed with calm interest that my body was standing. He guided me away from my bench, and — still holding me up — led me to a lounge chair a few feet away, at the sunny end of the deck. He lowered me into it, then pulled up a stool and sat down right in front of me, leaning one elbow on the end of the long table.

*He knows I can't move my head, so he's making sure he's within my field of vision.*

"Now, Alice," he said, speaking slowly, "I want you to concentrate on what my hand is doing. I'm putting my right thumb on top of the edge of this table, and my index finger on the bottom, and I want you to tell me how thick this tabletop is; how many inches are between my two fingers?"

*What the hell is he talking about? I'm sitting here, paralyzed and poisoned, and he's asking me to guess how thick a tabletop is! What's he DOING?"*

"I know this doesn't make sense, honey," urged Shura, "But please indulge me for a moment, okay? Just do your best to focus on my two fingers and tell me how many inches you think there are between them."

*Oh, God, I suppose I'm just going to have to play his silly game, because he's going to keep at me until I give him an answer. All right. Concentrate. How many inches of wood between the two fingers? Looks like two. Open my mouth and say the words.*

"Two," I heard my voice croaking, "Two inches."

Shura smiled and leaned forward to grasp my hands, "You did it! Now you can move! You're going to be okay!"

I looked at him in disbelief, but my arm had already gone up to protect my eyes from the sunlight, and I realized that he was absolutely right; the paralysis had gone. I sat back and smiled shakily at him.

"How did you do that? What was all that idiotic stuff about the thickness of a tabletop?"

"It's an old trick; if you can get yourself to focus on something, *really* focus your mind on a single point, you can break out of that kind of freeze. Maybe it has something to do with getting your ego back in control; I don't know. I only know it works!"

My irritation was beginning to dissipate. It should have been completely gone, but there was still a prickle left that was hard to shake.

*I'm going to have to appear grateful, because there's no excuse for being anything else, right now. Shura rescued me; he knew what to do and I'm going to be all right. But I'm still feeling pretty edgy.*

I smiled at him and gave myself a shake. I said, "Wow!"

"Come out of the sun, Alice," my tall magician said, and held out both hands to pull me up, and when I was sure I wasn't dizzy and could move without doing anything embarrassing, he walked me slowly between small clusters of people talking on the deck. They paid us no attention, for the most part, although there was an occasional friendly, "Hi!" Shura guided me to the shaded side of the deck, where there was a rainbow-colored hammock strung between a tree trunk and a heavy post. He settled me into a big Mexican cane chair next to the post, and wiggled himself down into the hammock. Then he leaned towards me, his hands on his knees, and opened his mouth to speak.

I was watching his face, wondering what he was going to say, when his color changed, and his hands flew apart to grasp the edges of the hammock. Then he was propelling himself like a rocket out of the big woven cradle, and I watched him run, staggering a bit, into the house.

It was probably no more than ten or fifteen minutes before he reappeared, but time was still a bit stretched, as it usually is with marijuana, and I felt as if it had been close to an hour. I hadn't minded, though; I'd been watching the other people on the deck, particularly one man who was acting strangely. He was alone, and all he seemed to want to do was hold onto the tree trunk growing through the floorboards. He had both arms around it, and from the look on his very pale face, I knew what he was going through.

*Looks like the black cigar got him, too, poor guy.*

Under normal circumstances, I would have gone over to him and tried to help in some way, but these weren't exactly normal circumstances, and my body had no intention of moving out of the chair until it had to.

*How am I feeling? Body recovering. Irritability fading. Why was I feeling that way, instead of being relieved and grateful when Shura got me out? Aaaah, of course! Loss of power, total helplessness; the recipe for resentment and anger. My emotions are still a bit flat, right now. So that explains the irritability; it was all I could feel of the anger underneath. Maybe I'll feel real anger later; I'm pretty sure I'll feel anger later.*

When Shura returned, he wasn't smiling. He didn't even make an effort to smile. I looked up and asked him if he was okay, and all he said was, "Let's get out of here."

I followed him into the house and through the crowded living room. We made no effort to find our hosts to say goodbye, on our way to the front door.

We climbed the hill to the parked car, slowly and in silence.

*Whatever happened to him must have been pretty bad, but he obviously doesn't want to talk right now, so I'll stay quiet.*

Shura backed the car out of the parking space very carefully, with several false starts and squeals of brake. Finally, we were on the narrow road, driving a bit faster than I thought wise. I was about to make a gentle suggestion that he slow down a bit, when he began to do just that. I breathed deeply and tried to relax.

After a few minutes, he said to me, "Could you watch — watch the road behind us? I can't look in the — the mirror, the rear — the rear-view mirror. I lose track of — uh — the — uh — where I'm going. Can't look in the mirror."

(He explained to me later that what he saw in the rear-view mirror became confused with the road ahead of him, that he couldn't tell which direction was which.)

"Oh, boy!" I muttered, then reassured him, "Don't worry, I'll turn around and keep my eyes on the road in back, so leave that part to me, and you can concentrate on what's in front."

*Boy-oh-boy-oh-boy! We should have stayed at the house until he was all right. Not too smart, driving when he's like this. Hope our guardian angels are on the job.*

I turned around in my seat so I could see through the rear window of the car, prepared to tell him whenever another car approached, but for some reason no one else was sharing our road at that particular time, so we didn't have to deal with traffic.

After about ten of the longest minutes in human history, Shura pulled to the side of the road and parked. I looked around. To our right I could see only trees, but across the road was a little outdoor cafe.

Shura said, "Let's go get ourselves a cup of coffee or something, okay?"

I smiled at him, "Sure. Looks like a nice place. I hope you want to sit outside."

"Yeah. Outside is fine with me."

*His voice is still a bit flat.*

We sat down at a table in the patio. There were no other customers in sight. Shura took my right hand, squeezed it gently, then let go. A stout man in a stained white apron appeared, carrying a small pad. When we both ordered coffee, he set his lips disapprovingly, but Shura repeated that all we wanted, for the moment, was coffee.

"I'd like to make him happy," said Shura, when the man had disappeared through the cafe door, "But I can't bear the thought of food, for the moment."

"Me, neither," I said, having already tested out images of sandwiches in my mind without noting any enthusiasm.

There was a moment's silence, and I openly searched his face, which was still set and grim, finally deciding it was time to try my first question.

"What happened to you?"

"Well, I was feeling pretty pleased with myself for having gotten you out of your bad place, and not being really much affected personally, then I sat in that damned hammock," he said, finally letting a small smile happen, "And — well — I suppose it was probably the swinging motion, just that bit of rocking back and forth; it wasn't much, but it was enough, and suddenly I knew I was about to vomit, and right on top of that, I had the sensation that — well, I figured I was going to let go at the other end, too, so I headed for the bathroom as fast as I could. Got there barely in time. Both ends exploded. Had to do some mopping up in that bathroom; it was a mess. That's what took me so long."

"How are you feeling now?"

He looked intently at my eyes and ground the words out, "I'm furious. Angry, angry. Mostly at myself, for having broken my own rule."

"Which is?"

"I think I mentioned it before. It goes: never take anyone else's drug in anyone else's house. And I broke it. And got slapped. What a damned fool I was!"

The grumpy man in the apron appeared with our coffees, and

waited stolidly while Shura got out his billfold and paid.

When we were alone again, we talked. We speculated on what might have been in the fat black cigar besides marijuana; the guesses ranged from PCP to exotic-sounding plants I had never heard of. Shura even expressed some doubt as to whether there had been any marijuana in it at all.

We drank from our cups and a small silence fell. I looked inward and concluded that I was experiencing a mixture of two states: pleasure at being with Shura, sharing a difficult experience, and on the other hand — a quietly growing awareness of my own outrage at what had happened.

*Well, if it WAS marijuana, then this will be the third time I've taken it and ended up being angry. Interesting.*

Shura hit his forehead and muttered, "Why didn't I pay attention to the nickname of that cigar!"

I heard myself actually laughing for the first time since the troubles on the deck. I had forgotten about that particular example of Truth in Advertising.

Shura looked at me and managed a wry smile.

Gradually, the conversation became broader and a bit less intense, as Shura found his way into reminiscences about previous near-death drug experiences, as he called them, and I discovered myself laughing again. We ordered more coffee. Finally, we examined each other's faces and eyes, and asked each other one more time, "How are you feeling now?" and decided we were back to baseline. Close enough, anyway, for the long drive north to San Francisco.

We saw Iolanthe. At least, everyone said we saw Iolanthe. I have never been able to remember a single moment of that performance. Total amnesia. Well, not really total. There is a faint impression of a blonde woman in pink, and a glitter of sequins. But that's all.

It was a very long time before we told Aaron and Grace what had happened that day, and why we both left so hurriedly. When we asked them, point-blank, if they knew what had been in that fat black cigar, they assured us that their friend had told them it contained nothing but a powerful African marijuana. Only one other guest, they said, reported having trouble with it (at which I nodded, remembering the man with his arms wrapped around the tree), and they were very sorry we'd had such a miserable experience.

We assured them we didn't hold them responsible, and Shura said, "Hey, no harm was done, my friends, and we both learned a valuable lesson, namely, pay attention to nick-names!"

The fourth and last time I tried marijuana finally gave me some-thing of great value. It was many years after the Dred and, again, with

Shura. A friend had given us what were, at that time, called Alice B. Toklas brownies, named after the friend and lover of the writer, Gertrude Stein. Ms. Toklas' marijuana brownies were famous. Neither of us had tried them before, and we told each other one Saturday evening that we owed ourselves one try of marijuana in this form, just to find out if there was any appreciable difference in its effects, compared with the smoke.

I had my bath, then Shura took a shower, and we met in the dining room in our dressing gowns. The two small brownies sat on a blue plate on the table. We looked down at the plate, we looked at each other, then Shura chuckled and I broke into frank laughter.

"Oh, boy!" I said, "Are we wary? Are we apprehensive? Are we chicken? Noooo. Not us, we aren't!"

"Well," Shura protested, "Do keep in mind that one of the measures of intelligence is supposed to be the ability to learn from experience, n'est pas?"

"Yes, indeedy, thy point is well made. But we've never tried this particular form of the stuff, have we? And as researchers, how can we express opinions on that which we tasteth not, et cetera, et cetera. Right?"

In reply, Shura picked up one of the innocent looking fudge squares, and handed it to me. He took the remaining one in his fingers and we touched brownies, as we would ordinarily have clinked glasses.

Waiting for the first signs of effects, we went to the bedroom and turned on the radio. Shura searched among our three available classical music stations until he found music we liked; a passionate piano concerto by Brahms. We lay back on the pillows and held hands.

When — about half an hour later — the experience began to blossom, I was aware of it mostly as a stretching of time, a slowing down of everything — thought, motion, the flow of life itself — which was certainly familiar enough. It wasn't any friendlier than before; there was again the push, the surge of sensation that made me uneasy, but I was reassured by Shura's presence and touch.

"How ya doin', buns?" asked my friend and lover.

"It's pretty strong, but I'm okay."

"Yeah, it does kind of come right at you, doesn't it."

"You all right?" I asked him, rolling over to nestle on his shoulder.

"I'm fine," he said, "But it still isn't my drug of choice."

After a while, I felt the pressure of a full bladder, and told Shura I would have to leave him for a moment. He got up with me and followed as I wobbled my way down the hall, through the dining room and kitchen, and into the bathroom. I called to him through the closed door, "I think that journey took about five days, give or take a week."

There was a brief silence beyond the door, then Shura said, "Hey, do you want to do an experiment?"

"Sure," I said, "What do you have in mind?"

"Wait a moment; I'm going to get a watch. Stay where you are, okay?"

"All right," I replied, "Don't take more than a month getting back to me."

I remember looking at myself in the mirror, combing my hair for what seemed like hours, then Shura's voice through the door, "Hey, still in there?"

"Uh-huh," I drawled, "I think so."

*I haven't the slightest idea whether I'm making sense or not, and it doesn't matter, because he hasn't the slightest idea either.*

The door opened and a mass of electrified silver hair, with Shura's bearded face beaming under it, poked itself into my field of vision.

"Hello!" I said, putting down the comb.

"Are you ready for some scientific research?"

"Absolutely! What do you want me to do?"

"I'm going to go back out and close the door, and I'll say 'Start,' and you keep doing whatever you're doing, then when I say 'Stop,' you tell me how many minutes you think have gone by since the 'Start.' Got it?"

The words crawled through my mind, occasionally taking a wrong turn or two through labyrinthian caverns, but eventually, I thought I understood what he'd said.

"All right," I nodded, "Go to it."

I turned to the mirror again and heard the word "Start," reverberating through the closed door. I looked at the eyes in the mirror and remembered being told that one should be careful, while under the influence of any psychedelic, not to look too long at reflected eyes, because it was easy to become hypnotized.

*What would happen if I got hypnotized? Would I stand here for hours and hours, my mind lost in hyperspace, or would it be like a state of sleep? I really should try it sometime, as long as Shura's around to rescue me.*

Images swam through my mind, and I sat down to pursue them. Planets, rivers, blackbirds cawing in dark woods —

*Ah, yes, that's England, the sound of those birds everywhere in the countryside.*

I remembered. Getting out of the downy bed, at the Bell Inn, the only place to stay in the village of Charlbury, my first morning in England, with Shura — all those years ago — going out onto the little porch and seeing the vegetable garden down below, and the stone wall and, across the fields, a wood full of loud blackbirds; standing there, watching the last of the morning mist curling around little cabbages, half expecting Peter Rabbit to trot into view any moment, wearing his blue jacket with the brass buttons. It was England as I'd imagined it all my life, a watercolor painted by Beatrix Potter, and all the bone-deep exhaustion of the previous day's travels was forgotten.

Suddenly, I heard Shura's muffled voice, "Stop!"

I opened the door.

"How long do you think it's been since I gave you 'Start'?"

I thought back, reviewing my movements from here to there, my thoughts and memories, and I said, "I would say at least twenty minutes."

Shura was obviously pleased. "That's a time-stretch of four to one! Pretty impressive!"

I poked his chest, "Well, fine, but how long was it really? You haven't told me!"

"Oh, sorry. It was all of five minutes."

"That's impossible!"

"Nope. Five minutes exactly," he grinned, waving a wristwatch.

"Boy," I muttered, "That's really hard to believe. Five minutes!"

The push of the unwelcome sensation that marijuana always imposed on me was less present, now. I could ignore it most of the time.

*Getting used to it. But it still isn't my ally, as Shura would say. No, not my ally.*

I was about to turn on heat under a pot of soup when Shura said, "Come here a minute, babe."

I turned to see him standing about a foot from the sink, looking at the large electric clock on the wall above the faucets. He motioned to me, so I joined him and put an arm around his waist. He whispered, "Look at the second hand."

"Okay, I'm looking," I said, not whispering.

"Notice anything?"

I watched the second hand and realized that it was moving very slowly, ridiculously slowly. I said so to Shura.

"Let's both concentrate on it," he said, "And see how much more slowing we can get."

We were focusing tightly on the second hand, willing it to hold back, slow down, when a surprising thing, a magically strange thing, happened. We both saw it at the same time: a curtain of translucent beads, threaded on lines of energy, between us and the clock face. The energy-curtain didn't block our view; we could see our second hand with absolute clarity, but I knew — I *knew* — that, in reaching through the curtain with our will, we were moving our entire selves — at least, mind and spirit — closer to going through the shimmering beads, into a very different place, a reality I couldn't conceive of.

This time it was I who whispered, "You see the curtain, too, don't you?"

"Of course I see it," he replied, almost impatiently.

The second hand was almost still. Almost unmoving. I was holding my breath, knowing that it was about to stop, when Shura broke the spell, loudly, "That's it! Now we know we can do it, we don't have to actually go all the way, right?"

"What are you *talking* about!" I asked, astonished, "Why did you pull back?"

There was something in his face, a look I couldn't decipher; at least, not until he said to me, "I don't like to admit it, but I suddenly got scared."

"Of what, honey?"

"Well, let me ask you this: what do you think happens when the second hand stops moving?"

I didn't have to think out the answer, "It probably means time has stopped."

"Exactly. And what happens to you and me when we find ourselves in a place where there is no time?"

I was beginning to understand, "We might get stuck and not be able to find our way out."

"See, once you're in a place with no time, no sequence of events, how can you even formulate the intent to get out?"

"Well, I must admit that the territory on the other side of the curtain did have a strange — ah — feel to it. Maybe next time, we'll have somebody babysit us; of course, I don't know what a third person could actually do, when you come down to it."

"I don't either." said Shura, then stooped to kiss me, "Do you forgive me, please?"

"Don't be silly, sweetheart; nothing to forgive. It's even possible you saved us both from a fate worse than — ," and it suddenly hit me, forcefully, that there really are fates worse than death, and that finding yourself trapped in timelessness might well be one of them.

On the way back to our bedroom nest, I told him that one of the most fascinating things about this experiment was the appearance of the energy curtain, because it was identical to the curtain I had told him about seeing on my life-changing peyote day, twenty-odd years ago, in the Natural Science Museum with Sam Golding.

"Remember I told you about the time when we walked into the dioramas, where there was nothing living — it was all steel and marble and glass— and after just a moment or two, I began coming down, do you remember?"

"Uh-huh, yes, I remember," said my man, "You said you saw a curtain —"

"It was exactly like this one tonight, only bigger, and it separated the two worlds, the one I had been in since eating the peyote, and the ordinary world I was falling back into. Same curtain, honey. I wonder what it is?"

Shura pulled me onto the bed, "Oh, it's probably just an ordinary worlds-separator curtain, kid; nothing to fuss about. They're a dime a dozen, where I come from. Now, how about taking off all that unnecessary clothing, hmm?"

*How wonderful, to end up with laughter instead of anger. It's the first time THAT'S happened, with pot. Maybe we should quit, while we're ahead. Find other ways to experience time-warping.*

And so, indeed, it came to pass. Clearly, marijuana was simply not our cup of tea, and we never took it again.

# CHAPTER 4.  THE BRAZIL CAPER

(Alice's voice)

In the mid 1980's, somewhere around the month of April, Shura received a phone call from a gentleman who introduced himself as Senhor Giorgio Paros, a businessman from Brazil.  He said, "I am here in the Bay Area to consult with an American company, and also to see you, Doctor Shura, on a very important matter."

Shura replied, "Well, Senhor — excuse me, could you repeat your name?"

The man gave his last name again and added, "Please call me Senhor Giorgio, Sir.  In Brazil, we do not use last names very much.  I would like also to bring with me a very good friend, Doctor Hector, the former Assistant Secretary of Housing and Transportation of Brazil, if that would be acceptable?"

Shura told me later, "He obviously didn't want to go into details on the phone, so I thought, what the heck, maybe you wouldn't mind making a few sandwiches for lunch tomorrow, and I invited them over. Is that okay with you?"

I laughed, "Sure. It sounds pretty intriguing, with a former — what was it? — assistant minister of something for Brazil, right?"

"Yeah," said Shura, "Transportation, I think he said.  Sounds as if it might be interesting.  And if it turns out to be a total dud, it'll only have cost us a couple of hours and a bit of lunch."

*Well, it's hard not to be impressed by a minister of anything of any country, when you get down to it.  Of course, this one's a Former, which isn't as good as a Presently, and he was only an Assistant, not the Main Man, but so what! Former Assistant Minister of anything coming to lunch is still pretty good, if you're an ordinary run-of-the-mill social climber.  Besides, it should make a good dining-out story, if nothing else.*

The next day, shortly after noon, the Boys from Brazil arrived with a bunch of flowers for the hostess, both of them carrying serious briefcases.

The businessman, Georgio, was a big, burly character who looked like an aging stormtrooper, with thinning hair and pale blue, penetrating eyes.

We sat down on the patio and talked, exchanging the necessary pieces of basic information. Sr. Giorgio, it turned out, had long been a major player in Brazilian radio as the owner of several stations, and was now moving into television. Despite the faintly threatening first impression, particularly when he scowled over some remembered annoyance, Giorgio gradually emerged as something of a pussycat, a bit sentimental and rather romantic in a way peculiar to Brazilians (as we were to discover later).

Giorgio's friend, Dr. Hector, was a small-boned man in his late sixties who seemed, at first, rather quiet for a politician; a bit self-effacing, in fact. But as the afternoon wore on, as we all became increasingly familiar with each other's faces and voices, Dr. Hector relaxed and smiled more often, and we began to understand his peculiar charm, the mixture of sincerity — sometimes approaching intensity — and humor which must have served him well in his government post.

But that's getting ahead of my tale. Back to the first few minutes of the meeting.

As I carried out plates of sandwiches to the patio, Giorgio was saying, "Even in the banks, they list customers under their first names! Yes, believe it, this is so!"

I didn't have to look at Shura to know what the expression on his face was: polite skepticism, mixed with frank amusement.

*I can't believe that, either. Must be a bit of exaggeration somewhere. But it does make a great Third World anecdote!*

I brought out a large pitcher of iced tea and some bottles of Calistoga water, then sat down and prepared to listen.

As background to their not-yet-specified proposition, Giorgio told us a story. It seems that, several years earlier, an American gentleman we will call Borch, who had relocated to Rio de Janeiro, and who could not fully explain to anyone's satisfaction why he was unable to return to the United States, married a wealthy Brazilian lady, and produced a couple of children. Then he moved his entire family to an island in the Caribbean whose authorities were notoriously friendly and accommodating towards foreigners with money, and within a few months, all his upper class acquaintances in Rio had received invitations to a new health spa. The brochure emphasized a kind of therapy not usually offered by spas: psychological, with emphasis on the resolving of marital discord and problems like alcoholism.

The Brazilians poured into the new spa. Every Wednesday, the owner, Mr. Borch, would bring out two vials from his private refrigerator. The fluid in the first vial was red; that in the second, yellow. Each client was given a carefully measured amount from one or the other of the vials, served in a beautifully designed miniature goblet, a small crystal bowl cradled in a network of pewter. Borch referred to the medicine as The Essence, and refused to further identify it.

The effect of the Essence medicine was astonishing, Georgio told us. "You had a feeling that God had entered your soul, and all was peace inside you," he said, "If you looked at somebody, you felt love for him, compassion, you understand? For married couples, it was miraculous. All the emotions — yes? — the feelings they had in the past for each other; all these returned, just like the day of their marriage."

Shura and I listened to the account in fascinated silence, but both of us were beginning to feel the pressure of questions needing to be asked, and I actually had my mouth open to say something, when Dr. Hector spoke up for the first time since the story began, and stunned us back into listening.

"Once, when I had expressed myself to Mr. Borch again," the grey-suited little gentleman said, "About wishing to know what was in the Essence, he told me that I could have faith in its value and its purity, because it had been created by one of the world's most respected scientists, a chemist called Alexander Borodin, and that it was not necessary for me to know anything else."

"Oh, my God!" I breathed, then laughed.

Shura protested, "I've never heard of anyone named Borch, and I certainly never supplied him with any drug!"

Georgio gestured impatiently, "Yes, yes, Hector and I decided this ourselves — that you had nothing to do with it — when we investigated and found out who you were."

*I wonder if he uses the word, "investigated," the same way we would use it. Sort of implies private detectives and all that sort of thing. Maybe better not to know.*

One burning question had arisen in my mind, and I decided now was the time to get an answer, before the conversation got any more complicated. I leaned forward in my chair and asked, looking from one to the other, "How much did these clients pay for the miraculous spa treatment, if you don't mind my curiosity?"

"Most of us paid twenty-five thousand dollars per week," said Giorgio.

Shura and I looked at each other, eyes wide.

"Oog," I said, brilliantly.

"Sounds like a pretty good scam," said Shura, nodding his appreciation.

"In the last week at the spa," said Hector, "Georgio and I managed to divert some of our Essence medicine, and we took the sample with us when we left. We had it analyzed in the United States. It was a drug called MDMA."

"Oh, boy," I said.

Shura just grunted.

Giorgio leaned forward, and I saw how the expensive suit pulled under his arms. I said, "Why don't you gentlemen take off your jackets; it's too warm to be formal."

They both smiled and followed my suggestion.

Sr. Giorgio leaned forward again, his elbows on the white patio table. He was wearing dark red garters around his shirtsleeves. His hands met each other in prayer position at the tip of his nose as he paused, obviously reviewing what was to come next.

Shura and I waited, respectfully. Dr. Hector sat back in his chair, eyes closed in the soft sunlight, apparently content to have his friend do the talking, for the moment.

Finally, Giorgio opened up Stage Two. "The reason we are here, Doctor Shura," he said, speaking slowly, "Is that we do not wish to go back to the Borch spa, for many reasons."

*Twenty-five thousand a week would be reason enough for me.*

Shura nodded.

"But we — all of my friends who have been there — believe that this medicine, this Essence — the MDMA — is of great value. We have a plan to open a clinic in Rio, where we live, and teach people to administer it to patients, yes?"

Shura shifted in his chair.

"We would like to do research," continued Giorgio, "And establish this medicine as a respected way to solve many problems for people who have pain in their souls. Do you understand?"

*He's hitting all the right buttons, so far.*

Shura said, "Do you have permission from the authorities in Brazil to do this?"

Dr. Hector spoke up, "Yes, we are working on that now. I have a good friend who has access to the President, and it will be only a matter of time."

Shura asked another blunt one, "What is the legal status of MDMA in Brazil?"

Giorgio looked over at Dr. Hector, then answered, "At the present time, it is not named in any of our laws. It is legal."

"You mean," said Shura, smiling gently, "It is not *illegal*, am I right?"

The light blue eyes squinted, then the big man laughed, "Yes, I suppose that is true. We hope to sanctify the use of this medicine by employing it in our clinic. Does this make sense to you?"

*Sanctify? Wow.*

"It sounds very interesting." replied Shura, cautiously. He paused for a moment, then asked, "And how can I be of help to you?"

"We would like," said Giorgio, glancing at Dr. Hector, who nodded, "To invite you — and your wife, of course — to come down to Rio and meet our friends, and talk to a group of doctors and psychiatrists about this medicine, and how it can be used. And we would like you to make a supply of MDMA for us, for our clinic, so that we can begin the good work."

"I would be most happy to do so," said Shura, courteously, even a bit formally, "As long as you can assure me that I will not be breaking any of the laws of Brazil. I have to have absolute certainty about that. At present, MDMA is not illegal in the United States, but I don't know anything about Brazilian drug law, and I cannot be put in the position of doing anything in a foreign country which is even slightly questionable, as I'm sure you understand."

"Absolutely!" declared Giorgio, while Dr. Hector murmured, "Of course, of course."

"By the time you get to Rio, my dear friend," assured Giorgio, "We will have copies of all Brazilian law that has relation to this project. But I can promise you already that you will not be breaking any laws of our country. We would not ask you to do such a thing. You are a great man, a great scientist, and we have deep respect for you, for your reputation. Be assured, all will be legal and honorable."

So we agreed to go to Rio de Janeiro.

When the airline tickets arrived in the mail, they were for mid-June, on Pan American, in first class for the first leg of the journey, and business class for the second. The return trip tickets were included in the package, for a date two weeks later, also Pan American, again first and business class.

"Oh, my God, Honey," I breathed, *"First class*! I've never flown first class in my life, have you?"

"Nope," said The Great Scientist, "And I don't expect to again, to tell the truth. Should be an interesting experience."

*"Interesting?"* I gasped, "You bet yore sweet bippy, it's gonna be interesting!" I got up and went around in back of him, and planted a loud, smoochy kiss on his neck. He kept his dignity, as usual, barely glancing up as I did a modified Bossa Nova past him, through the kitchen and into the hall.

FRIDAY          Rio de Janeiro, Brazil          10 p.m.

"It seems only wise to begin making notes now, considering the amount of activity that might continue for the rest of our stay. If today —

our first day here — is any indication, we are going to be inundated by people, energy, questions, enthusiasms, happy noise, food, sightseeing, and maybe even some chemistry."

The entire trip had been as comfortable and smooth as a long journey by air could possibly be. We had been in first class from San Francisco to Miami, a new experience, since each of us had always before traveled as a peasant among peasants. Both leg room and food are worlds better in first class. They gave us a menu from which to choose our main course (in this case for breakfast) and what we got was an omelet with an exquisite filet mignon and potatoes, along with fresh fruit, yeasty rolls, coffee and a choice of liquors and wines. I did a small double-take at the alcohol on the menu, right up there with eggs and strawberry jam.

*I wonder why they offer alcohol with breakfast; maybe a lot of people who fly first class are alcoholics; successful, driven people who can't relax unless they drink? And the airline wants those kinds of customers to feel that it's okay to order wine early in the day without being embarrassed or defensive?*

In Miami, we faced a seven-hour layover, which we spent in utter comfort in a room reserved for us at the Miami International Airport Hotel, where we fooled around on the fresh sheets as the air conditioning hummed away. All the hotel reservations, as well as the airline tickets, had been arranged and paid for by our Brazilian hosts. By the time our Pan Am flight to Rio was ready for boarding, we were refreshed, cleaned up and minimally tired.

All we knew about our next plane, Pam Am flight 441, was that we would be in something called Clipper Class. Turned out to be their term for what other airlines usually call business class, between first and peasant. We had never before flown *that*, either.

The leg room was still good, and the food only slightly less impressive than first, and we were perfectly content. My faith in Pan Am was, at that point, absolute.

Finally, we landed in Rio de Janeiro. The first proof of our hosts' influence and importance was in the way we went through immigration and customs. Dr. Hector met us coming off the plane and introduced us to two young men who apparently worked for the airport; one spoke good English, the other no English at all. While one of them stayed with us, obliging Shura's desire for a lesson in Portuguese (I was watching the carousel for our suitcases), the other went off with our passports and visas (Shura told me later that he felt a stab of panic as our vital papers disappeared in the hands of a stranger). Within a few minutes, the gentleman returned with our papers in order, properly stamped.

"Thus is the path smoothed for the Great One," I intoned, making a token curtsey, "And the Great One's humble and adoring wife."

"It certainly beats waiting in line," grinned Shura.

When the bags had been retrieved, we were shepherded past a line of waiting people and through an electronic gateway with a sign that said: "If you don't have anything to declare, push the green button and go through," which we did. At that point, we were apparently finished with any official procedures and free to leave the airport. I whispered to Shura, "Sort of like the King and Queen of California, yes?"

One could not help being impressed.

Once out of the Rio airport, in an area where cars picked up passengers, we saw Sr. Giorgio and his lovely wife, Lena, of whom he had spoken with some pride, and Dr. Hector's wife, Rita, who was equally attractive.

I wrote: "Both women are in their forties or maybe fifties, but the eyelids and dewlaps have been expertly taken care of by one or another of Rio's famous plastic surgeons. As we were to discover, it isn't considered something to be kept secret here, if you've had the signs of aging smoothed out; women boast about 'their' plastic surgeon, who is always the best and owns three homes in at least two countries to prove it."

There was an immediate sense of being welcomed without reservations, with none of the cool surveying, the critical inspection underneath the polite smiles, that would be expected from upper-class women in North America, meeting you for the first time. That isn't to say the inspection wasn't going on; after all, we look, we evaluate, we do a lot of comparing the first time we meet a stranger, no matter who we are or in what country. It's just that the instinct to make the new person welcome seemed uppermost at that moment, and the watchfulness less obvious.

We got into Giorgio and Lena's big American car, since it was their house (the "summer house") we were to stay in. Within a few minutes, I found myself regretting that I'd packed the camera in the back of the car; we were driving past the favelas — the shacks of the poor — climbing steeply up the hillsides. Red, blue, green, yellow, black and pink shacks, the paint scuffed and peeling. It was apparent that, in a reversal of what one finds in most countries, the Brazilian poor have the hills and the rich have the flatlands.

The famed Rio hills are quite extraordinary; they are like very large versions of the sharply up and down hills of China. Sugar Loaf is a massive, round-topped rock, a great solid piece, scored deeply on its sides as if it had risen in one huge, screaming up-thrust from the depths of the earth, eons ago.

Our car drove along the beautiful beachfront sidewalk familiar from photographs, with its lovely tilework in wave patterns, stretching as far as we could see.

Lena turned to me and said, regretfully, "You cannot go into the water. It is so pretty, but you cannot swim."

We asked why.

"It is poisoned," said Giorgio, "Because there are no sewers in the favelas, you understand? So the — everything — comes down the hills, and it all goes into the bay."

Shura was in the front passenger seat, but I knew we must be thinking pretty much the same thing.

*Jesus! That's what's meant by Third World. Instead of building sewers for the poor on the hill, they let the sewerage flow into their bay and ruin it, then they shrug and say what a pity it is, what a shame, as if it were all an act of God.*

I realized suddenly that I was extremely tired from the long trip, and would have to pay attention to what I said out loud, and the tone in which I said it.

*Keep your irritables to yourself, kid.*

There was a remark made by Giorgio, somewhere during the ride — perhaps while we were passing the clustered favelas up on the hillsides — about democracy being a fine idea, but it wasn't working here in Brazil; that things had been better controlled when the military was in power (although he added, perhaps out of courtesy to his guests, that he didn't feel comfortable with the idea of a military government). I think this was said just after he mentioned that the inflation rate was now one per cent every day.

The attitude expressed, during that car ride and afterwards, toward the people who live in the favelas was pretty much the same attitude to be found in every city when the rich are talking about the poor: resentment overlying anxiety and a certain chronic sense of guilt. It is a subject that outsiders are well advised to stay away from in any country, but especially in a place like Brazil, where there is not a large middle class, where there are, for the most part, only the very rich and the extremely poor.

On the beachfront, we passed huge hotels with carefully tended tropical gardens in front. Graffiti were everywhere, even on second and third stories of some of the tall buildings; many were faced with marble and all looked expensive. There were palm trees, fig trees, and one could glimpse carefully maintained miniature gardens between the hotels. Yet, despite the luxuriousness of this rich peoples' playground, I was aware of something typical of the tropics: an impression that decay was just around the corner, that if those in charge of maintenance failed for a week or two to make sure things were polished and cleaned, there would be a fast deterioration of surfaces, a growth of fungus in the crevices, grey-brown dust everywhere. It could have been an effect of the overcast sky, this sense-impression; perhaps it was the result of too few hours of sleep.

It was now winter in Brazil, which meant daytime temperatures in the 70's, for the most part, although sometimes it slipped into the low 80's. (We eventually got used to the Brazilians apologizing for the cold weather.)

What our hosts called the summer house had been built by Giorgio (he said) for Lena, and he complained during the drive there that, once it was built, she decided she didn't want to live in it, preferring their downtown apartment.

Lena looked over at me (we were in the back seat) and grinned. Giorgio's voice had conveyed a distinct touch of indulgence along with the exasperation, and I thought about Brazil being a man's world, and the subtle power games that go on between male and female in a patriarchal, machismo society.

It became clear, as the conversation continued, that the new place actually was used, despite Giorgio's complaints. They entertained there, because it had more room than their old apartment, and when friends from out of town came to stay, everybody moved into the summer house. The neighborhood was one of Rio's finest and most expensive, with brand new houses going up in every block. There was a watchman at the entrance gate and he was in charge of a movable crossing barrier, and there were speed bumps staggered on the pavement to insure that "unauthorized" vehicles would have a very tough time getting through. Authorized cars didn't exactly speed along, either.

Giorgio told us a story about life in the enclaves of the rich. He said, "Six months ago, we began to have many burglaries here, one house after another. Whenever the people would leave to go back to their apartments in the city, their house would become a victim. We were broken into, also. Finally, it was discovered that the watchman at the entrance gate was telling his friends which houses were empty, and they would come in at night and take everything. They could take their time, without fear, because the watchman always knew when the owners would return. That is part of his job, you see, to know which houses are empty, without servants, so he can keep his eye on them and protect them from thieves!"

We laughed, and Shura asked if the present watchman had been put through a very complete inspection before being hired.

"You bet," chuckled Giorgio, "He was investigated like he was taking a position in a bank vault. He is so clean, he has a halo over his head!" His booming laughter filled the car. Then we pulled into a driveway and parked.

The house was five stories (if you counted the little outlook on the top as a story), built of concrete and wood. Not particularly pretty outside, but very attractive inside, with white plaster walls and rich brown wood. Some delicious pieces of carved furniture — I was told they were Brazilian antiques — tempted me to stroke surfaces and edges. On one wall of the living room was a huge African ceremonial mask. Giorgio said this was in honor of his Negro blood (like many people in Brazil, and especially in Rio, he is a mixture of several races and proud of all of them). I noted some potted plants with thick trunks, their large green leaves climbing up the white walls. Big armchairs all over the room, and a long couch.

In the kitchen, we met Corazon, (which means "heart") who, Lena explained, was to be our cook, housekeeper and friend. She was a mixture of Portuguese, Italian, Negro (the Brazilians are comfortable with that word) and Amazonian Indian, and she had lived for four years in New York, so her English was very good. During our stay, she did our laundry with loving care, made the beds, cooked extraordinary meals, made constant strong Brazilian coffee for us, and interpreted the world around us when we needed to understand this very different culture.

She was also very, very pregnant.

On the second floor was our bedroom, very big, with furniture Shura finally, after some thought, identified as French moderne of the Jacques Tati era.

No facecloths anywhere. (I was to discover that facecloths are unknown in Brazil, as well as in many other countries, First as well as Third World.)

The bed had a hard mattress which Shura liked. The view from one side of the room, when we opened the sliding doors, was lovely: below us was the tree-lined cobblestoned street, and we could glimpse houses roofed in red tile on the other side of it. There were palms and mimosa trees growing in their gardens.

We slept for a couple of hours, then dressed for the first social obligation of our visit: meeting the "Family." This was what they called themselves, the group of about 35 people who took MDMA either once a week or perhaps only once a month. Giorgio explained that usually not all of them would be gathering together in the same house — eight to ten being considered the preferred maximum for the MDMA experience — but that this evening, in honor of our visit, the whole group had been invited for questions and answers and general celebration.

I wore a long, loose, white cotton dress with ruffles, comfortable and relatively graceful. Shura had already been told that ties simply were not worn in Brazil, except to the office when necessary and when meeting with VIP's of certain kinds, so he had on a sports shirt with his new dark pants.

The first lesson was in the ways of greeting. Women are welcomed in the French manner with a kiss on each cheek, kiss left then right; men shake hands with men or grip each other's arms or shoulders. Several of the guests did their best to confine themselves to the U.S. handshake, but we all soon adopted the nicer French double-buss. (By the time we fell into bed, Shura and I had kissed more cheeks and gripped more forearms than we would have believed possible in one single evening.)

Among the guests, this first time and the following day: Sr. Draggo (the only one of the Family known by his last name) who was lightly scarred from a crash in another South American country several years before. It seems he was in a limousine which was mistaken for that of the president, by some rebels or Communists or the CIA or whoever it is that's in the business of assassinating South American presidents. All in the car were killed but Sr. Draggo. We were informed that he was an importer whose specialty was trade with China, and that he owned four little companies of various kinds, all of them in Brazil.

Sr. Leo: heavyset, with a big round face I liked immediately; humorous, sad-funny and warm. He was also in business, import-export, and spoke French, English, Arabic, Portuguese and Spanish.

His wife, Anita, was quite pretty. She wore her very blond hair in a corona around her face, a style that I finally decided was old-fashioned Parisian.

Pierre and Helena, who stayed in the house next door (on weekends) with daughter Delia and her husband Tomas. They were French. Pierre owned half a dozen stores in Sao Paulo, all of them selling fabrics to interior decorators.

Sr. Waldo, masseur. He was present the following day, giving massages upstairs in the second-floor mini living room, but we weren't sure he had taken the MDMA. We speculated to each other that he probably couldn't afford it very often. (It had gradually become clear that our hosts charged for the MDMA, although we were never told the price, and didn't ask. They had to buy it from somebody, obviously, and Shura and I thought it likely that they had made some kind of arrangement with the infamous Borch — which would probably make it very expensive, indeed.)

Sr. Waldo was a gentle, sweet man who spoke no English. I made all kinds of passionate gestures and noises about the incense he was burning during the massages, and the next day he brought me several bundles of it, as a gift, along with some herbs, including one called Guarana (pronounced with emphasis on the last "a"), an herb which interested Shura very much, being apparently some kind of stimulant.

Doctor Roberto, plastic surgeon. A Good-looking, slender, tall and compulsively seductive man who appeared to be intelligent, and struck me as being somewhat calculating. He asked some sharp and insightful questions the first evening. Supposedly one of the best in his business.

Marina: a beautiful young woman, black haired, immature and lovable, very spontaneous and expressive. She was the mistress of Dr.

Roberto and the mother of his young daughter, Katya, who was also beautiful (we met her some days later). Roberto had a wife (whom we were to meet on Wednesday night at his birthday party) and two grown sons, one of them a doctor who assisted Daddy at the plastic surgery clinic. Mistress was a member of the MDMA family; wife was not. Marina was studying art.

(All this information was fed to us — with undisguised relish — by Giorgio and Lena, late that first night, after all the guests had gone.)

There were other people whose names were never quite made clear in the general cheerful confusion. One was a heavy-set mulatto woman with short hair and an open, friendly face, whose hobby was taking Kirlian photographs. She handed round a set of them which was quite impressive, showing before and after MDMA finger-tips from various family members. The "after" revealed expansion of the glowing halo around each fingertip, and the group responded to the photos with what sounded like expressions of admiration and congratulations in Portuguese.

Oh, yes, the multi-millionaire. One hundred and twenty million or so. Looked a lot like a certain handsome Spanish-American actor, and seemed gracious, observant and self-contained. Senhor Carlos. (One *always* finds out the name of a multi-millionaire.)

Another young plastic surgeon, dressed all in white, with his wife. Open-faced, nice, good-looking, rather boyish.

And others, whose names we did hear and didn't write down, but should have, because we couldn't remember any of them by the next day.

The gathering was in honor of us. We sat like royalty, side by side, and answered questions all evening. Each guest took a turn presenting himself, his business or profession, and history of MDMA use and benefits derived therefrom. Then came the questions and discussions, with either Giorgio or Dr. Hector translating when necessary. There seemed to be a willingness, even an eagerness, to confess to emotional problems worked through, marital problems straightened out, and weight problems overcome.

A great many of the guests had been introduced to MDMA by Mr. Borch, some others by members of the Family, we gathered. Although everyone present had left the Borch operation, he was still regarded with some reverence.

Shura and I had the impression that Mr. Borch was a consummate salesman and persuader, with a very strong, charismatic personality. Despite their expressed skepticism about this gentleman, our hosts still talked about him with a touch of awe. It seemed to me that all these people had given over a lot of their power to this would-be guru, and hadn't yet taken it all back.

We were still annoyed about his unauthorized use of Shura's name in connection with his MDMA, and had discussed the possibility of confronting him, but finally decided to forget the whole thing, because it simply wasn't worth the trouble. Besides, as Shura said at one point, "My name has probably been mis-used more times and by more con artists than I really want to know about, and I can't sue all of them. Better to let it go."

I agreed.

In any case, as Shura kept reminding me, we were well advised to be subtle about our opinions regarding Mr. Borch, since he was still an influence, even if only slightly so, among these rich and naive Brazilians. He said, "We should avoid making too many strong statements about somebody we've never met and hope never to meet."

That first evening, one of Shura's most important (and, to judge from the shocked silence, most surprising) bits of information to the group was his remark that the cost of a dose of MDMA (they used 125 milligrams, without supplement) was about a dollar. He felt it was a nice bit of data for them.

The gathering lasted many hours, with constant excited talk and the beginning of our multi-lingual experience. We found ourselves trying to communicate in every language we had between us, Shura being better at French and I at Spanish. Most of these people had some knowledge of one or both, along with their native Portuguese.

Questions about MDMA use ranged from whether there is neurological damage to humans from the drug, to why the first experience is never quite recaptured, and so on. The usual questions, in other words.

Shura's answer to the first was, "At the usual therapeutic dosage levels of between 100 and 150 milligrams per session, with or without a supplement of 40 or 50 milligrams, there is no scientific evidence that there is any neurological damage in humans. In certain laboratory animals, very high dosage levels — higher than any equivalent dose that would be given to humans — have shown damage, and in other lab animals, no damage at all."

His reply to the second question about the difficulty of recapturing the first wonderful experience was, "Nobody knows why, but it seems to be the case for most people I've talked to."

One of the guests, a man who had been identified by Lena as a psychiatrist, a middle-aged man with sharp, perceptive eyes in a kind face, came over toward the end of the evening and gave me that most wonderful of all compliments, telling me I was very "sympatico." My favorite word, in any language. Especially when applied to me. (We have no exact translation, but it means that you're sympathetic, empathetic, understanding and generally a nice, warm-fuzzy person.)

Then it was time to fold everything for the night, and we went through another round of kiss-kiss, hearty back-slaps (and occasional shy hugs between men), explosive appreciations and gratitudes and all that. We had begun what I later came to think of as The Week of Constant Smiling.

SATURDAY:

The day of the MDMA. The people from last night's group, plus some new ones who hadn't been able to come before. Perhaps thirty five people in all, give or take. Our hosts had made clear that they needed us to "oversee" their MDMA experience, which would be very different from what they were used to, in that the entire Family would be present, instead of the usual eight or ten. Some of them were, they said later, a bit nervous about the size of the group, but relaxed into it as time passed. We were not expected to take the "medicine," but just to be present and see if anything was being done unwisely, or should be changed. We were relieved, not having wanted to take anything at all, under any circumstances, down here. (The truth is, we usually did not participate in experiences with groups of people whom we didn't know very intimately, anywhere, in any country.)

After perhaps half an hour of very Latin noise and laughter, mouths moving and hands flying, our hosts quieted everyone down and the program began. First, they were each given 75 milligrams of the red MDMA. Then the gentle mulatto woman led what she called a meditation, in the softest of sing-song Portuguese. About thirty minutes after the first half of the dose, came the second half, 50 milligrams. People talked, or sat quietly by themselves, or wandered around, just like our own research group. Shura and I were kept busy by people asking questions or telling us their life stories and innermost secrets. Just like most people taking MDMA. In four languages.

*Well, there aren't that many advantages to growing older, when you get down to it, but now and then you do find yourself enjoying a situation that wouldn't have happened when you were young and beautiful. Here we are, Shura and I, being treated like Old Wise Man and Woman, being told things, being asked for our opinions, being looked at as if we know more than anyone else, as if we can solve what no one else can solve. We are the wise elders, and best of all, we're strangers, so we get all the juiciest positive projections. It's enough to turn your head, yes it is.*

I sat and talked for some time with a young man in his late twenties, who told me he'd had a terrible alcohol problem and a lot of depression and anger, which was relieved by MDMA (his parents joined us later and confirmed his story).

The weather was muggy and the sky slightly overcast. Somebody mentioned that it was one of the many Brazilian holidays, the feast of Saint

Somebody, and we began to hear the fireworks which continued, off and on, throughout the day.

Our group dispersed relatively early, after several hours of talk with people who had wanted to share intimate thoughts, or ask advice on some deeply personal problem, or even to say thank you to us for having come. More kiss left, kiss right, hugs, more, "See you tomorrow."

In the evening, we went for a ride with our hosts to the nearest beach, where we parked, locked the car and went down onto the fine sand to pick up tiny shells and watch the old fishermen sitting with their lines in the surf, lanterns glowing beside their chairs. As the stars began to appear, Shura and I had our first view of the Southern Cross. We stood, arms around each other's waists, looking at the unfamiliar constellations and marveling at their beauty.

Back at the house, we excused ourselves and while Shura wrote upstairs in the little not-quite-finished astronomy-study with its big windows, I unpacked some of our clothes and hung them up in the bedroom closet.

Peace and quiet for a while, then Dr. Hector arrived. People do that in Rio, we were told. They just arrive, expected or not. When we heard Giorgio's booming voice calling us downstairs to "Hear the good news that Doctor Hector has for you," we obliged with eagerness only slightly tempered by tiredness.

Shura had, by now, heard from several different sources that there were going to be two labs for the making of MDMA. The original plan, to use a lab in the university, had fallen through when the university went on strike, so there had been a search for a substitute. Of course, there were politics to be considered — the Family kind — (we didn't really know what they were, only that they existed, and we'd heard hints of concerns, such as how much of the magic alchemical procedure was to be made known to this person or that, and does half of the MDMA go to the use of the Family and the other half to the future clinic?). Shura had been getting increasingly anxious to know whether he would have to split the procedure between two labs, or whether he could do it in the most convenient way: in one place at one time.

But first and foremost, as he reminded me on our way down the stairs, he wanted definite word on the legal aspects of what he was being asked to do, and Dr. Hector was the person to give him answers.

In the big living room, we went through the usual hugs and greetings before settling into armchairs. In response to Shura's direct question, Dr. Hector smiled and told him that, after intensive investigation and consultation with friends in the government, he could say without hesitation that the proposed manufacturing of MDMA, especially for clinical use, was absolutely legal in Brazil. He added, "We will have final approval for our project in a few days, when my friend has a chance to talk to the right authorities, but that is only a formality."

Shura breathed a very audible sigh of relief, and thanked Dr. Hector for having cleared up the question of most importance to him, what he called the only remaining barrier to making MDMA for the Family and the shortly-to-be-launched clinic.

A sherbert-cool breeze was coming through the open doors, to my immense relief; I had been sweating in the earlier humid warmth, and now, finally, I was feeling comfortable.

Dr. Hector, looking even thinner than usual on the long, blue-and-green patterned couch, leaned forward and braced himself on his knees. He said to Shura, "We have decided we will use Doctor Roberto's laboratory, in his clinic where he does surgery, in the town of Niteroi. I think you will like it; it is a nice place."

Shura nodded, smiling, obviously relieved at hearing something that sounded like a plan taking shape. "It's all well and good," he'd told me earlier, "To be lionized and consulted and treated with respect and so on, but if I'm down here to make MDMA for a clinic which might actually produce some good publications, I'd like to get going."

Dr. Hector continued, "We will have our chemist, Doctor Sol — he speaks very good English — and he will bring all available equipment and basic chemicals. He can work with you and learn the procedures."

"Where does Doctor Sol usually work?" asked Shura.

"He is chief chemist at a large pharmaceutical company," said Dr. Hector, "And he is very intelligent, very *sympatico.*"

"Wonderful," beamed Shura, "I look forward to getting started."

Lena brought in a large pitcher of iced tea and glasses.

The discussion was now about the future clinic, and Shura was telling our three friends that he had brought with him some 2C-B, just enough for our hosts and wives to try, at least for now, and we talked about the use of 2C-B in psychotherapy. This time I joined in, because I was the only one who had actually used it with patients.

After mentioning the most practical aspect of 2C-B, its relative shortness, I explained that not as many patients would be able to benefit from 2C-B as from MDMA, "Because MDMA is not a true psychedelic, as you probably know. It opens the soul, or the psyche, to parts of itself that are not usually accessible — "

I paused for some iced tea, and to glance at the faces around me; no one looked particularly bored, so I continued.

" — and it allows for a dropping of fear, the fear of seeing something terrible inside yourself, so there can be a lot of insight work done. 2C-B, on the other hand, opens up a great deal more than that; it's a true psychedelic. I like to say that while MDMA opens up the mind and the heart, 2C-B opens up the gut, so to speak, the strong emotions, the great psychic energies, the unconscious images — what they call archetypes — and I really think that a patient should have worked with MDMA and intensive psychotherapy for at least six months before you begin thinking about introducing them to the different and deeper world of 2C-B."

*Was that understandable to people who don't speak English all that much? I've got to watch the words I use here, try to be clear to everyone.*

Suddenly, we were interrupted by the sound of loud firecrackers, very close by, and I remembered somebody telling us earlier that today was a saint's birthday. We trooped upstairs to the second floor and out onto a balcony, to see a fireworks display from a back yard two houses away, where they were having a big barbecue party with traditional miniature flags strung above the lawn.

No safe and sane firecrackers, these, but great whooshes of fire, thunking and crackling to make crazy the ears. Several pieces of flaming something fell back onto the tops of trees growing in the party yard and stayed there, burning happily away, while we speculated as to how much of the neighborhood was going to go up in smoke. Corazon, who had come onto the balcony behind us to see the sight, remarked that whatever parts of the tree had been burned would probably all grow back in a couple of days. (As it turned out, the next day there was no sign of tree damage at all.)

Lena pointed at balloons being sent up into the sky, and said, "You see there, they have tied paper sacks onto the balloons, and inside the sacks there are lighted candles, and they will wander all over the countryside like flying stars!"

*And set pretty little fires wherever they happen to come down.*

Shura chuckled, probably only half believing her, then asked, "Isn't that rather dangerous? I mean, what if they land on somebody's roof, or in a forest?"

Giorgio laughed, "Yes, yes, it is very dangerous, and every year there are fires, but nobody wants to stop the beautiful balloons, so what can you do?"

I could feel the Brazilian shrugs all around me, in the dark.

Finally, concluding that the neighborhood was going to stay intact, we all hugged and kissed goodnight and went to bed.

SUNDAY:

I wrote: "Warmer, maybe early 80's in mid-morning. What I could remember of my dreams last night had a negative, slightly anxious tinge, as if the unconscious had been working overtime, trying to deal with under-currents of doubt about this whole situation, as well as the constant need to interpret different languages, and fear of making social boo-boos."

We had breakfast with our hosts; there was a large plate of fruit of all kinds (I had read that in Brazil fresh fruit is eaten — usually — only for breakfast, but we were told that this just isn't so; it's used all the time in every kind of dish). There were pieces of pineapple, mango, papaya, some pear-oranges (there are many kinds of oranges here as well as ten varieties of bananas) and grapes. Coarse wheat bread, fine wheat bread, a kind of cinnamon roll bread and superb Provolone cheese. Corazon cooked excel-lent scrambled eggs with bacon. And there was plenty of the strong, addictive Brazilian coffee, which most people here took with a lot of sugar.

This was to be our sightseeing day. Despite Lena's worry about the probability that there would be too many tourists on Sugar Loaf, it was in the program, and Giorgio wanted to stick to it. (As it turned out, it was just as well he did, because the next day — and the next, and the next — we had rain.)

We reached the entrance to the Sugar Loaf ticket place, and when Giorgio parked his car and paid the car-person, he left his windshield wipers sticking up and out. This is the way, he explained, to indicate that one has already paid for parking.

We got into a gondola car running on cables, windows all around, which left us on top of an intermediate mountain, Urca. Somehow, Shura and I failed to understand from our friends that this was not the top of Sugar Loaf; just one of those small glitches in communication. We posed for each other's photos while a small mariachi band, dressed in dowdy Disneyland costumes (big mice and other strange animals) played what Shura de-scribed as "Execrable music, a Junior High School band before it knows which end of the instrument is up." Then we heard shouts from Giorgio, who waved us along and explained that we were only half way to Sugar Loaf. Oh. We hurried along to the next gondola car, amused at the pathway, which had been carefully set through the middle of the ultimate in souvenir tourist-traps, numerous little booths hawking everything from miniature flags to exercise videos.

On to Sugar Loaf. The top of the mountain, when we finally disembarked, revealed a view which must be absolutely unrivaled in the world. You couldn't possibly have a more fantastic bay. Its fame is totally justified. We just stood there, like all the other gawking tourists, and tried to take it all in. Giorgio and Lena watched us fondly, as we oohed and aahed and pointed and gaped in astonishment.

Back to the city and lunch at Porxo, (pronounced somewhat like Porshao) which is a chain of restaurants specializing in a great big salad-

and-vegetable bar, with waiters who come around to your table with various meats on metal skewers — chicken wrapped in bacon, several cuts of roast beef, sausages — and they keep coming back, until you've had your fill.

We were joined by Dr. Hector and his pretty wife, Rita, at Porxo. We ate, and ate, and ate. So far, Brazilian food had been totally irresistible. Now we were eating hearts of palm, superb vegetables and farinas. Brazilians like their food and rich Brazilians are gourmets; at least, *our* rich Brazilians were.

Then on again, driving to the only shopping open on Sunday, a spread of colored tents, striped awnings and handmade booths in a city park, called the Hippie Market. There, I found exactly the kinds of things I wanted to buy in Rio, including handmade clay pipes from the Amazon, decorated with bits of jaguar fur or teeth.

We drove home to get ready for an evening spectacular. Shura and I dressed up (no tie, of course) and were driven to a big theater called Scala. Our transportation was furnished by the daughter and son-in-law of the neighbors, Delia and Tomas. Delia spoke French and Portuguese, her husband only Portuguese, so Shura and I talked in French, with a bit of Spanish thrown in (usually by me) when in doubt.

Delia translated for Tomas. He had a few questions to ask about psychedelic mushrooms, which he had taken and liked. He wanted to know how to identify them, and Shura launched into one of his professorial expositions, speaking a bit slower than usual, because he had to explain everything in somewhat halting French; he also gave Tomas some information about poisonous species and their dire effects.

At Scala, which was an immense two-tiered tourist showplace, we had a long table right next to the stage. Our companions were the core members of the Family, again, with one new and welcome addition: Dr. Sol, the young chemist who had been assigned to assist Shura in the lab, and learn his method of making MDMA.

Sr. Leo bought a program for us and later insisted on paying for photos taken by the theater photographer. We had no Brazilian money, since we hadn't had a chance to change our American dollars, and Giorgio had told us to wait until Monday, when such exchanges would open again. In the meantime, everyone made clear, we should ask for anything we wanted and it would be provided. We had no choice, but promised each other we'd repay somehow.

The gold curtains parted, and the show, "Golden Brasil" began. Music very loud, costumes loaded with sequins, the showgirls' smiles glued in place, host of ceremonies in white satin with lots of dark face makeup and Las Vegas good looks. His smile was a dazzling gleam-o-rama of white teeth. Ziegfield Follies costumes, towering headdresses, feathers everywhere, even on the shoulders of the host of ceremonies. Bare breasts for most of the girls and minimum underwear, if any, under the satin pants of the young male dancers. My impression was that you could tell the status of the females by whether or not they wore something over their breasts. Claudia, the singing star, was fully dressed in satin, sequins and feathers.

Very pretty ladies, around 18 to 20 years old, good dancers. Some of them actually seemed to be enjoying themselves, during some of the acts, but most looked the way showgirls usually look — capped teeth fixed in professional smiles, eyes focused elsewhere. A few probably stoned. Excellent dancing.

The costumes emphasized the same thing that the mini-Bikinis of Rio emphasize: the derriere. (I had seen postcards of mini-clad bathing beauties on the beach, and not a single card showed any girl from the front.) Derrieres are very popular, and there was a lot of fooling around on the stage which emphasized the attraction of the "bum-bum," (pronounced "boom-boom,") as it's called in Brazil.

One thing was quite apparent on stage, as it is everywhere else in Rio: they are proud of their mixture of races, and like to draw attention to it. Which is very nice. The U.S. could use a bit of what they have here, in regard to race-mixing. People boast about their native Indian or "Negro" roots, and on the stage, the "naughty boys" running after the girls were black, and the most popular and acclaimed dancing group were the Mulattos.

The Mulattos did a real samba. The real samba is quite a dance. It's said that very few people can do it properly, since it takes a flexibility of joints, including hips, and an unbelievable quickness of foot. Whatever it takes, the Mulattos had it. One of the best parts of the show.

The second best part of the show was a bearded man who danced as The Gaucho (which is apparently Brazilian as well as Argentinian) and did extraordinary things with two strings tipped with small wooden balls, swinging them faster than the eye could see, the balls rattling in a fierce rhythm on the floor. Wonderful.

The loud, stomping, brassy show, the glittering tons of sequins, the Las Vegas atmosphere, reminded me of what we were already discovering about Brazil — at least, the Rio part of it — a lot of sparkle and activity overlying a great disquiet, anxiety and anger, because of the impossible and getting worse economic and political situation. I found myself thinking of the tall skyscraper apartment buildings set against the hills with their massed favela shacks, the poor living in utter deprivation, no sewage system, no running water, barely enough food to keep the children alive. And then, of course, the inflation, not as bad as Argentina, but bad enough to promise serious trouble very soon.

Corazon had told us, "Men work but sometimes they aren't paid. Eggs used to be, about a year ago, 10 cents a dozen; now they're a dollar. Often the workers can't afford the bus fare to get to their jobs."

Inevitably, as she explained it, a dreadful hopelessness sets in, and nobody cares any more, because even those with two or three jobs can't make enough to keep up with the inflation, so they stop trying to work hard. The increase in street crime reflects all this, and the increase in house break-ins.

Dr. Sol, Shura's new partner in chemistry, turned out to be young, funny, very bright, and slightly Americanized, having spent four years on the East Coast, where he studied. When the show ended, he said to Shura, "Since I am invited to your house this evening, perhaps you and your wife would like to go with me, in my car?" We accepted with pleasure.

During the drive, we were made aware of a quite different point of view, regarding the MDMA-making and the proposed clinic.

Shura began the conversation by saying, "Well, I am very happy to hear that you will be working with me in Doctor Roberto's hospital, making the MDMA. I've heard that you are a fine chemist, and it will certainly make my job easier to have you by my side!"

Dr. Sol smiled broadly and nodded, then turned serious, "I don't know if anyone has mentioned it to you, but my participation in this adventure must be kept — ah — as quiet as possible, because of my company, you understand?"

Shura said he understood, although I knew he didn't at all; neither of us did.

A small, uncomfortable silence settled in, and I decided to open up the subject and find out exactly why Dr. Sol was uncomfortable. I spoke up from the back seat, "Why would your company object to your involvement with this matter?"

His answer was a bit hesitant, as if he were searching for the right words, perhaps not wanting to offend, "The owners are American, and they are quite — ah — conservative. They would not be happy that I am doing chemistry work outside of the company." He paused, then continued, "And there is another concern. The legal status of MDMA is not clear in Brazil. But, in general, we follow the First World industrialized countries when it comes to recommendations on drugs, unless our government decides otherwise for reasons of its own."

*Uh-oh. That means nobody really knows for sure if making MDMA in Brazil actually is legal or just not illegal, or what. Maybe Giorgio and company are just being very optimistic, when they talk to us, and maybe it's not as clear-cut as they're making it seem.*

Shura shifted in his seat and tried to summarize, "So it's actually in limbo, not really clear, whether it's legal to make it here and use it in a clinic, is that what you mean?"

"As I understand it," said Dr. Sol, "It is important for our people to give good reasons, maybe like research in AIDS patients, or terminally ill people, and to get permission from somebody in the government to do this. But without such permission, it is, yes, a limbo situation. Unknown."

Another small silence. Then Shura said, "Do you know if anyone is actually proposing this plan to the right people in government, or are we hearing only intentions and hopes?"

Dr. Sol made a sharp right turn and I saw the familiar entrance gate to the Rich People's enclave where we were staying. In the headlights I caught sight of a large tree with immense white flowers, and caught my breath.

*These are the tropics, the* **tropics***; it's all so luxuriant, so rich, everything growing, growing, sometimes inches every day. Almost too much to take in.*

Dr. Sol slowed the car for the first speed bump within the compound, and replied to Shura's question, "Yes and no. Doctor Hector has a close friend who knows the right officials in the government, and I understand that he — the friend — is very soon going to talk to them and get approval for the clinic plans, so it seems to me logical that we can go ahead and prepare the MDMA for use, now that you are down here to show us the procedure."

I could feel Shura relaxing, letting it all go.

*We have to trust these people. After all, Giorgio and Dr. Hector are pretty powerful; they know important people, and they have access to them, so if they believe it's okay to go ahead, then we need to stop worrying about it and leave it in their hands.*

Back at the house, Dr. Hector and our hosts were already settling in on the big, comfy couch and chairs. Lena served iced tea and wine, and the conversation for the first few minutes was about the show at the Scala. After the laughter and reminiscences subsided, Giorgio leaned forward and said, "Now, I have some interesting pieces of information concerning Mr. Borch that Doctor Hector and I think you will want to hear."

Everyone looked at him, and in the sudden silence, I could hear the leaves of the house plants rustling slightly.

*It's so damned muggy; I hope that's the sound of moving air.*

"First," Giorgio said, "I read to you from a report by a private detective who was employed to find out why Mr. Borch left the United States, so many years ago." Our host, blue eyes hooded, looked around at the rest of us, his large face serious and intent.

*I'll bet he's enjoying the drama, though.*

"The subject," he read out loud, "Is suspected of having embezzled stock from a well-known investment firm in Chicago, and is still being sought for questioning in that matter."

*Oh, boy! That should do it for any lingering emotional ties to the charming Mr. Borch!*

Lena sat, hands to her face, looking truly shocked. She said something in Portuguese which I guessed meant, "My God!" Dr. Sol leaned back in his armchair and nodded thoughtfully, while Shura and I did our best to look grave and hide our satisfaction. (As we admitted to each other in private, later, we were relieved to hear some solid evidence of what had been mostly, up to now, only a continuing sense of unease and distrust, whenever we heard about the doings of Mister B.)

After some spirited talk about Mr. Borch, the Fugitive From Chicago, Dr. Hector came up with the gem of the evening, at least for Shura and me. He chuckled and said to Giorgio, "Do you remember when he told us that the Essence medicine at the spa had been made personally by Borodin, and I said that I wanted to go and find Alexander Borodin myself, to ask him questions about it? He told us that Borodin was 'the Pope' of this entire area of knowledge, do you remember, Giorgio? And he warned me that I should not try to see him under any circumstances, that this great scientist was unapproachable and high up and that only Borch himself had any chance of gaining admittance to that particular holy of holies!"

Shura was grinning, and I gave way completely to laughter, arms wrapped over my stomach, almost sliding off the chair. It just wasn't the moment to worry about being ladylike.

Shura asked, "Did he actually use the word, 'Pope?'"

Giorgio nodded vehemently, "Yes, yes, I swear to you!"

I managed to croak, "I especially like the idea of being the Pope's wife!"

On that supremely cheerful note, we called it a night.

MONDAY:

It was raining in Rio. We were alone with Corazon in the house, our hosts having gone back to their apartment in the city for the day. Over lunch, Corazon filled us in on the situation in Brazil as she knew or believed it, including who were the best and worst presidents (the current one was among the worst). She explained the virtues of the young man running for president in the November election, and told us about his idiotic mother, who made a television appearance and said all the wrong things about the blacks, the Indians and the poor. "But," she added, "People know that you can't be held responsible for your relatives. I do not think it will hurt him."

She believed that the former Brazilian presidents who died by "suicide" or "accident" were murdered (probably true). She told us about the "big hats," who are in positions of power, and who accumulate money without doing anything at all for the public. She said that all workers are paid at the end of the month — if they are paid, that is — because that way the employers can get the interest from the banks, which they don't pass on to the workers. Political corruption is rife, endemic, pervasive and all over the place.

Corazon talked about her good and wonderful former employers, the Draggo family (he was the one burned in the attempted assassination), who were not what she calls "uppy-noses," but very good people with good minds. And she warned us about shopping, "Look at the prices before you talk to the manager of the store to buy, because otherwise, they see your face, the price goes up."

*I guess she means they can tell you're a foreigner.*

She poured our second cups of coffee, cleared away the scrambled egg plates, and said, "Jacques Cousteau made a documentary about the cutting down of the Rain Forest, and made all Brazilians aware of the situation, and he is a great hero for doing this."

Shura and I exchanged glances and turned in our seats to face her, nodding encouragement. Neither of us had seen the documentary, but we were both deeply concerned about the Rain Forest and what was happening to it.

According to Corazon, Cousteau had made clear that the Indian tribes in the Amazon are or were being killed off or forced into 20th century ways of life, which was destructive to them. But Corazon believed that the real villains in the Amazon were not the Brazilian government people, but the "Spanish people." We understood that she meant the Spanish-speaking people, the non-Brazilians, who had come barging in from other South American countries to rape the Amazon Rain Forest of its wealth. She had apparently not heard that the Brazilians themselves, and their government, were doing most of the damage. What she had been told was that the poor government couldn't do anything, that it was powerless to prevent the trouble.

I suppose this was one place where we privately doubted Corazon's information, keeping in mind that most of the time we trusted her views more than those of the wealthy people who usually surrounded us. We had seen their response to the favelas, heard their theories about laziness and bad character being the cause of poverty and unemployment, and failed to hear a single word, so far, from any of those generous and thoughtful people, about the destruction of the great green Lungs-of-the-World to the north.

After breakfast, we retired to our little writing nest on the top floor, and did a bit of work, then felt sleepy (both of us tended to have moments like that, now and then, probably adjusting to the tropical humidity). We went to the bedroom and lay together on the bed, looking out through the open sliding door to the lovely view outside. Across the street, the colors of roof tiles (red) and tree leaves (yellow and green) were sharpened by the rain. We napped for a while.

Later, in the afternoon, Corazon enticed us into a superb dish she'd made for us, a chayote souffle, which I raved over, since I had long loved chayotes — called chou-chou in Brazil — but didn't really know how to use them well.

That evening, we were due to talk — both of us — to a roomful of people, including some VIP's, doctors and psychiatrists who were interested in the general area of psychoactive drugs. Dr. Hector would translate. Shura decided to wear a white shirt and tie for this event, and I agreed it was probably a good idea, tacticly speaking, when addressing a professional audience, even in relaxed, informally dressed Rio.

We drove to the Miramar Hotel with Pierre and Helena again, using our French. Actually, it was mostly Shura's French, but I chimed in every now and then, just to show that my heart was in the right place.

In the penthouse of the hotel, we were escorted into a room with large windows and a bar where I was able to get a glass of ice water, and there we met with some of the people who had come to hear from us about psychoactive drugs in general, and MDMA therapy in particular. Men, in this case, shook hands with Shura, North American style, while women did the kiss-kiss as usual. Dr. Hector introduced the people — several physicians among them — who spoke minimal or no English; those who spoke English well introduced themselves.

After about fifteen minutes of handshaking and smiling, we were shown to another room and a small stage, where a long table had been set up. There were three chairs for Shura, me, and our translator, Dr. Hector. I sat to his right, Shura to his left, and while he addressed the audience in Portuguese, I scanned the faces, recognizing our hosts and several people from the Saturday MDMA group, as well as the medical contingent we had just met in the other room.

It was my debut as an official speaker. I heard Dr. Hector introduce me as "Doctor Alice,"(despite my request not to) and prepared for someone in the audience, sooner or later, to ask whether I was a psychiatrist or a psychologist, at which point I was going to have to say, "Neither, just a therapist," which might or might not lead to even more probing questions.

Shura gave his presentation, having some difficulty with the brand new experience of being translated as he went along. It took a while for him to remember to deliver only a phrase or two before turning to Dr. Hector for the translation. Since Shura is used to talking to an audience at 150 mph, with digressions right and left, it presented him with some moments of frustration, until he got the hang of it. And it was certainly the first time I'd ever heard him talk at a normal rate of speed in public.

The usual questions came from all quarters. Now and then, when it was a matter of a therapeutic application of MDMA, for instance, Shura would turn to me, or Dr. Hector would. I found myself without the expected stage-fright, perhaps because I already knew a great many of the faces by then. But also, most probably, because I felt absolutely sure of what I was saying, and of how to say it. Nice feeling.

Halfway through the whole business, we got another translator who not only knew English better than Dr. Hector, he also had a gift of being able to present ideas — Shura's and his own — with great flair and poetry. He kept getting applause. This was Dr. Leon, whom we had not met before.

There were about twenty or so people in the audience, and the entire thing lasted, not the expected hour and a half, but a whole three hours. Toward the end, when I had been the recipient of the questions for some time, I felt my face flushing with the increased expectation of that dreaded confrontation, but it didn't happen. I was never asked for my credentials, heaven knows why.

When it was over, Shura came up to me and quietly said that he was very proud of me, that I had acquitted myself superbly, and a couple of other nice things along that line. It was the best compliment I could possibly have been given, and he was the one person from whom it was most meaningful.

We had supper in the hotel dining room with Dr. Roberto, the charming, shrewd plastic surgeon, his mistress Marina, and the young Dr. Leon, who had helped us out as second translator. He turned out to be the head of the department of pharmacology at one of the universities, and was apparently well respected by the medical community. He revealed that he had taken many psychedelics, having both good and bad trips, and he expressed to us his immense respect for their power, for what they made possible.

We went to bed late, knowing that — as Shura phrased it — "We done good, kid!"

TUESDAY:

Up at 6:00 a.m. for Lab Day. The original plan had allowed for three days, but that had been the plan attached to the early idea of two labs. Gradually, from odd conversations around us, we began to understand the two-lab plan as having been an effort on the part of Dr. Roberto and his allies to have MDMA synthesized in one lab for the use of an inner circle (chosen by Dr. Roberto from among his intimate friends) and another batch made in another lab for the clinic-to-be. Now it was one lab, one synthesis, and the battle between the two factions would take place without our participation; it wasn't our concern.

Giorgio was taking us in his car and, during the ride, the conversation turned to the driving of cars, and Giorgio filled us in on the rules of the road in Rio. First, he said, nobody pays attention to lane markings. You just sort of drive ahead, being careful to avoid everyone else who is just sort of driving ahead, too. Rio traffic is like traffic on the German Autobahn; those who are at the wheel are liable to be excellent drivers, because all others are either dead or in the hospital. Also, after 10 p.m., nobody stops for red lights, apparently to avoid being held up by robbers. The red lights are observed again after 7:30 a.m., when the rush hour begins, but in between, you simply watch out and drive carefully. (Especially when the light is green.)

We drove over the bridge to the city of Niteroi. It was raining, off and on, as it would all day — and the rest of the week. The tropics, I thought to myself, look most tropical in the rain. The poor-cousin city of Niteroi looked more genuinely Brazilian, somehow, than the glamorous Rio. There were more of the little cantinas with their bottled fruit drinks, and lots of small children in short pants and dirty undershirts. I glimpsed grey-white walls invaded by the ever-present fungus, and noted that the tall condominiums were fewer than in Rio. The graffiti were the same, though; no building was safe from them.

We arrived at a place on the far side of the city, in a suburb full of large, luxurious-looking houses.

The clinic building was large, and we were told that it was entirely devoted to plastic surgery. Its lobby had all the marble and leather appropriate to a place whose clientele is mostly wealthy women.

The lab turned out to be a recently abandoned one, a long, narrow room with a bench running its entire length, and a sink. Someone had boasted to Shura, the day before, that "The laboratory has running water!" Which had led us both to some feverish speculation as to how impossible this whole situation was going to be. We already knew that all, or most, of the lab equipment, glassware and essential chemicals, would be brought in by Dr. Sol, Shura's fellow chemist for the day — from his own company laboratory. What else we would find, what conditions, we were afraid to guess.

There were windows all along the bench-wall, and we opened most of them in anticipation of wild smells to come. Dr. Hector came in, then Sr. Draggo, then the handsome Dr. Roberto, who took my arm and said, "Come with me for a moment; I want you to see my new laboratory!" He led me upstairs to what turned out to be a very large, well-equipped lab indeed, and I expressed my surprise and admiration. He grinned proudly, then excused himself, "I have to leave you now; there is a breast-implant waiting for me. Please tell your husband I send to him my good wishes for his endeavors, and I will see all of you later!"

When I returned to the scene of the chemistry, Dr. Sol had arrived. Giorgio informed us that he, himself, would hang around to watch the proceedings until a bit later, when he had an appointment with a Brigadier General back in Rio.

Now and then, some stranger would pop in through the door and look around, then duck back out, but nobody paid any attention. I assumed they were clinic personnel who had heard rumors about something going on in the old lab, and wanted to see for themselves. Shura and Sol were already busy, unpacking equipment, and I heard the beginning of what would become a familiar accompaniment to the doings of the day — bursts of soft-voiced, sing-song cursing on the part of Shura, as he examined the equipment he was expected to use in making MDMA.

At one point, he called me over from my seat in the far corner of the lab, to look at a roll of aluminum foil, one of the essential ingredients in the process. It hadn't occurred to us that we perhaps should have brought our own aluminum foil from the United States, until we looked at the rolls they had there for our use.

Shura said to me, "Feel this, kid. It's thinner than the U.S. regular foil — much thinner." He looked concerned.

I crumpled a piece and agreed, "Yes, I see what you mean. But I don't understand; what difference does that make?"

"It's going to react faster and burn hotter, that's what it means."

"Oh," I said.

I don't know the first thing about chemistry, but I had learned some of the steps in making MDMA, many years ago; I'd done it not just to help make a good supply for the use of our therapist friends, but also to find out whether I had any unsuspected knack for chemistry. (It hadn't taken long for both of us to come to the conclusion that I didn't.)

One part of the process I remembered very well, the part where you weigh out a certain amount of cut aluminum foil into a big flask, then add a whole series of other chemicals and watch for heat to develop in the mixture, and as soon as it gets pretty hot, you dunk the glass flask into a pot of cold water, and you continue swirling the mixture and immersing the bottom half of the flask in the water until the heat begins to drop and the threat of a boil-over is gone.

I had volunteered to take care of this early part of the process, and I could visualize all too well what Shura was warning me about: rapid heat gain, boil-over, loss of too much valuable product, mess.

But first, we had to get to work, tearing strips of aluminum foil. Dr. Hector was drafted to help me, and had to suffer the inevitable teasing from both Sol and Shura, things like, "Who would have thought to see the former Assistant Minister of Transportation and Housing sitting on a stool in an old lab, tearing up aluminum foil! What is going on here?" And other such idiocies. To all of which he replied with a slightly conspiratorial smile, followed by even more diligent tearing.

Dr. Sol had carried in several cartons of equipment, some of it perfectly fine, some of it barely usable. There was an old rotary evaporator which wobbled alarmingly; Shura patched it with duct tape. There was a superb Buchner funnel among the treasures, but no sign of filter paper of the right size, so our boys cut out a substitute from a piece of paper towel.

Shura was beginning to go happily manic, and kept teasing Sol about Third World this and that, and the young chemist teased right back, caught in the energy. Hooking up, pulling down, fitting on, screwing in, both of them were delighted with the challenge one moment, despairing the next, hoping all over again, and mildly hysterical most of the time. They knew pretty well what they were dealing with, and what they would have to invent or do without, and — as Dr. Hector said later, reverently — "We were treated to a ballet of enthusiastic creativity, with Sol moving grace-fully, doing what he had to do, following Shura's directions and cautions, while Shura danced." Occasionally, when the Pope's eyes met mine, he rolled them wildly, and I grinned back.

I should note that our group of people (upper-crust? uppy-nose? The Rich?) not only didn't hesitate to refer to Brazil as Third World, they were almost eager to point out that that's what it was. However, after the day in the lab, I did suggest to Shura that perhaps he should tone down his references to Fourth, Fifth and Seventh World (this last being used to describe the balance brought into the clinic by Sol).

When it was time to manage the first reaction — by dunking the rapidly heating flask in a large stainless steel bucket of cold water at the appropriate time — I sat on the floor at the end of the lab, and soon discovered that I'd made a mistake. I was down in a corner, and there was no flow of air from the windows to dissipate the fumes. There wasn't much I could do about it for the moment, though; once the reaction was launched, it kept going, and had to be attended to.

Because of the thin-ness of the aluminum, the reaction was going hotter and faster than I'd ever seen it go before, and suddenly it boiled up and out of the top of the flask, although only a fraction of material was lost. I continued immersing it in the water, and the boiling subsided. As everyone was talking about getting ice-cubes from somewhere to keep the water cold, Dr. Hector, in shirtsleeves, came over and sat down beside me on the small stool he had used earlier. He produced a folded magazine and vigorously fanned my face, trying to get some air to me as I coughed — and laughed — in a cloud of methylamine.

For the second flask (we were only doing two), the chemists sat me up over the sink, and a fan was brought in to train on my face. The fan had no front guard; otherwise it was fine. The second flask heated much more slowly, with no boilover, and when I asked why it was going so much better, Shura said, "I made some adjustments," and I said, "Well, they seem to have worked."

Finally, I'd done my part, and I went on a brief exploratory journey down the corridors of the clinic, passing nurses and doctors and the occasional patient in bandages, before returning to the lab and its strange crew. Dr. Hector was still seated on his little stool, watching Shura and Sol as they measured, stirred and poured, occasionally grunting in code to each other.

I went over to Dr. Hector. He pulled my sleeve to bring my head closer to his, and whispered to me, "It is like being present at the birth of a royal baby." I smiled at him and patted his shoulder.

*He's such a funny, dear man; pretty romantic for a politician. But, then, this is Brazil; everything's a bit different in Brazil.*

Dr. Roberto dropped in again, this time with his physician son, both of them dressed for surgery, just to see that everything was proceeding well.

I kept feeding small cups of Brazilian coffee to the chemists and myself, then finally went off to a small room which Dr. Roberto had invited me to use if I wanted to rest. In the small attached bathroom, I washed my face and combed my hair and noted that there were no washcloths.

*I wonder if washcloths just aren't used in Brazil. Do other South American countries have them? Funny how you take little things like that for granted because you grow up with them, but washcloths aren't really essential to life, are they? They use these little handtowels instead, I guess.*

Dr. Roberto took us to lunch — Dr. Hector, Sol, Shura and myself — at another Porxo. This time, we ate more modestly. We talked briefly about what was happening in the Rain Forest, and Dr. Roberto dismissed all "rumors" about the killing of Indians. Never happened, he said, and we said Oh, happy to hear that, and didn't pursue the subject. The Rain Forest and its Indians were obviously not one of the great doctor's major concerns.

After lunch, he drove us to what I later decided was one of my favorite places of the entire trip. The drive was up a hill, past banana trees, which I'd never seen in person before. Small green bunches of ripening bananas were visible, with a large, wine-colored, heart-shaped pod hanging from each tree.

At the top of the hill, there was a crumbling cement overlook and the remnants of a spiral staircase to an upper level which no longer existed. The view was lovely, and we were surrounded by palm trees and flowering bushes of different kinds, and it was the tropics, the real tropics, again. I liked that place, with its quiet, and the humid air which had been cooled by the rain, and I would have liked spending some time there. But after a few minutes, we were off again, back to the Great Work. On the way down, Dr. Roberto pointed out a mango tree, which looked to me a lot like a mimosa, only not quite.

When we got back to the lab, I stood for a few minutes watching as the two chemists resumed work. Then I remembered that this was the 4th of July, and Shura's and my wedding anniversary.

*What better place to spend our anniversary than in a Third World clinic laboratory, making MDMA for research which might or might not ever actually take place, and if it did take place, might or might not ever produce an acceptable scientific paper; with an ever-changing audience watching two hilarious chemists wondering how they were going to manage with the antiquated equipment, trading friendly insults, thoroughly enjoying the challenge. No better place.*

I retired to my own personal room and went to sleep on the hospital bed. Slept soundly for a couple of hours.

When I returned to the lab, things were coming to an end. Shura told me that there was no proper distillation equipment, so Sol was going to take the product to his own company lab and complete the distillation there. Discreetly.

They started repacking the glassware and the chemicals in their cardboard boxes, while a tired audience watched. Now it was Dr. Roberto and Marina, with their little daughter, the beautiful Katya. Also Dr. Hector and Giorgio, and a young man who was introduced as an assistant to Sol.

Little bites of Brazilian pastry were brought up on a tray, and between mouthfuls, everyone talked and asked questions and laughed and offered congratulations.

Finally, the guests left for a while, and the two chemists were alone in the lab, cleaning up. I was outside the door, at that point, just standing there with another cup of the strong, fragrant coffee, when I heard loud yells from inside. Both Shura and Sol were shouting, "Gimme five! Gimme another five!" at the top of their lungs. I opened the door, stifling laughter, and reminded them, in a stage whisper, that this WAS a hospital, yes, and maybe a bit quieter, no? They put their fingers to their mouths like guilty schoolboys, and subsided after one last vehement slap of each other's palms.

Back home, our host and hostess settled in front of the television downstairs, to watch a Portuguese-dubbed re-run of the movie "Dune." I told them that my favorite person in the movie was the hero's baby sister, the blue-eyed, lisping little girl with telekinetic powers. This seemed to amuse them.

We went upstairs to write our notes for the day and fall into bed.

WEDNESDAY:

This was supposed to be a day of writing and quiet — nothing exciting going on — until the evening, when we would dress up for Dr. Roberto's birthday party at his home. So we were all alone in the house, both of us writing in the little study, with only Corazon downstairs. At around 11 a.m., we heard her feet on the stairs, and she appeared with a carafe of coffee and two mugs for us, moving slowly because she was seven months pregnant, going on eight. We thanked her effusively for having gone to all that trouble, then we asked her some questions about her young husband's new job in Mato Grosso, questions such as, is Mato Grosso a state or a town or both, and what kind of job, and she began telling us, tracing on the map the location of the town called Mato Grosso, talking a bit slower than usual.

Then, suddenly, she sat down on a chair beside me and said, "I have to tell you something. I am feeling very strange, and it is because I took some of the medicine that is in the refrigerator. Delia (next door) said that she took it when she had problems and it helped her very much, and that I should take some, just a little bit, so I did."

Shura and I looked at each other, then Shura asked her how much she had taken, and she tried to indicate with thumb and forefinger, then said she would show us in the refrigerator, so we all went very carefully down the stairs, Corazon holding onto my hand for dear life, until we reached the kitchen. We were making reassuring noises, telling her to go slowly, step over the telephone cord, be careful here, take it easy there.

In the refrigerator door, there were two bottles, one empty. The red liquid was gone; the yellow was left. Corazon showed us how much she had measured out in the bottle cap, and we later estimated that it might have been, probably, possibly, maybe about 150 milligrams of MDMA. We helped her recap the bottle and put everything back in the 'frig, telling her that this would remain a secret between the three of us, and she said thank you.

(That, of course, was a somewhat unrealistic promise, because eventually, someone would be sure to notice the empty bottle and probably ask questions, but for the moment, we were going to pretend that none of that would happen.)

We went into the living room, Corazon holding onto the back of my shoulders as I moved, saying to both of us, "I like you very much," to which we replied, truthfully, that we liked her very much, too. On the couch, she sat with her knee touching mine, holding onto my hand except when waving both of hers to illustrate a point. Her eyes were dilated and you could actually see the nystagmus, the eye-wiggle, if you watched for it. We told her it was normal with the medicine and would calm down, and not to worry about it. She laughed and told us it didn't bother her. Shura observed that she was talking through her teeth, and she laughed again when she realized he was right. We suggested a wet cloth (no washcloths in Brazil) and I brought her a handtowel to chew on. I told her that the grinding of teeth was normal, too, "It happens to everybody who takes this medicine for the first time, my dear — for the first few times, in fact — this and the eye wiggling; they won't hurt you, they're just annoying."

Corazon said she didn't mind any of it; it was all right. She added, "Everything is all right."

Yes, yes; she's getting that first magical gift of a good MDMA experience, the deep sense that the universe is in balance, that — despite all evidence to the contrary — all things really are going the way they're supposed to.

We sat there, Shura and I, gazing at the familiar features, now transformed. This was a different Corazon, her shining black hair framing a brown-skinned face softened and radiant as that of a girl of sixteen; frown lines had vanished from around eyes and mouth, and she was one of the most beautiful people I had ever seen. When I glanced at Shura, at the expression of awe on his face as he looked at Corazon, I knew he was seeing her as I did.

Then she said, "I want to tell you about myself, because you are good people, with good minds, and I do not want you to see me as just the maid and a good cook, you know? I want you to see me as a person."

We nodded and Shura replied, softly, "We are very glad to have the opportunity to know you as a person."

I smiled and squeezed her hand.

She had gone to New York, she said, when she was 16 or 17, and married a young Italian, a blond Italian whose family was very white and didn't like her because she was dark. "In my family," she said, "Because we are a mixture of races, some of my sisters are blond and some are dark like me, and I am proud of all the different bloods I have inside me."

But the Italian family treated her like dirt and kept telling the boy he should get rid of her and marry someone who didn't look like a Negro. She said she had never had this kind of treatment before in Brazil, and it was very hard, but she kept her pride.

One of the things she was proudest of, she told us, was her grandmother on her mother's side, who had been an Indian woman in the Amazon jungle, painted face and all, climbing trees for fruit, knowing about the uses of plants and leaves and roots and stems for different kinds of sickness.

"She was a wonderful, wise woman," said Corazon, "And I learned very much about that kind of medicine from her, and I wrote everything down in a little notebook that I keep always with me."

She said she had to work in New York and that her family in Brazil, which is very large, kept asking her to send money, and she sent all she could, but she had to live also, and she and her husband were very poor. Finally, she told us, the pressures got too much for her; the hard work, the discrimination, the hostility of her in-laws, the loneliness, the constant demands from her family back home. One day she'd had enough, she was too tired, always too tired so she couldn't think clearly anymore, and she climbed out of a window and let herself fall.

We didn't ask from what floor.

Corazon said, several times, emphatically, "I did not have the plan to kill myself. I just wanted a rest. I wanted everything to stop for a while, you know? So I could rest."

We both nodded.

She sustained fractures of most of her facial bones, hip and leg bones, and she was in the hospital for eight months. "I got the rest," she said. There was a good doctor who talked to her and gave her courage, and when she was healed, he got her a good job at a fancy restaurant, where she made decent money.

She told her husband that she was going back to Brazil, and asked him to come with her, but he didn't want to. She said, "We loved each other, but it wasn't enough." He told her he would go to Africa and marry another black woman (so there! to his parents) and she said goodbye and went back home.

She asked us if we would mind if she showed us something very personal, and we said go ahead. She released my hand and took out her upper teeth and her lower teeth, then popped them back in. Her jaw, she told us, was synthetic and her cheekbones were too. She pulled up her skirt, just far enough to show us the long, wide scar down the side of her right leg.

"You see?" she said, with an almost conspiratorial smile.

We told her, speaking the truth, that she was beautiful.

She reached over and took my hand again.

"When I returned to Brazil," she told us, "I took some of the money I saved from my good job in New York, and I went to the best cooking school in Rio." Now, in the town of Mato Grosso, where her new young husband had a job doing carpentry, some people who ran a ranch of some kind had asked her to train their kitchen staff. She was very pleased because it was something she knew she could do well. She was going to journey to Mato

Grosso as soon as this job — taking care of us — was over.

She said, "I want to learn everything I can while I am alive, and I like to spend time around people with good, rich minds, and you are people who have minds like that, and I am so glad I met you."

We told her we were learning a lot from her, more than from the other people around us, and Shura said, "Thank you for sharing so much with us — about Brazil and about yourself."

Corazon reached out with her free left hand, and Shura took it in both of his. His eyes were wet.

When she began coming down, we urged her to rest on her bed, while we dressed for our evening out. She said that the doctor had told her the baby was small, so she had to try to make it bigger before it was born. She asked if we thought she had done something wrong in taking the medicine, and we said no, it wasn't wrong (this was not the time for a lecture), but she shouldn't take anything like that again until after the baby was born and weaned. She said all right, she understood.

We hugged each other, and she went downstairs to her room.

"You never know —" said Shura, back in our bedroom, "— where the next lesson is going to come from."

"Wow," said I.

When we were dressed, we were picked up by Giorgio and Lena and driven to the home of Dr. Roberto. We were now going to meet his wife, the handsome, gracious (according to our hosts) Clara, who went through life admired by all who knew her, and never mentioned or in any way acknowledged the existence of the mistress, Marina, or the lovely little Katya.

Shura, seated in front because of his long legs, turned to Giorgio and said, "I remember, on the lab day, Dr. Roberto came in with his doctor son for a few minutes. Then, much later, when we were packing up, his mistress came in with the little girl. They must have met each other; I mean, the — Marina and her daughter and Roberto's son — "

Lena replied with a chuckle, "But it has not happened yet. And if it did happen, everyone thinks probably they would ignore each other."

I said what a pity that the adult sons and the young Katya could not form some kind of relationship; it seemed un-natural and sad that they pretended each other didn't exist. Our hosts said, but that's the way they are doing it, and yes, it is a pity.

Soap opera of Rio de Janeiro's Uppy-Noses.

Our surgeon's house was very large, with an immense living room whose walls were hung with paintings — good ones, mostly modern and by Brazilian artists, but one signed Klee — and we were greeted by the gracious Clara, who was, as advertised, a very handsome woman; she had a slim figure and was dressed in red and black sequins. Looking around at the roomful of expensively dressed women, one gathered that sequins were in, this season.

Outside the living room was a big deck with numerous tables set for guests. The deck ended at what I thought was a swimming pool (I hadn't realized we were on the bay), until I looked to the right and saw a yacht floating on the water. A large yacht. Shura came out onto the deck behind me, and I poked his arm and pointed. He whistled softly, and we both stood there, looking at the pretty boat in reverent silence.

"This," I remarked, "Is why people become plastic surgeons in Brazil."

"I do congratulate you," he said, "On a remarkable bit of insight."

A few minutes later, rain was beginning to fall. We sat at a table in a protected part of the huge deck with Giorgio and Lena, and soon Dr. Hector's wife, Rita, joined us. The rain was now coming down heavily and a strong wind was blowing, making the exposed part of the deck uninhabitable. Servants unrolled canvas walls with plastic windows in them, to shield us from the weather, and I saw lightning outside, to my great delight. I love lightning.

Our table now included the chemist, Sol, Sr. Draggo and his pretty young wife, Sonia, who was wearing a simple, expensive little dress of black velvet. Chairs were being borrowed from other tables and dragged over to ours, and the sounds of laughter and loud talk competed with the storm howling outside the canvas cover. I wondered how the yacht was doing.

There was a kind of musical chairs going on with the seat next to Shura. When one inhabitant got up to greet a friend, someone else would sit down. For a while, the young plastic surgeon we'd met the first night was there, talking and asking the usual questions. There was discussion of what everybody had heard about the ballet in the laboratory, the wonderful sight of Senhor Shura dancing around, showing the world that one's work should be joyful.

*Ah, yes; new legends are being born, even as we sit and drink our little drinkies.*

What looked like the rest of Rio's high society was pouring through the front door, visible through the glass wall behind our table. A middle-aged lady with dark hair worn in a tight bun sat at the table next to us, and Lena identified her as a very famous singer, but the name was scattered by a gust of wind. The singer was dressed in dark red sequins.

My ever-present little notepad was remarked on with amusement by all, and I explained that I was gathering names and addresses from our table-mates, omitting the fact that the rest of the notes were somewhat more personal and certainly not for public consumption.

Waiters served canapes, including (of course) caviar, and I watched people at other tables, the women loaded with what I guessed were genuine jewels, some watching our group and whispering discreetly among themselves. One of the late arrivals at our table (hugs and kiss-kiss all round) was the multi-millionaire, Sr. Carlos, and surely everyone at that party knew him by sight (one does not fail to recognize a man worth $120 million) and his affectionate greeting of Shura and me inspired more whispering.

The clothes were expensive and generally in good taste; the women did their hair in European styles, with no short hair that I could see. Figures were generally svelte, and when I remarked on this, Lena reminded me that most of the women there had had their plastic surgery done by Dr. Roberto, of course. And "lipo," she said, "Everyone loves to have lipo."

I muttered that I was beginning to seriously think about lipo (liposuction), myself. Not to speak of neck, jawline and eyelids. Shura gave me the expected dirty look.

I then said that Shura preferred that I remain my un-retouched self, which occasioned frankly pitying looks all round. They obviously didn't understand how that could be. At that point, neither did I. Ah, well.

There came a call to everyone to come and see the table in the dining room, to admire the setting and the food before the eating began. We all piled into the dining room and made appreciative noises at the beauty of it all, including a centerpiece of fruit and flowers that could well have served as a monument to harvest season at Rockefeller Center.

Then the serving people began filling plates. When I turned around to take mine back to our table, I saw Shura being drawn by Dr. Roberto to the side of the room, where a photographer waited. I smiled and let the crowd jostle me forward again, in the general direction of fresh air.

When Shura rejoined our group, about ten minutes later, I asked him what had happened.

"Well," he said, "Roberto asked me to pose for a picture for some society column, and I gather he was explaining to them about the great scientist from the United States — that's me — and then he took his arm from around my throat —"

I laughed.

"— and I went and got some supper, and here I am."

"Well, at least you're alive, and safe, and that's all that matters, right?"

"Just because you can't see any blood," mumbled Shura, "Doesn't mean there isn't serious trauma. Deeply buried, maybe, but trauma nonetheless."

"I'll keep an eye on you," I said, my mouth half full of asparagus, "Just in case there are symptoms."

Lightning continued to flash outside the walls of our deck, and gusts of wind flapped the canvas. It was a lovely storm.

Dr. Hector told me that he would like to bring two people over to the house on Friday, give them MDMA, and have me do therapy with them, with himself translating and watching, to "See how you do what you do." I explained, urgently, why I did not wish to do such a thing, pointing out that, first, I only work with one patient at a time and second, that whoever works with people who have problems (one of them was apparently his cousin, who has myasthenia gravis and is very depressed), should be the person who can continue working with them in the future, and I was going to be leaving in a few days.

My dear Dr. Hector thought for a while about what I'd said, then shrugged his disappointment and turned away.

(My reluctance was due, in no small part, to the idea of trying to communicate intently with a patient, using terms which are not part of the usual social vocabulary, with a translator between me and the person I'm trying to touch at a very deep level. Not the most satisfying image.)

When we were ready to leave, the handsome, suave Dr. Roberto wasn't around, but we bussed his wife and thanked her enthusiastically for the beautiful evening, while she nodded her head (graciously), probably understanding not a word (we'd been warned that she knew no English), but certainly getting the music, and we left.

THURSDAY:

Shura came upstairs with a cup of coffee for me, to help me wake up. This was to be the shopping day.

He sat on the edge of the bed and said, "Our hosts don't seem to quite understand me when I tell them that I don't necessarily want to buy things, just to 'go shopping.' They don't seem to understand the distinction between shopping and buying."

I told him, "You should have tried using the expression, 'window shopping,' but I'm not sure that would have been understood, either. It's okay, though," I added, "Because I fully intend to do buying."

Stopping at various bookstores to find something on the Amazon, Shura found two Portuguese-to-French dictionaries, which we couldn't get at home. I bought two Brazilian cookbooks. We went into a couple of souvenir stores, in which I found great little native nonsense to take home, over-priced. There were countless jewelry stores, some of them with barkers outside them, like North Beach exotic nightclubs, which seemed a bit strange. One is inclined to be suspicious of the quality of gems in a store that hires barkers.

Then up we went to Sonia's apartment to wait for Giorgio to join us, after his dentist appointment. The apartment was gorgeous, luxurious, full of Persian rugs of great quality, mostly Chinese furnishing and porcelain, reminders of Draggo's import and export connections.

Sonia insisted on giving us a gift of two lovely Chinese drawings on rice paper and a wonderful ashtray showing one of the "balagandans" (which means bunches) that the Indians make for good luck, like one I'd bought earlier that day. The Brazilians use them as coffee-table knick-knacks or to hang on the wall. They are usually a half-moon of tin or brass from which hang various symbolic fruits and a miniature fist with the thumb protruding between the first two fingers, always made of wood — the Brazilian (phallic) good-luck symbol.

In one corner of the large living room stood a most unusual statue. Shura told me, later, that it was one of probably only three or four in the world outside of China. A life-size-plus terracotta figure of one of the soldiers unearthed at Xian.

I liked Sonia. She had been patient and pleasant company, with Lena, on our shopping trip, and Corazon had spoken of her as a truly good person. And she'd been good to Corazon, which counted for much with Shura and me.

On the way back home there was a discussion in the car about the Family politics. Giorgio said, "You understand that Dr. Roberto wants use of the magic elixir kept for an inner circle of special people, mostly his friends, with almost nothing available for the rest of the Family. Of course, we don't agree."

*Neither do we, kiddo. Amazing, how some people who use MDMA for "spiritual enlightenment" can manage to forget everything they might have learned under the influence, once they're back in their normal state.*

Lena was saying, "— and everyone has a friend or relative who needs MDMA and should have it to help their problems."

Shura asked, "Does that mean he isn't interested in the new clinic and the research?"

Giorgio glanced at him, then back at the road, "Ah, but don't worry, my friend, because we are not going with Dr. Roberto's plan, as I already told you. It is just part of the story of what goes on in the Family."

*And we should keep in mind that we're only hearing one person's version of that story.*

FRIDAY:

At breakfast on Friday morning Giorgio told us that the new MDMA was to be brought over to the house on Saturday afternoon, and the

Family would gather to try it out. Lena patted Shura's arm and asked, "Do you mind if on Saturday evening we gather together, just a small group, to ask some questions?" Shura had replied, "Of course not."

*What the hell can they possibly ask that we haven't already answered? Oh, well. We're tired, at this point, and ready to go home.*

Shura and I remained upstairs, writing, until lunchtime, when we went down to the kitchen and joined our hosts. Corazon had cooked the national dish of Brazil, the feijoada (fey-joe-AH-dah). Black beans, vegetables, fruit and slices of meat. Wonderful. The kind of lunch that guarantees you won't eat supper. It was served in the longest baking dish I'd ever seen.

After lunch, we went with Giorgio to try to find a scale which could weigh milligrams. We went into jewelry stores, into health food stores. Nowhere, no-how. They wouldn't be able to weigh out their new MDMA without one, and now, with the failure of our expedition, Giorgio expressed the hope that Tomas, the next door neighbor, could get one in Sao Paulo in time for the Saturday gathering. My, oh my. The third world is such a mixture of have's and unexpected have-nots, and you can't predict what will or will not be available.

An interesting little incident happened during our expedition into the city with Giorgio to find a proper balance. There is a system in Rio whereby you keep your car protected from vandalism and theft (often of the entire car). When you park, there is always a man who offers to watch your car for you. When you come back, you tip him a couple of cruzados. It's the way he makes his living, and the way you keep your car out of the hands of the Paraguayan military (which is where stolen cars apparently end up).

Now, this time, when Giorgio, Shura and I returned to the car, the guardian was nowhere to be seen. Maybe off having coffee or taking a pee break. I thought, as did Shura, that Giorgio would simply drive off. But no, he looked all around for the man and, not finding him, flagged a policeman and told him that he had money for the man who watches the cars, and since he was absent, could he leave the payment with the policeman? The policeman (Giorgio told us later) said he didn't want to be seen taking money from somebody in a car, so Giorgio said, "Well, how about my shaking your hand; there's nothing suspicious about a handshake, is there?" During the handshake, the money was passed. Shura and I were impressed by the whole negotiation, especially by the desire of Giorgio to make sure the car man got paid.

In response to our obvious question, Giorgio said no, he was sure the policeman would pass on the money.

On we went to Dr. Hector's physiotherapy clinic, which was small but nicely furnished, with pleasant music playing in the background. (It simply hadn't occurred to me to wonder how, after his government service, he would be making a living.) There, we crowded into his little office and met the only representative of a group of three or four physicians who hadn't yet managed to make it to any previous presentation of ours, due to rainy weather, cold feet, or whatever. This turned out to be a cardiologist, Dr. Jorge, for whom we both felt an immediate liking. Tall, with thinning white hair and a shy, quirky smile, tailor-made to elicit maternal response, he had apparently asked Dr. Hector to arrange a personal meeting with us.

We sat alone with him for about an hour, as he talked about his background, and certain growing symptoms of depression. Shura sat back and nodded appropriately, but left the talking to me. Eventually, I suggested that hypnotherapy would probably be his best bet. He asked me whether he should take MDMA, and I told him that MDMA can be very helpful with depression, but that I would suggest trying trance work first, and emphasized the importance of finding a well-respected hypnotherapist with whom he could feel at ease.

When Shura asked me later why I'd dissuaded him from taking MDMA, I explained, "Well, the only people we know who have MDMA available are the so-called Family, and none of them are trained to do therapy with MDMA, even the psychiatrists; they just haven't the experience. Maybe they'll get it in the new clinic. If and when. But this guy needs a therapist who knows what he's doing, and can do it one-on-one, because a group session isn't the right thing for him, right now. If he can find a good hypnotherapist, he can probably get some real help immediately."

The nice Dr. Jorge volunteered another problem, which he said he hesitated to tell anyone, but after spending time with us, he thought we might understand. He said, "I have a trouble of many nights dreaming about my dead friends, who are loving and caring to me in the dream, but I have to fight their faces out of my mind in the morning. It is very hard for me to do this, and I am feeling too vulnerable and a little bit frightened."

I thought for a moment, visualizing this gentle man facing his bathroom mirror, half awake, with dear, dead faces crowding his mind, afraid of the pull to another world that they symbolized.

Going on plain old gut instinct, I said, "Instead of pushing your dead friends away when you wake up, try bringing them along as allies during the day. Any time you feel their presence, invite them to see through your eyes and feel through your skin, and enjoy being with you in what you are doing and experiencing. Think of them as occasionally coming in contact with you, especially in your dreams, to make sure you're all right, because they love you. They are not a danger to you, and after a while they'll go on with their other business and leave you to get on with your life. Does that make sense to you?"

He sat back in his chair, looking at me thoughtfully, then smiled and said, "That makes very much sense, as you say. It is true that I should not be afraid of them; why should I fear dead friends who love me?" He looked over at Shura and back at me, "Thank you very much, both of you."

*Good, good. The idea might have horrified him; thank heaven it didn't. Now, he can stop being afraid and feeling guilty because he's rejecting people he loved when they were alive.*

After the meeting at the clinic, we — Shura, Giorgio and I — stopped at one of the stands that sold coffee and beer and some food. We each had a small coffee, and to my great delight, I saw on the wall menu a listing for "Chisbuger."

SATURDAY:

We decided, right after breakfast, to give Corazon $40 (American), "for the baby." Just between her and us. The $40 would continually appreciate, because inflation in Brazil was about 40% a month, so if she was as wise as we believed her to be, she would resist changing it into Brazilian money for as long as she could.

The 13 people for the day's ceremony arrived late, of course, for the 11:30 a.m. start, but that's another Rio habit — being late.

The usual group, including the quiet sweet mulatto lady, and the modest masseur, Sr. Waldo.

The session was supposed to start at 11:30 a.m. and by 11:00 o'clock, Tomas had brought the promised balance scale (out of the turn of the century, said Shura), which was on loan from some friend of his in Sao Paulo. On this rather delicate-looking machine, the Pope — watched intently by Dr. Hector, Sol, Giorgio, Lena and the Pope's Wife — measured out 13 doses of 120 mgs. each. New material and a new way of taking it (powder, undisguised by colored liquids). I took pictures with our sturdy old camera, as the faces of our friends, wearing a mixture of expectancy and something close to reverence, clustered over the Great One's shoulder, observing every move.

It was almost noon before the rest of the group began arriving.

Sr. Leo and his Anita gave us a lovely table display of dried plants of Brazil, enclosed in a round plastic container, with a stand. The gentle masseur brought more guarana powder in a plastic wrap as a goodbye gift.

Shura and I ate lunch in the kitchen while the group was having its session. Corazon served us the remains of Friday's gorgeous feijoada, which tasted just as good as it had the day before. When we showed her the collection of Brazilian plants, she pointed at some tiny dried stems visible through the plastic and told us that these were called prickle-plants, and that if you touched one, and a little spine got into your skin, a mother-wart would form and send out roots, and another wart would grow, and another and another. She said her husband had them all over his body. Apparently they weren't toxic or dangerous, but a bloody nuisance, and once established, couldn't be removed.

We stared silently at the innocent-looking collection, resolving to never, never open the seal.

After lunch, I packed. In about an hour, the meditation and silence were over in the living room and people began talking and laughing. We were called down for photos by everybody's cameras and brief reports — all good, of course. A couple of the women had experienced a return of the early effect, which they had not been able to recapture since the first few times taking the Borch MDMA. Carlos (Lena told us) had refused to take Borch's stuff for some time, but said he wanted to take Shura's. Results were reported to be generally excellent. No one seemed to have had a bad experience.

When we were alone again, Shura said, grinning, "Why am I not surprised that everyone had a great time with the new stuff?"

I laughed and remarked that I couldn't imagine why, "But I suspect that you suspect that something called mind-set could be involved. Positive expectations, yes? Strong desire not to betray their faith in the sacred works of the Pope, no?"

"Uh-huh, could be, could be."

For now, we agreed, it was enough that there seemed to have been no negative effects, and that everybody seemed genuinely pleased.

We retired to our writing upstairs. We had both felt that our writing had been a Godsend to us (and to our hosts) because it had given us a valid reason to absent ourselves when we were tired of interacting with everybody (and it had given our hosts more time to themselves).

We worked until almost 5:00 p.m., when Giorgio called us downstairs to sit in the royal seats again, while Dr. Hector gave The Speech about how Shura (and Alice) led in important work for humanity, inspiring all of them to do the same, and so on. They were going to follow our example, he said, and help people instead of making money.

*Hooray, hooray. We are not cynical and we believe. We also hope. Whether the clinic will ever materialize, there's no way to tell, but Dr. Hector and Giorgio, particularly, seem to really want it to happen. So do we.*

Then Giorgio said more wonderful things, and we replied, Shura choking up a bit.

I did not choke up at all, feeling just the tiniest bit removed from all the heartfelt emotions, wondering how long all these idealistic plans and intentions would last, once we had left the scene.

SUNDAY:

We had coffee with our hosts and then the four of us took a walk up and down the street to take photos of the pretty houses and the magnificent flowers and trees, and of each other.

At 12:30 p.m. we loaded our packed bags into Giorgio's car and went to a big hotel on the beach, for a lunch given in our honor by Sr. Leo. A musical group played some Spanish songs, startling Shura, who realized that he could now tell the difference between Portuguese and Spanish, which he couldn't have done the week before. The musicians wore the kind of shirts I had expected to see all over Rio, and hadn't: colorful ones. These ones were bright red, with ruffles, embroidered in white. It turned out that all the music men were from Paraguay.

A fast-moving storm came on-shore, scattering Sunday strollers right and left on the tiled pavement and beach below.

A lawyer named Sr. Paro, who spoke no English, came over to us with Giorgio by his side to interpret. He was a stocky man with black hair turning grey at the sides, and a round face that showed both toughness and humor. He told Shura, through Giorgio, that he was extending to us an invitation to come down and stay with him in Manaos, on the Amazon River, for one week, sometime next year. He said, "I have much information on the use of the ayahuasca among the Indians in the forest, and I will take you to a ceremony so that you can see for yourself."

Shura stood up and shook the lawyer's hand. "We would be honored to have such an experience, Senhor. We are very grateful for the opportunity, and we look forward to hearing from you next year. Thank you very much for your kindness."

They bowed to each other, and Sr. Paro returned to his seat, Giorgio at his side.

After lunch, Dr. Hector informed us that Leo would drive us to the airport, and we would be on our way home.

My notes for that day include this:

"I had a dream last night of a big, big yellow tiger without stripes, asleep on the living room floor, his coat ragged and full of little pieces of white carpet fluff, his paws clutching a long pillow covered in faded blue cotton. Happy sleeping tiger. I thought, he needs brushing, but how does one safely groom a tiger, even if it's a pet? Occurred to me that I hadn't fed him for days. What was he eating? Ah hah — the leftover cat food (our cats at home were fed a lot of dry cat food while we were away).

"Okay. I suspect the tiger is the Brazil Caper, with all the doubts and suspicions which we had attached to it, (about the Brazilian drug laws, for instance, which were never fully explained, and the MDMA clinic, which might or might not ever come to be), which is now a happy, sleeping tiger who presents no problems, except that he is a bit dusty and needs brushing — but not now — and can be left in peace for the moment."

After a last go-round of hugs, we took off for the airport with Leo. When we arrived, he greeted a portly person with half his face showing signs of stroke. The man, we were told, managed to smooth the way of Leo every month or so, when he flew to various places around the world, and was given a tip of some kind. Leo asked him to attend to us, and told us to follow the man's lead. We found ourselves being pulled over into the First Class line, even though our tickets were for Business Class. Portly Person took our passports and the money for boarding passes and went ahead to take care of things. There were several people around the airport (Leo had told us) who specialized in doing just this sort of thing for people who could pay for the service. This one was pretty damned good. For a while, our new First Class seats were a half-plane apart, and the plane was oversold by 40 people — full load — yet somehow, he managed (after showing us to the VIP Lounge) to get us places only one seat apart. (On the plane, this resolved itself immediately, when the person who sat between us agreed to move, so we were finally seated side by side.)

We kept saying things to each other like, "I can't believe this whole trip!!" and from Shura, "Wait until I remark casually to Patrick (a good friend, an ethnobotanist, who was fascinated by the shamanic use of visionary plants) that we've been invited to explore the Amazon area by a lawyer who lives there and knows all about ayahuasca and is going to take us to a ceremony!"

"We'd better leave out the fact that the lawyer can't speak word One of English," I laughed.

We talked about the prospect of — next year — seeing the Orinoco River, which Shura said he'd always wanted to see; I reminded him that it was the favorite haunt of the piranha, but he wasn't fazed.

(I should add here that the Amazon trip hasn't yet taken place and perhaps never will.)

As we began to settle down, Shura sighed, "I wonder if that clinic will ever see the light of day."

"Somehow, I doubt it," I replied, "But, you know, maybe we'll be surprised, and the whole thing will actually happen. Giorgio and company really seem to want it; it's just that — well —"

"Things have a way of not quite getting done, in the Third World," finished Shura.

"Something like that," I shrugged a Brazilian shrug.

In Miami, we took our reserved room at the airport hotel again and slept like babes for a few hours, before the continuation of the flight to San Francisco. The TV in the room remained dark. I hadn't seen American television for 12 days, but the U.S. was apparently still around; everything else could wait until we got home.

My notes read: "From South America, the U.S. looks too powerful, too Big Brother, too willing to push other countries to do what it wants, too paranoid and dictatorial. However, it's no different, I suppose, from any other nation in a position of power. There is no such thing as a good, kind or altruistic country with a lot of power. Countries get nicer as they lose influence, when they have to sit back and watch and adapt and stay out of the way of whichever nations happen to be filling the roles of Big Boys at the time.

"In Rio, we were warned to be careful about guarding our pockets and purses on the street, but I noted with some amusement that the first thing I did, after we'd collected our suitcases in the San Francisco Airport, was to tie the top bags to each other and to the baggage cart, lest somebody run by and snatch, as tends to happen in the U.S.

"The Brazilians are aware of having parasites in their government who milk the economy and the people, and the men who run for high office do so on the one major promise of stopping corruption. But here in the good old U.S. of America, we are riddled with corruption, too, and anyone with any intelligence knows it.

"I have now — as does Shura — a different view of what it means to be Third World. For instance, the word 'inflation' will never be a dry, abstract economic concept again, for me. But, above all, this trip confirmed and made very real to me the idea that the nations of this planet are tied together with bonds of tremendous number and complexity and no one of them can stand outside the mesh. What one country does eventually affects every other, for good or for evil; it's as true for nations as it is for individuals. End of philosophical observations for the moment."

It was so good to be home. And to have a home to return to.

AFTERTHOUGHTS:

The clinic, to this day, has not been built. No therapy has been done in Brazil with MDMA; at least, none that has resulted in scientific papers written and published. The good, kind people who welcomed us in Rio and opened their hearts to us, went on to other interesting pursuits. Some of them left Brazil, fearing economic collapse; others joined new groups of spiritual seekers; a few discovered new drugs, such as 2C-B, and continued trying to understand and improve themselves.

They are intensely interested in matters of the spirit, those gentle people; I only wish that they, along with the rest of us who do our seeking with psychedelics, could find better ways of making changes in our world, starting with our immediate neighborhoods.

How many psychedelic users — in any country — actually give time to the local church soup kitchen, helping to feed the homeless and hungry? How many of us, having had the experience, under the influence of the visionary drugs, of seeing all human beings as incarnations of God, have gone down to the local hospital to give affection and a listening ear to lonely patients who need somebody to talk to? How many of us regularly visit a jail, to provide spiritual and emotional support to confused, damaged people who have grown up unloved, uneducated and unguided by their confused, damaged parents?

Have I done such kind and loving things for strangers? No, for the most part, I have not. Like most psychedelic seekers, I've been too busy with other matters. There are many excuses, many reasons, many good rational-izations. But the truth is, if we are to argue effectively for the value of these drugs and plants as spiritual openers, as keys to the doors of the soul, we must seriously consider how we should act, what we might do, and how we can manifest those values we like to think of as belonging to the psychedelic experience. Not just with our friends and families, but with our communi-ties, with the rest of our tribe.

And what are those values? They are, of course, the same ones expressed by the great religions and spiritual teachings of the world. They are the values of compassion, tolerance, forgiveness and the search for truth, respect for living things and for the great mother-planet on whose skin we walk and build our homes.

There has been a reassuring step taken in Brazil, since we were there: the use of the consciousness-altering brew called ayahuasca has been officially approved for use by two native religions, so at least this visionary plant mixture has been acknowledged as having a valid use for spiritual experience and growth.

We still do not know anything substantial about Brazilian drug law, and our impression is that none of our Brazilian friends do, either. We do know that the United States does its best to force its destructive War on Drugs on all the countries of South America, and as long as our country gives out money, the Third World will go along with some of the First World's agenda in this, as well as many other areas.

With the worsening of the Brazilian economy, the rich people we had met prospered, for the most part. The dear cook and housekeeper, Corazon, had a baby boy and moved from one job to another. We were in touch with her for a while, but haven't heard from her for a long time now. She taught us much of value, during those ten days, and we hope she and her child will be all right, in the confusion that is Brazil.

When I remember those ten days, among the images that present themselves are the faces of the chorus girls at Scala, the skewers of meat parading past us at Porxo, the wine-colored hearts hanging from the banana trees, the silent glory of the Southern Cross over the beach, and — above all — the radiant face of Corazon, that strange and unexpected day, her great dark eyes glowing with love and humor as she sat on the couch and looked at both of us, her slim hand firm and warm in mine, when she said, "It's all right. Everything is all right."

# CHAPTER 5. 'SHROOMS

(Alice's voice)

---

From my notes:

"1.5 Grams for each of us, of the type known as psilocybe cubensis, mixed with a few bits of another type, all crushed and eaten raw, at around 6:00 p.m. Taste was pleasant.

First effects felt at 10 minutes after eating the little devils. Shortly after that, the world erupted into patterns. Patterns over everything. They seemed to fill all the space between me and my surroundings. The most prevalent design was that of a sort of squarish amoeba with a central black dot, like a nucleus, repeated endlessly and in three dimensions. Actually, it began to look most of all like chickenwire, with a small black dot in the middle of each square. In three dimensions.

At this point, quarter to 8:00 p.m., we've plateau'd, I at plus three and Shura at around plus two (he speculates that an experiment two days ago probably softened his response).

I'm sitting at the computer, determined to get a head start on my notes, but it's getting increasingly difficult.

Well! I wanted a really intense psychedelic experience to write about, and here it is. Thank God we didn't take more. One and a half grams is quite enough to deal with."

---

I sat there, trying to see the room through the forest of lines and dots and bands of musty reds and greens. The world surrounding me had become strange, almost alien, and I had the sense of a personality present, and it wasn't particularly friendly. It felt unloving, emotionally cool, and it had a sense of humor which was not particularly kind.

I reminded myself, "This personality I'm feeling is my own projection. Necessary to own it. It's all me. Like it or not, it's me."

I squinted at the computer keyboard, did my best to focus, and managed to get out of Xtree (Hooray!) and back into WordStar. I opened a new file called 'shrooms, and typed in the date at the top of the blank page in the upper right-hand corner, but couldn't go any further. The keyboard had become impossible to see through the clusters of colored patterns imposed on it, and the part of me that gives words to things, and conceptualizes, was losing ground to another part which wanted only to immerse itself in the three-dimensional pattern world, or at least to find out how to relate to it. So I thought: later; I'll write later. No can do right now.

I went to the bedroom with my man. Everything was moving. The walls were moving, the sheets and blanket and pillows were full of moving chickenwire amoebas and black dots, interwoven with streamers of dusky colors, red and yellow, black and green and orange.

Shura took off his light robe and got under the sheets. I sat on top of the blanket, cross-legged, and talked to him about what was happening, what I was seeing. I realized — and told him — that, for the moment, I had no interest whatsoever in making love; things would have to calm down quite a bit before my thoughts might tend to drift in that direction.

Most interesting and disturbing of all, I explained to Shura, was the fact that I was having a lot of trouble finding words to describe what I was seeing. I simply could not connect easily with my own usually excellent ability to verbalize. Left brain? Right brain? Whatever. I said it felt like a distinct interruption between the sides of the brain, and those two aspects of me.

He suggested, "Well, why don't you close your eyes, and try to tell me what you see inside your eyelids."

I straightened my back and closed my eyes. What I saw against a black background were short, curved pieces of what looked like ribbon candy floating, and on the top edge of each ribbon were evenly spaced little squares, three to a ribbon, and both the ribbons and squares were variously colored greyish white, dark red, green and yellow, and the entire scene struck me as ugly and boring, like a very bad-taste 1930's linoleum floor pattern. I opened my mouth to give the picture to Shura, and could not talk. The strangest part of it was — as I then discovered — that I had no difficulty using words for anything else; anything other than the images I was seeing inside my head.

I said, "This is really weird; I can't describe it!"

Shura, quite understandably, misunderstood. He asked, very gently, "Are we talking ineffable, here? Is that what you mean?"

"No! Anything BUT ineffable! It's boring, uninspiring and painfully ordinary, but I simply cannot apply words to it; there's a total disconnect as soon as I try!"

"Well," he said, his voice warm and reassuring, "Stop trying and just let yourself experience for now. The words will come back."

"I know, I know; it's just so bloody ANNOYING, to be able to talk about anything else, but not be able to describe anything I see!"

I uncurled myself and lay down on my pillow, beside Shura.

*There's a part of me that's sort of wanting to float in the world of the images. It's kind of an ego-less feeling. That part doesn't care about getting control of this situation; it would just as soon wander around and — as Shura says — simply experience. The other part of me is really determined to get control, and it's pretty damned mad at not being able to do what it wants with words, especially. And I don't know which part to go with. Except that I don't have much choice, because there's this weird disconnect. I wonder if the two sides of my brain really are separated in some way!*

It occurred to me to try an experiment in control. I asked myself (speaking out loud all the time to Shura) whether, in case of a real-life emergency, I could — in the words he would use — screw myself down, back to baseline, in order to cope. It was instantly possible to do so. No problema. At least, not if I took it one moment at a time.

After a while, I found that my sense of Self, of being centered, was gradually increasing. And with it came an increase in fascination with whatever this interior world, this place, was. So far, I couldn't see what could be learned from it. The patterns were only the surface. Beneath all that was a state of being/knowing/seeing which was not to my liking.

*Why do I dislike it? Because it lacks most of the familiar emotions and feelings I'm used to. It's a place of strangeness for me. Alien.*

I searched the air above me. The patterns were still there, moving continuously between me and the ceiling.

*Which means I have to explore it, learn it, own whatever aspect of myself it represents. I wonder if it's just my Observer?*

There was music on the radio, and interestingly enough, I heard it without any particular increase of understanding or emotional relationship, as usually happens with other psychedelics. In this state, it was music and nice enough, but it had nothing to do with everything else that was going on. It was beside the point.

I looked at my beloved's face and saw it colored in mottled oranges, yellows and browns. Not beautiful, but certainly earthy, and I'd seen that kind of skin coloring before, during previous mushroom experiments.

*My face probably looks all mottled to him, too.*

Shura remarked, "It's Beethoven; are you comfortable with it?"

I nodded, "It really doesn't matter, but it's fine. And familiar."

But, even as I said it, I realized that I was no longer looking for anchors like familiar music, because I had begun to be more aware of the essential anchor within myself, and was very slowly beginning to feel less pushed at by the chickenwire squares and the restless streams of color, and increasingly stronger in my core.

I looked over at Shura. He was still my other Me, my essential person, skin of my skin and blood of my blood. There was no rush of emotion about him, just instant acknowledgement of who he was and what we were to each other.

I turned back to search the patterns filling the air above the bed, trying to feel out the nature of whatever form of consciousness was present. All I could sense was a mind whose view of the world with its contradictions and chaos was matter-of-fact; there was an attitude of "That's the way it is; you gain nothing by resisting or complaining; accept it." It wasn't unkind; just calm and cool, down-to-earth.

*Oh, yes. I know that one. That's just a version of my own Observer again. I'm projecting it onto something "out there," but it's part of my own psyche, like it or not.*

I lay on my back, gazing up at the frustrating tangle of lines and dots between me and the ceiling, wondering what in heaven I was supposed to do with any of it. I had recognized the projection of what I called my Observer, but beyond that, of what use was it?

*Owning it all as part of myself makes my sense of control better, but it doesn't do much to answer the question which continues to nag: what is this aspect of my mind? Is it also an aspect of the universal mind? Yes, of course. So I'm back in the old loop again. Whatever the universal consciousness is, our own is a mirror of it. The part of ourselves which we (most of us) prefer, feel comfortable with — the affectionate, loving, caring part — is balanced by other parts, including the one which emerged in this experience, which is characterized by cool knowing, acceptance, lack of emotional warmth or response. It isn't hostile to such feelings, but it isn't involved with them. And of course this describes my Observer, because its function is to observe and learn.*

We lay side by side, Shura and I, holding hands, listening now to one of my favorite pieces of music, Rachmaninoff's Symphonic Dances. The ceiling was still busy with slightly pulsing amoeba squares and their black nuclei, but I wasn't trying to learn anything from them any more.

Suddenly, I remembered something that had disturbed me the day before, and told Shura. I said, "I'm thinking about a dream I rediscovered on the computer. I'd written it down very carefully a long time ago, and as I read it over, I couldn't recall having had the dream at all. It was really strange, not being able to remember even a trace of it. It was like reading a stranger's account. It bothered me. And just now, it came to me that, since the dream had been totally understood at the time, and had been written down, there was no further need for me to remember the actual dreaming of it."

Shura prompted me, "What was it about?"

I summarized, "You were in it, and my children, and we were all interchangeable; we were all — we were each other. All of us were in this place, and there was a tremendous energy field; I mean, we *were* an energy field. A good dream. Actually, I think you'd call it a Samadhi dream, a bliss state."

We made some moves toward lovemaking, but my efforts were half-hearted, and I finally told Shura there was too much distraction going on, "I don't think I can focus enough, honey. Maybe later."

He pulled my head over to his shoulder, reassuring me, "You go with your instincts, babe. Just keep me abreast of what's happening."

It occurred to me, finally, to ask him what he was experiencing. He hesitated, then admitted, "I'm enjoying the music and I'm in a good place, but — believe it or not — I've had no visual effects whatsoever."

I raised my head and peered at him through mottled veils of color — mostly brown and dark red, at that point — and said, "Good grief, Charlie Brown; no visuals at ALL?"

He chuckled and shook his head, "I should have expected it, after the experiment earlier this week. It's okay, though. You seem to be having enough visuals for both of us!"

After cuddling beside him for some time, I told him I wanted to try writing again, if he didn't mind. He said, "Sure. Give it a go. I'm going to stay here awhile and listen to the music."

Walking down the hall towards the dining room, I realized how selfish I was being, how focused on my own experience, and wondered why I wasn't more empathetic with Shura. What was even more interesting was that my self-absorption didn't particularly trouble me.

*I don't think it would be right for me to pretend feelings that aren't genuine; he knows I love him; he knows I'm usually tuned into him. This is just the way it's going for me, this time, and I have to follow my instincts and not put on any kind of act; that would be insulting to him, a betrayal.*

This time, when I sat down at my computer, the keyboard was clearly visible and when I began describing the formerly undescribable, it was obvious that the separation within my mind which had so annoyed me earlier — the inability to apply words to what was being directly experienced — had changed. I was in charge again; I could use words to do anything I wanted. On the other hand, the patterns which had filled the air everywhere I looked, only half an hour ago, had faded. In fact, they were almost entirely gone. So there was nothing in the way of interior images for me to deal with anymore.

At around 1:30 a.m., we went back to the bedroom. Love-making flowed easily, but we couldn't manage orgasm, either of us. There was no distraction for me, this time; the visuals had disappeared. The music was a lovely Schumann thing we'd both known from childhood, and we hummed together through familiar passages. But still, I was aware of the fact that a large part of my mental and emotional focus was somewhere other than below my waist.

---

From my notes the next day:

"Sleep was pleasant, with dreams that were clear and clean in color, amusing and friendly. Completely unlike my usual post-2C-B dreams, which tend to be shallow, annoying and very repetitive.

After sleeping for a long time, during the entire next day I had energy and a quiet, calm pleasantness. No need for a nap, as after 2C-B. Wanted to write, looked forward to cooking, enjoyed whatever I was doing. Most unusual.

Bewildering experience, and I want to explore a different mushroom next time, at perhaps the same level, and see what comes up. This was difficult and frustrating, but it was also challenging, and in a strange way, rewarding. Much to learn."

---

Some time later, I was at a pot-luck dinner in a friend's house, with about forty members of what we call the Network — people interested in exploration of the human mind — and I was on the back deck, smoking and sipping a fruit drink. I was watching Shura through the big kitchen window as he gestured dramatically, engaged in intense conversation with a young blond man. I love watching him; with his enthusiasm, his pleasure in ideas, he is an 18 year-old soul radiating life in a 69 year-old body.

A friend of mine came onto the deck and headed toward where I was sitting at a big glass-topped patio table. She gave my shoulders a hug as she passed behind me. It was Sarah Vincent, another young soul in a middle-aged body, whose book on telepathy experiments had just been published.

Sarah was a completely extraordinary person. She'd been through marriage, divorce, motherhood, loss and triumph, and even now, in her sixties, with a full head of grey curls, she was usually involved in an affair, often with a man quite a bit younger than she. With her sharply intelligent eyes and lovely, animated face, she had the presence of a shaman and the warmth of an empathetic mother, and I always learned something from her. Sarah had been involved in the psychedelic movement from the beginning, and her fascination with the way the mind works, stimulated by what she had seen and experienced of the effects of psychedelic drugs, had led her to become involved in the study of brain waves and telepathy.

After we'd talked for a while about her book and the work that had gone into it, it occurred to me to ask Sarah if she could possibly help me understand the aspect of my mushroom experiment that had interested — and annoyed — me most: my inability, at the height of the effects, to describe what I was seeing.

"I could describe anything else, I could talk about anything else; it was just when I tried to apply words to whatever I was looking at, the patterns, the visuals, even the eyes-closed pictures — which were totally boring — I became wordless. Later on, as the images were beginning to fade, I could use words again and describe everything, no problem. But why that split, earlier?"

"The patterns, what were they like?" asked Sarah.

"Sort of traceries — no, not traceries; they were kind of like chicken-wire fencing, but the spaces weren't square, they were more like amoebas, and in the center of each space was a black dot, like the dark center of an amoeba. That's about as close as I can get."

"Flat or dimensional?"

"All the space around me was filled with them, with this stuff, you know, in three dimensions; I mean, the air was thick with them, everywhere I looked."

"Right, right."

"And everything was very dark — dark colors. It was not the most pleasant experience I've ever had, but — but the important thing was the inability to verbalize. I could tell Shura anything else, but I couldn't say a word about whatever I was seeing, and I thought that maybe there was some kind of — it felt to me as if there was a separation of parts of my brain, you know?"

"Yes, there is that," said Sarah, and took a drink from her glass.
"There is?"

*Surprise, surprise — does she really mean that?*

I asked, "Do you have any idea what happens — when everything you're looking at is perfectly simple, but you can't use the part of your mind — your brain — that finds words? And how come I could talk about anything else?"

"Well, focus of attention is important in this," said Sarah. "So often, when I want to say somebody's name, I will see that person; I will hear her talk; I will remember how she smells and how she's dressed. But I can't think of her name for anything!"

"Yes — "

"And part of that's because I am used to using the visual system as my dominant cognitive process, and it's not necessarily connected to the verbal. The stronger the visual, the less likely I will be able to name it."

"Yeah, yeah — "

"And there comes a separation — ," she closed her eyes as if to see better, "Even in our telepathic work, a person might draw one picture and give a different verbal report."

*She must mean when they're doing remote-viewing experiments.*

"And while one was attempting to receive, sometimes the picture would be right, and the words unrelated, and sometimes the words would be right and the picture unrelated."

"That's weird!"

"It is weird," she agreed, laughing, "And it's one of the things I want to go over with you. The verbal system can be quite independent of the visual system. There are people who use the verbal system most dominantly in their thinking processes, you know, and they'll often do word puns and you know, I'll miss those puns, because while they're talking, I'm visualizing — "

"Yes."

" — and all of a sudden, here comes this word pun, and I have to stop and shift thinking gears, 'Oh, yes, that must be a joke,' and it's just such a blank wall for me, at first — a non sequitur — because my dominant cognitive process is not verbal, but visual. So the punsters laugh about it, because I'm so slow at getting jokes, but it's because I'm not using that part of my brain in the same way."

"And the kind of visions that I'm describing — " I began.

"It's like you're projecting from the inside out. You're projecting onto the surface something that's going on in your visual processes, and if they're really, really dominant, they're not connected to the verbal, so you wouldn't be able to talk about them at the same time."

"But why could I — uh — why was I able to talk about anything else?"

"Because that's not the same process; you can — you see, you simply haven't made a verbal connection — "

"To what's going on visually," I finished.

*I could talk to Shura because it wasn't about things I was seeing, it was about ideas and feelings, nothing being visually experienced.*

Sarah went on, "You know, one of the difficulties in learning visual thinking, if you're not a visual thinker — "

"Yeah — "

" — you know, somebody's painting something, and they go —," she gestured in the air with an imaginary paintbrush, making little ch-ch-ch sounds to accompany the stabs of the brush, " — and the other person says, 'What's that?' because they have to put words to it — "

"Yes," I said.

" — because it has to be a leaf, or it has to be a — a SOMEthing, right?"

"You have to train them on Clyfford Still's paintings," I said, and was rewarded by Sarah's burst of laughter. She obviously knew Clyfford Still's work.

"If you're thinking in color," she said, "If your color-intelligence and your shape-intelligence are functioning, you don't need to have words for things at all."

"Ah."

Sarah continued, "If you're looking for Marianne Street, and you find Marine Street, you'll probably make the turn before you realize it was wrong, because you looked at the first letters and then you filled in what you expected to find — "

"Uh-huh!"

"So there's that — " Sarah was picking her words carefully, I thought, and wondered if she was sensing my confusion, " — that mixup in the area of intention."

"Intention," I repeated, "Meaning focus?"

"Well, like, you know, everything has to go through the thalamus — except smell — to get to the cortex, and the thalamus is the area of intention, as well as a switchboard; here it is, right here, in the center — half way between your eyes and the back of your head, half way between your ears, the switchboard — ," she demonstrated with a finger to her head, " — and sometimes there'll be synaesthesia, where you smell sounds — ," she illustrated with interweaving fingers, as I nodded enthusiastically, smiling because synaesthesia is one of my favorite experiences in the world.

" — and hear colors and that sort of thing. There's a whole section of the Tibetan Book of the Dead that Tim Leary and others translated; do you have that book around? They called it The Psychedelic Experience."

"The Tibetan Book of the Dead? Yes. I don't know exactly where in the house it is, but we do have it."

"Well, the way Leary and Alpert and Metzner translated that, it's one of the Bardos. When you see all these patterns and shapes and you're totally involved in these patterns and shapes, then that's one of the places you can go — "

I nodded.

"—and it's usually — ah — it's not a very advanced level, necessarily, and you may not even appreciate it, or like it."

"I didn't."

I thought for a moment, then added, "By the way, Sarah, these floating chickenwire sorts of things are familiar; I've seen them before. It wasn't that they were brand new or anything; they're like the snakeskin patterns, you know, that you can get with most real psychedelics."

"Yes," said Sarah, "We all know that one."

"So these amoeba kind of shapes — you've seen them?"

"I've seen something like it, yes. There are energy patterns around everything, and there are sort of these little transparent thingies — "

"Uh-huh."

"— and part of what you're seeing is from your pre-conscious, part is what you pick up from your environment, and part of what you're seeing is the projection of your rods and cones, and those are the patterns they make."

*Rods and cones, for Pete's sake!*

She sat back and smiled at me, "About four years ago, when I was teaching students who were eager to experience mind games, I used an old 16 millimeter projector as a mild strobe light in which the flicker rate could be changed to different frequencies to match the natural brainwaves. The old movies ran at 18 frames per second, which was fast enough for us to see the separate images as one image continuously moving. But at 13 frames per second, my students drew pictures of interference waveform patterns."

*Interference waveform — wonder what that looks like?*

"At around 6 to 10 frames per second — " continued Sarah, now completely caught up in her subject, eyes shining with pleasure and excitement, "— which matches the frequencies of the theta and alpha brainwave range — the majority of the students drew pictures of mandala patterns with polka-dots. They described the patterns as constantly moving, red to green, or red-orange to blue in opposite directions. You see, when you are sending a signal to the eye at the rate it 'sees' it, then you're looking *at* what you are looking *with*. I've collected about a hundred of these drawings, so you know I've studied the results."

"Yeah," I said softly, with just a tiny hesitation, letting her know I needed more explanation — just a bit more.

"In other words," said Sarah, slowing down slightly, "If you take a projector and project its own plain light on a wall, and then you close down the opening for the light, what you will see on the wall is the filament of the projector lamp itself! When you shine a light in somebody's eyes at the same rate as the brainwave of the visual cortex, it's like looking at the projector filament; the rods and cones are projected into the flickering light. Sometimes thought forms are projected into the middle of this as well."

*What? Thought forms?*

But Sarah was continuing, "The focus in the visual system becomes so intense that the pathways become dominant and the verbal system can seem to be unconnected to what you are seeing. Flickering lights are not the only way to stimulate this process; mind chemistry can also trigger strange activity of the visuals, as you know."

"Ah, yes!"

"So it's — part of what you're seeing may be related to the energy of the person you're looking at, and part of it is what you're looking with. It's a very, very primary state of vision."

"Yes, yes, right."

"And it's a very creative state of vision. Now, some of the other kinds of patterns that sort of dominate and seem to be meaningless, that's one of the Bardo's, and you can get stuck in it for a while."

"You used the word, 'creative,' though," I prompted, "Is it creative because it's down well beneath the intellect, and it's more open to the unconscious, so things can flow more freely?"

"Yes, that's one way of saying it; your pre-conscious is influencing what you're seeing, as well as the influences of the environment that's around you."

"Okay."

Sarah drank from her glass, then put it down and smiled at me, "One of the reasons I like to study telepathic imagery is because we are really scratching the surface of that creative space, and that brings deeper thoughts into conscious focus. I've collected over hundreds of telepathy trials between couples who just wanted to try to improve their communication with each other. They often find that the inner thoughts which they haven't confided to each other yet — or perhaps haven't admitted to themselves — are brought right up to the surface. The intelligence of the visual system is often more direct in exposing pre-conscious issues than the verbal system is."

"Well, now, with the business of — " I stumbled, "If you really wanted to, could you — by doing 'shrooms often enough, could you learn to translate what you're seeing and experiencing into the verbal, or do you just have to learn to wait until later, when the words can be found easily?"

"Ah —" began Sarah, but I interrupted.

"Is there any *point* in trying to learn to bring them — "

"To do it simultaneously? I don't think so. The non-verbal realms are their own reward."

"Okay, so it's more a matter of — it's a control issue."

"But you can recall it later on, just as you've done for me."

"Yes, oh yes, easily," I agreed.

"You know, if you're totally focused on making love, for example, you're not writing poetry."

"Yeah."

"That comes later," she chuckled, "And if you're totally focused on synchronizing your brain waves with somebody, then that's all you're doing and, like, if you do something else, you're not synchronizing any-more. If you talk about it, you've shifted the whole EEG, and you're no longer doing what you started out to do."

"So there really is no point to it."

"Not much. In hypnosis, I'll take a person into a deep space, watch the face very carefully, so I know when they're visualizing, I know if they've run into an emotional thing — "

I nodded firmly. I was remembering my own experience as a therapist, and how much I had learned from watching patients as they lay on the couch, dropping into the trance state as they'd been taught to do.

Sarah was saying, " — and at a certain point, I'll ask them to verbalize, in order to stabilize the memory for later, and to integrate the mental functions. But during the experience, there has to be a whole period of time when they're not verbalizing, because they have to be experienc-ing!"

I said, "Okay. I see what you mean. Trying to force verbalization blocks me from really experiencing, and there's nothing to be gained by all that effort, considering the fact that — eventually — the verbal ability returns, good as new."

Sarah reached across the table and patted my hand, "That's the way I see it, yes."

"Thanks, honey," I said, "I needed to find a different way of thinking about something I had assumed was a problem, and you've given it to me."

"You're welcome," she laughed, and we went on to talk about other things.

Thanks to Sarah, I've learned not to try to control experiences like these, but to go with what's being presented. I'm still not sure how to avoid being stuck in any of what the Buddhists call the Bardo's, which are usually described as being states through which a soul journeys after the body's death. The images in the Bardo's range from cartoon-like, silly figures without apparent meaning or depth, to demons and monsters which mirror the soul's unresolved dark side. I've always believed that what one is supposed to do in the Bardo's (whether one is a newly released soul or a psychedelic traveler) is confront and acknowledge these reflections of one's unconscious self, then move on.

But what in heaven's name could I possibly have done with floating bits of musty ribbon candy? Just wait it all out, probably, with patience and resignation. After all, everything transforms, if you give it enough time.

When I next see Sarah, I'll ask.

# CHAPTER 6.  PANSOPH-2

(Shura's voice)

I have never been particularly satisfied with my dream life. Not that it was uninteresting, it is just that I don't remember much of it. Oh yes, I have been told that if I were to ask myself immediately on awakening, "What were you dreaming?" I would be able to recall a lot of it. This is nothing more than exchanging one problem for another, since I can never remember to ask myself that question when I wake up.

There is one personal dream property of which I am pretty confident, however. I do not dream in color. When there is color called for by the plot, so to speak, it is intellectually supplied. Walk on the green light. I watch the light change, and I know that this is now the green light, and I walk. But the actual light itself is in shades of gray. Once in a long while something will colorize the scene, such as a field of flowers actually being yellow spots on a grey landscape, and I am awake immediately. It is as if I weren't allowed that particular modality.

An exception to the amnesia pattern occurred on the night following a group experiment with α,O-DMT. In the next day's reports, two of the participants mentioned having nightmares about cataclysmic events, with buildings toppling and people in agony. I can identify with these comments, since that very night I too had a most remarkable dream. And, completely unexpectedly, when I awoke I remembered the entire story with total clarity. This, I said to myself, will never be forgotten. It was structured like a movie script, with scenes all set and dialogue in place. Now, some fifteen years later, I am able to write it up from that still vivid memory. Even to the terrible pun built into the title, BARE-ASS as a play on the vehicle's name: PanSoph-2, or pants-off, too. Here is the story which, I note, might also be seen as a nightmare and even cataclysmic. But I found it totally entertaining. And it was, incidently, in black and white.

## BARE-ASS: A STORY ABOUT INFORMATION

## TUESDAY: A DAY OF CURIOSITY

The sky was an incredible expanse of black, peppered with count-less stars, scattered as if by some random process. Some looked like smudges; perhaps these were galaxies. Others were individuals and kept to themselves. None of the constellations that had been the sky-maps of generations of humans could be identified; the stars were surely still there somewhere, but the viewing perspective was new and always changing.

Willard was the son of the daughter of one of the original crew of the ship PanSoph 2. That launch had been 62 years ago, and his grand-mother Jane Willard Robertson was no more than a myth and a photograph on his desk. How strange and unnecessary, to have three names when you were, after all, just one person.

This had been his duty day for search and report. He had com-pleted the review of the recordings of possible responses from that morning's one hour beacon probe and it had been (as it had always been before and as it would probably be forever on) completely negative. So he drifted to the after lounge and settled back into the comfortable viewing chair. He brought the telescope view onto the screen, and reflected that one of these millions of points of light was the source of his blood line and the magical start of his life process, a source that he could never hope to see in reality. It was an unresolvable sadness that always touched him at this moment.

He covered the screen with the heliospectroscopic filter and quickly located the wanted pin-point dot, very near to the cross-hairs as always, that stayed lighted as all the others went dark. That was earth's sun; that was his origin.

He made the manual changes to bring the earth's sun exactly to the center, and carefully recorded the micrometer values used so that the earth-people could continue calculating the gravitational discontinuities that had introduced these errors. With the fine focusing optics moved into place, the recentering of the sun's dot provided the corresponding corrections of the positioning of the radio transceiver antenna, so that the link report could be made.

A very strange and sterile world it was for Willard, but he could not see it that way, for this world had been his entire life. He had been born here on the ship a couple of earth-decades ago, and had gone through the ritual vasectomy, clock-training, maternal linking and memory challenges. He was now one of the four navigators, each having one day on and three off, and all of them sharing the responsibilities of knowing where they were and where they were going. And why? In two years young Broderick would come of age and they would be back to a full complement of five again. And if Sara birthed a boy, there would be a sixth as backup in another couple of decades.

Once the locks were set on the radio antenna, he opened the receiving circuit for the earth message. It started precisely on time, at the calculated 14:22.37 on his watch and also, of course, in the small box in the lower right-hand corner of his start screen. He acknowledged the initial challenge with the completely familiar password, and saw the several lines of text, the news of the rest of the human race there on earth, unfold across the bottom of the screen. Another political challenge to the rulers of Serbia, a new approach proposed to the study of environmental changes, and the discovery of a new viral factor in a disease thought to be genetic. He would enter these bits of information into the transient encyclopedia; nothing, of course, was allowed to go into the basement computer.

He dumped the screen, switched to transmit, and sent the small fine-focusing corrections that he had made to center the sun, so that the people back there would be able to further map the small gravitational deflections the ship was experiencing in its present location. These calculations would take only a few minutes once the information got back there, but it would be more than three years for the signal to make the trip from PanSoph-2 to earth.

What Willard could not know was the tragic condition of life on earth, the changes and distortions that had occurred during the space ship's travels. The news messages were less than candid, as they were always framed in a structure which would use concepts that the crew could understand. The last living link with life other than the ship he had always known as his home, was the Mother Bess who had told unbelievable stories of her childhood. Although she was now dead, many of the tapes still existed, having been rerecorded many times. And the basement memory was replete with an overwhelming quantity of history, which could be copied and read at leisure. But it was, of course, current only at the time of their launch, many years ago. He was aware that the first of these information ships, PanSoph itself, had apparently been lost. At least its fate was unknown. That is why the daily link with the current ship #2 had been invoked as a fixed ritual.

It was the information in the basement that was, after all, the purpose of the ship and the sole reason for its existence. In this basement was a massive computer memory, with the entire inventory of factual knowledge, the history of the planet Earth, all scientific discovery and invention, as well as the complete art, music and writing of the human species. It was there in its entirety, guaranteed to be intact, potentially the remaining record of the human animal if earth were to be lost. Any amount of it could be decompiled and copied, and brought up by being transferred to the ship's top computer, its working computer, and used or enjoyed, then discarded. But it was one of the inflexible operational rules that nothing new should ever be sent down. More than a rule, this was sacred dogma. The basement memory bank was a record of earth as of the day of departure, and it must remain unchanged. It was a law that was not to be violated.

Just as the search for replies to the hour's beacon transmission was part of the day's routine (as was the focus and transmission to earth) so was the requirement that time be spent in some learning discipline to occupy the duty day. Willard was content in that he had completed his chores here in communication, and he knew that the pregnant Sara was busy in house-keeping. All the others were in suspension for the day. He made a quick run-down of all the control lights — gyro, $CO_2$ reducer, thrust pile, power to the basement memory and the sperm bank, delay tapes to the beacon probes — everything was green and quiet. So Willard relaxed and pursued his personal learning discipline, playing with pi in multidimensional matrices.

His current passion was to express pi in some even-numbered modulus and explore some form of walk in a dimensional system of half that number, basing everything on the actual value of pi. He had called up from the basement into the top computer (the encyclopedia, as they commonly called it) the value of pi that had been stored there as a quantum fact, known with complete accuracy to almost 10 to the 10th places. Then he manipulated it into modulo six. A magnificent collection of naughts and ones and twos and threes and fours and fives, all tumbling after one another in seemingly random patterns, but so exquisitely not-at-all random. Wherever he stopped, the next number was unknown to him, but he realized that by simply invoking any of several power series expressions, the next digit would be exposed. What it would be was totally unpredictable, but absolutely preordained. An eerie concept, the revealing of each new digit totally unknown to him, yet absolutely fixed in the infinite nature of things.

It was a moment of carelessness, of inattention, but a moment that would change the order of things in unexpected ways. Willard secured his day's number theory games by returning his slightly expanded value of pi to memory. It should have been discarded from top memory, or put into a personal folder there, as it now contained new information, but he had left the coding on it that identified it as galactic knowledge, and as such it was allowed back into basement memory. A fundamental rule had been violated.

WEDNESDAY: A DAY OF INEXACTNESS.

It was Charles the next day who conducted the beacon probes and went through the ritual (and again futile) search for replies. From the after lounge he called up the telescope projection and it was when he made the routine time check that the first hint was seen of something being amiss. The time on the screen was at the lower right, as always, but when he glanced at his watch, there was a three second discrepancy. He was fast! He queried the ship's computer; it was absolutely consistent with what he saw on the screen. He checked the battery of his watch; it had full power. So he touched it to the transfer plate of the terminal and reset it. His time was now corrected and there was, of course, agreement. Nonetheless he noted the event in the ship's log.

Receiving time for the day was set at the usual increment of advance, and was due for 14:23.37. The thought passed fleetingly through Charles' mind, should that time have been from his watch, or from the ship's computer? Well, they were now both the same, and of course the computer had to be correct. He filled the screen with the field that carried the earth's sun and, for the first time in his life, saw that none of the several stars in the center of the monitor were at all close to the cross hairs. Apparently some other error had entered the picture. The spectroscope filter quickly determined which of the several candidates was the proper sun, but it was much further off to the right than he had ever seen it before. Perhaps they were entering the gravitational field of some massive invisible body. He swung the field appropriately to bring the sun to the cross-hairs, but he carefully recorded the unusually large micrometer and vernier entries that were needed. He locked the scope, and as soon as the radio antennas had matched these bearings, he locked them as well.

The receiver was on, and he had yet another surprise. The earth message that was to be printed across the bottom of the screen had already started. Some of it had already been lost. At the end of the receiving, he noted that the amount lost was perhaps several seconds. With a shock he realized that it had not been his watch but, rather, the ship's computer, that had been in error with that morning's time check. Switching to transmission mode, he dumped back to earth the macro with the vernier readings, and the usual negative findings from the morning beacon probe. After a moment's hesitation he decided not to mention the clock discrepancy. And also not to mention the unusual shift of real position, from calculated position, of the earth's sun image. He would work around a bit with it first, and if there was some new gravitational attraction that was influencing their trajectory, he would be able to analyze it in a less hurried manner, and make any needed heading changes using the ship's existing programs rather than waiting for years for suggestions from Earth.

What was amiss? The fact that he had indeed found the sun (he had received Earth's transmission after all) suggested to him that the most rewarding first step would be to search out the clock mess-up. He brought up the exact time on the monitor from the ship's computer, and with his watch against the transfer plate, projected the exact time from it onto the screen as well. They were clearly printed one above the other, and again they did not show the same time. The watch was nearly a second fast. Again. Or the ship's computer was going slower yet. How could an entry into the gravitational field of some distant massive thing so dramatically influence the computer's timing crystal?

He went to the crew's suspension area, found Johnathan's bunk, moved his friend's arm out from under the covers, and carefully unstrapped his watch. Back at the main console, he projected its time onto the big monitor and, as he somehow knew it would be, the time was yet different from both his own watch and the ship's computer clock. The ship's clock was slowest, his own in-between, and Johnathan's the fastest. He went back to the suspension area and quickly gathered ten more watches, and brought them back and projected all of their times. Every one of them was absolutely identical, to a hundredth of a second. Identical to Johnathan's. It was his own that he had screwed up, in making those corrections needed to agree with the ship's top computer. The reference value in this computer was what was most certainly wrong.

What should he do? Try to reset the ship's clocks? That would be quite simple, but would simply hide the problem, not solve it. Run a system check on it; that would be a logical first step. The lines of verification rolled down the screen, but whereas under usual circumstances each line would compare exactly with its control form, Johnathan saw that there was not one, but two alerts. He had read about such things in the manuals, and knew the risks that can be associated with them, but in his entire life on the ship with his radio and navigation work he had never seen a true alert.

One was in the ship's top computer memory and the other, in the basement memory storage. That latter one could wait, as it clearly was not vital to the function of the ship. He thought about activating others in the crew and he knew he had to if this was a true emergency, but for the moment it just might be something related to a single failure, a failure of his personal watch, and he might be able to fix it himself. The first alert certainly made sense with the clock-watch discrepancy — there was a crystal failure in the primary chronometer. Thank goodness he had adjusted only his own watch to the faulted computer; the remaining watches all agreed with each other, and could serve as a reference for resetting things.

He logged deeper into the chronometer entry, to see just where the problem was located, and how he should go about repairing it. As more detailed screens came into view, it became apparent that the problem was not in the primary cesium oscillator, but in the program that translated its primary signal to seconds, and thence to minutes, hours and days. The error was not one of equipment but of calculation. Apparently the mechanics of the clock were intact. However, there was no hint that any of the circuit boards or chips were faulted. Try a sequential voltage check. All test points gave values comfortably within the allowed ranges. The hardware seemed to be perfect. Try a dynamic test.

Charles entered a challenge equation, and after a period of time that was almost, but not quite, outside the allowed limit, the calculation answer finally appeared in the answer box. It was wrong.

Something was very much out of control. He went immediately to the crew's quarters, and set in motion the procedure that would bring them all to consciousness and sensibility within a few minutes.

## THURSDAY: A DAY OF CHAOS

The entire crew was present, with the exception of the children and their nanny, and Jerome who had the beacon and transmission duty for the day. They sat around the large table in the central bulge. Hugo was the senior navigator and the leader of the discussion.

"Let me try to summarize where we are as of the moment. We have so far experienced four alerts in the top computer system; the clock is screwed up — that was the first problem spotted by Johnathan on his shift yesterday. And now faults appear to be present in some aspect of dead-reckoning, something in the Doppler analysis of the beacon responses, and something associated with the nuclear drive pile. Is this one thing wrong expressing itself in several ways, or is the whole ship falling apart all of a sudden?"

"Don't forget the alert from the basement system yesterday," added Charles.

"OK. Five alerts, then. What do they have in common?"

"They all involve calculations, maybe," suggested James.

"But calculations are basic activities of calculators. If the calculator is intact, the calculation gives the right answer." This, from Marie.

The comments flew in from all participants.

"But the answers are wrong."

"How do you know what the right answer is if the calculations are wrong? Maybe your 'right' answer is wrong."

"But they are inconsistent — calculate the same problem twice, and get two different answers."

"You haven't done that. You've compared the results with the published text."

"The watches are all consistent, except for Charles's. But they are different from the top computer's time."

"And the difference is getting absurd."

The free-for-all was interrupted by the appearance of a very disturbed Jerome.

"I can't find the sun at all. Nothing in the entire field has the right spectrum. I missed the transmission schedule. I can't find it!"

Hugo snapped back: "How would you know the right spectrum, if it has to be calculated for checking, and our calculators are screwed up?"

A chill settled over the group, as it became apparent that something was very wrong, and the trusted tools for isolating the source of the wrongness might themselves be faulted.

"That's it," came the voice of Willard. "Every wrong calculation invokes a power series calculation for its success. Maybe something is out to lunch with the power series part of the computer?"

"Well, how can that idea be checked?" asked Hugo.

"I can do it immediately from a pi calculation. I have the power series, and the correct answer in my personal satchel in top memory."

"How do you know just what the correct answer would be?"

"I have the accurate value up from basement, accurate to a gillion places."

"Then give it a try."

Jerome interrupted. "Would a couple of you come and help me on the earth screen. Look over my shoulder and see if I'm missing something."

The group broke up. No one noticed the soft hissing sound that filled the ship. At least no one commented on it. Willard opened his personal address on the nearest monitor, and called up the current power series he was using for new values of pi. In a moment, the screen was filled with a myriad of zeros and ones.

"The last form I had was modulo six, so let me convert this." A couple of strokes more, and the screen was now filled with digits from zero to five.

"See, it's working fine," he said with some satisfaction.

"Is it the right answer?" asked Hugo.

I'll make a subtraction check against the reference value." Another couple of strokes, but this time there was no change.

"My reference value is missing!"

"Did you erase it?"

"Of course not. I saved it."

"Where?"

"Right here in my ..." Willard stopped. A cloud went across his face. "Might it have been, somehow, saved to basement?"

Hugo immediately called up the system check screen, to look for any alert messages. The rules for bringing up and using information from the basement were clearly stated. All knowledge was of one of three classes:

Galactic knowledge. This was universal fact, which would be accessible to any and all intelligences anywhere in the universe. Here were the physical constances such as the speed of light and Planck's Constant. Here was the mass of the proton and the half-life of carbon-fourteen. On Arcturus 4B, as on earth, these numbers are identical. Such values went down to basement as class A information. They were uncensored and unrestricted, but they could only be entered with the quantum key. The value of pi was among these quantum facts.

Earth knowledge. Here were the facts that were uniquely those of earth. The physical scene, such as atmospheric oxygen concentration and the salinity of salt water. Chlorophyll and DNA. Other worlds might have, would most certainly have, similar numbers, but these were absolutely unique to earth, and reflected its evolutionary history. This material was factual, but not galactically universal. It was placed in the basement with the history key, and a copy could be brought up as wanted. It could never be changed from a distance. No alien intelligence could ever insert its own information, as there was no inherent truth in any alien numbers.

Human knowledge. This was the product of the intelligence of man. The history of the human animal, the writings of Shakespeare, the speeches of Cicero, the structures of psychoactive drugs, and the causes of depression. Again, initial information was put down with the mind key, but once there in basement, it was inviolate. If copies came up, they had to be kept in personal files or dumped.

The galaxy key, the history key, and the mind key. All had been used at the loading of the basement computer, the pan-sophistry repository of all human knowing, and all these keys remained on earth, so that this body of knowledge would be preserved intact for future scholars.

The hissing that seemed to come from everywhere was now quite a bit louder. Still, no one seemed to notice.

The checks that Hugo brought to the screen carried two alert messages. He opened immediately the basement alert that had been there from yesterday, but which had been totally ignored. It stated, quite simply:

"Unauthorized filing detected. System decompiling."

He clicked on the latter entry, and there appeared on the screen:

ALL DATA WILL BE DECOMPILED, MATERIALIZED, AND DUMPED

"What have we done here? Can this be stopped?"

The nanny from the nursery ran in, out of breath. "Sally has gone into what looks like a convulsion. Help me."

Johnathan ran out with her. Willard turned to Hugo, with a look of distress in his face. The hissing was quite a bit louder now.

"If I blew it with saving my pi game in basement, then at least I can call it up again and see if the numbers check."

"Try it," said Hugo. "I'll bet you can't find it."

Willard opened the read-only menu of basement, and scanned over to the number theory menu. It was blank. A message was all that remained, stating:

POWER SERIES BIN MATERIALIZED AND DUMPED

In a panic, he called up the master menu. The classical history and language files were also empty, and a red star lay alongside the biology file. He snapped this open, and found that the species file was active. In a moment of insight, he realized that all the recorded DNA was being dumped.

But it was all being materialized first. For some reason, certainly never to be known, the simplest forms were the first to be transformed from the genetic record to the actual expression of the entity. If there had been a million sets of nucleic code, a million living individuals were being created in exchange for the original record. And those million examples, be they pions or viruses or bacteria or yeast cells, were being materialized into the space all about him. There was the sense of a cloud, a grey transparent cloud, thickening all around him. The sounds became louder bit by bit, and the world about him became increasingly viscous.

The hiss was now a thing that could be felt as well, with a sound that resembled that of a smoke detector without the pulsing note. Simply a continuing whine. It built up yet more in intensity and he became aware of particulate things in the environment. Things that were spewing out of the bowels of the ship. First it seemed to be clumpy dust, but then it became more lumpy and had shapes that would have been familiar, if he'd been given the time to watch.

The hiss —

The hiss was now a roar. Willard backed away from the controls and screens, and took what comfort he could in having the ship's solid bulwark pushing against his back. He held his hands out in front of him, as if warding off aggressors that he couldn't see. He jerked aside as he felt some unknown life-form brushing his cheek. His mind said No! Then he realized that everything that had ever lived on earth, and for which the DNA code was known, was being re-created and released here aboard this isolated space ship. He screamed.

But his scream was never heard. The noise within the space ship had become deafening. Saber-tooth tigers and bats and spiders and buzzards; an unending variety of forms and identities spewed forth from the basement. In the last few seconds of his life, Willard realized that there would never be any further communication either to or from earth, and the fate of PanSoph 2 would never be known. Perhaps this is how the original PanSoph ended, an untellable story stemming from the curiosity and carelessness of one of its crew. Traits, both, that are exquisitely human.

In time, Willard's ship, leagues from it's origins, fell silent and continued its way as a hulk with a cargo of dead, outwards into the void where the concept of intelligence and knowledge and consciousness did not exist.

Some day there might be a new try, a PanSoph #3, but perhaps not. It might be that the wish to preserve the magic of the human animal, or the story of its creation and reason for being, had already been lost on earth.

# CHAPTER 7. STAMPS

(Shura's voice)

My most keen interests at the present time are drugs, especially drugs that can influence or modify the function of the mind. A much earlier area of compulsive enthusiasm involved the collection and study of stamps. I mentioned in *PIHKAL* my memories as a child living next door to an ancient man, a Mr. Smythe, who was a bookdealer. He received books by mail, thus there were stamps attached, and they of course came from everywhere around the world. He kept the books, but he gave me the stamps. I would take them all up to my bedroom, float them off their wrappers with cold water, press them dry with newspapers and blotters and heavy books for weight, and then identify them with my precious and personal copy of the 1930 Scott's Stamp Catalog. Actually, my mother had prepared me for this philatelic interest in an unusual way. She had traveled, as a visiting teacher, from school to school in the Nile basin during and just after the Great War (1914-1918) and had given me letters (boxes of them) that she had written home from there. Khartoum and Cairo were common names to me, and identifying numerals in Arabic was my first venture into foreign literacy. I got from her, and I still have squirreled away and waiting for some free time, quite literally hundreds of the 1914 Sphinx and Pyramid common issues, and a lot of larger stamps with camels on them, all on envelopes and with some unusual postmarks. That promised to be an area of exciting research.

At about the time of World War II (which effectively renamed the Great War as World War I) I discovered the Austro-Hungarian Empire, and the Zhemstvo postal system of Russia. This threw me back into the 19th century, and I decided that it would be completely cool and sophisticated to limit my philately to only those stamps that had been used prior to 1900. I put what money I could spare in the 1950's into buying many lots at auction, and I put together (but even today have not yet organized) a neat collection of old and lovely stamps. Newspaper stamps, steam-ship line stamps and, as it turns out, the very items that set the stage for this Washington, D.C. adventure: revenue stamps.

My compulsion in the area of the psychotropic drugs didn't become manifest until the 1950's when I participated in an experiment that involved the psychoactive drug mescaline. It caught my attention just as completely as had the Sudanese postal cards. I discovered that there were many simple things, in this case not stamps but chemicals, that could provoke changes of consciousness.

The passage of the Harrison Narcotics Act in 1915 created the first Federal law that illegalized drugs. There were two compounds specifically focused upon: cocaine (and the coca plant and its components) and heroin (and the opium poppy with its components and derivatives). For two decades these were the major, the only, pharmacological evils of our culture. There was no racism acknowledged; cocaine just happened to be the black man's problem, and opium just happened to be the Chinaman's problem. There were hot jazz clubs in New Orleans and opium smoking dens in San Francisco. The drug problem quickly became a legal concern instead of a medical one in that drug users were looked upon, legally, as criminals rather than as patients. Physicians were told to keep away from the treatment of addicts or they, too, would suffer legally. The law was cast in fiscal terms, not judicial, and it required permits and payments. Its enforcement was assigned to the Department of the Treasury rather than to the Department of Justice. One had to buy revenue stamps to possess these drugs, and it was the absence of these stamps that defined any crime that might be committed.

In the 1930's, another minority group population, the Mexican immigrants, served as the excuse for further Federal drug law change. The drug was marijuana. In 1932, the Federal Bureau of Narcotics was established within the Department of the Treasury, and it was responsible for the handling of any narcotics problems that might arise from the repeal of the alcohol prohibition amendment. The Commissioner of this Bureau, an ambitious politician named Harry J. Anslinger, saw the marijuana issue as an effective springboard to both power and fame, and personally launched a most disingenuous and dishonest propaganda campaign. The hysteria from the movies "Weed that Kills," and "Reefer Madness," is famous, and led directly to the passage of the Marijuana Tax Act of 1937, which was specifically modeled after the Harrison Narcotics Act of 1914. The medical usefulness of marijuana was openly acknowledged, and there could be no question but that physicians, dentists and veterinarians could continue to prescribe it; they would simply have to pay some revenue fee. Any physician who wished to use this drug in his practice had to respect these tax laws. Most states followed this Federal lead by the enactment of similar laws, and quite quickly legal access to marijuana by non-medical users was essentially terminated. This was the climate in the wake of the 1937 law, and the issuance of the Marijuana Tax Stamp in that same year.

It's here that the two areas of my personal interest — stamp collecting and research with psychoactive drugs — effectively overlap. As to the drug side of things, I wanted to answer questions that had never before been answered. Some of these questions had never even been asked before. Do the seeds of potent strains carry the essence of that potency, or is it the growing environment that effectively dictates the final plant? What is the relationship between the potency of a given strain of marijuana, and the components that can be shown to be in it? What is the contribution of the genetics of a given plant to its morphology? I decided to carry out several studies to address these questions, by actually growing marijuana on my farm. I needed the approval of the California Research Advisory Panel (whose name was finally shortened to Research Advisory Panel when the acronym of their original name became publicized). They reviewed my research protocol and approved it. I asked for, and received, a Federal drug license. So I planted and grew, and harvested, and analyzed a sizable crop of pot here on the farm where I live, all with the official organizations extending me blessings. But it became apparent that to learn from my findings I should make critical comparisons against the ultimate reference marijuana plant, the Federal Standard, which had been planted and raised in the Deep South.

So, I decided to begin exploring the world of administrative officialdom. Let's take advantage of my having the State's OK, and having a Federal license on the wall, and let's discover the moves needed to score a stash of Mississippi pot. I wrote to the appropriate authorities, and that is when I discovered that this was a revenue issue rather than a legal one, and there had to be Marijuana Tax Stamps involved in any such transactions. To receive legal marijuana, I had to pay for and receive the required Marijuana Tax Stamps, and then return them to the IRS office accompanying the actual order for the marijuana. So I played the game, and ordered two pounds of Mississippi marijuana, and four ounces of seeds and extracts. The first move of this transaction was the delivery to me of a massive sheet of Marijuana Tax Stamps, forty or fifty or so, at one dollar each, which was acknowledged and sent back with the actual order and a personal check as payment to effectively authorize their shipment of the marijuana. The plants arrived promptly. The stamps of course disappeared back into the maws of the system, but by good chance I had made a photocopy of them while they were in my hands.

It was about this time that I realized this was the ultimate, magical overlap, a synthesis of my two compulsions. It became apparent to me that the reward of this caper would be in the stamps, not the science. So I ordered another four ounces of Governmental grass, got the four one dollar Marijuana Tax Stamps of 1937 (one dollar per ounce plus two cents per form), paid for them, let my check clear, and then immediately abandoned the scientific questions and simply kept the stamps. I chose to add them to my stamp collection, expanding my Africas and my Austrias to now include four U.S. revenues.

This was in February, 1971. I had no way of foreseeing how such a trivial event could give rise to an unforeseeable cascade of consequences. The first step in this developing story was a request from a friend of mine about a year later. He was writing a book on the medical uses of marijuana and had heard that I had received some government marijuana via the Tax Stamp process of the Treasury Department. He wanted to include a photograph of the actual order form, with the stamps attached, in his book. I made a photostat of this order form with the four stamps, with my name and other details blanked out to protect my privacy, and this appeared in his book, *Marijuana Medical Papers 1839-1972* as a part of a chapter written by Dr. David Musto discussing the 1937 Marijuana Tax Act.

This 1973 book was apparently the spark that lit another fuse, bringing me first a phone call, then a visit in the 1980's, from a gentleman who claimed to be a pharmacist in Seattle. This young man was an avid collector of revenue stamps. He had seen the photograph of these four stamps in my friend's book, and had contacted him and succeeded in getting from him both my name and my address. This man flew down to visit me, and spent a half day discussing many aspects of drugs, philately and the law. He stated that he was interested in the legal marijuana situation since he was convinced that it had been used as a device for the manipulation of immigrants. But I personally believed that he truly wanted nothing more than the sensual pleasure of looking at these stamps, and maybe just touching them. Well, it worked out to his sorrow but very much to my own advantage (as became apparent later) that I had completely lost the IRS document with the stamps attached to it. I quite honestly had no idea where it was. Had it been taken by someone? Had it never been returned by my friend after he photographed it for his book? Was it simply buried under a mountain of papers which is the world I live and work in? Whatever. I could not put my hands upon it. Our pharmacist, obviously disappointed, returned to Seattle.

In the 1990's the issue came up again in a completely unexpected way. I received a call from a Special Agent Schmitz, of the Oakland office of the FBI, who said he would appreciate the chance to talk to me and ask a few questions. He came out to the farm, and the conversation went something like this:

"Do you happen to know a pharmacist from Seattle who was interested in the 1937 Marijuana Tax Stamp?"

"Yes, I do."

"Did he visit you?"

"Yes, he did."

"Did you sell him any such stamps?"

"No, I did not."

There were many additional questions, but slowly the story began to take form. I volunteered all of the information that I had, including the fact that the stamps were nowhere to be found, and that the curious philatelist had returned without having seen them. He asked if I could establish the date of the visit, and this proved to be easy, since I did know where my historic appointment books were kept, and I found the date of the visit. He borrowed the book, and it was promptly mailed back to me after being copied. All this took on the earmarks of a criminal action and, when I was asked by the FBI agent if I would be willing to give some sworn statement to them covering the details of the story, I assured them that I certainly would.

Things were to become more complex yet. A few months later I received a request to appear at a Grand Jury panel in Washington. To be exact, it was not a request, but a summons. You are not asked to come; you are told to come. I went, and spent a most informative afternoon with an Assistant U.S. Attorney who filled me in on many details of the story. Apparently there had been some strange goings-on at the Smithsonian Institution where the U.S. Government had put some of these 1937 Marijuana Tax Stamps on display. A young man had expressed keen interest in them and, having inspected them closely and carefully, left. But the stamps had apparently disappeared at about the same time. He had been observed attempting to swap them at a stamp fair in San Francisco, and when he was asked about them by Federal police he stated that he had bought them from me. But a bit of forensic detective work immediately established that the copies he had were the very ones that had been taken from the Washington Museum.

My testimony to the Grand Jury was to affirm that these stamps had not been provided to him by me. I so testified, sharing the sad fact with the jury that these were still lost items and I still held forth the hope that they might show up some day, as they might prove to be quite valuable. There was a feeling of indifference from the jury, as if they couldn't care less, but I had spoken honestly and was quite happy to return home and forget the matter.

Behind my desk I have a battery of filing cabinets, eight of them, each four drawers high, where I keep reprints, correspondence, and manuscripts. About two years ago I needed to file a letter and a reprint concerning a specific Psilocybe species, but I could not find my mushroom files. I knew that I had relocated the folder from one drawer to another because things were just too crowded. I found the folder one drawer down, and just behind it I saw an open pentaflex hanging folder that said, "Gov't letter re Pot." I pulled it out, and found that it contained the entire two decades of exchanges of correspondence with the FDA, the BNDD and DEA, and the IRS. With an eerie feeling of having come home again, I leafed through page after page of correspondence, of application forms and canceled checks. Towards the bottom of the file, there was a photocopy of the forty-or-so stamps and the order form for the two pounds of marijuana. My search was almost completed; there was one sheet left in the file. It turned out to be the unsent order form, and the four beautiful tax stamps were still neatly attached. I believe that I did not move for several minutes. The lost had been found, and I now had closure on a fascinating story of a completed era of pharmacological and fiscal history.

I have no idea how many of these stamps have ever made it into the public domain. I have personally seen fifty-one of them, and also there are these four I now hold which occupy a special page in my collection. It is just possible that they are the only copies that exist outside of the Smithsonian Institution or the IRS archives.

# CHAPTER 8.  LENINGRAD LETTERS

(Shura's voice)

It must be remembered that in 1985, the Soviet Union was still a most intractable police state; there were no signs of the fragmentation and diffusion of authority that now define the scene. There was (and for all I know perhaps still is) a rigid control of movement, speech, radio, television, and mail, along with a nearly pathological mistrust of strangers. This xenophobia did not generally show itself at the level of the common man, but grew as one went up the political and military hierarchy.

When the Leningrad letter arrived, it had a most unusual appearance. My name and address were clearly printed, in English, and the postage was, of course, paid for in Soviet stamps. The writer's return name, address, and Zip code were where they should have been. He was Anatole Zhoborov and (according to a Russian friend of mine) he lived on a rather fashionable avenue in Leningrad. It was at that point that all conventional appearance ended. The immediate unusual feature was the lettering that shone forth in brilliant red on the back of the envelope. A message was printed there, on the two edges of the sealing flap, and on the construction seams of the lower half, forming a sort of lurid St. Andrew's Cross. There, for all to read, was the message "SAVE ME GOD, IF YOU IS." And on the lower seams, "PEACE" and "NO WAR." I inspected the envelope most carefully, and even to my inexperienced eye there were obvious signs of entry. The gum of the flap was slightly misplaced, and a small scrap of selvage had been stuck exactly at the tip of the flap to re-seal the envelope. It even covered a small bit of the red message.

I opened the envelope with an extremely sharp knife, in order to do as little damage as possible. The text of the letter was written in a cursive style with the letters separated from one another, and it was in English. The content was clearly about drugs — drugs that have been classified in the United States as street, or illegal, drugs. There was information on the use and availability of opium and morphine (heroin was not mentioned), amphetamine (methamphetamine was not mentioned), PCP, mescaline, and hashish. Details were offered as to prices, availability, sources (at least the city of manufacture), and as to the popularity of each. All this from inside the Soviet Union. Wow. And all this from a country where there is no drug problem, at least according to the propagandists.

The accompanying text was equally sophisticated. Methods of manufacture were outlined, and the chemical structures had obviously been drawn by the hand of a person well studied in chemistry. The final line was a request for an exchange of correspondence. I was completely in a quandary as to just who this Anatole person was, and during the subsequent exchange of letters he never really told me, and I could only speculate with the few bits of the puzzle I had. He was knowledgeable about drugs. He wrote in rather good English. He showed a true Russian cultural background with the dropped articles in his writing and the added g. before the year of the date. He also appeared to be a person with some form of death wish, having written to me of such matters with an obvious flag on the back of his envelope.

Anatole was a person with consistent patterns, as I was to discover in the course of our developing correspondence. I tried to place him in a society with which I was not familiar. Was he indeed a young individual involved in the illicit drug scene? Was he a patient in some mental hospital who had once been involved in the illicit drug scene? Perhaps he was not a "he" at all, but a "them," a group of people at the KGB who had decided that it might be of value to appear to be a young individual, and initiate contact with an American who is knowledgeable about the American drug scene, for some future purpose? Or perhaps a group, not of the KGB but of the CIA with an agenda of its own, mailing strange letters from the Leningrad post office? Clearly his highlighting the envelope with the red writing had caught someone's attention, as the letter had been opened and presumably read. But it was sealed up again and sent on its way with no effort to hide the intrusion. The correctness of the postage indicated that if anything had been removed, it had been very light. It was weird, and I had no clue as to who or what Anatole represented. But I was certainly curious.

My answer to him was a model of circumspection and caution. All questions were answered with accuracy, supplemented with a carefully measured amount of unsolicited information. I volunteered the popularity of methamphetamine and of MDMA in the United States, and added that heroin and other synthetic substitutes were seen here more frequently than were opium or morphine. My letter was printed out from the computer, but I made a point of signing my name Shura in ink, and in cursive Cyrillic, to see if I might provoke some reciprocity in getting him to sign his own first name in some diminutive form. He never did. It was always presented in its full and proper form.

I sent my letter off, but I felt I should be equally diligent in flagging it. Why not play the game in the easterly direction as well? I used the old retired IBM Selectric typewriter to write his address on the left side of the front of the envelope in the typical American way, with the addressee's name first, followed by street number and name, then the city, and finally the country, USSR. Then, just to the right of that, I rewrote the address completely in Cyrillic, using the appropriate ball in the Selectric. But here it appeared not only in the Russian type font, but in the proper inverted Russian format as well. First the country, CCCP, then the city, the street name and number, and finally the name of the addressee. That, I felt, should be unusual enough to catch the eye of the CIA, or the KGB, or whoever else might be interested. I used exactly the right amount of air mail postage, and sent it off. Apparently my letter went right through.

The return letter from Anatole was considerably more detailed, and for the first time he ventured into the area of variously substituted Fentanyl compounds. Rather than providing some clues to help solve the enigma of who or what he was, this letter only added further fuel to the mystery. His mention of Fentanyl triggered some interesting thoughts and fun speculations in the area of pharmacology and chemical warfare.

A few years earlier, there had been a new form of "heroin" appearing on the streets of the larger cities of California. It was called China White, and it responded to none of the presumptive tests for heroin. And the overdosed users gave none of the usual measures of the presence of acetylmorphine or morphine, both standard metabolites of heroin, and routinely seen in the screening of patients. But the signs of heroin overdose were there — pin-point pupils, breathing problems, and narcosis. It was only with the use of a radioimmune assay designed for Fentanyl that the first clues as to the nature of the drug became apparent. It was not Fentanyl, but it was awfully close to Fentanyl. A sample went back to the research labs of the DEA (called Special Testing by its supporters, or Special Resting by those who had limited patience) and in good time the drug was identified as being a methyl homologue of Fentanyl. They said that, based on the presence of an extra carbon atom *here* in the molecule, the drug was a known thing, and was clearly being synthesized by some very sophisticated chemist somewhere. And with such extremely high potency (the active dose was down in micrograms) it should be easy to manufacture a great number of doses with only modest equipment. "A hundred million doses could be made with what could be bought at the hardware store for a few hundred dollars," was how one congressman put it.

Bang — it was made illegal. But the story quickly became more complex. It turned out that the initial China White really had the added carbon *there* in the molecule, but by the time the correction had been publicized within the forensic community, a sample had been seized from illicit sources with the added carbon placed in the *here* position, just where the Feds had originally thought. This "Son of China White" proved to be of similar extreme potency, and was soon followed by more and more Fentanyl analogues with other minor changes. There were methyl groups in yet other places, and carbon chains became different lengths, and new elements such as sulfur or fluorine were occasionally introduced.

Who was doing it? Was it all one person? Where was he located? There was quite an official effort made, but never were any completely satisfactory answers found by the authorities. I personally had been fantasizing a scenario that exploited the original name which contained the word "China." I had noticed that there had been quite a flurry of recent publications from Red China describing the synthesis and pharmacology of some fluorinated Fentanyls. This had followed an extensive quiet period, when almost nothing in this area had been published at all. Once before I had seen a similar quiet period followed by a burst of activity. This was in the Russian chemical literature in the area of quinuclidine chemistry. I suspect that the Soviet chemists were involved in research with compounds of this type in the area of Chemical Warfare, because only a short time after this quiet period ended, I learned from an inside source at Blackwood Arsenal that quinuclidine benzilate was unofficially described as an incapacitating agent in the U.S. arsenal.

Could China be developing, or better, had China been developing, some super-potent Fentanyl analogues as potential warfare agents? Let the fantasy roll. Maybe the Chinese were using second class citizens (the drug-using population of California) as guinea pigs for the initial human trials of their new drugs. After all, several pharmaceutical houses in the United States had also chosen to run the first human trials of the early contraception pills abroad, on what might be thought of, by some, as second class citizens (the fertile population of Puerto Rico). So, there was precedent.

The make-believe scenario rattled on — who would be the importers? Were the profits funneled back to Asia, or were they the pay-off for distribution and reporting? Were there any one-to-one correlations between Chinese scientific literature and the things seen here?

A second international connection was obvious in the fact that all the legitimate Fentanyl line came out of Belgium. There, research into the value of these compounds as anaesthetics was proceeding apace, with the development of new compounds that emphasized potency (which can be related to safety) and duration (short action was a virtue in surgical anesthesia). From these laboratories came such clinically useful inventions as Carfentanil, Sufentanil and Alfentanil. It was also observed, in connection with the radioimmune assay work being done in this country, that those Fentanyl analogues with a "second substituent in the piperidine 4-position" could not be seen by radioimmune assay. They were completely transparent, so there would be no way of spotting the use of such drugs by any standard urine screening analysis. This observation was never widely publicized, a point which made subsequent events even more intriguing.

Back to the Leningrad letters. Here in the second letter, I was getting quite a body of information on Fentanyl. Speculation is cheap, but it is fun. Could China be using some drug-users in Leningrad as an experimental population of second class citizens? Or was Leningrad merely the tip of an iceberg when it came to drug use in the Soviet system? I wanted more information from my correspondent concerning Fentanyl, so I asked some specific questions in my reply to him.

The third letter from him added yet more confusion to this already confused picture. In it, there was not a single mention of drugs. Everything was about explosives. Structures of great beauty and delicate complexity, with stated melting points, indicators of temperatures of detonation, discussion of bruissance — in all, completely sophisticated technological jargon that rang of competence. Why explosives? Why me? There was an intriguing hint at the end of the letter, in which Anatole (or KGB or CIA or whoever they were) asked me to send copies on to two people, both in the military in the United States. I was being asked to be the courier of some heaven-knows-what kind of military information between some Russian unknown and explosive experts here in the U.S. of A.? That was a little too much. I wrote to the people involved, and queried them as to whether they wished to received a letter from an A. Zhoborov in Russia with some information on chemical explosives. One letter was returned addressee unknown, and the other was never answered. And that particular letter from Leningrad, I too never answered. The subject of explosives never came up again.

Then a new bombshell. Again, with colorful alerting patterns of GOD SAVE US around the back flap, a registered letter from Leningrad. There could be no question of the attention-grabbing nature of the messages. The young lady at the post office asked me, with her eyebrows raised, "You mean that *this* came from Russia?" I assured her that it did, and that I didn't understand it either. And in that letter, I got Fentanyl information beyond all expectations. There was a recipe that explained how one could start with one and a half kilo of this and then add a liter of that, stir, cook, filter and so on, and all of this ending up with a half kilo of some substituted Fentanyl worth maybe $500,000 in the Swiss black market.

I was in awe. The details of large scale Fentanyl preparation. I mean, a half kilo of Fentanyl or one of its potent analogues, at maybe 50 micrograms a dose, is 10,000,000 doses. And even more provocative, he volunteered the information that if one were to put a second substituent on the 4-position of the piperidine, the compounds could not be picked up by radioimmune assay.

So he was not only privy to very sophisticated synthetic information, but to very sophisticated analytical information as well.

Our correspondence continued for another year. It was rich with stories of Anatole being called in to what he called "The Big House," to give information to the KGB authorities, his hiding in fear of his life, his going to Moscow for a week to avoid what he called "The Narco Mafia," or his simply traveling to the Baltics to observe how the big scale chemistry was progressing. He sent me a couple of dozen extraordinary text books and reference volumes that were currently being used in the colleges and in the industrial research labs in the Soviet Union. He spoke of his desire to travel, and of his plans for eventual expatriation. But in the next letter the flavor would shift back to his being the pursuer of information from me, rather than being pursued by the authorities or the Mafia. He never gave me a vision of being a completely "together" person, yet there was never an impression of being a completely scattered one, either.

Then everything changed. He apparently got an exit visa through the simple (clever?, accidental?) transliteration of his name into French, rather than into English, orthography. He was Juoboroff rather than Zhoborov, and there appeared to be absolutely nothing in the computer to stop his emigration. So now he is in a Western European country, still pursuing his dance between organic chemistry and law enforcement. Apparently he has some chemical connections with a commercial laboratory where he is acting as a technician, and he is also providing information to the state police concerning the Narco Mafia in his new country. I must conclude that there is some sort of drug underground everywhere in the world.

My interchange of letters has slowly dropped to a trickle. And I have no way of judging if the narcotics trade in the Soviet Union is proceeding apace (despite his disappearance) or has dropped to nothing (because of his disappearance). However, there is a small but real possibility that I may again be made privy to what is going on. Within three weeks of Monsieur Juoboroff's departure I received, from a person unknown to me, another first letter, again from Leningrad.

## CHAPTER 9.  LA RUTA DEL BAKALAO

(Shura's voice)

I have done a modest amount of traveling both inside and outside the United States.  The list of foreign destinations have included Asia (Turkey), Central America (Panama), South America (Brazil) and the South Pacific (Australia), but a majority of my overseas explorations have been in Western Europe.  The only countries I have missed until recently were, as I recall, Ireland, the Eastern European block (except for Czechoslovakia), Greece, San Marino, and Andorra.  And Spain.

But Spain was added to the list as a consequence of an invitation to lecture somewhere else.  In early 1992 I received a request to attend a meeting in Mexico, to give an opening address to a conference on Psychotropic Plants and Shamanism.  This was being held in the Fall, in the city and State of San Luis Potosí which was, I must confess, a place I had never heard of before.  There was to be a goodly collection of scholars and scientists there, in the areas of anthropology, botany, chemistry and pharmacology.  The conference languages offered were Spanish and English but, as it turned out, most of the talks were in Spanish.  And other than the two phrases "No tengo dinero" and "Hecho en Mexico por Mexicanos" (which I memorized during my one and only previous visit to Mexico in the late 1950's, the first for answering street urchins and the second from a back window sticker on a Ford) I did not know a single word of Spanish.

No, that is not entirely accurate.  My parents and I had driven in our brand new Model A Ford to Tijuana when I was perhaps four or five years old, and from that vacation there was one memory of Mexico.  We had driven into the hills, and were hurrying back on a nasty road to get to the border which at that time closed for the night at some early hour in the evening, 8 or 9 p.m. as I recall.  The road back was peppered with yellow and black traveler advisory signs that said simply "D.C."  We got to the border just after it was sealed up, so we spent the night in a hotel on the Mexican side of the border, and someone finally told me that D.C. stood for Desparados

Curvasos (literally Desperate Curves). And just now I remember something else. Something to do with my not knowing how to swim, and having been thrown, screaming, into the Pacific ocean by my father so that I would learn. This last item just now sprang into mind and, although it has nothing to do with the Spanish language, it may have something to do with the development of the relationship I had with my father. It's a memory that might be rewarding to pursue some day on an appropriate psychedelic drug.

Back to present day Mexico, in San Luis Potosí. My presentation went OK, considering that I was giving my talk from hand-written notes (in English) and each sentence was being translated into Spanish by Manuel Sanchez, in real time, by his deciphering of these very notes while seated alongside me. Alice and I became fast friends with him and his wife, Sophia.

The conference provided many free hours for exploring adventure. I remember having a terrible time orienting myself as to where I was in San Luis Potosí, even though I had a complete street map in my lap every time we went from our sleeping quarters (at the Cactus Motel) to the meal location (at the Motel Tuna), or to the meetings themselves at the Casa de la Cultura. I pride myself in always becoming oriented as to location in any new city within about 36 hours. But here, even though we took different routes each trip, in our private bus, I never could pin down just where on the map the Cactus place was. Then I discovered that my street map, which had all the major thoroughfares indicated in bright red, was a bit of a promoter's dream. These were the planned freeways, and they had not yet been constructed. Once I ignored them, I knew where I was.

Another magical tour was to the north (to Matahuala) and then west through Cedral to Real del Catorce which proved to be a former silver mine, now abandoned, and inhabited by a few hundred Indians, in total poverty. No, not total, as there were occasional satellite dishes and some well fed dogs, but this area appeared to be totally supported by a modest tourist trade coming to visit the area that is the Mecca of the Huichol pilgrimage. The mountains in this area are sacred, and it was not surprising that there was a quiet but inescapable street market, not only in bric-a-brac with a Christian motif, but also in freshly picked peyote buttons. Most of our party had chosen to meet in the parking area across from a deserted Catholic church and sense the history and magic of the fog-enshrouded terrain through the eyes of a non-scheduled alternative, 2C-B. We regrouped at about four in the afternoon at the only coffee shop in town, and made our way safely back to San Luis Potosí for dinner.

As with any meeting of this sort, the true value lay in the many personal interactions that took place. I received a tentative invitation from a totally charming philosopher/drug expert/writer named Antonio

Escohotado to teach in a Summer School in El Escorial, near Madrid, the following year, and perhaps to contribute to a second edition of this Shamanismo performance (in case it became a biannual tradition) in Barcelona, two years later. Suddenly there were two pentaflex folders for Spain hanging in my file drawer of future travels, where there had never been one before.

That wasn't all. As soon as Alice and I got home to the farm, we found a letter from a Spanish law firm asking for an opinion, in writing, as to the degree of harm that can visit the public by the use of MDMA. Well, such questions are pretty common, so off went a letter with a strongly worded opinion that MDMA is one of the safest drugs I have ever encountered. That, I felt, should put that matter to rest.

A formal invitation to teach at the Summer School came from Antonio in a few weeks. The class was to be held in the coming Summer, in the city of El Escorial, and was going to be on the subject of Civil Disobedience, Counter Culture, and Utopic Pharmacy. And there were the funds at hand for a second week repeat performance in the Canary Islands. I guess I had never really consciously thought of Spain as no longer being in the grip of Fascism and Franco, and I was certainly not expecting to find the government funding educational courses that included topics such as these. Again, it was an interaction largely in Spanish, and again a beautiful opportunity to expand yet further the circle of people we knew. Antonio was there as an organizer. Ott was there from Xalapa, and Thomas Szasz and Albert Hofmann. That was the faculty for this particular course. But there were peripheral treasures, such as Monica, Antonio's wife, and Josè Maria, a winsome psychiatrist, who invited me as a dinner guest to his home, an hour's drive away.

The structure of this Spanish Summer School system is totally remarkable, and would serve many other communities as a model for the use of funds for education. The lodging and meals (in an excellent hotel) are largely subsidized by the government, the expenses (travel and honoraria) of the faculty come from a 1% tax on some industry (in this case one of the banking systems) and the student gets all of this for something like $200 for the week. There are several of these courses going on at the same time in El Escorial, and they continue for perhaps ten weeks during the summer there, and at other locations. A tremendous reward at a remarkable bargain. Why can't we do something like this at home?

On returning from this trip, I decided that the logical thing to do was to begin serious study of the language for the Barcelona trip, just in case it really did come to be, in 1994. The language of the conference would probably be English and the local language, and, if past experience was any measure, Spanish would play a major role. It was at about this time that I discovered that the local language spoken in Barcelona (and all along the Costa Brava from the Pyrenees to Valencia, and in the Balearic Islands) is Catalan, so a fantasy flashed across my mind.

Many years ago I had the opportunity of hearing an address given at an international meeting by a famed French chemist. This just happened to be in London, where the official language of the conference was, of course, English. But, as of that time, the French Government had a rule concerning the conduct of its nationals when they were traveling abroad.

"I have been instructed by the French C.N.R.S.," the French scholar started, in French, "That any reports of research that have been subsidized by French funds, shall be reported in French regardless of where the talks are to be given."

The audience, largely non-French, groaned. M. le Professeur continued, still in French: "I have decided on a compromise. I will deliver it half in French and half in English."

A pause, then: "I have just completed the French half."

And the rest of the hour was in English, to the relief of the audience. My thought: to perhaps address the international crowd in the Barcelona meeting with a talk that at least started in Catalán, using the argument that I wished to extend this courtesy to our hosts, and then drop back into English for the rest of it. Pure fantasy, all, as there was as yet no invitation from anyone and there might never be one. Nonetheless I launched into tutoring lessons in spoken Catalán which I found to be a completely beautiful language.

Somewhere around here this Spanish connection began developing an aura of synchronicity. Everything sort of began converging. I received a fax from the law firm in Madrid that they wanted me to come to that city for a day or two to give testimony in an MDMA case. So I made a third Spain travel pentaflex, and wrote back that if I came to Spain I would need to travel by business class (uncrowded conditions and ability to move around) and that I would have to charge a handsome fee for the two days that I would be available for testimony. That should discourage the invitation, I thought. A check arrived promptly from a Bank in Puerto Rico, which cleared, and was used to cover a $4000 plane ticket. The fat was in the fire. I was going again to Spain.

The week before Christmas was about as full as a week can be. I was responsible for giving final exams to my 75 students at Berkeley, and getting the exams corrected and the results into the registrar's office by Friday at 4 p.m.; there were two Christmas dinners I was obliged to attend; I had to pack all the papers I might need for the Spanish court, and be ready at 5:00 a.m. for a taxi to take me to the airport. Ahead of me was the prospect of travel on four airplanes, consultations with lawyers in at least two languages (I could always hope that someone would speak French, because in Spanish I am helpless), and two days of total alertness and mental sharpness in a strange courtroom, attempting to unravel the mysteries of the Spanish legal system. I refused to even think about the jet lag, coming and going.

As is so often the case with the unknown, it started off on an up-beat note, and continued to get better and better. I knew that it would be a worth-while trip when I learned that my cab driver was an ex-speed chemist who abandoned the trade some seven years ago when he suddenly became a born-again Christian. We had a delightful hour's ride in the early morning's darkness with a conversation that bounced back and forth between 55-liter Pfaudler reaction vessels and the love of Jesus.

The first travel leg, from San Francisco to Dulles, was in the upper lounge of a 747, where I had the front seat (miles of leg room) and a young gentlemen at the window to my right whose two reading books were entitled *Synchronicity*, author unknown, and one of the early Castaneda books, *The Second Ring of Power*. In our conversation, Doug (his name) revealed that he had just evolved onto a path of self-discovery, knew of most of the writers of psychedelic texts, had heard of *PIHKAL* but didn't know how to find it, and very much wanted to buy a copy. I took down his name and address. The second half of the flight put me in the front of a 767, with a window seat companion named Anna, a young cardiologist who had married a Mexican man who gave her two children, but now she was returning to her home in Southern Spain to meet her family (minus the ex-husband, I think) and resume her medical career. Quite familiar with peyote and the Huichol Indians, Oaxaca mushrooms, ergot alkaloids, had heard of *PIHKAL* but had no idea of where to buy it. I took down her name and address. I just may have discovered a method of paying for my flights myself in the future!

In my talks with the lawyers involved with the MDMA case, I learned of the Spanish equivalent of the rave scene. The dance/music/drugs/no sleep party is not held in a single location as in England or the United States. Rather, it is more like a process that is a physical trip as well as a drug trip. It starts on a Friday evening, in Madrid, and strikes off for the nearest coastal city, which happens to be Valencia, to the East. The gathered masses stop at bars and dance locations along the way, to stoke up on more pills and buy water at $5 a bottle. The party may never get to Valencia, but does return to Madrid late Sunday night, or even Monday morning, exhausted and somehow making it back to school or work. They called the road from Madrid to Valencia the Ruta del Bakalao, the route of the cod. The entire British concept of the Acid House was re-named in Spain after a fish and I cannot find the reason, if there is one. The press is casting the scene in a completely negative light, saying that MDMA is corrupting their youth.

What drugs are actually involved has never been determined. I have been told that there is a lot of speed, and certainly alcohol and pot. But the catch word that sells newspapers is "extasis" and it is getting the credit for a lot of damage. And here I am to argue before three judges (who certainly read newspapers) that MDMA is not a drug that is "greatly harmful" from the health point of view. The defendant gets about ten years in prison for the several pills he sold if they contained an officially designated "very harmful" drug (like cocaine or heroin or LSD), and something like three years if the drug was not officially designated "very harmful" (like pot and hash). And he had already spent over two years in prison just waiting for this trial. With the broad negative publicity about MDMA and the Ruta del Bakalao, this was an inauspicious time for the trial to occur. I did not look forward to my cross-examination.

There was a much more personal route that I was offered by my dear friend Antonio, who somehow found out that I was going to be in Madrid. I can only call it La Ruta de las Tapas. Tapas is not a fish, but the Spanish word for bits. Little bits. It is a luncheon phenomenon that is, I suspect, exclusively Spanish. I had heard of it before, and it is highly recommended in the guide books, but nowhere had I seen an actual description of how one goes about it. My last time in Madrid, with Alice, along with our friends Manuel and Sophia, we went into what surely was a tapas bar, but all we saw were old-looking mayonnaisse-ish salads under a glass cover. Do you sit at the bar and point? Do you point and then find a table? Do you stake out a table and then browse the bar? We had no idea as to the custom, so instead of doing something wrong and making fools of ourselves, we opted to sit at a table and order some light meal from the dinner menu.

This spot where I was to meet Antonio (the Cuewllas Restaurante at Ferraz #5) was completely charming, just a few blocks from my hotel, and I was there ahead of him. I stood out of the way of the waiter's traffic, near the door, for ten minutes (the staff blessed me by ignoring me) and then sat on one of the bar stools and ordered a tinto (red wine). The glass was put in front of me, the wine poured from an unfamiliar label sporting the appropriate word, "Raijo" with a 1989 date, and was excellent. A small plate with two dollar-sized toasted flakes of French bread were placed alongside it; one was spread with something deep red in color, the other with something amber colored. I thought I had just eaten my first tapas, but I was soon to discover differently. They were strange and delicious, but they were indeed just snacks.

While waiting, I had a chance to get the feel of the place. It was class. The front room where I was seated was the bar/tapas waiting area, with a half dozen hand-made bar stools arranged around a polished bar-top, with a sealed-off glass counter at the back of the wooden surface. In this area were several plates, one with a collection of duplicates of the colored chips I had just eaten, another with fine narrow strips of white fish crossed with strips of brownish fish, yet others which were unidentifiable. On the wall at the back of the bar were rows of bottles of brandies and wines, reflected against a long mirror. There was a steady ebb and flow of white-jacketed waiters obviously coming from a kitchen and carrying strange foods through the front room and down stairs (there must have been tables there). There was a pair of draft beer handles and the bartender would periodically draw a draft into a glass of unusual shape. Glasses. There must have been dozens of types, all sparkling.

In a few minutes Antonio appeared, and joined me at the bar. The parking problem was terrible, he said (it is always terrible in downtown Madrid), and he sipped from the glass of red wine that was immediately put in front of him while he looked at the menu. He ordered a stop-gap plate of the red and cream-colored dollar sized things. The red proved to be pork loin, finely ground and spiced, with the fat included as a flavoring component; the other remained unknown.

Then Antonio ordered the first plate of the bona fide tapas, and demanded glasses of Chardonnay to come with it. I wondered if it was appropriate to have white wine following red, and he assured me that the food dictates the wine, never does the wine dictate the food. A plate appeared from the kitchen with six small French bread slices on it, with a creamy thick spread on each. They were a bit salty, sharply flavored, and totally delicious. The wine was cold and excellent. I learned that this tapas was a rough puree of sea urchin eggs, mixed with something. There followed more delectable mysteries in dark sauce, bits of goose liver, toasted French bread and a dry wine. Then, as a final dish, a small plate of jabon, thin slices of ham from pigs fed exclusively on acorns of a certain type of oak tree. This was accompanied by a sharper, darker red wine which must remain anonymous since I wasn't paying attention.

The finale: an espresso, and a generous offering of calvados in a large warmed snifter. This is the Spanish tapas. Snacks it is not. Feast it is. I don't think I could manage a daily lunch bill of $70, but if I could, this is the way I would do it.

Back to the hotel to await the call for the evening consultation.

I made arrangements to meet Mario, the defendant in the case, in a taxi at the front of my hotel at 9:45, but the famous Madrid traffic dictated the meeting to be 10:15, and we went directly to the courthouse. For the first time I actually made some personal connection with real people related to the defendant. His mother (striking, fiftyish), spoke fine English, lived in Puerto Rico, and was the source of my check for the air fare; brother (lived somewhere in US, spoke real American) and wife (slightly hippie, with beads, mousy, no English) were all in the lobby in the basement of the courthouse, just outside the courtroom. People kept coming, some were introduced to me as the six experts for one side or the other, and I met the young girl who was the court-appointed translator. The intended strategy was to ask the magistrates to allow all the experts (in Spain, they must come in pairs) to be seated together at the same time, rather than have them go in individually (the forensic toxicologists, then the clinical practitioners, and then the research scientists). The head tribunal gentleman said OK but in exchange, insisted on taking the lead in directing the questioning strategy. We sat outside and waited while our lead attorney, Jaime, was cross-examining the analytical team as to how they determined what drug was there and in what amounts. One of the analysts started to define MDMA as a highly dangerous drug, and was completely shot down. I was amazed to hear that challenges to the statements of prosecution witnesses were virtually unheard of. They are the authorities.

We finally went in. This was the second new interior I'd had the chance to see and describe, in as many days. A quality tapas bar it was not. The courtroom was drab, perhaps 40x40 feet square, with a 10x10 foot cage with bullet-proof glass walls located at the middle of the left side to contain a terrorist if one happened to be on trial. At the front was a U-shaped bench, raised a foot or two above floor level, with the three magistrate judges sitting facing the audience. All were in black robes, with an important patch of authority on the left breast, and with white lace wrist pieces coming up almost to the elbow. The center person was the principal magistrate, a clean-cut fifty year old with short peppery hair and beard formed into a goatee with an El Greco style white patch from the lower lip down to the chin. He was the only one who did any talking. On his right, stage left, was a dumpling old man with jowls and glasses who, most remarkably, seemed to be asleep most of the time without ever closing his eyes. And the third, stage right, was a 40 year old woman with brown hair, no makeup at all, a broad, tight-lipped mouth with an almost-smile on it, who kept moving her head and eyes about as if looking at everyone in the court, but never once made eye contact with anyone, at least not with me.

On the left side, the prosecutor, young, round-faced with a small black mustache, also with lace on the lower fore-arms. On the right, the defense attorneys, each with an outer garment cloak that was black and looked like satin. Three were up at the same height as the others, Jaime the closest, with his slightly long hair and scraggly beard. He was wearing a tie that was not quite in place, and a wrinkled shirt under his cloak. Number two and three were, respectively, a roly-poly man with a bushy mustache and a small, thin girl of around 25, who never participated in any way. As there were five defendants, there were five lawyers, and the remaining two were at a table that was an extension of the three-lawyer branch of the U-shape, but down at the main floor level, with the rest of us. The court-appointed translator, the concession to my ignorance of the Spanish language, sat alongside these lower two. And we, the six witnesses, sat on a bench and a couple of chairs, facing the magistrates, sort of completing a small rectangle. The defendants sat behind us with their protective bailiff, and the audience was on parallel benches towards the back of the room.

The mechanism of question/response was new to me. The chief magistrate asked a question, and each expert in turn took a portable microphone and replied. I, the sixth, was then informed by the translator what the question was that the others had answered, and had my turn. I had a preview of the length of the response of the others, but not the content. I felt very alone.

I really blew it on the last question before the coffee/smoking break, which was one of the first from the prosecutor rather than from the principal magistrate. It was whether I thought that there was any permanent damage resulting from the addiction to cocaine. I knew that the leitmotif of the defense was to build on the known subdivision of drugs in Spanish law as being either highly dangerous (like cocaine, heroin or LSD, thus long prison sentencing) or only slightly dangerous (like marijuana and hashish, thus short prison sentencing). MDMA had never been so classified, and if it were to fall into a low danger category, the defendant might get off for time served, but if MDMA were to be swept into an ugly status, he just might get another 10 years behind bars.

So, to the question, does addiction to cocaine lead to permanent damage, I answered honestly, but not helpfully that, except for possible erosion to the nasal mucosa, there were few long-term consequences. Everyone else had knocked cocaine, and I was (I found out) placed in a California-pro-drug-drugs-are-harmless image with my reply. I effected damage control my next time at the mike. I explained that I had understood the question to refer to the body status once the addiction phase had been treated and had become history. However, during the addiction phase for either cocaine or heroin, there is an extensive deterioration of behavior patterns that was dictated by the compulsive search for a continuing source of drugs. None of this was to be seen with MDMA, as there was no addiction. I found myself back on the righteous path, and would never stray again.

Things really tightened up nicely after that, and I felt increasingly comfortable. A few slips were made here and there , but they were not of my doing. My translator got the word primer mixed up with primal (I understand a weird sentence came out of that) and toleration and tolerance got garbled somehow. But more and more, the questions of both the magistrate and the defense lawyer were directed to me. It seems that I was the only one who had actually seen people in a clinical setting with known dosages of MDMA of known identity and purity. And it was never made obvious that my doctorate was not a medical one. I did not volunteer to correct this impression. Questions such as: should MDMA be in the most dangerous category of restriction? Absolutely not. Is there medical value intrinsic to MDMA? Yes, this is well established, and now clinical tests to evaluate that were being designed in several countries. Has the drug been shown to be dangerously lethal? It has been reliably estimated that up to 5,000,000 persons have used MDMA in England alone, and with only 5 deaths reported, I must conclude that MDMA is one of the safest drugs known today.

And: does MDMA cause a severe cardiovascular crisis? There is a small amount of cardiovascular push, but no more severe than a few cups of coffee or some vigorous exercise. This last contribution especially pissed off the medical toxicologist, who fumed to contradict this (slightly prejudiced) statement. The defense lawyer interposed with a nasty question, "Señor el Doctor: on what, besides the anecdotal review of Dr. Ron Seigel, do you base your opinions?" He had nothing and he became quiet again.

But the best was saved for last. The prosecutor finally entered the fray with a treasure that he had obviously been saving up. He announced that he had just received the most recent, up-to-date literature on MDMA, from the Spanish Health Council, provided them by UNESCO. He asked me if I was familiar with it. He gave a sheaf of a few papers to the bailiff to give to the translator. She looked at it, and began translating the first line into Spanish. It went:

"MDMA, Metilin-dioxi-metamphetamina —"

"No, no, no," said the prosecutor. "Translate the title of the publication."

"Pee-kal."

"Are you familiar with this information reference?" he asked me.

"My wife and I wrote it."

"You are the author?"

"Yes."

I caught a fleeting smile pass over the face of the principal magistrate (the first human response I had seen from him all day) and within twenty minutes I found myself, along with the entire witness and law party (the friendly ones at least), across the street from the courthouse building at a tapas place called "Rio Freo," enjoying a glass of tinto.

Six months later, I received a call from a friend in Madrid who informed me, with considerable relish, that my face was all over the newspapers and television, because MDMA had been officially categorized as an only slightly dangerous drug in Spain. We had won.

# Part Two:

# Psychedelics and
# Personal Transformation

# CHAPTER 10.  PLACES IN THE MIND

(Alice's voice)

Some form of alteration of consciousness can happen to anyone, anywhere, without warning and having no apparent cause.  It could range from an unfamiliar shift in perspective, creating a feeling of disorientation, lasting only a few minutes, to a profound change in perception and comprehension, persisting for days and even weeks. Understandably, most people who find themselves in such a state for the first time tend to get frightened.  Their fear and anxiety drive out whatever learning might have been possible if they had known from the beginning that, first, the altered state would be temporary and second, that such an experience does not imply sickness of either mind or body.

Of course, if there are indications of actual mental illness or brain disorder, such as intense headaches, noticeable changes of personality (for instance, episodes of violent behavior in a usually calm person) or other such symptoms well-known to the mental health community, there certainly should be an effort made to contact a psychologist or psychiatrist for an evaluation.  But what I am talking about in this chapter is a change in perception and perspective, not in social behavior or the ability to think rationally and logically.

Unfortunately, too many psychiatrists haven't the slightest idea of how best to handle an experience of this kind, which some people call a transformative process.  They tend to treat it the way they would treat psychosis (which this is not), and to prescribe tranquilizers or, worse, anti-psychotic drugs. The primary purpose of these drugs is to re-close the doors which have opened — unplanned and unbidden — between the conscious mind and the unconscious.

If the person who is undergoing an episode of this nature has heard of the "Spiritual Emergence Network," (see acknowledgements) he can at least hope to speak to a therapist of some kind (some psychiatrists are available) who will be understanding, reassuring and supportive, and not treat him as if he's mentally ill.

It is important to add here that whether or not a person experiencing this shift in perspective has ever taken a psychedelic drug in the past, this is *not* what is called a "flashback," and should not be dismissed as such. Genuine flashbacks are described in a later chapter.

As to why these spontaneous shifts in consciousness occur in some people, it seems to me that the human psyche has its own program, tucked away somewhere in what we call the unconscious mind. It has its own unpublished schedule, its own private plans for the learning and psychic stretching that is to be done, and often little, if any, concern about the inconvenience it may cause to have one's customary orientation to the world turned upside down, however temporarily.

Most difficult of all, the unconscious psyche doesn't seem to be interested in letting the conscious mind know what's going on, except in the language of dreams, and that language — when the dream can be remembered at all — is very hard for most people to decipher. Each human psyche has a personal dream language, and it isn't possible to accurately interpret somebody else's dreams without knowing him and his symbolic language intimately.

Although this isn't a book about dream analysis, there are a couple of things you might remember when trying to understand your own dreams. One: except for Big Dreams (as Jung called them) and lucid dreams, most dreams are status quo reports from the unconscious. Two: the important things about dreams are not usually the symbols or images chosen by the unconscious, but the feelings and emotions that pervade the dream. They are the clues to what is being reported. Three: interpretation is easier if you can keep in mind that the unconscious does not censor according to the rules or mores of your culture or religion; its job is to tell you what's going on inside you and what emotions are being felt; the approval or disapproval of your conscious mind is of no concern whatsoever to your unconscious. And finally, four: many people ask, "Why go to the bother of remembering or thinking about your dreams anyway?" One answer is simply, "To keep myself honest about myself." Another, of course, is, "To keep learning about the nature of the human mind."

So, if you are one of those who find themselves trying to deal with a breakthrough of the unconscious psyche into the everyday field of awareness, it is hard to know how to handle it, how to evaluate it, and how to get something positive out of the experience.

I would like to make some suggestions about coping with non-drug related alterations of consciousness. These experiences are not necessarily different from those resulting from psychedelic experimentation, except that the non-drug eruptions can sometimes last several days, while the psychedelic breakthroughs usually come to an end when the drug is no longer effective.

If you find yourself in one of these states, without having taken a drug shortly beforehand, remember that you're not "stuck;" remind yourself that it will pass, most likely in a few hours; at most, a few days. In the meantime, there are things you can do.

If you have a close friend who is available to stay with you until you are through the experience, call him or her and explain that you've suddenly been plunged into a strange, unfamiliar mental place, and you need the company of somebody who can watch over you with caring, and without being judgemental, since you have no way of predicting how this experience will play itself out, or what you will go through before it comes to an end. You can reassure your friend, however, that you can be depended on to conduct yourself in a way that will not endanger anyone else, and that this kind of altered state does NOT involve psychotic acting out of any kind.

Your friend can help you by cooking simple meals when you're hungry, answering your phone, taking care of your pets, and making sure that you feel safe in your home. And, above all, by listening to what you need to express, and being quietly supportive. Don't expect a friend to interpret anything you're seeing or feeling. That is, and will be, your job — if not immediately, then eventually.

(If you feel that you need more help than a friend can give, in managing this experience while it is going on, or help in understanding it after it is over, you can call the Spiritual Emergence Network, as I mentioned before. And the members of the organization known as Subud — if one is listed in your city directory — are also familiar with this territory, as are many spiritual teachers of all faiths. If you have no access to such people, your nearest public library may offer you the greatest variety of answers. Help can be found in the book, *Spiritual Emergency*, edited by Dr. Stanislav Grof, and Christina Grof, and in the other writings of Dr. Stan Grof. Also of value are the writings of Dr. C.G. Jung, Dr. John W. Perry and Aldous Huxley's *Doors of Perception, Heaven and Hell*, and *Moksha*.)

Whether or not you can find a friend to keep you company for a while, you should — if at all possible — excuse yourself from work (there's always a flu bug around to blame), because changes in your perceptions of space and time, and probably some increased sensitivity to sound, color and emotional fields, might make a normal work day difficult to maintain. Give yourself some quiet and privacy, and a chance to go along with whatever is flowing through you, so that you can learn as much as possible.

Some of us seem more prone to these kinds of breakthroughs than others, and, again, there is no way to know why. However, I tend to believe that the attitude of one's family (and of the society, the culture, in which that family has its place) toward matters non-physical and non-material may have something to do with it.

In other words, in a country like India, where numerous gods and goddesses are assumed to be involved in human affairs, the possibility of a drift into an altered state could be a lot less frightening to the average person than it would be in this country. Here, generally speaking, the spiritual world is considered either non-existent or safely confined to certain designated buildings, to be dealt with for only one or two hours per week, and even then with a mediator — a priest, minister or rabbi — running interference.

You might also fare better if your family is one in which dreams are often shared, and everyone understands them as being reports from the unconscious. When a child grows up among people who are fascinated — not frightened — by all aspects of the human mind, he stands a good (or at least better than average) chance of being able to get through a sudden, unplanned alteration of his normal consciousness with the least possible degree of anxiety and the maximum amount of learning.

It was at just such a time in my own life that I was told, by a wise old psychologist whom I have called Adam, "What you're going through is a process. All you have to do is not get in its way." He told me to learn everything I could while it lasted, and assured me that it wouldn't last more than a few days. This turned out to be the case, probably due to my unconscious mind having heard Adam's limited-duration prediction, and believing it, or perhaps just deciding it was a good plan to follow.

I would add this to Adam's admonition: take notes. As much as you can, write everything down as it happens; every feeling in body or mind, every concept, every shift of emotion. The notes could be of immense importance to you at some future time. However, the main value of keeping track of your experience, finding words to express what's going on, is that it will help you to assimilate the changes you're undergoing, and put them in perspective.

If you have had feelings of helplessness, of being out of control during your altered state, you'll find that focusing your thoughts on the words and phrases that best describe whatever is going on (it doesn't matter whether you use pen and paper or a tape recorder) will gradually bring back a sense of being in charge of what's happening within you and to you.

Why? Because you are taking input which is coming at you fast and with great intensity — colors, concepts, emotions, a sense of cosmic dimensions within the most ordinary objects, and a continuing sense of immense meaningfulness — and you're attempting to contain it as much as possible. Writing everything down, or talking into a tape recorder, are ways of imposing your own structure on interior chaos, and it will, bit by bit, give you a sense of participation to replace the feeling of being victimized. It will enable you to let go of fear, and perhaps open yourself to whatever it is that your psyche wants you to discover.

If, for any reason, you cannot or don't want to write or tape, then make use of whatever form of artistic expression you can: clay modeling, painting, anything that will express what you are experiencing and allow you to reshape and restructure it, thus helping you regain some sense of control.

For those who are used to praying, this is a good time to practice whatever you understand is meant by the word "prayer," asking your own higher Self — or God or your angel — for support, guidance and blessing.

In time, the shift in consciousness will right itself, and you'll be back to your normal baseline, or at least close enough to it to allow you to function comfortably in the world again. You should emerge from this kind of unexpected stretching of psychic muscles with a feeling of having opened up new dimensions within yourself, and an increased awe at the wealth of information that lies below the conscious mind in all of us. There are treasures of light and treasures of darkness within our souls, all of them wanting to be discovered and explored, and eventually understood.

Alterations of consciousness are inevitable if you are on a spiritual path using psychedelic drugs, visionary plants, or other methods such as, for instance, holotropic breathing, hypnosis or meditation.

You can find yourself (whether you are prepared or not) in a place inside your mind where familiar landmarks are nowhere to be found. Some of these places can infuse you with power and light; others will hold you in terror or sorrow. You must learn your way through each one because only by doing so can you begin to become familiar with the deeper levels of your own psychic interior; it is the only way to begin to understand who and what you are.

The choices you make, in all areas of life, help define who you are, not only as an individual human being, but as a member of your family and community. They form your personality, the part of you which other people know. Beneath this persona, however, is an essence which can never be completely known by another person, and it is the awareness of this core Self that will give you a psychic anchor if you should find yourself in a difficult, disorienting place, somewhere along the way. The core Self is not a personality; it is not a definable, stable *thing*; it is a form of spiritual energy, so it is never still, yet it remains the same. You will always recognize it as yourself, the essence of who you are, and you can seek it out and hold onto it when you're facing interior chaos.

I can only speak with authority about what I know personally. Many, though not all, of my most intense spiritual experiences have been brought about by the use of psychedelics — visionary drugs and plants. This method of learning has one great advantage: the experience has a beginning, a middle and an end. This means that, no matter how difficult my passage through a particular interior place may be, I know there will be an end to the fear or anxiety. As the effects of the drug wear off, I will find myself inevitably rediscovering my normal life and all the familiar, reassuring ways of being in that life.

The same can be said of the numerous other methods by which a person may pursue a deliberate path of spiritual exploration and learning. Most exercises taught by such methods have a beginning, middle and end, allowing for a predictable return to everyday life and awareness.

Let me take a moment here to say that, of the many inaccurate, uninformed and just plain wrong things that have been said about visionary or psychedelic drugs, the two most often heard are that they are addictive and that they are "escapist."

As to the first untruth, there are no known psychedelic drugs that cause physical dependence or addiction. There are, of course, many people who might be called "addictive personalities," and they tend to become psychologically dependent on any number of things, from food to gambling, but generally speaking, the psychedelics do not cause any kind of addiction or dependency.

As to the claim that the psychedelics are escapist drugs, I can say this: there are, indeed, moments of intense beauty and wonder as well as the occasional burst of laughter to be had during a psychedelic experience, but I have never gone through one that didn't involve some work.

I don't mean to imply that "escaping" is in itself wrong or destructive, if done occasionally and in balance with other aspects of one's life. After all, listening to music can be called escape; so can watching television, making love, reading a book, or taking a walk under the stars. All these can be thought of as escapes, especially if your view of life and what you call reality is generally grim and sour.

The young college-age psychedelic users who take drugs at rave dances might be said to be using them for escape, rather than for psychological or spiritual work. This is certainly not the highest and best use of these drugs, in the opinion of some. I'm not so sure. For many of the dancers at a rave, the combination of trance-inducing music and a (usually) low dose of MDMA, for instance, or LSD, creates an emotional openness and a sense of psychic participation with their fellow dancers. They sometimes experience a degree of euphoria which is absolutely unknown in their everyday lives. There is some question as to whether this state is induced as much by the trance-dancing as by any drugs they might have taken, but whether it is or not, I believe that euphoria is good for you, especially when it is achieved at no cost or pain to anyone else.

Most of the dancers at rave parties have spent a good part of their lives living in big cities, and they are not used to trusting or feeling affection towards strangers. In fact, life in most of the world's big cities, as a rule, demands continual caution and suspicion when one is outside the home. For some of these young adults, the only time they can let anxiety and fear of the stranger drop away is at a rave. There, they can experience trusting fellowship with many others, in a dancing situation which threatens no one and can, instead, open their hearts and give them a feeling of pleasure, companionship and hope.

As far as I'm concerned, none of this adds up to a threat to society.

Psychedelic exploration, for me, has always meant working, trying to come to terms with some aspect of my interior universe that makes me uncomfortable; dealing with insights into my own past or present behavior which may be disturbing; trying to dig out answers to basic questions about the nature of the world, the cosmos and whatever it is we call God. I have had well over a thousand exposures to these particular chemical tools. Escape is precisely what they have never given me, and my return to consensual reality — so-called ordinary life — has always been a pleasure, no matter how positive the psychedelic experience. But, then, I am blessed in having a good life to return to. For those whose everyday lives are not happy or fulfilling, the psychedelic experience can serve to renew their sense of meaningfulness and put them back in touch with wonder and joy.


## INFLATION

### (THE PRIESTESS)

I can still remember vividly the day I stepped into the inflation place. Shura and I were home on the Farm, and most of the research group was with us; only Dante and Ginger were absent. The experimental material was 2C-T-8, (which is short for 2,5-dimethoxy-4-cyclopropylmethylthiophenethylamine), and I had taken 42 milligrams about half an hour before. In previous trials, I had taken 35 mgs. and 40 mgs. and found it generally friendly.

(For most researchers, this material was not one of the great favorites; a few reported having had a hard time with it, but it hadn't given me any particular difficulties before the time of this experiment, aside from dampening erotic response in both Shura and me. One researcher loved it, since under its influence she produced more expressive and dynamic paintings than usual.)

This may be the moment to emphasize that the drug or visionary plant does not, in itself, contain any particular experience; each psychedelic drug simply makes it possible to open interior doors through which that experience might emerge. The doors opened by DMT tend to be quite different than those opened by mescaline, for instance, but once you are through those doors, what you encounter is part of yourself.

Our group had already gone through the ceremony of gathering in a circle, clinking glasses and blessing each other, and each of us had wandered off to find the right place in which to ride out the transition phase.

Ruth and George were on the couch, holding hands, as they often did during this stage, especially with a drug that was new to them. John was moving slowly through the house, hands in his pockets, peering at book covers, pausing to look at a bunch of daffodils in a vase. I found David seated at the dining room table, talking to Shura about their favorite subject and mutual passion — chemistry — and I saw through the dining room windows that Leah and Ben were heading down the path which leads to the old cow barn, their fingers interlaced.

Having walked through the house long enough to reassure myself that nobody was having problems, I did what I usually prefer to do during transition, whether the drug is an old friend or a new one: I looked for a place to be by myself.

I stepped outside and closed the front door quietly behind me. The air was fresh and sweet, tasting the way it does only in early spring. I walked down the short dirt path to what we call the barbecue patio, a half-circle paved with red bricks, set against a slope planted with ivy and geraniums. On the low brick wall at the bottom of the slope, I found myself a place, brushed a few twigs and leaves off the surface and sat down. Before me was a wide view of hills, still green after the winter rains, dotted with live oak trees. Looking beyond the hills, to the north, I could see the faint brown line of a fog-blurred horizon and, above it, the pale blue of the sky.

I straightened my back briefly, stretched both arms skyward, and relaxed again into a comfortable slump.

*Well, no question; I'm feeling it. Lots of body energy; foot wants to tap. Whole body wants to tap! Okay, though, so far.*

I reached into a pocket of my long grey-blue caftan, brought out a pack of cigarettes, and lit one. I kept my gaze focused on the curve of hill across the highway from us, where a large cluster of trees glowed like dark sculpture against a background of bright green.

*Better appreciate that color while we still have it; any moment now, the yellowing of the grass will begin, and after a while it'll be hard to remember how beautiful the hills were in spring.*

The sensation was on me before I had a chance to track it from its beginning as a burst of euphoria, deep in the gut. Suddenly it was there, radiating through every cell — pure power; I was sitting upright on a low brick wall, energy pouring into me, filling me. It brought with it a quieting of the desire to move around, tap feet, squirm on my ledge. The energy pulsed softly, and all of me was open to it.

I was full of strength and knowing, infinitely wise.

I sat quietly, radiating light and energy, noticing that, although my mind was suffused with something you'd have to call intense pleasure, each thought was distinct and clear; there was no confusion anywhere in my head, just as there was no illness or weakness within my body.

*Oh, my everlovin' God! This is what's meant by a bliss state. I'm a body of energy; my mind is like crystal; there's no question in the universe that I can't find the answer to. All I need in the world is myself, living in this serene rhythm, filled with livingness and knowledge.*

A tiny concern nibbled at the edge of the magnificence. What if somebody came out here to join me? Or even just to make sure I was all right?

*Don't want to scare people; I know anyone else coming out here would feel this power; it's too strong to be hidden. I'll have to gentle it out, somehow, if somebody turns up. Maybe I'll be lucky and no one will come.*

An image rose in my mind; it was the one and only thing I had left out of the description in PIHKAL of my first real psychedelic experience — with peyote — around thirty years earlier. I had considered including it, but somehow it just didn't get written, and I had finally acknowledged to myself that it still, after all this time, made me uncomfortable because it remained part of my dark side, and I still needed to keep an eye on it occasionally, especially during psychedelic sessions.

It had risen suddenly, clear on the mind's screen, during the early hours of the peyote day, while Sam Golding and I had been lying side by side on my bed. A few minutes before, we had both slipped into the full magic of the peyote world, and as I turned my head to say something to Sam, I saw an image of myself, seated on a throne, dressed in long robes — there was an impression of purple and blue — with a circlet of gold around my head. I was The Priestess, full of knowledge and power, seated above the rest of humanity, dispensing wisdom. It was a picture of supreme intellectual and spiritual arrogance, and although it was visible for only a few seconds, I had taken it as a warning: this was an aspect of myself that I had to keep under control.

Now, here I was, blazing with the fullness of this form of myself, knowing I needed nothing else and nobody else, and that I could continue being utterly sufficient unto myself — should I choose to stay in this place, in this state. I was complete.

*That's inflation. That's what my Priestess is. I disliked it — no, I hated it — all those years ago. I was ashamed of it. And now, here it is, here I am. I am*

*SHE, and the sense of wholeness, of utter fulfillment, is the most wonderful, delicious — I wonder if I can stay here forever, just basking, thrumming, swimming in this ocean of energy, my mind diamond clear.*

Somewhere, in the midst of the glory, a dialogue began. A part of me detached itself sufficiently from the radiance to ask questions and listen for answers from yet another part.

Q. What can possibly be negative about this place, this state?

A. Nothing. It's absolute heaven.

Q. Then why is there a faint uneasiness?

A. Because the Priestess is not what I've chosen to be.

Q. Why not?

A. Because she would have no use for anyone else in the world.

Q. What's wrong with that?

A. I prefer the version of me that likes people, interacts with the world, makes love with Shura; the one that mothers my kids.

This Priestess just isn't the person I want to become in this life. But, boy, does it feel GOOD! What a fantastic place to be in, even if only for a moment, and maybe only once; being a superhuman force, barely contained in a human body, does damn well have its points!

Q. So what are you going to do?

A. I'm going to get out of the Priestess.

Q. And you won't regret leaving all this behind?

A. Yes, I'll regret it, and I hope I can feel it again, just for a little while, perhaps. But it's pretty good, really, just being the usual me. And I enjoy relating to people, being a friend. I love Shura, and my children, and they like me being human.

Q. So we let the Priestess go. Goodbye, then, Great and Wonderful Lady! Hope to see you again, someday.

Now that the decision had been surely and firmly made, I was able to immerse myself in what was left of the euphoria, the energy, for a few minutes before there came a gradual softening of the image, a subtle, slow washing out of the magnificent state, like a vibrant watercolor painting being held under a fine misting spray.

Finally, feeling glowing streamers of the Priestess still clinging to my soul, I stood up and walked slowly toward the house, to reconnect with Shura and our friends.

Looking back on that day, the obvious question comes to mind: what would have happened if I had chosen to stay in the Priestess? I suspect that, within the hour, I would have found myself coming down, drifting out of that place, eventually understanding that I could not stay there forever.

In the meantime, of course, I might well have acted out of that archetype, to the considerable disturbance of the rest of the group — making pronouncements, delivering eternal truths, exercising my power and wisdom, and generally making an ass of myself. Even if I had experienced an hour or two of genuine inspiration, the expression of it would probably have caused no less discomfort to those around me. Playing the part of a seer — even for only a few minutes — isn't exactly the way to encourage your friends to feel relaxed and intimate in your company.

The Priest or Priestess is an archetype within the human unconscious, and I believe it's essential that it be experienced and worked through by anyone who wants to know all he can about the nature of his (and everybody else's) mind and psyche. The value of working through it is in the fact that it forces you to face the temptation, the seductiveness of that aspect of yourself. In gaining familiarity with it, you begin to understand, by contrast, the validity and value of the "normal," non-inflated personality you have developed throughout your life. This is the version of you that interacts and relates and listens to others, and admits to occasional mistakes, just like everyone else; the person you have chosen to be, who doesn't like arrogance in others, and certainly doesn't want to see it in her- or himself.

By "working through," I mean simply letting yourself go fully into the experience, enjoying the sense of power and wisdom and complete self-sufficiency. Resonate with it, let it fill you with its energy. If possible, go to some place where you can be alone; resist the temptation to communicate with others during the height of this marvelous state. Stay alone. After you've spent a bit of time enjoying the sensations and feelings, let yourself begin to pay attention to your Observer, the part of you that watches and keeps track and learns, but doesn't get swept away by feelings or emotions. This aspect of yourself will help to ground you, in the midst of the euphoria.

Recognize that this illuminated, powerful, totally self-sufficient being which you have become is valid, but it is only one version of yourself, and it is not what you have chosen to be in your everyday life.

Stay in the inflation place for a while, by yourself, then let it gradually subside. Understand that, seductive as it might feel, it cannot replace your usual, normal self, the one that has relationships, the one that is a social being, a friend, a sibling, a parent.

## CERTAINTY AND KNOWING

Absolute certainty, a feeling of knowing without any doubt what is true and not true about some particular thing, is a common experience to all adults. It's part of living, and ideally results from a process of questioning, testing, evaluating and eventually confirming.

The same feeling of absolute certainty, of complete conviction that your view of something (or everything, for that matter) is the ultimate truth, can and often does happen when you're under the influence of a psychedelic drug. It can be part of a state of inflation, as I've described above, or it might be just a momentary burst of enthusiastic self-validation.

There is a real problem associated with this sense of "knowing," when it is part of a psychedelic experiment. It feels good (certainty usually feels good), but the trouble is that it also feels, at the time, like a genuine experience of Truth. Your soul has no doubt at all; there is no question that your evaluation of whatever it is you feel certain about fills you with a sense of absolute "rightness."

If it remains a feeling and only a feeling, it can be enjoyable — like any other aspect of inflation — and will do no harm. If you act on it, however, you might find yourself saying things to those around you (for instance, analyzing the personalities of your friends) which you may regret intensely several hours later, when the inflation-certainty wears off with the drug effect.

The rule has to be: under the influence of a drug, do not make a phone call, do not write a letter and mail it, do not make pronouncements about anything at all. Enjoy the feeling, and tell others around you that you are experiencing a delicious inflation, then either leave the company of your friends until the all-knowingness begins to mellow out, or stay with them and just keep your mouth shut and your strong, wise opinions to yourself. You will be deeply grateful later.

Now, here comes the really hard question. How can you know if your certainty about something, during a psychedelic session, is or is not actually valid? Can you ever trust that certainty, that absolute knowing? The only reasonable answer I can give is this: wait until you wake up the next morning, presumably at baseline, and review the certainties of the day before. If you have, indeed, arrived at some solid truths, or some new (to you) concepts that have validity, they will have lasted through the night, and you will be able to enjoy them all over again in the morning, only this time without the inflation, and presumably with your normal common sense and humor restored.

## THE VOID

This is one of the terrible places. While it takes different forms for each person, the essentials of the experience tend to be the same. I call it the Void, because it involves facing a total loss of any sense of meaning. If it comes to you as part of a psychedelic experiment, you're lucky, because it should pass within a relatively short time. If you are in the company of other experienced travelers, someone else is sure to be familiar with it and can help you make your way through. If it happens spontaneously — without any drug use — as it sometimes does out of the blue, it is not only extremely frightening, it might lead to suicidal impulses in a sensitive person because whoever finds himself in this particular place is always convinced, at least temporarily, that what he is seeing and feeling is the basic truth about the world he lives in and the cosmos at large; that all life is absolutely meaningless.

This state of mind, if not drug-induced, is usually seen by the medical profession as a form of acute depression. If it persists beyond one day, and if there appears to be no progression towards some kind of resolution — a way out, a return to color and light — you should seek psychiatric help as soon as possible, because there are medications that will bring you back to normalcy. Keep in mind that acute depression is most probably the result of chemical imbalance in the brain, and can be treated.

If you have taken a psychedelic or visionary drug and find yourself in the Void (which has also been called the Sorrow Place or the Valley of the Shadow of Death) where everything feels gray, dirty and senseless, and the only emotions you experience are sorrow and total hopelessness, you must remember: it is *not* the final truth about the universe you live in; it's a genuine part of what is, but only a small part. It is no more the complete truth about life than Adolf Hitler and Vlad the Destroyer are the complete truth about the nature of the human race.

The second thing to remember is that you have no obligation to stay in this dark place. You have to know that it exists, and you should get the smell of it, for this reason, among others: a large number of people all over the world find themselves, perhaps for days, but sometimes for years, stuck in that hopeless, meaningless state, with no mental health professional or spiritual advisor available. You might find yourself able to be of help to some of them, if you know the territory and have found your way out of it.

One way to get free of this place is by focusing intently on certain images: perhaps the Laughing Buddha, or your favorite mental picture of Jesus the Christ, newborn babies being welcomed and adored by their parents, your own loving of your mate or your children, the music you like to hear, the deep pleasures of planting and harvesting, or whatever else you can remember of the beauty and joy in life. Concentrate on one of these, or let all of them parade through your mind, to the exclusion of everything else. See them clearly, your chosen good images, give them power by saying Yes to them, with all of yourself; let them radiate light within you. The Void, the hopeless place, will begin to disintegrate, color will gradually replace the dull grey, and meaningfulness will return.

Everybody's definition of "meaning," or "meaningfulness," is a bit different. My own is this: "meaningfulness" is the sense that everything that exists has a purpose, that there is a great story being told throughout the universe, and that each of us — along with every other form of life — is playing an important part in that story.

## PARANOIA

This unpleasant state often strikes people who experiment with marijuana; some (myself among them) do not outgrow this particular effect of the plant, and simply have to avoid exposing themselves to it. However, it can occur with any psychedelic or visionary drug. A single experience of paranoia under these circumstances can be of great value to you. For one thing, to be rather obvious about it, you'll know first-hand what is meant by paranoid thinking. You'll probably emerge from the drug effect with a greater understanding of what is called psychological "projection," and — ideally — an increased interest in understanding the deep-seated reasons for the shift that your mind took into distrust and suspicion.

If you find yourself feeling paranoid during a psychedelic experience, whether the drug involved is marijuana or something else, there are certain things to keep in mind. First, if you are seeing menace or hatred in the faces of people you know and love, try to activate your Observer, the part of you that watches, learns, and evaluates without emotion (although it does, at times, have a subtle sense of humor). The Observer is always present; remember it's there for you to use, and you must call it in. It should tell you something like this: "You have taken a drug, and it's changing your perceptions. Don't get trapped in this negativity and distrust. It's a part of your psyche, it's an aspect of your Survivor — the corner of your soul that assumes it's still living in the jungle, and senses danger everywhere — and what you're seeing has nothing to do with the truth about your friends or how they feel toward you; it has to do with projections from deep within your unconscious mind. Just ride it out, and it'll fade in a while."

Naming the state as paranoia does help you regain objectivity. No matter what drug you've taken, you may simply have to wait until it wears off, remembering not to act on the suspicion and fearfulness, reminding yourself continually that it's all the effect of a drug which is not friendly to you, and which you may not want to experiment with again. Also, consider the possibility that you are experiencing a one-time-only (it is to be hoped) exposure to a certain potential within all human beings to see their surroundings as dangerous.

If you are perceiving hostility in faces looking at you, or words said to you, remember that the perceived anger or disapproval — whether you feel it coming from people or trees or, for that matter, the sky — is a projection upon the outside world of negative judgements made upon yourself, tucked away in the unconscious mind. In other words, some part of you has learned, probably in childhood, to regard yourself as undesirable, bad, worthy of punishment, or worse. This is what you are seeing in the hostile faces of your friends or the menacing plants in your garden: a projection of the feelings of that judge and jury you have residing deep inside you.

Allow the paranoia to become a teaching about that part of your psyche and, when the drug session is over, discuss with others what you experienced. If the feeling of paranoia disturbed you with its intensity, perhaps consider going into therapy, if you can, to dig up that self-destructive unconscious programming and to consciously put it to rest.

## SELF-HATRED

For certain psychedelic explorers, there seems to be an early stage during which the overwhelming sense is one of self-rejection; in some cases, the strength of the negativity can be extreme enough for it to be called self-hatred. For these people, it can happen with a number of psychedelics, though seldom with all, and is usually part of the transition phase (from ingestion to full effect).

Again — as with paranoid thinking — self-observation and simple logic can help get you through it. Your Observer should be able to tell you (if you'll listen), that this kind of focus on only the warts, only the failures and inadequacies, is not coming from a perspective of balance and fairness, but from some part of you that has been programmed — probably by parents, peers, or other authority figures in your childhood — to make harsh and unforgiving judgements of yourself.

The question you must ask yourself, persistently, is: would I judge a good friend with this much implacable negativity? And if I wouldn't pass sentence on a dear friend this way, why am I doing it to myself? Where is compassion, understanding, patience, and just plain love? Don't I deserve as much of these as any friend of mine?

Watch and listen to the words and phrases you're using against yourself, and ask just where this hostility could have come from. Where did you learn it, and how can you supplant it with love, humor and tolerance for yourself?

In most psychedelic sessions, this stage passes within the first hour, and what takes its place is usually a mellow, good-humored self-acceptance. But it is because of the possibility of an eruption of childhood-programmed self-condemnation, or its cousin, paranoia, that your first experiment with a new (to you) psychedelic drug should always be in the company of an experienced guide, usually called a "babysitter." There should be someone present who can spot trouble and move in with sympathy and common-sense, to diffuse the potentially damaging self-rejection.

And by "potentially damaging," I mean that, in the case of self-hatred, if it is overwhelming and intense enough, and the researcher is not experienced, there can be an impulse to self-destruction. The damaged self-image is believed to be the ultimate truth, and no human being can tolerate living with an image of himself that is everything he hates and loathes.

Suicide is not liable to be a threat in the case of a person who is experienced with various psychedelics, because he's already gone through some version of this self-rejection and he's probably done some insight work and has come to understand this kind of eruption of self-loathing. It happens, in one form or another, to many people who experiment with psychedelics. The experienced traveler is certain, or has a pretty good idea, where the negative program originated, and he knows that it isn't even remotely the real nature of his soul. Experience has taught him that, if he gives himself whatever compassion he can and a little time, the dark state of self-hatred will dissipate and he'll find himself where he wants to be, possessed again of a sense of balance and humor and love for the totality of who and what he is.

The value of going through this horrible place is in coming face to face with childhood conditioning which has remained unconscious until opened up by the drug. Only when you are forced to acknowledge what you've been taught to believe about yourself, (almost always by parents and almost always unwittingly), can you begin the work necessary to the eventual transformation of your inner Beast into a Prince or Princess.

### THE OCEANIC EXPERIENCE

This is also known as *participation mystique* in the words of the great Mircea Eliade. It's as hard to find the right name for this state as it is to do it justice in words. For the serious explorer, it's usually one of the first places he'll find within himself. This experience will probably make a permanent change in his way of seeing his world, particularly his natural surroundings. I've discovered recently that I'm not the only psychedelic traveler who takes for granted that the beginning of the modern ecological awareness movement was not in Rachel Carson's important, ground-breaking book, *Silent Spring*, but in the psychedelic experimentation of the 1960's.

Young people who take psychedelic drugs solely for the purpose of partying and dancing at raves may indeed experience some of the heart-openness and warmth of feeling, empathy with others, and visual fun and games associated with some of these drugs, but they might not undergo the oceanic experience in its fullest, most complete form. For that place to open, it seems best to have quietness, both inside and outside, and to be in natural surroundings. However, there are no firm rules about the human psyche; if it is time for the oceanic experience to happen, it will happen, no matter where one is.

This state is characterized by a sense of connection — emotionally and spiritually — with all other living things, including the body of the planet itself. It is a place of exquisite joy; you feel immense gratitude for being alive and able to participate in an extraordinary natural system which is suffused with wisdom and an all-encompassing love. All plants, animals and insects appear as contributors to an immense tapestry of life, of which you yourself are a treasured and essential part.

There is a rare (at least, among the people I know) and more profound form of this experience which may involve you first in sorrow, before you are healed by joy and love. The sorrow is that of all living things caught in pain, fear and loss, everywhere in the world, and you will find yourself participating in their emotions, feeling what they feel, while simultaneously experiencing your own agonizing pity and compassion. After being in this place for a time, you will begin to be aware of an immense, boundless love permeating everything that exists, and with it, a growing sense of joy/euphoria/bliss. This bliss state does not negate the suffering you have participated in; it includes and contains it. You may find yourself on a cosmic knife-edge, with your soul balancing between vast, deep darkness on one side and an infinite stretch of light on the other. It is here, I believe, on this knife-edge inside us, that laughter is born.

One of the lasting effects of this experience is a sense of the livingness of everything around you, the *dearness* and even sacredness of all forms of life, including those you have never personally liked, and an abiding respect for them and their right to exist alongside you on the Earth.

The oceanic experience has happened upon people unexpectedly, without the aid of drugs or any other tools, probably from the beginning of our species. It is a deeply spiritual alteration of consciousness, and I have never heard or read of anyone who has regarded it as other than a priceless gift, even when it has happened without warning or anticipation. The poet, Edna St. Vincent Millay, described the more complete form of it in her superb poem, "Renascence." Here are three brief passages from different parts of a very long work:

> "...I saw and heard, and knew at last
> The How and Why of all things, past,
> And present, and forevermore.
> The universe, cleft to the core,
> Lay open to my probing sense...

> "No hurt I did not feel, no death
> That was not mine; mine each last breath
> That, crying, met an answering cry
> From the compassion that was I...

"The world stands out on either side
No wider than the heart is wide;
Above the world is stretched the sky,
No higher than the soul is high.
The heart can push the sea and land
Farther away on either hand;
The soul can split the sky in two,
And let the face of God shine through..."

I believe that it is impossible for a person who has found himself in this place of the soul to ever again think of a tree as just another "crop;" to deliberately set out to kill a wild animal without sending to that animal a conscious thought of respect and regret at having to take its life; to consider building a house without first listening to the sounds of insects and birds and the rustling of small ground animals in the field he is planning to invade.

To such a person, the news of the extinction of yet another species of animal or plant — however inevitable — brings a wave of regret bordering on sorrow. He knows that species have been born and later extinguished countless times in the history of this planet, long before man came along to accelerate the process, but he feels the loss as he would the death of a fascinating acquaintance whom he had hoped to get to know more intimately.

The person who has been in this place knows to his marrow that he is part of nature, not separate from it, and that the Earth itself, the great body beneath our feet, is a living entity with a consciousness all its own, of a kind far different from anything that can be understood intellectually. He has felt the edges of that planet-consciousness, so he knows that some part of his psyche is connected to it, and that this is true of every living thing in the world.

If you find yourself opening to this experience, whether it begins with suffering or goes directly to love and bliss, you will not need your Observer at all, because the entire process is a gift of Grace, and you will recognize it as such by the time it ends.

## SYNAESTHESIA

For people who experiment with psychedelics, this can be one of the most impressive and enjoyable aspects of the experience. The definition of synaesthesia in one dictionary is: "A sensation produced in one modality when a stimulus is applied to another, as when the hearing of a certain sound induces the visualization of a certain color." Under the influence of most psychedelic drugs, not only can music present itself to the listener in all shades of color, in all degrees of brightness and subtlety, but the reverse can also be true; colors can translate themselves into sound. There are sometimes such exotic interpretive changes as feeling emotions as textures, and intellectual concepts as three-dimensional shapes. Synaesthesia sometimes occurs in dreams, without any drug having been involved. It is something that all human minds do, usually unconsciously, and synaesthesia underlies all forms of creativity. Poets, artists and musicians may have experiences of synaesthesia while they are focusing intently on their work, probably because the creative experience usually involves an alteration of consciousness, a trance state. The taking of a psychedelic or visionary plant simply makes this interweaving of sensory modalities apparent to the conscious mind.

Many years ago, shortly before the birth of my first daughter, I had a Big Dream (the kind that C. G. Jung defined as a powerful, impactful dream which awakens the dreamer when it ends, and stays in memory for a long time, often for life). In my dream, I was standing in a garden, looking up at a tall, slender golden column. At its top, the column flared out to become a shallow bowl. Within that bowl I could see what I knew to be flower-fruits; round, succulent fruits with red, coral and purple colors, which were also, simultaneously, flowers. There was no division or difference between the two expressions of the plant; they were flower-fruits. To put this image in context, the rest of the dream involved my about-to-be-born daughter, who appeared as a young woman named Ann (which I of course named her when she arrived). The entire dream was vivid, detailed and extraordinary, but my amazement — when I woke up — was at the ability of my dreaming mind to accept without difficulty the merging of two states of plant life, flower and fruit, which is exceedingly hard to do when awake.

It is possible to get the intellectual *concept* of such a merging when one is awake, but only in a symbolic sense. In the dream — as in a psychedelic state — the experience is that of *feeling* the two as one entity.

The degree to which synaesthesia is experienced under the influence of a psychedelic depends on the nature of the drug, the dosage level at which the drug is taken, and finally, the receptivity and curiosity of the user; if he is inclined to explore new dimensions of his interior world, he will pay more attention to unusual and unexpected juxtapositions which may occur when his unconscious mind has the freedom to play these kinds of games with sensory input.

Here are a few excerpts from a letter written by a gentleman named Dan Joy:

"Synaesthesia is rich, resonant and meaningful. And it is

everywhere. In cartoons, you have the wiggly lines signifying motions or the lines splaying out from a trumpet, signifying its blast, sometimes accompanied by little musical notes... Drug experiences and phenomena are inseparable from the matrix/spectrum of human mental, sensory, perceptual, cognitive, etc., experience — *not* a distinct, self-contained cluster of anomalies. The vocabularies used for the different sensory modalities overlap, revealing an underlying synaesthetic sense in our language. For instance, both sounds and colors have 'tones' and 'overtones,' as do emotions; sonic tones, like color-spectral ones, can be 'bright' or 'dark;' sound tones can be 'high' or 'low,' language which synaesthetically connects them also to the kinesthetic and visual-spatial sensoria. It is known that *smells* vividly awaken the full sensory spectrum of memory, synaesthetically inclusive of visual, auditory and emotional aspects. All the 'separate' sensory channels, after all, feed into the same brain."

Synaesthesia produces a sense of *pleasure* in everyone I know who has experienced it. The human psyche seems to enjoy this melding of the senses. There are some people in this world who live with synaesthesia all the time; they apparently consider themselves among the luckiest human beings on the planet. I'm sure there are synaesthetic experiences which are dark and frightening, perhaps in nightmares or certain schizophrenic states, but I have never personally heard or read of such negative kinds of synaesthesia. For me, this is a place of great enjoyment and soul-satisfaction. Furthermore, it gives rise to a multitude of questions about the nature of the reality we perceive, or think we perceive, and the workings of our brains, minds and souls.

## LAUGHTER

Anybody who has enjoyed marijuana has had the giggles, and — since for most users marijuana is a social drug — he has probably been through one of those hilarious sessions where everything seemed tremendously funny to everyone involved, and people were laughing about the smallest, silliest remarks or events until they were gasping for breath. Marijuana is famous for inducing this kind of hilarity, but it can happen to users of other psychedelic drugs, particularly psilocybin, and often does. It may have something to do with the release of the usual social constraints which hinder most adults — at least in our western culture — in their expression of a good many of their feelings. Under the influence of these drugs, not only are repressed sorrows and angers sometimes released, so is humor and laughter.

Most of us have a lot of laughter inside us, but after childhood, we in the West learn to keep it to ourselves a good deal of the time. We let it loose — along with our sense of the ridiculous — when we've had some drinks which relax us, or a psychedelic which can serve the same purpose. And no matter how silly it may seem in retrospect, a bout of real laughter can strengthen the immune system, among many other good things, and should be treasured.

The question always comes up, eventually: what is laughter? It's a strange, choppy, spasmodic physical response to humor. So what is humor? A baby, when startled by a clown doll popping out of a box, will cry. The older child learns to suppress the startle response in favor of allowing something new and interesting into her world; she laughs and reaches out to grab the clown, to feel it and chew on it. Laughter, in child or adult, sometimes seems to be the result of this very rapid shuttling between fear and pleasure, or Yes and No.

But there are many kinds of laughter: bitter, sarcastic and cruel, as well as joyful and celebratory. The physical response may be basically the same, but the emotions that give rise to dark laughter are despair and anger, or simply the need to assert power and control. When we talk about "humor," or "laughter," most of us are thinking of that explosion of champagne bubbles that rises through stomach and chest, triggering an irresistible urge to open the throat and mouth and emit the odd staccato sound that expresses our pleasure.

The Laughing Buddha is an archetype, an illustration of what it is to stand on the knife-edge between Dark and Light, Death and Life, and to survey the universe from there. This is cosmic laughter, half pain and half bliss. One doesn't have to be a Buddha to know that place; it's inside every one of us mortals, and all that's needed is the willingness to open the door and step through.

## THE BETH STATE

Shura's name for this rare place is the Beth state, but it could also be thought of as a long-lasting threshold. We have experienced it only with a drug called Aleph-7, and Shura often wonders if it is exclusively a property of that particular material. Or, to put it more accurately, perhaps Aleph-7 is the only drug that opens that particular door in the psyche. And then again, perhaps there are others we don't know about.

His notes include the following: "Slow start at one hour, quiet.

Walking feels strange at three hours and twenty minutes; a feeling of something impending, but there are no handles, no way to place the intoxication. At four and a half hours, transition to a more familiar altered state, quite pleasant. The previous hour or so not unpleasant, just without definition."

In summary, the Beth state is one in which you are aware of being in an altered state of consciousness, but you can't pin down exactly how you know, since there are no visual changes, no emotional stimulation, no colorful patterns appearing in the mind, no nuthin'. And there it stays, and there you stay, for three to four hours. At least, that is the case with Aleph-7. It must be remembered, though, that if any single drug can elicit such a response as the Beth state, it means that the capacity for experiencing the Beth, for finding oneself in such a place, is intrinsic to the human mind. The only negative that could possibly be associated with the Beth place is the fear of dying of boredom.

## FLOODING

This can be one of the consequences of taking too high a dose of a psychedelic drug. It can also happen at a perfectly reasonable dosage level, but it is far less likely. You find yourself bombarded by a torrent of images, concepts and connections, all coming at you from your friendly neighbor-hood cosmos. The details of the experience will vary, of course, with every person who finds himself in this particular place in the mind, but the general feeling is one of being flooded by meaningful connections between every-thing in the universe and everything else. An experienced traveler, know-ing that this, too, will pass, might manage to relax and enjoy the complexi-ties of the onslaught, but to the naive experimenter, it can be overwhelming. The ego, the sense of core identity, might be hard to maintain; the sense of Self might be lost in the roaring noise of continual, intense input.

If you find yourself in this state, remember first of all that it's temporary. If you find it impossible to relax and swim with the roaring river, or simply need to recover your sense of identity and a bit more control over the experience, open your eyes (if you had them closed), then stand up and start moving around, trying your best to focus on what your body is doing. Watch yourself walking, and talk to yourself, using your Observer to remind you of who you are, what your immediate situation is, and what you are attempting to do. Something like this might result: "I am Jacob Smith, I took so-and-so milligrams of Whatchamacallit approximately an hour and a half ago; I'm being flooded by too much information and I am attempting to get grounded by having this silly conversation with myself."

If you can manage to see humor in anything you're experiencing, and especially if you can smile or laugh at yourself, you've won your battle. You may have hours of relative unease and mental overload still ahead of you, but if you can feel even the slightest little spurt of humor, you've recaptured the thread that will lead you back to your Self. When you can feel your own presence, when you can say to yourself, "I'm here, I'm ME," (never mind good grammar) your fear of dissolving into your surroundings, of losing track of your own existence, will gradually subside.

What you should be aiming for in such an experience is this: maintaining your sense of identity, your knowledge that you are a being distinct from other beings and from the world that surrounds you, while allowing the images and concepts and energies that are bombarding you to be what they are, to go where they are going, to flow through you and past you. After a while, everything will begin to soften and quiet, and the crashing flood of information will eventually become a trickle. One of the things you may be left with from this experience will be a new appreciation of what it means to live your life with a goal, a focus, an intent of some kind to help channel your energies and thoughts.

There's been much written over the years about the spiritual benefits of having your ego dissolve, of becoming part of the cosmos, of losing your sense of Self and experiencing the River of Life, the flow of universal spiritual energies, without the encumbrance of that separate identity, that "Me and I" thing, that terrible Ego, so beloved of individuals in the Western world.

I'm not comfortable with the way that concept is usually stated. For one thing, whose definition of "Ego" is being used? If what is meant is the "persona," the social face that all of us develop — and sometimes mistake for the real person inside — then yes, I couldn't agree more; anyone who wants to develop as a human being, as a soul, must be able to let the persona drop away at will.

But the Self, the core of you, the kernel of continually moving energy that is your essence, is not a burden. It's a piece of God, as tiny as a molecule and as large as infinity. It isn't necessary, I believe, to lose touch with it, in order to have the experience of dissolving into the stream of life; it should be your anchor, the place from which you launch into the interior cosmos, and the place to which you return.

There's a difference between an experience of overload or flooding, and one of mystical participation. Your instincts tell you when it's overload; you feel under attack, overwhelmed by too much, too much, and unable to learn anything of value (except, of course, that your dosage level of the drug was probably too high).

On the other hand, the experience of mystical participation, the oceanic experience — whatever you choose to call it — comes as a natural unfolding of the soul, deep and sweet, and often unaccountably familiar.

Again, and yet again, the experience that I call flooding is another reminder of why experienced researchers in the area of psychedelics always try to have another person, a babysitter, present, especially when trying a new level of a compound.

If flooding happens spontaneously, without a drug being involved, and if it lasts more than 24 hours, you may need professional help. Most psychiatrists will treat this as a form of psychosis, and will medicate you heavily. This may be appropriate if you are really overwhelmed by the input and get into a panic, but if the input is tolerable and can be handled by other means, keep in mind that anti-psychotic drugs make it impossible to process such an experience or to learn anything from it.

If you find yourself in this state, having taken no drug at all, you should get a friend to be with you, right away. With the friend's help, locate someone in your vicinity who is a spiritual guide of some kind; a priest or minister or a Buddhist teacher. If you happen to know of an older psychedelic explorer who has not only experience but also some degree of wisdom — a wise elder, in other words — ask that person to help you.

This state of being flooded by more information, more connections and concepts than you can handle, can teach you about that place in the psyche. It can also make clear to you why, as a human being, it is necessary for you to control the rate of that flow, at least to the extent that you can hold onto your Self, and give time to the exploration of a concept or series of connections. Only this way can you hope to learn something of value. In this case, at least, less is indeed more.

TIME DISTORTION

This is one of the most common effects of a psychedelic drug. Almost all of these drugs cause changes in one's time-sense; most of the time, there is a feeling of time stretching, but there can also be an experience of the opposite, a compression of time. This is not usually disturbing to the traveler, with one very distinct exception. I have heard of first-time psychedelic explorers who found themselves trapped in what they were sure was eternity, with no way out.

One lady, living alone in the woods of Northern California, took LSD (dosage level unknown) for the first time, and had the terrible experience of being in a profoundly altered state forever. *Forever.* She did finally come down, to her astonishment and intense gratitude, but an eternity had passed during those hours of consciousness change. Understandably, she says she will never take a psychedelic drug again.

I know of only one way to avoid such an experience, and that is to make sure that you take a relatively low amount of any psychedelic drug you haven't tried before. And when you are familiar with the drug, increase the dosage level very slowly, if at all. This is not an area in which being "macho" is advisable. You are experimenting with your own mind and with unknown levels of your own psyche, and it is best to go slowly and carefully, with great respect and humility.

If you do find yourself trapped in eternity, let your Observer remind you that it is a drug-effect, and that it will, indeed, come to an end when the drug wears off. In the meantime, make use of the state, in whatever way gives you most pleasure; writing notes, creating something of beauty out of clay or paint, sitting outside with growing things, and allowing yourself to look, listen and think. Keep reminding yourself that eternity, in this case, is temporary, and that you are experiencing a fascinating corner of your soul. Much can be learned from this experience about perceptions of time, about the nature of your Self, and about the extraordinary capacities of your mind.

## OUT OF BODY EXPERIENCES

The first problem I encounter, in trying to tackle this particular subject, is that of definitions. What is meant by an out-of-body experience? To the average scientist, for instance, a person trained in logic and what is called scientific thinking, and with no exposure to the world of the spiritual, the term OBE (out-of-body experience) is meaningless, because he has been taught to believe that the physical body is all there is, and the implication that one can have any kind of conscious experience separate from the body is ridiculous. To such a person, then, this whole discussion is meaningless. It is to others that these notes are addressed.

The expert on OBE's is generally believed to be Robert Monroe, who wrote the first books about the process, and founded an institute on the East coast of the United States to teach people how to journey out of their bodies at will.

There are many reports of OBE's under the influence of psychedelic drugs, but I have never had one, so I can't speak knowledgeably about it.

My stepson, Theo, had a classic OBE when he was in his twenties, unassociated with drugs. He used self-hypnosis (concentrating on a spot on the ceiling), and found himself floating above his bed, aware of a thin, strong life-line or umbilical cord connecting him to his body. From there, apparently without any fear or anxiety, he took off to find his girlfriend, who had gone with her family for the weekend to a cabin in the Sierras. He was there instantly, and observed her sitting on a small pier at the edge of a mountain lake. He took note of what she was wearing (a red sweater and blue jeans), then flew up to what looked like a small cloud, at which point he knew it was time to return to home base. "I just followed the cord — and, yes, it was sort of vaguely silver — and Wham! I was back in my bod," he told me.

Needless to say (I mean, I wouldn't be telling the story otherwise), when he later asked the girl if she had been in that particular place on that day, wearing those exact clothes, she said yes, she had been and how did he know? He sidestepped the question gracefully by laughing and changing the subject.

Theo stopped doing hypnotically induced OBE's only after a brief experience one day, when he concentrated on his favorite ceiling spot and, once out, went sailing into his father's bathroom, at the end of the hall. He drifted over to the mirror and looked in. There were the cabinets, the shower stall, the small shelf with Shura's shaving gear, all faithfully reflected. The only thing missing was his own face. There was simply no Theo in the mirror at all. For the first time since he had begun experimenting with OBE's, he became frightened. "I went back to my body immediately," he told me, "That was too much."

## HALLUCINATIONS

In Appendix C of this book, Shura and I define a hallucination, and I will repeat that definition here, adding only two brief clarifications.

> "An extremely rare phenomenon, in which a completely convincing reality surrounds a person, with his eyes open, a reality that he alone can experience and interact with. The inducement of hallucinations is a property that is commonly attributed to psychedelic drugs, but in reality is virtually non-existent in the use of such materials, unless there has been a massive overdose. In almost all psychedelic experiences undergone by normal, healthy people, using reasonable dosages, there is an awareness of real surroundings. Visual distortions are common, but they are not confused with objective reality by the subject; they are known to be visual distortions and appreciated as such. The delusional anesthetic drugs, such as scopolamine and ketamine, on the other hand, can and do produce true hallucinations."

Members of the medical (including psychiatric) community, being for the most part inexperienced in the use of psychedelic drugs, have gotten into the habit of using the word "hallucination" to describe an entire range of visual and auditory effects produced by such drugs, including many which have nothing whatsoever to do with hallucinations.

The important distinction is this: if you have taken a psychedelic drug and are, for instance, seeing increased brightness of color and richness of texture, interesting faces in large rocks, or kaleidoscopic imagery on your ceiling, and if you remain totally aware of the fact that such visual enhancements are due to your having taken a drug, you are NOT hallucinating.

On the other hand, if you have taken a drug and see a pretty blue horse prancing across your living room carpet, and are convinced that everybody else in your vicinity can also see the horse; if you make no association between the blue horse and the taking of a drug, but are certain that what you are seeing is part of consensual reality, then you are indeed hallucinating. It is the conscious awareness of cause and effect — the taking of a drug and the seeing of a blue horse — that makes the difference between experiencing visual effects or visual changes and real hallucinations.

I have had one experience of visual changes occurring as the result of an altered state without any drug being involved. I was attending a most unusual meeting at the home of a famous psychic in the city of Berkeley, years ago. There were many people present, including a group that was the focus of everybody's attention that evening: about ten psychic healers who were there to describe their methods and problems.

Present with his recording equipment was a well-known expert on out-of-body experiments, Dr. Charles Tart. He had done ground-breaking work in a university laboratory, placing electrodes onto people who claimed to be able to travel out of body almost every night, while retaining conscious control and memory of the experience. Dr. Tart assigned each subject specific tasks to accomplish while out of body in the lab; one assignment, for instance, was to float up to the ceiling, where there was a small placard with a name or series of numbers on it, placed out of sight of the awake subject. The subject was asked to report back when she awoke in the morning, as to what she had read on the placard.

Dr. Tart was the first university professor to publish the generally positive results of such research, and he was at this meeting to ask questions and tape-record answers from the healers.

The proceedings were taking place in a very large room with a wooden floor, and most of us were sitting on floor pillows against the walls. Everyone was quiet except the particular psychic healer whose turn it was to report into the microphone. Along with everyone else, I was concentrating on what was being said, and learning a great deal from each account, especially about the ways in which these people protected themselves from taking into their own bodies the illnesses of their clients.

Finally, bladder pressure made it necessary for me to get up and pick my way carefully over extended legs and feet on my way to the bathroom. Once inside the little room, I sat on the toilet and looked around me. To my surprise and delight, the shower curtain appeared to be rippling, the wallpaper was most certainly moving, and the faucets glinted with enthusiastic points of multi-colored lights. "Aha!" I thought, "What d'ya know! Never had this happen before. Maybe it's because of all that intense mental focusing. Wonder how long it'll last?"

Unfortunately, I was so impressed by this unexpected bit of fun and games that, when I returned to the big room, I lost my ability to fully concentrate on the continuing reports from the healers. By the time the meeting had broken up, all visual changes had disappeared, and things were back to normal.

In this case, I didn't think for one second that anyone else coming into that bathroom would see the movement of surfaces; I knew it was the result of changes in my own consciousness of a perfectly natural kind. Shura calls this, "Using the intellect as witness," and I call it using the Observer. When a person is having real hallucinations, his Observer has abandoned its post as reality checker, as witness, just as it does in the dream state.

If I had believed that the walls and shower curtain were really moving, and that the movements would be apparent to other people, i.e., part of consensual reality, it would have been an hallucination. I concluded then, and still do now, that it was a non-drug-induced alteration of perception produced by strong concentration; it was also thoroughly enjoyable, and I hope it happens again some day.

## THE KALI

This archetype is best known in India, where one can find numerous paintings which portray the Goddess Kali, wife of the God Shiva, usually as a grimacing black or blue female monster, wearing a necklace of skulls and dancing triumphantly on dead bodies. In one hand she brandishes a bloody sword; in the other, a bearded, severed head. Sometimes she is shown with four arms, the third carrying a trident and the fourth, a bowl which catches blood from the head.

In the book, *Dancing in the Flames*, by Marion Woodman and Elinor Dickson, (Shambhala Press, 1996) there are these comments:

> "At first glance, Kali comes across as a fierce embodiment
> of the devouring mother, who gobbles up everything, even
> her own children. A closer look, however, reveals a great
> halo around her head .... The halo attests to Kali's status as
> Goddess, to her need to be understood not only as de-

vourer, but also as transformer. She is black, dark as the matrix, from which all creation comes and to which it returns. To her devotees, she is like a black sapphire; radiance shines through her blackness."

"The mystery of Kali is that she is perpetually destroying and, at the same time, creating — destroying in order to create, creating in order to destroy, death in the service of life, life in the service of death. Kali is time, immanence, ceaseless becoming, nature as process. For Kali, all experience is one — life as well as death."

She is also understood to represent ego-death, which certain spiritual teachings believe to be an essential step on the pathway to illumination.

I've had two glimpses of The Kali, both of them astonishingly different from what I would have expected, and each giving rise to profound questions.

The first time was many years ago. It was in early summer, and I had taken around 20 milligrams of 2C-B in the early evening, while Shura was in San Francisco at the Owl Club, playing his viola in the orchestra, as he does every week.

At one point I went outside, climbed the brick steps and headed for my car to get something I needed. When I left the car and started back across the pavement towards the house, it was dark, except for the glow from the dining room below, illuminating the patio. Halfway to the steps, I suddenly stopped and stood riveted, my mouth open. About fifteen feet above the ground, glowing brightly against a shadowy mass of trees, was a large oval of light; seated cross-legged in its center was the figure of a lovely young woman. Her skin was the color of cream. Both arms were extended, hands open, as if to say, "Behold this!" She was surrounded by parts of dismembered human bodies — arms, legs, heads — lying on the ground, stretching as far as I could see. There was blood everywhere. What radiated from the vision was a feeling I can only describe as bliss.

The whole experience lasted barely two seconds, but I didn't move until it had faded out of existence, leaving me staring at the black outline of trees.

I walked slowly towards the stairs, thinking furiously.

*What WAS that? With all those — those pieces of bodies and the blood, it MUST be The Kali. But I've never heard of a beautiful Kali; all the paintings show monsters. And that feeling; how can a scene of bloody carnage give off such a sense of rightness? And bliss? I don't understand.*

I knew that I had just witnessed something not only important, but

sacred, and that it was part of the answer to my obsessive inner questions
about the nature of what we think of as good and evil. But I couldn't grasp
what it meant.

I hadn't yet solved the mystery, hadn't come to any satisfying
conclusions, when — seven months later — the second encounter occurred.
Shura and I were making love one night. He had taken 120 microgams of
LSD; I'd taken only 80 micrograms, because at higher levels, LSD is not
particularly my ally. I was doing dances with my tongue upon the body of
my love, when I saw in my mind's eye two figures far away, dressed in red,
against a background of light. They were embracing, and I knew instantly
that they were Death and Life, and suddenly they had melted into each
other and there was only one figure there, facing me, seated in a halo of soft
light, her clothes the color of blood.

This time, also, the duration of the vision was two or three seconds,
and it didn't fade, as the first one had, but simply ceased to exist.

*That's the level of the Gods. It isn't the human reality; we have to choose
between the life force and loving, and the other side, The Kali — destruction and
killing. How can that vision have any meaning for a human being?*

I turned my attention again to Shura, tucking away the memory of
the figures in red until later.

It took some time for me to acknowledge that my immediate
thoughts after the second experience had been simply avoidance, an effort
to postpone the work I was going to have to do to comprehend what I had
been shown.

Just a few weeks ago, I heard from a friend about her experience of
another form of the female destroyer archetype. It had come to her in a
dream, several years ago, and her description of the dream state makes it
clear that this was a "Big Dream," one which is vivid, numinous and always
remembered.

What my friend, Lara, saw in the dream state was the Goddess Pele,
sacred to the Hawaiians; she is the goddess of fire and volcanoes, and she
is also the patron goddess of the Hawaiian Islands. Pele appeared to Lara
as a magnificent being with a river of lava flowing around her. She spoke,
but what she said to the sleeping woman had nothing to do with destruction; it was about the sacredness of knowledge and the immense importance
of continual learning while in human form. Then she showed Lara the
creative side of her nature; she displayed the growth of new land that
results from the cooling of lava after a volcanic eruption, and invited her
to rejoice at the sight. Then the vision ended, and Lara awoke. "I lay
there in the dark," she told me, "And I felt this great happiness, and I went
over and over the memory of Pele and what she had said to me. It was
astonishing, and I am still feeling so grateful to her!"

I have gradually come to understand that all the dualities in the cosmos spring from a single Source, as does everything else; that duality, the dance of opposites, is necessary for life to exist, in any and all forms. I believe that, although perceptions of these archetypes may be possible only when one is in the God-space, the expression of these dual forces informs every second of existence, whether of plant, insect, animal or human.

My intellect can comprehend all this, but my heart and gut still rebel at grief, fear, pain, injustice and destruction. To work through that rebellion, I have to remind myself of certain things. For instance, although the great forces that shape all life can sometimes appear to the soul as serenely implacable and without mercy or love, this perception is not the truth. The archetype of Kwan Yin, the Chinese Goddess of Mercy, is also within us, as are numerous other archetypal images of loving, nurturing, creative energies.

As a species, we have always taken sorrow and transformed it into music and art; we have used experiences of pain to deepen our empathy and compassion for others; even fear and horror have had their uses, teaching us strength and will.

What we strive for, whether through the use of consciousness-altering drugs and plants or meditation and spiritual training, is to reach — however momentarily — that place inside us where there is true comprehension of the great dualities, and with it, a state of immense energy, acceptance and bliss. The Indian word for this place is "Samadhi," and a single experience of it will give life-long strength to your soul and spirit.

We, after all, along with all other life-forms, are pieces of the Source, expressions of the Source, so everything we do and feel is done and felt by the Source.

I am not stating any of the above as ultimate truth, but only as what I have experienced and learned. Every human being contains all of these places in his psyche; what he does with them, how he puts them together into a whole view of the universe and his role in it, will be unique to him and must be respected and honored.

## EUPHORIA

The first thing that can be said about this experience is: it's good and nourishing, food for our souls. Euphoria belongs in all our lives, as often as possible, because it feeds us with energy and hope.

A dictionary will give you the following definition of euphoria, and when you've read it, think about the implications. From the Random House Webster's College Dictionary, 1991, I get this simple one: "A strong feeling of happiness, confidence, or well-being." And, as Shura has said, many times, the prefix "eu-," means "normal," or "correct." The word, "euthy-roid," means a normally functioning thyroid. The opposite of "eu-," is "dys-," which means something *not* functioning normally. For instance, "dysphoria," means abnormal, as opposed to "euphoria," which means feeling well, normal and good. Thus, "hyperphoria" could be bliss, and "hypophoria" could be depression.

So, how have we come to be a society in which euphoria means "feeling too good, happier than you ought to, more confident than you deserve to," instead of what it ought to mean? Why is euphoria listed in the Physicians' Desk Reference as a possible *negative* side-effect of various drugs?

I wonder if we are, as a society, becoming so used to being in a state of mild depression most of the time, that feeling well, happy and full of energy engenders, in some people, a certain amount of suspicion and even disapproval. Perhaps some of this comes from the early Puritan and present Fundamentalist Christian teachings that Man is a sinner and true happiness and bliss can be expected only in heaven, if you've earned your place there by living a life full of self-sacrifice and a lot of suffering.

I have experienced euphoria and its higher spiritual form, bliss, as an upwelling of thanksgiving to the Source, by whatever name it is called. The feeling I have when giving whole-hearted Thank You to the universe is identical to that felt in a state of euphoria. Some evangelical Christians in their worship services seem to experience the two states as one. Perhaps they are.

As with all emotions felt by human beings, euphoria does not last, cannot be present all the time, and is not meant to be constant. Unless you have worked your way through to becoming an Initiate, a spiritual master, (in which case it may be possible to live in a state comparable to euphoria), for the most part you will have ups and downs, sun and shadow, pain and exhilaration. All we can hope for, both for ourselves and those we love, is that all of us will have more moments of euphoria than sorrow, and that we will be able to renew our hope and excitement about life as often as possible.

The only negative I can think of in regard to euphoria is that certain people may try to find a way of making it a permanent state of being. With or without drugs, it cannot be maintained constantly by most of us, any more than orgasm can be. There are stories — legends — of people who have slipped into a bliss state and remained there for the rest of their lives; Saint Theresa of Avila, for instance. However, if you want to remain in the world of human beings, to live a human life, to change, learn and transform, euphoria must be looked upon as a temporary gift and a reminder of your innate capacity for exquisite pleasure.

Psychedelic drugs can help open a person to an experience of euphoria, just as they can open him to deep sorrow, empathy and humor, cosmic meaningfulness and total confusion. Again, it isn't the drug that creates the experience; it's the drug that opens doors to what is already resident inside the person.

For those of us who live in the western industrialized countries, daily life tends to be busy, stressful and not conducive to the practice of insight or the fullest possible openness to emotions. Adults learn to repress, hide and even deny feelings that are uncomfortable or painful. Unfortunately, this results in a repression of feelings that are entirely positive, along with the negative ones. When we put a lid on anger and resentment, we are also making it hard to feel joy, deep love and humor. Everything gets dulled.

In the psychedelic experience, we can discover a clear, open channel to feelings and emotions again. It makes us more vulnerable to the world around us, but without that vulnerability, we cannot feel out truth and we can never hope to grow wise.

# CHAPTER 11. SEX, DRUGS, AND THE OLDER PLAYERS

(Alice's voice)

It's Saturday night, and Shura and I have each taken 100 micrograms of LSD, a rather low dose — not enough to stun the mind with too much input, but quite enough to open up lovemaking. It's June, and a warm night, so we don't need to get under the covers. I lie down beside him, and he turns off the bedside lamp. Now there's only the light from the radio, but it's enough to see each other by.

Shura turns his head and smiles at me, his hair standing out from his head like a corona, glinting silver and pink and orange in the half-light.

I raise myself on one elbow, and say, "How about searching the dial, see what our choices are?"

While he switches from one classical music station to another, I stroke his back and watch little rainbows erupting in the wake of my hand. Suddenly, Prokofiev's Second Piano Concerto brings a stop to the sampling of radio wares, and I give an approving pat to my favorite rounded portion of his anatomy, "Hey, we lucked out!"

Shura turns around, "Looks like it."

His hands move over my stomach and down one thigh, and I breathe out the breath I didn't know I was holding, as I let go of a week's concerns and frustrations. Most important of all, I'm letting go of fear that my body is not beautiful enough, not slim enough, not appealing enough. What grows in me — every time we make love — is a certainty that, in some way I can't understand with the self-critical part of my mind, Shura loves me anyway. Not despite, but including all the defects. It's easy for me to accept him, his body, the things that aren't perfect, but I'm always amazed that he accepts me in the same way.

What I love is the essence of the man inside, the male energy and its island of femininity. His body is the physical expression of his light and dark sides, sometimes in conflict and sometimes in balance, as is the case with all of us, I suppose.

We are affectionately amused by each other's less romantic signs of aging: the thinning of pubic hair, the rounding of tummies, the loosening of skin that was never supposed to be anything but taut and smooth. All of that, we gradually learn to allow in our own bodies, and love in each other's.

One of the things that makes it hard to see one's body getting older is that the soul, the sense of who we are, is never more than thirty-two or so. This is an uncomfortable thing for some people to hear, and they usually choose not to believe it, because it sounds too sad. They'd rather think that the spirit inside the shrunken, fragile grandmother lying against her pillows feels itself as ancient as her body. But it simply isn't so. And the idea of a young soul trapped in an old body isn't as tragic as it might sound. After all, aging happens very gradually, morning mirror by morning mirror, and after a while you learn to shrug resignedly at your reflection and avoid friends' cameras.

And there are compensations. In your thirties, you become aware that you are beginning to understand the rules of the game — the social, human relationship game. In your sixties and seventies, a new level of comprehension begins to make itself felt; occasionally, when you pay attention, you can hear the flow of life more clearly, sense it moving beneath and around you, feel yourself part of something immense and timeless, yet somehow intimately connected to you and everything you're doing and thinking.

Sexuality changes as we age. The body doesn't act or react the way it did twenty years earlier. If you and your lover have a good relationship you'll find that with the passing of the years, frequency is replaced by depth, subtlety and a new dimension of deliciousness. Love-making itself, the caressing and the imaginative uses of hands, mouth and tongue to play the beloved's body, whether or not there is final culmination, can become a pleasure undreamt of in the climax-driven world of the twenty-year-olds.

If you are familiar with certain psychedelics or visionary plants, and have experience in using them, love-making can become a truly multi-dimensional experience, sensuousness interwoven with spirit, jeweled images behind closed eyelids combining with the smell and feel of skin, and the orgasm flowering deep in the mind before it explodes — excruciatingly sweet and long — in the body.

But you should be familiar with the effects of the particular drug and be sure of the identity and quality of whatever you're using. The relaxing effects of certain psychedelic drugs may make it easier to find that erotic bud which can be urged into bloom, but it is important that you know enough about the effects of the drug to enable you to avoid taking too much. The reasons are obvious: with too high a dosage, the imagery filling the interior screen, and the conceptual complexities that may accompany them, could make it difficult to focus either mind or body on making love, if that is what you had intended. The emotional and spiritual closeness that such a shared experience might bring about would certainly be its own reward, but if your intent is love-making, a modest dosage level will serve you better than a high one.

Later that night, I am in a shadowed cave where Benjamin Britten's music is water over rocks, falling into a dark pool. A fine spray rises from the bases of two huge, rounded stones which are smooth as sculptured buttocks. The music flows through my breasts, an edge of violins raising questions in silver shading to pewter, answered by a moss-green cello in the depths of the pool. Red light glows from somewhere behind me, and there are glints of red-gold in the falling water, then Shura howls long, long, and I am rising, past the great rocks towards the night sky.

I lift my head and smile up at him; his hand strokes my hair. We are silent, at rest, listening to the music.

# CHAPTER 12. THE LIONESS AND
# THE SECRET PLACE

(Alice's voice)

It was a long time ago when I had my first terror dream.

I had heard vaguely of "hypnogogia," and not at all of its twin, "hypnopompia." The first word is used to describe a state in which one is descending into sleep and, as normally happens, control over the physical body has been turned off, but for unknown reasons, the mind lags behind the body in descending into that particular altered state known as sleep. The second word, "hypnopompia," is a similar state experienced in the process of waking up.

In both states, the dreamer's mind, his ego, is capable of being self-aware, basically oriented as to identity, place and time — although this awareness may fluctuate — but he is not able to control his body or open his eyes. It is in this disconnected, limbo situation that certain kinds of vivid dreams, certain kinds of spiritual attacks, if you will, can take place.

I think of this strange state as getting briefly caught between two worlds, and I should note that my experiences have been only in going to sleep.

The first time I experienced a dream of this kind occurred while I was living with my little son, Christopher, in the Sunnydale housing project, just below the city of San Francisco. I was around 21 years old, newly divorced, and my baby and I were very poor, as were all the residents of Sunnydale and other similar low-rent housing projects (nobody lives in such places by choice, after all). I was used to being, emotionally, in the grip of something grey and hopeless that I couldn't define — years later, I realized it was called clinical depression — but, after all, that state of mind wasn't unknown to many of those living in the projects.

One evening, I had put my baby to bed in his little room upstairs, and was settling myself down on the living room couch with a book from the library, when my mother phoned. After we'd exchanged family news and talked for a while, she mentioned that, for reasons I can't remember, she was memorizing Psalm 121, which begins, "I will lift up mine eyes unto the hills, from whence cometh my help." After we said goodnight, I opened up my old Bible to read the psalm, and decided I liked it enough to try to memorize it myself, which is something I often did in those days, with poems I particularly liked.

That night, as I lay upstairs in my bed, sprawled on my back in the dark, my mind beginning to drift, I became aware of a sound coming from the direction of the half-opened bedroom door. It was a sound of scratchy footsteps on the wooden stairs, and a surreptitious rustle of clothing, and I knew that there was a group of *things* on the stairs which looked much like the dwarves in fairy-tale books: small, chunky bodies, wearing ragged clothing and dark caps. I could see them in my mind. They were sneaking slowly up the stairs, and they intended to come into my room. Somehow, I knew their objective, which was quite simple: to cause me terror. They liked making human beings afraid. And they knew I was helpless.

From the moment I'd heard the first sounds, I had been trying to open my eyes. I knew that once I managed to do so, I would have control over the rest of my body. But I was stuck, just barely over that threshold which we all cross every night. My body was frozen, while my mind wandered, completely self-aware, in a strange territory which was not quite dream, but had some aspects of dream to it, such as sensing the general shape and size of my attackers, and knowing what they had come for.

As I lay there, my heart beating so hard it threatened to deafen me, I knew the first of the intruders was already through the door, and the group was continuing to edge ever closer, laughing silently at my panic. Then, the words of the psalm I had been reading rose in my mind, and I concentrated all my attention on them, saying them slowly and clearly in my head, "My help cometh from the Lord, which made heaven and earth." Suddenly, I had my eyes; they opened with a snap, and I could move my head, and then my hands. I breathed relief at being back in control of my body, flexed my fingers and smiled at the ceiling. Then I became aware that I was still hearing the rustling sound. I was fully awake, and by turning my head I could see an empty floor, but that menacing sound continued, gradually fading, in my ears for at least ten seconds.

I got up and went downstairs to make myself some hot tea, and sat on the couch with my cup and a cigarette, for a little while. I wondered what the intruders had been, whether they had — as I suspected — an independent existence on some unknown level of reality, and why they were so filled with malice. Why did they want to frighten humans? To what purpose? It never occurred to me, and it would not occur to me until ten or fifteen years later, that they just might be aspects of my own unconscious. And if it had, I would still have been completely bewildered.

I tucked my feet under me and curled my fingers around the

reassuring warmth of the cup.

*At least I've discovered something immensely valuable: if I get stuck in that region, that kind of place again, all I have to do is focus my attention very strongly on words — words which have meaning for me. The Lord's Prayer, or a psalm, like tonight. That focusing of the mind gives me back control, and I can open my eyes.*

For a very long time afterwards, I had no more dreams of that particular kind. I ascribed this — when I thought about it at all — to the fact that I knew how to bring myself out of paralysis, and whoever the dwarf critters were, they knew I had the secret and wouldn't be quite so frightened of them next time.

Then, in the late 1950's, I had a series of three terror dreams on three successive nights. I was working, at the time, as a medical transcriber in the Department of Pathology, at the huge medical complex on a hill called Mount Parnassus, in San Francisco. I lived in a tiny apartment, just two blocks downhill from the medical center. I usually got to bed at around 10:30 p.m. on weekday nights, because I had to get up at 6:30 in the morning and needed as much sleep as I could get, in order to function properly in a demanding, stressful job.

The night of the first dream, I found myself again in a state of awareness, conscious of the fact that I had just slipped out of my body, and couldn't control any part of it, but had apparently stalled on the way to full sleep. And something was moving in on me. The image came of myself standing on the roof of a tall building, looking up with horror at a monstrous face, the size of a house, coming up the side of the outer wall. Its immense mouth, lined with rotten teeth, gaped open. Its eyes were closed, and it seemed to be trying to smell me out. (Much later, I came across the famous painting by Goya, "Chronos devouring his children," and shuddered at the resemblance.) While all this was going on, I was trying to open my eyes, remembering vaguely that I was supposed to concentrate on magic words, focus on them, to the exclusion of everything else. The trouble was, I also had to move as fast as I could, away from the edge of the roof and the room-sized, distorted, hungry mouth that was searching for me. I was too busy being terrified to focus on anything except getting off the roof and staying alive.

I could see no exit, but I was able to run behind a square metal box or vent of some kind, well out of the reach of the blindly searching creature. It seemed, finally, to get tired of the pursuit and began to slither downward, toward the street below. I knew I wasn't yet safe; the atmosphere was still heavy with menace, and it was then that I collected myself enough to begin reciting the Lord's Prayer. Within a few seconds, I could open my eyes, and the horror was over.

The following night, it all happened again. I was suspended, just barely out of my body, unable to continue into sleep or to open my eyes. I was on a rooftop again, but this time something was coming toward me out of the sky: birds. Black birds, wave after wave of them, swooping low over my head. I knew they were birds of death; not omens, but actual embodiments of death. I recognized them as the birds flying over the field in van Gogh's last painting, the one he finished just before he killed himself.

I set to work as before, trying to open my eyes or lift a finger, to reassert control over any part of my body, while the malevolent birds flew closer and closer to my head. I did my best to ignore the terrified pounding of my heart, and concentrated on remembering the words of the Lord's Prayer, but what came into my mind instead was the gentle, familiar, "The Lord is my shepherd; I shall not want," and suddenly I was awake.

This time, although I had a workday ahead of me and needed my rest, I stayed up for half an hour, until something told me I wouldn't face danger again — tonight, anyway — if I tried to go to sleep.

The third night, there I was, unable to move, unable to open my eyes, helpless on my bed, and this time the attack was more direct, and there was no dream-world at all. I was lying on my back, and to my left, perched on the edge of the bed, were entities — I knew there were three of them — and they were doing something that seemed ridiculous; they were blowing air on me. One would blow a puff of air at my face, while the others blew on the skin of my arm, then there would be a brief pause, and they would do it again, watching me. The intent was exactly the same as that of the dwarf-like creatures, so many years before: to frighten me, to drive me into a state of helpless fear. They were small and evil, full of giggling maliciousness, and I was frozen, only inches away from them.

The fear, that night, was mixed with anger, and I tried to focus my thinking on some words that would get me out again, but this time, something completely new and shocking happened. I felt my neck muscles stiffen, and my head moved back on the pillow. My throat opened, and from it came a roar which originated deep in my solar plexus; it was directed at the creatures, and it kept going on and on. In that roar there was no fear at all, only murder. It was not a human sound, but it spoke an unmistakable message: "Get out of here, or I'll tear you to bloody pieces. OUT!"

(Later, I compared the way I had felt with being a lioness inside a cave with her cubs, roaring at a couple of small monkeys at the cave entrance, who had been making a nuisance of themselves.)

The visitors on my bed vanished. My neck muscles gradually softened, and the animal I had been slowly faded away, although her self-satisfied contentment lingered for a long time.

I could move my body again.

This time, I didn't get up to think about it. I knew, somehow, that this was the last time I would be attacked. Whatever it was, whatever had been going on for three nights, was finished.

I was right. The terror dreams were over. But I was left with a puzzle, a mystery. What had been activated that last night? From what part of me had that lioness roar come? What could possibly have happened, except the obvious: I had become a powerful, fearless animal for just long enough to scare the hell out of some sort of disembodied spirit-creatures who had nothing better to do than try to terrorize a vulnerable human being caught out of body. That roar had said STOP, or I will destroy you! And it had stopped.

It would be almost four decades before I would begin to understand that inner lioness, and her equivalent — gorilla, wolf, jaguar — inside every human being, and the new kind of psychotherapy which would know what to do with that part of us.

For now, I had only a great wonderment, a feeling of awe at what had happened, and, underneath it, a sense of strength and satisfaction. I turned over on my bed and let sleep search me out again, feeling neither hesitation nor fear. I knew I was safe.

To this day, I have had no more killer or terror dreams, not a single one. I've had ordinary nightmares, and I've experienced lucid dreaming, but I've never again found myself trapped in that strange and vulnerable out-of-body place, heart pounding, fighting for my life. I think it's because an unknown part of me activated my own self-protective killer, my beast ally in the deep interior cave of the unconscious, and I know that I can reach for its help instantly, if attacked. It might not always take the form of a lioness, but that isn't important; the knowledge that it's my utterly loyal, immensely powerful ally is. When I became a therapist, for a while, more than 20 years later, I came to call this part of the human psyche the Survivor. Others call it the Power-Animal. It is an aspect of the human Dark Side, or Shadow, that exists solely for the protection of its host.

And the attackers, the entities that like to terrorize, what have I concluded they are — or were? Until I have evidence to the contrary, I'll have to consider them aspects of my own unconscious psyche, perhaps symbolic images of things I hate and fear. If, in truth, they actually emerged from elsewhere than my own interior, they may have been "elementals," beings inhabiting the usually unseen country of nature spirits, visible occasionally to small children and inhabitants of Ireland. Perhaps they are twisted with anger at the ruination of so much of the planet, and are able to take their revenge only when one of my species gets stuck in a not-quite-connected place on the way into sleep. Or out of it. But I can't bring myself to think of nature spirits as malignant, for any reason; sad, yes; malicious and sadistic, no. So for now, I will say that they weren't nature spirits. Until

I'm convinced otherwise.

Recently, I've come to suspect that the entire series of terror dreams was a set-up, orchestrated by my own psyche to lead my unconscious to activate the Beast-Survivor; to come to know and recognize it as the ally it is meant to be. In a later chapter, The Intensive, I'll have more to tell about this.

---

I'd never had a lucid dream in my life until a few years ago, when I went through an incredible experience which I wrote about in *PIHKAL*. It lasted a week, and involved an altered state over which I had no control, and during which I was taught a great deal. Some of the teaching was done in two lucid dreams.

Lucid dreaming means that you are conscious during a dream; you know that you're dreaming, and the ego is intact. The most obvious difference between lucid dreams and hypnogogic/-pompic dreams is that, in lucid dreams, you have control over the general direction and content of the dreams. If things become difficult, dangerous or undesirable, since you know it is a dream, you can choose to get out or change it. You're never trapped, as in the terror dreams, because you are completely and continually aware of the nature of the experience.

After the first lucid dreams, during that extraordinary week, I was tremendously excited that this had finally happened to me, and hoped it would happen again. Months after the first two dreams, I had another. In this one I found myself seated in the lotus position, arms extended on either side, floating above a desert scene. There were red stone cliffs beneath me, on my left side, and a sandy desert floor far below. The entire dream lasted only a minute, but during that time I experienced myself as a body of energy, emitting energy, pulsing with energy, and the energy was joy, wide-awake completion, bliss.

I remember waking for a moment and saying to myself, "That's what is meant by Samadhi."

Something new was added just during the past two years, in my experiences of lucid dreaming. In all my reading about various spiritual practices, I had never come across a description of anything like it.

What happened was this: I began having occasional lucid dreams in which I experienced intense sexual energy, but not in the usual place — not in my genitals; I felt desire and a drive to orgasm in a part of my body located immediately above the pubic bone. Exactly where you can feel a full bladder if you push inwards. The first time it happened, I drove myself by sheer will to orgasm, and when it came, it was the most intense one I had ever experienced. In the dream, I was conscious and observant, and noted that there was no image of a partner, and no spiritualizing of the sexuality in any way; it was vivid and strongly felt, in a part of the body not usually associated with sexual impulses. The only reason for it happening at all — my instincts told me — was to re-affirm the strength of the life-force in my body and my soul. And to acquaint me with what is meant by an activation of the chakra (energy center) which is located right above the pubic bone.

This kind of lucid dream occurred every few weeks, and I always woke up afterwards. Sometimes I wasn't able to achieve orgasm, despite intense efforts to focus on that result; the lucidity would begin to slip away, and I would feel disappointment when I woke, usually attempting — without success — to go back into sleep to recapture the experience. But most of the time, the strange and marvelous dream would culminate in a glorious, completely selfish, self-affirming, body-shaking orgasm, comparable only to the best of those one can have making love under the influence of psychedelics, but even more piercingly intense, literally taking my breath away.

I shared all of this with nobody but Shura, although I wanted to find out whether it was known to others. But, whom can one ask? It might be considered, after all, a rather delicate subject.

Finally, I found the whom. Shura and I had met him about a year earlier at one of the pot-luck dinners we had every few weeks, at the house of my former husband, Walter Parr, to which people in the network — the consciousness and psychedelics network — would come to talk and make new friends. This gentle man, of medium height, with thinning blond hair and warm, amused blue eyes, introduced himself as "Karma Tendo," using his Buddhist name. When I looked a bit quizzical, he explained, "I know, I don't look Tibetan. Actually, I was born in London, but when I decided to study Buddhism, I changed my name. Okay?" I laughed and acknowledged that it did seem a bit unusual to see before you such a non-Oriental looking person and be given a name straight out of the Himalayas.

He told me that he was in training to become a lama.

"Lama?" I asked, being familiar only with the Dalai Lama.

"Lama means teacher. It's a common term among the Buddhists."

Shura and I developed great affection and respect for Karma. I had asked him a hundred questions and heard thoughtful, honest answers, including, "I don't know," and, "I really haven't a clue."

During a small party at the Farm on the Fourth of July (Shura's and my wedding anniversary), I sat with Karma at a table under the big market umbrella on the patio outside the dining room, and we talked about various practices and traditions of Buddhism. Most of the other guests had drifted out to the barbecue patio, on the other side of the house, and Karma and I didn't have to expect too many interruptions.

Eventually, we got onto the subject of chakras — those energy centers in the body which have been studied for centuries by Buddhist spiritual teachers, among others — and it occurred to me that this was the one person who might, just possibly, understand what I was talking about, if I told him about my lucid dreams of the sexual kind.

I introduced the subject by saying, "I have something rather interesting I'd like to describe to you. It's an experience I've shared only with Shura because it's a very personal matter, but perhaps you could tell me — ah — have you ever heard anything like this before?"

After I'd described the nature of the dream experience, I asked him, "Is there a name for this kind of thing; is it known to the Buddhists?"

Karma looked at me and nodded, smiling slightly, "That center, right above the pubic bone, is called the Secret Place, in Buddhism."

*Well, that isn't exactly what you'd call a startlingly original name, but so be it.*

"The Secret Place? And am I correct in assuming that this sort of intense sexual experience is — ummm — not unknown, then?"

"Well," said Karma, "Let me tell you about when it happened to me."

*Omigod! This, I didn't expect!*

"It was around six months ago," Karma said, "And I was fully awake. I'd gone off into the hills to have an LSD experience, and I was alone. Everything was especially rich and magical, and I was just sitting there, taking in the beauty, when suddenly I felt an extraordinary thing happening just — as you said — above the pubic bone. Nothing in the genitals. But it was a tremendous, fierce sexual desire, and a push to — to completion. And when the orgasm happened, it was certainly one of the most intense I've ever had. It left me feeling totally surprised and very good. In body and soul."

"Do you know what it means?"

Karma sat back and sighed, "Just an intuition, but I don't really know. Do you have any ideas?"

"Well," I said, "My answer is an intuition, too, but what I feel is that it was a message from the deep, wise part of my soul, reminding me that I'm alive and that there are extraordinary forces inside me, and — and that life really *is* worth living, all evidence to the contrary notwithstanding. Something like that."

Karma nodded thoughtfully, "And that we're basically healthy and functioning, no matter how depressed or tired we might feel sometimes. Yes."

I leaned forward over the table, under its big green umbrella, delighted at finally being able to share all this with somebody who had experienced it himself. I said, "I can't believe it! The first time I take a chance on telling somebody — I mean other than Shura — it turns out to be *exactly* the right person!"

Karma grinned, "By the way, this is the first time I've told anybody, too. After that day, I kept wondering whether it could happen the same way for a woman, and now I know. In fact, from your description, there's no difference at all!"

"Except that yours was fully awake! I've never had it happen except in dreams. Lucid dreams, but still dreams."

"The Secret Place," he repeated, "And I'm glad you got up the courage to ask me. We've both had some questions answered."

"Thank you, thank you," I laughed, "It's always good to have one's strange, solitary experience confirmed by someone else. Has it ever happened again, since that one time?"

"Never. I should make that 'Not yet' anyway,'" said Karma, "But I keep hoping. I keep hoping." He chuckled as I nodded my head vehemently.

"For Pete's sake, let me know if it happens to you again. I know that's a lot for me to ask, but I'm asking it anyway, because I have a lot of nerve, I guess, and I really want to know."

"If I'm graced with a repeat performance, I'll be happy to tell you. I don't mind at all."

So far, no news from Karma. And my own dreams of this kind are coming less frequently, now — perhaps about once every three or four months — but I'm grateful when I have one, and always wake from it with a sense of deep satisfaction and healthiness, and a feeling of what I can only describe as awe.

# CHAPTER 13.  FLASHBACKS

(Shura's voice)

There was a conference held in San Francisco, in approximately mid-December, 1991, dedicated to the topic of LSD.  It was hosted by the Drug Enforcement Administration, and invitations were extended not only to some of its staff, but to a number of officials of several police organizations around the world.  There were invitees from The Netherlands, Great Britain and Australia, amongst other countries.  The head count was around 200, and it was a two-day event.  The nominal host was Mr. Robert C. Bonner, who was at that time the acting head of the DEA.  And since many law enforcement administrators believed that the majority of the world's production of LSD actually took place in the San Francisco Bay Area, what better place could there be than San Francisco for a conference to discuss LSD problems?

Some time before the conference was to occur, I received word that I would probably be extended an invitation to present some of the history and background material as to the origin and early uses of the drug.  An actual invitation arrived about a month ahead of the meeting, from somebody in Washington I did not personally know.  However, my book PIHKAL had just appeared and I foresaw possible problems, not for myself necessarily, but for my acquaintance in the DEA who had suggested my name for the invitees' list in the first place.  I got back in touch with him and mentioned that there might be a few people in the law enforcement world who would view PIHKAL not as the wealth of factual information that it was (thus being of value to them) but as a work promoting the use of psychedelic drugs (thus being an offense to them).  In the latter case, there might be some question asked, like, "Who invited HIM here?" and this might put a bit of egg on my invitor's face.  I sent him a copy of the book making clear that, as far as I was concerned, there had been no actual, official invitation yet extended.

Apparently some discrete inquiries were made, and I received a call from my original contact saying, gently and diplomatically, that I had been dis-invited. The original invitation had apparently never been sent to me.

"Was it PIHKAL?" I asked.

"Not really. No one seemed to care, or even know about that."

"Why the no-show at San Francisco, then?" I asked, in as casual and unpushy a way as possible.

"Most divisions felt fine about it, in fact there was a general feeling that you could make a good contribution to the meeting. But one division was somewhat uncomfortable."

"Uncomfortable?"

"Well," he continued, "They were afraid that you might engage Bonner in a public debate that could prove embarrassing."

Indeed! I tried to visualize myself, a gray-haired old codger of an academic stripe, walking up to one of the most powerful law-enforcement men in the country, second only to the head of the FBI or the Attorney General, and initiating a verbal battle that would be embarrassing. To whom?, I asked myself. Somewhere, I thought, somebody has a very misguided opinion of someone! Was it the chief honcho who might be embarrassed by a debate with me? That doesn't speak well of their view of him. Were they afraid that I would be embarrassed? Why should anyone care how I felt? I could even see that there might be joy in certain quarters if I were to be tripped up and stumble into some public idiocy. Were they concerned that the Administration would be embarrassed? What was so fragile about their structure if one person could bring about such an imagined disgrace? And certainly it revealed the strange light in which some people view me, that they thought I would even consider such a stupid confrontation.

I did not participate, of course, but I did hear quite a bit, both officially and unofficially, about what went on. It turned out that the Angels had smiled upon me by keeping me home. It would have been more than just embarrassment. Had I been there, I would either have spoken up, and undoubtedly been most disruptive, or I would have kept quiet, and been completely ashamed of myself.

It seems that a holy war, a Jihad, was declared that day on LSD. It was portrayed as a thing of absolute evil which had to be eliminated at any cost. The Catholic Church had defined the witch as an enemy and death on the wheel was too kind a fate. The Muslim tribunal had decided that the heathen Christian devil was the embodiment of evil and was to be disemboweled. The law-enforcement powers that day had declared LSD to be an agent with unbelievably destructive potential which had to be eradicated.

I can't relate the actual texts that were delivered but let me try to give the flavor of this rampage. Much of the vitriol was directed at the people associated with the drug. There are the criminals who make it. According to the authorities, they are concentrated here in the San Francisco Bay Area, which is truly the head of this monster whose tendrils extend around the world. There are the "sociopathic therapists" who sneak out into the woods every week, to access their hidden supplies of the ergotamine tartrate precursor. There, they cook up what they need for distribution amongst other therapists, for the use of their patients, and for supplying others such as school kids. These misguided therapists continue to espouse the myth that LSD has some value in medical practice. This is, of course, a rationalization of their own shameful addiction to the drug.

But some of the anger was directed to the drug itself. One of the most outrageous properties given it was the capability of hiding away for years and years inside the human body, only to reappear after much time had passed and produce a flashback. The mechanisms that were offered to explain this event were so bizarre as to be humorous, had they only been offered in the spirit of comedy. Unfortunately they were presented and accepted in total seriousness. It was stated to the attendees that even a single exposure to LSD can squirrel away a few lingering molecules in the frontal lobes of the brain where they might well stay hidden for as long as twenty years. Then they can suddenly reappear, provoking what has been called, clinically, an LSD flashback, which can cause the victim to become psychotic. Obvious examples were evident right here in San Francisco, said these flashback advocates. In the late 1960's there was the Summer of Love, with the prodigious use of psychedelic drugs, especially LSD. And look at the streets of the city today! The homeless, the psychotic, the disenfranchised! The implied explanation was that they had taken LSD, and finally the tucked-away molecules had descended from the frontal lobes, bringing about this modern-day tragedy.

The truth is that once LSD is put into the body, it produces its effects, then it and its metabolites are washed out quickly. The half-life in the blood is less than three hours, which says that however much might be there initially, there will be only half that amount three hours later. Even if the metabolic machinery of the body ignored it, the dose would be over 99% excreted in a day. With a monster dose going in on Monday, there would be only one percent of it there on Tuesday, and there is no analytical tool known that could detect it on Wednesday. If any molecule of a drug, or if even a trillion molecules of a drug, can precipitate a psychotic state, then that drug is of unprecedented potency. This is simply fantasy. It has never been observed. It exists only in the dedicated minds of law enforcement and in the publications of those who make their living on the drug scare.

But, says the uneducated skeptic, maybe the LSD levels are dropping, not because they are being excreted into the urine and removed from the body, but because they are being absorbed and stored in the fatty tissue, and perhaps this fat depository is in the brain. Maybe it is in the frontal lobes! There is an earlier track record of the alleged brain fat and brain storage status, offered by a Presidential appointee, of another illegal drug. John Lawn, the head of the DEA under the Reagan administration, gave an address at the Commonwealth Club in San Francisco in February, 1986. In the question and answer session that followed, he received a written query from the floor.

"What's wrong with legalizing marijuana?" he was asked.

He replied without hesitation, "I think that if we decide upon legalization, we can forget democracy as we now know it. In experimental animals, mutations in the brain caused by marijuana are found not only in the user or the user's offspring, but in the offspring's offspring. The dangers associated with cannabis are different than those associated with alcohol. Marijuana is fat-soluble and one third of the brain is fat." According to this theory, the flashback (or here more likely a mutation) is seen not just twenty years later, but two generations later! Molecules are magically being shipped from father to son to grandson by some DNA process rather than by simple frontal lobe storage.

None of this information has ever been even remotely documented.

Flashbacks are real. Everyone has experienced them. They have no unique relationship to LSD. They have nothing to do with psychosis.

I had one recently, at the Spring concert weekend, at the redwood retreat of the Owl Club. The last selection that we were playing was a medley of the music of Duke Ellington. This was put together by a dear musician friend of mine from Los Angeles, and was entitled something like, "To Duke, With Love." While sawing away on my viola, I was suddenly reminded of a concert I had attended, in the winter of 1941 or 1942, in downtown Boston. It was a concert of Duke Ellington's music put on by The Duke himself and his band, and it was, at least for me, very impressive. I can't remember if it was the concert itself, or maybe it was the first number on the program, that was entitled, "Black, Brown and Beige." It had been snowing lightly during my long walk from Wigglesworth Hall (up in Cambridge, at Harvard, where there was at that time no obvious black, or brown, or beige) down to the Symphony Hall, and I had not thought to brush the collected snow out of my hair. As I sat in the crowded audience and the show got underway, the snow began to melt, and there was water trickling down my neck. I remember my intense embarrassment due to the fact that I did not dare shake my head (I would get all the surrounding people wet) and I could in no way stop the melting process. I was stuck, and destined to suffer the concert with a wet shirt.

And now here, over fifty years later, a remarkable event had occurred at my Owl Club retreat which was, for me, a flashback. As I swung into those themes from Duke Ellington's music, I felt water again trickling down my neck. Felt it with such authenticity that I actually had to put my hand up to my neck to check it out. Here I was, sitting in my present day world, in the direct sunshine, feeling my neck to see if it was wet! There was no LSD involved. If one wished to invoke past LSD use in any way as a contributing factor, then why not invoke any of the many other exposures I have had to remarkable phenomena? Maybe the climbing to the top of Mount Lassen, or piloting a Cessna 172 to Redding and refueling it there. Both of these occurred, and both were dramatic. It was the drama of the original event, and the trigger that allowed it to be relived, that provided the context of the flashback. Drugs need not be involved at all.

A few days later I was telling this story to a friend, and he gave me another example. His neighbor had been making his daily walk home from the train station following work, on the day of the Loma Prieta earthquake. He was about five minutes from his home when the earthquake struck. The ground ahead of him seemed to undulate up and down, and he became panicked as he thought he was experiencing a heart attack. It was only when he noticed that the telephone wires overhead were swaying back and forth that he realized the trauma was outside him, not within him. Nonetheless, the very next day, walking at the same time and at that very spot, he was hit with dizziness and light-headedness.

A flashback is triggered by some connection to a memorable event. And here was one certainly not involving LSD or any other "dangerous drug," as the man apparently was, and still is, a drug virgin.

Memorable? It is not really necessary that the remembered situation thought to be responsible for the flashback be documentably dramatic. Re-read Proust's *Swann's Way*. Nothing more was needed for his flashback than a bite of a madeleine that had been dipped in lime-blossom tea. Just a taste of this and he was catapulted back into an earlier time. A familiar smell, word, or sound, can catalyze a cascade of memories, which can be sufficiently intense to, in effect, allow some past event to be relived. And, without question, an intense LSD experience might focus your attention sharply on some sensory input. At some later time, a re-experiencing of that input might bring back the memory of the LSD event.

The event involved might be objectively trivial but, to you, important. Blame the brain and the marvelous workings of the mind for the phenomenon, but certainly don't blame the LSD. And, by all means, don't waste time looking for some lost molecule in the frontal lobes of the brain. It just ain't there.

# CHAPTER 14.  THE INTENSIVE

(Alice's voice)

Audrey Fenn Redman came into my life — and I into hers — in a way that one would have to describe as decidedly unusual. It was a spring day in the 1980's, and Shura answered the phone in his office. I was in the living room, sorting photographs for an album, when I heard the buzzer on my desk giving the code for, "Pick up the phone quietly, and listen in."

When I had the receiver to my ear, a woman's voice was saying, "Glad you remember that lunch, because it'll save a lot of time. I don't expect you to remember what we talked about, the three of us, but we had a lot of fun — "

Shura interrupted with a laugh, "We certainly did! We left poor Peter floundering, I'm afraid — all that bouncing around of crazy ideas. I don't know what got into us! How is Peter, by the way?"

The woman said, hurriedly, "He's fine, as far as I know, Shura. I haven't seen him in years, and we don't talk on the phone much, these days, but he's a full professor now, and seems to be pretty happy."

Shura must have heard the increasing stress in her voice, because he got to the point, "Well, Audrey, you began by saying that you've got an unusual problem, and I'm — "

Audrey interrupted him, "You're probably the only person I know who might make some sense of this. I realize that sounds strange, after years of hearing nothing from me, but I sent out a very strong request — I guess you could call it a prayer — for the universe to send somebody who could help me, and your face popped up on the mental screen. I mean, I certainly didn't expect that — especially considering that we only met once and don't really know each other — but that's what happened."

Shura grunted encouragement.

"So, here I am," the voice continued. "And it's such a weird story, I don't quite know how to — well, I'll just give you a bit of background, so you'll have some idea of where this all started."

"Go ahead," said Shura, and I could hear the creak of his leather office chair, which meant he was settling back in it. "I'm listening."

"I have a patient," began Audrey, then hastily interrupted herself. "Oh, I should remind you that I'm a psychologist and certified hypnotherapist, here in Marin County — I'm sure you know the town of Mill Creek?"

"Sure," said Shura.

"I also teach hypnotherapy; I have private patients and I conduct seminars; I've written a book and I'm doing very, very well."

"Great," said Shura cheerfully.

"I'm very good at what I do, okay?"

*Funny; why is she trying so hard to convince him?*

There was a fractional pause, then Shura said, "Okay."

Audrey went on, "I have one patient who has a problem of the type I don't usually deal with, and I suppose the reason I took her on was that it was a tremendous challenge, and I felt I had a lot to learn from trying to help her. It's a case of so-called demonic possession. It's nothing like the Exorcist, in case you ever read it or saw the movie — "

"Nope, never did," said Shura.

"Just as well. This lady is in her 20's, Catholic — and I've got to tell you that the majority of possession cases are female and Catholic, or were at least raised Catholic during their formative years."

Shura mumbled, "Uh-huh."

"Anyway," continued Audrey, "The only time the demonic stuff happens is during holy days — Christmas, Easter — and that's not unusual in these cases, either. All this has been going on for years, ever since she was a teenager. She's married to a very nice man who's genuinely worried about her. He's supportive and very patient, thank God; he just wants this whole business resolved."

"Yes, of course," said Shura.

"All right. Anyway. Now we get to the big day. It was just a few weeks ago. Easter. I got a call at home — I live in a big house that sometimes doubles as my office — and there was my client, Cherry, crying for help, obviously out of control, then her husband got on the line and asked if he could bring her to me, so I could see for myself what one of these — these attacks — was like. I'd never seen her in the middle of one with my own eyes. I told him to bring her over, if he thought it was safe to have her in the car in this state while he drove.

"As soon as he'd hung up, I phoned an old friend of mine who's a Jesuit priest, and told him that I was about to open my home to an apparent case of demonic possession, and I thought he might want to practice the rites of exorcism. I said it certainly couldn't hurt, and might help, because the victim was a Catholic. He said he'd never done one before, but of course he was intrigued and would gather up whatever he thought was necessary and hurry over."

"Oh, my!" said Shura, obviously getting involved, as was I.

Audrey paused, and I heard the sound of quick swallowing.

*Her throat is dry. Wonder if it's water or alcohol in the glass.*

"My friend the priest lives nearby, so he got to my house before the others; they live in the East Bay. He showed me his little bottle of holy water, and told me he would use the waiting time to bone up on the exorcism ritual. He was trying to be dignified and very serious, but I could tell he was excited at the prospect of actually seeing a case of possession — or presumed possession — live and in color, for the first time in his life, you know?"

"Yeah," said Shura, "I can imagine!"

"When Cherry arrived, her husband was with her. She was so pale, I wondered for a moment if she had any blood in her. I helped her onto one couch, and the husband and I sat on the other, and watched while my Jesuit friend got to work. He was very impressive, Shura. He'd done his homework, and he really rose to the occasion. A lot of intensity and passion and wonderful Latin phrases. And holy water, of course."

"Uh-huh," muttered Shura, "And — ?"

"It seemed to work. She stopped shaking, and the crying began to taper off. She was breathing more evenly, and there was more color in her face. All this took about an hour. And just as I was starting to relax, I caught sight of something out of the corner of my eye. It was a — an impression of a dark — a dark thing — a streak of black — moving very fast between Cherry's couch and the door to the dining room. An impression, you understand, too quick for me to turn and focus. Then my big dog, Hera, who is never, *never* spooked by anything, Shura — she's a true Buddha-dog — growled and got up from the carpet where she'd been lying all evening, and took off. I mean, she was going so fast, her nails slipped on the wooden floor, scrabbling desperately for purchase, then she was gone. She was terrified, Shura; she just wanted out of there. I've never seen her act that way, not in six years. Not even when we had a small earthquake; I've never seen her frightened of *any*thing!"

I heard another pause and a couple of swallowing sounds, then Audrey continued.

"In just a few minutes, everybody was fine; Cherry was back on her feet and full of smiles, thanking the priest; her husband hugged me; the only person there who wasn't completely satisfied with the whole thing was me. Or I. Whatever. But I got them all out the door, then I spent a lot of time calling for Hera, but she wouldn't come. She stayed out all night. That's the first time, Shura; she's never done that before."

Holding fingers over the mouthpiece of my phone, I reached for my coffee cup, sipped, then lit another cigarette.

"Okay," said Audrey, speaking slowly, "Now we get to the really difficult part, the truly weird part, Shura."

"I'm listening," he said.

*So am I, so am I.*

"Since that evening, I've been in a state — something happened to me that night. For one thing, I sense something here with me, in my house, and it's not benign. I don't feel it all the time, thank God, but when I get home from the office, my poor dog is a nervous wreck, and there's something — I think it's left over from the exorcism, Shura — and I don't know what I'm supposed to do with it. "

"Uh-huh," said Shura, almost absently. I knew he was thinking hard, as was I.

"But that's not the worst part. I haven't felt really normal since Easter. I feel as if I've taken some kind of strange psychedelic; I took a lot of them when I was in college, you know, and this is a state very much like being on a low dose of a drug. I know I'm supposed to learn something, or change something, or experience something, but I don't know what it is. I have questions like: am I supposed to resist this dark presence that seems to have attached itself to me; should I call back my friend the priest and have him exorcise a nice Jewish girl who seems to have adopted a Catholic demon? Or am I supposed to seek it out and learn its nature and discover what it wants to teach me? You see my dilemma?"

"I certainly can," said Shura, "And the fact that you seem to be in an altered state would imply, to me, that some sort of process is trying to work itself out. Have you talked to any of your peers? Other professionals who might — "

"I can't go to anyone I know, Shura. I don't have to tell you what they'd say. Psychotic episode. Treat with the usual tranquilizers. They aren't equipped to deal with this area, you know, the spiritual, the psychic. At least, none of the people I know would have the slightest idea how to go about handling this kind of thing. That's why I thought maybe you — "

"Well," interrupted Shura, and I could hear the chair creak as he sat forward, "How about coming up here and meeting my wife, Alice, and we can talk about it and see what we come up with."

There was a small pause, and when she spoke again I could tell from the tone of Audrey's voice that the introduction of an unknown stranger into the mix wasn't what she had expected, but she agreed to clear her calendar for Wednesday of the following week, when Shura would be home. After he had given her detailed directions to our place, the conversation ended with her intense whisper, "Thank you, Shura. Whether you can help me or not, thanks for listening to me. It feels good to have told somebody. It really does."

"See you next week, my friend. Let's see what we can do."

Shura hurried into the living room, grinning. "Well, how do you like *them* potatoes?"

"Pretty interesting. Pretty damned interesting," I smiled back, "And maybe you can fill me in on your lunch with her all those years ago; what was your impression?"

"Oh, yeah," Shura said, "There was an old student of mine, Peter Somebody-or-other — his name'll come back to me — and he phoned and said he wanted to collar me for lunch, and he'd have his girlfriend with him. So I went out to lunch with them in some place off-campus, and she turned out to be one of those super-smart, cocky young things who loves word-play and puns and all that kind of stuff. We had a ball — at Peter's expense, I'm afraid — just showing off to each other, you know, having fun with our own brilliance."

"What do you mean, 'at Peter's expense'?"

"Oh, I don't mean we ganged up on him; nothing like that. It's just that, after a while, I think he felt somewhat left out. He pretty much was. We just kind of ignored him. Not very nice, but we got caught up in our own little act, and it was hard to stop because we were both flying high. I felt a little bit ashamed afterwards, thinking about poor ole Peter with his big smile getting smaller, you know, as Audrey and I juggled our pretty balls in the air."

I chuckled at the mental picture, then asked for more details about Audrey.

Shura eased himself into the big comfy armchair next to the bookcase.

"I don't remember her that well, really," he said, after a moment's search through the memory bank, "But I have the impression of a very, very sharp mind, somewhat aggressive, not my type, I'm afraid, but a good sense of humor and a sparkle in the face. That's about it. Never heard from her again, until today. As a matter of fact, I don't think I heard from Peter again, either. I'm afraid I forgot about both of them."

"Tall, short, fat, blonde, dark hair—?"

"Uh — tall and skinny — yes, tall and thin and dark hair."

"Okay. I'll see for myself on Wednesday, I guess."

Audrey Redman arrived soon after noon, and I saw for myself. Taller than I, probably five feet six or seven, I thought, as I shook her hand. Somewhere in her late thirties. A heart-shaped face which, while it wasn't pretty, had an attractive aliveness, with deeply intelligent hazel eyes, under a curly cap of reddish-brown hair. When she smiled, it was only with the mouth, not the eyes.

*She's holding herself under strict control, this lady. Must be a lot of fear inside.*

After I'd done my hostess thing, serving iced tea and a plate of cookies, I sat down with both of them at the dining room table and we began to talk. Shura told Audrey that he had filled me in on the basic story, and I began asking questions.

Audrey's initial hesitation in talking about this private and difficult matter with a woman she'd only just met seemed to disappear as she heard in my voice no skepticism, no rejection of anything she was saying, only strong interest and acceptance, which was what I intended her to hear. The tension around her eyes smoothed out gradually, as we talked.

"I've never had anything like this happen before, I've got to tell you," she said with a short laugh, one hand making a gesture of emphasis, "And nothing I've experienced, in years of working with people's darker sides, prepared me for that — whatever that thing was which left Cherry and raced across the room. And which I think is still in my home. I wasn't ready for that. I'm not a Catholic, and I don't believe in the devil. But I do believe in the existence of evil, at least in the world of human beings. And something evil was made — well — almost physical, manifest somehow, in that room. And I'm still feeling a shadow of it — a piece of it — in my house."

All attempts at smiling, or sounding lighthearted, had been abandoned by now. Audrey's shoulders were slumped, and her hands gripped each other on the table; I wondered briefly if she was afraid they would shake if she let them loose.

She glanced up at each of us in turn, "What am I supposed to do with all of it? That's the major question. What do I do to get rid of this *entity* — or the residue that I keep sensing in my place, and that's still spooking my beautiful dog? Whatever it is — wherever it's from — what am I supposed to learn?"

"You teach hypnotherapy, Audrey," I said, "Have you tried getting into trance, to see what comes up?"

"Of course I have," she answered, with a touch of impatience, "And the results have been disturbing, to say the least. I think I told you, I'm going around in a state that feels pretty much off baseline, as Shura would say. As soon as I go into trance, all hell breaks loose. The mental screen fills up with images and they're all dark. I can't get any light in at all. I feel as if I'm under attack, as if something's sitting on my chest, weighing me down, pushing on me, demanding something, and I just have to get out."

I waited, feeling that there was more to come, not wanting to distract her.

"I have to admit I'm afraid," said Audrey, "The trance state makes me feel too vulnerable, so I've given up trying to get answers that way."

All three of us were silent for a moment.

At this time in my life I had begun, very slowly, during the previous year or so, learning how to guide people through an experience of MDMA, in order to gain insight into their problems. I saw very few people, perhaps one a week, and was gradually gaining a certain amount of confidence in myself as a therapist. I seemed to have an instinct for how to go about it.

I had gone through the inevitable mistakes and learned from them. I had even reached the point at which you understand that mistakes are going to happen, and the only thing that matters is being aware of them and admitting errors openly to yourself and the client, without defensiveness. So far, I had done no harm, and occasionally seemed to have helped a great deal. Every time I began work with a new client, I faced as calmly and honestly as I could my own lack of experience and inadequacy of knowledge; I was learning quite a lot of humility.

Shura and I had already discussed the possibility of my working with Audrey, using MDMA, if it seemed appropriate when I had a chance to talk to her. But now I was facing this sharp-edged, obviously intelligent woman, whose attitude and somewhat staccato way of talking managed to make it clear that she wasn't the type to suffer fools gladly. I felt a hollow in my stomach.

*This is the kind of female I stay away from. Judgmental, impatient, demanding; I could never work with someone like this; I'm simply not that sure of myself or what I know.*

Nonetheless, I heard myself saying, "Have you ever heard of a drug called MDMA, Audrey?"

"Yes, I've heard some mentions of it, but that's all. Why?"

"Well," I replied, "It's a quite extraordinary drug, not a psychedelic, but something else. It's a superb tool for psychotherapy. I have a paper I'll give you which describes its effects. I wrote this and a corresponding one on another drug called 2C-B, a few years ago, signed by the well-known Anonymous, and I think it might be of help to you."

"In what way?"

"Oh, yes, of course. I'm sorry, I didn't explain what I had in mind," I apologized, already feeling like the idiot I would undoubtedly prove myself to be if I tried working with this person.

*This is an animus woman, and I stay away from animus women; I certainly don't volunteer to do therapy with them. Especially considering the fact that she's a highly trained therapist, and I'm a highly untrained one.*

"What I had in mind was possibly trying a session with MDMA, with you, to see if you can get some new perspective on what's happening to you. It might help trigger some kind of breakthrough. If it doesn't work, then you certainly won't be the worse for it, anyway. What do you think? Want to give it a try?"

"Jesus," muttered Audrey, dropping her head into her hands. After a moment, she looked up and turned to Shura. "What do you think about this? Should I do it?"

"It's a good drug, Audrey. It works for an awful lot of people. And, as Alice says, it can't hurt you. At worst, you won't get any insights, and you may feel a bit tired the next day, but — after all — what can you lose? You seem to be up against a brick wall; at least, that's what it sounds like to me. Why don't you give it a try? Alice is pretty good at doing this kind of thing, or so they tell me."

"Who tells you?" I grinned at him.

"Oh — people. You know, the occasional grateful survivor!"

"Right!"

We both laughed and turned back to our guest, who was trying to smile and not quite managing it.

*Why am I doing this? I don't know if I like this lady, and I can't work with someone I don't like. On the other hand, she's really in a bind, and the whole demon thing is intriguing. It can't hurt to do one session and see what happens.*

Suddenly, Audrey's face brightened. She said, "I've brought a tape with me; it shows how I work. I tape some of my hypnotherapy sessions, to use in seminars, and I thought you might want to know that side of me."

"Sure, I'd love to see it," I nodded, feeling less than maximum enthusiasm.

*What if the tape confirms the aspects of her which already make me uneasy? I can't go back on my offer. It'll just make me that much more uncomfortable about the whole prospect. Oh, what the hell; may as well watch it and see what I can learn.*

"Let's take it into the living room," I said, rising, "That's where the TV is."

She followed me and watched while I took the tape from her and put it into the VCR.

"Make yourself comfortable on the couch, Audrey," I said, picking up the remote control and sitting myself down on a large floor pillow, facing the television.

During the next hour, I watched mesmerized as a completely different Audrey, a woman with the warmth of a loving mother, the intuition and instincts of a truly inspired therapist, and seemingly infinite patience, worked with a young man suffering from cancer, in a sunlit room in Arizona. Tears were drying on my cheeks when the tape ended.

"Hoo Boy!" I said, and blew my nose on a Kleenex.

"I just wanted you to see that side of me," said Audrey, quietly, her face showing relief and even pleasure at my response, "And how I work."

*This Audrey — the one on the tape — THIS Audrey I could work with!*

We made an appointment for an exploratory session using MDMA, in two weeks.

For the first time, as I always do with first times, I gave Audrey only 100 milligrams of the drug, because — although that amount is considered rather low — I've seen it result in a full-blown plus-three in a sensitive person. I told her, "Even if it turns out to be less effective than you might like, it'll give you a chance to know the material, get comfortable with it, and we can up the dosage level a bit next time."

I also reminded her that, at about the hour and a half point, she could have a supplement of 40 milligrams, which wouldn't increase the effect at all, but would simply stretch it out longer before it began declining. "If you really want the supplement — if things are going well for you, and you want it to continue at full effect for another hour — you can take it. But there's no obligation to do so, okay? The only negatives will be a slight increase in the jaw clench and nystagmus, but most people aren't that bothered by them."

I told her that she could do anything she felt like during the transition — sit, lie down, walk around — whatever was comfortable for her, and that she could talk or not, as she wished. I listened to my own voice, and noted that it had already softened, slowed and dropped slightly in pitch, as it tended to do during sessions.

Audrey chose to lie down on the couch during the transition, and spoke only to comment on the effects of the drug, as she became aware of them, "Yes, I see what you mean when you said it's like no other sensation you've ever had. It's coming in waves, very gentle. I think I like it."

I stayed silent, watching her. It took time for her hands to relax, but finally they lay at her sides as she breathed slowly, eyes closed.

*Wonder if she's letting herself go into trance?*

She was. It was my first experience with someone who was familiar with hypnotic trance, and the first clue that one could employ it successfully with MDMA.

We had begun.

Audrey came up to the Farm one day each week, and we would work together for around six hours, using MDMA at the level of 120 milligrams and adding a supplement of 40 milligrams, which she always chose to take at the appropriate time. She employed the trance state, which no longer threatened her. From the first session, the images had been clear and powerful, without any suggestion of the confusion and murky danger-ousness she had run into before. It was as if, once she had made the decision to uncover and understand her own buried darkness, her psyche opened and sent images of teachers, human and animal, to help the process.

If there was a crucial breakthrough in progress when the sixth hour ended, we would keep going until it was resolved. We called the sessions "intensives." I had been doing such sessions with other people, and had learned a great deal about many aspects of the human unconscious (including my own), but this was the first time I had worked in such depth with repressed dark side material — what Carl Jung called the Shadow — and it was both exhausting and tremendously exciting.

We dealt with the images and emotions that arose, most of them having to do with her childhood, growing up with an emotionally cold mother and a manipulative, judgemental father, trying to salvage what she could of self-validation, while her unconscious self-image grew darker and more twisted.

Over the weeks, she reported the gradual diffusion of the hostile strangeness which had haunted her house for the past many weeks.

"Hera's acting her old self, again," she told me cheerfully, one day, "I think the nasty from Easter has gone."

"Have any idea why it left?"

"Well," Audrey grinned, "It's beginning to look to me like it was a form of my own dark side, my own Beast. It was clamoring for my attention, needing to get resolved, and it took the exorcism as an opportunity to emerge. Now that I'm working it through, giving it that attention, there's no need for it to hang around. What do you think?"

"I suspect you're right on the money. And it must mean you're doing what your psyche wanted you to do with it."

"Yes," she said, "Oh, yes. Funny, how I've done dark side work with patients for years and years, and never stopped to realize I hadn't done my own!"

Early in our work, I had told her about my experience of my own dark side, what I called "The Maggot At The Bottom Of The Well," and the resolution — or the beginning of it, anyway — when I had visualized myself opening a door in my stomach and tucking inside it for warmth and nurturing the pathetic, cringing, self-hating, dirty little maggot-become-baby which was my unconscious self-image. Becoming mother to my rejected child-self.

I also gave her the image of the volcano, a mountain full of red-hot lava, which she could find just above her navel, where anger, old and new, could be located, and from whose top the lava of fury and outrage could be dribbled, safely, at a rate of her own choosing.

"When you practice letting that lava begin to flow, just a bit," I said, "And find out you can stop it whenever you want to, your unconscious begins to let go of the fear of having the whole world blow up, of getting lost in the firestorm, if any of that outrage is let loose."

Audrey nodded, "I can see how years and years of anger and frustration must have built up, to the point where my psyche felt it couldn't risk ventilating any of it, because there was just so much. As you said, there must have been a deep-seated fear that if it blew, it would take all of me with it!"

When, after months of work, Audrey finally faced her monster, it was a furry, black, spider-like entity which didn't expect to be seen, and had never before been looked at with the conscious mind. It kept trying to slide out of sight, until finally she trapped it and moved toward it. Then, deep in the trance state, she managed the most terrifying step of all — moving into the monster, looking out through its eyes — and discovered its exhilarating strength, its lack of fear, its determination to keep the entire structure, the entire identity that was Audrey, safe from harm, either physical or emotional.

"So the monster is also the Survivor, the part of you concerned only with keeping you alive and well," I said. "Once you get inside its skin, you can see that it can actually be your ally."

"My God," replied Audrey, opening her eyes, "What an amazing experience! I actually liked being inside it; there was no fear at all, just power — tremendous power!"

"How do you feel about it, now? Do you still hate it?"

"Yes. No. Not hate, anymore; dislike. It's a part of me that I can't help rejecting. It's still a monster, Alice. How can I like something like that — accept it — even if it serves a protective purpose?"

"It looks the way it does because it represents everything you were afraid you were, when you were a kid; your parents never validated you, honey. So, gradually, you developed an unconscious self-image of something unlovable, nasty, completely unacceptable. The little girl became a monster, because only a monster would have such a hard time getting anyone to show love and acceptance. Of course, once it settled in as resident beast, it had nothing to fear but being uncovered, so it became very, very strong. I mean, if you have to be a beast, yes?, may as well be the bestest beast on the block!"

"I know," said Audrey, "I understand all that, intellectually. But it's still hard to approach it with anything but disgust."

"That's okay, my dear," I reassured her, "You've done tremendous work today, and you deserve to pat yourself on the back for being a damned courageous, strong lady. This was tough stuff, and you did it!"

During the following weeks, we took the next step, moving slowly against Audrey's emotional resistance, working on having her take the spider thing into her arms, to feel the beginnings of compassion for it, some stirrings of pity for the unloved little girl who had grown to believe that this monster was who she was.

Finally, one extraordinary day, we both watched the black, filthy horror gradually transform into a huddled, grief-stricken child, and I moved over to the couch with Audrey and held her as she sobbed in my arms. I became the Good Mother she'd never had, rocking the long adult body which had been taken over by an agonized four-year-old. I cried with her.

Uncounted time later, I returned to my chair, leaving Audrey sitting up on the couch, beginning to smile, tears drying on her cheeks.

"Well, sweetheart," I said, grinning broadly, "It's done. You've done it. We're finished."

"Yes, I know we are," she said, smiling fully now. She stood up and held out her arms, and I went over to her and we held each other tightly.

Two weeks later, I had a phone call from Audrey. In reply to my question, she said, "I'm doing very well, in fact I'm doing beautifully. And I want to ask you something. Don't answer right away; give it some thought, okay?"

"Sure. What is it?"

"I want you to work with me. Be co-therapist with me, just for certain very special patients I've already gone a long way with; they're people I know can go further, if I can introduce them to MDMA. They've done their basic work, but they're capable of a lot of spiritual growth, and what you and I did together makes me believe it can be done with them."

"Well, m'dear," I said, "There's no reason you can't do it yourself, you know. I'll make sure you have the material; you know how to go about it."

"I want to work with you, Alice. I think we'd make a hell of a team. Just one or two patients a week, at the most. I'll pay you, you know. Not much, but something. You have a gift for it, and I think you'll find it tremendously exciting. Think about it, please. Take your time and consider everything. The one problem for you might be the distance you'll have to drive to get here. It's over an hour from your place, at the far end of the town. But please give it some real thought, okay? Phone me when you've made a decision."

I called her two days later, having talked it over with Shura. We had decided, as I told Audrey, that if for any reason I felt it was too much, or not working out for me, I would simply stop. But I knew there was a lot for me to learn, and this was the way to do it. "I'll give it a try, honey. Thank you for asking me. It's going to be very interesting, to say the least."

Thus began my two years of work as a co-therapist with one of the most gifted healers in this country, and the growth of one of the most extraordinary relationships I've ever had with another human being.

## DAN

Audrey lived in a sprawling, two-story Victorian house in the hills behind the town of Mill Creek. She met me at my car and pulled me by the hand through a short wooden gate to show me the large, carefully tended garden in back of the house.

Inside, there was a big kitchen, a dining room with an oval, highly polished table, and the living room where we would do our work. I saw two long, grey tweed couches at right angles to each other, facing a big, red brick fireplace. There were high windows on three sides of the room, and the light coming through them shone softly on the chestnut-satin surface of a long coffee-table. A grey-blue rug covered some of the parquet floor.

"How do you like it?" She was beaming at me, her face full of a child's transparent pride.

"Absolutely beautiful. It's a dream-house," I grinned back at her.

"Sit down, sit down. I'm usually on this couch, and I put my client on the other one."

"I thought you saw your patients — clients — in an office?"

"Most of them, yes. But there's an occasional one I'll do a long session with, you know — somebody who's ready for a breakthrough and needs to have more than the usual hour or two. That sort of thing. I usually have them come here."

I nodded.

Audrey put a hand on my arm, "Would you like some coffee?"

"Sure," I said, "Coffee would be great right now. Mornings are my worst time; I'm a night person, and my creative juices don't start flowing until after four in the afternoon, so a bit of caffeine is a help at whatever the hell hour this is in the morning."

"It's already nine, you ninny! Most of the world is hard at work, earning a living!"

I laughed, "Yeah, I suppose so. I used to be part of the rat-race, as a matter of fact, for more years than I care to remember."

I followed her into the kitchen and looked around while she set to work with an espresso machine sitting on the tile counter. On the refrigerator I saw several cartoons from various magazines, held in place by a variety of magnets, and laughed as I read them.

"You have my taste in humor, you'll be happy to hear!"

"Of course," she said, smiling, "How could it be otherwise?"

We took our coffee cups into the living room and curled up at opposite ends of her favorite couch, both of us dressed comfortably in blue jeans.

"Okay," said Audrey, "The reason I asked you to come an hour ahead of the patient is so that I could give you some background on him, and also, I thought we could talk about how best to go about doing this new — this kind of therapy."

"The intensive. I don't know what else to call it, do you?"

"The intensive seems the best term to use. The only other name that comes to mind is The Long, Long Session, or maybe The Never-ending Session!"

I chuckled, "Yeah, let's go with the dignified one."

"Okay, now, is there anything I don't already know from working with you?"

I sat forward, "Well, there are several things I'd like to go through with you, things I feel are really important, all right?"

"Go ahead," she said, picking up her coffee.

"Most details, we'll figure out as we go along," I began, "But there are a few absolute rules which have to be followed consistently, no exceptions. We can't be careless about them. By the way, I'll bring you the MDMA, enough for quite a few sessions, and you must put it in a safe place, somewhere very private.

"The first rule is that you must get the drug out ahead of time, before the client comes. Nobody should *ever* see where you keep it. MDMA's not illegal — and if the gods are on our side, it never will be — but that doesn't matter. We might want to use something someday that *is* illegal — one of the great classic psychedelics like LSD or mescaline or whatever — for people who are ready for it, and just in case we decide to do that, down the road, we need to have a system in place that'll protect you."

"Sure, okay," she smiled, "Secret panel behind toilet; deep hole between the dahlias. No problem."

"Doing psychotherapy with psychoactive drugs isn't exactly mainstream, after all, although a lot of therapists have been doing it for a long time. It's still something one has to be discrete about. More than discrete. It has to remain totally secret, at least for now. Someday, the political climate may change and we can all go public, but not yet."

"Yes, I know," Audrey nodded, "I can't afford to have any rumors going around that Doctor Redman is giving her clients mind-altering drugs, for God's sake!"

"No, you can't," I agreed, "And here comes rule number two."

I drank some coffee, then rummaged in my purse for a pack of cigarettes and lit one. There was a nice, big ceramic ashtray on the table, so I assumed it was all right to smoke.

"Okay," I said, "So when your patient gets here, have the MDMA already in a glass, and if it's the first time, tell him — or her — that it tastes awful by itself, and that most people like to mix it in fruit juice. Then you pour out his choice of juice into the glass and make whatever appropriate blessing you want, and tell him to drink it down.

"Now, the second rule is this: under no circumstances do you let him take his glass out of the room — which will probably be the kitchen — before he's emptied it; not to the bathroom, not out to the garden. He has to drink it down as you watch. Then you take his glass and rinse it out under the tap."

There was a brief silence, then Audrey said, "No traces of evidence, huh?"

"Yup. It's an unpleasant bit of paranoia, but it's necessary. You'll find that most people will go along with the little ceremony and not ask questions, so that you won't ever have to tell them that they're not allowed to drink it out of your sight. This rule has to be followed, even with someone you've known for years and trust absolutely. No exceptions. It means that you always have deniability."

She nodded, "Deniability. Yes."

"This way, no one can prove that you supplied the drug; the patient could have taken the MDMA or whatever before coming to your house. Okay? Deniability."

I took a moment to draw on my cigarette and sip my coffee, which was getting cool.

"The third rule," I went on, "Is my own personal one. It's not a safety thing, it's the way I want to do things. If a patient is on the edge of an important breakthrough, or if he's already launched into one, it doesn't matter how many hours have gone by, we keep on going until he's out the other side. We never leave a patient stuck in the middle of something important, regardless of how tired we are, okay?"

"I've always followed that rule," replied Audrey, "Most of my trance sessions are ninety minutes, but if something erupts at the end of that time, we just keep going and I apologize to the next patient — if I've got one waiting — or phone and shift later people around."

I beamed at her, "Oh, good, good!"

"The intensives have to be basically open-ended, in other words."

"Yes, exactly," I nodded, "Most of the time, as you know, six hours will be enough; the patient tends to get tired, and you begin to hear repetition instead of new stuff."

"Yeah," Audrey smiled and leaned forward over her knees, "But if the door's ready to open, you can *feel* it; there's all that energy flying around loose; you can smell it coming, like ozone in the air before a storm!"

"Uh-huh," I laughed, "We both know that one!"

She sat back against the couch, "I have no difficulty with any of those rules, Alice, none at all. They all make sense."

"The rest you know from your own experience." I said, "Everyone has to be reminded to drink something, water or juice, throughout the session; no one leaves until he's completely baseline, and if there's any doubt at all, he has to stay the night."

"Yes. I've explained all that to Dan, the patient you'll see today. I said he could take a taxi here and back home, instead of driving his own car, if he doesn't want to risk the chance of getting stuck overnight. And I told him he can't have a friend or relative pick him up, because that would mean involving another person in what's going on here, and that's a no-no."

I nodded, "I usually told the people I worked with that it was okay if they wanted to tell someone close to them about their experiences, *after* we were through working together, but they must never, never pin down exactly where or when it happened, and under no circumstances with whom."

"I've made all that absolutely clear to Dan. He understands."

"Good. Have you got Daniel's MDMA weighed out already, in the kitchen?"

"Yes, Mommy. Already done. One hundred twenty milligrams. And forty for a supplement if he wants one. He's a big, tall guy, so I thought one hundred might be a little light for him."

*He's her patient; I have to trust her instincts.*

I grinned approval. "Okay, then tell me about him; what should I know?"

"First, let me reiterate something I've already told you," said Audrey, putting her coffee cup down on the table, "Which is, that I will never bring up the subject of a psychoactive drug with a patient until I've worked with him, or her, for a minimum of six months — generally closer to a year — and I feel he's completed his basic work on whatever his problems are. By the end of that time, I can be pretty sure of whether or not we've got a good candidate, someone who can learn and keep growing."

I smiled, "Yes, it's a good rule. There may be exceptions, but I'll rely on you to really know your people very well before you make that decision. And, by the way, does Dan understand the precautions about talking on the phone?"

Audrey's face gave me the answer; she'd forgotten that part.

"Didn't mention that. I'll be sure to tell him today. Thanks for reminding me."

"No problem," I said, "Now, what do I need to know?"

Audrey started to answer, and caught herself. She looked intently at me and said, "You know, before I talk about Dan, I'd like to run this by you. I think it should be a part of the intensive."

"Yes, what's that?"

"A contract. It was taught me by one of my best teachers, years ago. Ruth drummed this into me, and I think it applies just as much to work with these drugs as it does to hypnotherapy alone."

"Who is this Ruth?" I asked.

"Someday, you've got to meet her. She lives far down on the

Peninsula, with some horses she loves like members of the family, and she's a tiny dynamo of a woman who knows more about hypnotherapy than anyone except the Founding Pillars, bless her. She's probably never even heard of MDMA or mescaline or any of those things, but she taught me the best of what I know about the use of trance."

I fastened my eyes on Audrey's face, listening intently.

"I always make a contract — a verbal contract — with my patients before beginning hypnotherapy," said Audrey. "And I insist that they repeat the words of the contract, the first time, thinking carefully about what they mean; I want to be sure that the unconscious mind hears all of it clearly. And they have to agree to each provision without reservations, or the therapy never gets going.

"The first rule," continued Audrey, "Is that, although any and all feelings of hostility can be freely expressed in the session, whether I am their object or not, the anger may not be physically acted out against me or my possessions. If the acting out of a traumatic event is needed, I will supply both the opportunity and the means. Otherwise, anger and hate will not cross the line into physical action."

"Let me ask a quick question," I interrupted, "What do you do for a patient who needs to act out something intense, like killing the bad parent, or the sexual abuser?"

Audrey nodded, "Yes. That often happens at a certain point in the therapy, and what I do is put a padded mat and a pillow on the floor and hand the client an old sheet — I have a stack of worn-out sheets and half-sheets in my closet, for exactly that purpose — and let him go to it, tearing the sheet, pounding the pillow, acting the whole thing out against the symbolic Bad Guys. I believe most hypnotherapists do something like that. It works."

"Great!" I said, nodding.

Audrey smiled and went on, "The second rule is exactly the same as number one, but applies to sexual feelings. No matter what the fantasy or urges or whatever, you can and should talk about it, but no physical acting out allowed.

"Finally, they must agree that, if an opportunity to go over the threshold into death presents itself in the trance state, and they're tempted, for any reason, they are not to do so. Or, to put it another way, 'You will not die on my time, in my house or office, because your death would cause me harm, and you will not cause me harm, as I will not cause you harm.'"

I nodded my head vehemently.

*Why didn't that occur to me? Of course, people have been known to meet up with the door to the other side — it happened to me that day on peyote — and they've been tempted to go through it. I wasn't, but somebody else might be. I didn't realize that could happen in trance, too.*

Audrey went on, "I know the way I said it sounds cold and uncaring, but you see, the client's reaction will be a sudden shock of understanding that we're talking about *real* life and death. His unconscious mind will register the fact that, no matter what might happen during the session, there are rules that have to be followed."

*And that death door is usually so friendly and welcoming. It doesn't entice you; it just says, "Here is the way back home, when it's time to return." For a deeply depressed patient, it can mean escape from pain and desolation. Without a contract, the temptation to go through could be overwhelming.*

"It's so obvious, when you put it into words," I said. "Of course, that's what should be done before any session with a psychoactive drug, as well as with trance work! I simply never thought of it in terms of an actual contract you could make with the patient, ahead of time. It's a great idea!"

Audrey waved a hand, "One of the advantages of having it spelled out that way, of course, is that the client unconsciously feels freer in expressing whatever heavy stuff comes up, because I've supplied a safe structure within which he can let loose. People with tremendous repressed rage are always unconsciously afraid of letting it out in some kind of explosion, because of the possibility — the probability, as the unconscious perceives it — of doing terrible damage to something or someone — "

"If that volcano erupts, it'll burn up the world," I said.

"— and having to hate and punish themselves for it forever after."

*She went through it, herself, when we worked together. She knows the fire mountain and the fear of letting the lava out.*

"Okay," I summarized, "We lay out the contract in detail before the first session. Since these people will all have worked with you for a long time, they'll already be familiar with it. We just say it again and emphasize that the rules of the contract apply to psychoactive drug therapy exactly as they do to hypnotherapy."

"Agreed," said Audrey, shifting her legs and raising one hand to check her watch, "Now, here's the background on Daniel. He's an engineer, and he works as a trouble-shooter for a large company with several branches across the country. He has to do a lot of flying. Just a few months ago, he told me he was having trouble with his legs, whenever he had to take a plane, and that this was a problem he'd never had before, and it had gotten so bad, he'd finally had to ask his doctor for a prescription analgesic. He asked me if I thought it might have anything to do with what we'd been working on in therapy."

"Hmmm. That's an interesting sort of question! Pretty insightful." I asked, "What *had* you been working on in therapy?"

"Well," replied Audrey, "His presenting complaint was a mild chronic depression which had been going on for years, with a couple of recent panic attacks which had gotten his attention. That's what led him to go looking for a therapist, to try to get a handle on what was happening."

"And you've worked with him —"

"For about seven months." she supplied, "There wasn't anything spectacular in his background; mostly it's a picture of a large family, middle class, in Pennsylvania, who adopted the father's military mind-set; you know, emotion is weakness, a real man doesn't display his feelings, and any attention at all to the workings of your own mind or psyche is self-indulgent poppycock. The kind of people who'll consult a psychiatrist only when a family member has gone totally bonkers and is running plumb naked down Main Street, shrieking that the Martians are chasing him, okay?"

I nodded.

"For ordinary problems of life," continued Audrey, "A 'real' man is expected to solve them solo or, if that's not possible, to use will-power and self-control and just get through the bad patches, without embarrassing himself or others. Et cetera."

I made a sour face in recognition.

"We'd been doing pretty well," continued Audrey, "Or so I thought; actually, we *were* doing pretty well, working on his relationship with his father, in particular."

"His father was in the military?"

"No, no!" She waved her hands, "I didn't mean he was — I said a military *mind-set*. He was actually the principal of an elementary school."

I smiled, "Okay, I understand."

"Then, eight weeks ago, Daniel came up with this leg problem. I've got some notes here, from the tapes of that session."

She leaned over and picked up an olive colored folder from the floor, opened it and removed a sheet of paper. She read to me, "It's my legs; as soon as the plane is airborne, they start hurting. A few months ago, it was just sort of an ache; you know, the kind of thing that makes you fidgety, 'cause you keep wanting to stretch them, and you can't walk up and down the aisles all the time — "

Audrey looked at me and put down the paper, "Then, apparently, the aches became shooting pains, and every time he flew — and it happened that he was doing a lot of flying at that point — it got more painful, until, as I said, he got himself a prescription for Percocet, I think. Yes, Percocet. He says he doesn't like taking it because it makes him feel groggy, and it doesn't knock the pain completely out — it just takes the edge off — and this whole business is beginning to affect his work because, as you can imagine, he's getting pretty reluctant to get on a plane, and his job depends to a great extent on his willingness to fly."

"And hypnosis hasn't cracked it?"

"Nope, but the message definitely came through that his unconscious feels there's something about his legs that's important, that he should
pay attention to. We haven't been able to dig up anything seminal about
legs in his childhood, although he said something really interesting in the
last session," she closed her eyes, trying to remember, "I think it was along
the lines of: 'I have this feeling that there's something I'm not supposed to
look at — taboo in some way — .'"

She opened her eyes and looked at me, "And that's why I thought
maybe we could give MDMA a try, see if there's anything down inside there
that can be shaken loose."

"How long does the pain last, after he's back on the ground?"

"He says it lingers for a few hours, then fades away completely."

"What makes you think," I asked her, "That it hasn't got something
to do with cabin pressure, or some other conditions on board the plane? I
mean, why do you — and he — think it's psychological?"

Audrey smiled, "He's pointed out, quite reasonably, that he's been
flying the same airlines, in the same kinds of planes, for over twenty years,
without any trouble. Then, all of a sudden, just when we've begun getting
into some very loaded areas of his childhood, this brand new problem starts
up. He says he senses there's something pushing at him from the inside, and
the leg pain is a way for his unconscious to get his attention."

She grinned at me, "Who am I to argue, eh?"

I laughed and said, for the second time, "Sounds pretty insightful,
your boy!"

Audrey said he was one of her favorite patients, "And it's probably
because this guy learns fast and has a lot of courage, and he's the kind who
makes use of everything I can give him. You know what I mean — he
doesn't waste anything he gets; he grows."

"What was his reaction when you brought up the subject of MDMA?"

"He was surprised, of course, but his body language was positive;
he leaned forward instead of sitting back, in other words," she smiled,
illustrating both reactions with some exaggeration, "And once I'd explained the effects, and told him about the jaw-clench and nystagmus —
especially the first time — he seemed mostly curious, and wanted to know
how soon we could do it!"

I smiled, "Good for him!"

"He did his share of experimentation in college," Audrey added,
"So the idea of altering his perceptions isn't a brand new one for him. And,
of course, when I was summarizing its effects, I emphasized the fact that
MDMA is not considered a psychedelic drug, and there is no loss of control

with it, as there can be with high doses of some psychedelics."

I asked, "What does he know about me, and how does he feel about having a stranger brought into this situation?"

Audrey smiled broadly, "I simply told him that you were my second mother, the good one, and that you had introduced me to this kind of therapy. I assured him that all he'd have to do is see your face, and he'd know he could trust you completely!"

I grinned, "Good grief!"

Audrey got up and gestured, "Come with me to the kitchen; I'm going to do a final check. He should be here any moment."

I sat down at the kitchen table, and watched Audrey as she brought out three bottles of juice from the refrigerator, naming them as she put them on the counter, "Tropical fruit, cranberry, Clamato. There — that pretty much does it!"

There was the sound of a door opening and closing in the front of the house, and a cheerful male voice called out, "Hey, Audrey? I'm here!"

"Come into the kitchen," Audrey shouted back.

I stood up and moved around the table, my eyes on the man coming through the door. He was tall and his body, in old jeans and a light blue cotton shirt, was obviously in good shape.

*Nice flat stomach. Intelligent face with clean bones, almost handsome. Grey in the hair; maybe mid-forties?*

He smiled at me, showing very white teeth, and searched my face openly while the introductions were being made, then leaned forward with a suggestion of a bow, and shook my hand. After that, he turned around to Audrey and gave her a big, rocking hug.

*Lovely smile, strong handshake. Eyes warm. Suspect he's got a good sense of humor.*

"Well, here I am!" he said, "Ready and willing — and starving, by the way — so I hope you have some coffee around because I need it, seriously!"

Audrey chuckled and handed him a mug of her morning brew, "Still up for it, huh?"

"Yup. My stomach's flip-flopping a bit, but that's to be expected, I guess."

"Sure," I said, "Anything new like this, your psyche has a big blank screen to project onto. All sorts of neat little anxieties tend to pop up when you're about to take a drug you haven't had before. By the way, I gather Audrey's told you that this material isn't a psychedelic. It does change consciousness, but you won't get any of the usual visual effects, unless you're a very rare bird indeed. There's a name for this kind of drug: entactogen. It means touching within."

"Entactogen?" said Dan, "Never heard the term."

"It was coined a very short time ago, and only a very, very few people have ever heard it. I like it, so I use it."

"Okay," said Daniel, agreeably, and sipped his coffee.

I continued, "Also, I'd like to reinforce what Audrey told you about this drug not threatening any loss of control; it just doesn't happen. It won't overwhelm you the way some of the psychedelics might. That just isn't the way it works."

Audrey asked him if he had made arrangements for getting himself home without having to drive. He said, "Yeah, all set. I got here by taxi, and I'll just call them when I'm ready to go. I didn't want to have to think up explanations for anyone I know. Six hours is a sort of unusually long time for a therapy session, and I could imagine a friend asking what the heck was going on, and why couldn't I just drive myself home, right?"

"Yes, of course," I said, "I think taxis are the best solution, as long as you don't live too far away."

Audrey took his empty coffee cup and patted his arm, "The fact is, honey, you'll probably be fine for driving when you're finished, but even when you're back to baseline there are sometimes light flashes at the edges of your field of vision, and they can be distracting. No use taking chances."

Daniel chose cranberry juice, and Audrey poured it carefully into the wine glass containing the MDMA powder. When she had finished, she handed the glass to Dan, and said directly to him, "I'm giving you exactly one hundred and twenty milligrams, which is the usual therapeutic dose; it should be enough to give you a full experience, but not enough to clobber you. Depending on how well you do with this amount, we can make adjustments in dosage for further sessions — if we decide to do further sessions."

I said, "After the first hour and a half, Dan, if you want to stay where you are for a while longer — if everything's working well for you — you can ask for a supplement, which is forty milligrams, and the only thing it'll do for you is simply extend the maximum effect, what we call the plateau, for another hour. It won't increase the effect at all, but it'll give you a longer plateau to work with. I should add: don't hesitate to turn it down; there are no have-to's in this experience, all right?"

"Right," said Dan.

There was a small silence, then Audrey handed me a tall glass of water with ice cubes in it, and raised one of her own, saying, "Blessings on us, and on this journey."

*Voice gentle; nicely spoken.*

When Dan had emptied his glass, Audrey rinsed it quickly under the tap. Then she took his hand and we all went into the living room, where the sunlight greeted us. Audrey patted the designated patient-couch and told him, "This is your place. You can sit or walk around — whatever you want to do is okay. You won't feel much of anything for about half an hour, so just do whatever makes you most comfortable."

I sat down on the second couch and drank some of my ice water.

Dan went over to the large window that overlooked the garden in back. "I think I'll just stroll around outside and look at your pretty flowers, if you don't mind?"

"Stroll ahead," said Audrey, smiling. Then she snapped her fingers and held out a restraining hand. "I almost forgot. Dan, sit down for a moment. We're going to redo the contract."

"Oh?" He sat on the edge of the couch, his eyes on Audrey. She lowered herself slowly into the corner opposite me and asked him, "Do you remember the contract you made with me the first day?"

"Yeah, pretty much. Not the exact words, but the idea."

"Tell me as much as you remember, please."

"Sure," said Dan, "The one that sticks in my mind was that, if I should be tempted to go to the other side, if I have a chance to go through an opening of some kind that I know leads me to — to death, I swear that I won't go through it. In other words, if I'm tempted to die, for whatever reason, I must agree that I won't do that, because it would cause serious problems for you, and do damage to you, and I agree that I won't do anything that puts you in danger. Have I got that one right?"

"Terrific," said Audrey, leaning forward on her knees, "You can tell me, talk to me about what you feel; just don't act on it. Now the other two — can you remember the other conditions?"

"Ummm — yeah, I think one had to do with getting aggressive. If I get very angry about something or feel real hostility toward you, for some reason, I can talk about it, I can yell or shout and make noise, if I need to, but I agree not to turn it into physical action, right?"

"You agree not to act out physically against me or my property, yes."

"And, if I remember correctly, the third rule had to do with sexual feelings. Same thing as the aggressive stuff. I can talk about it all I want, but I agree not to act out the feelings when I'm working with you."

"You've got it, honey. Now, what Alice and I need from you is an agreement that the contract applies also to this kind of session. When you're in an altered state brought on by a drug, the same rules apply as when your altered state is due to hypnotic trance."

Dan's face wore an expression of seriousness. He said, "Absolutely. Agreed." Then he looked over at me, and a hint of curiosity played in his eyes. I smiled very slightly and nodded my head, but said nothing.

"Oh, yes," said Audrey, "I almost forgot again. About phone calls."

She proceeded to give him the warning about discussing his own personal experience with this — or any other — drug over the phone. Dan said, "Sure. That's easy to remember."

"That's it," Audrey smiled, rising from the couch, "Wander around outside, if you'd like. Alice and I will be right here if you need us. After I get some juice and ice water out on the table, that is. Just take me a sec." And she was gone.

Dan paused at the back door and looked around the room, as if trying to memorize it. I knew he had been here before, so I guessed he might be looking at his surroundings with a view to having his perspective changed in some way by the drug.

By the time Audrey had reappeared with a full pitcher of ice water and the bottle of cranberry juice, Dan was outside. She put everything in the middle of the big coffee table and left the room again, returning with clean glasses, one of which she filled with water and placed on a small end table next to the patient couch.

I rose and went to the window, where Audrey joined me. Silently, we watched the lean figure, hands in pockets, moving slowly around the flowerbeds, occasionally stooping to inspect a plant or open blossom.

I met her eyes and grinned, "I like your Daniel, kiddo."

"Isn't he a sweetheart?" Suddenly, she whirled around and took off again, muttering something that sounded like, "Gotta get Mike."

*Who the hell is Mike?*

I had just curled up again in my corner of the couch when Audrey hurried in, her hands clutching a tangle of recording equipment, and I laughed.

"What?" She knelt at the coffee table and spilled the mess onto its top. She gave me a quick glance, "What's funny?"

"I just understood what you were mumbling about, that's all."

"Mumble? Me? I never mumble," she mumbled, taping the black metal stand of a microphone onto the table.

"Can I help?"

"No, no," Audrey said, "Almost done. Just have to attach the framdiddle to the whompus, and we're ready."

The back door opened and Dan came in. His face had changed. There was a suggestion of softness around the mouth, and expanding pupils made his eyes large and liquid. He made a small attempt at a smile, "Well, I guess I'm turning on. It sure isn't like anything I've felt before — it's really different."

Moving slowly, like a man with hurting bones, he let himself down onto the couch, and sat there, hands spread on his thighs.

*Body language says What the hell is happening to me?*

I spoke gently, "What you're feeling now is the strangeness of a sensation you haven't had before, Dan. If you were a child, it wouldn't seem so — so surprising, because everything's new in a child's world, but grownups don't have that experience very often. Just let yourself go with it; don't push against it. In a few minutes, as the feeling becomes more familiar, it'll mellow out."

Dan nodded. He had stopped trying to smile.

*Good — good. Dropping the social face, letting himself be real.*

Audrey, finished with hookups and recording machines, paused in front of me, her back to Daniel, and made a triumphant circle with forefinger and thumb, close to her waist, then took her place on our couch, feet curled up beneath her.

I continued speaking to Dan, a bit more slowly than usual, my voice gradually slipping into lullaby rhythm, in order to get through to the unconscious, "Remember you're in a safe place, Dan. You have all the time in the world to do whatever you want to do. There are no deadlines, no expectations. Let your body relax while you go through this transition phase. You're completely safe, and we're both here for you at all times."

*Stay with simple messages, right now, to reassure the child inside.*

I glanced at my watch. It had been forty minutes since the ceremony in the kitchen.

*He'll plateau pretty soon now.*

"How're you feeling, Dan?" Audrey's voice, too, had gone mother-soft.

He replied with a deep sigh, then eased himself back against the cushions and sat there, arms resting loosely at his sides. He looked at Audrey and me and smiled, and we both exhaled. The smile was full, unselfconscious, and told us exactly what we wanted to know.

We smiled back at him and at each other, then Audrey chuckled and I heard myself laugh in delight.

"Yes," said Dan, eyes smiling along with the mouth.

*Now Audrey and I can relax our own masks, and touch him directly with affection — and affirmation — and whatever else he needs.*

I looked down at my watch again and told him, "You've probably reached the plateau by this time. Which means that where you are now — the way you feel — is where you'll stay for the next hour. There won't be any further increase in the intensity."

"All right. Thank you. It's a great place to stay."

*As soon as he let himself go with the strange feeling — stopped fighting it — he opened up to this, this place of being at peace and blessed.*

"Let's get to work, my dear," said Audrey, very gently, "Time to stretch out there and let yourself go into trance."

I interrupted, "Before you get fully settled, Dan, please take a drink of water from that glass on the table near you, and we'll keep reminding you to drink, every now and then. MDMA can be quite dehydrating, so it's important."

After several healthy swigs from his glass, Dan lay down at full length on the couch, with a small throw pillow covered in Thai silk under his head. He closed his eyes.

*He's been doing this for a good part of a year, so he must be pretty good at it. The MDMA should make it easier for him to go way down.*

There was a sunlit silence in the large room and the sense of peacefulness was so complete, I wondered for a moment if Dan might fall asleep.

I looked at the way his body lay, hands relaxed, fingers loosely curled at his sides. His mouth was slightly open.

I focused all my attention on him, opening myself to whatever I could feel of his state, letting myself swim into the contact high.

From the garden, bird sounds rose and fell in long waves.

Audrey spoke softly, "How are your legs, Dan?"

We watched as his hands moved, hesitatingly, onto his thighs, then froze, fingers outspread.

Suddenly, he sat upright, eyes wide open, and exploded, "Jesus CHRIST!" He swung his legs onto the floor and sat there, on the edge of the cushion, leaning forward, his hands spread again on the tops of his thighs, his face showing astonishment as he gazed at something we couldn't see. Audrey and I waited quietly, watching him, barely breathing.

"How could I have forgotten it? How could I!" he exclaimed, his voice choked, "I can see it happening right in front of me, like it was just a couple of minutes ago."

"Tell us," whispered Audrey.

Dan had turned in our direction, but his eyes weren't seeing us.

"The roof fell in," he whispered, "No warning. We were sitting there at our desks and the ceiling came down on us."

He dropped his head into his hands, for a moment, then sat up straight and continued talking out loud, more to himself than to Audrey or me.

"Second grade. I was trapped under my desk. Both my legs were trapped; I couldn't pull them out. I remember choking on the white dust. People were crying all around. Guess I was crying, too. The next thing I knew, I was outside on the playground, and our teacher was making us line up — telling us to be quiet, everything was all right — and I can see the yellow collar of the boy in front of me in the line. There was a smudge of blood on the collar, and I was staring at it, not really thinking of anything at all, just doing what the teacher said. I guess I was in shock or something. I couldn't figure out how I got outside. Yes, I remember I was thinking, 'How did I get out? How did I get my legs out?' All I could remember was being down on the floor, with my legs hurting. Nothing else 'til I found myself here, standing in line."

*He's right there, reliving it. He's standing in that line, wondering what happened, looking at blood on the back of a friend's collar.*

I spoke quietly, not wanting to get in the way of his images, "You forgot all this?"

"In — in all these years — since the second grade, I haven't remembered it. How could I forget something so — so awful, so terrifying? How could a thing like that just disappear?"

Audrey and I exchanged glances, but kept quiet.

He sat for a moment with his head bowed, hands clasped together between his knees, then eased himself back again onto the couch, lying full length, eyes closed.

After a few moments of silence, Dan's hands went up to his head, feeling around, "I had a bandage on my head. A big bandage wrapped all around my head. It was on me for a long time. Oh, yes," he continued, urgently, "I remember the day they let me out of the house for the first time since I got hurt, and they told me I could walk down the porch steps, onto the front lawn, but only if I moved very slowly and carefully. I must have had a concussion; that would explain it." He paused, then went on,

"I thought I had to walk slowly because something was still wrong with my legs. I don't think I really paid much attention to my head at all."

He seemed to hesitate, then closed his mouth and swallowed.

*Dry throat. If I remind him to drink some water, it may interrupt the memories. Wait a bit.*

In the warm quiet of the room, I could hear the birds again. Then Dan spoke haltingly, "I can hear my mother's voice. At the table. We were eating supper, and my father — my father was the principal of the school, so it was a terrible thing for him, too, that ceiling coming down on all of us. And my mother is saying, 'We're going to forget all about what happened today. We will never talk about it, any of us. You children,' — my sister was sitting next to me, I remember — 'And your daddy and me. Nothing's to be gained by going over and over it. After today, it'll be like it never happened. Everything will be all right, if we just put it out of our minds.'"

I glanced at Audrey and caught her nodding to herself, then realized I was doing the same thing.

*Oh boy! You don't often get to hear the actual words of an early childhood programming!*

Dan sighed deeply again, and Audrey sat up, her mouth opening, but he spoke first, "I'm remembering something else, something that really bugged me after it happened, because I couldn't figure it out. I think I know what was going on, now."

Audrey silently clapped one hand over her mouth, then grinned at me and curled up again in her corner.

"When I was around sixteen, I got a summer job painting the old school — I thought of it as my father's school, because he was still principal — and I was working with my friend, Chuck, and one day I was supposed to paint the walls at the north end of the building and I just didn't want to do it; I had this weird sick feeling when I took my ladder over to that part of the school, and I couldn't figure out why, but I knew I couldn't paint there, and I told Chuck I would exchange with him. We usually flipped a coin to find out which of us would paint this or that, and he'd lost the last flip; he was stuck with the job of painting the basement, with all the pipes and stuff, and he couldn't understand why I'd want to work down there, when I could have the much easier job up on top. I couldn't explain it to him, because I didn't know myself; I only knew I didn't want to mess with that end of the building, like it was haunted or something. Now, for the first time, I understand what all that was about. It was the second grade classroom; that's where it was — at the north end. I didn't remember a damn thing about the roof falling on top of us, not one thing. I just knew I had to stay away from that part of the school."

"Wow," muttered Audrey, and I whispered to myself, "Yes, yes."

Silence settled on the room again. Then Dan spoke, hesitatingly, as if feeling out an idea, "You know, it may be just coincidence, but the only accidents I've had — the only times I've had something happen to me, to my body — it's always my legs that've been hurt. Always my legs. Like, once when I was a teenager and I was in a warehouse, with a friend of mine — we were fooling around in there, I don't remember how or why — and he got into this loader and fiddled around and it started up and he didn't know how to stop it, and just before he got the brakes working, he pinned me — the big metal lifter in front of it pinned my legs against a wall. He got hold of the brakes, and stopped the thing. All I got out of it were some bad bruises."

"What do you — " Audrey began, but stopped when Dan waved a hand in a gesture that said clearly, Wait, there's more.

"And then, about ten years ago, I was in a small plane crash in Oregon, and the only part of me that got hurt was my legs. Just bruising again, but not my shoulder, not my arm; again, it was my legs."

This time, we didn't interrupt the silence. Then, suddenly, he sat up, swung his feet to the floor again and sat there, looking directly at Audrey and me.

"This is amazing," he said, "Remembering this stuff. Bam, bam, bam! One memory after another. All about the legs."

"It sounds as if it's all about repressed memory, what it can do," said Audrey.

"Repressed memory has tremendous energy," I added, "When you put a lid on a powerful experience like that ceiling falling in, and your legs being trapped, the push of the feelings, the pressure of the emotions, remains in your psyche. And in your body. It looks as if that day in the second grade built up a hell of a charge inside you — the fear, the shock, anger at the helplessness — and with that lid on it, it couldn't disperse. If you'd been able to talk about it, relive it, over and over again, until it got to be old stuff, and boring — "

" — it's even possible that none of those later leg events would have happened," finished Audrey, adding, "Of course, that's a wild intuitive guess, and I can't support it logically, but it's interesting to speculate, just for the hell of it!".

"That's WEIRD," said Dan, grinning widely, "Real Twilight Zone. I guess we'll never know."

We spent the rest of the session listening to Dan as he relived in detail the newly opened memory of the original trauma, and all that had happened since that horrifying moment in the second grade classroom.

Neither Audrey nor I remembered to ask if he wanted a supplement of the MDMA until about two hours had gone by, when I happened to look at my watch and realized that the 1-1/2 hour point had long passed. Audrey and I embarked on an apology for having lost track of the time, but Dan interrupted us, waving a hand to stem the word-tide; "I'm just fine," he said, grinning, "This has been great, a fantastic experience, and I don't mind going without the supplement. I feel good, really at peace now with the whole thing. Going over it with you like this — that's what I needed to do, I know it. Maybe this'll stop the leg pains."

"It should," said Audrey, "I'd be very surprised if you have any more trouble when you fly. I can't wait to find out!"

I joined in the laughter.

Six weeks later, Audrey phoned me at home, and told me she had heard from Dan that morning.

"Yeah?"

"He told me he'd just returned from a round trip back east on United Airlines."

"And?"

"No pain. Not even a dull ache. He wanted me to tell you that he loves you, too!"

"Holy Christmas!" I said, "The great Snake Oil strikes again!"

"Snake oil?"

I explained, "Shura often says that MDMA reminds him of the old snake oil remedies traveling salesmen used to sell from wagons all across the country: good for whatever ails you!"

"Incredible stuff," agreed Audrey, "And he certainly used it, bless him. He dived — or is that 'dove' — right in, and got the job done."

"I think it may be 'dove,' kid," I said, "But I won't hold it against you."

"Thanks a bunch," she laughed, "Anyway, I thought you'd want to be the second to know."

"Thanks, honey. Looks like we done good, hey?"

Dan — as far as I know — never again took MDMA; he didn't ask for a second session, and neither Audrey nor I suggested one. It had opened up in him what needed to be opened, and allowed him to free himself of a subtle anxiety which had been a constant presence at the edges of his life for several decades. He told us that he was immensely grateful, and felt that he could now go ahead and finish his hypnotherapy with Audrey, and get on with his life, as he put it. And, with our blessings, that is what he did. Within a year, he had fallen in love with a co-worker in his company's main office and, the last time I heard about him, he was married and expecting his first child. His legs gave him no further trouble.

## REVIVING AN ANCIENT ART

Over the next two years, Audrey and I developed our own way of doing the intensives. We had no known model (except, of course, what we had experienced in working together); we came to hear of many (unnamed) others doing work of this kind, but none of those maverick therapists were publishing, either, so we had nobody to ask for advice. I have to admit that this didn't cause either of us much worry; we were growing confident in our own abilities and believed that our system worked exceedingly well.

Both of us were learning with every session; I, of course, had much more to learn than did Audrey, but doing the intensive work was new territory for both of us, so we often felt as if we were breaking new ground. Then, over time, it began to dawn on us that this kind of process was probably as old as mankind; it's just that the ancient practitioners called it by other names, and used local plants which were known to open the inner eyes and ears.

Eventually, most of our work came to be that of helping our patients deal with their Shadow (the term used by Carl Jung) or dark side, which I came to call the Beast-Survivor. It always begins as the primal Survivor, a part of the child that is concerned only with his own survival (physical and emotional), his comfort and his self-validation. It is a normal part of every one of us, and includes whatever we are born with that is instinctual, uncensored and "natural." Some of these energies — like anger and frustration — are potentially dangerous to others and the growing child must be taught to exercise control over them. Others are potential sources of creativity, and should be nurtured and developed.

As the child grows up and is increasingly shaped by the approval and censure of others, being reminded that This is Good and That is Bad, he gradually learns to control and repress many of the natural urges and impulses that his teachers and his particular culture consider unacceptable.

The Beast part of the Beast-Survivor begins to take shape if the parents and guides condemn not only the child's actions, but the child himself, instilling shame and self-rejection along with social instruction. Then the repressed feelings and urges begin to assume the outline of a terrible, hateful Thing in the dark cellar of the unconscious. In Audrey's own case, it had become a big, black, filthy spider. A strongly religious Catholic may unconsciously give his own Shadow the form of the Devil, itself.

In other words, if the child is taught with love and respect, by wise teachers, he will come to understand that it is necessary to control certain natural desires and instincts in order to become an accepted member of his family and tribe. But he will *not* be taught that these natural energies are wicked or shameful in and of themselves. As he grows, he will come to feel empathy with other beings — human and animal — which will give him further incentive to exercise control over certain impulses. His Shadow or dark side can be expected to serve him as a source of creative expression and new concepts, and the Survivor aspect of it will continue to function as the protector it was meant to be.

(There are many works of art, literature and music that illustrate and make use of the Shadow. The works of the artist H. R. Giger, who created the backgrounds and the ferocious monster in the movie, "Alien;" the stories written by Stephen King; the music of Igor Stravinsky, especially "Rites of Spring;" these are only three modern examples of creations by people who have had access — consciously or not — to their own dark sides.)

But if the child is taught to be ashamed and to see himself as inherently "evil," he will not just control his instinctual desires; he will eventually come to deny the very existence of those feelings within himself. Sometimes, this fearful repression can create in the unconscious an interior judge, jury, and potential executioner.

Spiritual growth must eventually involve a confrontation with the Beast-Survivor, which often takes the shape of a large, powerful animal. (Over the two years we worked together, Audrey and I met three wolves, five jungle cats, and two gorillas.)

The goal was to have the patient meet and get to know the hidden beast in the cellar, to move into it and feel its nature. This step in the process is one of the most terrifying things any human being can undertake, and requires great persistence and immense courage. The prospect of seeing what he unconsciously believes to be the core, the essence of himself as a horrendous, malignant, totally unacceptable entity, can bring about a state of fear that has no parallel in ordinary life.

No person can be asked to do the work of confronting his Shadow or beast without being told by his therapist, in advance, that what he will see and feel is *not* the whole truth about who he is, but only an important and essential part. There should be a great deal of discussion before any drug ingestion about the nature and function of the Beast-Survivor. The therapist should emphasize the patient's need to feel compassion for the innocent child he had been and to understand why and how that child developed certain habits of behavior and emotional response to his environment, in an effort to survive in a world he wasn't equipped to deal with or control.

All these explanations and reassurances should take place before the patient makes a final decision about taking MDMA or any psychedelic drug. It is essential preparation because, without it, the drug session might be wasted. When the unconscious psyche anticipates the possible destruction of a needed and long-nurtured positive self-image, when the Survivor hears footsteps outside the massive door that has guarded his monster aspect from view most of his life, one result may well be a complete lack of response to the drug. No insight, no images, no nuthin'. Or there may be the eruption of an acute anxiety state which thoroughly blankets any other effects and distracts the attention of everyone involved.

Having talked to a Jungian analyst about this whole process, I've concluded that there is one important way in which psychedelic exploration differs from Jungian analysis, when it involves facing and dealing with the Shadow. A Jungian therapist will encourage his client to see his Shadow as clearly as he can — see what shape it takes, sense what its qualities are — and then continue working on understanding its origins and functions. But a therapist working with MDMA or a psychedelic drug will gently help his patient to take one additional step. When the patient has full view of what I've been referring to as the Beast-Survivor or monster, he will then be urged to first face, then enter into the dark figure he is meeting; he must work to get inside its skin and look out through its eyes.

It is at this point that a battle may have to be fought, because not only does the conscious person have to fight his own revulsion, shame and fear of this forbidden aspect of himself, but he may project upon the monster an equal resistance to being made visible to the conscious mind. The more buried the monster is, the more power it gathers; only by staying in the cellar, unseen and unconfronted, can it continue having an influence on the patient's life, and it does not give up that power willingly.

Now and then, one finds a patient who seems to be able, once he has come face to face with this part of himself, to step right into it. Others must fight to get there, with strong, patient, loving support and encouragement from the therapist.

When the patient succeeds in deliberately stepping into his beast and looking out its eyes, his first response is usually astonishment at an unaccustomed absence of fear. The second is appreciation, then frank exhilaration at the sense of powerfulness that characterizes this creature. (This stage of getting to know the beast from the inside may take more than one session, but I have also seen the process finished in a single day.)

When this part of the work has been completed successfully, the patient begins learning to accept his beast and to understand how it took shape. Gradually, the Beast-Survivor begins to transform. With time and the support of his therapist, the patient allows himself to feel more and more compassion for the original child within the monster and, as he does so, the beast slowly disintegrates and only the hurt and fearful child remains. The rest of the work is gradual re-parenting and validation of the child, until he is able to merge with his grown-up self.

The Survivor, however, remains. When exposed to the conscious mind, and given respect and even possibly a bit of affection, it becomes the ally and protector it was intended to be. It is concerned only with the safety and welfare of its host. It will never be entirely housebroken or have good table manners, but it will be available as a totally loyal and devoted defender of the whole, integrated Self.

(In some cultures, this aspect of the psyche, when consciously understood and accepted, is called a "power animal.")

I developed a new respect for the old, classic fairy tales, coming to recognize certain ones as disguised descriptions of spiritual journeys and processes. The story most obviously applicable to dark side transformation work is "Beauty and the Beast." There are others, but that is the most outstanding example of a so-called fairy tale which describes coming to terms with one's Beast-Survivor, and the spiritual integration that results when the work is completed. ("They were married and lived happily ever after.")

Our intensives lasted a minimum of six hours. Neither of us took time out, except to go to the bathroom, or when Audrey would excuse herself for a few minutes, to make a sandwich in her kitchen so that she could maintain her energy. She always offered food to the client, but it was usually turned down. The patient was actively encouraged to sip water or juice all through the session to avoid dehydration.

We used MDMA with every one of these carefully selected patients.

Eventually, with certain ones who wanted to go deeper and further into their own interiors, we eventually tried 2C-B, (4-bromo-2,5-dimethoxy phenethylamine), which is a true psychedelic. It was also — at that time — not illegal. One of the advantages of working with 2C-B was that its effects were not as long-lasting as most other psychedelics, and the patient could usually expect to go home within eight to ten hours.

We thought of MDMA as the emotional and spiritual opener, the drug which allowed a patient to do intense insight work without fear of what he would find at the core of himself. MDMA had a particular magic; it gave the patient the ability to accept the whole of who he was — positive and negative, light and dark — without defensiveness. This enabled him to delve into his dark side, to explore the Beast-Survivor with minimum fear, and to eventually come to terms with that essential aspect of himself. MDMA was, indeed, penicillin for the soul.

I always thought of 2C-B as the gut-opener, in the sense that it opened up the deep energies of the psyche, and gave access to the part of the person that communicates with itself through archetypal imagery. It also emphasized the patient's connection with his body, since all the physical senses were sharpened. A good experience with 2C-B allowed for exploration and validation of the Survivor and its proper function as self-protector. Like most psychedelics, it brought the spiritual world into direct connection with the life of the body, and let the patient celebrate fully the fact that he was alive and healthy, a soul within a cherished human form.

In several cases, a single 2C-B session was used as a final experience for patients who had worked hard and courageously in the mine-fields of their own unconscious minds. They had used MDMA and the trance state to examine and acknowledge their long-hidden emotional programming from childhood, and they had learned how to change what needed changing. They were ready to move on by themselves, or perhaps to find new teachers for further spiritual growth.

Twice, the final session was not with 2C-B, but mescaline, which was illegal. Both Audrey and I considered this to be one of the most honored and respected Great Ones among visionary drugs. We used it with two people, both of whom had achieved deep, life-changing transformations after many months of intense and difficult work. The difference between 2C-B and mescaline, we felt, was a subtle but important one. While 2C-B unlocked doors to the archetypal images and the intense emotions that accompanied them, mescaline was even more of a spiritual opener and could introduce the patient to a landscape where light infused everything — people, plants and animals — and there was direct connection with what is called the "numinous."

When Audrey was working with a patient in the trance state, she spoke slowly, gently, unless there was reason to say something sharp and sudden. She was quietly persuasive and always prepared to stop talking if she detected an impulse to speak on the part of the patient. I was amazed at how acutely perceptive she was, and I found myself, over the months that we worked together, learning to watch the patient's face and body carefully, as she did, until I found myself picking up clues so subtle, I sometimes felt I was using some other sense than mere eyesight.

Somewhere during the second year, I learned to perceive emotional blocks in the body of a patient as he lay on the couch, deep in trance and the drug effect. I never saw colors, as many people do when they are sensitive to auras; what I saw — or felt — would usually be something like a grey, heavy mass located around the abdominal area, and what it meant to me was that the patient had a block formed by fear and sorrow, and deeply buried rage, which was making it hard for him to release negative emotions.

My response to such an impression would be to remind him that he was in a safe place, and — if it seemed appropriate for this patient — to tell him about the fire mountain located just above his navel. I would say something like this: "You can fly over the top of the volcano like a bird, and look down on it. Tell me when you're there."

When the patient said he was in the air over the volcano, I would go on.

"You'll see a small opening, and inside that opening is the deep red of the lava. Stay where you are, in the sky, looking down at that hole, and decide how much lava you want to release. The lava is rage and sorrow, and it's been gathering there for most of your life. You can make the opening as large or as small as you wish.

"I want you to know that you can safely let flow some of that burning fire, let it flow down from the top of the volcano, just as much or as little as you feel it's okay to let out. It won't burn up the world, it'll just burn bushes and trees on the side of the mountain, and that's okay. You have complete control over how much you let out, so you don't have to be afraid of the mountain exploding and destroying everything in sight; it won't. Just let flow as much as you want, and when you've released enough, you can close up the hole again, and stop the flow. It's your volcano; you can do whatever you wish with it."

This image proved to be one of the most effective for such patients, giving them conscious control over a needed but immensely frightening exposure to the searing heat of long-repressed rage, pain and grief.

An extraordinary relationship developed between Audrey and me as we sat at opposite ends of the therapist's couch; sometimes one of us would fall silent, momentarily at a loss for an appropriate response to something said by the patient; invariably, the other would find the answer rising instantly in the mind, emerging in exactly the right words. There were times when we seemed almost telepathic; we shared moments of knowing that we were, separately and together, a conduit, a means by which something Other, immensely loving and healing, was making itself felt and heard. When — now and then — it spoke through us, we could feel it happening. Then there would be a stillness, a sense of time having stopped, a peacefulness permeating the room.

I thought of it as an experience of the sacred, a gift of Grace. After such a moment out of time, the patient would usually sigh deeply, Audrey and I would nod to each other, and the work would continue.

To do this kind of psychotherapy, it is essential that the therapist lay aside all preconceived theories and belief systems, either psychological or spiritual, as much as possible. Her (or his) attitude must be that of a student, learning a new part of the universe, seeing it for the first time. The patient is a new world, unlike any other she has previously encountered, and the therapist must be ready to learn a language of symbol and imagery peculiar to that world. She has to keep her eyes and ears open and all her antennae alert, so that she might begin to get a glimpse of the emotional and spiritual structures and rules of survival that inform life in this unique human landscape.

It is important to remember that the patient's psyche contains a part which is a self-healer, and the patient should be told of the existence of that healer within because by telling him, the therapist will help activate it.

There is another rule which I believe must be observed by any therapist undertaking this kind of journey with a patient. She has to be able to feel something very close to love for the person she is guiding. There should be real caring, not simply an intellectual concern for the patient's welfare.

Real caring, like love, cannot be forced, as we all know, and the therapist should have sufficient insight of her own to be aware of what her feelings towards the patient really are. If there is even the slightest hostility or apprehension, she must be prepared to do the necessary insight work to discover the reason for those feelings, and to work on whatever projections may be involved. If she cannot completely resolve them, she should direct the patient to another therapist. I'm not talking about such feelings as momentary irritation or impatience; those can come naturally in response to many things, and don't negate basic love or caring.

It is in connection with this ability to affirm and care about her client that the therapist's own past training with MDMA and psychedelic drugs becomes important. If she has sufficient experience of her own with these tools, she will have — she should have — taken certain spiritual steps which will have brought her to specific places within herself. One of these interior places or states is the often-referred-to "participation mystique," and this frequently happens in the first MDMA or psychedelic experience, if the session is conducted (as it should be) in quiet natural surroundings. I have described this state in the earlier chapter, "Places in the Mind."

She will have felt the sense of kinship with every living thing, and she will have known — this is deep core knowing, not intellectual knowing — that every animal, plant and human being is related to her. She will have seen and felt that everything alive carries within it the God-essence, a spark of the Great Spirit, and that indeed we are all highly individual parts of one living, conscious Being. What may have appealed to her before as nothing more than a beautiful, poetic concept, will suddenly have taken the form of reality, and the profound impact of this realization will have become part of her for the rest of her life.

That is why, once she has had the privilege of being in this place in her soul, she will find it possible to feel true caring, even love, for a patient who is preparing to open himself to himself. She will know that this person she is working with is, in a spiritual sense, her parent, her brother, and her child.

I finally brought my participation in the intensives to an end when it became increasingly clear that doing them once or twice a week was extraordinarily draining of both physical and emotional energy, and I needed those energies for writing a book with Shura.

It's been many years since I worked as a psychedelic therapist, and Shura and I are still writing. I miss the excitement and continual learning, the exploration of other people's interior worlds, and helping them achieve clarity, self-love and integration. It has been a tremendous privilege to have participated in this kind of process, and I feel truly blessed.

But now I can talk about it, while those who are still quietly and secretly conducting these kinds of transformative sessions cannot speak out, and will not be able to share their experiences and accumulated knowledge until the current, unspeakably wrong laws regarding psychedelics and visionary plants are eliminated in the United States and everywhere else. Until then, an ancient healing practice in modern form will continue to be a criminal act, and the wisdom gained from it lost to all except a small group of therapists and their patients.

# Part Three:

# Tryptamina Botanica

# CHAPTER 15.  DMT IS EVERYWHERE

(Shura's voice)

Many, many years ago I put a Pendaflex folder into what was then my one and only filing cabinet (second drawer from the top as I remember) into which I would toss the occasional paper that I might come across that would mention DMT (N,N-dimethyltryptamine) as a component of some plant.  Then I would come across a couple of papers that described some pharmacology of DMT, and this called for a new folder.  Another paper would appear that discussed plant decoctions used in South American native rituals and ceremonies that could well involve DMT.  Some native brews clearly indicated the use of more than one plant.  Another folder?  Then, I found papers concerning anthropological studies of certain of these native peoples, involving other plant mixtures as sacraments, which did not even hint at any DMT content.  I began to appreciate the horrors associated with the filing of information when it can be interconnected by several organizing threads.  There is a drug (chemistry), and a plant (botany) that produces an effect (pharmacology) in some people out there (anthropology) that might have some healing use (medicine) or some spiritual impact (theology).

This introduction is an unfairly simplified presentation of factual information when one considers that all of these classes are indeed not simple, single entries but can, in fact, be multiple combinations. The "drug" can be a mixture of a number of chemicals, some of which may never have been identified, named, or even characterized.  The "plant" may be a mixture involving trees, or vines, flowers or grasses, none of which can be easily distinguished or identified. The effects observed can be complicated by the fact that they are reported within a cultural context involving superstitions, customs, tradition, and mythology, all without any written record.  And the description of the use was from an observer who stands outside of the cultural milieu of the event observed, who has a Western scientific knowledge of chemistry, botany, pharmacology, anthropology, medicine, or theology, and will see everything through his own set of glasses.

Many years ago my dream was to put together a complete review of the snuffing/drinking/smoking world of ethnobotany into one place, and write the total story. But even then, it was too complex and interdisciplinary, and I abandoned ship.

Today I have not just one folder, but a couple of file cabinet drawers filled with information about these areas. They include published reprints, literature searches, correspondence, and my own research notes. I am twenty-five years older, I have twenty-five times the quantity of data, and the area is twenty five times more complex and convoluted that was in one of my filing cabinets. No one can write a complete review of this area, and even if it were to magically appear, no one could read it to find just what he needed, as every reader has different needs.

Since I see myself as a chemist, I have decided to use the vocabulary of chemistry and let all the other structures of organization evolve as needed. Here is the major component of interest, there are the plants where it can be found, and finally this is the context of its usage. Perhaps this is an arbitrary hierarchy, but some hierarchy is needed and I have chosen this. So let me look on the turn-ons and the nostrums of the world first as chemical entities, and then explore the subtleties of interactions between them and their congeners (other things found alongside them), as contributors to the psychedelic scene.

What is on top of the pile? N,N-Dimethyltryptamine, or DMT, of course. A bit of chronological history of both the drug and the drug law might be appropriate here, as the year 1966 is an interesting point of confluence of both stories. DMT was first synthesized in 1931 by Manske. It was isolated from two plant sources independently in 1946 by Gonçalves de Lima (from *Mimosa hostilis*) and in 1955 by Fish, Johnson and Horning (from *Piptadenia peregrina*). Its human activity as a synthetic entity was first reported in 1956 by Szára. The first legal restrictions were placed on research with it in 1966 in response to its increasing popularity following the writings of Burroughs, Metzner, Leary and others in the early 1960's, and it was observed as being a component of the healthy human brain (and maybe a neurotransmitter) in 1976 by Christian.

The year 1965 launched the era of the use of initials as both drug and organization names in Federal law enforcement. It was then that the Drug Abuse Control Amendments were enacted and became effective, inspired to some measure by the psychedelic "hippie" movement in the younger generation at that time. This led to the formation of the BDAC (Bureau of Drug Abuse Control) which was put under the authority of the Food and Drug Administration (the FDA). These amendments were written to attempt to control non-narcotic drugs (called dangerous drugs) with examples offered such as DMT, LSD, DET, ibogaine, bufotenine, DOM, MDA, MMDA and TMA. This was a bureau that was parallel to, but non-overlapping, the already existing FBN (Federal Bureau of Narcotics), which was dedicated exclusively to the control of the three known narcotic drugs, heroin, cocaine and marijuana. In 1968, the BDAC (under the Department of HEW) was merged with the FBN (under the Department of the Treasury) to create the BNDD (Bureau of Narcotics and Dangerous Drugs) under the Department of Justice. At the time of the passage of the Controlled Substance Act (in 1970, the first new drug law since the Harrison Narcotics Act of 1914) a number of competing splinter groups were being formed such as ODALE (Office of Drug Abuse Law Enforcement) and ONNI (Office of National Narcotics Intelligence). In 1973, the BNDD, ODALE and ONNI, along with the enforcement and intelligence functions of the U.S. Customs, were melded into still another group, the DEA (Drug Enforcement Administration). And that is where things have rested up to the present time, except for a failed attempt (in 1982) to merge the DEA with the FBI. The latter group was to have run the show, and the DEA effectively rebelled.

In a sense, DMT is to the world of indolic psychedelics what mescaline is to the world of phenethylamine psychedelics. It is the starting point of both our classification and understanding of the hallucinogenic psychedelics, and from it our entire understanding of the relationship between structure and activity must evolve. So let me try an organizational scheme that asks; (1) what is the chemical? (2) where is it found? and (3) what does it do?

In answer to (1), the chemical is N,N-dimethyltryptamine (DMT) which is an in-house shortcut way of saying 3-(N,N-dimethylaminoethyl)-indole. It is N,N-dimethyltryptophan without the carboxyl group. It is bufotenine or psilocin without the hydroxyl group. (2), DMT is, most simply, almost everywhere you choose to look. It is in this flower here, in that tree over there, and in yonder animal. The whereness is, in effect, the stuff of this chapter. And (3), it is a relatively short-lived psychedelic compound that has a record of ancient and revered use in many cultures of the world. To some users, it is a connection to a vivid world of magic and mystical beings. To others, it is a dark exposure to the most negative aspects of the psyche. And everything in-between. This is discussed in greater detail in the recipe on DMT. This chapter is pretty much limited to a listing of some of the natural sources of this drug.

## MARINE WORLD

I am a bit uncomfortable in talking about alkaloids to be found in the marine world. There is no real agreement amongst chemists as to just what an alkaloid is. It is common to say that a natural product is an alkaloid if it meets a certain number of criteria, but there are so many devious exceptions that any definition can be voided. The accepted minimum is that it is a basic (in the chemical sense), organic compound that contains nitrogen, and comes from natural sources. Both the words alkali and alkaloid come from the Arabic "al-qili" meaning, literally, from the ashes. Often an added definition is that it should be modestly complex, as a way of excluding compounds such as cyanide and urea. Certainly they can be extremely weak bases, as with amides such as caffeine in coffee, or capsaicin in pepper. These are incontestably alkaloids even though they are substantially neutral. Quaternary amine salts such as candicine (from many cacti) or its positional isomer leptodactyline (from the skins of frogs) are actually acidic, but some insist that they are still alkaloids. Biological activity is not a useful criteria, as many natural alkaloids are without known pharmacology, and many pharmacologically potent compounds from nature don't even contain nitrogen. And many people assume that such a compound has to come from a plant source. Not so. There are many animals that carry tryptamines as part of their chemistry, and DMT is one of the most common of these.

A surprising number of natural products from the sea contain bromine. With chlorine being the most common halide in sea salt I have always been amazed that the supreme intelligence that designs and builds things such as alkaloids in the ocean would choose to use the bromine atom which is hundreds of times more scarce in sea water than is the chlorine atom. But the interesting question, "Why use bromine rather than chlorine in constructing marine alkaloids?" must wait its turn behind the even grander question of, "Why make alkaloids at all?" The answer to this is still unknown. It is just Nature's way.

Sponges have proven to be a source of brominated tryptamines. *Smenospongia maynordii* (a genus earlier known as *Polyfibrospongia*) has been shown to contain 5,6-dibromotryptamine and its N-mono-methyl homologue (dibromo-NMT). The corresponding DMT counterpart (5,6-dibromo-DMT) has been observed in *S. ehina*, and the more simple 5-bromo-DMT is found in *S. auria*. These Caribbean sponges solicited attention due to their anti-microbial properties, but it was found that the base extracts in a methanol solution upon reduction, with hydrogen gas and palladium on charcoal, gave pure DMT in a quantitative yield. And in the family of Thorectidae, the sponge *Smenospongia aurea* contains both of these brominated DMT derivatives.

An eerie cross-connection to the phenethylamines exists in the sponges, a connection to mescaline. The N,N-dimethyl homologue of mescaline has been called trichocereine and is an alkaloid found in the cactus *Trichocereus terschekii*. Two very closely related compounds have been isolated from species of the Caribbean sponge *Verongida* spp., which are the methonium salts of trichocereine where the two methoxyl groups have been effectively replaced with bromine atoms. The compound 3,5-dibromo-4-methoxy-N,N,N-trimethylphenethylammonium salt, and its O-demethylated counterpart, are marine antibiotics with an uncanny resemblance to active cactus phenethylamines. Searches in the families such as Niphatidae have been unsuccessful, but the Memosponga family (sponges) has an individual *Pachymatisma johnstonii* which contains yet another brominated material, an amino acid 6-bromo hypaphorine. This is a permethylated tryptophan precursor to the compounds mentioned in the biosynthesis section later. This same bromo-quat salt is in an Okinawan sponge of the genus *Aplysina*.

Another marine source of 5-bromo-DMT is an ascidian, specifically the tunicate *Eudistoma fragum*, which is a sea-squirt found in New Caledonia. An interesting tie-in with the ayahuasca world is to be found here with the simultaneous isolation of the identically brominated β-carboline, woodinine. This is the tetrahydroharman analogue, with a 6-bromo-substitution (that is in the same location as the 5-position in DMT) and an N-methylpyrrolidinyl-2 substituent at the carboline-1 position. It is a simple chemical maneuver to reduce the bromo group off with a little catalytic hydrogenation, but it is a real possibility that 5-Br-DMT might be active on its own account. Almost every other 5-substituted DMT is active. Another tunicate, of the genus *Lissoclinum*, contains 6-bromo-tryptamine.

A small phylum of sea-invertebrates are called bryozoans, and one of these has been reported to contain a brominated tryptamine. The organism *Flustra foliacea* has the N-formamide of 6-Br-NMT, which might also reduce to DMT with catalytic hydrogenation, as with the tunicate compound above.

And finally, there is a marine coral organism, a sea fan known as a Gorgonian, from the Bay of Naples in the Mediterranean, with the binomial name *Paramuricea chamaeleon*, which has been reported to have a number of indolic components present without any bromine at all. DMT is present, as is NMT. NMT is also in the related sea fan *Villagorgia rubra* from New Caledonia.

## THE MAGIC MUSHROOMS (The Families of the Order Agaricales)

There is an immense group within the world of all living things called the fungi. Many people hold this to be a kingdom in its own right, as its components are neither plant nor animal. They are everything else, from molds, to mushrooms, mildew, and bacteria. Probably they are closer to plants than to other things, but they do not have chlorophyll, so they aren't really plants, either. Some are parasites, growing in or on living stuff, and some are saprophytes that prefer dead matter. I have learned a lot from them about the balance of nature, by observing how they propagate and reproduce, but I have learned a lot more from them about the egocentric nature of man, simply by observing how the many experts in the field (called mycologists) seem to disagree, usually with vigor, as to how fungi should be classified. There are cliques, there are schools, there are societies, there are total philosophies that are convinced that they are completely right, and that all the others are completely wrong.

"This species must be moved to that genus, in yonder family, as noted in my most recent publication in Applied Mycologia Today."

"But, Dr. Rasputin, you already have tenure at the University, so let me use this genus for the title of an article in my new journal, Amanita Northwestica, and I will make you an Associate Editor. But will you drop your insistence for the renaming of the *Pholiota* group?"

"Yes, but you must allow me at least one race with my name attached to it, or allow me to identify this group as a new subspecies."

"But Dr. Sangfroid would object to that."

"Probably he would, but I hold Dr. Goodheart to be the defining authority." "Oh, really? Come to think of it, I'm not sure I have an editorial opening available at the moment."

In short, classification of these organisms has been a nightmare for many years and will, without doubt, remain a nightmare for many years to come. There is no right way. There is not even a currently accepted way. But I personally like things somewhat organized, even if incorrectly so, so here is a working pattern for the mushrooms that allows the placement of all dimethyltryptamines of interest, largely psilocybin and psilocin. I follow a rubric from high school that allowed me to memorize the Mendelian pattern: "I learned in my CLASS the ORDER of my FAMILY." The class name ends in "-etes," the ordinal name in "-ales," and the family name in "-eae" or perhaps just in "-ae."

Here is where I intend to list the families that contain the magic mushrooms (aka 'shrooms) along with a comment or two, and follow them with the known genera that contain active species. The compounds that are known to contribute to the central activity of these fungi are: psilocybin (4-hydroxy-DMT phosphate ester), psilocin (4-hydroxy-DMT), baeocystin (4-hydroxy-NMT phosphate ester) and norbaeocystin (4-hydroxy-tryptamine phosphate ester). An exhaustive and documented list of all active species is detailed in Jonathan Ott's *Pharmacotheon*, pp. 309-319, and need not be repeated here. What follows is not a keying structure to be used in the field, but just a collection of names to be enjoyed or avoided.

**CLASS:**

**Basidiomycetes** (including rusts, smuts, mushrooms, puff balls, everything with spores that are produced in specialized structures called bassifia. Two of the most common subclasses are:

**Gasteromycetes** and

**Hymenomycetes** which, in general, tell you where the spores are located. We are following the second subclass.

**ORDER:**

**Agaricales**, the gilled (agaric) and the tubed (bolete) fungi which we are following here, as opposed to the:

**Aphyllophorales**, the polyphores, the chanterelles, and the teeth and crust fungi, the:

**Boletales**, the boletes, now usually grouped in the order Agaricales, the:

**Tremellales** (the jelly fungi), and the:

**Dacrymycetales** (the tuning fork fungi) and the:

**Auriculariales**. These last three are often lumped together.

**FAMILY:**

**Strophariaceae** (the Stropharia family). *Psilocybe, Stropharia*

**Coprinaceae** (the Inky Cap Family). *Copelandia, Panaeolina, Panaeolus* and *Psathyrella.*

**Cortinariaceae** (the Cortinarius family). *Gymnopilus* (*Pholiota*) and *Inocybe.*

**Pluteaceae** (the Pluteus family, also called the Volvariaceae family). *Pluteus.*

**Bolbitiaceae**, (the Bolbitius family, known for its many LBM's or Little Brown Mushrooms). *Agrocybe, Conocybe.*

**Tricholomataceae** (the Tricholoma family). *Gerronema* and *Mycena.*

**Hygrophoraceae** (The Hygrophorus family, or the Waxy Caps). *Hygrocybe.*

That is pretty much the picture of the Magic Mushrooms. All of these contain 4-hydroxy-DMT compounds in various guises, but not one of them contains DMT, which I find to be totally amazing. Two additional families must be mentioned separately, for several reasons. One is:

**Amanitaceae** (the Amanita family).

The major genus is *Amanita* and some fifteen species have been explored chemically. All contain 5-hydroxy-DMT, or bufotenine. Some (*A. muscaria, A. pantherina*) also contain muscimol or ibotenic acid, as well as the cholinergic alkaloid, mescarine. Others (*A. phalloides*) are notorious for the presence of the deadly polypeptide hepatotoxins, phalloidin and amanitin. But again, as with the magic mushrooms, there is no report mentioning the presence of unsubstituted DMT or its 5-methoxy-analogue. The other is:

**Hypocreaceae** (the Ergot family).

Here the major genus is *Claviceps* which is the Mutterkorn of all the ergoline chemistry that has made both Sandoz and Albert Hofmann famous. Here is the raw material from which LSD and all of its remarkable extensions have come. And yet, there are no suggestions of DMT or any other simple tryptamines being present. And, as an extension of this fungal resource over into the dicotyledonous world of higher plants, there is the morning glory family, the Convolvulaceae, which is a treasure house of ergot-like alkaloids. Many species of *Ipomoea*, *Rivea*, and *Argyreia* are superb sources of ergot alkaloids that can be converted to lysergic acid as a synthetic intermediate, or are psychopharmacologically active as lysergamides in their own rights. There is a short, but rich chapter called MGS devoted to just to the seeds of these plants. An extremely rich collection that is, again, devoid of DMT or any of its interesting homologues.

### FROGS (Family Bufonidae)

There is a strange, almost surreal parallel between the chemistry of mushrooms (also called toadstools) and the chemistry of frogs (also called toads), when seen through the eyes of a person trying to paint a picture of the nature of plant or animal alkaloids. In fact, some insight can be gotten about the interests and prejudices of the person himself by his choice of names here. Frogs vs. toads. These are often used interchangeably, as both are defined as squat amphibians, without tails, which like to jump about, and have tadpoles. As differences go, frogs have smooth skins and are lumped into the aquatic world (there are some aquatic toads, however), and toads are warty and are assigned to the terrestrial world. The mushroom/toadstool distinction is just as arbitrary. Both are defined as fungi, usually with an umbrella-shaped cap called a pileus. The name a person chooses to use reflects his taste and opinions. He probably thinks that frogs are Frenchmen and toads are ugly. He feels that mushrooms are edible and toadstools are poisonous. But in truth, these two large groups of individuals are rich in pharmacologically active alkaloids which are closely related, structurally, to DMT. Yet neither frogs nor toads, mushrooms nor toadstools have been shown to contain this title compound.

With the mushrooms, the defining analogues were analogues of DMT which carried an oxygen atom in the 4-position, to provide the truly psychedelic compounds psilocybin and psilocin. Nature didn't show much imagination. There was not much variety, just a well-grounded capability of hydroxylating DMT at the 4-position. With these fungi, there was an occasional venturing into the 5-hydroxylation territory (to provide bufotenine), but interestingly this modification occurred only in those species that had to be left absolutely untouched because of the deadly peptides they contained. But with neither the 4-oxygenation species or the 5-oxygenation species was there any DMT to be found.

With the ergot fungi, nature showed almost too much imagination. From somewhere, a benign God conceived the lysergide ring structure, with a bewildering array of shrubbery on an exposed, vital carboxamide group which led to a treasure trove of natural alkaloids, as well as to a similar collection of synthetic allies. The morning glories provided more versatility, and from all this came LSD and the several variations that are detailed in the second half of this volume. All of these contain, in their structures, the tryptamine skeleton. And, a bit perversely, all of them also contain the phenethylamine skeleton. But none of these natural sources possess DMT.

With frogs, there is a sort of integration of both worlds, the specificity of the enzymatic hydroxylation capability, and the generality of structural imagination. As to positional specificity, it is simple and unambiguous. The frog will hydroxylate DMT at the 5-position rather than at the 4-position of the fungal world. The major alkaloid archetype is 5-hydroxy-DMT itself, bufotenine, and it is found throughout the frog world. *Bufo*, the prefix to bufotenine, is the major genus of frogs and, in fact, comes from the Latin word for toad. Putting a 5-hydroxy group onto a DMT molecule (to provide bufotenine) and in some instances to cap this hydroxy group with a methyl group (to provide 5-MeO-DMT), is, from the chemical viewpoint, the unimaginative part. The excitement is to be found in viewing the incredible wealth of bizarre chemicals that are to be found in the catalogue of poisons of the many tropical poisonous frogs. Complex alkaloids without precedent, strange, unexpected, with completely wild structures that are largely unrelated to any rational alkaloidal prototype. Most of them have been brought to our awareness by a little-recognized personal hero of mine, John Daly. And yet, even with this bountiful array of interesting compounds, one thing is lacking. There is no hint of DMT.

Thus, this is not the place for a review of the literature. Mushrooms are everywhere, and frogs are everywhere. And DMT is almost everywhere. They just don't happen to be in the same everywhere.

**GRASSES  The Grass Family, Gramineae (Poaceae)**

There are up to a thousand genera of grasses, with probably up to ten thousand species. There are many botanical families, and a lot of these contain plants that most of us would call grasses, but it is more comfortable for me to try to find common names for these groups. There are sedges (family Cyperaceae), bulrushes, and papyrus. There are similar hollow-stemmed rushes (family Juncaceae), and there are the bur reeds and cattails of the family Typhaceae. All of them are simple and ancient plants, but none of them have ever been reported to contain tryptamines.

But with the largest family of the grass-like plants, called Gramineae (sometimes called Poaceae), it is quite a different story. Here we find not only reeds but also the grains and forage foods used by both animal and man. There are soft flexible plants that are easily eaten by sheep and cattle. These are referred to as herbaceous, with leaves and soft tissue and nutritious seeds. There can be hard things like bamboo, reeds, and sugar canes, which are woody and have rigid stems. From these one can make furniture, arrows, spears, and clarinet and oboe reeds. Grasses are the mainstay of our diet, the rice and the corn and the wheat of life. But all of these foods, the hard and the soft, are nonetheless grasses and many of them are exceptionally rich sources of DMT and related tryptamines. Consider a most common name:

— Canary Grass          (*Phalaris* spp.)

I had a visit from a young ayahuasquero a year or so ago, who brought me a house gift of some liquid expressed from a grass that was presumably rich in DMT. Let me slow down for a minute. Just what, or who is an ayahuascero? He is a person who is knowledgeable in the making and offering of ayahuasca. In the Chapter "Hoasca vs. Ayahuasca" I try to lay out a definition of these two proper names. Both names apply (with appropriate attention paid to origins and professional territory) to a mixture of two things which are designed to interact to produce an active psychotropic drink. One component, usually containing DMT, is immediately inactivated by the body's chemistry if it is taken alone. The other component, usually containing harmine or harmaline, serves to inactivate the body's inactivating defenses, thus allowing the first component to become orally active. The second agent of the combination keeps the body from neutralizing the first. The combination, the inhibited and the inhibitor, is commonly called ayahuasca. The artist/craftsman/sage who can combine these two extracts together to create the material ayahuasca, is known as an ayahuasquero.

So, I had a visit by a young ayahuasquero who wanted to show me examples of ayahuasca that he had prepared. The first of these two components, the DMT-containing component, was an extract of a grass that had the proper name of *Phalaris*. He had gathered a handful of the grass (it apparently grows wild throughout most of the United States) and put it through something called a wheat grass juicer. This is a grinding instrument that can be obtained at the local health food store, and can reduce a pile of plant stuff to a glassful of liquid and some dry discards. The pale green watery liquid that came from this process could be consumed as part #1 of the ayahuasca combination, or it could be dried to a green brittle residue (evaporation of the contained water was achieved by pushing air over it with an electric fan) and smoked. About six tokes did it, or so he claimed.

So here I had a grass that was a DMT source and, according to him, a good one. I wanted to see what I could learn about it by snooping about in my library and doing a little bit of lab work. *Phalaris*. That is the only word I had to operate on. My U.S. government printing office publication (1950) on the grasses of the United States informed me that *Phalaris* is an old Greek name for grass. Fine. It is self-descriptive. However, my Webster's Collegiate Dictionary (which has few botanical aspirations) had another contribution in this area. Phalarope was a sandpiper-like bird named by combining phalaris and pod (according to them, phalaris is a Greek word for coot, and pod is a foot) so we have coot's feet. And coot is apparently a duck-like bird without pretensions. I was not making much headway, unless I wished to pursue haunts of coot and hern.

Everything fell completely apart after my ayahuasquero company had left, and I entered into a fine dialogue with my son, Theo. We tried to construct a botanical (not a classical) definition of *Phalaris*. Here are the first lines of the official definition from the U.S. Department of Agriculture text.

> "Spikelets laterally compressed, with (1) terminal perfect
> floret and (2) sterile lemmas below the rachilla disarticulat-
> ing above the glumes, the usual inconspicuous sterile

lemmas falling closely appressed to the fertile floret; glumes equal, boat shaped, often winged on the keel, sterile lemmas reduced to two small, usually minute, scales (rarely only one); fertile lemma coriaceous, shorter than the glumes, enclosing the faintly two-nerved palea."

We were doubled over in laughter. In the more advanced parts of First World countries there is a professional business phenomena known as the phone tree in which you will be presented with six choices following your initial inquiry, and each of these will, in turn, give you six additional directions to follow. In this *Phalaris* definition we have six words, each totally unknown, and each a part of the exclusive jargon of the botanists. Each one, when looked up, gave rise to new cascade of unknown words.

Glume: a chaffy bract. Chaff I know to be the dusty stuff that goes Southwards when you toss threshed wheat into the air with a North wind blowing. A bract I have always known as the brightly colored inside first leaf of the bougainvillea that is usually assumed, by most viewers, to be the blossom. And bracts comprise the bright red display of the Christmas poinsettia.

Lemma: the lower of the two bracts enclosing the flower of the spikelet of grasses.

Spikelet: one of the small few-flowered bracted spikes that make up the compound inflorescence of a grass or sedge.

I found myself becoming quite uncertain as to what even a grass was. The second of the two botanical words I ever learned as a precocious child was monocotyledon, a plant that first sprouts from the ground as a single-spiked, pointy thing.

This *Phalaris* is a foot-or-so high, a blooming grass, that likes a wet environment, and has an upside-down thimbly-shaped blossom that makes it stand out from other grasses. To use it you cut its tops, and leave the roots alone. So it is a regenerating crop.

The common name for the entire collection of these grasses is Canary Grass. I think I have discovered why. There is a commercial product called Canary Seed, a common food product for caged birds, that has for many years come from a plant that is known as Canary Island Grass, which is *P. canariensis*. This plant is an annual grass that had its origins in the Mediterranean area, largely through Southern Europe, and it has been raised both as bird seed and as a cereal. It was introduced years ago into the United States and is now to be found everywhere here. I have yet to find a report of any analysis of this archetypal Canary Grass showing DMT to be present in it, but I am not sure that anyone has ever looked there. However, its relatives warrant very close inspection as they are extremely rich sources of DMT, and each deserves to be highlighted.

— Reed Canary Grass    (*Phalaris arundinacea*)
                       (*Phalaris aquatica*)
— Staggers Grass       (*Phalaris tuberosa*)

The Reed Canary Grass (*P. arundinacea*) is a perennial grass. It is best known by its British origins as a reed grass that grows on the banks of British rivers and lakes. As an ornamental, it has often been called ribbon grass. A variety of it is widely scattered through the midwest part of the United States, its blades are striped with white, and it has been called Gardener's Garters. Four alkaloids are claimed to be present: DMT and the demethylated NMT, as well as the 5-methoxylated counterparts of both, 5-MeO-DMT and 5-MeO-NMT. But interestingly, there are reports that there is a simple beta-carboline present in this grass as well (2-methyl-1,2,3,4-THβC). Thus, depending on the amount there, this possible MAO inhibitor just might make the grass orally active. Another grass has the same species name, but is of a different genus. This is *Festuca arundinacea*, or the reed fescue, or alta fescue, and it is said to contain the simplest of the β-carbolines, βC itself. Its morphology is quite different from that of *Phalaris arundinacea*, so I must accept that it is a different grass.

There are a number of reports of DMT to be found in the literature on *P. aquatica*. I do not know of a common name for this grass. It appears to be a versatile source of alkaloids, containing not only DMT but also the mono-methyl analogue (NMT), and unsubstituted tryptamine as well. A thin layer chromatographic analysis of seedlings has shown the presence of six additional alkaloids, specifically the 5-hydroxy and the 5-methoxy derivatives of each of these three tryptamine alkaloids.

The third, and most controversial member of this genus of grasses, is the physically similar "Staggers Grass." It has been called Harding Grass and Peruvian Wintergrass. This is the plant *P. tuberosa*, which is also a perennial. It appeared in Australia early in this century, and in the United States a couple of decades later. This specific plant is a true bête noire of the agricultural community in that it is directly connected to the "staggers syndrome" in sheep. This is a tragic reality in that sheep will forage on grasses and in some cases undergo extreme muscular disturbance. The grass, "Staggers Grass", contains the three major tryptamines, DMT, bufotenine, and 5-MeO-DMT. It has been believed, and it has been pro-moted, that these chemicals are responsible for this syndrome. Not so. A direct administration of a major component, 5-MeO-DMT, did indeed seem to duplicate this syndrome, but the embarrassing point is that neither DMT nor 5-MeO-DMT is orally active, and as such should not affect sheep that take it in their food by grazing. If a drug is only active parenterally, the poisoned animal could not get the potentially active toxin via an oral route. Is there some enzyme discovery to be made here? This "staggers" story is extremely complex and, at the moment, there is no bottom line. Here is a quick overview of the staggers, and the poisons responsible for them, and the implicated plants from the fescues to the rye grasses to even the ergots, and no one knows yet just what is going on.

Pay careful attention. The earliest argument was presented that it was the high DMT level in *P. tuberosa* that caused the staggers in sheep. But as a preparation for what is to come, let me introduce a botanical reality called an endophyte. "Endo" means inside. "Phyte" means a plant. A plant within a plant. I am surprised to learn that there can be a plant of sorts, often a fungus, that can take up residence inside another plant and grow, through its entire life cycle, as an invisible parasite. About a decade ago this concept became widely accepted and appreciated, and this has led to some re-evaluations of the so-called toxic plants.

There is a form of the "staggers" called Fescue Toxicity (or Fescue Foot) in cattle, horses and sheep, which has been said to be caused by the grass called the Tall Fescue (or Reed Fescue). The plant has the name *Festuca arundinacea* and this species name is identical to the above-named *Phalaris* species, but this is not too surprising considering that "arundo" is the Latin word for reed. Inside this grass there is an internal fungus, an endophyte, which is carried (totally invisibly) from the seed stage clear through to the final adult. This organism was initially thought to be *Sphacelia typhina*, the asexual state of *Epichloë typhina*, a fungus known on many grasses and associated with the syndrome "Choke Disease." This fescue endophyte has been found to be sufficiently distinct to deserve a new name, *Acremonium coenophialum*, and the staggers syndrome may be the result of an ergot alkaloid present, ergovaline.

Pay more attention. Another family of grasses that cause animal problems is the rye-grass group. One of these, *Lolium temulentum*, (called darnel), actually has been connected with human intoxication. The toxic properties of yet another rye-grass, *Lolium perenne* (called English ryegrass, which just happens to contain β-carboline), has been explained by the presence of yet another parasite fungus, *Acremonium loliae*. Darnel is sometimes connected with the tare (the vetch seed), stated in the Parables of the Bible to have been sown by the enemy. But most scholars now believe that this poison weed was in fact a legume, the vetch *Vicia sativa* or *V. hirsuta*. Another grass, called "sleepy grass" which is largely narcotic to horses, is the needle grass *Stipa robusta*, which has been shown to contain lysergamide (ergine). Again there is a very strong reason to suspect that a fungus is present.

Pay yet more attention. A related plant, the vetch, is represented by a number of species of the genus *Cyperus*, which are known to be infested with the *Claviceps* fungi, perhaps the ergot individual called *Balansia cyperi*. These plants have spun their way into the medicine cabinets of several South American tribes for the treatment of postpartum hemorrhaging, as an abortifacient, as a general hemostatic agent, and for modifying the menstrual cycle. Ergots again are the prime candidates.

There is a final intimate marriage between grasses, staggers and the ergots. There is a grass called Dallis grass, that causes "paspalum staggers" and its botanical name is *Paspalum dilatatum*. This contains an infestation of *Claviceps paspali*, which is one of the most productive ergot cultures for the generation of lysergic acid propanolamide, a superb synthetic precursor to LSD.

I truly believe that the motor problem of staggers in sheep and other grazing animals is due to lysergic acid derivative poisoning, rather than tryptamine poisoning. I am totally convinced that DMT plays no role in this agricultural health problem. DMT is in these grasses, but DMT has no role in staggers. The efforts of the Government to breed grasses with low DMT content, to control these problems, has had no positive return. Such efforts will now be continued only for drug control reasons, not to protect grazing livestock. Let's get back to the rich Gramineae family of true grasses again.

There are a number of grasses that, because of their firmness and height, are commonly called reeds or bamboo. The best known genera, and of great interest to the searcher for plant sources of DMT or related tryptamines are:

| | |
|---|---|
| — Giant Reed | (*Arundo donax*) |
| — Common Reed | (*Arundo phragmites*) |
| | (or *Phragmites communis*) |
| | (or *Phragmites australis*) |
| — Bamboo | (*Phyllostachys* spp.) |

The giant grass *Arundo donax* is a tall, perennial reed of a bamboo-like nature. A number of studies have found this plant to be a rich tryptamine source. Almost all the published reports have located these alkaloids in the flowers or in the roots of the plant. The blossoms have both DMT and the 5-methoxylated N-demethylated analogue, 5-MeO-NMT. The roots are a rhizomal system and they not only contain these active tryptamines, but bufotenine as well. The quaternary methylated salt of DMT is in the flowers, and bufotenidine and the cyclic dehydrobufotenidine are in the roots. Another report puts 5-MeO-DMT in all of the plant's extracts.

The common reed can be found on banks of marshes, lakes, and streams, from the Arctic to the temperate zones. In Mexico it is called, simply, carrizo and it is used for making mats and screens, and nets for carrying things. One carefully studied individual is *Phragmites australis*, which is particularly rich in DMT in the root system, the rhizome. *Arundo phragmites* and *Phragmites communis* are old synonyms for this reed.

One of the earliest memories I have is of a plant called bamboo. It was a slender thing that grew very high, with round and hollow stalks — it always struck me as being unnatural, maybe man-made. To me it was a thick pile of vertical sticks that you did not go through, but which you had to go around. In Palenque, Mexico, I saw these in clutches many feet around, standing dozens of feet high, and always making squeaky sounds at the top as if their growing process was putting out noise. Most of our cultivated bamboos are from the Orient, but they have been transplanted around the world. The major tryptamine present in the bamboo species is serotonin, and of the twenty or more genera introduced to Western agriculture, most remain totally unexplored as to the alkaloids that might be present.

There are chemically less dramatic (but still widely distributed) grasses which are called the foraging grasses, or reed grasses. The list below includes these, as well as the grains we eat, which are further extentions of the grasses.

| | |
|---|---|
| — Reed Grass | (*Calamagrostis* spp.) |
| | (*Arundinella hirta*) |
| — Cogon Grass | (*Imperata cylindrica*) |
| — Reed Fescue | (*Festuca arundinacea*) |
| — Wild Rice | (*Zizania cacuciflora*) |
| — Rice | (*Oryza sativa*) |
| — Indian Corn | (*Zea mays*) |
| — Barley | (*Hordeum vulgare*) |
| — Oats | (*Avena sativa*) |

The various reed grasses, *Calamagrostis* spp., are just a little disappointing in that they contain mainly serotonin, as does the related *Arundinella hirta* and the Cogon Grass *Imperata cylindrica*. The reed fescue, *Festuca arundinacea*, which had been mentioned earlier, contains melatonin. Serotonin is an important neurotransmitter, and melatonin is a neutral compound that plays a role in the night and day functioning of the pineal gland. Neither of these is psychoactive. There is no pharmacological drama here; they are strictly the tryptamine building blocks of the simple alkaloids.

As for the grains, wild rice, *Zizania* spp., is a food source and contains serotonin. The common rice, *Oryza sativa*, is a rich source of melatonin, the sleep hormone. Melatonin is also in the seed-kernel of ordinary corn, *Zea mays*, along with a number of other N-substituted tryptamine amides which have not, to my knowledge, been explored as psychoactive chemicals.

The well-known cultivated barley, *Hordeum vulgare*, is the only agriculturally acceptable member of this lineage. The lesser varieties are considered weeds, especially the fox tail barley, *H. jubatum*, which has sharp-pointed spikes that can pierce the nose and mouth of foraging stock. But again, melatonin is present in the grain seed and the leaf also.

## LEGUMES  The Pea Family, Leguminosae (Fabaceae)

The legumes constitute probably the third largest family of plants, with upwards of a thousand genera, and over 10,000 species. The more exacting classifiers insist on a small cluster of sub-families which some botanists claim are families unto themselves, but for this chapter, the only family discussed will be the Leguminosae. I had always thought of legumes as things likes peas and beans that have funny root nodules with some bacteria in them, that can take atmospheric nitrogen and convert it to a chemical fertilizer form that is given to the soil and has the potential for enriching it. Nitrogen fixing, it is called. The legumes are also herbs and shrubs and trees. And they are one of the richest sources of tryptamines such as DMT. Some of the genera within the Leguminosae have many fascinating species, and some are monotypic, one of a kind.

One of the most bountiful of these, as far as tryptamine content is concerned, is the genus *Acacia*. Although many types of acacia can be found natively all around the world, there is one country that for over a hundred years has had an intimate identification with them. This is Australia, where there are more than 700 native species, and the common name for them is Wattle (which comes from an old Anglo-Saxon word meaning "flexible twig" as in the term, "wattle and daub").

Here I will digress for a moment into a bit of "Down-Under" history. Initially, the interest was a commercial one, as the bark of the Golden Wattle (*A. pycnantha* and the Black Wattle (*A. mearnsii*) contained almost 50% tannin. The closely related acacia (the Green Wattle, *A. decurrens*) was transplanted to large plantations in South Africa and, since these could be operated much more economically, the Australian industry pretty much disappeared by the end of the nineteenth century. But the fascination with the plant itself remained. The first Wattle Club was formed in 1899, and in 1910 the first national Wattle day was celebrated in Sydney,

Adelaide and Melbourne on September 1. Songs and poems were written, and sprigs of Wattle were worn on lapels. The movement grew like topsy. It was used for fund-raising for charities and for public morale connected with the World War I war efforts. There were Wattle queens elected and crowned, Wattle Day badges were worn, and every one pinned on a small sprig of it to wear to school. On the first of September, 1988, at a ceremony in Canberra, the Golden Wattle was officially proclaimed Australia's national floral emblem, exactly 75 years after the idea had been first proposed. Just recently I had the pleasure of being in Sydney, and heard from my Sydneysider host a nursery rhyme he had learned as a child:

> Here is the Wattle.
> The emblem of our land.
> You can stick it in a bottle
> Or hold it in your hand.

I don't remember any botanical poems from my childhood days in Berkeley, but I do remember that every spring there would be a burst of yellow trees on the hillsides all around us. The acacias were in bloom. In my naive innocence, the large, fluffy yellow blossom was the total definition of this plant, but I have now learned that there are many acacias and some of them look very different from these that I am familiar with. Some produce crops of economic importance such as Gum Arabic, and most of them are total dweebs, but there are surprises.

A couple of years ago I stopped alongside the Claremont Hotel on Fish Ranch Road in Berkeley and snagged a clutch of acacia leaf. I ground it up under some dichlor, filtered it, and evaporated the extract down to a smudge which I dissolved in a couple of drops of toluene/butanol. I shot a microliter of this solution into the GCMS looking for DMT. No DMT. I figured that our local acacia (*A. baileyana*, which is called the Cootamundra Wattle in its native Australia) was simply a Bay Area dweeb. But I shortly thereafter uncovered a surprising bit of information and learned a couple of lessons: (1), read the literature, and (2), nature is not simple.

Pursuing this plant in the botanical writings I discovered a paper written by a close friend of mine, published some twenty years earlier, who had performed and reported some careful work in contrast to my slap-dash one-shot deal. He selected one specific *A. baileyana* tree near his home, and took samples of its leaves in the spring, in the summer, and again in the fall. He carefully assayed these collections separately. The spring selection showed the 0.02% alkaloid content to be a mixture of tryptamine (not DMT but the parent, unsubstituted tryptamine) and β-carbolines, with tetrahydroharman being by far the major component. In the fall, this alkaloid fraction was exclusively tryptamine. The summer collection was devoid of any alkaloids whatsoever. If the botanist were to have made a single study of this plant, he would have missed the seasonal variation, and have come to a misleading conclusion as to its contents. And how many reports in the literature are based upon a single collection from a group of plants without the time of year even being recorded? Or perhaps even the time of day? If a psychonaut were to have made a single study of this plant, to have discovered activity he might have had to eat it in the spring, smoke it in the fall, and he would have found no activity in the summer months. But he may have tried it a single time, and might not have remembered just when this trial occurred, just as I cannot remember what time of year it was that I collected my own sample of acacia.

There are some pretty macho reports about a few of the other species. I have heard several interesting stories of experiences with the Australian Wattle tree, *Acacia maidenii*, or Maiden's Acacia. Early reports of DMT and NMT being components of the stem bark have been pharmacologically confirmed by a report made by some Sydney explorers who leached its bark with boiling methanol and, after evaporating the solvent, smoked the residue to successfully generate a dramatic DMT trip. There are quite a large number of other *Acacia* species that are well documented as containing methylated tryptamines, but few if any have histories of cultural use despite the presence of these compounds. There is DMT (or NMT, or T) reported in the following *Acacia* species: *A. albida* (DMT, in the leaf), *A. confusa* (DMT and NMT, in the leaf, stem and bark), *A. cultriformis* or Golden Glow or Knife-leaf Wattle (T, in the leaf and stem), *A. laeta* (DMT, in the leaf), *A. mellifera* (DMT, in the leaf), *A. nilotica* (DMT, in the leaf), *A. phlebophylla* or Buffalo Sallow Wattle (DMT, in the leaf), *A. podalyriaefolia* or Mt. Morgan's Wattle, or Queensland Silver Wattle (T, in the leaf), *A. polyacantha* (DMT, in the leaf), *A. senegal* (DMT, in the leaf), *A. seyal* (DMT, in the leaf), *A. sieberiana* (DMT, in the leaf), *A. simplicifolia* (DMT and NMT, in the leaf, stem and trunk bark), and *A. vestita* or Hairy Wattle (T, in the leaf and stem). *Acacia niopo* is an old name for the plant *Anadenanthera peregrina*, which is mentioned below.

There are two additional *Acacia* and Sydney comments, which must be offered here. The first is an Australian story. One of the early botanists exploring and identifying the many acacia trees discovered a new species, which he described and named. As is often the case, he gave it his name, which was Watts, and the plant is called *A. wattsiana*, and its common name is the rather remarkable Watts' Wattle. If this information were to become widely known down under, there in Sydney, one might hear a morning greeting between botanists at the University, "G'dye, myte; Watts' wattle!"

The second is an *Acacia* story. It deals with the acacias that are found in, and identified with, the ancient history of the Near East and Egypt. There was a balsam oil peddled to the priests of yore by the Bedouins, which was claimed to have come from the "original" "Tree of Knowledge," which existed at the lowest point on earth, near the Dead Sea and the Sinai Desert. This balsam oil was made from the *A. tortilis*, or the Umbrella Acacia.

There are three genera that are closely associated with the *Acacia* and with each other, and sometimes botanists exchange their genus names but they usually keep, thankfully, the species names intact. This is a sensible convention that has saved the amateur botanist much grief. Two of these related genera are named *Piptadenia* (originally *Niopa*) of which a number of species have slipped over into the second-named genus, *Anadenanthera*. The third genus is *Mimosa*.

One of the major legumes of interest in this nomenclature zoo is the plant *Piptadenia peregrina* (originally *Acacia niopo* or *Mimosa peregrina*), which is now generally known as *Anadenanthera peregrina*. Probably the earliest known active drug forms in the New World were the snuffs of the Amazon (known generically as paricá) and the West Indies (where the name cohoba was used). The snuff from the *A. peregrina* tree was called yopo, and it was made from the seed material from the tree's pods. These seeds of the Yopo Tree were moistened, fermented, mixed with lime (from snail shells), dried and finely powdered. This snuff apparently was used throughout the Northwestern part of South America, in Colombia, Venezuela, Peru, Bolivia, perhaps northern Argentina and certainly Brazil. There are a lot of conflicting data as to the addition of other plants into the yopo; certainly tobacco and virola resin were used. This latter material is the stuff of a snuff in its own right.

Here is a pristine example of the unresolvable conflict that I mentioned at the start of this chapter, the filing of complex things under simple headings. Do you focus on the drug concoction that is used, or its plant origins, as a means of organization? A given snuff may be associated with several plants; a given plant may be associated with several snuffs. I have chosen the plant and its components, and here we are discussing *Anadenanthera peregrina*. This plant is a Pandora's box of tryptamines, and they are to be found in every part of the plant. Bufotenine was the first alkaloid isolated from the seeds (over 40 years ago) and this was followed shortly by the discovery of a host of related alkaloids. Not only the seeds, but the leaf, the bark and the root, all contain DMT, NMT, tryptamine, bufotenine, as well as the two methoxylated analogues, 5-MeO-DMT and 5-MeO-NMT. There are even a couple of β-carbolines present. Several publications have described these analyses, and some of them give a quantitative measure of alkaloid content.

Other *Piptadenia* spp. are less well known, and less well studied. *Piptadenia macrocarpa* contains not only DMT, but bufotenine and its N-oxide as well in its seeds and pods. Further, the bark contains 5-MeO-NMT. *Piptadenia excelsa* also contains DMT, bufotenine and its N-oxide. Three species (*P. communis, contorta,* and *falcata*) contain bufotenine in their seeds. None of these plants have been explored as to their psychoactive potential.

A tree closely related to the *Piptadenia peregrina* (*Anadenanthera peregrina*) is the *A. columbrina* which is native to Peru, Bolivia, Southern Brazil and Northern Argentina. There are various local names for the snuffs from these trees such as vilca, huilca and cébil. The early studies on this particular species report many of the alkaloids that are present in *A. peregrina*, including DMT.

The third genus that is a close cousin to the *Acacia* is *Mimosa*. The Jurema Tree, known botanically as *M. hostilis*, has been used for centuries in northeastern Brazil as the source of an intoxicating drink, Vinho de Jurema. In early anthropological explorations, this plant was accepted as a narcotic plant, and called jurema prêta in popular language, but some felt that it was a bush and others, a tall tree. Names such as *Acacia jurema* and *Juremaprêta* were assigned to several candidates, but it was eventually determined that there were basically two kinds of jurema which were *M. nigra* and *M. hostilis*. The drink is made from the root of *M. hostilis* by boiling it a long time in water. The alkaloid that was found to be present, and accepted as the responsible intoxicating agent, was named nigerine and later identified as DMT. Since DMT is, by itself, not orally active, there is something unacceptable with this picture as it now stands; something is wrong. At least one of these statements must be changed: (1) *M. hostilis* is the single source of the orally active intoxicating drink Vihno de Jurema. (2) The plant that was used for the isolation of the alkaloid nigerine is *M. hostilis*. (3) This alkaloid is the sole active component in the drink. (4) Nigerine is DMT. It would be a fascinating project to look for accompanying minor alkaloids, or other clue indicators of origin, that might facilitate the connecting of the origins of this intoxicating drink to the jurema prêta, if it is still being used somewhere in Brazil.

There are several additional species of *Mimosa* that have been found to contain DMT. Another wine has been made from a plant called jurema branca which has been identified as *M. verrucosa*. It has a bark containing reasonably high quantities of DMT. Three closely allied plants contain alkaloids, but are not known as sources of drugs. *M. scabrella* has been reported to contain DMT and NMT as well as unsubstituted tryptamine itself. An even wider selection can be found in *M. somnians* where all of these are present plus bufotenine, 5-MeO-DMT and 5-MeO-NMT as well. And finally, traces of DMT have been reported from the trunk bark of *M. tenuiflora.*

There are a total of nine additional legumes that have been reported as containing DMT and other tryptamines. None of these, with one extraordinary exception, have shown a particularly high alkaloid content, and none have become popular as drug sources. Four species of the genus *Desmodium* demonstrate clear cases for their tryptamine content, in that all have DMT as a major component, all show examples of N-oxides of the more common alkaloids, and most of them contain pretty rich collections of tryptamine bases in general. *Desmodium gangeticum* is the classic model, with DMT and 5-MeO-DMT and their two N-oxides as the defining components of the leaf, the stem, and the root. *Desmodium pulchellum* has the same inventory, but with 5-MeO-NMT and bufotenine present in addition. *Desmodium triflorum* has all of the above, but some nor-bufotenine and bufotenine N-oxide as well. The roots of *D. caudatum*, on the other hand, simply contain DMT and bufotenine N-oxide. *Lespedeza bicolor* is a plant that has been studied as a uterine contractant. Its leaves and root bark contain a reasonable variety of tryptamines, however, including DMT and 5-MeO-DMT (and their N-oxides), and bufotenine. Another indolic alkaloid, lespedamine, is also present. The Indian plant *Mucuna pruriens* has the same inventory (DMT, 5-MeO-DMT and their N-oxides) and bufotenine in both the leaf and the fruit. *Petalostylis labicheoides* contains DMT and NMT in leaf and stem and, interestingly, also melatonin.

One very interesting plant is the Illinois Bundleflower, *Desmanthus illinoensis*. Its roots are a treasure house of tryptamines. As a DMT source, the entire root contains 2% by weight, and the actual root bark itself contains a whopping 25%. NMT is present in these tissues at 0.5% and 8% respectively. But there are other tantalizing goodies there. Both N-hydroxy-NMT and 2-hydroxy-NMT are present. Both are pharmacological unknowns, but it is interesting that N-hydroxy-NMT bears the same relationship to NMT that N-hydroxy-MDMA does to MDMA. And, since N-HO-MDMA is equipotent to MDMA, perhaps N-HO-NMT would be equipotent to NMT. But then, the human activity of NMT has not yet been confirmed.

One last legume problem remains, and I am not sure just how to deal with it. There are three more genera of the legumes that deserve special mention. None of them contain species that are sources of DMT, but they either contain tryptamine-like alkaloids or they are almost physically indistinguishable from their cousins that do, and all of them are very toxic and also have some passing reputation for producing a sort of psychotropic intoxication that is not well understood. This story involves the mescal bean history of the early Indian population of the United States and Mexico.

There have been red beans deeply involved in some ritual ceremonies throughout these areas for centuries, and they may well have been a prelude to the Peyote cultures which are now well established. As I explained to my dear step-daughter Wendy, there are reference books and photo-spreads and poison-plant manuals and ethnopharmacology theses, all referring to beans that are all red, to red things that are really brown, to the red things with black dots on them somewhere, to the red and black mixed half-and-half things, to simply the red beans found in the native marketplaces, all of which are part of the ceremonial and toxicological history of our early indigenous population. I told Wendy that all I really wanted to do was to steal from somewhere a paragraph that presents all of this complexity in simple language. I have looked quite widely, and I don't think that paragraph exists, so I have to write it myself. Here it is, an attempt to verify the botanical identity of the red beans reputed to have been used in Southwest Indian ceremonies for centuries. There are sections called "Probably Yes" and "Probably No," to be followed by an additional paragraph with other beans including teasers from Chiapas and from Australia entitled, "Most Certainly Not."

The "Probably Yes" deals with the story behind the Mescal Bean culture that existed for years in the Southwest United States and the Northern Sonora and Chihuahua desert of Mexico. Mescal is a tricky word with many connotations, and is often seen in Spanish as mezcal. It has been used for the strong distilled alcoholic drink made from the Century Plant or Maguey, known botanically as being of the genus *Agave*. One specific mescal drink, known as tequila, is made specifically from the species *A. tequilana*. It is a name that had been used mistakenly by the Bureau of Indian Affairs to identify the peyote cactus, *Lophophora williamsii*, and has contributed to the naming of its primary alkaloid as mescaline. The dried top of the cactus has been called a Mescal Button.

But the term "Mescal Bean" refers to the seed of the plant *Sophora secundiflora*, known popularly as the Texas Mountain Laurel or simply Wild Laurel. Its lavender blossoms are dramatic against the barren Southern Texas desert, and they themselves contain some of the alkaloids of the seeds and, if eaten, can make a person ill. It is the seeds themselves, the red beans, that are best known. They are called frijolillo, or frijolito, or frijol-rojo, or simply colorines. They are small, measuring 10 to 12 millimeters in length and from 8 to 10 millimeters in diameter. They are scarlet-colored, and have a centuries-old history of use in Indian culture, in a tradition known as the Deer Dance, or the Red Bean Dance. These seeds have an ancient reputation for being psychedelic, but they must be consumed with care, as there is a fine line between intoxication and poisoning. The alkaloid composition is complex, closely related to the piperidines and pyridinols rather than to the tryptamines, and can be located under the class name, cytisine.

The "Probably No" entry deals with two species of legumes known as *Erythrina*, widely recognized in folk medicine. They have seeds which are very easily confused with the *Sophora* seeds, and have been actually sold together, intermixed, in some native markets, as mescal beans, red beans, coral beans, and under the catch-all term, colorines. Here the alkaloid overlap with the tryptamines becomes quite strange. The class of alkaloids that are usually associated with the *Erythrina* collection are four ring systems, with a defining nucleus of a tetrahydro-isoquinoline. This latter unit is associated with the cactus alkaloids, and is the topic of an appendix to this book. There is a tryptamine connection, however, in that almost twenty species have been reported to contain hypaphorine, (N,N,N-trimethyltryptophan) in their seeds. This is the methyl quaternary salt of N,N-dimethyltryptophan, also known by the trivial names, lenticine and glyyunnanenine. This is a precursor to all sorts of potential tryptamine alkaloids discussed later under the section in this chapter called biosynthesis. Of the two species I have in my collection, the seeds of *Erythrina flabelliformis* are most similar to those of *Sophora secundiflora*. They are also red in color, slightly larger ratio of length to diameter, therefore appearing less spherical. Furthermore, they have a dark hilum (this is the navel-like spot where the seed is attached to the pod that sheaths it), whereas that of the mescal bean is cream colored. The other species of *Erythrina* I have is *E. herbocea*. These beans are again bright red, and have cream-colored hila, but they are quite a bit smaller, 6-12 millimeters in length, by average only half that dimension in diameter. I have one additional set of *E*. spp. ( I do not know the species) which has the same general dimensions, but with a coal-black hilum.

The "Most Certainly Not" listing deals with the little red seeds that have a black spot at the base that covers more of the surface of the seed than just the hilum itself. The best-studied member of this legume group has been called the Weather Plant, the Rosary Pea, or Indian or Wild Licorice, or simply the Jequirity plant. Its seeds have been called crab's eyes, rosary beans, or prayer or jumble beads. They have been used widely as necklaces in the Southwest and the corresponding seeds, in India, have been used as weight standards, with the name Rati. The plant has the binomial *Abrus precatorius*.

Two of the three interesting drugs derived from the seeds of this plant have similar names, although they have totally dissimilar chemistry. Abrin, also called toxalbumin, is an extremely toxic protein fraction, which can kill a mouse at a total dose of about 1 microgram. It has been said that one seed, well chewed, can be fatal to man. The second drug is abrine, which is N-methyl tryptophan, and a potential source (after decarboxylation) of

NMT. The third drug is, again, hypaphorine, the trimethyl quaternary salt of tryptophan. It is plentiful in the seeds, but there is a claim that the root of this plant contains as much as 7% of this tryptamine precursor.

There is more in this "Most Certainly Not" category. These are red beans that just might be confused with any of the above, but which cannot be in any way considered part of the Southwest United States or Northern Mexican cultures. They are here just because they are fun, and they deal with Indian cultures in their own way. While interacting with the Lacandon Indians in the Palenque Ruins last year, my wife bought a few necklaces that were strings of red Leguminosae beads. These were quite large beads, red and black (largely red), with a wandering line that separated the two colors. I asked my German botanist ally if he could give names to the plant, and I was informed that there were male and female names. The first of these are bright red in color, ellipsoid, fully a centimeter long, with a splash of black color on one edge that covers almost half the bean. The Lacandon name is, "äh äm u tooni" which is a huge legume tree assigned a male role, but which is unidentified! Yet I have also found a photograph in Emboden's "Narcotic Plants" that shows what appear to be these very seeds from a tree with the name *Rhynchosia pyramidalis,* and somewhat larger samples from the so-called necklace tree, *Ormosia monosperma.* I am totally befuddled. The Mexican seed used is bright red, almost circular, about a centimeter in diameter, and about 5 millimeters thick, and there is no black on it at all, but maybe a slight discoloration at the hilum. The Lacandon name is: "äh äm u ch'up" which is another closely-related gigantic legume tree, assigned the female role, but also unidentified! An interesting but different seed used in their necklaces is a small, black, spherical seed of about 5 millimeters in diameter, with no red on it at all. The Lacandon name is: "äh ch'änk'ala'" and it has the binomial of *Canna indica.*

Back to the DMT world. The heart of this section is the *Virola* plants, with the resins obtained from their bark, and with the snuffs that have been made from them. As to the plants, there are three that are well known and the most thoroughly studied; *Virola calophylla, V. rufula,* and *V. theiodora.* As to the plant parts that contribute to the drug, there is a blood-red resin that needs to be gotten one way or another from its bark. The bark can be taken from felled trees and, on being heated, will exude the red resin which on boiling down provides an amber-like solid, which on grinding becomes the snuff. Or, the inner surface of the bark can be scraped into shavings that can either be roasted and pulverized to form the snuff, or boiled with water, strained, and reduced to a sludge which is dried in the sun and then ground up to form the snuff. Some recipes call for the addition of plants outside of the *Virola* group.

What is it called? The snuff itself goes by many names, depending on the locale of its use.  The names paricá, epená (ebene) and nyakwana are heard in Brazil; yakee and yato are more common in Colombia.

How is it used?  In some cultures, the use of the snuff is restricted to the tribal elders, and the witch-doctors, to help in the diagnosis and treatment of their patients.  In others, its use is quite general and serves a social role in entertainment or in special ceremonies.  It is, however, generally restricted to the post-adolescent male population.  Two additional routes of using the *Virola* snuff must be seriously considered, as both are pharmacologically reasonable.  Some anthropological field notes have suggested that the dried inner bark might have been smoked, and DMT is well established as being active by this route.  Also, some of the claims of oral activity of the snuff may be explained by the reports of the presence of methoxylated beta-carbolines in several of the species.  The carboline chemical family contains a number of effective monoamine oxidase inhibitors which would allow the orally inactive tryptamines to show activity when taken by mouth.

The most thoroughly studied *Virola* plant is *V. theiodora* from the Brazilian Amazon.  Its bark can run as high as 0.25% DMT by dry weight, and the flowers can be twice this level.  5-MeO-DMT is also present at sizable levels, and both of the mono-methyl homologues, NMT and 5-MeO-NMT, have been found in various parts of the plant.  The bark is also a source of the carboline 6-methoxy-2-methyl-1,2,3,4-tetrahydrocarboline.

This exact same tryptamine content is present in the leaf, bark, and root of *Virola rufula* and, except for 5-MeO-NMT, in the bark and leaf of *V. calophylla*.  The five remaining *Virola* species that have been studied contain just DMT and 5-MeO-DMT in their leaf and bark (and root bark), and usually at levels too low for any serious consideration as a practical source of DMT.  These are *V. elongata, V. loretensis (= multinervia), V. pavonis, V. peruviana*, and *V. venosa*.  A rather complex assortment of alkaloidal components have been reported in *V. sebifera*.  DMT, NMT and 5-MeO-DMT are present, but so is the N-oxide of DMT and of 5-HO-DMT (bufotenine).  However, two unexpected amides are reported as being in this plant, the N-formyl and the N-acetyl derivatives of NMT.  These are probably not psychoactive, but their resemblance to melatonin is intriguing.

Final comments with the Myristicaceae.  Two *Virola* species (*V. calophylloidea* and *V. cuspidata*) have been reported as having positive color tests for alkaloids, but they have apparently never been analyzed.  Also, there are two relatively unknown stragglers of academic interest in the tryptamine world.  There is a Malaysian tree *Horsfieldia supurba* with 5-MeO-DMT reported in the leaves.  Also, there is a paper that discusses another *Myristica* relative, *Osteophloum platyspermum*, which contains abrine methyl ester, discussed later under biosynthesis.

## COFFEE, TEA, QUININE and PSYCHOTRIA   The Madder Family, Rubiaceae

I know that the world's coffee supply comes from the seeds of the plant *Coffea arabica, C. canephora* and *C. liberica* and the world's tea supply comes from the leaves of *Camellia sinensis*. These two drinks account for over 95% of the brewed caffeine drinks consumed in the world, and the bulk of the remainder is met by the seeds of the guarana plant *Paullinia cupana* and the yerba maté leaves of *Ilex paraguariensis*. There are four psychoactive drugs that are head and shoulders above all others, in that they can claim over a billion users each. Caffeine is one of them. Most people can guess that the second and third are alcohol and nicotine (from *Nicotiana tabacum* and *N. rustica*). But few would guess that the fourth was Betel nut. The nut itself is from *Areca catechu* with the active component arecoline, and the Betel leaf that is chewed with it is from the pepper, *Piper betle*. Amazingly, marijuana is way down there with cocaine and opium as runners-up. Quinine is mentioned here only because it is a standard diluent of heroin on the U.S. East Coast. This is due to the belief that pure heroin is bitter, and with the addition of quinine the diluted heroin is indeed bitter, thus taken as authentic. In the West, the mythology says that really pure heroin will numb the tongue, so there is the addition of benzocaine to the pile of sugar that surrounds heroin, that way it will pass the Western field test.

The only DMT-containing plants in this family are of the genus *Psychotria*. I find it totally amazing that the plant *Psychotria viridis*, whose leaves are an essential component of the two-part sacrament ayahuasca, was neither recognized nor described by botanists until only a few years ago. This is truly 50% of the ayahuasca world. Here is one of the most widely used plants in two of the accepted religions of Brazil, a rich and available source of DMT (and NMT and a little N-methyl-1,2,3,4-tetrahydro-$\beta$-carboline), and yet it had never been used for any of the snuff preparations. It has only been used in mixtures, never alone. There are many closely-related species of *Psychotria* that have been found and described in the Brazilian flora, and this would be a rich area for exploring the extent of alkaloid distribution. A quiet dream of mine is to get together a small but compatible team of curious scientists of several disciplines, equip a flat-bottomed barge with a pile of instruments, a good library, an OK kitchen and wine-cellar (if one could put one on a flat-bottomed barge), but no telephone or radio. Then, commit a year to wandering up the Amazon into the boondocks, just collecting and analyzing and recording for posterity. So many noble people are trying to stop the destructive trashing of the Amazon heritage through legal arguments, or with financial maneuvers, or by the restriction of the selling of chain-saws or matches. An innocent boat would be a totally different approach to the saving of the rain-forest.

The coryanthine and yohimbine alkaloids from the plant *Corynanthe johimbe*, and the mitragynine alkaloids of the *Mitragyna speciosa* are gathered here under this family name. Both of these have revealed compounds of central activity. which have been ignored. Their extracts are just now appearing as herbal medicines through the health food stores.

## LIMES, LEMONS, AND ANGOSTURA BITTERS: The Citrus Family Rutaceae

Here is a little known family that has everything and truly deserves to be at the forefront of the tryptamine literature. This is the family of many of the rich smells of the spice cabinet, and the oils on the palette of the artist making Screwdrivers and Bloody Marys. There are dozens of plants here that are super sources of both DMT and especially of 5-MeO-DMT. Let me take the DMT sources first, build it up from there with binomials and then with other alkaloids.

The women of Burma use a yellow face paint that is known by the native name, "tanaka." This powder comes from the stems of the tree that is known locally as the elephant-apple or the wood-apple, and botanically as *Limonia acidissima* (or *L. crenulata* or *Hesperethusa crenulata*). It has been found to be a substantial source of both DMT and the acetamide of NMT and, rather interestingly, of a carboline, vis., 2-methyltetrahydro-β-carboline. Both DMT and NMT are present in the leaves of *Zanthoxylum arborescens* and *Z. procerum*, both intimate cousins of the Prickly Ash. But it is the bark and berries of this latter plant (*Z. americanam*) which have the herb lore fame as a circulatory stimulant and for the relief of arthritis and rheumatism. I have heard the name Hercules' Club given this plant. A DMT-rich genus, and yet one I have trouble in really pinning down (called the *Vepris* spp.) is an unusually rich DMT source. There is one report that *Vepris ampody* contains over 0.2% DMT but there are several other species known to have medical use, and they contain alkaloids such as quinolinones and isoquinolines, but there is no further mention of tryptamines.

It is the 5-MeO-DMT that should be more closely identified with the Rutaceae. Many medical uses have evolved over the years with the rue plants of the genus *Evodia* (often spelled *Euodia*, from the Greek word for fragrance) because the teas made from the leaves or blossoms are extremely aromatic. They have a broad tradition from the Philippines, through Southeast Asia, and into China. Several contain alkaloids of the phenethylamine and carboline classes (synephrin and evodiamine) and the fruits and roots of *E. rutacarpa* are known to contain 5-MeO-DMT. The leaves of *Dutaillyea oreophila* contain hordenine and 2-methyl-6-methoxy-β-carboline in addition to 5-MeO-DMT, but the leaves of *D. drupacea* (an endemic New Caledonian shrub) contain only this latter base, and to the extent of over 0.4%. From a kilo of powdered leaves, there was actually isolated 450 mg of an alkaloid fraction that was 98% 5-MeO-DMT. The bark stem of both plants were rich in quinoline alkaloids, but no tryptamines were detected. A remarkably parallel story can be found with another New Caledonia plant, a one foot high bushy shrub that grows at the higher elevations of Mount Boulinda, known botanically as *Melicope leptococca*. The leaves contain the same spectrum of alkaloids, but 5-MeO-DMT, although present at the 0.2% level, is only 35% of the inventory. One of the other alkaloids in the leaves, however, presents an intriguing parallel to the cathinone story. This is the ketone analogue of 5-MeO-DMT, namely 3-(N,N-dimethylaminoacetyl)-5-methoxyindole. Admittedly, it is there in only a small amount but, pharmacologically, it is a completely unexplored tryptamine. One additional, unexpected occurrence of 5-MeO-DMT is in the leaves of *Pilocarpus organensis*. Perhaps a bit of caution is called for here, in that the closely related plant *P. jaborandi* is the source of the plant product Jaborandi, or Maranham. This contains the potent cholinergic drug Pilocarpine, which is a pretty heavy duty poison.

## HARMINE and HARMALINE (The Families Malpighiaceae and Zygophyllaceae

Here is the other half of the ayahuasca story. And I have offended a number of botanists by calling it the "Bad Pork group." I cannot pronounce either family name easily as I have always had some difficulty with the letter "h" to make something hard that would normally be soft. That, coupled with the fact that these families' names are words I have only read, never heard, makes it easy for me to fool around with them. "Mal-piggy" is just sitting there, and "zygo-fill" is not far behind! Just add "yea-see-ee" at the end, and you have it. Actually, the reputation these two families enjoy is in the role they play as activators of the DMT contained in other plants. In the story of the South American ayahuasca, the plant *Banisteriopsis caapi* plays a giant role, just as does the Syrian Rue (*Peganum harmala*) in the Northern Hemisphere. These are the two major contributors to this fascinating drink, and their contributions are due, exclusively, to the β-carbolines (the harmala alkaloids) that are in them. These serve as the inhibitors of the body's destructive enzymes that would normally keep us from experiencing any oral activity from DMT.

*Banisteriopsis caapi* (of the family Malpighiaceae) is a major source of harmine (telepathine, yageine), harmaline (harmadine) and tetrahydroharmine (leptaflorine). But it also contains a rich collection of other alkaloids, mostly carboline-related. A good rule of nomenclature to use as a guide in these alkaloidal areas is to respect that prefix, "harm." It means that there is a carbon atom, one carbon atom, attached to the 1-position, hanging down from the bottom of the right-hand ring of a carboline, at least the right-hand ring as the structure is usually drawn. Something in a way similar to the location of Tasmania, which is the island hanging down below the right-hand buttock of Australia, at least in the way that the map of Australia is usually drawn. Thus, in *B. caapi* there are several compounds with that "harm-" prefix, including the methyl ester of harmic acid and its amide, and the acid corresponding to harmaline (harmalinic acid). They all have that single carbon atom. The alkaloids present without that carbon atom on the 1-position usually have names with a "nor" in them which says that atom is not there. With a carbonyl group, one has ketotetrahydronorharmine; with an acetyl group, acetyl norharmine.

Several other species of *Banisteriopsis* have been studied, but mostly from the botanical view as ayahuasca components, rather than from curiosity about chemical composition. An exception is a species of great potential interest, *B. rusbyana*, sometimes called *B. cabrerana* and now commonly known as *Diplopterys cabrerana*. Here one finds, quite unexpectedly, a wealth of tryptamines with DMT leading the list. But there is also NMT present, as well as 5-MeO-DMT and bufotenine. And there is a charming bit of yin-yangness associated with these two quite opposite plants. Just as one finds a little island of yin in the middle of the yang, and vice versa, there is a trace of a carboline (N-methyl-tetrahydro-β-carboline) in the tryptamine fraction from *B. rusbyana* and a trace of 6-methoxy-tryptamine in the carboline fraction from *B. caapi*.

A second major natural source for harmala alkaloids is *Peganum harmala*, or Syrian Rue (of the Family Zygophyllaceae). It contains largely harmine and harmaline, but there are small amounts of many additional alkaloids present (things such as vasicine and related quinazoline compounds) as well as not only serotonin but the 6-hydroxy positional isomer of serotonin, 6-hydroxytryptamine. These have been mentioned in the Hoasca vs. Ayahuasca chapter, and probably do not contribute to the overall action of the plant extract. Certainly the use of Syrian Rue has become extremely popular in the structuring of new and novel combinations popularly known within our own domestic scene as ayahuasca. But, in the ayahuasca preparations used in present day Brazilian religious services, the DMT comes exclusively from *Psychotria viridis* (Rubiaceae) and the harmine/harmaline mixture comes exclusively from *B. caapi*.

## ONE SHOT FAMILIES

What I call one-shot families is a scatter of plants here and there which happen to contain DMT or a close relative, but nothing earth-shaking. Most of these have come to light, not because of biological activity, but due to a positive alkaloid color test, or as an unexpected bonus during a phytochemical study pursuing something quite unrelated.

The family Acanthaceae contributes a single active plant. Although most of the single plant sources of the South American snuffs have been named under the *Virola* collection above, there is a genus of plants, *Justicia*, that is well established as an active plant in its own right, or as an occasional additive to other plants in ceremonial use. Most members of this genus are herbs and shrubs, but a few are trees. The leaves of the best studied species, the one-foot high *J. pectoralis*, contains all the needed compounds for activity, NMT, DMT and 5-MeO-DMT. However, there are reports that this is used only as a flavoring agent for popular snuffs, so no one really knows, at the moment, the extent that these tryptamines might contribute to the overall activity.

The family Urticaceae is best known as the source of nettles. Several genera in this group have been studied as to their alkaloid content, but most have no tryptamines present other than the ubiquitous serotonin. Apparently *Urtica pilulifera*, the Roman Nettle, contains bufotenine, but none of the plants that were looked at contained DMT or 5-MeO-DMT.

The family Lauraceae contains the laurels and the bays. There is no mention of DMT here, but some of the closely related tryptamines are known to be present. The Brazilian variety, *Nectandra megapotamica* contains NMT largely in the bark, and the Oregon and California West Coast variety (*Umbellularia californica*) contains bufotenine. The several *Persea* spp. that have been looked at contain only serotonin.

The family Chenopodiaceae is composed of the goosefeet and pigweeds. Traces of NMT have been reported in several genera, here, including *Arthrophytum leptocladum, A. wakhanicum, Girgensohnia dipteria, Haloxylon scoparium* and *Hammada leptoclada* but only in very small amounts, not worth pursuing.

In the family Ochnaceae there is a Cameroon tree-shrub known as *Testulea gabonensis* which contains DMT as well as NMT (and its formamide) in the trunk bark. In the family Aizoaceae, DMT and NMT have been reported in some species of the genus *Delosperma*. Similarly, in the family Polygonaceae, there is a report of DMT in a species of *Eriogonum*.

In bringing one of the appendices up to date, I have just stumbled onto another family, Loranthaceae, which contains the parasitic plant, mistletoe. Its berries apparently contain 1-ethyltryptamine, of unknown pharmacology, but a true isomer of DMT with a 1-ethyl rather than an N,N-dimethyl.

I know of no native use of any of these. I am sure that there are small treasures scattered about here and there that I have missed, but in my own searching of the botanical literature, all the remaining families have been without anything close to DMT.

This has been a broad but brief overview of the ubiquitous nature of a very simple molecule, N,N-dimethyltryptamine, or DMT. It is amongst the smallest and simplest of the chemicals in the tryptamine world and it is, essentially, the "T" in the name of this book, *TIHKAL*. It has played and will certainly continue to play a pivotal role in the philosophy of drug definition and in the continuing dialogue between medicine and the law. For example:

Are "natural" drugs inherently safer or better than synthetic drugs? DMT was first synthesized in the laboratory and remained a "synthetic" drug for a couple of decades until it was identified from a plant source. Then, of course, it became a "natural" drug. Nothing changed except for the positions taken by the advocates on the two sides. A sample from either source, nature or the laboratory, can never be made sufficiently pure to eradicate all the trace tell-tale fingerprints of congeners that will forever define its origins. Yet these trace impurities will never be successfully argued as contributing to the action of the drug itself.

Will the natural sources of DMT eventually be exhausted or effectively removed from availability? Such an outcome is hard to imagine. This chapter alone gathers hundreds of sources of the drug and, by extrapolation, implies that there are hundreds more out there as yet unknown. The discovery process will remain difficult for the ethnopharmacologist as well as the prohibitionist, since the activity of a suspect plant found in the field cannot be quickly determined by tasting a leaf or nibbling a root. The fact that DMT is not orally active demands that some unusual degree of added sophistication must be used in surveying new candidates.

There are the ethnopharmacologists on the internet who are continually exploring and reporting new plant materials. There is an increased awareness of the Brazilian religious use of ayahuasca and the importation of these ideas into the United States and Europe. There is a proliferation of books by articulate authors such as McKenna, De Korne, Ott, Rätsch, Pendell, Stolaroff and many others. There is an open acknowledgment in several European countries of the validity, even the value, of scientific research and personal inquiry into the exploration of one's own consciousness by any of several means including the use of psychedelic drugs. This honest and healthy view will some day take root in the United States. Perhaps this review can provide some useful information.

If there is a role for DMT to play as a neurotransmitter or valid ligand in brain chemistry, will this be easily explored in future research? Not in the United States, in our lifetimes, I fear. Remember that unapproved research with it was prohibited several years before it was discovered to be a possible neurotransmitter, and that restriction has never been lifted. The first step needed would be to abandon the thoughtless compounding of drug laws and governmental control of medical and scientific research. Several grim stories have been told describing the complications faced in seeking official permission for any research with Schedule I drugs. There are no indicators that these requirements will lessen in the future. Perhaps progress will be made in some of the other Western countries where possession of and research with these chemicals is becoming more accepted. But within the United States, the political rewards derived from the increased demonizing of these chemicals far outweigh any conceived medical rewards that might come from the study of them.

## BIOSYNTHESIS

The conversion of a chemical "A" into another chemical "B" is the art of synthesis, and the person who achieves the conversion is called the chemist. The usual process followed is: the chemist gets "A," then finds a beaker, a stirrer, a flask, a steam bath and a reflux condenser, and boils "A" with this and that for some number of hours, then filters, extracts, concentrates, distills and crystallizes. I have succeeded, the chemist will say, in synthesizing "B" from "A" in the laboratory, in a 67% yield, using standard in vitro techniques. That is synthetic chemistry, at least to almost all of the chemists that you meet and talk to at the semi-annual American Chemical Society conference. The only living thing involved in the entire process is the chemist himself, who stands at the lab bench, weighs this and pipettes that, and takes his isolated product down the hall to the pharmacologist or to the patent attorney. The end product "B," the target achieved, has no other association with a living process, in that it was conceived on a cocktail napkin, and its uterus was a glass beaker.

But "A" just might have been converted to "B" by the chemist in quite a different way. What if he had dissolved "A" in a cup of water or packed it into a gelatin capsule, and swallowed it? His body is the beaker and his liver or lungs provide the synthetic capability for the wanted conversion. Then he collects his urine for the next 48 hours, and extracts, concentrates, distills and crystallizes. He has synthesized "B" from "A" in a 67% yield using standard in vivo techniques. There were almost no glass (vitro) containers used but rather the living body (vivo) was the beaker. All the biochemists and pharmacologists at the semi-annual Pharmacology and Experimental Therapeutics conference in Boston will discuss metabolism, bioconversion and the role of this isozyme and that enzyme promoter. It is still the art of synthesis, but it calls totally upon the living organism.

There are many in-between levels of chemical reaction where one might ask if a living process was indeed being used. This entire chapter is about living systems — fungi, coral, seaweed, grasses, flowers, trees, frogs.

You can learn from nature, you can study a tree to discover its patterns of growth and maturation, and become intimate with it through much patience. This is most certainly in vivo synthesis. You get to know the living entity, and choose to join it in its world. But what if one were to use a living individual, or some preparation that had once been a living system, but run the reaction in a non-living glass container? How about the making of wine by growing yeast in a sugar solution? Or the incubation of your starting material "A" with an otherwise discarded umbilical cord from a newborn sheep? What if you isolate the enzyme fraction from the liver of a living rabbit and use it as your chemical reagent? Are these in vivo or in vitro processes?

I want to close this chapter with three examples of twilight chemistry that are, in essence, illustrations of the imposition of the hand of man onto otherwise natural living systems. They are located somewhere in-between the natural world (in the living organism) and the inanimate laboratory world (in the flask on the steam bath).

Eloquent examples of this are the delightful reports of indole syntheses that were explored in Germany over the last few years. Visualize a vigorous growing mycelium culture that is synthesizing psilocin by bringing together the natural DMT in its diet with a vital but not-too-discriminating enzyme that has the capacity for putting a hydroxyl group onto a tryptamine. The mycelium has the knowledge of how to 4-hydroxy-late something, but it doesn't really care what that something is. The available target for this skill, in the natural mushroom, just happens to be DMT. The product is 4-hydroxy-DMT, or psilocin, and this is what the organism makes, because this is all that can be made. There is one starting material, there is one synthetic capability, and there is one product. And this product is what gives importance and substance to the biologically active magic mushrooms, be they grown in the field or in the lab. Now, let's manipulate things a little bit. Let's keep this little fungal factory going, but wash out the DMT and replace it with something like DET. The hydroxy-lating compulsion appears to be still there and is quite intact. What happens? The mycelium produces a bunch of 4-hydroxy-DET, an interesting compound and an active psychedelic, which was first reported by the Sandoz Laboratories, but a compound that is unknown in nature. I will wager that if the mycelia were to be sprinkled with MIPT, the enzyme system would produce 4-HO-MIPT which is fully as potent as psilocin, and unrecognized in any legal system in any country that I am aware of. You are exploiting a natural process by providing it with an unnatural starting material, and allowing it to generate a product that is intrinsically unnatu-ral. The mushrooms that are produced do not know that they are the vehicles of alien seed.

It has occurred to me that I have touched upon a fascination point of law. Federal law does not specify any mushrooms as being illegal. It is only the components of mushrooms, i.e., psilocin and psilocybin, that are explicitly specified in the statutes. There are only four plants named in the law itself, although two more have sneaked in by the dirty trick route. In the 1970 Controlled Substances Act these four plants are Peyote, Marijuana, Opium and Coca. Both *Tabernanthe iboga* and *Catha edulis* became listed through administrative maneuvering, and neither inclusion has been legally challenged. But mushrooms? *Psilocybe* spp. are not recorded anywhere in the law. They are not illegal. If they are things that contain illegal drugs (and indeed psilocin and psilocybin are named as Schedule I drugs) then they are the package in which these chemicals are transported or made available. But think for a moment. If a mushroom of a naughty genus had only non-scheduled indoles present in it, why could you not possess it with total immunity? The Controlled Substance Analogue Bill of 1986 might be an added hurdle, but the prosecutor would have to prove that there had been the production there of a chemical that you knew to be substantially similar, in action, to psilocin. And, for this synthetic act to constitute a criminal act, the product would have to be intended to be used in man. What an interesting argument of innocence. Perhaps they (the Suits) will quote this book? If they do, you can always argue that this book is a work of fiction.

Consider a second example in this in vivo/in vitro dialogue. One of my early mentors was a Professor of Medicinal Chemistry in San Francisco, who had spent some post-graduate time in Italy in the laboratory of a Professor of Microbiology. He was learning the process of making and using culture media for the growing of fungal clones. One of his discoveries was that there were unusual species within the Ergot world that could be easily grown in small broth vats. One of these was, as I remember, the ergot line called *Claviceps paspali*. A liter of sterile medium, inoculated with a clean probe of this organism, would produce hundreds of milligrams of the propanolamide of lysergic acid. As I remember (it has been a few decades) the boiling of this alkaloid in toluene would split off the aminoalcohol and produce lysergic acid which could be converted, with appropriate care, to a few hundreds of milligrams of LSD. My God. A quart of goop giving rise to a few tens of thousand doses of acid? My friend was not aware of this possibility, neither then nor even today, but it does indicate that access to foreign ergotamine tartrate is not an essential preliminary to illegal drug synthesis.

Yet another example. Virtually all the plant syntheses of interesting DMT derivatives have their origins in the amino acid tryptophan. To make this transformation, the plant must follow one of two possible paths.

There can be decarboxylation of tryptophan to produce tryptamine followed by methylation, or there can be methylation of tryptophan followed by decarboxylation. And if there is to be aromatic substitution (say, 5-hydroxylation) it can occur at any intermediate stage. Each of these two needed steps can be achieved by enzyme systems called, not surprisingly, decarboxylases and N-methyl-transferases. In short, one can go from tryptophan to DMT by some enzymatic process that adds methyl groups either before or after decarboxylation.

Tryptophan is the obvious starting spot for this particular form of bio-conversion to DMT. It is an essential amino acid, an archetypical protein building block, and a universally accepted safe sedative, available for many years, inexpensively, in every health food store. Then, a few years ago, a major Japanese manufacturer shortened its production recipe by one step, a reactive by-product was left in as a trace contaminant, and a toxic impurity was formed which led to a problem called eosinophilia-myalgia syndrome (EMS). People were hurt, the source was found, the short-cut was removed, and the product was again potentially available as a non-prescription health aid. But, during the period of contamination, a total restriction on the availability of tryptophan was ordered by the FDA on the sales of the amino acid and, despite the open acknowledgment that the crisis is past, sale to health food stores, or to the public at large without a prescription, is no longer allowed. All of this is discussed in the tryptamine recipe.

Consider the N-methylated tryptophans. The mono-methyl and the tri-methyl alkaloidal amino acids are most commonly found in the small tropical shrubs and vines of the Leguminosae. N-Methyltryptophan is called abrine. Both abrine and abrin come from the seeds of the very poisonous plant *Abrus precatorius,* which has been lumped together with several other red-seed plants in the Leguminosae section earlier. There I talked about seeds and plants; here I am talking about compounds. There are three very similar words here. "Abrine" is the amino acid. "Abrin" is a proteinaceous isolate. "Abrus" is the original British Pharmaceutical Codex name for the actual seeds and it is, of course, the genus name of the plant. Very little has been reported about the amino acid, abrine, except that it can be present in the seed to the extent of 5%, but the isolate abrin is composed of proteins that are quite specific as to their effectiveness in hemagglutination and cytotoxicity. The lethal dose of abrin to a single mouse, by injection, may be about one microgram. The lethal dose to man of this material has been said to be less than a milligram, or perhaps just the amount that is in one of these most attractive and colorful seeds.

Right on top of this one must reckon with the trimethylated tryptophan, N,N,N-Trimethyltryptophan quaternary salt, the betaine of tryptophan and the monomethyl counterpart abrine which is found in the

Jequirity seeds (*Abrus precatorius*). And also in the leaf, stem, and root of this plant. It is also in the seeds of the edible lentil *Lens culinaris*, *Pterocarpus officinalis*, and several species of *Erythrina* (of the red bean story) which are best known for a completely unrelated group of almost indole alkaloids known as the erythroidines. It is also known from several species of the unrelated Malvaceae genus, *Sida*. There are *S. acuta, S. cordifolia, S. rhombifolia,* and *S. spinosa*, all of the mallow family, all with Hypaphorine or its methyl ester in the root or stem or leaf. This quaternary derivative of tryptophan is especially toxic as a convulsive poison, and must be respected in any isolation manipulations that are conducted with the plants. Yet it can sneak in, in trace amounts, in familiar places such as the root of some of the Legumes of the genus *Glycyrrhiza* which is, on the one hand, the source of the sweet flavoring, licorice, and yet has been shown to contain sizable amounts of hypaphorine.

Both of these methylated tryptophans, the mono- and the tri-, have also been isolated from plant sources as their methyl esters. Abrine methyl ester is known to be in *Sida cordifolia*. Another possible rich source is the poison pea from Australia. There is a group of Legumes of the genus *Gastrolobium* that are known locally as the poison this and poison that; there is Poison Shrub, Narrow-leaf Poison, Champion Bay Poison, Burr Poison, Prickle Poison, Crump-leaved Poison. There is a report specifically on *G. callistachys* that has mentioned the presence of the methyl ester of abrine. Hypaphorine methyl ester has been isolated from *Abrus precatorius*. Interestingly, N,N-dimethyltryptophan, the homologue that would be the direct decarboxylation precursor, is quite rare in the plant world. I am aware of a single report of its methyl ester, occurring in the leaves and stems of the Legume *Pultenaea altissima*.

The parading of these methylated tryptophans is for the reinforcement of the argument that they might serve as biosynthetic precursors to the methylated tryptamines. There have been some promising reports of the synthesis of DMT from suspension cultures of selected cell lines of the periwinkle plant *Catharanthus roseus*, where "unnatural" use of specific enzymes have been employed in the in vitro synthesis of alkaloids that are not natural to the periwinkle. Even the betaine-type quaternary hypaphorine (in *Lens culinaris*) can eliminate trimethylamine metabolically, giving rise to a potential synthetic precursor, indoleacrylic acid.

A final comment. Almost forty years ago a researcher in the National institute of Mental Health, in Maryland, discovered an enzyme in rabbit lung that could transfer a methyl group to a tryptamine from the amino acid donor, S-adenosyl-methionine. With this system, serotonin gave N-methylserotonin, N-methylserotonin gave bufotenine, tryptamine gave N-methyltryptamine, and N-methyltryptamine gave DMT. What a fabulous black-box that would make. Get two enzyme preparations, one that can methylate S-adenosyl-homocysteine to S-adenosyl-methionine and another that can regenerate S-adenosyl-homocysteine by transferring the methyl group to an available amine. Two catalysts in a chamber heated to 37 °C, with a spigot adding tryptamine at the top, and another releasing DMT out the bottom. That's the science — I'll leave the details to the engineers.

---

This has been a multidisciplinary romp along many different paths of science. Each of them presents factual information that can be of value in the understanding of the relationship between us and the chemical, between us and nature. We tend to be discouraged when we see the barriers, legal and social, being continuously made more inflexible. But nothing is cast in immutable stone. The Berlin Wall could never fall. It fell. The Evil Empire of the Soviet Union was an overwhelming enemy. Today it does not exist. And the War on Drugs must be pursued with increasing vigor until it is won. Perhaps tomorrow it will be declared over, and whether it was won or lost will be left unannounced. Our efforts must be gentle but continuing. As Samuel Johnson once said, "Few things are impossible to diligence and skill."

# CHAPTER 16.  HOASCA VS. AYAHUASCA

(Shura's voice)

Let me start by explaining the title of this chapter, "Hoasca versus Ayahuasca." The distinction between these two names deals in part with past history and in part with current usage, and also with the need to canonize these materials with capital letters. Quite simply, but not completely accurately, the choice of the name to be used reflects where you are living. It just may be that hoasca is the Portuguese way of referring to the drink, and the original Spanish name for it was ayahuasca. I don't completely buy that, as I have heard both terms used widely by people expert in both languages. This is further complicated by the detail I have been told that the actual name "hoasca" is proprietary, owned by the UDV (União do Vegetal) church of Brazil. No sacrament, even made from the same plants by the same recipe, can have the name unless it has Mestre Gabriel's blessings, and is administered by some UDV Mestre in good standing. This may account for the use of the alternately spelled suffix of ayahuasca, "huasca," being used in synthetic terms such as pharmahuasca and gaiahuasca (non-hoasca combinations of plants), pharmahausca (combinations involving prescription drugs) and endohuasca (combinations of things already in the brain naturally). And I have recently seen this word creatively extended to terms such as acaciahuasca and mimosahuasca (made with leaves from the Acacia or the Mimosa tree). I will assume that if someone, somewhere, mixes yopo snuff with passion flower into an experimental drink, it will be called anadenantherahuasca or, perhaps, passafloraincarnatahuasca. Enough. I intend to use the term hoasca to represent the original beverage even without a papal OK, and use the term ayahuasca for things outside of the Amazon.

At a very recent meeting I heard a spokesman for one of the hoasca cultures pronounce this word not with two syllables (WAS-ka) or with four syllables (EYE-ah-WAS-ka) but with about two and a half syllables. It came out somewhere between ee-WAS-ka and eye-WAS-ka, but then he was from New York, and there was no way I could tell from the vowels of his particular Upper Manhattan accent just how he had perceived the Brazilian original.

Another direction that the separation of the words hoasca and ayahuasca has taken, and one which is the substance of this chapter, has been in the loosening of the identity of the composition of the drink. In its native use in the Amazon, in both religious and indigenous native cultures, it is referred to as ayahuasca, of course, but by many other names as well. There are names such as caapi, lagé, yajé, mihi, dapa, natema, and pinde, but some of these can be used to refer to not just the drink but to the components of the drink. The terms "daime" and "vegetal" are the informal names used within the two churches discussed below. Hoasca remains the most widely recognized name used within the modern-day Brazilian cultural setting, and it implies a rigidly prescribed composition. But as the popularity has moved abroad, and the concept of mixing two drugs together has become more widespread and corrupted, the term ayahuasca is the only one encountered. Over the last several years this term has spread widely, taking on an almost mystical connotation. The quantity of lay research in this area is staggering, and it is occurring today in many countries around the world, including the United States. Every month or so I learn of another combination of plants or chemicals or both, that has been tried and found valid. And is happily called ayahuasca. I can only guess as to the much larger number of unknown trials of home-designed ayahuasca that have been made and have failed.

An added popularity of the term ayahuasca has arisen, over the last few years, from a growing tendency of the "New Age" section of our society, those with the visionary-herbal-medicine-Gaia-natural-health-oriented philosophy, to look to the native cultures of the tropic forests or barren deserts as the last source of nature's wisdom. Books on alternate living styles, vision quests, and personal development have made words such as shamanism, curandero and ayahuasquero a part of our current vocabulary. Recently, several specialized books, such as, *Ayahuasca Analogues*, by Jonathan Ott and *Ayahuasca Visions*, by Luis Eduardo Luna and Pablo Amaringo, have appeared. I doubt that there has been a book written on the subjects of ethnobotany or shamanism in the last twenty years that does not have, if not a chapter, at least extensive discussion involving ayahuasca or the ayahuasqueros.

The origins of ayahuasca are very old; it has a tradition of use which predates written records. It is part of both the ancient religions and the healing customs of the native people who live throughout the Amazon area, from Brazil to the upper areas of Colombia, Equator and Peru. Many studies have been reported on its use in shamanism, and especially in healing rituals. Sadly, many of the people who have defined the culture there are today being disenfranchised as second-class citizens because they lack both Western language and political representation. No, it is worse than that. In the opinion of most South Americans, the native Indians are filthy, stupid and lazy, and are certainly holding up progress. There is little if any participation of this Indian population in the present-day religious ceremony.

There can be ambiguity with the use of the actual word, ayahuasca, itself. In the Peruvian Amazon, even today, the term can be used to represent a drink made just from the plant *Banisteriopsis caapi* alone, and the name is used to refer to the plant as well as its extracts. In fact, the origin of the word "ayahuasca" was from the Quichua Indians, to whom it means "vine of the souls" or "vine of the dead." There are other names found in other regions; yajé in Colombia has provided the name yageine for the alkaloidal extract (which has also been called telepathine, reflecting its presumed telepathic properties). The principal individual alkaloids that have been identified as present in the plant are harmine, harmaline and tetrahydroharmine. These compounds are described individually in the recipe portion of this book. There is no DMT present in yajé.

As a brew, ayahuasca is used widely in the Amazon area, in Peru, Ecuador, Colombia and Brazil. Its social and medical use depends more on its purgative properties than on visionary activity. It has been called "la purga" and "la limpia." Other names that have been used for ayahuasca, such as camaramti or chahua may reflect the ugly brown color of the final extract, or the addition of other plants, generically called "misha." In most cases, the field reports are social or anthropological, and the identities of any added plants are not documentable. An important point that should be made, is that it is necessary to distinguish the healing processes that are described in the shamanistic world from the religious use described below. In the original cultural format, it is the shaman who takes the ayahuasca for both diagnosis and treatment of the patient. Some of this is still seen in the present religious use (group healing) but in recent years the patient has himself more frequently participated in the healing by taking the brew.

Hoasca, a subset of the broad ayahuasca world, is the term that is associated with religious use. It is the admixture of two explicitly named plants. This tea is produced by boiling together the bark of the plant *Banisteriopsis caapi* and the leaves of the plant *Psychotria viridis*. Hoasca is quite simply the decoction that remains after the aqueous extracts have been decanted from the insoluble residues, and boiled down to a brown sludge. The best known practitioners of the making and using of hoasca are the members of several religious groups that are centered in Brazil. Two of the best known call themselves the UDV and the Santo Daime, and a revealing view of hoasca can be had by looking through the eyes of these two groups.

The larger of the two churches is the União do Vegetal, known popularly as the UDV. The Portuguese pronunciation of the abbreviation is OOH-day-VAY. A smaller organization is the Santo Daime (pronounced DYE-meh), and there are a number of yet smaller groups such as the Barquinia and the Comunidata 2000. These also use some form of the hoasca sacrament, but I will not discuss them here. The two major churches which I want to describe have their own philosophy, their own structure, and their own vocabulary.

The UDV was formed in the 1960's by a rubber trapper named Gabriel who observed ayahuasca and appreciated its magical properties. He inspired several associations of people from European, native Indian and Afro-American backgrounds, and these were collectively known as caboclos. By spinning together some fragments of early mythology with some aspects of not only the Catholic belief system but the jungle gods and spirits as well, a new church, the UDV, came into being. This has maintained an absolute confidence in the sacredness of the plants of the jungle. The symbol of this resynthesis is the sacred drink hoasca. The church has some 6000 members composed of an ever-growing number (currently 55) of separate churches or chapels called nucleos (the plural actually used for nucleus, rather than nuclei). The members of the UDV congregation are relatively upper middle class, with good incomes and good homes, and the leader of each congregation is known as a Mestre ( Master). The congregation includes physicians, lawyers, bankers, politicians, and other similar professional people. They pride themselves on having taken complete control over what they see as personality weaknesses, such as the use of tobacco and alcohol.

The Santo Daime church is a little older, having been founded in the 1930's, also by a group of caboclos. Its full official name is the "Doctrine of Santo Daime" and its members are called Daimistas. There are some eight or nine separate sects, whereas the UDV has just one, which is called the "União" (or Union). Each sect of the Santo Daime is composed of a number of communities, also called nucleos, which are maintained largely by agricultural activities, or by small or medium scale businesses. The leaders of each unit are called "Padrinhos" (or little Fathers) who are regarded as being more spiritually developed. The members tend more to the blue-collar class of society, and are a bit more casual in their social interactions, with guests more often brought to services and with a somewhat more lenient attitude towards tobacco and socializing. But the hoasca, the daime, still plays a dominant role, in place of alcohol, in this society. As with the UDV, healing is also held as the unifying goal of the church. Illnesses are much more than bodily events, since they are often recognized as coming from the mind and thus must be healed through the mind. I have asked several people as to the origin of the term Santo Daime, and have received several different answers. I have heard that it is really the name of a Saint. Or that it comes from the verb to give, and thus it really means Saint Give-unto-me, or perhaps, Saint Gimme. Or that Santo is a form of the word for sacred, or maybe even health, and the allusion is to the medical healing purposes, and stands for Give-me-health. The Daimistas call hoasca "Daime."

Although there is a history of a rather conservative administrative view of drugs and drug use in Brazil, the positive social position and the health stance of both churches, especially in light of their remarkable success in reducing or stopping the use of alcohol, have won them the governmental approval of hoasca as being a legally accepted religious sacrament. This de facto approval of the use of a drug in a religious context has been seen as a valuable precedent, by many in the United States, for the social acceptance of a similar philosophy in this country. There have been quiet moves made to form branches of these churches here. It goes without saying that there will be very little publicity on the hoasca aspect of these events until there is a general acceptance of these activities as bona fide religions.

There are two specific plants used in combination for the making of hoasca; these are *Banisteriopsis caapi* (originally, *Banisteria caapi*) and *Psychotria viridis*. *B. caapi* is a vine that is known within the UDV as the male component of hoasca and has been called "The Force." It has the popular name of Mariri. In the Santo Daime, it is called Jagube. It contains several β-carbolines that are monoamine oxidase inhibitors (MAOI-A) which effectively allow the DMT of the second hoasca component to express its action orally. The vine is beaten to a mixture of powder and pulp, called po and befeçao. I have recently learned that there are two distinct variants of *B. caapi* which possibly have not been described as separate individuals in the botanical literature. There is a smooth form of the vine called "tukunaca" which is predominately found in the cooler areas of Southern Brazil. Another variant has large nodes where the branching occurs; it is called caupurí and is found in Amazonia. When one vine is transplanted to the natural habitat of the other, the defining characteristics are maintained, suggesting true genetic distinction. The hoasca made from the caupurí provides a more severe spectrum of toxic symptoms than the tukunaca variation. The side-effects such as vomiting and diarrhea, nystagmus and muscular tremors can be extreme, suggesting a stronger, or even different alkaloid composition. This theory is presently being tested.

*P. viridis* is the second plant of hoasca. It is a shrub, and its leaves are considered the female half of the team. It has been called "The Light," and has a common name of Chacrona, or Chacruna, within the UDV. In the Santo Daime, the plant is called the queen (La Rainha) and its leaves are handled exclusively by women. It is the contributor of the N,N-dimethyltryptamine (DMT) component of the hoasca, which is the factor that is believed to provide its psychedelic effects.

The details of the hoasca preparation procedure (a ritual known as "Preparo" in the UDV and "Feitio" in the Santo Daime) varies from group to group, but the fundamental steps are simple and straightforward. These are extraction, separation, and concentration. The stems and branches of the *B. caapi* vine are beaten thoroughly to break loose the bark, and the pulped mass is combined with the leaves of the *P. viridis* in big pots which are usually aluminum. Water is added, and all is boiled until the extracts are dark and the pulp is spent. The liquid phase is separated, and the clear water extracts are boiled down to the dark, foul-tasting residue that is called hoasca.

The UDV refers to the effects produced by the completed hoasca as "burracheira" or the "Strange Force." The drink itself, the hoasca, is informally referred to as cha (tea) or vegetal. The quality of a batch of tea is usually discussed in terms of its force and/or light.

Although many analyses have been conducted on the two component plants of hoasca, the composition of the drug itself is relatively unknown. Such an analysis is a needed check on any possible changes to the alkaloid content that might occur in response to the extraction and concentration steps which are time-consuming and which are conducted at a rolling boil in the open air. Also, if the final hoasca is kept unrefrigerated for any time, fermentation from unexpected inoculations do indeed occur, but apparently there is no detectable change in the alkaloid content.

A number of analyses of daime from different Santo Daime sources have consistently shown the two carboline alkaloids harmine and tetrahydroharmine in major amounts, accompanied by lesser amounts of DMT. Much smaller amounts of harmaline have been seen, and noted. In one instance when a microscopic examination was made, considerable quantities of both yeast and fungal cells were present.

With the UDV, the tea is consumed only within the ritual context, called a session. These sessions take place about every two weeks. The presiding church leader, the Mestre, provides each participant with a single dosage of hoasca which is consumed at one time. The early part of the experience, conducted while seated, with eyes closed and in the presence of music, is when there might be visions experienced. It is here that the purgative effects of the hoasca are experienced; vomiting and diarrhea are common. The participant is attended to by a church member. After this, there takes place the "spiritual cleaning" that is the expression of the "force" component of the drink. This period is called the miração, and is considered a distraction; it lasts perhaps two hours. These factors become less intense with frequent exposure to the hoasca. The state of mind then becomes very clear, with a heightened sense of awareness usually accompanied by a muscular tremor. It is during this period that there is on-going interaction of the participants with each other, and with the Mestre. This is the "light" component of the drink. Questions are asked, answers are given; there is a continuing exchange of ideas, with the singing of songs and much laughter. The Mestre then brings the session to a close with a song. After this, there is time given to socializing and the congregation disperses at about the fourth hour.

The relationship of the miração period to the overall service can be seen by the comments of one user:

> "When I encountered the UDV I was amazed, and still am, with their level of organization, research, networking and loving brotherhood. I will always be grateful and indebted to them for the many things I learned and experienced. My first sessions were very powerful and, for me, synthesized together many aspects of all my preceding work. But as I continued I found that these intense experiences became decreasingly frequent. Most were mild. I began tracking the patterns of nausea and vomiting and began to question how this was related to a particular batch of tea. The orthodox church members feel that this nausea is a form of purification, detoxification, penance or even punishment, and I personally believe that the visuals distract me from hearing the message of the sacrament, and I must suffer them until the true voice is heard."

The services of the Santo Daime employ the same tea, called daime by them, but their structure is quite different. The ritual is called "hinário" and the daime is distributed at approximately two hour intervals. There is the collective singing of hymns throughout the services along with the constant movement of a synchronized and repetitive dance called the "bailado." Overseers prod the dancers when they begin to feel weary and want to rest. The hinário takes place around a central table in the shape of a six-pointed star. Special rituals occur periodically, which are called "Concentrations" and "Star Works." A concentration occurs twice a month and, as with the hinário, the daime is consumed at periodic intervals. The participants are seated in fixed positions (head up, back straight, uncrossed arms and legs) and maintain silence for periods of up to an hour. The energy that is thus allowed to pass freely though the body is directed in a general way to any who might be ill, either inside or outside of the community.

The ritual Star Works is dedicated specifically to an ill individual. The service often takes place in a "House of the Star" which is found only in the larger communities, and which is dedicated to curing rituals. This temple has a hexagonal shape and has a Star of David-shaped table in the center which holds incense sticks and revered objects such as paintings of Catholic saints and Christ, and of earlier Daimista leaders. Candles are everywhere. The congregation is divided by sex. Twelve chairs are put around this table for selected members, and the rest of the participants sit on benches. Daime is distributed, and the congregation alternates between silence and the singing of hymns. The padrinho delivers a sermon called a preleição which is interrupted regularly with the group's singing of additional hymns and the consumption of additional daime.

A contrast between the emphasis placed on the importance of the hoasca within the UDV, and the importance of group structure within the Santo Daime, is clear from a quotation from a Padrinho:

> "The ritual establishes everything. Ritual in each initiatory school is an element for grasping the material. I think that at the point at which we obtain spiritual evolution we are not going to need rituals anymore, for we will be the ritual. Christ did not need the ritual — Jesus was the ritual. He went there and showed the bread and wine. Today the ritual is Christ's force, so much so that in the Catholic Church, ritual is nothing more than the element to grasp and command faith. Ritual is like a bottle that contains the liquid of knowledge. It is only to give it form; it doesn't change the liquid, the content. The liquid is not altered. What purpose has ritual? It is in order to sit, to separate masculine and feminine energies. The person sits in concentration and drinks daime. It is not with one person head-bowed, another with legs up. Everything is in order. This is our ritual."

The public self-images of the two churches are quite different from one another. The UDV is a considerably more private group, tending to avoid publicity and outside interaction. They see themselves as playing a role in the development of a strong social structure of increasing value to the individual. The daimistas' view is more immediate. Salvation is to be found at the moment, as the world may end tomorrow. Both bring into their structures much of the Christian ethic, but from very different branches of it. "Onward Christian Soldiers" versus "Apocalypse Now." But both groups share the absolute belief that the sacrament hoasca allows access to the voice of God.

The ever-widening awareness of the psychopharmacological activity of the South American hoasca drink has led to a rapidly growing popularity of the concept of combining drugs. The current day exploration is truly world-wide, and extends well beyond the co-administration of these two specific South American plants. Not only are other active plants being combined with one-another, or active plants combined with synthetic drugs, but even the co-administration of two totally synthetic drugs is becoming an exploring ritual. This is all leading to a bewilderingly complex picture as there are so many variables that can be encountered.

Each of the two components of this on-going social experiment can be chosen from a long list of possibilities, making any organization of the situation a two-dimensional presentation rather than just a single list of the usual suspects. Each will have its own administration dosage, leading to both quantity and ratio as variables, and when plant extracts are involved, the concentrations of the active ingredient or ingredients are probably unknown. And the two materials may be administered in some timed sequence (which follow which, and by how long?). It is possible that there are no two experiments, anywhere, that will be duplicates of one another. I suspect that any attempt to organize this chaotic hodgepodge into a logical pattern and to come to a unifying conclusion is doomed. Even the underlying concept that one of the materials is a promoter of the other (something that inhibits the metabolic destruction of something else) is being lost in this complexity. And it must be remembered that most of these many research combinations are being referred to simply as ayahuasca.

Let me try to tell this expanded part of the story in a way that extends the picture outwards from the two specific plants of hoasca to the many, many substitutions for each of these two components, which I have here called ayahuasca. And, in this broadening, I will also elaborate on the replacement of plants (quite limited in numbers of species and intrinsically not reproducible) with chemicals (nearly unlimited in number, and intrinsically totally reproducible). Thus, there will be other plant-plus-plant combinations (only a few of these have been studied) and plant-chemical combinations, where either of the two original components is replaced by a chemical or a combination of chemicals. The chemical substitutes are more reasonably placed in the recipe portion of this book, and are not in this chapter.

There are a number of reports in the United States and in Europe of the employment of the exact plants that are the well established components of the South American hoasca. Both the UDV and the Santo Daime have formed churches outside of Brazil, and both churches are becoming increasingly accepted as recognized religions. The overall purpose and philosophy of each, both the Christian sub-structure and the emphasis on healing and health, are largely intact. So, too, is the role played by the definitional sacrament, hoasca. This material may be brought into the country from church-related sources in Brazil, but it may also be produced here from domestically raised plants. Both *B. caapi* and the *P. viridis* are legal, and are easily raised in the United States. An ever-increasing number of botanical supply houses are making seeds, cuttings or rooted starts available, as there is a steadily growing market to be filled.

But quite beyond this church and sacrament picture, there is an exciting renaissance in a discipline called ethnopharmacology. This is the exploring of one's environment for new things that have some instructive or beneficial action on an individual. This term has been reserved historically for the studies of the drug-oriented aspects of more remote cultures, past or present, in alien parts of the world. But today the term is fully applicable to many people in our Western world who are searching nature in the hope of an increased understanding of it, to be taught by it or to be entertained by it.

The exploration of pairs of plants other than the *B. caapi* and *P. viridis*, where one contains the inhibitor and the other contains the stuff to be inhibited, can be called botanical ayahuasca. I am using the term ayahuasca here with this very broad definition to maintain a distinction between new and novel mixtures and the more classical and rigidly defined drink, hoasca. The term ayahuasca is also becoming widely used to describe a mixture where at least one of the two components is a pure chemical rather than a plant. I have earlier mentioned some new and unexpected compound words involving the suffix huasca, but it seems that for this essay, ayahuasca is adequate.

Regardless of the name employed, there is a consistent role played by each of the two components. There is a thing that is intrinsically inactive but which inhibits the body's destruction of a drug that would normally be unavailable to the person. And there is a second thing that is intrinsically active but is rapidly and effectively destroyed metabolically. A potentiating, or allowing factor, and another that is potentiated or allowed. This is the combination that today answers to the term "ayahuasca."

Who are the players on these two pharmacological teams? The role of the *B. caapi* component of hoasca is being taken over, at least in the United States, almost exclusively by the plant *Peganum harmala*, although there are a number of alternate β-carboline sources such as the seeds of *Tribulis terristris* which have been used in man. *P. harmala* is a rich source of both harmaline and of harmine and is readily available from a number of domestic sources. If the local Indian/Arab retail store does not recognize this binomial, try another name for this product: "esfand." You may be surprised to find that they sell this incense in one pound packages, even in five pound packages. Since this seed contains most of the same alkaloids that are in the *B. caapi* component of hoasca, the choice of this plant as a substitute has a certain authenticity.

The search for plants to play the role of *P. viridis* in hoasca has called for much more imagination. In principle, any plant that contains DMT could be used, to maintain the effect of the original hoasca. There are many botanic sources of this ubiquitous alkaloid, and some of these have been mentioned in the Chapter "DMT is Everywhere." A wide variety of grasses, roots, bark and leaves have been explored. Another alkaloid that needs inhibition of its destruction is 5-MeO-DMT, which is also widely found in many natural sources. It, too, is not normally active orally. Recently, however, there has been a move to explore many other well known drugs as this second component, perhaps illogically in that all these are well established as being orally active. For this second part of ayahuasca, I have heard of trials with materials such as LSD, mescaline, mushrooms, datura, and even dextromethorphan. It is almost as if the *P. harmala* is being called upon to play a role of modifier or enhancer (or even to an extent, contributor) of activity, rather than one of being a simple revealer of activity. This brings up a vital question: If *P. harmala* can directly contribute to the action of another drug by some process other than that of potentiation or synergism, or by simply allowing this other drug to become orally active due to its presence, then it would have a pharmacological action in its own right. What is the action of *P. harmala* all by itself?

At this point, let me open a can of worms just enough to introduce you to the rather incredible color and magic of the territorial rights and egos of the academic world. There has been a question bounced about for many years in the area of the history of pharmacy. In the Rg Veda, the earliest scripture of the Hindus, there are numerous references to an intoxicating plant-derived drink known as Soma. The evolving palaver has been centered on the attempt to identify just what plant Soma really was. I have a number of friends who have or have had very strong opinions as to how this question should be answered. And, believe me, not all of these opinions are the same!

Let me introduce you to R. Gordon Wasson. He was one of the most extraordinary explorers, adventurers and authors that I have ever known. His professional training was as a financier and banker but, in alliance with his wife Valentina, he discovered the world of magic mushrooms, and the rest is history. He followed a number of excellent clues which led him to the Mexican state of Oaxaca, to the Mazatec world of Maria Sabina, and to the explosive announcement in Life Magazine, almost forty years ago, of the existence and impact of the psychopharmacological activity to be found in the Genus *Psilocybe*. I have quibbled as to whether he should be called a mycological scientist or a mycological scholar, but there is no question that he must be called a mycological amateur in the truest English sense of that word. Having been seduced into the mycophile world by his wife, he became a devotee of the discipline. It became for him an adventure rather than a profession. And it strongly encouraged him to seek out a mushroom motif in everything that his research touched upon. I remember a meeting that we both attended, in Port Townsend, Washington, where he presented a scholarly essay on the prevalence of the mushroom icon in the early history of central Mexico. During a lecture, he showed a hemispherical stone figure that looked for all the world like a mushroom's fruiting body. This, he said, is proof that the mushroom was a sacred entity in Mexican culture and religion. A question from the audience suggested that since this figure was almost exactly the diameter of the sporting balls used in the Aztec games contests, that perhaps, just perhaps, the stone figure might be a mold upon which the rubber balls were cast. If you took two rubber half-spheres and glued them together, you would get one rubber ball. The question was not answered, nor even acknowledged. For Wasson, there was no question but that the stone image was a mushroom. As to the identity of Soma, when the clues all led him to the conclusion that the Hindu plant was the fly agaric mushroom *Amanita muscaria*, not surprisingly, he found the total body of the accumulated evidence completely supported this assignment.

Let me introduce you to David Stophlet Flattery. He, too, is a scientist and scholar, and the author of a remarkable book, *Haoma and Harmaline*. Here, an equally persuasive argument is made that the Soma of yore might well be the seeds of *Peganum harmala*, harmel, mountain rue or wild rue. It is now commonly called Syrian Rue, but older texts call it African Rue, the "semen Harmalae sive rutae sylvestris" of the early European Pharmacopoeias, or the Haoma of early Middle Eastern Folklore, which are known by the common name of esfand. Its properties match, equally satisfactorily, the generalized descriptions of the Soma plant in the original Rg Veda. It was a shrub in the Asian Steppes and the Persian Plateau as well as in Afghanistan and Northern Tibet, so it can meet the geographic demands of the ancient Soma fields. It has been the classical source of a deeply colored dye known as Turkey Red which has been used in the coloring of fezes and carpets in both Turkey and Iran. The seeds also provide an oil popular in Egypt as "Zit-el-Harmel" which is sold as an aphrodisiac and narcotic. The consumption of the actual seeds themselves has a well established reputation for giving rise to an intoxication that might answer the tantalizing clues of the Rg Veda.

Some caution should be taken with the old literature, because in the original Persian biology classifications the term "rue" has been used in quite a general way. It used to be that *Peganum harmala* and *Ruta graveolens* were considered the wild, and the cultivated, variations of the same plant. The classic origins of the two generic names are parallel; "peganon" was the Greek word for rue, and in Latin "rue" was simply rue. Today these plants are classified as being in completely separate botanic families (Zygophyllaceae and Rutaceae) and they are morphologically quite different. The present day *R. graveolens* is called the common rue, or the herb of grace. It is considered a European plant that was involved in mediaeval medicine as a stimulant and an irritant, and was claimed to have been used by witches and as a symbol of repentance. It is commonly cultivated as a garden herb. In fact, the sample I have in my garden was bought at a Mexican market on 24th street in San Francisco. Its leaf has a sharp smell which some people like, and which others claim reminds them of cat urine. It certainly has a following due to its food use, but I would hardly call it an intoxicant.

So, just what is the action of *P. harmala* seeds alone when they are not used in admixture with some other component? There is indeed something there but it takes a lot of seed. There are several reports of explorers taking many grams of straight seed, usually ground up and then boiled in quite a lot of water (which sometimes contains something acidic) into a tea. But by definition, if the plant alone is a candidate for the Soma role, then it should have some kind of noteworthy activity without any second component, to warrant its historic position in so many cultures.

Here is a description of a recent trial, which highlights some of its properties:

> "I boiled one ounce (28 grams) of viable *Peganum harmala* seed for seven hours in a liter of water, removed the seeds, and boiled the extract down to half its volume. The mixture was brown, and bitter, and I drank it down. In about forty-five minutes, a pleasant lassitude took me over, and I sat so as to observe my environment. I noticed that the objects in my vision seemed to have multiple contours surrounding them. Even small body motions suggested nausea to me, so I retired to quiet, empty darkness. There commenced a gentle upwelling of hypnogogic imagery that was quite different from anything I was familiar with. There was a vision of seemingly abstract fractal patterns that quickly evolved into what reminded

me of foliage that started close to me and then grew to fill the whole visual field. The original spiral patterns of organization evolved into realistic images (in shades of blue and green) of buses speeding through city streets, street corners, a busy supermarket. This visual phase lasted for almost an hour, at which point the nausea returned very strongly. Following vigorous vomiting, I felt quite relaxed again, but the visionary phase of the experiment seemed to have come to a close."

One must keep in mind that there is also harmaline as well as harmine present in sizable amounts in these seeds, as compared to the largely harmine contribution of *B. caapi* to native ayahuasca. In the one assay I have run, they are present in pretty much equal quantities. Both are effective inhibitors of the amine oxidase enzyme system of the body, which is nature's own way of protecting us from poisons such as DMT. There are many styles of oxidation inhibition, and I must admit that I don't know one from another. There is an amine oxidase inhibitor system that is called an "A" inhibitor, and another that is called a "B" inhibitor. Then the picture is further confused with a claim for a non-specific oxidase inhibitor. It is a fact that there are foods that are toxic if you have inhibited your detoxification mechanisms. There have been problems with foods such as pickled herring, red wine, and particular cheeses when a person is being medicated with certain serotonin receptor drugs which act as enzyme inhibitors. There are many clinically employed anti-depressant drugs that show their activity through this monoamineoxidase inhibition mechanism, and these could be very threatening to a person using ayahuasca. Some of these prescription drugs, given in the treatment of clinical depression, have been used as substitutes for the *B. caapi* component of ayahuasca. The pure chemicals themselves, harmaline or harmine, are discussed in the appropriate recipe part of this book.

I had intended to share a few ayahuasca reports involving Syrian Rue and any of several other amines, with the rue expressed as an approximate quantity of harmaline and/or harmine. This plan suddenly became terribly misleading when I learned that there are some other, very different alkaloids in the seeds. Tetrahydroharmine is pretty well known, and of course might play some role in the action of the plant. But non-tryptamine, non β-carboline alkaloids? I was totally ignorant of these. I was looking by GCMS at a pH 9 methylene chloride extract of a certain batch of *P. harmala* seeds, to verify the approximate ratio of harmine to harmaline, and I noticed a big and broad peak that had the molecular weight equal to that of the simplest hydroxy tetrahydro-β-carboline (7-HO-THβC, $C_{11}H_{12}N_2O$). And there was a smaller, earlier, sharp peak that lacked the hydroxy group. Could this be the simplest possible tetrahydro-β-carboline, just THβC itself? I did not remember these ever having been reported in *P. harmala* before. In fact, I would need a trip to the library to see if they had been reported in any plant before. Both 6-HO-THβC and THβC have been formed from serotonin and tryptamine (with formaldehyde) and have been reported to be found in rat brain, often in association with the pineal gland. And there had been assigned to the latter compound the totally unappealing name of tryptoline. At least that allows the serotonin numbering system to be used, but gives rise to yet more outlandish chimera such as methtryptoline as a literature synonym for tetrahydroharman. But all of this is in rats which are animals, not plants or people.

There is an old saying in chemistry (and I am sure also in physics and any other exploratory technical discipline) which is an important caution: "Wait until tomorrow before you publish your discovery." I remember the time a couple of decades ago that David Ladder and I were up to our ears (figuratively) in poison oak. I had made a hexane extract (with some care as I used to be very sensitive to it) and we had put it into the chemical ionization mass spectrograph. Well, everyone knows that the C-15 family of phenolic alkanes and alkenes characterizes poison ivy, and the C-17 family is the hallmark of poison oak. And there they were. There was the expected neat cluster of nice peaks, all with their different degrees of unsaturation, at the C-17 location. Then, we both noticed a similar cluster at the position of C-21. There were four additional carbon atoms in each molecule. Wow. Has no one seen this before? Had no one run the mass that high, and these new things had simply escaped observation? The discovery of the century! But the next day, pinning down all alternate explanations, we asked the operator of the CIMS what carrier gas he had been using. Isobutane, he said, which just happens to contain four carbon atoms. Why, he asked? We told him, and he re-ran our sample with ammonia instead. The C-21 area was totally clean.

Back to the hydroxy-THβC story. I looked under this empirical formula in the Merck Index, and there was listed a compound which I had never heard of before, called vasicine. It is a quinazoline alkaloid, also called peganine, that had been isolated from *P. harmala* by Späth in 1934. And the alkaloid without the hydroxy group was also known, and had the named desoxypeganine. And there is a ketone peganine which has a structure closely resembling methaqualone; I have put the appropriate pictures in the discussion part of the recipe for harmaline.

Looking again at the cracking patterns of my "new" THβC's, they are very reasonable for these well known quinazoline bases. And there appears to be a vasicinone and a desoxyvasicinone present in these seeds as well. It was a personal disappointment to realize that I had not discovered a new alkaloid in Syrian Rue. But it was exciting to realize that this compound was there in pretty good quantities, and could very well contribute to an unpredictable extent to the pharmacology either of *P. harmala* itself, or of its combination with other plants or chemicals.

So, since I was thirsty for another drink from the Pierian spring, I dove into the literature to learn what I could about the pharmacology of these, to me, new alkaloids. My God, they do everything! Whereas harmine, and especially harmaline, are inhibitors of the monoamine oxidase enzyme, keeping amines such as DMT from being destroyed (the underlying basis of action of ayahuasca) it turns out that desoxypeganine is a potent inhibitor of an entirely different enzyme, one that is called acetylcholinesterase. This is the body's detoxification operator for getting the neurotransmitter acetylcholine out of the synapse when it is no longer needed to conduct a signal from one nerve to another. If the transmitter cannot be destroyed after it has functioned, the nerve system keeps firing and produces what is called parasympathetic toxicity. There can be cardiac depression, vasodilatation, and the flow of saliva and tears. Anticholinergics are members of a pharmacological classification which includes the best of our insecticides and nerve gases. Vasicine is perhaps a tenth as effective as desoxypeganine as an anticholinergic, but it appears to be a good bronchodilator in man, as well as a uterotonic and abortifacient in test animals. These alkaloids are also found in other plants, such as *Adhatoda vasica* which is the origin of the name vasicine. The leaves and flowers of the closely related *A. vasicina* have an ancient native reputation for effective use in the relief of colds, coughs and bronchitis. And it has come to light that a forage legume, *Galega orientalis*, is a well established source of vasicine and by an intriguing twist of fate, it also has a common name of a rue, Goat's Rue! The urge to pursue every factoid until it leads to another factoid is difficult to resist. It is obvious that this kind of botanical and chemical-free association will quickly lead into fascinating areas that have absolutely nothing to do with South American religious sacraments. And religion and religious sacraments are what this chapter is all about. There is even serotonin itself present, as well as a positional isomer of 6-hydroxytryptamine, which has a distinct pharmacological profile of its own.

So enough already. To be too thorough or specific about the possible side-effects of minor components in a plant material is to establish a place for them in the subconscious mind of the user, and this could subtly lead to his experiencing them as "unexpected" complications. The amounts of all the alkaloids in *P. harmala* other than the β-carbolines, those that are directly responsible for its virtue as a substitute for the *B. caapi* component of ayahuasca, appear to be pharmacologically trivial. Nonetheless, I decided not to use estimates of these two alkaloids as a measure of this component, but to stick with the actual weight of the seeds that had been used. There is simply too much variation in the alkaloidal composition to allow such a calculation to be of value.

How much of these several β-carbolines does a given weight of *P. harmala* seeds represent? The alkaloid content has been reported to cover quite a wide range (from as low as two and as high as six percent), so a gram of seed has potentially twenty to sixty milligrams of the desired alkaloids. But here, suddenly, there is a new and treacherous variable. There is a difference between weights and volumes; grams are weights and the kitchen containers are volumes. From one individual seed, to a level teaspoonful of seeds, to a one-shot saki tumbler full of seeds, one will have a dry gross weight of from two and a half milligrams to three milligrams, to maybe three grams, to a half ounce (almost fifteen grams). The alkaloidal content will be in the ballpark range of a tenth of a milligram, to something over a hundred milligrams, to something over a half gram for each of these measuring units. So, a typical individual dosage of *P. harmala* seeds for an ayahuasca experiment would be a level teaspoonful, or three grams, or something over a thousand seeds if you have tweezers and patience rather than a kitchen. This is certainly a sloppy ruler for measuring things, but it works. A small tally of the activity of the extracts of the seeds alone is included in the harmaline recipe in the second half of the book. Also there, please find an algorithm for converting teaspoonfuls to grams.

The action of *P. harmala* seed extracts when used not alone, but in concert with some other amine factor, can be quite dramatic at a much lower dosage. And this higher potency means that much less of the seed extract is really needed than when one makes use of the *B. caapi*. So, what is the action of *P. harmala* seeds when they are in admixture with some other component? I had met an enthusiastic researcher when I was recently at a conference in Göttingen, Germany, who had devised a most remarkable structure for studying these aspects of ayahuasca. He said that he had developed a grid containing a number of component cells, labeled horizontally with the names of potential inhibitors (six of them, the 6-methoxy and 7-methoxy substituted derivatives of harman, harmalan, and tetrahydroharman) and vertically with the two basic parenterally active tryptamines (DMT and 5-methoxy-N,N-dimethyltryptamine). Each display cell contained a plot of the doses of the appropriate combinations that one member of his research group had chosen to explore, and following his trial he would place a green, yellow or red star there, noting the exact quantities taken, and whether the effects he had experienced could be classified as inactive, or maybe active, or really active. His plan was to allow each member of his experiment research group to choose a cell (defining the drugs to be used in combination that day) and a dosage level that appealed to his curiosity for the day. After the experiment was done, he would place his personally initialed star, with the appropriate color, within the appropriate cell. It was a fine idea, and the results would certainly have been a treasure of information, but I never saw any of them. I have no idea if the whole story was fact or fantasy.

The majority of all ayahuasca trials that I am aware of have been between the seeds of *P. harmala* and purified DMT, both taken orally. There are several dozen such trials that I know about, some in the literature (largely taken from Ott's *Ayahuasca Analogues*) or from personal communications to me from a lot of people out there. In the absence of green, yellow and red stickers, I will paint a word-picture of these results. A prototype experiment might go as follows:

(1) The experimental subject consumes three grams of *P. harmala* seeds that had been lightly ground (to break the husks) and placed in gelatin capsules. An alternate and more cumbersome preparation is the boiling of the seeds in a water suspension, which might be lightly acidified with lime or lemon juice. Sometimes they have been ground, sometimes not.

(2) About an hour following the consumption of the *P. harmala* seeds, seventy five milligrams of N,N-dimethyltryptamine (DMT) are taken, also contained in capsules. The time interval between the *P. harmala* seeds and the DMT can be quite variable. In many regimens all the capsules are taken at the same time, and sometimes there is a gap of ten or twenty minutes between them. One hour appears to be a satisfactory period allowing release and absorption of the β-carboline alkaloids. The use of one hundred milligrams of DMT rather than seventy five leads to a somewhat stronger, but completely acceptable experience.

I have heard very mixed reports from trials employing *P. harmala* and the second of the biotic tryptamines, 5-methoxy-N,N-dimethyl-tryptamine, or 5-MeO-DMT. Apparently, modest amounts of both components gives a modest experience, but I have had two reports of truly toxic crises with larger quantities. There is one report of a dosage of about five grams of *P. harmala* seed (water extract) followed in thirty five minutes with ten milligrams of 5-MeO-DMT. The toxicity presented in two phases:

> "In a half hour there was a mild hallucinosis noted which in another half hour deepened considerably. There was an uncharacteristic body rush but in another two hours all effects were waning to my relief. This relief was short lived as some thirty minutes later there was a very abrupt onset of problems. There was a very rapidly build-ing sympathomimetic situation and for the next three hours I was subjected to intense stimulation with rapid

pounding heart-beat and a strange hallucinosis. These effects came in waves: ten minutes of extreme adrenergic stress without appreciable psychic component, followed for a minute or two where I would feel basically 'normal' which would, in turn, be followed by a hallucinosis similar to but more intense than when massive amounts of **P. harmala** seed had been consumed as a single entity. Strangely there was no body strain the next day despite my conviction at the time that I'd have a heart attack or massive cerebral aneurysm."

A second report I have recently read about, with almost exactly the same exposure to *P. harmala* and to 5-MeO-DMT, led to vomiting, temporary blindness, and amnesia followed by extensive sleeplessness. Yet another report with unstated quantities of both drugs indicated a cardiovascular incident similar to the quoted one above. The three of these together support a strong word of caution that perhaps 5-MeO-DMT cannot be interchanged casually with DMT in these calculations, based solely on the dosages used in parenteral studies. Other ayahuasca studies, employing *P. harmala* or the carbolines themselves, with xenobiotic tryptamines (other than the natural DMT and 5-MeO-DMT) are tucked away in the recipe part of this volume.

A small scattering of reports exist in the evaluation of ayahuasca mixtures using *P. harmala* as the deaminase inhibitor and plants or plant extracts as the DMT source. This is probably one of the most "pure" of the ayahuasca analogue studies in that it is truly a mixture of plants as in the prototypic vegetal, but it has been little studied. In most cases the inhibitor is the staunch standby, *P. harmala*, but the other component is any of several reasonably popular *Psychotria viridis* substitutes. In a study with a tea made from actual *P. viridis* leaves, there was a disappointing absence of any effects. Similarly, root bark extracts of *Desmanthus illinoensis* gave modest activity, but when consumed along with grass extracts of the *Phalaris* spp., there was a duplication of the characteristic hoasca magic.

I have been led to believe that if the amount of the inhibitor is adequate (three grams of *P. harmala* seems to be quite enough), then the intensity of the experience depends totally on the amount of the DMT-containing plant that is consumed. It must always be remembered that the alkaloid content of a plant that has been reported to be such-and-such in the scientific literature, can be something entirely different if the botanical material is gathered at different times of the day, the growing cycle, the seed-producing cycle or, for that matter, if it grows on the North or the South side of the hill. If a lot of DMT goes in, in the ayahuasca trial, and there is an adequate amount of the inhibitor on board, the experience can be extraordinary and quite frightening.

Let me quote at some length from a plant/plant combination experience that I heard about a while ago, which beautifully portrays the agony and the ecstasy of ayahuasca. This follows the consumption of about three grams of *P. harmala* followed with an unknown (but obviously large) quantity of extract from the leaves of the tree, *Acacia phlebophylla*. Look at the world and at reality through the eyes of a young adventurer during the course of about two hours at home, with both the "force" and the "light" guiding him in his quest.

"At 2:15 a.m. on Saturday morning I ingested (rather quickly) a heaped teaspoonful of ground harmala seeds, and I flushed it down with water. Ten minutes later, I drank a cup full of the brew, also rather quickly. Fifteen minutes later things got really, really weird.

"Three of us were sitting in the front room of my house. This is where I kept a spare mattress and all of my musical gear, and it was the furthest room from where my girl friend was trying to sleep. I was told to get comfortable so I brought in a bean bag from the living room, and I lay on that. I was on the bean bag, describing a dull cramp in my stomach to my friends. I glanced over at the curtains which are a see-through material with a floral pattern. They started moving. The flowers on the curtain seemed as though they were at a different distance from the material itself. They looked different, almost brighter. The Venetian blinds, behind the curtains were breathing. There was no shading, no shadows, no scratches, no texture. Just a single color for every single object.

"The flowers on the curtain were shimmering, the curtains started breathing, and then they flowed down onto the floor, just like the smoke from a spilt bottle of liquid nitrogen flows down stairs. Then the eyes-closed visuals started. I felt that this was about as much as I could handle at that moment, and if the trip stopped there I would have heaps to talk about. But no ....

"I felt vaguely nauseous, and I didn't want to throw up later because I didn't know what to expect: my expectations were exceeded even at this early stage through the trip (it had been only five minutes since the onset of effects). I forced myself to throw up in a clear Tupperware container thing. I was beginning to hallucinate strongly, and had lost the ability to distinguish between visuals experienced with the eyes closed and those with the eyes open. I didn't know what I was doing at the time. I felt some bowel movement, and asked if I had defecated. Apparently I was OK, but I thought it'd probably be best if I went to the toilet, 'just in case.'

"Things went up a level. It was no longer my house I was in. I was walking down some hallway thingy but I didn't know where any of the doors led to. Someone must have gotten to the bathroom before me because the light was on, but I went in there anyway. I was now experiencing full on hallucinations, but I didn't think it was a case of bad timing and I didn't attempt to abort the toilet visit. I had no sense of time at all. The bathroom certainly wasn't mine. Yes, there was a basin, and a bathtub, and there was also a strange door that someone opened for me. I was only vaguely aware that I had to do something here. The hallucinations were pretty heavy before I sat down, somehow I managed to unzip myself and to drop my trousers, and sit down. Then the universe changed ...

"I left my body sitting on the toilet and was thrown into a universe where nothing seemed to make any sense. The eyes-closed visuals were absolutely outstanding, freeforming, morphing from one complex scene to another. I went through huge sliding doors, traveled in space vehicles, saw incredibly complex and insane roads and highways, floating through space I could never fully describe. Beings were present, gray munchkin-like things with yellow stripes, and there were snake objects too. And, especially, eyes. Peeking out of every bend in the road, off every snake, under every door. They didn't frighten me. I was just curious to know what they all were doing, and what they all were seeing.

"These visuals came on with such an incredible intensity it was simply neuronically impossible to process all of them. I remember thinking that nothing made sense, so I must've analyzed these images at one point, although I can never remember specifically doing so. The colors for my eye-closed visuals remained the same throughout all the trip; striking pinks, gray, vivid yellows, deep dark blues, purple, red. All tones had terrific contrast. There were no 'boring colors;' colors seemed to be like some weird arcade game.

"My 'field of vision' had significantly changed too.

In the normal state I can usually only look at one thing at a time, but now my field of vision had become an entire hemisphere, and my body (rather, my being) became a point in this crazy universe. The point didn't have a body, it just floated around in this virtual brain space. I could accept input from this visual hemisphere, but there was no way I could ever come close to processing it. It was just too fast, too complex, and too intense.

"In the meantime, my body was trying to have a shit. I don't know if that eventually happened, but I thought I would give myself a wipe anyway. I turned to where I thought the toilet paper was, on the right, and the Valhalla poster was on the left. What a mess. There were these letter things all over it, and I could see the words, but I couldn't read. I couldn't attach any meaning to the lettery things. Directly in front of me was a blank, white wall. I stared at this for a while but I cannot remember what I saw. I finally got to the toilet paper, but couldn't find the end of the roll. I grabbed it, clawed at it, but it felt like smoke. I eventually managed to grab a fistful, and looking down at my hand I couldn't see anything, but I knew I had the paper. I managed to wipe somehow, and while glancing down I noticed that my legs had disappeared. Oh, no, its OK. There they are. No, they're gone again. How am I supposed to wipe when everything keeps disappearing. Somehow my hand completed the task. I don't remember standing up, zipping up, washing my hands or anything like that. But I remember telling the guys that I wanted my favorite chair. Somehow I ended up seated in it. I had somehow ended up with a clean bucket in my lap, so I didn't have to worry about throwing up on my self.

"I didn't have anything to throw up. I hadn't eaten anything since 1 p.m. on Friday, and it is now 3 a.m. on Saturday. And the morning's experience started at 2:40 a.m., just twenty minutes ago!

"After a little while the visuals started to decrease in intensity, and I tried communicating with my baby-sitter. We mainly giggled a lot, and we seemed to spend more time actually working out if we could communicate than actually communicating. We were both going to be OK. I occasionally tried to keep my own checks on my body. One of the hardest things was actually trying to figure out if I was breathing. There was a vague sound somewhere that sounded familiar. Audio was basically annoying — there was no correlation between the audio and the visuals. Taste was not there (I couldn't taste the vomit), smell likewise, and I couldn't feel anything. But there was endless 'visual noise' that was continuously confusing. Seashell noise. Everything looked as if it were made of a flexible membrane (single color, of course) and there were all these moving seashells underneath the surface.

"The visuals themselves were very, very geometric, although like nothing ever constructed by humans before. But throughout the whole thing, not a single element of chaos. No fractals, nothing irregular. Everything perfect and geometric. I wonder what it would be like to see a tree under DMT? Being a fractal person, I'm doing the next trip during the day, where I can try and interpret nature.

"Nothing short of the most amazing and intense experience of my life to date."

This was an extremely long experience that lasted less than two hours. This abbreviated version of the complete report is a rich introduction to the complexities of DMT, the light of the hoasca, that can become apparent with the expression of a material that is protected from the body's urges to destroy it quickly.

A final comment. I was asked recently by a person in law enforcement to give him a definition of just what the term "ayahuasca" stood for, since it apparently had been encountered in connection with some drug-related incident. I wrote the following short essay, which was published in a journal called CLIC, and is reproduced here with permission.

## AYAHUASCA

Until recently, the term "Ayahuasca" was seldom seen or heard outside of reports that originated in the Amazon basin. This plant decoction has found wide use throughout northern South America in healing, prophesy, initiation, and as a sensory intoxicant. Depending upon its area of origin, it has also been called caapi, natema, or yaje.

In the last decade or two, it has appeared more and more frequently in non-Indian settings. It has become a component of a religious movement in Brazil, and it is provoking broad curiosity in Europe and in the United States.

Its composition is extremely variable, depending upon the personal choice of the curandero-shaman-healer-practitioner-physician who prepares it. It can be composed entirely of plant materials, or of synthetic compounds, or of combinations from both sources. Invariably, ayahuasca is a mixture of two components. One is an enzyme inhibitor, a factor that will block the deamination of an amine. The other is the amine that is protected from metabolic destruction. As a rule, neither component is particularly active alone, orally, but in combination the deamination inhibitor allows the amine to show oral activity.

The monoamineoxidase inhibitor can be from plant sources, or it can be an appropriate pharmaceutical agent. The chemicals that are usually found in the plant products are harmine, harmaline, or tetrahydroharmine, all 7-methoxy-beta-carbolines. In the Amazon, plants of the *Banisteriopsis* Genus are common, including species such as *B. caapi* or *B. inebrians*. In Europe and the Southern United States and Mexico, one can find several species related to *Peganum harmala*, or Syrian Rue, being used as a source of these carbolines. The positional isomers, 6-methoxyharman and its hydrogenation products, have also been employed in this enzyme inhibitory role. Even prescribable antidepressant MAOI drugs such as tranylcypromine (Parnate) have been used in this role of activator.

The amine being allowed oral availability by this deaminase activity can be from an even wider collection of sources. The simplest tryptamines such as N,N-dimethyltryptamine (DMT) or 5-methoxy-N,N-dimethyltryptamine (5-MeO-DMT) are common. There are many plants that have been used for this component. The extracts of the leaves of *Psychotria*, a shrub of Amazonian origin but now found throughout the world, are active and often employed. Acacia species from Australia (the Wattle tree) or China, the snuff sources derived from *Anadenanthera*, the roots of *Mimosa hostilis* or from grasses found in the midwest, the various Virola bark resins from the Amazon, or even from the poison glands of the *Bufo alvarius* frogs of the Southwest, all contain tryptamine alkaloids that become orally active when mixed with a MAOI companion.

But the amine being protected from metabolic destruction can be from many other sources. I know of mushroom extracts, some of the *Psilocybe* line, some from *Amanita*, some from *Inocybe*, that have been used. There can be extracts of plants of the Solonaceae, the *Datura* group, or belladonna, henbane, or mandrake, or extracts of the *Brugmansia* that are the South American relatives of the *Datura*. Here, the active agents are atropine and scopolamine. Although many of these amines are quite active by themselves, they have nonetheless been explored as the "second half" of the ayahuasca.

Most often, the patient/recipient has no idea of the composition of the ayahuasca brew. If these are plants, their identities might be uncertain due to the use of native names. Even the person who assembles and provides the active mixture might be unable to accurately acknowledge its components, as he may be using extracts and concentrates of plants of unknown origins.

Thus, ayahuasca can be a capricious combination of either plant extracts or specific compounds. It can be encountered as a viscous oil that can vary from amber in color to tarry black. It is neither consistent in composition, nor is it reproducible as to pharmacological activity. An illicit drug may be present in a given sample (DMT, psilocybin, or possibly bufotenine) but these explicitly scheduled drugs may not be there at all. Most exhibits will be complex mixtures that will be challenging to analyze.

This brief introduction to the area, just cited above, was written for an audience that would be largely forensic chemists, so I emphasized the uncertainties and complexities that might be encountered in their laboratory work. Perhaps this broad and somewhat diffuse definition might provide a bit more time for these religious and spiritual seeds to germinate in the United States. And a bit more time to learn the remarkable world that can be revealed from within ourselves.

To me, there is something of great potential value in these particular tools, and I would like to see research with it get started and flourish.

# CHAPTER 17. MGS

(Shura's voice)

I pride myself on being pretty much up to speed concerning the plant sources for psychedelic drugs. But morning glory seeds were an item that took me completely by surprise. Oh, the scientific papers were there in the older literature — in fact, one of the earliest was a short report published in 1941 by Richard Schultes, describing the use of the seeds of a morning glory by Mexican Indian groups following a tradition that dated back to Aztec time. This was the plant *Rivea corymbosa* or *Turbina corymbosa*, and the seeds were called ololiuqui. A couple of decades later, another report appeared in a Mexican anthropological journal, of a similar plant with a similar action. This was another morning glory which had seeds called "tlitliltzen" by the Aztecs. The botanical binomial for this plant was *Ipomoea violacea* or *I. tricolor.*

I do not read either the monographs from the Botanical Museum of Harvard University, or the Boletin del Centro de Investigaciones Anthropológicas de Mexico with any regularity. But part of my daily reading ritual does include the San Francisco Chronicle, and this of course included the daily offering of the columnist, Herb Caen.

It was over my morning coffee, in 1963, that I was captivated by a column devoted to a pile of rumors that involved the latest drug in the San Francisco scene, MGS. During World War II there was a vigorous cigarette advertising promotion for Lucky Strikes that exploited the change of package color from green to white. It went, "Lucky Strike green has gone to war." After the war, this dropped away, but there appeared the slogan, LS/MFT, or Lucky Strikes Means Fine Tobacco. And the caption that caught my eye in the Herb Caen column was, LS/MGS. Apparently, the real swingers (so the column said) were abandoning peyote and LSD, in favor of chewing a hundred morning glory seeds. People were ordering 25 lb. sacks of seeds from whomever sold them. In the middle of May, 1963, a vice president of a major supplier, the Ferry Morse Seed Company, began to get suspicious. Although morning glory seeds were one of their five most popular items, he said, their sales had leapt to 50 times normal. The three most sought-after varieties had the unbelievable names, Heavenly Blue, Pearly Gates, and Flying Saucers.

Suppliers quickly removed the seeds from the market with the explanation, "We want to be sure." The state narcotics chief said that it was just a rumor. A spokesman from the FDA said that he didn't think there was anything to it but he remembered that, as a kid, he had been told never to chew on morning glory seeds. The medical director of the Menlo Park International Foundation for Advanced Study reported the experiences of test subjects, with 50 to 500 seeds each, lasting five to eight hours. The FDA started their own investigation, and there was the suggestion that this could prompt Congressional action: an anti-morning glory seed bill.

Were these reports all valid? Yes, they were. The most remarkable chemist Albert Hofmann, the ergot expert who was the first to synthesize LSD and to eventually discover its activity, undertook the challenge of exploring the seeds of the morning glories and he discovered, to his amazement, that they contained alkaloids that were previously known only amongst the ergot fungi. The presence of these complex alkaloids (widely believed to be unique to the ergot world) in higher plants such as these Convolvulaceae, was initially disbelieved. It was suggested that since there certainly were all sorts of fungal ergots adrift in Hofmann's lab, there obviously had to have been some cross-contamination. But others found the same results and this remarkable parallel between the lowly fungus and the pretty sophisticated plants (from the botanical point of view) proved to be correct.

Everyone climbed on the bandwagon, and there was a wealth of publications in the 60's. The scientists wanted to pursue the holy grail by finding new morning glory plants and new components, but at the same time they had to distance themselves from the reality that these plants were pharmacological turn-ons. One of my most cherished quotes comes from a paper published in 1966, sponsored by the NIMH (National Institute of Mental Health, of the U.S. Department of Health) which informed the scientific community that, "Law enforcement officers and garden seed companies in the United States have recently become concerned because of reports in the lay press that students, psychologists and maladapted persons of Bohemian habits ('beatniks') were ingesting seeds of cultivated morning glories sold in garden supply shops." They spoke of suicide attempts, and severe reactions with dosages of 250 seeds that required hospitalization. There was fear that a potentially dangerous psychoactive drug abuse problem might be arising in he United States.

They were probably quite correct. There has been an ever increasing volume of questions and answers on the internet over the last few years, with interest focused on these morning glory plants. "Where do the seeds come from?" "What are their names?" "How many do I use?" "How do I prepare them?" "What sort of effects should I expect?" I am again confronted with my classical dilemma: how do I present my scattered notes and thoughts to make them most useful when there is no obvious organizational structure? Should I organize the sources as botanical individuals (which fits with native use) or as chemical individuals which might be responsible for the biological activity? Either choice will offend the purists in the other camp. So let me start with the plant, which will allow a little of the componentry to be listed and perhaps associated with the action of the whole entity, and then let me bring together some of the potential active components, the "usual suspects," which might contribute to the overall effects. These issues are far from being resolved; they will never be resolved. The plants will be in part defined by the compounds within them, and these very compounds will be used to identify the plants that contain them. There will never be an acceptable hierarchy of ordering.

The plant that started all of this notoriety was *Rivea corymbosa* (or *Turbina corymbosa* or *Ipomoea sidaefolia*). The Nahuatl name for the plant in Mexico is "coaxihuitl" (the snake plant) and they called the seeds ololuiqui (small round things). They are small and spherical, brown colored, and they appear one to a capsule. The Zapotec name for them is "badoh." This was the first of this botanical group to be analyzed for its alkaloid content, which proved to be only a fraction of that of the tlitliltzen group mentioned below, and contained levels that measured some 0.01% by weight in the fresh seeds.

There is the second morning glory with the botanical name of *Ipomoea violacea* (or *I. tricolor* or *I. rubrocaerulea*). It has large five-petaled blossoms that last just one day before changing into a seed capsule that contains three seeds. These are black, rice-grain sized, with a distinct tapering bulge towards one end. The Zapotec name for them is "badoh negro" and the Aztec name, tlitliltzen, means "little black one." It takes about 25 seeds to weigh a gram, and the alkaloid content of the fresh seeds, by weight, runs between 0.02 and 0.10 %.

There was a third morning glory that came into popular notoriety a couple of years later. This was the Hawaiian baby wood rose known botanically as *Argyreia nervosa*. Although there is no shamanic reputation for this plant in the history of Mexican native use, there certainly developed quite a notoriety in our own western culture. My first encounter with this plant was at the opening of a new Standard Oil gas station in Berkeley, where each customer was given a small bouquet of dried flowers as a thank you for coming by and buying gas on the first day of business. The flower?

A bunch of hard, wood-like blossoms called wood roses. Here the seeds are larger than those of the usual morning glories; they are four to a capsule, running perhaps 10 seeds to the gram. They have an alkaloid content of up to almost 1%. Thus they are perhaps one or two dozen times more potent on a per-seed basis than the *Ipomoea* and *Rivea* species mentioned above. A second wood rose is a pharmacological disappointment, the just plain Hawaiian wood rose, *Ipomoea tuberosa*. The seeds of this beautiful flower are immensely larger, over a gram apiece, but they are devoid of alkaloids.

How active are the seeds pharmacologically? There is a small scattering of somewhat objective reports in the early medical literature, and a vast outpouring over the last few years of completely subjective anecdotal reports from the internet. The medical reports usually involved a hundred or more of either the badoh or the badoh negro seeds, and usually described effects that covered the range from apathy and listlessness, to increased visual sensitivity, to a feeling of well being, to no effect at all. Even with dosages up to 300 seeds there were very few positive effects reported, usually only sedation and nausea. Isolated extracts of the seeds (2 milligrams of the extract) led to some alterations of color perception and the appearance of objects, and a generalized dreamy state. In the more recent popular reports, quite often there are effective efforts made to extract the alkaloids from the raw plant material, to lessen the gastric distress that reflects the massive amount of plant material that is consumed.

What is in these seeds that makes them psychoactive? The major alkaloidal components in most of the seeds are the two isomeric amides of lysergic acid, lysergamide (ergine, LAA, LA-111) and isolysergamide (isoergine, iso-LAA). They represent perhaps a half of the alkaloid content of the two badoh's and they are a smaller but sizable component of the baby wood rose. It has been found that the acetaldehyde adduct of these two amides, the N-(1-hydroxyethylamides) accounts for some of the isolated ergines, as this material is quite unstable and is easily converted in the process of isolation. The only other amide of lysergic acid that is present in these plants is ergometrine. All of these are known to have activity in man, and they are specifically described in the commentary located in the LSD recipe in the second half of this volume.

The four lesser alkaloids that are present are all alcohols, reflecting the reduction of the acid group of lysergic acid. The primary reduction product is elymoclavine and the isomer with the double bond moved into conjugation with the aromatic ring is lysergol. This can further hydroxylate to provide penniclavine. And the complete opening of the fourth "D" ring yields chanoclavine. A number of trace alkaloids are also known.

What are the virtues and what are the risks associated with the exploration of morning glories and their contents? The virtues are many, both as a natural intoxicant with an ancient history of use in the traditions of shamanism and spirituality, and as a raw material source of ergot alkaloids. Historically, there is a rich lore of medical and religious value that has been part of the Meso-American culture for many generations.

As far as the raw material aspect is concerned, it must be noted that some of the alkaloids that are present are of nuisance value only, as they are chemical modifications of lysergic acid. These are the alcohols and open ring compounds with intriguing structures in their own rights, but they cannot be brought around into anything of immediate value by easy synthetic manipulation. The major alkaloids are, however, the amides of lysergic acid and of isolysergic acid, and the fragile 1-hydroxyethylamide precursors to them. All these are of interest as themselves, being psychoactive in different ways to different people.

A second value is that all these will hydrolyze to the corresponding lysergic acids (LA and iso-LA) with strong base treatment. This mixture is the immediate synthetic precursor to the mixture of LSD and iso-LSD which, on chromatographic fractionation, will provide LSD itself. To be able to go from the local nursery, in two steps and one fractionation, to LSD, would certainly appear to be a virtue to some people.

The risks? They are also very worthy of caution. It must always be remembered that these chemicals are ergot alkaloids, and as such have profound effects on the uterus and can be extremely damaging to hormonal balance. The history of ergotism is well known, both as to the gangrenous and the convulsive possibilities. Probably the single most dangerous aspect of the isolates from the morning glory seeds is the fact that both lysergamide (ergine, the natural alkaloid present) and lysergic acid (the hydrolysis product of it mentioned above) are Schedule III drugs according to the present listings in the Controlled Substance Act (see Appendix B).

The continuum from innocent behavior to criminal behavior is relatively undefined and must be viewed through the eyes of someone who may not approve of your behavior. One should visualize a sequence, the stations of the psychedelic intent so to speak. It starts with the possession of a package of Flying Saucer seeds, and progresses to an isolate of those seeds, to a hydrolysate of that isolate, to a coupling of that hydrolysate to diethylamine, to a separation of the resulting mixture into two components, one of which is LSD. This is a transition from total innocence to felonious behavior. The law is vague. The enforcement of it is capricious and usually harsh. Intent to commit a crime is today itself a crime, even if no overt act has been made. If you involve a buddy, there are equally punitive con-spiracy laws.

I had a dear friend who always traveled in his car with a pocket full of nasturtium seeds. Anywhere he would see a pile of garbage alongside the road, or an ugly ditch or perhaps a barren mud slide, he would throw a handful of seeds there, and he knew that next year the eyesore might well be a little less ugly as it would be a mass of nasturtium leaves and blossoms. Maybe somewhere there is a Johnny Ipomoea seed scatterer. His fifty pound gunny sack of morning glory seeds is dedicated to environmental reconstruction. If you were to ask him, "Do you use these as a drug?" He would say, "Drugs? Moi? You've got to be kidding. I'm just into growin' flowers."

# Part Four:

# Time and Transformation

# CHAPTER 18.  WHAT BIG BANG?

(Shura's voice)

Sometimes when I am working late in my laboratory I have problems finding an OK radio station.  On KNBC, at 740, there is a continuing
reiteration of the day's news which I hear repeated almost verbatim every
few hours, and I lose interest.  And then, up the dial a little bit, I find Morten
W. on KGO at 810.  He is a knowledgeable scientist explaining such weird
stuff as, for example, why green water is coming out of the water pipes over
in Danville.  He always explains such things well, but with a tone of
superiority and arrogance that I find humorous rather than impressive.  But
when I go from 740 to 810, I pass a station at 770 or 780 that is devoted to the
Bible and Christian fundamentalism, and finding that has proven to be a
total treasure.  A stanza that I learned in childhood comes to mind,
"Whenever I go to Severn along the Erie Tract, I pass by a poor old farmhouse whose shingles are broken and black."  This religious farmhouse on
the way to KGO along the AM dial is often my retreat from the boredom
of both replayed news and omniscience.

It is here that I have learned much of what I know about creation-
ism.  Most of the speakers hold to the seven-day model of Genesis, a week
of God's work, ending with an earth, the sun and, for all I can tell, the rest
of the universe.  Since this is the text of the Bible, and the Bible is the word
of God, it serves well as a fait accompli explanation of our origins.  Given
the premise of divine origin, everything holds together remarkably well.
Oh, there are a few things that are awkward, such as fossil records and
partially decayed radioactivity, but if you accept the cosmology of creation-
ism, then you can find ways of accepting and living with its troublesome
contradictions.  Once the shift is made from a process of reason to one of
faith, everything can be made to fit your thesis.  Things such as dinosaurs
and uranium, things that give the illusion of ancient times, are also the
products of that busy week, and all were the handiwork of the Creator.

Those who see themselves as being scientifically sophisticated will smile with patient and quiet amusement upon those whom they see as present-day champions of a Middle Ages philosophy. Those who wish to enter into a dialogue will support their arguments with the hard, cold facts of science, the rewards gained from the application of the "scientific method." And the creationists quite rightly argue back, that these scientists are defending their positions with the same blend of theory and observation that they themselves employ. Neither camp will gracefully admit that there are many embarrassing observations that are being ignored. In my lecturing at Berkeley, I enjoy the disruption that will inevitably follow some offhand comment I might make concerning the arguments that favor the one-week origin that took place some maybe ten thousand years ago.

As a person who identifies himself with the scientist side rather than the creationist side of this polemic, I find myself quite irritated when I hear the theory of the big bang being accepted by the scientific community as an item of faith. This is the current myth in vogue that deals with the origin of the universe. One of the most predictable questions each of us has asked of our elders, at one time or another in our youth, is, "Where did I come from?" As individuals we cannot remember back to our birth — our memories are sadly incomplete and we seek the input from others who may fill in the details. As a species we ask the same question over an immensely broader time base, "Where did we come from? Was there a beginning? What was there before that?"

Embarrassing stuff, here, since there is no available parent to help us find answers when the question is asked in cosmological terms. The religious fundamentalist says, God created us all out of his infinite good will, in early March, 8065 B.C. Or thereabouts. The learned astrophysicist says the big bang created us all in late September, 14.3 billion years B.C. Or thereabouts. There is no record of this event that is unambiguous, so the acceptance of the big bang myth is every bit as much an act of faith as is the acceptance of the Genesis myth. To keep things in perspective, I should capitalize Big Bang so that it looks as important as God.

Not that I want to knock God. As this fun essay progresses, I hope to offer an alternative to the concept of origin. There might have been no origin. Our universe has always been here, it is infinitely old, and so God just might have been with us much longer than anyone ever suspected. All the weird observations that are part of our science will fit another explanation just as well, or even better, but the veil of prejudice must be put aside for a moment for us to see it. More of this iconoclasm later.

Let me paint a brief word picture of the Big Bang religion first, using the vocabulary of the faithful. We have interpreted the evidence from our instruments to support a theory that the universe is expanding, and expanding at a remarkably rapid rate. And the further away something is, the faster it is moving away from us. This is our way of being at peace with the observation that the further away a light source is, the more the spectrum of that light is shifted to the red. This relationship, between how far away the light emitter is from us, and the red shift of the light emitted, is called the Hubble constant. The resemblance between this dynamic picture and an explosion has provided us an irresistible model for the origin of our universe. This is portrayed as a super explosion, and what we see now is the debris, the shards and fragments, still flying away in every direction. With this model in front of us, let us pretend that we can watch the passing of time in the reverse direction. Let's run the movie projector backwards. Each frame takes you to an earlier point in time, so that the flying fragments appear to be coming together again, with the volume of the universe getting progressively smaller and the matter (or whatever it is) that is in it getting progressively hotter. As the film continues to roll backwards, everything appears to condense to a smaller and smaller volume, and then even this shrinks further to what looks like a point and that point is so hot that matter can't even exist at all. Stop the projector right there. Look at that birth frame. If you closely inspect the image before you, you should see an extremely small something, at a temperature of a fantastically large number of degrees centigrade. The movie is said to have started from this point in the normal time direction and that is what the physicists call the Big Bang. From that minuscule source came all the stuff that constitutes this universe: the energy, the eventual mass, the stars and the galaxies, the forces of gravity and of life.

I recently read a review by Rem B. Edwards (published in the International Journal for Philosophy of Religion) of a book written by two physicists, who argued as to whether the Big Bang cosmology provided evidence for the existence of God. It stated that both authors agreed that our universe emerged as a cataclysmic explosion from an initial singularity, understood in contemporary astrophysics as a state in which the mass/energy of the universe is condensed into an infinitely dense, infinitely hot, infinitely small (zero diameter), infinitely curved, pointlike dimension. If those were the true dimensions of our origin as shown on that birth frame, then even if that "cataclysmic explosion" were to increase that original diameter a zillion-fold it would still be zero, if the temperature were to drop a zillion-fold, it would still be infinite. Anything times zero is still zero. Infinity divided by anything is still infinity. In short, the second frame, and the thousandth frame of our movie would appear identical to the first one, and there would be no stars or galaxies. We would not exist.

But here is the faith aspect of this particular cosmological religion. Look at that one frame again, the first frame with the very small speck that is so very hot, and ask to look at the frame that immediately precedes it. To make that request is to immediately offend all the anticreationists, and you will find yourself confronted by an army of the astronomically faithful who will leap to the defense of their theory.

The question has no meaning, some will say. According to Stephen Hawking, "That is like asking what lies five miles North of the North Pole." Others will talk about singularities involving unbelievably large accumulations of mass produced from some form of a black hole environment where the rules of light and energy are nonexistent and there is no meaning to time. "Without the passage of time, there is no meaning to the word 'before'." But, you say, if there is no before, and there is no time, then nothing can get started and there can be no after. And furthermore, you can't have it both ways. If all is energy, and energy is mass, then you would have nothing but a single black hole, and there could be no way to "Big Bang" your way out of it. If time can't move, then the film can't be run either way. But if the mass equivalency doesn't apply, there can be no black hole, and you can't invoke your time suspension rules, and our movie frames can indeed be viewed in sequence. But the devotees of quantum mechanics will say, oh yes, you can indeed have it both ways, because both extremes are really expressions of the same state. But this still avoids the origin question. From whence? What lit the fuse? Who said, "Let the games begin." Listen carefully and you just might hear someone speak the name so frequently invoked by the biblical creationists: God.

So the Big Bang is presented within our present day science as a miracle, nothing more and nothing less. It is a pleasure to watch the contortions that our revered scientists go through in their compulsion to fit all observations into a theory that will support, or at least be at peace with, this Big Bang miracle.

One of the most amusing examples involves the determination of the presence of a background radiation that is uniform in all directions in the heavens. Some few years ago a couple of scientists, at Bell Laboratories as I remember, received the Nobel Prize for the discovery that there was an absolutely uniform level of radiation to be found in the sky, regardless of which direction you happen to look. Homeostasis. A flat, constant coldness at around 3° Kelvin. The fact that it was both smooth and exactly the same in every direction was the killer observation that finally provided the ultimate proof of the Big Bang origin of the universe. Or so they said. And then, a few years later, some super detectors were put up in orbit with orders of magnitude greater sensitivity. You know what they observed? That flat background radiation wasn't really flat, but had undulations and unevennesses in it. The fact that it was, in its fine detail, uneven and variable was then advanced as the ultimate proof of the Big Bang.

Examples abound of the capitulation of the scientific community to this canonical cop-out. Two recent articles appeared in the local San Francisco Chronicle that are superb illustrations of this mind set.

On March 4, 1995, there was reported the discovery of the sixth and last quark, the top quark. I do not wish to detract in any way from the beautiful story of fundamental particles, the various forces, the laws of physics and all the related entities that are the ultimate building blocks and operative rules of the matter that constitute the universe. I'm all for chemistry, and physics, and thermodynamics and quantum mechanics. They are real; they are essential; they are inescapable. What I am against is the blind attachment of everything to the Big Bang nonsense. Let me make a parallel between the biased reporting that is so much in vogue now (let's call it Big Bang Bias, or BBB), and how it might have been phrased in non-biased language (called IOU for Infinitely Old Universe), in the matter of this quark report.

> BBB "Scientists have managed to isolate a bit of matter providing a major clue to the origin and evolution of the universe."
> IOU "Scientists have managed to isolate a bit of matter providing a major clue to the structure of the universe."

> BBB "Quarks vanished as independent entities at the very beginning of time when the original Big Bang that created the universe began to cool."
> IOU "Quarks have never before existed as independent entities, as the extreme conditions of heat and energy needed to release them are not known in nature."

> BBB "... have found the missing link in our theoretical model that tries to understand how the universe evolved from its birth."
> IOU "... have found the missing link in our theoretical model that tries to understand what the universe is and of what it is made."

The article has a climax sentence that is directly comparable to the Catholic Church's Sunday mass. "In the instant of the Big Bang the universe was a soup of quarks and leptons and radiation, but then as the universe cooled down in seconds and minutes, and as its temperature cooled to 2,000 trillion degrees, it lost its quarks." That one I cannot paraphrase, although the expression "lost its marbles" is very tempting. As I would with the personal viewing of the second coming of Christ, I must rest in awe of

2,000 trillion degrees temperature.

My dear wife Alice uses the term "factoid" to represent something that is accurate and totally trivial. Big numbers, certainly those that I lump together under the term zillion which I have used a couple of times already in this chapter, certainly fit into this classification. Just how big is a trillion? The American system is based on the old French system. But the French recently changed their system to correspond to the German and British systems, so again we stand alone. Since this is, both figuratively and literally, a hot topic, let me continue this trivial aside. Going up in factors of one thousand, there is:

| how many zeros | American | British |
|---|---|---|
| 3 | thousand | thousand |
| 6 | million | million |
| 9 | billion | milliard |
| 12 | trillion | billion |
| 15 | quadrillion | thousand billion |
| 18 | quintillion | trillion |

and with a little etymological looseness, in either country;

| | |
|---|---|
| with a lot of them | zillion |
| with a 100 of them | googol |
| with a googol of them | googolplex |

So, is that the American one thousand million equals a billion world, or the British one million million equals a billion world? This is important. It is, incontestably, the difference between 2,000,000,000,000,000 °C and 2,000,000,000,000,000,000,000 °C. Or with the addition of 273 degrees as minor correction, you get °K (Kelvin), the thermometer preferred by physical scientists. And since the mythology claims that it was at this moment of cooling that the quarks all went out to lunch, never to be seen again, it becomes a crucial point in the cosmic history. The new article concludes: "The Standard Model is correct when it describes the fundamental particles and forces of the universe — and that science is on the right track." I am strangely not convinced.

A second article appeared, in the same paper, exactly five months later, to the day. There were presented some recent findings from the Hubble telescope that, if taken as being correct, deal a killing blow to the Big Bang theory. The essence and the irony can be seen in a single paragraph from this report:

"The basic theory of cosmology, that the universe burst forth in a Big Bang from a tiny volume long ago, remains intact. But the details must be revised, or explanations of stellar physics changed, to get stars older than the universe."

Let me sum up the paradox in a single sentence. The astronomers are finding 16 billion year-old globular clusters in an 8 billion year-old universe. Note the rigid, blind adherence of the faithful in that above paragraph, "The basic theory of the Big Bang ... remains intact." How do the true believers get out of this most recent contradiction? There were other embarrassing details accumulating. Most of them use terms and vocabulary that I cannot even pretend to understand. Terms such as Grand Unified Theory, magnetic monopoles, anti-matter, domain walls, symmetry breaking, Higgs fields, all led to a single, very disturbing contradiction to the Big Bang model. The time scale was all screwed up. Everyone had always looked at the early seconds of this event. But when you got into the very, very early pictures, an early microscopic fraction of a second immediately following this moment of ultimate origin, things didn't make sense. If the mass was what they said the mass had to be, then the whole shooting match would have fallen back upon itself, collapsed into some revisitation of the original point of origin, a Big Crunch, a singularity to end all singularities, or maybe even a black hole, in a few tens of thousands of years. But it didn't. Here we are, not thousands or millions, but billions of years later (in the American, not the British sense), and we are not yet sure, even today, if we are closed (some day to recollapse), open (or forever expanding to infinity) or magically neutral (on to a point of ultimate balance). Something new was needed to maintain the faith.

Inflation was found. By ignoring the rules of physics for a millionth of a millionth of a millionth of a millionth of a second (I kid you not) just after the incredibly dense, incredibly hot Big Bang went off, you have to allow the exploding thing to expand at $10^{25}$ times the speed of light (some suggest maybe $10^{50}$ times as fast) to achieve the organization and the mass distribution needed to accommodate the galaxies and the big attractors as we know them today. The rewards of this sleight-of-hand are many — atomic ratios are reasonable now, as are some of the questions as to anti-matter — and include, most importantly, an effective insulation from having to address the questions of just what that preinflation world really looked like. By the very act of inflation all earlier records have been lost.

So here a second miracle is needed to explain the universe. A neat article appeared in the journal "The Sciences" some twenty or thirty years ago, giving about fifteen criteria for determining if the author of some extraordinary discovery was a genius or a crack-pot. A few years ago a couple of well known scientists somewhere in the U.S. made a claim of having observed room-temperature fusion. I applied these criteria to their reports and about twelve of them failed. The impossibility of applying experimental challenges to the Big Bang makes this test largely pointless, but one criterion I remember very clearly: "Is there more than one miracle being claimed?" There is the first miracle — a small, dense, hot thing that came from nowhere and started our clock. And now, to justify that first one, we have to have a second miracle — a magical suspension of the laws of physics for a while so that everything can expand at a zillion times the speed of light. Two is one too many.

What a wealth of richness in vocabulary and esoteric thought has now become available to us, from this Big Bang affair. In fairness I will admit that I am not sufficiently in the know to follow the jargon of this new-age science, but let me quote one example to give you the music. This is from a chapter in a text-book entitled *The New Physics* as part of the explanation of the inflation concept:

> "The most peculiar property of the false vacuum is prob-
> ably its pressure, which is both large and negative."

And it just might be that the groundwork is being laid for a third miracle, to address the question of just how stars can be older than the age of the universe. Cosmologist Hogan of the University of Washington suggests that the most likely way is to:

> "... drastically change the way the age of the universe is
> calculated. Among the possibilities are that the universe is
> far less massive than the experts believe, so that its gravity
> has barely slowed it down since the Big Bang, or that some
> strange anti-gravity force ... has actually accelerated its
> growth over time."

How much simpler life would be if we just dropped the concept of the Big Bang, and the insistence upon there being a point of origin. Rather than continue a search for a beginning, simply assume that everything has always been here. And rather than fret over when it all might crunch, simply assume that everything will always remain here. Our space and cosmos has been around forever, and will stay with us forever.

Something in this direction was proposed by the Hoyle group some years ago, invoking the continuing generation of mass to account for the retreating of the outermost limits. But still there is the embodied assumption that there is expansion (the red shift observations) and thus some earlier time there was something smaller, and hence (at some time in the past) maybe there was an origin.

To me, there is a fine alternative explanation of what we are and why we appear as we do (universe-wise) with the simple replacement of one assumption with another. A lot of bizarre inconsistencies suddenly become quite reasonable. The assumption to be discarded: the idea that there was a Big Bang with a zillion degrees of temperature in a tiny location somewhere, and that it came from nowhere. The assumption to be accepted in its place: the idea that time is continuously speeding up, and that newly emitted photons move faster than older photons.

I will elaborate fully on just one point of this IOU hypothesis, the Infinitely Old Universe cosmology. This is a consideration of the Hubble constant I mentioned earlier, proposed in the 1920's as a measure of the expansion of the universe, the argument that single-handedly brought the Big Bang theory into being. A good correlation has been established between how far away a star, or galaxy, is from us, and to what extent its light has been shifted towards the red. This is the famous "red-shift" and it has been used for decades both as a measure of the distance of a light source, and the rate of its recession from us. That is the equation that is the Holy Grail of the BBB's, the Big Bang Bias cosmologists; that the distance from us of a light source can be determined with reasonable accuracy by the rate of its recession. The further away, the faster it is receding. Distances are independently determined by a variety of clues, from energies of quasars to the periodicity of certain stars that vary regularly in their brightness. But the dogma is: the further away, the faster the retreat. This shift is akin to the Doppler effect so familiar to us as the change in pitch of the whistle of a train coming towards us, or going away from us. As the approach becomes a retreat, the pitch drops in frequency. The high note WEEE becomes a low note WAAH as the train zips past us in the station with its whistle blaring. Light plays by the same rules, in that if its origin is coming towards us, its frequency is higher (shift to the blue) and if its origin is going away from us, its frequency is lower (shift to the red).

No revision need be made to the distance of stars and galaxies from us, so there is no revision needed as to the apparent size of the universe. They, the energy emitters, are as far away as their red shifts say they are. The point of issue taken here is that the red shift is due to something emitting its photons at a slower time scale, rather than at the same time scale but with the emitter actually moving away from us. They are relatively static as to position, it is just that we are seeing them as they were billions of years ago, functioning on a slower physical time base, and they are not receding at all. Nothing is receding. The universe is what it has been (big) and what it is now (just about as big) and what it will be a lot of years in the future (still pretty much the same big) except that every year we let pass us by, the bits of energy we emit as photons (in TV broadcasting radio waves and with solar flares from our sun) will be cast in a slightly faster time scale. Our reality is speeding up.

Some one mentioned to me that there was once a cosmic hypothesis that had been called "tired light," but that it had been discredited. That phrase is not in the indices of any of my reference books on the subject, and maybe this is a repetition of that idea. I would love to know just what it implied, and especially just how it became discredited.

Subjectively all of us admit this apparent speeding up of time — that things seem to be happening at a faster and faster rate, almost as if time is passing us by. But physically, there is no way of determining any absolute standard. The rate of change is so small, there is no practical way to measure the photon speed of old versus new photons. Bounce them off the mirrors we have left on the moon? They come back to us in seconds, practically virgins. Where do you find old photons, so you can measure their speed? From distant stars of course, and we already know that they are moving on a slower time base, since we already know that they are shifted to the red. The whole concept of an old, really old, universe presents the same self-satisfying supports and reinforcements that the Big Bang and the newly born universe presents. What is rough for one proves to be good for the other, and vice versa.

Suddenly a number of things that seemed to be uncomfortably hurried in the BBB world become quite relaxed in the IOU world. The most obvious of these issues is the question of the origin of life.

The time period allotted for the creation of life, in our current philosophy, is absurdly small. This carries the arguments that presume the origins to be on earth. We have an extraordinarily complex DNA system that encodes the ultimate details of the living organism. It is complex today, and there are indicators that three billion years ago, when the earth was just cooling down enough to support life, it was just as complex. When did it have time to evolve from something simple to something less simple to something as complex as it is today (just as it was back then)? If you accept evolution, then you must assume that we leapt from a zero level (no life) to a ten level (life as we know it today) with the nine level having been reached while the earth was still new and relatively uninhabitable.

This problem can be deferred, but not necessarily solved, by calling upon a second and longer time period. There are the pan-spermia arguments of the Watsons and the McKennas of our time. Life didn't form on earth, but it formed somewhere else, and spores (or some similar sort of seeding material) were cast from these sites of synthesis out upon the vast stellar reaches, and over the billions of years needed to wander from galaxy A to galaxy B, fluttered down onto earth to successfully root at the time that the earth proved fertile. But doubling the 4 billion year earth life-span to an 8 billion year universe life span might, at best, give us the time to drop to an eight level in the zero to ten time scale in the reckoning of the development of our DNA sophistication. But this gives no grace period for intergalactic travel of the genetic material.

So, what a delightful comfort one can find by considering a third time period proposal for the creation of life. An infinitely old universe, with all the time in the world (literally) to explore the many combinations of molecules (mostly failures, with an occasional success) that would lead us slowly towards our present living structure. There is a glib axiom in mathematics. If something is conceivable, then given infinite time it becomes inevitable. No, I am afraid that is not quite correct. I am sure there are infinite sets that do not contain all possible combinations. This is too severe a claim for nature. But it somehow has a valid ring to it. I have the gut instinct that since life is certainly conceivable, its turning up in an infinitely old universe just might be a pretty common event. And this might be in a lot of places and at a lot of different times. The purists will soften this bravado by arguing that the universe may be infinitely old, but it is not infinitely large, so there are not an infinite number of places available. But I appeal to the knowledgeable physicists amongst you, the readers. To what extent does our confidence that the universe is 10 to some big-number-power grams in mass, rather than being infinite, depend upon our assumption that there was at one time, a Big Bang? And it is true, life may have become extinguished, or may have extinguished itself many, many times, as might ours in time. But the comforting side benefit of this infinitely old universe theory is that it allows us to say with quite a bit of confidence that we are not alone.

Big Bang? *Requiescat in pace.*

# CHAPTER 19.  THREE PHOTOGRAPHS

(Shura's voice)

Hollyhock Farm is a young institution located on the Southeastern tip of a Manhattan-sized island smack in the middle of Georgia Straits, between the Canadian mainland and the island of Vancouver. It has been compared with Esalen, an older institution on the Pacific Ocean some hundred miles south of San Francisco and, although there are many differences, there clearly was the image of Esalen in mind during the setting- up of Hollyhock Farm.

There is, each year, a program of meetings and conferences that extends through the summer months. The overlying leitmotif is pretty much New Age, with seminars relating to self-analysis, dream interpretation, personal discovery, and many related topics that always appeal to those with the chop-wood-fetch-water philosophy. And, in keeping with this view and in keeping with the prototype model of Esalen, they raise their own food and set a superb table with few, if any, equals. There are meeting rooms that have been constructed with a hand that shows both skill and taste. There is a lodge with a piano and a fireplace. Private living quarters are Spartan, clean, and quiet. The garden outside the lodge, which clearly provides the bulk of the substance for the kitchen, is also a floral treasure. Even the compost area and the sewage disposal mechanisms have been well thought out and reward anyone who inspects them closely.

Alice and I had arrived on a mid-afternoon in August, 1988, having flown in from Seattle by float-plane. This was her second flight in a small, six-seat plane, and it was not yet a familiar vehicle of transportation for her. The first, ever, trip on such a plane was in connection with our first river rafting experience. This Salmon River adventure required that we get somehow from a metropolis called Boise to a hamlet called Salmon, and the available transportation was a small Cessna plane. As we walked up to it, Alice comforted herself by making it known that she would prefer a window seat. As the plane was only two people wide, she got her wish.

On the other hand, I was invited to sit as co-pilot, as I had years ago managed to put together most of the skills needed to fly a small plane. I allowed myself to indulge in the fantasy game of taking over the controls if I had to (the unexpected heart attack of the pilot who collapses in his seat and the naive passenger who saves everyone). As we flew along just skimming the tops of the Sawtooth Range, I looked for and located every dial and gauge that I needed, except for the carburetor heat control. I asked, and was told, that a fuel injection engine doesn't have one. So I shut up, and passively watched as the pilot picked his teeth with the pointy end of the claw of his removable bridge, and managed the plane with total competence. A smooth landing on the grass runway of the town of Salmon was anticlimactic.

But back to Canada. On one of the last evenings in Hollyhock, I was asked by my host if I would consider giving an additional short lecture, perhaps on the relationship between psychochemistry, time, and the aging process. I immediately confessed that although each of these subjects had been of personal interest to me, I had never thought of tying them all together. Together, the time and aging themes suggested to me an interesting direction to take, without the need to invoke any chemistry at all. I told him I would be happy to give it a try and see what would happen.

The get-together for the talk was quite well attended and went smoothly. As I had to give it a title, I called it "Three Photographs," and organized it using that metaphor. Of course, I didn't actually have any photographs with me, so they had to be drawn with word pictures. And, as I gave the descriptions, it became apparent that there was in fact only a single scene which had been photographed at three different times. I described those photographs in some detail. It was a picture that presented quite a cross-section of people. Some of them were small children in their pre-teens, some were mature adults in their thirties and forties, and yet others were the older folk in their sixties and seventies. A spanning of at least three generations.

In the first picture I was a child who was ten years old. It was taken in the large living room in the home of a close friend of my parents. This friend was a lecturer in the Department of Comparative Linguistics at the University of California and his name was, as best as I can recall from my mother's description, Reico Ratsche. He was an untenured faculty member, he could speak with ease in some sixteen languages, and was completely fluent in six of them. And he had a reputation as a Don Juan, vis-à-vis the unattached other sex. Perhaps even vis-à-vis the attached other sex. In this picture there was a dramatic but unposed central display of the young adults, all gathered together and quite obviously engaged in enthusiastic conversation. It was a beautiful exhibition of the socially successful. These were the people who were important. I was in the background with a small group of other children of the "successful adults," most of them about my own age. There were two of my cousins, Sally and Terri, and there were the sisters Nadya and Tanya and Olya, and there was Jimmy. We were playing a game of Monopoly on the floor in front of the davenport. And on the far right, there were several grandparents who were the chaperones and the necessary representatives of the older generation. They were the quiet ones who were always there, and who were respected for their genetic input to the group, but somehow never really made any difference in the flow of things. I remember the picture well, in that I had just discovered how to calculate the odds at Monopoly and could take a little advantage of the others of my own age.

Now here was that very same picture but it carried quite a different set of identifiers the next time that I saw it. This was taken at the Gordon Research Conference at Colby College, in New Hampshire, some thirty years later. The backdrop was a collection of brick buildings and green lawns, but in my eyes it was exactly the same picture as the one I had seen much earlier. This time I found myself located amongst the adults in the center, surrounded closely by my scientific peers, and all of us were the ascending stars in the professional world of scientists. I was with those I wished to know better, and who might help me advance into a more influential position in the arena of scientific competition. There were some small kids in the background who appeared to be playing catch with a baseball. They had obviously been required to come here to New London as part of their parents' vacation, but were totally indifferent to the importance of this gathering. And gathered about, not in any way an essential part of the photo, were the oldsters, the old guard, the has-beens, those who were respected for their scientific contributions to the group and who may well have played a major role in the development of this current state of knowledge, but were now bits of history. It is so marvelous that they could come to the meetings, and be complimented for their past contributions. But I was where it was at. I was with my colleagues here who had found the cutting edge of science and technology. The oldsters somehow appeared to be tired and so gray.

And, as I tried to explain to the assembled group, that very same picture was here, yet again, at Hollyhock Farm. An identical photograph, except for minor background details. The same people, and all of them standing in about the same places. There is a group of doers and swingers, those who will uncover new paradigms in science and resounding psychological truths. They will occupy center stage and present the themes and theses which will define the path that must be followed. And yet, earlier tonight, up in the lodge with the piano and the fireplace, I saw a couple of young children playing a quiet game of chess with perhaps a touch of boredom. They are here because their parents are here. And I stand over to the side, as one of the old people, one of the gray observers, who is both respected and complimented for some seminal contributions to some area, but who is not really part of the current dynamics of creativity or the mainstream of research and development by the young adult movers and shakers who are here. What a fascinating series of photographs, one from Berkeley, one from New England, and one from here in Canada, each and every one the same photograph, and yet in each I see myself first in one role, then in a second, and then a third. The picture does not change. It is my position in the picture that has changed. The innocent, the hero and, finally, the observer.

What an interesting view of the story of man! One always looks to the moving scene — the emergence of a personality, a savior, a villain — and tries to understand the nature of the human animal by observing his birth, his life, and his death. But, maybe the whole world is nothing but a painting by Breugel, with the child feeding from its mother over there on the left, the drunken ne'er-do-well in the center, and the toothless ancient stooped and silent over here on the right. The history of man is this same painting again and again and again, but simply with the players on the stage moving from over there, to center stage, to over here for the final exit. Only the costumes change, as there will always be something de rigeur and something else passé and outré.

OK. So, I will try to put my thoughts together as one of the old ones. Let me chatter for a while and tell you just what I see from this most unusual vantage point of being one of the ancients. I didn't choose this role, and I wasn't expecting to have to play it. It was not part of my plan. It just quietly came upon me, and here I am.

Let me put things into perspective. I will never lead a revolution down the street to storm the door of an oppressor. My enlightened role, if it is wanted, would be to suggest what street to use, based on the knowledge of the history of which streets have failed. I cannot personally mount an attack on an infringement of Constitutional rights. All I can do is to make note that such an infringement has taken place. The potential loss of any of the freedoms in our society calls for battle by alert activists. My contribution is to support and encourage the battler by keeping him aware of the other freedoms that we have already lost. At my gentle age of retrospect, I am realizing that, to be effective, I must know where I am inside myself. Wisdom, as has been said by someone, is the art of understanding others. Enlightenment is the art of understanding yourself.

This was the reason, quite simply, why I taught at Berkeley for years. How many people can one person get to and influence, and at what cost? The people in control of the world, from the highest (the national military or elected dictators) clear down to the lowest (the martinet who controls the issuance of local business permits) all maintain their power by enforcing their opinions and prejudices as law. Their success must be weighed against the fact that they are targets as well. There will always be someone who wants their position, and will use whatever weapon he might require to get it. The price you must pay: you may be on top and should be looking forward, but you must always be looking behind you, over your shoulder, to see who is the second runner so you can neutralize him. One wrong move and you are no longer effective. Or there will be that one person in a thousand, that sociopath, who can never be in the position of second runner, so declares you to be the devil incarnate and tries to assassinate you. You must always have protection against this small but real threat, so you can never experience a truly private life. And there are yet more subtle challenges. Your ability to get others to accept your opinions and prejudices requires the support of many underlings, and you have to mold your expressed opinions to incorporate theirs. As the statement of your opinion changes, so gradually does the opinion itself change. It is a loss that cannot be easily recovered.

This is why I preferred being a teacher rather than an administrator. The one-on-one approach was my preference. It is a joy to have a class of young students in front of you, each with his opinions still in the forming stage, and each with personal biases not yet cast in concrete. My once-a-year class at Berkeley was a total pleasure for me and, from the evaluation sheets that are anonymously handed in each year, it was equally satisfactory for the students. It was nominally a course in forensic toxicology, described in the University catalogue as a presentation of the analytical procedures needed in the identification of drugs in pills and powders, body fluids, and tissues. Pretty dull stuff. But the course was really an exploration into the excitement of science and of learning. The lecture detail had all been written out ahead of time, and it was suggested that the students could read the day's lecture before coming to class. I asked, "Are there any questions?" And, as a rule, there were no questions. This then gave me the license to use the printed lecture as a point of departure, and to sail off into the stratosphere. It took about three lectures for most of my students to realize that I was not totally off the wall, and that I would eventually bring this lecturing diversion back to the point from which I had departed. But they came to enjoy the flight with me. There were always a few that couldn't hack this different style, and they split the scene. But always, in their place, an equal number wandered in as the word spread that this was one loose class. It started maybe twenty years ago with about ten students and the body count went up every year. In the last year

I taught, before the State cut funds to the University so severely that I could not continue, the enrollment hit almost a hundred. I expressed my love for organic chemistry, and insisted that it was really an art form rather than a science, and treated it as such. So I asked my class about chemistry and discovered, each year, that almost every student felt an intense dislike for it.

"Why?" I asked.

"Because," I was told, "It is taught as a course in memory. Here's a typical assignment. For next week memorize pages 89 to 146 and there will be a quiz on Monday."

They had come to expect midterms with true-false questions that can be graded by computer. Instead, they found that I asked questions for which I myself had no answers. No one could cheat on the midterms, since they were all open book — bring all the references you want, and if there is something unclear, ask me and I will try to share an explanation with everyone. And, if the hour might be used better with active lecturing rather than passive sitting around writing in blue-books, why not take the exams home to complete, and hand them in next week.

"But how do you know we won't get help in finding out the answers?"

"Get help if you need to. I want you to find out the answers."

Each year, I started with a very simple request. Get three, maybe four, concepts into your awareness. I don't mean simply to "learn" these things. I mean really and truly get them to become part of you. Live with them until they become obvious and inescapable. There will be that light that goes on overhead with an explosive "Ah Hah" being the expression of understanding. "Of course!" "How obvious!" I told them that if they got these concepts, they would pass the course with an excellent grade. And those who didn't would fail the course. Well, maybe not really fail, but we would both be disappointed. These concepts are extremely simple, but they would not have been easily stated, or even easily conceived of, when I was younger. Sometimes I wonder if you have to get to a certain age before you can be comfortable with some truly simple realities. In any case, I was going to do my best to make them clear to my students.

Let me give one example of such a concept: no fact can ever be proved. Some people today accept as fact that the earth is round. But you cannot perform an experiment that will prove it. Any number of experiments can be designed and performed which, if just a single one is successful, will disprove it. And as they fail, one by one, the reality of the earth's being really round will emerge as an ever stronger hypothesis. But it takes only a single experiment that fails, and the hypothesis is out the window. The earth is not round. It must be something else. Never forget that it was only the day before yesterday (so to speak) that it was accepted as a fact that the earth was flat.

This is the thesis that was named "Inductive Inference" by the great Elizabethan scholar, Francis Bacon. His recipe for the establishment of the truth of a fact was deceptively simple. State the "fact" as a hypothesis, and design an experiment that will show this hypothesis to be wrong. Carry out the experiment. If you fail, then there is a little more reason to believe that the fact is indeed fact. But it is still not proven. If you succeed with your experiment, then the fact goes down in flames, and your efforts now can be directed to the search for a different, and perhaps better, hypothesis. It is only the failure to disprove a hypothesis that can lend weight to its validity. But proof? That is not obtainable. Many years ago I had a quiet dinner with a research person from the FDA, who told me that marijuana would never be approved for popular use until it had been proven safe.

"What," I asked him, "would be the final experiment that would prove its safety?"

"Well," he admitted, "there isn't really any definitive experiment that would answer that concern."

"Then, I must assume that marijuana will never be approved by the FDA?"

"I guess you're right."

This is an example of the Bacon thesis from the world of the reâlpolitic. You cannot prove safety. You can only fail to demonstrate danger. Marijuana is still illegal and I suspect will remain so for a very long time.

Another true pleasure in teaching, especially when you are an old person, is that you can get away with murder. As a young professor, you see your lecture topic in terms of details, but as you age you appreciate that the overall music is more important. Details can be gotten from reference texts. But there is no incentive for the student to search them out unless he is interested, and it is this interest that must be kindled. But just as you might be able to present a broader picture of something that is intrinsically complex, you can lose the sense of urgency for presenting it at all. Phrases such as, "Why bother?" or, "Who really cares?" are dangerous to say because, with sufficient repeating, they become increasingly believed by you. How often have you heard someone say, "I'm so tired," and watch them use this as a justification for slowing down and doing less. Or to continue to use the cane that was called for with some past injury, because it elicited sympathy and attention. Patterns establish reality, so break all patterns. Do it one way today, and another tomorrow. Periodically break all habits, regardless of how good they are. Learn something new.  Teach by example.  And share the excitement of discovery with a child by letting him see your own genuine excitement in discovery.

You realize now that the rules are really quite simple.  You are at peace with your beliefs, and can quietly act out of them.  You may appear to be the gray has-been at the outer fringes of the group picture, but you are as alive as any of them, and can be extraordinarily effective by cycling back to the youngsters. Catch their attention. You see them, and for a magic moment they see you.  Be a teacher, and you will be eternal.

# CHAPTER 20.  DESIGNER DRUGS

(Shura's voice)

The world of chemistry is, to me at least, without any question the most exciting of all the disciplines of science.  It is developing with extraordinary rapidity, it is continuously providing discoveries that are unexpected, and there seems to be no logical limit as to where it might go. Astronomy, mathematics, archeology, all continuously reward us with the discovery of the unknown.  The things discovered have always been there. It is just that we did not know them.

Chemical syntheses also provide discovery of the unknown, but all the unknowns are without any earlier history, at least here on earth.  Each new compound produced by a chemist is a glimpse into a universe of the unprecedented, without any history and without any agenda.  As far as we know, at the moment before its creation, no hint of it existed anywhere in the cosmos.  At the moment of its creation, it exists in full beauty.  This is why I am totally captivated by the art of chemistry, and why I say it is the most exciting of all the scientific disciplines.  Everything that is newly created in my laboratory is also new in the known universe, as far as I am aware, and therefore there can be no one who can advise me as to what its properties will be.  There is a thrill in creating new things.  Let me to share this excitement with you.

There are millions and millions of compounds that are known, that have been described in the literature and that constitute our chemical heritage.  Who knows the extent of undiscovered treasures all around us? We have not yet looked in the right place.  Like a mummy in an undiscovered tomb, or a star in some undescribed galaxy, they may be unknown to us, but they might be present in a tree leaf, or a moss spore.  But if we are diligent, and keep searching, they can be found because in this very moment, they do indeed exist.  It is a process of discovery, not of invention.

These many compounds can be discovered in the world of animals around us.  There are the biochemicals of the life process.  There are foods, and metabolites, hormones, enzymes, and minerals that in essence define us. In some ways we share common molecules; we all produce the same urea. In some ways, we are totally unique; we each produce different DNA. These compounds can have their origins in the world of plants. There are the alkaloids in the plants. There are the steroids, the terpenes, the sugars and the essential oils as well, and all can influence our behavior. These many compounds have had their origins in the yet simpler forms of life, which are anything but simple: the fungi, the bacteria, the molds and yeasts and viruses, that have provided us with our poisons and our anti-poisons, from the time of life's origins. Here one can often find that the bug which is so threatening to us can be closely related to a cousin bug that just might provide a curative antibiotic which could control the threatening bug.

But these compounds of nature, these treasures from the world about us, are only a small part of this chemical heritage. It is the discovery part. Many, many more of the known compounds are from the imagination — and the diligence — of man. This is the invention part. The technology of controlling, of directing chemical reactions, has created an ever-expanding collection of new molecules. None of them have been seen before in nature. Therefore they have no obvious role in the natural process. They can have no evolutionary significance as their reason for being. Let us look at new and novel chemicals with new and novel structures. Let us see how they have come to be.

How does a chemist make, or describe, or define a new compound? In the early days, new compounds were produced by accident or by luck. Through the middle of the last century, more and more organic compounds became known; the count soared dramatically. As the number of compounds known increased rapidly, the number of possible combinations of these compounds increased exponentially. From the systematic study of these combinations, there emerged an awareness of the rules of reactivity. And with the increased accuracy of reaction predictions, and the development of tools such as spectroscopy and chromatography, there came forth the concept of molecular structure. The last 100 years of chemistry can be seen as the century of creation rather than of discovery.

This "creativity" concept has given rise to the philosophy that there can be target compounds. There can be synthetic strategies, rather than simply cooking things together, and observing the results. There has been a shift from: "Let's throw this together with that, with a pinch of something else, and see what comes out of it," to: "Let's see if we can create something new."

This is a new definition of the research approach. Instead of asking: "What have we done?" we can now ask: "What can we do?"

With the concept of a molecular structure as a device for looking at a compound, in the case of these compounds being drugs, it was a natural development to study the relationship between structure and activity. The concept of the designing of a drug for a specific purpose had suddenly become very real, and very desirable.

There are two concepts used presently in our country, that should be held separate. On the one hand, there is the "designing of drugs" which describes an exciting and socially acceptable research process. Through "drug design" one can conceive of, synthesize and define new drugs that are related to old drugs. On the other hand, there is the term "designer drugs." A clothing company called "Levi's" had a popular product, a line of blue, washable pants, that were known as "Blue-jeans." A fad started up for well known people to add a little bit of personal identification to otherwise "normal" jeans, and attach their names to the product. And sometimes to sell them for twice the usual price. One could find "Gloria Vanderbilt" jeans and "Calvin Klein" jeans. These became known as "Designer Jeans" which was a term of merchandising and promotion. When a series of unrecognized variations of the narcotic Fentanyl appeared on the street as substitutes for heroin, the term "Designer Drugs" was coined by Professor Gary Henderson, at the University of California at Davis, to refer to these substitutes. However, there were no well-known people associated with the new drugs. The only names associated with them were street slang terms such as "China White." The term "Designer Drugs" became a term of condemnation, and was used to imply an attempt to circumvent the law. It says, "I will get around your careful definition of explicitly defined illegal drugs, and I will provide new drugs that fall outside of that definition."

What are the motives for designing new chemicals? There are three that are obvious to me: the circumvention of drug law, the circumvention of patent claims, and the development of research tools. And each of the motives presents the researcher, the scientist, the inventor in a distinct and well-defined role. The effort to evade the explicit letter of the law is the act that gave rise to the actual term, "Designer Drugs," and it is used in the United States only in its most negative sense. The average citizen, on hearing the phrase, will immediately assume the target to be bad. The chemist involved is believed to be trying to develop something that would bypass the existing narcotics laws. He will be assumed to be engaged in some unacceptable behavior, and the authorities will try to stop him and then punish him. The drugs themselves will be branded as being evil, having been made only for the purpose of appealing to the drug user, to the anti-social drop-out, to those who define the worst of our society.

The second reason for the designing of new chemicals is quite the opposite. It celebrates all of the acceptable attributes of our Western capitalist philosophy. The rationale for the designing of new drugs goes something like this: "Our competition is making piles of money with its sales of one of the most in-demand products of the year." For a pharmaceutical company, this might be a popular antidepressant. For an agricultural industrial corporation, this might be a potent and highly selective insecticide. For a tobacco company, this might be an additive that makes smoking more pleasant or less painful. Each of these products will certainly be protected by an air-tight patent. How does a competing company break into a highly successful monopoly? It tells its research chemists to go into the laboratory and design a new molecule that will get around the letter of the patent law. Go and invent something to make and sell, that would not be specifically illegal. The chemist involved will try to develop something that would not be in conflict with the existing patent laws. Society responds to this example of circumvention of the law in a totally positive way. This behavior is always applauded as being completely correct. The intellectual environment that surrounds the search for these drugs, these new industrial discoveries, is held in the highest esteem. This type of drug design is considered to be totally appropriate. The chemist involved in this kind of search is seen as being engaged in the most noble of scientific work, and his employers will reward his successes.

And as to the drugs themselves? The drugs themselves could well be accepted as being of great social value, in that they could contribute to a better standard of living. But remember that, although the reasons that justify these two very different philosophies for the designing of drugs are completely opposite, the goals were the same. The motive is to get around the law. And to make money in the process. They are different only as to their acceptance by our society. The procedures actually employed in each are identical. In each of the two cases, the inventor explores a path of discovery that follows closely to what is known, and he learns from it, and perhaps even steals from it, but he always takes care not to make anything so similar to it that the law (be it narcotics law or patent law) will pay too much attention to what is being done.

The third technique for the designing of new drugs contains elements of both of these earlier examples, the modification of known things to make unknown things, and yet it has a purpose all its own. This is the design of instruments of research, the design of instruments of inquiry. Here one can create chemicals for the use of researchers, tools that might answer questions about uniquely human capabilities such as logical thought, self-esteem (or lack of it), motivation (or lack of it), joy, euphoria, despair, schizophrenia. How can one design a probe that will reveal some detail of the human mind? One must always remember that here one is not speaking about the brain. The brain has been looked at in great anatomical detail over the years. It has been the target of a great deal of recent-day study in biochemistry, neurotransmitter receptors, actions of agonists and antagonists. But the brain that is most often used is the brain of the rat, as that is the only presently acceptable workplace for the neurochemists. But I am speaking here about the mind. This is found only in humans. How does one design the tools for exploring the normal function of the human mind? Or for exploring the possibilities of repairing problems with mental functions, not brain functions, so as to bring them back to the normal? Or for exploring, or even extending and elaborating upon these mental functions, to extend them beyond what we presently accept as the normal?

Some of these designs may lead to a molecule that acts in some way like an illegal drug. And legal authorities might believe that you are violating the narcotics laws. Society might frown upon you, and perhaps try to punish you. And there may be action taken, to make your invention illegal.

Some of these designs may produce therapeutic drugs that might well be commercially useful. And industry will come to you with offers of patenting, and of exploitation. And society will smile upon you, and perhaps try to reward you. And there will be moves to protect, and thus hide, your discovery under patent law.

But most often, these drugs that have been targeted for exploring the mind are neither abusable nor exploitable. They are simply what they are; research tools that are interesting only in man.

This is the work that I choose to do, in this third area of the designing of drugs; one which I have found to be unbelievably exciting. I want to describe to you a little bit of this particular world of tools. I will use the vocabulary of a tool-maker. When you design a new tool, a new compound, a potential drug, you are playing very much the role of an artist. You have a blank canvas in front of you. You have a pallet of oil paints, which is your collection of chemicals, and solvents, and catalysts, and reagents. You have the skill and talent in your hands of creating. With the artist, this is painting; with the chemist, this is synthesizing. And you have an inspired image of what the final picture might be. You have a target. You may be quite surprised as to where you eventually get to, but you indeed have a goal. Let me give one example of this form of artistry. I would like to walk you through the act of creation, from the initial design, to the actual birth of the new drug, to the introduction and getting-to-know this new individual, and up to the final definition and understanding of the completed product.

The example I have chosen is a research drug called N,N-diisopropyl tryptamine, or DIPT for short. As to the initial design consideration, I had a pretty good vision of what I wanted to create. I have produced my most satisfying creations using one of two types of canvases, the nucleus of phenethylamine or the nucleus of tryptamine. Here I knew that a tryptamine was needed, but how was I to embroider it? My past work had assured me that if I were to put lots of bulky stuff on the basic nitrogen, I might get a compound with oral activity. Should I place a group on the aromatic ring? Nah. Keep it simple. Go for a simple product, and maybe it just might be a clean and instructive product. Forgive me the mixing of the metaphors of artist and chemist but many of the concepts of designing a painting or a compound are identical.

Let me continue the mental picture. What kind of chemical shrubbery should I put on the right hand side of the canvas, on that basic nitrogen? How about a couple of isopropyl groups? They have never been used in this particular situation and they have an appealing, interlocking three-dimensional nature. A nice kind of bulkiness. Once the concept, the design, is pretty much complete, it's time to put oil to canvas. This stage of the process can be difficult, or it can be straightforward. But it always gives promise of being instructive. It can be especially informative when everything goes wrong. It is then that new and unexpected things can be learned about chemistry. In this particular case, however, there were no surprises. In the tight jargon of the world of chemistry, let me sum up the "how" part by simply stating that the indole was converted — via oxalyl chloride and diisopropylamine — to the glyoxamide — which was reduced with LAH to give me DIPT. The hydrochloride salt was a fine white solid.

So, having designed a potential drug and given it birth, so to speak, I now must meet it and get to know it. Looking at these fine white crystals is, in one way, like looking at a newborn baby. Either one, the compound or the baby, is a total unknown. True, I know the structure of the compound, and its obvious physical properties, but in no way do I really "know" the chemical. The structure it possesses is only one of the many brushes that I have used in this creation process. I must begin to interact with my creation by employing a mixture of caution, curiosity, and excitement. I will learn from this creation, and it will learn from me. It is a truly mutual development. With time I will gradually discover the inherent properties, the unique nature of this compound. But as I learn, I always become aware that some of these very properties that I am observing have been instilled into it by me. It is by this give and take interaction that we become familiar with one-another. The first clue of the nature of this friendship between DIPT and me was when I became aware of the fact that I was listening to a recording of "The Young Person's Guide to the Orchestra" on the radio in my study. It sounded absolutely terrible. I had accepted some 18 milligrams of DIPT into my body a short time earlier, and I now had my first hint as to just how it might become a useful tool someday. Its value might be in learning how we interpret sounds.

I knew that there was no way possible that any symphonic group could be so awful and still be tolerated in the recording of this little gem of Benjamin Britten. I began to pay attention to what was inside me, not outside me. Somehow, a certain number of cycles were being removed from the perceived sound, so that a lowering of the apparent pitch was being experienced. Different notes were distorted to different extents. It was not like putting your finger on the edge of a record player turn-table, and slowing it down. There was no distortion of the sense of time. But there was a complex distortion of chords, and that which would otherwise have been an acceptable harmonic relationship sounded terrible. This type of highly specific distortion gives promise of a tool for looking at the interface between an actual physical sound and how we hear it. These two realities, what actually goes into the ear, and what we think went into the ear, can be very, very different. A recent study has established that DIPT is primarily associated with the auditory process and that this property can be demonstrated in others. Two subjects with absolute pitch were able to state what the exact pitch was of any one of several single musical notes that were generated for them by an independent observer. They provided their opinions before, during, and after exposure to DIPT. Their assignments were very accurate before the drug was given and quite inaccurate while the drug was present inside them, then accurate again after the effects of the drug had dissipated. This allowed an objective time-curve of effects to be constructed, and satisfactorily confirmed this unique property of the drug.

Here is a potentially superb tool to explore and begin to understand one of the complex functions of the human mind. Perhaps it can be defined pharmacologically by the neurotransmitters it replaces or interferes with. Perhaps it can be labeled with carbon-11 and its dynamics observed with a PET camera in a human subject. What would be the scan of its distribution in a tone-deaf subject? What would be its effect on a schizophrenic subject who is hearing the voice of God?

And the most exciting part of any discovery such as this, is that perhaps this tool might be a prototype for another. You must ask yourself a sequence of questions. What do you want from a new drug or a new tool? How would you design it? How can you learn what you have? And having learned this, now what new tool do you want to create? This cycle can be repeated as often as you wish. Nothing might come out of this series of questions, the next time around. But just maybe, out of it might come some totally different and unexpected tool; one that might someday be used to explore a little further into the miracle of the human mind.

This is the true magic that is to be found in the concept of "Designer Drugs."

# Part Five:

# Drugs and Politics

# CHAPTER 21.  COULD WE?  SHOULD WE?

(Shura's voice)

I was driving back up to the Owl Club annual encampment a week or so ago, with Martin, and we got into a discussion about one of the lakeside talks by an oncologist from Texas. He was an unexciting but very well organized speaker, who spoke about environmental origins of cancer, and especially about preventable cancer. There was no surprise that much of his presentation concerned the use of tobacco, and the public health problems that have been a consequence of smoking.

I forget the statistics, but they were impressive. Lung cancer has come from a virtually unknown diagnosis at the turn of the century to a major killer in society. In recent years this has become true for women as well as for men. And heart attacks and emphysema are both undeniably associated with smoking. And there is a good argument for bladder cancer. In short, the use of cigarettes represents one of the major preventable sources of cancer and its tragic economic and social consequences.

So we got into a fun discussion — could one by law stop the use of cigarettes?

It became something of a game — I would propose some restriction or control, and he would adjust it a bit to soften the edges. Then he would add another idea, and I would move it around a bit. But it went something like this:

First, let's put a ten year scale to the program. Start by phasing out the government's subsidy to the tobacco growers over the course of ten years, so that some alternate crops might be found. There would be a more than modest savings for the taxpayer right there. And pass some sort of an ordinance that smoking in public is a minor crime. Say, a five dollar fine and the confiscation of the cigarette butt on the spot. But with a receipt so that if there is a medically valid reason requiring continuous smoking, the courts could refund the fine (and the butt). This is, after all, the way they effectively stopped the use of horns in Paris. They outlawed horns along with the threat of arrest, and then they outlawed horns with the threat of arrest and court-imposed fines. Nothing happened. Still a din in traffic. Then a simple ordinance — one honk and you are fined 5000 francs ON THE SPOT with a receipt. In 24 hours, virtual silence. So — no smoking in public. Still OK in cars, in the home, in the rest-rooms and the telephone booths of the country, but not where others gather.

And then, we went on, once that has sort of worn itself into the behavior patterns, a move could be made to allow tobacco sales only in state or government stores. That would allow an eventual restriction of hours and, as was found in Sweden with the nationalization of the pharmacy profession, considerable additional profit to the government. As was done there, the rationalization would be that the excess funds coming in could be used for medical research. Perhaps even cancer research. No one could really complain.

Our enthusiasm rolled on unabated. After a couple of years, tighten the screws a bit more. Make it a misdemeanor to have an opened pack of cigarettes in your possession in public! This would drive the poor addicted person closer and closer to either quitting for good (our benevolent goal) or truly withdrawing from social intercourse (at least it would get them out of sight). And if, in conjunction with a legal search within one's home, an opened pack of cigarettes were to be found, then this too would constitute evidence of criminal behavior.

Oh yes, there would probably be an ongoing black market for cigarettes smuggled in from across the border because of the profits that would accompany illegal sales, but in due time the problem, and the human suffering, and the social expenses associated with tobacco use would be brought down to acceptable levels.

A very impressive social program.

And I said to Martin, "I really think we could do it!"

"Yes, but it would be a pretty heavy scene from the law enforcement point of view."

"But should we do it?" I asked him.

He thought for a few seconds, smiled, and shook his head.

"No. We have a pretty good system of personal liberties as we are right now, and this might be a valid process if seen simply from the health and welfare point of view but it flies in the face of our civil rights."

We drove a bit in silence. Then I asked him, "Then why is heroin illegal?"

To this, he found no answer.

# CHAPTER 22.  BARRIERS TO RESEARCH

(Shura's voice)

Scientific literature has become unmanageable.  Every year more and more journals pop up like mushrooms, dedicated to the publication of papers of an increasingly narrow scope and appealing to an audience with correspondingly narrow interests.

Some of this is a product of the publish-or-perish ethic of the academic world, where a faculty member will be weighed for his worth in tenure by the number of publications he has amassed.  The push to publish, to get another paper out, is a tremendous driving force behind every young scientist who wishes to create a slot for himself in his university department or to receive a priority on his pending grant application.  The pressure is expressed in a joke told about pharmacologists by those who are not pharmacologists.  What is the definition of a pharmacologist?  A laboratory person who, upon injecting a compound into an animal, produces seven publications.  This is sometimes, sadly, referred to as "Salami Science."  Paper after paper is published, each looking at substantially the same research work, but through an ever-changing lens.  Inject a drug into a pregnant female mouse.  Run a maze, and publish a paper on drug discrimination.  Collect a dropping, and publish on metabolic transformation.  Collect a second dropping and report pharmacodynamic kinetic curves.  Let nature take its course and hatch the young, then put a note into a teratogenicity speciality journal.  And on and on and on.  Sometimes the single "injecting of a compound" is cleverly disguised in the experimental section; sometimes the authors simply don't bother to hide their sloth.  They assume, and quite rightly, that no one out there has either the time, the energy, or the interest, to read all of the literature.

But some of this mushrooming of the scientific literature is the product of an ego expression of a different sort.  As an example of this type, consider the aging and not-too-widely acknowledged Dr. Angst, Professor of Botany at Silverdale, who asks himself how many scientists are aware of the seminal work that he had done, some twenty years ago, in defining the Genus Xelorhrobida in the area of the Euphorbia? "Maybe the time is right," he will say to himself, "to start a research journal, which I'll call 'Xelorhrobida Letters', and probably I can get Pergamon to publish it if I could guarantee two hundred subscribers. I will call my buddies and get them to promise to submit a research paper in the near future. I'll make sure by appointing them all associate editors, and giving them free subscriptions."

The average citizen has no idea how much of his income tax dollar goes to just this sort of vanity stroking. Every month there are a half dozen new journals being published that are designed to appear six times a year (the issues may be some 50 pages each) for an outrageous annual subscription rate of $320 to institutional libraries. And so often the journal predictably fades from sight at the conclusion of Volume 2. Many of the publication vehicles here can be called the hyphenated journals, things that require an overlap of normally separate disciplines, giving rise to names such as: *Psychoneuroendocrinology*, *In Vitro Cellular and Developmental Biology*, and *Journal of Neurology, Neurosurgery and Psychiatry*. Occasionally one finds an obscure and totally in-house name such as *MacGuires Comments*. They come, they go. But they fill a need for someone, somewhere. This is the bottom level of published scientific literature.

The middle level consists of journals that offer to publish the research findings of scientists within a given discipline. This is a large body of publications, appearing at regular intervals, presenting reports that are directed to readers of a specific discipline. Some of the titles name the discipline, e.g., *Toxicology*, *Phytochemistry*, *Analytical Chemistry*, *Journal of Pharmacy and Pharmacology*, and *Neurology*. Many of the journals of specific professional societies serve a second level of communication — not only an exchange of scientific information, but a comfortable way of staying in touch between the mandatory national meetings. Examples are: *The Journal of the American Chemical Society* and the *Journal of the Royal Society of Medicine*. There are also the publications of societies that promote themselves as being the organizations that define the scientist. Are you a pharmacologist? Of course. I am a member of the Society of Pharmacology and Experimental Therapeutics, and I have published in JPET. Oh! Then you must be a pharmacologist! It is through publication at this middle level that most of the quality research discoveries are presented to the scientific community.

But what about that highest level of publication, the interdisciplinary journal which is devoted to any and all fields that are collected under the broad umbrella of scientific observations and factual reporting? When I was young, and blossoming forth into this exciting world, I had been taught that every major country (one with some self-image of being "first world" in the areas of research) had its own journal that could serve as a sort of national emblem. These were the ne-plus-ultra of class and prestige. To publish in such a journal was a mark of international recognition and acceptance by your peers. England had its *Nature*, the United States had *Science*, Switzerland had *Experientia*, France had the *Comptes Rendu*, and Germany had its *Naturwissenschaften*. Each of these maintained the principle of multidisciplinary reporting as a founding heritage, but each of them has found that such an ideal does not bring in enough subscriptions. And so, each of them has become more and more specialized, at the cost of losing all appeal to a broad interest amongst its readership.

Science, the weekly publication of the American Association for the Advancement of Science, is an excellent example. Years ago, articles involving archeology, geology, astronomy, mathematics, and embryology would compete equally for space on its pages. Recently, sadly, the editorial staff has chosen to go the genome route, and a disproportionate number of pages deal with genotypes and DNA sequencing. With a $10,000,000,000 encouragement to be realized over several years from several governmental agencies for the unraveling of the human genome, I can't fault their specialization. That's where the money is. There's where the public acclaim will come from. The advertising revenue reflects this specialization. Yet, I am sad to say that I believe this is prostitution at its most blatant, and I have let my membership in the AAAS lapse.

So, it was with some surprise that I received an invitation to attend, and address, an AAAS meeting in San Francisco. The topic of the symposium was "Designer Drugs" but it was made known to me that there would be quite a bit of freedom extended, allowing discussions to involve related topics. I assumed that there would be much mention of MDMA, since that drug had just been swept into the Schedule I classification by the invocation of the Emergency Scheduling Act of 1984. And, as this move would effectively stop any and all research on its use in clinical practice, I knew that this would be the area I would have to address. Since there had been no medical utility acknowledged for MDMA, it was placed in the most restricted category, Schedule I. As such, it was substantially untouchable in the research environment, and it would be most difficult to discover medical value. I saw a mindless iron hand removing some of the freedoms of research, and somehow, this loss had to be exposed. Why not use the invitation from the AAAS gene cowboys to the San Francisco Annual meeting, in early 1989, as an opportunity to discuss this situation? Why not, indeed!

What follows is the text of my presentation. I thought of creating a completely nasty title such as "Psychedelics and the Genome," but I abandoned the idea. So my presentation was more modestly titled; it was given to an audience of perhaps 400 individuals and largely ignored.

## BARRIERS TO RESEARCH

In a paper that I presented a few years ago to the California Association of Toxicology, I stated that we were blessed in this country with what could be considered among the best narcotics laws in the world. Approximately 250 drugs, and four plants, had been brought under Federal control and were specifically and explicitly named. There was rarely any ambiguity in the courts as to whether a material was or was not an illegal drug.

The procedure for adding new materials was well defined. When the Federal authorities became aware of a drug which they felt might present a potential public health hazard if it remained unregulated, a published announcement was made through the Federal Register. This action started a sixty-day process, and at the end of that time, the drug would either be placed in a schedule, in keeping with the degree of its danger and the presence or absence of medical utility, or hearings would be set up to help decide these issues.

There were many in the law enforcement community who felt that this process was too time consuming. Congress was asked to authorize that the hearings process be deferred, and in 1984 it passed an emergency scheduling act that allowed the temporary placement of a drug into Schedule I without hearings and with only a thirty-day notice. This was to apply only to drugs which were felt to be an imminent hazard to public safety. But please note that the drugs involved were still explicitly named, and the hearings could still be held if specifically requested.

Fentanyl is a synthetic narcotic with many years of proven medical usefulness, and it served as the focal point of the Analogue Enforcement Act of 1986. A great number of structural modifications of Fentanyl had been synthesized by Janssen Pharmaceutica in Belgium. Some of them, compounds such as Alfentanil, Sufentanil, Lofentanil, and Carfentanil, have been incorporated successfully into medical and veterinary practice. All of these are morphine-like narcotics that differ from one-another largely in their potency and duration of action. A very large number of additional structural modifications of this parent drug have been explored in the academic community.

Then, a few years ago, one of these synthetic variants of Fentanyl appeared in the street heroin trade. Almost as soon as it had been identified, a second and different one appeared, instilling a legitimate concern within the law enforcement community. The Drug Enforcement Administration (DEA) expressed its fear that these new drugs, cleverly named "designer drugs" in imitation of the "designer jeans" fashion concept, could continue to appear, one after another, and effective enforcement would be impossible. Although the Emergency Scheduling Act of 1984 was fully in force, it was stated that a general, rather than a specific, law was needed.

As an aside, let me ask you to put a moment's thought into the phrase "designer drugs." How could we, as scientists, have allowed such an idiotic, pejorative term to be used in our hearing more than once, without having immediately torn it to bits and shown it to be completely meaningless! Every one of us knows perfectly well that when you synthesize a new potential drug, whether you work for Ciba or for the CIA, what you come up with is a designer drug. Designed to do something new. Perhaps designed to avoid patent law. Maybe designed to allow a new scientific paper to be published. Almost every new and unknown drug is a variation on an old, known drug.

Congress was given carefully worded suggestions by the DEA, through the offices of the Attorney General. These concerned the need for a "Designer Drug Law" that could be used as a blanket control covering any new drug that could be abused, if it lay outside of the medically approved pharmacopoeia. In other words, Congress was provided a written outline that would establish legal control over any "designer drug."

The recommendations of the DEA were followed nearly verbatim, and Federal law was written and passed to attempt to control anything and everything that might appear on the illicit drug scene. This legislation is called "The Controlled Substance Analogue Enforcement Act of 1986" and is part of Public Law 99-570. It was signed into law on October 27, 1986, just days before the national elections, and the news and ramifications of it have been largely lost in the noise and drama of the political events of the time. I personally believe that this law presents a shameful barrier to a very important segment of scientific research.

Let me dissect this law into its two major parts. What is an analogue? And what is the behavior, involving an analogue, that is criminal?

According to this law, a drug is an analogue if it meets any one of the following criteria:

First, the chemical structure of the drug is considered. The compound is an analogue if its structure is substantially similar to the structure of any listed Schedule I or II drug. Just what are the structures of the drugs that are contained in these two schedules? You can find a complete spectrum of functional groups. All four types of amines are present; primary amines, secondary amines, tertiary amines, and quarternary ammonium salts. All three types of alcohols are present; primary alcohols, secondary alcohols and tertiary alcohols. There are acids, esters, ethers, amides, ketones, and nitriles.

There are examples of all the most common heterocyclic ring systems, such as pyridines, piperidines, pyrrolidines, indoles, imidazoles, morpholines, thiophenes, furans, pyrans, quinazolines, dioxoles, oxazolines, pyrimidines, and purines. And of course, there are simple benzene-ring aromatic compounds and there are simple non-benzene-ring aliphatic compounds including cyclopropyl rings, cyclobutyl rings, cyclopentyl rings and cyclohexyl rings. One would be hard put to find a structure of any drug, anywhere, which could not be argued by some person, somewhere, as being in some way structurally related to a Schedule I or a Schedule II drug.

And what was the reason for the use of the intentionally vague phrase "substantially similar?" There is a term in rhetoric known as a disclaimer, a word introduced as a hedge or qualification, a word chosen to allow a certain freedom of interpretation. Words or phrases such as *almost, probably, approximately, in a few days, in two weeks at the latest,* are disclaimers. There is a measured ambiguity in the phrase "similar to" and there is a measured ambiguity in the phrase "substantially the same as." But what is to be inferred from "substantially similar?" Suddenly, the exactness, the precision of the original Controlled Substances Act, with its explicitly named drug targets, had been totally compromised.

A second, independent definition of an analogue deals with its pharmacological action. A drug is to be legally considered as an analogue if it has a stimulant, depressant, or hallucinogenic action that is substantially similar to that of a Schedule I or Schedule II drug. In short, any drug which affects the CNS (central nervous system) in any of these ways, or in ways that could be construed as being "substantially similar" to those evoked by a scheduled drug, becomes an analogue within this legal definition. Again, the vague double disclaimer "substantially similar" must be reckoned with as part of the description.

A third definition is an extension of this, and involves the way a drug is represented. If a material is intentionally represented as having a stimulant, depressant, or hallucinogenic action substantially similar to that of a Schedule I or Schedule II drug, it becomes an analogue.

It is generally accepted that if two of these three definitions are met then the chemical or drug in question becomes a controlled substance analogue. The law explicitly states that there are four criteria, any of which will exclude it from becoming an analogue; if it is already a controlled substance, if it has an approved drug application, if a particular person has an exemption allowing him investigational use of that drug in question, or it is not intended for human consumption.

And what is the nature of one's behavior with an analogue that shall constitute a criminal act? It is the intent to make it available for human consumption. And if such were to occur, the analogue would be treated as if it were a Schedule I drug.

As to what human research studies may or may not be performed, this law has given the authority for the decision directly to governmental administrative bodies, where it had never before rested.

The function of the Food and Drug Administration (FDA) has evolved over the years into one of safeguarding the public from exposure to medicines that have disproportionate hazards, or that are ineffective, or that are mislabeled. And the evaluation of protocols for the determination of actions and risks of medicines is clearly the FDA's major contribution to the protection of the public from any inadequate evaluation of these risks. But this role has heretofore been restricted to the weighing of the virtues of a drug versus the risk of using it as a medicine. What are the virtues being claimed? What is the basis for these claims?

The FDA has always carefully avoided any act that could be interpreted as directing the practice of medicine. That was the province and the responsibility of the physician. And they have always avoided any intimate involvement in the structure of academic research, as this was the province and the responsibility of the individual researcher. The officials of the FDA had never before been given the role of judging the merits of research, or been put in a position of having the power to allow or disallow the pursuit of a research question. That has classically been a matter involving the relationship between the researcher, his professional peers, and his experimental subjects.

The placement of medical research approval within law enforcement, the DEA, is unthinkably stupid and inappropriate, and cannot be tolerated.

We, as the research community, have largely accepted this complete somersault over the age-old traditions of exploratory research. We have quietly acceded to a non-scientific authority that can oversee and, to an increasing degree, influence the direction of our inquiry. Somewhere along the line in this country, within the past five years, we have begun to lose that sense of independent looking, asking, searching, and questioning, and the insistence upon being personally responsible for what we do in our search and how we conduct that search.

I am making a heart-felt plea for the changing of these drug laws; laws which take the research initiative concerning human studies away from scientists and give it to politicians and bureaucrats.

I know that there will be a number of questions and arguments. Let me try to anticipate them.

Q:   THERE HAVE BEEN REMARKABLE SUCCESSES IN THE DEVEL-
OPMENT OF ANIMAL MODELS FOR HUMAN ILLNESSES. WHY NOT
USE THEM AND AVOID THE RISKS IMPLICIT IN HUMAN EXPERI-
MENTATION?

Indeed, many human illnesses now have superb animal models.
Agents that relieve pain can be screened for, and evaluated in, animals
which have been given painful stimuli.  Agents that can reduce blood
pressure or cholesterol levels can be titrated in animals that have high blood
pressure or high cholesterol levels.  Toxic side-effects can be detected in
animals.  These are areas where animal research is indispensable in the
discovery of new medicines, and in the evaluation of their safety and
potential usefulness.

There are numerous areas where animals can be valuable in the
search for drugs that are needed for the treatment of non-animal illnesses
such as depression, anxiety, and psychosis.  For these, the animal models
that are used can be based on the animal responses to drugs known to be
effective in man in the relief of human symptomatology.  But the animal
models that are used are not intrinsically valid, since these diseases do not
exist naturally in the animal.  For example, an antipsychotic drug known to
be effective in man might induce a characteristic behavior pattern or a
consistent biochemical change in an experimental animal.  And similar
changes by a completely different drug would imply that it, too, might
possess an antipsychotic action.  The screening of drugs with such animal
models can provide leads to new and potentially interesting families of
antipsychotic drugs, but the validation of the action must take place in the
psychotic human subject.  The animal model may even serve research needs
by providing an access to receptor site studies or neurochemical research
which can be used to explain psychosis in man.  Yet, intrinsically, the model
in animals is a forced one.  There are no spontaneously psychotic rats.

There are, however, many aspects of the human mind for which no
animal model is conceivable.

Consider things such as empathy, imagination, ego inflation, creativity, the anticipation of mortality, and the search for meaning, all of
which are unique products of the human mind.  Not a single one of these
qualities can be demonstrated believably in a rat.  And I am completely
convinced that none of them will be satisfactorily explained by the study of
the distribution of neurotransmitters in a rat's brain.  So, how can one use
a rat as an experimental animal for the discovery of a drug that might
influence or touch upon these aspects of human mental and emotional
experience?  If these areas are to be explored, they can only be explored in
man.

Q:     BUT THE GOVERNMENTAL REVIEWING AGENCIES ARE COMPOSED OF RESPECTED SCIENTISTS WITH UNQUESTIONED STANDING IN THE PROFESSIONAL COMMUNITY. HOW CAN YOU OBJECT TO THEIR EVALUATIONS OF RESEARCH PROJECTS?

I can object with a simple, straight-forward answer. A person who has integrity, be he explorer, scientist, or philosopher, cannot tolerate another person's usurping his right to ask his question in his own words. If the question is badly asked, or if the answer is sought in sterile ground, the man of integrity takes full responsibility for his own errors or his mistakes. And he learns from them. He will formulate his own questions and he will evolve his own answers, in his own time and way.

In my opinion, the present reality is that permission to conduct certain kinds of scientific research — the kinds that must be done in human beings and cannot be done in any experimental animal — is, for the most part, now given or withheld according to reasons of politics, not of science.

Q:     DO YOU ADVOCATE DISCARDING LAWS CONCERNING HUMAN EXPERIMENTATION?

Of course not. There must be laws because there are people who seem unable to empathize with others and who apparently do not care about other people's fear or pain. We must protect the innocent from them. We have known of such people in Hitler's Third Reich and we have known of them in our own CIA. There must be laws that protect the helpless from those persons who would misuse power. There must be laws to punish the abuser of children or the drunk driver. I believe that laws must be at hand which insist upon the three traditional principles of human experimentation: obtaining informed consent, seeking peer review, and the acceptance by the researcher himself of personal responsibility. But all other drug laws must be repealed. Not decriminalized or legalized. These are merely new laws over old ones. Laws involving drugs must, in general, be repealed.

It is within the concept of informed consent that one can find the best answer to society's need to protect its innocent against a potentially abusive member of the research community. When you give informed consent it means that, first of all, you are a fully responsible adult, not a child. Second, that you are aware of yourself, your surroundings, and your social context. And third, that you agree without any kind of coercion (such as rewards or threats) to whatever activity it is that you have decided to participate in.

Peer review represents the establishment of a close liaison with knowledgeable and interested colleagues. It is through the consensus of a peer group that society is protected against the manipulations of the crackpot, the sociopath, or the seductive charmer who might be able to coerce a naive and unsophisticated individual into giving his informed consent.

The ultimate responsibility for any inquiry must be assumed by the researcher himself. He should be able to speak from personal experience when he states that his new and experimental drug is not life-threatening. He should be able to say with confidence that it is free from disturbing side effects, since he himself has tried it at or above the intended dosages. In the area of psychopharmacology, especially in research with exploratory drugs which may affect the state of mind, I hold that it is irresponsible to give to another person any drug which you have invented or discovered, unless you have personally experienced that drug's effects.

This is a form of ethics that is gradually but steadily disappearing from the research scene. We call upon the government authorities for permission to perform our experiments, as if their blessing somehow assured us of safety, and freedom from risk. There has always been risk in using drugs to probe the machinery of the human mind, just as there has always been risk in using drugs to affect the physical body. There always will be.

If one looks at the basis of this entire business of laws, regulations, and losses of scientific courage, one is confronted with some profound questions. How afraid are we of truly looking at and into the mind? Are we all so distrustful of what we suspect we might find in exploring the human mind and spirit that we must pass laws against certain kinds of investigation?

What is the inevitable future of research into the mind, as opposed to simply the chemistry of the brain, if the laws now on the books are allowed to remain unchanged? The investigation into the nature of mind started with the appearance of man, and it will continue in its many ways as long as man is curious. The tools will remain the same as they have always been. These include the use of meditation, the study of dreams and sleepwalking states, exploration by means of hypnotic trance, and the use of psychoactive substances that bring about alterations in perceptions and states of consciousness.

It would be a tragic development if we were to see the dissemination of knowledge accumulated by such investigations revert to the old system of word-of-mouth, or perhaps underground pamphlets — shades of the Dark Ages. The information which should, in this day and age, be published openly by reputable and responsible scholars in good, respected journals will instead be lost to the scientific community at large. It will again become a new form of arcane, occult knowledge. This is already happening, as a matter of fact. We are becoming a society of respectable establishment journals, increasingly separated from an underground of mystical-psychological-alchemical knowledge that is being transmitted, not from laboratory to laboratory, but from bookstore to bookstore.


Q:      WHAT IS THERE TO BE LOST BY WORKING WITHIN THE FRAMEWORK OF THESE NEW REGULATIONS?

There is everything to be lost. As to drug research that might involve the exploration of a normal, healthy person's state of consciousness, the official position is clear. We are told that, as there is no virtue to be gotten from any such experiment, and since no answer to any valid question can be expected, there can be no risk tolerated. Thus, no experiment can be approved.

I believe that it is more important today than ever before in human history that we begin to try to understand the human mind. The human brain is now very popular, and it is surrounded on all sides by questioners and probers, by makers of positron-emitting ligands that will locate receptor sites that are begging to be named, by analysts with exquisitely sensitive spectrographs which can measure the slightest hints of metabolites in body fluids. The human mind, on the other hand, has always been surprisingly unpopular. It is to many scientists an object of distrust, awe, and apprehension. In many parts of the scientific community, there is an absolute refusal to acknowledge that it exists at all. The only people who seem to be making a living out of trying to understand any part of the mind are psychotherapists, terrorists, and the makers of horror movies.

I am deeply committed to the concept that the art of chemistry can provide superb tools for use in this area of research. Over the last thirty years I have devoted a major part of my efforts to the task of making sense of the human mental processes by the designing of research probes that in some way influence them. The technique I have used follows a logical series of steps: There is the conceptualization of a potential probe that can be argued as having some possible constructive or disruptive effect on a person's psyche or sensorium, it is synthesized, and then it is evaluated through graded dosages in self-experimentation until there is some indication of biological activity noted, or until the assay is deemed — for whatever reason — to be no longer worth the time and risk.

Needless to say, most materials have proven to be of no great value, but some few have made the search worthwhile. With them, a careful clinical trial amongst a small and experienced group of subjects serves to define the action with considerable exactness, and the findings are then published in an appropriate medical or pharmacological journal so that the compound can be explored by other researchers in the area.

Through just this form of research, several tools and potential pharmaceuticals have come into the hands of researchers. The prototype hallucinogen DOM (STP), the serotonin receptor ligands DOI and DOB, the auditory distortant DIPT, were all discovered by these techniques. There would have been no other way to have discovered them.

I am making an appeal here, very simply, for a resumption of this kind of courage. I am speaking for the removal of artificial restraints that are, if not completely prohibitory of such research, at least casting a heavy chill on it. In the present social and political climate, such a chill is enough to discourage many researchers from these avenues of exploration, avenues which I strongly feel must be travelled. Let me consider a single example, one which was the focus of intense interest at the American College of Neuropsychopharmacology (ACNP) meetings not long ago in Puerto Rico. This is the remarkable and controversial drug MDMA.

Here is a drug that has the unusual property of, more often than not, freeing a patient in psychotherapy from the anxiety and lack of trust that often prevents the emotionally fragile person from expressing his feelings to another. And, as has been attested to by many therapists and patients, MDMA allows a personal perspective, which is called "insight," with a minimum amount of fear and self-censoring. All of this without any loss of self-control or rationality.

The recent flood of primate research with MDMA has shown that there are long-term changes in the serotonin systems in the brains of some animal species, although there is as yet no clinical study which has shown that such changes occur in man.

I am completely convinced that this is the type of tool that must be developed and explored as a possible adjunct to psychotherapy. The official line is, at the moment, that MDMA has a large risk factor, and no medical utility. That is, in my opinion, totally incorrect. The extent of risk to humans can only be extrapolated from animal experiments, and MDMA has been shown to have less toxicity than the FDA-approved appetite suppressant fenfluoramine. But there is a real medical utility and an immense medical promise. The FDA has not allowed any IND (Investigation of New Drug) application to be effective and so, to the extent that the term "currently accepted medical use" means FDA approval for medical use, there can be no medical use. The fact remains that MDMA has proven extraordinarily effective in many clinical applications and therapeutic interventions.

However, since it came to administrative attention at the same time that the Fentanyl analogues became notorious, it was labeled a designer drug, and condemned as an abuse drug that had no virtue. The DEA holds that it is a hallucinogen, which is simply untrue. MDMA is not a hallucinogen.

How might a compound with similar action be discovered and developed for potential medical utilization? By definition, thanks to the present Analogue Amendments currently in force, such a drug would be an analogue (it would have an action substantially similar to a Schedule I or II drug) and it would be a felony to explore it in man without prior FDA approval. And I know of no animal screening, from behavioral screening to drug discrimination studies, which could demonstrate those subtle properties that separate MDMA from any of the structurally related stimulants which do not share those properties.

This is simply one example of the many paths through the unknown territory of the human mind that must be pursued and which are currently very difficult to explore in light of our present scientific and political attitudes.

In an effort to facilitate law enforcement, and in the pursuit of an ideal of rational social behavior, we have allowed laws to be passed which have robbed us of our freedom to inquire. To accept these laws without argument and without protest means not only a further loss of our integrity but also — as I said earlier — a continuing loss of essential information to the scientific community and society at large.

Discoveries about the functioning of the human mind and psyche must be made in the open — not in hiding. The effort to develop a working vocabulary for various levels of mental experience and the sharing of information and theories about what is discovered — all this must be done out loud, not in conspiratorial whispers and anonymous underground publications.

The continuation of the human species itself obviously requires that we get to work very quickly indeed to understand as much as we can about how the human mind functions. We must use all possible tools toward that end, and we must use them with care, with love, and with respect.

## CHAPTER 23. WHO IS JOHN JONES?

(Shura's voice)

In another chapter in this volume (DMT is Everywhere), I mentioned having had the pleasure of being in Australia and enjoying the pursuit of Wattle trees, and Acacia species, and the total pleasure of exploring and discovering Sydney. But I did not talk about my reason for being there.

I was the guest of the attorney for a defendant in the Crown Court case involving some allegedly improper activity with a drug called Nexus. This had been identified as 2C-B and, as I had been the first person to have thought of it, synthesized it, and published its properties and activity, I had been invited to provide factual material to the court in its search for justice. Alice and I were given first class accommodations in a clean, stylishly furnished hotel room in downtown Sidney, in the many-star Sheridan on the Park. The entire structure of the court system there, and the roles of barristers and solicitors, was new and totally fascinating. The scheduled time for our appearance for testimony was being continuously delayed by the Crown, which gave us a fine opportunity to explore the city and become comfortable with the typical Sydneysider and his behavior.

We found, among other things, an intense relationship with the telephone, and an unexpected terminology for coffee. I have never seen so many cellular phones in my life. Walking up the street we would approach a frail grandmother who was pulling her grocery cart behind her and talking on a cellular phone. Going up to the top of the Centerpoint tower, with sixteen people on the elevator, we saw four using their cellular telephones. An unexpected cultural difference is the way they say phone numbers. If we have two of the same numbers in a row, we will say, 4-2-2-7, for example. In Sydney, it is 4-double-2-7. How about 1-1-1-3? It becomes triple-1-3. I asked my barrister ally, what if there are four? Such as 2-5-5-5-5-8? It becomes 2-double-5-double-5-8. I tried for sequences of 5 identical digits in a row but never got an answer.

Then there was the matter of coffee ordering and coffee service which deserves comment. I drink black coffee, and Alice has cream in hers. To order a black coffee in Sydney, you ask (without hand gestures, please) for a long black. A coffee with cream is a flat white. Exploring this further, we found that an espresso is a short black, and a cappuccino is, rather unimaginatively, a cappuccino. Quite unexpectedly, one does not get any benefit from the request for a "topping-off," or a little more. If you want more coffee, you get a second cup, saucer and all, for another two dollars.

Two aspects of the criminal case that brought us to Australia became important to us, one informative and the other provocative. Both dealt with *PIHKAL*, the predecessor to this book that Alice and I wrote a few years ago. The informative point was the discovery that there are censorship laws in Australia, and the provocative point was the anonymous nature of the censor.

In the United States, there is a most remarkable amendment to our Constitution that protects our right to speak and write as we wish. And, although there are continuous efforts to circumvent this protection, the courts have, to a large measure, reiterated and respected it. I used to believe, along with many of my countrymen, that such rights are shared by many of the other developed nations but, in fact, the United States is virtually unique in having this concept as an operating principle. This issue became quite apparent with our publication of *PIHKAL*, and the encountering of some difficulties in distributing it in several countries. I knew that Nicholas Saunders had had an unpleasant interaction with the Customs people in Australia over the seizure of a shipment of his popular book, *E for Ecstasy*. He was told that it was not allowed to be imported due to its provocative nature. A court action would be required to contest the act of seizure, and the costs of the battle would far exceed the value of the books. In effect, this was an act of censorship.

I was curious about this Australia vs. England nastiness. Some years ago a book was written about the inner workings of British intelligence, MI-5 and/or MI-6, and it was not too complimentary. It was not allowed in to be sold in England, but it was published in paperback in Australia and everyone who returned home from there to England brought back 10 copies. They were theoretically banned from importation, probably through the invocation of National Security restrictions which is a common ploy used by a country that wishes to continue looking liberal to the rest of the world. But after a very large number of copies flooded back in, the authorities said to hell with it, and the importation barrier was removed. So, there is a listing of banned books in England too. Germany is not free of these restrictions either. I had an offer from a very enthusiastic bilingual German to translate *PIHKAL* into German. I queried my German publisher friend who told me that although there would be no censorship imposed on a German edition, it would nonetheless be "indexed," and this would effectively keep it from the open market there.

I was told that, in Australia, *PIHKAL* was on some official list of banned books, but I found that a bit hard to believe as I'd had several large mail shipments go right through into the country. Many had been individual mailings, and maybe the return address that had been used was not the one that had been recorded with the authorities. I know that quite a bit of raw stuff (sex, pornography and terrorism; what else is there?) was easily available in Sydney, as I had snooped in the off-color portion of the basement of a large bookstore called Dymick's, not far from the children's section. There I had found illustrated photo-books on sexual mutilation, and a couple of handbooks designed for anarchists. Maybe it's the drug theme that is of most interest to the censors. A chemist who works for the Government (and who has appeared on numerous occasions as an expert witness in court cases) told me that when he needs to make reference to *PIHKAL* in court he has to add the qualifier that he has access to the book only by some special legal dispensation. The book, he tells the court, is not publicly available in Australia. Indeed?

During this visit I was invited to give a short lecture to the members of a forensic society made up mostly of chemists and toxicologists from Australia and New Zealand. Initially my reception was a bit cool, quite reasonably, as I had been invited by the defense and some of them would certainly be providing testimony in conflict with mine. But our interaction warmed up quickly once I started talking and, when there had developed an easy give and take, I mentioned some chemical detail out of *PIHKAL*. On impulse I asked, out of curiosity, how many of them had their own copy. Most people guardedly raised their hands. In court, Madame Crown apparently had her own copy. The defense barristers also had their own copies. The defendant had his own copy. I doubt that they all had some official dispensation. So what is the nature of this censorship? On returning from Sydney, I mailed six copies that I had promised to new acquaintances I had met while there, and all went off by airmail with my home return address on the cover, and each clearly marked as being a book. None returned.

The existence of some form of national censorship, in itself, did not surprise me too much. What I found much more provocative was my inability to find out what had been censored. I had to assume that the listing of the books denied entry is itself a confidential matter, constituting yet another example of censorship. And, more important, who is the anonymous John Jones who decides what that list should contain? What is the identity of the person who wields the power to say what can or cannot be read? His beliefs and prejudices will achieve wide currency with the exercise of this power. Are these choices confirmed by some sort of consensus? Is there a committee? Who elected them, or are they appointed? Are there guidelines that are to be followed and, if so, who wrote them and who approved them? In the case of books, are they read before being condemned, or are there key words or ideas that are the kiss of death?

There are subtle pressures that can be brought to bear against the free expression of controversial ideas even in a Constitutionally defined and protected society such as ours here in the United States. Referring again to one of my favorite topics, the ongoing polemic concerning drug legalization, free speech may not be disallowed but it can be effectively discouraged. The main equation for those who would wish to limit the freedom of expression is based on a faulted application of the truth table structure. Those who are not against something must be in favor of it. There is a classical logic form called the dilemma: either $a$ or $b$, not $a$ implies $b$. This line of thought in its pure form applies to a logical and inanimate world without people or choice. If it is either red or blue and it is not red, then it has to be blue. No morality is involved, no sermon is delivered, and there is no hidden message. But this becomes quite distorted when applied to the real world. And the flaw comes in the division of the world into just red or blue when there are many other colors. Either you do love your wife, or you do not love your wife. No consideration is taken of the possibility that you are not married.

It is with this kind of reasoning that the drug law arguments are presented. Any suggestion of softening the law is seen as the advocacy of drug use. Even the statement "the need for discussion in these areas" is condemned as being, de facto, drug advocacy. The phrase, "Harm Reduction," is equated to "Legalization." All the world is either just say "no" or just say "yes," and not "no" implies "yes." This is why the politicians feel that ever louder "no's" must be enacted into law, to assure their constituency that they are not saying "yes."

One likes to think of controversy as being largely middle ground, with extreme positions representing small populations at the outer edges of the distribution. But in situations where no compromise is sought, the population is usually gathered at the two extreme positions with only a few of the middle-of-the-roaders occupying neutral ground. Two phenomena contribute to this and effectively exacerbate it. One, the more widely acknowledged, is called the hostile media effect. Even if a discussion on a controversial topic is balanced, as fairly judged by neutral evaluators, a listener from side A will tend to simply accept the presented arguments of the side he favors, but be unduly offended at the arguments favoring side B, which he sees as wrong and unfair. A sees the media as presenting an argument to a large measure in favor of B; B sees the media as favoring side A. Both see the media as being unfair and prejudiced though it may be quite neutral.

A second phenomenon is less widely appreciated, but is just as effective in separating people ever further from considering the poorly populated middle ground. It is the polarization effect. When an effort is made by a neutral person to temper an opinion of an A-side believer, especially in a public situation, it is seen as an attack, and A's conviction can be made even more extreme. B-sides will respond similarly. This is truly an "us against them" distribution and, without some overriding acknowledgment of a need for compromise, none can ever be found.

A sizable amount of public funds is used to emphasize this dichotomy in respect to the war on drugs. There are anti-drug programs bringing police into our schools to instruct our children in the badness of drug use, and it is called education; they have their staunch advocates and their equally vigorous opponents. There are many research grants awarded from our health service institutions to search out explanations of neural damage and addiction associated with illegal drugs. This of course reinforces the public opinion that there are only negative consequences stemming from drug use. Pamphlets are available from the DEA giving public speakers clues on holding their own in public debates with people advocating drug legalization. One of the precipitating factors in the firing of Jocelyn Elders from the position of Surgeon General was her remark that we should discuss the question of drug legalization. Even though she said discuss, not promote, her comments were held as "sending the message" that drug use was OK, and she eventually had to resign her position. There is the pervasive use of the pejorative word "abuse" in association with drug use, when the drug in question is one that the speaker does not approve of.

There are effective ways of constraining and limiting one's freedom of speech which lie completely outside the protection of the Bill of Rights amendments to the Constitution. If you express opinions that are not liked by your employer or, say, the Dean of your University, you may be called up to a critical panel to provide an apology or a recantation, with the threat of public condemnation or job loss if you don't. This process was honed to a fine art a few centuries ago and is known as an inquisition. Not judgment by legal powers, but judgment by societal powers. This can serve as an effective deterrent to the expression of your opinion.

But back to Australia, and the matter of John Jones' identity. How can you get answers to such questions? The first of my usual approaches in this kind of exploration is through the briar patch of administrative obfuscation. Ask someone in a governmental position just who it is you should ask. Ask in several places to start with. Maybe the National Committee on Arts and Letters, or the Customs Service Office in Canberra, or the librarian at the Sydney Police Centre. Try all three. Ask each one for the correct place to write for this information. If you follow such a plan for a few steps, using the previous person contacted as an introduction to the new one, sometimes you get somewhere. My second approach is more indirect and usually more successful. Ask writers, and radio and TV news people, and newspaper investigative reporters. Again, let each lead you to another, and the chain of introductions will in time get you your answer. And with either approach, if the answer is that the answer is not known or not to be told, your search has then revealed the threads of a police state in the making, and this is even a more valuable bit of information concerning a culture. A man of John Jones' degree of empowerment deserves to be publicly known and publicly acknowledged, and to share with everyone his philosophy and the tenets of his operating agenda. He is certainly influencing his own nation and, indirectly, all other nations which have diplomatic interactions with it.

I will try each of these processes for information gathering. I would love to be able to say who John Jones really is, his source of authority, and his personal philosophy. I intend to do my best to find out.

# CHAPTER 24.  CUI BONO?

(Shura's voice)

When an official investigation is conducted to address a criminal event, an arson fire, a bomb explosion, a homicide, any crime for which there is no apparent suspect, the attention of law enforcement is always first focused on who might have been rewarded by the crime. I'd had this concept in my mind as "Qui Bono," or, "who benefits?" I searched in all the thesauri and classical quotations for the phrase, to no avail. Then a linguistic scholar friend of mine paraphrased the 1992 Clinton political catch-phrase involving the economy, by telling me, "It's the dative, stupid." And indeed it turns out to be "Cui Bono," "to whose benefit?" It is instructive to apply this question to the entire "War on Drugs" scene.

Look about you and observe just which institutions are the most vocal in demanding that, rather than considering a stopping or even softening of the war, it must be continued and even exacerbated. Look at the specific way each particular institution benefits from the war. How much is it worth, and to whom, to continue the war? What would they lose if the war were to cease? And it is not just the dollars and cents to be considered but also the power and authority to control behavior that accrue to the war and its warriors. That is the heart of this chapter. In a word, what is the size of the industry that is, in fact, the "war on drugs?" How much benefit is there to be realized in maintaining and expanding this war? The picture is not particularly pretty, but it must be painted, and I will try to do so here.

The measurement of the size of a corporation can be reckoned as a dollars thing. How much income is there? How many expenses? Add up profits, sales, dividends, imports and exports. Count up the number of shares listed on the NYSE and the cost per share. Such and such corporation is worth $40 billion according to its current financial records. This is what I call the world of the bean-counters. But that is the measure of a company, not an industry. The influence of the transportation industry is not measured by the gross income of a bunch of airlines. The power of the communications industry is much more than the gross income of the television and radio corporations. One must measure the industry's inter-actions with society and its ability to affect politics. How extensive is its control of human behavior? This is the true measure of its power. And the war on drugs is indeed an industry. The size of it is a measure of the power and influence it has both on Congress and public opinion, and on its immunity from close inspection and change. Let me try to take its measure.

I saw a fascinating short clip on television some time ago. The Pentagon, rather proudly, made a public release of some film footage of periscope viewings from one of its nuclear submarines. It had been tracking a trawler presumably carrying cocaine from a South American port towards the United States. It showed an image of the trawler targeted by the cross-hairs, with a voice-over making a claim that for a mere $23,000 an hour, the Navy can not only maintain its tracking skills but also provide valuable information in the war on drugs. The latter is achieved by alerting the Coast Guard as to where and when smuggling boats will reach American ports. This one little film clip brought two totally ugly facts into mind. One, the Navy here is being encouraged, perhaps required, to pay attention to the "war" aspect of the war on drugs. And two, this activity is being made to appear trivial by a bean-counting manipulation that considers only some of the beans, not all of the beans. How much does this military involvement contribute to the drug war industry?

I was sitting around the campfire last year with my Owl Club friends at the annual two-week get-together of my favorite conservative gentlemen's club group. During a lull in conversation I asked them what they thought the cost was of operating a nuclear submarine, on full duty, for one hour? Oh, wow; this got a heated discussion started. The sales tag of $23,000 was less than the lowest estimate, and was dismissed as only the cost of potato chips and toilet paper, and maybe salaries for the crew for that 60 minute period along with a pro-rata share of the necessary land-based controlling operation structure. That would be the money out of pocket for that hour. Perhaps this estimate was from a commissary analyst, thinking in terms of hour by hour, with accounting claims made by the first of next month. The two engineers who were there saw the costs in a very different light, considering the essential returns to port at frequent intervals to repair, replace, and renew. New rods must go into the reactor pile, and new tritium must be supplied to the nuclear warheads. This takes expensive manpower and expensive materials. Millions of dollars of nuclear stuff. And this must be pro-rated over that entire cruise at sea while you were looking at cocaine boats. Many millions of dollars a year for maintenance adds much to that hourly potato chip rate.

Then the one physicist who was in the circle said, "Hold it. You are out of your skulls. How much money did it take to create that initial breeding pile of isotopically enriched uranium? Where was this done, and with what, made where? How were the fuel rods moved to the site where the submarine was being made? How often were they replaced? And, again, by whom and with what, made where? Where were the spent rods taken? How will they be disposed of? And, in a few years, how will we successfully hide, forever, the spent carcass of this fiercely radioactive submarine, so that it will not be a lingering poison for decades on our children's doorsteps? We are into many, many more millions of dollars of unacknowledged obligations, all of which must be pro-rated into the hourly costs of that cocaine snooper." His guess was the cost of that sub might be a million bucks an hour. Then one additional comment made shambles of the entire discussion. "How much is it worth to us, to be protected from being destroyed by someone like the Soviet Union? Without this weapon being available and at the ready, we are of an increased vulnerability to any enemy. Even if it is not being used, just having that machine is most valuable in the front line as protection against any unknown threat to our nation. That transfers some of your war on drugs dollars over to National Defense."

Unknown billions of dollars, divided into a few decades of operation, put a monster cost on the operation of a submerged surveillance submarine. There is no accurate way to come to a final dollar total on this, or most of the other matters discussed in this chapter, so I won't try. It is easy to lose sight of the dollar cost of a detail, in an effort to measure the dollar size of an industry. Forgive me if I say stuff like "a few billions," or "lots of billions." It is clear that no exact costs can be gotten here, and that same uncertainty will apply to all efforts to measure the size of this particular "war" industry. The war is being waged by a large number of unrelated interests, by millions of people, and it is being fought largely within the United States. It is the first full-scale instance of American citizens fighting American citizens in a battle fought on domestic soil in over a century. The last conflict of this size was the 1861 Civil War, or the War between the States, which consumed our energies and wealth, and destroyed so many of our youth in that four year period. But our present war has been underway now for well over a decade, and there is no victory in sight. The intensity and costs have been continuously increasing, and the suffering and damage from it is without precedent.

The Military Component:

The submarine example makes the discussion of the military a logical starting point. After the Civil War (the first Civil War, not this war on drugs), there was passed by Congress in 1878, and signed by President Rutherford Hayes, a law called the Posse Comitatus Act. This was a reconstruction measure designed to stay the hand of the Northern troops in seeking either revenge or influence in the restructuring of the Southern states. This law prohibited, and still prohibits, any military involvement in police action or law enforcement with the civilian population. Exception is allowed only if a National Emergency is declared to address a crisis that demands control of civilians.

I know of one try by Congress to write such a statement into proposed drug control legislation, but it was softened with some appended conditional words which would have provided a compromised and partial measure. At present, there is no such declared emergency and, by Federal law, the military cannot be legally involved.

A very large percentage of our annual budget of over a thousand billion dollars goes to the military. We must have enemies, and we must be prepared to fight them on demand. With the loss of the Soviet Union as a major foe, and with the subtle shift from big national antagonists to the more elusive and ephemeral uglies such as terrorists and rogue dictators, there was nothing large and obvious to justify hundreds of billions of dollars annually for Star Wars and stealth bombers. A new enemy was needed, and drugs fit the bill perfectly. The submarine example earlier is trivial. Ask, rather, how much of our influence and effectiveness in South and Central America, and in Asia, is directly correlated to our policies on illegal drugs such as cocaine and heroin? What is the level of military cooperation, or effective economic stability, that comes from our government's acceptance of the Mexican army's role as one of the major producers and distributors of marijuana in the Western Hemisphere? There are many suggestions of alliances between agencies such as the CIA and cocaine transport. Look at our relationships with Central America, and with Asia in the Golden Crescent and the Golden Triangle. If only a few of the many rumored military, political, and intelligence conspiracies were valid, we (America) would have a multi-billion dollar contribution to the war on drugs industry.

But just such involvement is today a de facto reality, as both the Coast Guard and the National Guard have been brought in to help police our borders. Originally their participation was justified by the understaffing of the customs and immigration services, but in recent years the role that drugs play in defining their participation has become quite blatant. Their usual duties (safety violations, current registration, identification papers) have become thinly-disguised excuses for drug searching. Recent seizures of boats or vehicles under authority of the rules of civil forfeiture regulations clearly define the civil law aspect of their actions. The only way such action could have been rationalized under the Posse Comitatus Act would have been to declare these groups not to be part of the U.S. Military. Instead, their participation was never challenged. This tacit approval met the legal needs for a while and, although they call for tactical support from the Army or Navy (helicopters, airplanes), they were officially not to be considered a part of the Pentagon empire. But that sham is pretty well exposed with the submarine tracking incident I mentioned above. The military continues to consume an outrageous percentage of our national wealth. In 1990, the following of cocaine trawlers would have been a throw-away hiccup on the edge of the tracking field of a high resolution spy satellite. Our casual justification of an immense military budget used to depend upon our unquestioning acceptance of the Soviet threat to national security. But with the Soviet threat now being history, we have had to find other threats to our nation in order to continue to maintain our declared objective of being capable of fighting two wars simultaneously. Thus, this domestic war, our war on drugs, has become an economic life-saver for the military budget.

Does the Navy use taxpayers' funds for other submarines to follow traffic in and out of other ports, foreign or domestic, that might be involved in drug transactions? What about the Army (or the Navy or the Air Force?) as the source of the planes and pilots for drug-related operations in the interior of Colombia (or Bolivia, or Burma, or any other country the United States may wish to exert influence over) using the enforcement of drug laws (theirs or ours) as a rationalization? What about within the United States itself? Who runs, or at least provides, the machinery for the observation and documentation of illegal crops, especially marijuana growing? How can one begin to estimate the financial bookkeeping entries for items that have, until very recently, never even been acknowledged?

The Political Component:

Similar difficulties arise in trying to determine the profit the war on drugs provides to the State Department and its strategists, because the drug trade is an international phenomenon. This trade, and the laws against it, allows an easy entry into foreign, clandestine operations, and an ever greater influence in shaping other governments' policies. Always remember that, to a major extent, the enactment of the domestic drug laws of many of the countries around the world has been at the encouragement, or insistence, of the United States. The Single Narcotics Convention Treaty was crafted and written within the United States and, as it has been signed by many of the members of the United Nations, it has effectively provided a structure that has directed the writing of their laws.

What is this sort of influence, this entry into the politics of other countries, worth? Perhaps an idea might come from guessing how much would be lost if drug laws were repealed, and this entry denied to our Government.

"War on drugs" is a misleading name for this conflict. That kind of title brings to mind an image of a platoon of infantrymen all lined up with loaded rifles, firing round after round of bullets into stacks of gelatin capsules and glass ampules. It is certainly obvious that the drugs are not protecting themselves by firing back or running away, so drugs as such cannot be the enemy. Drugs are not good or bad. There is nothing that is intrinsically either sacred or evil in a crystal of white solid or a drop of aqueous solution. As you read the continuous news reports from the battlefields you will realize that our nation is not making war against drugs as such but, rather, against the people who use drugs. It perhaps should be called a "war on drug users," and not all drug users but, specifically, those people who use drugs that our legislative spokesmen disapprove of. This disapproval stems, in turn, from their belief that these opinions are shared by those who might elect them back into office.

However, when you look between the lines of these reports from the front, a much more complex picture becomes apparent. There really is no war at all, neither against drugs (of course), but for all intents and purposes not even against the many, many people who use them. There are no legions with cohorts gleaming in purple and gold and there are no bullets or bombs of righteousness. There are no "God is on our side, not on yours" pronouncements. Oh yes, there are skirmishes, nasty interactions between the authorities and the little people, between the police (Federal, State and local) and the largely defenseless minorities, be they dealers in dope or simply part of an unenfranchised population. Certainly, the drug motif is frequently used to justify the profound changes that are taking place in our society, but these us-versus-them interactions are side-shows to the actual process that is currently underway. The phenomenon is much more sinister and far-reaching than would be inferred from the newspaper headlines, which mention only the ephemeral, drug-related events. A local arrest here and a related raid there are the reminders to the public that the evils of drug use are all about us, and that we need ever stronger measures to be taken in the name of this war.

But these increasingly strong measures constitute the heart of the true threat, and it can only be through the analysis of them, and of their reasons for being and the reasons for their continuation and amplification, that the size and the end-goal of this threat can be determined. What are the changes that are being made under the guise of the war on drugs? What are the real reasons for their being instituted? And of especially revealing importance, who gains power or wealth from these changes? To whose benefit? Cui bono?

My thesis is this: The war on drugs has little to do with drugs and drug users. It exists and is promoted largely as a means to accumulate power in the form of money and in the gaining of control over individual citizens. This centralization of power will be at the cost of personal freedoms, and represents a dire threat to the nature of our republic. The process is well underway, and it has progressed much further than most people realize. To stop it now would prove to be very difficult. The end state will be a complacent and obedient society (the terms "Police State" and "Totalitarianism" are too loaded to use casually but they are completely applicable) with no effective Constitutional rights and with a Congress which has an ineffective voice. The war on drugs is a cover for these transformations. I want to explore the nature of the beast.

I believe the most direct way to effect such an exploration is to look at this war as an industry, and to analyze it as such. How large is it? How effectively diversified is it? How much public support does it currently have, and how is this being increased? How much wealth have the several individuals and corporations that make up this industry already accumulated, and how is this power being invested in the continuation of this transformation? The war-on-drugs industry is more than a drug bust and a police raid. Let me try to unravel this monster a piece at a time, beginning with an attempt to estimate the size of this industry. Originally I had started to record big chunks of money as a measure of the size of this phenomenon, $20 billion here and $40 million there, and quickly realized that I was, indeed, becoming another bean counter. No. Better to ask who is involved, who reaps the rewards, who gets both power and control over others, from the operation? Let me look at the several components in a broad sense, which are only in part measurable in dollars. Let me recapitulate the argument above, along with some information that will be of value to the reader.

The Prison Component:

Many years ago, President Dwight Eisenhower referred to the economic structure of our country as the military/industrial complex. This enlightened term has proven to be completely appropriate — for the complex is not two separate components working separately; it is not two separate components working in sympathy; it is a single thing, a single entity, that directs the economy and thus effectively defines both the domestic as well as the international image of the United States. Recently a friend of mine paraphrased this as the industrial/military/prison complex, and I found myself making an uncomfortable connection between the recent Soviet nation and the present American one. The Stalinist prison camps, the Gulag world, the Siberian labor camps, are all well documented as having been isolated dumping areas for people who were not part of the desired social structure. Some were real criminals with proven records of sociopathic behavior that constituted a true risk to society. But most were victims of a strategy designed to achieve a political goal by the designation of carefully chosen social patterns as being criminal activity. The crimes were speaking badly of the state, or choosing not to work at meaningful jobs, or being homosexual, or acting in some way that could be interpreted as being anti-establishment. The vast majority of the criminal class, defined as being in prison for the commission of crimes against the state, were violators of laws that were political devices created solely for the cleaning up of unwanted minorities and for the effective consolidation of power. The Soviet Union had, until recently, the largest per capita prison population of any industrial country in the world.

Look now at our own domestic situation. Change a few of the defining criteria, and you will find a remarkable parallel between the former Soviet Union and the present United States. We also have the statistically valid number of sociopaths, and we protect our society from their offenses in the generally accepted way, by protective incarceration. These are the killers, the molesters, the rapists and thieves deemed worthy of removal from our society. But how have we rationalized the removal of the masses of people who are not a functional part of our society, who might be misfits or present difficulties to the consolidation and centralization of power? For us these are not the Trotskyites and antisocial revolutionaries; they are the racial minorities, the urban gangs and "welfare parasites." We cannot use the excuse of lawlessness and anarchy as the rationalization for prosecution and imprisonment. What we can do is take advantage of the fact that there has always been, and there will always be, a small but real percentage of our population that finds some reward from the use of drugs. Then we can shine an ever-more intense spotlight on this behavior through the escalation of laws and penalties, the promotion of a civilian propaganda campaign generating social disapproval, with everything done, of course, in the name of purifying the culture and ridding our society of a vicious, destructive plague. Our progress can be documented by the fact that over half — *over half!* — of our prison population consists of people who violated our drug laws, or commited crimes that existed only by virtue of our drug laws. We now have the world's largest per capita prison population, and Russia is no longer in the running.

Estimating the costs of prisons is somewhat straightforward, in that contracts are signed and structures are built. Each person who is in prison requires a cell, guards, medical attention and food, and is estimated to cost our taxpayers $30,000 a year. With a nation-wide population of over a million prisoners, over half of whom are in some way casualties of the war on drugs, a rough figure of some $20 billion appears to be a good guess for this component of this industry. But this is the potato chips and toilet paper cost.

There is not enough space. There is the insistent pounding of the spoon against the dish by hungry Oliver; more, more, more. The prison building contractors are active in construction with dozens of new prisons currently being built and many more in the bidding stage. Maybe a few more tens of billions of dollars? So much money has successfully gone into lobbying by the prison interests this year, in California, that the budget for prison maintenance and construction has, for the first time, exceeded the State budget for education.

But again, there are dollar estimates which are difficult to make even with prisons and law enforcement. If you put a man in prison for any reason, he may well leave behind a wife and two children who cannot support themselves. How can one even guess at the economic chaos that is a direct consequence of having the bread-winner removed from his dependent family by conviction and incarceration for a drug crime?

Also do remember the necessary machinery for the determination of guilt or innocence. What are the costs associated with the staffing and operating of all the Federal Courts, the State courts, the county and munici-pal courts, with judges and juries and bailiffs and janitors? A large percentage of this is directly or indirectly related to drug law violation and has to be reckoned into the calculation. And let us not forget the mon-strously large legal profession. The nation has almost a million lawyers, many of whom are employed exclusively in drug law violation defenses, and most of them charge somewhere around 200 dollars per hour. Some thousands of drug lawyers, serving many thousands of clients involved in charges of drug-related behavior, comprise a multi-billion dollar compo-nent in this industry.

We cannot forget domestic law enforcement. There is an ever increasing annual budget for the Federal Drug Enforcement Administra-tion, and each of the fifty states has its own Bureau of Narcotics Enforcement empire which is also paid from public funds. And, of course, there are thousands of municipal narcotics task forces and marijuana search teams. Adding these into our estimate, the law-enforcement branch of our argu-ment swells this industry by many additional billions of dollars.

The Asset Seizure Component:

Remember a rapidly growing off-shoot from this giant, one which started small but which is compounding at a rate of over 100% per year. This is the area of criminal forfeiture and asset seizure. Just in the last year there were over $2 billion in contested seizures and many more that were accepted as a fait accompli. This is at the Federal level.

Most of the states are also on the take, but they are without the need of accountability or auditing, so the volume can only be guessed at. Maybe add another $10 billion to the punishment-associated "lots of billions of dollars." The following article by Joyce Rosenwald appeared in a recent issue of Media Bypass, and says it more completely than I could. It is reprinted here with permission.

Forfeiture: The New American Evil

> "Forfeiture appears to be the newest weapon in the legal arsenal of the U.S. government unleashed upon the American people. It is used in the politically correct 'war on drugs' against every segment of society. The American people have come to fear the word 'forfeiture.' Forfeiture is a creature of statute, law made by man. It was generously given to the American people by their elected public servants in the federal congress and senate. It was then codified into state law by their duly elected public servants who were placed in office to protect the inalienable rights of the people from harm.

> "The forfeiture provision of the U.S. drug law allows the government to seize property when it is believed to have been used, or intended to be used, in a drug offense. Every type of property, real or personal, tangible or intangible may be subject to confiscation under forfeiture law. Motor vehicles, boats, and homes are the most common items subject to seizure of the tangible items. But, the most important and least publicized are the intangibles. These are your basic rights, privileges, interests, claims and securities. The money from illegal drug transactions and all property believed to have been bought with that money, are also subject to confiscation.

> "The government doesn't have to actually find any drugs. Forfeiture can occur if the government believes the owner merely intended to use the property to commit a crime involving drugs. Some time after the government has taken everything you own, they will bring a forfeiture lawsuit to permanently deprive the owner of his or her property. In some cases, criminal or civil charges are never brought against an individual.

"The basic belief of all Americans in questions of law has always been that you are innocent until proven guilty. Forfeiture law inverts this principle. Americans have also believed that in civil law, there must be a victim who will come forward and bring charges against you. Forfeiture law also changed that belief. Today government is the victim, which is a new principle of American law. Today you are guilty, with perhaps no opportunity to prove your innocence, and without any assets to pay for your defense.

"Actually, forfeiture is a relic of the medieval law of 'deodand'. Law of deodand evolved from the legal superstition that an inanimate object can itself be guilty of wrongdoing. So, if a man fell from a tree and died, the tree was chopped down as a deodand. The tree was believed to be guilty of murder. In early English common law, an animal, or any weapon or other object that caused the death of a human being was confiscated as a deodand, and then sold with the proceeds going to the family of the deceased. The same principle applied today would be if a death resulted from an automobile accident. The automobile would be confiscated and sold as a deodand with the proceeds going to the family of the deceased. The automobile would be considered the offender, not the driver. The automobile would be forfeited, i.e. the deodand.

"Today, when government claims to be the victim in a civil or criminal crime, under forfeiture (deodand) law, it receives the proceeds from the sale of the offending property.

"Although deodand forfeitures were common in the early American colonies, they appear to have been abolished by the time of the American Revolution or shortly thereafter. In colonial America, common law forfeiture was rare. During the Revolution, some of the states enacted provisions forfeiting the land and goods of those sympathetic to the Crown. After the Revolution the Constitution restricted the use of forfeiture unless congress passed a statute (law) allowing for its special use.

"Today 'Civil' forfeiture is termed as an 'in rem' proceeding. This means your property, as in English deodand, is the

defendant and the burden of proof rests on the party claim-
ing ownership. The innocence of the owner is of no importance. All that is necessary for prosecution is that the
property was involved in a violation to which forfeiture is
the penalty. 'Criminal' forfeiture on the other hand today,
is an in personam proceeding, and confiscation is only
possible upon the conviction of the owner or user of the
property.

"Most state and federal forfeiture statutes (laws) call for civil
forfeiture, which as proceedings in rem (property) allows
the court to take your property as the first step in confiscation proceedings. The United States Constitution prohibits
confiscation of property without 'DUE PROCESS.' Under
forfeiture law, due process requires that those with an
interest in the property be given reasonable notice and
opportunity for a hearing on the property seizure.

"This does not mean that pre-seizure notice and hearing is
required. Pre-seizure notice before confiscation of property
does not always take place. Although confiscation of property without 'Due Process' blatantly violates the United
States Constitution and the Constitutions of most of the
United States, court challenges have been mostly unsuccessful.

"Once property has been forfeited to the sovereign, (U.S.
government) the statutes (laws written by congress) may
authorize use of the property by the seizing agency, (Department of Justice). Distribution of the proceeds from the
sale of the property may then go to the seizing agency, (local
law enforcement or Justice Department, to informers, or to
the sovereign's general fund, the U.S Treasury Department)
who will then have the funds to hire more government
agents to make it easier to start forfeiture proceeding against
your neighbors or you.

"The newly passed crime bill creates hundreds of new
crimes, many falling under penalty of forfeiture. The bill
also allows for the hiring of 10,000 new police officers. It
would appear that along with 'the war on drugs' and 'the
war on crime' your government has just declared 'War On
Property Ownership in America'."

Please do remember the following two quotations: "The right of the people to be secure in their persons, houses, papers, and effects, against unreasonable searches and seizures, shall not be violated ... " U.S. Constitution, Amendment IV; "... nor be deprived of life, liberty, or property, without due process of law ..." U.S. Constitution, Amendment V.

The Industrial Component:

The industrial and corporate division of this extraordinary war on drugs touches, in one way or another, the entire civilian population.

One of the most pernicious and unjustified insults to the average person has been the increasingly wide-spread demand for urine tests for evidence of guilt or innocence as to the use of drugs. The concept probably had its origins with the use of alcohol in connection with driving. If a person is, through some erratic behavior, thought to be driving after having been drinking, he could be asked to provide a body fluid sample, blood or urine. Blood was preferred, as it is quickly drawn, and the state of being "under the influence" is defined by blood levels. With urine, on the other hand, a twenty minute waiting period is required following the emptying of the bladder, to assure a sample that most closely reflects the blood level. But the information was supplementary to a "field sobriety test" which carried much weight. All of this, following an observation that justified a "for cause" argument.

The "on demand" without "due cause" urine test has quietly grown to monster proportions over the last decade. Initially it was a search of a person involved in some accident, some unexpected event, for evidence that his actions might be explained by drug use. Then it became extended to a precautionary move to assure an increasingly propagandized public that those in positions of public service (pilots, train engineers, bus drivers) would not put us at risk.

This was then promoted into the concept of a "drug-free workplace" through a dishonest interpretation of the findings of a well-known research institute on the East Coast. The negative correlation part of this report, that implied a decrease of work performance with the use of certain drugs, was amplified to apply to all drugs, then expressed in dollars, adjusted for inflation, and extrapolated to the total employed population of the country. The summed total, $60 billion dollars, was pronounced as the annual loss to our productivity due to drugs. From this evolved an unprecedented, but now widely accepted, procedure used by many companies. You must provide a urine sample when you are applying for employment, and you must agree to a random test at any time, if you are hired. And with many of these employers, if you fail your test or refuse to take a test, you can be fired.

But, sadly, the quality of these urine tests can be very low. The presumptive test is an inexpensive screen, sometimes an antigen/antibody assay, or perhaps a thin layer chromatography procedure. The purpose of a screen is, primarily, to spend a few dollars to determine if an excellent but much more expensive assay known as gas chromatography mass spectroscopy would be justified. Spend ten bucks to save a couple of hundred bucks. These screening tests have frequent false positives, meaning that a signal is obtained that implies drug use when in fact there has been no drug exposure at all. There can be many reasons. These can include unusual dietary factors, erroneous responses due to prescription drugs, misreading or misrecording of the measuring instrument, or simply a mix-up of sample identities or laboratory cross-contamination. The only believable value that these presumptive tests have is to exonerate the subject from the need of any further testing. However, in the interests of economy or due to indifference, some employers act directly on the results of this initial screen. With a false positive rate of maybe 3% (quite a conservative number) about one in thirty employees will be labelled as being a drug user, even though he is completely innocent of such behavior.

These drug-testing procedures used to be the exclusive province of the forensic chemists, who assay seized evidence for testimony in criminal law cases. The Federal government has a few labs across the country, the States have one or several, and there are many in the more populated counties or cities. But in the last few years, an entire industry of analytical services has materialized, involving screening for drugs, or confirming the presence of drugs in urine, blood, sweat or hair. As many of these require a $50,000 GCMS, this is a bonanza for the scientific equipment manufacturer, and represents a rapidly growing investment in the war on drugs.

President Clinton had proposed, as a re-election ploy, the urine testing of all teen-age applicants for driver's licenses. But apparently no one had thought this through to its end point. How many of our youth have their 16th birthday in a given year? Five million? Even if every one were absolutely drug free, at $10 a pop and with a 3% false positive rate there would be 150,000 false positive results, 150,000 of our innocent youth immediately branded with a narcotics record, at the cost of $50 million dollars. And this error would cost all of these young people access to a driver's license. Many lives ruined, future careers jeopardized, without a single drug user being validly identified. Much would be lost, and absolutely nothing gained. Of course, confirmatory tests by GCMS will catch some of these mistakes, with the annual expenditure of about twice this amount of money. That was a very destructive proposal, but it is still alive and being actively demanded by the drug warriors. Sadly, the ancient aspect of the British law that extended an individual the presumption of innocence is neither in our Constitution nor in our legal statutes. There is only the 5th Amendment to the Constitution that protects our citizens from being required to testify against themselves. Random urine tests, or blanket urine tests, performed in the absence of cause, are simply not acceptable in our republic.

As an added thought in passing, how does one measure the loss of self-esteem, or self-respect, of a person who has just been handed a Dixie cup by his boss and told to go over there and pee into it, and in front of a witness yet? No urine? No job. It is not your skill or performance that keeps you employed — it is the degree to which you hew to the dictated morality and behavior patterns suggested by your superiors. They may not have to share this indignity, but you do. You are not trusted. In their eyes you are a second-class citizen.

Another component of the war on drugs industry represents a very large and totally unguessable amount of money. What is the loss of taxes that could accrue to the public's benefit, from this vast volume of sales of illegal drugs? At the present time there is no revenue at all. Were they in the legitimate market, there could be some measure of regulation and control and, as with alcohol and tobacco, some equation could be found for a tax that would produce a reasonable return and which would still keep the black market at a modest level. A regulated market in marijuana alone might be a multimillion dollar source of tax money with little increase in the volume of use over the present illicit level.

The Academic Component:

The two levels of our academic institutions are both severely impacted by the war on drugs and, in their very different ways, they both contribute hugely to the size of this industry and to the welfare of those who are benefiting from it. There is the K to 12 school student population, and there is the world of higher education.

The teen age and pre-teen age crowd is being hard hit by a propaganda campaign that can be summed up in a cute phrase, "Just say no." There are television ads of the Partnership for a Drug Free America, the PDFA, which is a source of a dedicated effort to demonize all illicit drug use. For them, drug free means illegal drug free, and there should be no surprise in learning that most of the economic support comes from the major legal drug providers, the alcohol and tobacco industries. These are the groups whose monopolies of legal drug sales would be the most eroded if any of the currently illegal drugs were to be made legally available.

There is also a second assault on our young school children by an equally ineffective, but much more insidious, program called D.A.R.E.

(Drug Abuse Resistance Education). This is a government funded project that brings policemen into our schools as instructors sharing factual information concerning the use of drugs. The meta-message is that the popular illicit drugs are bad and law enforcement, in its curtailment of all illicit drug use, is a positive factor in the promotion of social values. A small but real percentage of the youngsters are coerced into sharing information about their parents' private drug lives, and family tragedies have resulted from subsequent police action.

I have a good friend who went to a DARE meeting as a surrogate for his buddy whose son was in the class. He told me with much humor of his interactions with the instructor. He said to the officer, "I am a pharmacologist. How would you accept me at the police academy if I came as a teacher to your classes on arresting procedures and the processing of prisoners?" He told me that the policeman admitted he would probably dismiss him as being unqualified. He asked, "Then how are you, as a policeman, qualified to be a teacher of pharmacology?" He did not receive an answer.

The world of higher education contributes to this war on drugs in quite a different way. Much of the research work in the Universities is funded by grants from the Government. The National Institutes of Health (NIH) through the National Institute of Drug Abuse (NIDA) and several related agencies, is one of the major sources of support for graduate and postdoctoral research grants. In addition there are a number of so-called center grants maintained at the major Universities, to set up and maintain medical and pharmacological research. There is always a keen competition for this support money, and the proposed topics are chosen and crafted with care. The structure of a grant application revolves about a research question which will be looked at favorably by the grant reviewers. Often, abuse drugs, or illegal drugs, are the subject of the application and, not unexpectadly, the questions asked suggest that the answers which might be found could be useful in advancing the anti-drug stance. Note the fine distinction between, "Is MDMA neurotoxic in the salamander?' and "What are the neurotoxic changes produced by MDMA in the salamander?"

This is only a small contributor to the difficult task of evaluating the size of this part of the war on drugs industry. There are public health problems associated with the war on drugs that extend far beyond medical research in academic areas. The spread of AIDS through needle sharing; the need for medical intervention in the many cases of drug dependency and addiction; the shocking disregard of the families left behind when the breadwinner is thrust into prison for some trivial drug crime. There is a generalized condemnation of all aspects of drug use even when factual information is available. There is no permission given for research to be done that might weigh the virtues against the risks of drug use. There are few acknowledged virtues. Most questions along these lines are unanswered because they are not allowed to be asked. Listen to the voices which say, "We cannot allow any legal use of some given drug until more research has been done," and then say, "It is not in the public interest to allow such research." Or, "We cannot use a given drug medically until it has been proven safe," and then admit that there can be no body of evidence of any size that could ever completely prove safety.

But back to the title of the chapter. To whose benefit does all of this inhumane, irrational attitude accrue? Is there a person or a system that will be the eventual benefactor? Cui bono? There is a lot of power being amassed very rapidly in this war on drugs, and the industry that is associated with it is growing daily.

I am convinced that there will be an eventual polarization of this rush to a police state, but I have no insight as to what form it will take.

Perhaps there is a cabal of unknown people — a behind the scenes council — of a dozen or so super-egos, who will exploit some minor tragedy within this highly charged drug hysteria with a move to force the President to declare a national emergency, effectively suspending the remaining fragments of the Constitution. This would automatically institute a state of martial law, and that would allow the inclusion of the military forces in the corralling and sequestering of any particular segments of the civilian population.

Perhaps some charismatic military person might emerge from behind the wizard's curtain and win national approval in demanding, and obtaining, a referendum to take whatever steps might be called for, to return our society to the stable and secure condition that is our national self-image.

Perhaps a persuasive advisor could convince a suggestible president that he and he alone has the divine empowerment to save the country, and have him set into action the several executive orders that are sitting at the ready on his desk, to precipitate this nation into a dictatorship, in order to save it from some more heinous fate.

If any of these irreversible events occur, it will be too late to alter our course and the fate of this nation will be sealed in concrete. The changes that are needed to avert these possibilities must be made now. With every month that passes, the task will be harder. It is becoming increasingly unpopular to suggest changes, and increasingly difficult to find a way of making them. In a few years the goal will be lost from view and the task will be impossible. We will be the Fourth Reich, and we will admire and celebrate our own Hitler. We will have ceased to be a republic.

Perhaps it is already too late to end this pernicious war on drugs, but maybe a pause could be effected. I would like to quote yet another bit of writing, this from a group that calls itself "Family Council on Drug Awareness." At a recent "State of the World Forum" in San Francisco, I received a leaflet handout with a beautifully phrased appeal for rationality and sanity in this increasingly mad race to national disaster. I feel it makes an appropriate closure to this chapter.

### A CALL FOR A DRUG WAR TRUCE WITH PEACE NEGOTIATIONS

**Preamble:** No civilized nation makes war on its own citizens. We, the people, did not declare war on our government nor do we wish to fight its Drug War. Hence, we now petition for redress of grievances, as follows:

**Whereas** any just government derives its authority from a respect of the People's rights and powers; and

**Whereas** the government has resorted to unilateral military force in the Drug War without any good faith effort to negotiate a peace settlement;

**Therefore,** we hereby call for a Drug War Truce during which to engage our communities and governments in peace negotiations, under the following terms:

**Article 1:** The United States shall withdraw from, repudiate, or amend any and all international Treaties or agreements limiting its ability to alter domestic drug policy.

**Article 2:** No patient shall be prosecuted nor any health care professional penalized for possession or use of any mutually agreed upon medications.

**Article 3:** Drug policy shall henceforth protect all fundamental rights, as described below:
    **1.** Each person retains all his inalienable Constitutional, and Human Rights, without exception. No drug regulation shall violate these rights.
    **2.** The benefit of the doubt shall always be given to the accused and to any property or assets at risk. Courts shall allow the accused to present directly to the jury any defense based on these Rights, and explanation of motive,

or any mitigating circumstances, such as religion, culture, or necessity.

     **3.** No victim: no crime. The burden of proof and corroboration in all proceedings shall lie with the government. No secret witness nor paid testimony shall be permitted in court, including that of any government agent or informant who stands to materially gain through the disposition of a drug case or forfeited property. No civil asset forfeiture shall be levied against a family home or legitimate means of commercial livelihood.

     **4.** Issues of entrapment, government motive, and official misconduct shall all be heard by the jury in any drug case, civil or criminal. Government agents who violate the law are fully accountable and shall be prosecuted accordingly.

     **5.** Mandatory minimum sentences undermine our system of justice. The jury shall be informed of all penalties attached to any offense before deliberating a verdict. Courts shall have the discretion to reduce penalties in the interest of justice.

**Article 4:** We propose a Drug War Truce and call for the immediate release of all non-violent and, aside from drug charges involving adults only, law-abiding citizens.

**Article 5:** No non-violent drug charges involving adults only shall be enforced or prosecuted until all parties have agreed to, and implemented, a drug policy based on full respect for fundamental Rights and personal responsibility.

Of course, all this is simply making a restatement of the rights that have been our heritage from the Magna Carta, British common law, and our own Constitution. This truce sounds like a fine idea to me. There is a lot to gain, and nothing to lose.

     Please listen.

# Epilogue

# CHAPTER 25. GALILEO

(Shura's voice)

There are interesting parallels to be drawn between the Holy Writ of 350 years ago, and that of the present day.

| THEN | NOW |
|------|-----|
| The earth is the center of the universe, and anyone who says otherwise is a heretic | All drugs that can expand consciousness are without medical or social justification, and anyone who uses them is a criminal |

and shall be imprisoned.

I was sitting in the Owl Club orchestra pit at my music stand during an especially long pause in the dress rehearsal for the musical "Galileo," when this fascinating train of thought came to mind. The stage scene was an interaction between the young Galileo and the cardinals of the Inquisition. The question put to him was quite simple: "Are you engaging in heretical teachings along the lines of Copernicus, in contradiction to the facts known and taught by the Catholic church?" He had made a promise that he would not act in violation of the faith.

The authorities said:

| | |
|------|-----|
| We do not need to actually look through that mysterious contraption | There is no need to actually taste those mysterious compounds |

of yours to see what is fact and what is fiction. We know what is real and we know what is not real. It is written in all the texts and no recourse to such artificial means is needed. To entertain such notions is contrary to nature and is to manifest the work of the devil.

How dare you claim that the earth
is not the center of the universe?
Your looking glass, your moons
around Jupiter, and your navigation
tables prove nothing. Your heresy
is an affront to the church, and to
God who made the earth the center
of the universe and gave us the
sun as our clock.

How dare you claim that an
understanding of God is to
be found in a white powder?
This talk of communication
with the inner self, the finding
of one's way into the hidden
reaches of the unconscious, is
New Age nonsense and simply
an excuse to use dangerous drugs.

It has been almost four centuries

It has been many decades

since the original pronouncement had been made that the reality as seen through these evil instruments had no merit. The authority as invested in the church (then) has admitted that it had been wrong. The authority as invested in the government (now) has not yet made this statement. In time, it will.

# BOOK II

# THE CHEMISTRY
# CONTINUES

Justice is incidental to Law and Order.
Law and Order is the be-all and end-all.

Attributed to John Edgar Hoover (1895-1972)
FBI Director 1924-1972

---------------

It is dangerous to be right in matters on which
the established authorities are wrong.

François Marie Arouet Voltaire (1694-1778)
Writer

# A SHORT INDEX TO THE TRYPTAMINES

This short index to the tryptamines lists the fifty-five chemical entries by their code names followed by a compact chemical name. All numbers, letters and atom symbols are ignored in the alphabetization. The abbreviation T is for tryptamine, C is for β-carboline, L is for lysergamide and NL is for 6-norlysergamide. The long index includes all synonyms and is to be found in Appendix F.

# TRYPTAMINES

## #1. AL-LAD: 6-NORLYSERGIC ACID, 6-ALLYL-N,N-DIETHYLAMIDE; 6-NORLYSERGAMIDE, 6-ALLYL-N,N-DIETHYL; N,N-DIETHYL-NORLYSERGAMIDE, 6-ALLYL; N-(6)-ALLYLNORLYSERGIC ACID, N,N-DIETHYLAMIDE; 9,10-DIDEHYDRO-6-ALLYL-N,N-DIETHYL-ERGOLINE-8β-CARBOXAMIDE; N-ALLYL-NOR-LSD

SYNTHESIS: To a solution of 66 mg nor-LSD (see under ETH-LAD for its preparation) in 2 mL freshly distilled DMF under a nitrogen atmosphere, there was added 48 mg anhydrous $K_2CO_3$ and 30 mg allyl bromide. When TLC analysis indicated that the nor-LSD had been consumed (30 min) all volatiles were removed under a hard vacuum. The residue was solubilized in $CHCl_3$ (5x5 mL) and the pooled extracts dried over anhydrous $Na_2SO_4$ which was removed by filtration. The filtrate was stripped under vacuum leaving a residual white solid. This was separated into two components by centrifugal chromatography (alumina, $CH_2Cl_2$, nitrogen and ammonia atmosphere), the first of which was the major product. After removal of the solvent, this was dissolved in hot benzene, filtered and cooled. The addition of hexane prompted crystallization of AL-LAD (N-allyl-nor-LSD) as a white crystalline product weighing 66 mg (88%). It had a mp of 88-90 °C and an $[\alpha]_D + 41.8°$ (c 0.44, EtOH).

DOSAGE:  80 - 160 micrograms, orally

DURATION:  6 - 8 h

QUALITATIVE COMMENTS:  (with 50 µg, orally)  "I am aware in twenty minutes, and am into a stoned place, not too LSD like, in another hour. I would very much like to push higher, but that is not in the cards today and I must acknowledge recovery by hour eight."

(with 80 µg, orally) "I had a mild effect, although the doors to my repressed feelings somehow really became opened up. There was nothing transcendental here, but there were moments where I felt a conscious separation from the world about me. None of the profound meanings that I had hoped to have explained were explained."

(with 150 µg, orally) "I felt it in less than a quarter hour, and was shooting up past a +++ in another quarter hour. Fast. Just like LSD but without the vaguely sinister push. A little time slowing, randy, no body disturbance. Dropping at six hours and totally tired and going to sleep at twelve hours. I will repeat."

(with 150 µg, orally) "Simply beautiful. Erotic and music absorption after second hour. Clear thinking with superb imagery and good interpretation. Easy, gentle sleeping. Next day — serene, clear-thinking peacefulness. One of the best materials ever."

(with 160 µg, orally) "I took 160 micrograms at 11 AM on an empty stomach and lay down to listen to a hypnotic relaxing tape, with eye shades and headphones. The onset was very gradual over two or three hours. There was some visual distortion similar to LSD, but mild. I decided that this was about as intense as it was going to get, so I lay down in the living room with the others. The experience continued to intensify over the next hour in intermittent waves. I had to verify that I was actually in a physical room rather than in the music I was hearing. There was never any fear or panic, but I chose to retreat to a private place for the next couple of hours. Soon I started to feel worse and I tried to gain some insight and relief from my negative attitude. I prayed, and I cried, and I began to feel calmer and had more positive thoughts as to how to deal with the others, but I was still afraid to go out into the group. I was afraid that my hopelessness would bother them but I eventually went back out at about the five hour point and the rest of the day was spent pleasantly and smoothly. I took 2.5 g of L-tryptophan to sleep, and I slept well, waking twice."

(with 160 µg, orally) "I pretreated myself with 40 milligrams of Inderal 40 minutes beforehand, took the AL-LAD, and went to bed with eye-shades and ear-phones. There was a very slow onset. The effects were best described as very short bursts of loss of contact with my body, which became increasingly intense and frequent as things progressed. It became really trippy, like acid. There were no visuals with my eyes closed, but when I removed my eye-shades the floors were melting, and the wall patterns and the wood ceiling really flowed. My body felt very blob-like, and I had to get help from my sitter to get up so I could pee. I was very affected by music. There was a very long down-ramp, with physical excitation appearing to linger longer than psychic excitation. Pretty much out of it by 12 hours and I felt well the next day."

(with 200 µg, orally) "This was taken on the tail end (seventh hour) of an MDMA experience. I felt it quickly, but it never got to a super level. Complicated erotic, good talking, looked pretty stoned, and yet I still had cognitive integrity."

EXTENSIONS AND COMMENTARY: This is one of the several very potent compounds in a large series of analogues of nor-LSD alkylated on the nitrogen at the six-position. Most of them proved to be less potent than LSD, and considerably less dramatic. The Inderal mentioned in one of the comments is a trade name for propranolol, an antihypertensive that reduces nervousness.

A comment is appropriate concerning the use of the prefix "nor," as in the name of this material N-allyl-nor-LSD and of its immediate precursor, nor-LSD. Its exact meaning is that there is an alkylated nitrogen atom somewhere that has lost an alkyl group. The original term is from the German phrase "N-ohne-Radical" meaning N (the nitrogen) without the radical (meaning the alkyl group). The removing of the N-methyl group of LSD to form the N-H counterpart is a text book example of this usage. Unfortunately its use has slopped over to embrace the removal of an alkyl group from a heteroatom of any sort. Recently I learned of a metabolite of ibogaine that has lost a methyl group from the indolic oxygen atom (a methoxy has become a hydroxy) and the compound was called noribogaine. The correct term, to retain the use of the parent ibogaine word in its name, would have been desmethyl ibogaine. The removal of something is usually indicated with a "de" or a "des" prefix ahead of the item that has been lost, as in deoxy (or desoxy) ribonucleic acid, DNA, which is ribonucleic acid (RNA) missing an oxygen atom.

## #2.    DBT:    TRYPTAMINE,   N,N-DIBUTYL;    INDOLE,   3-[2-(DIBUTYLAMINO)ETHYL];   N,N-DIBUTYLTRYPTAMINE;   3-[2-(DIBUTYLAMINO)ETHYL]INDOLE

SYNTHESIS: To a well-stirred solution of 10 g indole in 150 mL anhydrous $Et_2O$ there was added, dropwise over the course of 30 min, a solution of 11 g oxalyl chloride in 150 mL anhydrous $Et_2O$. Stirring was continued for an additional 15 min during which time there was the separation of indol-3-ylglyoxyl chloride. This intermediate was removed by filtration as used directly in the following step. It was added, portionwise, to 20 mL stirred anhydrous dibutylamine. There was then added an excess of 2N HCl, the mixture cooled, and the resulting solids removed by filtration. These were recrystallized from aqueous EtOH to give, after air drying, 19.7 g (77%) indol-3-yl-N,N-dibutylglyoxylamide with a mp 131-132 °C.

A solution of 19 g indol-3-yl-N,N-dibutylglyoxylamide in 350 mL

anhydrous dioxane was added, slowly, to 19 g LAH in 350 mL dioxane which was
well- stirred and held at reflux temperature under an inert atmosphere. After the

addition was complete, refluxing was maintained for an additional 16 h, the reaction mixture cooled, and the excess hydride destroyed by the cautious addition of wet dioxane.
The formed solids were removed by filtration, washed with hot dioxane, the filtrate and washings combined,
dried over anhydrous $MgSO_4$, and the solvent removed under vacuum. The residue
was dissolved in anhydrous $Et_2O$ and saturated with anhydrous hydrogen chloride.
The solids that formed were recrystallized from benzene/methanol to give 12.6 g
(64%) of N,N-dibutyltryptamine hydrochloride (DBT) with a mp of 186-188 °C.

EXTENSIONS AND COMMENTARY: The earliest reports that mention any
human responses to DBT suggested that with an i.m. injection of 1 mg/Kg there was
less effect than with DMT or DET. This report was discussed in the commentary
on DMT, and it was stated that the dihexyl- homologue (DHT) was without any
activity at all. The monohexyl-homologue (NHT, see below) has been described as
being "inactive in a few patients," but has not been systematically studied.

What kinds of homologues of DMT can exist out there on that tryptamine
nitrogen? Methyls, ethyls, propyls, butyls? These are already part of this story,
known as DMT, DET, DPT and DBT. The di-iso-butyl analogue of DBT may best
be called DIBT and it comes from indo-3-yl-N,N-di-(i)-butylglyoxylamide and
LAH in a manner parallel to the DBT procedure given above. The HCl salt has a
mp of 202-204 °C. The pairs of alkyl groups can go on and on forever, but the
activity seems to drop off as they get longer. How about a pair of 5-carbon chains?
Diamyltryptamine? DAT? I certainly can't use the alternate name dipentyl-
tryptamine, as that would be in conflict with DPT which has already established a
prior claim for use with dipropyltryptamine. And there is still some possible
ambiguity in that there is one mention in the literature that N,N-diallyltryptamine
is active, but neither dosage nor route was mentioned. Maybe it should be DALT.
For carbon chains that are 7-carbons long, there can only be DST for diseptyl-
tryptamine. The synonymous diheptyltryptamine would require DHT, and this has
already been usurped by the 6-carbon job, dihexyltryptamine.

And as to trying to name anything higher, such as the N,N-dioctyltryptamine,
forget it. The code would have to be, following all this logic, DOT. That term, at
least its use as a code for a psychedelic drug, is already assigned to ALEPH in the
phenethylamine series. There it stood for DesOxyThio, the DOM analogue with a
sulfur atom put in the place of an oxygen atom at a critical substitution position. So
that pretty much cools any efforts to get ever longer chains on that nitrogen atom.
They simply cannot be named. After all, there are only 26 to the third power

combinations of the letters of the alphabet, around 17,000 possible three letter codes. I remember a statistical challenge from many years ago, sort of an intellectual's party game: how many people would you need to invite to your party to guarantee that there would be a 50:50 chance that two of your guests had the same birthday? Not any specific day; just the same day. My gut instinct was to say maybe half as many people as there were days in the year. Something over a hundred? But the answer was more like 23 or so. So, how many drugs with three-lettered codes would you have to create, to have a 50:50 chance of having two with the same code? I have totally lost the technique for making the calculations, but I'll bet it might be fewer than a thousand. This particular difficulty may well soon arise, as we are already into the hundreds. One final thought. The group one longer than the octyl (8) is the nonyl (9) chain. And if one could create a meaning for a tertiary nonyl group, it would produce TNT as an abbreviation, and nothing much would dare ever go wrong with it.

But the DNA-like triplet code has other complications. What happens when there is just one substituent group on the tryptamine nitrogen atom? Mono-this and mono-that. Monomethyltryptamine has occasionally been called MMT but that might be seen as standing for two methyl groups. In this one case the compound with two methyl groups, DMT, already has a well established identity. But, as was discussed under N-ethyltryptamine, it is safer to reserve the two letters of a three letter code in front of the "T" for the two alkyl groups, when they are different. N-methyltryptamine (monomethyltryptamine) then becomes NMT and dimethyl-tryptamine stays as DMT. N,N- as a prefix is assumed and is simply left out. MMT looks like methyl methyl tryptamine (which is already called DMT). For consistency, abandon the modest literature convention and use NMT. And the potential conflict between S for secondary and S for septyl is easily resolved by simply not making compounds with any alkyl substituents that are longer than six carbons.

Let me make a table to help unravel the codes used for variously substituted tryptamines. First, there can be the numbers, those things that are never considered in alphabetizing, things that are locators of groups, and they always come first in any code. And, the numbers precede the Greek letters, which precede the atom symbols, all separated by commas. As examples:

| | | |
|---|---|---|
| 1 | $\alpha$ | N |
| 2 | $\beta$ | O |
| 3 | $\gamma$ | S |
| 4 | $\delta$ | |
| 5 | $\omega$ | |
| 6 | | |

Then comes the name of the compound itself containing, as a rule, either three or four letters. The first letter either tells the number of the groups present, or it can be the first of these groups. As to number:

N   is for nitrogen to which a single group is attached — indicates mono-
        substitution
D   is for di-substitution
T   is for tri-substitution

As to group names:

aliphatic alkyl groups        groups with hetero-atoms

M is for methyl               HO is for hydroxy
E is for ethyl                MeO is for methoxy (or dimethoxy if
P is for propyl                        preceded by two numbers)
IP is for isopropyl           MeS is for methylthio
B is for butyl                MDO is for methylenedioxy
IB is for isobutyl
SB is for secbutyl
TB is for tertbutyl
A is for amyl
AL is for allyl
H is for hexyl

And the last letter defines the parent skeleton:

T is for tryptamine
C is for carboline
S is for serotonin

In this way, a monster such as 5,$\alpha$,N-TTBT becomes, quite obviously, a
tryptamine with three tert-butyl groups attached, one at the 5-position, one at the
alpha-carbon next to the amine, and one on the amine nitrogen atom itself.
        A last comment. Remember that many drugs have code names all their
own and none of the above lettering applies. Examples are such as LSD, AL-LAD,
pyr-T and even T itself.


**#3.    DET;    TRYPTAMINE, N,N-DIETHYL;    INDOLE, 3-[2-
(DIETHYLAMINO)ETHYL];   N,N-DIETHYLTRYPTAMINE;   3-[2-
(DIETHYLAMINO)ETHYL]INDOLE;   T-9**

SYNTHESIS:  (from indole) To a well-stirred solution of 10 g indole in 150 mL
anhydrous $Et_2O$ there was added, dropwise over the course of 30 min, a solution of
11 g oxalyl chloride in 150 mL anhydrous $Et_2O$.  Stirring was continued for an

additional 15 min during which time there was the separation of indol-3-ylglyoxyl chloride. This intermediate was removed by filtration and used directly in the following step. It was added, in small portions, to 20 mL anhydrous diethylamine. There was then added an excess of 2N HCl, the mixture cooled, and the resulting solids removed by filtration. These were recrystallized from MeOH to give, after air drying, 19.4 g (93%) indol-3-yl-N,N-diethylglyoxylamide, mp 175-177 °C.

A solution of 19 g indol-3-yl-N,N-diethylglyoxylamide in 350 mL anhydrous dioxane was added, slowly, to 19 g LAH in 350 mL dioxane which was well-stirred and held at reflux temperature under an inert atmosphere. After the addition was complete, reflux was maintained for an additional 16 h, the reaction mixture cooled, and the excess hydride destroyed by the cautious addition of wet dioxane. The formed solids were removed by filtration, washed with hot dioxane, the filtrate and washings combined, dried over anhydrous $MgSO_4$, and the solvent removed under vacuum. The residue was dissolved in anhydrous $Et_2O$ and saturated with anhydrous hydrogen chloride. The white, solid product was recrystallized from benzene/methanol to give a yield of 14.7 g (75%) of N,N-diethyltryptamine hydrochloride (DET) with mp of 170-171 °C.

(from tryptamine) To a solution of 1.6 g tryptamine base in 20 mL isopropanol, there was added 5.5 mL diisopropylethylamine and 2.3 mL ethyl bromide. After stirring at room temperature for 36 h the volatiles were removed under vacuum on the rotary evaporator and the light brown residue (5.17 g) was treated with 5 mL of acetic anhydride and heated in the steam bath for 5 min. After coming to room temperature, 3.5 mL ammonium hydroxide was added, and the exothermic reaction was allowed to return to room temperature. The reaction mixture was suspended in 150 mL 0.5 N $H_2SO_4$, and washed with 3x40 mL $CH_2Cl_2$. The pooled washes were again extracted with 150 mL 0.5 N $H_2SO_4$ and the aqueous phases again washed with $CH_2Cl_2$. The aqueous phases were combined, made basic with 6 N NaOH, and then extracted with 3x40 mL $CH_2Cl_2$. The pooled extracts were stripped of solvent under vacuum, and the residue (1.49 g of a dark oil with a sharp smell) was distilled at the KugelRohr. The product, N,N-diethyltryptamine, distilled at 175-185 °C at 0.05 mm/Hg to yield a white oil weighing 1.02 g, which spontaneously crystallized. This product was dissolved in 20 mL boiling hexane, cooled to room temperature, and seeded. There was thus obtained 0.72 g of a white waxy crystalline material melting at 84-87 °C. IR (in cm$^{-1}$): 741, 804, 970, 1018, 1067, 1090 and 1120. MS (in m/z): $C_5H_{12}N^+$ 86 (100%); indolemethylene$^+$ 130 (6%); parent ion 206 (1%). The hydrochloride salt (crystallizing spontaneously from an IPA solution of the base treated with a few drops of concentrated HCl) had a mp 169-171 °C, and the following fingerprint: IR (in cm$^{-1}$): 717 (br.), 759, 847, 968, 1017, 1110. This salt appears to be unstable, darkening with time.

DOSAGE:  50-100 mg, orally

DURATION:  2 - 4 h

QUALITATIVE COMMENTS:  (with 44 mg, orally) "I was in a public place, and might have had to interact with someone at any moment, which probably accounted for a grim paranoia and wish to retreat. I had my full effect in just over an hour, with almost no visual or physical properties, but a crashing fear of interacting. I had to retreat to a private place to read and appear deeply involved, but in another hour I found it an increasingly easy task to pretend to be normal. I carried it off, OK. Good sleep, no residues."

(with 75 mg, orally) "Onset seemed to be at 40 minutes, which were mostly physical symptoms, which seemed to fade away at 1.25 hours. All in all, an absolutely profound, enriching experience with both Brahms (G-minor piano quartet) and Verdi (requiem) contributing mightily. All over in 3.5 - 4.5 hours and a delightful afterglow."

(with 150 mg, orally) "There was a slow onset. It was more than an hour before something started, which I didn't believe at first but which became completely undeniable. I was heading toward an appointment, and walked right past the meeting place. I was unable to concentrate on just where I was and where I was hoping to go. With enormous effort I located my appointment coordinates but the sidewalk was doing funny things and I again managed to miss my target. I sat down to try to manage things, but I couldn't."

(with 150 mg, orally) "The effects were manifestly notable in 50-60 minutes, quite intense from hour one to hour three. Then there is an hour when trailing is still perceptible. By hour five it is all over. There appeared to be 'vegetative effects' as they used to say. I definitely noted sweating of hands and feet. There was a hollowness in the chest. There was an insignificant presser response, but pronounced tachycardia, with my normal resting pulse in the 60's going up above 100 for a while. I think that 150 milligrams is a little too much."

(with 400 mg, orally) "Too much."

(with 40 mg, smoking) "I have found that ten milligrams of DET is the size of a match head, so I smoked four of them. The taste of the stuff is terrible — it smells like burning plastic — but I don't care. The onset was gentle, in about five minutes, euphoric and empathogenic, and there was an immediate camaraderie with the group I was with (they were using between twenty and forty milligrams apiece). I found myself stroking a calico cat, and asked a friend, 'Do people purr?' and was told, 'Sure, if you know how to listen.' We began scratching one another's backs, and made vaguely purring noises."

(with 90 mg, smoking) "This was with 3x30 milligrams, at ten minute intervals. It took almost too much concentration for the last toke. Too stoned. Some emotional insights, but I can't remember them to write them. Fine muscular tremor. Some hangover the next day, lassitude, fine edge of thought was blunted."

(with 40 mg, subcutaneously) "There was a slight burning and a numbness of both the hands and feet some twenty minutes. A few minutes later I felt an alcohol-like intoxication and a slight drifting of thoughts. Music was slightly enhanced and eyes-closed patterning was noted, with a predominance of greens and oranges. No music, no patterns. The effects peaked at 30 minutes, but the numbness I felt lasted up to three hours. Overall, this was somewhat disappointing."

(with 60 mg, intramuscularly) "The yellow walls with many windows in them, massing over one another, appeared in increased intensity, had an air of medieval mood about them. The ornaments, painted white, on the roof and eaves had a particularly strong decorative effect. A test subject, without a painter's fantasy, must certainly be greatly impressed by this depth and colorfulness. I felt as I did when I began to learn painting, when I tried to look at things consciously with a painter's eye. I felt that the drug acted on fantasy, in the first place, increasing its dynamism. On a subject with normal mind, this experience will certainly have an astonishing and marvelous effect. An artist with creative mind and fantasy will be less impressed."

(with 60 mg, intramuscularly) "About 15 minutes after the injection came the same vegetative symptoms seen with DMT. The illusions and hallucinations were the same. But the alteration of the surrounding world and the emotional reaction to them were strong and impressive. The mask-like faces of the persons, the dream-like mysteriousness of the objects in the room gave me the feeling that I had arrived in another world, entirely different and queer and full of secrecy and mystery. The wonderful but strange world attracted me at one moment, but the next moment I did not want to accept it. I became perplexed; I did not know what I ought to do. I began to walk anxiously up and down, and said, 'I ought to do something, I must!' There was a peculiar double orientation in space and time: I knew where I was, but I was inclined to accept this strange world as a reality, too. The dusk of the room was lightened for some minutes, and again the light was switched off, and that seemed to me as if this period might be an entire epoch, filled with events and happenings, but at the same time I knew that only several minutes had passed."

(with 60 mg, intramuscularly) "The vertigo is gone — now comes the attraction. I have the honor of seeing the elements of the universe in this moment. As if I saw algae, flagellates under the microscope, in black and white. Now I see some colours, too. As if I saw a shell, the rainbow colours are disintegrating rapidly. One's consciousness becomes air-like. From the neck upward I am feeling a shapeless lightness. If we could inoculate this into all men, human interrelations would undoubtedly improve greatly."

(with 60 mg, intravenously) "I was looking out of the window. I was seeing the leaves of a tree, the color of the grass, people walking to and fro utterly without thinking, like a small child staring at things. I felt as if I were discovering the world anew."

(with 60 mg, intravenously) "The objects opened up their essence to me, I was feeling as if I knew them as they really are, I live in them and was in direct contact with them. I felt an enormous drive to write, to put down the marvelous feelings. The associations came spontaneously, but I was unable to concentrate in a way required for working. Anyway, I did not want to miss one moment of the visions."

EXTENSIONS AND COMMENTARY: I have to bear the responsibility for much of the mythology that maintains that DET is only active by some parenteral route. All of the published human studies that explicitly mentioned dose and dosage, involved intramuscular administrations. Most of the people with whom I had private conversations about this material had evaluated it through the smoking route. It was only recently that I began to hear of oral trials. I had assumed that it was inactive orally, and had said so in a number of reviews that I had published over the years. As they say in Latin, *mea culpa*. There was one mention of oral activity that had been made, in one table written by Steve Szara, in 1969, presented at a meeting that we both participated in, at Irvine, California. I gave the opening overview, and deferred tryptamine questions to Steve, later, in his talk. And in this talk, he presented a Table that referred to DET as being active at a dose of 60 mg, i.m. or p.o. The latter is Latin for *per os*, and means that it was orally active, but he had never mentioned it explicitly to me, and I had never asked. Some 25 years later, we met again and rehashed old times, and at this meeting I gave yet another review paper with the parenteral restriction on DET activity, and he never mentioned anything. And yet, the damned thing is indeed orally active, and since I have said otherwise in publications, I accept the responsibility for the error. Apparently the MAO systems do not chomp up the dialkylamines higher than methyl. Certainly the dipropyl and the diisopropyl are active by mouth, and so is the diethyl.

Several clinical studies were conducted in the late 1950's and early 1960's. They employed the oppressive research environment that was considered scientific at that time, and there were variable results. One study involved ten physically normal subjects, who were unemployed men from a depressed mining area. The DET was administered in i.m. injections and trials were conducted in a partially soundproofed experimental clinic equipped with a one-way mirror and microphones. The subjects were subjected to a battery of psychological tests and body function measurements at frequent intervals. The consensus expressed was one of dysphoria. Neurological signs varied from slight generalized tremors to gross athetoid movements. Among the bizarre somatic complaints were such as: "Air is rushing through my body," "My chest is empty and there is a jelly ball in my spine," "My hands aren't there, my whole body feels funny." All subjects experienced dizziness and increased sweating. Six of the subjects stated that the experience was an unpleasant one, three of them markedly so. There was no enthusiasm in the group for a repetition of the experience, and several stated that they would leave the clinical center before submitting to it again. A similar study with ten chronic paranoid schizophrenic patients (in the same setting and with the same dosage) produced similar effects. Most became pale, shaky, and either complained of feeling sick or actually vomiting. Several also developed tremors. In general, these were pretty negative experiences, and contribute to the negative medical and scientific opinions that are held concerning these drugs.

Another study was carried out in an entirely different, informal setting, with professional colleagues, with other professionals and with artists. These were with personal friends of the research scientists, rather than strangers to them. The observed mood changes (produced, in this study, by the i.m. administration of 0.70 to 0.80 mg/Kg of DET) were described as being in the direction of euphoria; the subjects generally enjoyed the experience and wished to repeat it. The volunteered comments under the drug tended towards the mystical and philosophical, and several of these experimental subjects responded to music and art in ways that were new to them.

In the earliest research with DET and the related dialkyltryptamines, the chemistry of metabolism was studied for any clues that could explain the activity of these materials. It must be remembered that this was in the heyday of the concept of psychotomimesis, the search for drugs that would imitate the psychotic state. What an appealing concept, that there might be a drug that could produce the syndrome of mental illness and thus be an accepted model for designing some treatment for it. There was a delicious search made at that time (the 1950's) for names that could be given to these remarkable substances, names which would obscure any spiritual or positive aspects, so that one could present one's findings into the orthodox medical literature. At that time, I chose to use the name psychotomimetic in the titles of my publications, because I knew it might deflect criticism from the medical community for the findings that I described. But such a variety of names were used as keywords to these studies. In my notes I find: "delirients," "delusionogenics," "dysleptics," "misperceptinogens," "mystico-mimetics," "phanerothymes," "phantasticants," "pharmakons," "psychosomimetics" (an "s" for the "t"? why?), "psychotaraxics," "psychoticants," "psychotogens," "psychogens," "psychotoxins" and "schizogens." Not a very appealing collection from which to choose a week-end trip.

In 1956, Humphry Osmond suggested at a New York Academy of Science meeting that it might be less pejorative to soften the prefix that was used to relate to the mind from psychoto- or psycho- (used in medical diagnoses that are largely negative) to a misspelled but softer alternative, psyche- (which had not yet been tarred by the image of medical pathology). His suggestion, "psychedelic," was aped in many trials with such creations as "psychephoric" (mind-moving), "psychehormic" (mind-rousing), "psycheplastic" (mind-molding), "psychezymic" (mind-fermenting), "psycherhexic" (mind-bursting-forth) and "psychelytic" (mind-releasing). But, psychedelic (mind-manifesting) has weathered all storms, and is now a fixed component of our vocabulary. Several recent contributions for possible class names for some of these compounds, such as entheogen (God-created-within), entactogen (touching-within) or empathogen (the discovery of empathy), are creations that try to address the integrity and warmth that can be part of the psychedelic experience. Each uses the suffix, "-gen," that suggests genesis, or creation. Each has its use, and each has its limitations. One must remember that none of these terms describe what occurs within an experience. Their value is limited to the search for a label for the drugs that allow these experiences to happen.

Back to the metabolism discussion. And to the search for the actual drug, the magic bullet, that actually precipitated a model schizophrenic state. If one were to find it, one could look skillfully for the counterpart in the human animal, the one that simply appeared on the scene from some mismanaged metabolic process, and thus could be blamed for mental illness. It had been observed that the longer the chains on the N,N-disubstituted tryptamine, the less the potency. And the longer the chains, the less of the drug was excreted as the 6-hydroxyl metabolite. This focused attention on the hydroxy metabolites of the two simplest and most potent of the dialkyltryptamines, DMT and DET.

6-HO-DET has been observed to be a minor human metabolite of DET, with the excretion of about 20% of the administered dose as the glucoronide conjugate. In a study with normal and schizophrenic patients, a positive correlation was observed between the amount of 6-HO-DET excreted and the intensity of the experience. Also, there was a suggestion that the schizophrenics produced greater amounts of this metabolite. This led to a hypothesis that perhaps it was an active factor in the generation of the intoxicated state. In principle, as with bufotenine, the bare, exposed polar hydroxyl group should make its entry to the brain quite difficult. But, on the other hand, if it were generated there from DET after it had gotten into the brain, entry would not be a concern and the lipophilic barrier could serve to make its exit difficult. Then, if it were an effective compound, it might well be a long acting one. There is an early report of the self-administration intramuscularly, to a single subject, of 10 milligrams 6-HO-DET with the description of what appeared to be DET-like effects from about the second to fourth hour. Although this report suggested that it was several times more potent than DET, it has never been replicated and it does not jibe too well with the 6-HO-DMT report below.

As a challenge to the hypothesis that hydroxylation at the 6-position of the N,N-dialkyltryptamines might play some role in the expression of the activity, this position was metabolically blocked by the insertion of a fluorine atom there, giving 6-F-DET. This compound, with DET as the control, was studied in some twelve hospitalized alcoholics at doses of about 60, 80 and 100 mgs intramuscularly. It "does produce autonomic effects, pupillary changes, blood pressure changes; but it does not produce the drifting away into a dream world and other phenomena characteristic of most hallucinogenic compounds." The experimenters considered its possible experimental role as an "active placebo" but nothing more was done with it.

6-HO-DMT is a minor metabolite of DMT in man, and it was studied for the same reasons. Could this compound play a role in explaining the activity of the parent dialkylamine? It was explored in a series of subjects who had responded spectacularly to DMT. The five volunteers in this study were former opium addicts who were serving sentences for violation of United States narcotics laws. They were administered 6-HO-DMT at either 0.75 mg/Kg (one subject) or 1.0 mg/Kg (four subjects) and reported no differences from the inactive placebo control. The objective measures (blood pressure, respiration and heart rate, pupillary dilation) confirmed the absence of activity at this level. The active control drug was DMT itself, and it showed the expected responses in all regards.

I have always been just a little embarrassed that so many of these early studies used hospitalized patients, schizophrenics, alcoholics, and prisoners as subjects. These latter experiments were carried out at the Lexington, Kentucky Public Health Service Hospital. This has been for years a major site for human research in the area of addictive or psychotropic drugs. But it cannot be forgotten that it was first, and foremost, a prison and the people there were prisoners. Complete objectivity of reporting, from a person who is in custody and who might wish to please his jailers, is unlikely. The whole scene started shortly after the Harrison Narcotics Act passed back near the time of World War I. The medical profession held that narcotics addiction was a medical problem, and the legal authorities held that it was a legal problem. In other words, was a heroin user sick, or was he a criminal? The law enforcement viewpoint prevailed, the physicians who objected went to jail, and the addicts went to what were called "narcotics farms." They were indeed prisons, but the name carried the politically correct suggestion of rehabilitation. And it was at the last of these, at Lexington, that this hydroxylated DMT study was done.

The results were negative, to the disappointment of the researchers. It is pretty generally accepted that 6-HO-DMT is inactive. I am not too surprised. There are so few things with open and exposed hydroxyl groups that succeed in making it through the lipid barriers that protect the brain.

### #4. DIPT; TRYPTAMINE, N,N-DIISOPROPYL; INDOLE, 3-[2-(DIISOPROPYLAMINO)ETHYL]; N,N-DIISOPROPYLTRYPTAMINE; 3-[2-(DIISOPROPYLAMINO)ETHYL]INDOLE

SYNTHESIS: (from indole) To a well-stirred solution of 10 g of indole in 100 mL MTBE, cooled to 0 °C with an ice bath, there was added 11 g oxalyl chloride. The reaction mixture was stirred for 0.5 hr, and the solids removed by filtration and washed twice with 50 mL MTBE. This acid chloride was added to 20 mL anhydrous diisopropylamine with good stirring. There was then added an excess of 2N HCl, the mixture cooled, and the resulting solids removed by filtration. These were recrystallized from MeOH to give, after air drying, 11.4 g (49%) indol-3-yl-N,N-diisopropylglyoxylamide with a mp of 200-202 °C.

A solution of 11 g indol-3-yl-N,N-diisopropylglyoxylamide in 350 mL anhydrous dioxane was added, slowly, to 19 g LAH in 350 mL dioxane, which was well-stirred and held at reflux temperature under an inert atmosphere. After the addition was complete, reflux was maintained for an additional 16 h, the reaction mixture cooled, and the excess hydride destroyed by the cautious addition of wet dioxane. The formed solids were removed by filtration, washed with hot dioxane, the filtrate and washings combined, dried over anhydrous $MgSO_4$, and the solvent removed under vacuum. The residue was dissolved in anhydrous $Et_2O$ and saturated with anhydrous hydrogen chloride. There were formed crystals which were recrystallized from benzene/MeOH to give 4.5 g (40%) of N,N-diisopropyltryptamine hydrochloride (DIPT) with a mp of 198-199 °C.

(from tryptamine) A solution of 1.60 g tryptamine base in 10 g melted sulfolane was treated with 8.5 g isopropyl iodide and 6.5 g diisopropylethyl amine, and held at steam bath temperature for 12 h with occasional shaking to mix the two phases. This mixture was then added to 100 mL $H_2O$, and extracted with three 30 mL portions of hexane. These were combined and, after removal of the solvent under vacuum, the residue was distilled at the KugelRohr to give an off-white oil boiling at 170-185 °C at 0.05 mm/Hg weighing 1.37 g (56%) that spontaneously crystallized to a solid, mp 69-71 °C. Recrystallization of a sample from hexane produced a white product with a mp of 72-74 °C. IR (in $cm^{-1}$): 742, 791, 1009, 1133, 1162, 1198. MS (in m/z): $C_7H_{16}N^+$ 114 (100%); $C_4H_{10}N^+$ 72 (38%); indolemethylene$^+$ 130 (18%); parent ion 244 (<1%). A solution of 0.50 g of the free base in 2.5 mL isopropanol was treated with 0.5 mL concentrated HCl and slowly diluted with $Et_2O$ with good stirring. There was thus obtained, after filtering, washing and air drying, the hydrochloride salt with a mp of 192-193 °C. The infra-red spectrum of this salt was the same from either source; IR (in $cm^{-1}$): 752, 773, 935, 972, 1138, 1183.

DOSAGE:  25 - 100 mg, orally

DURATION:  6 - 8 h

QUALITATIVE COMMENTS:  (with 18 mg, orally) "Wild effects noted in an hour. Remarkable changes in sounds heard. My wife's voice is basso, as if she had a cold — my ears with slight pressure as if my tubes were clogged but they aren't. Radio voices are all low, music out of key. Piano sounds like a bar-room disaster. The telephone ringing sounds partly underwater. In a couple more hours, music pretty much normal again."

(with 25 mg, orally) "Within the first hour I noted changes already, and my hand-writing became very poor. I cannot seem to measure the rate of the drug's effects as there is no obvious window through which I am moving. Abrupt sounds have golden spikes attached to them as after-sounds, but I can't focus in on any other sensory changes. I moved into a completely quiet environment and there don't appear to be any effects of any kind. If I were deaf, this would have been an inactive compound. How many other drugs have appeared to be inactive because I didn't know where to look for effects?"

(with 50 mg, orally) "Everything was auditory, and I can only describe it with a '!'"

(with 100 mg, orally) "Nothing until 35 minutes when a definite change in hearing was observed. There was a decrease in high frequency acuity with an unusual tonal shift of all frequencies to a lower pitch. Voices sounded very similar to a single side-band radio signal which had been mistuned to the low side of the center frequency. All familiar sounds became foreign, including the chewing of food. No effects were noted with respect to clarity of speech, and both comprehension and interpretation were normal. Music was rendered completely disharmonious although single tones sounded normal. There were no changes in vision, taste, smell, appetite, vital signs, or motor coordination. The effects began to fade at four hours post-ingestion, and were completely gone at eight hours. Mild diarrhea occurred from five to ten hours post-ingestion but was not a significant problem."

(with 250 mg, orally) "Shortly after I ingested the substance I heard a spirit say, 'Once in a lifetime.' She encouraged me to believe that I would have more life after the experience. But, there was a feeling of foreboding. The light was there, but DIPT was the body of Satan. The voices of people were extremely distorted — males sounded like frogs — children sounded like they were talking through synthesizers to imitate outer space people in science fiction movies. In fact I felt that I was somehow sent into an anti-universe where everything looked the same as normal but was a cold and empty imitation. I felt I was a fallen angel."

(with 8 mg, smoked) "In four minutes I was aware of things going on, and by eight minutes, I was at a plus 2. My tongue was numb, and my ears felt plugged up although my hearing was keen and there was a background hissing sound."

EXTENSIONS AND COMMENTARY: Most psychedelic drugs affect, primarily, the visual sense, but here is one that shows its effects primarily in the auditory system. And it screws it up in a most unlinear manner, in that there is not just a simple decrease in pitch which would be as if someone had his thumb against the LP record and made everything come out at a 3/4 speed text, or a 1/2 speed text. Actual proportionality is lost, so there is complete harmonic distortion.

A physician friend of mine has expressed it using a neurological vocabulary: "If it [the drug] delayed only the neural response to a stimulus, then pitch might have been shifted down, and yet harmony between notes should have been preserved. A variable delay related to the pitch of the stimulus would produce the disharmony but would not explain the preservation of normal relationships between single tones. It seems clear that this compound affects the auditory processing centers in the brain in a complex way which deserves further scientific study. The lack of significant toxic effects should make this compound useful for further studies."

I am in absolute agreement. Here is a drug that goes directly after the hearing system, rather than the seeing system. Let's stick a carbon 11 on one of those isopropyl groups, and see where the drug goes using the positron emission tomography camera. Will we highlight the auditory cortex? Or maybe some association area? But if we are indeed dealing only with musical pitch, not musical structure, there might be only a small part of that cortical region visible. This could well be a tool for two things. First, the localization of the pitch center in the brain. And second, it is a prototypic drug that might allow structural modification in several directions with several augmenting atoms. Some simple homologue might well have even more remarkable and specific properties. If you don't look, you won't find.

I have been told by an adventurous graduate student that a study has been made with two subjects who had absolute pitch, with either a piano or a sinewave generator as a sound source. He wanted to explore the possibility that some relationship could be developed between the pitch of the note provided and the apparent pitch of the note perceived. No meaningful relationship was found, except for the reinforcement that the observed drop in pitch was not linear, in that true distortion rather than simple pitch dropping was always observed. Most interesting was the plot of the error for each trial against the elapsed time. This provided what could be seen as an almost-quantitative measurement of the drug's intensity and chronology. Pretreatment with relatively small amounts of MDMA (35 milligrams, at between 1.5 and 2.5 hours before DIPT, at 55 milligrams) led to an exaggerated distortion, with an enhanced intensity that verged on being painful.

The homologue with only one isopropyl group on the nitrogen, N-isopropyltryptamine or IPT, has been made according to the same recipe, with the indol-3-yl-N-isopropylglyoxalylamide (mp 199-200 °C from MeOH) obtained in a 98% yield, and the amine hydrochloride (mp 245-246 °C from benzene/MeOH) obtained in a 60% yield. The free base distilled at 130-140 °C at 0.1 mm/Hg to give a fraction that spontaneously crystallized to a very hard solid. MS (in m/z): $C_4H_{10}N^+$ 72 (100%); indolemethylene$^+$ 131 (60%), 130 (32%); parent ion 202 (3%). No active level has yet been found in man, to my knowledge.

#5.  α,O-DMS; 5-MEO-α-MT; TRYPTAMINE, 5-METHOXY-α-ME-THYL; INDOLE, 3-(2-AMINOPROPYL)-5-METHOXY; SEROTONIN, α,O-DIMETHYL; 5-METHOXY-α-METHYLTRYPTAMINE; 3-(2-AMINOPROPYL)-5-METHOXYINDOLE; α,O-DIMETHYLSEROTO-NIN; ALPHA-O

SYNTHESIS: To a solution of 2.0 g 5-methoxyindole-3-carboxaldehyde in 25 g nitroethane there was added 0.5 g anhydrous ammonium acetate, and the mixture held at reflux for 1.5 h on the steam bath. The excess nitroethane was removed under vacuum yielding a wet, orange solid. This was dissolved in 20 mL boiling isopropanol which, after cooling, deposited bright orange crystals. These were removed by filtration, washed with cold isopropanol, and air dried to provide 1.56 g 1-(5-methoxyindol-3-yl)-2-nitropropene mp 179-180 °C (lit. 182-184 °C). Evaporation of the filtrates gave 0.81 g crude product which was recrystallized from 10 mL EtOH giving a second crop as dull gold crystals. This weighed, after EtOH washing and air drying, 0.57 g (80% total yield), with a mp of 178-179 °C.

A solution of 1.54 g 1-(5-methoxyindol-3-yl)-2-nitropropene in 60 mL anhydrous THF was added dropwise to 50 mL 1 M LAH in THF, well-stirred, in an argon atmosphere. Each drop generated a red color which immediately discolored. The addition took 0.5 h and the reaction mixture was held at reflux for 18 h, then allowed to stir at room temperature for 7 days. There was added, in

sequence, 1.6 mL $H_2O$ in 10 mL THF (much gas evolution), 1.6 mL 15% aqueous NaOH (no more gas) and finally 5 mL $H_2O$. The $Al_2O_3$ was removed by filtration, washed with THF, and the combined filtrate and washing stripped of solvent under vacuum. The residue (1.83 g of a clear oil) was dissolved in 300 mL dilute HCl, washed with 3x50 mL $CH_2Cl_2$, made basic with 25% NaOH, and extracted with 3x50 mL of $CH_2Cl_2$. The extracts were stripped of solvent under vacuum, and the 1.13 g residue distilled at the KugelRohr. A fraction that distilled at 145-155 °C at 0.2 mm/Hg was a white oil that spontaneously crystallized, mp 95-96 °C. MS (in m/z): $C_2H_6N^+$ 44 (100%); methoxyindolemethylene[+] at 161/160 (88%, 43%, here, as with the secondary amines, this primary amine has the 161 greater than the 160, nonmethoxylated tryptamines, the 131 greater than the 130); 146 (22%); parent ion 204 (4%). These solids (0.51 g) were dissolved in 5 mL boiling isopropanol, neutralized with several drops of concentrated HCl, and diluted with $Et_2O$. The solution became turbid and scratching produced a fine, white crystalline product. After 20 min standing this was removed by filtration, washed with $Et_2O$, and air dried. There was obtained 0.44 g 3-(2-aminopropyl)-5-methoxyindole hydrochloride (α,O-DMS) as white crystals, with a mp of 216-218 °C. A sample prepared some 20 years earlier (brown as the salt, not distilled as the base, mp 220-222) now melted at 215-217 °C. The residue from the aqueous acid wash above contained no additional α,O-DMS as assayed by TLC (19:1; $CH_3CN/NH_4OH$). The infra-red spectra are different for these two materials, indicating polymorphism. The new white crystals; IR (in $cm^{-1}$): 805, 816, 872, 1023, 1055, 1102, 1169, NH at 3300. The old brown crystals; IR (in $cm^{-1}$): 809, 839, 1021, 1041, 1080, 1112, 1170, NH at 3250. The brown morph, upon recrystallization from IPA/$Et_2O$ had an IR identical to the new white material.

DOSAGE:  2.5 - 4.5 mg, orally

DURATION:  12 - 18 h

QUALITATIVE COMMENTS: (with 2.0 mg, orally) "Initial anxiety about getting nauseated or having diarrhea was almost immediately dissolved after ingestion. It took a little while before I felt the energy. By the way, before I took the medicine, I had read some lurid details about other people's experiences, and was rather anxious about it, because there was a lot of diarrhea and vomiting mentioned. But it didn't happen. Matter of fact, I felt really good afterwards. The dosage level seemed just right. I had a very enjoyable day. Communication was easy and fun. Sleep was easy to reach and it was great. Next morning, feel wonderful. Would I repeat? Yes. At about the same level."

(with 2.3 mg, orally) "It has been an hour and a half, but now I am really turning on. Physically, I have had some pretty thorough diarrhea, but mentally I am still waiting for some sensory or perceptual, or conceptual event to occur. At the sixth hour I think I am clearing, and I don't know what it was all about. It was as if I was in a state of preparedness like a plate of sterile agar waiting to provide nutrition to whatever was to be introduced into it. But there was no inoculation. I didn't contribute my share. A good argument for threshold being a better measure of drug potency than a full dose. Had a slight fragile headache the next AM — gone by noon."

(with 2.5 mg, orally) "Came on fairly nicely, but at about 40 minutes, began to feel slightly nauseous. This stuck with me for a couple of hours. I could get out of it by concentrating, so it wasn't debilitating. But then, as I began to come out of that, felt a nice warm glow, and a nice centered feeling, and felt really good the rest of the day. Evening was very tired, and had a difficult time going to sleep because there was still a powerful push from the substance. In fact, I think it's the most tenacious stuff I've taken, and I never could detect much let-up during the afternoon. Then, I don't think I got into good sleep until about 2 a.m. No problem after that. Good sleep. Next morning, felt good. Still a bit languid. Today feels good. Everything looks and feels fine, but I'm not a ball of energy. At the moment, haven't fully integrated it all. No great enthusiasm about taking it again."

(with 3.0 mg, orally) "Just over an hour into it, some mild vomiting relieved my nausea and I began building into a wild ASC. With my eyes closed the clouds are rolling and I have strange imagery. I am going into a zombie place, my walk is a bit Frankensteinish, the piano keys are unreal, the typewriter keys are unreal — music and text that comes out has little bearing on my intentions. The most fun was writing with the power off; no inhibitions, no record. Tried a bit with the power on, and this is an exact copy of what came out: what an alien keyboard - what will it produce? anilan alina anein alein alean ailean alain alein wow - wowowow owow. The face on the lion's chair is many things, cheeks become boxing gloves, mouth talks but no words are evident, entertaining but not profound. Such mileage from just three milligrams of C, H, N & O. Obviously it is my own energy pool that has been tapped. Fourth hour, diarrhea again — modest — just symbolic. All through the last two hours — in addition to the interpretive changes, there were wild visual distortions. Things tended to flow — not bothersome — but I know I couldn't drive a car. By the fifth hour, I was mending; the physical zombie is not there anymore. I can ignore the crawling. At the ten hour point I am still dilated, and teeth rubby, and hypoxic. Something is still poisonous. Sleep not satisfactory. Restless, with strange mental interpretations. The next day, I am clear and totally without residues. This α,O-DMS is probably the most potent indolic psychedelic yet uncovered, at least via the oral route. Any higher dose would require a baby-sitter, and I must remember that there is a big toxic component that is part of this trip."

(with 3.5 mg, orally) "I started with 2.5 milligrams followed in two hours by 1 more. Never got above 1.75 plus. Not much insight. Pleasant generally, but essentially non-productive. Slept easily at post-lunch nap time. Had trouble sleeping near midnight. Had to take a Restoril. Sleep okay, but like 2C-B, dreams slightly annoying and repetitive."

(with 4.0 mg, orally) "Slight nausea with no problem at an hour, and then developed to a plateau for about a ++ for the three to seven hour slot. I slept but was still not baseline at the 16 hour point. A wonderful drug for interacting with others and formulating ideas. It bestows a remarkable ability to multi-task mental activities. No hang-over the next day, in fact quite the reverse. Can't wait to try 5 milligrams."

(with 4.5 mg, orally) "I started with 3.0 milligrams and with the complete absence of physical malaise I supplemented with 1.5 milligrams at two hours. There were some shakes appearing, but there was a super window-state that developed, not intellectual, not psychotic, but things are crawling. At five hours fully +++ but it is beginning to drop, but dropping very slowly. The mental memory was there still at nine hours and the mental memory at twelve hours. There was teeth clench."

(with 0.8 mg. of the R-isomer, orally) "I feel excellent, but I felt excellent before the experiment. No drug effect."

(with 1.5 mg of the R-isomer, orally) "There is a faint light-head-light-body feel about two hours into it. And light diarrhea at the fourth hour. Certainly nothing at 6 hours."

(with 3.0 mg of the R-isomer, orally) "I am aware at one hour, and to a real plus one at three hours. Still real at four hours, vaguely pleasant, and the diarrhea is right on schedule. Pretty much out of whatever this was, by eight hours."

(with 0.8 mg of the S-isomer, orally) "There is an honest threshold, a real tingle at one hour. This clearly is the active isomer. At 2 1/2 hours, this is pushed up to a plus one, not just in the body but there is something active in the head. At the third hour, everything seems stable, there is complete diarrhea, the body knows that it has been affected, but there is some mental still. Six hours dropping, eight hours clear, but there are body memories."

(with 2.4 mg of the S-isomer, orally) "I took 1.5 milligrams initially, and was aware in a half hour. No nausea, but diarrhea. Stuck at a mental plus two at three hours, so I augmented this with another 0.9 milligrams. The supplement became apparent in another half hour, and I was at a +++ in short order. Not too much in the way of eyes-open visual effects, but there was a thorough intoxication that lasted for another three hours. Attempted sleeping at fifteen hours failed — I am far too guarded to sleep. Finally OK, but I don't remember my dreams. Next morning, the body still not completely baseline. Is this ever the active isomer!"

EXTENSIONS AND COMMENTARY:   From the point of view of the neuropharmacologist, this has to be one of the most appealing and seductive of compounds. Serotonin (5-HT) is the "in" neurotransmitter, and it is the first receptor system that is looked at in any research lab working with psychedelic drugs. An association with serotonin is a strong justification for grant writing and funds solicitation from the mother of most medical research funding, the branches of the National Institutes of Health in Washington. Although this specific neurotransmitter is a big item in the brain, if you feed it to a person, or put it into him via the blood or tissue, it can't get there. It has no way of moving this specific molecule from the outside of the brain (the periphery) into the brain itself (the central Kingdom).

Two obstacles effectively prohibit this availability. Serotonin has a free hydroxy group (the 5-hydroxy which is the H of 5-HT). This is a big polar water-loving pimple which denies it any passage across the brain's defensive Maginot Line, the blood-brain barrier. And there is the second problem. There is an exposed amino group, the amine of T of 5-HT, the tryptamine, which is immediately removed by the body's monoamine oxidase enzyme. In short, it is blocked from entry into the brain because it is both too polar and too metabolically fragile.

The structure of alpha-O is designed to overcome these two restrictions. A methyl group on the oxygen (the O-methyl) removes the polarity restriction. A methyl group next to the amine function (the alpha-methyl) protects the molecule from enzymatic attack. With the two obstacles removed, this compound apparently has easy access directly to the brain. Hence, alpha,O-dimethylserotonin ($\alpha$,O-DMS) goes directly into the central nervous system and has proved to be one of the most potent tryptamines yet described. And it is active following oral administration, which exposes it to all of the body's protective machinery.

I have been sent one report from an anonymous source, that told me that the compound did not have any increased potency when it was smoked. His report was with 5 milligrams, and said: "Not too intense a smell, but it has quite a bite. Slow onset, unlike DMT. After a few minutes there was some dizziness, light giddiness, dysphoria, stretching of the limbs, some gastrointestinal disturbances, a sense of the body floating, and pupil dilation. Even with the eyes closed, and concentration, there were only indistinct visual hallucinations. With the eyes open, a strong intensification of colors, and a harmonization of visual impressions just like everything was 'velvet coated and has its own mystical movement.' Sleep was restless and on the next day there were some remaining effects with tiredness and mental exhaustion." If the oral and a parenteral route indeed both produce the same effects and show the same potency, the argument against metabolic catabolism may be valid. This would be an interesting experiment to repeat.

An additional complication and opportunity is provided by the fact that the placement of the methyl group on the alpha-position introduces a chiral carbon. The R- and S-isomers have been compared (see in the Qualitative Comments section) and the S-isomer is clearly three or four times more potent that the R-isomer. These were assayed completely blind, with the code having been broken only after the completion of the study. The dramatic differences in potency let the assignment of the more active isomer be made without hesitation. This S-isomer is the d- or dextrorotary one, and has the absolute configuration of the more active member of the isomer pairs of amphetamine, of methamphetamine and of MDMA. All the psychedelic amphetamine derivatives (all that have been assayed, that is) have the R-isomer as the more potent one.

Some half of the subjects I specifically queried as to their sleeping patterns confirmed my own observation that the dreams were generally negative. A few actually had memories of catastrophes or high danger. This, coupled with the extremely high potency of this compound and many options for structural variation, allows a treasure trove of speculation. The 5-methoxy group is in every way the pharmacological analogue of the 4-substituent in the phenethylamine world. Would the 5-ethoxy, the 5-isopropoxy, the 5-something-else-oxy provide psyche-delic compounds? Would alpha-ethyl or higher provide anti-depressants, as had been seen with Ariadne and related phenethylamines? Would N-substitution (N-methyl, N-isopropyl, N,N-dimethyl, N-methyl-N-isopropyl) lead to orally active things with increased potency or increased drama? Would any of these changes improve the ratio of mental effects over the body toxicity? Are the occasional nightmares reported with sleep following alpha-O unique to this compound, or might a specific dream-modifying agent be uncovered with structural modifica-tions?

I am aware of one of these modifications, specifically on that magical 5-methoxy-position. This is the sterically similar, but metabolically totally dissimi-lar fluorine analogue, 5-fluoro-alpha-methyltryptamine, or 5-F-α-MT. The fluo-rine atom is the darling of the manipulators of molecular structure in that it is a form of fake hydrogen. True, as an atomic lump on an aromatic ring it is a lot larger and a lot heavier, but it is a lump that doesn't like to associate with anything else. Its bonding with a ring carbon is the same sort of two-electron bond that the hydrogen atom makes, but it cannot be oxidized off in the same way. So, when a drug has a position of sensitivity to oxidation, and that oxidation is thought to be responsible for some particular pharmacological property, put a fluorine there and you will deny the drug that property. This was discussed in the section on DET where the metabolism attacks a 6-position hydrogen.

And it may play such a role here. When one balances the sort-of stimulant nature of α-MT with the potent psychedelic properties of α,O-DMS, one can ask if the oxidation of the tryptamine system at this 5-position can be of some significance. Tryptamine becomes serotonin by this action. DMT becomes bufotenine by this action. If there is some extension of this to the α-MT world, then the placement of a fluoro group at that position of attack would be interesting. 5-F-α-MT has been made, and it appears to be of reduced activity in man. But it has proven to be an extremely potent monoamineoxidase inhibitor, and strongly influences the brain serotonin levels. The 6-fluoro isomer, 6-F-α-MT, is also effective.

This kind of molecular manipulation is the ultimate treasure of the research pharmacologist: the taking off of one atom and the replacement of it with another. This is the simplest single maneuver that can be done to a drug, and any change in the observed pharmacology must be the result of that change. Some of the explorations described in this book are of exactly this nature. Some have been tried. Most have not and are completely unknown. All must eventually be explored if we ever hope to learn what is going on up there in the human mind.

### #6.   DMT;   TRYPTAMINE, N,N-DIMETHYL;   INDOLE, 3-[2-(DIMETHYLAMINO)ETHYL];   N,N-DIMETHYLTRYPTAMINE;   3-[2-(DIMETHYLAMINO)ETHYL]INDOLE;   DESOXYBUFOTENINE; NIGERINE

SYNTHESIS: (from N,N,N-trimethyltryptammonium iodide, dimethyltryptamine methiodide, DMT·CH$_3$I): This quaternary salt is prepared from tryptamine and methyl iodide. To a stirred solution of 3 g tryptamine in 30 mL IPA there was added 10 g methyl iodide. Cream-colored solids appeared immediately and, after 12 h stirring at room temperature, these were removed by filtration, washed twice with warm IPA, and air dried to constant weight. There was thus obtained 1.81 g N,N,N-trimethyltryptammonium iodide. Recrystallization of an analytical sample from acetonitrile gave a white crystalline product with a mp of 210-211 °C. IR (in cm$^{-1}$): 767, 919, 953, 978, 1105, with a sharp stretch at 3400. In principle, DMT is contained in the filtrate along with NMT and tryptamine itself. The tryptamine can be removed based on its ether insolubility and the NMT by its conversion to the benzamide with acetic anhydride or benzoyl chloride. The remaining basic material is largely DMT which can be further purified as the picrate salt. The yield is minuscule, and better results are obtained by the demethylation of this salt.

The demethylation of the iodide salt: Under an inert atmosphere, a solution of 0.40 g N,N,N-trimethyltryptammonium iodide in 5 mL THF was treated with 1.5 mL of 1M LiEt$_3$BH in THF and held at reflux temperature for 9 h. After cooling, the mixture was acidified with dilute HCl and the THF removed under vacuum. The residue was suspended in dilute NaOH and extracted with Et$_2$O. The extracts were pooled, and the solvent removed under vacuum to provide a residue of 0.12 g N,N-dimethyltryptamine (DMT) as a crystalline solid, with a mp of 57-59 °C. IR (in cm$^{-1}$): 732, 740, 811, 859, 1011, 1037, 1110, 1171. The MS is discussed below.

The demethylation of the chloride salt: A hot aqueous solution of N,N,N-trimethyltryptammonium iodide was treated with an excess of freshly precipitated AgCl, and all was boiled gently for 15 min. The mixed silver halides were removed by filtration, and the filtrate stripped of $H_2O$ as rapidly as possible. To the residue there was added a small amount of MeOH follow by acetone until the crystallization of N,N,N-trimethyltryptammonium chloride was complete. It had a mp of 193 °C (80%), and was considerably more water soluble than the starting iodide. This salt was pyrolysed under hard vacuum and the residue distilled. This distillate was dissolved in a small amount of MeOH and acidified with dilute nitric acid. A small amount of insoluble material was removed by filtration, the aqueous phase washed with CHCl$_3$, made basic with aqueous NaOH, and extracted with CHCl$_3$. The solvent was removed under vacuum, and the residue treated with a hot solution of picric acid. This was decanted from a little insoluble material, and slowly cooled to provide the picrate of DMT as yellow needles with a mp of 167 °C. An aqueous suspension of this picrate was made basic with an excess of aqueous NaOH, extracted with Et$_2$O, and the solvent removed under vacuum to provide a pale, yellow residue that crystallized. This was pressed on a porous plate and washed with petroleum ether to give N,N-dimethyltryptamine (DMT) as an off-white solid with a mp of 47 °C.

The demethylation of the thiophenolate salt: A suspension of 2.5 g N,N,N-trimethyltryptammonium iodide in 25 mL MeOH was brought into solution by heating, and treated with 1.0 g Ag$_2$O. The mixture was heated for 10 min on the steam bath, the solids removed by filtration and washed with an additional 20 mL MeOH. The MeOH solutions were treated with 1.0 g thiophenol and the solvent was removed under vacuum. The resulting viscous oil (2.12 g) was heated with a flame to the reflux point and there was extensive bubbling. After 5 min, the light colored reaction mixture was cooled to room temperature, dissolved in 50 mL CH$_2$Cl$_2$, and extracted with two 25 mL portions of dilute HCl. These were pooled (pale yellow color), made basic with 5% aqueous NaOH and extracted with 3x25 mL CH$_2$Cl$_2$. After removal of the solvent from the pooled extracts, the residue (an amber oil, 1.04 g) was distilled at the KugelRohr. A white oil distilled over at 130-140 °C at 0.1 mm/Hg, and crystallized spontaneously. This distillate weighed 0.77 g, and was recrystallized from boiling hexane after decanting the solution from a small amount of insolubles. There was thus obtained 0.40 g of dimethyltryptamine (DMT) with a mp 67-68 °C. The distillate contained about 3% of 2-Methyl-1,2,3,4-tetrahydro-β-carboline (parent peak mass 186, major peak mass 143) as an impurity which was lost upon recrystallization.

(from tryptamine and ethyl formate) A suspension of 1.0 g tryptamine in 50 mL ethyl formate was held at reflux for 15 h during which time the mixture became homogeneous. The volatiles were removed under vacuum, yielding an oily residue of the formamide. This may be purified by distillation but this unpurified product can serve satisfactorily in the following reaction. This residue was dissolved in 50 mL anhydrous THF and added, dropwise, to a solution of 1.0 M LAH in THF (40 mL, 40 mmole) which had been diluted with another 50 mL THF. After the addition was complete the reaction mixture was heated under reflux for 15 hours. Reflux was continued as a solution of 40 mL 1.0 M freshly distilled ethyl formate in THF was added dropwise over the course of 2 h. Heating was discontinued and the reaction mixture was quenched by the addition of excess solid sodium sulfate decahydrate at room temperature. The reaction mixture was filtered and the filtrate was concentrated under vacuum to yield 1.15 g pure N,N-dimethyltryptamine as an oil which solidified upon storage in the freezer. The material can be recrystallized from hexane to give white crystals with a mp of 67 °C.

(from indole) To a well-stirred solution of 10 g indole in 150 mL anhydrous $Et_2O$ there was added, dropwise over the course of 30 min, a solution of 11 g oxalyl chloride in 150 mL anhydrous $Et_2O$. Stirring was continued for an additional 15 min during which time there was the separation of indol-3-ylglyoxyl chloride as a yellow, crystalline solid. This intermediate was removed by filtration and washed with $Et_2O$. It deteriorates at a significant rate at room temperature, and should be used as soon as possible after preparation. The diethylether in this synthesis can be replaced advantageously with t-butylmethylether (TBME) which works well as a solvent in this reaction, but which avoids the potential danger associated with peroxide formation. The above indol-3-ylglyoxyl chloride was added to 20 g anhydrous dimethylamine in 150 mL cold, stirred anhydrous $Et_2O$. When the color had largely been discharged, there was added an excess of 2N HCl, the mixture was cooled, and the resulting solids were removed by filtration. These were recrystallized from EtOAc to give, after air drying, 14.6 g (79%) indol-3-yl-N,N-dimethylglyoxylamide with a mp of 159-161 °C.

A solution of 14 g indol-3-yl-N,N-dimethylglyoxylamide in 350 mL anhydrous THF was added, slowly, to 19 g LAH in 350 mL THF which was well-stirred and held at reflux temperature under an inert atmosphere. After the addition was complete, reflux was maintained for an additional 16 h, the reaction mixture cooled, and the excess hydride destroyed by the cautious addition of wet dioxane. The formed solids were removed by filtration, washed with hot THF, the filtrate and washings combined, dried over anhydrous $MgSO_4$, and the solvent removed under vacuum. The residue was dissolved in hot petroleum ether. On cooling, crystals of N,N-dimethyltryptamine (DMT) were formed, filtered free of solvent, and air dried, weighing 11.1 g (91%). There have been reports of byproducts from this LAH procedure when performed in $Et_2O$ that can compromise the purity of the final product. To obtain the HCl salt of DMT, the residue was dissolved in anhydrous

Et$_2$O and saturated with anhydrous hydrogen chloride. The resulting crystals were recrystallized from benzene/methanol to give N,N-dimethyltryptamine hydrochloride with a mp of 165-167 °C. The yield from 14 g of the amide was 13.3 g of the salt.

There are several comments to be made as to salts, melting points, and spectra.

As to salts, this last recipe above, taken from the literature, is the only claim of a valid hydrochloride salt of DMT. In the original synthesis, by Manske, the following description appears. "The hydrochloride could be obtained only as a pale yellow resin which, when dried in a vacuum desiccator over potassium hydroxide, became porous and brittle." I have found no attempts at its synthesis in the literature, and I have personally had no success at all. The picrate salt is well defined, used mostly for isolation and purification. The oxalate is used occasionally in animal studies. Early human studies involved the injection of solutions of the hydrochloride apparently made by dissolving DMT base in dilute aqueous HCl, and neutralizing this with base to achieve an end pH of appropriate 6. The fumarate is the salt specifically approved by the FDA for human studies, and this was the form used for human intravenous injection employed in the recent New Mexico studies.

As to melting points, some in the literature are of plant isolates and others are of synthetic samples. A brief and incomplete survey has revealed the following numbers, all in °C: 44, 44.6-46.8, 46, 47, 48-49, 49-50, 56-57, 57-59, 58-60, 64-67, 67 and 67-68. The 58-60 and 64-67 values are from the Aldrich Chemical Company, samples bearing the purity claims of "puriss" and 99+% "Gold Label" resp. The Merck Index gives the very early, very low values of 46 °C and 44.6-46.8 °C and claims that the bp is 60-80 °C with atmospheric pressure being implied. It is clearly in error on both matters. No evidence has been published suggesting polymorphism. The published mp values for the trimethyl quaternary iodide span the range from 188 °C to 233 °C, including in-between values of 197 °C and 216-217 °C. This physical property is of limited value.

As to spectra, the EI-MS of DMT presents no surprises. MS (in m/z): C$_3$H$_8$N$^+$ 58 (100%), indolemethylene$^+$ 130 (10%); parent ion 188 (4%). DMT had a CI-MS (with NH$_3$) with the expected M+1 at mass 189 and a fragment at mass 166.

DOSAGE:  >350 mg (orally)
            60 - 100 mg (intramuscularly)
            60 - 100 mg (subcutaneously)
            60 - 100 mg (smoked)
            4 - 30 mg (intravenously)

DURATION:  Up to 1 h

QUALITATIVE COMMENTS: (with 150 mg, orally) "No observable psychic or vegetative effects."

(with 250 mg, orally) "It was inactive."

(with 350 mg, orally) "Completely without effect either physiological or psychological."

(with 100 mg, via the buccal mucosa) "Numbness at the site, but no central effects."

(with 20 mg, intramuscularly) "I began to see patterns on the wall that were continuously moving. They were transparent, and were not colored. After a short period these patterns became the heads of animals, a fox, a snake, a dragon. Then kaleidoscopic images appeared to me in my inner eye, fantastically beautiful and colored."

(with 30 mg, intramuscularly) "There was eye dilation and, subjectively, some perception disturbances."

(with 50 mg, intramuscularly) "I feel strange, everything is blurry. I want my mother, I am afraid of fainting, I can't breathe."

(with 60 mg, intramuscularly) "I don't like this feeling — I am not myself. I saw such strange dreams a while ago. Strange creatures, dwarfs or something; they were black and moved about. Now I feel as if I am not alive. My left hand is numb. As if my heart would not beat, as if I had no body, no nothing. All I feel are my left hand and stomach. I don't like to be without thoughts."

(with 75 mg, intramuscularly) "The third or fourth minute after the injection vegetative symptoms appeared, such as tingling sensation, trembling, slight nausea, mydriasis, elevation of the blood pressure and increase of the pulse rate. At the same time, eidetic phenomena, optical illusions, pseudohallucinations, and later real hallucinations, appeared. The hallucinations consisted of moving, brilliantly colored oriental motifs, and later I saw wonderful scenes altering very rapidly. The faces of people seemed to be masks. My emotional state was elevated sometimes up to euphoria. At the highest point I had compulsive athetoid movements in my left hand. My consciousness was completely filled by hallucinations, and my attention was firmly bound to them; therefore I could not give an account of the events happening to me. After 3/4 to 1 hour the symptoms disappeared, and I was able to describe what had happened."

(with 80 mg, intramuscularly) "My perceptual distortions were visual in nature and with my eyes closed I could see colored patterns, primarily geometrical patterns moving very fast, having sometimes very deep emotional content and connotation. My blood pressure went up and my pupils were dilated."

(with 30 mg, smoked) "I spread it evenly on a joint of *Tanacetum vulgare* and melted it with a heat lamp. In about 30 seconds a strong light-headedness started, with a feeling of temporal pressure. Some yellowing of the visual field. There was nothing for me to do because I had to turn complete control over to the drug. Off the plateau in 3-4 minutes and the fact that the radio was on became apparent. I was out in a few more minutes."

(with 60 mg, smoked) "We did it together. Swift entry — head overwhelmed — elaborate and exotic. Slightly threatening patterns — no insight — slight sense of cruelty and sharpness between us, but enjoying. His face, as before with MDA, demonic but pleasantly so. He said he saw my face as a mask. He asked me to let him see my teeth. I laughed — aware that laughter was slightly not-funny. Heavy, massive intoxication. Time extension extraordinary. What seemed like 2 hours was about 30 minutes."

(with 60 mg, smoked) "Rapid onset, and in a completely stoned isolation in about a minute for about three minutes. Slow return but continued afterglow (pleasant) for thirty minutes. Repeated three times, with no apparent tolerance or change in chronology. Easily handled. The intoxication is of limited usefulness but the residues are completely relaxing,"

(with 100 mg, smoked) "As I exhaled I became terribly afraid, my heart very rapid and strong, palms sweating. A terrible sense of dread and doom filled me — I knew what was happening, I knew I couldn't stop it, but it was so devastating; I was being destroyed — all that was familiar, all reference points, all identity — all viciously shattered in a few seconds. I couldn't even mourn the loss — there was no one left to do the mourning. Up, up, out, out, eyes closed, I am at the speed of light, expanding, expanding, expanding, faster and faster until I have become so large that I no longer exist — my speed is so great that everything has come to a stop — here I gaze upon the entire universe."

(with 15 mg, intravenously) "An almost instantaneous rush began in the head and I was quickly scattered. Rapidly moving and intensely colored visuals were there, and I got into some complex scenes. There were few sounds, and those that were there were not of anyone talking. I was able to continue to think clearly."

(with 30 mg, intravenously) "I was hit harder than I had ever been when smoking the stuff. The onset was similar, but the euphoria was less."

EXTENSIONS AND COMMENTARY: There is a staggering body of information on the subject of intoxicating snuffs and their use throughout the area of the Caribbean, the Amazon, and on to the west, past the Andes, in Colombia and Peru. The literature that has accumulated over the last forty or so years is fascinating, but extremely difficult to organize. The problem lies in deciding which discipline shall dictate the hierarchy of classification. Does one organize by snuff name? But each different tribe will use a different name. Does one classify by the plants employed? This requires actual observation in the field, but a given plant may have several native names. And one snuff may use any of several different plants or plant combinations, depending on cultural tradition. To add uncertainty to this complexity, these traditions are being rapidly lost, with the eradication of folklore. So perhaps one should turn to the snuff itself, and classify according to the chemical composition. This is appealing in that there are many museum samples available, as well as a host of anthropological artifacts such as snuff trays and botanical residues that can be identified. But that is a luxury that requires the sophistication of the laboratory, and precludes any botanic assignment.

No matter which system might eventually prove to be the best, the use of a chemical assignment of drug structure to the active components allows some form of clinical challenge to the native use in the field. DMT and 5-MeO-DMT are the mainstay chemicals in most snuffs, and can be introduced into the product from any of several plants.

A major plant source for one of the best studied of the snuffs, cohoba, are the ground beans of the *Piptadenia peregrina*. There are two alternative generic names, *Anadenanthera* and *Mimosa,* which may represent the same, or similar, plants, but this is the stuff for battles between botanical taxonomists. There are several species in this classification, and the alkaloid content amongst them is most variable. With *P. peregrina* and *P. macrocarpa*, the major contents of the beans and their pods appear to be bufotenine, its N-oxide and the oxide of DMT. It may be only the pods of the seeds that contain the DMT. And the bark seems to be the major source of N-methyltryptamine, of 5-MeO-NMT (its 5-methoxy analogue) and of 5-MeO-DMT itself. The species *P. columbrina* is reported to have bufotenine in its seeds as the only active component. This plant, in Argentina, occurs in only two major species, *P. macrocarpa* and *P. excelsa*, and the composition seems to parallel that of the Amazonian counterparts. Other forms, (*P. rigida, P. paraguayensis,* and *P. varidiflora)*, are without any alkaloid content.

The native intoxicant search becomes even cloudier as one goes from snuff to decoction. There are several drinks, sometimes described as "narcotic" and sometimes as hallucinogenic or dream-inducing, that come from closely related plants. The roots of the acacia-like tree, *Mimosa hostilis,* are reputed to be the source of the drink jurema, or vihno de jurema. But the only alkaloid present, originally called nigerine, has proved to be DMT, and this is not orally active. There are pasture grasses, such as reed canarygrass, that can produce a central nervous system disruption in grazing sheep. Chemical analyses of these plants (such as *Phalaris tuberosa, P. arundinacea,* and *P. aquatica)* have revealed the presence of alkaloids like DMT and 5-MeO-DMT, but these compounds require intravenous administration to duplicate the toxicity symptoms. The observation of 5-MeO-NMT being present does not help explain the toxicity. How can something that is not orally active be orally active? A possible explanation is the presence of another indole with a one-carbon shorter chain. This is gramine, or 3-(N,N-dimethylaminomethyl)indole which is synthesized in the plant with an entirely different set of enzymes. Its human pharmacology is not known. Incidently, a related homologue, one carbon longer, is the three-carbon chain compound 3-[3-(dimethylamino)propyl]indole, produced by the Upjohn Company. It has been studied clinically under the code name U-6056, at levels of up to 70 milligrams in 10 subjects, by i.m. injection. There were no reports of visual, auditory or tactile disturbances. Physically, there was a slight increase in blood pressure and pulse rate. Certainly there were no psychological effects. It, however, is a synthetic laboratory product and does not have any botanical source.

The drink ayahuasca is also a DMT-containing decoction, but the presence of some harmaline-containing plant is required to make it active by mouth. This area is discussed under harmaline, although there is some information to be found in the 5-MeO-DMT commentary section. And there are several species of *Acacia* found in both Africa and Australia that contain DMT, but there is no native medical use that suggests psychotropic action. These concepts are the part and parcel of two chapters in the first part of this book, "DMT is Everywhere" and "Hoasca vs. Ayahuasca." There is no reason to repeat it all here.

In the early clinical studies of DMT and DET, frequent use was made of schizophrenic patients, in the belief that if these drugs imitate the mental disorder in normal subjects, the use of schizophrenic populations might be especially informative, either through some enhanced response or perhaps a lack of response. One clinical study with a group of female patients (with 1.0 or 1.5 mg/Kg DMT being administered, presumably by intramuscular injection) showed a delayed onset (doubling of time), a relative freedom from autonomic effects, and an absence of hallucinations. I truly admire the logic patterns that allow the construction of a research study that will have it either way. Positive effects, our hypothesis is supported. Negative effects, our hypothesis is supported. Do schitzies get better or do they get worse? See? We were right.

A study conducted on 40 normals, this in Hungary some 30 years ago, found the administration of 40 mg of DMT alone to be symptom-free. With several of the experimental subjects in this study, the DMT was preceded by the administration of 1-methyl-d-lysergic acid butanolamide (UML-491), a potent serotonin antagonist. This was given either orally (1-2 mg 30 to 40 minutes before) or intramuscularly (0.5 mg 10 minutes before). This served to greatly amplify the effects of the DMT, with vivid and agitated hallucinations, highly intensified colors, and a more extreme loss of time and space perception. It was assumed that UML-491 was inactive, but recent trials indicate that there can be central effects produced. This ergot derivative is discussed in the entry for LSD.

DMT is the only psychedelic tryptamine that has recently been taken through the Kafkaesque processes for approval for human studies (via the FDA, the DEA, and the other Health agencies of the Government) and is one of the few Schedule I drugs that is being looked at clinically in this country today. It has been studied in Albuquerque, New Mexico. The first published results of this study show a smooth grading of subjective effects as a function of injected dose. The lowest dose (i.v.) was 0.05 mg/Kg, about 4 milligrams, and it could not be distinguished from placebo. At 8 milligrams, there were the physical effects without the mental. At 15 milligrams (the threshold psychedelic dose) nearly all subjects had visual hallucinations, but auditory changes were rare. At 30 milligrams, the effects were overwhelming both in speed and in intensity. The rush, the freight-train as several subjects call it, was underway well before the 45 second infusion was complete. A study of repeated administrations of dosages of 16 mg i.v., at half-hour intervals, was made to explore the possible development of short-term tolerance and none was observed.

In the definition of DMT either as an endogenous psychotogen or, equally appealing, as a natural neurotransmitter, it would be desirable to show that the body does not build up long-term tolerance to it (otherwise the psychotic would spontaneously repair, and the brain would spontaneously shut down). To address this, four subjects were given some 50 mg of DMT intramuscularly, twice daily, for 5 days. The blood levels that were achieved, and the picture of autonomic effects (both in mydriasis and in cardiovascular function) were not changed. No tolerance was seen. The psychological conclusions were a little bit less convincing. Several subjects said that the "high" was diminished, but others seemed to feel a maintenance of subjective responses. The jury is still out on this one.

Thanks to the developement of ever-increasingly sensitive scientific instruments, the search of body fluids for possible psychedelics has brought forth a number that appear to be natural components of the human animal. DMT has been reported to be in the urine of schizophrenic patients, and so have 5-MeO-DMT, bufotenine, and its demethylated homologue N-methylserotonin. The levels are increased with the administration of monoamineoxidase inhibitors. A methylating enzyme has been found in blood, capable of forming DMT in plasma, and it is present in both normal subjects and schizophrenics. It is not surprising that studies comparing DMT blood levels between patients (psychotic depression, acute and chronic schizophrenia) and normal subjects have shown no differences. The ubiquitous nature of DMT touches upon a couple of delicate points. It was first a man-made compound, synthesized in Canada in the early thirties. Then some twenty years later it was discovered in the plant world as a natural product. This puts a delicate weapon in the hands of the "natural is better than synthetic" argument often voiced. Then, as mentioned here, it has proven to be a natural, normal component of human metabolism, making the wording of Federal Drug law interesting, as the section in the Schedule I hallucinogens implies (in a phrase that lacks a verb and hence a specific meaning) that the possession of any quantity of any form of any listed substance (such as DMT) is illegal. Our brains are illegal?

The principal reason that DMT must be administered parenterally is its rapid and efficient metabolism. It can be oxidized to the N-oxide. It can be cyclized to β-carbolines, both with and without an N-methyl group. It can be N-dealkylated to form NMT and simple tryptamine itself. Best known is its oxidative destruction, by the monoamine oxidase system, to the inactive indoleacetic acid. There is a wild biochemical conversion process known for tryptophan that involves an enzymatic conversion to kynurenine by the removal of the indole-2-carbon. A similar product, N,N-dimethylkynurenine or DMK, has been seen with DMT, when it was added to whole human blood in vitro.

Several simple substitution derivatives of DMT are known. Those that are known to be psychedelic have their own recipes, of course, but the others will be summarized here. The 1-methyl homologue of DMT (1,N,N-trimethyltryptamine) can be prepared from DMT in KOH and DMSO, with $CH_3I$. It forms a picrate salt which melts at 175-179 °C, and bioxalate, mp 174-176 °C. It is more toxic than DMT in rats, but has an identical serotonin binding capacity. The compound with a methoxy group substituent at the 1-position is called Lespedamine, 1-MeO-DMT. With an NO bond, this should be classified as a substituted hydroxylamine. I would love to know if anyone anywhere has ever tried smoking it. I suspect it might very well be active, but it is, to my knowledge, untried. I wonder why it deserves a trivial name, vis., Lespedamine? Two additional ring-substituted derivatives of DMT come from the marine world. 5-Bromo-DMT and 5,6-dibromo-DMT are found in the sponges *Smenospongia auria* and *S. echina*, resp. I have no idea if they are active by smoking (the 5-Br-DMT just might be) but they are quantitatively reduced to DMT by stirring under hydrogen in methanol, in the presence of palladium on charcoal. A very closely related sponge, *Polyfibrospongia maynardii*, contains the very closely related 5,6-dibromotryptamine and the corresponding monomethyl NMT. I have the fantasy of trying to scotch the rumor I'm about to start, that all the hippies of the San Francisco Bay Area were heading to the Caribbean with packets of Zig-Zag papers, to hit the sponge trade with a psychedelic fervor. This is not true. I refuse to take credit for this myth.

The demethylated homologue mentioned above is N-methyltryptamine (NMT) and it is also widely distributed in nature. It has a synthesis in an entry of its own.

Both the N-hydroxy and the 2-hydroxy analogues of NMT are found in another legume, *Desmanthus illinoensis*, but have not been pharmacologically evaluated. Another provocative mono-alkyl analogue of DMT is N-cyclopropyltryptamine, made from indole-3-yl-glyoxyl chloride and benzyl cyclopropylamine with eventual hydrogenolysis of the benzyl group; mp 180-182 °C. This compound, as with the 5-methoxy and the 7-methoxy counterparts, is a potent monoamineoxidase inhibitor, and it has also been reported to have hypoglycemic activity. The 2-methyl-homologue of NMT was made from 2-methyl-3-(2-bromoethyl)tryptamine and methylamine. This is 2,Me-DMT (or 2,N,N-TMT). Both it and tryptamine itself (T) have their own entries.

Before this is closed, three points can be made regarding nomenclature. Older literature uses alpha for the 2-position of the indole ring. Thus, alpha-methyltryptamine, in early literature, refers to the indole-2-methyl, not to a side-chain methyl derivative. Throughout *TIHKAL*, the numbers are devoted to the indole ring, and the alpha and beta terms to the side-chain. And the use of the letter N refers to the side-chain amino nitrogen atom. The pyrrole nitrogen is the indole position 1. And finally, I found in my old files a news announcement (dated March 25, 1974) that Hercules Chemical Company intends to build a big DMT plant in the Southern United States, with an annual capacity of 800 million pounds a year. In the industrial world, DMT can also stand for dimethylterephthalate.

**#7.  2,α-DMT; TRYPTAMINE, 2,α-DIMETHYL; INDOLE, 2-METHYL-3-(2-AMINO)PROPANE; 2-α-DIMETHYLTRYPTAMINE; 2-METHYL-3-(2-AMINO)PROPYLINDOLE; 2-Me-α-MT; ALPHA-2**

SYNTHESIS: A solution of 4.78 g 2-methylindole-3-carboxaldehyde in 18 mL of nitroethane was treated with 0.77 g anhydrous ammonium acetate and heated on the steam bath for 2 h. The excess nitroethane was removed under vacuum and the residual orange-red solids were removed and washed with $H_2O$. After drying these were triturated under 25 mL MeOH, filtered and air-dried to constant weight. There was thus obtained 3.8 g (59%) of 1-(2-methylindol-3-yl)-2-nitropropene with a mp 146-148 °C.

To 250 mL of a room-temperature 1.0 M solution of LAH in THF, well-stirred and under $N_2$, there was added a saturated solution of 3.6 g 1-(2-methylindol-3-yl)-2-nitropropene in warm THF. The addition took place over 1.25 h, the reaction mixture was stirred for an additional 8 h, and then held at 40 °C for 8 more h. The slurry was then cooled in an ice bath and decomposed by the slow, sequential addition of 30 mL isopropyl acetate, 20 mL $H_2O$ and, finally, 20 mL of 20% aqueous NaOH. The resulting alkaline suspension was extracted with 3x100 mL isopropyl acetate. The extracts were pooled, washed with 3x50 mL 10% aqueous NaOH, then extracted with 10% aqueous acetic acid. This extract was washed with isopropyl acetate, made basic with 20% aqueous NaOH, and extracted with 3x50 mL $CHCl_3$. These extracts were pooled, dried with anhydrous $Na_2SO_4$ and, after removal of the drying agent by filtration, the solvent was removed under vacuum. The residual yellow oil was distilled under vacuum, at 150-160 °C at 1.8 mm/Hg, to give a pale yellow product. This was dissolved in a few mL MeOH and neutralized with a solution of fumaric acid in MeOH. The clear solution was heated and diluted with two volumes of hot isopropyl acetate. On cooling, fine white crystals of α,2-dimethyltryptamine fumarate (2,α-DMT) were deposited. These were removed by filtration, and air-dried to constant weight. The yield was 1.64 g (60%) of a product with a mp of 209-211 °C.

DOSAGE:  300 - 500 mg, orally

DURATION:  7 - 10 h

QUALITATIVE COMMENTS:  (with 200 mg, orally) "I feel just a little bit intoxicated. Probably few if any effects."

(with 300 mg, orally) "It was an hour before I realized that something was happening. Very subtle, some tingling of the face, the lights are somehow brighter. Really laid back, try to let my fantasy go with closing my eyes and sitting quietly, but it mostly just felt good to sit quiet. I feel that I am on the edge of something here, but I see it slipping away. "

(with 450 mg, orally) "It was almost as if I had had a drink too many. I was feeling good, but I tried turning the dial on the radio to find music, and the fine motor coordination in my hands was not there. My thinking was completely clear, and the music I finally found was fine for day-dreaming. There were some flashes on the edge of my visual field and things seemed to feel softer and richer. Eating was quite an adventure in tastes, but I really couldn't eat much. Very peaceful, and an easy sleep took over at about the 13th hour. Next day, still pretty dehydrated. All in all, it was a very nice experience."

EXTENSIONS AND COMMENTARY: I do love the satisfying feeling that comes with the successful assignment of a pharmacological change as a function of a single structural change. This is the holy grail of every SAR enthusiast (SAR = Structure Activity Relationship). Make a change in structure, see a corresponding change in activity. There is a correlation. There is causality. And there you have a new, firmly established fact of science to add to the understanding of the universe.

A case in point. What happens when you put a methyl group on the two-position of the indole ring of a tryptamine? In the three examples, examples of the best-studied tryptamines that were not active orally, they all became orally active. DMT, DET and 5-MeO-DMT, the three major parenterally-only active psychedelics, all blossomed into orally active compounds with the addition of a simple methyl group to that indole 2-position. As I had smugly argued in the discussions of 2-Me-DMT, 2-Me-DET and 5-MeO-TMT, it is as if that bit of bulk got in the way of the destructive amine oxidases, and protected the molecule from its expected first-pass metabolic destruction.

So what happens here? You take a compound, α-MT, that is already immune to this oxidase system and is already orally active. Add a 2-methyl group to give 2-Me-α-MT (or 2,α-DMT). And what happens? The potency goes down, not up, and by a factor of 10 times. And it ends up being more of a sedative than a stimulant. It would be neat to take advantage of the chiral center (as with α,O-DMT) and see which optical isomer has the sedative properties.

So much for generalities. I suspect that I do not understand the universe nearly as well as I thought I did.

## #8.    α,N-DMT;    TRYPTAMINE,    α,N-DIMETHYL;    INDOLE,    3-[2-(METHYLAMINO)PROPYL];    α,N-DIMETHYLTRYPTAMINE;    3-[2-(METHYLAMINO)PROPYL]INDOLE;    ALPHA-N

SYNTHESIS: (from indoleacetone) To a solution of 1.55 g NaOAc in 5 mL acetic anhydride there was added 2.0 g 3-indoleacetic acid and the mixture was heated at

135-140 °C for 18 h. Removal of all volatiles on the rotary evaporator under vacuum produced a pale yellow residue that was the 1-acetylindole-3-acetone. This was dissolved in MeOH to which 0.93 g MeONa was added, and the solution held a reflux several hours. After removal of the solvent under vacuum, the residue was suspended in $H_2O$ and extracted with several portions of $Et_2O$. These extracts were pooled, and removal of the solvent under vacuum gave 0.41 g (21%) indole-3-acetone as a white solid, mp 115-117 °C. MS (in m/z): indolemethylene$^+$ 130 (100%); parent ion 173 (16%). IR (in cm$^{-1}$): 691, 753, 761, 780, 1017, 1110, 1172, and a broad C=O at 1710.

To 1 g shredded aluminum foil there was added a solution of 20 mg $HgCl_2$ in 15 mL $H_2O$. After 15 min the amalgamated aluminum was drained free of the mercury solution, well washed with fresh $H_2O$, and shaken as dry as possible. There was then added, in sequence, a solution of 1.5 g methylamine hydrochloride in 2 mL $H_2O$, 3 mL of 25% NaOH, 5 mL of IPA, and finally 1 g of indol-3-ylacetone in 20 mL IPA. This was stirred for 1 h, then heated briefly on the steam bath. After cooling, the reaction mixture was filtered and the solids washed with MeOH, the washing and filtrate combined, and stripped of solvent under vacuum. The residue was dissolved in 200 mL $H_2O$, made acidic with HCl, washed with $CH_2Cl_2$, treated with aqueous NaOH to a pH of greater than 9 (becomes cloudy), and extracted with 2x50 mL $CH_2Cl_2$. Removal of the solvent from the combined extracts gave a light brown oil which distilled at 125-135 °C at 0.4 mm/Hg to give 0.74 g of a viscous oil. This was dissolved in 5 mL IPA, neutralized with concentrated HCl and diluted with anhydrous $Et_2O$ to the point of turbidity. After standing, the solids were removed, washed with $Et_2O$ and air dried, to yield 0.87 g of $\alpha$,N-dimethyltryptamine hydrochloride ($\alpha$,N-DMT) as white crystals. MS (in m/z): $C_3H_8N^+$ 58 (100%); indolemethylene$^+$ 131-130 (19, 14%); parent ion 188, just above noise level.

Alternately, the indol-3-ylacetone can be catalytically reduced in the presence of methylamine. A solution of 3.3 g indol-3-ylacetone in 100 mL EtOH was hydrogenated over Pd-C catalyst in the presence of an excess of methylamine. After 2 h the catalyst was removed by filtration, the filtrate stripped of solvent under vacuum, the residue dissolved in $H_2O$ and made acidic. After washing with $Et_2O$, the aqueous phase was made alkaline, and the solids that formed were removed by filtration and recrystallized from a mixture of hexane and THF. The product, $\alpha$,N-dimethyltryptamine ($\alpha$,N-DMT), was a tan solid that weighed 2.2 g and had a mp of 93-94 °C. The picrate is brick red from EtOH, and melted at 207-208 °C.

(from $\alpha$-MT) A solution of 4.4 g alpha-methyltryptamine ($\alpha$-MT) in 5.5 g acetic anhydride containing 3.1 g HOAc and 2.4 g $HCO_2H$ was stirred at room temperature for 18 h. All volatiles were removed under vacuum at a temperature of less than 40 °C which left a syrup as a residue. To this was added 100 mL $H_2O$ and extracted with several portions of $Et_2O$ which were combined and the solvent removed under vacuum. There remained 4.9 g (95%) of α-methyl-N-formyltryptamine which was used as such in the next step. This was dissolved in 30 mL anhydrous THF and this solution was added to a gently refluxing suspension of 3.7 g LAH in 30 mL THF, under nitrogen, and the reflux was continued for 16 h. After cooling, the excess hydride was destroyed by the careful addition of wet THF followed by sufficient aqueous NaOH to produce a solid that can be easily removed by filtration. After filtration, the filtrate was stripped of solvent under vacuum and the residue (4.3 g) crystallized from benzene/petroleum ether to give 2.5 g (56%) of α,N-dimethyltryptamine (α,N-DMT) as a solid with a mp of 90-91 °C. The N-ethyl homologue, made in a similar way from α-methyl-N-acetyltryptamine, had a mp 187-189 °C.

DOSAGE: 50 - 100 mg, orally

DURATION: 6 - 8 h

QUALITATIVE COMMENTS: (with 50 mg, orally) "Something was going on, and it was rather strong a couple of hours into it, but there doesn't seem to be anything particularly psychedelic here. I am wakeful and alert, maybe a little bit starry-eyed as if I were wearing glasses with the wrong prescription. Maybe a little bit light-headed as well. It was several hours before these physical discomforts disappeared."

(with 75 mg, orally) "Compulsive sneezing, and quite uncomfortable. Urpy. Tried eating some quiche, and couldn't do it — no appetite at all. Pulse seems to be proper, but it is almost as if I were using speed without any of the stimulant virtues. After about three or four hours I am losing the buzziness property and am pretty much normal in three or four more hours. Still some teeth clench. Sleep OK. I'm not sure that going higher is worth it. Or even repeating it. Why?"

EXTENSIONS AND COMMENTARY: The relationship between α-MT (alpha-methyltryptamine) and this compound, α,N-DMT (alpha,N-dimethyltryptamine) is exactly analogous to that seen with the phenethylamine counterparts, between amphetamine (alpha-methylphenethylamine) and methamphetamine (alpha,N-dimethylphenethylamine). Both the primary and the secondary amine compounds retain activity. In the amphetamine camp, both compounds are dramatic stimulants showing a complete spectrum of sympathomimetic properties including cardiovascular excitement, loss of appetite, and sleeplessness. Here, the tryptamine counterparts are similar to one another, but it is not as clear that they are stimulants. In animal studies, they have been compared with each other and with amphetamine. Except for the speed of onset, both tryptamines caused amphetamine-like behavior in activity cages, but required some 10 times the dosage of amphetamine. In man there are some suggestions of this, the loss of appetite, the buzzy lightheadedness, and the absence of any of the usual suggestions of psychedelic action.

I mentioned an appealing hypothesis in the commentary on α-MT, and it is applicable here. Both of these materials, α-MT and α,N-DMT, are effective monoamine oxidase inhibitors. Both of these materials show some of the syndrome that has been described for the monoamine oxidase inhibitors of the beta-carboline family. It would be interesting to design and conduct a study into the role that either of these might play in promoting the oral activity of the materials of ayahuasca that are deaminated and thus deactivated when taken alone. This entire argument could and should embrace the methoxylated counterpart, α,N,O-TMS. I am not aware of any studies that have been made as to its deaminase enzymatic effectiveness, but it too fulfills that nausea, discomfort, un-psychedelic pattern shown here. The expected increase in potency due to the 5-methoxy group is proper, making it a more potent compound than either of these two. It has its own entry.

In all of these cases, the adding of an additional methyl group to the nitrogen atom makes a tertiary amine. In the phenethylamine analogy, one gets N,N-dimethylamphetamine. This compound appeared in a couple of clandestine methamphetamine laboratories a few years ago, as a result of the cooks substituting N-methylephedrine for the customary precursor, ephedrine. Although animal studies on N,N-dimethylamphetamine showed it to have little if any stimulant properties, the authorities reasoned that since it had appeared in an illicit context (potentially being peddled as a street drug) it had a real abuse potential. And since it had no recognized medical utility, its obvious resting spot was in Schedule I of the Controlled Substances Act. And there it was, indeed, placed.

The application of this structural modification to the tryptamine area gives alpha,N,N-trimethyltryptamine (α,N,N-TMT). The tertiary amine in the phenethylamine, N,N-dimethylamphetamine, showed a loss in its stimulant nature. Here, the adding of that additional methyl group gives a tertiary amine that has the skeleton of DMT. This base has been reported as having been made by either of two different routes, both starting with indole. Reaction with propyleneoxide gave the 1-(indol-3-yl)-2-propanol which was treated first with PBr$_3$ followed by dimethylamine. Or, reaction with chloropropionyl chloride gave a 1,3-bis interme-diate which was converted to the amino ketone 3-[2-(dimethylamino)propionyl]-indole with dimethylamine. This was reduced to the same product, α,N,N-TMT, with LAH. The bimaleate salt had a mp of 139-140 °C.

Another parallel exists between the amphetamine world and the tryptamine world. Rather than adding a second methyl group to the terminal nitrogen, simply keep the one methyl group that is there and lengthen it by another carbon atom. Make the methyl into an ethyl. With the amphetamine/methamphetamine proto-type, this extension provides the homologue N-ethylamphetamine and by further extension, N-propyl, N-butyl, N-etc. amphetamines. With the same manipulation, again in the phenethylamine world where there is a 3,4-methylenedioxy substitution on the aromatic ring, one gets the MDA, MDMA, MDE, MDPR series of com-pounds. The exact same world exists with the tryptamines. Lengthening the N-methyl group of α,N-DMT leads to compounds that are known and potentially active in man, but which have not yet been explored.  As discussed under DPT, the presence of two different alkyl groups on a tryptamine are best named for those two groups, with their locations given as numbers or letters as prefixes in front of the initialed code.  But here the convention becomes hopelessly ambiguous.  What is to be done if one of the prefixes belongs to one group, and the other to the other?  One has to break them up, of course.  But then something else like α-M-N-ET becomes a nightmare to be properly located in the long index.  Let's compromise with α-MET, where the M belongs to the α, but the E (ethyl) is on the T (tryptamine) nitrogen atom where it belongs.  So, the N-ethyl compound (alpha-methyl-N-ethyltryptamine) becomes α-MET and it forms readily through the reductive alkylation of indol-3-ylacetone with ethylamine (HCl salt, mp 187-189 °C, picrate mp 203-205 °C), and the N-isopropyl analogue (alpha-methyl-N-isopropyltryptamine) becomes α-MIPT and it results from the reductive alkylation of indol-3-ylacetone with isopropylamine (HCl salt, mp 229-230 °C, picrate mp 219-220 °C).  Their pharmacology in animals is not exciting, but they are untried in man.  Well, maybe they are untried.  An early patent (1962) that gives the synthesis for both the N-methyl and the N-ethyl compounds (α,N-DMT and α-MET) claims that they both have psychostimulant properties.

And, as a final note, be careful.  The code TMT has two meanings.  In the phenethylamine area it identifies the mescaline analogue, 3,4,5-trimethoxy-tranylcypromine (or trans-2-(3,4,5-trimethoxyphenyl)cyclopropylamine).  This is entry #56, page 607 of *PIHKAL*, and check there for further details.  Here, entries of trimethylated tryptamines will be preceded by the specific locations of the methyl groups prefixes with numbers, Greek letters, and/or N for nitrogen.

### #9.   DPT;   TRYPTAMINE, N,N-DIPROPYL;   INDOLE, 3-[2-(DIPROPYLAMINO)ETHYL];   N,N-DIPROPYLTRYPTAMINE;   3-[2-(DIPROPYLAMINO)ETHYL]INDOLE

SYNTHESIS: (from tryptamine) A solution of 1.6 g tryptamine base in 10 mL IPA was treated with 5.1 g propyl iodide and 5.2 g diisopropylethyl amine, and stirred at room temperature for 36 h.  The volatiles were removed under vacuum, and the residue was partitioned between $CH_2Cl_2$ and $H_2O$ made basic with NaOH.  The organic phase was separated, the aqueous phase extracted with two additional portions of $CH_2Cl_2$, the extracts pooled and the solvent removed under vacuum.  The residue, a fluid brown oil weighing 2.75 g, was treated with 5 g acetic anhydride and heated on the steam bath for 20 min.  After cooling, a small amount of ammonium hydroxide was added, and the mixture added to 200 mL 0.5 N $H_2SO_4$.  This aqueous solution was washed three times with $CH_2Cl_2$ and then made basic with 25% NaOH.  This was extracted with 3x40 mL $CH_2Cl_2$, the extracts pooled, and the solvent removed under vacuum. The oily residue was distilled at 145-155 °C at 0.08 mm/Hg to give 1.14 g N,N-dipropyltryptamine base as a white oil. This was dissolved in 5 mL IPA, acidified with concentrated HCl, and diluted with 20 mL anhydrous $Et_2O$ to give N,N-dipropyltryptamine hydrochloride (DPT) as a fine white powder. Yield was 1.10 g (39%) with a mp of 174-176 °C. IR (in cm$^{-1}$): 759, 774, 831, 987 (br.), 1084, 1101. The replacement of the organic base diisopropylethyl amine with an equivalent amount of $NaHCO_3$ yielded the same product but with a yield of less than 10%.

(from indole) To a well-stirred solution of 10 g indole in 150 mL anhydrous $Et_2O$ there was added, dropwise over the course of 30 min, a solution of 11 g oxalyl chloride in 150 mL anhydrous $Et_2O$. Stirring was continued an additional 15 min during which time there was the separation of indol-3-ylglyoxyl chloride. This intermediate was removed by filtration and used directly in the following step. This was added, in small increments, to 20 mL anhydrous dipropylamine which was being stirred. There was then added an excess of 2N HCl, the mixture cooled, and the resulting solids removed by filtration. These were recrystallized from aqueous EtOH to give, after air drying, 13.2 g indol-3-yl-N,N-dipropylglyoxylamide, mp 95-96 °C. A solution of 13 g indol-3-yl N,N-dipropylglyoxylamide in 350 mL anhydrous dioxane was added, slowly, to 19 g LAH in 350 mL dioxane which was well-stirred and held at reflux temperature under an inert atmosphere. After the addition was complete, refluxing was maintained for an additional 16 h, the reaction mixture cooled, and the excess hydride destroyed by the cautious addition of wet dioxane. The formed solids were removed by filtration, washed with hot dioxane, the filtrate and washings combined, dried over anhydrous $MgSO_4$, and the solvent removed under vacuum. The brownish residue was dissolved in anhydrous $Et_2O$ and saturated with anhydrous hydrogen chloride. The resulting crystals were recrystallized from benzene/methanol to give 11.9 g (49%) of N,N-dipropyltryptamine hydrochloride (DPT) with a mp of 178-179 °C.

DOSAGE:  100 - 250 mg, orally

DURATION:  2 - 4 h

QUALITATIVE COMMENTS:  (with 200 mg, orally) "This started sooner and was a lot stronger than I had expected. I had trouble talking and I felt very uncomfortable. I think physically I was in a chair but I was on a kind of mountain surrounded by clouds. And the clouds talked to me."

(with 250 mg, orally) "I was seeing the Light real strongly. The Light sort of looked like bright bursts of Light but also like a kind of Spiritual Tunnel, and it seemed at one point, along with that, I saw a Human form, but the Vision seemed like I was sort of inside the Being and outside, and the Human was inside me and appeared to be outside, but I didn't see the being's face or clearly see the various limbs because the Being seemed to be the tunnel of Light that I was inside in the Vision, and seemed much larger than me.  As King Jesus said: (St. John 6:56) 'Whoever eats my Flesh and drinks my Blood lives in me and I live in them.'"

(with 275 mg, orally) "I have smoked this amount one time some while ago, and this is a lot more interesting. And a lot more intense. With smoking, there was a body rush that was uncomfortable, and you never really know how much went into you, what with pyrolysis and all."

(with 500 mg, orally)  "This was intensely visual, and it lasted an exhausting 12 hours. I prefer the smoking route."

(with 100 mg, smoked) "The entire experience lasted only 20 minutes. I found the visual experience to be everything.  It was a lot more benign than mushrooms with pretty much no toxic things, more like mescaline."

(with many mg, smoked) "I saw this vision of two hearts rotating. They were shaped like the usual heart shape (like a valentine).  They filled most of my vision and were rotating one inside the other. Around the outside of the hearts there were sparkling jewels or crystals of light of different colors, maybe four rows deep surrounding them all around.  This vision was totally clear.  When I saw this vision, time was very full and long and complete."

(with 80 mg, intramuscularly) "I feel light and nervous.  I'm way off in a big castle with beautiful colors and scenery.  I'm back with the girl who accused me of fathering her child.  It's peaceful.  She had everything she wanted.  My aunt made sure we went to church on Sunday.  I see the devil in front of my face.  Everything is going fast.  Too fast.  It's not pleasant.  Things are going zig-zag.  Feels like I'm tired.  I feel like an old man in a rocking chair sitting in front of a phonograph.  Everything is so mixed up.  I'm trying to get myself together.  I have a vibrating feeling.  It makes me feel as though I'm not here."

(with 100 mg, intramuscularly) "I was being led by the hand of a wise old man who I know was God, and we went off to the front of the synagogue.  I was handed a Torah for me to carry as a sign that I had been accepted, and forgiven, and that I had come home."

(with 12 mg, intravenously.)  "We were using an i.v. drip with sodium ascorbate which affected the timing, of course. This was strong at this level.  I was set to go to a target dosage of 60 milligrams, but decided to stop at 12. It was strong, real strong."

(with 36 mg, intravenously) "This was administered as a sterile solution of the fumarate salt, so the actual weight of the drug used is somewhat less.  This was a very intense experience, every bit as powerful as this amount of DMT."

EXTENSIONS AND COMMENTARY: The earliest reports of human activity, at 1 mg/Kg, are mentioned under DMT.  The clinical trials, from which the 80 mg comment above was entered, were conducted on a population of physically sound alcoholics. It was not only a study to define the nature of action of DPT, but to challenge the idea that the metabolism of the dialkyltryptamine on the 6-hydroxyl position might give rise to active metabolites. This challenge was in the form of assaying 6-fluoro-N,N-diethyltrypamine in the same subjects, to see if it might be an active placebo. This is discussed under that specific compound, DET. Incidentally, the actual amount of DPT used was originally published as being 1.0 mg/Kg body weight, and I am guessing that the subject might have been of average weight, about 175 lbs. In these studies, dosages were taken up to as high as 1.3 mg/Kg, which resulted only in a prolongation, not an intensification, of effect. In all trials, the onset of effects occurred between 10 and 15 minutes following injection.

Studies using lower dosages of DPT (15-30 mg intramuscularly) have been explored as adjuncts to psychotherapy with alcoholic patients. The enhancement of recall of memories and experiences, the greater emotional expressivenes and self-exploration, coupled with a consistently short duration, made the drug very attractive. Higher doses, up in the 100 milligram range, have been explored in psychotherapy, in the quest for peak experiences. In yet another study, exploring the interaction of therapy counseling and DPT-induced peak experiences with patients who are dying, the i.m. dosage range was between 75 and 125 milligrams.

There is a rather remarkable religious group known as the Temple of the True Inner Light, in New York City, which has embraced as its Eucharist DPT, which they refer to as a powerful Angel of the Host. Their communion is confirmed by either the smoking or the drinking of the sacrament, and they have been totally unbothered by any agency of the Federal Government, as far as I know. It is not as if they were unknown. Quite on the contrary, I had on one occasion received a request for information on the drug from a reporter who was writing a story on DPT and its use in the church. I asked him just how he had gotten my name, and he told me that he was given it by someone within the DEA. Someone, sometime, should write an essay on contemporary religions, as to why DPT has flown, why peyote forever struggles, and LSD and marijuana have bombed out, when tied to religion. Is there something about a faith being an "approved" religion? Who gives his approval? Who decides the applicability of the first amendment, which explicitly states that "Congress shall make no law respecting an establishment of religion, or prohibiting the free exercise thereof"?

I wish the True Inner Light congregation Godspeed, if you will excuse the expression. My impressions of them from our correspondence have left me totally convinced of their integrity and dedication. It is an intriguing fact that this tryptamine was commercially available for a while from at least one small independent supplier of chemical novelties, but I believe that this is now no longer a valid source.

An intriguing (and perhaps theoretical) homologue of DPT is the 1-propyl counterpart, 1,N,N-tripropyltryptamine, referred to as PDPT. It has been claimed that simply reacting tryptamine with an excess of propyl bromide put an alkyl group on the indolic 1-position (as stated also for the ethyl counterpart, sometimes referred to as EDET). In my own experiments with this reaction, I have yet to see any suggestion of 1-alkylation.


#### #10. EIPT; TRYPTAMINE, N-ETHYL-N-ISOPROPYL; INDOLE, 3-[2-(ETHYLISOPROPYLAMINO)ETHYL]; N-ETHYL-N-ISOPROPYL-TRYPTAMINE; 3-[2-(ETHYLISOPROPYLAMINO)ETHYL]INDOLE

SYNTHESIS: (from indole): To a well-stirred solution of 1.6 g indole in 30 mL anhydrous $Et_2O$ there was added, dropwise over the course of 30 min, a solution of 3.8 g (2.6 mL) oxalyl chloride in 30 mL anhydrous $Et_2O$. Stirring was continued for an additional 15 min during which time there was the separation of indol-3-ylglyoxyl chloride as a crystalline solid. This intermediate was removed by filtration and washed with $Et_2O$. It was used directly in the following step. This solid acid chloride was added to 3.6 g anhydrous ethylisopropylamine in $Et_2O$, followed by the addition of an excess of 2N HCl. The mixture was cooled, and the resulting product, N-ethyl-N-isopropylindol-3-ylglyoxylamide, was removed by filtration. The air-dried product weighed 2.2 g (62% yield) and had a melting point of 149-151 °C.

A solution of 2.0 g N-ethyl-N-isopropylindol-3-ylglyoxylamide in 50 mL anhydrous THF was added, dropwise, to 1.5 g LAH in 50 mL anhydrous THF which was well-stirred under an inert atmosphere. This was brought to reflux and held there for 3 h. The reaction mixture was cooled, and the excess hydride destroyed by the cautious addition of wet THF. A 15% NaOH solution was then added until the solids had a loose, white cottage cheese character to them, and the mobile phase tested basic by external damp pH paper. These formed solids were removed by filtration, washed first with THF and then MeOH. The filtrate and washings were combined, dried over anhydrous $MgSO_4$, and the solvent removed under vacuum. The residue set up to a crystalline mass weighing 1.6 g (90%). This was recrystallized from pentane to provide N-ethyl-N-isopropyltryptamine (EIPT) as a free base with a mp of 71-73°C. Indole can also serve as a precursor to NET, which is easily transformed into EIPT.

(from N-ethyltryptamine, NET): To a solution of 0.33 g N-ethyltryptamine base (see NET recipe) in 4 mL IPA there was added 1.5 g isopropyl iodide and 1.2 g diisopropylethylamine, and this was held at reflux for 36 h. The volatiles were removed under vacuum, and to the residual black oil there was added 100 mL 15% aqueous NaOH. This was extracted with 3x50 mL $CH_2Cl_2$, the extracts pooled, the solvent removed, and the residue distilled at the KugelRohr to give 0.24 g (59%) of N-ethyl-N-isopropyltryptamine as a pale amber oil, bp 150-160 °C at 0.11 mm/Hg, that did not crystallize. MS (in m/z): $C_6H_{14}N+$ 100 (100%); $C_3H_8N+$ 58 (58%); indolemethylene+ 130 (11%); parent ion 230 (1%). This base was converted to the hydrochloride salt, as described above.

DOSAGE:   24 - 40 mg, orally

DURATION:   4 - 6 h

QUALITATIVE COMMENTS: (with 24 mg, orally) "There is something strange going on, and I am feeling quite urpy, but I feel quite horny at the same time. What would it be like to be making love and vomiting at the same time? Something is not at peace with itself. No way. And then suddenly I am baseline, and there is nothing left."

(with 40 mg, orally) "I see some similarities with DET and MIPT orally, not too pleasant with somewhat dysphoric components and visual effects more in the background. Michael Valentine Smith described a 'little elephant' as a thing to be found in 5-MeO-DMT. And a little of this is to be found in this drug."

(with 40 mg, orally) "Within a half hour, I have sparkling and a very unsure tummy. This is, on one hand, strangely not erotic, and yet I am completely functional, sexually. Remarkable orgasm. But still not erotic. No visuals, no sound enhancement, no fantasy, so why is it up there at a plus 2? I don't know, and I am pretty much baseline by the fifth hour."

(with 40 mg, orally) "In an hour, a very mild pre-nausea, which passed off in about 45 minutes. No visual effects at all. The dreams that night weren't quite as satisfying as the excellent, nice, clear, pretty dreams with an earlier 30 mg trial. The night was full of chopped-up sleep, since I was up about once an hour to pee. Observation: there is some diuretic component to this material. Barely plus 1. Would not bother taking it again."

EXTENSIONS AND COMMENTARY: Clearly this is not an exciting compound. So why go to the extensive bother to make it and test it? For the single reason that the diisopropyl analogue is totally weird, one of the two weird tryptamines that need to be explored. If everything went as predicted, then nothing would ever be discovered. One must look always for the aberration that will demand that you change your working hypotheses and become responsive to unexpected and unexplainable things. 5-MeO-DET has an unexpected property, a lightheadedness and vertigo at a very small dosage. This may prove to be its value in research, and this is discussed in its own entry. Here is a response to another unexpected observation. N,N-diisopropyltryptamine causes extraordinary auditory distortions. What about this molecule does this thing? Are both isopropyl groups needed? Is only one needed? Might neither be needed, but simply to have something equally massive stuck to that nitrogen atom? This compound, EIPT, is an essential brick in this wall that will contain, define, and describe the fine details of this remarkable CNS property.

This is why EIPT is interesting. Let me itemize these close relatives of the diisopropylamine analogue, maintaining one isopropyl group but letting the other be something different. What can be seen from all of this exploration?

| N1 | N2 | name | action |
|----|----|------|--------|
| methyl | isopropyl | MIPT | It seems to be psychedelic in the 25 mg area, but it has not been brought up to the 40 mg level. |
| ethyl | isopropyl | EIPT | An uncomfortable nausea and uncomfortable trip, but no auditory disruptions. |
| propyl | isopropyl | PIPT | (not yet evaluated) |
| isopropyl | isopropyl | DIPT | Intense auditory distortion at the 40 mg level. |
| butyl | isopropyl | BIPT | (not yet evaluated) |

If it turns out that the diisopropyl substitution is an absolutely essential structural component of this sensory phenomenon, then it will become one of the most remarkable tools known for the study of the human auditory association area in the brain.

This is why all of this research is important. You can never tell what a new compound will do. So you must continue to make new compounds and you must continue to be the observer. It is truly an exciting world.

#### #11.  α-ET; ALPHA-ETHYLTRYPTAMINE; INDOLE, 3-(2-AMINO-BUTYL); TRYPTAMINE, ALPHA-ETHYL; 3-(2-AMINOBUTYL)INDOLE; ETRYPTAMINE; MONASE

SYNTHESIS: To a 50 °C warmed mixture of 60 mL glacial acetic acid and 18 mL acetic anhydride, there was added 66 g crystalline ammonium acetate, and stirring continued until solution was complete (20 min). To this there was added a solution of 87 g indole 3-carboxaldehyde (see under α-MT for preparation) and 300 mL nitropropane in 360 mL acetic acid. The mixture was held at reflux temperature for

3 h, cooled, and diluted with 360 mL $H_2O$. After standing at 10 °C for several additional hours, the solids were removed by filtration and recrystallized from 600 mL of 40% EtOH to give, after filtering and drying to constant weight, 44.5 g of 1-(3-indolyl)-2-nitrobut-1-ene-1 ($\alpha$-ethyl-$\beta$-indoleninidenium ethyl nitronate) which had a mp of 128-131 °C. Anal. ($C_{12}H_{12}N_2O_2$); C: calcd, 66.64; found 67.54: H,N.

A suspension of 31.7 g LAH in 300 mL anhydrous THF, stirring under an inert atmosphere, was treated by the addition of a solution of 36 g 1-(3-indolyl)-2-nitrobut-1-ene in 285 mL anhydrous THF. This was added dropwise over the course of 3 h, while the mixture was being brought up to reflux temperature. The reaction mixture was held at reflux for an additional 2 h, then allowed to return to room temperature. After standing overnight, the excess hydride was destroyed by the cautious addition of 500 mL wet $Et_2O$, followed with 70 mL $H_2O$, 100 mL THF, and finally 20 mL 50% NaOH. After 1 h additional stirring, the solids were removed by filtration, washed with 1.5 L $Et_2O$, the combined filtrate and washings dried over anhydrous $K_2CO_3$, and the solvent removed under vacuum. The residue, 78 g, was dissolved in 100 mL MeOH, treated with 12 mL acetic acid, stripped of volatiles under vacuum, redissolved in a mixture of 250 mL ethyl acetate and 30 mL MeOH, concentrated to a volume of about 100 mL, and again treated with 2 mL acetic acid. The product, $\alpha$-ethyltryptamine acetate ($\alpha$-ET), separated as a solid with a mp of 164-165.5 °C. Anal. ($C_{14}H_{20}N_2O_2$); H: calcd, 8.11; found 7.60: C,N. It can be recrystallized from ethyl acetate/MeOH, which increased and tightened the mp to 165-166 °C. The free base, from ethyl acetate/petroleum ether, had a mp 97-99 °C. The hydrochloride salt has a mp 215.5-218 °C. The picrate had a mp 165-166 °C.

DOSAGE:  100 - 150 mg, orally

DURATION:  6 - 8 h

QUALITATIVE COMMENT:  (with 50 mg, orally) "No effects of any kind were felt with 50 milligrams, orally."

(with 100 mg, orally) "A nearly imperceptible feeling of well-being and pleasure was noted about 80 minutes later, and seemed completely gone at three hours."

(with 105 mg, orally) "Very slowly soluble in water and mildly bitter. I was aware of something just before a half-hour, and at one hour I had a light-headed sparkle and felt light of body. It is like speed without the cardiovascular, or like a psychedelic without the visuals. I can see how it was sold in Chicago as MDMA. At two hours, a slight cooling of the feet, a bit of unsureness in the gut, a tendency to squeeze the teeth together, a trace of eye-wiggle, and a tendency to talk with my ears popped. Four and a half hours, largely out, with some residue in eyes and teeth.

Six hours baseline, and fine sleep. No residue."

(with 110 mg, orally) "I am in a very different place. It's exciting but at the same time I don't know what to do with the energy. It makes my eyes want to close."

(with 120 mg, orally) "Very keen, pure euphoria, feels great. Reaches +3 in about one hour. Sharply focused feelings very strong, strong energy push. Keeps rising until it goes over the top and begins to break up. The pure tone of euphoria gets joggled with other feelings, like a bit too much to handle. Not really uncomfortable, but not as nice as the earlier +2 stage. A wall seems to grow around me. I am being shut off from intimate contact with others. But in a couple of hours the push of the drug diminishes, and I get more comfortable. The day ended beautifully."

(with 130 mg, orally) "There was a smooth onset of relaxation at about 55 minutes with only a trace of motor intoxication. Both radio and television seemed more enjoyable than normal and there was a definite enhancement of the beauty of instrumental music. The effect seemed to peak at about 150 minutes and was essentially gone at the five hour point. There were never any visuals nor any type of sensory distortions, just warm, pleasant feelings. No interference with sleep was noted, and there were no after-effects the next day."

(with 150 mg, orally) "My dosage level was the highest of the group, but, to my surprise, it had almost no effect whatsoever. A plus-one, if anything. After the peak, as I was slowly coming down, I was aware of feeling slightly depressed. This state continued until I achieved baseline, but was not severe enough to prevent me from participating in the general good spirits of the group. There is a real possibility that my weekly use of MDMA for writing might have built up a tolerance to the stimulation of this material. I think that that may be close to the answer. Would I take it again? Not with much enthusiasm. It didn't give enough exciting rewards."

(with 160 mg, orally) "A strong feeling of being-at-peace was evident in an hour, although there was some concentration required to do things in a coordinated way. I wouldn't want to drive a car. There seemed to be very easy drifting of thoughts but no visuals or sensory distortions. There were no GI disturbances anywhere along the line except for some loose stools the next morning. Appetite was slightly depressed, but food tasted very good. Sex at the 2-hour point showed some difficulty in reaching orgasm but significantly enhanced pleasure during orgasm once it was attained. A very slight tremor could be detected in the fingers around the peak of the experience. There was a desire to talk with friends somewhat reminiscent of MDMA; I am sure that this drug could be quite a social-enhancing material. The effects wore off gradually and were essentially gone by the six hour point. Sleep was unaffected; however, the next morning there was a slight feeling of dullness and possibly hang-over which quickly wore off."

EXTENSIONS AND COMMENTARY: This base, $\alpha$-ET or etryptamine, was a promising anti-depressant, explored clinically as the acetate salt by Upjohn under the name of Monase. Its central stimulant activity is probably not due to its monoamineoxidase inhibition activity, but appears to stem from its structural relationship to the indolic psychedelics. It was withdrawn from potential commercial use with the appearance of an unacceptable incidence of a medical condition known as agranulocytosis, but the extramural research into its action, among the lay population, goes on.

One property has been mentioned more than once in anecdotal reports. It appears to serve well, with short term dosage regimens, as an effective tool in kicking dependency on opiates. In chronic use, there is a rather rapid tolerance built up over four or five days, that allows a dosage escalation to a daily load of a gram or more. There might be some discomfort such as sores in the softer tissues of the mouth, but apparently the withdrawal from heroin is easy and effective. Here is a potential tool in addiction treatment that might warrant closer investigation.

Other homologues of α-ET have been synthesized. The α-propylhomologue (α-PT) has been made from tryptophan, and the acetate salt was recrystallized from ethyl acetate/MeOH and melted at 158-158.5 °C. It has not, to my knowledge, ever been tasted. But I suspect that it will take a pretty hefty dosage to get some CNS effect based on the loss of potency with the similar homologation in the Muni Metro series related to MDMA. Rather than lengthening the chain on the alpha-position, some studies have exploited the known potency enhancement that comes from putting a methoxyl group on the 5-position of the indole. This compound, 5-MeO-α-ET, has been made from the 5-methoxyindole-3-aldehyde by coupling with nitropropane (with ammonium acetate) to form the nitrobutene which is a reddish, crystalline material, mp 114-116 °C from ethanol. LAH reduction in $Et_2O$/ THF gave the desired 5-MeO-α-ET in a 72% yield, mp 201-203 °C, as the hydrochloride salt. There is an alternate synthesis that avoids LAH which involves the conversion of 5-methoxyindole to the nitrobutane with 2-nitro-1-butene, followed by reduction with nickel boride to give 5-MeO-α-ET, as the free base in a 52% yield, mp 110-112 °C. As might have been predicted, it was more potent than α-ET by a factor of two with 70 milligrams orally producing a trippy feeling that lasted several hours accompanied with an increased heart beat and difficulty in sleeping. There were no psychedelic effects as such, and no unpleasant side effects. Another compound that has been closely associated with α-ET is a carboline. If a molecule of acetone is brought to react with the amine group and the indolic 2-position, in a condensation that is called a Pictet-Spengler reaction, there will be formed 1,1-dimethyl-3-ethyl-1,2,3,4-tetrahydro-β-carboline. This is a chemical ally of the harmine family of alkaloids, but I have not heard of its having been explored psychedelically. It has been reported to be an impurity of commercial α-ET (including the pre-scheduling product from the Aldrich Chemical Company) to an extent of some 30%. At these levels, it was suggested that it might play some role in the central action of the parent tryptamine.

α-ET has played yet another role in the evolution of our drug laws, a role that will be found to be of extraordinary importance once it becomes more widely known. This compound may prove pivotal in our ultimate definition of the Analogue Drug Law. I want to talk about: (1) The Controlled Substance Analogue Drug Bill; (2) What happened in a trial in Denver; and (3) What happened in a District Court in Colorado.

During the most political period of the War on Drugs Congress passed and the president signed a new law every two years, on the even-numbered years (the years of congressional re-election), that increased either the definition of what were illegal drugs, or the penalties that follow a conviction for having been associated with them in any way. In 1986, there was a proposed draft of a bill called the "Designer Drug Bill" that had been created within the DEA, and sent on to the Justice Department who, in turn, submitted it to Congress as desired legislation. This was a proposal that would make it illegal to tinker with the structure of a molecule of an illegal drug, to change it in a way that would make it fall outside of the explicit listings of illegal drugs but without significant changes in its pharmacological effects. It was the first time a drug law would define a crime by the activity of a compound as well as by chemical structure. The proposal went to the appropriate legislative committee and, with some modifications, it became law in 1986. There was considerable celebration within the DEA, expressing a "We did it!" kind of satisfaction.

The first three Articles of the Constitution of the United States are entitled: Article. I. The Legislative Department; Article. II. The Executive Department; and Article. III. The Judicial Department. The first of these consists of Congress, which has the role of writing law and defining the military structure of the nation. The second of these defines the president, who approves the laws of Congress and is the highest military officer. The third of these is invested in the enforcement of these laws. The three departments were defined in a way to assure a balance of power. It is a dangerous step towards a totalitarian state when one special interest group (here the DEA) can, in effect, both write the law and then enforce it.

(1)   The Controlled Substance Analogue Drug Bill. This is contained within Public Law 99-570, the Controlled Substances Analogue Enforcement Act of 1986. This is the so-called "Designer Drug" bill which was intended to allow the prosecution of any act associated with an unscheduled drug, if that drug is analogous either in structure or in action to a scheduled drug, and if it is intended for use in man. Here is the exact wording of this amendment:

(32)(A) Except as provided in subparagraph (B), the term 'controlled substance analogue' means a substance —
   "(i)  the chemical structure of which is substantially similar to the chemical structure of a controlled substance in schedule I or II;
   (ii)  which has a stimulant, depressant, or hallucinogenic effect on the central nervous system that is substantially similar to or greater than the stimulent, depressant, or hallucinogenic effect on the central

nervous system of a controlled substance in schedule I or II; or

"(iii) with respect to a particular person, which such person represents or intends to have a stimulant, depressant, or hallucinogenic effect on the central nervous system that is substantially similar to or greater than the stimulant, depressant, or hallucinogenic effect on the central nervous system of a controlled substance in schedule I or II.

"(B) Such term does not include —

"(i) a controlled substance;

"(ii) any substance for which there is an approved new drug application;

"(iii) with respect to a particular person any substance, if an exemption is in effect for investigational use, for that person, under section 505 of the Federal Food, Drug, and Cosmetic Act (21 U.S.C. 355) to the extent conduct with respect to such substance is pursuant to such exemption; or

"(iv) any substance to the extent not intended for human consumption before such an exemption takes effect with respect to that substance.".

"SEC. 203. A controlled substance analogue shall, to the extent intended for human consumption, be treated, for purposes of this title and title III as a controlled substance in schedule I.".

This is the exact wording of the law, and I have discovered that the more times I read it the more convinced I become that, whatever the original intent might have been, it was structured in a way to promote vagueness. I have written elsewhere about the rhetorical nightmare of a double disclaimer, "substantially similar." "Similar" means "pretty much the same." "Substantially identical" would means "pretty much the same." But what does "substantially similar" mean? I like the analogy of seeing two cut glass shakers in the center of the fancy table, one with small holes in the silver screw-down cap containing salt, and the other with slightly larger holes containing pepper. Are these two items substantially similar? If you happen to be a collector of antique crystal glassware, these items are completely identical. If you happen to need to add a condiment to your entree these items are totally different. You must know whose eyes are being looked through to approach the question of "substantial similarity." At a trial a few years ago in Southern California the issue was settled once and for all for a confused jury when a forensic chemist gave an expert opinion that two things were substantially similar when they were greater than 50% identical. Is the right hand more than 50% identical to the right foot? This opinion was patently absurd.

(2) What happened in a trial in Denver? A few years ago a young man

discovered that the Aldrich Chemical Company offered alpha-ethyltryptamine acetate as a fine chemical. He could buy it in 100 g quantities, and package it in 150 milligram capsules to be sold to the street trade as Ecstasy, or MDMA. He could and he did. His actions came to the attention of Law Enforcement, and an opinion was obtain from a DEA chemist that α-ET was not an analogue substance. So the prosecutor decided against pressing charges. But not every one agreed with this not-analogue opinion.

So the chemist solicited the thoughts of his professional colleagues and the answers came back with as many no's as yes's. The no's were from those who reasoned objectively (scientific, compare the structures) and the yes's were from those who reasoned subjectively (abuse potential, compare the action).

The adventurous α-ET peddler continued, and was again brought to task. The analytical duties went to another chemist, and charges were finally brought under the Analogue Drug Bill. But the earlier opinion was in the record, and the first chemist was brought in by the defense to present these findings at the trial. Clearly there was uncertainty if this was an analogue of anything that was scheduled. The research toxicologist for the home-office of the DEA gave testimony that it was, without question, an analogue. But on cross examination, he was asked just how many times, and for for how many different drugs, he had been asked that same question, as an expert witness at a criminal trial. Perhaps twelve, he said. And how many times had he offered the conclusion that the proposed compound had been an analogue of a scheduled drug? In every case. The judge decided that there were some conflicting opinions here, amongst the experts, and dismissed the charges. The defendant was given the warning that this kind of leniency was not common, and told to behave himself in the future.

(3) The text of the appellate decision in this matter is a valuable lesson in the fine aspects of grammatical analysis. This all is from 806 F.Supp. 232 (D.Colo., 1992). In way of background it emphasizes that the purpose of the controlled substance analogue statute is to attack underground chemists who tinker with molecules of controlled substances to create new drugs that are not yet illegal. In this case, the defendants were not chemists who created or marketed a designer drug but rather allegedly purchased and distributed a substance that preexisted drugs to which it was a purported analogue. This was probably, in and of itself, sufficient reason to deny the appeal. But the argument developed marvelous new texture as things progressed. As a reminder of the wording of the law (here SS is, of course, substantially similar but this terminology is not addressed in the decision), the three phases of the definitional part of the law can be summarized as follows:

|      | (i)   | a chemical structure which is SS to ... ; |
|------|-------|-------------------------------------------|
|      | (ii)  | which has an effect that is SS to ... ;   |
| or   | (iii) | which is represented as having an effect that is SS to ... |

The prosecution's reading and analysis of this definition:

"The government's reading of the analogue definition has superficial appeal. As a matter of simple grammar, when an "or" is placed before the last term in a series, each term in the series is usually intended to be disjunctive. Under this reading, α-ET would be an analogue if it satisfies any of the three clauses; however, this reading ignores other grammatical principles that apply in favor of defendant's construction. The operative segments of clauses (ii) and (iii) both begin with the word 'which,' signaling the start of a dependent relative clause modifying a previous noun. In each case the precedent noun is 'chemical structure' found in clause (i). Because both clauses (ii) and (iii) can be read to modify clause (i) the statutory language can be fairly read as requiring the two-pronged definition asserted by the defendants."

The defendant's reading and analysis of this definition:

"Defendant's reading is also bolstered by a deeply rooted rule of statutory construction. A statute must be construed to avoid unintended or absurd results. If I adopt the government's construction and read clause (ii) independently, alcohol or caffeine would be controlled substance analogues because, in a concentrated form, they can have depressant or stimulative effects substantially similar to a controlled substance. Likewise, if I read clause (iii) independently, powdered sugar would be an analogue if a defendant represented that it was cocaine, effectively converting this law into a counterfeit drug statute. In both cases the defendant could be prosecuted for selling a controlled substance analogue even though the alleged analogue did not have a chemical structure  substantially similar to a schedule I or II controlled substance. Therefore, to prevent this unintended result, clause (i) must apply to any substance that the government contends is a controlled substance analogue."

There is a most instructive bit of history to be considered. In July, 1986, the House of Representatives considered the Designer Drug Enforcement Act of 1986 (H.R. 5246). As with the Senate, the House bill focused on underground chemists who seek to evade the drug laws by slightly altering a controlled substance. The House proposed a two-pronged definition of "analogue" that is virtually identical to the construction advocated by the defendants here. The House bill contained the same three clauses as the current statute, but added the word "and" after clause (i). Congress ultimately adopted the analogue statute as part of the comprehensive "Anti-Drug Abuse Act of 1986." Inexplicably, the analogue definition enacted by Congress dropped the word "and" after clause (i).

This pretty well defines the legislative intent of Congress, and I would give a pretty penny to meet the writer who happened to delete that "and," the one critical word that changed the heart of the law. I would like to know to whom he answered.

Here is a masterpiece of logic which makes some sense out of sloppy law. It must be remembered that the purpose of all of this is to determine if one, or two, or three definitions must be applied to establish just what is an analogue. This court declared that a substance may be a controlled substance analogue only if it satisfies clause (i) and at least one of clauses (ii) or (iii).

There is a fascinating, and potentially most disruptive, appeals ruling made in 1996 concerning the interpretation of this law, in this case involving aminorex and phenethylamine as being analogues of 4-methyl aminorex and methamphetamine, respectively, and thus chargeable as a crime under this analogue statute. This is from the United States District Court for the District of Minnesota, No. 95-2132. In this ruling the Analogue Drug Bill is paraphrased with the following text: "... a drug becomes a controlled substance if it has a chemical structure substantially similar to that of a controlled substance, and either has a substantially similar effect on the user's central nervous system, or a relevant someone represents that it has or intends it to have such an effect." This is fascinating in that the source cited for this quote, 21 U.S.C. SS 802(32)(A), has no such text. And it is potentially disruptive for two reasons. It suggests that an analogue shall become a controlled substance, rather than be treated as if it were a controlled substance. It also introduces a new and undefined term, a "relevant someone." I do not have the legal background to guess the extent that this statement can influence future court challenges in the area of controlled substances analogues. Do, always, keep in mind that the finding that a chemical, in a given situation, is a controlled substance analogue does not make that chemical a controlled substance. The analogue status exists for just the single instance, and the next time the arguments all start over again.

Back to the case involving α-ET. The DEA retreated, licking its wounds, and got its own back by immediately proposing the placement of α-ET into Schedule I. They succeeded, and Monase is today no longer an FDA-approved antidepressant but it is, instead, a drug with a high potential for abuse. One of the more unexpected forms of abuse can be seen in the costs to the researcher who wished to study it in some legal way. Before it became a scheduled drug, alpha-ethyltryptamine was what is known as a "fine chemical" and was listed in the catalog of a major chemical company (1993) for a modest $60.90 for a hundred grams. It became a Schedule I drug by emergency scheduling that same year. Recently (1995) I noted that the chemical has been discontinued (as a fine chemical) but has appeared in a catalog from a major supply house for neurological chemicals. Alpha-ethyl tryptamine now requires a DEA license for purchase, and retailed at $424.00 for 100 milligrams. That calculates out at $424,000.00 for a hundred grams, a price inflation of a factor of almost 7000, or a 700,000% increase. Now THAT is truly drug abuse.

**#12.   ETH-LAD;   6-NORLYSERGIC   ACID,   6-N,N-TRIETHYLAMIDE;
6-NORLYSERGAMIDE, 6,N,N-TRIETHYL;   6,N,N-TRIETHYLNOR-
LYSERGAMIDE;  N-(6)-ETHYLNORLYSERGIC ACID, N,N-DIETHYL-
AMIDE;        9,10-DIDEHYDRO-6,N,N-TRIETHYLERGOLINE-8β-
CARBOXAMIDE; N-ETHYL-NOR-LSD**

SYNTHESIS: A solution of 0.323 g of lysergic acid diethylamide (LSD) in 10 mL
$CHCl_3$ was diluted with 70 mL $CCl_4$ and added over the course of 1 h to a refluxing
solution of 0.44 g BrCN in 30 mL $CCl_4$ in a nitrogen environment and protected
from direct illumination. After the addition was complete, the reaction was held at
reflux for an additional 6 h, allowed to cool, and washed with an aqueous solution
of tartaric acid. The organic solvents were removed under vacuum, and the residue
dissolved in 70 mL $CH_2Cl_2$ and washed with 50 mL additional tartaric acid solution.
The $CH_2Cl_2$ phase was dried with anhydrous $Na_2SO_4$, and after removal of the
drying agent by filtration, the solvent was removed under vacuum. The residue was
cleaned up by passage through 5 g of neutral alumina being eluted with a 9:1 $CH_2Cl_2$
/MeOH mixture. Centrifugal chromatography with alumina and $CH_2Cl_2$, under a
nitrogen atmosphere containing ammonia, provided a solid product. After recrystallization from IPA or EtOAc, there was obtained 0.24 g (71%) 6-cyano-nor-LSD
(9,10-didehydro-N,N-diethyl-6-cyanoergoline-8β-carboxamide) with a mp of 190-
191 °C.

To a solution of 0.33 g 6-cyano-nor-LSD
in a mixture of 3 mL acetic acid and 0.6 mL $H_2O$,
under a nitrogen atmosphere, there was added
0.6 g powdered zinc and the stirred mixture was
heated for 4 h with an external oil bath maintained at 130 °C. The reaction mixture was
cooled to ice-bath temperature, diluted with an
additional 3 mL $H_2O$, and brought to an alkaline
pH with the addition of concentrated $NH_4OH$.
This suspension was extracted with $CH_2Cl_2$
(5x10 mL), the pooled extracts dried with anhydrous $Na_2SO_4$, and the solvent removed (after
filtration) under vacuum providing a tan solid.
Centrifugal chromatography (with alumina and a 9:1 $CHCl_3$/MeOH elution solvent
under an ammonia vapor environment), followed by the removal of the solvent
under vacuum, yielded a solid product which was recrystallized from EtOAc/
hexanes. There was thus obtained 0.19 g (61%) of tan crystals of nor-LSD (9,10-
didehydro-N,N-diethylergoline-8β-carboxamide) with a mp of 196-198 °C (dec.).

To a solution of 66 mg nor-LSD in 2 mL freshly distilled DMF under a
nitrogen atmosphere, there was added 48 mg anhydrous $K_2CO_3$ and 38 mg ethyl
iodide. When TLC analysis indicated that the nor-LSD had been consumed (4 h)
all volatiles were removed under a hard vacuum. The residue was solubilized in

CHCl$_3$ (5x5 mL) and the pooled extracts dried over anhydrous Na$_2$SO$_4$, cleared by filtration, and the solvent removed under vacuum. The residue was separated into two components by centrifugal chromatography (alumina, CH$_2$Cl$_2$, nitrogen and ammonia atmosphere) the first of which was the major product. After removal of the solvent, this was dissolved in hot benzene, filtered and cooled. The addition of hexane prompted crystallization of N-ethyl-nor-LSD (9,10-didehydro-N,N,6-triethylergoline-8β-carboxamide) as a white crystalline product weighing 66 mg (61%) after drying. It had a mp of 108-110 °C and an [α]D + 40.5 (c 0.46, EtOH).

DOSAGE: 40 to 150 micrograms, orally

DURATION: 8 - 12 h

QUALITATIVE COMMENTS: (with 20 μgs, orally) "This has a very real effect at this level, whereas I have no response at all from LSD at 20 mikes."

(with 50 μgs, orally) "This is already coming on in fifteen minutes, and is completely developed in another hour. Very few visual changes or distortions but easy eyes-closed imagery. Pretty much out after ten hours; it was a good, repeatable experiment."

(with 60 μgs, orally) "In about an hour or so, gentle movements of the house plants were noted. The painting of the walkway above the fireplace changed as if the sunny spots were moving ahead. The visual aspects became more LSD-like after a couple more hours, though in a very gentle way. The spider windowpane looked three-dimensional: at first I thought the windows were double-paned, but they were not. Stones, rocks and glass had a magical look to them, but tree bark looked like tree bark. Occasionally, a dark streak (spot) would go through the visual field and a page of a book would move sharply without effort. These aspects were very pleasant to me."

(with 75 μgs, orally) "I am up to a ++ within the hour and am feeling lazy. It is very diuretic and certainly not anorexic. Have been dieting strenuously for the past 4 days, but could definitely be interested in food. Also a decongestant. Body feels balanced. Thinking easy. Concepts easy to follow through. Mind and feelings together as should be. Definitely a plus two, no further. I wonder if it would be possible, at any level, to attain that blurring of boundaries that is the plus three at its best? My mind was at all times capable of realistic and down-to-earth thought, this is not a material that will allow you to float two inches off of the floor."

(with 100 μgs, orally) "It sort of sneaks up on you. Certainly not the push of LSD and, sadly, not the sparkle either. Possible time slowing. Easy sleep and no price to pay the next day."

(with 150 μgs, orally) "Extraordinary experience, none of the demands of LSD, just a completely together trip. There were hints of tummy discomfort and some chills early in the trial, but they were trivial and quickly passed. Fine music, and fine sex."

EXTENSIONS AND COMMENTARY: What a remarkable compound. It is a little more potent than LSD, but much less aggressive in the nature of its action. There appears to be little if any of the push, the taking control nature, of LSD and a greatly modified degree of visual distortion. The warmth and humor appears to be there, but all seems more allowing rather than demanding.

I suspect that this material is rather unstable in solution, even as the tartrate in dilute saline, although I cannot guess why that should be. A few months in the dark, at zero degrees and in the absence of air, led to a very real drop in potency, measured by a control assay of a freshly made solution of the same nominal concentration.

What a difference a single atom makes, an ethyl rather than a methyl group at the ring-D nitrogen atom. The absence of any group there (a hydrogen atom rather than the methyl group of LSD or the ethyl group of ETH-LAD) is nor-LSD, the synthetic intermediate mentioned in the preparation recipe above. It has no activity at all, even at a half a milligram. The allyl group at this location gives AL-LAD and the propyl group is PRO-LAD, and both of these are active and have their own individual entries.

## #13.    HARMALINE;   β-CARBOLINE, 3,4-DIHYDRO-7-METHOXY-1-METHYL; 3,4-DIHYDRO-7-METHOXY-1-METHYL-β-CARBOLINE; 3,4-DIHYDROHARMINE; 7-METHOXYHARMALAN; HARMADINE

SYNTHESIS: To a solution of 0.033 g 6-methoxytryptamine in 3.5 mL 0.1 N HCl, there was added 0.011 g glycolaldehyde and the mixture was heated on the steam bath for 1.5 h. The solution was then made basic with 10 mL 0.5 N NaOH, and extracted with $Et_2O$ on a continuous extractor. The $Et_2O$ extracts were pooled, dried over solid KOH, the solvent removed under vacuum. The residue was an oil that crystallized to give a solid, mp 170-175 °C, presumably a hydrate of 1-hydroxymethyl-

7-methoxy-1,2,3,4-tetrahydro-β-carboline. This was treated with 2.5 mL 90% $H_3PO_4$ and heated on the steam bath for 2 h. After dilution with $H_2O$, this was made alkaline with aqueous NaOH and extracted with $Et_2O$. The pooled extracts were stripped of solvent under vacuum, and the residue distilled to give a fraction (bp 120-140 at 0.001 mm/Hg) that weighed 0.027 g (72%). MS (in m/z): Parent ion -1, parent ion, 213, 214 (100%, 89%); 198 (29%); 201 (23%); 170 (22%); 173 (19%). IR (in cm$^{-1}$): 817, 832, 916, 1037, 1139, 1172. Harmaline hydrochloride dihydrate; IR (in cm$^{-1}$): 820, 841, 992, 1022, 1073, 1137.

There is a little bit of interesting history connected with the melting point of harmaline. A report appeared that described an alkaloid from *Peganum harmala* that looked like harmaline but which melted 18 °C too high, and so it was thought to be an isomer and was given the name harmadine. This was all cleared up a few years later when it was observed that on an open melting point block, harmaline had a mp 242-244 °C (with beginnings of sublimation at 189 °C) and harmadine had the values of 241-243 °C and 178 °C. In a capillary tube, harmaline melted at 256°C and harmadine at 257 °C. So, harmadine is now a synonym for harmaline.

DOSAGE:  150 - 300 mg, orally

DURATION:  5 - 8 h

QUALITATIVE COMMENTS:  (with 100 mg, orally) "I have tried this on two occasions, essentially without effect."

(with 150 mg, orally) "In an hour and a quarter, there was a rapid-onset intoxication and I felt a little unstable. And a little bit numb. There was an unusual shimmering in my lateral vision when I turned my head to the side. Everything was just a little bit down. Music was pretty much normal but I was missing the higher frequencies. Even light food sat heavily, and I wasn't too hungry (and I was remembering to watch what I eat, with this monoamineoxidase stuff). Sex was difficult — probably due to some reduced sensations. I feel that this compound is unlikely to be attractive to most people, as its major effects are an intoxication with a clouding of thoughts and some disruption of musical relationships."

(with 175 mg, orally) "After about one hour I found myself becoming relaxed and a bit sloppy. By the end of the second hour, I had peaked, and was pretty much at baseline after five hours. At the peak, three areas of disturbance were obvious. There were obvious tracers — when looking at a bright object, and moving your eyes to the side, the image of the object lags in its leaving the visual field, and it leaves in the opposite direction. As to the auditory, it seemed as if the higher frequencies of music were attenuated, and the lower frequencies amplified. And as to touch, there is a definite numbing. I had no appetite, and the little I ate didn't taste particularly good."

(with 200 mg, orally) "At about the two hour point I remember three things. The first was the effort to bring into reality the visual image of a face that was playing with my eyes-closed imagery. I got the mouth and, after a bit of work, I got the eyes. So I concentrated on the nose and it came into view, finally, but it was upside down. The second and third things were more easily defined. Nausea and diarrhea. Fortunately they alternated. This is not my trip of choice."

(with 300 mg, orally) "I was in a psychotherapy environment, so there were some suggestions and leading that influenced my responses. But I have great difficulty reliving my experience, in fact I don't remember anything. I have only disconnected images. There is a girl — me — in front of a church on a dusty road, myself at communion, receiving the Host from an invisible hand at a grandiose altar. I feel that I am going crazy. Something inside. It is not anxiety. It is not depression.

It is some of each, plus irritation and disorientation. I am dead but still have to come back to life. I am facing a reality of mine that I cannot accept."

(with 400 mg, orally) "This is Fluka material, and has a nasty taste. I felt completely immobilized and sick to my stomach. Closed eyed visuals yielded native women, 'organic' colors and shapes, and a black panther! I would like to do DMT and Harmaline together, but am put off by the nausea."

(with 500 mg, orally) "I took a half gram of pure synthetic harmaline after fasting for over a day. The resulting nausea was greatly attenuated after I vomited. At this dose there were intense and annoying visual disturbances, and complete collapse of motor coordination. I could barely stagger to the bathroom, and for safety's sake locomoted by crawling. Tracers and weird visual ripplings disturbed my sight with open eyes. With eyes closed, there was eidetic imagery. It had no symbolic significance, just bothersome disjointed sequences that lacked a relevant theme. They proceeded to transform so slowly (in comparison to the speed of my thought) that they were predictable and boring. Throughout the experience I just lay hoping it would end soon. It did not seem as though I had encountered intrapsychic material which was being expressed through somatic symptoms. Rather, I felt that I was struggling to metabolize a chemical disruption of my physiological functions. Although the session was not enjoyable, I was satisfied at having educated myself about the effect produced by a penalty dose of this compound."

(with 2 g *Peganum harmala* seeds, ground, in capsules) "No effects."

(with 5 g *Peganum harmala* seeds, ground, in capsules) "At about 1:45 tinnitus was obvious. At 2:00 precise movements were problematical and nystagmus was noticeable. Mild nausea and diarrhea, but no vomiting. I was sensitive to light and sound, and retired to a dark room. Hallucinations were intense, but only with the eyes closed. They consisted, initially, of a wide variety of geometrical patterns in dark colors, getting more intense as time went on. They disappeared when the eyes were opened. Although the loose bowels and nausea were pretty constant through the first part of the trip, I was not afraid. It was as if the "fear circuits" in the brain had been turned off. The geometric shapes evolved into more concrete images, people's faces, movies of all sorts playing at high speed, and animal presences such as snakes. It was like vivid and intense dreaming except that I remembered most of it afterwards. In another hour things became manageable and I could go out in public. My sex drive was pleasantly enhanced, and I slept very well."

(with 7 g *Peganum harmala* seeds, ground, in capsules) "Very sick for 24 hours."

(with 20 g *Peganum harmala* seeds, as extract) "This is equivalent, probably, to a gram or so of the harmala alkaloids. This was ground up material extracted with hot dilute lemon juice. Within a half hour, I found myself both trippy and sleepy. Then I became quite disorientated, nauseous, and with an accelerated heart beat. I had the strong sensation of moving backwards, drifting, with faint visuals under my eyelids. Restraining the vomiting urge was an ongoing problem.

I could have gone out of body quite easily, except that I was completely anchored by the nausea. After about three hours, I knew that it had peaked, and I went to sleep and experienced intense and strange dreams. The entire experience was a conflict between tripping and being sick. I want to explore this more."

(with 28 g *Peganum harmala* seeds, as extract) "I sat up late one night drinking gulp after gulp of tea from about an oz. of seeds, periodically adding more water and simmering. This process took several hours, and though I had read up on harmaline, I didn't know quite what to expect. Suddenly it hit me like a wall. It was starting to get light outside and as I shifted my gaze, zebra-like stripes of light and dark spiraled off the perimeter of the window silhouettes. Every time I shifted my focus my visual field would shudder and swirl before settling down. This visual effect had a physicality unlike those of any other entheogen I'd experienced. Rather than patterns revealing greater order in sensation, these were waves of chaos revealing no particular order and urging the mind to retreat from the disturbing realm of sensation. Accompanying this was a pronounced auditory buzz. Lying down and closing my eyes I left the physical symptoms behind and explored the vivid spontaneous imaginations evoked by this state. Unfortunately, it was getting light, which made it harder to shut out the distracting world of sensation. I resolved to conduct future sessions in the night-time (and always in a quiet, undisturbed place).

"A second trial was made at the same level. This time it came on very fast. That tremendous buzz on the other side of which are the wondrous realms of the subconscious. The most memorable impressions from this trip were of weird animals. I imagined myself spinning on a merry-go-round of strange winged creatures. I started to feel very sick and negotiated my way to the bathroom to face the inevitable — voiding from both orifices simultaneously. It proved cathartic, and released me to experience the state more fully. I remember traveling to jungle-like places, full of imagery of vines, fountains, and animals. Minutes seemed like hours as I roamed in these spaces. Though the sensory effects were very disturbing when I got up, given the high dose level, I could easily ignore my body when laying down and traveling in my mind."

EXTENSIONS AND COMMENTARY: Right off the bat, I must make an apology, in that I have commingled reports employing harmaline as a single chemical, with reports employing seeds from *Peganum harmala*. This is, of course, pharmacological nonsense in that harmaline is a pure chemical substance, whereas the seeds of the *P. harmala* contain harmine as well, along with a lot of other alkaloids that could well play some role in its psychopharmacology profile.

There is a valid reason for this commingling of the reports of the effects of this chemical and plant, however. In many people's minds, the two materials are felt to be exclusively monoamineoxidase inhibitors, and to be interchangeable. I recently read the following bit of advice somewhere on the internet. "If you really want to get off on 'shrooms, take some harmaline or Syrian Rue seeds along with them." This one phrase embodies a number of popular myths in the psychedelic drug subculture. Let me try to unravel this tangled knot.

Some drugs are metabolized by the removal of the needed amine function. This deamination results from the action of an enzyme system that is called a monoamineoxidase, or a MAO. If this enzyme system is inhibited, then the drug would be destroyed to a lesser extent, and would have a greater potency. The material that protects the drug from this erosion is called a monoamineoxidase inhibitor, or a MAOI. As a result, some drugs that do not show any oral activity (such as DMT) become available when the oxidizing enzymes are made dysfunctional by an inhibitor. This is the heart of the chapter Hoasca vs. Ayahuasca, where this argument is treated at length. But, there is a general inference that the MAOI is, itself, without action and this is simply not correct. They might show some activity in that there are a lot of dietary amines, some of them pretty toxic things, that normally do not bother us since our body defenses can destroy them. Take away that defense, and they can express their toxicity. But I truly believe that there can be a complex spectrum of pharmacological properties that are intrinsic to the inhibiting drug. A goodly number of our prescription anti-depressants on the market today have exactly this mechanism of action.

That is the reason for the presentation of the effects of harmaline by itself, and of *Peganum harmala* seeds, just by themselves. They are very different from oneanother, although both can be pretty rough on the body.

Now, I would like to reenter the qualitative comments mode, this time with the use of harmaline or *Peganum harmala* in conjunction with a second drug. In some of these examples, the inhibitor was taken ahead of the actual tryptamine, as indicated by the time statement.

FURTHER QUALITATIVE COMMENTS:

WITH DMT

(with 20 mg harmaline and 55 mg DMT) "There was nothing for three hours, and then I became aware of some eyes-closed hypnogogic abstractions. The peak was slightly longer with adrenergic push somewhat more intense than what the mild psychic effects would suggest. The come-down was equally drawn out. It all was certainly less intense than when the DMT is smoked."

(with 50 mg harmaline, 60 mg DMT [20 min]) "No effects were noted except for perhaps a brief suggestion of some increase in motor activity."

(with 80 mg harmaline, 40 mg DMT [60 min]) "There was quite a bit of visual activity. The onset was subtle, but the drop-off was quick."

(with 100 mg harmaline, 120 mg DMT [10 min]) "It was not until 80 minutes into the experiment that it became clear that CNS effects were occurring. Initially this was felt as clarity of detail of everything around me followed by slight time distortion. There was no loss of reality but closed eye imagery developed rapidly, later becoming present even with eyes open, even though less intense. Images were initially very colorful, consisting of sheets of patterns infinitely repeated with some gentle waviness, somewhat like looking through a kaleido-scope. Deliberate shifting of attention was possible at all times and although gait was mildly affected it was possible to perform any given task with concentration. There was no loss of identity or reality. Pupillary movements did not change the area of focus of my 'sight,' which was surprising. Images could be willfully dismissed as desired with eyes open. Music became another world with headphones on, and 'Hearts of Space' albums easily became voyages which could be interrupted at any desired point with eyes opening. The effects began to recede at the two and a half hour point. The bright colors and patterns had shifted to less intense scenery in a calm, peaceful way. At no time was there any noticeable amphetamine jaw-clenching, hyperactivity, or restlessness. The entire episode had ended at the four hour point leaving an intense feeling of happiness and amazement. Sleep was easy at five hours, and yet for the subsequent 30 hours my concentration was noticeably impaired. There were no motor problems or incoordination, yet short-term memory was significantly disrupted, requiring deliberate concentration on minor things. At 38 hours my mental condition seemed back to normal. The only criticism I might make of this experience was that there seemed to be none of the insight that I had experienced with TMA-2. This seems, however, to be a very psychologically safe experience for almost anyone and was very enjoyable."

(with 150 mg harmaline, 35 mg DMT [20 minutes]) "Initial effects were noted at 70 minutes, characterized by feelings of mild intoxication followed by significant visual distortions and inability to focus thoughts. By two hours, colored patterning was present with eyesclosed, but the images flashed through conscious-ness so quickly that they could not be considered or analyzed. There was a pronounced sensation of being cold that was difficult to change, despite a very warm heating blanket. An interesting finding was that I was unable to visually "picture" some desired scene. In other words, I could verbally say that I wanted to visualize a forest, or a horse, or a tree, but none of these items could be brought forward. The rapid flood of thoughts quickly became exhausting and there was a strong desire to avoid all stimuli, including music, TV, or any other sounds. The effects began declining at the three-hour point and were essentially gone at five hours. I am beginning to reach the conclusion that DMT has few redeeming qualities. So far, it cannot compare with the insight and clarity of thought which occur with some of the phenethylamines and phenylisopropylamines. This potent activity at the 35 milligram level suggests that the 150 milligrams harmaline dose is highly effective as an MAO blocker."

(with 150 mg harmaline, 80 mg DMT [20 min]) "At just about an hour into it there was a rapid onset intoxication with some staggers and difficult walking. During the next half hour, there were closed-eye visuals along with nausea and a severe depression. I turned on all the lights in the room for security, although I do not like bright lights. I considered calling a friend on the phone, but then I realized that nothing could reassure me at this point. Intellectually I knew that I was safe, but psychologically there was overwhelming loss of self worth and a feeling of despair. This was a severe ego-smashing experience which might have been diagnosed as psychosis if a psychiatrist had been present. The effects lasted longer than anticipated, with a gradual return to normality at the fifth hour, and an hour later I slept. Despite the negative experience, the next day I realized that I had viewed many aspects of my life with extraordinary clarity and insight, and as a result of this experience I intend to try to change several of these personal flaws."

(with the extract of 3 g *Peganum harmala* seeds, 40 mg DMT) "The DMT was noticeably effective just over an hour following ingestion, and it built up to a peak rather quickly. It stayed there for an hour, then dropped off. I would call the overall effect mild."

(with the extract of 5 g *Peganum harmala* seeds, 20 mg DMT [0 min]) "There was a feeling of aliveness and excitement, above and beyond the effects of this amount of harmel seeds alone."

WITH 5-MeO-DMT

(with 70 mg harmaline, 10 mg 5-MeO-DMT [0 min]). "I felt changes in pressure around the eyes at 18 minutes, and there was a floating feeling when walking. I had peaked at an hour and a half, probably at a plus three, with no visuals, no emotionals, no intellectuals, no negative, no positive. A little nausea. I am not sure why I am at a +++ but I am. By the 2 hour point I am coming down. At three hours, I noticed a complete change of character, the harmaline was beginning to kick in. This grew in intensity for several hours, with quite a bit of nausea. This was fully equivalent to 300 mg. harmaline alone, but without the physiological noise. At 12 hours I got a little sleep with a lot of dreams."

(with 80 mg harmaline, 10 mg 5-MeO-DMT) "This was conceptually very active. Extremely rewarding. Remarkable difference from the harmaline alone, or the tryptamine alone, neither of which would have been active taken this way, orally."

(with 150 mg harmaline, 25 mg 5-MeO-DMT [60 min]) "In about 15 minutes I began to feel the typical effects of 5-MeO-DMT, a gradually building emotion of solid, somewhat boiling, turbulent feeling. I began to feel like vomiting so I did so, several times. Waves of the inner feeling would approach, completely removing my awareness of the physical world, but it never reached that point as it does when I have smoked 12 milligrams of 5-MeO-DMT alone. The experience was quite intense but I never felt a great deal of fear. I consciously debated whether or not to smoke some 5-MeO-DMT in order to break through this 'middle' level of experience into a complete transcendent state as I had experienced in the past. But the complexities of asking for the pipe and managing to smoke it seemed too much, even with assistance. I abandoned the idea.

"I started to come 'down' into a more differentiated consciousness, and the first thing I felt was a powerful, aggressive sexual feeling. I was not wearing any clothes and I spent a long time, over an hour, writhing around, occasionally uttering phrases of one or three or four words of a very hostile and/or sexual nature. I remember saying I hated my sitter (a female) and God, but it was quite clear that it was the sexual/maternal image of the sitter that I hated as something that I desired and felt dependent upon while resenting that I needed something I did not have within myself. The next phase found me physically calm and quiet. Finally, after four hours, I felt sleepy and comfortable. I ate well, and was in a good mood.

"I do not feel that taking a higher dose orally would necessarily have pushed me through to the state achieved by smoking because the onset was so, so slow. I don't think I'll repeat this combination."

## WITH TMPEA

(with 150 mg harmaline, 200 mg TMPEA (2,4,5-trimethoxy-phenethyl-amine) [20 min]) "A very faint peripheral visual flicker was noted at 40 minutes. By 80 minutes, a decrease in coordination was apparent and walking required somewhat more attention than normal. This incoordination increased gradually, peaking at three hours. By this time the visual latency characteristic of harmaline was pronounced (when rotating the head or gazing quickly in a different direction, the prior images exit the visual field in a multiple wave fashion in a direction opposite to the motion). At no time were there any detectable effects on thought, and there was no open- or closed-eye imagery, with or without music. No effects were detectable at the five hour point and sleep was easily achieved shortly thereafter. In summary, there was nothing there that could not be explained by the harmaline alone."

## WITH MESCALINE

(with 100 mg harmaline, 60 mg mescaline (3,4,5-trimethoxy-phenethyl-amine) [20 min]) "At two hours I was in a pleasant state of physical relaxation, a fine sense of well being, and I found music most enjoyable. From then to the fourth hour, thoughts flowed freely, and it became obvious that insight was a major part of this experience. Normally unconscious thoughts were easily available. It was as if I could observe my mind in operation, as facts were weighed to form conclusions. By the sixth hour music was a thing of beauty, with the higher notes crisp and clear. The harmaline has probably worn off. Sleep at eight hours, and the next day was without any adverse effects. This was a remarkable experience, the insight of TMA, and the relaxation of MDMA."

(with 150 mg harmaline, 100 mg mescaline [15 min]) "A stomach ache developed at about 45 minutes, followed by a mild nausea which occurred intermittently throughout the next six hours. I felt comfortable, although there was a slight discoordination at about two hours. Walking was never a problem but did require more concentration than normal. Colors on the television were obviously more intense, and highly saturated at this point, and moderate photophobia developed. Even a fire in the fireplace was distracting, and stereo was best enjoyed in the dark. Attempts at sleep did not work until the ninth hour. Upon awakening there was a feeling of dehydration but otherwise no ill effects. Mild looseness of stools was present later that morning. Since experiments using only mescaline at doses between 80 and 120 milligrams resulted in no CNS effects at all, it seems clear that the MAO blocking effects of the harmaline were crucial to this experience.

FURTHER EXTENSIONS AND COMMENTARY: There is a fascinating unanswered question that I had to ask myself a little while ago. It is a question that, if ever answered accurately, just might throw the entire area of the pharmacology of harmaline into a delightful disarray. I received a small quantity of documented seeds of Syrian rue and I was curious to see, in my hands, what its alkaloid content was. This is, after all, a well-known source rapidly increasing in popularity as the inhibitor component of ayahuasca. So I ground a few of them up in a mortar under DMF and carbonate, spun down the extract, dissolved a drop of it in a milliliter of 90:10 toluene/butanol, and shot a microliter into the GCMS. As expected, there were two major peaks, and an intriguing scatter of small things. The spectrum of the first was clearly that of harmaline, and of the second, that of harmine. The literature is correct.

Then, to tidy up a bit and make absolutely sure of the relative retention times, I decided to run standards from my reference collection. Reference harmine gave the second peak with identical retention time and MS spectrum. It was when I injected a sample of my reference harmaline that I got my surprise. Here, a sample of E. Merck AG, Darmstadt yellow crystalline material labeled Harmalinhydrochlorid, was very much looking as if it was a mixture of about two parts harmaline and one part harmine. Only 70% pure? Wow.

Three explanations popped into mind. (1) Maybe the harmine was being generated from harmaline, somehow, in my analysis. So I tried another reference sample, one recently purchased, and it gave a single peak. So it was not an artifact arising from some quirk of my analytical process. (2) Maybe the Merck sample, which I had obtained in the early 1960's (and of course I had no way of knowing how old it was when I got it) had come from plant sources, maybe even *P. harmala* itself. Maybe the analytical tools at the time were inadequate to detect and identify this amount of harmine as an impurity. This is not comfortable, in that these two alkaloids were first isolated, and separated from oneanother, from plant sources some 150 years ago. I am sure my sample is not that old. I am not sure that even E. Merck AG is that old. The tools of analysis have been around a long time. Anyway, I wrote to them, and they answered me with the elliptical statement that they had never had harmaline in their catalog, only harmine. And thus, they would have no way of knowing what was in the bottle. Of course they could have distributed research samples of many things, of stuff that was never in their catalog, but by replying in this way they are absolved of all guilt. And of all legal responsibility as well, of course. OK.

This leaves (3). Maybe over the years, harmaline spontaneously loses a molecule of hydrogen, and becomes harmine. Not an easy thing to reckon with, chemically, but I am running out of possibilities. I was led to a comment that had been once made by a quiet hero of mine, Bo Holmstedt in Sweden, concerning the analysis of an ancient sample of plant material from *Banisteria caapi* (now known as *Banisteriopsis caapi*). The herbarium specimens he was looking at had been collected by the 19th century plant explorer Richard Spruce in the Rio Negro area of South America and had, after a few years of storage in a moist and mildewy hut a few miles down river, been rediscovered and sent on to the Kew Botanical Museum where they had quietly rested for over a hundred years. When Holmstedt worked them up some 30 years ago, he reported that the alkaloid content was 0.4%. This was virtually identical to a newly collected, botanically verified specimen of *Banisteriopsis caapi* which he analyzed at the same time and found to contain 0.5% alkaloids. The latter material contained, as described by many authors, the main alkaloids harmine, harmaline and tetrahydroharmine. By contrast, the alkaloid content of the Spruce material consisted exclusively of harmine. It is open to question whether the samples collected by Spruce in 1853 originally contained only harmine or, perhaps more likely, that harmaline and tetrahydroharmine have with time been transformed into the chemically more stable aromatic $\beta$-carboline harmine.

How can this enigma be answered? Put away a sample of pure harmaline, with its spectral identification, onto the shelf for 50 or 100 years, and then re-analyze it? Who knows, but what might be needed for this conversion is heat, or a bit of iron catalyst, or some unknown species of South American mold. Acid is certainly known to promote this oxidation. It would be very much worth while to answer this question because some, perhaps much, of the results of human pharmacological studies that involve harmaline as a metabolic poison may be influenced by the independent action of harmine as a harmaline contaminant.

If, indeed, the use of *Peganum harmala* becomes increasingly popular as a harmaline source, some help might be useful for those who do not have balances and need to call upon volumes instead. I decided to make an equivalency table between weights, and volumes, and quantities, and laboratory numbers, and kitchen things, so that some consistency might be found in the measurement of the botanical materials that are being used. In short, how heavy is something or how bulky is it? My starting point was the most frequently used tool that is mentioned, continuously, in the lay press dealing with drugs and drug use. It is the teaspoon. How much stuff is there in a teaspoon? Just how big is a teaspoon? What is a teaspoon? Is it a small semi-spherical metal scoop hanging from a ring that has other scoops of different dimensions attached, that is found in the knife and cork-puller drawer in the kitchen? Or is it a schluppy thing, with an artistic handle on it, that adds sugar to your coffee and does the stirring? Do you heap stuff up on it, or do you level it off by smoothing it flat with your finger? The dictionary says that a teaspoonful contains exactly 1.333 fluid drams. Indeed! Let's look it up. You will discover that this is a total cop-out if you read the dictionary definitions of dram: (1) 1.771 grams if you are using the avoirdupois system, or (2) 3.887 grams if you are using the apothecaries system. So, how does a non-pharmacist person, without an analytical scale or an immediate command of the avoirdupois versus apothecaries vocabulary, measure a wanted quantity of *Peganum* seeds?

I would suggest using the following scale, remembering that, with water, weights can be easily interchanged with volumes, since water has a weight that is equal to its volume. In both of these scales, the water and the rue, the teaspoon is the small semi-spherical thing in the cork-puller drawer, leveled off:

—— This is for water ——

| | | | | |
|---|---|---|---|---|
| 1 teaspoon water = | | | | 0.16 ounces (5 grams) |
| 3 teaspoons = 1 tablespoon = | | | | 0.5 ounce (14 grams) |
| 2 tablespoons = | | | | 1 ounce (28 grams) |
| 4 tablespoons = | 1/4 cup = | | | 2 ounces |
| 16 tablespoons = | 1 cup = | 1/2 pint = | | 8 ounces |
| | 2 cups = | 1 pint = | | 1 pound |
| | | 2 pints = | | 1 quart |
| | | 4 quarts = | | 1 gallon |

or, as I had learned as a childhood rhyme: a pint's a pound, the world around.

You must remember, this volume thing has its own traps. When you start using the volume measurement for things such as seeds, or bark, or leaves, or other biological things that are not of the density of water, they possess varying degrees of fluffiness, and the weights will be less than the volumes. The Rosetta stone translation that is appropriate here is based on the fact that the *Peganum harmala* seeds are just over half the density of water. And, since they may contain from 2 to 6% their weight in alkaloids, the following equations are useful:

—— This is for the seeds of Syrian rue ——

| | | |
|---|---|---|
| 1 teaspoon rue seeds = | 3 grams = | 60-180 mg alkaloids |
| 1 tablespoon rue seeds = | 9 grams = | 200 - 600 mg alkaloids |
| 1 large (OO) gelatin capsule | | |
| with ground rue seeds = | 0.7 gram = | 15-45 mg alkaloids |

But do remember, with the harmaline and harmine content of the seeds of *Peganum harmala*, you are also accepting an equal weight of quinazoline alkaloids with pharmacological properties that are quite different from those of the carbolines.

### #14.    HARMINE;    β-CARBOLINE,   7-METHOXY;   7-METHOXY-β-CARBOLINE;    BANISTERINE;    YAGEINE;    TELEPATHINE; LEUCOHARMINE

SYNTHESIS: To a solution of 0.5 g harmaline hydrochloride dihydrate in 8 mL EtOH containing 8 mL concentrated HCl there was added a solution of 0.25 mL concentrated $HNO_3$ in 7 mL EtOH. This was heated on the steam bath until an exothermic reaction set in, with considerable bubbling. Heating was continued for 0.5 min, and then the reaction mixture was cooled, producing a crop of fine crystals, which were removed by filtration and washed lightly with EtOH. With air drying, there was thus obtained 0.31 g (67%) harmine hydrochloride monohydrate which was dissolved in 3.1 mL $H_2O$ and neutralized with a few drops of concentrated $NH_4OH$. There separated a fine, pale cream solid that was removed by filtration and air dried, to give 0.22 g (89%) harmine base as an off-white powder. MS (in m/z): parent ion 212 (100%); 169 (67%); 197 (24%). IR (in $cm^{-1}$): 819, 951, 1037, 1110, 1138, 1165. Harmine hydrochloride hydrate, IR (in $cm^{-1}$): 737, 800, 821, 1021, 1076, 1110, 1138, 1162.

DOSAGE:  unknown

DURATION:  unknown

QUALITATIVE COMMENTS:  (some reports paraphrased from literature summations)

(with 25-75 mg, s.c.)  L. Lewin found this to produce euphoria which Turner et al. insisted should not be regarded as a hallucinogenic reaction.

(with 35 mg, orally, and separately intranasally) "In neither occasion was a notable psychoactive or somatic effect felt, and harmine could not be detected in any of the plasma samples."

(with 35-40 mg, i.v.) "The most frequent symptoms were bradychardia, trouble in focusing the eyes, tingling, hypotension, cold extremities and light-headedness. All symptoms disappeared within 45 minutes after the injection except bradychardia in two subjects and drowsiness in three subjects."

(with 40 mg, orally) "There was an immediate sensation of excitement with difficulty remaining in one place. Restlessness was the predominant symptom. All activity was performed as if with greater ease, and no clouding of the senses was described. It appeared to be a consequence of 'central cortico-motorstimulation.' I felt as if consciousness was packed with ether. When lying on a sofa, the lightness increased to a feeling of a fleeting sensation, and the weight of the body was subjectively less."

(with >40 mg, orally) "The excitement I felt was increased even in a belligerent way. Although it is not my nature, I started a fight with a man in the street where I was the one who attacked. Even though, according to the circumstances, the prospect for me was unfavorable."

(with 140 mg, orally) "There was no stimulation, no suggestion of entheogenic response, perhaps a little bit of sedation which was still evident several hours later. It was sufficiently mild as to make me forget I had ingested anything."

(with 150-300 mg, i.v. [clinical distillation of Pennes and Hoch]) "With this route, 5 of 11 subjects reported visual hallucinations of varying degrees of complexity and organization. Bradycardia and hypotension occurred with all doses of intravenous harmine despite a 20 to 30 minute injection time, thereby limiting maximum dosage to 300 mg. Recovery occurred in about 30 minutes. The drug was hallucinogenic by oral or subcutaneous routes."

(with 300 mg, sublingually) "I found myself pleasantly relaxed and withdrawn from my environment. There was a slightly diminished capacity to concentrate."

(with 300-400 mg, orally [undocumented claim by Clarke]) "Produces psychotic symptoms."

(with 750 mg, sublingually) "Dizziness, nausea and ataxia were the neurological symptoms observed. I do not choose to go any higher — there must be other substances that are responsible for the hallucinogenic effects of Ayahuasca."

(with up to 900 mg, orally [clinical distillation of Pennes and Hoch]) "Visual hallucinations might have occurred."

EXTENSIONS AND COMMENTARY: Here I am being just a bit nasty. What a hodge-podge of published reports which are, in several cases, simply quoted here from the literature. Up the nose, down the throat, under the tongue, in the arm. Claims of irrational aggression at about 30 milligrams can be contrasted with claims of virtually nothing happening at all at up to a gram. I have no choice but to give the dosage as "unknown" and to let the reader pick and choose what fits his fancy. One of the most dramatic syntheses of chemistry with medicine can be found in a viewing of the treatment of the symptoms of Parkinson's Disease. The clinical course of PD had been well characterized by the turn of the century. One of the more bizarre aspects of the syndrome is the alternation of periods of total immobility with those of easy movement. To the extent that these changes might be part of willful action, it was suspected by some physicians that the disease might have psychological components, and be a kind of neurosis. This led to the exploring of a number of psychotropic agents in the search for therapies.

It was Louis Lewin, of *Phantastica* fame, who first suggested that banisterine might be useful in the treatment of diseases of the nervous system. And it was Kurt Beringer, of *der Meskalinrausch* fame, who ran the first clinical study using banisterine on 15 patients with postencephalitic parkinsonism, in 1928. Other studies reinforced the virtues of this drug. Initially, doses of 20 or 40 mg were administered intramuscularly, and within 15 minutes the patients had less motor rigidity and were able to move more freely. Even when used orally, at 10 mg thrice daily, the responses were remarkable. In some cases the tremor was diminished, and in others it was exaggerated, but in general the mental status of the patients was brightened, without producing "psychic" effects. Banisterine became the wonder drug of the year, the feature stuff of the Sunday Supplements.

Then, through a series of events, it fell out of favor just as rapidly. A large study involved patients who had been controlled rather well with scopolamine. They were withdrawn from treatment for a week, deteriorated rather badly, and to a large measure failed to respond to banisterine. And at about this time another researcher, a German physician Dr. Halpern, involved herself in self-experimentation (the physician of the 40 and >40 milligram quote above) and published these findings at the time of this excitement. Belligerency is not necessarily a good property for a drug to have in the treatment of sick people. Then it became popularized that banisterine is really an old and well-known plant product called harmine. The pharmaceutical industry was evolving into the preference for synthetic materials that were patentable, and losing interest in natural products that were not patentable. What a short but fascinating bit of medical history.

There is a strange overlap between the chemistry of harmine and that of a botched synthesis of a meperidine analogue. During the illicit synthesis of what was called the reverse ester of meperidine, the propionate esterification of 4-phenyl-4-hydroxy-N-methylpiperidine, dehydration occurred instead, producing a compound called 4-phenyl-N-methyl-1,2,3,6-tetrahydropyridine, or MPTP. This wrong product was injected as if it were meperidine, and produced immediate and irreversible Parkinsonism in the user. What happens in the brain is that the material is aromatized to form a quaternary salt, called MPP+, a toxic metabolite. If a N-methyl bridge were to be put between the two rings of MPP+, one would have a carboline, one that could in theory be produced from harmine. This material, 2,N-dimethylharmine has been synthesized, and vies with MPP+ as a neurotoxin. What is it we can't see, here? Harmine can serve as a treatment for Parkinson's disease, and a dimethylated harmine can be a potential causative agent for Parkinson's disease.

As with harmaline, a number of drug combinations have been studied using harmine as the potential deaminase inhibitor. This is much closer to the basic structure of ayahuasca, where the plant *Banisteriopsis caapi* is the native inhibitory component, and it contains much more harmine than harmaline. In measured experiments, the use of harmine in the 140 to 190 milligram range, administered with 35 to 40 milligrams DMT, produced unmistakable effects lasting from one to three hours. Trials with smaller amounts, with 120 to 140 milligrams of harmine and 30 milligrams of DMT, produced no signs of central activity at all. Harmine apparently is an effective, although modest, promoter of oral activity of DMT. At least this occurs at levels where it itself is substantially without action, so here it may truly be a facilitator rather than a participant.

### #15.   4-HO-DBT;   TRYPTAMINE, N,N-DIBUTYL-4-HYDROXY; 4-INDOLOL, 3-[2-(DIBUTYLAMINO)ETHYL];   N,N-DIBUTYL-4-HYDROXYTRYPTAMINE; 3-[2-(DIBUTYLAMINO)ETHYL]-4-INDOLOL

SYNTHESIS: A solution of 0.50 g 4-acetoxyindole (see under 4-HO-DET for its preparation) in 5 mL Et$_2$O was stirred and cooled to 0 °C with protection from atmospheric moisture. There was then added 0.5 mL oxalyl chloride. The reaction mixture was stirred for an additional 30 min, and the intermediate indoleglyoxyl chloride separated as a yellow crystalline solid but was not isolated. This was treated with a 40% solution of dibutyl amine in anhydrous Et$_2$O, dropwise, until the pH was 8-9. The reaction was diluted with 100 mL CHCl$_3$ and shaken with 30 mL of a 5% aqueous NaHSO$_4$ followed by 30 mL of a saturated aqueous NaHCO$_3$ solution. After drying over anhydrous MgSO$_4$, the organic solvents were removed under vacuum.   The residue was recrystallized from cyclohexane/hexane

to give 0.78 g (77%) of 4-acetoxy-indol-3-yl-N,N-dibutylglyoxylamide with a mp 123-125 °C. Anal: C,H,N.

To a stirred suspension of 0.50 g LAH in 10 mL anhydrous THF stirred under nitrogen, at room temperature, there was added a solution of 0.75 g 4-acetoxyindol-3-yl-N,N-dibutylglyoxylamide in 10 mL anhydrous THF. This was added dropwise at a rate that maintained the reaction at reflux. When the addition was complete, the reflux was maintained for an additional 15 min and then the reaction was cooled to 40 °C. The excess hydride and the product complex were destroyed by the addition of 1.0 mL EtOAc followed by 3.0 mL H$_2$O. The solids were removed by filtration, the filter cake washed with THF, the filtrate and washings pooled, and the solvents removed under vacuum.   The residue was distilled at the KugelRohr and the distillate recrystallized from EtOAc/hexane. Thus there was obtained 0.19 g (35%) of N,N-dibutyl-4-hydroxy-tryptamine (4-HO-DBT) with a mp 74-75 °C. C,H,N.

DOSAGE: >20 mg, orally

DURATION: unknown

QUALITATIVE COMMENTS: (with 20 mg, orally) "No effect."

EXTENSIONS AND COMMENTARY: This was a total disappointment. With the remarkable activity of the diisopropyl compound (4-HO-DIPT) this seemed to be a promising candidate for activity. Especially interesting would be the di-sec-butyl isomer with the same branching of the chain right at the position of attachment to the basic nitrogen atom.

Allow me a moment to present to the non-chemist a lay definition of what is being talked about here. This is one of the most exciting, and most annoying, tidbits of what could be called isomeric aliphatic chain branching. Please, all non-chemists, forget that I used that phrase. Let me give a simple demonstration of the weird terms (such as methyl, ethyl, propyl, butyl) and prefixes (such as normal, iso, secondary, tertiary) that have been part and parcel of this second half of the book. Let me give you, hypothetically, any number of tennis balls (my metaphor for carbon atoms) from one (initially) to four (at which point I will abandon ship). You are to put them (however many you have) up against the tennis net in every possible way.

You have one tennis ball. There is only one way you can do it. There is the net (the nitrogen atom with an implacable point of attachment, that can touch only one ball at a time, at least in this example), and here is the ball (the carbon atom that has to be attached to it):

N - C                          one carbon is methyl,
                               there's only one way it can be attached.

Now you have been given two tennis balls:

N - C - C                      two carbons is ethyl,
                               there is only one way you can attach them.

Now you have been given three tennis balls:

N - C - C - C                  three carbons is propyl,
                               this is one way they can be attached
                               (known as propyl).

But a second possibility emerges:

N - C - C                      the third tennis ball can touch the first,
   |                           rather than the second ball
   C                           (known as isopropyl).

Now you have been given the fourth tennis ball:

N - C - C - C - C              four carbon atoms is butyl,
                               this is one way they can be attached
                               (known as normal butyl),

```
N - C - C - C          the fourth ball can touch the first,
      |                this is another way they can touch
      C                (known as secondary butyl, or s-butyl),


N - C - C - C          the fourth ball can touch the second,
      |                this is yet another way they can touch
      C                (known as iso butyl, or i-butyl),
```

(of course, if the fourth ball touches the third, you have the normal butyl, as shown before)

```
      C                the third and fourth ball can touch the first one,
      |                this is the fourth way they can touch
N - C - C              (known as tertiary butyl, or t-butyl).
      |
      C
```

You can have one of the four tennis balls touching two of the others at the same time (as well as touching the nitrogen); this formation is known as a cyclopropyl ring. Four of them all touching one another gives a cyclobutyl ring. You can see that when the number of tennis balls gets into the many dozens, the isomer count gets into the many millions, because there can be not just straight out, but ups and downs as well, and little rings and big rings and multiple rings, and cross-linking and everything and anything that can be imagined. That, in a word, is what makes chemistry fun. When two groups that are the same are both attached to the nitrogen atom, you have a di-compound, and with this four-tennis ball analogy, you can have dibutyl, or di-i-butyl, or di-s-butyl or di-t-butyl tryptamine and, of course, all possible mixtures.

Back to the rational world. Two n-butyl groups gives the compound 4-HO-DBT, the theme of this recipe. It is not active at 20 milligrams, but I suspect that it will be so at a somewhat higher dose. There is the secondary-isomer, 4-hydroxy-N,N-di-s-butyltryptamine (4-HO-DSBT, an oil that never crystallized) which should be an isomer of increased activity, but it has not been assayed. The iso-isomer (4-HO-DIBT, mp 152-154 °C) should be yet less active as the steric mess around that important nitrogen atom is much larger, and indeed it is not active at the same 20 milligram level. The tertiary isomer (4-HO-DTBT) has yet to be made and, as it is extremely crowded around that innocent nitrogen atom, it may be unmakable. The activity is unknown, as the compound itself is unknown. The four methyl butyl possibilities are all known, and are mentioned in the recipe for 4-HO-MPT.

#### #16.    4-HO-DET; TRYPTAMINE, N,N-DIETHYL-4-HYDROXY; 4-INDOLOL, 3-[2-(DIETHYLAMINO)ETHYL]; N,N-DIETHYL-4-HYDROX-YTRYPTAMINE; 3-[2-(DIETHYLAMINO)ETHYL]-4-INDOLOL; CZ-74

#### 4-HO-DET PHOSPHATE ESTER; TRYPTAMINE, N,N-DIETHYL-4-PHOSPHORYLOXY; 4-INDOLOL, 3-[2-(DIETHYLAMINO)ETHYL], PHOSPHATE ESTER; N,N-DIETHYL-4-PHOSPHORYLOXYTRYPT-AMINE; 3-[2-(DIETHYLAMINO)ETHYL]-4-INDOLOL, PHOSPHATE ESTER; CEY-19

SYNTHESIS: To a solution of 5.0 g 4-hydroxyindole in 20 mL pyridine there was added 10 mL acetic anhydride and the reaction heated on the steam bath for 10 min. The reaction was quenched by pouring over chipped ice to which was added an excess of $NaHCO_3$. After being stirred for 0.5 h the product was extracted with EtOAc and the extracts washed with brine and the solvent removed under vacuum. The residue weighed 6.3 g (95%) which, after crystallization from cyclohexane, had a melting point of 98-100 °C. IR (in $cm^{-1}$): 1750 for the carbonyl absorbtion.

To a solution of 0.50 g 4-acetoxyindole in 4 mL $Et_2O$, that was stirred and cooled with an external ice bath, there was added, dropwise, a solution of 0.5 mL oxalyl chloride in 3 mL anhydrous $Et_2O$. Stirring was continued for 0.5 h and the intermediate indoleglyoxylchloride separated as a yellow crystalline solid but it was not isolated. There was then added, dropwise, a 40% solution of diethylamine in $Et_2O$ until the pH was raised to 8-9. The reaction was then quenched by the addition of 100 mL $CHCl_3$, and the organic phase was washed with 30 mL of 5% $NaHSO_4$ solution, with 30 mL of saturated $NaHCO_3$, and finally with 30 mL of saturated brine. After drying with anhydrous $MgSO_4$, the solvent was removed under vacuum. The residue set up as crystals and, after recrystallization from $Et_2O$, provided 0.62 g (72%) 4-acetoxyindol-3-yl-N,N-diethylglyoxylamide with a mp of 150-151 °C.

A suspension of 0.5 g LAH in 10 mL anhydrous THF was held in an inert atmosphere and vigorously stirred. To this there was added, dropwise, a solution of 0.6 g of 4-acetoxyindol-3-yl-N,N-diethylglyoxylamide in 10 mL anhydrous THF at a rate that maintained a gentle reflux. After the addition was complete, the refluxing was maintained for an additional 15 min, cooled to 40 °C, and the excess hydride killed by the addition of 1.0 mL EtOAc, followed by 2.3 mL $H_2O$. The reaction mixture was filtered free of solids under a $N_2$ atmosphere, washed with THF, and the filtrate and washings combined and stripped of solvent under vacuum. The residue was distilled in a KugelRohr apparatus and the solid distillate recrystallized from EtOAc/hexane to give 0.24 g (52%) 3-[2-(diethylamino)ethyl]-4-

indolol (4-HO-DET) as white crystals with a mp of 103-104 °C. The product discolored quickly in the presence of air, and was best stored under an inert atmosphere at -30 °C. Conversion to the phosphate ester was achieved by reaction of the sodium salt of 3-[2-(diethylamino)ethyl]-4-indolol with dibenzyl-chlorophosphonate, followed by the reductive removal of the benzyl groups with catalytic hydrogenation, as described for psilocybin.

DOSAGE:  10 - 25 mg, orally (as the indolol, the acetate or the phosphate)

DURATION:  4 - 6 h

COMMENTS:  (with 15 mg indolol, orally) "This was in a gelatin capsule and it came on from a half hour to the three-quarter hour point like gang-busters. Time really slowed down, with sparkly-ness, interesting, and yet there was a touch of sadness. The intense visuals held the scene, and there was the compulsion to talk and to interact and to share stuff, but the erotic was not to be found. I slept OK but there was something uncomfortable at a deep level. Am OK."

(with 15 mg phosphate ester, orally) "It is meaningful to say that I ceased to exist, becoming immersed in the ground of Being, in Brahman, in God, in 'nothingness,' in Ultimate Reality, or in some similar religious symbol for oneness. The feelings I experienced could best be described as cosmic tenderness, infinite love, penetrating peace, eternal blessing and unconditional acceptance on one hand and, on the other, as unspeakable awe, overflowing joy, primeval humility, inexpressible gratitude and boundless devotion. Yet, all of these words are hopelessly inadequate and can do little more than meekly point toward the genuine, inexpressible feelings actually experienced. It is misleading even to use the words, 'I experienced,' as during the peak of the experience (which must have lasted at least an hour) there was no duality between myself and what I experienced. Rather, I was these feelings, or ceased to be in them and felt no loss at the cessation. Four days after the experience itself, I continue to feel a deep sense of awe and reverence, and am simultaneously intoxicated with an ecstatic joy. This euphoric feeling is in no sense analogous to hebephrenic giddiness; it includes elements of profound peace and steadfastness, surging like a spring from a depth of my being which has rarely, if ever, been tapped prior to the drug experience."

(with 20 mg indolol, orally) "I felt this faster than psilocin, but being twenty mg this is probably less potent."

(with 20 mg acetate ester, orally) "A mild stomach discomfort for twenty minutes, followed by intoxication to the 40 minute point. A strange mixture of things at one hour, sedation, jaw-tightening, and a generalized body tremor. The light from the fireplace gave me bursts of color. Music let me drift with my thoughts. Anorexia was intense, in fact there was some gut disturbance throughout the day, plus a lot of diuretic effect. Four hours into it I was fine on the telephone to a friend who knew nothing about the day."

(with 25 mg acetate ester, orally) "There was nausea and motor incoordination going into this. And my blood pressure went up a bit. The mental part of it all peaked at 90 minutes and all closed-eye effects had stopped after three hours. Another couple of hours and the body seemed to be OK again. Sleep OK, too. I am not impressed with this stuff."

EXTENSIONS AND COMMENTARY: On the topic of psilocybin and psilocin, one of the most frequent questions I am asked is, "Isn't it true that psilocybin is immediately converted to psilocin in the blood stream, and so the two chemicals are in essence identical, molecule for molecule?" At this moment I always suppress a brief sense of mental fragmentation, with the automatic reply, "Where is the evidence that psilocybin is converted to psilocin in man?" If it exists, I certainly do not know of it. This clears my conscience. I really do not know the answer. But I have a tremendously strong suspicion that it really does. Any such ester, be it the phosphate, the sulfate, or the acetate, would all be easily split to the archetypal indolol by the ubiquitous esterases in the body. I do indeed believe, in my inner heart, that they all act upon the brain as the same end product, psilocin. And here, with the N,N-diethyl homologue, the same arguments probably hold as well.

The ratios of molecular weights for these ethyl homologues, 314 for the phosphate (CEY-19), the same for the sulfate (by the way, it's not yet explored in man, to my knowledge), 276 for the acetate and 234 for the free phenol (CZ-74), all fall into a pretty narrow range, from about 4 to 3. So, the weight of the ester component in the actual molecule being considered is a relatively minor factor in the dose calculation. I am at peace with the hypothesis that all four compounds are interchangeable in potency.

Some fascinating studies have been done in Germany where the metabolically active mycelium of some Psilocybe species have been administered diethyltryptamine as a potential diet component. Normally, this mushroom species dutifully converts N,N-dimethyltryptamine (DMT) to psilocin, by introducing a 4-hydroxyl group into the molecule by something that is probably called an indole 4-hydroxylase by the biochemists. You put DMT in, you get 4-hydroxy-DMT out, and this is psilocin. Maybe if you put Mickey Mouse in, you would get 4-hydroxy-Mickey Mouse out. It is as if the mushroom psyche didn't really care what it was working with, it was simply compelled to do its sacred duty to 4-hydroxylate any tryptamine it came across. It was observed that if you put N,N-diethyltryptamine (DET, which has not yet been found in nature) into the growing process, the dutiful and ignorant enzymes would hydroxylate it to 4-hydroxy-N,N-diethyltryptamine (4-HO-DET) a potent drug also not known in nature. This is the title drug of this commentary. Yet another beautiful burr to thrust into the natural versus synthetic controversy. If a plant (a mushroom mycelium in this case) is given a man-made chemical, and this plant converts it, using its natural capabilities, into a product that had never before been known in nature, is that product natural? What is natural? This is the stuff of many long and pointless essays.

A valuable concept was championed by one of the most respected psychotherapists and academicians in recent years, Hanscarl Leuner, the Chairman of the Psychotherapeutic Department of the University of Göttingen, Germany. Leuner was convinced that the value of the psychedelic drug was in the opening of the psyche with repeated modest exposures, with therapy carried forth over a period of time. This is the "psycholytic" approach to therapy. An opposite approach is called "psychedelic." Here there is what might well be a one-time interaction, in which the patient is blasted into orbit with the hopes of his confronting his problem and also finding its solution. When LSD is used in the former approach, in psycholytic dosages, one would expect levels of between 50 and 150 micrograms to be used; in the latter (psychedelic) approach, the dosage would be in the 500 to 1500 microgram range. The first calls upon the activation and development of a process of understanding; the second can be seen as a religious crisis, or a conversion event. In Europe, the first was favored, but there were strong advocates (Unger, Pahnke, Grof) in the United States favoring the latter process. Here, CZ-74 was thought to be suitable only in the psycholytic role, in that it was too short lived and, at high doses, there was a restlessness and body disturbance that was not usually seen with LSD.

There is a second instructive point to be learned from Leuner. It was he who had made early observations of the psychological effects of CZ-74 in man (within two years of the reported synthesis in about 1959) and had carried out the most extensive clinical studies ever conducted, involving at least 160 trials in human volunteers. He presented two separate reports in 1965, to two very different audiences. To the psychotherapeutic audience there was a strong emphasis made of the psycholytic virtues to be found in CZ-74, including its very short duration and the positive nature of the experience. The sessions were called "overwhelming and ecstatic" with the "elimination of the hangover of LSD — or any pathological after-effects — even with dosages of up to 40 milligrams." The plaudits continued: "Thus, this drug must be considered to be particularly safe and suited for ambulant psycholytic treatment and use by psychiatrists in their practices." Almost every-thing was positive.

However, in addressing a neurosciences conference, also in 1965, and referring to the same studies and the same experimental population, he reported some pretty heavy-duty neuropharmacological negatives. "In all sessions there were disturbances of body image, illusions, pseudo-hallucinations and hallucina-tions. In 50% of [the] cases, motor restlessness, aphasia, loss of concentration and temporal and spatial disorientation could be clearly observed. In 25% of the cases there was loss of impetus, derealization and acoustic hallucinations. More rarely and only with the highest doses did extreme psychotic symptoms occur, with increased volubility, depersonalization, cosmic-mystic experiences, delirium, schizo-phrenic behavior with catatonic fits and temporary paranoia." Almost everything was negative.

At a banquet associated with an international conference on the study of consciousness, held in Göttingen a few years ago, Alice and I had the pleasure of sitting at the table with Hanscarl Leuner and his wife. He thanked me for inventing 2C-D, which he and his students had been exploring as an adjunct to psychotherapy. They had renamed it, initially DMM-PEA and then LE-25, and had apparently explored it at dosages that reached into the hundreds of milligrams. In *PIHKAL*, I had offered an effective range for this drug of from 20 to 60 milligrams. It would seem that in his later years, Dr. Leuner chose to move from the psycholytic camp over to the psychedelic camp.

One final comment. When you read a paper or listen to a lecture offered by a researcher of impeccable qualifications, take a moment to look about you to see who is alongside you in the audience that is being addressed. Who else is reading his paper? Who else is hearing his lecture? How might the presentation be tailored to fit the interests of the recipients? The identification and recognition of your neighbors should play a role in your evaluation and acceptance of the presentation.

## #17. 4-HO-DIPT: TRYPTAMINE, N,N-DIISOPROPYL-4-HYDROXY; 4-INDOLOL, 3-[2-(DIISOPROPYLAMINO)ETHYL]; N,N-DIISOPROPYL-4-HYDROXYTRYPTAMINE; 3-[2-(DIISOPROPYLAMINO)ETHYL]-4-INDOLOL

SYNTHESIS: A solution of 0.50 g 4-acetoxyindole (see under 4-HO-DET for its preparation) in 5 mL $Et_2O$ was stirred and cooled to 0 °C with protection from atmospheric moisture. There was then added 0.5 mL oxalyl chloride. The reaction mixture was stirred for an additional 30 min, and the intermediate indoleglyoxyl chloride separated as a yellow crystalline solid but not isolated. This was treated with a 40% solution of diisopropyl amine in anhydrous $Et_2O$, dropwise, until the pH was 8-9. The reaction was diluted with 100 mL $CHCl_3$ and shaken with 30 mL of a 5% aqueous $NaHSO_4$ followed by 30 mL of a saturated aqueous $NaHCO_3$ solution. After drying over anhydrous $MgSO_4$, the organic solvents were removed under vacuum. The residue was recrystallized from EtOAc/hexane to give 0.33 g (35%) of 4-acetoxyindol-3-yl-N,N-diisopropylglyoxylamide, mp 204-206 °C. Anal: C,H,N.

To a stirred suspension of 0.25 g LAH in 10 mL anhydrous THF, stirred, under nitrogen and at room temperature, there was added a solution of 0.30 g 4-acetoxyindol-3-yl-N,N-diisopropylglyoxylamide in 10 mL anhydrous THF. This was added, dropwise, at a rate that maintained the reaction at reflux. When the addition was complete, the reflux was maintained for an additional 15 min and then the reaction was cooled to 40 °C. The excess hydride and the product complex were destroyed by the addition of 0.5 mL EtOAc followed by 1.5 mL $H_2O$. The solids were removed by filtration, the filter cake washed with THF, the filtrate and washings pooled, and the solvents removed under vacuum. The residue was distilled at the KugelRohr and the distillate dissolved in 1 mL MeOH. One equivalent of dilute HCl was added, and the volatiles were removed under vacuum. The solid residue was recrystallized from MeOH/$Et_2O$ to give 0.12 g (44%) of 4-hydroxy-N,N-diisopropyltryptamine hydrochloride (4-HO-DIPT), mp 263 °C with decomposition. Anal: C,H,N.

DOSAGE: 15 - 20 mg, orally

DURATION: 2 - 3 h

QUALITATIVE COMMENTS: (with 10 mg, orally) "I feel it in my legs! Within the hour I have leg tremors, a mild physical awareness for another hour. Mentally, probably nothing."

(with 15 mg, orally) "There was an alerting, noisy and nice, in 30 minutes. I swear I am already there. Nice friendly place. Perhaps some light tension, like a chill, maybe my body temperature response is confused. At the two hour point I am substantially out of the experience. Short, intense experience, basically enjoyable. Another hour and I am back to where I started in every way."

(with 20 mg, orally) "It has a bitter taste. Early signs noted at 15-20 minutes which include mild sensation of central stimulation, 'loosening' of muscles in arms, legs, and neck. Mild distortion of objects and slight color effects, typically 'rainbow halos' around objects. Plateau reached in 20 minutes. Mild elation with relatively simple intellectual musings about the nature of the compound and how one could describe the nature of the state of mind and body caused by this material. 2.0 hours, mild effects. 2.5 hours, nearly normal. Mild but entirely pleasant experience with rather abrupt termination of effects. Could be a good candidate for psychotherapy sessions, certainly good for 'novice' introduction to hallucinogens."

(with 20 mg, orally) "Fifteen minutes, it starts and develops fast — very nice — some leg tremor. Thirty minutes, I am already well over a plus 2. Speed of onset is incredible — I could not drive — I feel robbed of voluntary action. Forty minutes, this could not get any deeper. Fifty minutes, incredible orgasm. Fifty five minutes, I struggle to put a name to it, just +++ smashed — with eyes closed very little — I am somewhat chilled — no visual, no sensory, this seems like an extreme Aleph-7 Beth state (see Places in the Mind, chapter 10). One hour ten minutes, Rubenesque fancy — no sex but back-to-mother cuddly imagery — removed from physical angles. One hour thirty minutes, go for two very significant pieces of wood for the fireplace — if all my actions are preprogrammed and I am following commands, then I have no free will — if the command is 'to have free will', then I obey. Whom? Who? Why obey an undefined, unheard commander? Still +++. Nothing is inventive, all is preprogrammed. One hour forty minutes, back to ++, still very much in the grips of 'lack of self determination.' I could function rationally in the lab, but following 'whose' directions? Is this finally God? Is this a religious experience? One hour fifty minutes, down to +. This has to have been a religious awakening. Two hours, still a little zombie-like, but largely down. Two hours twenty minutes, I am still shaken to my roots by these realizations. Three hours, completely together."

EXTENSIONS AND COMMENTARY: I truly doubt that there is another psychedelic drug, anywhere, that can match this one for speed, for intensity, for brevity, and sensitivity to dose, at least one that is active orally. These reports have been taken from different experimenters, but they share some rather consistent features:

Speed: The effects are noted within a quarter hour following ingestion. LSD is one of the few psychedelic drugs that can show its early effects in the first few minutes. This suggests fundal absorption.

Intensity: The second 20 milligram report sounds as if there was some flirting with the magical plus-four transcendental peak experience. I happened to be the subject, and I was impressed.

Brevity: To be on a trip and then to be back pretty much in two hours and really baseline in another hour? Most unusual. If there will ever be an acceptance of drugs such as these, in a psychotherapeutic context, a short duration is of extreme value to both the patient and the therapist.

Sensitivity to dose: There have been a number of trials at and below the 10 milligram bottom, and most have been substantially without activity. And yet, there have been no trials at higher than 20 milligrams, as far as I know. That is a lot of steepness in the dose-response curve.

And similar comments can be made regarding the consistency of physical side-effects. There seemed to be a muscular tremor, and a vague body malaise, that is part of the trip. At least when the psyche got going, the body was less noticeable.

An interesting sideline. This is the same nitrogen substitution pattern, N,N-diisopropyl, that is present in the rather dramatic sex-enhancer 5-MeO-DIPT. I wonder what might come out of an exploration of this substitution pattern in the world of the phenethylamines? As a rule, most phenethylamines lose their appeal with substitution on the nitrogen atom. But has anyone tried to make an N,N-diisopropyl homologue of MDMA, for example? Or of mescaline? Or of DOM? It would be interesting to explore these areas.

**#18.  4-HO-DMT;  TRYPTAMINE, 4-HYDROXY-N,N-DIMETHYL;  4-INDOLOL, 3-[2-(DIMETHYLAMINO)ETHYL];  N,N-DIMETHYL-4-HY-DROXYTRYPTAMINE; 3-[2-(DIMETHYLAMINO)ETHYL]-4-INDOLOL; CX-59; PSOH; PSILOCIN**

**4-HO-DMT PHOSPHATE ESTER;  TRYPTAMINE, N,N-DIMETHYL-4-PHOSPHORYLOXY;  4-INDOLOL, 3-[2-(DIMETHYLAMINO)ETHYL], PHOSPHATE ESTER;  N,N-DIMETHYL-4-PHOSPHORYLOXY-TRYPTAMINE; 3-[2-(DIMETHYLAMINO)ETHYL]-4-INDOLOL, PHOS-PHATE ESTER;  CY-39;  PSOP;  PSILOCIN, PHOSPHATE ESTER; PSILOCYBIN**

SYNTHESIS: To a solution of 0.50 g 4-acetoxyindole (see preparation in the recipe for 4-HO-DET) in 4 mL Et$_2$O that was stirred and cooled with an external ice bath there was added, dropwise, a solution of 0.5 mL oxalyl chloride in 3 mL anhydrous Et$_2$O. Stirring was continued for 0.5 h and the intermediate indoleglyoxyl chloride separated as a yellow, crystalline solid but it was not isolated. There was then added, dropwise, a 40% solution of dimethylamine in Et$_2$O until the pH came to 8-9. The reaction was then quenched by the addition of 100 mL CHCl$_3$, and the organic phase was washed with 30 mL of 5% NaHSO$_4$ solution, with 30 mL of saturated NaHCO$_3$, and finally with 30 mL of saturated brine. After drying with anhydrous MgSO$_4$, the solvent was removed under vacuum. The residue set up as crystals and, after recrystallization from THF, provided 0.61 g (80%) 4-acetoxyindol-3-yl-N,N-dimethylglyoxylamide with a mp of 204-205 °C. Anal: C,H,N.

A suspension of 0.38 g LAH in 10 mL anhydrous THF was held in an inert atmosphere and vigorously stirred. To this there was added, dropwise, a solution

of 0.55 g of 4-acetoxyindol-3-yl-N,N-dimethylglyoxylamide in 10 mL anhydrous THF at a rate that maintained a gentle reflux. After the addition was complete, the refluxing was maintained for an additional 15 min, the reaction mixture cooled to 40 °C, and the excess hydride destroyed by the addition of water diluted with a little THF. The reaction mixture was filtered free of insoluble material under a N$_2$ atmosphere and the resulting solids washed with THF. The filtrate and washings were combined and stripped of solvent under vacuum. The residue was distilled in a KugelRohr apparatus and the solid distillate recrystallized from EtOAc/hexane to give 3-[2-(dimethylamino)ethyl]-4-indolol (4-HO-DMT, psilocin) as a white oil which solidified. Recrystallization from EtOAc/hexane gave white crystals which had a mp of 103-104 °C. The final weight was 0.23 g (yield 56%). IR (in cm$^{-1}$): 686, 725, 832, 991, 1040 and 1055; the OH stretch is at 3240. MS (in m/z): C$_3$H$_8$N$^+$ 58 (100%); parent ion 204 (15%); indolemethylene+ 146 (3%); 159 (2%).

Most of the early syntheses of psilocin and psilocybin use the O-benzyl ether as a protecting group. This provides more stability to the chemical intermediates, but also requires the additional step of reductive debenzylation. The flow chart of this process is: conversion of 4-hydroxyindole to 4-benzyloxyindole via the sodium salt, with benzyl chloride; the conversion of this with oxalyl chloride to 4-benzyloxyindole-3-glyoxylchloride; the conversion of this to 4-benzyloxyindole-3-(N,N-dimethyl)glyoxamide with anhydrous dimethylamine; the conversion of this to 4-benzyloxy-N,N-dimethyltryptamine with LAH in dioxane; and finally the conversion of this to 4-HO-DMT (psilocin) with hydrogen with a Pd catalyst on $Al_2O_3$. The phosphate ester, psilocybin, requires two additional steps: the conversion of 4-HO-DMT (as the sodium salt) to 4-(O,O-dibenzylphosphoryloxy)-N,N-dimethyltryptamine, with dibenzyl chloro-phosphonate, followed by the catalytic removal of the benzyl groups with hydrogen and Pd on $Al_2O_3$ to give the phosphate ester of 4-HO-DMT (psilocybin). This product is much more stable in air than psilocin, and is water soluble. The yields of this conversion are, however, very bad, often less than 10%, and the two products appear to be pharmacologically equivalent. Further, I have heard that the phosphorylating agent dibenzyl chlorophosphonate must always be used in solution as it is quite unstable as a pure reagent. The fingerprint infra-red spectrum for psilocybin shows (in $cm^{-1}$): 752, 789, 806, 858, 925 and the P=O stretch at 1110; the acidic OH stretches are broad peaks at 2400, 2700 and 3200. The mass spectrum is identical to that of psilocin.

DOSAGE: 10 - 20 mg, orally (as the indolol, the acetate or the phosphate)

DURATION: 3 - 6 h

QUALITATIVE COMMENTS: (with 6.6 mg phosphate ester, orally) "Something has started but I decide to join in a full dinner anyway. The effects develop right through the meal, with some hints of animal faces in the pork-chop bones. No movement, nothing flows, but it probably wouldn't take much effort. Another hour and I am dropping off already. The food? Somehow I doubt it. I would be completely unable to tell this from, say, 80 milligrams of MDMA except that I had a good appetite."

(with 7 mg, orally) "Basically I am not in a pleasant place — quite neurotic — inwardly turned — a touch of despair — considerable visual activity and if I were with someone I might find some sort of reinforcement. The apathy and unpleasantness is ebbing now. My mood might have been negative, and the psilocybin simply amplified everything. There was some intensification of the lights and darks around me."

(with 10 mg, orally) "Approximately forty minutes after the start, there was a flutter and a very high, stimulated feeling, and gradually things began to move very rapidly. It was astounding. When I closed my eyes I saw so many fantastically beautiful patterns, textures, colors. Everywhere I looked, eyes open, colors were brilliant. The house looked absolutely gorgeous, nature was simply spectacular. It was a little frightening, almost too exciting, after the gentleness of other substances. I could not believe that I was doing it, and that I had the power within myself to see such beauty. I don't know how long this went on but the motion was so rapid that I felt a sort of motion sickness. Then I became quite nauseated and remained nauseated the rest of the day, until things quieted down in the evening, and then I felt absolutely wonderful."

(with 15 mg, orally) "My 'early warning system' alerted me at fifteen minutes, then all was quiet for a while. I start building up again, and I am awfully glad that I am familiar with this transition. Visual distortions. Things distract me. I can't find the cap to my pen — must I keep writing forever? At this point I couldn't drive, let alone write, and it is just a bit more than a half hour since I took it. The furniture in my office is moving up and down. I lie down, and close my eyes. THIS is where it is at. Visuals are wild. Even with eyes open, with no visual target, there are imaginative visual effects. I imagine a dark room with a fire place going in the middle of the night, with no other inputs, and with my eyes closed I have the body image of being seated in front of that fire and I am amazed by the hallucinations and distortions I am seeing there only there is no fireplace as I am still lying in my darkened bedroom. Sort of a 2x removed hallucination. This is a night-time drug — the day-light washes everything out. I tried but could not repeat the fireplace thing, and must be dropping rapidly. At three hours I ask if I would try some other experiment. OK, but there are some reservations. At four hours, no reservations."

(with 15 mg, orally) "As soon as I felt the chill and the alert, I lay down and closed my eyes. Indian motif. Abundant fruits, vegetables, leaves, straw, wood, vines. Very responsive sexually. Beautiful, stern, rich encounter with livingness and Indian Gods and serenity. Color and peacefulness. A couple of hours, then elaborateness dropped slightly. At this point top of temple easy, but it was a South American temple, with earth floor, straw, vines full of fruit. Familiar feeling. We are naked and we are children-adults, daring to be there, regarded benignly (stern, amused) (rising through the floor). This is one of the true ones, this plant experience.

(with 12 mg phosphate ester, intramuscularly) "This is strong. There were a lot of wild images in about two hours, and I thought that the day would never end. At about six hours I knew it would, but in fact in the evening I took 100 milligrams of Seconal which allowed me to drift into a fine sleep. The next day I was fine."

(with 3 mg phosphate ester, intravenously) "The effects are immediate (in 30 seconds) and I did not have the time to build up any worry — it was simply too fast. In about an hour I was back where I started from."

(with 12 mg phosphate ester, intravenously) "I had had eight milligrams earlier, with a very good reaction. Here, today, I feel that everything has disintegrated, and I am extremely anxious. I am very confused."

*Psilocybe cubensis*: (with 1.5 g, orally) "At best, some speckled patterning with my eyes closed, and in general a light intoxication. Certainly not the sparkle of LSD. Dropped quickly and felt heavy and tired, good sleep."

(with 3.5 g, orally) "Took a gram to start with, and it started in ten minutes, but not strong enough, so did the other 2.5 grams. Everything was coming at me in waves, boxing me in, the visuals were in waves and in dark earth colors, orange and brown, not the wide spectrum of acid. I was sea-sick, and vomiting helps some, and a little dope quieted the tummy. Started dropping, and everything became very good, and by midnight I was out. No hangover at all."

EXTENSIONS AND COMMENTARY: There are two generalizations implicit here, one of which I am quite at peace with, but the other is both complex and disturbing. The OK item is the casual equation between the hydroxy compound psilocin, the acetate ester, and the phosphate ester, psilocybin. As I had discussed in the CZ-74 to CEY-19 entries in 4-HO-DET, there is no proof that the ester goes to the indolol metabolically, but it is a good guess, and there have been no demonstrated differences in their pharmacology. Ditto here, with psilocin and psilocybin. I have explored both of them as pure chemicals, and I find them completely interchangeable as to their pharmacological properties.

The second generalization is more difficult and leads into some uncomfortable areas. This is the effort to equate the chemicals, psilocin and psilocybin, with their natural sources, the mushrooms. Part of the uncertainties I feel are related to the unknowns that are intrinsic to the plant sources. There are many species that have been offered and accepted as magic mushrooms. Identification in the field is one thing, but what can be said of dried, ground up plant material of unknown sources? What are they? How have they been preserved? What is their composition? The older samples may be reasonably free of the rather unstable psilocin, but psilocybin is much more stable and may persist. But so might its congeners such as baeocystin and norbaeocystin which are scattered in widely different proportions in many species, and which are quite unexplored pharmacologically. The same instability certainly applies to the dephosphoralated psilocin analogues 4-HO-NMT and 4-HO-T. These both could well be metabolites of psilocin in man. There are so many uncontrollable variables in the mushroom area that here I cast my vote for exploration with the chemicals themselves. They can, at least in principle, be analyzed, and weighed. But this is a luxury not available to many, as the synthesis of these alkaloids is difficult, and woefully illegal.

Which brings us back to the mushrooms, and the topic of the law. In the original writing of the Controlled Substances Act of 1970, our Federal drug law, there are only four plants listed as being "Scheduled Drugs." In Schedule I there was Marijuana (later defined as the plant *Cannabis* spp.) and Peyote (later defined as the botanical *Lophophora williamsii*); in Schedule II there was Opium poppy and poppy straw, and Coca leaves. It is generally known that commercial opium comes from the plant *Papaver somniferum* and that commercial coca comes from the plant *Erythroxylum coca*, but I am not aware of either of these botanical binomials having been explicitly named in the statutes. A couple of quickies were slipped in, not completely properly, in the giving of the binomial of *Tabernanthe iboga* as a synonym for ibogaine, and the giving of the binomial of *Catha edulis* as a synonym for cathinone, both Schedule I drugs. So there are definitely four, and maybe six, plants that can be considered scheduled drugs.

But nowhere in the legal archives of current drug statutes can you find mention of Genera such as *Psilocybe, Stropharia, Paneolus* or *Inocybe*. Nor of the dozens and dozens of species that stem from them. So, you would logically conclude that these magic mushrooms are not illegal? Well, yes and no.

No, in the letter-of-the-law sense that they are not explicitly named as illegal entities. But yes, in the *de facto* exercise of the law. With the inescapable fact that both psilocin and psilocybin are named as Schedule I drugs, and the acknowledgment that there are some mushrooms that might contain these drugs, then these botanical entities become legal complications. Might the dried fruiting bodies be seen as packaging strategy for the sale and delivery of a Schedule I drug? Might the growing of them be seen as a production strategy for the manufacture of a Schedule I drug? Of course it might be, as the law has stated that the manufacture and sale of Schedule I drugs is a Federal felony. "Your Honor. I gathered these things out there in the field for my dinner salad. I had no idea that they contained something illegal." A reasonable defense, and it may well work today, along with the argument that opium poppy pods are buyable at the Farmer's Market as floral decorations, and morning glory seeds can be bought at the local nursery for next Spring's garden. Innocence may be a virtue for a while, as it is not widely recognized that these decorative poppies are in fact Schedule II opium capsules and those *Ipomoea* seeds in fact contain ergine, a Schedule III depressant. But that is today. What happens tomorrow?

Today, to a large measure, the burden of proof still falls upon the accuser, and that ephemeral and undocumented "presumption of innocence" concept provides some measure of protection. They, the accusors, must prove you are guilty. But, as the legal structure drifts from the criminal statutes to the regulatory statutes, this protection is lost. You must prove that you are innocent. The perfect example is the random urine test, which demands, without any probable cause, that you prove that you do not have drugs in you. There is no presumption of innocence. This has been the sad state of our income tax laws for years, and now it is becoming a reality in our drug laws. Prove to the court that you didn't know that these mushrooms were psychoactive! Shades of the Inquisitions of a few hundred years ago. Or the Salem travesties of more recent times. Prove to us you are not a witch.

There is quite a body of scientific literature that discusses the changes (increases and well as decreases) of psilocybin and psilocin content in mushrooms as a function of their nutrient diet. And, under the 4-HO-DET entry, I mentioned that the inclusion of an unnatural component into the diet just might produce an unnatural alkaloidal product, with an exploitation of the natural and available enzyme systems that are part of the mycelial structure.

Another aside. There is a trivial, and fun, bit of nomenclature which I have used for years. I have, in my notes, referred to psilocybin as PSOP (because of the phosphate thing) and psilocin as PSOH (because of the exposed OH group). I have gotten into the habit of referring to the acetate as PSOA, the O-methyl ether as PSOM and the chemical intermediate O-benzyl ether as PSOB. I know that this will never catch on, but I still do it because it is convenient and a bit campy. One code that is not mine, but Sandoz's, is CMY for 1-methyl-psilocin. I know it has been looked at in a clinical environment, but I have no idea as to its activity. It is a straightforward thing to make. I would love to know what it does.

## #19. 5-HO-DMT; TRYPTAMINE, N,N-DIMETHYL-5-HYDROXY; INDOL-5-OL, 3-[2-(DIMETHYLAMINO)ETHYL]; N,N-DIMETHYL-5-HYDROXYTRYPTAMINE; 3-(2-DIMETHYLAMINOETHYL)INDOL-5-OL; N,N-DIMETHYLSEROTONIN; BUFOTENINE; MAPPINE

SYNTHESIS: A solution of 0.67 g 5-hydroxyindole (indol-5-ol) in 10 mL dry MeOH was treated with a solution of 0.30 g NaOMe in MeOH, followed by 0.70 g benzyl chloride. The mixture was heated on the steam bath for 0.5 h, and the solvent removed under vacuum. The residue was suspended between $H_2O$ and $CH_2Cl_2$, the organic phase separated and the aqueous phase extracted once with $CH_2Cl_2$. The combined organics were stripped of solvent under vacuum, and the residue distilled. A colorless fraction came over at 170-190 °C and spontaneously crystallized in the receiver. There was obtained 0.90 g (80%) 5-benzyloxyindole with a mp 81-86 °C which increased, on recrystallization from toluene/hexane, to 94-96 °C. A sample prepared from the decarboxylation of 5-benzyloxyindole-2-carboxylic acid has been reported to have a mp of 102 °C from benzene.

A solution of 1.0 g 5-benzyloxyindole in 20 mL $Et_2O$ was cooled to 0 °C, vigorously stirred, and treated with 0.6 g oxalyl chloride in 10 mL $Et_2O$, added dropwise, over the course of 0.5 h. About half way into the addition a pale red solid appeared. The stirring was continued for an additional 0.5 h and the solids were removed by filtration and washed with a small amount of $Et_2O$. This acid chloride had a mp of 149-151 °C and was used without further purification or characterization in the following reaction. It was added in small increments to 1.2 mL of a 33% aqueous solution of dimethylamine, diluted with acidified $H_2O$, and the resulting solids removed by filtration. These were washed with $H_2O$, and then $Et_2O$ and air dried. The product,

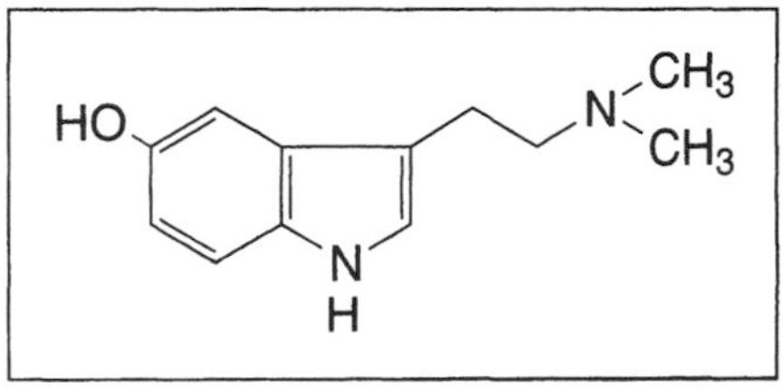

5-benzyloxy-N,N-dimethyl-3-indoleglyoxylamide weighed 1.18 g (82%) when dry and had a mp of 185-187 °C.

To a well-stirred suspension of 1.0 g LAH in 40 mL Et$_2$O there was added a solution of 1.0 g 5-benzyloxy-N,N-dimethyl-3-indoleglyoxylamide in 15 mL THF. When the addition was complete, the mixture was held at reflux temperature for 6 h, cooled, the excess hydride and reaction complex cautiously decomposed by the addition of H$_2$O, and when the hydrogen evolution ceased the mixture was made basic with concentrated NH$_4$OH. The solids were removed by filtration and the filter cake washed with THF. The filtrate and washings were combined, and the solvents removed under vacuum to give a clear residue that was dissolved in Et$_2$O and acidified with a solution of oxalic acid in Et$_2$O. The formed crystals were removed by filtration, washed with Et$_2$O and air dried to yield 1.0 g (84%) of 5-benzyloxy-N,N-dimethyltryptamine oxalate with a mp of 178-180 °C after recrystallization from MeOH. The hydrochloride salt has a reported mp of 154-155 °C, and of 162-163 °C.

The benzyl group was removed by hydrogenation of a solution of 0.8 g 5-benzyloxy-N,N-dimethyltryptamine oxalate in 5 mL MeOH containing 0.1 g 10% Pd/C catalyst. The mixture was shaken under three atm hydrogen for 6 h, and the solids removed by filtration. Evaporation of the solvent under vacuum gave a residue that was dissolved in anhydrous Et$_2$O and acidified with a solution of oxalic acid in Et$_2$O. There was thus obtained, after filtration, Et$_2$O washing, and air drying, 0.53 g (87%) bufotenine mono-oxalate as pink needles, with a mp 93-94 °C. A mp of 178 °C in the literature may be of the bioxalate. The free base has been reported to have a mp of 125-126 °C or 146-147 °C.

DOSAGE:  8 - 16 mg, intravenously

DURATION:  1 - 2 h

QUALITATIVE COMMENTS:  (with 1 mg, intravenously, over a three minute period) "Within a minute (from the start of the injection) I had a tight feeling in my chest and my face felt as if it had been jabbed by nettles and this lasted for about 6 minutes. I had fleeting nausea."

(with 2 mg, intravenously, over a 3 minute period) "I felt a tightness in my throat and stomach and it seemed that my pulse was racing, although apparently there was no change in either my pulse or blood pressure."

(with 4 mg, intravenously, over a 3 minute period) "During the injection, I first felt a burning sensation in my face, then a load pressing down from above, and then a numbness of the entire body. I saw red and black spots — a vivid orange-red — moving around. Apparently my purplish face color lasted some 15 minutes, well after my visual things had disappeared."

(with 8 mg, intravenously, over a 3 minute period) "I became lightheaded as soon as the injection started, and then my face turned purple and I became nauseated and I felt I couldn't breathe. I see white, straight lines with a black background. I can't trace a pattern. Now there are red, green and yellow dots, very bright like they were made out of fluorescent cloth, moving like blood cells through capillaries, weaving in and out of the white lines. In another two minutes, everything was pretty much gone."

(with 10 mg, intravenously, over a 50 second period) "My face was suddenly very hot. I could not breathe fast enough."

(with 10 mg, intravenously, over a 77 second period) "There were no psychological changes."

(with 16 mg, intravenously, over a 3 minute period) "Almost immediately I felt a burning sensation in the roof of my mouth and I felt a tingling all over my body. My face turned purple, and my chest feels crushed. Everything has a yellow haze, and I was sweating heavily and I vomited. Words can't come. My mind feels crowded. When I start on a thought, another one comes along and clashes with it. I can't express myself clearly. I am here and not here. It has now been forty minutes and I feel better, but I still feel like I would like to walk it off, like a hang-over."

EXTENSIONS AND COMMENTARY: This is a presentation of the very earliest studies done with bufotenine with human subjects, studies with 14 schizophrenic patients at a state mental hospital and with two convicts in a state prison. The two convicts were injected over the course of three minutes, with a solution of bufotenine as the salt. This single observation, a description of hyperserotoninemia (a release of serotonin in the blood, called a carcinoid flush) was all it took, at the right time and the right place, to put bufotenine on the books as a "dangerous drug" by FDA classification. And with the passage of the Controlled Substance Act of 1970, it was placed in Schedule I as a hallucinogen, with a high abuse potential and no accepted medical utility. Whatever the actual activity of bufotenine might be, and what role it could play in explaining the complex role of serotonin in the human animal, today it would be extremely difficult to study, because of the flushing of the face of an experimental subject in a prison in Maryland in a study that occurred at just the wrong time.

But that is the politics of the drug. I cannot help but comment on some aspects of the medical ethics that accompanied these studies. Here were a collection of 14 schizophrenic patients— experimental cattle is the analogy that comes to mind — into which the researching physicians injected their drug. Listen to the account of one lady, following a rapid intravenous injection of bufotenine. "There was intense salivation. She could easily have drowned in her own saliva, and she had to be turned on her side. The pulse rate rose slightly during the period extending from the end of the injection until some 10 minutes later, but without much change in blood pressure. Responsiveness returned in about 23 minutes, at which time the patient was entirely lucid and, in response to a query related to a preinjection suggestion, spoke of a long-repressed memory from the age of three years, when she came into the bathroom and saw her mother dying of a uterine hemorrhage. This was told without affect and had no therapeutic consequences." HOLY COW! A schizophrenic victim volunteers a long-repressed memory of her mother's traumatic death. And with the state of the healing art in the mental hospitals of that time, two physicians effectively ignored what today would be considered a dramatic breakthrough in therapy. Another of their trials was acknowledged as being nearly fatal, requiring artificial respiration as intervention. This is research in the healing art of medicine?

So much for the politics, and for the medical ethics lecture. What can one say about the drug itself? This is an example of a very rare breed of active compounds, one that can be found in both the animal and the vegetable kingdoms. From toads to toadstools. There are a number of extremely close structural relatives out there in the wild world. Bufotenine must first and foremost be seen as an extremely close relative to serotonin (one of our principal neurotransmitters) of which it is the N,N-dimethyl homologue. There are many modifications of it in nature (found most frequently in the skins of frogs), and these all have deceptively similar names. It is helpful to me to tally them.

**Bufoviridine:** This is the 1:1 ester of bufotenine with sulfuric acid. It is yet more polar than bufotenine, and correspondingly less likely to get into the brain. If the bisulfate acid position were itself esterified in some biologically stable manner, then this compound just might be centrally active, but probably only via a parenteral route as seen with 5-MeO-DMT. The exposed dimethylamino group would still make it an easy substrate for MAO's.

**Bufotenidine or Cinobufagine:** This is the quaternary amine internal salt, 5-hydroxy-N,N,N-trimethyltryptammonium salt. It also is frequently found as a hydrogen sulfate ester, but this latter has no trivial name. Mention has been made of bufotenidine and its sulfate ester as an occasional companion of histamine analogues found in frog skins. See the appendix on histamines.

**Dehydrobufotenine:** There is a covalent bond formed between the dimethylated nitrogen atom and the indolic 4-position, by the theoretical removal of a molecule of hydrogen. It is no longer a simple tryptamine but as it is a commonly found component of the chemistry of several toads, and a few giant reeds as well, it is included here. It is, by definition, a quaternary amine salt. The original structure assigned it was that of a vinylamine (with the loss of a hydrogen molecule from the alpha/beta chain positions). This was shown to be incorrect.

**Bufothionine:** This is the hydrogen sulfate ester of dehydrobufotenine.

**O-Methylnordehydrobufotenine:** This is a rearrangement product of dehydrobufotenine, which may be a natural product or it may be an artifact of analysis.

**O-Methylbufotenine:** This represents a true crossover alkaloid, found in many plants as well as in the toad family. It is entered as a recipe under the synonym 5-MeO-DMT.

**Norbufotenine** (5-hydroxy-N-methyltryptamine, N-methylserotonin, 5-OH-NMT): This base is scattered in both the animal and the plant kingdoms. It has been found in quite a few toads and in barley shoots. It has been isolated from the herb *Desmodium pulchellum*. This is an interesting twilight compound lying half way between a notorious toxin (bufotenine) and a vital neurotransmitter (serotonin). And it is unexplored, for shame. It has been detected in the urine of schizophrenic subjects, but that doesn't say anything about its potential activity. That bare hydroxyl group may make it difficult to get into the brain, probably as difficult as bufotenine itself proved to be. The removal of the second methyl group reveals serotonin.

**Bufogenins or Bufagins**: These are nitrogen-free steroidal lactones that are heart toxins found in toad venom. They have no chemical resemblance to bufotenine whatsoever. Examples are bufogenin B, bufotalin and bufotalinin.

**Bufotoxins**: These are steroidal bufagins, usually linked via an hydroxyl suberic acid which is, in turn, bound by a peptide link to arginine.

There are two structural variations of bufotenine that I feel would be interesting to explore. One deals with the ethers of the 5-hydroxyl group. The O-methyl ether is, of course, 5-MeO-DMT. It is mentioned above under the name O-methylbufotenine. What about the obvious O-ethylbufotenine, 5-EtO-DMT? It had once been synthesized from 5-ethoxytryptophol in a physostigmine study, and had been converted to bufotenine with aluminum chloride. If the analogy from the phenethylamines applies here (MEM is as potent as TMA-2) then 5-EtO-DMT should be as potent as 5-MeO-DMT. And probably would have to be smoked for the very same reasons. Another variation deals with possible esters on that 5-hydroxyl group. Finding activity in things like the bisulfate bufoviridine would be unlikely, but perhaps an acetate ester (easily made from bufotenine and acetic anhydride) would allow it to make it into the CNS, in a manner similar to the acetate of the 4-hydroxy analogue, psilocin.

There once was (and maybe still is) a group called The Institute of Current World Affairs who gave grants to people to allow them to travel and write on topics of cultural interest. I was on their mailing list, which gave me a fabulous collection of essays and vignettes written by Andy Weil, who later spun some of them together into a book called, *The Marriage of the Sun and Moon*. In trying to organize and understand the pharmacology of bufotenine I was pleasantly reminded of the essays Andy devoted to the magic of Uri Geller.

He was initially completely entranced by the way this young man from Israel could muster the psychic energy of an audience to bring about some remarkable phenomena. It was not just the bending of keys and spoons, but it was remote viewing and mind-reading as well. It was the stuff of the miraculous.

Andy was a total convert, but then there was an abrupt erosion of certainty that began with Andy's meeting with a skeptic called the Amazing Randi, who could duplicate most of the illusions with his sleight of hand mastery. Andy went from total belief to total disbelief in a very short period of time. It seemed that his earlier conviction was wrong and that all was indeed misrepresentation. This change in position of course managed to offend both camps. Then he came finally to a middle ground. The status of Uri Geller may be essentially unanswerable. Psychic phenomena are believed by some. Are these things factual? Who is judging it all, and from what point of view?

And so it is with bufotenine. Is it an active psychedelic? Absolutely yes, absolutely no, and maybe yes and maybe no.

The early reports used the "psychotomimetic" term and pushed for a psychedelic interpretation of the observations. Observers saw colored spots, straight lines against a black background. "Words can't come. My mind feels crowded." These and similar descriptions are often encountered as components of psychedelic experiences. And yet a skeptic would point to the terms that are closely associated with toxic effects, and peripheral poisoning: my face turned purple and I became nauseated, I could not breathe fast enough. Lacrimation and tachycardia. These all are excerpts from the small selection of comments given above. In the period that has followed the earliest studies described in the "Qualitative Comments" section above, there have been about a dozen additional reports that could be offered that describe the same scatter of ups and downs, employing different modes of delivery. With insufflation, I have one that claims a feeling of fear, a flushing of the face, lacrimation and tachycardia, with ten milligrams. Another report states that after snorting forty milligrams, he observed neither objective nor subjective effects. Some clinicians declare that the compound is unquestionably a psychotomimetic and it must be catalogued right up there along with LSD and psilocybin. Others, equally sincere, present human trials that suggest only peripheral toxicity and conclude that there is no central action to be seen. And there are many who state that there are no effects at all, either inside or outside the CNS. The psychopharmacological status of bufotenine, like that of Uri Geller, may be essentially unanswerable.

Two recent publications provide new and provocative input to this dialogue. One of these involved a series of appearances of a reddish substance on the East Coast called Chinese Love Stone, Black Stone, Rock Hard or Stud 100, being sold as aphrodisiacs. They were to be moistened and rubbed on the genitals, but as might be expected, quite a few were eaten and eventually smoked. They contained steroidal toxins, and were possibly related to some frog origins, but they were claimed to be bufotenine and indeed contained bufotenine in addition to several cardiotoxins as well as 5-MeO-DMT.

A second report carries, at least for me, much more impact. A study of the use of the seeds of a South American legume, *Anadenanthera columbrina* var. Cebil by the Argentine Shamans in Chaco Central, shows them to be dramatically psychedelic. And yet, extremely sophisticated spectroscopic analysis has shown them to contain bufotenine and only bufotenine as their alkaloid component.

The bottom line: I do not really know if bufotenine is a psychedelic drug. Maybe yes and maybe no.

## #20. 4-HO-DPT; TRYPTAMINE, N,N-DIPROPYL-4-HYDROXY; 4-INDOLOL, 3-[2-(DIPROPYLAMINO)ETHYL]; N,N-DIPROPYL-4-HYDROXYAMINOTRYPTAMINE; 3-[2-(DIPROPYLAMINO)ETHYL]-4-INDOLOL

SYNTHESIS: A solution of 0.50 g 4-acetoxyindole (see under 4-HO-DET for its preparation) in 5 mL $Et_2O$ was stirred and cooled to 0 °C with protection from atmospheric moisture. There was then added 0.5 mL oxalyl chloride. The reaction mixture was stirred for an additional 30 min, and the intermediate indoleglyoxyl chloride separated as a yellow crystalline solid but was not purified. This was treated with a 40% solution of dipropyl amine in anhydrous $Et_2O$, dropwise, until the pH was 8-9. The reaction was diluted with 100 mL $CHCl_3$ and shaken with 30 mL of a 5% aqueous $NaHSO_4$ followed by 30 mL of a saturated aqueous $NaHCO_3$ solution. After drying over anhydrous $MgSO_4$, the organic solvents were removed under vacuum. The residue was recrystallized from $Et_2O$/cyclohexane to give 0.73 g (78%) of 4-acetoxyindol-3-yl-N,N-dipropylglyoxylamide with a mp 130-131 °C. Anal: C,H,N.

To a stirred suspension of 0.50 g LAH in 10 mL anhydrous THF, stirred, under nitrogen and at room temperature, there was added a solution of 0.66 g 4-acetoxyindol-3-yl-N,N-dipropylglyoxylamide in 10 mL anhydrous THF. This was added dropwise at a rate that maintained the reaction at reflux. When the addition was complete, the reflux was maintained for an additional 15 min and then the reaction was cooled to 40 °C. The excess hydride and the product complex were destroyed by the addition of 1 mL EtOAc followed by 3 mL $H_2O$. The solids were removed by filtration, the filter cake washed with THF, the filtrate and washings pooled, and the solvents removed under vacuum. The residue was distilled at the KugelRohr and the distillate recrystallized from EtOAC/hexane. Thus there was obtained 0.27 g (51%) of N,N-dipropyl-4-hydroxytryptamine (4-HO-DPT) with a mp 96-97 °C. Anal: C,H,N.

DOSAGE: unknown

DURATION: unknown

QUALITATIVE COMMENTS: (with 20 mg, orally) "Possible threshold, nothing more."

EXTENSIONS AND COMMENTARY: Here is another case where there just aren't enough observations to determine at what level the activity will be seen, or what form it will take. The track record is pretty well established with the oxygen-free analogue DPT, and it would be hard to imagine a loss of potency by incorporating the "psilocin signature," the 4-hydroxy group. This threshold suggests something is nearby. It is a shame that the compound is rather difficult to make.

### #21. 4-HO-MET; TRYPTAMINE, N-ETHYL-4-HYDROXY-N-METHYL; 4-INDOLOL, 3-[2-(ETHYLMETHYLAMINO)ETHYL]; N-ETHYL-4-HY-DROXY-N-METHYLTRYPTAMINE; 3-[2-(ETHYLMETHYLAMINO)-ETHYL]-4-INDOLOL

SYNTHESIS: A solution of 0.50 g 4-acetoxyindole (see under 4-HO-DET for its preparation) in 5 mL $Et_2O$ was stirred and cooled to 0 °C with protection from atmospheric moisture. There was then added 0.5 mL oxalyl chloride. The reaction mixture was stirred for an additional 30 min, and the yellow crystalline solid was removed by filtration and dissolved in 10 mL of anhydrous THF. This was treated with a 40% solution of methylethyl amine in anhydrous $Et_2O$, dropwise, until the pH was >10. The solvents were removed under vacuum and the residue dissolved

in 200 mL $CHCl_3$. This was washed first with 50 mL 0.1 N HCl and then with 50 mL of saturated aqueous NaCl. After drying with anhydrous $MgSO_4$ and filtration, the solvent was removed under vacuum. The residue was recrystallized from $Et_2O$ to give 0.60 g (yield 73%) of 4-acetoxyindol-3-yl-N-ethyl-N-methylglyoxylamide with a mp 179-180 °C. Anal: C,H,N.

To 10 mL of a stirred solution of LAH (1 M in THF under $N_2$), there was added dropwise a solution of 0.57 4-acetoxyindol-3-yl-N-ethyl-N-methyl-glyoxylamide in 10 mL anhydrous THF. When the addition was complete, the reaction mixture was brought to a reflux for 15 min. After cooling to 40 °C, sufficient water was added to decompose both the reaction complex and the excess hydride. After filtration through Celite (under an $N_2$ atmosphere), the solvent was removed under vacuum, and the solid residue recrystallized from EtOAc/hexane to provide 0.18 g (41%) N-ethyl-4-hydroxy-N-methylindole (4-HO-MET) with a mp 118-119 °C. Anal: C,H,N.

DOSAGE: 10 - 20 mg, orally

DURATION: 4 - 6 h

QUALITATIVE COMMENTS: (with 20 mg, orally) "Qualitatively a lot like psilocin. It started within the first half-hour, and at the max, I felt the same alteration of color and form, and at times, sound was felt. As with psilocin, the experience was wave-like, with an alteration of effects between near-normal perception at one minute, only to be swept up in a swirl of altered concepts the next minute."

EXTENSIONS AND COMMENTARY: First, an apology for just a single entry in the comments section. This, and several other of these substituted hydroxy and methoxy tryptamines, had had earlier evaluations, but the notes are not at hand and cannot be used. Much will have to come back from memory, and there must be an appropriate fuzziness allowed for the concluded generalization as to dose and duration. With this particular compound, some of the original observations suggested that it was more potent than psilocin, certainly more dramatic. But at the bottom line, I doubt that this ethyl homologue, or the isopropyl homologue 4-HO-DIPT for that matter, could be distinguished from the methyl counterpart psilocin in any blind clinical study.

What's to choose between them? From the viewpoint of synthesis, the cost and availability of the secondary amine will certainly be a factor. Both methylethyl amine and methylisopropylamine are available, but are quite expensive. Dimethylamine, on the other hand, is dirt cheap but it is a recognized precursor to DMT and thus is difficult to find. In any event, the dimethyl compound is widely available in the mycological arena, and I suspect it would be simplest to stay with nature.

## #22. 4-HO-MIPT; TRYPTAMINE, 4-HYDROXY-N-ISOPROPYL-N-ME-THYL; 4-INDOLOL, 3-[2-(ISOPROPYLMETHYLAMINO)ETHYL]; 4-HYDROXY-N-ISOPROPYL-N-METHYLTRYPTAMINE; 3-[2-(ISOPROPYLMETHYLAMINO)ETHYL]-4-INDOLOL

SYNTHESIS: A solution of 0.50 g 4-acetoxyindole (see under 4-HO-DET for its preparation) in 5 mL $Et_2O$ was stirred and cooled to 0 °C with protection from atmospheric moisture. There was then added 0.5 mL oxalyl chloride. The reaction mixture was stirred for an additional 30 min, and the yellow crystalline solid was removed by filtration and dissolved in 10 mL of anhydrous THF. This was treated with a 40% solution of methyl isopropylamine in dry $Et_2O$, dropwise, until the pH of the reaction mixture was >10. The solvents were removed under vacuum and the residue dissolved in 200 mL $CHCl_3$. This was washed first with 50 mL 0.1 N HCl and then with 50 mL of saturated aqueous NaCl. After drying with anhydrous $MgSO_4$ and filtration, the solvent was removed under vacuum. The residue was recrystallized from $CHCl_3$/hexane to give 0.68 g 4-acetoxyindol-3-yl-N-isopropyl-N-methylglyoxylamide with a mp 211-212 °C (79%).

To 10 mL of a stirred solution of LAH (1 M in THF under $N_2$), there was added, dropwise, a solution of 0.60 mg 4-acetoxyindol-3-yl-N-isopropyl-N-methylglyoxylamide in 10 mL anhydrous THF. When the addition was complete, the reaction mixture was brought to a reflux on the steam bath for 15 min. After cooling to 40 °C, sufficient water was added to decompose both the reaction complex and the excess hydride. After filtration

through Celite (under an $N_2$ atmosphere), the solvent was removed under vacuum, and the solid residue recrystallized from EtOAc/hexane. There was thus obtained . 34 g (74%) of 4-hydroxy-N-methyl-N-isopropyl-tryptamine (4-OH-MIPT) with a mp of 123-124 °C. 4-HO-MIPT discolors quickly if it is not kept in an inert atmosphere and in a freezer. Anal: C,H,N.

DOSAGE:  12 - 25 mg, orally (as the indolol or the acetate)

DURATION:  4 - 6 h

QUALITATIVE COMMENTS:  (with 9 mg, orally) "I am stuck just part way on. There is some retinal activity with my eyes closed. Maybe I am a little light-headed, a little starry. Nothing much."

(with 12 mg, orally) "It was just an hour ago that I swallowed the capsule, and everything is happening. It was completely developed at 45 minutes. The imagery with my eyes closed is vivid. The music is exceptionally sensual. I notice a tendency to twitch but it doesn't bother me. Everything is rolling — how can they allow an erotic piece like the Saint-Saëns second piano concerto to ever appear in public, let alone over the radio? A very rapid decline between the third and fourth hour. A rich day for love, insights, fantasy, and for retreating into one's mind. A rich day for discovery."

(with 12 mg, orally) "I suspended the solids in water, and a drop of HCl put it into solution immediately. The first awareness was unmistakable at twenty minutes, and from there it was a rapid and noisy development ending at about an hour. But this lasted for only another 40 minutes, and then dropped off quite rapidly. The erotic was excellent, but there were few visuals and I had difficulty connecting fantasy to music. Good appetite afterwards, and I had no trouble getting to sleep."

(with 15 mg acetate ester, orally) "An interesting mixture of intoxication and sedation, progressing to a very relaxed state with some motor incoordination. Just a little bit like alcohol. There was no drifting of thoughts nor any gut disturbance at any time, although I wasn't very hungry. Conversation was easy."

(with 20 mg, orally) "Early signs (muscle sensations) were noticed in 10 minutes. In another 10 minutes a rapid heightening of all senses ensued, reaching a plateau in 40 minutes and beginning to decline in 3 hours with a return to near normal in 5-6 hours. The intensity of the experience is marked. At the plateau, communication (verbal) is difficult with intense alteration in the sense of time and distance. Multiple and overlapping wave forms occur with an extremely intense color alteration. Drifting in and out of the body is common with an increased sense of body processes, i.e., blood flow in vessels. Muscular sense is increased and a feeling of soaring in bodiless flight is experienced. A mild vertigo was felt with attempted walking but is not associated with nausea. Some anxiety was experienced initially, but could be interpreted as a reaction to the extremely powerful onset. A curious, probably idiosyncratic effect, was of possessing the essence of sexual power associated with being a large jungle cat. The idea was prominent for some time. Conservatively, this compound is at least twice as active as psilocin at comparable doses, in terms of plateau or peak effect. External stimuli, especially light, were distracting to the point of annoyance. Sounds can be seen, words explode into showers of bright points with eyes closed. Other eyes-closed imagery is prominent with patterns (in color); at times soaring clouds dominate the eyes-closed scenery. I cannot overemphasize the intensity of the experience. I would not want to go much higher than 20 milligrams (50 milligrams of psilocin is not as intense)."

(with 30 mg acetate ester, orally) "It was as if I had downed a few martinis in a hurry — except that there were eyes-closed visuals in a lot of different colors, especially metallic greens. I had jaw clenching and a body tremor, reminding me of ecstasy except it was not in any way stimulating. I listened to music in front of a fireplace in a darkened room and I saw bright, colorful, unstructured patterns. Seven hours and I fell into an easy sleep and was fine the next day."

EXTENSIONS AND COMMENTARY: This is a two-carbon homologue of psilocin and, as the latter chemical is orally active, it is not surprising that this is, as well. One direct comparison between the two materials, on widely separated days and at very high levels, indicated that 20 milligrams of 4-HO-MIPT was fully equivalent to 50 milligrams of psilocin, in one report. And yet, in another report with 30 milligrams of the acetate ester, things were considerably more modest. At these higher levels, the onset was noted well within the first half hour.

Here, as with the 4-HO-DMT (psilocin) and the 4-HO-DET entries, some care must be made with the use of the term "acetate" or "phosphate." As these materials are both bases (tertiary amines) and acids (hydroxy indoles), they are, in effect, internal salts. For stability, they are usually converted into salts (at the amine end) or esters (at the phenolic end), or both. In this context, the term "acetate" can mean either modification, a salt or an ester involving acetic acid. And, of course, a phosphate can be either a salt or an ester. I will try to append the additional term "salt" or "ester" whenever this ambiguity is possible. In all of these studies, the acetate is the ester, and some of these are free bases, some are the hydrochloride salts and some are the fumarate salts.

A large number of related homologues of psilocin have been synthesized and described, and some of them tasted to varying degrees, but none of them to a degree of definition to justify a recipe devoted just to them. With the 4-hydroxyl group assuring some measure of oral activity, all of these could serve as a structural activity relationship gestalt to selectively, and specifically, evaluate the geometric nature of the nitrogen substituents.

If one were to be a complete perfectionist in these areas of chemistry, one should actually make the phosphate ester of 4-HO-MIPT, as this would be the exact homologue of psilocybin. But that would be a great amount of additional work, just to have the body chop off the ester group as soon as it had the chance. The current thinking is that there would be the same activity with either compound, making allowances for the change in molecular weight. But at least it might be a lot more stable for storage. What about the sulfate ester? It should be a very stable salt, and the body has sulfatases just as it has phosphatases. Maybe the ubiquitous non-specific esterases would work as well. A number of studies have been made with the acetate ester (some mentioned here) and it should whap off immediately once it's inside you.

A careful clinical comparison of the acetate ester of psilocin with the phosphate ester and the free phenol might help resolve this question. The ideal way of resolving this would be to run pharmacokinetic studies on blood levels of these three materials, in parallel with studies of the psychopharmacological responses. I feel that this is not likely to be done in the foreseeable future.

### #23.  4-HO-MPT;  TRYPTAMINE, 4-HYDROXY-N-METHYL-N-PRO-PYL;  4-INDOLOL, 3-[2-(METHYLPROPYLAMINO)ETHYL];  4-HY-DROXY-N-METHYL-N-PROPYLTRYPTAMINE;  3-[2-(METHYL-PROPYLAMINO)ETHYL]-4-INDOLOL

SYNTHESIS: A solution of 0.50 g 4-acetoxyindole (see under 4-HO-DET for its preparation) in 5 mL Et$_2$O was stirred and cooled to 0 °C with protection from atmospheric moisture. There was then added 0.5 mL oxalyl chloride. The reaction mixture was stirred for an additional 30 min, and the yellow crystalline solid was removed by filtration and dissolved in 10 mL of anhydrous THF. This was treated with a 40% solution of methylpropyl amine in anhydrous Et$_2$O, dropwise, until the pH was >10. The solvents were removed under vacuum and the residue dissolved in 200 mL CHCl$_3$. This was washed first with 50 mL 0.1 N HCl and then with 50 mL of saturated aqueous NaCl. After drying with anhydrous MgSO$_4$ and filtration, the solvent was removed under vacuum. The residue was recrystallized from EtOAc/hexane to give 0.54 g (63%) of 4-acetoxyindol-3-yl-N-methyl-N-propylglyoxylamide with a mp 94-95 °C. Anal: C,H,N.

To 8 mL of a stirred solution of LAH (1 M in THF under $N_2$), there was added, dropwise, a solution of 0.48 4-acetoxyindol-3-yl-N-methyl-N-propylglyoxylamide in 8 mL anhydrous THF. When the addition was complete, the reaction mixture was brought to a reflux for 15 min. After cooling to 40 °C, sufficient water was added to decompose both the reaction complex and the excess hydride. After filtration through Celite (under an $N_2$ atmosphere), the solvent was removed under vacuum, and the oily residue dissolved in MeOH, neutralized with HCl, and $Et_2O$ added until crystallization started. Thus there was obtained 0.23 g (54% of theory) 4-hydroxy-N-methyl-N-propylindole hydrochloride (4-HO-MPT) with a mp 162-163 °C. Anal: C,H,N.

DOSAGE: unknown

DURATION: unknown

QUALITATIVE COMMENTS: (with 8 mg, orally) "There is a very mild visual distortion, and a prominent vertigo without nausea. In the second hour there is still some enhancement of visual detail, but I am not endowed with the flight of ideas or philosophical concepts as with psilocin. I am rapidly subsiding and I am able to eat normally. Residual insomnia lasted eight hours."

EXTENSIONS AND COMMENTARY: As with the discussion presented with the lower homologue, 4-HO-DET, there is not enough here to give a fair estimate of either dose or duration. In my file under this compound I can find only this one report. Extrapolation suggests that this might be yet another material active in the psilocin range of somewhere up to 20 milligrams, all orally. Maybe it is a generality that anything with up to six carbons attached one way or another to the tryptamine nitrogen atom (and all sporting a 4-hydroxy group, of course) will be active in the 10 to 20 milligram range. This certainly holds for the methyl-methyl, methyl-ethyl, methyl-propyl, methyl-isopropyl, diethyl, dipropyl and diisopropyl. That makes it a pretty good generalization.

How far can this argument be pushed? What about one of the N-alkyl groups having four carbons? Keeping the other N-alkyl group as the smallest and most simple methyl group, all four isomeric compounds are known. There is the n-butyl isomer (4-HO-MBT, an oil), the isobutyl isomer (4-HO-MIBT, mp 142-145 °C), the secondary butyl isomer (4-HO-MSBT, mp 138-140 °C) and the tertiary butyl isomer (4-HO-MTBT, mp 225-226 °C). Of these four materials only 4-HO-MTBT has been looked at as a possible psychedelic. Some 15 milligrams produced virtually no effects, maybe a hint of something in a few minutes and then nothing. Probably pure placebo response.

Many yet heavier substitution patterns are in the literature but they, too, are unexplored. The symmetrical disubstituted isomers are listed separately in these recipes.

**#24.    4-HO-pyr-T;    TRYPTAMINE,4-HYDROXY-N,N-TETRAMETH-YLENE;  4-INDOLOL,3-[2-(1-PYRROLIDYL)ETHYL];  PYRROLIDINE, 1-[2-[3-(4-HYDROXY)INDOLYL]ETHYL];    4-HYDROXY-N,N-TETRA-METHYLENETRYPTAMINE;    3-[2-(1-PYRROLIDYL)ETHYL]-4-INDOLOL;    1-[2-[3-(4-HYDROXY)INDOLYL]ETHYL]PYRROLIDINE; "4-HYDROXYPYRROLIDYLTRYPTAMINE"**

SYNTHESIS:  A solution of 0.50 g 4-acetoxyindole (see under 4-HO-DET for its preparation) in 5 mL $Et_2O$ was stirred and cooled to 0 °C with protection from atmospheric moisture. There was then added 0.5 mL oxalyl chloride. The reaction mixture was stirred for an additional 30 min, and the intermediate indoleglyoxyl chloride separated as a yellow crystalline solid but was not purified. This was treated with a 40% solution of pyrrolidine in anhydrous $Et_2O$, dropwise, until the

pH was 8-9. The reaction was diluted with 100 mL $CHCl_3$ and shaken with 30 mL of a 5% aqueous $NaHSO_4$ followed by 30 mL of a saturated aqueous $NaHCO_3$ solution. After drying over anhydrous $MgSO_4$, the organic solvents were removed under vacuum. The residue was recrystallized from $CHCl_3$/hexane to give 0.47 g (55%) of 4-acetoxyindol-3-yl-N,N-tetramethyleneglyoxyl-amide with a mp 174-176 °C. Anal: C,H,N.

To a stirred suspension of 0.25 g LAH in 10 mL anhydrous THF, under nitrogen and at room temperature, there was added a solution of 0.30 g 4-acetoxyindol-3-yl-N,N-tetramethyleneglyoxylamide in 10 mL anhydrous THF. This was added, dropwise, at a rate that maintained the reaction at reflux. When the addition was complete, the reflux was maintained for an additional 15 min and then the reaction was cooled to 40 °C. The excess hydride and the product complex were destroyed by the addition of 0.5 mL EtOAc followed by 1.5 mL $H_2O$. The solids were removed by filtration, the filter cake washed with THF, the filtrate and washings pooled, and the solvents removed under vacuum. The residue was recrystallized from EtOAc/hexane to give 0.12 g (50%) of 4-hydroxy-N,N-tetramethylenetryptamine (4-HO-pyr-T) with a mp 193-195 °C. Anal: C,H,N.

DOSAGE:  >20 mg

DURATION:  unknown

QUALITATIVE COMMENTS:  (with 20 mg, orally) "This substance proved to be quite unlike psilocin and bordered on the bizarre. There was a latency period of about three hours after ingestion before the onset was noted. Visual disturbances were minimal; no alteration in colors or objects occurred. The nature of this compound was characterized by the heightening of the intellectual process, but not to the extent seen with psilocin. The entire experience was more 'stimulant-like' rather than hallucinogenic. A very unpleasant ride. Have no desire to go deeper or, indeed, to look at the other cyclic analogues."

EXTENSIONS AND COMMENTARY: There are three pyrrolidine amines in this tryptamine compilation, and all three are simply weird and illogical. Both the simple "pyrrolidyl tryptamine" (pyr-T) and the 5-methoxy counterpart (5-MeO-pyr-T) caused physical distress, and this one (4-HO-pyr-T) seems to be more of a stimulant than a psychedelic. In all three cases (and with the 5,6-methylenedioxy example as well) the other two-ring systems that often accompany the pyrrolide example as a "set" were simply not explored. This is due, largely, to the unexpected and generally negative responses to the pyrrolidine archetype. The piperidine homologue (4-HO-pip-T) is a white crystalline solid with a mp of 180-181 °C. The morpholine analogue (4-HO-mor-T) is also a white crystalline solid with a mp of 177-178 °C.

### #25. IBOGAINE; 12-METHOXYIBOGAMINE

SYNTHESIS: There have been three total syntheses of ibogaine reported in the chemical literature. The first of these was a thirteen-step process published about 30 years ago. The chemistry lab can serve a fine function for both isolation and purification of ibogaine from plant sources, but in the real world, there is no practical way to start from a bottle of nicotinic acid and actually prepare useful amounts. The parent ring system contains two chiral centers, neither of which is amenable to easy manipulation. Because of these two separate and largely inaccessible

chiral centers there are, in theory, four distinct isomers of ibogaine which are difficult to resolve. When the term "synthetic" is used in regard to ibogaine in the scientific journals, it usually applies to the resynthesis of the parent alkaloid from the demethylated metabolite. For reference purposes, here are the fingerprint numbers from the infrared spectra: for the free base: IR (in $cm^{-1}$): 741, 799, 830, 1037, 1111, 1148; mp 152-153 °C. For the hydrochloride salt: IR (in $cm^{-1}$): 638, 810, 832, 925, 1031, 1149; mp 299-300 °C (dec).

DOSAGE: (from hundreds of milligrams up to a gram or more, orally)

DURATION: (quite long)

EXTENSIONS AND COMMENTARY: Here is an example of a most remarkable material that has allowed people to have some rather complex and dramatic experiences. Any effort to present a fair overview of its action, through a selection of individual responses in the "extension and commentary" format would fail, as it would ignore the impact of the set and setting on the subject. Here I will mention a few of these different sets, and a leading author who gives more detail.

There is a well studied history of the use of the iboga plant in the religious rituals in Gabon and its neighboring countries, from the early part of the 19th century. The Buiti religion calls for the use of the root bark of *Tabernanthe iboga* as a sacrament, and the reports of its psychopharmacological effectiveness reflect these needs (see Samorini).

Another area of reports that can be called upon reflects the exploration of the isolate from this plant, or the isolated active component ibogaine itself, in the study of its use with psychotherapy. Here the reports reflect the physician/patient interaction with an emphasis on early memory and the reliving of past experiences (see Naranjo). In clinical studies such as these, a typical dose would be four hundred milligrams of the chemical, twice this weight of the crude isolate, and perhaps ten times this weight again if the actual root bark is used.

Yet another source of reports is to be found in some studies that are exploring ibogaine as a treatment for heroin dependency (see De Rienzo and Beal). This end-goal of retrieving evidence of addiction confrontation and addiction control can certainly color any published reports in its own way. Here, it is only the chemical ibogaine that is used, and typical dosages are at or above 1000 milligrams.

There is no question but that ibogaine is a rough trip, physically as well as mentally. Here is one report that shows the body aspects of its use.

(with 200 mg, orally) "Subjectively, the most unpleasant symptoms were the anxiety, the extreme apprehension, and the unfamiliar mood associated with visual and bodily hallucinations. The visual hallucinations appeared only in the dark and consisted of blue disks dancing up and down the walls. Dysesthesia of the extremities, a feeling of light-weightedness, and hyperacusis were other symptoms noted. Autonomic signs, such as dryness of the mouth, increased perspiration, slight pupillary dilation, and increase in pulse rate, as well as extrapyramidal syndromes (fine tremors, slight ataxia, enhanced tendon reflexes and clonus) were also present. The peak effect was reached at about 2 hours after swallowing the drug; it subsided gradually, leaving as a residue complete insomnia. No undesirable after-effects, such as exhaustion or depression occurred."

As was pointed out in a pharmacological review (see Popik et al.), as the hallucinogenic dose appears to be several times higher than the stimulant dose, the user must endure intense and unpleasant central stimulation in order to experience the hallucinogenic effects.

But as fascinating as the pharmacology of ibogaine, it is the chemistry of this alkaloid that is overwhelmingly awesome. The presence of four isomers was mentioned in the chemistry section above, but this fact was not appreciated until the 1960's and even then, a couple of troublesome errors were made that confused the absolute configuration picture quite badly. The story has been accurately told in a (nearly) hundred page review chapter (see Cordell) which is a must for anyone who wants to risk understanding some pretty far-out chemistry. Oh my, there are a lot of closely related alkaloids. As to indolic alkaloids in general, there are well over two thousand of them, with a few dozen added every year. And most of these are kosher tryptamines in that they carry the tryptamine structural skeleton. And, in turn, a great number of the tryptamine alkaloids are found in the remarkable family Apocynaceae, which is the ultimate treasure-trove of alkaloids, probably the richest single source of pharmacologically active compounds in the entire plant kingdom. It is made up, largely, of tropical shrubs of the dogbane group, which almost always ooze out a sticky sap when you break off a twig. They have showy flowers, and the reputation of being very poisonous.

And this all leads smoothly to the botany, which is almost as convoluted as the chemistry. Here, let me list the plants that contain ibogaine, or that should contain it. Allow me a brief run-down of binomials. There is a number of species that are, or have been, classified as belonging to the *Tabernanthe* genus and which are reasonable sources of ibogaine, and which are logical alternatives, psychopharmacologically, to the iboga plant itself.

*Tabernanthe iboga.* This is the major source of ibogaine and is found in Gabon, mentioned above.

*Tabernanthe orientalis.* This plant is now called *Ervatamia orientalis*, and is found in Western Australia. The leaves contain ibogaine, along with six minor alkaloids that are closely related, structurally.

*Tabernanthe pubescens.* This is found in Zaire, and contains a number of alkaloids closely related to ibogaine in structure, as well as ibogaine itself.

*Tabernaemontana* spp. This genus is from a tribe within the family Apocynaceae that is called the Tabernaemontaneae. As an official sub-family it would be called Tabernaemontanoideae. It is because of the casual use of names such as these that botanical binomialists are rarely invited to social functions. It (this Genus, that is) contains several dozen species, some with ibogaine, many with analgesic or sedative action in experimental animals, and some with quite a history of native usage either in Africa or Southeast Asia.

And there are many plants in the Apocynaceae family that carry fascinating alkaloids that are closely related in structure to ibogaine and which, potentially, might have a similar psychopharmacology. In most of these, ibogaine is present in very small amounts, if at all.

> *Anacampta* spp. have usually been published as *Tabernaemontana* spp., as have been species originally published as part of the Genera *Bonafousia, Capuronetta* (which has become the species *capuronni* under this Genus), *Conopharyngia, Ervatamia, Gabunia, Hazunta, Muntafara, Pagiantha, Pandaca, Peschiera, Phrissocarpus,* and *Stenosolen.* All of these contain alkaloids related to Ibogaine.
>
> *Callichilia barteri* has appeared as *Hedranthera barteri,* but *C. subsessilis* demands the name *Tabernaemontaneae subsessilis* in the presentation of its alkaloid content.
>
> *Creoceras, Rejoua, Schzozygia, Stemmadenia* and *Voacanga* have, with all their species, remained intact with their original names.
>
> *Peschiera echinata,* this is one of some ten species within the Tabernaemontaneae classification, with some 2% alkaloid content in its leaves. Ibogaine is present.
>
> *Voacanga schweinfurthii* var. *puberula* (known in the older literature as *Voacanga puberula*) contains some ten related alkaloids. The major one, found in the seeds, and is tabersonine, is present at a rather remarkable 3.5%. Ibogaine is present in the root bark but, at a concentration of 200 mg/Kg (0.02%), it is truly a minor constituent.

## #26.    LSD-25; ACID; LYSERGIDE; D-LYSERGIC ACID DIETHYLAMIDE; METH-LAD; D-LYSERGAMIDE, N,N-DIETHYL; N,N-DIETHYL-D-LYSERGAMIDE; 9,10-DIDEHYDRO-N,N-DIETHYL-6-METHYLERGOLINE-8β-CARBOXAMIDE

SYNTHESIS: A solution of 6.7 g KOH in 100 mL $H_2O$, under an inert atmosphere and magnetically stirred, was brought to 75 °C, and 10 g ergotamine tartrate (ET) added. The reaction mixture turned yellow as the ergotamine went into solution over the course of 1 h. The stirring was continued for an additional 3 h. The reaction mixture was cooled to about 10 °C with an external ice bath, and acidified to a pH of about 3.0 by dropwise addition of 2.5 N $H_2SO_4$. White solids began to appear early in the neutralization; approximately 60 mL of sulfuric acid was required. The reaction mixture was cooled overnight, the solids removed by filtration, and the filter cake washed with 10 mL $Et_2O$. The dry solids were transferred to a beaker, suspended in 50 mL 15% ammonia in anhydrous ethanol, stirred for 1 h, and separated by decantation. This extraction was repeated, and the original decantation and the second extract combined and filtered to remove a few hundred milligrams of unwanted solids. The clear filtrate was stripped of solvent under vacuum, the residual solids dissolved in 50 mL of 1% aqueous ammonia, and this solution was acidified as before with 2.5 N $H_2SO_4$. The precipitated solids were removed by filtration and washed with $Et_2O$ until free of color. After drying under vacuum to a constant weight, there was obtained 3.5 g of d-lysergic acid hydrate, which should be stored in a dark, sealed container.

A suspension of 3.15 g d-lysergic acid hydrate and 7.1 g of diethylamine in 150 mL $CHCl_3$ was brought to reflux with stirring. With the external heating removed, there was added 3.4 g $POCl_3$ over the course of 2 min, at a rate sufficient to maintain refluxing conditions. The mixture was held at reflux for an additional 5 min, at which point everything had gone into solution. After returning to room temperature, the solution was added to 200 mL of 1 N $NH_4OH$. The phases were separated, the organic phase dried over anhydrous $MgSO_4$, filtered, and the solvent removed under vacuum. The residue was chromatographed over alumina with elution employing a 3:1 $C_6H_6$/ $CHCl_3$ mixture, and the collected fraction stripped of solvent under hard vacuum to a constant weight. This free-base solid can be recrystallized from benzene to give white crystals with a melting point of 87-92 °C. IR (in cm$^{-1}$): 750, 776, 850, 937 and 996, with the carbonyl at 1631. The mass spectrum of the free base has a strong parent peak at mass 323, with sizable fragments at masses of 181, 196, 207 and 221.

This base was dissolved in warm, dry MeOH, using 4 mL per g of product. There was then added dry d-tartaric acid (0.232 g per g of LSD base), and the clear, warm solution treated with $Et_2O$, dropwise, until the cloudiness did not dispel on continued stirring. This opaqueness set to a fine crystalline suspension (this is achieved more quickly with seeding) and the solution was allowed to crystallize overnight in the refrigerator. Ambient light should be severely restricted during these procedures. The product was removed by filtration, washed sparingly with cold MeOH, with a cold 1:1 MeOH/$Et_2O$ mixture, and then dried to constant weight. The white crystalline product was lysergic acid diethylamide tartrate with two molecules of MeOH of crystallization, with a mp of about 200 °C with decomposition, and weighed 3.11 g (66%). Repeated recrystallizations from MeOH produced a product that became progressively less soluble, and eventually virtually insoluble, as the purity increased. A totally pure salt, when dry and when shaken in the dark, will emit small flashes of white light.

DOSAGE: 60 to 200 micrograms, orally

DURATION: 8 to 12 h

QUALITATIVE COMMENTS: In the case of LSD, it seems presumptuous to attempt to select typical comments for quotation. Literally thousands of reports are in the literature, from early exploratory research, to clinical applications for treatment of autism, of alcoholism, or mental illness, to assisting in psychotherapy and in the dying process, to the adventures of the military in both intelligence and chemical warfare, to innumerable anecdotal tales of pleasure and pain. Dozens of books have been devoted to these topics.

EXTENSIONS AND COMMENTARY: LSD is an unusually fragile molecule and some comments are in order as to its stability and storage. As a salt, in water, cold, and free from air and light exposure, it is stable indefinitely. There are two sensitive aspects of its structure. The position of the carboxamide attachment, the 8-position, is affected by basic, or high pH, conditions. Through a process called epimerization, this position can scramble, producing isolysergic acid diethylamide, or iso-LSD. This product is biologically inactive, and represents a loss of a proportionate amount of active product. A second and separate point of instability is the double bond that lies between this 8-position and the aromatic ring. Water or alcohol can add to this site, especially in the presence of light (sunlight with its ultraviolet energy is notoriously bad) to form a product that has been called lumi-LSD, which is totally inactive in man. Oh yes, and often overlooked, there may be only an infinitesimal amount of chlorine in treated tap water, but then there is only an infinitesimal amount of LSD in a typical LSD solution. And since chlorine will destroy LSD on contact, the dissolving of LSD in tap water is not appropriate.

There are many synthetic methods developed and reported for the preparation of LSD. All of them start with lysergic acid, and for that reason it has been listed as a Schedule III controlled drug, as a depressant, under Federal law. The amide lysergamide, a component of several varieties of morning glory seed, is also a controlled drug and, by law, a depressant. The earliest syntheses of LSD involved the use of an azide intermediate (the original Hofmann process, 1955), mixed anhydrides with trifluoroacetic anhydride (1956) or sulfuric anhydride ($SO_3$-DMF on the lithium salt, 1959), with the peptide condensation agent N,N'-carbonyldiimidazole (1960), or with the acid chloride as the active intermediate with $POCl_3$, $PCl_5$ or thionyl chloride (1963) or just phosphorus oxychloride (1973). Most methods are faulted due to excessive moisture sensitivity, generation of side-products, or epimerization or inversion at the 8-position carbon to form d-iso-LSD. The $POCl_3$ procedure is clean and fast, and is the preferred process today for the synthesis of a wide variety of substituted lysergamides.

The term "LSD" comes from the initials of the German for lysergic acid diethylamide, or LyserSäure Diäthylamid. The number "25" following it has many myths attached to it, such as: it was the 25th form of LSD that Hofmann tried, or it was his 25th attempt to make LSD. From my own experience with chemical companies that are allied with pharmaceutical houses, I had assumed that the chemical name (which might be a mouthful for the pharmacologist) was simply replaced with a pronounceable code number equivalent. But the answer here is yet simpler. Hofmann, in his *LSD, My Problem Child* wrote: "In 1938, I produced the twenty fifth substance in a series of lysergic acid derivatives: lysergic acid diethylamide, abbreviated LSD-25 ... for laboratory usage."

Within a few years of the discovery of the extraordinary potency of LSD, a large number of close analogues were synthesized by Hofmann and his allies at Sandoz. Over the following decade many were tested in humans, both in patients and healthy subjects, with the qualitative descriptions and dosages published in the medical literature.

------

A number of analogues of LSD have maintained the diethylamide group unchanged, but additions or changes have been made in the pyrrole ring.

|  --- indole-ring substituent --- | | |
| --- | --- | --- |
| at N-1 | at C-2 | code |
| -H | -H | LSD-25 |
| -COCH$_3$ | -H | ALD-52 |
| -CH$_3$ | -H | MLD-41 |
| -CH$_2$OH | -H | |
| -CH$_2$N(CH$_3$)$_2$ | -H | |
| -H | -Br | BOL-148 |
| -H | -I | |
| -CH$_3$ | -Br | MBL-61 |
| -CH$_3$ | -I | MIL |

**ALD-52.  1-Acetyl-N,N-diethyllysergamide.**  This material has been explored in the 50-175 microgram range and there are a number of human trials reported, with varying conclusions.  One found that there was less visual distortion than with LSD and it seems to produce less anxiety and was somewhat less potent than LSD.  Another report claimed it was more effective in increasing blood pressure.  Yet another could not tell them apart.  ALD-52 just may have been the drug that was sold as "Orange Sunshine" during the "Summer of Love" in the late '60's.  Or "Orange Sunshine" may have been, really, LSD.  This was the focus of a fascinating trial where two defendants were accused of distributing LSD, whereas they claimed that it was ALD-52, which was not an illegal drug.  The prosecution claimed that as it hydrolyses readily to LSD, for all intents and purposes, it was LSD, and anyway, you had to go through the illegal LSD to get to ALD-52 by any of the known chemical syntheses.  The defendants were found guilty.  And yet, I do not know who has actually measured the speed or ease of that reaction. If ALD-52 hydrolyses so easily to LSD, and the body is indeed a hydrolytic instrument, then these two drugs should be absolutely equivalent in every particular. This is the ergot equivalent of the psilocybin to psilocin argument, except this is an acetamide rather than a phosphate ester.

**MLD-41.  1-Methyl-N,N-diethyllysergamide.**  The 1-methyl homologue of LSD has more of a somatic than sensory effect, has fewer visuals, and is less well accepted than LSD, with the range of dosages being from 100 to 300 micrograms. This indicates that it is perhaps a third the potency of LSD, which is in accord with both pupilary dilation and reflex action. However, the cardiovascular responses are actually increased. Besides being less potent than LSD, it appears to have a slower onset but is equally long lived. There is cross-tolerance between MLD-41 and LSD.

**BOL-148.**  2-Bromo-N,N-diethyllysergamide.  This synthetic ergot derivative, along with its 1-methyl homologue MBL-61 (mentioned below) should be used as powerful tools for studying the mechanism of action of LSD in the human animal. It does not have LSD-like effects in man. At 6 to 10 milligrams orally, there are some mental changes noted. But in another study, 20 milligrams a day was administered to a subject for 7 days, and there were no reported effects. And yet it is as potent a serotonin agonist as is LSD. How can serotonin be argued as a neurotransmitter that is a major player in explaining the action of psychedelic drugs, when this compound is nearly without activity?

There are some suggestions that an intravenous route may be more effective. I have heard of effects being noted at maybe a milligram and a short (2-3 hour) intoxication following 20 milligrams administered over a 20 minute period. I was involved many years ago in a study of radio-labelled BOL-148 which was made by the bromination of LSD. I was quite sure that the only radioactive material present was BOL-148, but there could well have been some unreacted LSD still present which would, of course, still be psychoactive. The synthesis is not clean — I was tempted to make an entry for this compound if only to reproduce Albert Hofmann's original published experimental procedure. He reacted 13.2 grams of N-bromosuccinimide (in 400 mL dioxane), with 1.2 liters of dioxane containing 25 grams of LSD. This gave 11 grams of crude product which had to be recrystallized. The radioactive synthesis used effectively elemental bromine, and gave yields of from 5 to 15%. Visualize that reaction! A warm flask containing over a quart of warm solvent in which there were maybe half a million doses of LSD.

**1-Hydroxymethyl-LSD, 1-dimethylaminomethyl-LSD and 2-iodo-LSD.**  These three additional compounds are shown here because they were described in a synthetic flurry that followed the discovery of the activity of LSD. But at the moment I know neither their internal Sandoz codes nor if they had ever been explored in man. This is a kind of frustrating catch-all entry, in that the long index will send you here, and once here you realize that nothing is known. Well, at least the compounds are known, and perhaps there is something in the Sandoz vaults that might be interesting. I do not have access to them.

**MBL-61.** 2-Bromo-N,N-diethyl-1-methyllysergamide. This is the compound BOL-148 (mentioned above) with a methyl group attached to the 1-position of the indole ring (LSD has a hydrogen there). This would be an even more tantalizing challenge to the serotonin theory for central activity of the psychedelics, in that it is without any activity in man at an oral dose of 14 milligrams (similar to the inactivity of the BOL-61 compound, but it is some five times more potent as a serotonin agonist. With it, as with the iodinated analogue MIL, there are many examples of the compromising of scientific integrity in the quest for funds and recognition. Both compounds are as effective as LSD itself in displacing labelled LSD that is bound to the post-synaptic serotonin receptor sites in animal brains. But neither of them show any LSD-like activity. But both have been labelled with $^{11}$C or $^{122}$I to give positron emitting forms that can be administered to man and localized in a positron emission tomography instrument (a PET scanner).

I was at a meeting of a NIDA study section a few years ago, where someone presented some findings with a group of subjects who were complaining of continuing mental problems allegedly due to LSD exposure. A chart was put up showing the outline of the brain with the locations of the EEG foci that were observed in one of these subjects. Alongside it was a PET scan showing the distribution of radioactive LSD in a subject. The purpose was to discuss the similarities and differences of the coordinates of electrical activity and radio-isotope concentration. I innocently asked what positron isotope had been used, as I did not know of any successful positron labelling of LSD. Carbon 11, I was told. Where in the molecule was the label incorporated, I asked. In the 1-position methyl group. It was finally acknowledged that the compound that had actually been used was 2-iodo-1-methyl-LSD, our MIL compound, which is quite a different world. A pharmacologist might say that they are similar in action (looking at serotonin, not psychedelic action), and a chemist might say they are of similar structure (looking at the upper 80% of the molecule). But they are different compounds. This is a most subtle form of deceit. It is, in fact, out and out dishonest, but it looks good up there on the screen at a lecture.

Let me mention in passing, that there are three stereoisomers possible for d-LSD. There are d-iso-LSD, l-LSD, and l-iso-LSD. The inversion of the stereochemistry of the attached diethylcarboxyamido group of d-LSD gives the diastereoisomer (d-iso-LSD) which is a frequent synthetic impurity of d-LSD itself. The corresponding optical antipodes l-LSD and l-iso-LSD are also known and have been tasted. All three are completely inactive: d-iso-LSD shows no psychological changes at an oral dose of 4 milligrams; l-LSD none at up to 10 milligrams orally; and l-iso-LSD none at 500 micrograms orally. These dramatic decreases in potency show both the stereoselectivity of the native LSD molecule in producing its central effects, and the LSD-free purity of these isomers.

The second major location of variations in the structure of LSD has been in the nature of the alkyl groups on the amide nitrogen atom. Some of these are Sandoz syntheses, some are from other research groups, and a few of them are found in nature. Some of these have been studied in man, and some have not. A few of the original clutch of Sandoz compounds have both 1-substituents and amide alkyl (R) group variations:

| indole | —— amide nitrogen substituents —— | | code |
|--------|-----------------------------------|--------|------|
| R= | R= | R= | name |
| -H | -H | -H | LA-111 |
| -H | -CH$_3$ | -H | |
| -H | -CH$_2$CH$_3$ | -H | LAE-32 |
| -H | -(CH$_2$)$_2$CH$_3$ | -H | |
| -H | -CH(CH$_3$)CH$_2$OH | -H * | Ergonovine |
| -H | -(CH$_2$)$_3$CH$_3$ | -H | |
| -H | -CH(CH$_3$)CH$_2$CH$_3$ | -H * | |
| -H | -CH(CH$_2$CH$_3$)CH$_2$OH | -H * | Methergine |
| -H | -(CH$_2$)$_4$CH$_3$ | -H | |
| -H | -CH(CH$_3$)CH$_2$CH$_2$CH$_3$ | -H * | |
| -H | -CH(CH$_2$CH$_3$)$_2$ | -H | |
| -H | -(CH$_2$)$_5$CH$_3$ | -H | |
| -H | -CH(CH$_3$)CH$_2$CH$_2$CH$_2$CH$_3$ | -H * | |
| -H | -(CH$_2$)$_6$CH$_3$ | -H | |
| -H | -CH(CH$_3$)CH$_2$CH$_2$CH$_2$CH$_2$CH$_3$ | -H * | |
| -H | -CH$_3$ | -CH$_3$ | DAM-57 |
| -H | -CH$_2$CH$_3$ | -CH$_3$ | |
| -H | -(CH$_2$)$_2$CH$_3$ | -CH$_3$ | LAMP |
| -H | -CH(CH$_3$)$_2$ | -CH$_3$ | |
| -H | -CH(CH$_3$)CH$_2$C$_6$H$_5$ | -CH$_3$ * | |
| -H | -CH$_2$CH$_3$ | -CH$_2$CH$_3$ | LSD-25 |
| -H | -(CH$_2$)$_2$CH$_3$ | -CH$_2$CH$_3$ | |
| -H | -(CH$_2$)$_2$CH$_3$ | -(CH$_2$)$_2$CH$_3$ | |
| -H | -CH(CH$_3$)$_2$ | -CH(CH$_3$)$_2$ | |
| -H | -CH$_2$CH=CH$_2$ | -CH$_2$CH=CH$_2$ | DAL |
| -H | -(CH$_2$)$_3$CH$_3$ | -(CH$_2$)$_3$CH$_3$ | |
| -H | -CH$_2$CH$_2$CH$_2$CH$_2$- | | LPD-824 |
| -H | -CH$_2$CH=CHCH$_2$- | | |
| -H | -CH$_2$CH$_2$CH$_2$CH$_2$CH$_2$- | | |
| -H | -CH$_2$CH$_2$OCH$_2$CH$_2$- | | LSM-775 |
| -CH$_3$ | -CH$_2$CH$_3$ | -H | MLA-74 |
| -CH$_3$ | -CH(CH$_2$CH$_3$)CH$_2$OH | -H * | UML-491 |

| -COCH$_3$ -CH$_2$CH$_3$ | -H | ALA-10 |
| -CH$_3$ | -CH$_2$CH$_2$CH$_2$CH$_2$- | MPD-75 |

In the amides marked with "*" there has been the introduction of a new asymmetric center, which of course doubles the number of isomers that is possible. In each case the resulting two optical forms were prepared separately, and evaluated separately as to their pharmacology.

This listing is not intended to be thorough, but it is shown to suggest the amount of synthetic effort that has been made towards exploring and understanding the high potency associated with those two remarkably important ethyl groups on the amide nitrogen of LSD. I have given the Sandoz code names, again, as far as I know them. Although none of these really warrant a dedicated recipe, there is sufficient animal and human pharmacology reported to justify listing them below as separate items. Most of these reports appeared in the mid-1950's, but some studies are still being done, and papers are published even today with new ideas but, sadly, only with animal pharmacology. I have been as guilty as the next person who has tried to mount all these compounds into a table with a "human potency" factor that compares them directly to LSD. This is an uncomfortable simplification. Here are the actual reported observations, and I'll let the reader provide his own potency index.

**LA-111, ergine, d-lysergamide**. This is an active compound and has been established as a major component in morning glory seeds. It was assayed for human activity, by Albert Hofmann in self-trials back in 1947, well before this was known to be a natural compound. An i.m. administration of a 500 microgram dose led to a tired, dreamy state with an inability to maintain clear thoughts. After a short period of sleep, the effects were gone and normal baseline was recovered within five hours. Other observers have confirmed this clouding of consciousness leading to sleep. The epimer, inverted at C-8, is isoergine or d-isolysergamide, and is also a component of morning glory seeds. Hofmann tried a 2 milligram dose of this amide, and as with ergine he experienced nothing but tiredness, apathy, and a feeling of emptiness. Both compounds are probably correctly dismissed as not being a contributor to the action of these seeds. It is important to note that ergine, as well as lysergic acid itself, is listed as a Schedule III drug in the Controlled Substances Act, as a depressant. This could be, in all probability, a stratagem to control them as logical precursors to LSD.

**LAE-32, N-ethyllysergamide**. Different people have observed and reported different effects, with different routes of administration. Subcutaneous administrations of from 500 to 750 micrograms have been said to produce a state of apathy and sedation. Clinical studies with dosages of 500 micrograms i.m. were felt to be less effective than the control use of 100 micrograms of LSD. And yet, oral doses of twice this amount, 1.6 milligrams, have been said to produce a short-lived LSD-like effect with none of these negatives.

**LPD-824, N-Pyrrolidyllysergamide**. Five trials at a dosage of 800 micrograms orally led to the reporting of a fleeting effect that was similar to one tenth this amount of LSD.

**LSM-775, N-Morpholinyllysergamide**. There are conflicting reports; one states that 75 micrograms is an effective dose, comparable to a similar dose of LSD, and the other stated that between 350 and 700 micrograms was needed to elicit this response, and that there were fewer signs of cardiovascular stimulation and peripheral toxicity.

**DAM-57, N,N-Dimethyllysergamide**. This compound did induce autonomic disturbances at oral levels of some ten times the dosage required for LSD, presumably in the high hundreds of micrograms. There is some disagreement as to whether there were psychic changes observed.

**DAL, N,N-Diallyllysergamide**. As the tartrate salt, there is at best a touch of sparkle seen at 600 micrograms orally, but there is a sedation also reported. It is certainly an order of magnitude less potent than LSD itself.

**UML-491, Methysergide, Sansert**. This is the synthetic homologue of methergine (1-methyl) and is employed clinically as a treatment for migraine headaches. When the usual therapeutic dosage of two milligrams is scaled up by a factor of ten, there is a profound LSD-like response described by most subjects. A number of these ergot analogues from nature can be considered as potential precursors for the preparation of LSD. But here, there is a 1-methyl group that is effectively permanently attached, so it cannot play this role.

The third location of structural modification of the LSD molecule has been at the 6-position in ring D. This is the LAD series, with any of several alkyl groups attached to the nitrogen atom. The methyl group is found with LSD itself, and is the reason for using METH-LAD in the title as a synonym. The ethyl, allyl and propyl substitutions provide ETH-LAD, AL-LAD, and PRO-LAD, and each of these commands a separate entry.

The most frequently encountered precursor for the manufacture of LSD is ergotamine, a major alkaloid of the ergot world. It is totally unknown in the morning glories. The usual commercial form is the tartrate salt, and is often referred to under the code abbreviation of ET, for ergotamine tartrate. It has found medical use in the treatment of migraine headaches, and as an oxytocic (an agent that is used in childbirth to stimulate uterine contractions). Care with the ET terminology must be taken, in that in the drug world it has two additional associations; α-ET for alpha-ethyltryptamine and NET for N-monoethyltryptamine.

Ergonovine is a naturally occurring, water-soluble ergot alkaloid, found in both ergot preparations and in many species of morning glory seeds, and there are several reports of LSD-like action at oral levels of between two and ten milligrams. It has an important use in obstetrics, again as an oxytocic, at about a tenth of this dose. This pharmacological potential must be respected in psychopharmacological trials. The one-carbon homologue (the butanolamide rather than the propanolamide) is called methergine or methylergonovine. It is a synthetic ally and is orally effective as an oxytocic at a dosage of 200 micrograms. It also has an LSD-like action at ten times this level.

Although there are many other chemical treasures in the ergot fungal world, I would like to wrap this commentary up with a return to the topic of morning glory seeds. Four additional alkaloids of the ergot world must be acknowledged as being potentially participating factors in the MGS story. With each of these, the primary ergoline ring system is largely intact but the amide function is completely gone. The carboxyl group has been reduced to the alcohol to give elymoclavine. There is the related molecule present which is the isomer with the double bond moved to be conjugated with the aromatic ring; it is called lysergol. There is the same molecule but with a hydroxy group attached to the 8-position carbon atom (an ethyleneglycol!); it is called penniclavine. And lastly, that D-ring can actually be opened between the 5 and 6 positions, to give us a secondary amine tryptamine derivative, chanoclavine. To be completely anally retentive in this Ipomoea inventory, mention must be made of five alkaloids that are present in truly trace amounts, all of which have no oxygen atoms present whatsoever on that substitution on the ergoline 8-position. These are the 8-methyl isomers agroclavine, setoclavine, festuclavine and cycloclavine, and the methylene analogue lysergene. These structures in effect define absolute obscurity, and most probably do not contribute to the morning glory intoxication state. But the others, some present in sizable amounts, may someday help explain why the pharmacology of these seeds is so different than that of the major isolates, the ergines.

### #27.   MBT;   TRYPTAMINE, N-BUTYL-N-METHYL;   INDOLE, 3-[2-(BUTYLMETHYLAMINO)ETHYL];   N-BUTYL-N-METHYLTRYPT-AMINE;  3-[2-(BUTYLMETHYLAMINO)ETHYL]-INDOLE

SYNTHESIS: To a well-stirred, ice cold solution of 5.0 g indole in 75 mL TBME, there was added a solution of 6.35 g oxalyl chloride in 25 mL $CH_2Cl_2$, dropwise, over the course of 15 min. Stirring was continued for an additional 10 min, and the resulting solids were removed by filtration and washed with 15 mL cold TBME. This solid amide was, in turn, added portionwise over a period of 10 min to a well-stirred, ice cold solution of 15 mL N-butyl-N-methyl amine in 100 mL $CH_2Cl_2$. The clear, red solution that resulted was stirred for a few additional minutes, washed in sequence with $H_2O$, 1% aqueous hydrochloric acid, and then $H_2O$. Following drying with solid anhydrous $Na_2SO_4$, the solvent was removed under vacuum, yielding a thick red oil. Upon dilution with 20 mL cold EtOAc an off-white solid was produced. This was recrystallized from 100 mL boiling EtOAc producing, after cooling, filtering and air-drying to constant weight, 5.82 g of N-butyl-N-methyl-indoleglyoxylamide with a mp of 128-130 °C. A second crop of 0.6 g was obtained from the filtrate, for a total yield of 58%.

A stirred suspension of 6.3 g of N-butyl-N-methyl-indoleglyoxylamide in 150 mL dry toluene, in a three-neck, round-bottomed flask and under a $N_2$ atmosphere, was cooled with an external ice bath. A total of 30 mL of a 65% RED-AL solution in toluene was added slowly by syringe, and there was immediate gas evolution. After the addition was complete, the stirring was continued for an hour, then the flask was gradually warmed to 40 °C, and the stirring continued for an additional 2 h. After cooling again to ice temperature, the excess RED-AL was decomposed by the dropwise addition of first IPA followed by (after conspicuous gas evolution had ceased) $H_2O$. The inorganic aluminum salts were removed by filtration of the resulting suspension, and the filter cake was washed with isopropyl acetate. The filtrate and washings were combined and washed thoroughly with $H_2O$. The product was then extracted into 1 N hydrochloric acid, the pooled extracts washed twice with $CH_2Cl_2$, made basic with 20% aqueous KOH and extracted with $CH_2Cl_2$. After washing with $H_2O$ and drying with anhydrous $Na_2SO_4$, the solvent was removed under vacuum to yield a light yellow oil with a bluish florescence. The free amine did not crystallize but was dissolved in MeOH and titrated to a slightly basic end-point with a methanolic solution of fumaric acid. The solution was heated to the boiling point, and slowly diluted with two volumes of hot isopropyl acetate. Slow cooling yielded beautiful light yellow crystals of N-butyl-N-methyltryptamine fumarate (MBT). A recrystallization from MeOH/isopropyl acetate gave 5.83 g (69%) of product with a mp 148-150 °C.

DOSAGE:   250 - 400 mg

DURATION:   4 - 6 h

QUALITATIVE COMMENTS: (with 130 mg, orally) "Perhaps a subtle intoxication at two hours, and certainly nothing at five hours."

(with 175 mg, orally) "Some mild incoordination and concentration difficulties, all trivial, and a good sleep and a good day the next day."

(with 250 mg, orally) "At 75 minutes there was the prompt development of an intoxicated state primarily characterized by fine motor impairment. Nothing remotely resembling any type of hallucination. Appetite was normal and food and water were consumed without difficulty. Most activities were uninteresting, even dull. The effects lasted about five hours."

(with 400 mg, orally) "It hit in just over an hour, and it quickly became difficult to keep both eyes focused on the point of gaze. There was no actual double vision, but things were not quite right. In a few more minutes an apparent motion became apparent with fixed objects, and shortly thereafter there was a faint 'retinal circus' that was reminiscent of DMT but less compelling. Subject matter could not be chosen, but rather came on its own. At this point, walking required great concentration, and lying on a bed was a much better choice. Music seemed to encourage the drifting of thoughts, but all the eyes-closed effects faded quite quickly. I felt overheated, sweat a lot, was intensely dehydrated, and drank quantities of water all night, and still felt dehydrated. Urine output was low. Not my choice of drug; the intoxication is too much for the visual stuff."

EXTENSIONS AND COMMENTARY: This is a pretty heavy body trip for a modest mental return. As with any tertiary amine, one cannot help but speculate what role the deamination enzyme systems of the liver have in compromising the results that are being experienced. Here is a compound with five aliphatic carbon atoms hanging out there on the basic nitrogen. No branched chain; everything straight chain. How can this be compared with other tryptamines with a straight-chain on that nitrogen atom? DMT has two such carbon atoms. DET has four, DPT has six and DBT has eight. With a tally of five, MBT should lie in-between DET and DPT. Both of these show oral activity in the 300 milligram range (as does MBT) but at least DET has some five-fold increased potency if given parenterally. I really would like to see this particular compound explored by smoking, or injection, or even orally with some effective monoamine oxidase inhibitor on board (a dose of *P. harmala,* maybe) and see if there can be more mental effects and fewer toxic effects at a lower dose exposure. There is certainly good precedent for it, amongst the other dialkyl tryptamines.

A structural isomer has been made, with the butyl group branched at the nitrogen atom. This is N-s-butyl-N-methyltryptamine, or MSBT. It came from a two-pass alkylation of N-methyltryptamine (NMT) with s-butyl bromide in isopropylalcohol in the presence of solid potassium iodide. It remained an oil, but was over 90% pure by GCMS, with unreacted NMT being the major impurity. MS (in m/z): $C_6H_{14}N+$ 100 (100%); indolemethylene+ 130 (8%); parent ion 230 (1%). It has been assayed in man, but it remains an unknown.

**#28.    4,5-MDO-DIPT;    TRYPTAMINE, N,N-DIISOPROPYL-4,5-METHYLENEDIOXY; INDOLE, 3-[2-(DIISOPROPYLAMINO)ETHYL]-4,5-METHYLENEDIOXY;   N,N-DIISOPROPYL-4,5-METHYLENE-DIOXYTRYPTAMINE;    3-[2-(DIISOPROPYLAMINO)ETHYL]-4,5-METHYLENEDIOXYINDOLE;    5H-1,3-DIOXOLO-[4,5-E]INDOLE-7-ETHANEAMINE, N,N-DIISOPROPYL**

SYNTHESIS: A solution of 4.8 g 4,5-methylenedioxyindole (see under 4,5-MDO-DMT for its preparation) in 60 mL anhydrous $Et_2O$ was stirred and cooled with an external ice bath. There was added, dropwise, a solution of 5.0 g oxalyl chloride in $Et_2O$ so that the temperature did not exceed 5 °C. The intermediate acid chloride separated as a red solid, and was removed by filtration and washed with $Et_2O$. It was then suspended in 60 mL cold anhydrous $Et_2O$, treated with 14 mL diisopropylamine and the mixture stirred for 30 min. The solvent was decanted from the crude solids that formed, and they were suspended in 50 mL $H_2O$. The product was removed by filtration and vacuum-dried to provide 5.3 g (56%) N,N-diisopropyl-4,5-methylenedioxyindole-3-glyoxylamide as white solid, with a mp 260 °C (dec).

To a stirred and cooled solution of 3.8 g LAH in 100 mL anhydrous THF there was added, over the course of 1 h, a solution of 4.70 g N,N-diisopropyl-4,5-methylenedioxyindole-3-glyoxylamide in 500 mL anhydrous THF. After 1 h reflux, the cooled reaction mixture was treated with 3.8 mL $H_2O$, followed by 3.8 mL aqueous 5% NaOH and then by an additional 10.4 mL $H_2O$. The solids were removed by filtration and washed with THF. The combined filtrate and washings were dried ($MgSO_4$) and the solvent removed under vacuum. The residual oil was distilled at the KugelRohr (0.5 mm/Hg at 100 °C) to give a distillate that solidified. This was crystallized from benzene/hexane to provide 1.34 g (31%) of N,N-diisopropyl-4,5-methylenedioxytryptamine (4,5-MDO-DIPT) with a mp of 109-113 °C. Anal: C, H. N.

DOSAGE:  > 25 mg, orally

DURATION: unknown

QUALITATIVE COMMENTS:  (25 mg, orally) "Nothing much happened for about 3 hours, and then I suddenly shot up. I was at the plateau for a fair time, the recovery was difficult to define chronologically. This was in daylight; I was reminded very much of LSD."

EXTENSIONS AND COMMENTARY: This is one of the two tryptamines reported here with the most appealing methylenedioxy ring bridge located at the two most sensitive ring positions of the indole nucleus. It, too, is an unknown entity. There is a single observation of an oral trial, and it suggests something of interest at 25 milligrams. Higher dosages might prove most interesting. There is no question that the methyl isopropyl homologue of this compound, 4,5-MDO-MIPT, would be a rewarding compound to assay. As of the present moment, it has not yet been synthesized. It should be a relatively easy one to make.

There is an interesting parallel to be seen here. This methylenedioxy hetero-ring is snuggled as closely as possible to the ethylamine chain of the indole (the 4-position occupied by the nearer oxygen atom, and the indole chain at the 3-position). The same intimacy is possible in the phenethylamine world. This would be realized by moving the methylenedioxy ring of MDA (3,4-methylenedioxyamphetamine) to the 2,3-location. Here, again, the nearer oxygen would be as close as possible to the ethylamine chain at the 1-position. This compound, 2,3-methylenedioxyamphetamine, has been made by several research groups, and has been looked at in man. At 50 milligrams, orally, it produced some pretty strong stimulatory effects, with no sleep found to be possible during the following 24 hours. But, on the other hand, it seemed to be devoid of MDA-like effects. This positional isomer was mentioned in PIHKAL.

There is no way to meaningfully extrapolate from this phenethylamine analogue, 2,3-MDA, to 4,5-MDO-DIPT, but it does present a very close structural relationship that could be used to justify a clinical study of this unusual tryptamine.

## #29. 5,6-MDO-DIPT; TRYPTAMINE, N,N-DIISOPROPYL-5,6-METHYLENEDIOXY; INDOLE, 3-[2-(DIISOPROPYLAMINO)ETHYL]-5,6-METHYLENEDIOXY; N,N-DIISOPROPYL-5,6-METHYLENEDIOXY-TRYPTAMINE; 3-[2-(DIISOPROPYLAMINO)ETHYL]-5,6-METHYL-ENEDIOXYINDOLE; 5H-1,3-DIOXOLO-[4,5-F]INDOLE-7-ETHANE-AMINE, N,N-DIISOPROPYL

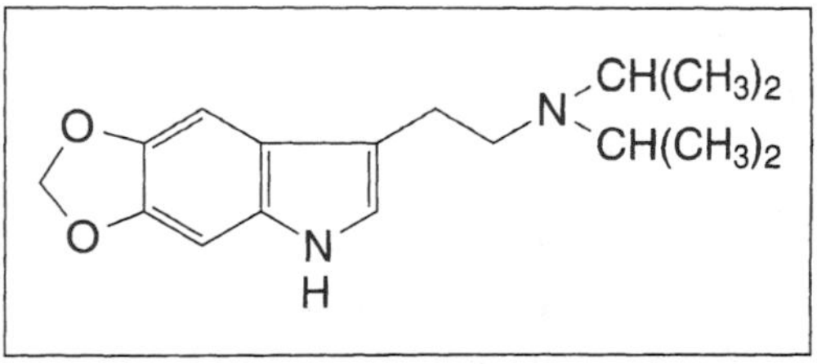

SYNTHESIS: To a well-stirred, cold solution of 1.61 g 5,6-methylenedioxyindole (see under 5,6-MDO-MIPT for its preparation) in 20 mL anhydrous $Et_2O$, there was added dropwise a solution of 1.75 mL oxalyl chloride in 5 mL $Et_2O$. The addition took 20 min. After an additional 20 min stirring in the external ice bath, the red crystals that formed were removed by filtration, washed with 2x5 mL $Et_2O$, and dried under vacuum for 0.5 h. This crude acid chloride was dissolved in 100 mL anhydrous THF and cooled, under $N_2$, to 0° C. An $Et_2O$ solution of diisopropyl-amine was added until the reaction mixture remained basic (pH >9 to external pH paper). The solvents were removed under vacuum, and residue treated with 100 mL each of $H_2O$ and $CHCl_3$. The organic phase was separated, the aqueous phase extracted with additional $CHCl_3$, the pooled extracts dried over anhydrous $MgSO_4$, filtered, and the filtrate evaporated under vacuum. The residue was recrystallized from ethyl acetate/hexane to yield 1.20 g N,N-diisopropyl-5,6-methylenedioxyindol-3-ylglyoxylamide with a mp 278-280 °C (38%). Anal: C,H,N.

To a well-stirred suspension of 0.77 g of LAH in 40 mL dry THF, there was added, dropwise, a solution of 0.95 g N,N-diisopropyl-5,6-methylenedioxyindol-3-ylglyoxylamide in approximately 100 mL of anhydrous THF. The mixture was brought to reflux temperature and held there for 2 h, and allowed to return to room temperature. It was hydrolyzed by the cautious addition of 0.8 mL $H_2O$, followed with 2.4 mL 10% aqueous NaOH, and finally an additional 0.8 mL of $H_2O$. The inorganics were removed by filtration through Celite, and the filtercake was washed with additional THF. After removal of the solvent of the combined filtrate and washings under vacuum, the residue was distilled by KugelRohr and the colorless distillate recrystallized from a mixture of $Et_2O$/hexane. There was thus obtained 0.52 g N,N-diisopropyl-5,6-methylenedioxytryptamine (5,6-MDO-DIPT) with a melting point of 93-94 °C (60%). Anal: C,H,N.

DOSAGE: Unknown

DURATION: Unknown

EXTENSIONS AND COMMENTARY: So why enter an entry into a listing of active compounds when it is simply not known if it is active or not? The truth is that none of these three 5,6-methylenedioxy-N,N-disubstituted tryptamines (this one, or 5,6-MDO-DMT or 5,6-MDO-MIPT) have been explored up to an active level, but they are appealing targets in that they have the progression of nitrogen substituents that has proven so valuable in similar sequences of compounds. This is the pattern dimethyl, methylisopropyl and diisopropyl. With both the unsubstituted, and the 5-methoxy-substituted groups, the activity goes from quite potent but requiring parenteral administration, to highly potent and orally active, and back to quite potent and orally active, as the methyl groups are progressively replaced with isopropyl groups. It would be instructive to see if this arrangement was maintained with this methylenedioxy trilogy.

The three kinds of closed-ring substituents mentioned in the pyr-T recipe have also been described with this 5,6-methylenedioxy ring substitution. These could be named 5,6-MDO-pyr-T (the pyrrolidine analogue, mp 110-112 °C), 5,6-MDO-pip-T (the piperidine analogue, mp 150-152 °C) and 5,6-MDO-mor-T (the morpholine analogue, mp 117-119 °C). To my knowledge, none of these have ever been put into man.

**#30. 4,5-MDO-DMT; TRYPTAMINE, N,N-DIMETHYL-4,5-METHYLENEDIOXY; INDOLE, 3-[2-(DIMETHYLAMINO)ETHYL]-4,5-METHYLENEDIOXY; N,N-DIMETHYL-4,5-METHYLENE-DIOXYTRYPTAMINE; 3-[2-(DIMETHYLAMINO)ETHYL]-4,5-METHYLENEDIOXYINDOLE; 5H-1,3-DIOXOLO-[4,5-E]INDOLE-7-ETHANEAMINE, N,N-DIMETHYL**

SYNTHESIS: To a well-stirred $H_2O$ suspension (160 mL) of 3.7 g methyl-trialkylammonium chloride (Adogen 464) and 138 mL $CH_2Br_2$ (under nitrogen), there was added a solution of 100 g 3-methylcatechol in 400 mL $H_2O$ containing 80 g NaOH, over the course of 2 h. Stirring was continued for 1 h, then the reaction mixture was subjected to steam distillation. The distillate was cooled, and the phases separated. Extraction of the aqueous phase with $CH_2Cl_2$, pooling of the organic phases, and removal of the solvent under vacuum, yielded 85 g (78%) of 2,3-methylenedioxytoluene as a colorless oil.

A mixture of 21 g 2,3-methylenedioxytoluene and 1 g $Hg(OAc)_2$ in 60 mL acetic acid was stirred and heated to 80 °C. To this there was added, dropwise, 12.8 g of concentrated nitric acid. Heat-ing and stirring was continued for 2 h. The reaction mixture was quenched by pouring it into ice-$H_2O$, and extracted with $Et_2O$. The extracts were pooled, dried with anhydrous $MgSO_4$, and the volatiles removed under vacuum. The orange solid residue was recrystallized from EtOH to provide 20 g (58%) of a mixture of the ortho- and meta-products, 2,3-methylenedioxy-5-nitrotoluene and 2,3-methylenedioxy-6-nitrotoluene, with a mp 65-67 °C. This unresolved mixture was employed in the next step without further purification.

In a flask equipped with a total reflux packed column and a variable take-off head, 15.0 g of the 2,3-methylenedioxy-5-nitrotoluene/2,3-methylenedioxy-6-nitrotoluene mix was added to a mixture of 100 mL freshly distilled DMF and 12.8 g of N,N-dimethylformamide dimethyl acetal. The reaction mixture was heated to a controlled reflux that kept the head temperature at 50 to 70 °C, allowing the removal of MeOH. After 4 h, 90% of the theoretical amount of MeOH (7.4 mL) had been distilled off, and the residual solvent (DMF) was removed under vacuum. The dark residue was dissolved in benzene, washed with $H_2O$, dried with anhydrous $MgSO_4$, and the solvent removed under vacuum. The crude crystalline product was recrystallized from hexane/benzene to provide 4.8 g (50%) of 2,3-methylenedioxy-6-nitro-beta-dimethylaminostyrene as red needles with a mp 126-128 °C.

A solution of 3.5 g 2,3-methylenedioxy-6-nitro-beta-dimethyl-aminostryrene in 200 mL benzene was placed in a Parr hydrogenation bomb and treated with 0.35 g of 10% Pd/C. The mixture was shaken for 7 h under 3 atm $H_2$.

The catalyst was removed by filtration, and the filtrate was washed first with 2N $H_2SO_4$, followed by aqueous $NaHCO_3$ and $H_2O$. This was dried and the solvent removed under vacuum to give 1.2 g (50%) of 4,5-methylenedioxyindole as a residue. After crystallization from benzene/petroleum ether, it had a mp 111 °C. Anal: C,H,N.

A solution of 4.8 g 4,5-methylenedioxyindole in 60 mL anhydrous $Et_2O$ was stirred and cooled with an external ice bath. There was added, dropwise, a solution of 5.0 g oxalyl chloride in $Et_2O$ so that the temperature did not exceed 5 °C. The intermediate acid chloride separated as a red solid, and was removed by filtration and washed with $Et_2O$. It was then suspended in 60 mL cold anhydrous $Et_2O$, treated with 7 mL dimethylamine and the mixture stirred for 30 min. The solvent was decanted from the crude solids that formed, and they were suspended in 50 mL $H_2O$. The product was removed by filtration and vacuum dried to provide 5.7 g (77%) N,N-dimethyl-4,5-methylenedioxyindole-3-glyoxylamide as a white solid with a mp 240-243 °C.

To a stirred and cooled solution of 3.8 g LAH in 100 mL anhydrous THF there was added, over the course of 1 h, a solution of 3.7 g N,N-dimethyl-4,5-methylenedioxyindole-3-glyoxylamide in 500 mL anhydrous THF. After 1 h reflux, the cooled reaction mixture was treated with 3.8 mL $H_2O$, followed by 3.8 mL 5% NaOH and then by an additional 10.4 mL $H_2O$. The solids were removed by filtration and washed with THF. The combined filtrate and washings were dried ($MgSO_4$) and the solvent removed under vacuum. The residual oil was distilled at the KugelRohr (0.5 mm/Hg at 100 °C) to give a distillate that solidified. This was crystallized from benzene/petroleum ether to provide 0.25 g (8%) of N,N-dimethyl-4,5-methylenedioxytryptamine (4,5-MDO-DMT) with a mp of 93-95 °C. Anal: C, H. N.

DOSAGE: unknown

DURATION: unknown

EXTENSIONS AND COMMENTARY: The two aromatic ring positions that are associated with human psychedelic activity are the 4-position (of psilocybin fame) and the 5-position (of 5-methoxy-this-and-that fame). Here is a compound with both positions oxygen-substituted (with the methylenedioxy ring that is so effective in the phenethylamine world) and it has not been looked at in man, to my knowledge. I snooped around in the literature associated with this kind of DMT substitution, and the world of di-oxygen substitution to be found at these two potent focal points is almost unknown. Aside from the 4,5-methylenedioxy-diisopropyltryptamine, described here in the recipes (under 4,5-MDO-DIPT), there are only five of these dioxygenated compounds known. 4-benzyloxy-5-methoxy-tryptamine is the precursor of the DMT and DET homologues with a 4-hydroxy group exposed after hydrogenation. But nowhere is there a 4,5-dimethoxy pattern.

In fact the methoxy group is unknown in the 4-position in this simple system.

I have been told that Mark Julia, in France, had made the 4-hydroxy-5-methoxy compound with a methyl and an ethyl on the tryptamine nitrogen. If so, it certainly is not in the literature abstracts and thus is of unknown properties. I want to search this out.

#### #31.    5,6-MDO-DMT;    TRYPTAMINE, N,N-DIMETHYL-5,6-METHYLENEDIOXY; INDOLE, 3-[2-(DIMETHYLAMINO)ETHYL]-5,6-METHYLENEDIOXY;    N,N-DIMETHYL-5,6-METHYLENEDIOXY-TRYPTAMINE;    3-[2-(DIMETHYLAMINO)ETHYL]-5,6-METHYLENE-DIOXYINDOLE; 5H-1,3-DIOXOLO-[4,5-F]INDOLE-7-ETHANEAMINE, N,N-DIMETHYL

SYNTHESIS: To a well-stirred, cold solution of 1.61 g 5,6-methylenedioxyindole (see under 5,6-MDO-MIPT for its preparation) in 20 mL anhydrous $Et_2O$, there was added, dropwise, a solution of 1.75 mL oxalyl chloride in 5 mL $Et_2O$. The addition took 20 min. After an additional 20 min stirring in the external ice bath, the red crystals that formed were removed by filtration, washed with 2x5 mL $Et_2O$, and dried under vacuum for 0.5 h. This crude acid chloride was dissolved in 100 mL anhydrous THF and cooled, under $N_2$, to 0° C. An $Et_2O$ solution of dimethylamine was added until the reaction mixture remained basic (pH >9 to external pH paper). The solvents were removed under vacuum, and the residue treated with 100 mL each of $H_2O$ and $CHCl_3$. The organic phase was separated, the aqueous phase extracted with additional

CHCl3, the pooled extracts dried over anhydrous $MgSO_4$, filtered, and the filtrate evaporated under vacuum. The residue was recrystallized from ethanol/EtOAc to yield 1.07 g N,N-dimethyl-5,6-methylenedioxy-4-indoleglyoxylamide with a mp of 225-226 °C (yield 41%). Anal: C,H,N.

To a well-stirred suspension of 0.77 g of LAH in 40 mL dry THF, there was added, dropwise, a solution of 0.87 g N,N-dimethyl-5,6-methylenedioxy-4-indoleglyoxylamide in approximately 100 mL of anhydrous THF. The mixture was brought to reflux temperature, held there for 2 h, and allowed to return to room temperature. It was hydrolyzed by the cautious addition of 0.8 mL $H_2O$, followed with 2.4 mL 10% aqueous NaOH, and an additional 0.8 mL of $H_2O$. The inorganics were removed by filtration through Celite, and the filtercake was washed with additional THF. After removal of the solvent of the combined filtrate and washings under vacuum, the residue was distilled at the KugelRohr and the colorless distillate recrystallized from a mixture of EtOAc/hexane. There was obtained 0.30 g (38%) N,N-dimethyl-5,6-methylenedioxytryptamine (5,6-MDO-DMT), mp 115-117 °C.

DOSAGE: Greater than 5 mg

DURATION: Unknown

QUALITATIVE COMMENTS: (with 5 mg, smoked) "Nothing."

EXTENSIONS AND COMMENTARY: Up until 15 years ago, there had been no research published describing any simple N,N-disubstituted tryptamines carrying the methylenedioxy substitution pattern on the indole ring. This is interesting in that the activity of the methylenedioxy substituted phenethylamine MDA had been well documented almost 40 years ago, and its N-methyl homologue MDMA has been of known human activity for about 25 years. Then, within a year, two papers appeared in the literature describing both this compound (5,6-MDO-DMT) and the corresponding N,N-diisopropyl homologue, 5,6-MDO-DIPT. As to the position of this five-membered ring, there are two appealing locations. The 5,6-pattern has an appealing symmetry to it, being closely parallel to MDA, with a sort of long axis extending through the tryptamine molecule from the 3-position (where the side chain is attached), across the indole ring, coming out between the 5- and 6- positions. This certainly feels like the most natural analogue to MDA or MDMA. It has the plus of having the important 5-position occupied, but there might be a bit of a negative effect due to its having something at the 6-position. A more exciting possibility would be the 4,5-disubstitution, which would involve the favorite 5-position along with the site of the oxygen atom of psilocin and psilocybin. This compound has been made and is the preceding recipe, 4,5-MDO-DMT, #30.

As to the nature of the nitrogen substituents, this N,N-dimethyl compound is directly analogous to its 5-methoxy or 5-hydrogen counterparts. In behavioral studies, it is less potent than either of these simpler compounds, 5-MeO-DMT or DMT. In human studies these latter two chemicals are both active at levels of a few milligrams, and a trial with 5,6-MDO-DMT showed no activity at all at a five milligram trial. More studies are needed, and I am sure that, in time, they will be carried out.

### #32.   5,6-MDO-MIPT;   TRYPTAMINE, N-ISOPROPYL-N-METHYL-5,6-METHYLENEDIOXY;   INDOLE, 3-[2-(ISOPROPYLMETHYLAMINO)-ETHYL]-5,6-METHYLENEDIOXY;   N-ISOPROPYL-N-METHYL-5,6-METHYLENEDIOXYTRYPTAMINE;   3-[2-(ISOPROPYLMETHYL-AMINO)ETHYL]-5,6-METHYLENEDIOXYINDOLE; 5H-1,3-DIOXOLO-[4,5-F]INDOLE-7-ETHANEAMINE, N-ISOPROPYL-N-METHYL

SYNTHESIS: To 500 mL concentrated nitric acid, stirred and cooled with an external ice-bath there was added, a bit at a time, 50 g of finely powdered piperonal. The temperature must not be allowed to rise above 0 °C during the addition. After two hours of additional stirring, the reaction was poured over chipped ice, the product removed by filtration and washed with $H_2O$ to remove all traces of acid. After recrystallization from a 50/50 mixture of EtOAc and EtOH, the

product, 2-nitro-4,5-methylenedioxybenzaldehyde, was obtained as lemon-yellow colored crystals that weighed 47 g when dry, and had a mp of 97-98 °C.

A solution of 43.8 g 2-nitro-4,5-methylenedioxybenzaldehyde in 225 mL glacial acetic acid was treated with 66.2 g nitromethane followed by 29.2 g anhydrous ammonium acetate. After being held at reflux for 2 h, the volume was reduced to approximately half by distillation, and the residues poured into ice water. The solids were removed quickly by filtration, washed well with $H_2O$, and air-dried. An analytical sample of 2,2'-dinitro-4,5-methylenedioxystyrene was obtained as yellow crystals by crystallization from EtOH and had a mp of 121-122 °C. The unpurified isolate can be used directly in the next step.

A round-bottom flask was equipped with a mechanical stirrer, a reflux condenser, and a means of cooling with an external water bath. To 165 mL glacial acetic acid there was added 21 g 2,2'-dinitro-4,5-methylenedioxystyrene and 82 g powdered elemental iron. With good stirring, gentle heating was applied until an exothermic reaction set in, and this was maintained at a controlled pace with external cooling. When the spontaneous reaction had subsided, the reaction was brought to reflux for 15 min, then quenched by addition to a solution of 120 g NaOH in 500 mL $H_2O$. The reaction mixture was subjected to steam distillation and the distillate (25 L) was extracted several times with $Et_2O$. These extracts were combined, the solvent removed under vacuum, and the residue crystallized from petroleum ether. There was thus obtained 4.7 g of 5,6-methylenedioxyindole as colorless plates with a melting point of 108-110 °C, for a yield of 33% of theory. Catalytic hydrogenation is an alternate process for reduction. To a solution of 19.12 g 2,2'-dinitro-4,5-methylenedioxystyrene in a mixture of 55 mL absolute EtOH, 40 mL acetic acid and 300 mL EtOAc, there was added 4 g 10% palladium on charcoal and the reaction was shaken under 55 psi hydrogen for 45 minutes. After filtration through Celite under an inert atmosphere, the filtrate was treated with a suspension of 40 g $NaHCO_3$ in 100 mL $H_2O$. The organic phase was dried over anhydrous $MgSO_4$, then the solvent was removed under vacuum. The greenish-black residue was triturated with 4x100 mL portions of boiling cyclohexane. The extracts were combined and cooled, allowing the crystallization of the product 5,6-methylenedioxyindole as a solid with a mp of 107-110 °C. The yield was 8.3 g (64%).

To a well-stirred, cold solution of 1.61 g 5,6-methylenedioxyindole in 20 mL anhydrous $Et_2O$, there was added, dropwise, a solution of 1.75 mL oxalyl chloride in 5 mL $Et_2O$. The addition took 20 min. After an additional 20 min stirring, the red crystals that formed were removed by filtration, washed with 2x5 mL $Et_2O$, and dried under vacuum for 0.5 h. This crude acid chloride was dissolved in 100 mL anhydrous THF and cooled to 0° C with stirring under $N_2$. An $Et_2O$ solution of N-isopropyl-N-methylamine was added until the reaction mixture remained basic (pH >9 to external pH paper). The solvents were removed under vacuum, and the residue treated with 100 mL each of $H_2O$ and $CHCl_3$. The organic phase was separated, the aqueous phase extracted with additional $CHCl_3$, the pooled extracts dried over anhydrous $MgSO_4$, filtered, and the filtrate evaporated under vacuum. The residue was recrystallized from acetone to yield 1.47 g N-isopropyl-N-methyl-5,6-methylenedioxy-3-indoleglyoxylamide with a mp 203-204 °C. Anal: C,H,N.

To a well-stirred suspension of 1.15 g of LAH in 60 mL dry THF, there was added, dropwise, a solution of 1.44 g N-isopropyl-N-methyl-5,6-methylenedioxy-3-indoleglyoxylamide in approximately 150 mL of anhydrous THF. The mixture was brought to reflux temperature, held there for 2 h, and allowed to return to room temperature. It was hydrolyzed by the cautious addition of 1.15 mL $H_2O$, followed with 3.5 mL 10% aqueous NaOH, and finally an additional mL of $H_2O$. The inorganics were removed by filtration through Celite, and the filtercake was washed with additional THF. After removal of the solvent of the combined filtrate and washings under vacuum, the residue was distilled at the KugelRohr and the colorless distillate recrystallized from a mixture of benzene and cyclohexane. There was thus obtained 0.43 g N-isopropyl-N-methyl-5,6-methylenedioxytryptamine (5,6-MDO-MIPT) with a melting point of 87-89 °C (33%). Anal: C,H,N. MS (in m/z): $C_5C_{12}N^+$ 86 (100%); indolemethylene$^+$ 174 (7%); parent ion 260 (9%).

DOSAGE:  > 50 mg, orally

DURATION: Unknown

QUALITATIVE COMMENTS: (with 35 mg, orally) "Some paresthesia noted. Nothing else."

(with 50 mg, orally) "Maybe a trace of activity after an hour. Certainly nothing at three hours."

(with 60 mg, orally) "There is something going on there, but I can't tell what it is. Very vague."

(with 75 mg, orally) "Just a teasing smell of light-headedness in twenty minutes, and maybe a bit more light-headedness in an hour. I can suspect the chronology, but the character of the effects remains nebulous. It is certainly less dramatic than the 5-methoxy-compound."

EXTENSIONS AND COMMENTARY: I must continuously struggle with the reality that the substitutions on the indole ring demand an analogy to those on the phenethylamine ring. Clearly the 4-substituent is important, and the 5-substituent calls the shots (as with the 4-substituent in the phenethylamines). But is it possible that anything at the six-position is the kiss of death?

Both the 4,5-dimethoxy and the 5,6-dimethoxy-analogues are well established, and they would be fantastic tools to help unravel this problem. Clearly the 5,6-methylenedioxy materials are not too interesting, whereas the 4,5-methylenedioxy-counterparts have the rich smells of interest.

A totally compelling incident occurred in the course of writing this commentary. I decided not to assume that the reader had access to commercially available 5,6-methylenedioxyindole, but just might want to make it himself. It has been prepared from piperonal, and I said to myself, why not put into the recipe a dull but useful preparation from the ancient literature? So, let's find the 1967 article in the *Monatsh. Chem.* and translate the original German instructions into English for the readers. Simple and straight-forward? Yes? No!

A bit of background. Years ago, the fantastic library at the Medical School at San Francisco got into a bit of space and storage problems, and had to put its older reference issues in some sort of storage status, and it became necessary to get volumes brought out of hiding as you needed them. OK. We don't have the space. I can buy that. Let's get the space. So, a new library was designed to bring all reference material into one location and thus allow the researcher access to anything and everything he needed. Big money was asked for and big money was gotten. Finally, a single research source was created that appeared to meet all these needs. It was a multi-story giant across the street from the old medical school buildings. A treasure for the medical center, with all things for all people. So I tried to find Volume 98 of *Monatsh. Chem.*, published in 1967, with the details of the nitration of piperonal. No problem. The call number was W1 MO 343, so I go down three floors into the W1 territory, and I discover that there is nothing in the MO 343 section. Nothing but empty shelves. I find a helpful man who confirms that the volumes are missing, and then he asks me, "Are they pre-1975?" "Well, yes, they are." "Are they in a foreign language?" "Yes, in German." "Well," he says, "They have probably been moved over across the bay to Richmond, for safe keeping." "Is it a space problem?" "No, it deals with preservation and deterioration." "You are saying that older German text journals are more fragile than English counterparts?" "Well, it's a precautionary move."

The next day, I phoned in my needs to Richmond and was assured that when I got there the volume I needed would be immediately available at noon as I had asked. I made two errors in navigation in my search for the Richmond Agricultural Field Station, and located the Earthquake Research Library first. But I was met with total courtesy and was supplied with improved directions. It turned out that the field library had a Xerox machine than needed nickels, and I happened to have a pile of nickels. And I now have my recipe for the nitration of piperonal firmly in hand. But I also got a feeling that the priorities of those who needed to use reference libraries might be in conflict with the priorities of those who controlled these reference libraries.

I plead a most simple case to all of these authorities. I will in the future, on occasion, need a reference. Please let me have access to that reference when I need it. I see all these obstacles you might raise to my free access to any particular reference as a form of censorship, and I see it as a small but real measure of the superimposition of your principles upon mine. In a word, Mr. University, let me find what I want to find. Let me read what I want to read. Let me copy what I want to copy. In short, Mr. University, play the role that your founders intended you to play. My taxes paid for you; stay out of my way.

### #33.   2-Me-DET; TRYPTAMINE, N,N-DIETHYL-2-METHYL; INDOLE, 3-[2-(DIETHYLAMINO)ETHYL]-2-METHYL;   N,N-DIETHYL-2-METHYLTRYPTAMINE; 3-[2-(DIETHYLAMINO)ETHYL]-2-METHYL-INDOLE

SYNTHESIS: To an ice-cold and stirred solution of 6.56 g 2-methylindole in 75 mL TBME there was added, over the course of 20 min, 35 mL of a 2.0 M solution of oxalyl chloride in $CH_2Cl_2$. The glyoxyl chloride formed immediately and was removed by filtration and washed with 20 mL cold TBME. A solution of 16 mL diethylamine in 50 mL $CH_2Cl_2$ was prepared, cooled in an external ice bath, and vigorously stirred. To this, the solid glyoxyl chloride was added in small increments, producing a yellow solution. The reaction mixture was washed successively with $H_2O$, 0.5 N HCl, and again with $H_2O$. After drying over anhydrous $Na_2SO_4$, the solvent was removed under vacuum, providing an orange solid as residue. This was recrystallized from boiling THF and, after filtration and air drying to constant weight, provided N,N-diethyl-2-methylindoleglyoxylamide with a mp 170-172 °C.

To a stirred and cooled solution of 7.4 g N,N-diethyl-2-methylindole–glyoxylamide in 80 mL dry toluene under an inert atmosphere, there was added 31 mL 65% RED-AL in toluene, at a slow rate. After 20 min the ice bath was removed and the reaction allowed to stir for 2 h, and finally an additional 3 h at 60 °C. The light yellow solution was cooled again in the ice bath, and the excess hydride destroyed by the slow addition of 15 mL IPA followed by 50 mL $H_2O$. The solids were removed by filtration and washed with toluene. The combined filtrate and washings were repeatedly washed with $H_2O$ and then extracted twice with 0.5 N

HCl. The aqueous extracts were pooled, washed with $CH_2Cl_2$, and made basic by the addition of 25% NaOH. The precipitate that formed was extracted into several small portions of $CH_2Cl_2$ which were pooled and dried with anhydrous $Na_2SO_4$. After removal of the drying agent, the solvent was removed under vacuum. To the residue there was added a 1.0 M solution of HCl in anhydrous $Et_2O$ until the mixture was neutral, as determined by external, damp pH paper. The resulting solid was removed by filtration and twice recrystallized from a MeOH/acetone mixed solvent. There was thus obtained N,N-diethyl-2-methyltryptamine hydrochloride (2-Me-DET) as white crystals with a mp 214-216 °C.

DOSAGE: 80 - 120 mg, orally

DURATION: 6 - 8 h

QUALITATIVE COMMENTS: (with 70 mg, orally) "A very subtle onset characterized most notably as a mild stomach ache that lasted a short while. There was a sort of vague unreal feeling at an hour, but my thought pattern seemed to be quite clear. In another hour I noticed that higher pitches of the music on the radio were being muffled and the tones seemed to be shifting to lower frequency. I phoned a friend, and first the dial tone, and then her voice sounded wrong. The sense of touch (the phone receiver) was normal and my conversation flowed easily. Television seemed amusing, but perhaps it really was amusing. Soup tasted fine, and there was no appetite suppression. No GI problems, no next-day negatives."

(with 120 mg, orally) "My thoughts became quite cloudy, increasingly so for several hours. And somehow slower than usual. Reading didn't seem to connect, and I had to turn the radio off as it was lousy. Texture, not content. I could type OK, and did, so my body was OK, but things came to me slowly. I wasn't very hungry but food tasted OK. The 'cloudy' was pretty much gone after six hours. I don't particularly want to repeat this, as there isn't much here that I enjoy."

EXTENSIONS AND COMMENTARY: There is an interesting idea tucked away here in what seems to be an uninteresting compound.

The sound distortion, mentioned in both of these reports, brings to mind DIPT, where it is the major indicator of intoxication. With some people, it is the only change observed. With DIPT, there are two isopropyl groups on the basic nitrogen atom; here there are two ethyl groups. One might speculate that there might well be some optimum group geometry that would make the auditory to visual distortion ratio as high as possible. There were no suggestions that there were any auditory changes with DET so perhaps the added mass of that methyl group at the 2-position brings the molecular weight into some "auditory window." A compelling compound would be, of course, N,N-diisopropyl-2-methyltryptamine (2-Me-DIPT), but I don't believe that it has ever even been synthesized as of the present moment. It would certainly be a simple compound to make from the above indole.

**#34.   2-Me-DMT;   2,N,N-TMT;   TRYPTAMINE, 2,N,N-TRIMETHYL;
INDOLE, 3-[2-(DIMETHYLAMINO)ETHYL]-2-METHYL;   2,N,N-
TRIMETHYLTRYPTAMINE;   3-[2-(DIMETHYLAMINO)ETHYL]-2-
METHYLINDOLE; DESMETHOXY-INDAPEX**

SYNTHESIS: To a stirred, ice-cooled solution of 1.31 g 2-methylindole in 30 mL
TBME, there was added 7.5 mL of a 2M solution of oxalyl chloride in $CH_2Cl_2$,
dropwise. An orange-red precipitate formed when the addition was half complete.
The solid product was removed by filtration,
and washed with another 30 mL of cold
TBME. This material was added, in small
portions, to an ice-cold mixture of 3.5 mL
40% aqueous dimethylamine and 30 mL
$CH_2Cl_2$ that was being vigorously stirred.
The acid chloride faded to a pale yellow immediately on contact with the reaction
medium. After the addition was completed, the organic phase was washed with
$H_2O$, dilute HCl, and again with water. After drying over anhydrous $Na_2SO_4$, the
solvent was removed under vacuum to yield a yellow glass as residue. Scratching
with a warm isopropyl acetate cyclohexane mixture successfully induced crystallization, and there was thus obtained 0.84 g of 2,N,N-trimethylindoleglyoxylamide
with mp 167-170 °C.

A stirred solution of 3.8 g 2,N,N-trimethylindoleglyoxylamide in 70 mL
dry toluene was placed under a nitrogen pad and cooled with an external ice bath.
There was then added 25 mL of a 60% solution of sodium bis(2-methoxyethoxy)–
aluminumhydride in toluene (RED-AL). The stirring was continued at 0 °C for
30 min, then brought to room temperature for an additional 2 h. After cooling again,
the excess hydride was destroyed by the dropwise addition of IPA, and (when the
gas evolution had ceased) $H_2O$ was added with caution. The aluminum salts were
removed by filtration, and washed with isopropyl acetate. The filtrate and washes
were combined, washed with $H_2O$, then extracted with dilute HCl. After washing
the aqueous phase with $CH_2Cl_2$, it was made basic with 20% aqueous KOH, and
extracted with $CH_2Cl_2$. The pooled extracts were washed with $H_2O$, dried over
anhydrous $Na_2SO_4$, and the solvent removed under vacuum. The residue was
dissolved in a small amount of MeOH and brought to a neutral pH with the careful
addition of fumaric acid in MeOH. Removal of the solvent under vacuum gave a
white crystalline residue which was washed with isopropyl acetate, and recrystallized from a MeOH/isopropyl acetate mixture. There was thus obtained 1.8 g
2-methyl-N,N-dimethyltryptamine fumarate (2-Me-DMT) as colorless crystals
with mp 205-208 °C.

The compound has also been synthesized from 2-methylindole-3-acetic acid
via the ethyl ester, to the ethanol with sodium and alcohol, to the ethyl bromide with
$PBr_3$ in $Et_2O$, to the product (2-Me-DMT) with dimethylamine. The reported mp

of the free base is 97-98 °C.

DOSAGE: 50 - 100 mg, orally

DURATION: 4 - 6 h

QUALITATIVE COMMENTS: (with 50 mg, orally) "There was tingling everywhere but it faded after about three hours. Nothing else."

(with 75 mg, orally) "Very mild stomach rumbling during the first hour, with no other effects until the 65 minute point. Then there was the onset of a very mild relaxed feeling followed by intermittent skin alerting, especially on the head and neck. No visuals. Sexual activity at 90 minutes showed marked enhancement of both the pre-climactic and orgasmic phase, which was confirmed by repeat activity at 120 and 180 minutes. When I switched on TV to a familiar news announcer, I thought that he had a cold because his voice sounded lower than normal, and throaty. Later I picked up a phone to call a friend and both the dial tone and the touch-tones sounded very unusual. Music at this point sounded normal, but I am sure that some tonal perception was altered by this drug. The effects seemed almost gone by 4 hours and were undetectable by 5 hours. Appetite seemed unaffected throughout, and dinner at the 5-hour point was very good. No GI problems occurred, and there were no after effects the next day."

(with 90 mg, orally) "The entire body was becoming activated (in a good way) but not much going on in the head. I am mentally clear but with the entire touch system a bit more activated than I would choose. This peaked at 3 hours, and was gone in another 3 hours. Everything is tactile."

(with 120 mg, orally) "There is as much to be said for what didn't happen as for what did. No visual changes. No cloudiness of the thought processes. No motor impairment what-so-ever. There was some down-shifting of music, with some distortion, which was overall more annoying than interesting. But I am glad I am alone because I cannot wear clothing. Anything touching the skin makes all my hair stand on end. The erection of my nipples is almost painful. Exploring sexual stimulation seemed a little dangerous but explored anyway. The climax was disappointing. Too much activity of a slightly scary sort. Never again at this level."

EXTENSIONS AND COMMENTARY: How does one classify this kind of compound? It doesn't seem to be a psychedelic, at least at the levels reported. A stimulant? There were no mentions made of any increase in cardiovascular activity. It sounds like an example of a tactile stimulant, not for treatment of impotence but with the potential of augmenting and enhancing sexual pleasure.

From the structure activity point of view, it seems that the methyl group on the indolic 2-position again allows oral activity of something that, without it, would not be. Here, the parent compound is DMT, and the other examples were

2-Me-DET and 5-MeO-TMT. But of these, 2-Me-DMT seems to be the most free of "negative" side-effects, except for the sound distortion (and as for the sexual stimulation, there might be an occasional shaker manqué amongst us who would consider that also as a negative).

#35. MELATONIN; TRYPTAMINE, N-ACETYL-5-METHOXY; IN-DOLE, 3-(2-ACETAMIDOETHYL)-5-METHOXY; SEROTONIN, N-ACETYL-O-METHYL; ACETAMIDE, N-[2-(5-METHOXYINDOL-3-YL)ETHYL]; N-ACETYL-5-METHOXYTRYPTAMINE; 3-(2-ACETAMIDOETHYL)-5-METHOXYINDOLE; N-ACETYL-O-METHYLSEROTONIN; N-[2-(5-METHOXYINDOL-3-YL)-ETHYL]ACETAMIDE; REGULIN

SYNTHESIS: To a well-stirred solution of 10 g 5-methoxyindole in 150 mL anhydrous $Et_2O$ there was added, dropwise over the course of 30 min, a solution of 11 g oxalyl chloride in 150 mL anhydrous $Et_2O$. Stirring was continued for an additional 15 min during which time there was the separation of 5-methoxyindol-3-ylglyoxyl chloride as a tomato-red solid. This intermediate was removed by filtration, and used directly in the following step. To 40 mL of concentrated $NH_4OH$, which was being vigorously stirred, there was added as a solid, a bit at a time, the above glyoxyl chloride. This red solid gradually became yellow. After 15 min, there was added 200 mL 1 N HCl and the stirring continued, with the mechanical breaking-up of lumps, until the product was loose and finely dispersed. This was removed by filtration and washed with $H_2O$. After drying, this crude isolate weighed 8.2 g (55%) and was recrystallized twice from EtOH. The product, 5-methoxy-3-indolylglyoxylamide, was a fine, white crystalline material and had a mp of 245-247 °C.

To a well-stirred, warm suspension of 6.0 g LAH in 100 mL anhydrous dioxane, there was added a warm solution of 3.2 g of 5-methoxy-3-indolylglyoxylamide in 100 mL of anhydrous THF. The mixture was held at reflux for 38 h, cooled, and the excess hydride decomposed by the sequential addition of wet dioxane followed by 10 mL 5% aqueous NaOH. The resulting solids were removed by filtration, and extracted several times with boiling dioxane. The filtrate and washings were combined, dried over solid KOH, and stripped of solvent under vacuum, yielding an oily residue. This was dissolved in

80 mL warm benzene, decolorized with charcoal, and the filtered solution treated with an anhydrous solution of HCl in EtOH until it was acidic. The precipitate that formed weighed, after air drying, 1.1 g (29%) with mp 230-235 °C. This solid was recrystallized from EtOH, which provided the product 5-methoxytryptamine-hydrochloride with a melting point of 247.5-248.5 °C. Treatment with aqueous NaOH, followed by the extraction and isolation of the free base, provided a fine solid that could be recrystallized from CHCl₃ or EtOH, with a mp of 121-122 °C. This product has been obtained by two other procedures. The above starting indole, 5-methoxyindole, can be converted to the corresponding gramine with dimethylamine and formaldehyde, and this is converted easily with cyanide to the nitrile, 5-methoxy-3-indoleacetonitrile. This can be readily reduced to 5-methoxytryptamine with LAH. Another published procedure starts with the aldehyde of the indole, 5-methoxyindole-3-carboxaldehyde, which is coupled with nitromethane to form the nitrostyrene analogue, which has been reduced in turn to the above amine with LAH. In all cases, this intermediate amine was acetylated as described below.

To a solution of 0.2 g 5-methoxytryptamine in 4 mL of glacial HOAc there was added 2.0 mL acetic anhydride and heated at steam-bath temperature for 1 min. The volatiles were removed under vacuum and the residue was ground up under a mixture of EtOH and petroleum ether to yield 0.2 g (82%) of a white solid. This, after recrystallization from an ethanol/petroleum ether mixture, provided N-acetyl-5-methoxytryptamine (melatonin) as a white crystalline solid with a mp 116-118 °C. MS (in m/z): 173 (100%); indolemethylene⁺ 160 (97%); parent ion 232 (28%). IR (in cm⁻¹): 713, 794, 825, 925, 1042, 1101, 1177.

DOSAGE:  1 - 10 mg, orally

DURATION:  a few hours

QUALITATIVE COMMENTS:  (with 2.5 mg, orally) "I took one tablet sub-lingually just before I lay down to sleep, and slept very well. I was not tired the next day."

(with 5 mg, orally) "I cannot distinguish it from placebo."

(with 10 mg, orally) "For over a month I would take 10 milligrams every night, or 5 or 2.5 milligrams. More 10's than 2.5's. I slept well and then I stopped it all, and still had no trouble sleeping. Why waste the money?"

EXTENSIONS AND COMMENTARY: This is a difficult drug to try to determine the active level. It is late. You want to sleep. You take a tab of melatonin and you sleep well. Or you don't take a tab of melatonin and still you sleep well. Or perhaps you sleep poorly — what connection can be drawn from the melatonin usage? The end-point of these studies is not the enhancement of consciousness but the loss of consciousness. I truly cannot say what the active level might be, because I do not know what positive experience might be expressed with an active level. In my notes is a report of a person who took 80 milligrams, orally. "Apparently I drifted quite quickly and smoothly into sleep, which was sound and which felt natural. On awakening, both my mood and performance seemed enhanced over my usual state." Is that a positive response? Melatonin has been espoused as a cure for jet-lag. But when I try to record the doses and times and effects, there is quite a bit of looseness. It is being sold in tablets (sometimes for sublingual use, why, I do not know) at dosage units from 300 micrograms to 10 milligrams. I know of one very modest i.v. trial (with 25 micrograms, at 0.10 micrograms/minute). "No subjective effects were noted."

Melatonin is found in many areas of many animals. It is involved in the skin coloration of amphibians, and in the thermal or motor regulation in some higher animals. Its major regulatory role is in response to light and, in man, it is the major hormone produced by the pineal gland. This popular gland in the brain (incidentally the only unpaired site in the brain) has long been the darling of the new-age set as it is the so-called third eye. Its primary hormone, melatonin, has been the subject of many studies related to brain function. It has effects on other brain bodies that are themselves involved in hormone secretion. It has been implicated in behavioral and emotional changes in man, including anxiety, seasonal depression, and delayed sleep-phase syndrome (DSPS, with a delay in getting to sleep, and delay in coming awake). Its function is strongly affected by exposure to light, and it has been referred to as the body's hormone of darkness. And there is no question but that the biochemistry of the brain allows it to know what time of day it is. Studies with the pineal in the rat have shown that the enzymatic activity needed to run the acetylation reaction (using N-acetyltransferase, which produces melatonin from its original serotonin precursor) is 45 times more active at 10:00 PM than it is at 10:00 AM.

There has been no satisfactory pharmacology ascribed to melatonin. At low dosages it certainly decreases sleep latency. It is not a sedative at the low milligram levels (which achieves blood levels in the physiological range) but rather is a factor that might guard the user from the disruptions known as jet-lag, which is certainly a close cousin to the DSPS. Here the dosages usually explored are in the 2 to 10 milligram range. It is invariably offered as a dietary supplement rather than a sleep aid (which would be a medical claim) but a side-effect that the user is warned against is drowsiness. One popular brand I know of is available in 2.5 milligram tablets recommended for sub-lingual use. I inquired of them to learn what studies were available that indicated any virtue the sublingual route might have over direct oral use, and I learned nothing. Just a few days ago I was shown a fascinating sham offering in the OTC world. Alice brought home from the local branch of a national chain drug store a container containing 120 tablets that contained 300 micrograms each. The label said, "University Tested Strength" and "Preferred Dosage." The recommendation was for the user to take from one to three tablets (still less than a milligram). This is an example of drug-abuse at the corporate level. At relatively large dosages (75-80 milligrams) it appears to produce an increase in total sleep, along with a decrease in daytime sleepiness. This is all without hangover. It appears to be a sleep catalyst at modest levels, and a soporific at higher levels, where it can be administered chronically (75 mg/day) for a couple of weeks with satisfactory effects. There is a paucity of reports at intermediate dosage levels. Whatever the effective dosage might be, the sales of melatonin are truly booming in the health food stores. Genzyme, a major manufacturer of melatonin, estimates that 20 million people in the United States bought melatonin for the first time in 1995, and it places the retail sales at between $200 million and $350 million per year.

In an entirely different area of pharmacology, one of the most effective protections against external radiation is a simple sulfur compound, mercaptoethylamine, commonly called MEA. This is a fascinating compound with the common name of cysteamine, and it has a wide variety of biological effects, both as a poison in that it causes ulcers, and as a treatment for poisoning in overdose cases involving acetaminophen (Tylenol). One of its most broadly studied properties is that of protecting an experimental animal against the damage of being exposed to radiation. It was unexpectedly observed that our essential and favorite neurotransmitter serotonin was every bit as effective as a radioprotective agent. In efforts to make this natural compound more accessible to the damaged animal, it was studied as the unacetylated O-methyl ether. This simple compound, 5-methoxytryptamine (5-MeO-T, or Mexamine) has been mentioned under the recipe for 5-MeO-DMT in its possible effects in potentiating CNS-active drugs. But here it deserves to be highlighted for its protection against radiation.

Two structural modification directions of 5-methoxytryptamine have been thoroughly explored. The Russians have published many years of work where they have modified that methyl group on the oxygen and have studied these changes in structure to changes in activity. In the United States, the research direction has exploited the observation that the acetamide derivative is also a good protective agent against radiation. And that amide is our title compound, melatonin. Extending the carbon length of the acetyl out to the amides in the hexanoic and octanoic area increases the prophylactic virtue, as does the making of an amide with a heptofluorobutyroyl group. The bigger the amide, the better the protection. Another study has shown melatonin to be very protective of the DNA in human white blood cells from gamma irradiation, even at very low concentrations. This may be due to the strong anti-oxidant properties of melatonin. And then, there are claims that exposing animals to low, chronic levels of melatonin can affect their life span.

Could all of these actions of melatonin be connected? When one is flying at high elevations for long periods of time, one is exposed to quite a bit of solar radiation, and one also tends to get jet-lag. Melatonin, a natural hormone of the pineal gland, both protects against radiation and defuses jet-lag. Might there be a closer connection between the nuisance of jet-lag with the high altitude aspect of trans-Atlantic flights, rather than with the time-zone passage of trans-Atlantic or trans-Pacific flights? Personally I don't think so, as I don't get jet-lag (much) traveling in the Westerly direction, and I cross just as many time-zones and fly at similar altitudes. And I have not heard of jet-lag at all on North-to-South flights that may be just as long, but which do not cross many, if any, time zones. New York to Santiago, or London to Cape Town, for example.

This is all pharmacology. These are answers to the question, what does the drug do? A second point must be loudly mentioned here, one that concerns the questions, "How does it do what it does, and where does it go to do it?" Allow me to tell a tale based on an old, made up, Sufi legend.

The master asked the student, "How do you follow a guide who cannot be seen, who walks through a dark forest in the middle of the night?"

The student answers, "It is simple. Let him carry a light."

"But then," answers the teacher, "He is no longer the guide who cannot be seen."

"True, but at least I can now follow it, and I know where the light goes."

"You must be aware you are following a different guide?"

The student thinks for a minute, and then says, "Yes, of course I know that, but what else can I do?"

This is the sad plight of the research pharmacologist, who is trying to plot the in vivo course of a biochemical that cannot be followed. It must be labeled somehow, with a radioactive element, but nature demands that it is one that is not a normal part of its makeup. So he says, I would like to follow melatonin through the darkness of the body but I cannot see it as there is no light. I will attach a brilliant radioactive label to it, something like an iodine 125, so I can follow it as it goes here and there. The iodine is the light that the melatonin molecule is carrying, and the light can indeed be followed, but it is a different molecule. It is no longer melatonin; it is now 2-iodomelatonin. It is a completely different guide.

It is a sad story to tell, but this subtle shape-shifting is all too often invisible to the researcher. We will learn what melatonin does, by studying its radio-iodinated derivative. We will determine the quality of our synthetic analogues by measuring the displacement they make of iodinated melatonin from the melatonin receptor. Iodomelatonin is not melatonin. It is a different compound. It has a different biochemistry and a different pharmacology. It is used in melatonin studies only because it can be seen. Melatonin itself is, by its nature, a dark traveler in a dark forest, and we still do not know how to study it directly.

There is a third point, an additional fillip that is associated with the popular use of melatonin; the history of the transition of any interesting drug up the historic ladder, from availability to promotion, to broadcast usage, to spectacular claims, to prohibition, to illegality. This has always been seen as a pattern controlling drug use in our society. But will this apply to melatonin? We are midstride in this process, today. Its reputation as a sedative and life-extender within the health food store circuit grew quickly in the early 90's. A sleep article in the magazine "Esquire" (Michael Segall, October, 1994) advanced the expected warning of not knowing enough about it. "Until more is known, though, it's probably not a good idea to self-medicate your jet lag with melatonin. No one knows how much you should take nor about the potential side effects." So far, right on schedule. Although a great deal is known, and potential side effects have been examined, the restrictive warning label must be voiced. But just recently, a feature article has appeared in another magazine ("Newsweek," August 7, 1995, by Geoffrey Cowley) that expands on its potential additional virtues, such as preventing pregnancy, boosting the immune system, preventing cancer, and extending life span. Heavy duty. It will be interesting to see if this precipitates an FDA control action in light of potential medical claims, or a DEA control action in light of an abuse potential. Maybe the sales of the chemical will have to hit something in the megatonage area first. I have just ordered a few grams from the Aldrich Chemical Company and I can state that its availability remains intact for the moment. But, if it is restricted, thus withdrawn and made illegal, its popularity will grow with renewed vigor, and it will be instructive to observe in just what way the dynamics of the illicit market will evolve!

This is a present day example of a problem in the making, one that law-makers and regulatory administrators have had to face again and again since that moment that the government decided it was necessary to make a pretense of controlling the relationship between its citizens and their drugs. In the name of drug control, melatonin will eventually become illegal, and it will then pass totally out of any semblance of control. The fact that it is a natural component of the healthy human body will probably carry little weight in any attempt to thwart its becoming outlawed. Compounds such as bufotenine and DMT are normal components of our nervous system, but they are currently Schedule I drugs due to their reputed abuse potential and the absence of any accepted medical use.

A few words are needed here concerning the neurotransmitter serotonin. It is the immediate precursor to melatonin in the brain, and it is the, no, **THE** neurotransmitter that is the sine qua non of the brain. Everything centers on it, everything is explained by it, and all virtue and all damage that occurs there is because of it. It is not a brain chemical from outside the body. If you swallow a bunch of it, it passes on through the body without making it to the brain, because it is too polar to get through what is called the "blood-brain barrier." But maybe an enabled precursor just might make it. Recently there has been a wide promotion of 5-hydroxytryptophan that just might play this role. If it were to be actively transported into the brain, it might produce cerebral serotonin. But maybe not. I am just a bit overwhelmed by the beneficial steroids that are not steroids, and the smart drug that may or may not make you smart, of the hormone substitutes that might or might not make you a sexy octogenarian. The over-the-counter world is awash with materials that appear to be virtuous but which are carefully presented as being without any medical claims. Back to serotonin. It is an essential factor in our brain chemistry. Since it cannot be made elsewhere and be moved to where it is needed, it must be made on location. Most drugs are judged good or bad by their influence on the changes made of serotonin levels. This is the guide we follow because he is carrying the light. What is really happening in the brain is happening in darkness, because we have no way of seeing it.

It is my quiet hope that the psychedelic drugs will give us that guidance towards the understanding of the mind. They just might let us see that trail through the dark forest where most of the people who search choose to follow the lighted path.

### #36.   5-MeO-DET;   TRYPTAMINE, N,N-DIETHYL-5-METHOXY;   IN-DOLE, 3-[2-(DIETHYLAMINO)ETHYL]-5-METHOXY;   N,N-DIETHYL-5-METHOXYTRYPTAMINE;   3-[2-(DIETHYLAMINO)ETHYL]-5-METHOXYINDOLE

SYNTHESIS: (from 5-methoxytryptamine) A solution of 0.95 g of free-base 5-methoxytryptamine was dissolved in 10 mL warm IPA and, after returning to room temperature, treated first with 2.8 mL diisopropylethylamine followed by 1.2 mL bromoethane. After 3 days, TLC showed considerable starting material, so there was added an additional 2.8 g of the amine and 1.2 g of the bromide and the room-temperature stirring continued for an additional 3 days. The volatiles were removed under vacuum, and the residue treated with 1.6 g acetic anhydride, and heated on the steam bath for 20 min. The excess anhydride was destroyed by the addition of 3 mL concentrated $NH_4OH$, followed by dilution with 100 mL 0.5 N $H_2SO_4$. The aq-

ueous phase was washed with 3x50 mL $CH_2Cl_2$, made basic with 6N NaOH and extracted with 3x25 mL $CH_2Cl_2$. The solvent from the pooled extracts was removed under vacuum, and the residue distilled at the KugelRohr.

A fraction boiling at 190-200 °C at 0.5 mm/Hg providing 0.45 g of a white oil. This was dissolved in 2.5 mL IPA, acidified with approximately 8 drops of concentrated HCl, which produced spontaneous crystallization. There was added, slowly and with good stirring, 20 mL of anhydrous $Et_2O$ to yield beautiful white crystals of N,N-diethyl-5-methoxytryptamine hydrochloride (5-MeO-DET), weighing 0.50 g (35%) and with a mp 190-191 °C. IR (in $cm^{-1}$):  817, 830, 930, 1109, 1185. MS (in m/z):  $C_5H_{12}N^+$ 86 (100%), $C_3H_8N^+$ 58 (12%); indolemethylene$^+$ 160 (4%); parent ion 246 (2%).

The pooled extracts of the $CH_2Cl_2$ washings of the acidified aqueous phase above gave, upon removal of the solvent under vacuum, a brownish residue that crystallized. Recrystallization of this from MeOH gave 0.44 g of N-ethylmelatonin as a white crystalline solid. IR (in cm$^{-1}$): 790, 829, 929, 1031, 1068,1108, 1182, 1199. MS (in m/z): 173 (100%); indolemethylene$^+$ 160 (67%); parent ion 260 (14%). This amide proved extremely difficult to hydrolyze.

(from 5-methoxyindole) To a well-stirred solution of 1.5 g 5-methoxyindole in 15 mL anhydrous Et$_2$O there was added, dropwise over the course of 30 min, a solution of 1.4 g oxalyl chloride in 15 mL anhydrous Et$_2$O. Stirring was continued for an additional 15 min, during which time there was the separation of 5-methoxyindol-3-ylglyoxyl chloride as a red crystalline solid. This intermediate was removed by filtration and washed with Et$_2$O, and was used directly in the following step. This was added in small dabs to 2.0 g anhydrous diethylamine, cooled and well-stirred. The off-white resulting solids were suspended in 100 mL 1 N HCl, stirred until it was a loose and creamy texture, then filtered and washed with H$_2$O. Recrystallization from acetonitrile gave 2.24 g (80%) N,N-diethyl-5-methoxyindol-3-ylglyoxylamide as white solids, with a mp of 158-160 °C.

A solution of 2.1 g N,N-diethyl-5-methoxyindol-3-ylglyoxylamide in 35 mL anhydrous THF was added, slowly, to 3.2 g LAH in 60 mL THF which was well-stirred and held at reflux temperature under an inert atmosphere. After the addition was complete, reflux was maintained for an additional 16 h, the reaction mixture cooled, and the excess hydride destroyed by the cautious addition of wet THF. Aqueous 15% NaOH was added cautiously until the solids had a loose, white cottage cheese character to them, and the mobile phase tested basic by external damp pH paper. These solids were removed by filtration, washed with first THF and then with MeOH. The filtrate and washings were combined, dried over anhydrous MgSO$_4$, and the solvent removed under vacuum. The residue was distilled, yielding a fraction boiling at 190-200 °C at 0.5 mm/Hg that weighed 1.45 g and was a white oil. This was dissolved in 8 mL IPA, acidified with concentrated HCl until it was acidic to external damp pH paper, and diluted with Et$_2$O and stirred until crystallization appeared to be complete. N,N-diethyl-5-methoxytryptamine hydrochloride (5-MeO-DET) was obtained as white crystals, weighing 1.60 g (74%).

DOSAGE: 1 - 3 mg, orally

DURATION: 3 - 4 h

QUALITATIVE COMMENTS: (with 2 mg, orally) "My tinnitus is really out there, and there is no way of getting away from it. Light-headed in a funny way — no hypotension, not dizzy — maybe something to do with the inner ear? It is in the head, I am attentive, and I am not comfortable. Three hours into it I am down, and I have a bit of wine, and I am aware of it. Am I drunk? Was I drunk earlier? I was intoxicated, to be sure."

(with 3 mg, orally) "It hit in a half hour, and the thought that came to mind was the phrase from my days at college, "Boy, I really felt that drink!" I may be sloppy, but let me explore the sexual. Wow. I may be spacey in the head, but my body knows where it is at. The next day was normal. I don't think I want to do this again."

(with 3 mg, orally) "Effect felt within 20 mins, mainly light-headedness, almost dizziness. This blocked anything else. Just wanted to stay quiet and hope it would all go away as soon as possible. During the next hour, lying beside husband (who was experiencing the same effect but not minding it as much), I became aware of another dimension behind the dizziness. I could sense enough of it to believe that it would have been interesting to explore, but that there was no way to get through the dizzies, which effectively blocked anything else. At approximately the hour and a half to two hour point, I felt a faint lessening of the head-fuzzies, and tested it out by walking to the living room. Felt it necessary to walk carefully. Body felt heavy and mood was rather dark, verging on depressed. After that, attempted love-making, which was extraordinarily successful for husband. For myself, there was still a reluctance to let down my guard. My back problems had been bothering me quite a bit, during all of this, and even two Bufferins didn't help as much as I would have liked. It's quite obvious that, if it were possible to remove the part of the molecule that causes the dizzies, this would be one of the best drugs for erotic stuff imaginable. And if wishes were horses, etc. Too bad. Would I try this again? And at a higher dosage? No, and No. "

(10 mg, smoked with peppermint leaves) "After a few minutes a high feeling with some dizziness, intense heartbeat, trembling, anxiety, restlessness, cold sweating, paleness and weak belly cramps. There were some visions I could not concentrate on because of the strong side-effects. I felt sick, went to bed, and was very glad when the effects disappeared after about one and a half hours."

EXTENSIONS AND COMMENTARY: The is one of the most provocative temptresses I have ever encountered in the tryptamine world. It is a case of having a protégé that you absolutely know will be a success if allowed to come to fulfillment, and yet you know that uncontrolled circumstances will prevent that fulfillment.

Here is a simple, easy to make compound that lies in-between the lower homologue, 5-MeO-DMT (active at 10+ milligrams by any parenteral route) and 5-MeO-DIPT (active at 10+ milligrams orally). The most rudimentary logic demands, yea, screams, that 5-MeO-DET should be active at 10+ milligrams, probably also by the oral route. That is the clear potential of this individual. But, at a fraction of this dosage, an unexpected new property is apparent, one that suggests neurotoxicity, and thus will preclude the achievement of that 10 milligram psychedelic potential. There is a light-headedness, a vertigo and intoxication, a warning of fragility, that pretty effectively blocks any exploration into areas that might be psychologically virtuous. This is reinforced by a report I had received from a person who had smoked some 10 milligrams of it. His report is in the qualitative comments above. He described it as a "torture psychedelic."

This is a new and totally unexpected negative activity that may well be unique to this particular diethyl material — it certainly was not reported with either of the immediate homologues, the dimethyl or the diisopropyl. And, as an intriguing corollary, could the unexpected new activity property that brought the physical concern also be the thing that brought the terrific erotic enhancement? Are they tied together as a single new component of action? Or might there be two new components of action, the scary vertigo and the friendly sexual?

To me, an obvious bridge to help explain this seeming discontinuity would be the dipropyl analogue. I made the compound, and explored it up to its active levels. It is an easy compound to make, and has been known in the scientific literature for many years. My quandary was how to present it in this book. Should I make it a recipe in its own rights, giving the detailed synthesis and a formal position as an active tryptamine? Its actions are ambiguous, and not totally positive, making an argument for its inclusion as a footnote in some other, more interesting recipe. It is this latter route that I have chosen, so here is the 5-MeO-DPT story, both chemical and pharmacological, tucked away in the bigger 5-MeO-DET

CHEMISTRY: To a warm solution of 0.9 g 5-methoxytryptamine in 10 mL IPA there was added 2.8 mL diisopropylethylamine and 1.5 mL propyl iodide, and the mixture was heated on the steam bath for 5 h. TLC analysis at this time showed the presence of both the mono- and the dialkylamines, but there was no indication of the presence of unreacted 5-methoxytryptamine or of the quaternary salt. After removal of the volatiles under vacuum, a $CH_2Cl_2$ solution of the residue was treated with 1 g acetic anhydride (on the steam bath for 5 min) followed by 2 mL ammonium hydroxide. Extraction of this solution with 1 N $H_2SO_4$ proved to be almost worthless, as the extracts after separation, alkalinification with 6 N NaOH, extraction with $CH_2Cl_2$ and distillation of the residues following removal of the solvent, provided only a few milligrams of the desired product. The product had remained in the $CH_2Cl_2$. The solvent was removed under vacuum, and the residue partitioned between MeOH (containing a small amount of aqueous NaOH) and hexane. The hexane fraction was concentrated under vacuum to provide 0.54 g of an almost colorless oil which was distilled by KugelRohr. A white oil was obtained, boiling at 170-180 °C at 0.04 mm/Hg, which weighed 0.49 g. This was dissolved in 2.5 mL IPA and neutralized with 8 drops of concentrated HCl. The solution was diluted with 25 mL anhydrous $Et_2O$ to provide 5-methoxy-N,N-dipropyltryptamine hydrochloride as a white crystalline salt. This was removed by filtration, washed with $Et_2O$, air dried to constant weight, and weighed 0.54 g. The mp was 193-194 °C. IR (in cm$^{-1}$): 811, 828, 929, 1079, 1103, 1186. MS (in m/z): $C_7H_{16}N^+$ 114 (100%); methoxyindolemethylene$^+$ 160 (13%); parent ion 274 (3%).

QUALITATIVE COMMENTS: (with 4.0 mg, orally) "Within the hour there is something and after another hour there is nothing. Happy to go on up."

(with 6.0 mg, orally) "I am up above baseline for sure. Maybe to a ++, erotic maybe, and not too much light-headedness. It is comfortable. Completely out before the fourth hour."

(with 8.4 mg, orally) "Aware in 12 minutes, some head noises at 20 minutes. These noises are reminiscent of the 5-MeO-DET in that they were "bells" which were bad and the underlying "turn-on" which was good. But the "bells" were outweighing the "turn-on." Let's ride it out but then, for that matter, what choice is there! At the 25 minute point the turn-on now outweighs the bell noise. But these keep alternating. Pulse 84; no cardiovascular. But for the next half hour, the bells > the turn-on. At three hours, almost baseline, and I eat modestly. I have better things to do with my time."

------

There is the irrepressible fascination of this type of research. Could one tinker with the molecule to emphasize one new property and de-emphasize another? Here is the theoretical conundrum stripped of arcane chemical words and put into non-technical symbolism. Give a single letter to a substitution group, increasing as the group increases in size. Here is the code:

A = hydrogen
B = methyl
C = ethyl
D = propyl
E = isopropyl
F = butyl
G = s-butyl

And let's arrange the 5-methoxylated tryptamines in order of increasing mass, and see if there is a pattern apparent as to the quantity or quality of action.

| | | | | |
|---|---|---|---|---|
| A | A | 5-MeO-T | anti-radiation, not a psychedelic | ? |
| A | B | 5-MeO-NMT | unknown activity | ? |
| B | B | 5-MeO-DMT, | positive, psychedelic, out-of-body | 6-20 mg |
| B | E | 5-MeO-MIPT | mixed, complex | 4-6 mg |
| C | C | 5-MeO-DET | negative, vertigo, erotic | 2-3 mg |
| C— C | | 5-MeO-pyr-T | very negative, amnesia | 0.5-2 mg |
| D | D | 5-MeO-DPT | neutral, balance, good and bad | 6-10 mg |
| E | E | 5-MeO-DIPT | positive, LSD-like psychedelic | 8-12 mg |
| F | F | 5-MeO-DBT | known compound, unknown activity | ? |
| G | G | 5-MeO-DSBT | unknown compound | - |

So, I ask, how could C C be modified to eliminate the vertigo component, maintain the erotic component, perhaps even maintain the psychedelic component, and certainly maintain the orally active property? Clearly, tying them together in the form of a pyrrolidine ring didn't do it. Only one of these listed 5-methoxy's of known activity is asymmetric, the methyl isopropyl analogue. It is probably through this device of mixing and comparing that our answer will be found. Some guide might come from the 5-hydrogen counterparts, more of which have been explored in man. The variations with a constant isopropyl group have been organized in the recipe for EIPT. Here is the rest of the story.

| B | C | MET | positive, psychedelic | 80-100 mg |
|---|---|---|---|---|
| B | D | MPT | unknown | > 50 mg |
| B | E | MIPT | mixed, complex | 10-25 mg |
| B | F | MBT | mixed | 250-400 mg |
| B | G | MSBT | unknown | ? |
| C | E | EIPT | mixed | 24-40 mg |

My hope is that getting leads from the second list (no substituent at the indolic 5-position) could help guide the choice of asymmetric substituents for the first list (a methoxy group at the 5-position) that would lead to an expected increase in potency but to an unexpected change in quality of action.

Kierkegaard probably summed it up best. "Life is not a problem to be solved, it is a mystery to be lived." That's chemistry, friends; that's life!

## #37. 5-MeO-DIPT; TRYPTAMINE, N,N-DIISOPROPYL-5-METHOXY; INDOLE, 3-[2-(DIISOPROPYLAMINO)ETHYL]-5-METHOXY; N,N-DIISOPROPYL-5-METHOXYTRYPTAMINE; 3-[2-(DIISOPROPYL-AMINO)ETHYL]-5-METHOXYINDOLE

SYNTHESIS: To a solution of 3.0 g 5-methoxytryptamine (see under melatonin for its preparation) in 20 mL sulfolane (tetramethylenesulfone) there was added 8.2 g diisopropylethyl amine and 10.7 g 2-iodopropane, and the two-phase mixture was heated on the steam bath with frequent shaking. After 3 h, the mixture was brought back to room temperature and stirred vigorously for an additional 16 h. After the removal of all volatiles under vacuum, the res-

idue (30 g) was diluted with 100 mL H$_2$O, which gave a clear solution. The addition of 10 mL 5% aqueous NaOH produced a cloudy suspension that was extracted with

3x40 mL hexane. These pooled extracts were stripped of solvent to yield 1.0 g of an almost colorless oil that was distilled at the KugelRohr. A small cut at 100 °C (at 0.01 mm/Hg) proved to be largely residual sulfolane (about 0.01 g) and the bulk of the product distilled at 140-150 °C to give a viscous white oil, 0.80 g. This was dissolved in 3.5 mL IPA and neutralized with 15 drops of concentrated HCl. The addition of five drops of anhydrous $Et_2O$ instigated crystallization, and the product was removed by filtration, washed with 4:1 $IPA/Et_2O$ mixture, and air-dried. There was thus obtained 0.85 g of a fine white crystalline product, N,N-diisopropyl-5-methoxytryptamine hydrochloride (5-MeO-DIPT), with a mp 181-182 °C (17%). IR (in cm$^{-1}$): 731, 809, 826, 931, 1035, 1064, with an NH at 3165. MS (in m/z): $C_7H_{16}N^+$ 114 (100%); $C_4H_{10}N^+$ 72 (31%); indolemethylene$^+$ 160 (12%); parent ion 274 (<1%). There was no detectable 5-MeO-NIPT by GC (<1%).

DOSAGE:  6 - 12 mg, orally

DURATION:  4 - 8 h

QUALITATIVE COMMENTS:  (with 6 mg, orally)  "Effects were present in twenty minutes, and I took my portable radio into the garden at forty minutes just to pull weeds. Each weed had special significance, and my cat joined me and agreed with me. This is excessively strange. The radio was discussing a President Ford fund-raiser, and continued with word sequences such as fund, fun, profun, pro-found, profane, refrain, and on and on. A car drove by with sitar music playing on its radio! Why not. And by my hour number three, I am back where I started. That was quite a morning."

(with 6 mg, orally)  "Talking wasn't really interesting, music wasn't interesting, nothing was very interesting. One hour in and I felt turned on as if a wave passed over my body, and then the wave went back to the ocean, or wherever waves go. I was getting hungry but I didn't want to go to the kitchen, as I didn't want to interact with anyone I might encounter. What remained with me the longest was the awareness of vibrations, and what felt best was the stillness. Was back to baseline in 4 hours."

(with 7 mg, orally)  "In one hour I was in a marvelous, sexy place. Everything was shaded with eroticism. Sex was explosive, and in another three hours I was completely ready for the outside, public world. As a short term aphrodisiac, this leaves 2C-B in the dust."

(with 10 mg, orally)  "Colors on the edges of the wiggles of the eye, a sort of Jessie Allen running design with color contrasts and sparkle. People's faces were interesting, quite serious, and not completely friendly. Well after everything had cleared, later in the evening, there was a residual, good clean feeling. This is a definite sense-distorter. I am not completely sure I like it."

(with 10 mg, orally)  "We found it to be outstanding — combining the best

characteristics of two other like products while contributing a penetrating efficaciousness of its own."

(with 12 mg, orally) "Had prepared for this experience during the day, and
was looking forward to the time with my partner. Flowers, candles, fluffy pillows,
arranged for food, etc. Large pillar-type candles and the glow was nice and warm.
Warm was comfort and comfort was good. Warm led into a wonderful sexual turn-
on, where my entire body was alive and alert. This was one hour into the trip. This
sexual turn-on was the feeling of a bud about to unfold into a full-blown, beautiful
flower, which happened during love-making. The flower continued to fill out fuller
and fuller for a couple of hours, and then just remained a full-blown, beautiful,
wonderful flower, and I fell asleep with this feeling."

(with 12 mg, orally) "Remembering how hungry I got during my last 6 mg.
experience, and without any dietary restriction, I ate a vegetarian burrito four hours
earlier. It took an hour for me to turn on. I have never experienced such an increase
of the peristalsis process in moving the burrito through my colon and with each
defecation I would become a little more turned on. As I became more turned on, the
greater I felt the sense of hypertension. A mind/body load became uncomfortable.
It was never psychedelic in the way of acid or psilocybe. My muscles, gluteus
maximus, the lateral rotators that connect to the trochanter and the large muscles that
connect to the hamstrings, all contracted and spasmed. Psychologically it was as
though my conservative instinct, my sense of Being, became extremely agitated. I
felt completely unnerved, and the only relief offered was by having sex. As the
effects of this material were rather extreme, I never felt as though I was having a
psychedelic experience. Maybe because it was all about dealing with body load and
discomfort."

(with 12 mg, orally) "There was a very strange, almost paranoid session
of listening to music, about an hour and a half into it. The program was a program
of Irish music called "The Thistle and Shamrock," but I had paid no attention to the
announcement. What was being played were three nativity pieces with song and
words, from strange places. What I heard were three distant, fraudulent selections
with generically meaningless words, mumbled so as to sound authentic. Everything
was faked. It was "Hearts of Space" music in the worst possible taste. My neutral
observer was completely taken in by it all, and quite enjoyed it. It turned out that
I was wrong; the music was strange but of good quality. It was my interpretation
that was screwed up."

(with 12 mg, orally) "My experience with this material was different in its
action than anything I had tried in the past — it came on quicker but with much less
intensity. I really enjoyed the mellowness, and it sort of waved in and out. I came
down after almost an hour, smoked a little marijuana, and went back up to where I
had been previously. I could do this around my children, and they would know I was
happy but I doubt they would realize just exactly what was up. I liked it and would
consider a public event (craft fair, street fair, window shopping) very adventurous.

No hangover; sleep excellent."

(with 12 mg, orally) "Awful, awful taste. Quickly aware and in the second half hour I rapidly shot up to a +++ in a very LSD-like manner, without the visuals. Time was quite slowed down during this come-on. Erotic world was fantastic, explosive, almost scary. Rapid drop-off, and by the fourth hour I am clear of any effects."

EXTENSIONS AND COMMENTARY: Here is a rather fast-acting psychedelic-like drug, with suggestions of LSD action but with essential differences. It has a lot of things going for it. It is short-lived, a virtue in many people's minds. It may vie with 2C-B as a potential aphrodisiac. It is reasonably easy to synthesize. It is of a pretty high potency. The physical side-effects are minimal. These are the positive points.

But there are points that are neutral or actually negative, and they must be considered. A fair number of people who have explored 5-MeO-DIPT have said that there are some uncomfortable aspects with the experience. Not only are there few if any visual enhancements, but the altered state they entered was one that they simply couldn't use. They couldn't make intuitive leaps. They were wasting their time.

On the neutral, but scientifically exciting edge, there is again some musical sound distortions that remind one of the actions of the analogue without the 5-methoxy group, DIPT. With DIPT, there was a physical, harmonic distortion of the sounds that were heard. With 5-MeO-DIPT (again, two isopropyl groups on the basic nitrogen) these perversions involved musical character and interpretation. None of the comments suggested harmonic structure. I do believe that these two drugs, having such an intimate structural resemblance but with their different distortions of music interpretation, would be rewarding to explore more fully with the view of objectively defining these changes. 5-MeO-DIPT is a mixed bag. But it is a bag that I predict will demand a great deal of interest sometime in the future, especially if the erotic enhancement at a low dose proves to be a consistent property.

There is an interesting story associated with the first publication of the chemistry and pharmacology of this compound, in 1981. My co-author was a Michael Carter, in England. We had discussed a number of potentially interesting tryptamines and agreed upon making a small handful to evaluate. We had, some six years earlier, co-published a paper describing a new and exciting phenethylamine which we called 2C-B, and we expected to work together, in our separate labs, on a number of research projects. And indeed, I heard from Michael from a new address, and he sent me his samples and reports of the new compounds we had decided to make, including 5-MeO-DIPT. Our synthetic materials were spectro-scopically identical and the human trials had shown that they were very similar. Along with the samples and a letter there came the draft of a possible paper. I wrote back to Michael my own version of the paper, to his new address, and the letter was returned as undeliverable — no forwarding address available! Again I sent it back, with full first-class postage and a clear request to forward it if necessary — and this time it simply never came back at all.

The issue sat there for a year or two, and I hoped that something would occur. Nothing. I finally wrote to the telephone company in London (Michael had said something about eventually moving up to London) and asked if they could possibly send me the addresses of all the Michael F. Carter that had telephone service in the greater London area. Bless their hearts, they sent back a list of twenty names. And a statement that they were appreciative of having the middle initial, as without that the list would have been in the hundreds.

I wrote to each and every one of these Michael F. Carter's the same letter phrased in a way that required no answer if it was the wrong person, but which would inspire immediate answer from the right Michael F. Carter's. No answer. Was he alive? Could some unthinkable thing have happened to him associated with his drug experimentation, either personally or legally? There was absolutely no way to tell, so Michael, somewhere out there, if you read this please drop me a note if you wish to and are able to.

So I left the paper pretty much with his ideas in it, crossed my fingers as I used my address for both authors, and sent it off for publication. The paper appeared and I sincerely hope that I did the right thing.

**#38.    5-MeO-DMT;   TRYPTAMINE,   5-METHOXY-N,N-DIMETHYL; INDOLE,    5-METHOXY-3-[2-(DIMETHYLAMINO)ETHYL];        5- METHOXY-N,N-DIMETHYLTRYPTAMINE;       5-METHOXY-3-[2- (DIMETHYLAMINO)ETHYL]INDOLE;    N,N,O-TRIMETHYLSERO- TONIN;    N,N,O-TMS;    BUFOTENINE   METHYL   ETHER;    O- METHYLBUFOTENINE;   OMB**

SYNTHESIS: To a cooled and well-stirred solution of 16 g 5-methoxyindole in 200 mL anhydrous $Et_2O$ there was added, dropwise, 25 g oxalyl chloride. Stirring continued for an additional 10 min, then the red solids were removed by filtration, washed lightly with $Et_2O$, and returned to the reaction beaker as a suspension in 200 mL fresh anhydrous $Et_2O$. To this there was added a solution of 8.5 g dimethyl-

amine in 25 mL anhydrous $Et_2O$ which discharged the red color. Stirring was continued for an additional 0.5 h, and the solids were removed by filtration and washed with $Et_2O$. These were suspended in $H_2O$, filtered, and washed alternately with $H_2O$ and $Et_2O$. Recrystallization from $THF/Et_2O$ provided 20 g (75%) 5-methoxy-N,N-dimethylindol-3-ylglyoxylamide, mp 223-223.5 °C, as fine white crystals.

To a well-stirred suspension of 11.7 g LAH in 350 mL anhydrous $Et_2O$ there was added, in small portions, a suspension of 18.5 g 5-methoxy-N,N-dimethylindol-3-ylglyoxylamide in 200 mL hot benzene. The last of the solids were rinsed out with anhydrous $Et_2O$ and the mixture held at reflux for 1.5 h. After cooling with an external ice bath, the reaction complex and excess hydride were decomposed by the cautious addition of $H_2O$. The inorganic solids were removed by filtration, the filter cake washed with additional $Et_2O$, the filtrate and washing were combined and dried over anhydrous $MgSO_4$, and the solvents removed under vacuum. The residue was distilled at the KugelRohr to provide a colorless fraction, distilling at 160-170 °C at 0.6 mm/Hg, that crystallized on cooling. There was thus obtained 12.8 g (78%) 5-methoxy-N,N-dimethyltryptamine (5-MeO-DMT) which on recrystallization from hexane, had a mp 69-70 °C. The hydrochloride salt can be made by passing a stream of hydrogen chloride gas through an $Et_2O$ solution of the base. It, upon recrystallization from $EtOH/Et_2O$, had a mp of 145-146 °C.

DOSAGE:   6 - 20 mg, smoked; 2 - 3 mg, i.v.

DURATION:   1 - 2 h

QUALITATIVE COMMENTS:  (with 6 mg, smoked) "I felt it in a minute — not really light head, but the head feels close to the lower parts of the body — close to the ground — knees weak — distinct shakes. I peaked at 2 or three minutes. It was quite intense, but not the max of DMT at 30 milligrams and no sensory close-out. Slight nausea on the drop-off — I am glad I had not eaten anything. Overall comparison to DMT, more potent, slightly faster, but like DMT is largely a simple, stoning drug with no sensory contribution, no intellectual contribution. It's greatest contribution might be to provide a subject the vocabulary of an altered state of consciousness so that, with interesting and constructive drugs, these effects will be familiar, and thus not distractions."

(with 8 mg, smoked) "I was blown away, far away I might add, but only for 10 minutes and effects were gone by half an hour. During this episode mental activity was almost absent. I can't say I wasn't 'impressed' in some way, though it wasn't exactly what I expected. I had read reports with statements varying from 'dwarfs + elves' to 'conk on the head,' the latter of which relates more closely to my experience."

(with perhaps 10 mg, smoked) "Onset was gentle, perhaps over 15 minutes. I felt like all of my blood had turned to concrete. There were no noticeable visual effects, but my hearing was slightly diminished. The whole experience was over after 1 hour."

(with perhaps 15 mg, smoked) "I took a hit from the pipe with five-methoxy in it, and after the 8 to 10 seconds it took to carry the chemical to my brain I remember starting to fall over from my sitting position. My normal physical perceptions dissolved away from my awareness. My ears started to ring and I started to float off. I was acutely aware of a certain resonation of my aural perception, an electrical buzzing that fluctuated in synch with my visual perception. What I saw can only be described as a fantastically subtle multicolored phosphene, completely filling every area visually available. I say it in this way because I was simultaneously losing contact with my body, I could not tell if my eyes were open or shut, although I initially had the feeling that they were darting back and forth, from side to side. These feelings and sensations built up in intensity very quickly, a matter of seconds: I can remember this feeling of building intensity up to a point, and then I was not there in my body or in time. In the 10 to 15 minutes that my body was under the influence of the drug my mind was completely referenceless, there was no way for my consciousness to limit or gauge the stimuli my being was barraged with. I remember switching to a perception where the endless and intricate phosphene was love and the energy of light. I called upon those forces within my being to realign and submit, to let go of all the cogent fears and just exist ... and that innate decision saved me a lot of psychic damage. What is most outstanding about the way it feels is an inability to judge in any way, by any method of the mind ... it is unconquerable, as deep and profound as a totally unconditional love that is life. What a trip, huh?"

(with 15 mg, smoked) "At about 60 seconds after I smoked this free-base, I beheld every thought that was going on everywhere in the universe and all possible realities while I was wracked out with this horrible ruthless love. It scared the hell out of me. When I could see again (15 minutes later) it was almost as if there was an echo of a thought in my head saying that I was given an extremely rare look at the true consciousness of it all. I've never been hit this hard since then. A definite ++++."

(with perhaps 20 mg, smoked) "This is a very strong hallucinogen. A twenty minute experience. For me it was like adding the MDMA experience to DMT. DMT for me is terrifying (I still go back though) and I must really think about it before proceeding. The 5-MeO-DMT was much more relaxed, a kind of cosmic consciousness type of experience. I broke into a space similar to DMT but it was more like receiving grace. I felt a little shaky (tremor-like) coming down."

(with 25 mg, smoked) "I placed 25 mg of 5-methoxy-DMT in a stainless steel one-quarter teaspoon and vaporized it over a cigarette lighter collecting the smoke in an upside-down funnel. All smoke was inhaled; the taste was mild — none of the plastic taste of DMT. About 10 seconds or so after inhaling the last of the smoke, it began with a fast-rising sense of excitement and wonder, with an undertone of "Now you've done it," but dominated by a sense of, "WOW, This Is IT!" There was a tremendous sense of speed and acceleration. In perhaps 10 more seconds these feelings built to an intensity I had never experienced before. The *entire universe* imploded through my consciousness. It's as if the mind is capable of experiencing a very large number of objects, situations and feelings, but normally perceives them only one at a time. I felt that my mind was perceiving them all at once. There was no distance, no possibility of examining the experience. This was simply the most intense experience possible; a singularity, a white-out (as opposed to a black out). I have little memory of the state itself. I have no memory, for example, of whether my eyes were opened or closed. After some seconds or minutes, it started to fade and came to resemble a merely intense psychedelic state. Here I had the feeling, a visualization of being part of the universe of beings, all active in our daily, interwoven tasks, still moving at an incredible rate, and with a longing for a single group/organism awareness and transcendence. In a few more minutes it faded to an alert (+ one) state with an additional sense of awe and wonder, relief, and a strong feeling of gratitude toward the universe in general, for the experience."

(with 30 mg, smoking) "I placed approx. 30 mg of 5-MeO into a pipe, and smoked it, in one toke, without a second thought. An instant later, I was crawled up on my bed (in the fetal position) with my eyes closed, squirming around, screaming (in my head) 'Fuck! You killed yourself!' I repeated this several times, very fearful of death. I didn't see anything, while my eyes were shut, except for a bright white light, that which you see after staring at a bright light. The only other "vision" was one in my mind -- I came to the realization that my life would be wasted if I died there. This showed me all of my scripts being discarded and nothing good happening ever again. It was a glimpse into my future, if I died. I concentrated on breathing and that helped me survive (mentally). I walked into the living room and placed a CD into the stereo, and as the first song started, my attention span disappeared, and I walked back into my bedroom. To my surprise, forty minutes had passed, in what I remembered as mere seconds. This scared me, thinking that maybe I had blacked out. I felt the effect for about an hour, then it slowly faded away."

(with an unknown but large amount, smoked) "I observed the subject pass very quickly into an almost coma-like state. Within seconds his face became purple and his breathing stopped. I pounded his chest, and breathed for him, and he seemed to emerge in consciousness, with the comment, 'This is absolute ecstasy.' He stopped breathing a second time, and both heart massage and mouth-to-mouth resuscitation was provided. Again, he recovered and managed to maintain a continuing consciousness and achieve a partial recovery. In the awake condition he was increasingly lucid, but on closing his eyes he became possessed with what he called "The energy of terror." He could not sleep, as upon closing his eyes he felt threatened in a way he could not tolerate. Three days later, medical intervention with antipsychotic medication was provided, which allowed the recovery of an acceptable behavior pattern in a few more days."

(with 35 mg, orally): "No activity."
(with 0.25 mg, intravenously): "A real effect."
(with 0.5 mg, intravenously) "I felt the effects distinctly within a minute,

along with some pain at the injection site. In a few minutes I felt a very distinct calming and stilling of my mind. While I could have carried on a conversation about anything and didn't feel the least bit stoned, I found the feeling very recognizable."

(with 0.7 mg, intravenously): "This was basically a +1 experience. After a few instances I felt its motion, very gentle waves. I was thinking about thinking about the experience, about writing about it, and so I was experiencing myself as both observer and editor. This was not overwhelming, but gentle."

(with 1.3 mg, intravenously) "In a few seconds I was participating in exquisite, full body, teeth-chattering shivers that lasted in all about 10 minutes, nearly the duration of the effects. The sensations seemed to come more from my head region, whereas my 'full blown' experiences of smoked 5-MeO-DMT seemed to emanate from my center and heart."

(with 2.3 mg, intravenously) "I remember having a perspective of knowing I was aware and, if not from the start of the experience then very soon into it, knowing I knew I was aware. I thought I was an ocean. I don't remember where I first lost continuity of consciousness (this is a little like a black-out from hard liquor) but I remember being aware of the sounds I was making apparently some time after I began vocalizing. Around the time I thought to change these sounds as I pleased, I also noted with brief wonder that the sound was continuous, not changed by my breathing. I sang my way back."

(with 3.1 mg, intravenously) "I vocalized effortlessly. I was getting in touch with my body. I said, 'Turn off the lights,' and 'I love you,' and then I lost it. I was amazed later to find a roomful of people who had been frightened by the noises they had been amazed to hear, and I was amazed to be told I had made."

EXTENSIONS AND COMMENTARY: This is, like DMT, another naturally occurring alkaloid that is not orally active. And, as with DMT, it is almost always smoked. This is the reason that both there and here, there are several entries with the word "perhaps" in the dosage statement. When the transportation vehicle is a rolled joint containing some inert plant carrier, or a glass pipe heated with a torch, who can accurately say how much of the drug was actually volatilized and drawn into the lungs? Further, from the qualitative range of responses, one can truly say, it is different things to different folks. I don't know of any active oral level (I have been told of it being tried at 35 milligrams) but a number of experiments with oral 5-MeO-DMT preceded by harmaline have shown activity in the 10 - 25 milligram area. These are discussed in the Hoasca vs. Ayahuasca chapter. Some trial i.v. experiments with radioactively labeled and unlabeled materials showed no effects at 100 micrograms, but real effects at 250 micrograms. Higher levels have convincingly established the enhanced potency that is the result of this route. The injection process is faster than the smoking process, and it avoids the smoke's odd flavor.

5-MeO-DMT was first observed in a member of the Rue family (Rutaceae) called *Dictyoloma incanescens*. Now it is recognized as a major component of a number of South American snuffs. The snuff called cohoba is generally associated with plants of the *Piptadenia* and *Mimosa* genus, and as they are largely DMT-containing, they are discussed under that entry. But there are other snuffs, such as yakee and yato (in Colombia) and paricá, epená and nyakwana in Brazil, which should probably be discussed here. The plants used are of the *Virola* genus, containing trees most plentifully found in the Amazon basin.

There has been a long-standing and never-to-be-resolved disagreement amongst botanists as to the best way of classifying plants. There are the morphotaxonomists, who insist that species assignment should be based primarily on appearance, and there are the chemotaxonomists who feel that the natural composition should be a deciding factor in the distinction between species. But the ultimate requirement for morphology is to find the plant in bloom, and for chemistry, to have some analytical capabilities. Often, neither luxury is available in the jungles of the rain forest. A major contributor to the *Virola* snuffs, *Virola theiodora*, is a good case in point. Two plant sources, both gathered in Brazil, have been found to have radically different compositions. In one, 5-MeO-DMT is substantially the only alkaloid found in the bark, whereas in the other, DMT is the major alkaloid. But both have DMT almost exclusively in the young green shoots. Are they the same species? Another plant used in some of the snuff preparations is *Virola calophylla*, where the bark, root, leaves and shoots all run about 90% DMT as the alkaloid content. Yet, the alkaloids in the root and bark of *Virola rufula* consist of some 95% 5-MeO-DMT.

The inquiries into metabolic 6-hydroxylation as a prelude to biological activity have been made with both 5-MeO-DMT and the corresponding primary tryptamine (see below). 6-HO-5-MeO-DMT has been shown in several animal models to be pharmacologically less active than its parent compound. See the discussion under DET for the role that this metabolism played in some early clinical studies.

Removing one of the N-methyl groups provides N-methyl-5-methoxytryptamine (5-MeO-NMT), which has its own entry. Removal of both methyl groups from the nitrogen gives 5-methoxytryptamine (5-MeO-T) which has been explored most extensively by Soviet researchers as a treatment for exposure to radiation; this aspect of its action is discussed and expanded upon in the commentary under Melatonin. It is also known by the trade name Mexamine and has been looked at as a potentiator of centrally active drugs. Here, as with the simpler N,N-dialkyltryptamines, the metabolic introduction of a hydroxyl group at the 6-position (to give 6-HO-5-MeO-T) leads to a lowering of pharmacological potency. And again, no human studies have been reported.

A true academic challenge exists with the many studies of 5-methoxy-DMT (as has been mentioned under DMT, different drug, same problem) which have involved drug mixtures. The second drug, added to the tryptamine, is almost always a monoamineoxidase inhibitor such as harmaline, either as a chemical (in most clinical studies in the Northern Hemisphere) or as the plant decoction (in most jungle uses in the Southern Hemisphere). The challenge is, just how should one classify these observations? Under the first drug modifying or being modified by the second? Under the second drug modifying or being modified by the first? Or should the mixture be treated as a variable thing in its own right?

Since the mixture invariably shows properties that neither component can show alone, it is obvious that the combination is a major classification component. When the harmaline component is a plant mixture containing harmaline, a common name that is used is Ayahuasca. This can be any of a large number of carboline-containing plants (or even harmaline itself) combined with a really wide variety of amines, ranging from the tryptamines to mushrooms, to such diverse materials as Jimpson Weed components. These combinations are usually unknown as to exact composition, and they will be discussed in a chapter devoted to just this combination, entitled "Hoasca vs. Ayahuasca." On the other hand, when the components are discrete compounds, the process is much more controlled (in the experimental sense rather than in the effects sense) and these combinations are gathered in the recipe for harmaline.

There are a couple more entries for 5-MeO-DMT, one very important, and the other quite trivial. There is a drug-use phenomenon that is often referred to by the popular title of "toad-licking." The toad involved is the Sonora Desert Toad, also called the Colorado River Toad, and carries the binomial *Bufo alverius*. It is not the closely related marine toad *Bufo marinus,* as some people have insisted, prompted by the early Olmec and Mayan iconography. Of course the licking myth is newspaper hype — it is the venom that is active, and it is smoked. When the desert toad is stroked near the parotid glands in the neck region, there is the squirting out of this venom and when it is allowed to dry on a hard surface it takes on the texture of rubber cement. It contains up to 15% 5-MeO-DMT, as well as N-methyl-5-methoxytryptamine, 5-MeO-NMT and Bufotenine, which have their own entries.

And here is the trivial entry. I involved myself in a small Australia/toad incident when I recently visited Sydney. There is a consistent historical record of the axiom "the road to Hell is paved with good intentions" in the effort to import solutions to problems that were the unforeseen consequences of earlier imported solutions. I can't recall the decade-by-decade record but, as I remember, it involved, amongst other things, dogs, rabbits, viruses to control rabbits, and maybe mongooses. And cattle. Cattle had been imported mid-century as a desired agricultural commodity, but it could not be predicted that their cow-plops would not deteriorate. There were domestic dung beetles, but they appreciated kangaroo droppings (raisin-sized) rather than cow-plops (birthday-cake sized). So the eggs of a cow-oriented dung beetle were brought in about 1970 and, after weathering the usual quarantine, were released into the ecosphere. Another beetle came in without invitation with the importation of agricultural cane. Hitch-hiking along with the cane was a cane beetle, and it had no natural enemies. The beetle proliferated, and as a solution to this infestation there was brought in a "cane toad," the *Bufo marinus* (the marine toad, not the desert toad, to the eventual disappointment of the drug-oriented subculture) which was believed could provide some control over them. Well, it turned out that the beetles lived at the top of the cane stalks, and the frogs lived at the bottom. The toads didn't eat the beetles, but they did successfully reproduce and multiply because they, too, had no natural enemies. They are today sweeping across north-eastern Australia.

In the middle of downtown Sydney, right alongside Hyde Park at Williams and College, there is the Australian Museum, with a superb library of natural history which I wished to use in the pursuit of the Aborigine use of red beans. And there was a special exhibit on display of the frogs and toads of Australia, with histories, photographs, and occasional soundtracks of croakings. I spotted a panel devoted to the origins and short history of the *Bufo marinus*. And right in front of it was a little old lady diligently reading the text which said, approximately, that a virus was being developed at some research laboratory in South America that would be specific for this toad, and which would bring the problem under control. I wondered to myself, but just loud enough for her to hear, if this was the same virus that could cause the AIDS syndrome in the Wallaby?

She looked at me for a moment, turned, and walked away. Maybe, just maybe, another rumor of unknown origin has been launched.

### #39.  4-MeO-MIPT;  TRYPTAMINE, N-ISOPROPYL-4-METHOXY-N-METHYL;  INDOLE, 3-[2-(ISOPROPYLMETHYLAMINO)ETHYL]-4-METHOXY;  N-ISOPROPYL-4-METHOXY-N-METHYLTRYPTAMINE; 3-[2-(ISOPROPYLMETHYLAMINO)ETHYL]-4-METHOXYINDOLE

SYNTHESIS: A solution of 4.0 g of 4-methoxytryptamine in 50 mL toluene was combined with another containing 5.52 g $K_2CO_3$ in 50 mL $H_2O$ and vigorously stirred at room temperature. To this there was added, dropwise, a solution of 3.0 mL benzyl chloroformate in 20 mL toluene. Stirring was continued for 15 h, then the reaction was treated with 200 mL EtOAc, the organic layer separated, and dried with anhydrous $MgSO_4$. After filtration, the solvent was removed under vacuum, and the solid residue recrystallized from $Et_2O$/hexane to give 3.9 g N-(benzyloxycarbonyl)-4-methoxytryptamine with a mp of 84 °C. Anal: $C_{19}H_{20}N_2O_3$. C,H,N.

A suspension of 0.76 g LAH in 50 mL THF was stirred under an inert atmosphere, and treated with the dropwise addition of a solution of 2.5 g

N-(benzyloxycarbonyl)-4-methoxytryptamine in 30 mL anhydrous THF. The reaction mixture was held at reflux for 30 min, then cooled to 40 °C and the excess hydride destroyed with the addition of 50% aqueous THF. The solids were removed by filtration, washed with THF, the filtrate and washings combined, and the solvent removed under vacuum. The residue, impure 4-methoxy-N-methyltryptamine, was dissolved in 50 mL EtOH, treated with 1.0 mL acetone, then with 0.5 g 10% Pd/C, and the reaction mixture shaken under a $H_2$ atmosphere at 50 psi for 15 h. The catalyst was removed by filtration through a bed of Celite, the filtrate stripped of solvent under vacuum, and the solid residue recrystallized from $Et_2O$/hexane to give 0.51 g N-isopropyl-4-methoxy-N-methyltryptamine (4-MeO-MIPT) which had a mp 80-81 °C. Anal: $C_{15}H_{22}N_2O$. C,H,N. MS (in m/z): $C_5H_{12}N^+$ 86 (100%); indolemethylene$^+$ 160 (4%); parent ion 246 (6 %).

DOSAGE: 20 - 30 mg, orally

DURATION: 4 - 6 h

QUALITATIVE COMMENTS: (with 10 mg, orally) "In 30-40 minutes, I found I could get some distortions of objects around me, if I really tried hard. There are no color changes. It is unexpectedly mild, and I have no anxiety, no tachycardia. At the two hour point, the peak must be past, and I feel somehow disappointed. I am not sure, in retrospect, if there was ever anything there at all."

(with 17 mg, orally) "I am aware of this at 40 minutes, and was in a very light but not very well defined place for about two hours. It was neither good nor bad. It kind of drifted away and I was not sure when I regained baseline."

(with 26 mg, orally) "I took this orally, in dilute hydrochloric acid so that it would be in solution going down. I was aware in 20 minutes, and went right up to a +3 within the hour. That was quite a bit of change in a half hour. Extremely erotic, but absolutely no visuals to music, either with eyes open or with them closed. I know I am at +3 since there is no way I could drive a car, not for anything in the world, but why not? Don't know, but no way. Cold gaspacho tastes superb, but one cup is enough, and the croissant seems dry and hard. By seven hours I am back where I started from again. Pity."

(with 26 mg, orally) "This is my first try with this drug, ever. First indications of effects in twenty minutes. Quiet onset, no remarkable visuals, in fact no particular visuals at all. To a + 2 within about ten or fifteen minutes more. Body is comfortable, mind-set pretty much unchanged from baseline. No euphoria, no insights. But also, no discomfort. Erotic was extremely successful, and orgasm seemed easier than with other materials. Still no visuals but seemed to be a soft +3. Music fine. Hard to define exactly how we knew we were in an altered state, because of the lack of visual clues. Body aware more than mind. Would like to explore this further. Perhaps for writing? Nice material. Maybe higher next time?"

EXTENSIONS AND COMMENTARY: It seems to me to be somehow a pivotal compound, in that it carries the pattern of nitrogen substituents that appears to be the most effective orally (the methyl group and the isopropyl group) and it is oxygenated in the aromatic ring. Both the 4-hydroxy analogue (4-HO-MIPT) and the 5-methoxy analogue (5-MeO-MIPT) are very active at these levels. Perhaps if the oxygen is in the 4-position it must be exposed as in psilocin to reveal an active zwitterion. And if the oxygen is in the 5-position, it must be masked as a methyl ether to hide its intrinsic polarity. But these are observations, not explanations. Why is this compound, 4-MeO-MIPT, so seductive and appealing a hybrid, not as potent as one might expect? The remaining two, the 6-isomer and the 7-isomer, are described in the recipe for 5-MeO-MIPT.

A similar discussion could be made about the corresponding compounds that possess the N,N-dimethyl pattern of DMT. Again, there are a total of four possible ring-methoxylated isomers. The 5-substituted compound is 5-MeO-DMT and, as it is remarkably potent, it is given its own entry. However, the other three monomethoxy analogues, 4-methoxy-, 6-methoxy- and 7-methoxy-N,N-dimethyltryptamine, remain relatively unknown.

The 4-methyl ether of psilocin, 4-MeO-DMT, is especially appealing, in that it is a simple homologue of psilocin and it is quite stable. But the methyl group as an ether link lacks the lability of the phosphate or acetate esters, and it cannot be easily hydrolyzed off to form psilocin. The immediate homologue is 4-MeO-DET, which is completely without action either orally or by smoking at dosages up to 30 mgs. The two remaining DMT isomers are with the methoxy at the 6-position (to give 6-MeO-DMT, originally thought to be a minor alkaloid in B. caapi) and at the 7-position (to give 7-MeO-DMT, which was observed as a minor impurity in the preparation of 7-MeO-MIPT). Some rat studies were performed in the mid 60's on all three of these compounds. A couple of years later the 4-isomer was studied in the squirrel monkey and found to have weak central activity (size discrimination studies with rewards of grapes, underwater maze running with rewards of simply being allowed to survive). These studies suggested that it was not very potent, certainly much less potent than 5-MeO-DMT, but no trial has as yet been reported in man for any of these three isomers. If this lower potency were to hold up in human trials, it would give additional support to the positional parallels between the "4-position" of the phenethylamines, and the "5-position" of the tryptamines. That is where, indeed, the action is to be found. All of these methoxylated DMT analogues will probably be pretty easily destroyed metabolically, so some parenteral route might have to be used in exploring them. Right here, in the above preparation, 4-methoxy-N-methyltryptamine (4-MeO-NMT) has been made as a chemical intermediate, but it was not characterized, and no spotlight was put on it as a potential drug in its own rights. It is the ether that corresponds to the natural ester baeocystin, and it probably wouldn't come off gracefully, either chemically or metabolically. There is yet another mushroom analogue here. The starting material is the bare tryptamine itself, 4-MeO-T, which is the ether counterpart to norbaeocystin.

## #40. 5-MeO-MIPT; TRYPTAMINE, N-ISOPROPYL-5-METHOXY-N-METHYL; INDOLE, 3-[2-(ISOPROPYLMETHYLAMINO)ETHYL]-5-METHOXY; N-ISOPROPYL-5-METHOXY-N-METHYLTRYPTAMINE; 3-[2-(ISOPROPYLMETHYLAMINO)ETHYL]-5-METHOXYINDOLE

SYNTHESIS: To a solution of 1.40 g 5-methoxy-N-methyltryptamine (5-MeO-NMT, see separate recipe) in 50 mL methanol there was added 1.0 mL acetone and 0.5 g 10% Pd/C. This mixture was shaken under a $H_2$ atmosphere at 50 psi for 15 h. The catalyst was removed by filtration through a bed of Celite, the filtrate stripped of solvent under vacuum, and the solid residue recrystallized from $Et_2O$/hexane to give 1.45 g N-isopropyl-5-methoxy-N-

methyltryptamine (5-MeO-MIPT). This was isolated as the hydrochloride salt by dissolving it in a small amount of IPA, neutralization with concentrated HCl, and dilution with $Et_2O$. This had a mp 162-163 °C. Anal: $C_{15}H_{23}ClN_2O$. C,H,N. MS (in m/z): $C_5H_{12}N^+$ 86 (100%); indolemethylene$^+$ 160 (5%); parent ion 246 (4%).

DOSAGE: 4 - 6 mg, orally;
        12 - 20 mg, smoked

DURATION: 4 - 6 h

QUALITATIVE COMMENTS: (with 1.5 mg, orally) "In 15 minutes I was already off baseline, and by an hour it is unquestionably real. There is no visualization to music, but a general turned-on randiness. Dropping at an hour and a half, and out by three hours. Modest but real."

(with 4 mg, orally) "Up very fast, to a +2 in an hour. Absolutely no visuals, but over the next two hours an ease of interpretive fantasy, almost dream-like, and easy eroticism. Food tasted marvelous, but there was no appetite. Easy, normal sleep and good spirits in the AM."

(with 5 mg, orally) "Extremely bitter taste. Some stimulation and tingling at 10 minutes, and I am apprehensive at this rapid onset. There are no visual symptoms at all, but the stimulation of conceptual thought is intense. Depth perception is slightly altered and a very minor wave pattern can be noticed in the peripheral vision, but no major object or color distortion. Minor enhancement of auditory acuity. Philosophical concepts about this and other substances seem important. I wonder what the value of writing about, or attempting to describe, their effects really is. At the second hour, the effects are subsiding, and for another three hours there are tailings and insomnia, but I am able to eat normally. There is a certain amount of 'negativity' about this compound. The dose is satisfyingly small, but I wonder if it is worth it. Somewhat of a disappointment. Have no desire to experiment further."

(with 6 mg, orally) "Rapid development to 45 minutes, some shakes, uneven handwriting, and hints of time slowing. Extremely erotic. Full plateau at a +3 at the 2 1/2 hr. point, then a graceful and rather rapid drop. Easy, restful sleep. Absolutely no visuals or related sensory effects — what does one call this stoned state? Very pleasant, music extremely acceptable, tactile extraordinary. I feel that higher dosages would not contribute anything more."

(with 12 mg, smoked) "I was able to take 4 or 5 puffs, and to hold off the onset until then, then I couldn't anymore. Powerful, tremendous rush, but all along maintaining body-ego awareness, unlike 5-MeO-DMT where the world appears to utterly dissolve. I was aware of doing a lot of groaning, writhing, shaking around; headphones and eyeshades kept it completely internal. Not too much visual, but lots of disorientation. Early on there was a lot of emotional lability, laughing, crying, 'Oh God' kinds of outbursts.

"At an hour and a half, I was down enough that I tried smoking the remainder of the bowl without much additional effect. A typical psychedelic afterglow and in the morning ate a big breakfast and felt essentially normal. In summary, I took too little, I was in a bad mood, and felt myself to be in a rushed environment. The experience seemed to me like a hybrid between CZ-74 and 5-MeO-DMT; the trippiness of the former and the rush (although not as intense) of the latter."

(with 20 mg, smoked) "Most all of it was smoked in about three or four inhalations before I felt it coming on so strongly that I lay down. Within less than a minute after I lay down, with my eyes closed, my visual field was filled with brilliant geometric, patterned lines of different colors that were slowly moving. There were several sets of parallel and curved lines superimposed upon each other. Soon after that, probably within a minute or two, I became extremely disoriented from my normal sense of being a person in a body; I was lost in an undifferentiated mass of feeling and non-specific sensation. It was similar to the overwhelming feeling of 5-MeO-DMT in quality and, as with that material, the peak phase lasted less than 30 minutes.

"Then I began to think more coherently, but intense waves would return every 5 to 15 minutes. In between, my perception and thinking would be fairly normal, but with the waves I would be swept up in imagery or memories heavily laden with emotional content. After two hours I was joined by my wife. We spent some very intimate time together, and I remember asking her who she was and she replied, 'Your wife.' This was very powerful to me since I did not really know what it meant, except that it seemed to be the best combination of mother, lover and friend, and that it was an entirely new kind of relationship that we would be creating for the rest of our lives together.

"After three or four hours, the waves had virtually stopped, and I remained oriented to the present and my immediate surroundings. I stayed under a mild influence until I ate supper, around 7 hours. I felt tired, had trouble falling asleep, but awoke refreshed."

EXTENSIONS AND COMMENTARY: In my lecturing at the University, every couple of years or so some student uses the term "more unique than" or "relatively unique." This immediately triggers a reflex response from me, to emphasize the simple definition that something that is unique is something that is one of a kind, and that all one-of-a-kind things are different from all other one-of-a-kind things. All drugs are unique. Every drug is different from all other drugs. 5-MeO-MIPT is unique.

The last two entries in the "Qualitative Comments" section are longer than usual, but even at that they have been trimmed down from reports sent to me that were each over three pages in length. A thread common to each of them is the comparison of the effects of smoking 5-MeO-MIPT to those from smoking 5-MeO-DMT. The speed of onset, the intense depersonalization and loss of immediate contact with one's surroundings, the impressive recall of early memories and the significance of these memories, make the drugs appear similar to one another. And the fact that they are of similar potency when smoked (5-MeO-DMT is perhaps a tad more potent) makes the relationship more comfortable. And then, with the eye of a chemist making further comparisons, the whole structure-activity relationship falls into place. The formulae are identical, except that one of the N-methyl groups of 5-MeO-DMT is extended by a couple of carbon atoms, to an isopropyl group in 5-MeO-MIPT. They are almost the same. They have almost the same action when smoked. They are "unique and similar" and together they appear to be quite different from the rest of the pack. Nope, that is just not so! They are totally different from one another.

All you need to do, to see that clearly, is to look at that one additional observation involving oral activity. This drug, 5-MeO-MIPT, is several times more potent when taken orally than it is when smoked. 5-MeO-DMT is much less active orally than when it is smoked. As a matter of fact, it is not active at all when taken orally. No active oral level has ever been found. What a rich area for speculation. Preferential metabolism? First pass goings-on? Chemical change from pyrolysis in the pipe? Different receptors? Lipophilicity? I am reminded of the quote from Mark Twain: "I like science because it gives one such a wholesome return of conjecture from such a trifling investment of fact."

Might the observations of the remaining oxygen-substituted MIPT's provide additional clues? There are four possible mono-methoxylated MIPT's; all have been synthesized and all have been explored in man. The 4-methoxy-isomer was of modest activity and deserves, and has received, a recipe of its own. The 5-methoxy-isomer is the one described here, and is extremely potent (orally, but less so parenterally). But as one goes to the 6- and 7-positional isomers, the two remaining positions, the psychopharmacological activity seems to be lost. This is a humorous reminder of the British idiom, to be at 6-'s and 7-'s about something.

6-MeO-MIPT was made from the corresponding indole, by reaction with 2-nitroethyl acetate, the resulting 3-nitroethylindole catalytically hydrogenated to 6-MeO-T, which was converted to the N-benzyloxycarbonyl derivative. This was reduced to 6-MeO-NMT, which was in turn reductively coupled with acetone to provide 6-MeO-MIPT, with a mp of 89-91 °C and an overall yield of 9%. MS (in m/z): $C_5H_{12}N^+$ 86 (100%); indolemethylene$^+$ 160 (7%); parent ion 246 (4%). In human trials there was one report of some kind of neurological twinge at a 16 milligram level, but nothing else at trials of up to 50 milligrams and it has been shelved as being inactive.

The isomeric 7-MeO-MIPT was synthesized by the exact same five-step reaction sequence starting with 7-methoxyindole, in an overall yield of 24%. The actual reaction conditions for this conversion are detailed in the recipe for 4-MeO-MIPT. The mp of 7-MeO-MIPT was 72-73 °C and its MS (in m/z): $C_5H_{12}N^+$ 86 (100%); indolemethylene$^+$ 160 (5%); parent ion 246 (4%). Gas chromatographic analysis indicated that the product was only 80% pure, and three of the impurities were identified. One was 7-MeO-NIPT with MS (in m/z): $C_4H_{10}N^+$ 72 (100%); indolemethylene$^+$ 161/160 (13, 8%); parent ion 232 (4%). Another was 7-MeO-DMT with MS (in m/z): $C_3H_8N^+$ 58 (100%); indolemethylene$^+$ 160 (6%); parent ion 218 (9%). The third was 7-MeO-NMT with MS (in m/z): $C_2H_6N^+$ 44 (100%); indolemethylene$^+$ 161/160 (82, 39%); parent ion 204 (5%). These three impurities represented approximately 5%, 3%, and 4%, resp., of the isolated product's final weight. It showed something going on at 20 mg orally with perhaps a little distortion in the visual field. And, separately, at 70 milligrams orally there might have been a light-headedness after a few minutes. Nothing more. It, too, has been given the kiss of death by being declared inactive at the 50 milligram level.

The last of the Mohicans, the tribe of compounds with the remarkably potent, orally active, N-methyl-N-isopropyl system on the tryptamine nitrogen atom, was the dimethoxy analogue with both the 5- and the 6-positions occupied with methoxy groups. This specific compound has its own recipe as it raises specific questions that deserve direct attention. The very close relative with the methylenedioxy group at this 5,6-location also has a separate recipe.

Two final laments. Remember that all these beautiful compounds are unique. Why do they behave the way they behave? I have no idea, and there never are enough data to explain everything. I hate the fact that the word data is plural. But singular or plural keep collecting it (them), and keep trying to make sense of everything. And, a small point from my infancy. *The Last of the Mohicans* was one of the very first books I read, and I had very innocently accepted the footwear of these Indians as being the metaphor for the people themselves. I had seen that title as, "The Last of the Moccasins." This is a pair of words that I still interchange without any defense, along with shoulder and soldier, avatar and atavar, and especially annoying when lecturing, irrelevant and irreverent.

## #41.    5,6-MeO-MIPT;   TRYPTAMINE, 5,6-DIMETHOXY-N-ISOPRO-PYL-N-METHYL;   INDOLE, 5,6-DIMETHOXY-3-[2-(ISOPROPYL-METHYLAMINO)ETHYL];   5,6-DIMETHOXY-N-ISOPROPYL-N-METHYLTRYPTAMINE;   5,6-DIMETHOXY-3-[2-(ISOPROPYL-METHYLAMINO)ETHYL]INDOLE

SYNTHESIS: To a suspension of 0.88 g 5,6-dimethoxyindole in 50 mL Et$_2$O, stirred and cooled with an external ice bath, there was added, dropwise, a solution of 0.87 g oxalyl chloride in 5 mL Et$_2$O over the course of 20 min. The mixture was stirred for an additional 20 min, and then the glyoxyl chloride was removed by filtration, washed with Et$_2$O, and dried under vacuum. A suspension of this red solid in 50 mL of ice-cold dry THF, under nitrogen, was treated with the dropwise addition of a 30% solution of methyl isopropyl amine in Et$_2$O, until the pH exceeded 9. The solvents were removed under vacuum, and the residue partitioned between CHCl$_3$ and H$_2$O. The organic phase, after decolorization with charcoal, was stripped of solvent under vacuum and the solid residue recrystallized from EtOAc/hexane. There was thus obtained 0.61 g 5,6-dimethoxy-N-isopropyl-N-methylindoleglyoxylamide, with mp 204-206 °C (yield 40%).

A well-stirred suspension of 0.55 g LAH in 25 mL anhydrous THF was treated, dropwise, with a solution of 0.53 g 5,6-dimethoxy-N-isopropyl-N-methylindoleglyoxylamide in 75 mL anhydrous THF. The reaction mixture was brought to reflux temperature, held there for 30 min, and cooled to about 40 °C. There was added 0.55 mL H$_2$O followed by 1.65 mL 10% aqueous NaOH and an additional 0.55 mL H$_2$O. The solids were removed by filtration and the filter cake washed with THF. The combined filtrate and washings were stripped of solvent under vacuum. The oily residue was crystallized from hexane to give 0.34 g (yield 71%) 5,6-dimethoxy-N-isopropyl-N-methyltryptamine, mp 71-73 °C. MS (in m/z): C$_5$H$_{12}$N$^+$ 86 (100%); indolemethylene$^+$ 190 (4%); parent ion 276 (9%).

DOSAGE: > 75 mg, orally

DURATION: unknown

QUALITATIVE COMMENTS: (with 35 mg, orally) "Nothing at all."

(with 75 mg, orally) "There was a vague awareness of something at about the one-hour point. Not enough to even be called a threshold effect."

EXTENSIONS AND COMMENTARY: This compound, having no detectable activity even at the milligram/kilo level, pretty much condemns the 5,6-dimethoxy indole pattern. Quite a few closely related derivatives have been made; there is the N,N-dimethyl (5,6-MeO-DMT), the N,N-diethyl (5,6-MeO-DET), the N,N-dibutyl (5,6-MeO-DBT) and the three famous heterocyclic ring compounds, the pyrrolidyl (5,6-MeO-pyr-T), the piperidyl (5,6-MeO-pip-T) and the morpholyl (5,6-MeO-mor-T) compounds. They were all synthesized and characterized in the 1960's, but I have no record of any having been tried in man.

One desoxy analogue warrants mention. This is known as 5-methoxy-6-methyl-DMT (5,6-MeOM-DMT) or as 5-methoxy-6,N,N-trimethyltryptamine (5-MeO-6,N,N-TMT), where the 6-methoxy group is, in effect, replaced with a 6-methyl group. Having a DMT skeleton, it was assayed parenterally, and even at 15 milligrams (smoking) there was nothing noted. This is a level that would have been dramatic had there been no substitution at that 6-position. Some of the historical background of an oxygen at this position is discussed in the 6-HO-DMT recipe.


#### #42.  5-MeO-NMT;  N,O-DMS;  NOR-5-MeO-DMT;  TRYPTAMINE, 5-METHOXY-N-METHYL;  INDOLE, 5-METHOXY-3-[2-(METHYL-AMINO)ETHYL];  SEROTONIN, N,O-DIMETHYL;  5-METHOXY-N-METHYLTRYPTAMINE;  5-METHOXY-3-[2-(METHYLAMINO)-ETHYL]INDOLE;  N,O-DIMETHYLSEROTONIN

SYNTHESIS: (from 5-MeO-DMT). To a solution of 0.10 g 5-methoxy-N,N-dimethyltryptamine (see 5-MeO-DMT) in 5 mL benzene there was added 0.5 g 2,2,2-trichloroethyl chloroformate, and the resulting solution was held at reflux temperature for 2 days. After cooling there was added 5 mL Et$_2$O and the organic phase washed with 2x20 mL 3N HCl followed by 20 mL H$_2$O. The solvent was then removed under vacuum. The residue (N-(2,2,2-trichloroethoxycarbonyl)-N-methyl-5-methoxytryptamine, 0.12 g) was dissolved in 2 mL acetic acid and treated with 0.15 g powdered zinc. After stirring for 4 h at room temperature, the reaction mixture was filtered and the filtrate made basic with 3N NaOH. This was extracted with 3x20 mL Et$_2$O, the extracts pooled, and the solvent removed under vacuum. The residue was purified by preparative TLC, using a BuOH/AcOH/H$_2$O (12/3/5) solvent for development. There was thus obtained 0.013 g of 5-methoxy-N-methyltryptamine (5-MeO-NMT) as a solid with a mp of 90-93 °C.

(from 5-MeO-T) A solution of 0.086 g 5-methoxytryptamine (5-MeO-T) in 1 mL dioxane containing 0.5 mL of 2N NaOH was cooled to 0 °C and well-stirred. There was added, at the same time, 0.2 mL benzyl chloroformate and 0.25 mL 4N NaOH. This was allowed to come to room temperature and the stirring was continued for an additional 10 min. There was added concentrated HCl, followed by 10 mL $H_2O$. This mixture was extracted with 3x20 mL $Et_2O$, the extracts pooled, and the solvent removed under vacuum. The crude carbamate was purified by silica-gel column chromatography using n-hexane/$CH_2Cl_2$ (1/9) as an eluting solvent. After removal of the chromatographic solvent under vacuum, the residue was dissolved in 10 mL anhydrous THF and added slowly to an ice-cold, well-stirred suspension of 0.178 g LAH in 10 mL anhydrous THF. After being brought to reflux and held there for 4 h, the mixture was cooled and acidified with 1N HCl. The THF was removed under vacuum, and the aqueous residue washed with $Et_2O$. This was then treated with solid $NaHCO_3$ and extracted with 3x50 mL $Et_2O$. The solvent from the combined extract was removed under vacuum, and the residue purified by preparative TLC as described above. There was thus obtained 0.016 g of 5-MeO-NMT with a mp of 88-91 °C.

DOSAGE:  (not known)

DURATION:  (not known)

EXTENSIONS AND COMMENTARY: This base is the botanically and pharma-cologically famous 5-MeO-DMT, missing one of its two N-methyl groups. Sort of a nor-5-MeO-DMT. Its human exploration has just been started, but the expected vulnerability of it to metabolic oxidative deamination makes it a good guess that it (as seen with the dimethyl homologue) will only be active parenterally, or when the body's destructive enzymes are held at bay by effective monoamine oxidase inhibition. This base has been found in several *Virola* species but, as it is always accompanied by 5-MeO-DMT, its contribution to the psychoactivity of the result-ing snuff is completely unknown. It has also been found in the skin of the *Bufo alvarius* at the trivial level of 20-23 micrograms per gram, compared to skin levels of 1.0 to 3.5 mg/g of 5-MeO-DMT.

A fascinating cyclization product of this "nor-compound" is a cyclic dehydrogenation product where there is a direct coupling of the tryptamine nitrogen to the 4-position of the indole ring. This tricyclic material, O-methyl-nordehydrobufotenine, proved to be of comparable activity to DMT in rat studies, but has not apparently been studied in man.

**#43.        5-MeO-pyr-T;      TRYPTAMINE, 5-METHOXY-N,N-TETRAMETHYLENE; INDOLE, 5-METHOXY-3-[2-(1-PYRROLIDYL)-ETHYL]; PYRROLIDINE, 1-[2-(5-METHOXY-1H-INDOL-3-YL)ETHYL]; 5-METHOXY-N,N-TETRAMETHYLENETRYPTAMINE; 5-METHOXY-3-[2-(1-PYRROLIDYL)ETHYL]INDOLE; 1-[2-(5-METHOXY-1H-INDOL-3-YL)ETHYL]PYRROLIDINE;      "PYRROLIDYL-5-METHOXY-TRYPTAMINE"**

SYNTHESIS: To a well-stirred solution of 1.25 g 5-methoxyindole in 15 mL TBME there was added, dropwise, a solution of 1.1 g oxalyl chloride in 15 mL TBME, over the course of 20 min. Stirring was continued for an additional 10 min during which time there was the separation of 5-methoxyindol-3-ylglyoxyl chloride

as a tomato-red crystal, which was removed by filtration and washed with a small amount of TBME. The loose crystals were added, a bit at a time, to 2.0 mL well-stirred pyrrolidine, and the stirring continued until the red color had dissipated and the solids had returned to room temperature as a cream-colored paste. There was then added 80 mL of 1 N HCl which produced a product with a loose crystalline texture. This was removed by filtration, yielding, after air drying at 100 °C to constant weight, 1.13 g of a cream colored material with a mp in the 180-195 °C area. Recrystallization from 15 mL of boiling MeOH gave, after cooling and filtering, 5-methoxy-indol-3-yl-N,N-tetramethyleneglyoxylamide as a white crystalline solid weighing, after air-drying to constant weight, 0.65 g (28%) with a mp of 211-212 °C. IR (in $cm^{-1}$): 700, 741, 792, 1013, 1150, 1188, with a broad carbonyl centered at about 1620 and the indolic NH stretch a broad peak at 3160.

A solution of 0.52 g 5-methoxyindol-3-yl-N,N-tetramethylene-glyoxylamide in 15 mL anhydrous dioxane was added, slowly, to 0.80 g LAH in 15 mL dioxane, which was well-stirred and held at reflux temperature under an inert atmosphere. After the addition was complete, reflux was maintained for an additional 16 h, the reaction mixture cooled, and the excess hydride destroyed by the cautious addition of wet dioxane. The formed solids were removed by filtration, washed with hot dioxane, the filtrate and washings combined, dried over anhydrous $MgSO_4$, and the solvent removed under vacuum. The pale amber residue was distilled at the KugelRohr at 160-170 °C at 0.05 mm/Hg to give 0.11 g (23%) of 5-methoxy-N,N-tetramethylenetryptamine as an off-white oil that did not crystallize. MS (in m/z): $C_5H_{10}N^+$ 84 (100%); indolemethylene$^+$ 160 (4%); parent ion 244 (6%). The hydrochloride salt was prepared by treating an $Et_2O$ solution of the free base with anhydrous hydrogen chloride gas, and recrystallizing the formed solids from MeOH/benzene. The mp was 164-167 °C.

DOSAGE:  0.5 - 2 mg, orally; 2 -3 mg, smoked

DURATION:  several hours

QUALITATIVE COMMENTS:  (with 0.5 mg, orally) "This stuff is an absolute poison. Within minutes I noticed what can only be called ear-ringing without any ear-ringing. Intense tinnitus with no sound, most uncomfortable. There were two waves of nausea and vomiting of yellow bilious stuff, with thick mucus for saliva. I can't think straight — muddled. I can't get answers to questions because I simply cannot form the questions. Eyes closed to music gave no images, but the music sounded OK. Recovery was quite rapid, and I was together again in a few hours. Never again."

(about 1 mg, smoked) "I managed to vaporize about a milligram of the material, and there was nothing profound. There was a slight feeling of calmness. As I felt sure that this material would be a quieting agent, I managed to vaporize and inhale what might have been up to another milligram. There were no psychedelic effects manifested, and I fell asleep easily 10 minutes later."

(with 3 mg, smoked) "Initially the compound exhibited a 5-MeO-DMT-like effect. There was a total loss of self-identity in a nearly instantaneous rush. I felt as if the top of my head was blown off at the onset of the drug experience. My observers told me that I had been unconscious for four hours. I remember reentering with the feeling 'God is Love.' After completely coming to, I felt very nauseous, and threw up in the bathroom several times. I felt drained and sick for the rest of the evening as well as mentally slow. By the next morning I was more alert and responsive. I have absolutely no memory of anything that transpired while I was on the compound."

(with 3 mg, smoked) "I inhaled the vaporized sample at 10 past noon. There was quite a rush. There were none of the shifting shapes, colors and forms of DMT. Nor was it acute with clarity or energy as with my many experiences with 5-MeO-DMT. The effect was intense but not terrifying, with a full body buzz and with humming resonance as I fell backwards into something where all memory was lost. I was told that at 18 past noon, I was unconscious. Something over an hour later, I started flailing, rolling about, quivering and shaking, and had very constricted pupils. In another hour I was able to talk lucidly, but quietly. In yet another hour, I was nauseous and tried for the bathroom, but didn't make it. The people who were watching me were alarmed. My actions were scary. And my skin looked funny for several days afterwards. There are long-lasting properties of this. My first exposure was with perhaps a milligram (smoked, also) and the effects were substantial, with rough edges and minor dysphoria."

(with 4 mg, smoked) "This was the free base. I remember the pipe, and the inhalation and, with the pouring of a small glass of scotch, I settled down in front of the TV to watch a re-run of Star Trek. That was it. I came to some time later in the front room of a professional ally of mine, who had by chance discovered me walking down the street near his house. I do not recall, nor have I been able to regain, any memories of the time I was 'out there.' I apparently experienced no physical discomfort from the drug. In fact I distinctly remember feeling very comfortable when I awoke. Clearly this compound is some weird-ass shit."

EXTENSIONS AND COMMENTARY: Again, as with other compounds in these writings, there is an irresistible urge to present generalizations. But with this particular material, there are obvious unresolved problems with both dosage or duration, and I am limited to the few comments provided above. Dosage? A very few milligrams parenterally, but with smoking such small amounts it is hard to accurately estimate the actual dosages received. Duration? One subject could be fine the next morning, and another could be still aware of wrongness a week later. I am uncomfortable with any compound that seems to be widely variable in its impact on different people.

The qualitative aspects of these (and other) reports imply some individual variability. It is always easy to look at tryptamines such as this one, or the others in these recipes, and say, "We know that they are psychedelics. And maybe good ones or maybe bad ones. So we should look at them with that preconceived notion in mind." But looking objectively at this particular compound, 5-MeO-pyr-T, we are far away from any vocabulary of psychedelics. How is it different from, say, what one might expect from a Fentanyl analogue? Here is a collection of trials that describe parenteral administration and the quick development of an anesthesia. This compound may not be the new Fentanyl because of the nausea during what would be the recovery period. But what are the chances that, perhaps not with this compound, but with any of the obvious analogues that are screaming to be assayed, there just might be a useful clinical tool?

There is another message of warning. Here one must accept the eloquent argument that, for the structuring of an experiment with an unknown and thus undefined new drug, there must be observers present who are both sober and sympathetic. The heroic and macho "I'll do it my way" can lead to both psychological problems and physical risks. As with scuba diving, always work with a partner.

With both pyr-T and 4-HO-pyr-T, there are two additional ring analogies that are natural companions to 5-MeO-pyr-T. These are the piperidine and the morpholine counterparts, 5-MeO-mor-T and 5-MeO-pip-T. Both compounds are in the literature, and an entry reference to them can be gotten from the "known tryptamines" appendix. Along with the pyrrolidine material I had made a reasonable supply of the amides for these other two, both by way of the 5-methoxyindole and oxalyl chloride procedure given above. With piperidine, there is 5-methoxyindol-3-yl-N,N-pentamethyleneglyoxylamide, mp 167-169 °C and IR, (in cm$^{-1}$), 730, 780, 811, 928, 1033, 1161, a broad carbonyl at 1600 and a broad indolic NH stretch at 3190. With morpholine, the corresponding glyoxylamide melted at 193-194 °C, with an IR spectrum (in cm$^{-1}$), of 747, 791, 856, 925, 976, 1043 and 1122, the carbonyl at 1620 and the broad NH at 3150.

With the rather unexpected, and unencouraging descriptions of the pyrrolidine tryptamines in general, and this one in particular, I was not in too blinding a hurry to explore the two heterocyclic analogues. The amides are still on the shelf in the lab. If some good reason comes forth to assay the final amines, they can be made with a dash of lithium aluminum hydride, but until then I have other things to do.

#### #44.  6-MeO-THH;  HARMAN, 6-METHOXY-1,2,3,4-TETRAHYDRO;  β-CARBOLINE,  6-METHOXY-1-METHYL-1,2,3,4-TETRAHYDRO;  6-METHOXY-1,2,3,4-TETRAHYDROHARMAN;  10-METHOXY-3,4,5,6-TETRAHYDROHARMAN;  6-METHOXY-1-METHYL-1,2,3,4-TETRAHYDRO-β-CARBOLINE;  1-METHYLPINOLINE;  ADRENOGLOMERULOTROPIN;  ALDOSTERONE-STIMULATING HORMONE; MCISAAC'S COMPOUND

SYNTHESIS: (from melatonin): To a gently refluxing solution of 1.6 g melatonin in 120 mL dry xylene there was added in small portions 14 g $P_2O_5$ over the course of 45 min. The solvent was removed under vacuum, and the residue treated with $H_2O$, then made basic with dilute NaOH, and extracted with $Et_2O$. Removal of the solvent from the pooled extracts and recrystallization of the residue from EtOH gave 1 g 6-methoxyharmalan with a mp 205-207 °C. High vacuum sublimation gave a product with a mp 208-209 °C. IR (in cm$^{-1}$): 801, 824, 849, 990, 1031, 1076, 1182. MS (in m/z): Parent ion -1, parent ion 213, 214 (100%, 83%); 170 (22%); 195 (19%). This base can be dehydrogenated by heating 0.7 g with 3 g of Pd-black in a sealed tube for 30 min at 200 °C. The reaction mixture was treated with hot EtOH, filtered, and the filtrate stripped of solvent under vacuum. This gave 0.4 g 6-methoxyharman with a mp 266-267 °C from aqueous EtOH. The mp after recrystallization from MeOH is reported to be 273-274 °C. IR (in cm$^{-1}$): 621, 698, 835, 1028, 1075, 1184. MS (in m/z): 197 (100%); parent ion 212 (66%); 169 (37%).

To a solution of 0.10 g 6-methoxyharmalan in 5 mL dilute HCl there was added 10 mg $PtO_2$ followed by the dropwise addition of 40 mg $NaBH_4$ dissolved in 1 mL of $H_2O$. The solids were removed by filtration through paper, and the cream-colored filtrate made basic with 5% NaOH and extracted with 4x20 mL portions of $CH_2Cl_2$. The extracts were pooled, the solvent removed under vacuum, and the solid residue recrystallized from MeOH to give, after air drying to constant weight, 75 mg of free base 6-methoxytetrahydroharman (6-MeO-THH) as a white solid. IR (in cm$^{-1}$): 797, 832, 975, 1112, 1121, 1148. MS (in m/z): 201 (100%); 186 (43%); parent ion 216 (38%); 172 (21%); 144 (16%).

(from 5-methoxytryptamine) A solution of 1.00 g 5-methoxytryptamine in 25 mL $H_2O$ was brought to a pH of 4 with 0.1 M HCl and placed under a $N_2$ atmosphere. There was then added a solution of 1.5 g acetaldehyde in 15 mL of 85% aqueous EtOH. The solution was stirred for 2 days at room temperature, and then made basic and held at 0 °C, allowing crystallization. There was thus obtained 175 mg (19%) of 6-methoxytetrahydroharman (6-MeO-THH) as a white solid, with a mp 160-161 °C. The literature also reports a mp of 224-226 °C.

EXTENSIONS AND COMMENTARY: I have decided to completely eliminate the dosage, duration, and qualitative comments for this compound, and all related harman analogues. The reason is painfully obvious — virtually nothing is known about their psychopharmacology. Despite their enormous potential for someday being understood as possible intermediates in brain chemistry, they remain almost unexplored. I was working closely with Dr. C. Naranjo in the middle '60's in this area, on a study we were considering co-authoring, to be entitled, "Hallucinogenic Properties of a Pineal Metabolite, 6-Methoxytetrahydroharman." This was recorded in the *Ethnopharmacologic Search for Psychoactive Drugs* book of Daniel Efron, as being in Science, in press. But, the paper was never in press, as it had never been submitted for publication, as it had never been written. All of this for the very simple reason that the research for it was never completed. It had just been started. Claudio had explored both 6-methoxytetrahydroharman and the corresponding harmalan in the 100-150 milligram area, and was finding some activity. I was running parallel studies and had gotten up to about 100 milligrams and had not found anything. We both saw this as being a rich and promising virgin field for exploring human pharmacology. It still is rich and promising. And it still is virgin.

Before any particulars, let me offer some rather broad generals about nomenclature. This world of carbolines is a total bear as to the assignment of chemical names, and this is a logical place to talk about it. Many terms will be encountered. Some are totally trivial, such as a specific compound that has been given a name from the binomial of the plant where it had been discovered, as in Leptaflorine from *Leptactinia densiflora*. Some are based on the completely general parent ring system itself, beta-carboline. Many compounds have many synonyms, and the carboline appendix in the back of this book would be a good place to save these names as you find them. For me, I look for middle territory. I look for two clues. The first is a sound that catches my attention immediately, the prefix, "harm-." This demands that there is a methyl group in the molecule and that it is at the 1-position. The second clue is the vowel that follows the harm-. It will usually be an "a" or an "i" or occasionally an "o." The harma- things have nothing on the aromatic ring, and the harmi- things have a 7-methoxy group there, and the harmo-

things are usually phenolic, with an oxygen attachment there. And the numbering systems can be totally off the wall.

Let me try to organize the "harm" chaos first, always with that methyl group at the C-1 position of the carboline ring. The second collection has a hydrogen atom there.

indole sub.   aromatic ($H_0$)   dihydro ($H_2$)      tetrahydro ($H_4$)

with a 1-methyl substituent

| | | | |
|---|---|---|---|
| Ar-H | **harman** | harmalan | **tetrahydroharman** (THH) |
| Ar-6-OH | 6-harmol | 6-harmalol | **6-tetrahydroharmol** |
| Ar-6-OMe | 6-MeO-harman | **6-MeO-harmalan** | **6-MeO-tetrahydroharman** |
| Ar-7-OH | harmol | harminol | **tetrahydroharmol** |
| Ar-7-OMe | harmine (a) | harmaline (a) | tetrahydroharmine (a) |

with a 1-hydrogen substituent

| | | | |
|---|---|---|---|
| Ar-H | βC | DHβC | **THβC (tryptoline)** |
| Ar-6-OH | 6-HO-βC | 6-HO-DHβC | **6-HO-THβC** |
| Ar-6-OMe | 6-MeO-βC | 6-MeO-DHβC | **6-MeO-THβC (pinoline)** |
| Ar-7-OH | 7-HO-βC | 7-HO-DHβC | 7-HO-THβC |
| Ar-7 -OH | 7-MeO-βC | 7-MeO-DHβC | 7-MeO-THβC |

(a) has its own recipe
**bold,** included in this recipe

Some minor stumbling blocks remain in this system. βC (beta-carboline) has been called nor-harman, since it is harman without the methyl group. This is incorrect in theory in that the prefix "nor" implies that the lost group comes from a nitrogen. Incorrect, but common. Many additional synonyms and botanical locations are given in the carboline appendix. And throughout this discussion, I will totally ignore the chemically correct way of naming beta-carboline, which is 9H-pyrid-[3,4-b]-indole.

A brief comment on the numbering systems that can be found. The procedure used here and in the appendix starts counting at the carbon atom of the pyridine ring that is closest to the indole nitrogen. The pyridine nitrogen atom becomes two, and on around, hitting every substitutable atom ending on the indole nitrogen as the 9-position. However, as usually in the older literature but still seen sometimes today, the indole nitrogen is the 1-position (as it still is when a structure is seen as an indole) and then every atom, substitutable or not, is numbered sequentially. This brings the 7-substitution identifier of harmine (which is the indolic 6-position) up to the number 11. This makes harmine 3-methyl-11-methoxy-beta-carboline. Some years ago the general term "tryptolines" was introduced to embrace the family of compounds with no methyl group on the 1-position. The numbering required that the pyridine nitrogen be called the 1-position, effectively maintaining the position numbers of the parent indoles, but it turns out that the original 1-position, now without a number, has to default to the end of the line, to the rather sad 9-position name.

Back to the individual chemical stories. This commentary will cover the scatter of beta-carbolines that might play some major role in the human nervous system, other than the harmine trilogy. Harmine, harmaline and tetrahydroharmine all have the oxygen at the 7-position, and mostly have their origins in the botanical world. The 6-position oxygen can come directly from serotonin or hydroxy-tryptophan, and are found both in plants and animals. Similarly, the hydrogen derivatives (unsubstituted) derive from tryptamine and tryptophan, again from both plants and animals.

**6-Methoxytetrahydroharman (6-MeO-THH)** is the title chemical of this recipe. This particular β-carboline is a focal point of an ongoing controversy. To put all the cards directly on the table, this compound can in theory be made easily in the body and thus it could be present as a normal component in the brain. It has been synthesized by McIsaac, in Texas, under physiological conditions, with acetaldehyde and 5-methoxytryptamine. And, so the reasoning goes, if it can be made under these conditions in the laboratory, why not in the brain? He was completely convinced that it would be found some day to play an important role in mental health, just as he was convinced that it would prove to be a psychoactive compound. Perhaps it would be the product of some psychological trauma, or maybe the source of such a trauma. He once told me (at a meeting years ago, over a quiet breakfast) that one of his ambitions was to assay the brains of people who were in all different kinds of mental states at the time of their deaths, and to correlate the carboline levels with that mental state. I asked him if he had personally tasted the material, and apparently he had not.

**6-Methoxytetrahydro-β-carboline (6-MeO-THβC, pinoline)** is a naturally occurring component of human blood and cerebral spinal fluid. Like 6-MeO-THH, it is readily formed from 5-methoxytryptamine, but with formaldehyde rather than with acetaldehyde. The levels have been found to be similar in schizophrenics and psychiatrically healthy patients, suggesting that it is not a factor in the chemistry of mental illness. It is a natural component of the human pineal gland and is quite effective in binding to serotonin sites in human platelets. It has been suggested that the balanced interplay between melatonin and pinoline in the manipulation of serotonin levels might be an explanation of the sleep/dream state. The carbolines just might play an endogenous role in creating dreams, our "asleep" visual tripping.

**6-Methoxyharmalan (6-MeO-DHH)** was the chemical intermediate in the synthesis given above. Its main claim for attention is that it is the immediate result of the removal of a molecule of water from melatonin, which is a major actor in the biochemistry of the pineal gland. It is also a pretty effective monoamineoxidase inhibitor.

**Harman** is the simplest of the carboline alkaloids, and also one of the most widely distributed throughout the plant world. Many of its common names derive from these sources, such as loturine, aribine and passiflorin. In tasting trials with the alkaloid alone, there are no effects noted at even up to 250 milligrams orally. Rather surprising, even though it has been shown to be a good monoamineoxidase inhibitor, a 250 milligram trial followed in 20 minutes with 35 milligrams of DMT also had no effects. Clearly, harman does not share pharmacological similarities with its methoxylated cousins. Harman is the prototype alkaloid of the β-carboline class and has been found in many plants although not usually a contributor to the action for which they are best known.

It is a component of the bark of the legume *Arariba rubra* (*Sickingia rubra*), native to the Bahia state in Brazil, as well as from the bark of *Symplocus racemosa*. This tree was introduced into Goa in the mid-nineteenth century, and from it has come a drug called Araroba powder (or Goa Powder, Brazil powder, or Ringworm powder). This turn of the century drug of commerce contains the non-nitrogenous anthracene Chrysarobin, isolated commercially from the closely related legume, *Andira araroba* (*Vouacapoua araroba*). It has been used in the treatment of ringworm and a number of skin diseases. Harman plays no part in this medical use. I have not been able to pin down just why harman has been given the name Loturine. Some Genus, no doubt, but I don't know what it is.

It is, however, a recognized component of the extracts of the passion flower *Passiflora incarnata*, but the much more plentiful inventory of flavinoids present in this marvelously named plant seem to be the agents that are responsible for its sedative properties. Again, harman is probably not an active contributor to the reported pharmacological action. In fact, it has been spotted as a component of cigarette smoke, and here it certainly cannot be a factor that contributes to the virtues of smoking.

**Tetrahydroharman (1-methyl-1,2,3,4-tetrahydro-β-carboline)** has been the topic of many animal studies, but within the last few years it has demanded attention in an unexpected way. A couple of years ago there was a rash of medical problems that occurred and that were ascribed to an impurity found in certain supplies of the amino acid tryptophane. The chemical twist is that the causal impurity appears to be the product of cyclizing tryptophane with acetaldehyde. The product of this reaction is 1-methyl-1,2,3,4-tetrahydro-β-carboline-3-carboxylate (tetrahydroharman-3-carboxylate, THH-3-COOH). It has been generated in experiment animals which have been fed tryptophane, ethanol, and cyanamide (a drug that, by interfering with the normal metabolism of alcohol, allows an accumulation of acetaldehyde in the body). The introduction of a new chiral center into an already asymmetric system gives promise of a challenging research problem, involving, in any body fluid assay, an interesting analytical problem. Anyway, this amino acid decarboxylates to give tetrahydroharman, which was under some suspicion as being involved. Well, it wasn't involved, and the story itself has been discussed in the recipe for tryptamine. It is a story of politics, not of chemistry. Another 3-carboxylic acid derivative, the totally aromatic material without the 1-methyl group, has been found as a natural material in trace amounts in human urine. In fact, the yield was a total of 1.78 milligrams from 1800 liters. This is the ethyl ester of βC-3-carboxylic acid. It is an extraordinarily potent inhibitor of brain benzodiaz-epine receptors but, surprisingly, totally without any affinity for serotonin recep-tors. The hydrogenated version, THβC-3-COOH, as well as the harman analogue above (THH-3-COOH) are normal components of both beer and wine, being present at the several ppm level.

Since tetrahydroharman can come from the union of tryptamine and acetaldehyde, and since both of these compounds are natural components in the body, it is not surprising that tetrahydroharman is also a natural body factor. And, since ethanol is metabolized by way of acetaldehyde, the body level of tetrahydroharman closely reflects the amount of alcohol that has been consumed. A parallel reaction takes place in the human body between acetaldehyde and the neurotransmitter serotonin. This material, **6-tetrahydroharmol**, or 5HMTLN (5-hydroxy-9-methyltryptoline) employing the cute tryptoline nomenclature, also reflects alcohol consumption. The levels are, however, unreasonably high for the amount of free acetaldehyde normally adrift in the sober body and so it is suspected of having an alternate synthetic origin, perhaps involving pyruvate. The positional isomer with the hydroxyl group at the 7-position, **tetrahydroharmol**, is noteworthy for two reasons. A minor one, to let it be known that it, too, as with almost all possible combinations of natural tryptamines and aldehydes and acids looked for with diligence and sufficient sensitivity, has been found in human urine. The more impressive item: The use of the "tryptoline" word. Here is a view of an extreme cul-de-sac that was created by this procedure. This is all taken directly from the mass spectroscopy paper published in 1986. The problems arose from the fact that the methyl group of the harmine/harman world could not be slipped into the name, as its position had no logical number. And that there was no abbreviation for tryptoline that could be distinguished from tryptamine. Either could be "T." The paper discussed the hydroxylation metabolism of MTLN (methyltryptoline, in reality tetrahydroharman) to give the 6- and 7-hydroxylated derivatives. I would call these 6-tetrahydroharmol and tetrahydroharmol. But in this research paper, having been committed to the tryptoline word, these metabolites came out as 5HMTLN and 6HMTLN. The "5" and "6" represent the 6 and 7 positions on the carboline ring. The "H" is the hydroxyl group. The "M" is the methyl group which they do not choose to locate, but in the only offered numbering system it would be in the 9-position. And, of course, TLN is the abbreviation for tryptoline (MT was spelled methtryptoline in the title). I do believe that 6-H-9-M-TLN is harder to understand than tetrahydroharmol.

Serotonin, in an enzymatic interaction with the methyltetrahydrofolate one-carbon source, gives rise to the beta-carboline analogue, **6-HO-THβC**. This happens also to be the plant alkaloid plectomine as well as a metabolite of THβC in the rat. Attempts to make DMT from methyltetrahydrofolate and N-methyltryptamine (NMT) gave rise exclusively to the carboline 2-Me-THβC.

**Tetrahydro-β-carboline (THβC, tryptoline)** has also been demonstrated as being formed in the brain by the simple fusion of tryptamine with formaldehyde from methyltetrahydrofolate, and it is a normal component of human urine. It is the structural icon of the family of tetrahydro-β-carbolines without the methyl group at the 1-position, the "tryptolines," mentioned above. It, and the 2-methyl homologue mentioned just above, are both natural metabolites of DMT. I had the lucky timing to be present at a seminar at the Department of Pharmacology, at the U.C. Medical School in San Francisco, when the crowd from Stanford came up to give the first San Francisco unveiling of the "tryptoline" word. I remember that I was not the only chemist in the audience who groaned at the use of a totally unneeded and artificial name. But these researchers did a lot of work and a lot of publishing, and the term is now pretty well established in the literature. A cautionary note is appropriate here. It is essential, in abbreviating this material as THβC that the "beta" be included. Without it, the code "THC" will be assumed immediately to stand for tetrahydrocannabinol, the active component of marijuana.

#### #45.   5-MeO-TMT;  TRYPTAMINE, 5-METHOXY-2,N,N-TRIMETHYL; INDOLE, 3-[2-(DIMETHYLAMINO)ETHYL]-5-METHOXY-2-METHYL; 5-METHOXY-2,N,N-TRIMETHYLTRYPTAMINE; 5-METHOXY-2-ME-THYL-DMT;   3-[2-(DIMETHYLAMINO)ETHYL]-5-METHOXY-2-METHYLINDOLE; INDAPEX

SYNTHESIS: To a stirred solution of 7.16 g of 1-(p-chlorobenzoyl)-5-methoxy-2-methylindole-3-acetic acid (indomethacin) in 150 mL CHCl$_3$ there was added, dropwise, 4.4 mL oxalyl chloride and the reaction mixture held under reflux conditions for 2.5 h. Removal of the solvent under vacuum produced a thick yellow oil which was dissolved in 150 mL of CH$_2$Cl$_2$. There was then added, in small portions, 40% aqueous dimethylamine until the aqueous phase remained basic to pH paper. The phases were separated, and the organic phase was washed sequentially with H$_2$O, dilute HCl, and finally saturated saline, then stripped of solvent under vacuum. The residue was dissolved in 20 mL EtOAc and after a few minutes, the product crystallized out. This was recrystallized from a hot acetone/$H_2O$ mixture yielding, after filtration and air drying to constant weight, 5.08 g 1-(p-chlorobenzoyl)-5-methoxy-2,N,N-trimethylindole-3-acetamide as pale yellow, fine needles.

To a suspension of 5.0 g of 1-(p-chlorobenzoyl)-5-methoxy-2,N,N-trimethylindole-3-acetamide in a mixture of 80 mL IPA and 20 mL $H_2O$ there was added 1.0 g KOH and the mixture was stirred at room temperature for 1.5 h. The starting material gradually dissolved over this period. The excess IPA was removed under vacuum, and the residue partitioned between EtOAc and $H_2O$. The organic phase was separated, then washed sequentially with $H_2O$, dilute HCl, $H_2O$ and finally saturated brine. After drying with anhydrous $Na_2SO_4$, the evaporation of the solvent yielded a white product that was recrystallized from a small quantity of boiling EtOAc that was allowed to cool slowly. There was obtained, after filtration and air drying, 1.44 g of 5-methoxy-2,N,N-trimethylindole-3-acetamide as white crystals.

To 40 mL of stirred anhydrous THF in a round-bottomed flask equipped with a reflux condenser and in an atmosphere of argon, there was added 2.70 g 5-methoxy-2,N,N-trimethylindole-3-acetamide. There was then added 20 mL of 1.0 molar $LiAlH_4$ in THF (there was a rapid evolution of bubbles) and the reaction mixture was held at reflux conditions for 2.5 h. The mixture was cooled to room temperature and treated with 8 mL of a 1:1 solution of IPA and $H_2O$. There was then added 2.0 mL 15% aqueous NaOH followed by an additional 2.0 mL $H_2O$. The suspension was filtered, the solids washed with 2x20 mL THF, the filtrate and washings combined, and the solvent removed under vacuum. The solid residue was dissolved in 25 mL 0.5 molar HCl, washed with $CH_2Cl_2$, made basic with 25% aqueous NaOH, and extracted with 3x40 mL $CH_2Cl_2$. Removal of the solvent under vacuum yielded a light yellow oil. This was distilled at 0.25 mm/Hg to yield a fraction boiling at 155-160 °C, weighing 1.52 g that was a pale yellow oil. This slowly set up as a milky crystalline solid, 5-methoxy-2,N,N-trimethyltryptamine (5-MeO-TMT) which had a mp of 90-92 °C.

DOSAGE: 75 - 150 mg, orally

DURATION: 5 - 10 h

QUALITATIVE COMMENTS: (with 65 mg, orally) "I felt the first intoxication at an hour. I was relaxed along with subtle day-dreaming to "Hearts of Space" music. I was sexually stimulated, with some heightening of intensity of orgasm. At the three hour point I seemed pretty much baseline. The rest of the day went without difficulty."

(with 90 mg, orally) "This was ingested in a capsule. Effects were first noted at 55 minutes with a feeling of relaxation and a mild impairment of fine motor skills. Sexual activity was initiated at the 90 minute point. Spinal tingles were felt and, although erection may have been slightly more difficult than normal to maintain, orgasm was phenomenal. This potentiation was confirmed three more times over the next three hours! Mild stomach fullness was felt but no other GI problems were noted. Significant appetite suppression was noted for the first five hours, after which food tasted fine. Music evoked closed-eye drifting of thoughts but no true visuals occurred with eyes open or closed. A faint tremor of the jaw and fingers could be noted with careful examination. The effects were barely noticeable at the five hour point, and were completely gone at seven hours. Sleep was broken by awakening every few hours with moderate thirst, and dream activity seemed enhanced. There were no side-effects the following morning."

(with 120 mg, orally) "Unlike what I was told might happen, no sexual feelings were even remotely felt at any time during this experience. Thoughts seemed poorly connected and there was a feeling of being drugged with a sedative. Moderate chills and cold sensations occurred for several hours, requiring first a jacket and later a heating blanket. Time seemed moderately slowed and both respiration and pulse were reduced. Mild stomach fullness was noted, with indigestion. I was not hungry. No other GI problems occurred. Everything faded at about the five hour point, when I got very hungry and thirsty. My sleep was not comfortable, and the next morning I was still a little bit jittery."

(with 150 mg, orally) "No effects were felt until the 55 minute point, when a mild degree of intoxication began. At seventy minutes mild nausea and gastric fullness was apparent. There was a loss of fine motor skills and I found it hard to walk. My peripheral visual field had a waviness to it. Both television and a radio talk show became completely uninteresting and difficult to follow, and a feeling of sadness and despair became overwhelming. No music could change these feelings, although there definitely were pronounced closed-eye visuals by the 100 minute point. Emotions were extremely labile, going from profound crying to calm and back in a period of twenty minutes. I saw every defect and failure in my life and, although very sad, I recognized some things that I will correct in the future. Apparent body temperature fluctuations were continuous, going from being hot to chilled over and over again (actual body temperature was not measured). It was impossible to get comfortable for several hours. The stomach distress continued throughout the entire experience, with a moderately severe stomach ache during the third and fourth hours.

"By the sixth hour I could again watch television, and I did so while waiting for the experience to end. Some residual effects were still present at nine hours, but sleep thereafter was uneventful. No eating, or even drinking of water, was possible until the eighth hour, at which time small sips of water were tolerated. I awoke several times during the night and took in additional small amounts of water, but still arose the next morning very dehydrated. There were no other apparent hang-over effects."

EXTENSIONS AND COMMENTARY: This is certainly a hallucinogenic at a dosage of 150 mg orally, and can be compared with 300 mg of mescaline hydrochloride. This exact same chemical, if you were to remove that tiny, little, itty-bitty methyl group at the indolic 2-position, would become the remarkably potent material 5-MeO-DMT. But this latter stuff must be smoked or injected to show any activity at all. It is known that a methyl group on the alpha-carbon of a tryptamine blocks access of a deaminating enzyme allowing oral activity. I wonder if the methyl group on the 2-position is doing the same job of getting in the way.

At modest dosages in the 70-80 mg area orally, 5-MeO-TMT is both relaxing and sexually stimulating. The highest dosages studied seem to reveal a toxic component, and few subjects chose to repeat these levels.

### #46.  5-MeS-DMT;  TRYPTAMINE, N,N-DIMETHYL-5-METHYLTHIO; INDOLE, 3-[2-(DIMETHYLAMINO)ETHYL]-5-METHYLTHIO;  N,N-DIMETHYL-5-METHYLTHIOTRYPTAMINE;  3-[2-(DIMETHYL-AMINO)ETHYL]-5-METHYLTHIOINDOLE

CHEMISTRY: To a solution of 5.0 g of 5-methylthiotryptamine as the free base (the hydrochloride, with mp 252-254 °C or 263-265 °C, is dissolved in $H_2O$, made basic with aqueous NaOH, extracted with $CH_2Cl_2$, and the solvent removed under vacuum) in 250 mL MeOH, there was added 4.0 g $NaHCO_3$ and 6.8 g MeI. This was held at reflux for 72 h, with the addition of 1.5 g more MeI at both 24 and 48 h. Removal of the volatiles under vacuum produced a white residue which was dissolved in 300 mL boiling EtOH, insolubles were removed by filtration of the hot solution, and the filtrate allowed to cool. Fine white crystals appeared which were removed by filtration, and air-dried to produce 3.22 g (53%) of N,N-dimethyl-5-methylthiotryptamine methiodide with a mp 177-179 °C.

A suspension of 3.0 g N,N-dimethyl-5-methylthiotryptamine methiodide in 50 mL DMF was treated with 1.9 g 1,4-diazobicyclo[2.2.2]octane and held at reflux for 3 h. The reaction mixture was diluted with 300 mL $H_2O$, extracted first with 200 mL EtOAc followed by 400 mL benzene. These extracts were combined and back-extracted with 10% HCl. This aqueous phase was made basic with 5N NaOH, and extracted with several portions of EtOAc. The organic extracts were pooled, dried with $MgSO_4$, and the solvent removed under vacuum to give a residue that was a dark gold oil. This was distilled at the KugelRohr to give a fraction that boiled at 130-140 °C at 0.01 mm/Hg which was a yellow solid, with mp 94-97 °C.

This was recrystallized from benzene/petroleum ether to give 1.41 g (76%) N,N-dimethyl-5-methylthiotryptamine as colorless needles, with a mp 97-100 °C.

DOSAGE: 15 - 30 mg, smoked

DURATION: < 1 h

QUALITATIVE COMMENTS: (15 mg, smoked) "Consumed it over 75 seconds, 15 seconds later I noticed it. Light, no visual, rather pointlessly stoned. In another 5 minutes I am starting to clear, and in another 5 I am repaired."

(with 20 mg, smoked): "Coming on very fast, quite intense, and within half an hour I am clear. I suspect 30 mg would be effective."

EXTENSIONS AND COMMENTARY: Sulfur lies in the very same column of the periodic table as oxygen, in the location directly below it. Therefore there are many similarities as to chemical bonding, making things like thioethers which are true analogues of ethers. A sulfur atom is put between two carbons rather than an oxygen atom. But the polarity and lipophilicity properties are different and the pharmacology is, of course, different. In the phenethylamine series, as reported in *PIHKAL*, there can be a considerable increase in potency: with the basic skeleton of 2,5-dimethoxyamphetamine, the replacement of a 4-methoxy group (giving TMA-2, active level 20-40 mg) with a 4-methylthio group (giving Aleph-1, active level 5-10 mg). The corresponding change for the ethyl counterparts (from MEM to Aleph-2) is an increase from an active level of 20-50 mg to one of 4-8 mg.

The 5-position on the indole ring of the tryptamine family is analogous to the 4-position in the phenethylamine family. And yet, here, with the 5-methoxy group of 5-MeO-DMT being replaced with the 5-methylthio group of 5-MeS-DMT, the activity actually seems to decrease by a factor of two, rather than increase by a factor of four. Is this a generality of the tryptamines, or is this an anomaly of this one pair of compounds?

There is the raw stuff potentially available to answer this question. There are a couple of compounds known with the sulfur in the 4-position, which is the location of the oxygen atom in psilocybin. The 4-thio analogues have been synthesized from 4-methylthio-indole, via the oxalyl chloride method and reaction with the appropriate amine. With dimethylamine, the indoleglyoxylamide was made in a 43% yield and had a mp 163-164 °C. With diisopropylamine, the amide was made in a 27% yield and had a mp 190-192 °C. The final amines were prepared by the reduction of these amides with LAH in THF. N,N-Dimethyl-4-thiotryptamine (4-MeS-DMT) was obtained in a 68% yield and melted at 108-110 °C; N,N-diisopropyl-4-methylthiotryptamine (4-MeS-DIPT) was obtained in a 61% yield and melted at 92-94 °C. In animal studies of behavioral disruption with these three compounds, there was systematic drop of potency in going from the 5-MeS-DMT to 4-MeS-DMT to 4-MeS-DIPT.

The challenge would be to see what the activities would be in man. And, of course, to make a direct comparison to the oxygen counterparts. The 5-MeO-DMT has already been mentioned, and the remaining two would be 4-MeO-DMT and 4-MeO-DIPT. The former is a known compound but has not been measured in man. The latter is not a known compound.

### #47.  MIPT;  TRYPTAMINE, N-ISOPROPYL-N-METHYL;  INDOLE, 3-[2-(ISOPROPYLMETHYLAMINO)ETHYL];   N-ISOPROPYL-N-METHYLTRYPTAMINE;   3-[2-(ISOPROPYLMETHYLAMINO)-ETHYL]INDOLE

SYNTHESIS: (from tryptamine via NMT): A solution of 3.36 g tryptamine in 50 mL toluene was combined with another solution containing 5.52 g $K_2CO_3$ in 50 mL $H_2O$ and vigorously stirred at room temperature. To this there was added, dropwise, a solution of 3.0 mL benzyl chloroformate in 20 mL toluene. Stirring was continued for 15 h, then the reaction was treated with 200 mL EtOAc, the organic layer separated, and dried with anhydrous $MgSO_4$. After filtration, the solvent was removed under vacuum, and the solid residue recrystallized from $Et_2O$/hexane to give 5.25 g (85%) N-(benzyloxycarbonyl)tryptamine with a mp of 84-86 °C. Anal: C,H,N.

A suspension of 0.76 g LAH in 50 mL anhydrous THF was stirred under an inert atmosphere, and treated with the dropwise addition of a solution of 2.27 g N-(benzyloxycarbonyl)tryptamine in 30 mL THF. The reaction mixture was held at reflux for 40 min, then cooled to 40 °C and the excess hydride destroyed with the addition of 50% aqueous THF. The solids were removed by filtration, washed with THF, the filtrate and washings combined, and the solvent removed under vacuum. The residue was impure N-methyltryptamine (NMT) and could be used without purification in the following alkylation. The isolation, purification and characterization of this intermediate amine is described in the NMT recipe, and of course the pure NMT can be used in the following reductive alkylation.

The crude N-methyltryptamine obtained above (for which one can substitute 1.20 g of pure NMT, as described in the NMT recipe) was dissolved in 50 mL EtOH, treated with 1.0 mL acetone, then with 0.5 g 10% Pd/C, and the reaction mixture shaken under a $H_2$ atmosphere at 50 psi for 15 h. The catalyst was removed by filtration through a bed of Celite, the filtrate was stripped of solvent under vacuum, and the solid residue recrystallized from $Et_2O$/hexane to give 0.93 g

N-isopropyl-N-methyltryptamine (MIPT) which had a mp 82-83 °C. From the benzyloxycarbonyltryptamine, the yield was 56%. From NMT the yield was 62% of theory. Anal: $C_{14}H_{20}N_2$. C,H,N. MS (in m/z): $C_5H_{12}N^+$ 86 (100%); indolemethylene$^+$ 130 (10%); parent ion 216 (2%). Efforts to isopropylate NMT with an excess of isopropyl iodide in IPA gave a 51% yield of a distilled product that did not crystallize.

(from N-isopropyltryptamine, NIPT): A solution of 0.47 g of N-isopropyltryptamine hydrochloride in 50 mL $H_2O$ was made basic with 5% aqueous NaOH, and extracted with 3x40 mL $CH_2Cl_2$. The pooled extracts were stripped of solvent and the solid residue was dissolved in 25 mL IPA and treated with 0.35 g $CH_3I$. After 3 h at reflux, an additional 10 mL IPA and 0.14 g $CH_3I$ were added and the reflux continued for 6 h. After removal of the solvent under vacuum, the residue was partitioned between dilute base and $CH_2Cl_2$. Removal of the solvent under vacuum yielded 0.29 g of an oil that was shown chromatographically to be a mixture of NIPT and MIPT in a 3:2 ratio. This was treated with 0.35 g $CH_3I$ in 25 mL IPA and allowed to stand at room temperature for several days. A small quantity of crystals separated (N,N-dimethyl-N-isopropyltryptammonium iodide) which were removed by filtration. The filtrate was stripped of solvent under vacuum, and the residue again partitioned, as above, between aqueous NaOH and $CH_2Cl_2$. After removing the organic solvent, the residue (0.23 g NIPT to MIPT ratio 2:3) was treated with 0.5 g acetic anhydride, heated on the steam bath for 1 h, diluted with 5% aqueous NaOH and stirred for 2 h. This was extracted with 3x40 mL $CH_2Cl_2$, the extracts were pooled, and then extracted with 3x40 mL 1 N $H_2SO_4$. The pooled acid extracts were made basic with NaOH, reextracted with $CH_2Cl_2$ which, on pooling and the removal of the solvent under vacuum, gave 0.12 g of a colorless oil. Distillation at 0.1 mm/Hg (140-150 °C) gave 0.06 g (a 15% yield) of N-isopropyl-N-methyltryptamine as a colorless oil that spontaneously crystallized.

DOSAGE: 10 - 25 mg, orally

DURATION: 3 - 4 h

QUALITATIVE COMMENTS: (with 5 mg, orally) "Maybe a hint towards the end of an hour. Nothing further. Slept soundly."

(with 10 mg, orally) "There is no question but that this is active. I felt it just a half hour after taking it, and was somewhat disappointed to see it disappear over the next couple of hours. A very good feeling, quite randy."

(with 10 mg, orally) "Definitely active, mild excitement, dry mouth, some muscle tension in the back of the neck. At 75 minutes, definitely rolling, but still no visual effects. Finally subsiding. Not unpleasant, although a feeling of restlessness persists. Tailing insomnia for 6-8 hours."

(with 20 mg, orally) "My handwriting is shot. There are almost no visuals, so why am I at a plus two? I feel very alert. Tried to sleep and ended up talking for quite a while instead. The overall experience can best be described as 'mild.'"

(with 25 mg, orally) "Quite an active dose. Same initial effects as with 10 milligrams, but considerably more excitement, central stimulation. At an hour, the effects seem to have plateau'd. Enhancement of visual field, i.e., brightened colors, clearly defined objects. Definite auditory effects, and I can pick out each sound with clear definition. Very 'heady,' but still remarkably free of visual distortion. Slight mydriasis. As it subsides, there is some muscle tension in the jaws, but much milder than with MDA or even psilocin."

(with 20 mg, by insufflation) "Immediate onset (less than a minute) and to ++. A little dizziness. My first thought is, 'This is definitely psychedelic.' Everything looked brighter, and vision was tinted orange. Everything appeared as if under an orange overlay. No other visual changes to speak of. Skin, hearing, sensitive. All-in-all, however, sensory changes were minor. The effects on thought were more typically psychedelic. The spin-offs, tangents, and implications of different threads of thought became apparent, and I could watch them unfold with my mind's eye. These effects gradually tapered off over the next three and a half hours or so. During this time, interaction with my companions was facile, and we had a good conversation. This compound seems to emphasize 'psychedelic' effects over 'hallucinogenic' effects."

EXTENSIONS AND COMMENTARY: This is the simplest tryptamine with the somewhat magical pair of nitrogen substituents, a methyl group and an isopropyl group. Why should this combination allow a molecule to be orally active, even though the conventional thinking is that if there is a methyl group there, the amine oxidases will destroy it? My sense is that it is the N-small-group that does the job in the brain, and it is the N-big-group that keeps the inactivating oxidase enzymes away from the nitrogen atom. This is consistent with the N,N-dimethyl compound (DMT) not being orally active. Lying midway between DMT and DIPT is the ethyl compound, N-ethyl-N-methyltryptamine, or MET. It can be made by adding ethyl acetate to a reaction mixture where the formamide of tryptamine (see under NMT) has been reduced to NMT but there is still a goodly excess of hydride still remaining. The free base, as an oil, shows oral activity in the eighty to one hundred milligram range, so going from a methyl to an ethyl does indeed protect the compound from total enzymatic annihilation when taken orally.

The isomer of MIPT, with a considerably less bunched-up propyl group, is N-methyl-N-propyltryptamine, or MPT. This was made via the amide from indoleglyoxyl chloride and methylpropylamine, and reduction with LAH. MS (in m/z): $C_5H_{12}N^+$ 86 (100%); indolemethylene$^+$ 130 (8%); parent ion 216 (1%). Several human trials, up to twenty milligrams orally, showed no effects of any kind, so the activity, if there is any, is definitely less than that of MIPT. So the lumpiness of the isopropyl may be playing some role. There is no other way that is obvious of challenging this without adding more carbon atoms, and that would introduce another variable. This same decoration scheme has been used successfully in several other tryptamines in this story.

A couple of points of passing interest. As to stability: many of the free-base tryptamines are sensitive to air oxidation, some of them extremely so. This particular base, standing for a goodly number of years with no particular protection from air, has remained almost colorless, with no apparent signs of decomposition. And as to subjective effects: there is almost a total lack of visual phenomena. There were no wave-forms, color distortion or object shape changes, and no eyes-closed imagery, unlike most N,N-disubstituted tryptamines.

#48.   α-MT;   TRYPTAMINE, ALPHA-METHYL;   INDOLE, 3-(2-AMINOPROPYL);        ALPHA-METHYLTRYPTAMINE;         3-(2-AMINOPROPYL)INDOLE;   IT-290;   3-IT

SYNTHESIS: There was prepared a solution of 25.75 g indole in 100 mL DMF. A second solution was also prepared by cooling 80 mL DMF in an external ice bath (internal temperature about 12 °C), stirring well, and adding 20 mL POCl$_3$ dropwise over the course of 30 min. This was then warmed to 25 °C and the first solution of indole in DMF was added, dropwise (with continued stirring), over an additional 30 min. Stirring was continued for yet another 45 min, during which time the temperature was raised to 40 °C. Yellow solids formed during this period. The reaction mixture was poured onto chipped ice, which produced a clear red solution. This was made basic with the addition of 200 mL 5 N NaOH, which allowed the separation of a yellow solid. This was diluted by the addition of 200 mL hot H$_2$O and, after cooling again, the product was removed by filtration and washed with cold H$_2$O. This can be recrystallized from aqueous DMF to yield, after air drying, 24.5 g (84%) of indole-3-carboxaldehyde as faint orange needles.

A solution of 4.35 g indole-3-carboxaldehyde in 17.2 mL nitroethane was treated with 0.77 g ammonium acetate and heated, with occasional swirling, on the steam bath for 2.5 h. The excess reagent was removed under vacuum and the resulting yellow solids washed with H$_2$O and air dried. Trituration under 25 mL dry MeOH, filtration, and air-drying gave 5.22 g (86%) 1-(3-indolyl)-2-nitroprop-1-ene as a yellow powder with mp 190-192 °C.

A suspension of 10.7 g LAH in 100 mL anhydrous THF was placed under an inert atmosphere, stirred, and treated, dropwise, with a solution of 10 g 1-(3-indolyl)-2-nitroprop-1-ene in anhydrous THF over the course of 2.5 h. The reaction mixture was brought to reflux temperature, held there for 2 h, and then returned to room temperature. The excess hydride was destroyed with an aqueous THF solution (80 mL of 25% solution) and there was then added 10 mL of 50% NaOH. There was added 150 mL Et$_2$O, and the stirring was continued until no more solids formed. The reaction mixture was filtered and the filter cake washed with 150 mL Et$_2$O. The filtrates and washings were combined, dried over K$_2$CO$_3$, and the solvent removed under vacuum. The residue weighed 9.2 g and was distilled at 130-140 °C at 1 mm/Hg to give a white oil that crystallized and had a mp of 96-98 °C. This was recrystallized from an ethyl acetate/petroleum ether mixture, and had a mp of 97-100 °C. The yield was 6.3 g (73%). IR (in cm-1): 750, 818, 911, 933, 1093, 1111. MS (in m/z): C$_2$H$_6$N$^+$ 44 (100%); indolemethylene$^+$ 130, 131 (44%, 43%); parent ion 174 (2%). A sample dissolved in 10 volumes of methanol, treated with one equivalent of glacial acetic acid, and taken to dryness under vacuum gave the acetate salt which, on recrystallization from ethyl acetate and air drying to constant weight, yielded the product α-methyltryptamine (α-MT) as fine white crystals with a mp of 143-144 °C. The fumarate salt, formed by the addition of ethyl acetate to a hot solution of free base α-MT in methanol which had been neutralized with fumaric acid, was isolated as fine white needles with a mp of 200-203 °C.

DOSAGE   15 - 30 mg, orally;
              5 - 20 mg, smoked

DURATION   12 - 16 h

QUALITATIVE COMMENTS:   (with 15 mg, orally) "I got a strong psychedelic experience that lasted about twelve hours, but an unexpected relief from my chronic depression that lasted for four days."

(with 20 mg, orally) "Nothing happened for three hours — I thought I had drawn a blank. Then I became a little uncomfortable, restless, this delayed action is new to me. I feel completely washed out, exhausted. And I had a hangover the next morning."

(with 30 mg, orally) "It felt a little like speed, strong speed. Yet I found myself yawning and in sort of a dreaminess state and quite lethargic. It lasted a long time."

(with 30 mg, orally) "Effects were first noted in just over an hour, a general numbness and a mild loss of motor coordination. This all became more pronounced over the next half hour, but my thoughts remained clear. A hand tremor and jaw tightness persisted throughout the experience. Music was OK but I didn't really connect with it. There were no open or closed-eye visuals, but there was a moderate light sensitivity that lasted the day, and the visual field was altered such as the outside world did indeed appear unreal and alien. Were there any positive aspects to the day? I talked with a friend for two hours on the telephone, with ease. And I had no appetite. But there seems little else to recommend this compound. I slept well at the 12th hour."

(with 80 mg, orally) "I shot up in an hour, and by another hour I was vomiting worse than with mescaline. Absolutely no visuals, no hallucinations, but extreme depersonalization. Thirteen hours into this and it is still go, go, go. Out with a bit of pot."

(with 100 mg, orally) "There was pupillary dilation, jaw clenching, tachycardia and vomiting. Too much. But I really liked this compound at lower dosages."

(with 4 mg, smoked) "It burns and smells bad. It took quite a while to come on. After a half hour, BINGO, there was a very slow building of a definite psychedelic. It builds slowly but strongly for another few hours to a plateau at maybe four hours after which a very slow decline sets in. But even after 18 hours following input, and after 7 hours of sleep, I awoke still feeling the effects."

(with 5 mg, smoked) "Qualitatively it was milder and less intense than mushrooms, but much longer lived. Not complex, but just a lot of very good spirit, energetic feeling, enhanced colors, attractive rhythms in music. Party stuff."

(with 6 mg, smoked) "Onset was immediate, with heart racing, enhancement of surroundings. Taste? Pee-yew!"

(with 10 mg, smoked) "While there are no true visuals to speak of, the overall picture of things seemed grainy — as if filmed on low quality, color 16mm film. There is an energized eeriness about inanimate objects. This lasted three hours."

(with 20 mg, smoked) "I inhaled several hits from my vaporizer and sat back. I felt head-pressure and uneasiness, then suddenly I became very fast. My mind was moving fast, and my body was speeding along with it in an unconscious way. Several hours into it, I began to notice more of a psychedelic effect beginning to manifest. It seemed as if the speedy part was becoming less predominant and the psychedelic visual effects were starting to kick in. I went back to my room to watch the distinctive waves of soft red/orange visuals. They were similar to colors of LSD. It gradually increased to a level of intensity similar to perhaps 0.5 - 1.0 g *P. cubensis*, and after several more hours it was clear that I had reached the plateau. Feeling fairly tired and ready for bed, I decided to call it a night. Quite to my surprise, when I awoke four hours later I was at the same level as when I went to sleep. Gradually, over the next day, I returned to baseline and I was left feeling quite euphoric with a pleasant afterglow."

EXTENSIONS AND COMMENTARY: In the 1960's there was quite a bit of interest at a couple of pharmaceutical houses in the indole analogues of amphetamine. Both the alpha-methylated tryptamine (this compound, $\alpha$-MT) and the alpha-ethylated homologue ($\alpha$-ET, see its separate recipe) were found to be effective monoamine oxidase inhibitors, and both were clinically studied as potential antidepressants. The ethyl compound became a commercial drug, offered by the Upjohn Company as Monase, but now is considered to be without medical use and is a Schedule I drug. It is interesting that this methyl compound, $\alpha$-MT was also a medically available antidepressant in the Soviet Union in the 1960's and was sold under the name of Indopan, in 5 and 10 milligram tablets.

There is quite obviously a wide range of reported effects described for α-MT, indicating much individual variability. For some it has a fast onset, for others a slow one. Some find it a good psychedelic, others are disturbed by the negative physical side-effects. This is all a bit reminiscent of harmaline, where the spectrum of responses also range from 1 to 10 on a scale of 1 to 10. Perhaps this is a reflection of the monoamineoxidase inhibition property, and if so, perhaps low levels of α-MT might serve the harmaline role of inhibiting the metabolic destruction of DMT in some form of a pharmahuasca.

I have always been intrigued by a fascinating bit of speculation. Ken Kesey had his own nest in a log cabin down in La Honda, back in the '60's. This was given fame mostly by Tom Wolfe's *The Electric Kool-Aid Acid Test,* where it was well described. At that time, Kesey served as an experimental subject for a number of studies involving psilocybin, Ditran, and α-MT. Shortly after these were completed, he left and took the role of "The Chief" of his band of "Merry Pranksters" who traveled far and wide around the U.S. in the now famous bus, the "Further." I had heard as a rumor that the research supply of α-MT had disappeared at about the same time, and the thought occurred to me that maybe the drug consumed on the tour was not LSD but α-MT. I made gentle inquiry of the research director, whom I knew personally, if this might be so, and his opinion was that the material used by Kesey and the pranksters was probably LSD, as it was so widely available at that time.

There is another parallel to the ethyl homologue, α-ET. In the commentary under α-ET, I had mentioned how industry was benefiting economically in the War on Drugs, by charging inflated prices for reference and research samples. Here, there just might be political counterpart. There are several commercial sources for α-MT, with catalog prices ranging from $50 to $150 per gram. I bought a gram from Acros Organics and it was delivered with dispatch. I also received the MSDS sheet (Material Safety Data Sheet, a listing of physical hazard information now required to accompany all chemicals purchased) and it not surprisingly had no mention of any known hazard. Imagine my surprise when I received the invoice only to find that there was a $6 surcharge as a hazardous shipping charge. Some three 800-number phone calls later, I got to a person at Fisher Scientific who told me that this was a result of the State of California placing this compound on a Classification #110 listing. I had previously received solvents from Acros that were inflammable, volatile, bad smelling and rather toxic, and had never before had to pay a hazard fee. I suspect that someone in Sacramento has discovered that this compound has a wide acceptance as a stimulant and somewhat psychedelic, and is effectively capitalizing on it before it becomes illegal. One of the commercial suppliers, a mail-order operation called CRSB, provides drug precursors (not illegal) and actual drugs (not illegal) as long as no illegal use will be made of them. The demand for α-MT is very high, second only to gamma-butyrolactone which can be converted to GHB with sodium hydroxide (the #3 item in their sales volume listing).

There is some interesting biochemistry and pharmacology all around the edges of α-MT. The 4-hydroxy analogue of α-MT has been looked at in human subjects. It is reported to be markedly visual in its effects, with some subjects reporting dizziness and a depressed feeling. There were, however, several toxic signs at doses of 15 to 20 milligrams orally, including abdominal pain, tachycardia, increased blood pressure and, with several people, headache and diarrhea. The 5-hydroxy analogue of α-MT is also a well-studied compound, but not, to my knowledge, in man. It can be called α-methylserotonin (α-M-5-HT or α-MS), and it is an effective inhibitor of 5-hydroxytryptophan decarboxylase, which is the immediate precursor to serotonin (5-HT). The amino acid tryptophan, without the 5-hydroxy group but with an α-methyl group, is α-methyltryptophan, and it is readily metabolized by the rat to α-MS. In the pineal, it mimics serotonin rather than melatonin, and there is no evidence that it is acetylated on to a melatonin analogue. This α-methyl blocking of the amine group from metabolic deamination represents a half-way step in the modification of serotonin to allow it to enter into the central nervous system, i.e., the protection of the amine group from deamination because of its alpha-methyl substituent. The rest of the needed modification is the methylation of the 5-hydroxy group as well. This yields alpha,O-dimethylserotonin which allows the entry of this serotonin-like product (α,O-DMS) directly into the brain. In all this casual use of the Greek letter alpha to indicate the carbon atom next to the nitrogen atom of the tryptamine side-chain, readers of the very old literature should remember that the letter alpha used to be used to indicate the 2-position of the pyrrole ring.

A few more compounds can be considered as part of this territory. The addition of a methyl group to the indolic 1-position gives rise to 1,α-DMT. This has been prepared from the 1-methylindole-3-carboxyaldehyde via the intermediate nitrostyrene reduced, in turn, with LAH. It represents the MLD-41 to LSD relationship, where there was some three-fold drop in potency. The alpha,alpha-dimethyltryptamine homologue (α,α-DMT) is also known. It represents the phentermine to amphetamine relationship where, again, there is a three-fold drop in potency. It would be a fair hypothesis to expect either of these "DMT's" to be active stimulants at reasonable dosages, but neither has been explored in man. The analogue with the methyl group relocated to the indolic 4-position (4,α-DMT) has been looked at in man. At an oral dose of 20 milligrams, there are reports of feelings of unreality. External body signs include flushing, muscle tightness, and eye dilation.

There are five possible chain relocations, from the normal 3-position to the 2-, the 4-, the 5-, the 6- or the 7-positions. All five "α-methyltryptamine" isomers are known, but only one is known to be active in man as a CNS active material. This is the 5-isomer, 5-(2-aminopropyl)indole or 5-IT, which, at 20 mg orally, is a long-lived stimulant producing increased heart-rate, anorexia, diuresis, and slight hyperthermia for about twelve hours.

### #49. NET; N-ETHYLTRYPTAMINE; TRYPTAMINE, N-ETHYL; INDOLE, 3-[2-(ETHYLAMINO)ETHYL]; 3-[2-(ETHYLAMINO)ETHYL]-INDOLE

SYNTHESIS: (from indole) To a well-stirred solution of 1.6 g indole in 30 mL anhydrous $Et_2O$ there was added, dropwise over the course of 30 min, a solution of 3.8 g (2.6 mL) oxalyl chloride in 30 mL anhydrous $Et_2O$. Stirring was continued for an additional 15 min, during which time there was the separation of indol-3-ylglyoxyl chloride as a yellow crystalline solid. This intermediate was removed by filtration and washed with $Et_2O$. It was used directly in the following step. This solid acid chloride was added to 3.6 g anhydrous ethyl amine in $Et_2O$ and stirred until the color had largely faded. Then there was added 100 mL of 2 N HCl. The mixture was cooled, and the resulting product N-ethylindol-3-ylglyoxamide was removed by filtration. The air-dried product was obtained in a 67% yield (mp 208-210 °C from benzene).

A solution of 1.6 g N-ethylindol-3-ylglyoxylamide in 50 mL anhydrous THF was added, dropwise, to 1.5 g LAH in 50 mL anhydrous THF which was well-stirred and under an inert atmosphere. This was brought to reflux and held there for 3 h. The reaction mixture was cooled, and the excess hydride destroyed by the cautious addition of wet THF. A 15% NaOH solution was then added until the solids had a loose, white cottage cheese character to them, and the mobile phase tested basic by external damp pH paper. These formed solids were removed by filtration, washed with first THF and then MeOH. The filtrate and washings were combined, dried over anhydrous $MgSO_4$, and the solvent removed under vacuum. The residue set up to a crystalline mass. This was converted to the hydrochloride salt (mp 188-190 °C from benzene/MeOH) in a 35% yield.

(from tryptamine) To a well-stirred solution of 16.0 g tryptamine base in 25 g triethylamine, there was added, dropwise, 11.2 g acetic anhydride. The mixture was heated on the steam bath overnight, then the volatiles were removed under vacuum. The residue was dissolved in 100 mL $CH_2Cl_2$ and washed with 100 mL dilute aqueous HCl. The water phase was extracted twice with additional $CH_2Cl_2$, the organic phases were combined, washed with aqueous $NaHCO_3$ solution, and the solvent removed under vacuum. The resulting residue (12.5 g of a dark viscous oil) was distilled at the KugelRohr to give N-acetyltryptamine as a viscous amber oil boiling at 185-200 °C, which set to a fused glass at room temperature. It weighed 9.45 g, for a yield of 47% of theory. This glass-ground under hexane had a mp of 70-73 °C and formed white crystal from toluene, mp 73-74 °C. IR (in $cm^{-1}$) 756, 810, 1022, 1073, 1103, C=O at 1640. MS (in m/z): indolemethylene+ 130 (100%); 143 (86%); parent ion 202 (7%).

A solution of 2.31 g of N-acetyltryptamine in 30 mL anhydrous THF was added, dropwise, to 60 mL of 1 M LAH in THF and held at a reflux under argon. After 12 h reflux, the reaction was returned to room temperature and the excess hydride destroyed by the addition of 20 mL of 50% aqueous THF. The mixture was filtered through paper, washed with 3x25 mL THF, and the combined filtrates and washings stripped of volatiles under vacuum. The remaining pale cream-colored oil was distilled at 0.1 mm/Hg to give a white oil, bp 125-135 °C, 1.58 g (73%). This free-base product spontaneously crystallized to a white, waxy solid, with a mp of 80-81 °C. IR (in cm$^{-1}$): 751, 887, 940, 1021, 1051, 1118. MS (in m/z): $C_3H_8N^+$ 58 (100%); indolemethylene$^+$ 131, 130 (48%, 33%); parent ion 188 (2%). N-ethyltryptamine base, dissolved in 5x its weight of IPA, acidified with concentrated HCl, and Et$_2$O added dropwise, yields the hydrochloride salt, N-ethyltryptamine hydrochloride or NET, with a mp of 181-182 °C. IR (in cm$^{-1}$); 750, 761, 825, 1020, 1108, 1142.

## NIPT; TRYPTAMINE, N-ISOPROPYL; INDOLE, 3-[2-(ISOPROPYL-AMINO)ETHYL]; N-ISOPROPYLTRYPTAMINE; 3-[2-(ISOPROPYL-AMINO)ETHYL]INDOLE

SYNTHESIS: To a solution of 3.2 g tryptamine base in 25 mL IPA there was added 6.8 g isopropyl iodide and the solution was held at reflux for 36 h. All volatiles were removed under vacuum, and the residue suspended in dilute aqueous NaOH and extracted three times with 40 mL portions of CH$_2$Cl$_2$. These extracts were pooled and, after removal of the solvent, yielded 2.19 g of a dark oil which crystallized on standing. This was distilled at the KugelRohr at 130-150 °C at 0.08 mm/Hg to give 1.51 g of a white oil that set to a solid in the receiver. An analytical sample was recrystallized from IPA, and had an mp 94-95 °C. A solution of the free base in 10 mL warm IPA was treated with concentrated HCl, dropwise, until the solution was red to external damp pH paper. The spontaneous crystals that formed were diluted, with stirring, with 20 mL anhydrous Et$_2$O, the resulting curdy, crystalline mass removed by filtration, washed with additional Et$_2$O, and air dried to constant weight. Thus there was obtained 1.58 g N-isopropyltryptamine hydrochloride (NIPT) as fine white crystals, mp 224-227 °C. MS (in m/z): $C_4H_{10}N^+$ 72 (100%); indolemethylene$^+$ 131,130 (50%, 35%); parent ion 202 (2%). IR (in cm$^{-1}$): 751, 860, 1024, 1036, 1112.

EXTENSIONS AND COMMENTARY: Why two complete recipes, for two monoalkyltryptamines which have received only modest human trials but which have yet to have any active levels discovered? For several very good reasons.

First, these two monosubstituted tryptamines described here are easily made as pure entities, in acceptable yields.

Secondly, they are prepared here by completely different processes, each of which is amenable to modification to other, potentially useful mono-substituted tryptamines (NRT'S, where the R is a sizable alkyl group). There is the oxalylamine route and the acylation route (used here with ethylamine for NET), and the alkyl halide route (used here with isopropyliodide for NIPT, but which proved to be rather useless in making NET, where the major product was the quaternary salt). With these two procedures available, there is almost no limit to the potential identity of that mono-group on the nitrogen atom of tryptamine. Quite a few have already been made. Let me list some examples.

The normal-propylamine NPT has been made by the oxalylamide route, with the amide having a mp 179-181 °C (75%) from benzene and NPT hydrochloride mp 186-187 °C (33%) from MeOH/benzene. An attempt to make NPT by the alkyl halide procedure failed. Using these same ratios of reactants, there was the formation of a sizable quantity of DPT with appreciable unreacted tryptamine presence (T:NPT:DPT/1:5:4). A recycling under the same conditions gave T:NPT:DPT/0:3:7 and a third cycle gave only DPT, but with a loss of almost 90% of the material, presumably to quaternary salt formation. Interestingly, NPT is less toxic than DPT in experimental mice, but has not yet been assayed in man.

NBT (N-butyltryptamine) is also an oxalylamide product. The amide has a mp 167-169 °C (81%) from benzene, and NBT hydrochloride has a mp 203-205 °C (13%) from benzene/MeOH.

The two geometric isomers, mono-isobutyl and mono-sec-butyl tryptamines are best called NIBT and NSBT. They also have been made by the oxalylamide route and the hydrochloride salts melt at 150-151 °C and 175-177 °C resp. Interestingly, NSBT is one of the two mono-substituted tryptamines that just might have CNS activity. It has shown a generalized and somewhat diffuse intoxication with several studies covering the 25 to 75 milligram range. Short lived, intellectual excitement with some modest sensory enhancements. Promising, but no plus three's, yet.

The tertiary-butyl analogue, NTBT, is the remaining mono-substituted tryptamine that just might have psychotropic potential. In the 5 to 20 mg area, there is a light-headed intoxication that is a totally pleasant buzz, but nothing more profound than that. Wouldn't it be fascinating if it turned out that all of the mono-tryptamines (the NRT's) were GHB-like intoxicants, and totally devoid of psyche-delic activity? That would be a true challenge to the SAR crowd.

Both the mono-amyl and the mono-hexylamines have been described (NAT and NHT), both having been made by the glyoxylamide process. These, too, as has been mentioned above, appear to be inactive in man, as reported by Stephen Szara at the famous "Ethnopharmacologic Search for Psychoactive Drugs" confer-ence, organized by the late Dan Efron of the National Institute of Mental Health, in San Francisco, in 1967.

Thirdly, this is where the staggering potential power of this recipe comes into focus. One can make, easily, pure mono-ethyl, mono-propyl, mono-isopropyl, mono-n-, s-, i- and t-NBT's. And using these directions, one can systematically react these mono's with every different alkyl halide. Thus, there suddenly becomes available "this" times "that" squared possibilities of new tryptamines, every one easily made, every one potentially psychoactive, and almost every one totally unknown to the scientific literature. The oxalylamide process goes out to lunch when one considers the unlikelihood of finding N-s-butyl-N-i-butyl amine as a commercially available product. It is no longer required. Make IBSBT (how would you ever encode that product?) by the simple treatment of one of these mono's with an appropriate alkyl halide, and clean up the mess with a dash of acetic anhydride.

Fourthly, and most important, every one of these adventures has an exact counterpart with the inclusion of that magical 5-methoxy group. Whatever is found with the 5-H archetype is certain to be more potent, and correspondingly unpredictable, with a 5-methoxy-substituent. Some have already been made. Most have not. This is open territory. Go West, young man!

Back to the mundane. I really have to justify the "N" in the NET. I will try to hold to the convention that is expanded on at length in the recipe for DBT, that if there is one alkyl group (a monoalkyl tryptamine) then it is N-alkyl-tryptamine, with the reserving of M for methyl rather than for mono, even in the case of monomethyltryptamine. There is wide use of MMT for monomethyltryptamine in the literature, but the ambiguity comes from the higher mono-substituted homologues, and this makes NMT a much safer name. As there can be several places for the ethyl group, perhaps it is best to give the location as a number or letter, such as 1, 2, $\alpha$ (for alpha) or N.

A detail for spectroscopists amongst us. With the mono-N-substituted tryptamines, there is always a 131 e/m mass peak, larger than the 130 e/m mass peak. This peak is a minor one with the disubstituted analogue. The same relationship exists with the 5-methoxy analogues, where N-monosubstituted compounds have a 161/160 m/e fragment (the 5-methoxymethylene indole fragment), with the 161 m/e peak always the larger. The primary amine shows this same character. The disubstituted analogue has only the 160 m/e fragment.

### #50. NMT; TRYPTAMINE, N-METHYL; INDOLE, 3-[2-(METHYLAMINO)ETHYL]; N-METHYLTRYPTAMINE; 3-[2-(METHYLAMINO)ETHYL]INDOLE

SYNTHESIS: A suspension of 10 g tryptamine base in 10 g butyl formate was held at reflux for 24 h. The resulting clear solution was stripped of volatiles under vacuum, and the residue partitioned between dilute HCl and $CH_2Cl_2$, and the aqueous phase extracted twice with additional $CH_2Cl_2$. The pooled organic extracts were washed once with dilute aqueous HCl, once with dilute aqueous NaOH, and the solvent removed under vacuum to give a black oil. This was distilled at the KugelRohr to give 9.05 g (77%) of

N-formyltryptamine as a clear oil, boiling at 170-190 °C at 0.1 mm/Hg which set to a glass. MS (in m/z): indolemethylene$^+$ 130 (100%); 143 (57%); parent ion 188 (15%). This amide slowly crystallized on standing, but was used as the glass in the reduction described below.

A solution of 1.88 g N-formyltryptamine in 40 mL anhydrous Et$_2$O was added to 60 mL of a 1 N solution of LAH in THF, well-stirred under argon, and was held at reflux for 24 h. After cooling to room temperature, the excess hydride was destroyed by the addition of 20 mL of 50% aqueous THF. The resulting solids were removed by filtration, and the filter cake washed repeatedly with damp THF. The basic filtrate was stripped of solvent under vacuum to give 1.39 g of a pale oil which started to crystallize. After distillation at 135-145 °C at 0.1 mm/Hg, there was obtained 1.22 g (70%) of N-methyltryptamine as a white oil which spontaneously set up to white crystals of the free base. These rapidly darkened on exposure to air. The IR (in cm$^{-1}$): 740, 1018, 1103, 1132, 1161. The literature mp is 90 °C. A 0.22 g sample of darkened base in 1.0 g IPA was neutralized with concentrated HCl (using external, moistened pH paper as a titration guide) with the development of an intense blue-green color with the addition of each drop of acid. The acidified solution (now a stable blue-green color) was diluted with diethyl Et$_2$O (about 1 mL). This cloudy solution, upon scratching, set to crystals which, upon removal by filtration, Et$_2$O washing, and air drying to constant weight, weighed 0.18 g and had a mp of 178-180 °C. N-methyltryptamine hydrochloride (NMT) IR (in cm$^{-1}$): 748, 850, 1009, 1104, 1119, 1136. MS (in m/z): C$_2$H$_6$N$^+$ 44 (100%); indolemethylene$^+$ 131, 130 (61%, 51%); parent ion 174 (2%).

EXTENSIONS AND COMMENTARY: N-Methyltryptamine (mono-methyltryptamine, NMT) is an alkaloid that has been found in the bark, shoots and leaves of several species of Virola, Acacia and Mimosa. However, the major snuffs associated with these plant have been shown to also contain 5-MeO-DMT and are discussed there. NMT has been synthesized in a number of ways. One can react 3-(2-bromoethyl)indole with methylamine. NMT can be isolated as the benzoyl derivative from the methylation of tryptamine with methyl iodide followed by reaction with benzoyl chloride, with the hydrolysis of this amide with alcoholic KOH. It can also be synthesized from indole with oxalyl chloride, with the resulting glyoxyl chloride reacting with methylamine in ether to give N-methylindol-3-ylglyoxalylamide (mp 223-224 °C from IPA) which is obtained in a 68% yield. This is reduced to NMT to give the amine hydrochloride (mp 175-177 °C from EtOH) in a 75% yield. The most simple and direct synthesis is the formamide reduction given above.

To my knowledge there have been no reports of oral activity of NMT, although its wide availability from botanic sources has encouraged some explorers to assay it. I have had one report that the smoking of 50-100 mg gave visuals that lasted for maybe 15 seconds. The N-hydroxy analogue has been noted as being found in plants, in the "DMT is Everywhere" chapter.

## #51. PRO-LAD; 6-NORLYSERGAMIDE, N,N-DIETHYL-6-PROPYL; 6-NORLYSERGAMIDE, N,N-DIETHYL-6-PROPYL; N,N-DIETHYL-NORLYSERGAMIDE, 6-PROPYL; 6-PROPYLNORLYSERGAMIDE, N,N-DIETHYL; 9,10-DIDEHYDRO-6-PROPYL-N,N-DIETHYLERGOLINE-8β-CARBOXAMIDE; 6-PROPYL-NOR-LSD

SYNTHESIS: To a solution of 66 mg nor-LSD (see under ETH-LAD for its preparation) in 2 mL freshly distilled DMF under a nitrogen atmosphere, there was added 48 mg anhydrous $K_2CO_3$ and 41 mg propyl iodide. When TLC analysis indicated that the nor-LSD had been consumed (9 h) all volatiles were removed under a hard vacuum. The residue was solubilized in $CHCl_3$ (5x5 mL) and the pooled extracts dried over anhydrous $Na_2SO_4$, cleared by filtration, and the solvent removed under vacuum. There was a residual white solid. This was separated into two components by centrifugal chromatography (alumina, $CH_2Cl_2$, nitrogen and ammonia atmosphere) the first of which was the major product. After removal of the solvent, this was dissolved in hot benzene, filtered and cooled. The addition of hexane prompted crystallization of N-propyl-nor-LSD (9,10-didehydro-6-propyl-N,N-diethylergoline-8β-carboxamide) as a crystalline product weighing 54 mg (72% yield dry). It had a mp of 87-88 °C.

DOSAGE: 100 - 200 micrograms, orally

DURATION: 6 - 8 h

QUALITATIVE COMMENTS: (with 80 µg, orally) "I am aware of some change within a quarter hour, and then nothing more for quite a while. Certainly no visuals, almost like MDMA in that I am not really sure that this is even psychedelic — it does not have any of the flavor of LSD. I want to try it at a higher dose some day."

(with 135 µg, orally) "A strange development into a sort of paranoia place, without any reasonable dialogue with my partner. A light-headed experience of a different kind, but we did not find common space. Not too comfortable — emotions are dull. At about mid-experience, considerable visuals came into play, with easy fantasy interlocking with music. Brüchner's "Viola quintette in A" produced extraordinary castle frames within castle walls. Emotions were reknit, food was good, and sleep fine at the 8th or 9th hour. It is not up to LSD (if that is your standard) because it is basically not like LSD."

(with 175 μg, orally) "This is an intellectually clear material, but it is a funny material. I am certainly at a +++ or at least I was a couple of hours ago. How does one describe PRO-LAD? It's not-quite-this and not-quite-that sort of stuff. Or, to borrow from Winnie-the-Pooh, 'It's not at the bottom, and it's not at the top (but this is the stair where I always stop)' — oh, never mind. I mean, I'm not sure how to categorize this material. It's pleasant, it's fine for fooling around, it's good for humor, even excellent. It's very good for clear thinking, although not cosmic-type particularly. It's a sort of nice, comfortable, middle-American, July-Fourth-Picnic, apple-pie with ice cream sort of psychedelic, the kind that you can wrap up in gold and white striped paper for your youngest aunt, the one who likes to think she's really a bit <u>wild</u>, you know — the kind of psychedelic that's a bit much for your Dad or Mom, but it's just jazzy enough to keep some younger relatives happy with you for a few months. However, I must tell you, kid, if you try to bring this to the Big Town, well... It is pretty much dropped off, now. Ah'm gonna lie mahself on down."

EXTENSIONS AND COMMENTARY: With success in the preparation of the rather stable nor-LSD intermediate, any number of 6-substituted nor-LSD homologues and analogues can be synthesized. Simply use the appropriate alkyl bromide or alkyl iodide and the desired product will be in hand, after a modest amount of rather sophisticated purification at a micro scale. Several analogues are in the chemical literature, and some of them have been explored in direct comparison to LSD. Here are a few examples:

N-Propynyl-nor-LSD (PARGY-LAD). Some activity at 160 micrograms. Active at 500 micrograms.

N-Butyl-nor-LSD (BU-LAD). Something at 500 micrograms.

N-Phenethyl-nor-LSD (PHENETH-LAD). Nothing at 500 micrograms.

As these substituents get heavier and heavier, the potency of the products drop by an order of magnitude or so, or even more. But here, in this N-substituted nor-LSD family, there is a fantastic research opportunity just waiting to be exploited, an exact parallel to the radio-iodine labeling of DOI as was described in PIHKAL. It is a good guess that this position is one of good metabolic stability. So what about putting on a small group that can be labeled with a reasonably long-lived positron isotope? A specific proposal: N-(2-fluoroethyl)-nor-LSD with an $^{18}$F radio-label. The compound should be makable rather quickly (nor-LSD and $^{18}$FCH$_2$CH$_2$I in DMF with potassium carbonate) and cleanly purified by centrifugal chromatography, all well within the almost two hour half-life considerations of radio-fluorine. Here is a group that would be (in theory) intrinsic to the central activity of the end product, N-(2-fluoroethyl)-nor-LSD. The end compound could be synthesized, purified, characterized and sterilized quickly, allowing its brain localization and central dynamics to be determined by PET scanning, with virtually no risk to the subject. Let's call it FLUORETH-LAD.

**#52. pyr-T; TRYPTAMINE, N,N-TETRAMETHYLENE; INDOLE, 3-[2-(1-PYRROLIDYL)ETHYL]; PYRROLIDINE, 1-[2-(3-INDOLYL)ETHYL]; N,N-TETRAMETHYLENETRYPTAMINE; 1-[2-(1H-INDOL-3-YL)-ETHYL]PYRROLIDINE; 1-[2-(1-PYRROLIDYL)ETHYL]INDOLE; "PYRROLIDYLTRYPTAMINE"**

SYNTHESIS: To a well-stirred solution of 1.0 g indole in 15 mL TBME there was added, dropwise over the course of 20 min, a solution of 1.1 g oxalyl chloride in 15 mL TBME. Yellow crystals of indol-3-ylglyoxyl chloride appeared at about the half-addition point. Stirring was continued for an additional 10 min. This intermediate was removed by filtration, washed sparingly with TBME, and used directly in the following step. The above indol-3-ylglyoxyl chloride was added, a bit at a time, to 2.1 mL anhydrous pyrrolidine that was being vigorously stirred.

The color was discharged, and reaction mixture became almost colorless. To this there was added 80 mL of 1 N HCl, the mixture cooled, and the resulting solids removed by filtration, washed with $H_2O$ and air-dried. This was recrystallized from 30 mL boiling $CH_3CN$ (slow to dissolve and crystallize out) to give, after filtration, $CH_3CN$ washing, and air drying, 0.87 g (42%) of indol-3-yl-N,N-tetramethylene-glyoxylamide with a mp of 219-220 °C. The literature reports a mp 224-225 °C. IR (in cm$^{-1}$): 753, 789, 834, 1143, 1161, 181, C=O 1615 (br), NH at 3150.

A solution of 0.76 g indol-3-yl-N,N-tetramethyleneglyoxylamide in 15 mL anhydrous dioxane was added, slowly, to 0.8 g LAH in 15 mL dioxane which was well-stirred and held at reflux temperature under an inert atmosphere. After the addition was complete, reflux was maintained for an additional 16 h, the reaction mixture cooled, and the excess hydride destroyed by the cautious addition of wet dioxane. The formed solids were removed by filtration, washed with hot dioxane, the filtrate and washings combined, dried over anhydrous $MgSO_4$, and the solvent removed under vacuum. The residue was distilled at the KugelRohr at 0.05 mm/Hg, yielding a fraction boiling at 170-180 °C which spontaneously crystallized. Thus, there was obtained 0.35 g (52%) of N,N-tetramethylenetryptamine (pyr-T) with a mp 114-115. IR (cm$^{-1}$): 740, 784, 807, 886, 1011, 1108. MS (in m/z): $C_5H_{10}N^+$ 84 (100%); indolemethylene$^+$ 130 (7%); parent ion 214 (3%). A solution of this base in $Et_2O$ treated with anhydrous HCl gave the hydrochloride salt which, on recrystallization from MeOH/benzene, had a mp 193-194 °C.

DOSAGE: unknown

DURATION: unknown

QUALITATIVE COMMENTS: (with 25 mg, orally) "There was a general malaise without any particular spiritual or noble side to it. I was sick."

(with 50 mg, orally) "There is maybe something here, but it is unpleasant. Salivation, muscle and joint pains. I tried smoking it earlier and it was almost inactive. Certainly less potent than DMT or DET."

(with 70 mg, smoked) "This smells like a mixture of DMT and naphthalene. The effects began very soon, and led to an intense, but a little bit uncomfortable, high. I was distinctly dizzy, and the visuals were minor. I would classify this compound in the 'not too pleasant' category, certainly not colorful."

EXTENSIONS AND COMMENTARY: First of all, the name pyr-T, which is an abbreviation for "pyrrolidinyltryptamine," is out-and-out wrong. There is just one single nitrogen at the end of the tryptamine chain and it cannot be claimed by both halves of the name. It is intrinsic to the name pyrrolidine as well as to the name tryptamine. This is why the name is in quotation marks. This drug has occasionally been called PT in the popular literature, but choosing to spell it out as pyr-T allows a parallel code to be used with the piperidine and morpholine analogues. These two analogues are both described in the literature. The piperidine material (pip-T) is made via the glyoxylamide (mp 182-183 °C) which is reduced with LAH to the target amine (mp 149-150 °C, HCl salt 220-221 °C). The morpholine analogue (mor-T) also came to be via the glyoxylamide (mp 187-188 °C) and the reduction to the amine which can be an oil, but which has been reported to have a mp 145-147 °C. The only trials I know of with either of these is with mor-T which, as the fumarate salt, had no effects at all upon the i.m. injection of a 30 milligram bolus.

Actually, this neat trilogy of heterocyclics, the pyrrolidine ring, the piperidine ring, and the morpholine ring, have been the chemist's favorite for many years. Leaf through the "Known Tryptamines" appendix, and see how often you see stretched between the nitrogen substituents the phrases:

$$— CCCC —$$
$$— CCCCC —$$
$$— CCOCC —$$

These are the exact rings. They are easy to make; they add a sense of sophistication to an otherwise pedestrian scientific paper; and they often represent the inactive extremes in a receptor-site study of structure activity relationships of CNS-active agents. But the compounds represented here appear to have simply the wrong properties, somehow, and should not really be seriously considered in the quest for understanding of the remarkable actions of most of the psychedelic phenethylamines and tryptamines.

And yet no observation, favorable or unfavorable, deserves to be discarded. The very failure to act in an expected way might, if completely understood, add to our intimate understanding of the mystery of why these materials do what they do.

#### #53. T; TRYPTAMINE; INDOLE, 3-(2-AMINOETHYL); 3-(2-AMINOETHYL)INDOLE

SYNTHESIS: (from indole) To a cold solution of approximately 25% aqueous dimethylamine (most easily made by dissolving 20 g dimethylamine hydrochloride in 20 g cold 50% NaOH) there was added 30 mL acetic acid followed by 17.2 g 37% HCHO. This mixture was added to 23.4 g indole crystals, and the combination was allowed to stir overnight. This reaction was then quenched by pouring into 40 g KOH in 300 mL $H_2O$. A yellowish gum settled out, slowly solidified, and was washed with 2x100 mL $H_2O$. The yellow solids were dissolved in 100 mL $CH_2Cl_2$ and extracted with 2x200 mL 1 N $H_2SO_4$, the extracts pooled, and washed with an additional 50 mL $CH_2Cl_2$. The nearly colorless, aqueous phase was made basic with 25% NaOH, and extracted with 3x75 mL $CH_2Cl_2$. Removal of the solvent under vacuum yielded a white, solid residue which, on recrystallization from acetone, yielded 11.0 g 3-(dimethylaminomethyl)indole (gramine) as a loose white crystalline product with a mp 131-132 °C. IR (in $cm^{-1}$): 749, 832, 868, 1000, 1040, 1119 and 1174. MS (in m/z): indolemethylene+ 130 (100%); parent ion 174 (21%). The yield is very dependent on the amount of $H_2O$ present and the temperature of the reaction. Here, with $H_2O$ intentionally introduced as a simplification, there was the generation of some 1,3-bis-(dimethylaminomethyl)indole (MS (in m/z): $C_3H_8N^+$ 58 (100%); indolemethylene+ 129 (7%); parent ion 231 (3%)), considerable yellow gum not soluble in either $CH_2Cl_2$ or $H_2O$, and considerable recoverable indole. This yield (here, 32%) has been reported to approach quantitative with the use of anhydrous dimethylamine and only acetic acid as a solvent. To a solution of 15 g NaCN in 30 mL $H_2O$ there was added a solution of 10.0 g 3-(dimethylaminomethyl)indole in 100 mL EtOH, and the reaction held at reflux for 80 h. The solvent was removed under vacuum and the semi-solid residue dissolved in $CH_2Cl_2$ and washed several times with dilute HCl (caution, HCN evolved). After removal of the solvent, the residue was distilled at the KugelRohr to give 7.1 g (yield of 79%) of indole-3-acetonitrile (bp 140-150 °C at 0.1 mm/Hg) as a white oil. IR (in $cm^{-1}$): 751, 824, 930, 1017, 1070, 1103; CN at 2265, NH at 3420. MS (in m/z): parent ions 155, 156 (100%, 66%); indolemethylene+ 130 (56%). The product is a crystalline solid (mp 35-37 °C) but was used in the following reaction without further purification. From the distillation pot, the by-product indole-3-acetamide could be obtained, with a mp 150-151 °C from aqueous EtOH.

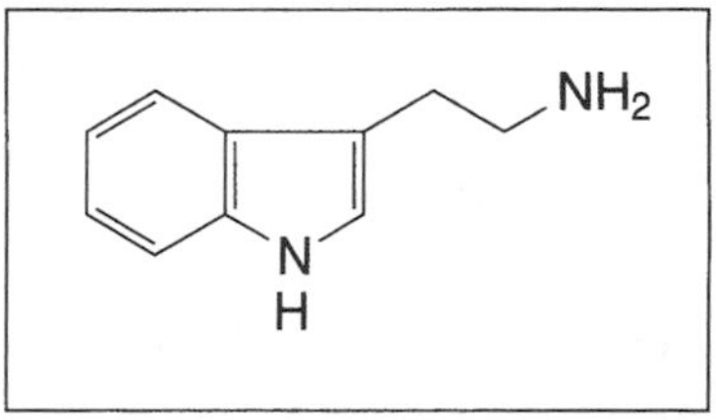

A solution of 6.0 g indole-3-acetonitrile in 15 mL anhydrous THF was added, dropwise, to 160 mL of a 1 M solution of LAH in THF, stirred and held under reflux conditions. After an additional 8 h reflux, the reaction was cooled, and the excess hydride and reaction complex were decomposed by the careful addition of wet THF until the evolution of hydrogen ceased, then 25 mL 5% aqueous NaOH was added, followed by sufficient $H_2O$ to leave the inorganic solids with a filterable texture (about 15 mL additional).  These solids were removed by filtration, the filter cake washed with THF, the filtrate and washings combined, and the solvent removed under vacuum.  The solid residue was recrystallized from $CH_3CN$ to provide 5.3 g (86%) tryptamine as a cream colored crystal with a mp 112-114 °C. IR (in $cm^{-1}$): 751, 811, 882, 941, 1014, 1112 and 1128.

This synthetic scheme is probably not needed by the chemist.  There are many commercial sources of indole and, for that matter, for gramine, for indoleacetonitrile, and for tryptamine itself.  In general, the commercial price goes up modestly with each material named in this reaction scheme.  Tryptamine itself, as the hydrochloride salt, is disproportionately expensive and, in most reactions, must be converted back to the free base before use.

DOSAGE:  250 mg, intravenously

DURATION:  Very short

COMMENTS: (with up to 10 mg, intravenously) "There were no changes in blood pressure or self-rating scores."

(with 250 mg, intravenously) "Tryptamine was infused intravenously over a period of up to 7.5 minutes.  Physical changes included an increase in blood pressure, in the amplitude of the patellar reflex, and in pupillary diameter.  The subjective changes are not unlike those seen with small doses of LSD.  A point-by-point comparison between the tryptamine and LSD syndromes reveals a close similarity which is consistent with the hypothesis that tryptamine and LSD have a common mode of action."

EXTENSION AND COMMENTARY:  This quotation is from a paper by Martin and Sloan, published almost thirty years ago, that stands as our only measure of the human response to tryptamine.  The first of the two reports in the comments took place 5 years earlier, with depressed patients and at very low levels of drug administration.  It had already been established in rat and dog studies that tryptamine was known to enter the brain but, due to rapid metabolism, had only a short duration of central activity.  Hence, the researchers in both these studies chose to employ an intravenous route of administration.  There are a number of valuable points to be made in this latter report describing the 250 mg. study.

Clearly, the model drug in vogue at that time for central action was LSD, and all researchers felt that comparisons should be made to it, as sort of a gold standard.  It was acknowledged that the setting in which an experiment took place could influence the outcome.  Many studies with LSD were conducted in an environment that was quite different (in private living rooms, with good music and friendly faces) than these tryptamine experiments conducted in a clinical ward of the Lexington Addiction Center, with automatic patellar reflex hammer strokes and polygraphic pupillary diameter measurements, conducted in what was in fact a narcotics prison.

Most instructive was the statement that the tryptamine syndrome was similar to the LSD syndrome. This equation has been broadly quoted, but it is valuable to read, first hand, the explicit observations of central activity that supported this conclusion. These are quoted here:

"Shortly after the onset of the infusions, three of the patients became aware of the experimental setting and complained of a heaviness, tiredness or numbness of the limbs which subsequently became generalized to other parts of the body. With continued infusion, a variety of other visceral symptoms and signs emerged which have been previously described following administration of LSD and mescaline, including nausea, vomiting, dizziness, sweating, acute or dulled hearing, metallic taste, and a heaviness of body. Further, in 2 of the 4 subjects, there were visual changes (subsequently described as a heaviness behind the eyes, a clouding of vision, and lines or cobwebs)."

The tryptamine experience sounds pretty heavy, and it is almost as if every negative LSD or mescaline property was exhumed and displayed, to justify tryptamine as being similar to this widely accepted psychedelic drug.

Why is tryptamine of any interest at all? Just as the simple compound phenethylamine was the nucleus for all of the potential psychedelic compounds in *PIHKAL*, so tryptamine plays a similar role as the nucleus of all drugs discussed in this volume. These are the structural basic-skeleton archetypes of these two corresponding classes of psychedelic drugs. Both are widely scattered throughout the plant kingdom, and they are both normal components of the human animal. They both have amino acid origins, phenylalanine for phenethylamine and tryptophan for tryptamine, and these amino acids are extremely important factors in human biochemistry. And they, each in turn, can only provoke pharmacological effects when administered parenterally at very high levels.

Tryptophan, the metabolic precursor to tryptamine, is itself a centrally active amino acid. There is a complex and little appreciated story associated with it as to its human psychopharmacology. Although tryptamine is only active parenterally, tryptophan is active orally and is directly converted to tryptamine, the two compounds must be considered in concert. What is the action of tryptophan, taken orally? Here are some quotations from the published literature, mostly with the voice of the giver, not the taker, with some copy taken from health-food store fliers of a decade ago.

COMMENTS: (with 2 g, orally) "I administered two grams to 7 normal subjects, and 5 of them became drowsy after 1-2 hours."

(with 2 g, orally) "The amino acid tryptophan is a safe, non-addictive sleeping aid which works because it is made into serotonin in the brain. Serotonin is the neurotransmitter which initiates sleep. Tryptophan is found in milk and bananas and can sometimes be purchased in pill form. Two grams of tryptophan just before bed is very helpful in getting to sleep. For best results take it on an empty stomach. Although milk contains tryptophan, the pure amino acid is more effective."

(with 5 g, orally) "I took five grams orally several times over a period of days (to study urinary metabolites) and I did not expect any psychological effects. Within an hour, there was a slight dizziness, a feeling of light-headedness and some euphoria which was comparable to whiskey."

(with 6 g, orally) "We gave six grams tryptophan orally to seven subjects. All became listless and yawned frequently, and five of them slept between the periods of testing. Three were unable to remain awake for more than a few minutes. All were easily aroused however, and then felt euphoric and were unusually voluble and overactive. One showed marked social disinhibition in his behavior. Two were clumsy in turning and tandem walking. One had a frontal headache and another was dizzy without vertigo."

(with 10 g, orally) "We gave our sixteen normal subjects 10 g d,L-tryptophan orally. All experienced symptoms such as changes in perception (lightheadedness and dizziness) and changes in mood, mainly euphoria. None of the thirty-four chronic alcoholic subjects noted any symptoms at this dosage level."

(with 15 g, orally, with 150 mg iproniazid) "This was a daily treatment given to schizophrenic patients, tryptophan along with an antidepressant which is a monoamine oxidase inhibitor. Most showed marked changes such as an elevation in mood, an increased involvement with other people in their ward, and an increased extrovertism. A separate study of this combination with the addition of the amino acid L-methionine produced in about half of these patients a toxic or delirioid state."

CONTINUING COMMENTARY: Look at this fabulous story that unfolded some twenty years ago. It is completely coherent, and it is totally exciting. Let me try to distill the human information given above into a logical flow. Tryptophan, a natural and nutritionally essential amino-acid, is a centrally active intoxicant and sleep-provider in man. It is converted metabolically to tryptamine, which is a little bit psychedelic. When administered with methionine (another amino-acid known to methylate things) it produces methylated tryptamines, the two best-studied being N-methyltryptamine (NMT) and N,N-dimethyltryptamine (DMT). The effects that result are hard to categorize, reflecting the diagnostic status of the patient. But something happens. In short, tryptophan, alone or in combination with MAO inhibitors or methyl donors, is a fabulous tool for exploring brain function. And it was an easily available research tool, openly explored by many private individuals. It was inspiring a broad curiosity as to meeting a large number of human inadequacies.

Then, an incident occurred in 1989, at the Showa Denko company in Japan, where a change in the manufacturing procedure produced an impure product. The impurity led directly to a health problem, a condition with a flu-like syndrome called

Eosinophilia-Myalgia Syndrome (EMS), which caused some 1500 incidents in the United States, including 38 deaths. The FDA quite rightly removed tryptophan from the market on the 17th of November, 1989, and banned its distribution. The source of the health problem was quite quickly identified, and the production operation was changed back to the original process, and the tryptophan product was again available free of any toxic impurity. This freedom from any impurity was acknowledged by the FDA, but they transferred the toxic aspect of the substance from the impurity contained within it (now no longer present) to the substance itself. The implied declaration was that tryptophan was intrinsically toxic.

The sale of tryptophan as dietary supplements for man is now illegal. Dietary supplements to animal stock feed is okay. Tryptophan is available to hospitals for use in critical situations. Tryptophan is available as a prescription drug. But it is not available in the health food stores and so cannot be explored by the lay researcher. The world of inquiring into the action on normals, schizophrenics, alcoholics, people who are overweight, people who are depressed, is denied both to the private individual and to the clinical researcher. There are commercially available drugs, all approved, that can play the same role. Within four days of the announced ban of tryptophan (after the problem had been resolved and corrected) a broad promotion of Prozac (an antidepressant similar in action to Tryptophan) appeared in Newsweek (March 26, 1990). Prozac is still widely promoted. Tryptophan is still not available to the private individual. Both can play the role of being an effective sedative.

A quotation from the FDA "Dietary Supplement Task Force Report," page 2, June 15, 1993, deserves careful reading.

> "The [FDA] Task Force considered various issues in its delibera-
> tions, including ... what steps are necessary to ensure that the
> existence of dietary supplements on the market does not act as a
> disincentive for drug development."

What are dietary supplements? How might they get in the way of pharmaceutical industry creations? Where is the line to be drawn between nature and big business? What plants are there that might serve as health adjuncts? I truly think that we are being had by the powers that be, who are authorized to control our access to medicines. Today we cannot eat ABC because it contains an outlawed drug. Tomorrow we cannot eat DEF because it is suspected of containing an outlawed drug. The day after tomorrow, we cannot eat GHI because it has not been shown to be free of outlawed drugs. And yet, everything in the drug store had its origins somewhere in a botanist's observation or in a chemist's mistake. Where does this oppression stop? When do we say, hold, enough?

We must be free to eat this plant, and smell that flower, as we choose to. To deny us this right is to deny us a simple and basic freedom that is our Constitutional heritage. If I want to continue to eat bananas and drink milk, I will do so, and get off my back. If I want to consume tryptophan because I feel it brings me closer to God and Jesus, or makes me sleep better, I will consume tryptophan. You, the empowered authority, will not tell me not to. As was so eloquently expressed in Leonard Bernstein's "West Side Story," when the group of heroes came up against the authorities, they said, "Hey, Officer Krupke, krup you!"

There are a pile of pharmacological details that should be collected and disposed of. For example, L-tryptophan is the natural and normal amino acid and yet it is more toxic than the unnatural d-isomer. The rat data would suggest that it might be a problem at something over a 100 gram dose, although I know no one who has nibbled that high. In fact, L-tryptophan is the most toxic of all the natural dietary amino acids (in rats at least). Interesting. But, so what? There is a botanical side to all of this. Gramine is a synthetic precursor of tryptamine, and yet it has been reported here and there as a natural plant component. The same is true for indole-3-ethanol. Yet, both of these can serve you in the laboratory for the synthesis of tryptamine and, of course, of DMT. The plant world seems to be fully aware of these same processes.

A final comment to connect man and plant. The primary animal metabolite of both tryptamine and of DMT is the corresponding indoleacetic acid which is itself a potent plant hormone. This just happens to be one of the most thoroughly studied plant growth hormones, and has been isolated from a number of natural sources. Less well studied is the reduction product of the intermediate aldehyde, by the action of monoamine oxidase, to the corresponding alcohol, indole-3-ethanol, or tryptophol. This rather rare plant stimulant has been found in cucumber seedlings, but has also been shown to be present in trace amounts (along with the hormone indoleacetic acid, MMT and DMT) in at least one Ayahuasca component, the Illinois Bundle-flower legume, *Desmanthus illinoensis*. Another circle has closed upon itself in an interesting way.

## #54. TETRAHYDROHARMINE; HARMAN, 7-METHOXY-1,2,3,4-TETRAHYDRO; HARMINE, 1,2,3,4-TETRAHYDRO; β-CARBOLINE, 7-METHOXY-1-METHYL-1,2,3,4-TETRAHYDRO; 7-METHOXY-1,2,3,4-TETRAHYDROHARMAN; 1,2,3,4-TETRAHYDROHARMINE; 7-METHOXY-1-METHYL-1,2,3,4-TETRAHYDRO-β-CARBOLINE; 7-MEO-THH; LEPTAFLORINE

SYNTHESIS: A stirred solution of 1.0 g harmaline hydrochloride in 25 mL $H_2O$ was covered with a pad of Argon, and there was added 0.1 g $PtO_2$ followed by the dropwise addition of 0.4 g $NaBH_4$ in 4.0 mL $H_2O$ over the course of 20 min. The pH was determined periodically and the reaction mixture was kept acidic during this period by the addition of 1 N HCl as needed. The catalyst was removed by filtration through paper with H₂O washing, and the pale yellow filtrate made basic with the addition of aqueous NaOH. The cloudy basic suspension was extracted with 4x25 mL CH₂Cl₂, these extracts were pooled, and the solvent removed under vacuum. There was thus obtained 0.88 g of crude tetrahydroharmine as a white solid. A 0.25 g sample was recrystallized from MeOH to give a reference sample as white crystals with a mp 187-190 °C, IR (in cm⁻¹): 804,

902, 922, 943, 1036, 1157. MS (in m/z): 201 (100%); parent ion 216 (33%); 172 (20%). The remaining crude sample (0.60 g) was dissolved in 12 g IPA and treated with 8 drops of concentrated HCl (acidic to external pH paper) and allowed to stand for a day. There were deposited crystals which were removed by filtration, lightly washed with IPA, and dried at 100 °C to give tetrahydroharmine hydrochloride 0.53 g (75%) as a fine solid, with a greenish tinge, mp 232-234 °C. IR (in cm⁻¹): 789, 804, 816, 838, 1033, 1160.

DOSAGE: 300 mg, orally

DURATION: unknown

QUALITATIVE COMMENTS: (with 300 mg, orally) "At this dosage level there were subjective effects similar to what I had experienced with 100 milligrams of harmaline."

EXTENSIONS AND COMMENTARY: This one comment is the sum total of what I can find in the literature concerning the human activity of tetrahydroharmine. It was a study done with the synthetic racemate, whereas the natural isolate is the dextrorotatory isomer. It was a single trial. It was carried out in a single volunteer. There is no information given as to what this person's response had been to 100 milligrams harmaline. Tetrahydroharmine could very well be an extremely important factor in the study of plants known to promote materials such as DMT to oral activity. It is present (along with harmaline and harmine) in *Peganum harmala*, and has been reported as being present in levels equal to those of harmine in the analyses of ayahuasca samples (where harmaline itself is usually present in rather small amounts). And it is an effective monoamineoxidase inhibitor. The material is easily synthesized and it should not be difficult to resolve it into its optically opposite forms. Clinical studies would be extremely informative. In balance, the psychopharmacological activity of this plant isolate must be accepted as being essentially unknown.

The first isolation of tetrahydroharmine from the botanical world has an interesting story attached to it. The major alkaloid known to be in *Banisteriopsis caapi* (back in 1920's when the Genus was still called *Banisteria*) was harmine. Some reports a few years later reported the presence of harmaline, but it was not until the 1950's that a careful chromatographic analysis of the plant revealed a third alkaloid. The apparent optical activity was discounted, and the isolated material was thought to be 6-methoxy-N,N-dimethyltryptamine (6-MeO-DMT). This was synthesized, and it wasn't quite right. In chemistry, not quite right means out and out wrong. Then the racemic (optically inactive) form of tetrahydroharmine was synthesized and not only was it spectroscopically identical to the dextrorotatory plant isolate ($[\alpha]_D$ +32°) but it had an identical infra-red spectrum, an identical melting point, and no depression with a mixed melting point. There are precious few optical isomers and racemates that can make that claim.

There are a number of other plants that are known to contain tetrahydroharmine and to have been used in various native preparations. I have recently learned of analysis of an Ayahuasca brew that had used the plant *Calliandra pentandra* as a component, instead of the usual *Psychotria viridis*. Ott's magnificent compendium *Pharmacotheon* makes mention of a *Calliandra augustifolia* as a component of ayahuasca, but there is no mention of this *pentandra* species. The preliminary analysis that I have been given of this decoction is that a component that had initially appeared to be DMT by HPLC analysis had proven to be tetrahydroharmine when assayed by GCMS. There was no detectable DMT present. And yet the material appears to have psychopharmacological activity.

More studies on tetrahydroharmine are absolutely imperative.

#### #55. α,N,O-TMS; TRYPTAMINE, 5-METHOXY-α,N-DIMETHYL; INDOLE, 5-METHOXY-3-[2-(METHYLAMINO)PROPYL]; 5-METHOXY-α,N-DIMETHYLTRYPTAMINE; 5-METHOXY-3-[2-(METHYLAMINO)-PROPYL]INDOLE; α,N,O-TRIMETHYLSEROTONIN; SEROTONIN, α,N,O-TRIMETHYL

SYNTHESIS: To a solution of 1.21 g 5-methoxyindole-3-carboxaldehyde in 15 mL nitroethane there was added 0.3 g anhydrous ammonium acetate, and the mixture was held at steam-bath temperature. Periodic assay by TLC showed the reaction to be complete in 1.5 h. The volatiles were removed under vacuum, and the residue (1.58 g of rusty red crystals) was recrystallized from 15 mL boiling IPA. After filtration and air-drying, there was obtained 1.24 g (82%) of 5-methoxy-3-(2-nitropropenyl)indole as dull gold crystals with a melting point of 178-179 °C. The literature value is 182-184 °C.

A suspension of 1.7 g electrolytic iron dust in 10 mL of 80% aqueous acetic acid was heated on the steam bath until there were clear signs of hydrogen evolution.

To this stirred suspension there was added 0.50 g 5-methoxy-3-(2-nitropropenyl)indole a bit at a time, over the course of 2 min. The heating and stirring was continued for 30 min, by which time TLC analysis (CH$_2$Cl$_2$/hexane, silica) showed the starting material to be gone, and there were two new spots, one slower moving and one at the origin. The reaction mixture was poured into 100 mL of a H$_2$O/CH$_2$Cl$_2$ mixture, and filtered through paper. The two phases were separated, and the aqueous phases extracted with an additional 2x50 mL CH$_2$Cl$_2$. The pooled organic extracts were washed once with saturated aqueous K$_2$CO$_3$, and the solvent removed under vacuum. The resulting residue was distilled at 0.08 mm/Hg to give 5-methoxyindol-3-yl acetone as a colorless oil which came over at 215-230 °C. The product weighed 0.24 g, had a carbonyl absorption at 1710 cm$^{-1}$, and had an acceptable fragmentation pattern by GCMS.

To 20 mL methanol, there was added 1.17 g of 5-methoxyindol-3-yl acetone, 4.3 g CH$_3$NH$_2$ hydrochloride, 0.5 g NaCNBH$_3$ and sufficient concentrated HCl/MeOH to bring the pH down to a yellow color on damp, broad range pH paper. The reaction was stirred at room temperature, with periodic addition of more acid as needed, over the course of several days. The reaction mixture was poured into dilute sulfuric acid, washed twice with CH$_2$Cl$_2$, made basic with dilute NaOH, and extracted with 3x50 mL CH$_2$Cl$_2$. After the removal of the solvent under vacuum, the residue (0.76 g) was distilled at 180-190 °C at 0.05 mm/Hg to give 0.65 g α,N,O-trimethylserotonin (α,N,O-TMS) as a colorless oil. It did not crystallize, nor were any solid salts of it obtained. MS (in m/z): C$_3$H$_8$N$^+$ 58 (100%); indolemethylene$^+$ 161/160 (19, 7%); parent ion 218 (<1%).

DOSAGE: 10 - 20 mg, orally

DURATION: 6 - 8 h

QUALITATIVE COMMENTS: (with 16 mg, orally) "It was maybe a plus two, but there wasn't really much of anything. My body felt safe, was safe. The only strong negative, negative only to me, was the nature of my dreaming that night; shallow, a faint metallic flavor, a distinct lack of depth or dimension. A waste of good dreaming time."

(with 16 mg, orally) "I got as far as this would go, at about an hour and a quarter. There was nothing in the visual field, but I was unquestionably somewhere. I was quite horny, and the erotic was both excellent and satisfying. Tried writing, and it seemed easy. There was no fantasy, no color enhancement, and not much in the way of eye-dilation or appetite loss. Nothing much anywhere at all. As with Oakland, no there, there. And by the seventh hour, there was baseline, with a residual feeling of having been cleansed."

(with 20 mg, orally) "I was in quite a depressed state, but I don't think it was the α,N,O-TMS. But it certainly didn't lift the depression. Everything I saw confirmed my growing despair about the human race and I concluded, after a few hours, that we have doomed ourselves. I am tired at being angry at it all. Enough already."

EXTENSIONS AND COMMENTARY: There is a sadness felt with most of the published efforts to form sweeping correlations between the structure of a molecule and its biological activity. This relationship is called a SAR, or a Structure Activity Relationship, and there are journals that are dedicated to just this form of analysis. One needs a large collection of compounds of known structure, and all of them must be of known pharmacological activity. And one needs a computer of some sort. One considers all aspects of the structure such as bond energies, electronic charge densities, molecular lengths, widths and thicknesses, degrees of freedom or of constraint, anything that can be calculated or measured. Then one assigns an independent variable coefficient to everything, constructs some additive equation where these coefficients equal something else, and then compares that something else to the biological activity. Push the "go" button on the computer, and let everything be varied clear across the map, until the calculated solution of the equation makes the best match with the value of pharmacological activity. Then one has a SAR with a statistical measure of goodness of fit, and it then can be used to predict the activity of new structures, which are yet untried, pharmacologically.

And there is the essence of why this entire process is ineffective. Prediction is the heart of this procedure, and prediction is never brought to bear. Let us take a new structure that is not in the original collection of structures, and let us make a prediction as to its, let us say, psychedelic potency. But no one ever tries it out for any of a number of reasons. Maybe the new compound is never synthesized. Or maybe it is synthesized, but never evaluated pharmacologically. The synthesist does not care, or is uninterested, or is restrained by the legal complications that might ensue. Or he does explore it, but chooses not to publish. Almost never is a prediction tested. What is more likely to happen is that a new input of biological activity and structure variation is uncovered (for which there is no published prediction) and this data is tossed into the mill, and a new set of "more valid" coefficients is calculated, and the SAR becomes touted as a more accurate predictor. But, always remember that without prediction and challenge, there is no inventive value from the SAR game. It simply organizes what is known, but creates nothing new.

This is a role that I would have loved to see α,N,O-TMS play. At the time of its first synthesis its biological activity was, by definition, completely unknown. Let's cast its shadow up against the structures that were known, and with known activity. What would you predict? The most logical archetype to use as a starting point is the primary amine homologue, α,O-DMS. This is an extremely potent, quite long-lived tryptamine that still ranks up there as the most potent, or nearly so, of all the simple substituted tryptamines. It is orally active. It lasts for many hours. It is completely wild as to visual distortions and illusions. It consistently leads to dramatic, perhaps frightening, but certainly memorable dreams. Three or four milligrams are unmistakably adequate. I would have loved to have had an SAR jock predict what changes would come from the simple addition of an N-methyl group. No one out there predicted this for me, and I have now completely abandoned the art of prediction, at least via the SAR technique. My motto is, make 'em and taste 'em.

To base structures that are stimulants (amphetamine, for example) an added N-methyl group enhances potency and richness. With MDA, for example, one gets MDMA, not more potent, but of an entirely different form of psychological magic. However, with all the other explored primary amine phenethylamine psychedelics, the potency and the quality of action are effectively lost. With tryptamines, however, the N-methyl groups appear to be needed for full, robust activity. Here, the loss of an N-methyl group might well detract from full potency, and the final unmethylated product (DMT becoming simply tryptamine) will be relatively weak and uninteresting. If α,N,O-TMS had been active at one milligram, then the MDMA explanation is obviously correct. If α,N,O-TMS had been active only at a meager level of twenty milligrams, then the DMT explanation would appear to be correct. It is much less active. It is not spectacular. All you SAR scientists, take this new data, toss it into the maws of computer calculation, and come out with better coefficients.

With this, now, as a challenge, predict for me the potency of α,N,N,O-tetramethylserotonin. Here is a compound that has not, to my knowledge, been synthesized. It carries the second N-methyl group (closer to DMT at the nitrogen atom, and probably more potent) and yet a structural kiss of death (as to potency) in the MDA/MDMA world. Will it be up? Will it be down? I am afraid that the "make 'em and taste 'em" procedure is the only one that I can trust.

Good luck.

# APPENDIX A:   BILL OF RIGHTS

## AMENDMENTS TO THE CONSTITUTION OF THE
## UNITED STATES OF AMERICA

### AMENDMENT I  RELIGIOUS AND POLITICAL FREEDOM

**86. Congress Must not Interfere with Freedom of Religion, Speech or Press.** Congress shall make no law respecting an establishment of religion, or prohibiting the free exercise thereof; or abridging the freedom of speech, or of the press; or the right of the people peaceably to assemble, and to petition the Government for a redress of grievances.

### AMENDMENT II  RIGHT TO BEAR ARMS

**87. Congress Must Not Deny the States a Militia.** A well regulated Militia, being necessary to the security of a free State, the right of the people to keep and bear Arms, shall not be infringed.

### AMENDMENT III  QUARTERING SOLDIERS

**88. Congress Must not Quarter Soldiers on the People.** No Soldier shall, in time of peace be quartered in any house, without the consent of the Owner, nor in time of war, but in the manner to be prescribed by law.

### AMENDMENT IV  SEARCHES AND SEIZURES

**89. Federal Officials Must not Authorize Unreasonable Searches.** The right of the people to be secure in their persons, houses, papers, and effects, against unreasonable searches and seizures, shall not be violated, and no Warrants shall issue, but on probably cause, supported by Oath or affirmation, and particularly describing the place to be searched, and the persons or things to be seized.

### AMENDMENT V  RIGHTS IN CRIMINAL PROSECUTION

**90. Federal Courts Must not Violate Certain Rights of the People.** No person shall be held to answer for a capital, or otherwise infamous crime, unless on a presentment or indictment of a Grand Jury, except in cases arising in the land or naval forces, or in the Militia, when in actual service in time of War or public danger; nor shall any person be subject for the same offence to be twice put in jeopardy of life or limb; nor shall be compelled in any criminal case to be a witness against himself, nor be deprived of life, liberty, or property, without due process of law, nor shall private property be taken for public use, without just compensation.

## AMENDMENT VI  RIGHTS IN CRIMINAL PROSECUTION

**91.  Federal Courts Must Guarantee Certain Rights to the Accused.**  In all criminal prosecutions, the accused shall enjoy the right to a speedy and public trial, by an impartial jury of the State and district wherein the crime shall have been committed, which district shall have been previously ascertained by law, and to be informed of the nature and cause of the accusation; to be confronted with the witnesses against him; to have compulsory process for obtaining witnesses in his favor, and to have the Assistance of Counsel for his defence.

## AMENDMENT VII  RIGHT TO TRIAL BY JURY

**92.  Federal Courts Must Guarantee Jury Trial in Civil Suits.**  In Suits at common law, where the value in controversy shall exceed twenty dollars, the right of trial by jury shall be preserved, and no fact tried by a jury, shall be otherwise reexamined in any Court of the United States, than according to the rules of the common law.

## AMENDMENT VIII  EXCESSIVE BAIL, FINES AND PUNISHMENT

**93.  Federal Courts Must Avoid Excesses.**  Excessive bail shall not be required, nor excessive fines imposed, nor cruel and unusual punishments inflicted.

## AMENDMENT IX  UNENUMERATED RIGHTS OF THE PEOPLE

**94.  The Federal Government Exercises no Power over the Unenumerated Rights of the People.**  The enumeration in the Constitution, of certain rights, shall not be construed to deny or disparage others retained by the people.

## AMENDMENT X  POWERS RESERVED TO STATES OR PEOPLE

**95.  All Undelegated Powers Remain with the States or the People.**  The powers not delegated to the United States by the Constitution, nor prohibited by it to the States, are reserved to the States respectively, or to the people.

# APPENDIX B: CURRENT DRUG LAW

I was asked by a friend the other day if I could read Tolstoi's War and Peace in a week. I shuddered as I recalled the massiveness of that book, but said that, yes, I probably could. He smiled and said, "If you were to read the current law of the land, the body of statutes and regulations that are presently in effect, at the same rate, it would take you 25,000 years."

The drug component is but a small chunk of this, but it is still one of the most complex and self-serving bodies of legal aggression that exists anywhere in the world. I would like to give a brief history of how we got to where we are, and then a brief examination of our situation today.

Look at where Mexico is presently in its attitude to drugs. You buy what you want at a pharmacy (at your doctor's suggestion) and most drugs are used as needed. There is almost no drug abuse problem, and the only legal complications have resulted from their relationship with the United States. This is just where the United States was a hundred years ago. There was no Federal drug law, although some States did have restrictions of various sorts, usually anti-opium smoking laws that reflected an anti-Chinese racist mood. Opium was openly dispensed to patients, and the patent medicine world was alive with Pectorals and Soothing Syrups. But there was only modest abuse, and no criminal aspect to it all. Opium was domestically grown, or legally imported. The non-medical use of drugs was, although legal, deemed to be improper, and it was rather well contained by societal pressures. There was a broad recognition of the addictive nature of the most widely used drug, opium, but it was felt not to present any threat to our society. The following is a brief chronology (with commentary) of the changes seen over the last hundred years.

1906: Passage of the Pure Food and Drug Act was an effort to address opium use through truth in labelling. This direction produced the FDA (Food and Drug Administration) whose objectives evolved from finding out what is there, to how much is there, to its purity, to its efficaciousness. The FDA world and the narcotics world did not reconnect for sixty years, until the BDAC was created, as mentioned below.

1914: Passage of the Harrison Narcotics Act. This was an anti-opium and anti-cocaine law that effectively emasculated the 1906 food and drug law, in that since opium was now made illegal, the value of labelling how-much and how-pure was lost. Three new definitions became evident. First, this Act was a racist response to the Chinese social patterns of use. Secondly, this was a fiscal measure (reporting to the Department of the Treasury) that made it a crime to not have a tax-stamp for specific drugs, and this was addressed by treasury agents rather than by police. A third change was in the legal viewing of addiction. The physicians had said that it was a medical problem. The treasury men said it was a criminal matter. The medical community lost the battle.

1922: Cocaine was officially declared as narcotic (it was closely associated with the black community) and its importation was restricted as severely as was opium. Again a tax matter, not a criminal matter and, again, there were clear racial overtones.

1937: Passage of the Marijuana Tax Act, responding to the image of marijuana as a social problem leading to crime and insanity. The head of the newly created BN (Bureau of Narcotics), Henry Anslinger, invoked yet another racial connection, the immigrants from Mexico, as a negative factor. Again, all of this was a tax matter, a concern of the Treasury Department. The pattern of legal intensification continued with the Opium Poppy control act of 1942, a war-time effort to separate us from overseas sources. The Narcotics Act of 1946 had its emphasis on controlling the synthesis of narcotic drugs. In 1951 the Harrison Act was amended to demand prison sentences for offenders, and the Narcotics Control Act of 1956 made these sentences mandatory through the elimination of probation and parole. Amphetamines were a new focus at this time, with the Narcotics Manufacturing Act (1960) and the RICO laws (1962) defining racketeering and organized crime as part of the problem.

1965: The Drug Abuse Control Amendments brought the FDA back into the picture by the making them a law enforcement agency (the Bureau of Drug Abuse Control, BDAC). They were to go after dangerous drugs (largely the psychedelics of the Summer of Love in San Francisco) rather than the famous narcotic drugs (heroin, cocaine and marijuana).

1968: The rivalry between the BDAC group (FDA, under Health, Education and Welfare, dangerous drugs) and the BN group (under the Department of Treasury, narcotics) was resolved with the formation of the BNDD (Bureau of Narcotics and Dangerous Drugs) under the Department of Justice.

1970: Passage of the Controlled Substances Act (The Comprehensive Drug Abuse Prevention and Control Act) effectively ended the Harrison Act and laid the groundwork for the legal situation we have today.

1973: The Drug Enforcement Administration (DEA) was created, effectively merging a host of independant but scattered agencies (ODALE, the Office of Drug Abuse Law Enforcement, ONNI, the Office of National Narcotics Intelligence, and of course the BNDD which was a merger of the BDAC and the BN). This congealed everything into the ultimate law-enforcement monolith that we currently enjoy. All subsequent legislation has been dedicated to the confirmation and empowerment of this law enforcement group. Below are a few of the many laws that have helped achieve this goal.

1978: Passage of the Psychotropic Substances Act (an amendment to the 1970 law above) which contained a section called "Forfeiture of Proceeds of Illegal Drug Transactions." This is the original justification for the now common procedure of seizing personal property and assets.

1981: Passage of the "Department of Defense Authorization Act" revised the Posse Comitatus statute which had prohibited any military involvement (except in the case of a National Emergency) in civil law enforcement.

1984: Passage of the Comprehensive Crime Control Act which allowed the DEA to place new "designer drugs" temporarily into Schedule I without the need of following the usual procedures. It also provided the first equations that tied the penalties for drug-related crimes to the quantity of the drug involved.

1986: Passage of the Anti-Drug Abuse Act which contained a subtitle E, Controlled Substance Analogue Enforcement Act of 1986. The law, quoted in full in the extensions and commentary part of the α-ET entry (page 437), allows the prosecution to charge and bring to trial anyone who is involved with any chemical at all, if that chemical can be defined (structure, action, or intended action) as a controlled substance analogue. It does not become a Scheduled drug; it is merely treated as if it were one. That same year, President Reagan signed a National Security Decision Directive which stated that drug trafficking constitutes a threat to the national security of the United States.

1988: The Anti-Drug Abuse Act of 1988 brought precursors and essential chemicals (not drugs themselves but things associated with drug synthesis) under legal recognition. Two statements of Congressional policy were entered into this law, both rather interesting. "The Congress finds that legalization of illegal drugs, on the Federal or State level, is an unconscionable surrender in a war in which, for the future of our country and the lives of our children, there can be no substitute for total victory." And, "It is the declared policy of the United States Government to create a Drug-Free America by 1995." In that Act, as in almost every one following, there has been a consistent increase in the powers given the authorities, and the penalties imposed upon the offenders.

The following is the current status of the scheduled hallucinogens under Federal law, including the DEA Controlled Substance Code Number. There is also a listing of the non-drug chemicals that command the DEA's interests. These latter chemicals, when found side by side even when no drug is found, can be used as evidence supporting the charge of the *intent* to violate the law. The term "list I chemical" was previously called "listed precursor chemical," and the term "list II chemical" was "listed essential chemicals." The text contains the exact words used by the legislatively chosen authorities. When there is an out-and-out chemical misspelling, the intended version follows in parenthesis, underlined. The commas, semi-colons and unexpected spaces (or lack of them) are as in the original.

(from the Code of Federal Regulations 1997)

§ 1308.11
    Schedule I
        (d) *Hallucinogenic substances.* Unless specifically excepted or unless listed in another schedule, any material, compound, mixture, or preparation, which contains any quantity of the following hallucinogenic substances, or which contains any of its salts, isomers, and salts of isomers whenever the existance of such salts, isomers, and salts of isomers is possible within the specific chemical designation (for the purposes of this paragraph only, the term "isomer" includes the optical, position and geometric isomers):

(1) Alpha-ethyltryptamine 7249 Some trade or other names: Monase; α-ethyl-1H-indole-3-ethanamine; 3-(2-aminobutyl)indole; α-ET; and AET

(2) 4-bromo-2,5-dimethoxy-amphetamine 7391 Some trade or other names: 4-bromo-2,5-dimethoxy-α-methylphenethylamine; 4-bromo-2,5-DMA

(3) 4-bromo-2,5-dimethoxyphenethylamine 7392 Some trade or other names: 2-(4-bromo-2,5-dimethoxyphenyl)-1-aminoethane; alpha-desmethyl DOB; 2C-B, Nexus

(4) 2,5-dimethoxyamphetamine 7396 Some trade or other names: 2,5-dimethoxy-α-methylphenethylamine; 2,5-DMA

(5) 2,5-dimethoxy-4-ethylamphet-amine 7399 Some trade or other names: DOET

(6) 4-methoxyamphetamine 7411 Some trade or other names: 4-methoxy-α-methylphenethylamine; paramethoxyamphetamine, PMA

(7) 5-methoxy-3,4-methylenedioxy-amphetamine 7401

(8) 4-methyl-2,5-dimethoxy-amphetamine 7395 Some trade or other names: 4-methyl-2,5-dimethoxy-α-methylphenethylamine; "DOM"; and "STP"

(9) 3,4-methylenedioxy amphetamine 7400

(10) 3,4-methylenedioxymethamphetamine (MDMA) 7405

(11) 3,4-methylenedioxy-N-ethylamphetamine (also known as N-ethyl-alpha-methyl-3,4(methylenedioxy)phenethylamine, N-ethyl MDA, MDE, MDEA 7404

(12) N-hydroxy-3,4-methylenedioxyamphetamine (also known as N-hydroxy-

alpha-methyl-3,4(methylenedioxy)phenethylamine, and N-hydroxy MDA 7402

(13) 3,4,5-trimethoxy amphetamine 7390

(14) Bufotenine 7433 Some trade and other names: 3-($\beta$-Dimethylaminoethyl)-5-hydroxyindole; 3-(2-dimethylaminoethyl)-5-indolol; N,N-dimethylserotonin; 5-hydroxy-N,N-dimethyltryptamine; mappine

(15) Diethyltryptamine 7434 Some trade and other names: N,N-Diethyltryptamine; DET

(16) Dimethyltryptamine 7435 Some trade or other names: DMT

(17) Ibogaine 7260 Some trade and other names: 7-ethyl-6,6$\beta$,7,8,9,10,12,13-octahydro-2-methoxy-6,9-methano-5H-pyrido [1',2':1,2] azepino [5,4-b] indole; Tabernanthe iboga

(18) Lysergic acid diethylamide 7315

(19) Marihuana 7360

(20) Mescaline 7381

(21) Parahexyl 7374; Some trade or other names: 3-Hexyl-1-hydroxy-7,8,9,10-tetrahydro-6,6,9-trimethyl-6H-dibenzo[b,d]pyran; Synhexyl.

(22) Peyote 7415 Meaning all parts of the plant presently classified botanically as *Lophophora williamsii Lemaire*, whether growing or not, the seeds thereof, any extract from any part of such plant, and every compound, manufacture, salts, derivative, mixture, or preparation of such plant, its seeds or extracts (Interprets 21 USC 812(c), Schedule I(c) (12))

(23) N-ethyl-3-piperidyl benzilate 7482

(24) N-methyl-3-piperidyl benzilate 7484

(25) Psilocybin 7437

(26) Psilocin 7438

(27) Tetrahydrocannabinols 7370 Synthetic equivalents of these substances contained in the plant, or in the resinous extractives of *Cannabis* sp. and/or synthetic substances, derivatives, and their isomers with similar chemical structure and

pharmacological activity such as the following:

Δ1 cis or trans tetrahydrocannabinol, and their optical isomers

Δ6 cis or trans tetrahydrocannabinol, and their optical isomers

Δ3,4 cis or trans tetrahydrocannabinol, and its optical isomers

(Since nomenclature of these substances is not internationally standardized, compounds of these structures, regardless of numerical designation of atomic positions covered.)

(28) Ethylamine analog of phencyclidine 7455 Some trade or other names: N-ethyl-1-phenylcyclohexylamine, (1-phenylcyclohexyl)ethylamine, N-(1-phenylcyclohexyl)ethylamine, cyclohexamine, PCE

(29) Pyrrolidine analog of phencyclidine 7458 Some trade or other names: 1-(1-phenylcyclohexl)-pyrrolidine, PCPy, PHP

(30) Thiophene analog of phencyclidine 7470 Some trade or other names: 1-[1-(2-thienyl)-cyclohexyl]-piperidine, 2-theinyl analog of phencyclidine, TCPC, TCP

(31) 1-[1-(2-thienyl)cyclohexyl]pyrrolidine 7473 Some other names: TCPy

§ 1308.12

Schedule II

(f) *Hallucinogenic substances.*

(1) Dronabinol (synthetic) in sesame oil and encapsulated in a soft gelatin capsule in a U.S. Food and Drug Administration approved drug product 7369 [Some other names for dronabinol: (6a*R-trans*)-6a,7,8,10a-tetrahydro-6,6,9-trimethyl-3-pentyl-6*H*-dibenzo[*b,d*]pyran-1-ol, or (-)-delta-9-(trans)-tetrahydrocannabinol]

(2) Nabilone 7379 [Another name for nabilone: (±)-*trans*-3-(1,1-dimethylheptyl)-6,6a,7,8,10,10a-hexahydro-1-hydroxy-6,6-dimethyl-9H-dibenzo[b,d]pyran-9-one]

(g) *Immediate precursors.* Unless specifically excepted or unless listed in another schedule, any material, compound, mixture, or preparation which contains any quantity of the following substances:

(1) Immediate precursor to amphetamine and methamphetamine:

(i) Phenylacetone 8501 Some trade or other names: Phenyl-2-propanone; P2P; benzyl methyl ketone; methyl benzyl ketone

(2) Immediate precursor to phencyclidine (PCP):

(i) 1-phenylcyclohexylamine 7460

(ii) 1-piperidinocyclohexanecarbonitrile (PCC) 8603

§ 1308.13
    Schedule III
        (c) *Depressants*. Unless specifically excepted or unless listed in another schedule, and material, compound, mixture, or preparation which contains any quantity of the following substances having a depressant effect on the central nervous system:

(6)  Lysergic acid  7300
(7)  Lysergic acid amide  7310

---

From the Federal Register 62:13938 1997, and from the U.S. Code Title 21 Food and Drugs § 802.33, § 802.34 and § 802.35:

(33)  The term "listed chemical" means any list I or any list II chemical.

(34)  The term "list I chemical" means a chemical specified by regulation of the Attorney General as a chemical that is used in manufacturing a controlled substance in violation of this subchapter and is important to the manufacture of the controlled substances, and such term includes (until otherwise specified by regulation of the Attorney General, as considered appropriate by the the Attorney General or upon petition to the Attorney General by any person) the following:
        (A)  Anthranilic acid, its esters , and its salts.
        (B)  Benzyl cyanide.
        (C)  Ephedrine, its salts, optical isomers, and salts of optical isomers.
        (D)  Ergonovine and its salts.
        (E)  Ergotamine and its salts.
        (F)  N-Acetylanthranilic acid, its esters and its salts.
        (G)  Norpseudoephedrine, its salts, optical isomers, and salts of optical isomers.
        (H)  Phenylacetic acid, its esters, and its salts.
        (I)  Phenylpropanolamine, its salts, optical isomers, and salts of optical isomers.
        (J)  Piperidine and its salts.
        (K)  Pseudoephedrine, its salts, optical isomers, and salts of optical isomers.
        (L)  3,4-Methylenedioxyphenyl-2-propanone.
        (M)  Methylamine.
        (N)  Ethylamine.
        (O)  Propionic anhydride.

(P)  Insosafrole. (Isosafrole*)

(Q)  Safrole.

(R)  Piperonal.

(S)  N-Methylepherdrine. (N-Methylephedrine*)

(T)  N-methylpseudoephedrine.

(U)  Hydriotic acid. (Hydriodic acid*)

(V)  Benzaldehyde.

(W)  Nitroethane.

(X)  Any salt, optical isomer, or salt of an optical isomer of the chemicals listed above in subparagraphs (M) through (U) of this paragraph.

(35)  The term "list II chemical" means a chemical (other than a list I chemical) specified by regulation of the Attorney General as a chemical that is used in manufacturing a controlled substance in violation of this subchapter, and such term includes (until otherwise specified by regulation of the Attorney General, as considered appropriate by the Attorney General or upon petition to the Attorney General by any person) the following chemicals:

(A)  Acetic anhydride.

(B)  Acetone.

(C)  Benzyl chloride.

(D)  Ethyl ether.

(E)  Repealed. Pub. L. 101-647, title XXIII, Sec. 2301(B), Nov. 29, 1990, 104 Stat. 4858. (this used to be hydroiodic acid, which is now a list I chemical)

(F)  Potassium permanganate.

(G)  2-Butanone. (*)

(H)  Toluene.

(I)   Iodine. (**)

(J)  Hydrochloric gas. (**)

* The three chemical terms were corrected in Public Law 104-237 (Oct. 3, 1996). In this law there was added a synonym for 2-Butanone, Methyl Ethyl Ketone.

** In Public Law 104-237 (Oct. 3, 1996) these two chemicals were added to the list II chemicals. (Presumably Hydrochloric gas should be Hydrogen chloride gas).

# APPENDIX C:  GLOSSARY

This is a dictionary of terms that have commonly been used in and about the area of psychedelic drug experimentation. It was an appendix in *PIHKAL* and several people expressed the hope that it might be included in this book. Many of these are common words, but in immediate application to this particular area of inquiry, they can carry different meanings than usual. These are our definitions of terms we have used in both books.

Ambrose Bierce composed a Devil's Dictionary over the course of 25 years, at the turn of the last century. His definition of a dictionary is most apt:

> DICTIONARY, n. A malevolent literary device for cramping the growth of a language and making it hard and inelastic. This dictionary, however, is a most useful work.

Jonathan Ott turned the coin over with his neologistic *Angels' Dictionary* which appeared in 1995, and which precipitates the reader into his entheogenic world. Our offering is more modest that these others, but we hope that it proves useful. It is an effort to give simple descriptions of what can be complex concepts and should serve to clarify what we have written.

---

ACUTE, adj. A single exposure to a drug.

AFTERGLOW, n. A state of total peace and tranquility that can follow a psychedelic experience. There is a well-known term, POT, or post-orgasmic tranquility, that implies a drifting, a de-stressed period of inattention and reflection, a calmness and placidity; this can also be a major part of the drop-off and recovery period following the use of a psychedelic. It is the smile on the face of the Buddha.

ALERT, n. The first clue that a drug will show activity. Each researcher, with experience, comes to recognize his own personal alert. It may be a tinge of lightheadedness, a chill, or a brief raising of the hair on his neck, and simply serves as a reminder that he took something half an hour (or a couple of hours) ago. Sometimes an alert can follow very soon after the taking of the drug, without any further effects becoming apparent until some time later. Each person's alert tends to be experienced consistently, regardless of the nature of the drug being researched.

ANOREXIC, adj. Or anorectic, is related to anorexia, meaning loss of appetite. Some of the psychedelic drugs, especially those with a considerable stimulant component, can quite effectively wipe out all desire to eat (temporarily). Unfortunately (for most of us), there are others, especially those with a strong sensory component, which achieve quite the opposite effect.

ASC   Altered state of consciousness.

ASSAYING, *see* RUNNING UP.

AWARENESS, *see* ALERT.

BASELINE, n. The normal psychological and physical state of a person prior to the start of an experiment which, once regained, marks the end of that experiment.

BODY LOAD, n. Any sense of unease in the physical body, such as nausea, aching, heaviness, or the feeling of being "wired," or over-stimulated. For some people, diarrhea is considered a form of body load, while for others it is an expected part of most psychedelic experiments, and is regarded as a welcome cleaning out of the system. One elderly and very experienced psychologist considered nausea and vomiting to be a positive event; he welcomed it as a sign that the experimental drug was active, and for him, it meant the beginning of his experience. His attitude, however, was very much the exception and we haven't heard of anyone else doing this research who regards nausea quite that fondly.

CENTRAL NERVOUS SYSTEM (CNS), n. The part of the nervous system that involves the brain, the brain stem, and the spinal column. It is to this system that all senses connect (the afferent pathways) and it is from this system that all motor commands emanate (the efferent pathways).

CHRONIC, adj. Repeated exposure to a drug.

CLEAN, adj. To be in that state of body which results from having declined the use of any psychoactive drug for a period of time. For some people, that might well be months, or even years, but for those who are continuously experimenting with new materials, and who are primarily worried about the masking of effects due to tolerance or refractoriness, it is more likely to mean a period of four or five days.

CNS, *see* CENTRAL NERVOUS SYSTEM

CONSCIOUS, adj. Used most commonly in phrases such as "the conscious mind," or "being conscious of." It is the term applied to that part of the human psyche which is aware of its surroundings, and is capable of being aware of its own existence and observing its own functioning. It has been speculated that the conscious mind also serves as a filter, to prevent the activities of the unconscious psyche from flooding the field of waking awareness. In sleep, the conscious, self-aware mind is usually, for the most part, at rest, and the unconscious part of the psyche becomes activated.

CONTACT HIGH, n. A common occurence in a group experiment with a psychedelic drug is that a drug-free observer becomes aware that he is experiencing some effects of the material being used by the others. The altered state has become contagious. Animals in the household are especially prone to this kind of unintentional participation, usually appearing to enjoy it immensely. There is no known scientific explanation for this phenomenon.

CROSS-TOLERANCE, n. The decrease or loss of response to a drug due to recent (or prolonged) exposure to a different drug that displays some pharmacological similarities. *see also* TOLERANCE.

DARTING, n. A sudden and unexpected neurological firing that produces a momentary contraction of the musculature. It may occasionally occur when falling asleep while still at a plus two level of effect. It also occurs under normal conditions involving no drug at all.

DECLINE, n. or v. The period that follows the plateau, during which there is a loss of the drug's effects and an eventual recovery of one's baseline state. From person to person, this is the most variable in length of the time periods in a drug experiment. It has also been called recovering, tapering off, or dropping off.

DEVELOPING, v. The period of change from the onset of effects to the achievement of the plateau. It is also called the transition. The temporal sequence terminology is: taking the drug, alerting, developing, plateauing, declining, and reestablishment of (or being at) baseline.

DROPPING, *see* TAKING, *also see* DECLINING.

DRUG-DRUG INTERACTIONS *see* PIGGYBACKING, PRIMER *and* SYNER-GISM.

DRUG-FREE, *see* CLEAN.

ENERGY TREMOR, n. A sensation of heightened responsiveness and sensitivity which may be actually experienced as a fine body tremor with visible shaking, or simply felt as excitement.

EUPHORIA, n. "Eu-" is a prefix that means "normal." Euphoria is from the Greek, euphoria, literally a "bearing well," from eu, meaning well, and pherein, to bear. The original meaning is a normal state of feeling, as opposed to dysphoria, which means an abnormal state of feeling. In the field of medicine, to give another example, the term euthyroid means a normal, healthy state of the thyroid gland, as opposed to dysthyroid, which indicates an abnormal condition of that gland (usually either hyper- or hypothyroid).

The fact that the word euphoria has come to mean a state of feeling better — or much, much better — than usual, should give us pause. The implication is that our customary state is one of dysphoria, and that what has come to be considered the proper and normal way to feel in our everyday life is, in actuality, a state of depression.

This term must not be confused with U-4-E-uh, a name given to the drug 4-methylaminorex.

EXPERIENCED TRAVELER A person who can remember to feed the cats while under the influence of a psychedic drug.

FANTASY, n. The eyes-closed construction of an interior world which can become believable to the point where the subject confuses it with objective reality, until and unless he opens his eyes. At high dosage levels of a psychedelic drug, some subjects may forget to open their eyes occasionally, and may find themselves totally captured by and immersed in the fantasy landscape and interactions, as happens in normal dreaming.

FLASH-BACK, n. The rare but not unknown recapitulation of a psychedelic experience at a time when there is no drug present. A reasonable explanation is that there had been, during a past psychedelic experience, some unusual stimulus which had become associated with it, and that, at some subsequent time, a re-experiencing of that unusual stimulus could reprecipitate the psychedelic state. The main reason that the average man views this phenomenon as something negative, is that the average man has been taught to view the psychedelic state as something negative.

FUGUE STATE, n.  A transient disorientation that separates the cognitive part of oneself from the sensory part. There is a loss of understanding of the symbolic interpretations of words and things, with only the literal and tangible meanings left for personal use. This is our definition of the word, not that of the medical profession.

GRAM, n.  The basic unit of weight on the metric scale, a system used for weights and distances and volumes in all countries other than the United States and, I believe, Brunei. The common subdivisions of the gram is into a thousand parts called milligrams, or a million parts called micrograms.  Imagine that you are sitting down to eat a couple of eggs over easy. You take the salt shaker, and give three or four light shakes of salt over the surface of your breakfast. That is about a fourth of a gram of salt, or 250 milligrams. This is equivalent to the weight of a typical dose of mescaline.  And in that 250 milligrams of salt there are maybe 5,000 grains, or individual crystals. Each grain weighs maybe 50 micrograms, which is equivalent to the weight of a typical dose of LSD.

HALLUCINATION, n.  An extremely rare phenomenon, in which a completely convincing reality surrounds a person, with his eyes open, a reality that he alone can experience and interact with.  The inducement of hallucinations is a property that is commonly attributed to psychedelic drugs, but in reality is virtually non-existent in the use of such materials.  In almost all psychedelic experiences undergone by normal, healthy people, there is an awareness of real surroundings. Visual distortions are common, but they are not confused with objective reality by the subject; they are known to be visual distortions and appreciated as such. The delusional anesthetic drugs, such as scopolamine and ketamine, on the other hand, can and do produce true hallucinations.

HALLUCINOGENS, n.  A misleading and inaccurate synonym for psychedelic drugs.

HAND IN THE AIR  In any psychedelic experience involving two or more people, there can be a shifting of one's reality reference point and a concomitant potential for mental game-playing.  In our research group, a phrase that is unquestioned as being a prelude to a not-game comment is, "Hand in the air." It means that whatever follows is a serious, non-stoned, non-mind-fuck statement. "I smell smoke" could be the entry to an editorial on cigarette smoking or a remark on some aspect of politics. But, "Hand in the air; I smell smoke," is intended to cut right through any fantasy or game and must be taken seriously. It is accompanied by an actual raising of the hand. This particular agreement, or rule, is never violated.

HARDHEAD, n. There is an occasional person who requires 200 milligrams of MDMA, or 400 micrograms of LSD, just to get some beginnings of effect. Whatever the drug might be, he will need twice or five times the dosage required by most other people. This may be due to psychological barriers that must be overcome, or it may be due to the fact that he was born with a nervous system and physical chemistry which is unusually insensitive to the effects of drugs. The term hardhead implies a thick, tough skull, of course, and is often used by such subjects to describe themselves, always with a certain amount of pride.

HITCHHIKING, v. Sometimes an innocent, drug-free person will find himself strangely disturbed or uncomfortable in the presence of an experimental subject who is, unknown to him, experiencing the effects of a psychedelic drug; for instance in the checkout line at the supermarket. This unconscious awareness (or contact high) can produce a feeling of irritation, or even overt hostility, in the inadvertent hitchhiker, and his or her distress is all the worse for having no apparent or understandable cause. The responsible psychedelic researcher does not go out in public when under the influence, or if he must do so, he takes care not to risk such intrusion on the unconscious psyches of strangers.

IDIOT, n. A person of either sex who drives a car, motorcycle, or even a bicycle, for that matter, on a public road while under the influence of a psychedelic drug. Most researchers in this area have done it at least once, sometimes in an emergency, but only in a life-and-death situation is it excusable.

IMAGERY, n. Figures, lines and shapes of all kinds, including fine filigree and intricate patterns, superimposed on the dark visual field behind closed eyes. Music can serve as a template for the construction of these images. There is no confusion of realities as can happen with fantasy, but instead, a continuing complexity and richness of design. Such images disappear upon the opening of the eyes. To be precise, they should be referred to as eyes-closed imagery. Patterns and movements seen with the eyes open are called visual changes or visual images.

INFLATION, n. An exhilarating sense of self-importance, self-validation and fearless power. It is essential that any researcher seeking insight into the workings of the human mind experience this radiant state at least once, in order to learn its nature and, by contrast, the nature of a normal, well- balanced state of integration and self-validation. It is also important to his/her understanding of psychological inflation in emotionally disturbed people and in the rulers of certain nations.

INGESTION, *see* TAKING

INTOXICATION, n. This word has the same general meaning in the psychedelic area as it has among drinkers of alcohol and people in love.

KETAMINE STATE, n. Used to indicate a state of consciousness alteration which involves a large degree of dissociation from the body. Users of ketamine can become adept at remaining integrated with their physical world by carefully monitoring their dosage levels and keeping them low, but most ketamine use tends to result in separation from the body and its concerns. We are strongly prejudiced against psychedelic drugs which cause such mind-body separation, as we are against any drug which causes separation from feelings and emotions. However, we acknowledge that the ketamine state can be highly instructive for researchers trying to understand the functions of the human mind.

LAUNCHING, *see* TAKING

MACHO, adj. This describes a person of either sex who pushes his limits too much in experimentation with psychedelics. He always strives to take a higher and yet higher dosage, to prove that he can weather the storm. Such a person should be encouraged to do some intensive insight work into his compulsion, which is essentially self-destructive.

MINUS, n. On the quantitative potency scale ( -, ±, +, ++, +++), there were no effects observed.

MYDRIASIS, n. Enlargement of the pupil of the eye.

NAIVE, adj. An adjective used to describe a person who has had no personal experience with any psychedelic drug. More properly, the term used should be "drug-naive."

NIBBLING, v. This is a jargon term for running up, in small increments, the human evaluations of a new compound. (See under "running up")

NOISE, n. A term used in describing the inner busyness of the mind, the excessive or annoying mental input, produced by certain psychedelic drugs, or characteristic of the initial — transition — stages of some of these drugs. It can also result simply from too high a dosage level.

OFF BASELINE, *see* ALERT

PARESTHESIA, n.  A peripheral response to a drug which can be felt as tingling, pins-and-needles, or hair standing on end; it might take the form of a chill (even if the air is warm), or a feeling that one's skin is crawling.

PIGGYBACKING, v.  A study of the interaction of two different drugs, the second being administered in place of a supplement to the first.  Any deviation from the effects that would have followed a supplement of the original drug will give additional information as to the nature of the second drug.

PLATEAU, n. or v.  The period of time spent at the level of maximum effect of whatever drug has been ingested, at the particular dosage given.  It is preceded by the transition and development, and is followed by the decline.  As a verb, "to plateau" means to reach that level of drug effect.

PLUS/MINUS, n. ($\pm$)  The level of effectiveness of a drug that indicates a threshold action.  If a higher dosage produces a greater response, then the plus/minus ($\pm$) was valid.  If a higher dosage produces nothing, then this was a false positive.

PLUS ONE, n. (+)  The drug is quite certainly active.  The chronology can be determined with some accuracy, but the nature of the drug's effects are not yet apparent.

PLUS TWO, n. (++)  Both the chronology and the nature of the action of a drug are unmistakably apparent.  But you still have some choice as to whether you will accept the adventure, or rather just continue with your ordinary day's plans (if you are an experienced researcher, that is).  The effects can be allowed a predominent role, or they may be repressed and made secondary to other chosen activities.

PLUS THREE, n. (+++)  Not only are the chronology and the nature of a drug's action quite clear, but ignoring its action is no longer an option.  The subject is totally engaged in the experience, for better or worse.

PLUS FOUR, n. (++++)  A rare and precious transcendental state, which has been called a "peak experience," a "religious experience," "divine transformation," a "state of Samadhi" and many other names in other cultures.  It is not connected to the +1, +2 and +3 of the measuring of a drug's intensity.  It is a state of bliss, a *participation mystique*, a connectedness with both the interior and exterior universes, which has come about after the ingestion of a psychedelic drug, but which is not necessarily repeatable with a subsequent ingestion of that same drug. If a drug (or technique or process) were ever to be discovered which would consistently produce a plus four experience in all human beings, it is conceivable that it would signal the ultimate evolution, and perhaps the end of, the human experiment.

POTENTIATION, n. The influence of an inactive drug on the effects realized from an active drug.

PRIMER, n. A word used in the study of the interaction of two different drugs, one of them without activity. The inactive, "primer," drug is administered and, while it is still in the system, the second, "primed," drug is given. Any activity observed which is different from that expected from the primer drug alone will be a measure of potentiation. The effect may be one of enhanced action; it may be that of decreased action; it may be a change in either quality or duration of activity.

PRIMING, see PRIMER

PRODRUG, n. A chemical that is intrinsically without activity at a receptor site, but which is converted (activated) by the metabolic processes of the body.

PSYCHE, n. A term used to encompass the non-physical human mind, conscious and unconscious, including feelings and emotions. The word "psyche" has come into modern use as substitute for the more ancient, but scientifically unapproachable, concept of soul.

PSYCHEDELIC, n. or adj. As an adjective, meaning pertaining to a change in the normal state of consciousness, usually with some accompanying changes in the acuity of the senses. Also, "mind-manifesting." As a noun, a drug that can allow such changes to occur. The word was coined by Doctor Humphrey Osmond in the 1950's.

PSYCHOTOMIMETIC, n. or adj. A name given to the psychedelic drugs to emphasize some supposed similarities between certain of their effects and the psychotic state. The word unites the prefix *psychoto-* (referring to psychosis) with the suffix *-mimetic* (meaning imitation). It was one of the earliest terms used for these drugs, and one which implied medical approval of the use of such drugs, at least as research tools.

RECOVERY, *see* DECLINE

REFRACTORY, adj. The state of showing a reduced response to the action of a drug. This may be due to tolerance resulting from recent exposure, the action of some inhibitor, or a condition of health or expectation that interferes with the expected action.

RUNNING UP, v. The process of searching for activity in a new drug by a strategy of taking incrementally larger and larger doses, at time intervals which are calculated to minimize the development of tolerance. A usual pattern is an increase of either 60% or 100% of the previous dosage, following a clean period of several days, until activity is detected. There are many popular terms for this titration process, such as nibbling, assaying, or tasting.

SAMADHI, n. A word in the terminology of the Yoga which represents a direct union with ultimate reality, allowing the dissolving of the ego and an achievement of a state of bliss. Used by western researchers, the word does not necessarily imply a dissolving of ego, but a transformation of it.

SCRUDGE, n. (Defined in *PIHKAL*, entry #176)

STARTING, *see* TAKING

STONED, adj. This generally means being under the influence of a psychoactive drug. It is a widely used word, and we have employed it in our story as carelessly as most people do. However, in writing a report on the effects of an experimental drug, there is actually an important difference between being "stoned" and being "turned-on," and the researcher should make a distinction between them. A stoning effect is one in which there is awareness of a strongly altered state of consciousness; it may be pleasurable or unpleasant. It is characterized, usually, by a general inability and disinclination to deal with concepts or to employ insight. In other words, one finds it difficult to learn anything of value. On the other hand, being turned on is simply to be aware of a change in one's mind and/or body in the direction of an increased sense of physical and mental energy. Being turned on is usually thought of as positive, whereas there are many researchers who do not enjoy being stoned at all.

STRAIGHT, adj. The state of being at baseline, with no psychedelic drug present in the body,

SUBACUTE, adj. An occasional or short-term exposure to a drug.

SUPPLEMENT, n. or v. The administration of a second dose of an active drug, during the drop-off phase of the activity of an initial dosage. The usual consequence is a prolongation of effect, with a concomitant increase in signs of toxicity.

SYNERGISM, n.  The interaction of two drugs, often administered at the same time, which produces a response that is not simply additive.  The summed responses may be exaggerated (positive synergy), or attenuated (inhibition).

SYNESTHESIA, n.  An activation of two or more senses simultaneously; for instance, sound may be "seen" in the mind as being composed of color and shape, or a color may be "heard" as a musical note or harmony.  There are innumerable examples of this melding together of the senses, and the experience is generally considered one of the most treasured effects of a psychedelic drug.  There are many people who live in a world of synesthesia continuously, without benefit of drug, having been born with this ability.  For the most part, they regard themselves as profoundly blessed.

TAKING, v.  The actual ingestion of a drug.  When there are several persons involved, any of several rituals can be followed; a toasting and clinking of glasses, the recital of an favorite prayer, or a touching of hands and brief silence.  The taking of a drug has also been called "launching," "dropping," "taking off" or, simply, "starting."

TAPERING OFF,  *see* DECLINE

TASTING,  *see* RUNNING UP

THRESHOLD, n.  A dosage of a drug that gives some detectable change from baseline.  A minimum detectable effect of a drug.

TIME-DISTORTION  A mis-perception or distortion concerning the subjective passage of time.  With psychedelic drugs, there is almost always a sense that time is passing more slowly than usual.  This may be recognized at the global level (you mean it's only been an hour since we took this stuff?), at the clock-watching level (I've been watching the second hand and I've found I can really slow it down), or at the afferent level (where, for instance, the radio pitch and the pulse rate might appear to have dropped considerably).

TITRATE, v.  To determine the effective level of a drug by the sequential taking of graded doses, at separated intervals.  *see* RUNNING UP.

TOLERANCE, n.  The decrease or loss of response to a drug, due to recent or prolonged exposure to it.

TOMSO, n. or v. Used as a noun: a sulfur-containing drug, described in detail in *PIHKAL*, entry #173. Used as a verb: to instigate or promote an altered state of consciousness during exposure to an ineffective dosage of a psychedelic drug, by the absorption of a modest amount of alcohol.

TRANSITION, *see* DEVELOPING

TRAVELER, n. A person who explores the effects of psychedelic drugs.

TURNED-ON, *see* STONED

UNCONSCIOUS, n. or adj. As an adjective, this is a simple word, meaning not being conscious. As a noun, it is a most complex word, meaning that part of the psyche which contains the building blocks of each individual identity, not accessible for most people in the everyday waking state. The sources, shapes and origins of these blocks, these components, are — to varying degrees — available to us in sleep, in certain states of mental disturbance, in hypnotic trance, meditation, artistic inspiration, and with the use of certain drugs. Intentional and conscious access to unconscious material can be achieved with the aid of psychedelic drugs, which is one of the values — and risks — of such exploration.

VISUALS, n. Changes in the visual area that are usually among the effects of a psychedelic drug. There may be an enhancement of colors, an exaggeration of light-dark contrast, a sparkling of lights, or a change in the visible texture or quality of an object. Some of the changes may reflect the mydriasis (enlargement of pupils) that is often one of the effects of such a drug. The term "visual effects" is also used to describe the apparent movement of objects in one's surroundings which may be seen with the eyes open, usually at higher than plus-two dosage levels of a psychedelic drug. These are not hallucinations, since they are known by the subject to be apparent and not objectively real, which is not the case in an hallucinatory experience.

WIRED, adj. A condition of intense neurological alertness, which suggests that the response to a given stimulus might be exaggerated by an overly sensitive nervous system.

# APPENDIX D:  ACKNOWLEDGMENTS

Abramson, H.A., *The Use of LSD in Psychotherapy and Alcoholism*. The Bobbs-Merrill Company, Ed., 1967.

Abramson, H.A., Sklarofsky, B., Baron, M.D. and Fremont-Smith, N., Lysergic Acid Diethylamide (LSD-25) Antagonists. II. Developement of Tolerance in Man to LSD-25 by Prior Administration of MLD-41. A.M.A. Arch. Neurol. Psychiat. **79** 201-207 (1958).

Abramson, H.A., Response Index as a Measure of Threshold Activity of Psychotropic Drugs in Man. J. Psychol. **48** 65-78 (1959).

Abramson, H.A., Rolo, A., Sklarofsky, B. and Stache, J., J. Psychol. **49** 151 (1960).

Abu Zarga, M.H., Three New Simple Indole Alkaloids from Limonia acidissima. J. Nat. Prod. **49** 901-904 (1986).

Adachi, J., Ueno, Y., Ogawa, Y., Hishida, S., Yamamoto, K., Ouchi, H. and Tatsuno, Y., Acetaldehyde-Induced Formation of 1-methyl-1,2,3,4-tetrahydro-beta-carboline-3-carboxylic Acid in Rats. Biochem. Pharmacol. **45** 935-41 (1993).

Agurell, S., Holmstedt, B., Lindgren, J.E. and Schultes, R.E., Alkaloids in Certain Species of Virola and other South American Plants of Ethnopharmacologic Interest. Acta Chem Scand **23** 903-916 (1969).

Akkerman, A.M., de Jongh, D.K., and Veddstra, H., Synthetic Oxytocics: I. 3-(1-piperidylmethyl)indoles and Related Compounds. Rec. Trav. Chim. **70** 899-916 (1951).

Aldrich Handbook of Organic Chemicals, Aldrich Chemical Company, 1972.

Al-Shamma, A., Drake, S., Flynn, D.L., Mitscher, L.A., Park, H.Y., Rao, G.S.R., Simpson, A., Swayze, J.K., Veysoglu, T. and Wu, S.T.S., Antimicrobial Agents from Higher Plants. Antimicrobial Agents from *Peganum harmala* Seeds. J. Nat. Products **44** 745-747 (1981).

Andlerová, E., Ernest, I., Hnevosová, V., Jélek, J., Novák, L., Pomykácek, J., Rajsier, M., Sova, J., Vejdelek, Z. and Peotiva, M., Synthetische versuche in der Gruppe Hypotensive Wirksamer Alkaloide VIII. Synthese Einiger Tryptaminederivate in Stelung. Col. Czech. Chem. Commun. **25** 783-796 (1960).

Anonymous. Catalog Handbook of Fine Chemicals, Aldrich Chemical Company, page 610 (1992-1993).

Anonymous. Neurotransmissions, Research Biochemicals International. Volume XI, Number 2, page 9 (April 1995).

Anonymous. The Entheogen Review **4** No. 4, p. 8 (1995).

Arnold, O.H., N,N-Dimethyltryptamin: Einige erste Vergleichsergebnisse. Arzn. Forsch. **25** 972-974 (1975).

Bacon, C.W., Lyons, P.C., Porter, J.K. and Robbins, J.D., Ergot Toxicity from Endophyte-Infected Grasses. A Review. Agromomy J. **78** 106-166 (1986).

Bacq, Z.M., Acta Radiol. **41** 47 (1954).

Bailey, K., Verner, D. and Legault, D., Distinction of Soom Dialkyl Amides if Lysergic and iso-Lysergic Acids from LSD. J. A. O. A. C. **56** 88-99 (1973).

Baldini, R.M., Revision of the Genus *Phalaris* L. (Gramineae). Webbia **49** 265-329 (1995).

Balsam, G. and Voigtlander, H.W., A Psychotropic Alkaloid from *Pilocarpus organensis*. Arch. Pharm. **311** 1016 (1978).

Barker, S.A., personal communication

Barker, S.A., Monti, J.A. and Christian, S.T., Metabloism of the Hallucinogen N,N-Dimethyltryptamine in Rat Brain Homogenates. Biochem. Pharmacol. **29** 1049-1057 (1980).

Barlow, R.B. and Khan, I., Action of Analogs of 5-Hydroxytryptamine on the isolated Rat Uterus and the Rat Fundus Strip Prepns. Brit. J. Pharmacol. **14** 99 (1959).

Baudouin, G., Tillequin, F., Koch, M., Pusset, J. and Sevenet, T., Plants of New Caledonia. LXXII. Alkaloids of *Dutaillyea oreophila* and *Dutaillyea drupacea*. J. Nat. Prod. **44** 546-550 (1981).

Bauml, J., personal communication.

Beck, O., Faull, K.F., Barchas, J.D., Johnson, J.V. and Yost, R.A., Chiral Analysis of Urinary 5-Hydroxymethyltryptoline: Implications for Endogenous Biosynthesis and Formation During Ethanol Intoxication. *Aldehyde Adducts in Alcoholism*, Alan R. Liss, Inc. 1985. pp. 145-160.

Beck, O., Repke, D.B. and Faull, K.F., 6-Hydroxymethtryptoline is Naturally Occurring in Mammalian Urine: Identification by Combined Chiral Capillary Gas Chromatography and High Resolution Mass Spectrometry. Biomed. Environ. Mass Spectr. **13** 469-472 (1986).

Bellman, S.W., Mass Spectral Identification of Some Hallucinogenic Drugs, J.A.O.A.C. **51** 165-175 (1968).

Benington, F., Morin, R.D. and Clark, J., Synthesis of O- and N-Methylated Derivatives of 5-Hydroxytryptamine. J. Org. Chem. **23** 1977-1979 (1958).

Bentov, M., Kaluszyner, A. and Pelchowicz, Z., 6-Fluoroindole and its Derivatives. J. Chem. Soc. 2825 (1962).

Bentov, M., Penchowicz, Z. and Levy, A., 4-Fluoroindole and Derivatives. Israel J. Chem. **2** 25 (1964).

Beringer, K., Der Meskalinrausch seine Geschichte und Erscheinungsweise. Berlin 1927.

Beringer, K., Über ein Neues, auf das Extrapyramidal-motorische System wirkendes Alkaloid (Banisterin). Nervenarzt. **1** 265-275 (1928).

Bernauer, K., Notiz über die Isolierung von Harmin und (+)-1,2,3,4-Tetrahydro-harmine aus einer indianischen Schnupfdroge. Helv. Chim. Acta **47**, 1075-1077 (1964).

Bickel, P., Dittrich, A. and Schoepf, J., Eine experimentelle Untersuchung zur bewußtseinsverändernden Wirkung von N,N-Dimethyltryptamin (DMT). Pharmakopsych. **9** 220-225 (1976).

Bigwood, J., Ott, J., Thompson, C. and Neely, P., Entheogenic Effects of Ergonovine. J. Psychedelic Drugs **11** 147-149 (1979).

Blickenstaff, R.T., Brandstadter, S.M., Reddy, S. and Witt, R., Potential Radioprotective Agents. 1. Homologs of Melatonin. J. Pharm. Sci. **83** 216-218 (1994).

Blickenstaff, R.T., Reddy, S. and Witt, R., Potential Radioprotective Agents- V. Melatonin Analogs. Oral Activity of p-Aminopropiophenone and its Ethylene Ketal. Bioorg. Med. Chem. **2** 1057-1060 (1994).

Boehme, W.R., 5-Benzyloxyindole. J. Am. Chem. Soc. **75** 2502-3 (1953).

Bonson, K., personal communication.

Bosin, T.R., Campaigne, E., Dinner, A., Rogers, R.B. and Maickel, R.P., Comparative Toxicological Studies of Indole, Benzo[b]thiophene, and 1-Methylindole Derivatives. Tox. Environ. Health **1** 515-520 (1976).

Bosin, T.R., Krogh, S. and Mais, D., Identification and Quantitation of 1,2,3,4-Tetrahydro-ß-carboline-3-carboxylic acid and 1-Methyl-1,2,3,4-tetrahydro-ß-carboline-3-carboxylic acid in Beer and Wine. J. Ag. Food Chem. **34** 843-847 (1986).

Böszörményi, Z., Creative Urge as an After Effect of Model Psychosis. Confin. Psychiat. **3** 117-126 (1960).

Böszörményi, Z. and Brunecker, G., Dimethyltryptamine (DMT) Experiments with Psychotics. *Psychotropic Drugs*. Ed. S. Garattini and V. Ghetti. Elsevier Publishing House, Amsterdam. pp. 580-581 (1957).

Böszörményi, Z. and Szara, S., Dimethyltryptamine Experiments with Psychotics. J. Ment. Sci. **104** 445-453 (1958).

Böszörményi, Z., Der, P. and Nagy, T. Psychotogenic Effect of N,N-Diethyltryptamine. A New Tryptamine Derivative. J. Ment. Sci. **105** 171-181 (1959).

Braestrup, C., Nielsen, M. and Olsen, C.E., Urinary and Brain ß-Carboline-3-

carboxylates as potent inhibitors of Brain Benzodiazepine Receptors. Proc. Natl. Acad. Sci. USA **77** 2288-2292 (1980).

Brimblecombe, R.W., Hyperthermic Effects of some Tryptamine Derivatives in Relation to their Behavioral Activity. Int. J. Neuropharmacol. **6** 423-429 (1967).

Brimblecombe, R.W., Downing, D.F., Green, D.M. and Hunt, R.R., Pharmacological Effects of a Series of Tryptamine Derivatives. Brit. J. Pharmacol. **23** 43-54 (1964).

Brimblecombe, R.W. and Pinder, R.M., *Hallucinogenic Agents.* Wright-Scientechnica, Bristol (1975).

Brown, J.B., Henbest, H.B. and Jones, E.R.H., 3-Indolylacetaldehyde and 3-Indolylacetone. J. Chem. Soc. 3172-3176 (1952).

Buck, J.S., Hjort, A.M. and DeBeer, E.V., Relative Anesthetic Effects of Various Ureas. J. Pharmacol. **54** 188-212 (1935).

Callaway, J.C., A Proposed Mechanism for the Visions of Dream Sleep. Medical Hypotheses **26** 119-124 (1988).

Callaway, J.C., personal communication.

Cannon, J.G., Lee, T., Ilhan, M., Koons, J. and Long, J.P., 6-Hydroxy-4-[2-(di-n-propylamino)ethyl]indole: Synthesis and Dopaminergic Actions. J. Med. Chem. **27** 386-389 (1984).

Cannon, J.R. and Williams, J.R., The Alkaloids of *Gastrolobium callistachys*. Aust. J. Chem. **35** 1497-1500 (1982).

Carlsson, A., Corrodi, H. and Magnusson, T., Basic Derivatives of 4,5,6-Trimethoxyindole and 3,4,5-Trimethoxyphenol. Helv. Chim. Acta **46** 1231-1235 (1963).

Carpenter, W.T., Fink, E.B., Narasimhachari, N. and Himwich, H.E., A Test of the Transmethylation Hypothesis in Acute Schizophrenic Patients. Am. J. Psychiat. **132** 1067-1071 (1975).

Cassady, J.M., Blair, G.E., Raffauf, R.F. and Tyler, V.E. The Isolation of 6-Methoxyharmalan and 6-Methoxyharman from *Virola cuspidata*. Lloydia **34** 161-2 (1971).

Cassidy, J.M., Tyler, V.E., Blair, G. and Williams, M., Tryptamines and Carbolines from *Virola* species. Lloydia **32** 523 (1969).

Chapman, N.B., Clarke, K. and Hughes, H., Synthesis of some 5-Substituted-2-methyl-tryptamines and their N-Mono and N,N-Dialkyl Derivatives. J. Chem. Soc. 3493 (1965).

Christian, S.T., Harrison, R. and Pagel, J., Evidence for Dimethyltryptamine (DMT) as a Naturally Occurring Transmitter in Mammalian Brain. Alabama J. Med. Sci. **13** 162-165 (1976).

Cimino, G. and De Stefano, S., Chemistry of Mediterranean Gorgonians: Simple Indole Derivatives from Paramuricea Chamaeleon. Comp. Biochem. Physiol. **61** 361-362 (1978).

Clarke, E.G.C., *Isolation and Identification of Drugs in Phamaceuticals, Body Fluids and Post-Mortem Material.* The Pharmaceutical Press, London, 1969. pp. 359.

Coddington, J., personal communication.

Coddington, R., personal communication.

Collins, M.A., Neafsey, E.J., Matsubara, K., Cobuzzi Jr., R.J. and Rollema, H., Indole-N-methylated ß-Carbonium Ions as Potential Brain-bioactivated Neurotoxins. Brain Research **570** 154-160 (1992).

Comings, M., personal communication.

Cooper, D.A., Proceedings of the International Symposium on the Forensic Aspects of Controlled Substances, U.S.D.O.J., U.S.G.P.O., 1998.

Coppen, A., Shaw, D.M., Malleson, A., Eccleston, E. and Gundy, G., Tryptamine Metabolism in Depression. Brit. J. Psychiat. **111** 993-998 (1965).

Costa, C., Bertazzo, A., Allegri, G., Curcuruto, O. and Traldi, P., Indole Alkaloids from the Roots of an African Plant *Securidaca Longipedunculata.* I. Isolation by Column Chromatography and Preliminary Structural Characterization by Mass Spectrometry. J. Heterocyclic Chem., **29** 1641-1647 (1992).

Coutsoftides, M., personal communication.

Cozzi, N., personal communication.

Crockett, E.L., personal communication.

Crookes, D.L., Parry, K.P. and Smith, G.F., 2-(indole-3'-yl)-2-hydroxy-N,N-dimethylethylamine (4) and 2-(indole-3'-yl)-2-(3"-[2'''-N,N-dimethylamino-ethyl]indole-2"-yl)-N,N-dimethylethylamine (1), by products in the LAH reduction of 3-indoleglyoxyl-N,N-dimethylamide... Polish J. Chemistry **53** 73-79 (1979).

Culvenor, C.C.J., Dal Bon, R. and Smith, L.W., Occurrence of Indole Alkylamines Alkaloids in *Phalaris tuberosa* and *arundinacea*. Australian J. Chem. **17** 1301 (1964).

Dallacker, F. and Bernabei, D., Derivate des Methylenedioxybenzols. Monatsh. Chem. **98** 785 (1967).

Daly, J,W, and Witkop, B., Chemistry and Pharmacology of Frog Venoms, *Venomous Animals and their Venoms*. Bucherl and Buckly, Eds. Vol 2, Academic Press, New York (1971).

Davis, W. and Weil, A.T., Identity of a New World Psychoactive Toad, Ancient Mesoamerican **3** 51-59 1992.

Debitus, C., Laurent, D. and Pais, M., Alkaloids from an Ascidian of New Caledonia, *Eudistoma fragum*. J. Nat. Prod. **51** 799-801 (1988).

De Budowski, J. Marini-Bettolo, G. B., Delle Monache, F. and Ferrari, F., On The Alkaloid Composition of the Snuff Drug Yopo from Upper Orinoco (Venezuela). Farmaco. Ed. Sci. **29** 574 (1974).

Deguchi, T. and Axelrod, Diurnal Changes of Acetyltransferase in Rat Pineal. Anal. Biochem. **50** 174-178 (1972).

Deitrich, R., Biogenic Amine-Aldehyde Condensation Products: Tetrahydroisoquinolines and Tryptolines (ß-Carbolines). Ann. Rev. Pharmacol. Toxicol. **20**, 55-80 (1980).

Delaney, J., personal communication.

De Moraes, E.H.F., Alvarenga, M.A., Ferreira, Z.M.G.S. and Akisue, G., Nitrogenated Bases Of Mimosa Scabrella Quim. Nova **13** 308-309 (1990).

De Rienzo, P. and Beal, D., *The Ibogaine Story; Report on the Staten Island Project*. Autonomedia, New York. (1997).

Der Marderosian, A.H., Pinkley, H.V., Chao, K.M. and Goldstein, F.J., The Use of Hallucinatory Principles of the Psychotropic Beverage of the Cashinahua Tribe (Amazon basin). Drug Dependence **5** 7-14 (1970).

Der Marderosian, A.H., Pinkley, H.V. and Dobbins, M.F., Native Use and Occurrence of N,N-dimethyltryptamine in the leaves of *Banisteriopsis rusbana*. Lloydia **31** 430 (1968).

De Smet, P. and Rivier, L., Intoxicating Parica Seeds of Brazilian Maue Indians. Econ. Bot, **41** 12-16 (1987).

De Smet, P., *Ritual Enemas and Snuffs in the Americas*. Amsterdam, pp. 111-112 (1985).

Dolan, C., personal communication.

Donnell, M., personal communication.

Dorjé, K.T., personal communication.

Djura, P., Stierle,, D.B., Sullivan, B., Faulkner, D.J., Arnold, E.V. and Clardy, J., Some Metabolites of the Marine Sponges *Smenospongia aurea* and *Smenospongia (Polyfibrospongia) echina*. J. Org. Chem. **45** 1435-41 (1980).

Drug Policy Foundation, Washington, DC. We wish to acknowledge a generous grant from this group that greatly facilitated the production of this book.

Ehmann, A., N-(p-Coumaryl) Tryptamine and N-Ferulyltryptamine in Kernels of *Zea mays*. Phytochemistry **13** 1979-1983 (1974).

Ely, H., personal communication.

Ely, R., personal communication.

Erspamer, V., Vitali, T., Roseghini, M. and Cei, J.M., Identification of Histamine Derivative in the Skin of *Leptodactylus*. Experientia **21** 504 (1965).

Eve, M., personal communication.

Fabing, H., Hawkins, J.R., Intravenous Bufotenine Injection in the Human Being. Science **123** 886-7 (1956).

Faillace, L.A., Vourlekis, A. and Szara, S., Paper presented at the Fifth International

Conference of the Collegium Internationale Neuro-Psychopharmacologicum, Washington, DC (1966).

Faillace, L.A., Vourlekis, A. and Szara, S., Clinical Evaluation of Some Hallucinogenic Tryptamine Derivatives. J. Nerv. Ment. Dis. **145** 306-313 (1967).

Fan, J. and Yao, X., (in Chinese) J. Shenyang College of Pharmacy **9** 144-151 (1992).

Fauteck, J.D., Lerchl, A., Bergmann, M., Møller, M., Fraschini, F., Wittkowski, W. and Stankov, B., The Adult Human Cerebellum is a Target of the Neuroendocrine System Involved in the Circadian Timing. Neuroscience Lett. **179** 60-64 (1994).

Fish, M.S., Johnson, N.M. and Horning, E.C., *Piptadenia* Alkaloids. Indole Bases of *P. Peregrina* (L.) Benth, and Related Species. J. Am. Chem. Soc. **77** 5892-5895 (1955).

Fisher, J., personal communication.

Flattery, D.S. and Schwartz, M., *Haoma and Harmaline*. U.C. Press, Berkeley, California, 1989.

Frey, A. U.S. Patent 3,084,164 (1963).

Gallagher, C.H., Koch, J.H. and Hoffman, H., Poisoning by Grass. Int. J. Neuropharmacol. **6** 223 (1967).

Gallagher, C.H., Koch, J.H., Moore, R.M. and Steel, J.B., Toxicity of *Phalarais tuberosa* for Sheep. Nature **204** 542 (1964).

Gander, J.E., Marum, P., Marten, G.C. and Hovin, A.W., The Occurrence of 2-Methyl-1,2,3,4-tetrahydro-ß-carboline and Variation in Alkaloids in *Phalaris arundinacea*. Phytochem. **15** 737-738 (1976).

Garbrecht, W.L., Synthesis of Amides of Lysergic Acid. J. Org. Chem. **24**, 368-72 (1959).

Garfinkle, S., personal communication.

Gersch, C., personal communication.

Gessner, P.K., Godse, D.D., Krull, A.H. and McMullan, J.M., Structure-Activity Relationships Among 5-Methoxy-N,N-Dimethyltryptamine, 4-Hydroxy-N,N-

Dimethyltryptamine (Psilocin) and other Substituted Tryptamines. Life Sciences **7** 267-77 (1968).

Geyer, M.A., Warbritton, J.D., Menkes, D.M., Zook, J.A. and Mandel, A.J., Opposite Effects of Intraventricular Serotonin and Bufotenine on Rat Startle Response. Pharmacol. Biochem. Behav. **3** 687 (1975).

Ghorbel, N., Damak, M., Ahond, A., Philogène, E., Poupat, P. and Jacquemin, H., Study of American *Tabernaemontana*. IV. Alkaloids from *Peschiera echinata*. J. Nat. Products **44** 717-721 (1981).

Ghosal, S. and Bhattacharya, S.K., Desmodium Alkaloids. Part II. Chemical and Pharmacological Evaluation of *D. gangeticum*. Planta Medica **22** 434-440 (1972).

Ghosal, S. and Bhattacharya, S.K., Mehta, R., Naturally Occurring and Synthetic ß-Carbolines as Cholinesterase Inhibitors. J. of Pharmaceut. Sci. **61**, 808-810 (1972).

Ghosal, S., Chaudhuri, R.K. and Dutta, S.K., Alkaloids of the Flowers of *Arundo Donax*. Phytochemistry **10** 2852 (1971).

Ghosal, S. and Mukherjee, B., Indole-3-Alkylamine Bases of *Desmodium Pulchellum*. J. Org. Chem. **31** 2284- (1966).

Ghosal, S. Mazumder, U.K. and Bhattacharya, W.K., Chemical and Pharmacological Evaluation of *Banisteriopsis argentea*. J. Pharm. Sci. **60** 1209 (1971).

Ghosal, S., Singh, S. and Bhattacharya, S.K., Alkaloids of *Mucuna Pruriens*. Chemistry and Pharmacology. Planta Med. **19** 279 (1971).

Gill, S., personal communication.

Gillin, J.C., Kaplan, J., Stillman, R. and Wyatt, R.J., The Psychedelic Model of Schizophrenia: The Case of N,N-Dimethyltryptamine. Am. J. Psychiat. **133** 203-208 (1976).

Glennon, R.A., Quantum Chemical Investigation of the pi-electronic Structure of the Hallucinogenic N,N-dimethyltryptamines. Res. Comm. Chem. Path. Pharm. **9** 185-188 (1974).

Glennon, R.A. and Gessner, P.K., The Electronic and Serotonin Receptor Binding Affinity Properties of N,N-Dimethyltryptamine Analogs. J. Med. Chem. **22** 428-432 (1979).

Glennon, R.A., Gessner, P.K., Godse, D.D. and Kline, B.J., Bufotenine Esters. J. Med. Chem. **22** 1414-1416 (1979).

Glennon, R.A., Hong, S.S., Bondarev, M., Law, H., Dukat, M., Rakhit, S., Power, P., Fan, E., Kinneau, D., Kamboj, R., Teitler, M., Herrick-Davis, K. and Smith, C., Binding of O-Alkyl Derivatives of Serotonin at Human 5-HT1Dß Receptors. J. Med. Chem. **39** 314-322 (1996).

Glennon, R.A., Schubert, E., Jacyno, J.M. and Rosecrans, J.A., Studies on Several 7-Substituted N,N-Dimethyltryptamines. J. Med. Chem. **23** 1222-1226 (1980).

Glennon, R.A., Young, R., Benington, F. and Morin, R.D., Hallucinogens as Discriminative Stimuli: A Comparison of 4-Methoxy and 5-Methoxy-N,N-dimethyl Tryptamine with their Methylthio Counterparts. Life Sciences **30** 463-467 (1982).

Gogerty, J.H. and Dille, J.M., Pharmacology of d-Lysergic Acid Morpholide. J. Pharm. Exp. Therap. **120** 340-348 (1957).

Golden, J., personal communication.

Goldsmith, N., personal communication.

Gonçalves de Lima, O., Observaçoes Sôbre o Vihno da Jurema Utilizado Pelos Indios Pancarú de Tacaratú (Pernambuco). Arquiv. Inst. Pesquisas Agron. **4** 45-80 (1946).

Goto, M., Noguchi, T. and Watanabe, T., Useful Components in Natural Sources. XVII. Uterus Contracting Ingredients in Plants. 2. Uterus Contracting Ingredients in *Lespediza bicolor* var Japonica. Yakugaku Zasshi **78** 464-467 (1958).

Greenwood, J., personal communication.

Grina, J.A., Ratcliff, M.R. and Stermitz, F.R., Constituents of Zanthoxylum. Part 7. Old and New Alkaloids from *Zanthoxylum arborescens*. J. Org. Chem. **47** 2648-2651 (1982).

Grob, C.S., personal communication.

Grob, C.S., McKenna, D.J., Callaway, J.C., Brito, G.S., Neves, E.S., Oberlaender, G., Saide, O.L., Labigalini, E., Tacla, C., Miranda, C.T., Strassman, R.J. and Boone, K.B., Human Psychpharmacology of Hoasca, A Plant Hallucinogen Used in Ritual

Context in Brazil. J. Nerv. Ment. Dis. **184** 86 (1996).

Grof, S., Soskin, R.A., Richards, W.A. and Kurland, A.A., DPT as an Adjunct in Psychotherapy of Alcoholics. Int. Pharmacopsychiat. **8** 104-115 (1973).

Grof, S., Soskin, R.A., Richards, W.A. and Kurland, A.A., J. Rel. Health **17** #2 (1978).

Gross, D., personal communication.

Gross, P., personal communication.

Grotjahn, D.B., Synthesis and Characterization of 5H-1,3-Dioxolo[4,5-indoleethylamines. J. Heterocyc. Chem. **20** 1031-1036 (1983).

Gupta, M.P. and Arias, T.D., Lloydia **42** 234-236 (1979).

Gupta, M.P., Arias, T.D., Etheart, J. and Hatfield, G.M., The Occurrence of Tryptamine and N-Methyltryptamine in *Mimosa Somnians*. J. Nat. Prod. **42** 234 (1979).

Gynther, J., Peura, P. and Salmi, S., Electron Impact and Chemical Ionization Fragmentation of 5-Methoxytryptamine and Some 6-Methoxy-ß-carbolines. Acta Chem. Scand. **39** 849-859 (1985).

Halpern, L., Über die Harminwirkung im Selbstversuch. Dtsch. Med. Wochenschr. **56** 1252-1254 (1930).

Haney, D.R., personal communication.

Harsh, M.L. and Nag, T.N., J. Nat. Products **47** 365-367 (1984).

Hatfield, G.M., Valdes, L.J. and Smith, A.H., The Occurrence of Psilocybin in Gymnopilus Species. Lloydia **41** 140-144 (1978).

Hattori, A, Migitaka, H., Iigo, M., Itoh, M., Yamamoto, K., Ohtani-Kaneko, R., Hara, M., Suzuki, T. and Reiter, R.J., Identification of Melatonin in Plants and its Effects on Plasma Melatonin Levels and Binding to Melatonin Receptors in Vertebrates. Biochem. Mol. Biol. Int. **35** 627-634 (1995).

Heagy, J.A., Allen, A.C. and Sorgen, G.J., Paper presented at the1986 Spring meeting, NWAFS, Bend Oregon. 1986.

Heinzelman, R.V., Anthony, W.C., Lyttle, D.A. and Szmuszkovics, J., The Synthesis of α-Methyltryptophans and α-Alkyltrypamines. J. Org. Chem. **25** 1548-1558 (1960).

Herbert, N., personal communication.

Hjort, A.M., DeBeer, E.J., Buck, J.S. and Ide, W.S., Some Unsymmetrical Alkylanyl Ureas Preparation, Physical Properties and Hypnotic Effects. J. Pharmacol. **55** 152-172 (1955).

Ho, B.T. and Walker, K.E., Org. Syn. **51** 136 (1964).

Hochstein, F.A. and Paradies, A.M., Alkaloids of *Banisteria caapi* and *Prestonia amazonicum*. J. Am. Chem. Soc. **79**, 5735-5736 (1957).

Hodson, H.F. and Smith, G.F., Structure of Folicanthine. Chem. Ind. (London) 740 (1958).

Hoffer, A. and Osmond, H., . Chapter IV. Indole Hallucinogens Derived from Tryptophan, *The Hallucinogens*, Academic Press, p. 445, 468. 1967.

Hoffman, A.J. and Nichols, D.E., Synthesis and LSD-like Discriminative Stimulus Properties in a Series of N(6)-Alkyl Norlysergic Acid N,N-Diethylamide Derivatives. J. Med. Chem. **28** 1252-1255 (1985).

Hoffman, J.T., personal communication.

Hofinger, M., Monseur, X., Pais, M. and Jarreau, F.X., Further Confirmation of the Presence of Indolylacrylic Acid in Lentil Seedlings and Identification of Hypaphorine as its Precursor. Phytochemistry **14** 475-477 (1975).

Hofmann, A., personal communication.

Hofmann, A., Psychotomimetic Drugs: Chemical and Pharmacological Aspects. Acta Physiol. Pharmacol. Neerlandica **8** 240-258 (1959).

Hofmann, A., Chemical Aspects of Psilocybin, the Psychtropic Principle from the Mexican Fungus, Psilocybe mexicana Heim. *Neuro-psychopharmacology*. Ed. P.B. Bradley, P. Deniker and C. Radouco-Thomas, Elsevier, Amsterdam pp. 446-448 (1959).

Hofmann, A., The Active Principles of the Seeds of *Rivea Corymbosa* and *Ipomoea Violacea*, Psychedelic Review **1** 302-316 (1964).

Hofmann, A., *LSD - Mein Sorgenkind*, (LSD - My Problem Child) German Edition, 1979, English translation by Jonathan Ott, Tarcher Press, 1983.

Hofmann, A. and Troxler, F., Esters of Indoles for the Treatment of Mental Disturbances. U.S. Patent 3,078,214, Feb. 19, 1963.

Hollister,. L.E., personal communication.

Hollister , L.E., Prusmack, J.J., Paulsen, J.A. and Rosenquist, N., Comparison of the Three Psychotropic Drugs (Psilocybin, JB-329, and IT-290) in Volunteer Studies. J. Nerv. Ment. Dis. **13** 428-434 (1960).

Holmstedt, B., personal communication.

Holmstedt, B., Tryptamine Derivatives in Epena; An Intoxicating Snuff Used by some South American Indian Tribes. Arch. Int. Pharmacodyn. Ther. **156** 285-305 (1965).

Holmstedt, B., Betacarbolines and Tetrahydroisoquinolines: Historical and Ethnopharmacological Backround. *Beta-Carbolines and Tetrahydroisoquinolines*. Eds F. Bloom, J. Barchas, M. Sandlet and E. Usdin, Alan R. Liss, New York (1982). pp. 3-13.

Holmstedt, B., Lindgren, J.E., Rivier, L. and Do Valle, J.R., Ayahuasca, Caapi or Yagé - Hallucinogenic Drink of Amazonian Basin Indians (Brasil). Cienc. Cult. (Sao Paulo) **31** 1120-1124 (1979).

Honecker, H. and Rommelspacher, H., Tetrahydroharmane (Tetrahydro-ß-Carboline), a Physiologically Occurring Compound of Indole Metabolism. Arch. Pharm. **305** 135-141 (1978).

Hoshino, T. and Shimodaira, K., Sythese des Bufotenins und über 3-Methyl-3-ß-oxyäthyl-indolenin. Ann. **520** 19 (1935).

Hoshino, T. and Shimodaira, K., Über die Synthese des Bufotenin-methyl-äthers (5-Methoxy-N-dimethyl-tryptamine) und Bufotenins. Bull. Chem. Soc. Japan **11** 221-224 (1936).

Hryhorczuk, L.M., Rainey Jr., J.M., Frohman, C.E. and Novak, E.A., A New Metabolic Pathway for N,N-Dimethyltryptamine. Biol. Psychiatry **21** 84-93 (1986).

Hsu, L.L., *In vivo* Formation of 1,2,3,4-Tetrahydro-ß-carboline from [14C]-

Tryptamine in the Brain. IRCS Med. Sci. **13** 1054-1055 (1985).

Hsu, L.L., Mandell, A.J., Regional Formation of 6-Methoxy-1,2,3,4-Tetrahydro-ß-Carboline in Rat Brain Extract. Res. Commun. in Chem. Pathol. and Pharmacol. **12**, 355-362 (1975).

Hunt, R.R. and Brimblecombe, R.W., Synthesis and Biological Activity of Some Ring-Substituted Tryptamines. J. Med. Chem. **10** 646-648 (1967).

Huss, K., invaluable help.

Iacobucci, G.A. and Rúveda, E.A., Bases Derived from Tryptamine in Argentine *Piptadenia* Species. Phytochemistry **3** 465-467 (1964).

Isbell, H. and Gorodetzky, C.W., Effects of Alkaloids of Ololiuqui in Man, Psychopharmacologia **8** 331-339 (1966).

Isbell, H., Miner, E.J. and Logan, C.R., Relations of Psychotomimetic to Antiserotonin Potencies of Congeners of Lysergic Acid Diethylamide. Psychopharmacologia **1** 20-28 (1959).

Isbell, H., Rosenberg, D.E., Miner, E.J. and Logan, C.R., Neuropsychopharmacology. Proceedings 3rd Internat. Congress, Munich, 1962.

Isbell, H., Wolbach, A.B., Wikler, A. and Miner, E.J., Cross Tolerance Between LSD and Psilocybin. Psychopharmacologia **2** 147-159 (1961).

Iyer, V.V.S. and Robinson, R., ind-N-Methylharmine, J. Chem. Soc. 1635-1637 (1934).

Jacobs, P. III, personal communication.

Jacobs, W.A. and Craig, L.C., The Ergot Alkaloids. II. The Degredation of Ergotinine with Alkali Lysergic Acid. J. Biol. Chem. **104** 547-51 (1934).

James, B., personal communication.

Janiaud, P., Neuroendocrin. Let. **9** 311 (1987).

Jarvik, M.E., Abramson, H.A. and Hirsch, M.W., Comparative Subjective Effects of Seven Drugs Including Lysergic Acid Diethylamide (LSD-25). J. Abnorm. Soc. Psychol. **51** 657-662 (1955).

Jenks, C., personal communication.

Jesse, R., personal communication.

Jibuike, U., personal communication.

Johnson, F.N., Istvan, I.E., Teiger, D.G. and Kassel, R.J., Emetic Activity of Reduced Lysergamides. J. Med. Chem. **16** 532-537 (1973).

Jossang, A. Jossang, P. Hadi, A. Sevenet, T. and Bodo, B., Horsfiline, an Oxindole Alkaloid from *Horsfieldia superba*. J. Org. Chem. **56** 6527-6530 (1991).

Julia, M. and Manouri, P., Research in the Indole Series. XIII. 5- and 6-methoxytryptamines. Bull. Soc. Chim. France, **5** 1411-17 (1965).

Julia, M. and Pascal, Y.R., Recherches en Série Indolique. XXII. Nouvelle Synthèse du Noyau Indole, Application à la Psilocine. Bull. Chim. Ther., pp 279 (1970) #4.

Kalir, A. and Szara, S., Synthesis and Pharmacological Activity of Alkylated Tryptamines. J. Med. Chem. **9** 341-344 (1966).

Kalir, A. Balderman, D., Edery, H. and Porath, G., Israeli J. Chem. **5** 129-136 (1967).

Kantor, R.E., Dudlettes, S.D. and Shulgin, A.T., 5-Methoxy-a-methyltryptamine (a,O-Dimethylserotonin), A Hallucinogenic Homolog of Serotonin. Biol. Psychiatry **15** 349-352 (1980).

Kawanishi, K. and Hashimoto, Y., Flavonolignan from the Bark of *Virola sebifera*. Proc. Int. Cong. Nat. Prod. Res. p-59 (1988).

Katt, E., personal communications.

Kawanishi, K., Uhara, Y. and Hashimoto, Y., Alkaloids from the Hallucinogenic Plant *Virola sebifera*. Phytochemistry **24** 1373-1375 (1985).

Kennedy, A.B., Ecce Bufo: The Toad in Nature and in Olmec Iconography. Current Anthropology **32** 273-290 (1982).

Khalil, S.K.W. and Elkheir, Y.M., Dimethyltryptamine from the Leaves of Certain *Acacia* Species of Northern Sudan. Lloydia **38** 176-177 (1975).

Kline, T.B., Structure-activity Relationships of N,N-Dialkyltryptamines Substituted in the Benzene Moiety. PhD Thesis, University of Alabama in Birmingham. 1980.

Kline, T.B., Benington, F., Morin, R.D. and Beaton, J.M., Structure-Activity Relationships in Potentially Hallucinogenic N,N-Dialkyltryptamines Substituted in the Benzene Moiety. J. Med. Chem. **25** 908-913 (1982).

Kondo, H., Kataoke, H., Hayashi, Y. and Dodo, T., Serotonin and Related Compounds. Itsuu Kenkyusho Nempo **10** 1-9 (1959).

Kondo, K. Nishi, J. Ishibashi, M. and Kobayashi, J.I., Two New Tryptophan-Derived Alkaloids from the Okinawan Marine Sponge *Aplysina* sp. J. Nat. Prod. **57** 1008-1011 (1994).

Kotake, Y., Tasaki, Y., Makino, Y., Ohta, S. and Hirobe, M., 1-Benzyl-1,2,3,4-tetrahydroisoquinoline as a Parkinsonism-Inducing Agent: A Novel Endogenous Amine in Mouse Brain and Parkinsonian CSF. J. Neurochem. **65** 2633-2638 (1995).

Kühn, H. and Stein, O., A New Gramine Synthesis. Ber. **70B** 569 (1937).

Kutney, J.P., Choi, L.S.L., Kolodziejczyk, P., Sleigh, S.K., Stuart, K.L., Worth, B.R., Kurz, W.G.W., Chatson, K.B. and Constabel, F., Alkaloid Production in Catharanthus Roseus Cell Cultures. V. Alkaloids From The 176g, 299y, 340y and 951g Cell Lines. Nat. Prod. **44** 536-540 (1981).

Laakso, I., Virkajärvo, P., Airaksinen, H. and Varis, E., Determination of Vasicine and Related Alkaloids by Gas Chromatography-Mass Spectrometry. J. Chromatog. **505** 424-428 (1990).

Lai, A., Tin-Wa, M., Mika, E.S., Persinos, G.J. and Farnsworth, N.R., *Virola peruviana*, A New Hallucinogenic Plant: Phytochemical Investigation. Lloydia **36** 437-438 (1973).

Lamphere, J., personal communication.

Lee, F.G.H., Dickson, D.E., Suzuki, J., Zirnis, A. and Manian, A.A., Synthesis of 5,7- and 6,7-Disubstituted Tryptamines and Analogs. J. Hetero. Chem. **10** 649-654 (1973).

Legler, G. and Tschesche, R., Isolation of N,methyltryptamine, 5-Methoxy-N,methyltryptamine and 5-Methoxy-N,N-dimethyltryptamine from the bark of

*Piptadenia peregrina.* Natturwiss. **50** 94 (1963).

Lenz, B.C., personal communication.

Leuner, H., personal communication.

Leuner, H., Present State of Psycholytic Therapy and its Possibilities, *The Use of LSD in Psychotherapy and Alcoholism*, H.A. Abramson, Ed., Bobbs-Merrill, Co., New York (1967). pp. 101-116.

Leuner, H. and Baer, G., Two New Short-acting Hallucinogens of the Psilocybin Group. *Neuro-psychopharmacology.* 471-474 (1965). Elsevier, Amsterdam. Ed: D. Bente and P. B. Bradley.

Levit, C., personal communication.

Lewin, L, *Phantastica; Die Betäubenden und Erregenden Genußmittel.* Berlin. 1927.

Lewin, L., Untersuchungen über *Banisteria caapi* Spr. (ein südamerikanische Rauschmittel). Arch. Exp. Path. Pharmakol. **129** 133-149 (1928).

Liu, K-C, Chou, C-J and Lin, J-H., (in Chinese) Hua Hsueh **1** 15-16 (1977).

Lloyd, D.H. and Nichols, D.E., Nickel Boride/Hydrazine Hydrate: Reduction of Aromatic and Aliphatic Nitro Compounds. Synthesis of 4-(Benzyloxy)indole and a-Alkyltryptamines. J. Org. Chem. **51** 4294-4295 (1986).

Lyttle, T., personal communication.

MacDougall, T., *Ipomoea tricolor*, A Hallucinogen Plant of the Zapotecs, Boletin del Centro de Investigaciones Anthropológicas de México, No. 6. March 1, 1960.

MacFarlane, J.G., Cleghorn, J.M., Brown, G.M. and Streiner, D.L., The Effects of Exogenous Melatonin on the Total Sleep Time and Daytime Alertness of Chronic Insomniacs: A Preliminary Study. Biol. Psychiat. **30** 371-376 (1991).

Majak, W. and Bose, R.J., Further Characterization and Quantitative Determination of 5-Methoxy-N-Methyltryptamine in *Phalaris arundinacea.* Phytochemistry **16** 749-752 (1977).

Makino,Y., Ohta, S., Tasaki, Y., Tachikawa, O., Kashiwasake, M. and Hirobe, M., J., A Novel and Neurotoxic Tetrahydroisoquinoline Derivative in Vivo: Formation of 1,3-Dimethyl-1,2,3,4-tetrahydroisoquinoline, a Condensation Product of Ampthetamines, in Brain of Rats under Chronic Ethanol Treatment. Neurochem. **55** 963-969 (1990).

Malitz, S., Wilkins, B., Roehrig, W.C. and Hoch, P.H., Psychiat. Quarterly **34**, 333-345 (1960).

Mandel, L.R., Rosegay, A., Walker, R.W. and Vanden Heuvel, W.J.A., 5-Metehyltetrahydrofolic Acid as a Mediator in the Formation of Pyridoindoles. Science **186** 741-743 (1974).

Manders, D.W., The FDA Ban of L-Tryptophan: Politics, Profits and Prozac. Social Policy, **26** 35-37 (1995).

Manske, R.H.F., A Synthesis of the Methyltryptamines and Some Derivatives, Can. J. Research **5** 592-600 (1931).

Markus, M., personal communication.

Martin, W.R. and Sloan, J.W., Effects of Infused Tryptamine in man. Psychopharmacologia **18** 231-237 (1970).

Martin, W.R. and Sloan, J.W., Relationship of CNS Tryptaminergic Processes and the Action of LSD-like Hallucinogens. Pharmacol. Biochem. Behav. **24** 393-399 (1986).

Mathis, C.A., Hoffman, A.J., Nichols, D.E. and Shulgin, A.T., Synthesis of High Specific Activity $^{125}$I- and $^{123}$I- Labeled Enantiomeres of 2,5-Dimethoxy-4-iodophenylisopropylamine (DOI). J. Labelled Cmpds. Radiopharmaceuticals **25** 1255-65 (1988).

Maurer, M., Symposium on Current State of Research in the Field of Psychoactive Substances; Ed. H. Leuner and M. Schlichting, 1985 p. 169.

McKenna, D.J., personal communication.

McKenna, D.J. and Towers, G.H.N., Biochemistry and Pharmacology of Tryptamines and beta-Carbolines A Minireview. J. Psychoactive Drugs **16** 347-358 (1984).

McKenna, D.J., Towers, G.H.N. and Abbott, F.S., Monoamine Oxidase Inhibitors in South American Hallucinogenic Plants Part 2. Constituents of Orally-Active Myristicaceous Hallucinogens. J. Ethnopharmacol. **12** 179-211 (1984).

McKenzie, E., Nettleship, L. and Slaytor, M., New Natural Products from *Peganum Harmala*. Phytochemistry **14** 273-275 (1975).

Meckes-Lozoya, M., Lozoya, X., Soucy-Breau, C., Sen, A. and Arnason, J.T., N,N-Dimethyltryptamine Alkaloid in *Mimosa Tenuiflora* Bark (Tepesco-Huite). Arch. Invest. Med. (Mex) **21** 175-177 (1990).

Meller, E., Friedman, E., Schweitzer, J.W., Friedhoff, A.J., Tetrahydro-ß-Carbolines: Specific Inhibitors of Type A Monoamine Oxidase in Rat Brain. J. Neurochem. **28** 995-1000 (1977).

Meltzer, Pahnke, Kurland and Henkin, Serum CPK and Aldolase Activity in Man Following Controlled Administration of Psychotomimetic Drugs. Psychopharmacologia **16** 419 (1970).

Meyer, J.B., personal communication.

Miles, D.H., Ly, A., Randle, S.A., Hedin, P.A. and Burks, M.L., Alkaloidal Insect Antifeedants from *Virola calophylla* Warb. J. Agr. Food Chem. **35** 794-797 (1987).

Misztal, S., Synthesis of New Indole Derivatives with Biological Activity. Dissertations Pharm. **14** #3 305-14 (1962).

Monte, A.P., Marona-Lewicka, D., Kanthasamy, A.M., Sanders-Bush, E. and Nichols, D.E., Stereoselective LSD-like Activity in a Series of d-Lysergic Acid Amides of (e)- and (s)-2-aminoalkanes. J. Med. Chem. **38** 958-966 (1995).

Montgomery, R., invaluable help.

Montine, T.J., Missala, K. and Sourkes, T.L., Alpha-Methyltryptophan Metabolism in Rat Pineal Gland and Brain. J. Pineal Res. **12** 43-48 (1993).

Mosley, W., personal communication.

Mulamba, T., Delaude, C., LeMen-Olivier, L. and Lévy, J., Alkaloids from *Tabernanthe pubescens*. J. Nat. Products **44** 184-189 (1981).

Mulvena, D.P. and Slaytor, M., Separation of Tryptophan Derivatives in *Phalaris aquatica* by Thin-Layer Chromatography. J. Chromatog. **245** 155-157 (1982).

Murphree, H.B. and Bircher, R. Psychotomimetic Drugs, Chapter 24, *Drill's Pharmacology in Medicine*, page 449. McGraw Hill. 1971.

Murphree, H.B., DeMarr, E.W.J., Williams, H.L. and Bryan, L.L., J. Pharm. exptl. Therap. **122** 55a-56a (1958).

Murphree, H.B., Dippy, R.H., Jenney, E.H. and Pfeiffer, C.C., Effects in Normal Man of α-Methyltryptamine and α-Ethyltryptamine. Clin. Pharmacol. Therap. **2** 722-726 (1961).

Murphree, H.B., Jenner, E.H. and Pfeiffer, C.C., Comparison of the Effects of Congeners of Lysergic Acid Diethylamide and Tryptophane in Normal Human Volunteers. The Pharmacologist **2** 64 (1960).

Nagatsu, T. and Yoshida, M., An Endogenous Substance of the Brain, Tetrahydroisoquinoline, Produces Parkinsonism in Primates with Decreased Dopamine, Tryosine Hydroxylase and Biopterin in the Nigrostriatal Regions. Neurosci. Lett. **87** 178-182 (1988).

Nakagawa, H., Makino, Y., Yoshida, Y., Ohta, S. and Hirobe, M., Biol. Pharm. Bull. **16** 579-582 (1993).

Naranjo, C., Psychotropic Properties of the Harmala Alkaloids, *Ethnopharmacologic Search for Psuchoactive Drugs*. Ed: D.H. Efron, Public Health Service Publication #1645. 1967. pp. 385-402.

Naranjo, C., Psychotherapeutic Possibilities of New Fantasy-Enhancing Drugs. Clin. Toxicol. **2** 209-224 (1969).

Naranjo, C., Ibogaine, Fantasy, and Reality, *The Healing Journey: New Approaches to Consciousness*. Pantheon Books, New York. 1973. pp. 174-228.

Naranjo, C., Harmaline and the Collective Unconscious, *The Healing Journey: New Approaches to Consciousness*. Pantheon Books, New York. 1973. pp. 124-173.

Naranjo, C., personal communication.

Nichols, D.E., personal communication.

Nichols, D.W., Frescas, S., Marona-Lewicka, D., Huang, X., Roth, B.L., Gudelsky, G.A. and Nash, J.F., 1-(2,5-Dimethoxy-4-(triflouromethyl)phenyl)-2-aminopropane: A Potent Serotonin 5-HT2A/2C Agonist. J. Med. Chem. **37** 4346-4351 (1994).

Nógrádi, T., Investigations into Rauwolfia-alkaloid Models. I. Tryptamine and Gramine Derivatives. T. Monatsch. Chem. **88** 768-777 (1957).

Oberlender, R.A., Pfaff, R.C., Johnson, M.P., Huang, X. and Nichols, D.E., Stereoselective LSD-like Activity in d-Lysergic Acid Amides of R- and S-2-aminobutane. J. Med. Chem. **35** 203-211 (1992).

O'Connell, P.W., personal communication.

Ohta, S., Kohno, M., Makino, Y., Tachikawa, O. and Hirobe, M., Biomed. Res. **8** 453-456 (1987).

Olson, R.E., Gursey, D. and Vester, J.W., Evidence for a Defect in Tryptophan Metabolism in Chronic Alcoholism. N. England J. Med. **263** 1169 (1960).

Ono, M., Shimamine, M., Takahasi, K. and Inoue, T., Hallucinogens. V. Synthesis of Psilocybin. Eisei Shikenjo Hokoku **92** 41-3 (1974).

Ott, J., *Pharmacotheon: Entheogenic Drugs, Their Plant Sources and History.* Natural Products Company, Kennewick, Washington. 1993.

Ott, J., *Ayahuasca Analogues.* Pangaean Entheogens. Natural Products Company, Kennewick, Washington. 1994.

Ott, J., *The Age of Entheogens & The Angels' Dictionary.* Natural Products Company, Kennewick, Washington. 1995.

Ott, J. and Neely, P., Entheogenic (Hallucinogenic) Effects of Methyl-ergonovine. J. Psychedelic Drugs **12** 165-166 (1980).

Ott, J., personal communication.

Pachter, I.J., Zacharias, D.E. and Ribeiro, O., Indole Alkaloids of *Acer saccharinum* (the Silver Maple), *Dictyoloma incanescens*, *Piptadenia colubrina*, and *Mimosa hostilis*. J. Org. Chem. **24** 1285-1287 (1959).

Palla, S., personal communication.

Parker, M., personal communication.

Paul, R. and Anderson, G.W., N,N-Carbanyldiimaidazole, Peptide Forming Reagent. J. Am. Chem. Soc. **82**, 4596 (1960).

Pearson, D. and Shaw, S., *Life Extension.* Warner Books, Inc., New York (1982). Part III, Chapter 2: "Revitalizing your Brain Power." p 179.

Pelchowicz, Z., Klauszyner, A. and Bentov, M., N-Alkylated 5-Fluorotryptamines. J. Chem. Soc. 5418 (1961).

Pendell, D., personal communications.

Pennes, H., Hoch, P.H., Psychotomimetics, Clinical and Theoretical Considerations: Harmine, Win-2299 and Nalline. Am. J. Psychiatry 113 887 (1957).

Perlman, D., S. F. Chronicle, March 4, 1995.

Perrine, D. M., personal communication.

Perry, J.W., personal communication.

Petit, C., S. F. Chronicle, August 4, 1995.

Petrie, K., personal communication.

Petrova, M.F., Kaverina, N.S. and Men'shikov, G.P., Synthesis of 7-Methoxy-4,5-dihydroharman and 7-Methoxyharman from Serotonin. J. Gen. Chem. USSR 33 1303-1304 (1963).

Pioch, R.P., U.S. Patent 2,736728 (1956).

Pollin, W., Cardon, P.V., Jr. and Kety, S.S., Effects of Amino Acid Feedings in Schizophrenic Patients Treated with Iproniazid, Science 133 104 (1961).

Popik, P., Layer, R.T. and Skolnick, P., 100 Years of Ibogaine: Neurochemical and Pharmacological Actions of a Putative Anti-addictive Drug. Pharmacological Reviews 47 235-253 (1995).

Pouchert, C.J., Aldrich Library of Infrared Spectra, Aldrich Chemical Company, (1970).

PSR Research Group, Ltd., Speculations on 1-Substituted Tryptamines, P. M. and E., Vol. 6 pp. 159-162 (1993).

Racette, D.L., personal communication.

Rasmussen, A., invaluable help.

Rätsch, C., personal communication.

Rausch, P., personal communication.

Raverty, W.D., Thomson, R.H. and King, T.J., Metabolites from the Sponge *Pachymatisma johnstoni*: L-6-Bromohypaphorine, A New Amino-Acid (and its Crystal Structure). J. Chem. Soc., Perkin Trans. 1204 (1977).

Ray, T., personal communication.

Reeve, C.B., personal communication.

Repke, D.B., personal communication.

Repke, D.B. and Ferguson, W.J., Psilocin Analogs. III. Synthesis of 5-Methoxy- and 5-Hydroxy-1,2,3,4-tetrahydro-9H-pyrido[3,4-b]indoles. J. Heterocyclic Chem. **19** 845-848 (1982).

Repke, D.B., Ferguson, W.J. and Bates, D.K., Psilocin Analogs. I. Synthesis of 3-[2-(Dialkylamino)ethyl]- and 3-[2-(Cycloalkylamino)ethyl]indol-4-ols. J. Heterocyclic Chem. **14** 71-74 (1977).

Repke, D.B., Ferguson, W.J. and Bates, D.K., Psilocin Analogs. II. Synthesis of 3-[2-(Dialkylamino)ethyl]-, 3-[2-(N-Methyl-N-alkylamino)ethyl]-, and 3-[2-(Cycloalkylamino)ethyl]indol-4-ols. J. Heterocyclic Chem. **18** 175 (1981).

Repke, D.B., Grotjahn, D.B. and Shulgin, A.T., Psychotomimetic N-Methyl-N-isopropyltryptamines. Effects of Variation of Aromatic Oxygen Substituents. J. Med. Chem. **28** 892-896 (1985).

Repke, D.B., Leslie, D.T. and Guzmán, G., Baeocystin in *Psilocybe*, *Conocybe* and *Panaeolus*. Lloydia **40** 566-578 (1977).

Repke, D.B., Mandell, D,M, and Thomas, J.H. Alkaloids of *Acacia baileyana*. Lloydia **36** 211-213 (1973).

Resch, S., personal communication.

Rhead, J.C., Soskin, R.A., Turek, I., Richards, W.A., Yensen, R., Kurland, A.A. and Ota, K.Y., Psychedelic Drug (DPT)-Assisted Psychotherapy with Alcoholics: A Controlled Study. J. Psych. Drugs **9** 287-300 (1977).

Richard, B., Delaude, C., Massiot, G. and Le Men-Olivier, L., Alkaloids from *Voacanga schweinfurthii* var. puberla. J. Nat. Products **46** 283-284 (1983).

Richards, W.A., Counseling, Peak Experiences and the Human Encounter with Death: An Emperical Study of the Efficacy of DPT-assisted Counseling in Enhancing the Quality of Life of Persons with Terminal Cancer and their Closest Family Members. Ph.D. Thesis, The Catholic University of America, 1975. p. 291.

Richards, W.A., Rhead, J.C., DiLeo, F.B., Yensen, R. and Kurland, A.A., The Peak Experience Variable in DPT-Assisted Psychotherapy with Cancer Patients. J. Psychedelic Drugs **9** 1-8 (1977).

Rimón, R., Airaksinen, M.M., Kari, I., Gynther, J., Venäläinen, E., Heikkilä, L., Ryyppö, J. and Palo, J., Pinoline, a ß-Carboline Derivative in the Serum and Cerebrospinal Fluid of Patients with Schizophrenia. Ann. Clin. Res. **16** 171-175 (1984).

Rivier, L., Indole Protoalkaloids Metabolism In *Anadenanthera Peregrina* Seeds. Planta Med **39** 215 (1980).

Rivier, L. and Lindgren, J. E., "Ayahuasca." The South American Hallucinagenic Drink: An Ethnobotanical and Chemical Investigation. Econ. Bot. **26** 101-129 (1972).

Robertson, J., Uncontainable Joy, *The Ecstatic Adventure: Reports of Chemical Explorations of the Inner World.* Metzner, R., ed. Macmillan, New York, 1968. pp. 87-88.

Robinson, B., Characterisation and Identification of Harmadine as Harmaline. Chemistry and Ind. 605 (1965).

Rosenberg, D.E., Isbell, H. and Miner, E.J., Comparison of a Placebo, N-Dimethyltryptamine, and 6-Hydroxy-N-dimethyltryptamine in Man. Psychophamacologia **4** 39-42 (1963).

Rosenberg, D.E., Isbell, H., Miner, E.J. and Logan, C.R., Effect of N,N-Dimethyltryptamine in Human Subjects Tolerant to Lysergic Acid Diethylamide. Psychopharmacologia **5** 217-227 (1964).

Rosenberg, D.E., Wolbach Jr., A.B., Miner, E.J. and Isbell, H., Observations on Direct and Cross Tolerance with LSD and d-Amphetamine in Man. Psychopharmacologia **5** 1-15 (1963).

Rosengarten, H., Meller, E. and Friedhoff, A.J., Possible Source of Error in Studies of Enzymatic Formation of Dimethyltryptamine. J. Psychiat. Res. **13** 23-30 (1976).

Rosenwald, J., Forteiture: The New American Evil. Media Bypass, June (199?).

Ross, L., Nibett, R., *The Person and the Situation*. McGraw Hill, 1991.

Rothlin, E., Lysergic Acid Diethylamide and Related Substances. Ann. N.Y. Acad. Sci. **66** 668-676 (1957).

Rovelli, B. and Vaughan, G.N., Alkaloids of Acacia I. $N_bN_b$-Dimethyltryptamine in *Acacia phelebophylla* F. Muell. Aust. J. Chem. **20** 1299-1300 (1967).

Saavedra, J.M. and Axelrod, J., Psychotomimetic N-Methylated Tryptamines: Formation in brain *in vivo* and *in vitro*. Science **175** 1365-1366 (1972).

Sahelian, R., *Melatonin, Nature's Sleeping Pill*. Be Happier Press, Marina del Rey, 1995.

Sai-Halasz, A., The Effect of Antiseotonin on the Experimental Psychosis Induced by Dimethyltryptamine. Experientia **18** 137-138 (1962).

Sai-Halasz, A., Brunecker, G. and Szara, S., Dimethyltryptamine- Psychotic Agent. Psychiat. Neurol. **135** 285 (1958).

Samorini, G., The Buiti Religion and the Psychoactive Plant *Tabernanthe Iboga* (Equatorial Africa). Integration #5 105-114 (1995).

Sanchez-Ramos, J.R., Banisterine and Parkinson's Disease. Clin. Neuropharmacol. **14** 391-402 (1991).

Sann, R., personal communication.

Salsbury, P., personal comunication.

Savinelli, A., personal communication.

Schlichting, M. and Leuner, H., "Psychotropic Effects of a New Orally Active Phenethylamine (DMM-PEA) and its Use as an Adjunct to Psychotherapy." Poster presentation at the International Conference on New Directions in Affective Disorders. Jerusalem, April 5 to April 10, 1987.

Schneckloth, R., Page, I.H., del Greco, F. and Concoran, A.C., Effects of Serotonin Antagonists in Normal Subjects with Carcinoid Tumors. Circulation **16** 52 (1957).

Schneider, J.A. and Sigg, E.B., Pharmacologic Analysis of Tranquilizing and

Central Stimulatiung Effects. In: *Psychopharmacology; Pharmacologic Effects on Behavior.* Ed. H.H. Pennes, Hoeber, New York. 1958. pp 75-98.

Schultes, R.E., *A Contribution to our Knowledge of Rivea corymbosa, The Narcotic Ololiuqui of the Aztecs.* Botanical Museum of Harvard University, Cambridge, Massachusetts, 1941.

Schultes, R.E. and Hofmann, A., *The Botany and Chemistry of Hallucinogens.* C.C. Thomas, Publ., Springfield, 1980.

Schultes, R.E., Holmstedt, B. and Lindgren, J.-E., De Plantis Toxicariis e Mundo Novo Tropicale Commentationes III. Botanical Museum Leaflets Harvard University 22 121-132 (1969).

Schultes, R.E., Holmstedt, B., Lindgren, J.-E. and Rivier, L., Phytochemical Examination of Spruce's Ethnobotanical Collection of *Anadenanthera peregrina.* Botanical Museum Leaflets, Harvard University 25 273 (1977).

da Selva, P., personal communication.

Shan, Y., personal communication.

Shields, J., personal comunication.

Shulgin, A.T., The Distortion of Music. Reality Hackers, #6 (Winter, 1988) pp. 27.

Shulgin, A.T., and Carter, M.F., Centrally Active Phenethylamines. Psychopharm. Commun. 1 93-98 (1975).

Shulgin, A.T., and Carter, M.F., N,N-Diisopropyltryptamine (DIPT) and 5-Methoxy-N,N-diisopropyltryptamine (5-MeO-DIPT). Two Orally Active Tryptamine Analogs with CNS Activity. Commun. Psychopharm. 4 363-369 (1981).

Shulgin, A. T. and Shulgin, A., *PIHKAL, A Chemical Love Story.* Transform Press, Berkeley, 1991.

Shulgin, T.A., personal communication.

Skaltsounis, A.L., Tillequin, F. and Koch, M., Plants of New Caledonia. Part LXXXIII. Alkaloids from the Leaves and Stems of *Melicope leptococca.* J. Nat. Prod. 46 732-735 (1983).

Skylla, personal communication.

Slotkin, T.A., DiStefano, V., Au, W.Y.W., Blood Levels and Urinary Excretion of Harmine and its Metabolites in Man and Rats. J. of Pharmacol. and Exp. Therapeut. **173** 26-30 (1970).

Smith, B. and Prockop, D.J., Central-Nervous-System Effects of Ingestion of L-Tryptophan by Normal Subjects. N. England J. Med. **267** 1338 (1962).

Smith, T.A., Tryptamine and Related Compounds in Plants. (Review) Phytochemistry **16** 171-175 (1977).

Snow, P.J.D., Lennard-Jones, J.E., Curzon, G. and Stacy, R.S., Lancet, 1955 II, 1004-1009.

Snyder, H.R. and Katz, L., Alkylation of Aliphatic Nitro Compounds with Gramine-Synthesis of Derivatives of Tryptamine. J. Am. Chem. Soc. **69** 3140 (1947).

Solms, Von H. Schweiz., Lysergic Acid Ethylamide (LAE), A New, Strong Sedative, Psychotic Agent from Ergot. Med. Wochen. **83** 356-360 (1953).

Somei, M., Sato, H. and Kaneko, C., A Short Step Synthesis of Lespedamine. Heterocycles **20** 1797-1799 (1983).

Soskin, R.A., Grof, S. and Richards, W.A., Low Doses of Dipropyltryptamine in Psychotherapy. Arch. Gen. Psychiat. **28** 817-821 (1973).

Spadoni, G., Stankov, B., Duranti, A., Biella, G., Lucini, V., Salvatori, A. and Fraschini, F., 2-Substituted 5-Methoxy-N-acyltryptamines: Synthesis, Binding Affinity for the Melatonin Receptor, and Evaluation of the Biological Activity. J. Med. Chem. **36** 4096-4074 (1993).

Späth, E. and Lederer, E., Synthesen von 4-Carbolinen. Ber. **63** 2102—2111 (1930).

Speeter, M.E. and Anthony, W.C., The Action of Oxalyl Chloride on Indoles: A New Approach to Indoles. J. Am. Chem. Soc. **76** 6208-6210 (1954).

Spenser, A.D., A Synthesis of Harmaline. Can. J. Chem. **37** 1851-1858 (1959).

Spiritual Emergence Network (located in Santa Cruz, CA): 408-426-0902.

Stolaroff, J., personal communication.

Stolaroff, J., personal communication.

Stoll, A. and Hofmann, A., Ergot Alkaloids. XXXVIII. Amides of Stereoisomeric Lysergic and Dihydrolysergic Acids. Helv. Chim. Acta **38** 421 (1955).

Strassman, R.J., personal communication.

Strassman, R.J., Peake, G.T., Qualls, C.R. and Lisansky, E.J., A Model for the Study of the Acute Effects of Melatonin in Man. J. Clin. Endocrin. Metabol. **65** 847-852 (1987).

Strassman, R.J., Clifford, R. and Qualls, C.R., Dose-Response Study of N,N-Dimethyltryptamine in Humans. Arch. Gen. Psychiatry **51** 85-97 (1994).

Strassman, R.J., Qualls, C.R. and Berg, L.M., Differential Tolerance to Biological and Subjective Effects of Four Closely Spaced Doses of NB,N-Dimethyltryptamine in Humans. Biol. Psychiat. **39** 784-795 (1996).

Strassman, R.J., Clifford, R., Qualls, C.R., Uhlenhuth, E.H. and Kellner, R., Dose-Response Study of N,N-Dimethyltryptamine in Humans. Arch. Gen. Psychiatry **51** 98-108 (1994).

Strassman, R.J., Human Hallucinogenic Drug Research in the United States: A Present-day Case History and Review of the Process. J. Psychoactive Drugs **23** 29-38 (1991).

Stuart, R., personal communication.

Supniewski, J. and Misztal, S., Bull. Synthesis of Melatonin 5-Methoxy-N-acetyltryptamine. Acad. Polon. Sci. **8** 471-481 (1960).

Szara, S., Dimethyltryptamine: Its Metabolism in Man; the Relation of its Psychotic Effects to the Serotonin Metabolism. Experientia **12** 441-442 (1956).

Szara, S. in *Psychotropic Drugs*. Ed. Garattini, S. and Ghetti,V. Elsevier, Amsterdam, 1957. pp. 460-467

Szara, S., Correlation between Metabolism and Behavioral Action of Psychotropic Tryptamine Derivatives Biochem. Pharm. **8** 32 (1961).

Szara, S., in *Ethnopharmacologic Search for Psychoactive Drugs*. 1967. Discussion on the Psychoactive Action of Various Tryptamine Derivatives. Ed: D.H. Efron. pp. 374-382.

Szara, S. and Hearst, E., 6-Hydroxylation of Tryptamine Derivatives: a Way of

Producing Psychoactive Metabolites. Ann. N.Y. Acad. Sci. **96** 134-141 (1962).

Szara, S., Rockland, L.H., Rosenthal, D. and Handlon, J.H., Psychological Effects and Metabolism of N,N-diethyltryptamine in Man. Arch. Gen. Psychiat. **15** 320-329 (1966).

Szmuszkovics, J., Anthony, W.C., and Heinzelman, R.V., N-Acetyl-5-methoxytryptamine. J. Org. Chem. **25** 857-9 (1960).

Taborsky, R.G., Delvigs, P. and Page, I.H., 6-Hydroxyindoles and the Metabolism of Melatonin. J. Med. Chem. **8** 855-858 (1965).

Taborsky, R.G., Delvigs, P., Palaic, D. and Bumpas, M., Synthesis of Pharmacology of Some Hydroxylated Tryptamines. J. Med. Chem. **10** 403 (1967).

Tadano, T., Neda, M., Hozumi, M., Yonezawa, A., Aral, Y., Fujita, T., Kinemuchi, H. and Kisara, K., Alpha-methylated Tryptamine Derivatives Induce a 5-HT Receptor-mediated Head-twitch Response in Mice. Neuropharmacology **34** 229-234 (1995).

Takahashi, T., Takahashi, K., Ido, T., Yanai, K., Iwata, R., Ishiwata, K. and Nozoe, S., [11]C-Labeling of Indolealkylamine Alkaloids and the Comparitive Study of their Tissue Distributions. Int. J. Appl. Isot. **12** 965-969 (1985).

Tanimukai, H., Ginther, R., Spaide, J., Bueno, J.R. and Himwich, H.E., Occurrence of Bufotenine (5-hydroxy-N,N-dimethyltryptamine) in Schizophrenic Patients. Brit. J. Psychiat. **117** 421-430 (1970).

Tasaki, Y., Makino, Y., Ohta, S. and Hirobe, M., 1-Methyl-1,2,3,4-tetrahydroisoquinoline, Decreasing in 1-Methyl-4-phenyl-1,2,3,6-tetrahydropyridine-Treated Mouse, Prevents Parkinsonism-like Behavior Abnormalities. J. Neurochem. **57** 1940-1943 (1991).

Taylor, D.L., Tansey, W., Cook, J.M. and Ho, B.T., Evaluation of Two Distinctive Beta-carbolines on Serotonin Binding in Human Platelets. Res. Commun. Chem. Path. Pharm. **47** 133-136 (1985).

Temple of the True Inner Light, personal communication.

Thieltges. R., personal communication.

Thompson, A.C., Nicollier, G.F. and Pope, D.F., Indolealkylamines of *Desmanthus illinoensis* and their Growth Inhibition Activity. J. Ag. Food Chem. **35** 561 (1987).

Torres, C.M., personal communication.

Torres, C.M. and Repke, D.B., The Use of *Anadenanthera columbrina* var. Cebil by Wichi (Mataco) Shamans of the Chaco Central, Argentina. Yearbook for Ethnomedicine and the Study of Consciousness **5** Berlin (1997).

Trout, K.O., personal communication.

Troxler, F. and Hofmann, A., Ergot Alkaloids. XLV. Substitution in the Ring System of Lysergic Acid. 3. Halogenation. Helv. Chim. Acta **40,** 2160 (1957).

Troxler, F., Seeman, F. and Hofmann, A., Synthetic Indole Compounds. II. Psilocybin and Psilocin Modifications. Helv. Chim. Acta **42** 2073 (1959)

Turner, W.J. and Merlis, S., Effect of Indolealkamines on Man. Arch. Neurol. Psychiat. **81** 121-129 (1959).

Turner, W.J., Merlis, S., Carl, A., Concerning Theories of Indoles and Schizophrenigenesis. Am. J Psychiat. **112** 466-467 (1955).

Ueno, A., Ikeya, Y., Fukushima, S., Noro, T., Morinaga, K. and Kuwano, H., Studies on the Constituents of *Desmodium Caudatum*. Chem. Pharm. Bull. **26** 2411-2416 (1978).

Utiger, R.D., Eng. J. Med. **327** 1377-1379 (1992).

Uyeno, E.T., 6-Hydroxylated N,N-Dimethyltryptamines and Hallucinogenic Potency. Proceedings of the Western Pharmacology Society **12** 118-123 (1969)

Uyeno, E.T., Alteration of a Learned Response of the Squirrel Monkey by Hallucinogens. Int. J. Neuropharmacol. **8** 245-253 (1969).

Uyeno, E.T., Relative Potency of Amphetamine Derivatives and N,N-Dimethyltryptamines. Psychopharmacologia **19** 381-387 (1971).

Van De Voorde, A., Catch Me if You Can. Westworld, pp 13-20 November 11-17, 1992.

Van Heiden, S.A., personal communication.

Van Lear, G.E., Morton, G.O. and Fulmor, W., New Antibacterial Bromoindole Metabolites from the Marine Sponge *Polyfibrospongia maynardii*. Tetrahedron Lett. 299 (1973).

Van Rhijn, C.H., Variables in Psycholytic Treatment, in *The Use of LSD in Psychotherapy and Alcoholism.* Edited by, H.A. Abramson, The Bobbs-Merrill Company, Ed., 1967. pp. 208 et sec.

Vijayalaxmi, Reiter, R.J. and Meltz, M.L., Melatonin Protects Human Blood Lymphocytes from Radiation-Induced Chromosome Damage. Mutation Research **346** 23-31 (1995).

Vilenskaya, L., personal communication.

Vinkers, H.M., personal communication.

Vitali, T. and Mossini, F., Sulla Preparazione di alcune Triptamine N'-disostituite [°]. Boll. Sci. Fac. Chim. Ind. Bologna **17** 84-87 (1959).

Waldhauser, F., personal communication.

Waldhauser, F., Saletu, B. and Trinchard-Lugan, I., Sleep Laboratory Investigations on Hypnotic Properties of Melatonin. Psychopharmacology **100** 222-226 (1990).

Wallace, R., personal communication.

Wasson, R.G., "Seeking the Magic Mushroom." Life, May 13, 1957; "En Busca del Hongo Mágico." Life en Español, June 10, 1957.

Weil, A., *The Marriage of the Sun and Moon.* Houghton Mifflin, Boston, 1980.

White, G., personal communication.

Wieland, H., Konz, W., Mittash, H., Ann. **513** 23 (1934).

Wieland, H., Hesse, G., Mittash, H., Toad Poisons. V. Basic Constituents of the Skin Secretion of the Toad. Ber. **64**, 2099-2103 (1931).

Wilcox, J.A., J. Psychoactive Drugs. **27** 181-182 (1995).

Wilkinson, S., 5-Methoxy-N-methyltryptamine: A New Indole Alkaloid from *Phalaris arundinacea.* J. Chem. Soc. 2079-81 (1958).

Willaman, J. J. and Li, H.L., Alkaloid-Bearing Plants and their Contained Alkaloids, 1957-1968. Lloydia **33** 1-286 (1970).

Winn, M., Horrom, R.W., Rasmussen, R.R., Chappell, E.B. and Plotnikoff, N.P., N-Cyclopropyltryptamines, Potent Monoamine Oxidase Inhibitors. J. Med. Chem. **18** 437-438 (1975).

Wohlrab, H.F., personal communication.

Wolbach Jr., A.B., Isbell, H. and Miner, E.J., Cross Tolerance between Mescaline and Lysergic Acid Diethylamide with a Comparison of the Mescaline and Lysergic Acid Diethylamide Reactions. Psychopharmacologia **3** 1-14 (1962).

Wolfson, P., personal communication.

Wu, F-E., Koike, K., Nikaido, T., Sakamoto, Y., Ohmoto, T. and Ikeda, K., New ß-Carboline Alkaloids from a Chinese Medicinal Plant, *Arenaria kansuensis*. Structures of Arenarines A, B, C, and D. Chem. Pharm. Bull. **37** 1808-1809 (1989).

Wulff, P., Carle, J.S. and Christophersen, C., Marine Alkaloids. Part 4. A Formamide, Flustrabromine, from the Marine Bryozoan *Flustra Foliacea*. J. Chem. Soc., Perkin Trans. 2895-2898 (1981).

Wyatt, R.J., Mandel, L.R., Ahn, H.S., Walker, R.W. and Vanden Heuvel, W.J.A., Gas Chromatographic-Mass Spectrometric Isotope Dilution Determination of N,N-Dimethyltryptamine Concentrations in Normals and Psychiatric Patients. Psychopharmacologia **31** 265-270 (1973).

Wyatt, R.J., Erdelyi, E., DoAmaral, J.R., Elliott, G.R., Renson, J. and Barchas, J.D., Tryptoline Formation by a Preparation from Brain with 5-Methyltetrahydrofolic Acid and Tryptamine. Sciences **187** 853-855 (1975).

Wyatt, R.J., Saavedra, J.M and Axelrod, J., A Dimethyltryptamine-Forming Enzyme in Human Blood. Am. J. Psychiat. **130** 754-760 (1973).

Young, E.H.P., The Synthesis of 5-Hydroxytryptamine (Serotonin) and Related Tryptamines. J. Chem. Soc. 3493-3496 (1958).

Zhang, F. and Dryhurst, G., Effects of L-Cystine on the Oxidation Chemistry of Dopamine: New Reaction Pathways of Potential Relevance to Idiopathic Parkinson's Disease. J. Med. Chem. **37** 1084-1098 (1994).

# APPENDIX E:  CACTUS ALKALOIDS

## TETRAHYDROISOQUINOLINES
## AND PHENETHYLAMINES

This is an index of the tetrahydroisoquinolines (THIQ's), dihydroiso-
quinolines (DHIQ's) and aromatic isoquinolines (IQ's) as well as the phenethylamines (PEA's) that are natural components of the cactii. This collection is from
my old mescaline files, from NAPRALERT, and from the Chemical Abstracts.
Plant sources other than Cactaceae may be mentioned, but not detailed, and if an
interesting synthetic analogue is reported in the literature, it will be noted.

An exception to this limitation is when a tetrahydroisoquinoline has been
found in the human nervous system and may well play some pharmacological role
there. The biosynthesis of most of the human "alkaloids" follows a single type of
chemistry. A phenethylamine (this can be phenethylamine itself, or any of the many
substituted phenethylamines that are known to populate the human brain, or even
the exogenous amines such as amphetamine or substituted amphetamines which get
there from outside the body) condenses with a carbonyl group (usually formaldehyde from folic acid, acetaldehyde from the metabolism of ethanol, pyruvic acid
from the metabolic pool, or occasionally a phenylacetaldehyde from one of the
above amines, formed by the action of a monoamineoxidase) to form a tetrahydroisoquinoline. This chemistry is illustrated in Appendix G. It seems inescapable that
these endogenous compounds play some role in our sickness and health, and these
natural compounds deserve companion status to the plant materials that are
exogenous to our nervous system, at least initially.

Let me use the mysterious syndrome of parkinsonism to illustrate such
role-playing with the very simplest possible phenethylamines and simple aldehydes. The first three entries, below, illustrate this complexity. Phenethylamine (a
component of several cacti, and of many other plants, and a well established natural
brain amine) condenses with formaldehyde to give the simplest possible
tetrahydroisoquinoline. This base produces the symptoms of parkinsonism in
animals, but in the human the brain levels are the same in both the diseased people
and in normals. When the condensing aldehyde is acetaldehyde (a major alcohol

metabolite) the product is 1-methyltetrahydroisoquinoline. This base was found at only a low level in both populations, and the level dropped with age. But, in experimental animals, pretreatment with this compound completely prevented the development of some of the damaging parkinsonism symptoms normally produced by either THIQ or the notoriously pathological drug MPTP. And when phenethylamine condenses with its own metabolite, phenylacetaldehyde, 1-benzyl-THIQ is formed. This material is much higher in the CSF of parkinsonism patients than in normals but its role with this disease, if any, is a mystery. So these three THIQ's, very closely related as to structure and *in vivo* synthesis, all have very different properties in the brain.

Many tetrahydroisoquinoline-3-carboxylic acids, the simple cyclization products of amino acids and aldehydes, are known both synthetically and from plant sources. None have been reported to occur in the cacti, and none are entered here.

Most of these alkaloids are 1,2,3,4-tetrahydro, and the convention that will be used with the carbolines to indicate the degree of unsaturation in the piperidine ring is also used here. The tetrahydro, dihydro and totally aromatic isomers are indicated with an $H_4$, $H_2$, and $H_0$, respectively, in the "other" column.

---

## 1,2,3,4-TETRAHYDROISOQUINOLINES (THIQ's)

——————— Ar unsubstituted ———————

| 1 | 2 | other | |
|----|----|-------|---|
| H | H | $H_4$ | THIQ |

Not reported in cacti. This is a normal component of human brain and urine. It is the reaction product of phenethylamine and formaldehyde.

| | | | |
|----|----|-------|---|
| H | Me | $H_4$ | isokairoline |
| | | | 2-methyl-THIQ |

| | | | |
|----|----|-------|---|
| Me | H | $H_4$ | 1-methyl-THIQ |

Not reported in cacti. This is a normal component of human brain and urine. It is the reaction product of phenethylamine and acetaldehyde.

Me      H       H₄      3-Me                              1,3-dimethyl-THIQ

Not reported in cacti.  When amphetamine is fed to rats and chronically exposed to alcohol, this is formed.  It is quite toxic, it causes tremors, and it produces a Straub tail response.

Bz      H       H₄                                       1-benzyl-THIQ

Not reported in cacti.   It is the condensation product of phenethylamine with its metabolite phenylacetaldehyde, and is found at elevated levels in Parkinson's disease patients.

Its inclusion in this collection is symbolic.  There are a great number of plant alkaloids that contain the carbon skeleton of a 1-benzylisoquinoline.  There are the curare paralytics from the South American arrow poisons from species of *Strychnos* and *Chondodendron*. There are the bridged pavine alkaloids from the laurels.  There are the antibacterials and anti-everything-else alkaloids of the berberine group from the roots of the holly-leafed barberry and the stems of the indian barberry.  There are the tetracyclic lycorine alkaloids from the bulbs of a variety of species of *Narcissus*, *Amaryllis* and *Lycoris* genera (the latter should not be confused with licorice which is a root extract flavoring from Leguminosae), not the Amaryllidaceae.  There are the squished four-ring systems of the *Erythrina* alkaloids of the jaiquery red-bean fame.  There are the tetracyclic apomorphine alkaloids (the synthetics from the alkaloids of opium), the natural neurotransmitter agonist bulbocapnine from species of *Corydalis,* and the quaternary magnoflorine from the magnolia.

The opium allusion is a fine starting point for a more complete explanation of just how the opium alkaloids (all of them are also 1-benzyl-substituted isoquinolines) can give rise to a thread of continuity that embraces not only the simple, almost cactus-like tetrahydroisoquinolines but the phenethylamines, as well.  The alkaloid fraction of opium (*Papaver somniferum*) is about 50% morphine and, of the remaining, about half is the alkaloid narcosine.

Narcosine is a 1-benzyl-tetrahydroisoquinoline with three noteworthy structural peculiarities.  The aromatic ring in the isoquinoline part of narcosine has the 3,4-methylenedioxy-5-methoxy substitution pattern on the aromatic ring, identical to that which is found in myristicin and in the phenethylamine MMDA.  The aromatic ring of the benzyl part of narcosine (attached to the 1-position of the THIQ, thus affording a chiral center) has the 3,4-dimethoxy-substitution pattern found in the phenethylamines DMPEA, and MDA.  And there is a carboxyl function at the 2-position of that benzene ring connected back to the benzylic carbon in the form of a lactone, which introduces a second asymmetric center. This big, fairly simple four-ring system is a super cough suppressant.  It was first isolated and described almost 180 years ago and, being an isoquinoline, is explicitly exempted from the illegal opium alkaloid constellation. It has also been called narcotine, but for political reasons many years ago (to be used as an antitussive but not to carry the pejorative "narc" prefix) it was renamed noscapine. The racemized isolate has been called gnoscopine.

When narcosine is treated with dilute nitric acid, two rings are torn away leaving the isoquinoline skeleton intact with the formation of cotarnine, 6,7-methylenedioxy-8-methoxy-1-hydroxy-2-methyl-THIQ. The shifting of a hydrogen atom from the 1-hydroxy group to the 2-nitrogen gives a differently named, tautomeric structure, 6,7-methylenedioxy-8-methoxy-1-oxyanionic-2-methylcationic 3,4-dihydro-IQ, which is still cotarnine. Gentle reduction provides the more prosaic compound hydrocotarnine, 6.7-methylenedioxy-8-methoxy-2-methyl-THIQ, that is missing that 1-hydroxy group. More strenuous reduction (elemental sodium in alcohol) actually removes the 8-position methoxyl group as well, giving rise to hydrohydrastinine, 6,7-methylenedioxy-2-methyl-THIQ. This base is the normal endpoint when these reactions start with hydrastine, the analogue of narcosine that never received an 8-methoxy group from nature in the first place. It is a hemostatic principle of **Hydrastis canadensis**, and is oxidized easily to hydrastinine, the 8-hydrogen-substituted tautomeric isomer of cotarnine above. This can, similarly, be reduced to hydrohydrastinine. These four isoquinolines are entered in this collection at their appropriate substitution pattern locations. Although none are from the cacti, all are plant related, largely from opium. Incidentally, the third most plentiful alkaloid in opium is also a 1-benzyl substituted isoquinoline. This is papaverine, 6,7-dimethoxy-1-(3,4-dimethoxybenzyl)-IQ.

Just as hydrastine is the methylenedioxy/dimethoxy non-opium analogue of narcosine (at the isoquinoline-6,7 and the benzyl-3,4 positions, resp.), two additional narcosine wannabes have been well studied as plant products. The corresponding methylenedioxy/methylenedioxy analogue is called adlumidine. The d-isomer is in **Adlumia fungosa**, and in the prolific genus **Corydalis** (**C. incisa** and **C. thalictrifolia**). The l-isomer (called capnoidine) is found in **C. crystallina**, **C. scouleri** and **C. sempervirens**). The stereoisomeric cis-isomer (called bicuculline) is in **Dicentra cucullaria** as well as in several of the **Corydalis** species. The corresponding dimethoxy/methylenedioxy analogue is called adlumine. The d-isomer is from **Adlumia fungosa** and the l-isomer is found in a variety of **Corydalis** species.

The connection of all of this to the phenethylamines comes from the reaction of hydrastine (as the quaternary methyl chloride salt) with strong alkali to form narceine, a tri-substituted phenethylamine which was explored commercially (as the ethyl ester) as an antitussive called Narcyl. The ultimate approach to the PEA world is the observation that 3,4-methylenedioxy-N-methylphenethylamine is also an antitussive in human studies. It is a direct imitation of part of the narceine structure. It is a kissing cousin of 3,4-dimethoxy-N-methylphenethylamine, which is a common component in many cacti, and it lacks just one methyl group (the alpha-methyl) to become the structure of MDMA (Ecstasy). It would be instructive to do a clinical study of MDMA to explore any antitussive action (amongst other things).

―――――――――――― Ar-6-substituted ――――――――――

| 6 | 1 | 2 | other | |
|---|---|---|---|---|
| HO | H | Me | H$_4$ | longimammosine<br>6-hydroxy-THIQ |

*Dolichothele longimamma*

| MeO | H | H | H$_4$ | longimammatine<br>6-methoxy-THIQ |
|---|---|---|---|---|

*Dolichothele longimamma*
*Dolichothele uberiformis*

| MeO | H | Me | H$_4$ | 6-hydroxy-2-methyl-THIQ |
|---|---|---|---|---|

Not reported in cacti. It is a synthetic isomer.

―――――――――――― Ar-7-substituted ――――――――――

| 7 | 1 | 2 | other | |
|---|---|---|---|---|
| MeO | H | H | H$_4$ | weberidine<br>7-methoxy-THIQ |

*Lemaireocereus weberi*
*Pachycereus weberi*

| MeO | Me | H | H$_4$ | isoweberidine, 1-methyl<br>x-methoxy-1-methyl-THIQ |
|---|---|---|---|---|

*Pachycereus weberi*

The position of the methoxy group has not been established with certainty.

——————————————— Ar-8-substituted ——————————

| 8 | 1 | 2 | other |
|---|---|---|---|

| HO | H | Me | H₄ |  | longimammidine |

longimammine
8-hydroxy-2-methyl-THIQ

*Dolichothele longimamma*
*Dolichothele uberiformis*

| HO | H | Me | H₄ | 4-HO | longimammamine |

4,8-dihydroxy-2-methyl-THIQ

*Dolichothele longimamma*
*Dolichothele uberiformis*

——————————————— Ar-5,7-disubstituted ——————————

| 5 | 7 | 1 | 2 | other |
|---|---|---|---|---|

| MeO | HO | H | Me | H₄ | uberine |

5-methoxy-7-hydroxy-2-methyl-
                                        THIQ

*Dolichothele uberiformis*

——————————————— Ar-6,7-disubstituted ——————————

| 6 | 7 | 1 | 2 | other |
|---|---|---|---|---|

| HO | HO | H | H | H₄ | norsalsolinol |

6,7-dihydroxy-THIQ
Not reported in cacti. This is a chemical found normally in the human brain.

| HO | HO | H | Me | H₄ | 6,7-dihydroxy-2-methyl-THIQ |

Not reported in cacti, but a brain component in both normals and in Parkinson's disease patients, whose dopamine cells have been studied as targets for this compound.

| HO | HO | Me | H | H₄ | salsolinol |

6.7-dihydroxy-1-methyl-THIQ
Sal
Not reported in cacti, although salsolinol is quite wide-spread

elsewhere in the plant world.  It is generated in man through the coupling of dopamine and acetaldehyde.  It is short-lived, being readily oxidized.  It has been given the nickname "Sal" by those studying the biochemistry of parkinsonism.

HO      HO      R       H       $H_4$      R = a substituted benzyl group

Many compounds have been synthesized and studied that are the products of the fusion of dopamine with a biologically generated phenylacetaldehyde.  Many are very active drugs, but none of them are plant products.  An example, from dopamine and deamination product of mescaline 3,4,5-trimethoxyphenylacetaldehyde, is the commercial bronchorelaxant Trimetoquinol.

HO      HO      Me      Me      $H_4$      6.7-dimethoxy-1,2-dimethyl-THIQ
                                            methyl-Sal

Not reported in cacti, but again a chemical in the human brain, both in normal subjects and in Parkinson's disease syndrome patients.  Only the "R" isomer is taken up in dopamine cells.

HO      HO      Me      Me      $H_0$      6,7-dihydroxy-1,2-dimethyl-
                                            isoquinolium quaternary
                                            salt

Not reported in cacti, but this quaternary salt has been identified in the brains of parkinsonism patients.  It apparently is not taken up in dopamine cells.

HO      MeO     H       Me      $H_4$      isocorypalline
                                            6-hydroxy-7-methoxy-2-
                                            methyl-THIQ

Not reported in cacti, although it has been identified in a number of other plants.

HO      MeO     Me      H       $H_4$      salsoline
                                            6-hydroxy-7-methoxy-1-methyl-
                                            THIQ

*Echinocereus merkerii*
*Pachycereus pecten-aboriginum*

It has been demonstrated that 3-MeO-4-OH-PEA gives rise to salsoline in the plant.  In radiolabelled studies with the N-acetyl analogue in *E. merkerii* cultures incorporated no radioactivity, so this expected cyclization may not occur in nature.  Interestingly, the name salsoline comes from the thistle *Salsola richteri*, where it was first discovered.

HO      MeO     Me      Me      H$_4$      1,2-dimethyl-6-hydroxy-7-
                                                    methoxy-THIQ

Not reported in cacti, nor in any other plant source, apparently. This is a synthetic compound.

MeO     HO      H       Me      H$_4$      corypalline
                                                    7-hydroxy-6-methoxy-2-methyl-
                                                    THIQ

*Islaya minor*

This alkaloid is present in a number of species of the genus *Corydalis*, called the fume warts, and is the source of a number of four-ring (or almost four-ring) fused THIQ's like corydaline and corycavidine. In fact, it is a good bet that any natural product with a name that starts with cory-something other than "n" comes from some *Cordalis* species. The coryn- prefix is largely reserved for the *Corynanthe* spp. alkaloids such as corynanthine and yohimbine.

MeO     HO      H       Me      H$_2$      pycnarrhine
                                                    7-hydroxy-6-methoxy-2-methyl-
                                                    3,4-dihydro-
                                                    isoquinolinium quaternary
                                                    salt

This is a partially oxidized form of corypalline, again associated with the *Cordalis* genus, but it does not occur in cacti.

MeO     HO      Me      H       H$_4$      isosalsoline
                                                    7-hydroxy-6-methoxy-THIQ

*Pachycereus pecten-aboriginum*

Take care: the name isosalsoline has been used in the literature to represent the "S" isomer of salsoline.

MeO     HO      Me      Me      H$_4$      1-methylcorypalline
                                                    N-methylisosalsoline
                                                    1,2-dimethyl-7-hydroxy-6-
                                                    methoxy-THIQ

This dextro-rotary isomer of this alkaloid occurs in several plant systems, but the levo-isomer is only known synthetically. Neither has been reported in cacti.

MeO     HO      CH$_2$OH Me     H$_4$      hedycarine
                                                    7-hydroxy-1-hydroxymethyl-6-
                                                    methoxy-2-methyl-THIQ

Not reported in cacti.

MeO    HO    i-Bu    Me    H$_4$        lophocerine
                                                    1-(i)-butyl-7-hydroxy-6-methoxy-
                                                        2-methyl-THIQ

*Lophocereus schottii*

There is a report of the isolation from this cactus of a compound, lophocine, which is a dimer of lophocerine. It is a biphenyl nucleus with a carbon-carbon bond connecting the 8,8' positions and the formation of two new six-membered rings with an ether link formed by the oxidative coupling of the 7-hydroxyl group to the 1-position. It is thought to be an artifact of isolation.

MeO    O-8 trimer  i-Bu   Me   H$_4$        pilocereine

*Lophocereus australis*
*Lophophora gatesii*
*Lophocereus schottii*
*Pachycereus marginaatus*

Pilocereine is a trimer of lophocerine, having a structure wherein the three molecular units are connected with two ether links from the oxygen at the 7-position of one, to the aromatic 8-position of the next. The corresponding dimer is called isopilocereine, containing just one such 7- to 8- ether link. This dimer is a synthetic compound and apparently does not occur in these cacti.

MeO    MeO    H    H    H$_4$        heliamine
                                                    6,7-dimethoxy-THIQ

*Backebergia militaris*
*Carnegiea gigantea*
*Lemaireocereus weberii*
*Pachycereus pecten-aboriginum*
*Pachycereus pringlei*
*Pachycereus weberi*

MeO    MeO    H    H    H$_2$        1,2-dehydroheliamine
                                                    3,4-dihydro-6,7-dimethoxy-IQ

*Backebergia militaris*
*Carnegiea gigantea*
*Pachycereus weberi*

MeO    MeO    H    H    H$_0$        backebergine
                                                    1,2,3,4-dehydroheliamine
                                                    6,7-dimethoxy-IQ

*Backebergia militaris*
*Pachycereus weberi*

| MeO | MeO | H | Me | $H_4$ | N-methylheliamine |
| | | | | | O-methylcorypalline |
| | | | | | 6,7-dimethoxy-2-methyl-THIQ |

*Backebergia militaris*
*Lemaireocereus weberi*
*Pachycereus weberi*
*Pilosocereus guerreronis*

| MeO | MeO | H | Me | $H_0$ | 1,2,3,4-dehydro-N-methylheliaminium quat salt |
| | | | | | 1,2,3,4-dehydro-O-methylcorypallinium quat salt |
| | | | | | 6,7-dimethoxy-2-methyl-isoquinolium quat salt |

This quaternary salt is not found in any cactus but it is in the fruit of the meadow rue *Thalictrum revolutum*. It is easily reduced (NaBH$_4$) to give 6,7-dimethoxy-2-methyl-THIQ which is, indeed, a cactus alkaloid.

| MeO | MeO | Me | H | $H_4$ | salsolidine |
| | | | | | 6,7-dimethoxy-1-methyl-THIQ |

*Carnegiea gigantea*
*Pachycereus pecten-aboriginum*

| MeO | MeO | Me | H | $H_2$ | 1,2-dehydrosalsolidine |
| | | | | | 3,4-dihydro-6,7-dimethoxy-1-methyl-THIQ |

*Carnegiea gigantea*
*Pachycereus weberi*

| MeO | MeO | Me | H | $H_0$ | isosalsolidine |
| | | | | | 1,2,3,4-dehydrosalsolidine |
| | | | | | nigellimine |
| | | | | | 6,7-dimethoxy-1-methyl-IQ |

*Pachycereus weberi*

| MeO | MeO | Me | -O | $H_0$ | nigellimine N-oxide |
| | | | | | 1,2,3,4-dehydrosalsolidine-N-oxide |
| | | | | | isosalsolidine N-oxide |
| | | | | | 6,7-dimethoxy-1-methyl-IQ N-oxide |

Not reported in cacti, although present in other plants.

MeO   MeO      Me      Me      H$_4$       carnegine
                                          pectenine
                                          6,7-dimethoxy-1,2-dimethyl-THIQ

*Carnegiea gigantia*
*Pachycereus pecten-aboriginum*
*Pachycereus weberi*


MeO    MeO     Me      Me      H$_4$  4HO
This is the first structure to be assigned to gigantine, but now the hydroxy group is known to be on the 5-position.


MeO    MeO     HO      H       H$_2$       corydaldine
                                          6,7-dimethoxy-1-oxo-THIQ
                                          3,4-dihydro-6,7-dimethoxy-1-
                                                    hydroxy-IQ
Two small problems here. This is a cyclic amide which is tautometric with a vinyl alcohol where an oxygen atom and a tertiary nitrogen atom share a double bond. One name refers to one structure, a carbonyl group bonded to an NH, and the other to a carbinol double bonded to a tertiary amine. The structures are identical, being tautomeric forms of one another. The atoms as well as the electrons move about a bit. The second problem is, why is this with a trivial name? The coryd- prefix reminds me of the naming argument following the corypalline entry above. But this was synthesized early in the century. Not a cactus component, but what is it?


MeO    MeO     HOCH$_2$ H      H$_4$       calcotomine
                                          6,7-dimethoxy-1-hydroxymethyl-
                                                    THIQ
Not reported in cacti, but present elsewhere in the botanic world.


-OCH$_2$O-      H       Me      H$_4$       hydrohydrastinine
                                          2-methyl-6,7-methylenedioxy-
                                                    THIQ
This compound is not found in any cactus, but it is a most important alkaloid in the area of plant chemistry. It is the reduction product of hydrastinine, the immediately following entry.


-OCH$_2$O-      HO      Me      H$_2$       hydrastinine
                                          1-hydroxy-2-methyl-6,7-
                                                    methylenedioxy-THIQ

3,4-dihydro-2-methyl-6,7-
methylenedioxy-
isoquinolium hydroxide

This product is, again, a tautomer mess, to which the last two
names offered will attest. It is not a cactus alkaloid, but a marvelous bridge
compound between complex alkaloids (here, hydrastine) and the THIQ's
and the PEA's. These two compounds are discussed under 1-benzyl-
THIQ above.

——————————— Ar-7,8-disubstituted ———————————

| 7 | 8 | 1 | 2 | other | |
|-----|-----|-----|-----|-------|---|
| HO | HO | H | Me | H$_4$ | 7,8-dihydroxy-2-methyl-THIQ (synthetic) |
| HO | MeO | H | Me | H$_4$ | 7-hydroxy-8-methoxy-2-methyl-THIQ (synthetic) |
| MeO | HO | H | Me | H$_4$ | 8-hydroxy-7-methoxy-2-methyl-THIQ (synthetic) |
| MeO | HO | Me | H | H$_4$ | arizonine 8-hydroxy-7-methoxy-1-methyl-THIQ |

*Carnegiea gigantea*
*Pachycereus pecten-aboriginum*

| | | | | | |
|-----|-----|-----|-----|-------|---|
| MeO | MeO | H | H | H$_4$ | lemaireocereine 7,8-dimethoxy-THIQ |

*Backebergia militaris*
*Lemaireocereus weberi*
*Pachycereus pringlei*
*Pachycereus weberi*

| | | | | | |
|-----|-----|-----|-----|-------|---|
| MeO | MeO | H | H | H$_2$ | 1,2-dehydrolemaireocereine 3,4-dihydro-7,8-dimethoxy-IQ |

*Backebergia militaris*
*Lemaireocereus weberi*
*Pachycereus weberi*

| MeO | MeO | H | H | H$_0$ | isobackebergine |
|-----|-----|---|---|-------|-----------------|

1,2,3,4-dehydrolemaireocereine
7,8-dimethoxy-IQ

*Backebergia militaris*
*Pachycereus weberi*

| MeO | MeO | H | Me | H$_4$ | N-methyllemaireocereine |
|-----|-----|---|----|-------|--------------------------|

7,8-dimethoxy-2-methyl-THIQ

*Backebergia militaris*

| MeO | MeO | Me | Me | H$_4$ | tepenine |
|-----|-----|----|----|-------|----------|

7,8-dimethoxy-1,2-dimethyl-THIQ

*Pachycereus tehuantepecanus*

——————— Ar-5,6,7-trisubstituted ———————

5 — 6 — 7 — 1 — 2 — other

| HO | MeO | MeO | Me | Me | H$_4$ | gigantine |
|----|-----|-----|----|----|-------|-----------|

6,7-dimethoxy-1,2-dimethyl-5-
hydroxy-THIQ

*Carnegiea gigantea*
      The earliest isolation reports assigned the OH group to the 4-position, but this 5-position is now preferred.

| HO | MeO | MeO | HOCH$_2$ | Me | H$_4$ | deglucopterocereine |
|----|-----|-----|----------|----|-------|---------------------|

6,7-dimethoxy-5-hydroxy-1-
hydroxymethyl-2-
methyl-THIQ

*Pterocereus gaumeri*

| HO | MeO | MeO | HOCH$_2$ | Me | H$_4$ | 2-O |
|----|-----|-----|----------|----|-------|-----|

deglucopterocereine N-oxide
6,7-dimethoxy-5-hydroxy-1-
hydroxymethyl-2-
methyl-THIQ N-oxide

*Pterocereus gaumeri*

| O-glu | MeO | MeO | HOCH$_2$ | Me | H$_4$ | pterocereine |
|-------|-----|-----|----------|----|-------|--------------|

6,7-dimethoxy-5-glucosyloxy-1-
hydroxymethyl-2-methyl-
THIQ

*Pterocereus gaumeri*

| | | | | | | | |
|---|---|---|---|---|---|---|---|
| MeO | MeO | MeO | H | H | $H_4$ | | nortehuanine<br>5,6,7-trimethoxy-THIQ |

*Lemaireocereus weberi*
*Pachycereus weberi*

| | | | | | | | |
|---|---|---|---|---|---|---|---|
| MeO | MeO | MeO | H | H | $H_2$ | | 1,2-dehydronortehuanine<br>3,4-dihydro-5,6,7-trimethoxy-IQ |

*Pachycereus weberi*

| | | | | | | | |
|---|---|---|---|---|---|---|---|
| MeO | MeO | MeO | H | H | $H_0$ | | isonortehuanine<br>1,2,3,4-dehydronortehaunine<br>5,6,7-trimethoxy-IQ |

*Pachycereus weberi*

| | | | | | | | |
|---|---|---|---|---|---|---|---|
| MeO | MeO | MeO | H | Me | $H_4$ | | tehuanine<br>2-methyl-5,6,7-trimethoxy-THIQ |

*Lemaireocereus weberi*
*Pachycereus pringlei*
*Pachycereus tehuantepecanus*
*Pachycereus weberi*

| | | | | | | | |
|---|---|---|---|---|---|---|---|
| MeO | MeO | MeO | H | Me | $H_4$ | 2-O | tehuanine N-oxide<br>2-methyl-5,6,7-trimethoxy-THIQ<br>N-oxide |

*Pachycereus pringlei*

──────────── Ar-6,7,8-trisubstituted ────────────

6 — 7 — 8 — 1 — 2 — other

| | | | | | | | |
|---|---|---|---|---|---|---|---|
| HO | MeO | MeO | H | H | $H_4$ | | isoanhalamine<br>7,8-dimethoxy-6-hydroxy-THIQ |

*Lophophora williamsii*

| | | | | | | | |
|---|---|---|---|---|---|---|---|
| HO | MeO | MeO | H | Me | $H_4$ | | isoanhalidine<br>7,8-dimethoxy-6-hydroxy-2-<br>methyl-THIQ |

*Lophophora williamsii*

| | | | | | | | |
|---|---|---|---|---|---|---|---|
| HO | MeO | MeO | Me | H | $H_4$ | | isoanhalonidine<br>7,8-dimethoxy-6-hydroxy-1-<br>methyl-THIQ |

*Lophophora williamsii*

| HO | MeO | MeO | Me | Me | H4 | isopellotine<br>7,8-dimethoxy-6-hydroxy-1,2-<br>dimethyl-THIQ |

*Lophophora diffusa*
*Lophophora williamsii*

| MeO | HO | HO | H | H | H4 | 7,8-dihydroxy-6-methoxy-THIQ |

Not reported in cactii.  Synthetic material.

| MeO | MeO | HO | H | H | H4 | anhalamine<br>6,7-dimethoxy-8-hydroxy-THIQ |

*Gymnocalycium gibbosum*
*Lophophora diffusa*
*Lophophora williamsii*

3,4-Dimethoxy-5-hydroxy-PEA has been shown to be a bioprecursor of anhalamine.  One report claims anhalamine to be hallucinogenic, but there is no follow-up information.

| MeO | MeO | HO | H | H | H2 | 1,2-dehydroanhalamine<br>3,4-dihydro-6,7-dimethoxy-8-<br>hydroxy-THIQ |

*Lophophora williamsii*

| MeO | MeO | HO | H | CHO | H4 | N-formylanhalamine<br>6,7-dimethoxy-2-formyl-8-<br>hydroxy-THIQ |

*Lophophora williamsii*

| MeO | MeO | HO | H | COCH3 | H4 | N-acetylanhalamine<br>2-acetyl-6,7-dimethoxy-8-hydroxy-<br>THIQ |

*Lophophora williamsii*

| MeO | MeO | HO | H | Me | H4 | anhalidine<br>6,7-dimethoxy-8-hydroxy-2-<br>methyl-THIQ |

*Lophophora williamsii*
*Pachycereus weberi*
*Pelecyphora aselliformis*
*Stetsonia coryne*

MeO  MeO  HO   H       Me    H$_2$   1,2-dehydroanhalidinium quat salt
                                     3,4-dihydro-6,7-dimethoxy-8-
                                            hydroxy-2-methyl-IQ

*Lophophora williamsii*

MeO  MeO  HO   H     (Me)$_2$$^+$ H$_4$   anhalotine iodide
                                     anhalidine methiodide
                                     6,7-dimethoxy-2,2-dimethyl-8-
                                            hydroxy-1,2,3,4-
                                            tetrahydroisoquinolium
                                            salt

*Lophophora williamsii*

MeO  MeO  HO   Me      H     H$_4$   anhalonidine
                                     6,7-dimethoxy-8-hydroxy-1-
                                            methyl-THIQ

*Lophophora diffusa*
*Lophophora williamsii*
*Pachycereus weberi*
*Stetsonia coryne*
*Trichocereus pachanoi*

　　　If 3,4-dimethoxy-5-hydroxy-PEA does indeed give rise, biosyn-
thetically, to anhalonidine in *Lophophora williamsii*, it does not get there
by way of the cyclization of the logical corresponding N-acetyl derivative.

MeO  MeO  HO   Me      H     H$_2$   1,2-dehydroanhalonidine
                                     3,4-dihydro-6,7-dimethoxy-8-
                                            hydroxy-2-methyl-IQ

*Lophophora williamsii*

MeO  MeO  HO   CO$_2$H  H    H$_4$   peyoxylic acid
                                     1-carboxy-6,7-dimethoxy-8-
                                            hydroxy-THIQ

*Lophophora williamsii*

MeO  MeO  HO   Me(CO$_2$H)  H  H$_4$   peyoruvic acid
                                     1-carboxy-6,7-dimethoxy-8-
                                            hydroxy-1-methyl-THIQ

*Lophophora williamsii*

MeO  MeO  HO   Me      Me    H$_4$   pellotine
                                     N-methylanhalonidine

6,7-dimethoxy-1,2-dimethyl-8-
hydroxy-THIQ

*Islaya minor*
*Lemaireocereus weberi*
*Lophophora diffusa*
*Lophophora fricii*
*Lophophora jourdaniana*
*Lophophora williamsii* 3,4-Dimethoxy-5-hydroxy-PEA has been shown
   to be a bio-precursor of pellotine in this cactus.
*Pachycereus weberi*
*Pelecyphora aselliformis*

MeO  MeO  HO  Me  Me  $H_2$    1,2-dehydropellotinium quat salt
                            3,4-dihydro-6,7-dimethoxy-1,2-
                                dimethyl-8-hydroxy
                                isoquinolium salt

   *Lophophora williamsii*

MeO  MeO  HO  Me  (Me)$_2$  $H_4$    peyotine iodide quat salt
                            pellotine methiodide
                            6,7-dimethoxy-2,2-dimethyl-8-
                                hydroxy-1-methyl-1,2,3,4-
                                tetrahydroisoquinolium
                                salt

   *Lophophora williamsii*

MeO  MeO  HO  Me  CHO  $H_4$    N-formylanhalonidine
                            2-formyl-6,7-dimethoxy-8-
                                hydroxy-1-methyl-THIQ

   *Lophophora williamsii*

MeO  MeO  HO  R  R  $H_4$    R-R= -CH$_2$CH$_2$C(O)-
                            peyoglutam

   *Lophophora williamsii*

MeO  MeO  MeO  H  H  $H_4$    anhalinine
                            6,7,8-trimethoxy-THIQ

   *Lophophora diffusa*
   *Lophophora williamsii*
   *Trichocereus pachanoi*

MeO  MeO  MeO  H  CHO  $H_4$    N-formylanhalinine
                            2-formyl-6,7,8-trimethoxy-THIQ

*Lophophora williamsii*

| MeO | MeO | MeO | Me | H | $H_4$ | O-methylanhalonidine<br>1-methyl-6,7,8-trimethoxy-THIQ |

*Lophophora williamsii*

| —— | (MeO)$_3$ | —— | Me | H | $H_2$ | 1-methyl-trimethoxy-3,4-DHIQ<br>(methoxy positions undetermined) |

*Pachycereus weberi*

| —— | (MeO)$_3$ | —— | Me | H | $H_4$ | 1-methyl-trimethoxy-IQ<br>(methoxy positions undetermined) |

*Pachycereus weberi*

| MeO | MeO | MeO | CO$_2$H | H | $H_4$ | O-methylpeyoxylic acid<br>1-carboxy-6,7,8-trimethoxy-THIQ |

*Lophophora williamsii*

| MeO | MeO | MeO | Me(CO$_2$H) | H | $H_4$ | O-methylpeyoruvic acid<br>1-carboxy-1-methyl-6,7,8-<br>    trimethoxy-THIQ |

*Lophophora williamsii*

| MeO | MeO | MeO | Me | Me | $H_4$ | O-methylpellotine<br>1,2-dimethyl-6,7,8-trimethoxy-<br>    THIQ |

*Lophophora diffusa*
*Lophophora williamsii*
*Pachycereus weberi*

| MeO | MeO | MeO | Me | CHO | $H_4$ | N-formyl-O-methylanhalonidine<br>2-formyl-1-methyl-6,7,8-<br>    trimethoxy-THIQ |

*Lophophora williamsii*

| MeO | MeO | MeO | R | R | $H_4$ | R-R= -CH$_2$CH$_2$C(O)-<br>mescalotam |

*Lophophora williamsii*

| -OCH$_2$O- | MeO | H | Me | | $H_4$ | hydrocotarnine<br>8-methoxy-2-methyl-6,7-<br>    methylenedioxy-THIQ |

This compound is not found in any cactus, but it is a most important alkaloid in the area of plant chemistry. It is the reduction product of cotarnine, the immediately following entry.

-OCH₂O-   MeO   HO   Me   H₂     cotarnine
                                 1-hydroxy-8-methoxy-2-methyl-
                                       6,7-methylenedioxy-THIQ
                                 3,4-dihydro-8-methoxy-2-methyl-
                                       6,7-methylenedioxy-
                                       isoquinolium hydroxide

This product is, again, a tautomer mess, to which the last two names offered will attest. It is not a cactus alkaloid, but a marvelous bridge compound between complex alkaloids (here, narcosine) and the THIQ's and the PEA's. These two compounds are discussed under 1-benzyl-THIQ above.

MeO   -OCH₂O-   Me   H   H₄     anhalonine
                                6-methoxy-1-methyl-7,8-
                                      methylenedioxy-THIQ

*Gymnocalycium leeanum*
*Lophophora williamsii*
*Trichocereus terscheckii*

MeO   -OCH₂O-   Me   CHO   H₄     N-formylanhalonine
                                  2-formyl-6-methoxy-1-methyl-7,8-
                                        methylenedioxy-THIQ

*Lophophora williamsii*

MeO   -OCH₂O-   Me   COCH₃   H₄     N-acetylanhalonine
                                    2-acetyl-6-methoxy-1-methyl-7,8-
                                          methylenedioxy-THIQ

*Lophophora williamsii*

MeO   -OCH₂O-   Me   Me   H₄     lophophorine
                                 1,2-dimethyl-6-methoxy-7,8-
                                       methylenedioxy-THIQ

*Gymnocalycium gibbosum*
*Gymnocalycium leeanum*
*Lophophora diffusa*
*Lophophora williamsii*

MeO   -OCH₂O-   Me   (Me)₂   H₄     lophotine iodide
                                    lophophorine methiodide

6-methoxy-7,8-methylenedioxy-
    1,2,2-trimethyl-
    tetrahydroisoquinolium
    quat salt

*Lophophora williamsii*

MeO   -OCH$_2$O-   Me   Et   H$_4$   peyophorine
                                    2-ethyl-6-methoxy-1-methyl-7,8-
                                        methylenedioxy-THIQ

*Lophophora williamsii*

——————— Ar-5,6,7,8-tetrasubstituted ———————

5 — 6—— 7 —— 8 — 1—2 — other

HO   MeO MeO MeO H   Me   H$_4$   O-demethylweberine
                                    5-hydroxy-2-methyl-6,7,8-
                                        trimethoxy-THIQ

*Pachycereus weberi*

MeO MeO MeO MeO H   H   H$_4$   norweberine
                                    5,6,7,8-tetramethoxy-THIQ

*Pachycereus weberi*

MeO MeO MeO MeO H   H   H$_2$   1,2-dehydronorweberine
                                    3,4-dihydro-5,6,7,8-
                                        tetramethoxy-IQ

*Pachycereus weberi*

MeO MeO MeO MeO H   H   H$_0$   isonorweberine
                                    5,6,7,8-tetramethoxy-IQ

*Pachycereus weberi*

MeO MeO MeO MeO H   Me   H$_4$   weberine
                                    2-methyl-5,6,7,8-tetramethoxy-
                                        THIQ

*Lemaireocereus weberi*
*Pachycereus pringlei*
*Pachycereus weberi*

MeO MeO MeO MeO Me   H   H$_4$   pachycereine
                                    1-methyl-5,6,7,8-tetramethoxy-
                                        THIQ

*Pachycereus weberi*

| MeO | MeO | MeO | MeO | Me | H | $H_2$ | 1,2-dehydropachycereine |
|-----|-----|-----|-----|----|----|-------|---|

3,4-dihydro-1-methyl-5,6,7,8-
tetramethoxy-IQ

*Pachycereus weberi*

| MeO | MeO | MeO | MeO | Me | H | $H_0$ | isopachycereine |
|-----|-----|-----|-----|----|----|-------|---|

1,2,3,4-dehydropachycereine
1-methyl-5,6,7,8-tetramethoxy-IQ

*Pachycereus weberi*

| MeO | MeO | MeO | MeO | Me | Me | $H_4$ | N-methylpachycereine |
|-----|-----|-----|-----|----|----|-------|---|

1,2-dimethyl-5,6,7,8-tetramethoxy-
THIQ

*Pachycereus weberi*

## PHENETHYLAMINES

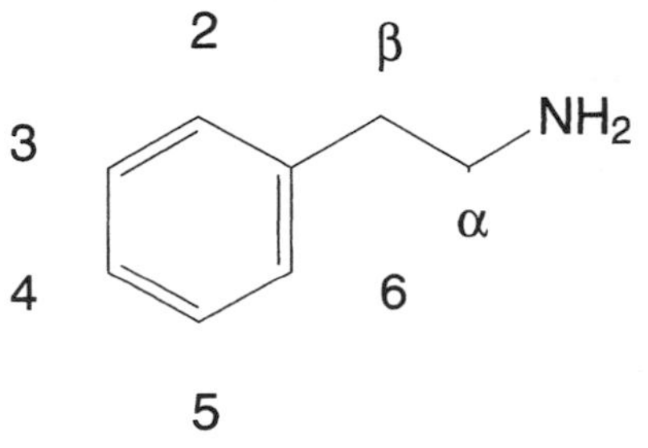

------------ Ring unsubstituted phenethylamines ------------

N ——— β

| N-H | β–H | phenethylamine |
|-----|-----|----|
|     |     | PEA |

*Islaya minor*
*Pereskia pititache*
*Pereskia tampicana*
*Pereskiopsis chapistle*

| N-Me | β–H | N-methyl-PEA |
|------|-----|----|

*Dolichothele sphaerica*

*Dolichothele surculosa*

N-(Me)₂ β–HO                              ubine
                                         N,N-dimethyl-β-hydroxy-PEA

*Dolichothele uberiformis*

N-(Me)₃ β–MeO                            β-methoxy-dehydroxycandicine
                                        coryphanthine
                                        β-methoxy-N,N,N-trimethyl-PEA

*Coryphantha greenwoodii*

——————— 4-Substituted phenethylamines ———————

4 —      N —      β

4-HO     N-H      β-H                    tyramine
                                        tyrosamine
                                        4-hydroxy-PEA

*Azureocereus ayacuchensis*
*Cactus grandiflorus*
*Cereus forbesii*
*Cereus glaucus*
*Cereus jamacaru*
*Cereus peruvianus*
*Cereus peruvianus monstruosus*
*Cereus valadus*
*Coryphantha missouriensis*
*Coryphantha pectinata*
*Echinopsis rhodotricha*
*Espostoa huanucensis*
*Gymnocalycium leeanum*
*Gymnocalycium saglione*
*Islaya minor*
*Lobivia allegriana*
*Lobivia aurea*
*Lobivia backebergii*
*Lobivia binghamiana*
*Lobivia huashua*
*Lobivia pentland*
*Lophophora williamsii*
*Mammillaria microcarpia*
*Melocactus delessertianus*

*Melocactus maxonii*
*Obregonia denegrii*
*Opuntia clavata*
*Opuntia ficus-indica*
*Opuntia imbricata*
*Opuntia invicta*
*Opuntia kleiniae*
*Opuntia schottii*
*Opuntia spinosior*
*Opuntia stanlyi var. kunzei*
*Opuntia stanlyi var. stanlyi*
*Opuntia versicolor*
*Pereskia aculeata*
*Pereskia autumnalis*
*Pereskia corrugata*
*Pereskia cubensis*
*Pereskia godseffiana*
*Pereskia grandifolia*
*Pereskia pititache*
*Pereskia tampicana*
*Pereskiopsis chapistle*
*Pereskiopsis scandens*
*Pilosocereus maxonii*
*Pseudolobivia kermisina*
*Trichocereus bridgesii*
*Trichocereus camarguensis*
*Trichocereus candicans*
*Trichocereus courantii*
*Trichocereus cuzcoensis*
*Trichocereus fulvilanus*
*Trichocereus knuthianus*
*Trichocereus macrogonus*
*Trichocereus manguinii*
*Trichocereus pachanoi*
*Trichocereus peruvianus*
*Trichocereus purpureopilosus*
*Trichocereus santiaguensis*
*Trichocereus skottsbergii*
*Trichocereus species*
*Trichocereus strigosus*
*Trichocereus tunariensis*
*Trichocereus werdermannianus*

4-HO    N-Me    β-H                        N-methyltyramine
                                          4-hydroxy-N-methyl-PEA

*Ariocarpus fissuratus*
*Ariocarpus kotschoubeyanusz*
*Ariocarpus lloydii*
*Ariocarpus scapharostrus*
*Ariocarpus trigonus*
*Coryphantha calipensis*
*Coryphantha missouriensis*
*Coryphantha cornifera*
*Coryphantha cornifera var. echinus*
*Coryphantha durangensis*
*Coryphantha elephantidens*
*Coryphantha ottonis*
*Coryphantha pectinata*
*Coryphantha poselgeriana*
*Coryphantha radians*
*Coryphantha ramillosa*
*Coryphantha runyonii*
*Dolichothele sphaerica*
*Dolichothele surculosa*
*Dolichothele uberiformis*
*Espostoa huanucensis*
*Gymnocalycium leeanum*
*Islaya minor*
*Lobivia allegriana*
*Lobivia aurea*
*Lobivia backebergii*
*Lobivia binghamiana*
*Lobivia huashua*
*Lobivia pentland*
*Lophophora williamsii*
*Pilosocereus maxonii*
*Mammillaria microcarpia*
*Obregonia denegrii*
*Opuntia clavata*
*Opuntia ficus-indica*
*Opuntia invicta*
*Opuntia kleiniae*
*Opuntia schottii*
*Opuntia stanlyi var. kunzei*
*Opuntia stanlyi var. stanlyi*

*Opuntia versicolor*
*Solicia pectinata*
*Trichocereus camarguensis*
*Trichocereus candicans*
*Trichocereus courantii*
*Trichocereus fulvilanus*
*Trichocereus manguinii*
*Trichocereus purpureopilosus*
*Trichocereus schickendantzii*
*Trichocereus skottsbergii*
*Trichocereus thelegonus*

4-HO    N-(Me)$_2$  β-H

hordenine
anhaline
eremursine
peyocactine
4-hydroxy-N,N-dimethyl-PEA

*Ariocarpus agavoides*
*Ariocarpus fissuratus*
*Ariocarpus kotschoubeyanus*
*Ariocarpus lloydii*
*Ariocarpus retusus*
*Ariocarpus scapharostrus*
*Ariocarpus trigonus*
*Cactus grandiflorus*
*Cereus alacriprotanus*
*Cereus glaucus*
*Cereus peruvianus*
*Coryphantha bumamma*
*Coryphantha calipensis*
*Coryphantha cornifera*
*Coryphantha cornifera var. echinus*
*Coryphantha durangensis*
*Coryphantha elephantidens*
*Coryphantha greenwoodii*
*Coryphantha missouriensis*
*Coryphantha ottonis*
*Coryphantha pectinata*
*Coryphantha poselgeriana*
*Coryphantha radians*
*Coryphantha ramillosa*
*Coryphantha runyonii*

*Coryphantha vivipara*
*Dolichothele surculosa*
*Dolichothele uberiformis*
*Echinocereus merkeri*
*Echinopsis eyriesii*
*Echinopsis rhodotricha*
*Espostoa huanucensis*
*Gymnocalycium leeanum*
*Gymnocalycium saglione*
*Helioanthocereus huascha*
*Helioanthocereus pasacana*
*Helioanthocereus poco*
*Islaya minor*
*Lobivia allegriana*
*Lobivia aurea*
*Lobivia backebergii*
*Lobivia binghamiana*
*Lobivia huashua*
*Lobivia pentland*
*Lophophora diffusa*
*Lophophora williamsii*
*Mammillaria microcarpia*
*Notocactus ottonis*
*Obregonia denegrii*
*Opuntia aurantiaca*
*Opuntia clavata*
*Opuntia invicta*
*Opuntia maldonadensis*
*Opuntia schottii*
*Opuntia versicolor*
*Opuntia vulgaris*
*Pelecyphora aselliformis*
*Pelecyphora pseudopectinata*
*Selenicereus pteranthus*
*Solicia pectinata*
*Trichocereus andalgalensis*
*Trichocereus candicans*
*Trichocereus lamprochlorus*
*Trichocereus manguinii*
*Trichocereus pachanoi*
*Trichocereus santiaguensis*
*Trichocereus schickendantzii*

*Trichocereus species*
*Trichocereus strigosus*
*Trichocereus taquimbalensis*
*Trichocereus thelegonoides*
*Trichocereus thelegonus*
*Trichocereus tunariensis*
*Turbinicarpus pseudomacrochele*
*Wigginsia erinacea*
*Wigginsia macrocantha*
*Wigginsia tephracantha*

4-HO    N-(Me)$_3$   β-H                    candicine
                                          hordenine methiodide
                                          4-hydroxy-N,N,N-trimethyl-PEA

*Denmoza rhodacantha*
*Echinocereus merkeri*
*Gymnocalycium saglione*
*Lobivia formosa*
*Opuntia hickenii*
*Trichocereus andalgalensis*
*Trichocereus candicans*
*Trichocereus pasacana*
*Trichocereus species*
*Trichocereus strigosus*

4-HO    N-Me     β-HO                     synephrine
                                          4,β-dihydroxy-N-methyl-PEA

*Coryphantha cornifera*
*Coryphantha cornifera var. echinus*
*Coryphantha durangensis*
*Coryphantha elephantidens*
*Coryphantha greenwoodii*
*Coryphantha ottonis*
*Coryphantha pectinata*
*Coryphantha poselgeriana*
*Coryphantha ramillosa*
*Coryphantha runyonii*
*Dolichothele sphaerica*
*Dolichothele surculosa*
*Dolichothele uberiformis*

4-HO    N-Me   β-MeO                          β-O-methylsynephrine
                                             4-hydroxy-β-methoxy-N-methyl-
                                                    PEA

    *Coryphantha cornifera var. echinus*
    *Coryphantha greenwoodii*
    *Coryphantha pectinata*
    *Coryphantha ramillosa*
    *Dolichothele sphaerica*


4-MeO   N-H    β-H                            O-methyltyramine
                                             4-methoxy-PEA

    *Coryphantha cornifera*
    *Coryphantha ottonis*
    *Coryphantha poselgeriana*


4-MeO   N-Me   β-H                            N-methyl-4-methoxy-PEA
    *Ariocarpus retusus*
    *Coryphantha bumamma*
    *Coryphantha cornifera var. echinus*
    *Coryphantha macromeris*
    *Coryphantha pectinata*
    *Coryphantha ramillosa*
    *Dolichothele uberiformis*


4-MeO   N-(Me)$_3$  β-H                       O-methylcandicine
                                             4-methoxy-N,N,N-trimethyl-PEA

    *Coryphantha greenwoodii*


4-MeO   N-H    β-HO                           β-hydroxy-4-methoxy-PEA
    *Coryphantha cornifera*
    *Coryphantha cornifera var. echinus*
    *Coryphantha elephantidens*
    *Coryphantha pectinata*
    *Pereskia grandifolia*
    *Pereskia tampicana*
    *Pereskiopsis chapistle*


4-MeO   N-Me   β-HO                           β-hydroxy-4-methoxy-N-methyl-
                                                    PEA

    *Dolichothele uberiformis*

——————— 3,4-Substituted phenethylamines ———————

3 —— 4 —— N —— β

3-HO   4-HO   N-H   β-H          dopamine
                                       3,4-dihydroxy-PEA

*Carnegiea gigantea*
*Lophophora williamsii*

3-HO   4-HO   N-Me   β-H       epinine
                                       desoxyepinephrine
                                       3,4-dihydroxy-PEA

*Lophophora williamsii*

3-HO   4-MeO   N-H   β-H      isohomovanilylamine
                                       3-hydroxy-4-methoxy-PEA

*Pachycereus pecten-aboriginum*

3-MeO   4-HO   N-H   β-H      homovanilylamine
                                       3-methoxytyramine
                                       3-methoxy-4-hydroxy-PEA

*Backebergia militaris*
*Echinocereus merkeri* Studies with [14]C labelled N-acetyl 3-MeO-4-
      HO-PEA did not provide labelled salsoline, the biological
      cyclization product, in culture studies with this cactus.
      Another intermediate is obviously responsible.
*Islaya minor*
*Lophophora williamsii*
*Opuntia imbricata*
*Opuntia spinosior*
*Opuntia subulata*
*Pereskia corrugata*
*Pereskia grandifolia*
*Pereskiopsis chapistle*
*Pachycereus pecten-aboriginum*
*Trichocereus bridgesii*
*Trichocereus camarguensis*
*Trichocereus courantii*
*Trichocereus cuzcoensis*
*Trichocereus knuthianus*
*Trichocereus macrogonus*
*Trichocereus manguinii*

*Trichocereus pachanoi*
*Trichocereus peruvianus*
*Trichocereus taquimbalensis*
*Trichocereus werdermannianus*

3-MeO   4-HO   N-Me   β-H            3-methoxy-N-methyltyramine
                                     4-hydroxy-3-methoxy-N-methyl-
                                          PEA

*Lophophora williamsii*
*Pilosocereus maxonii*
*Trichocereus courantii*

3-MeO   4-HO   N-Me   β-HO           metanephrine
                                     4,β-dihydroxy-3-methoxy-N-
                                          methyl-PEA

*Coryphantha runyonii*

3-MeO   4-HO   N-(Me)₂   β-H         N,N-dimethyl-3-methoxytyramine
                                     N,N-dimethyl-4-hydroxy-3-
                                          methoxy-PEA

*Ariocarpus agavoides*
*Lophophora williamsii*
*Pilosocereus maxonii*

3-MeO   4-OH   N-(Me)₂   β-HO        N-methylmetanephrine
                                     4,β-dihydroxy-N,N-dimethyl-3-
                                          methoxy-PEA

*Coryphantha runyonii*

3-MeO   4-MeO   N-H   β-H            DMPEA
                                     3,4-dimethoxy-PEA

*Backebergia militaris*
*Carnegiea gigantea*
*Echinocereus blankii*
*Echinocereus merkeri*
*Islaya minor*
*Lophophora williamsii*
*Mammillaria microcarpia*
*Melocactus maxonii*
*Neoraimondia arequipensis var. roseiflora*
*Opuntia acanthocarpa*
*Opuntia echinocarpa*
*Opuntia exaltata*

*Opuntia imbricata*
*Opuntia ramosissima*
*Opuntia spinosior*
*Opuntia whipplei*
*Pachycereus pecten-aboriginum*
*Pelecyphora aselliformis*
*Pereskia corrugata*
*Pereskia tampicana*
*Pereskiopsis scandens*
*Pilosocereus maxonii*
*Polaskia chende*
*Pseudolobivia kermisina*
*Pterocereus foetidus*
*Pterocereus gaumeri*
*Stenocereus beneckei*
*Stenocereus eruca*
*Stenocereus stellatus*
*Stenocereus treleasei*
*Trichocereus bridgesii*
*Trichocereus camarguensis*
*Trichocereus courantii*
*Trichocereus macrogonus*
*Trichocereus pachanoi*
*Trichocereus peruvianus*
*Trichocereus taquimbalensis*
*Trichocereus werdermannianus*

3-MeO   4-MeO   N-Me   β–H          N-methyl-DMPEA
                                     3.4-dimethoxy-N-methyl-PEA

*Ariocarpus agavoides*
*Ariocarpus fissuratus*
*Ariocarpus retusus*
*Ariocarpus scapharostrus*
*Ariocarpus trigonus*
*Backebergia militaris*
*Coryphantha bumamma*
*Coryphantha calipensis*
*Coryphantha cornifera*
*Coryphantha cornifera var. echinus*
*Coryphantha durangensis*
*Coryphantha elephantidens*
*Coryphantha greenwoodii*
*Coryphantha missouriensis*

*Coryphantha pectinata*
*Dolichothele uberiformis*
*Echinocereus cinerascens*
*Echinocereus merkeri*
*Mammallaria heyderi*
*Pelecyphora aselliformis  (trace)*
*Pilosocereus guerreronis*
*Pilosocereus maxonii*
*Pilosocereus chrysacanthus*

3-MeO  4-MeO  N-Me    β-HO          normacromerine
                                    3,4-dimethoxy-β-hydroxy-N-
                                        methyl-PEA

*Coryphantha calipensis*
*Coryphantha greenwoodii*
*Coryphantha runyonii*
*Dolichothele longimamma*
*Dolichothele uberiformis*

3-MeO  4-MeO  N-Me    β-MeO         calipamine
                                    O-methylnormacromerine
                                    N-methyl-β,3,4-trimethoxy-PEA

*Coryphantha calipensis*
*Coryphantha greenwoodii*

3-MeO  4-MeO  N-(Me)$_2$  β-H       N,N-dimethyl-DMPEA
                                    3,4-dimethoxy-N,N-dimethyl-PEA

*Ariocarpus scapharostrus*
*Backebergia militaris*
*Coryphantha greenwoodii*
*Echinocereus cinerascens*
*Echinocereus merkeri*
*Pilosocereus guerreronis*

3-MeO  4-MeO  N-(Me)$_3$  β-H       coryneine
                                    3,4-dimethoxy-N,N,N-trimethyl-
                                        PEA
                                    N,N-dimethyl-DMPEA methiodide

*Stetsonia coryne*

3-MeO  4-MeO  N-(Me)$_2$  β-HO      macromerine
                                    3,4-dimethoxy-N,N-dimethyl-β-
                                        hydroxy-PEA

*Coryphantha cornifera var. echinus*
*Coryphantha elephantidens*
*Coryphantha macromeris*
*Coryphantha pectinata*

3-MeO  4-MeO  N-(Me)₂  β-MeO      N,N-dimethyl-β,3,4-trimethoxy-
                                                    PEA

*Coryphantha calipensis*
*Coryphantha greenwoodii*

3-MeO  4-MeO  N(Me)CHO  β-HO      N-formylnormacromerine
                                            3,4-dimethoxy-N-formyl-β-
                                                    hydroxy-N-methyl-PEA

*Coryphantha runyonii*

3-NO2  4-HO  N-H     β-H          3-nitrotyramine
                                            4-hydroxy-3-nitro-PEA

*Cereus valadus*

──────── 3,4,5-Substituted phenethylamines ────────

3 ── 4 ── 5 ── N

3-HO  4-HO  5-MeO  N-H           3,4-dihydroxy-5-methoxy-PEA
*Lophophora williamsii*

3-HO  4-MeO  5-MeO  N-H          3-demethylmescaline
                                            4,5-dimethoxy-3-hydroxy-PEA

*Lophophora williamsii*
*Pelecyphora aselliformis*
*Trichocereus cuzcoensis*
*Trichocereus pachanoi*

3-HO  4-MeO  5-MeO  N-CHO        4,5-dimethoxy-N-formyl-3-
                                                    hydroxy-PEA

*Lophophora williamsii*

3-HO  4-MeO  5-MeO  N-COCH₃      N-acetyl-4,5-dimethoxy-3-
                                                    hydroxy-PEA

*Lophophora williamsii*

Radiolabelled N-acetyl-4,5-dimethoxy-3-hydroxy-PEA was
shown not to undergo the expected cyclization as a bioprecursor of
anhalonidine in feeding experiments with *L. williamsii*, although the

parent amine is probably incorporated in this alkaloid. This is amazing, as both this acetylated PEA and the end THIQ are known components of peyote.

3-HO    4-MeO  5-MeO  N-Me              4,5-dimethoxy-3-hydroxy-N-
                                                    methyl-PEA

        *Lophophora williamsii*

3-HO    4-MeO  5-MeO  N-(Me)$_2$        3-demethyltrichocereine
                                        4,5-dimethoxy-N,N-dimethyl-3-
                                                    hydroxy-PEA

        *Lophophora williamsii*
        *Pelecyphora aselliformis*

3-MeO   4-HO   5-MeO  N-H              3,5-dimethoxy-4-hydroxy-PEA
        *Escontria chiotilla*
        *Melocactus maxonii*
        *Neoraimondia arequipensis  var. roseiflora*
        *Opuntia acanthocarpa*
        *Opuntia basilaris*
        *Opuntia echinocarpa*
        *Opuntia exaltata*
        *Polaskia chende*
        *Pterocereus foetidus*
        *Pterocereus gaumeri*
        *Stenocereus beneckei*
        *Stenocereus eruca*
        *Stenocereus stellatus*
        *Stenocereus treleasei*
        *Trichocereus pachanoi*
        *Trichocereus peruvianus*
        *Trichocereus werdermannianus*

3-MeO   4-MeO  5-MeO  N-H              mescaline
                                       3,4,5-trimethoxy-PEA

        *Gymnocalycium gibbosum*
        *Islaya minor*
        *Lophophora diffusa*
        *Lophophora echinata*
        *Lophophora fricii*
        *Lophophora jourdaniana*
        *Lophophora williamsii*
        *Myrtillocactus geometrizans*

*Opuntia acanthocarpa*
*Opuntia basilaris*
*Opuntia cylindrica*
*Opuntia echinocarpa*
*Opuntia ficus-indica*
*Opuntia imbricata*
*Opuntia spinosior*
*Pelecyphora aselliformis*
*Pereskia corrugata*
*Pereskia tampicana*
*Pereskiopsis scandens*
*Polaskia chende*
*Pterocereus gaumeri*
*Stenocereus beneckei*
*Stenocereus eruca*
*Stenocereus stellatus*
*Stenocereus treleasei*
*Trichocereus bridgesii*
*Trichocereus cuzcoensis*
*Trichocereus fulvilanus*
*Trichocereus macrogonus*
*Trichocereus pachanoi*
*Trichocereus peruvianus*
*Trichocereus strigosus*
*Trichocereus taquimbalensis*
*Trichocereus terscheckii*
*Trichocereus validus*
*Trichocereus werdermannianus*

3-MeO  4-MeO  5-MeO  N-Me          N-methylmescaline
                                   N-methyl-3,4,5-trimethoxy-PEA

*Pelecyphora aselliformis*
*Lophophora diffusa*
*Lophophora williamsii*

3-MeO  4-MeO  5-MeO  N-CHO         N-formylmescaline
                                   N-formyl-3,4,5-trimethoxy-PEA

*Lophophora williamsii*

3-MeO  4-MeO  5-MeO  N-COCH$_3$    N-acetylmescaline
                                   N-acetyl-3,4,5-trimethoxy-PEA

*Lophophora williamsii*

3-MeO  4-MeO  5-MeO  N-R          R = -CH$_2$CO$_2$H
                                  glycine, N-(3,4,5-
                                          trimethoxyphenethyl)

*Lophophora williamsii*

3-MeO  4-MeO  5-MeO  N-R          R = -CH(CH$_3$)CO$_2$H
                                  alanine, N-(3,4,5-
                                          trimethoxyphenethyl)

*Lophophora williamsii*

3-MeO  4-MeO  5-MeO  N-(Me)$_2$   Trichocereine
                                  N,N-dimethyl-3,4,5-trimethoxy-
                                          PEA

*Trichocereus terscheckii*

3-MeO  4-MeO  5-MeO  N-R$_2$      R = -COCH$_2$CH$_2$CO-
                                  mescaline succinimide

*Lophophora williamsii*

3-MeO  4-MeO  5-MeO  N-R$_2$      R = -COCH$_2$CHOHCO-
                                  mescaline malimide

*Lophophora williamsii*

3-MeO  4-MeO  5-MeO  N-R$_2$      R = -COCH=CHCO-
                                  mescaline maleimide

*Lophophora williamsii*

3-MeO  4-MeO  5-MeO  N-R$_2$      R = cyclic imide with citrate
                                  mescaline citrimide

*Lophophora williamsii*

3-MeO  4-MeO  5-MeO  N-R$_2$      R = the lactone of the cyclic imide
                                          with citrate
                                  mescaline isocitrimide lactone

*Lophophora williamsii*

3-MeO  4-MeO  5-MeO  N-R$_2$      R = N-pyrrole derivative
                                  peyoglunal

*Lophophora williamsii*

3-MeO  4-MeO  5-MeO  N-R$_2$      R = -pyrrole carboxylate
                                  peyonine

*Lophophora williamsii*

──────── 2,3,4,5-Substituted phenethylamines ────────

2 —— 3 —— 4 —— 5 —— N

2-Cl    3-MeO  4-MeO  5-MeO  N-H     2-chloro-mescaline
                                     2-chloro-3,4,5-trimethoxy-PEA

*Trichocereus peruvianus*

This compound was isolated from the alkaloid fraction of this cactus, but was determined to be an artifact of extraction. Chloroform was used as a solvent, and it apparently provided the chlorine atom. This compound was not seen when non-chlorinated solvents were used.

# APPENDIX F:  CARBOLINES

This is an effort to tabulate all the biologically interesting beta-carbolines, with a statement of their plant origins if they are natural, or their reasons for being interesting, if synthetic. The references are not included here. However, the compounds are connected to the plants, and either one will allow the interested reader to get started in his literature search.

There are a few misleading chemical clues that should be recognized when they are seen. Carbazole is a similar name and a similar ring system, but it lacks a nitrogen atom in the right-hand ring. There are other Greek letters that define the nitrogen position in the carboline ring, as shown in the structure below. Many of these are known chemically, and some of them are found in botanical sources, and some are pharmacologically active, but none of them have any connection to the tryptamines.

Let me define my classification of substitution patterns. Ar- is the substitution system on the aromatic ring, positions 5,6,7 or 8. The locators 1- and 2- show substituents on these positions of the piperidine or pyridine ring as seen in the structure. $H_x$ is the degree of hydrogenation of this right hand ring, with $H_4$ being the tetrahydro, $H_2$ with the double bond at the 1,2-position (the dihydro) and $H_0$ is the totally aromatic pyridine ring. "Other" locates unusual groups elsewhere on the piperidine ring or on the indolic 9-position. The listing of compounds is alphabetized from right to left, by and large, and the $H_x$ progresses from $H_4$ to $H_2$ to $H_0$. And, it must be remembered that the placement of an H on the 2-position of a completely aromatic $H_0$ structure indicates the absence of any substitution.

This compilation is not an exhaustive review by any means, but rather a collection of tidbits intended to serve as a guide for further searching. Also, I apologize for the absence of Family names here and there. I don't know them.

The true reward from this kind of searching is the discovery of some sort of chemical insight that is not at all obvious. Here, I was surprised to learn of two styles of attachment of a pyrrole ring (via its 2-position) to the β-carboline. It can go to the carboline 1-position, to provide a host of alkaloids found in the genus

*Eudistoma* from tunicates (little marine chordate animals found in the Caribbean and off Okinawa), or to the 4-position, to give alkaloids found in Russian sedges. The former are antiviral compounds and the later are uterine contractants. Names were given for some of these in the Napralert files but no structures, and they are best found by plowing through Chemical Abstracts. But even there you must put up with the variability of the numbering of the N and the tetrahydro locations. A good start is 9H-pyrido[3,4b]indole but it changes regularly from page to page. There is a moral here: no search is complete, not even this one. Learn what you can from others, come up with a new idea, and then create something unexpected all on your own.

The β-carboline numbering system is shown below. Numbers in parentheses are those that are used in tryptolines or on the indole aromatic ring.

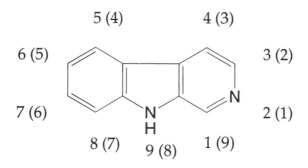

---

UNSUBSTITUTED AROMATIC RING (5, 6, 7, 8 = H)

| 1 | 2 | H$_X$ | other |
|---|---|-------|-------|
| H | H | H$_4$ | — |

1,2,3,4-tetrahydro-β-carboline
tryptoline
THβC
noreleagnine

*Commelina communis* (Commelinaceae)
*Eudistoma glaucus* (Ascidiacea)
*Lolium perenne* (Gramineae)
*Phalaris arundinacea* (Gramineae)
*Strychnos johnsonii* (Loganiaceae)
*Testulea gabonensis* (Ochnaceae) trunkbark
*Villagorgia rubra*

THβC is the simplest of the tryptamines and is a normal component of rat brain and urine, and it has also been found in human blood platelets, plasma, and urine. It was given the trivial name of tryptoline probably out of ignorance, rather than by design. It forms spontaneously from the interaction of tryptamine and a one-carbon unit such as formaldehyde. Also, in brain biochemistry, both THβC and the N-methyl homologue 2-Me-THβC are normal metabolites of DMT. In the rat THβC also gives rise to a mixture of 6- and 7-hydroxy-THβC, the 1-keto-amide, and to β-carboline as well. The nomenclature using the 9H in the synonym above for THβC is offered as an explanation as to why there will be no more Chem. Absts. proper names offered. They are a bit too long, and they do not make things clearer.

| H | H | H$_4$ | 3-Me | 3-methyl-1,2,3,4-tetrahydro-β-carboline |
|---|---|---|---|---|

3-Me-THβC

***Arthrophytum leptocladum*** (Chenopodiaceae)
***Hammada leptoclada*** (Chenopodiaceae) aerial parts

| H | H | H$_4$ | 3-CO$_2$H | 1,2,3,4-tetrahydro-β-carboline, 3-carboxylic acid |
|---|---|---|---|---|

TCCA
THCA

***Aleurites fordii*** (Euphorbiaceae) L-isomer, seed
***Allium tuberosum*** (Liliaceae) leaf

The cyclization product of the amino acid tryptophan and formaldehyde. This has been reported as a component of wine. It is also present in saki and soy sauce.

| H | H | H$_2$ | 9-COCH$_3$ | 9-aceto-3,4-dihydro-β-carboline |
|---|---|---|---|---|

***Adhatoda vasica*** (Zygophyllaceae) root

| H | H | H$_0$ | — | beta-carboline |
|---|---|---|---|---|

β-carboline
βC
norharman

***Acraea andromacha*** (Nymphalidae) butterflies
***Cannabis sativa*** (Cannabinaceae) in smoke condensate
***Carex brevicollis*** (Cyperaceae)
***Catharanthus roseus*** (Apocynaceae) leaf
***Cichorium intybus*** (Compositae) root
***Cinchona ledgeriana*** (Rubiaceae) suspension culture — conversion of tryptophan to carbolines.

*Codonopsis lanceolata* (Campanulaceae) root
*Commelina communis* (Commelinaceae) aerial parts
*Desmodium gangeticum* (Leguminosae)
*Desmodium pulchellum* (Leguminosae)
*Didemnum species* (Didemnidae) marine
*Festuca arundinacea* (Gramineae) the same species name as *Phalaris arundinacea*, but a different grass, I believe.
*Heliconius cydno-galanthus* (Nymphalidae)
*Heliconius erato-petiverana* (Nymphalidae)
*Heliconius ethilla-eucoma* (Nymphalidae)
*Heliconius melpomene-rosina* (Nymphalidae)
*Heliconius sara-thamar* (Nymphalidae)
*Heliconius wallacei-flavescens* (Nymphalidae)
*Lolium perenne* (Gramineae) a grass associated with toxicity, see the "DMT is Everywhere" chapter. In the aerial parts.
*Nicotiana tabacum* (Solanaceae) leaf. This is also reported as a component of cigarette smoke.
*Nocardia species* Strain P-9 (Nocardiaceae) culture filtrate
*Noctiluca miliaris* (Noctilucaceae) first ever isolation of a carboline from a marine source — a dinoflagellate — in 1980 — all because its cells showed fluorescence! Harman is here as well.
*Panax ginseng* (Araliaceae) root
*Phaseolus vulgaris* cv. Red Kidney Bean (Leguminosae) suspension culture
*Pinellia pedatisecta* (Araceae) Both the plant and its bulbs contain β-carboline.
*Polygala tenuifolia* (Polygalaceae) rhizome
*Rauwolfia caffra* (Apocynaceae)
*Rauwolfia sumatrana* (Apocynaceae) leaf
*Ritterella sigillinoides*
*Strychnos johnsonii* (Loganiaceae) rootbark
*Strychnos potatorum* (Loganiaceae) rootbark
*Tribulus terrestris* (Zygophyllaceae) entire plant

This is the parent aromatic alkaloid that defines the β-carboline family of alkaloids. It has been a popular exploration to evaluate analogues and homologues of β-carboline as monoamine oxidase enzyme inhibitors, but the bottom line seems to be that the unsubstituted, totally aromatic parent β-carboline itself is a potent enzyme inhibitor. It has also been found in saki and soy sauce.

H      H      $H_0$      $3\text{-}CO_2CH_2CH_3$    3-carboethoxy-β-carboline
                                                ethyl β-carboline-3-carboxylate

ethyl norharman-3-carboxylate

β-CCE

*Picrasma quassioides* (Simaroubaceae)

This aromatized, cyclized tryptophan product has been extensively explored as a benzodiazepine receptor ligand. It has been isolated from human brain and urine, although the ester itself may be an artifact of isolation. SAR studies of many analogues show that the 1,2,3,4-dienes are more potent than the saturated counterparts, and that the 3-carbonyl group is desirable for maximum potency.

H     H     $H_0$     4-(1-methyl-2-piperidinyl)

4-(1-methyl-2-piperidinyl)-

β-carboline

homobrevicolline

*Carex* spp.  (Cyperaceae)

H     Me     $H_4$     —          2-methyl-1,2,3,4-tetrahydro-β-

carboline

2-methyl-1,2,3,4-

tetrahydronorharman

2-Me-THβC

*Acacia simplicifolia*  (Leguminosae) The leaves and the bark of this tree were analyzed and found to contain NMT, DMT, N-formyl-MMT and 2-Me-THβC. A study on the stem bark reports that there is a 3.6% total alkaloid content, with 40% NMT, 22.5 % DMT and 12.7% 2-Me-THβC. Leaf, stem and trunkbark.

*Anadenanthera peregrina*  (Leguminosae) seed

*Arthrophytum leptocladum*  (Chenopodiaceae) entire plant

*Banisteriopsis rusbyana*  (Malpighiaceae) see *Diploteris cabrerana*.

*Desmodium gangeticum*  (Leguminosae) leaf and stem

*Desmodium pulchellum*  (Leguminosae)

*Diploteris cabrerana*  (Malpighiaceae) contains 2-Me-THβC in trace amounts. DMT is the major alkaloid present to the extent of up to 98% of the leaf alkaloid content, or about 0.5% of the dry weight. There is also present NMT, 5-MeO-DMT and bufotenine.

*Elaeagnus angustifolia*  (Elaeagnaceae) entire plant

*Fluggea microcarpa*  (Euphorbiaceae)

*Gymnacranthera* spp.  (Myristicaceae)

*Hammada* spp.  (Chenopodiaceae)

*Limonia acidissima*  (Rutaceae) stem

*Mimosa scabrella*  (Leguminosae) bark. Presence of T, NMT, DMT and 2-Me-THβC in the bark. This is another of several plants mentioned here with tryptamines and β-carbolines occurring naturally together. If the right example were chosen, it could well serve as a one-step source of ayahuasca.

***Palicourea marcgravii*** (Rubiaceae) leaf

***Papaver pavoninum*** (Papaveraceae) entire plant

***Papaver rhoeas*** var. Chelidonioides (Papaveraceae)

***Phalaris arundinacea*** (Gramineae) aerial parts. 2-Me-THβC and variations are reported in this grass.

***Polyalthia acuminata*** (Annonaceae) bark and leaf

***Psychotria carthaginensis*** (Rubiaceae) The leaves of this plant contain DMT, and as well, NMT and 2-Me-THβC.

***Psychotria viridis*** (Rubiaceae) The leaves of this plant contain DMT, and as well, NMT and 2-Me-THβC. It is one of the two defining plants of ayahuasca.

***Securinega virosa*** (Euphorbiaceae) leaf

***Testulea gabonensis*** DMT, N-formyl-NMT and 2-Me-THβC are present, but the major alkaloid, 90% of total, is NMT. Bark.

***Virola sebifera*** (Myristicaceae) bark. This plant contains NMT, its formamide and acetamine, DMT and its N-oxide, and 2-Me-THβC.

***Virola theiodora*** (Myristicaceae) Also contains 2-Me-6-MeO-THβC as well as the DMT, 5-MeO-DMT, and NMT as a major component.

2-Me-THβC is a metabolite of DMT, and thus it is a natural component of human biochemistry. It is a member of a small group of β-carbolines called "mammalian THβC's" in that they can and do arise as normal blood and urine materials in man. A more subtle source in man might be from the use of poorly synthesized DMT, as 2-Me-THβC is an established side-reaction product.

The structure of 2-Me-THβC is, with the exception of a simple -NH- bridge, precisely that of MPTP, N-methyl-4-phenyl-1,2,3,6-tetrahydropyridine. This was the impurity in a synthetic heroin substitute that gave rise to an irreversible parkinsonism syndrome in both man and primates. The story is well presented in a film, "The Frozen Addict." Studies in owl monkeys of this carboline gave some effects similar to those produced by MPTP but there was neither a parkinsonism syndrome nor any brain pathology observed.

| H | Me | H$_4$ | CO$_2$Me | 3-carbomethoxy-2-methyl-β-carboline |

***Gastrolobium callistachys*** (Leguminosae)

| H | Me | H$_0$ | — | 2-methyl-β-carbolinium quat salt |

***Desmodium gangeticum*** (Leguminosae)

***Desmodium pulchellum*** (Leguminosae)

*Strychnos usambarensis*  (Loganiaceae)

This aromatic extension of 2-Me-THβC is a very close structural analogue to the Parkinson toxin MPP+, the oxidation product of MPTP that is probably the active factor in the achieved tragic fame as a mis-synthesized heroin substitute mentioned above. This carboline is highly toxic by intranigral injection, but not as potent as MPP+.

| =O | Me | H4 | — | 2-methyl-3,4-dihydro-β-carbolone-1 |
|    |    |    |   | strychnocarpine |

*Strychnos elaeocarpa*  (Loganiaceae) bark
*Strychnos floribunda*  (Loganiaceae)

| Me | H | H4 | — | 1-methyl-1,2,3,4-tetrahydro-β-carboline |
|    |   |    |   | 1-Me-THβC |
|    |   |    |   | tetrahydroharman |
|    |   |    |   | methtryptoline |
|    |   |    |   | 9-methyltryptoline |
|    |   |    |   | calligonine  (racemate) |
|    |   |    |   | elaeagnine  (racemate) |
|    |   |    |   | eleagnine  (racemate) |

*Acacia baileyana* (Leguminosae) leaf
*Acacia complanata* (Leguminosae) leaf
*Amsonia tabernaemontana*  (Apocynaceae) green parts, roots
*Arundo donax*  (Gramineae) flowers
*Banisteriopsis argentea*  (Malpighiaceae)
*Burkea africana*  (Leguminosae)
*Calligonum minimum*  (Polygonaceae) aerial parts and root
*Desmodium pulchellum*  (Leguminosae)
*Elaeagnus angustifolia*  (Elaeagnaceae) entire plant
*Elaeagnus spinosa*  (Elaeagnaceae) bark
*Guiera senegalensis*  (Combretaceae) root
*Haloxylon scoparium*  (Chenopodiaceae) aerial parts
*Hammada articulada* Var. scoparia (Chenopodiaceae)
*Hammada leptoclada*  (Chenopodiaceae) aerial parts
*Leptactinia densiflora*  (Chenopodiaceae)
*Peganum harmala*  (Zygophyllaceae)
*Petalostylis cassioides* (Leguminosae) (the butterfly bush) contains some 0.5% alkaloids, mostly tryptamines including DMT. Tetrahydroharman is present in the leaves and stems.
*Petalostylis labicheoides*  (Leguminosae) leaf and stem
*Polyalthia acuminata*  (Annonaceae) dl-racemate bark and leaf
*Prosopis alpataco*  (Leguminosae) bark

*Prosopis nigra*  (Leguminosae) leaf
*Prosopis ruscifolia*  (Leguminosae) bark
*Prosopis sericantha*  (Leguminosae) bark
          Besides tetrahydroharman being in many plant species, it is a potent monoamine oxidase inhibitor which is interesting in that it can occur in plants associated with DMT.  Infusion into rats encourages alcohol consumption and it may be a metabolite of alcohol, but look under harmalan below for a note of caution.  Further metabolism adds a 6-hydroxy group, to form tetrahydroisoharmol.  As to the biosynthetic formation of tetrahydroharman, its origins are clearly from tryptamine, but studies in *Elaeagnus angustifolia* cultures have shown that the most logical compound, N-acetyltryptamine, does not play this role.  It is a normal component of wine and a natural component of both human brain and urine, independent of any ethanol being consumed.

Me       H       H$_4$       3-CO$_2$H          1-methyl-1,2,3,4-tetrahydro-β-
                                                          carboline, 3- carboxylic acid
                                                MTCA
                                                TCCA
                                                EMS factor

*Amanita muscaria* (Amanitaceae)
*Eleocharis dulcis*  (Cyperaceae) entire plant (the 1-S, 3-S isomer)
          The reaction between the amino acid tryptophan and acetalde-hyde produces a number of toxic compounds, including MTCA and its metabolic precursor 1,1'-ethylidinebis (tryptophan), the so-called peak E associated with an eosinophilia-myalgia syndrome (EMS).  See the tryptamine recipe for more information on this political issue.  Interestingly, MTCA is formed from native acetaldehyde (and tryptophan) in the normal wine-making processes and it is also present in saki and soy sauce.

Me       H       H$_2$       —                  dihydroharman
                                                harmalan

*Burkea africana*  (Leguminosae)
*Elaeagnus angustifolia*  (Elaeagnaceae) entire plant
*Flindersia laevicarpa*  (Rutaceae) leaf
*Peganum harmala*  (Zygophyllaceae)
          Harmalan levels reflect the consumption of alcohol.  Acetalde-hyde is a metabolite of ethanol, and readily condenses in vitro to yield harmalan.  However, a second biochemical role of acetaldehyde is to inhibit the disposition of pyruvic acid, a material which reacts with tryptamine to give tetrahydroharman-1-carboxylic acid which on decar-boxylation and sequential dehydrogenation gives rise to the β-carboline

cascade, tetrahydroharman, harmalan and harman.

The naming convention in the world of the harmane alkaloids (see under harman) is to indicate that two hydrogen atoms have been added to the molecule by the insertion of the letters "al" into the name. Dihydroharman becomes harmalan, dihydroharmine becomes harmaline, and dihydroharmol becomes harmalol. It is quite similar to the insertion of the literary factor of "p-something" to completely hydrogenate one-ring nitrogen heterocyclics. Hexahydropicolinic acid becomes pipecolinic acid, hexahydropyrazine becomes piperazine, and hexahydropyridine becomes piperidine.

Me      H       $H_2$      9-COCH$_3$          acetyldihydroharman
                                              acetylharmalan
*Flindersia laevicarpa*  (Rutaceae) leaf

Me      H       $H_0$      —                   harman (harmane)
                                              1-methyl-β-carboline
                                              1-Me-βC
                                              aribine
                                              loturine
                                              passiflorin
                                              galligonum base-4
                                              zygofabagin
*Acraea andromacha*  (Nymphalidae) butterflies
*Arariba rubra*  bark
*Burkea africana*  (Leguminosae)
*Calligonum minimum*  (Polygonaceae) aerial parts and root
*Calycanthus occidentalis*  (Calycanthaceae) leaf
*Cannabis sativa*  (Cannabinaceae) smoke condensate
*Carex brevicollis*  (Cyperaceae)
*Cephalanthus natalensis*  (Rubiaceae) leaf
*Cichorium intybus*  (Compositae) root
*Cinchona ledgeriana*  (Rubiaceae) suspension culture
*Commelina communis*  (Commelinaceae)
*Costaticella hastata*  (Vittaticellidae)  A marine bryozoan, which also
            contains three 2-carbon homologues, the ethyl, the hydroxyethyl
            and the vinyl
*Cribricellina cribraria*   (Mucronellidae), from the marine world of
            bryozoans — also contains the 1-ethyl and 1-vinyl β-carbolines.
*Desmodium pulchellum*  (Leguminosae)
*Elaeagnus angustifolia*  (Elaeagnaceae) aerial parts and rootbark
*Fagonia arabica*  (Zygophyllaceae)

*Fagonia bruguieri* (Zygophyllaceae)
*Fagonia cretica* (Zygophyllaceae)
*Fagonia glutinosa* (Zygophyllaceae)
*Fagonia mollis* (Zygophyllaceae)
*Fagonia parviflora* (Zygophyllaceae)
*Festuca arundinacea* (Gramineae) This grass has a name temptingly
     close to *Phalaris arundinacea*, which is a major source of DMT,
     and is discussed in the "DMT is Everywhere" chapter. One
     wonders if one gathered "things-arundinacea" the carbolines
     would allow the tryptamines to be orally active, à la ayahuasca.
*Grewia bicolor* (Tiliaceae) root
*Grewia villosa* (Tiliaceae) root
*Guiera senegalensis* (Combretaceae) root (sometimes spelled *Giera*)
*Heliconius cydno-galanthus* (Nymphalidae) more butterflies
*Heliconius erato-petiverana* (Nymphalidae)
*Heliconius ethilla-eucoma* (Nymphalidae)
*Heliconius melpomene-rosina* (Nymphalidae)
*Heliconius sara-thamar* (Nymphalidae)
*Heliconius wallacei-flavescens* (Nymphalidae)
*Hippophae rhamnoides* (Elaeagnaceae) flowers, fruit, root, stembark
     and leaf
*Kochia scoparia* (Chenopodiaceae)
*Lolium perenne* (Gramineae)
*Mitragyna hirsuta* (Rubiaceae) leaf, stem
*Myxococcus virescens* Strain MX-V-48 (Myxococcaceae) bacterial
     culture filtrate
*Nauclea diderrichii* (Rubiaceae)
*Niesosperma glomerata* (Apocynceae) bark
*Nicotiana tabacum* (Solanaceae) leaf. This can be detected in the smoke
     of cigarettes.
*Nocardia species* Strain P-9 (Nocardiaceae)
*Noctiluca miliaris* (Noctilucaceae) cells. This, and norharmine, are the
     first of these alkaloids to have been isolated from the marine
     environment.
*Newboldia laevis* (Bignoniaceae) roots
*Ochrosia nakaiana* (Apocynaceae) bark
*Opiorrhiza japonica* (Rubiaceae)
*Opiorrhiza kurolwai* (Rubiaceae)
*Palicourea alpina* (Rubiaceae)
*Panax ginseng* (Araliaceae) root
*Passiflora alata* (Passifloraceae) leaf
*Passiflora edulis* var. Flavicarpa (Passifloraceae) fruit juice, leaf and stem

*Passiflora edulis* (Passifloraceae) fruit, leaf, root and seed. Interestingly, in experiments with radioactive tryptophan feeding, the labeled isotope is found almost exclusively in harman.

*Passiflora incarnata* (Passifloraceae) aerial parts and stem. This is the passion flower and it contains harmine as well.

*Pauridiantha callicarpoides* (Rubiaceae) bark

*Pauridiantha lyalli* (Rubiaceae)

*Pauridiantha viridiflora* (Rubiaceae) bark

*Peganum harmala* (Zygophyllaceae) root and suspension culture.

*Phaseolus vulgaris* cv. Red Kidney Bean (Leguminosae) suspension culture. The two major metabolites of tryptophan were harman and nor-harman.

*Polygala tenuifolia* (Polygalaceae) rhizome

*Prosopis nigra* (Leguminosae) leaf

*Pyricularia oryzae* (Hyphomycetes) culture filtrate

*Rauwolfia psychotrioides* (Apocynaceae) leaf and rootbark

*Rauwolfia sellowii* (Apocynaceae) root bark

*Rauwolfia sumatrana* (Apocynaceae) leaf

*Rauwolfia viridii* (Apocynaceae) leaf

*Sickingia klugei* (Rubiaceae) bark

*Sickingia rubra*, see *Arariba rubra*

*Sickingia tinctoria* (Rubiaceae) stembark

*Sickingia williamsii* (Rubiaceae) stembark

*Simira maxonii* (Rubiaceae) root

*Simira mexicana* (Rubiaceae) stembark

*Simira salvadorensis* (Rubiaceae) bark

*Strychnos johnsonii* (Loganiaceae) rootbark

*Strychnos usambarensis* (Loganiaceae) rootbark and stembark

*Symplocus racemosa* (Symplocaceae)

*Tribulus terrestris* (Zygophyllaceae) the aerial parts, entire plant, leaf, root and seed

*Uncaria attenuata* (Rubiaceae) leaf

*Uncaria canescens* (Rubiaceae) leaf

*Uncaria orientalis* (Rubiaceae) leaf

*Zygophyllum fabago* (Zygophyllaceae) aerial parts and stem

It is noteworthy that, although harman is a very effective monoamine oxidase inhibitor, oral dosages as high as 250 milligrams followed with oral doses of DMT, did not produce any effects. This level of harmaline or harmine would have effectively protected the DMT from metabolic attack. The name "harmane," sometimes found as a synonym for harman, is usually used in the phrase "harmanes" or "harmane alkaloids," to define the subgroup of the β-carbolines that have a methyl group at the 1-position. In most scientific usage the terminal "e" is now dropped. Harman is a natural component of mammalian brain and blood. It is also a component of cigarette smoke and, as with so many others of the carbolines, it is in saki and in soy sauce.

Me      H      $H_0$      2-O                    1-methyl-β-carboline N-oxide
                                                harman N-oxide
                                                harmanine
*Calligonum minimum*  (Polygonaceae) aerial parts, roots

Me,$CO_2H$  H   $H_4$    3-$CO_2H$              1-methyl-1,2,3,4-
                                                        tetrahydro-β-carboline, 1,3-
                                                        dicarboxylic acid
        The sulfuric acid hydrolysis of casein (25%, 80°C) gives rise to several carbolines, including harman, harmalan, 3-carboxyharmalan, and the corresponding tetrahydroderivative. This same spectrum of products is obtained from the parallel hydrolysis of this dicarboxylic acid formed from tryptophan and pyruvic acid. See the discussion under harmalan.

Me      H      $H_0$      3-$CO_2H$              1-methyl-β-carboline, 3-carboxylic
                                                        acid
                                                harman, 3-carboxylic acid
*Aspidosperma polyneuron*  (Apocynaceae)
*Aspidosperma exalatum*  (Apocynaceae)
        This compound has been identified in the milk, urine and rumen of cows.

Me      H      $H_0$      3-$CO_2CH_3$           1-methyl-3-carboxymethyl-β-
                                                        carboline
*Nauclea diderrichii*  (Rubiaceae)

Me      H      $H_0$      3-$CO_2CH_2CH_3$       1-methyl-3-carboxyethyl-β-
                                                        carboline
*Aspidosperma rhombeosignatum*  (Apocynaceae) bark

Me      H      $H_0$      4-Me                   1,4-dimethyl-β-carboline
*Kitasatosporia setae*  antifungal, antibiotic

Me      H      $H_0$      4-$(CH_2)_4NHCH_3$
                                                "brevicarine"
*Carex brevicollis*  (Cyperaceae)
*Carex parva*  (Cyperaceae)

Me      H       $H_0$      4-$(CH_2)_4$N(CH3)COCH3
                                    "brevicarine"
*Carex parva*  (Cyperaceae)

Me      H       $H_0$      4-$(CH_2)_4$N(CH3)2  "brevicarine"
*Carex brevicollis* (Cyperaceae)
     I have seen the common name brevicolline used for any of the three open-chain amines

Me      H       $H_0$      4-(N-methylpyrrod-2-yl)
                                    brevicolline
*Carex brevicollis*  (Cyperaceae)  leaves
     What an extraordinary group of 4-substituted β-carbolines from a pair of sedge plants in Russia. Brevicolline is a potent vasodilator, inhibits peristalsis, and is a uterine contractant. And there is a second unexpected surprise. Draw out the structure, and white-out the indole ring and the 1-methyl group. What is left? The molecule nicotine. Someone, somewhere, is trying to tell us something.

Me      H       $H_0$      9-CHO          9-formylharman
                                            9-formyl-1-methyl-β-carboline
*Codonopsis lanceolata*  (Campanulaceae) root
*Lycium chinense*  (Solanaceae) fruit
*Panax ginseng*  (Araliaceae) root
*Polygala tenuifolia*  (Polygalaceae) rhizome

Me      Me      $H_4$      —              1,2-dimethyl-1,2,3,4-tetrahydro-β-
                                            carboline
                                            1,2-Me-THβC
                                            2-methyl-1,2,3,4-tetrahydroharman
                                            leptocladine
*Acacia complanata*  (Leguminosae) There is present in this plant
    leptocladine (1,2-DiMe-THβC, 0.3%, in leaf and also in stem)
    and eleagnine (1-Me-THβC, trace amount in leaf).
*Arthrophytum leptocladum*  (Chenopodiaceae) entire plant
*Banisteriopsis argentea*  (Malpighiaceae) leaf A03231 (+) isomer
*Desmodium gangeticum*  (Leguminosae) DMT, 5-MeO-DMT, and their
    two N-oxides are the tryptamines isolated from this Indian shrub.
    There are two carbolines, 1,2-DiMe-THβC and 6-MeO-2-Me-
    carbolinium salt. The tryptophane quaternary salt was also
    observed, as were several phenethylamines including cathinone.
*Desmodium pulchellum*  (Leguminosae)
*Guiera senegalensis*  (Combretaceae) root

*Hammada leptoclada* (Chenopodiaceae) aerial parts
*Hammada vakhanica* (Chenopodiaceae)

Me      Me      $H_0$      —                    1,2-dimethyl-β-carbolinium salt
                                                2-methylharmanium salt
                                                melinonine-F

*Desmodium gangeticum* (Leguminosae)
*Desmodium pulchellum* (Leguminosae)
*Strychnos melinoniana* (Loganiaceae)
*Strychnos usambarensis* (Loganiaceae)

This quaternary β-carboline is one of several alkaloids from this plant, originally named from this species. Melinonine G is a crynantheine called flavopereirine, also from the *S. melinoniana* (see the alkaloid families related to the carbolines at the end of this appendix). Melinonine A is a five-ring vinyl lactone ester, a closely-related extension of melinonine G. Strychnine, although a tryptamine alkaloid, is a distant cousin of these compounds at best, and comes from the seeds of *S. nux-vomica* and the beans of *S. ignatti*.

Me      COMe    $H_4$      —                    2-aceto-tetrahydroharman
                                                2-AcO-1-Me-THβC

This is a synthetic derivative of tetrahydroharman (1Me-THβC) which was assayed as a monoamine oxidase inhibitor. It was inactive. It has not yet been reported in nature.

Me      -O      $H_0$      —                    harman-N-oxide

*Calligonum minimum* (Polygonaceae) aerial parts, roots

Me,Me   H       $H_4$      3-$CH_2CH_3$         1,1-dimethyl-3-ethyl-1,2,3,4-
                                                        tetrahydro-β-carboline
                                                cyclized alpha-ethyltryptamine/
                                                        acetone adduct

This adduct between alpha-ethyltryptamine (α-ET) and acetone has been considered by law enforcement to be a possible intoxicant, as it has been found to be a 30% impurity in commercial alpha-ethyltryptamine. It is not a natural material.

Me,$CO_2H$ H    $H_4$      —                    1-methyl-1,2,3,4-
                                                        tetrahydrocarboline, 1-
                                                        carboxylic acid

This is the natural adduct of pyruvate to tryptamine; see discussion under harmalan, above. It is converted to harmalan and harman in *Passiflora edulis* and *Elaeagnus angustifolia*.

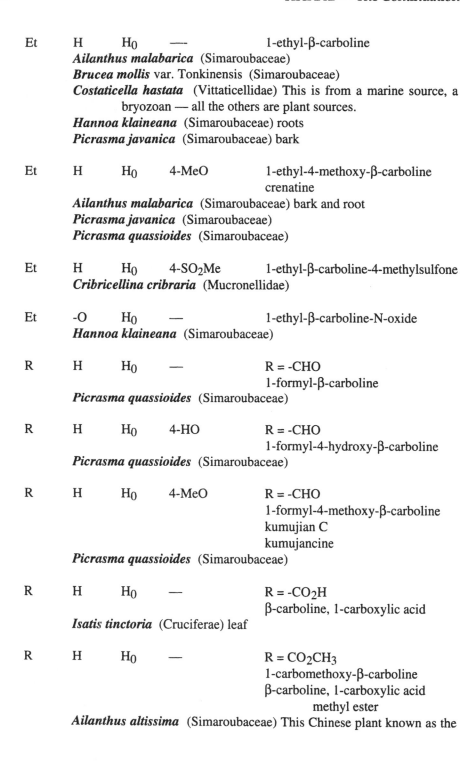

Et        H        $H_0$        —                          1-ethyl-β-carboline
*Ailanthus malabarica* (Simaroubaceae)
*Brucea mollis* var. Tonkinensis (Simaroubaceae)
*Costaticella hastata* (Vittaticellidae) This is from a marine source, a
      bryozoan — all the others are plant sources.
*Hannoa klaineana* (Simaroubaceae) roots
*Picrasma javanica* (Simaroubaceae) bark


Et        H        $H_0$        4-MeO                      1-ethyl-4-methoxy-β-carboline
                                                          crenatine
*Ailanthus malabarica* (Simaroubaceae) bark and root
*Picrasma javanica* (Simaroubaceae)
*Picrasma quassioides* (Simaroubaceae)


Et        H        $H_0$        4-$SO_2$Me                 1-ethyl-β-carboline-4-methylsulfone
*Cribricellina cribraria* (Mucronellidae)


Et        -O        $H_0$        —                         1-ethyl-β-carboline-N-oxide
*Hannoa klaineana* (Simaroubaceae)


R        H        $H_0$        —                           R = -CHO
                                                          1-formyl-β-carboline
*Picrasma quassioides* (Simaroubaceae)


R        H        $H_0$        4-HO                        R = -CHO
                                                          1-formyl-4-hydroxy-β-carboline
*Picrasma quassioides* (Simaroubaceae)


R        H        $H_0$        4-MeO                       R = -CHO
                                                          1-formyl-4-methoxy-β-carboline
                                                          kumujian C
                                                          kumujancine
*Picrasma quassioides* (Simaroubaceae)


R        H        $H_0$        —                           R = -$CO_2$H
                                                          β-carboline, 1-carboxylic acid
*Isatis tinctoria* (Cruciferae) leaf


R        H        $H_0$        —                           R = $CO_2CH_3$
                                                          1-carbomethoxy-β-carboline
                                                          β-carboline, 1-carboxylic acid
                                                                    methyl ester
*Ailanthus altissima* (Simaroubaceae) This Chinese plant known as the

Tree of Heaven has been reported to have this ester, along with
its 4,8-dimethoxy analogue, in its leaves and root bark.

*Ailanthus malabarica* (Simaroubaceae) bark and root
*Alstonia constricta* (Apocynaceae) stembark
*Arenaria kansuensis* (Caryophyllaceae)
*Codonopsis lanceolata* (Campanulaceae) root
*Commelina communis* (Commelinaceae)
*Lycium chinense* (Solanaceae) fruit
*Picrasma quaissioides* (Simaroubaceae) contains this ester in the heart
     wood portion of the plant
*Pleiocarpa* spp. (Apocynaceae)
*Polygala tenuifolia* (Polygalaceae) rhizome
*Quassia amara* (Simaroubaceae)


R       H       $H_0$     4-MeO       R = $-CO_2CH_3$
                                      1-carbomethoxy-4-methoxy-β-
                                         carboline
                                    4-methoxy-β-carboline, 1-
                                         carboxylic acid methyl ester

*Ailanthus altissima* (Simaroubaceae) contains this β-carboline in its root
bark.  It also has been studied as a suspension culture.


R       H       $H_0$     —          R = $-CO_2CH_2CH_3$
                                        1-carboethoxy-β-carboline
                                      β-carboline, 1-carboxylic acid
                                           ethyl ester
                                      kumijian A

*Panax ginseng* (Araliaceae)
*Picrasma quassioides* (Simaroubaceae) stem and heartwood
*Polygala tenuifolia* (Polygalaceae) rhizome


R       H       $H_0$     —          R = $-CO_2(CH_2)_2CH_3$
                                        1-carbopropoxy-β-carboline
                                      β-carboline, 1-carboxylic acid
                                         propyl ester

*Hannoa chlorantha* (Simaroubaceae)


R       H       $H_0$     —          R = $-CO_2(CH_2)_3CH_3$
                                        1-carbobutoxy-β-carboline
                                      β-carboline, 1-carboxylic acid
                                         butyl ester

*Polygala tenuifolia* (Polygalaceae) rhizome

R      H      H$_0$      —                    R = -CONH$_2$
                                             1-carbamoyl-β-carboline
                                             β-carboline-1-carboxamide
*Ailanthus altissima* (Simaroubaceae) rootbark
*Ailanthus malabarica* (Simaroubaceae) bark and root
*Nauclea diderriccii* (Rubiaceae)
*Neisosperma kilneri* (Apocynceae)
*Odyendea gabunensis* (Simaroubaceae)


R      H      H$_0$      —                    R = -CH$_2$OH
                                             1-hydroxymethyl-β-carboline
*Brucea mollis* var. Tonkinensis (Simaroubaceae)
*Odyendea gabunensis* (Simaroubaceae)
*Picrasma quassioides* (Simaroubaceae)


R      H      H$_0$      —                    R = -CH$_2$OCH$_3$
                                             1-methoxymethyl-β-carboline
*Eurycoma longifolia* (Simaroubaceae) bark


R      H      H$_0$      —                    R = COCH$_3$
                                             1-aceto-β-carboline
*Picrasma quassoides* var. Bennet (Simaroubaceae)


R      H      H$_0$      3-CO$_2$CH$_3$       R = COCH$_3$
                                             1-aceto-3-carbomethoxy-β-
                                                  carboline
                                             1-acetyl-β-carboline, 3-carboxylic
                                                  acid methyl ester
*Vestia lycioides* (Solanaceae) leaf and stem


R      H      H$_0$      4-MeO                R = COCH$_3$
                                             1-aceto-4-methoxy-β-carboline
*Ailanthus altissima* (Simaroubaceae) in root bark
*Ailanthus malabarica* (Simaroubaceae)
*Picrasma javanica* (Simaroubaceae)


R      H      H$_0$      R = COCH$_2$OCH$_3$
                                             1-methoxymethylcarbonyl-β-
                                                  carboline
                                             arinarine-A
*Arenaria kansuensis* (Caryophyllaceae) whole plant


R      H      H$_0$      —                    R = -CH=CH$_2$

1-vinyl-β-carboline
pavettine

*Costaticella hastata* (Vittaticellidae)

*Cribricellina cribraria* (Mucronellidae) This and the above entry are marine Bryozoans. This material is quite cyctotoxic, and with the hydroxy group in the 8-position (also in this animal) is much more so.

*Hannoa chlorantha* (Simaroubaceae) rootbark

*Panetta lancelata*

*Soulamea fraxinifolia* (Simaroubaceae)

| R | H | $H_0$ | 4-MeO | R = -CH=CH$_2$ |
|---|---|---|---|---|

4-methoxy-1-vinyl-β-carboline
dehydrocrenatine

*Ailanthus altissima* (Simaroubaceae)
*Ailanthus malabarica* (Simaroubaceae)
*Hannoa chlorantha* (Simaroubaceae) rootbark
*Picrasma javanica* (Simaroubaceae) bark
*Picrasma quassioides* (Simaroubaceae) wood

| R | H | $H_0$ | 9-MeO | R = -CH=CH$_2$ |
|---|---|---|---|---|

9-methoxy-1-vinyl-β-carboline

*Picrasma excelsa* (Simaroubaceae)

| R | H | $H_0$ | 4,9-(-MeO)$_2$ | R = -CH=CH$_2$ |
|---|---|---|---|---|

4,9-dimethoxy-1-vinyl-β-carboline
picrasidine D

*Picrasma quassioides* (Simaroubaceae)

| R | H | $H_0$ | — | R = -CHOHCH$_3$ |
|---|---|---|---|---|

1-(1'-hydroxyethyl)-β-carboline

*Costaticella hastata* (Vittaticellidae)

| R | H | $H_0$ | — | R = -CH$_2$CH$_2$OH |
|---|---|---|---|---|

1-(2'-hydroxyethyl)-β-carboline

*Brucea mollis* var. Tonkinensis (Simaroubaceae) rootbark
*Soulamea fraxinifolia* (Simaroubaceae) stembark

| R | H | $H_0$ | 4-MeO | R = -CH$_2$CH$_2$OH |
|---|---|---|---|---|

1-(2'-hydroxyethyl)-4-methoxy-β-carboline

*Ailanthus altissima* (Simaroubaceae) root bark

R     H     H$_0$     4-MeO          R = -CHOHCH$_2$OH
                                     1-(1',2'-dihydroxyethyl)-4-methoxy-
                                                β-carboline
*Ailanthus altissima*  (Simaroubaceae) root bark.

R     H     H$_0$     —              R = -CHOHCH$_2$OCH$_3$
                                     1-(1-hydroxy-2-methoxy)ethyl-β-
                                                carboline
                                     ariarine B
*Arenaria kansuensis*  (Caryophyllaceae) whole plant

R     H     H$_0$     4-MeO          R = -CHOHCH$_2$OCH$_3$
                                     1-(1-hydroxy-2-methoxy)ethyl-4-
                                                methoxy-β-carboline
*Ailanthus altissima*  (Simaroubaceae)

R     H     H$_0$     —              R = -CH(OCH$_3$)CH$_2$OCH$_3$
                                     1,2-dimethoxyethyl-β-carboline
                                     arenarine B
*Arenaria kansuensis*  (Caryophyllaceae)

R     H     H$_0$     —              R = -CH=CHCH$_3$
                                     1-(1-propenyl)-β-carboline
*Nicotiana tabacum*  (Solanaceae) smoke condensate

R     H     H$_0$     —              R = -CH$_2$CH$_2$CO$_2$H
                                     β-carboline, 1-propionic acid
*Ailanthus altissima*  (Simaroubaceae)
*Aerva lanata*  (Amaranthaceae)
*Ailanthus malabarica*  (Simaroubaceae)
*Brucea mollis* var. Tonkinensis  (Simaroubaceae)
*Eurycoma longifolia*  (Simaroubaceae)
*Hannoa klaineana*  (Simaroubaceae) root
*Picrasma quassioides*  (Simaroubaceae)
*Quassia africana*  (Simaroubaceae) root

R     H     H$_0$     —              R = CH$_2$CH$_2$CO$_2$Me
                                     β-carboline, 1-propionic acid
                                                methyl ester
                                     infractine
                                     kumujanrine
*Cortinarius infractus*  (Cortinariaceae)
*Picrasma quassioides*  (Simaroubaceae)

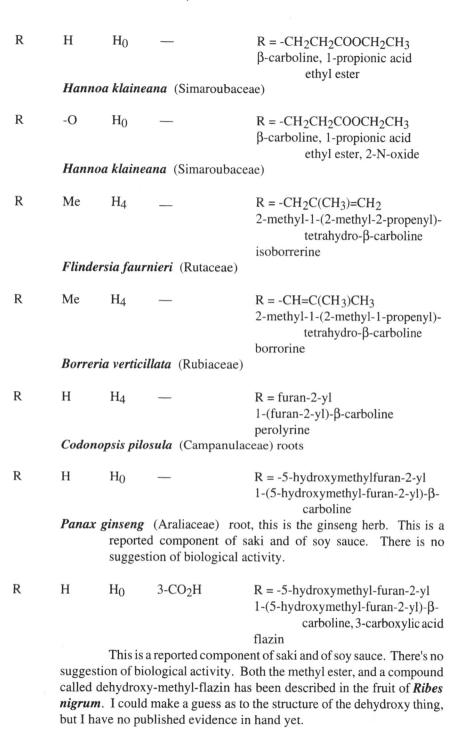

R    H    $H_0$    —                    R = -$CH_2CH_2COOCH_2CH_3$
                                        β-carboline, 1-propionic acid
                                                ethyl ester

*Hannoa klaineana*  (Simaroubaceae)

R    -O   $H_0$    —                    R = -$CH_2CH_2COOCH_2CH_3$
                                        β-carboline, 1-propionic acid
                                                ethyl ester, 2-N-oxide

*Hannoa klaineana*  (Simaroubaceae)

R    Me   $H_4$    —                    R = -$CH_2C(CH_3)=CH_2$
                                        2-methyl-1-(2-methyl-2-propenyl)-
                                                tetrahydro-β-carboline
                                        isoborrerine

*Flindersia faurnieri*  (Rutaceae)

R    Me   $H_4$    —                    R = -$CH=C(CH_3)CH_3$
                                        2-methyl-1-(2-methyl-1-propenyl)-
                                                tetrahydro-β-carboline
                                        borrorine

*Borreria verticillata*  (Rubiaceae)

R    H    $H_4$    —                    R = furan-2-yl
                                        1-(furan-2-yl)-β-carboline
                                        perolyrine

*Codonopsis pilosula*  (Campanulaceae) roots

R    H    $H_0$    —                    R = -5-hydroxymethylfuran-2-yl
                                        1-(5-hydroxymethyl-furan-2-yl)-β-
                                                carboline

*Panax ginseng*  (Araliaceae)  root, this is the ginseng herb.  This is a
reported component of saki and of soy sauce.  There is no
suggestion of biological activity.

R    H    $H_0$    3-$CO_2H$            R = -5-hydroxymethyl-furan-2-yl
                                        1-(5-hydroxymethyl-furan-2-yl)-β-
                                                carboline, 3-carboxylic acid
                                        flazin

This is a reported component of saki and of soy sauce.  There's no
suggestion of biological activity.  Both the methyl ester, and a compound
called dehydroxy-methyl-flazin has been described in the fruit of *Ribes
nigrum*.  I could make a guess as to the structure of the dehydroxy thing,
but I have no published evidence in hand yet.

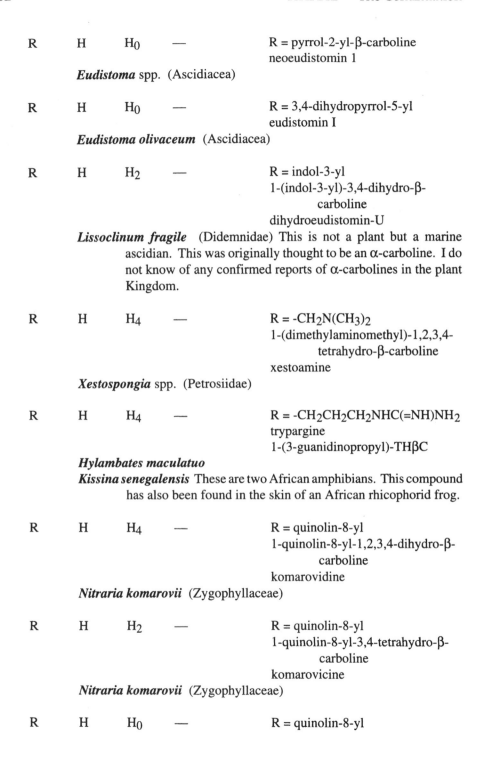

R    H    H$_0$    —          R = pyrrol-2-yl-β-carboline
                              neoeudistomin 1

*Eudistoma* spp. (Ascidiacea)

R    H    H$_0$    —          R = 3,4-dihydropyrrol-5-yl
                              eudistomin I

*Eudistoma olivaceum* (Ascidiacea)

R    H    H$_2$    —          R = indol-3-yl
                              1-(indol-3-yl)-3,4-dihydro-β-
                                   carboline
                              dihydroeudistomin-U

*Lissoclinum fragile* (Didemnidae) This is not a plant but a marine ascidian. This was originally thought to be an α-carboline. I do not know of any confirmed reports of α-carbolines in the plant Kingdom.

R    H    H$_4$    —          R = -CH$_2$N(CH$_3$)$_2$
                              1-(dimethylaminomethyl)-1,2,3,4-
                                   tetrahydro-β-carboline
                              xestoamine

*Xestospongia* spp. (Petrosiidae)

R    H    H$_4$    —          R = -CH$_2$CH$_2$CH$_2$NHC(=NH)NH$_2$
                              trypargine
                              1-(3-guanidinopropyl)-THβC

*Hylambates maculatuo*
*Kissina senegalensis* These are two African amphibians. This compound has also been found in the skin of an African rhicophorid frog.

R    H    H$_4$    —          R = quinolin-8-yl
                              1-quinolin-8-yl-1,2,3,4-dihydro-β-
                                   carboline
                              komarovidine

*Nitraria komarovii* (Zygophyllaceae)

R    H    H$_2$    —          R = quinolin-8-yl
                              1-quinolin-8-yl-3,4-tetrahydro-β-
                                   carboline
                              komarovicine

*Nitraria komarovii* (Zygophyllaceae)

R    H    H$_0$    —          R = quinolin-8-yl

1-quinolin-8-yl-β-carboline
komarovine

*Nitraria komarovii* (Zygophyllaceae)
The 1-substituted β-carboline with the quinoline bonded at its 6-position is known as komarovinine, at its 5-position it is known as isokomarovine, and at its 2-position it is known as nitramarine. All come from *Nitraria komarovii.*

Ar-5-substituted

| 5 | 1 | 2 | $H_X$ | other | |
|---|---|---|---|---|---|
| 5-HO | R | H | $H_0$ | 4-MeO | R = -CH$_2$CH$_3$ |

1-ethyl-5-hydroxy-4-methoxy-β-carboline

*Picrasma javanica* (Simaroubaceae)

| 5-HO | R | H | $H_0$ | 4-MeO | R = -CH=CH$_2$ |
|---|---|---|---|---|---|

5-hydroxy-4-methoxy-1-vinyl-β-carboline

*Picrasma javanica* (Simaroubaceae)

| 5-MeO | Me | H | $H_4$ | — | |
|---|---|---|---|---|---|

5-methoxytetrahydroharman
5-MeO-1-Me-THβC
*Banisteriopsis argentea* (Malpighiaceae) leaf

| 5-MeO | Me | Me | $H_4$ | — | |
|---|---|---|---|---|---|

5-methoxy-1,2-dimethyl-1,2,3,4-tetrahydro-β-carboline
5-methoxy-2-methyltetrahydroharman
5-MeO-1,2-dimethyl-THβC
*Banisteriopsis argentea* (Malpighiaceae)

| 5-MeO | HO | H | $H_2$ | — | |
|---|---|---|---|---|---|

1-hydroxy-5-methoxy-3,4-dihydro-β-carboline
1-oxo-5-MeO-THβC
1-oxo-5-methoxy-1,2,3,4-tetrahydro-β-carboline
*Alstonia venenata* (Apocynaceae) rootbark
A tautomer, in chemistry, is a structure that can be drawn in two ways, by the casual rearrangement of hydrogen atoms and electrons. The structure of this compound can be drawn as a -CO-NH- (1-keto, with a

single bond to a nitrogen atom that has a hydrogen attached) or as -C(OH)=N- (1-hydroxy, double bonded to a bare nitrogen). This is simply two different ways of drawing the same molecule. The first is probably what it would look like under a hypothetical microscope, but the second is much easier to list in a table that allows only one substituent to a ring position. This subtlety cannot exist in those β-carbolines that are substituted on the 2-position nitrogen.

Also there is a numerical trap here; the ring positions are misleading. These "5-substituted" carbolines have the substitution at the "4-position" of the indole ring. When one uses a certain number to indicate a substitution position as an indole, it is one larger as a carboline. A "4-substituted" indole such as psilocybin becomes a "5-substituted" carboline once that third ring is formed. The substitution is in the same place — it is just that the numbering system has shifted up by one. Serotonin, a 5-hydroxyindole becomes 6-hydroxytetrahydroharman when it is cyclized with acetaldehyde. The oxygen does not move. It is the numbering system that moves. However, beware. When a tryptoline name is used for a β-carboline, the numbering rule reverts to the indole system.

---

Ar-6-substituted

| 6 | 1 | 2 | Hx | other | |
|---|---|---|---|---|---|
| 6-HO | H | H | H4 | — | 6-hydroxy-1,2,3,4-tetrahydro-β-carboline<br>6-OH-THβC<br>5-hydroxy-tryptoline<br>plectomine<br>plectocomime |

**Plectocomiopsis geminiflorus**

Here is another "mammalian THβC," in this case the cyclization product of the neurotransmitter serotonin with a one-carbon unit such as formaldehyde. It may be viewed as a tryptoline analogue. It occurs as a trace component in beer. It is a normal component in human urine, apparently independent of diet. It has been found in the rat brain and the rat adrenal gland. It is, along with the 7-hydroxy analogue, a metabolite of THβC in the rat.

| 6-HO | H | H | H4 | 3-CO2H | 6-hydroxy-1,2,3,4-tetrahydro-β-carboline, 3-carboxylic acid |
|---|---|---|---|---|---|

*Agropyron repens*  (Gramineae) rhizome and root

| | | | | | |
|---|---|---|---|---|---|
| 6-HO | H | H | $H_0$ | — | 6-hydroxy-β-carboline<br>6-OH-βC |

*Plectocomiopsis geminiflorus*

| | | | | | |
|---|---|---|---|---|---|
| 6-HO | Me | H | $H_4$ | — | 6-hydroxy-1-methyl-1,2,3,4-<br>tetrahydro-β-carboline<br>6-OH-1-Me-THβC<br>6-hydroxy-tetrahydroharman<br>tetrahydroisoharmol |

*Shepherdia canadensis*  (Elaeagnaceae)

Yet another "mammalian carboline," this time the cycle between serotonin and acetaldehyde. It is probably also a normal component in human metabolism and it definitely is a metabolite of ethanol in man. Very small levels are found in beer (a fraction of a milligram per liter) and lesser amounts in fruits and vegetables, so it can be called a trace component in some plants. Metabolically, it can be oxidized to a quinonic dione which reacts with glutathione. This compound has been associated with alcohol use and with neuronal loss.

| | | | | | |
|---|---|---|---|---|---|
| 6-HO | Me | H | $H_0$ | — | 6-hydroxyharman<br>isoharmol<br>6-hydroxy-1-methyl-β-carboline |

*Grewia bicolor*  (Tiliaceae) root
*Grewia mollis*  (Tiliaceae) root
*Grewia villosa*  (Tiliaceae)
*Opiorrhiza japonica*  (Rubiaceae)

| | | | | | |
|---|---|---|---|---|---|
| 6-HO | R | H | $H_0$ | 4-MeO | R = -CH=CH$_2$<br>6-hydroxy-4-methoxy-1-vinyl-β-<br>carboline |

*Picrasma javanica*  (Simaroubaceae) stembark

| | | | | | |
|---|---|---|---|---|---|
| 6-HO | R | H | $H_0$ | — | R = -CH$_2$CH$_2$CO$_2$H<br>6-hydroxy-β-carboline, 2-propionic<br>acid |

*Cortinarius infractus*  (Cortinariaceae)

| | | | | | |
|---|---|---|---|---|---|
| 6-HO | R | H | $H_0$ | — | R = -pyrrol-2-yl<br>6-hydroxy-1-(pyrrol-2-yl)-β-<br>carboline<br>eudistomin M |

*Eudistoma olivaceum*  (Ascidiacea)
    This compound has been patented for the treatment of viral infections.

6-HO    R      H      $H_0$              R = -(3,4-dihydro)[2H]pyrrol-5-yl
                                        6-hydroxy-1-(3,4-dihydro[2H]
                                            pyrrol-5-yl)-β-carboline
                                        eudistomin Q
*Eudistoma olivaceum*  (Ascidiacea)

6-MeO   H      H      $H_4$      —       6-methoxy-1,2,3,4-tetrahydro-β-
                                            carboline
                                        6-MeO-THβC
                                        5-MeO-tryptoline
                                        pinoline
*Anadenanthera peregrina*  (Leguminosae) Bufotenine was the first alkaloid isolated from this plant.  Then came DMT, 5-MeO-DMT, DMT-N-oxide and bufotenine-N-oxide.  The bark also contains NMT and 5-MeO-NMT, 5-MeO-DMT, and two β-carbolines, 6-MeO-THβC and 6-MeO-1,2-dimethyl-THβC. This is a loaded plant from the alkaloid point of view.
*Nectandra megapotamica*  (Lauraceae) bark
*Virola rufula*  (Myristicaceae) Various parts of the plant have been shown to contain DMT, NMT, 5-MeO-DMT, 5-MeO-NMT, and 6-MeO-THβC
*Virola theiodora*  (Myristicaceae) The snuff of the Waiká Indians in the Amazonian basin is prepared only from the resin of this plant. It is another alkaloid-loaded plant, mainly 5-MeO-DMT, and lesser amounts of DMT, NMT, 5-MeO-NMT, and 6-MeO-THβC.

This carboline is found as a normal component in the human body, in the pineal gland of both chicken and man, and the retina of rabbits, pigs and man. It is a cyclization product of O-methylated serotonin, which is well represented in the plant Kingdom.  The coining of the unneeded word "pinoline" for this methylated serotonin cycle product suggests a territorial effort to win some points from the folks who felt that "tryptoline" could promote the importance of THβC in brain chemistry.  Neither word contributes to a better understanding of carboline chemistry.

6-MeO   H      H      $H_0$      —       6-methoxy-β-carboline
*Phalaris arundinacea*  (Gramineae)

6-MeO  H        Me      H₄      —       6-methoxy-2-methyl-1,2,3,4-
                                                tetrahydrocarboline
                                        6-MeO-2-Me-THβC

*Anadenanthera peregrina*  (Leguminosae) bark
*Antirhea lucida*  (Rubiaceae) root
*Desmodium pulchellum*  (Leguminosae)
*Dutaillyea oreophila*  (Rutaceae) leaf
*Horsfieldia superba*  (Myristicaceae) leaf
*Meconopsis horrida*  (Papaveraceae) entire plant
*Meconopsis napaulensis*  (Papaveraceae)
*Meconopsis paniculata*  (Papaveraceae) entire plant
*Meconopsis robusta*  (Papaveraceae) entire plant
*Meconopsis rudis*  (Papaveraceae) entire plant
*Melicope leptococca*  (Rutaceae) leaf and stem
*Nectandra megapotamica*  (Lauraceae) entire plant
*Papaver rhoeas*  (Papaveraceae) root
*Phalaris arundinacea*  (Gramineae) aerial parts
*Phalaris arundinacea*  Clone R-5  (Gramineae) aerial parts
*Phalaris arundinacea* var. Ottawa Synthetic C  (Gramineae) entire plant
*Virola calophylla*  (Myristicaceae) wood
*Virola rufula*  (Myristicaceae) bark and root
*Virola theiodora*  (Myristicaceae) bark

A number of these plants, especially the *Phalaris* spp. and the *Virola* spp., are known to contain DMT, and/or NMT, and/or 5-MeO-DMT, as well as other β-carbolines. If this specific β-carboline were to be effective as a monoamine oxidase inhibitor, then these plants could be seen as self-contained ayahuasca sources. Only one plant might be needed, not a mixture of two plants.

6-MeO  H        Me      H₄      9-Me    2,9-dimethyl-6-methoxy-1,2,3,4-
                                                tetrahydro-β-carboline

*Phalaris arundinacea* var. Ottawa Synthetic C  (Gramineae) entire plant

6-MeO  H        Me      H₀      —       6-methoxy-2-methyl-β-
                                                carbolinium ion
                                        6-MeO-2-Me-THβC quat salt

*Desmodium gangeticum*  (Leguminosae)

6-MeO  H        COCH₃   H₄      —       2-aceto-6-methoxy-1,2,3,4-
                                                tetrahydro-β-carboline
                                        2-Ac-6-MeO-THβC

A synthetic cyclic analogue of serotonin which was assayed for enzyme inhibition activity, which it largely lacked.

6-MeO   Me      H       H$_4$        —          6-methoxy-1,2,3,4-
                                                    tetrahydroharman
                                            6-MeO-1-Me-THβC
                                            adrenoglomerulotropin
                                            aldosterone-stimulating hormone
                                            ASH
                                            McIsaac's Compound

*Virola cuspidata* (Myristicaceae) leaf and stem.

This is the major component of the alkaloid fraction of this plant. Since the processing of plant extracts as snuffs demands boiling as a step for concentration, this pure material was boiled for eight hours in water. There was partial conversion to both the dihydro (harmalan) compound and the totally aromatic harman isomer below.

This is a simple β-carboline which deserves some additional discussion. It is a normal component of the pineal gland of both the dog and the human. (The pineal is the "third eye" in the brain that is associated with melatonin secretion and with Eastern philosophy.) It is easily synthesized from 5-methoxytryptamine and acetaldehyde under physiological conditions in vitro, just as melatonin is the union of 5-methoxytryptamine and acetic acid. A friend of mine, William McIsaac, was completely convinced that this material: (1) could be made spontaneously in the human brain under certain circumstances from 5-methoxytryptamine, and: (2) its sudden and unexpected generation just might be the trigger for a psychotic episode. He was saddened by his inability to show this hormone to be either psychoactive or present in unusual amounts upon autopsy of victims of fatal accidents who were floridly schizophrenic at the moment of death.

6-MeO   Me      H       H$_2$        —          6-methoxyharmalan
                                            6-methoxy-1-methyl-3,4-dihydro-β-
                                                    carboline

*Virola cuspidata* (Myristicaceae) leaf and stem

This is a minor component of this plant. The quintessence of mammalian tetrahydro-β-carbolines is the cyclization product of plain and simple melatonin. This is the primary hormone in the pineal gland and its simple cycle should be an important factor in brain chemistry. It has been synthesized, explored a little bit biochemically, and is basically unknown pharmacologically.

6-MeO   Me      H       H$_0$        —          6-methoxyharman
                                            isoharmine

*Grewia bicolor* (Tiliaceae)
*Grewia villosa* (Tiliaceae)

***Peganum harmala*** (Zygophyllaceae)
***Virola cuspidata*** (Myristicaceae) leaf and stem
This compound has been named as isoharmine with "iso" having the meaning of "the other way about." Harmine is the 7-MeO isomer counterpart, so here it means a group relocation rather than a rearrangement within a substituent group. This compound, a monoamineoxidase inhibitor, has been reported to be formed by dehydrogenation of 6-methoxy-1,2,3,4-tetrahydroharman by simply being boiled in water, as mentioned above. This makes one wonder what chemistry might be going on in the preparation of ayahuasca by the protraced boiling of the extracts in the open air.

| 6-MeO | Me | Me | H$_4$ | — | 1,2-dimethyl-6-methoxy-1,2,3,4-<br>tetrahydro-β-carboline<br>1,2-Me-6-MeO-THβC<br>6-methoxy-2-methyl-1,2,3,4-<br>tetrahydroharman |

***Anadenanthera peregrina*** (Leguminosae) The bark contains a number of tryptamines, like 6-MeO-THβC and 1,2-DiMe-6-MeO-THβC.
***Desmodium pulchellum*** (Leguminosae)

| 6-Br | H | H | H$_0$ | — | 6-bromo-β-carboline<br>eudistomin N |

***Eudistoma olivaceum*** (Ascidiacea)

| 6-Br | Me | H | H$_0$ | — | 6-bromo-1-methyl-β-carboline |

***Aglaophenia pluma*** (Plumulariidae)

| 6-Br | Et | H | H$_0$ | — | 6-bromo-1-ethyl-β-carboline |

***Aglaophenia pluma*** (Plumulariidae)

| 6-Br | R | H | H$_0$ | — | R = -3,4-dihydropyrrol-5-yl<br>6-bromo-1-(3,4-dihydropyrrol-5-yl)-<br>β-carboline<br>eudistomin H |

***Eudistoma glaucus*** (Ascidiacea)
***Eudistoma olivaceum*** (Ascidiacea)

| 6-Br | R | H | H$_4$ | — | R = N-methylpyrrolid-2-yl<br>6-bromo-1-(N-methylpyrrolid-2-yl)-<br>1-2-3-4-tetrahydro-β-carboline<br>woodinine |

***Eudistoma gragum*** (Ascidiacea)

Ar-7-substituted

| 7 — | 1 — | 2 — | H$_x$ — | other |
|-----|-----|-----|---------|-------|
| 7-HO | H | H | H$_4$ | — | 6-hydroxytryptoline |

7-hydroxy-1,2,3,4-tetrahydro-β-
        carboline

7-OH-THβC

This is a metabolite of THβC in the rat, but has not been reported from any plant source.

| 7-HO | Me | H | H$_4$ | — | 7-hydroxy-1-methyl-1,2,3,4- |

tetrahydro-β-carboline

7-OH-1-Me-THβC

tetrahydroharmol

*Elaeagnus angustifolia*  (Elaeagnaceae)
*Peganum harmala*  (Zygophyllaceae)
*Shepherdia argentia*  (Elaeagnaceae)
*Shepherdia canadensis*  (Elaeagnaceae)
    This material is found as a normal component in human urine.

| 7-HO | Me | H | H$_2$ | — | 3,4-dihydro-7-hydroxy-1-methyl-β- |

carboline

7-hydroxyharmalan

harmalol

*Amsonia tabernaemontana*  (Apocynaceae) green parts, roots
*Apocynum cannabinum*  (Asclepiadaceae) roots
*Grewia villosa*  (Tiliaceae) root
*Hippophae rhamnoides*  (Elaeagnaceae) twigs, leaves
*Passiflora incarnata*  (Passifloraceae) aerial parts
*Peganum harmala*  (Zygophyllaceae) entire plant, including leaf, root,
    seed and stem.  Both suspension cultures and hairy root cultures
    have been successful.
*Tribulus terrestris*  (Zygophyllaceae) entire plant

| 7-HO | Me | H | H$_0$ | — | 7-hydroxy-1-methyl-β-carboline |

7-hydroxyharman

harmol

*Banisteriopsis caapi*  (Malpighiaceae) stem
*Carex brevicollis*  (Cyperaceae) leaf
*Elaeagnus angustifolia*  (Elaeagnaceae) aerial parts and rootbark
*Grewia villosa*  (Tiliaceae) root

*Hippophae rhamnoides* (Elaeagnaceae) entire plant and root
*Passiflora edulis* var. Flavicarpa (Passifloraceae) fruit juice
*Passiflora incarnata* (Passifloraceae) aerial parts
*Peganum harmala* (Zygophyllaceae) callus tissue, seed and suspension
      culture
*Tribulus terrestris* (Zygophyllaceae) entire plant and root
*Zygophyllum* spp.

| | | | | | |
|---|---|---|---|---|---|
| 7-HO | Me | Me | $H_4$ | —– | 1,2-dimethyl-7-hydroxy-1,2,3,4-tetrahydro-β-carboline |

    1,2-Me-7-OH-THβC
    2-methyl-tetrahydroharmol

*Elaeagnus* spp. (Elaeagnaceae)

| | | | | | |
|---|---|---|---|---|---|
| 7-HO | Me | Me | $H_0$ | — | 1,2-dimethyl-7-hydroxy-β-carbolinium ion |

    2-methylharmol quaternary salt

Here is another connection to Parkinson's disease, a very close analogue of MPTP which leads directly to this syndrome. This compound has not been reported in nature.

| | | | | | |
|---|---|---|---|---|---|
| 7-HO | R | H | $H_0$ | — | R = -COCH3 |

    1-aceto-7-hydroxy-β-carboline
    arinarine-D

*Arenaria kansuensis* (Caryophyllaceae) whole plant

| | | | | | |
|---|---|---|---|---|---|
| 7-MeO | H | H | $H_0$ | —– | 7-methoxy-β-carboline |

    7-MeO-βC
    norharmine

*Peganum harmala* (Zygophyllaceae) contains this compound in its seeds.

    The use of the prefix "nor" here to indicate the removal of a methyl group is not correct, just as it was not correct with the term "norharman" used earlier. In these cases, the compounds are missing the methyl from the 1-position carbon atom. But "nor" comes from the German phrase, "N-ohne-radical" or N-without-radical, insisting that the methyl group should have been removed from a nitrogen atom. And there are no N-methyl groups in any of these compounds. The proper names should have been "desmethyl harmine" here, and "desmethylharman" earlier.

| | | | | | |
|---|---|---|---|---|---|
| 7-MeO | H | CHO | $H_4$ | — | 2-formyl-7-methoxy-1,2,3,4-tetrahydro-β-carboline |

    harmalicine

*Peganum harmala* (Zygophyllaceae) seed contains this minor alkaloid.

This trivial name, harmalicine, is close in sound but far away in structure to the compounds harmalidine and harmalacidine. The first of these latter two names belongs to a tetrahydro-β-carboline with a two carbon bridge between the 1 and the 9 positions, creating a five-membered ring. The second name is a common name for the 7-methoxy-1-keto-β-carboline mentioned below.

| 7-MeO | Me | H | H$_4$ | — | 7-methoxy-1,2,3,4-tetrahydroharman |
|---|---|---|---|---|---|

7-methoxy-1,2,3,4-
       tetrahydroharman
7-methoxy-1-methyl-1,2,3,4-
       tetrahydro-β-carboline
7-MeO-1-Me-THβC
1,2-dihydroharmaline
tetrahydroharmine
leptoflorine

*Banisteriopsis argentea* (Malpighiaceae) leaf
*Banisteriopsis caapi* (Malpighiaceae) This plant also contains harmine as a major alkaloid. This is the (+) isomer.
*Banisteriopsis inebrians* (Malpighiaceae)
*Calliandra pentandra* (Fabaceae)
*Elaeagnus* spp. (Elaeagnaceae)
*Leptactinia densiflora* (Rubiaceae) The origin of the name leptaflorine.
*Peganum harmala* (Zygophyllaceae) seeds
*Tribulus terrestris* (Zygophyllaceae)

Tetrahydroharmine, harmine, and harmaline below, are probably the major active principles in the promotion of DMT to oral activity in the South American drink, ayahuasca. Care should be taken with the names tetrahydroharmine and leptoflorine. There is a chiral center in this molecule (the 1-position) and sometimes the term leptoflorine has been used to specify the natural product. In some isolates the optical integrity has not been determined. The two names have been used interchangeably.

7-MeO Me H H$_2$ — 3,4-dihydroharmine
3,4-dihydro-7-methoxy-1-methyl-β-
       carboline
7-methoxyharmalan
harmalol methyl ether
harmidine
harmaline

*Banisteriopsis argentea* (Malpighiaceae) leaf
*Banisteriopsis caapi* (Malpighiaceae) stem
*Banisteriopsis inebrians* (Malpighiaceae)

*Grewia villosa*  (Tiliaceae) The root also contains harmine
*Hippophae rhamnoides*  (Elaeagnaceae) flowers, fruit, leaf and stembark
*Nicotiana tabacum*  (Solanaceae)  in smoke condensate
*Passiflora edulis*  (Passifloraceae) fruit
*Passiflora incarnata*  (Passifloraceae) aerial parts and seed
*Peganum harmala*  (Zygophyllaceae) aerial parts, callus tissue, fruit, leaf,
    stem, root.  The seed is an especially rich source with many
    assays showing between 3 and 4 % content by weight.  Suspen-
    sion cultures have been successful.
*Peganum nigellastrum*  (Zygophyllaceae) roots
*Tribulus terrestris*  (Zygophyllaceae) entire plant
*Uncaria* spp.  (Rubiaceae)
    Harmaline has the reputation of being a major contributor to the
oral activity of DMT-containing plants, but this may not be totally
justified.  It certainly is active as an amineoxidase inhibitor when used
from *Peganum harmala*, or when used as a pure compound.  Old reference
samples of harmaline may contain sizable quantities of harmine.  The
reason is unknown.  See the discussion in the harmaline recipe.

7-MeO   Me     H     $H_0$      —      7-methoxyharman
                                        7-methoxy-1-methyl-β-carboline
                                        7-MeO-1-Me-βC
                                        telepathine
                                        banisterine
                                        yageine
                                        leucoharmine
                                        harmine

*Acraea andromacha*  (Nymphalidae) butterflies
*Amsonia tabernaemontana*  (Apocynaceae) entire plant
*Arenaria kansuensis*  (Caryophyllaceae) whole plant
*Banisteria* spp.  Now commonly called *Banisteriopsis* spp.
*Banisteriopsis argentea*  (Malpighiaceae) leaf
*Banisteriopsis caapi*  (Malpighiaceae) leaf, root and stem.  This plant also
    contains harmaline and several other alkaloids, which are listed
    here.  A century-old sample from South America contained no
    harmaline, but only harmine.
*Banisteriopsis inebrians*  (Malpighiaceae) The leaf and stem have been
    said to contain harmine but no harmaline or tetrahydroharmine.
    But some botanists consider it to be synonymous with *B. caapi*,
    so this composition contradiction is yet to be resolved.
*Banisteriopsis rusbyana*  (Malpighiaceae) see *Diploteris cabrerana.*
*Cabi paraensis*  (Malpighiaceae)
*Calligonum minimum*  (Polygonaceae) aerial parts and root

*Calycanthus occidentalis* (Calycanthaceae) aerial parts and leaf
*Diploteris cabrerana* (Malpighiaceae) is listed here largely to keep
    company with the other *Banisteriopsis* species. It may not
    contain harmine, it has been reported to contain only trace
    amounts of one β-carboline (2-Me-THβC, q.v.) but it does have
    1.3% DMT, and so can be mixed with the other *Banisteriopsis*
    spp. for making ayahuasca or yajé. DMT is the major alkaloid
    present, but there is also present NMT, 5-MeO-DMT and
    bufotenine. The harmine contribution is controversial.
*Elaeagnus angustifolia* (Elaeagnaceae) aerial parts and root
*Fagonia cretica* (Zygophyllaceae) entire plant
*Galium aparine* (Rubiaceae) aerial parts
*Grewia villosa* (Tiliaceae) root
*Heliconius cydno-galanthus* (Nymphalidae)
*Heliconius erato-petiverana* (Nymphalidae)
*Heliconius ethilla-eucoma* (Nymphalidae)
*Heliconius melpomene-rosina* (Nymphalidae)
*Heliconius sara-thamar* (Nymphalidae)
*Heliconius wallacei-flavescens* (Nymphalidae)
*Kochia scoparia* (Chenopodiaceae) arial parts
*Nicotiana tabacum* (Solanaceae) in tobacco smoke
*Oxytropis puberula* (Leguminosae) aerial parts
*Passiflora edulis* var. Flavicarpa (Passifloraceae) fruitjuice
*Passiflora edulis* (Passifloraceae) in seed and root
*Passiflora incarnata* (Passifloraceae) leaf, seed and stem
*Peganum harmala* (Zygophyllaceae) aerial parts, callus tissue, flowers,
    fruit, stem and especially the root. Both hairy root cultures and
    suspension cultures have been made. This plant is also a rich
    source of harmaline.
*Peganum nigellastrum* (Zygophyllaceae) aerial parts
*Thalictrum foetidum* (Ranunculaceae) root
*Tribulus terrestris* (Zygophyllaceae) entire plant and seeds
*Uncaria* spp. (Rubiaceae)
*Zygophyllum fabago* (Zygophyllaceae) entire plant

A discussion of the brief history of harmine as a treatment of Parkinson's disease is offered in its recipe. It has been a major contributor to the action of ayahuasca. Mention was made under harmaline of an ancient sample of *B. caapi* sent out of South America by the botanist Richard Spruce. The fact that it contained only harmine, whereas fresh samples contain both harmine and harmaline, has been suggested as an argument for an oxidative deterioration with time.

7-MeO  R       H       $H_0$      —       R = -CH$_2$CH$_2$CO$_2$H
                                          7-methoxy-β-carboline, 1-
                                                    propionic acid

***Eurycoma longifolia*** (Simaroubaceae) root

7-MeO  OH      H       $H_2$      —       1-oxo-1,2,3,4-tetrahydronorharmine
                                          1-hydroxy-3,4-dihydronorharmine
                                          1-oxo-7-methoxy-1,2,3,4-
                                                    tetrahydro-β-carboline
                                          1-hydroxy-7-methoxy-3,4-dihydro-
                                                    β-carboline
                                          harmalacidine

***Banisteriopsis caapi*** (Malpighiaceae)

The two names for this compound reflect a tautomeric relationship, as has been explained above for 1-oxo-5-methoxy-THβC. The pairs
of oxo/hydroxy names are interchangable, and represent a single compound. The similarity of the name harmalacidine to either harmalicine or
harmalidine has been mentioned earlier, under harmalicine above. This
and harmalicine are a couple of the rare exceptions to the rule that the use
of the prefix "harm" means a methyl group in the 1-position.

7-MeO  Me      Me      $H_0$      —       2-methylharminium iodide
                                          1,2-dimethyl-7-methoxy-β-
                                                    carbolinium quat salt

A synthetic analogue of MPP+ (the toxic factor from MPTP as an
instigator of Parkinson's Disease, see 2-methyl-β-carbolinium iodide
above) which is as effective an inhibitor of mitochondrial respiration as is
MPP+ itself. It has not yet been observed in nature.

7-MeO  Me      -O      $H_0$      —       harmine N-oxide
***Banisteriopsis caapi*** (Malpighiaceae)

7-MeO  R       H       $H_2$      —       R = -CO$_2$H
                                          harmalinic acid
***Banisteriopsis caapi*** (Malpighiaceae)

7-MeO  R       H       $H_0$      —       R = -CO$_2$CH$_3$
                                          1-carbomethoxy-7-methoxy-β-
                                                    carboline
                                          harmic acid methyl ester

***Banisteriopsis caapi*** (Malpighiaceae) leaf and stem

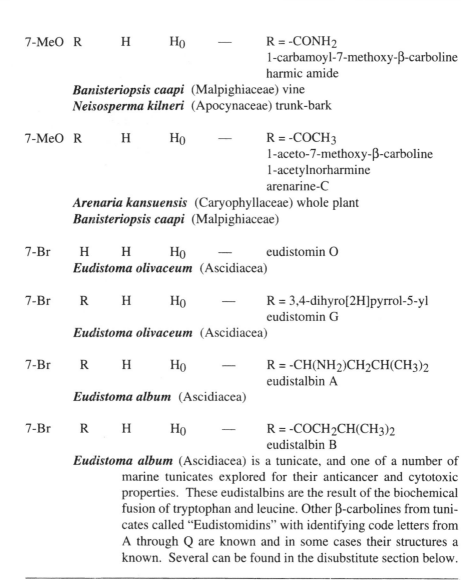

7-MeO   R        H        $H_0$        —          R = -$CONH_2$
                                                  1-carbamoyl-7-methoxy-β-carboline
                                                  harmic amide
   ***Banisteriopsis caapi***  (Malpighiaceae) vine
   ***Neisosperma kilneri***  (Apocynaceae) trunk-bark

7-MeO   R        H        $H_0$        —          R = -$COCH_3$
                                                  1-aceto-7-methoxy-β-carboline
                                                  1-acetylnorharmine
                                                  arenarine-C
   ***Arenaria kansuensis***  (Caryophyllaceae) whole plant
   ***Banisteriopsis caapi***  (Malpighiaceae)

7-Br    H        H        $H_0$        —          eudistomin O
   ***Eudistoma olivaceum***  (Ascidiacea)

7-Br    R        H        $H_0$        —          R = 3,4-dihyro[2H]pyrrol-5-yl
                                                  eudistomin G
   ***Eudistoma olivaceum***  (Ascidiacea)

7-Br    R        H        $H_0$        —          R = -$CH(NH_2)CH_2CH(CH_3)_2$
                                                  eudistalbin A
   ***Eudistoma album***  (Ascidiacea)

7-Br    R        H        $H_0$        —          R = -$COCH_2CH(CH_3)_2$
                                                  eudistalbin B
   ***Eudistoma album*** (Ascidiacea) is a tunicate, and one of a number of
       marine tunicates explored for their anticancer and cytotoxic
       properties. These eudistalbins are the result of the biochemical
       fusion of tryptophan and leucine. Other β-carbolines from tuni-
       cates called "Eudistomidins" with identifying code letters from
       A through Q are known and in some cases their structures a
       known. Several can be found in the disubstitute section below.

---

### Ar-8-substituted

8 —— 1 —— 2 —— Hx —— other

8-HO    R        H        $H_0$        4-MeO    R = -$CH_2CH_3$
                                                  1-ethyl-4-methoxy-β-carboline
                                                  picrasidine J
   ***Picrasma quassioides***  (Simaroubaceae)

8-HO    R       H       $H_0$      —          R = -CH=CH$_2$
                                              8-hydroxy-1-vinyl-β-carboline
                                              8-hydroxypavettine
                                              picrasidine I

*Catenicella cribraria*  (Vittaticellidae)
*Cribricellina cribraria*  (Mucronellidae) The high cytotoxicity of this
        compound led to its isolation from this marine bryozoan. The
        methyl ether and the acetate ester are also active, but the hydro-
        genation of the double bond drops the potency considerably. See
        pavettine.
*Picrasma quassioides*  (Simaroubaceae)


8-OH    R       H       $H_0$      4-MeO      R = 2-dimethylaminoethyl
                                              1-(2-dimethylaminoethyl)-8-
                                                      hydroxy-4-methoxy-β-carboline
                                              picrasidine K

*Picrasma quassioides*  (Simaroubaceae)


8-MeO   H       H       $H_4$      4-MeO      4,8-dimethoxy-1,2,3,4-tetrahydro-β-
                                                      carboline
                                              picrasidine P

*Picrasma quassioides*  (Simaroubaceae)


8-MeO   Et      H       $H_0$      4-MeO      4,8-dimethoxy-1-ethyl-β-carboline
                                              crenatidine

*Ailanthus malabarica*  (Araceae) bark and roots
*Picrasma javanica*  (Simaroubaceae)
*Picrasma quassioides*  (Simaroubaceae) roots


8-MeO   R       H       $H_0$      4-MeO      R = -CH=CH$_2$
                                              4,8-dimethoxy-1-vinyl-β-carboline
                                              kumujian G
                                              dehydrocrenatidine

*Ailanthus malabarica*  (Araceae)
*Picrasma quassioides*  (Simaroubaceae) stem
*Quassia amara*  (Simaroubaceae)


8-MeO   R       H       $H_0$      4-MeO      R = -CO$_2$CH$_3$
                                              1-carbomethoxy-4,8-dimethoxy-β-
                                                      carboline

*Ailanthus altissima*  (Simaroubaceae)


8-MeO   R       H       $H_0$      4-MeO      R = -CH$_2$CH$_2$OCH$_3$

4,8-dimethoxy-1-(2-methoxyethyl)-
β-carboline
*Picrasma quassioides* (Simaroubaceae) roots

8-MeO   R        H        $H_0$    4-MeO    R = -COCH=CHCO$_2$CH$_3$
*Picrasma quassioides* (Simaroubaceae)

Ar multisubstituted

Ar —— Ar —— 1 —— 2 —— $H_x$

5-Br    6-HO   H        H        $H_0$    5-bromo-6-hydroxy-β-carboline
                                          eudistomin D
*Eudistoma glaucus* (Ascidiacea)
*Eudistoma olivaceum* (Ascidiacea)

6-HO    7-Br   H        H        $H_0$    7-bromo-6-hydroxy-β-carboline
                                          eudistomin J
*Eudistoma olivaceum* (Ascidiacea)

6-HO    7-Br   R        H        $H_0$    R = pyrrol-2-yl
                                          7-bromo-6-hydroxy-1-(pyrrol-2-yl)-
                                              β-carboline
                                          eudistomin A
*Eudistoma olivaceum* (Ascidiacea)
      This compound is patented for the treatment of viral infections.

6-HO    7-Br   R        H        $H_0$    R = 3,4-dihydro[2H]pyrrol-5-yl
                                          7-bromo-1-(3,4-dihydro[2H]pyrrol-
                                              5-yl)-6-hydroxy-β-carboline
                                          eudistomin P
*Eudistoma olivaceum* (Ascidiacea)

6-MeO   7-MeO  Me       H        $H_4$    6,7-dimethoxy-1-methyl-1,2,3,4-
                                              tetrahydro-β-carboline
                                          6-methoxy-1,2,3,4-
                                              tetrahydroharmine
*Roemeria hybrida* (Papaveraceae)

6-MeO   7-MeO  Me       H        $H_0$    6,7-dimethoxy-1-methyl-β-
                                              carboline
                                          6-methoxyharmine

6,7-dimethoxy-harmane
roeharmine

*Roemeria hybrida* (Papaveraceae)

6-MeO  7-MeO  R  H  H$_4$  R = 4-hydroxybenzyl
6,7-dimethoxy-1-(4-hydroxybenzyl)
1,2,3,4-tetrahydro-β-carboline
norroecarboline (+)

*Roemeria hybrida* (Papaveraceae)

6-MeO  7-MeO  R  Me  H$_4$  R = 4-hydroxybenzyl
roecarboline (-)
6,7-dimethoxy-1-(4- hydroxybenzyl)
2-methyl-1,2,3,4-
tetrahydro-β-carboline

*Roemeria hybrida* (Papaveraceae)

6-MeO  7-Br  R  H  H$_0$  R = 1,3-dihydro-3-methoxy-
[2H]pyrrol-2-yl
7-bromo-1-(1,3-dihydro-3-methoxy-
[2H]pyrrol-2-yl)-6-
methoxy-β-carboline
eudistomin B

*Eudistoma olivaceum* (Ascidiacea)

6-Br  7-HO  R  H  H$_0$  R = pyrrol-2-yl
6-bromo-7-methoxy-1-(pyrrol-2-yl)-
β-carboline

*Eudistoma olivaceum* (Ascidiacea)

6-Br  8-HO  R  H  H$_0$  R = 3,4-dihydropyrrol-5-yl
6-bromo-1-(3,4-dihydropyrrol-5-yl)-
8-hydroxy-β-carboline
eudistomidin A

*Eudistoma olivaceum* (Ascidiacea)

6-Br  8-Br  Et  H  H$_0$  6,8-dibromo-1-ethyl-β-carboline
*Aglaophenia pluma* (Plumulariidae)

7-MeO  8-O-glu  Me  H  H$_0$  8-hydroxyharmine glucoside
8-hydroxy-7-methoxy-1-methyl-β-
carboline glucoside
8-glucosidyl harmine

*Peganum harmala* (Zygophyllaceae) seed

| 7-MeO | 8-O-glu | Me | H | H₄ | dihydroruine |

7-MeO  8-O-glu  Me    H    H$_4$    dihydroruine
                                    8-hydroxy-7-methoxy-1-methyl-
                                        1,2,3,4-tetrahydro-β-
                                        carboline glucoside
                                    8-glucosidyl-tetrahydroharmine

*Peganum harmala* (Zygophyllaceae) callus tissue and entire plant

7-MeO  8-O-glu  Me    H    H$_2$    ruine
                                    8-hydroxy-7-methoxy-1-methyl-
                                        1,2,3,4-3,4-dihydro-
                                        β-carboline glucoside
                                    8-glucosidyl-7-methoxy-1-methyl-
                                        3,4-dihydro-β-carboline
                                    8-glucosidylharmaline

*Peganum harmala* (Zygophyllaceae)

There is ambiguity here. Some references give the dihydroruine/ ruine as being the tetrahydro/dihydro pair as shown here. Others accept the relationship as being a dihydro/aromatic pair.

---

RELATED ALKALOID FAMILIES
(through botany, pharmacology or chemistry)

CARBAZOLES: These are compounds with structures that are isosteric with the β-carbolines; the pyridine ring nitrogen atom is missing.

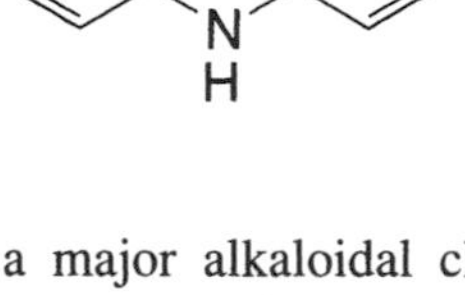

QUINAZOLINES: This is a major alkaloidal class found alongside the β-carbolines in seeds of the currently popular plant, Peganum harmala. The structure of these is a two ring benzopyrimidine, a naphthalene system with nitrogen atoms at the 1- and 3-positions, chemically unrelated to the carbolines. It is rather sly of nature to give the parent alkaloid of this group, desoxypeganine, and of the congener carboline group, THβC, the same empirical formula, $C_{11}H_{12}N_2$. Vasicine (peganine) is illustrated here.

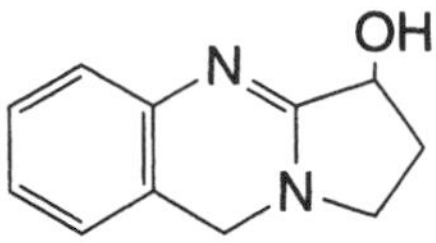

**HARMALIDINES:** These are β-carbolines with a five membered ring tying together the 1- and the 9-positions.

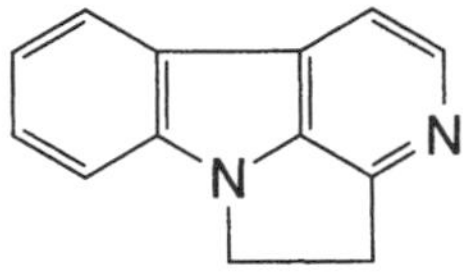

**CANTHINONES:** These are β-carbolines with a six membered ring tying together the 1- and 9-positions.

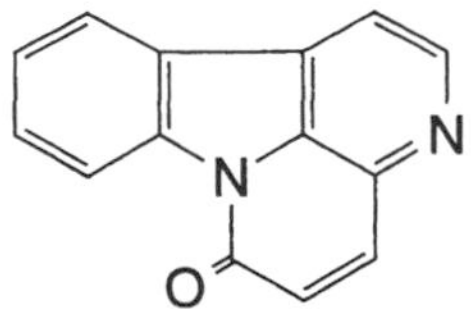

**CARYNANTHEINES:** These are β-carbolines with a six membered ring tying together the 1- and 2-positions.

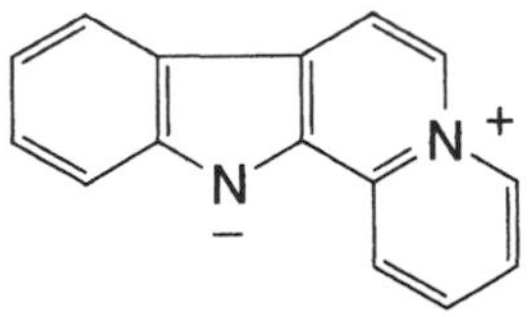

# APPENDIX G:  HISTAMINES

There are no psychoactive imidazolethylamines (IEA's or histamines) or tetrahydroimidazopyridines (THIP's or spinaceamines), to my knowledge. So, why is there an appendix devoted to these families of chemicals? Because I am quite convinced that some day they will be intimately involved in the understanding of the actions of psychedelic drugs. This may be either through direct or indirect action. These speculations are supported by some remarkable parallels between their chemistry and that of the widely recognized active materials.

(1) There are three natural neurotransmitters in the human brain that are derived from amino acids by decarboxylation, and that contain a molecular skeleton that can be described as an aromatic ring (a diffuse or broad base) separated by two carbon atoms from a nitrogen atom (a localized or focused base).

There is phenethylamine, from phenylalanine, which provides the skeleton of dopamine and norepinephrine (noradrenalin) and with appropriate substitution gives rise to the compounds described in PIHKAL.

There is tryptamine, from tryptophan, which provides the skeleton of serotonin and melatonin and with appropriate substitution gives rise to the compounds described in this book, TIHKAL.

There is histamine which is derived from histidine. Perhaps with appropriate substitutions this might give rise to compounds described in some future book called HIHKAL! (?)

(2) Each of these three neurotransmitters is metabolized into a biologically inactive product, each by an enzymatic oxidative deamination. Phenethylamine yields phenylacetic acid, tryptamine yields indole-3-acetic acid and histamine yields imidazoleacetic acid.

(3) Each of these three neurotransmitters is methylated by specific N-methyl transferase enzymes; norepinephrine yields epinephrine (adrenalin), tryptamine yields N-methyl and N,N-dimethyltryptamine (NMT and DMT) and histamine yields $N^\tau$-methylhistamine.

(4) Each of these three amines can close, with an appropriate carbon atom,

to form a new six membered ring, and each of these conversions is known to occur in the normal brain. Phenethylamine will close this ring to form a tetrahydroisoquinoline, tryptamine will close this ring to form tetrahydro-β-carboline and histamine will close this ring to form tetrahydroimidazopyridine.

Phenethylamine (PEA)                    Tetrahydroisoquinoline (THIQ)

Tryptamine (T)                          Tetrahydro-β-carboline (THβC)

Histamine (H)                           Tetrahydroimidazopyridine (THIP)
Imidazoleethylamine (IEA)                        (spinaceamine)

(5) The relationships between the parent, open-chain amine and the cyclized product are complex, and they can often afford a different class of action, sometimes a complimentary form of action. With the tetrahydroisoquinolines, there has yet to be a definition of the role that they play in the action of the many cacti where they are major alkaloids. With the tetrahydro-β-carbolines, the action is that of facilitation. The carbolines serve as the enzyme inhibitors that allow the tryptamines to show their central action via an oral route of administration. Within the histamine/THIP compounds, no roles have yet been assigned, but there are suggestive hints. For example, there have been a number of studies of $N^\tau$-

methylhistamine levels in the brain reflecting the administration of certain centrally active psychotropic anesthetics. In cats the brain level of this metabolite goes down following the administration of phenobarbital or chloral. But with the administration of ketamine, the blood level shoots up by a factor of some 12 fold. Could it be that this $N^\tau$-methylhistamine in the brain is the active contributor to the complex action of ketamine, and is promoted into this role by the actual drug's administration? Do anesthetics that function by afferent blockade, such as ketamine or PCP, function by changing the brain $N^\tau$-methylhistamine levels? The level also goes up with the administration of drugs such as pargyline and tranylcypromine. Just possibly, could the harmine alkaloids be expressing their action through this medium of producing buckets of $N^\tau$-methylhistamine inside the brain? This area cries out for research.

Another off-the-wall bit of information. As noted below, the salamander is a valuable source of members of the spinaceamine world. Just a short time ago I proof-read a paper for a colleague from Slovenia, who wanted to submit it to an ethnopharmacology journal for publication. It described the local traditional custom of making salamander brandy, by allowing the distillate to flow down a string to which was attached a live salamander. The mucus was washed off the animal and carried into the brandy, and with the death of one animal, another was used in substitution. The result was a strange and admired drink, and I wonder if it could contain cyclized histamines as unexpected additives.

Do remember that this short appendix is intended to be more provocative than informative. This world started in 1964 with the observation of spinaceamines as an isolate from frog skins, along with bufotenine and some phenethylamine quarternary salts. This area is too new to have much data yet discovered, so I will use this opportunity to try to unravel some of the nomenclature and tautomeric complications associated with the imidazoles that have, in a subtle way, discouraged more than one chemist from exploring this area.

There are only a few entries, so I will be a bit pedantic with each one, and try to address tautology and the nomenclature assignment in what is one of the more tricky areas of organic chemistry. The use of the Greek letters simplifies things. The two structures shown here are different only in the location of the hydrogen atom on the imidozole ring, and the position of the double bonds. These are known as

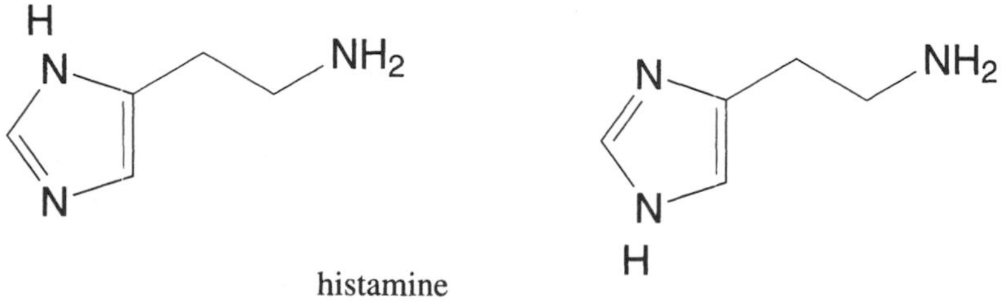

histamine
decarboxylated histidine
1-H-imidazole-4-ethanamine

tautomers, and are indistinguishable from one another. The hydrogen atom is basically unassigned, and can be here or there and it doesn't really matter -- it's all the same, since the hydrogen-nitrogen bond is a rather casual one and, when in solution, is in an easy interchange with water. Given: the NH is the position defined as the 1-position, and given: one assigns ring numbers to positions from the NH through the tertiary N, and this latter must be at the 3-position. Hence the first drawn structure could be seen as being 1-H-imidazole-4-ethanamine and the second as being 1-H-imidazole-5-ethanamine. But since these are two ways of drawing the same molecule, one simply takes the lower number, and 4-substitution is the name that is needed. However, when these nitrogen atoms are locked into non-interchangeable definition with methyl group substitution, things lose this casual freedom.

Here are the four methylated histamines that are often confused with oneanother. The three nitrogen substituted isomers are found in nature, but the chain

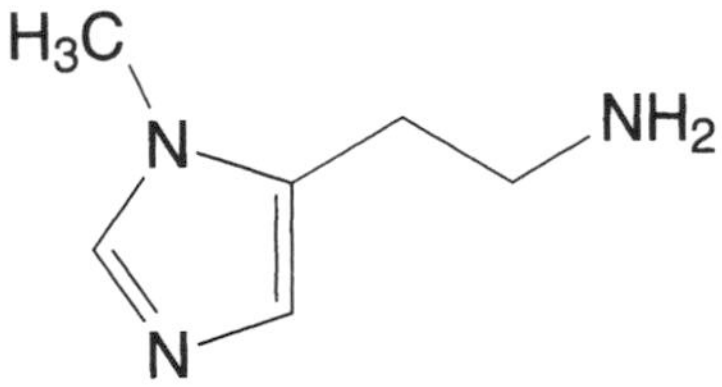

$N^{\pi}$-methylhistamine
proximo-methylhistamine
1-methylimidazole, 5-(2-aminoethyl)

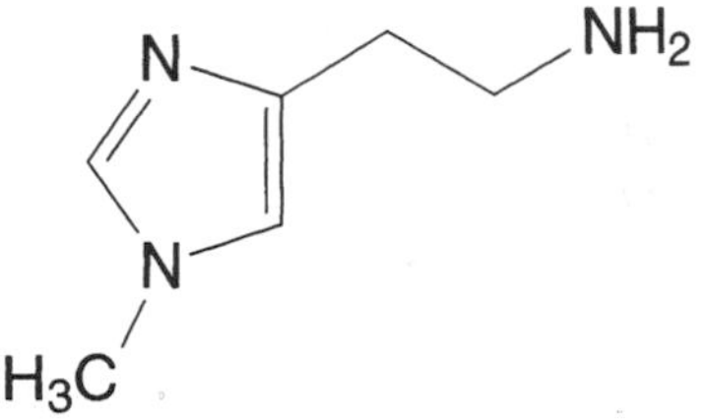

$N^{\tau}$-methylhistamine
tele-methylhistamine
1-methylimidazole, 4-(2-aminoethyl)
1-methylhistamine

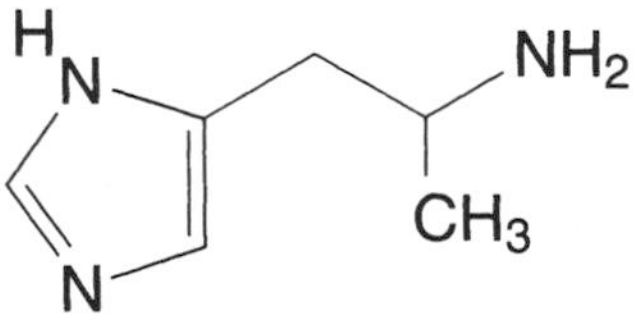

α-methylhistamine

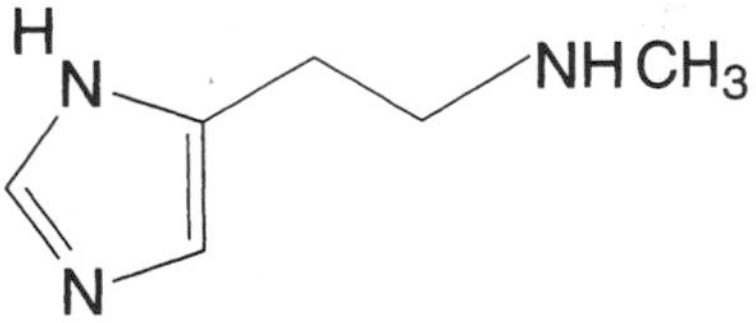

$N^{\alpha}$-methylhistamine

homologue is synthetic. There are three more synthetic isomers that are not known in nature. The carbon position between the two nitrogen atoms of the imidazole ring is called the 2-position, the remaining position is the 4-position, and the carbon atom that attaches the side-chain to the ring is the β-position, sometimes called the omega position in the older literature. Thus one can encounter the positional isomers, 2-methylhistamine, 4-methylhistamine and β-methylhistamine (or ωmethylhistamine). The synthetic α-methylhistamine and the two dimethyl compounds, $N^\alpha,N^\alpha$-dimethylhistamine (natural, see below) and α,β-dimethylhistamine (synthetic) are remarkably potent agonists at the histamine H-3 receptor. In other words, they act as if they were indeed histamine.

Most of the sources of these histamine analogues have been various marine animals such as frogs and sponges. In browsing the literature one routinely encounters other, provocative compounds that somehow tie in to the topics touched upon in this book. In the assaying of frogs you will frequently come across, as expected, both bufotenine and its trimethylammonium salt bufotenidine (it is mentioned in the bufotenine recipe). And there is an unexpected connection with the cactus in that both tyramine (4-hydroxyphenethylamine) and candicine (the trimethylammonium quaternary salt) are rather wide-spread amongst certain frogs. These are frequently encountered in a number of the cacti. A most remarkable compound, the trimethylammonium quaternary salt of meta-tyramine is called leptodactyline and was first seen as a natural product in the *Leptodactylus spp.* of frogs.

But the listing below is organized by compound, not source, and any additional detail will follow the source mentioned within the appropriate histamine homologue paragraph.

$N^\tau$-**Methylhistamine**: This is one of the major metabolites of histamine in man, but its distribution and dynamics have been studied mostly in the rat. As has been mentioned above, its levels are strongly influenced by a number of drugs. The positional isomer, $N^\pi$-histamine is believed to be a minor metabolite, but it has not been as well studied.

$N^\alpha$-**Methylhistamine**: This is a normal, but minor metabolite found in man. But it is a major alkaloid of the sponge *Verongia fistularis* and with the $N^\alpha,N^\alpha$-dimethyl homologue mentioned below, is responsible for its reported cardiotonic activity. Nomenclature alert! A purist will insist that the term "alkaloid" should be restricted to those basic nitrogen-containing organic compounds found in seed-bearing plants. I have already used the term with spore-bearing mushrooms, and here I will extend its use to include animals. I am not a purist. Of a number of species of the frog genus *Leptodactylus* there is only the one example, *Leptodactylus pentadactylus labyrinthicus* that has a skin that is blessed with four of these alkaloids, the $N^\alpha$-methyl and $N^\alpha,N^\alpha$-dimethylhistamines, the cyclic spinaceamine and its methyl homologue 5-methylspinaceamine.

$N^\alpha$-**Acetylhistamine**: In a number of amphibians, this amide is found accompanying either those that contain one or more of the group $N^\alpha$-methylhistamine, $N^\alpha,N^\alpha$-dimethylhistamine, spinaceamine and 5-methylspinaceamine, or those that contain bufotenine and bufotenidine. There is little overlap between the two groups of amphibians. There have been other amides found in animal species. The isovaleramide has been found in *Dolichothele sphaerica,* for example, where it has been given the name of dolichotheleine.

$N^\alpha,N^\alpha$**-Dimethylhistamine**:  All of the frogs mentioned in the above entry on $N^\alpha$-methylhistamine also contain this dimethyl homologue.  This tertiary amine is also present in the sponge *Ianthella* sp. and is stated to be the hypotensive principle there.  The analogy to the methylation of tryptamine to the mono- and the dimethylhomologues is inescapable.  DMT is now unquestionably accepted as a normal component of our central nervous system.  There is an almost incestual aura to the report of this alkaloid as a component in the cactus *Echinocereus triglochiditus.* Might this dimethylhistamine counterpart of DMT be there in the brain as well?  If so, why?  If you were to smoke it, would it have some effect?  If you were to consume it in some pseudohoasca brew with some deaminase inhibitor such as *Peganum harmala*, would it become orally active?  But if it did, and it has the cardiotoxic effects noted in the sponges, might it not be of enhanced toxicity?  Or, if it is indeed hypotensive (as in the above sponge) might it be of medical value?  Maybe by blocking the imidazole active hydrogen with one further methylation and putting some exciting group in the 2-position (an alkyl, or maybe a trifluoromethyl, or a thioether) the effects might be quite changed, for the better.  What a fertile area for research!

**Spinaceamine (4,5,6,7-tetrahydro-1-H-imidazo[4,5-c]pyridine)**:  Although some 75% of the skin-gland secretion alkaloids of the fire salamander *Salamandra maculosa* is composed of the two magnificent five-ring alkaloids samandarine and samandarone, in the remaining inventory there are both spinaceamine and the 5-methylhomologue below.  All of this might have given sparkle to that salamander brandy of Slovenia.  As mentioned above, the cutaneous gland secretions of the frog *Leptodactylus pentadactylus* contains this alkaloid along with bufotenine.  See the 5-methyl entry below for some comments concerning the naming of these alkaloids.

**5-Methylspinaceamine (5-methyl-4,5,6,7-tetrahydro-1-H-imidazo-[4,5-c]pyridine)**:  The first report of the existence of this cyclized histamine compound was in 1964, with the description of four alkaloids from the skin of the *Leptodactylus pentadactylus labyrinthicus*, namely $N^\alpha$-methylhistamine, $N^\alpha,N^\alpha$-dimethylhistamine, spinaceamine and 5-methylspinaceamine.  The tautomer discussion above for histamine (where the hydrogen is) applies equally here.  The numbering in the piperidine ring is dictated by just where the hydrogen atom is.  Some literature references say this compound is the 6-methyl isomer.  Same compound, differing numbering system.  By the way, the word "spinacene" is a synonym for squalene from the shark, but there is no conceivable connection between sharks and frogs.  At least none that is obvious to me.

# APPENDIX H:  KNOWN TRYPTAMINES

This is a listing of all of the known tryptamines that are, or may be, of interest psychopharmacologically.  The criteria for inclusion on this list are:

(1)     There is a indole nucleus present to which there is attached at a single site a carbon chain with a basic nitrogen separated by two carbon atoms from the indole ring.  Alkyl and alkoxy substituents on these carbon atoms are allowed, alpha and beta, but no added funtionality.

(2)     An additional ring may be attached to this skeleton only if it can be removed metabolically or chemically (such as a benzyl group attached to a heteroatom).  All benzyls are included except for those with a C-C bond attachment.  Rings such as a piperazine which usually lead on to bigger things disqualify a compound.  There are no bis-compounds (with two or more aminoethyl chains attached.

(3)     No extremely polar groups are included, unless there is the potential for facile conversion to less polar analogues metabolically (such as an N-oxide or the O-ester).  Also excluded are bis-things such as dimers. Amides are OK as long as the tryptamine nitrogen remains basic; melatonin and its allies are thus excluded.

(4)     Derivatives that are prepared for chromatography, such as trialkyllsilyls or perfluoracid amides or ethers, are excluded.

(5)     There are no rings that connect the tryptamine nitrogen to the 2-carbon chain.

(6)     The only hetero-rings included are the pyrrolidine, piperidine and morpholine types that involved the basic tryptamine nitrogen atom.

(7)     There are no phenyl derivatives except for the benzyl on a heteroatom.
        There are no fused heterocyclic rings attached, or fused rings (such as
        furonyl, furfuryl, pyridinyl, pyranyl).

---

        Barring these negatives as to central activity, every trytpamine that is in the
chemical literature is included in this compilation. For well-known and well studied
compounds, a single citation is pointless. There are over a hundred citations a year
to tryptamine itself, and even the less common plant compound 5-MeO-DMT can
show ten or twenty a year. It is only if a compound has been reported only a few
time, an early citation or a citation giving a preparation procedure will be given. In
either case this will give immediate access to the CAS number. The style of the
naming of tryptamines was changed in 1972, and care must be taken in following
searches that straddle this date. As an example, the chemical names for DMT,
bufotenine (5-hydroxy-DMT) and methylenedioxy-DMT are given. Note that in
the pre-1972 form, the amine nitrogen is incorporated as a part of the substituent;
in the post-1972 form, it has become a part of the nucleus that is being substituted.
Also, early citations are more prone to file articles under trivial names. The actual
written forms are here and be used as guides:


DMT             (pre-1972)      Indole, 3-($\beta$-dimethylaminoethyl) and later,
                                Indole, 3-(2-dimethylaminoethyl) and later,
                                Indole, 3-[2-(dimethylamino)ethyl]-
                (1972 on)       1H-Indole-3-ethanamine, N,N-dimethyl-

5-HO-DMT        (pre-1957)      5-Indolol, 3-(2-dimethylaminethyl)-  see bufotenine
                (to 1961)       Indol-5-ol, 3-(2-dimethylaminethyl)-  see bufotenine
                (to 1966)       Indol-5-ol, 3-[2-(dimethylamino)ethyl- see bufotenine
                (to 1972)       Indol-5-ol, 3-[2-(dimethylamino)ethyl-
                (1972 on)       1H-Indol-5-ol, 3-[2-(dimethylamino)ethyl}-

4,5-MD-DMT                      6H-1.3-dioxolo[4,5-e]indole-8-ethanamine, N,N-
                                    dimethyl
5,6-MD-DMT                      5H-1,3-dioxolo[4,5-f]indole-7-ethanamine, N,N-
                                    dimethyl

---

Here are, for reference purposes, the common groupings of Chemical Abstracts as to volumes, as to dates, and as to the numbering of the collected indices:

| Vol.   1 - 40:   | 1907-1946 |                       |
|------------------|-----------|-----------------------|
| Vol.  41 - 50:   | 1947-1956 | 5th Coll. Index       |
| Vol.  51 - 55:   | 1957-1961 | 6th Coll. Index       |
| Vol.  56 - 65:   | 1962-1966 | 7th Coll. Index       |
|                  |           | (now two volumes/year) |
| Vol.  66 - 75:   | 1967-1971 | 8th Coll. Index       |
| Vol.  76 - 85:   | 1972-1976 | 9th Coll. Index       |
| Vol.  86 - 95:   | 1977-1981 | 10th Coll. Index      |
| Vol.  96 -105:   | 1982-1986 | 11th Coll. Index      |
| Vol. 106 -115:   | 1987-1991 | 12th Coll. Index      |
| Vol. 116 -125:   | 1992-1996 | 13th Coll. Index      |

In this appendix each section is defined by the number of nuclear substitution, and the last section by the position of the relocated ethylamine chain. Each section is alphabetized, generally, from left to right within this order: numerical substituent position, indolic substituent by chemical priority (see below), nitrogen substituents by chemical priority. These N-groups are, always, arranged with the larger of the two first being increased step by step in size but then held unchanged at each step until the second substituent has brought up to this size. With each entry, a single, early CA citation is given, and if there are many such entries, a "many" will be entered. If the only appearance is in this volume, it will say "TIHKAL."

The chemical priority observed in the following bonding priorities:

| Carbon       | Oxygen | Halide | Nitrogen | Heteroatom |
|--------------|--------|--------|----------|------------|
| H-           | HO-    | F-     | -NH$_2$  | HS-        |
| Me-          | MeO-   | Cl-    | -NO$_2$  | MeS-       |
| Et-          | EtO-   | Br-    |          | EtS-       |
| Pr-          | RO-    | I-     |          | RS-        |
| iPr-         |        |        |          | RSe-       |
| Allyl-       |        |        |          |            |
| Propynyl-    |        |        |          |            |
| Cyclopropyl- |        |        |          |            |
| Bu-          |        |        |          |            |
| Bz-          |        |        |          |            |
| CF$_3$-      |        |        |          |            |
| MeCO-        |        |        |          |            |

## UNSUBSTITUTED TRYPTAMINES:

| N | N | | CA CITATION | CODE |
|---|---|---|---|---|

### 2-CARBON CHAIN

| N | N | | CA CITATION | CODE |
|---|---|---|---|---|
| H | H | | — many — | T |
| Me | H | | — many — | NMT |
| Me | Me | | — many — | DMT |
| Me | Me | N-oxide | — many — | |
| Et | H | | — many — | NET |
| Et | Me | | 64:19542b | MET |
| Et | Et | | — many — | DET |
| ethylidine | - | | 124:146544f | |
| ethylidine | - | N-oxide | 103:160749z | |
| ß-F-Et | H | | 77:P126425a | |
| ß-Cl-Et | H | | 92:128821k | |
| (MeO)$_2$CC | H | | 115:256446x | |
| Pr | H | | 53:20559c | NPT |
| Pr | Pr | | — many — | DPT |
| iPr | H | | 61:11207g | NIPT |
| iPr | Me | | 103:184h | MIPT |
| iPr | Et | | (TIHKAL) | EIPT |
| iPr | iPr | | 61:11207g | DIPT |
| isopropylidine | - | | 61:13293h | |
| allyl | H | | 100:6900y | |
| allyl | allyl | | 54:19644b | DAT |
| propynyl | Me | | 82:156005j | |
| propynyl | Et | | 82:156005j | |
| propynyl | iPr | | 86:P106379w | |
| propynyl | propynyl | | 77:P126425a | |
| cyclopropyl | H | | 83:705x | |
| propylidine | - | | 124:146544f | |
| propylidine | - | N-oxide | 103:160749z | |
| Bu | H | | 61:11207g | NBT |
| Bu | Bu | | 54:19644b | DBT |
| butylidine | - | | 118:192065z | |
| sBu | H | | 61:11207g | NSBT |
| iBu | H | | 61:11207g | NIBT |
| iBu | iBu | | 61:11207g | DIBT |
| isobutylidine | - | | 118:192065z | |
| tBu | H | | (TIHKAL) | NTBT |

| | | | |
|---|---|---|---|
| cyclopropylmethyl | H | 83:705x | |
| Pe | H | 93:P220719b | |
| Pe | Pe | 60:6078a | |
| pentadienyl | H | 111:114991q | |
| pentylidine N-oxide | - | 113:78193m | |
| cyclopentyl | H | 76:25136f | |
| cyclopentylidine | - | 76:25136f | |
| 1-prenylidene | - | 119:250218k | |
| C≡CC(C)$_2$- | H | 123:P256342a | |
| 5,5-(EtO)$_2$-Pe | H | 86:72950h | |
| =CC=C(C)C | | 95:115194v | |
| He | H | 64:17522d | NHT |
| He | He | 60:6078a | DHT |
| cyclohexyl | H | 76:25136f | |
| cyclohexylidine | - | 76:25136f | |
| cyclohexylmethyl | H | 93:P220719b | |
| 2-ethylcyclopentylidene | - | 100:139430s | |
| Bz | H | — many — | |
| Bz | Me | 66:27488q | |
| Bz | Et | 67:107054f | |
| Bz | iPr | 86:P106380q | |
| Bz | cyclopropyl | 83:705x | |
| Bz | propynyl | 82:156005j | |
| Bz | iBu | 64:5032f | |
| Bz | Bz | — many — | |
| benzylidine | - | 68:39406r | |
| cycloheptyl | H | 76:25136f | |
| cycloheptylidine | - | 120:217334t | |
| octylidine | - | 120:299048q | |
| cyclooctylidine | - | 120:217334t | |
| — CCCC — | | 48:12931f | |
| — CCCCC — | | 46:8115a | |
| — CCOCC — | | 58:13895c | |
| — C(C)=CH-CH=C(C) — | | 113:155f | |
| HO | H | 64:5032g | |
| HO | Me | 83:203236t | |
| HO | Pr | 63:P2959e | |
| HO | iBu | 63:P2959f | |
| MeO | H | 119:95257b | |
| (MeO)$_2$-CCCCO | H | 114:P247324h | |
| NH2 | H | 55:P3615d | |

## 3-CARBON CHAIN

### α-METHYL

| | | | |
|---|---|---|---|
| H | H | — many — | α-MT   IT-290 |
| Me | H | 57:P12438f | N,α-DMT |
| Me | Me | 79:42276f | N,N,α-TMT |
| Et | H | 57:P12438g | |
| Pr | H | 64:5032f | |
| iPr | H | 64:5032f | |
| propynyl | Me | 99:101449c | |
| Bu | H | 64:5032f | |
| Bz | H | 64:5032f | |
| HO | H | 112:158703x | |
| MeO | H | 119:95257b | |
| benzylidine | - | 77:48135q | |
| NH$_2$ | H | 55:P3615d | |

### β-METHYL

| | | |
|---|---|---|
| H | H | 48:692f |
| Me | H | 93:94740m |

### α,β-METHYLENE

| | | |
|---|---|---|
| H | H | 56:P15484f |

## 4-CARBON CHAIN

### α,α-DIMETHYL

| | | |
|---|---|---|
| H | H | 42:1933f |
| Me | H | 64:5032f |
| phenyl | H | 98:P125870p |

### β,β-DIMETHYL

| | | |
|---|---|---|
| H | H | 57:9788i |

### α-ETHYL

| | | | |
|---|---|---|---|
| H | H | — many — | α-ET |
| Me | Me | 65:16929g | |
| Et | H | 61:633a | |

### α,β-DIMETHYL

| | | |
|---|---|---|
| H | H | 59:2753 |

## 5-CARBON CHAIN

α-PROPYL

| H | H | 55:8382c |

α-ISOPROPYL

| H | H | 53:21876b |

β-PROPYL

| H | H | 57:5988i |

ß-ISOPROPYL

| H | H | 57:9788i |

α-METHYL-α-ETHYL

| H | H | 81:P3767p |
| Me | H | 81:P3767p |
| Bz | H | 81:P3767p |

α,α,β-TRIMETHYL

| H | H | 62:11022a |

## 6-CARBON CHAIN

α-BUTYL

| H | H | 64:6602h |

α-METHYL-α-PROPYL

| H | H | 81:P3767p |

α,α-DIETHYL

| H | H | 81:P3767p |

α-i-BUTYL

| H | H | 75:19394b |

α-t-BUTYL

| H | H | 53:21876d |

β,β-DIETHYL

| H | H | 57:9788i |
| Et | Et | 68:84583g |

β-tert-BUTYL
H                    H                    76:126827n

α,β-TETRAMETHYLENE
H                    H                    58:5614b

## 7-CARBON CHAIN

α-ISOAMYL
H                    H                    75:19394b

α-ISOPRENE
H                    H                    58:8182b

## 8-CARBON CHAIN

α,α-DIPROPYL
H                    H                    81:P3767P

## MONOSUBSTITUTED TRYPTAMINES:

| RING | N | N | | CA CITATION | CODE |
|------|---|---|---|-------------|------|

### 2-CARBON CHAIN

| RING | N | N | | CA CITATION | CODE |
|------|---|---|---|-------------|------|
| 1-Me | H | H | | — many — | 1-MT |
| 1-Me | Me | H | | 51:15516i | 1,M-DMT |
| 1-Me | Me | Me | | 81:145588e | |
| 1-Me | Me | Me | N-oxide | 82:57133t | |
| 1-Me | Et | H | | 83:178702g | |
| 1-Me | Et | Et | | 57:9785a | |
| 1-Me | iPr | H | | 86:P106380q | |
| 1-Me | propynyl | Et | | 83:178702g | |
| 1-Me | propynyl | iPr | | 83:178702g | |
| 1-Me | benzylidine | - | | 68:39406r | |
| 1-Me | Bz | H | | 83:178702 | |
| 1-Me | Bz | propynyl | | 86:P106380q | |
| 1-Me | Bz | Bz | | 55:21155h | |
| 1-Me | — CCCCC — | | | 58:10251e | |
| 1-Me | HO | H | | 113:115654k | |
| 1-COC- | HO | H | | 109:149183p | |
| 1-Et | H | H | | 48:692h | |
| 1-Et | Et | Et | | 57:9785b | |
| 1-vinyl | H | H | | 124:P131483m | |
| 1-COCC- | H | H | | 120:P8937c | |
| 1-CCOC- | Me | Me | | 56:6595d | |
| 1-iPr | H | H | | 78:124389p | |
| 1-iPr | iPr | H | | 115:105458b | |
| 1-allyl | H | H | | 121:179446s | |
| 1-propynyl | H | H | | 64:2041e | |
| 1-Bu | Me | Me | | 92:215199g | |
| 1-cyclopropylmethyl | H | H | | 121:179446a | |
| 1-cyclopentyl | H | H | | 120:P8937c | |
| 1-Bz | H | H | | — many — | |
| 1-Bz | Me | H | | 48:P5230e | |
| 1-Bz | Me | Me | | 56:440g | |
| 1-Bz | Et | H | | 83:178702g | |
| 1-Bz | Et | Me | | 78:147730g | |
| 1-Bz | Et | Et | | 78:147730g | |
| 1-Bz | i-Pr | H | | 83:178702g | |
| 1-Bz | propynyl | Me | | 86:P106380q | |

| | | | | |
|---|---|---|---|---|
| 1-Bz | propynyl | Et | 83:178702g | |
| 1-Bz | Bz | H | 83:178702g | |
| 1-Bz | iPr | propynyl | 83:178702g | |
| 1-Bz | Bz | propynyl | 83:178702g | |
| 1-(CO)₂CCC- | allyloxy | H | 123:33485y | |
| 1-(CCO)₂CCCC- | allyloxy | H | 123:33485y | |
| 1-(CCO)₂CCCC- | Bz | H | 123:33485y | |
| 1-(CCO)₂CCCCC- | allyloxy | H | 123:33485y | |
| 1-MeCO | H | H | 111:58083f | |
| 1-MeCO | Me | Me | 78:3422k | |
| 1-CF₃CO | Me | Me | 88:117167t | |
| 1-propionyl | Me | Me | 89:99491h | |
| 1-HO | Me | Me | 122:161008m | |
| 1-MeO | H | H | 103:123301b | |
| 1-MeO | Me | H | 90:71992u | |
| 1-MeO | Me | Me | 62:14740c | Lespedamine |

---

| | | | | |
|---|---|---|---|---|
| 2-Me | H | H | 50:1759i | |
| 2-Me | Me | H | 62:10398e | |
| 2-Me | Me | Me | 54:13555g | |
| 2-Me | Et | Et | 44:10721c | |
| 2-Me | Pr | Pr | 53:20559g | |
| 2-Me | cyclohexyl | Me | 93:107063v | |
| 2-Me | Bu | Bu | 93:107063v | |
| 2-Me | benzylidine | - | 68:39406r | |
| 2-Me | — CCCCC — | | 58:10251e | |
| 2-Me | — CCOCC — | | 72:66865d | |
| 2-Et | H | H | 64:9697f | |
| 2-Et | Me | Me | 69:86857u | |
| 2-C=C- | H | H | 117:7726j | |
| 2-Pr | H | H | 116:213769h | |
| 2-propynyl | propynyl | Me | 82:156005j | |
| 2-propynyl | propynyl | Et | 86:P106379w | |
| 2-propynyl | Bz | propynyl | 82:156005j | |
| 2-Bz | H | H | 64:9697f | |
| 2-Bz | Me | H | 63:14834c | |
| 2-CF₃ | H | H | 105:P78834f | |
| 2-HO | H | H | 80:146391b | |
| 2-HO | Me | H | 91:5443k | |
| 2-HO | Me | Me | 91:5443k | |

| 2-Cl | Et | Et | 80:P82649g |
|------|-----|-----|------------|
| 2-Br | Me | Me | 122:161008m |
| 2-Br | Et | Et | 80:P82649g |
| 2-I | H | H | 103:215112u |
| 2-I | Et | Et | 80:P82649g |
| 2-MeS | H | H | 74:P87824w |
| 2-MeS | Me | Me | 78:52823a |
| 2-MeS | Et | Et | 74:P87824w |
| 2-MeS | — CCCC — | | 74:P87824w |
| 2-MeS | — CCOCC — | | 74:P87824w |
| 2-EtS | Me | Me | 85:21008d |
| 2-EtSO | Me | Me | 85:21008d |
| 2-BzS | — CCCC — | | 74:P87824w |

---

| 4-Me | H | H | 50:1759i |
|------|-----|-----|------------|
| 4-Me | Me | Me | 54:18772f |
| 4-prenyl | H | H | 67:79993r |
| 4-HO | H | H | — many — |
| | | | norbaeocystin is the phosphate ester |
| 4-HO | Me | H | — many — |
| | | | baeocystin is the phosphate ester |
| 4-HO | Me | Me | — many —     psilocin |
| | | | psilocybin is the phosphate ester |
| 4-HO | Et | H | 72:130696d |
| 4-HO | Et | Me | 95:61908k |
| 4-HO | Et | Et | — many —     CY-74 |
| | | | CEY-19 is the phosphate ester |
| 4-HO | Pr | H | 87:39215v |
| 4-HO | Pr | Me | 103:184h |
| 4-HO | Pr | Pr | 87:39215v |
| 4-HO | iPr | H | 87:39215v |
| 4-HO | iPr | Me | 95:61908k |
| 4-HO | iPr | iPr | 103:184h |
| 4-HO | Bu | H | 87:39215v |
| 4-HO | Bu | Me | 95:61908k |
| 4-HO | Bu | Bu | 87:87:39215v |
| 4-HO | iBu | H | 95:61908k |
| 4-HO | iBu | Me | 98:61908k |
| 4-HO | iBu | iBu | 113:155f |
| 4-HO | sBu | Me | 98:61908k |

| | | | | |
|---|---|---|---|---|
| 4-HO | sBu | sBu | 113:155f | |
| 4-HO | tBu | Me | 95:61908k | |
| 4-HO | cyclopentyl | Me | 95:61908k | |
| 4-HO | — CCCC — | | 87:39215v | |
| 4-HO | — CCCCC — | | 87:39215v | |
| 4-HO | — CCOCC — | | 87:39215v | |
| 4-MeO | H | H | — many — | |
| 4-MeO | Me | H | 103:184h | |
| 4-MeO | Me | Me | — many — | 4-MeO-DMT |
| 4-MeO | ethylidene | - | 96:104449b | |
| 4-MeO | iPr | Me | 103:184h | |
| 4-EtO | H | H | 74:3458u | |
| 4-EtO | Me | Me | 74:3458u | |
| 4-iPrO | Me | Me | 80:145952y | |
| 4-BzO | H | H | 50:5631d | |
| 4-BzO | Me | H | 54:18473b | |
| 4-BzO | Me | Me | 50:5360e | |
| 4-BzO | Et | H | 54:18473b | |
| 4-BzO | Et | Et | 54:18471i | |
| 4-BzO | iPr | H | 54:18472e | |
| 4-BzO | — CCCCC — | | 54:18471i | |
| 4-F | Me | Me | 60:15815a | |
| 4-F | Et | Et | 60:15815a | |
| 4-F | — CCCCC — | | 60:15815a | |
| 4-F | — CCOCC — | | 60:15815a | |
| 4-Cl | H | H | 71:88200q | |
| 4-Cl | Me | Me | 59:11399f | |
| 4-Br | H | H | 107:4667y | |
| 4-Br | Me | Me | 54:18772f | |
| 4-NH$_2$ | H | H | 112:199014s | |
| 4-NH$_2$ | Me | H | 85:87116u | |
| 4-NH$_2$ | Me | Me | 59:11399f | |
| 4-NH$_2$ | Et | Et | 96:97144t | |
| 4-NO$_2$ | H | H | 59:11399f | |
| 4-NO$_2$ | Me | Me | 59:11399f | |
| 4-MeS | H | H | 70:69283g | |
| 4-MeS | Me | Me | 65:P15377a | |
| 4-MeS | iPr | iPr | 97:56085b | 4-MeS-DIPT |
| 4-BzS | H | H | 65:P15337a | |
| 4-BzS | Me | Me | 65:P15336h | |

| | | | |
|---|---|---|---|
| 5-Me | H | H | — many — |
| 5-Me | Me | Me | 55:8384h |
| 5-Me | iPr | Me | 113:155f |
| 5-Me | Bz | H | 94:P30565w |
| 5-NH$_2$CH$_2$- | H | H | 121:256302w |
| 5-NH$_2$CH$_2$- | Bz | H | 97:P6148d |
| 5-(Me)$_2$NCH$_2$- | H | H | 121:256302w |
| 5-Et | H | H | 79:19057b |
| 5-Et | Me | Me | 124:21939g |
| 5-CNCH$_2$- | H | H | 119:203336n |
| 5-CNCH$_2$- | Me | Me | 119:203336n |
| 5-CH$_2$=CF- | H | H | 124:316929e |
| 5-CH$_2$=CF- | Pr | Pr | 124:316929e |
| 5-Pr | H | H | 96:28265w |
| 5-iPr | H | H | 121:P134097n |
| 5-iPr | Me | Me | 121:57264k |
| 5-Bu | H | H | 96:28265w |
| 5-tBu | H | H | 121:P134097n |
| 5-Pe | H | H | 79:19057b |
| 5-cyclohexyl | H | H | 121:P134097n |
| 5-hexyl | H | H | 79:19057b |
| 5-phenyl | H | H | 106:98661w |
| 5-C$_{10}$ | H | H | 124:21939g |
| 5-MeCO | H | H | 124:21939g |
| 5-HO | H | H | — many —   serotonin |
| 5-HO | Me | H | — many —   norbufotenine |
| 5-HO | Me | Me | — many —   bufotenine |

bufoviridin is the sulfate ester

| | | | | |
|---|---|---|---|---|
| 5-HO | Me | Me | N-oxide | — many — |
| 5-HO | Et | H | | 58:2632f |
| 5-HO | Et | Et | | 58:4936d |
| 5-HO | Pr | Pr | | 76:148759u |
| 5-HO | iPr | H | | 61:16041h |
| 5-HO | iPr | iPr | | 113:155f |
| 5-HO | Bu | H | | 66:27488q |
| 5-HO | Bu | Me | | 66:27448q |
| 5-HO | Bu | Bu | | 56:6595d |
| 5-HO | sBu | H | | 61:16042a |
| 5-HO | CCCC(C)- | H | | 61:16042a |
| 5-HO | CCCCC(C) | H | | 61:16042a |
| 5-HO | CCCC(CC) | H | | 61:16042a |
| 5-HO | CCCCCC(C) | H | | 61:16042a |

| | | | | |
|---|---|---|---|---|
| 5-HO | CCCCCCC- | Me | 66:27488q | |
| 5-HO | CCCCCC(CC)- | H | 61:16042a | |
| 5-HO | CCCCCCCCC- | H | 104:28942y | |
| 5-HO | CCCCC(CCC)- | H | 61:16042a | |
| 5-HO | — CCCC — | | 122:23213y | |
| 5-HO | — CCCCC — | | 58:13895e | |
| 5-HO | — C(C)CCC(C) — | | 112:198126t | |
| 5-HO | — C(C)CCCC(C) — | | 122:23213y | |
| 5-HO | — CCOCC — | | 58:13895e | |
| 5-HO | NO$_2$ | H | 61:16042b | |
| 5-MeO | H | H | — many — | 5-MeO-T |
| 5-MeO | Me | H | — many — | 5-MeO-NMT |
| 5-MeO | Me | Me | — many — | 5-MeO-DMT |
| 5-MeO | Me | Me | N-oxide — many — | |
| 5-MeO | Et | H | 56:3438f | 5-MeO-NET |
| 5-MeO | Et | Me | 68:103533j | |
| 5-MeO | Et | Et | 61:16038e | 5-MeO-DET |
| 5-MeO | COCC- | H | 85:142945r | |
| 5-MeO | Pr | Pr | 63:8295f | 5-MeO-DPT |
| 5-MeO | iPr | H | 63:8295f | 5-MeO-NIPT |
| 5-MeO | iPr | Me | 103:184h | 5-MeO-MIPT |
| 5-MeO | iPr | iPr | 62:7716d | 5-MeO-DIPT |
| 5-MeO | cyclopropyl | H | 83:707x | |
| 5-MeO | Bu | H | 63:8295f | 5-MeO-NBT |
| 5-MeO | Bu | Bu | 63:8295f | 5-MeO-DBT |
| 5-MeO | cyclohexyl | H | 86:151135x | |
| 5-MeO | Bz | H | 73:P45340j | |
| 5-MeO | Bz | cyclopropyl | 83:707x | |
| 5-MeO | Bz | Bz | 80:P120759c | |
| 5-MeO | benzylidene | - | 77:48135q | |
| 5-MeO | — CCCC — | | 67:107054f | |
| 5-MeO | — CCCCC — | | 121:207078k | |
| 5-MeO | — CCOCC — | | 58:13895d | |
| 5-MeO | HO | H | 113:24306g | |
| 5-EtO | H | H | — many — | |
| 5-EtO | Me | H | 91:P5216p | |
| 5-COCCO | H | H | 86:42660w | |
| 5-CCOCCO | H | H | 85:142945r | |
| 5-NCCO | H | H | 86:42660w | |
| 5-NCCS | H | H | 118:233816r | |
| 5-PrO | H | H | — many — | |
| 5-C$_2$NCCCO | H | H | 74:50313c | |

| | | | |
|---|---|---|---|
| 5-allyl-O | H | H | 101:146879u |
| 5-propynyl-O | H | H | 101:146879u |
| 5-iPrO | H | H | 62:15243c |
| 5-CCOCCCO- | H | H | 101:146879u |
| 5-BuO | H | H | — many — |
| 5-PeO | H | H | 124:21939g |
| 5-HeO | Et | H | 64:P11180g |
| 5-cyclohexyl | H | H | 122:P31501f |
| 5-BzO | H | H | — many — |
| 5-BzO | Me | H | 50:5630h |
| 5-BzO | Me | Me | 49:15852i |
| 5-BzO | Et | H | 50:5630h |
| 5-BzO | Et | Me | 64:19541h |
| 5-BzO | Et | Et | 50:5630h |
| 5-BzO | iPr | H | 51:P15588h |
| 5-BzO | iPr | iPr | 53:20560a |
| 5-BzO | Bu | Bu | 50:P16870a |
| 5-BzO | 3-pentyl | H | 51:P15588i |
| 5-BzO | Bz | H | 52:P3866f |
| 5-BzO | Bz | Bz | 49:15852h |
| 5-BzO | 4-heptyl | H | 51:P155881 |
| 5-BzO | 2-methyloctyl | H | 66:27488q |
| 5-BzO | — CCCC — | | 58:13895e |
| 5-BzO | — CCCCC — | | 50:5630i |
| 5-BzO | — CCOCC — | | 58:13895e |
| 5-$C_6$O | H | H | 123:P56363w |
| 5-$C_7$O | H | H | 124:21939g |
| 5-$C_8$O | H | H | 123:P56363w |
| 5-CCCCOCCCCO- | H | H | 123:P56363w |
| 5-CCOCCCCCCO- | H | H | 123:P56363w |
| 5-$C_9$O | H | H | 121:170371f |
| 5-$C_9$O | Me | Me | 124:21939g |
| 5-$C_9$O- | Bu | H | 124:21939g |
| 5-$(C)_2C_6$O- | H | H | 124:21939g |
| 5-$(C)_2C_6$O- | Bu | H | 124:21939g |
| 5-$(C)_2C_6$O- | Me | Me | 124:21939g |
| 5-$(C)_2C_7$O- | H | H | 123:P56363w |
| 5-$(C)_3C_6$O- | H | H | 124:21939g |
| 5-$(C)_3C_7$O- | H | H | 124:21939g |
| 5-$(C)_3C_8$O- | H | H | 124:21939g |
| cyclohexylCCCCO- | H | H | 124:21939g |
| 5-$(C)_3C_8$O- | H | H | 123:P56363w |

| | | | | |
|---|---|---|---|---|
| 5-C$_{10}$O | H | H | | 124:21939g |
| 5-C$_{11}$O | H | H | | 124:21939g |
| 5-MeCOO- | Me | Me | | 124:21939g |
| 5-EtCOO- | Me | Me | | 124:21939g |
| 5-iPrCOO- | Me | Me | | 124:21939g |
| 5-tBuCOO- | Me | Me | | 124:21939g |
| 5-C$_3$F$_7$COO- | Me | Me | | 71:629c |
| 5-C$_8$H$_{17}$COO- | Me | Me | | 124:21939g |
| 5-F | H | H | | — many — |
| 5-F | Me | H | | 97:85103m |
| 5-F | Me | Me | | 56:12835b |
| 5-F | Et | Et | | 56:12835b |
| 5-Cl | H | H | | — many — |
| 5-Cl | Me | Me | | 70:114926g |
| 5-Cl | Me | Me | | 55:8384h |
| 5-Cl | Et | H | | 95: P150981w |
| 5-Cl | Et | Et | | 77:P101381v |
| 5-Cl | Bz | H | | 99:P139925t |
| 5-Cl | Bz | Me | | 123:P313758s |
| 5-Br | H | H | | — many — |
| 5-Br | Me | H | | 68:49392x |
| 5-Br | Me | Me | | 68:49392x |
| 5-Br | MeCH= | - | N-oxide | 114:62452e |
| 5-Br | Et | Et | | 68:49392x |
| 5-Br | Pr | H | | 119:63691x |
| 5-Br | Pr | Pr | | 68:49392x |
| 5-Br | Me$_2$C= | - | N-oxide | 114:62452e |
| 5-Br | Bz | H | | 96:P35713u |
| 5-Br | Bz | Me | | 123:P169499p |
| 5-Br | — CCCC — | | | 68:49392x |
| 5-Br | HO | H | | 111:214791t |
| 5-I | H | H | | — many — |
| 5-I | Me | Me | | 70:114926g |
| 5-NH$_2$ | H | H | | — many — |
| 5-NH$_2$ | Me | Me | | 48:4513b |
| 5-NH$_2$ | — CCCCC — | | | 47:10734a |
| 5-NMe$_2$ | H | H | | 64:9670b |
| 5-NMe$_2$ | Me | Me | | 64:9670b |
| 5-NO$_2$ | H | H | | 82:139888g |
| 5-NO$_2$ | Me | Me | | 48:4512g |
| 5-NO$_2$ | Pr | Pr | | 64:8123d |
| 5-MeS | H | H | | 53:21873h |

| | | | |
|---|---|---|---|
| 5-MeS | Me | H | 64:9670a |
| 5-MeS | Me | Me | 64:9670a |
| 5-NH$_2$CCS- | H | H | 86:42660w |
| 5-BzS | H | H | 62:7716h |
| 5-BzS | Me | H | 64:9670a |
| 5-BzS | Me | Me | 64:9670a |

---

| | | | |
|---|---|---|---|
| 6-Me | H | H | — many — |
| 6-Me | Me | Me | 93:197541b |
| 6-Me | Et | Et | 68:68815d |
| 6-Me | HO | iBu | 63:P2959f |
| 6-Et | H | H | 64:5032f |
| 6-CF$_3$ | H | H | 68:68815d |
| 6-CF$_3$ | Me | Me | 68:68815d |
| 6-HO | H | H | — many — |
| 6-HO | Me | H | 90:201093q |
| 6-HO | Me | Me | — many — |
| 6-HO | Et | Et | 68:33151g |
| 6-MeO | H | H | — many — |
| 6-MeO | Me | H | 63:8295f |
| 6-MeO | Me | Me | 52:4668b |
| 6-MeO | Et | H | 63:8295f |
| 6-MeO | Et | Et | 63:8295f |
| 6-MeO | Me$_2$C= | - | 61:16415d |
| 6-MeO | Pr | Pr | 63:8295f |
| 6-MeO | iPr | Me | 103:184h |
| 6-MeO | iPr | iPr | 63:8295f' |
| 6-MeO | Bu | Bu | 63:8295f |
| 6-MeO | Bz | H | 52:5477f |
| 6-MeO | — CCCC — | | 67:107054f |
| 6-EtO | H | H | 53:21873i |
| 6-EtO | Et | H | 56:3438h |
| 6-iPrO | H | H | 55:P24808d |
| 6-BuO | H | H | 55:P24808a |
| 6-BzO | H | H | 50:1760e |
| 6-BzO | Me | Me | 50:5630e |
| 6-BzO | Et | Et | 64:17522d |
| 6-F | H | H | 55:P11436h |
| 6-F | Me | Me | 57:8531g |
| 6-F | Et | Et | 57:8531h |

| | | | |
|---|---|---|---|
| 6-F | — CCCCC — | | 57:8531h |
| 6-F | — CCOCC — | | 57:8531h |
| 6-Cl | H | H | — many — |
| 6-Cl | Me | Me | 55:8385e |
| 6-Br | H | H | 102:221046w |
| 6-I | H | H | 113:55090m |
| 6-NH$_2$ | H | H | 59:1392e |
| 6-NH$_2$ | Me | Me | 59:11399f |
| 6-NMe$_2$ | H | H | 55:P12430i |
| 6-NO$_2$ | H | H | 59:11399f |
| 6-NO$_2$ | Me | Me | 59:11399g |
| 6-SMe | H | H | 55:2364c |
| 6-SMe | Me | Me | 97:155950m |

---

| | | | |
|---|---|---|---|
| 7-Me | H | H | — many — |
| 7-Me | Me | H | 45:7576i |
| 7-Me | Me | Me | — many — |
| 7-Me | Et | H | 85:40641w |
| 7-Et | Me | Me | 93:197541b |
| 7-Pr | H | H | 62:P1700g |
| 7-HO | H | H | — many — |
| 7-HO | Me | Me | 67:1848c |
| 7-HO | Et | H | 96:97144t |
| 7-HO | Et | Et | 67:108512r |
| 7-MeO | H | H | — many — |
| 7-MeO | Me | H | 96:97144t |
| 7-MeO | Me | Me | 61:14623d |
| 7-MeO | Et | H | 85:87116u |
| 7-MeO | Et | Et | 63:8294f |
| 7-MeO | iPr | Me | 103:184h |
| 7-MeO | cyclopropyl | H | 83:707x |
| 7-MeO | Bz | Me | 80:15097n |
| 7-MeO | Bz | cyclopropyl | 83:707x |
| 7-MeO | — CCCC — | | 67:107054f |
| 7-BuO | H | H | 55:P24808a |
| 7-BzO | H | H | 49:12438e |
| 7-BzO | Me | Me | 54:18471h |
| 7-F | H | H | 122:P31501f |
| 7-Cl | H | H | — many — |
| 7-Br | H | H | 78:124389p |

| 7-Br | Me | Me | 93:197541b |
| 7-NH$_2$ | H | H | 62:7717a |
| 7-NO$_2$ | H | H | 97:92714q |
| 7-NO$_2$ | Me | Me | 90:187197t |
| 7-MeS | H | H | 53:21873h |

## 3- CARBON CHAIN

α-METHYL

| 1-Me | H | H | — many — | 1,α-DMT |
| 1-Pr | H | H | 113:224121e | |
| 1-iPr | H | H | 79:19057b | |
| 1-Pe | H | H | 113:224121e | |
| 1-cyclopentyl | H | H | 123:9837u | |
| 1-Bz | H | H | 60:7976b | |
| 1-octyl | H | H | 113:224121e | |
| 1-MeO | H | H | 90:71992u | |
| 2-Me | H | H | 55:5459f | |
| 4-Me | H | H | 66:74683j | MP-809 |
| 4-Me | Me | H | 64:5032f | |
| 4-HO | H | H | 66:p18670r | |
| 4-HO | Me | Me | 61:P4319o | |
| 4-MeO | H | H | 109:22749x | |
| 4-BzO | H | H | 54:18472d | |
| 4-BzO | Me | Me | 61:P4319c | |
| 4-BzO | Et | H | 61:P4319e | |
| 4-F | H | H | 71:49693h | |
| 4-Cl | H | H | 57:P16564g | |
| 4-Br | H | H | 57:P16564g | |
| 4-MeS | H | H | 66:P94909r | |
| 4-BzS | H | H | 66:P94909r | |
| 5-Me | H | H | 72:130696d | |
| 5-Et | H | H | 53:7138h | |
| 5-iPr | H | H | 68:11415u | |
| 5-HO | H | H | — many — | α-Me-serotonin |
| 5-MeO | H | H | — many — | α,O-DMS |
| 5-MeO | Me | H | 64:5032f | |
| 5-EtO | H | H | 60:15816c | |
| 5-BzO | H | H | 53:7138h | |
| 5-C$_9$O | H | H | 124:21939g | |
| 5-F | H | H | — many — | |
| 5-Cl | H | H | — many — | |

| | | | |
|---|---|---|---|
| 5-Cl | Me | H | 64:5032f |
| 5-Br | H | H | 60:7976b |
| 5-Me$_2$N | H | H | 64:9670b |
| 5-MeS | H | H | 64:9669h |
| 5-MeS | Me | H | 64:9670a |
| 5-MeS | Me | Me | 64:9670a |
| 5-BzS | H | H | 64:9669h |
| 5-BzS | Me | H | 64:9670a |
| 6-Me | H | H | 66:74683j |
| 6-Me | Me | H | 64:5032f |
| 6-CF$_3$ | H | H | 95:110796h |
| 6-HO | H | H | 72:130696d |
| 6-MeO | H | H | 56:P458d |
| 6-MeO | Me | H | 64:5032f |
| 6-MeO | HO | H | 64:5032g |
| 6-BzO | H | H | 64:5032f |
| 6-F | H | H | — many — |
| 6-Cl | H | H | — many — |
| 6-Cl | Me | H | 64:5032f |
| 7-Me | H | H | 66:74683j |
| 7-Pr | H | H | 113:224121e |
| 7-Pe | H | H | 113:224121e |
| 7-CF$_3$ | H | H | 58:12497h |
| 7-HO | H | H | 72:130696d |
| 7-MeO | H | H | 62:P7731c |
| 7-Cl | H | H | — many — |

### β-METHYL

| | | | |
|---|---|---|---|
| 1-Me | H | H | 118:P59581y |
| 1-Bz | H | H | 57:9788h |
| 2-Me | — CCCC — | | 52:P10202h |
| 2-Me | — CCCCC — | | 52:P10202i |
| 4-BzO | H | H | 54:18473b |
| 4-BzO | Me | Me | 62:P16201a |
| 4-NO$_2$ | H | H | 64:8122e |
| 5-HO | H | H | 95:35348h |
| 5-MeO | H | H | 57:8532g |
| 5-F | H | H | 57:15058b |
| 5-Cl | H | H | 57:15058b |
| 5-Br | H | H | 57:15058b |
| 5-Br | — CCCC — | | 69:P27242s |
| 5-MeS | H | H | 64:9669h |

| | | | | |
|---|---|---|---|---|
| 5-MeS | Me | H | 64:9670a | |
| 5-BzS | H | H | 64:9669h | |
| 6-MeO | H | H | 53:12325b | |

## 4- CARBON CHAIN

### α,α-DIMETHYL

| | | | | |
|---|---|---|---|---|
| 1-Me | H | H | 92:121569a | |
| 2-Me | H | H | 98:P125870p | |
| 5-HO | H | H | 56:6595d | α,α-DMS |
| 5-MeO | H | H | 64:5032f | |
| 5-MeO | Me | Me | 94P:156744x | |
| 5-F | H | H | 110:23668c | |
| 5-Cl | H | H | 62:H1763d | |
| 5-Br | H | H | 62:11763d | |
| 5-MeS | Me | H | 64:9679a | |
| 6-MeO | H | H | 100:P209642p | |
| 6-F | H | H | 123:P285773x | |
| 6-Cl | H | H | 66:74683j | |
| 6-Cl | Me | H | 64:5032f | |
| 7-MeO | H | H | 98:P125870p | |

### β,β-DIMETHYL

| | | | |
|---|---|---|---|
| 1-Me | H | H | 58:P3398d,f |
| 1-Me | Me | H | 114:121936r |
| 1-Bz | H | H | 57:9788h |
| 6-MeO | H | H | 57:9788i |

### α,β-DIMETHYL

| | | | |
|---|---|---|---|
| H | H | H | 66:74683j |
| 5-MeO | H | H | 59:2754a |
| 5-MeS | H | H | 64:9669h |
| 5-BzS | H | H | 64:9669h |

### α-ETHYL

| | | | |
|---|---|---|---|
| 1-Me | H | H | 61:633a |
| 1-BzO | H | H | 65:16929g |
| 2-Me | H | H | 61:633a |
| 4-Me | H | H | 72:130696d |
| 4-HO | H | H | 66:P18670r |
| 4-BzO | H | H | 62:P16197g |
| 4-Cl | H | H | 57:P16564 |
| 4-Br | H | H | 57:P16564g |

| 4-NH$_2$ | H | H | 74:40779v |
|---|---|---|---|
| 5-HO | H | H | 56:6595d |
| 5-MeO | H | H | 58:P9029b |
| 5-Cl | H | H | 59:2752f |
| 6-HO | H | H | 74:40779v |
| 6-MeO | H | H | 74:40779v |
| 6-BzO | H | H | 61:633a |
| 6-F | H | H | 74:40779v |
| 6-Cl | H | H | 59:2752f |
| 6-NH$_2$ | H | H | 63:633a |
| 7-Me | H | H | 61:633a |
| 7-Cl | H | H | 59:2752f |

### β-ETHYL

| 1-Me | H | H | 118:59581y |
|---|---|---|---|
| 5-MeO | H | H | 58:P7910f |
| 5-Cl | H | H | 57:P7332e |
| 6-MeO | H | H | 57:P15076e |

## 5-CARBON CHAIN

### α-PROPYL

| 1-Bz | H | H | 65:P691d |
|---|---|---|---|

### α-ISOPROPYL

| 1-Me | H | H | 60:14500f |
|---|---|---|---|
| 4-Me | H | H | 66:74683j |
| 5-MeO | H | H | 54:9881e |
| 6-Me | H | H | 66:74683j |
| 6-MeO | H | H | 66:74683j |
| 6-Cl | H | H | 66:74683j |
| 7-Me | H | H | 66:74683j |

### β-ISOPROPYL

| 1-Me | H | H | 118:P59581y |
|---|---|---|---|
| 1-Bz | H | H | 57:97 |

### α-METHYL-α-ETHYL

| 1-Me | H | H | 81:P3767p |
|---|---|---|---|
| 5-HO | H | H | 57:P7235b |
| 5-MeO | H | H | 81:P3767p |
| 5-F | H | H | 81:P3767p |

α-ETHYL-β-METHYL
| | | | |
|---|---|---|---|
| 5-MeO | Et | H | 65:P691d |

## 6-CARBON CHAIN

α-BUTYL
| | | | |
|---|---|---|---|
| 5-HO | H | H | 57:P7235b |

α-s-BUTYL
| | | | |
|---|---|---|---|
| 6-Me | H | H | 76:113384r |

α-t-BUTYL
| | | | |
|---|---|---|---|
| 5-MeO | H | H | 54:9881g |

α,α-DIETHYL
| | | | |
|---|---|---|---|
| 5-HO | H | H | 57:P7235b |

β-BUTYL
| | | | |
|---|---|---|---|
| 1-Me | H | H | 118:P59581y |

β,β-DIETHYL
| | | | |
|---|---|---|---|
| 1-Me | H | H | 118:P59581y |
| 1-Bz | H | H | 57:9788h |

## 8-CARBON CHAIN

α,α-DIPROPYL
| | | | |
|---|---|---|---|
| 5-HO | H | H | 57:P7235b |

α,α-DIALLYL
| | | | |
|---|---|---|---|
| 1-Me | H | H | 118:P59581y |

## 10- CARBON CHAIN

α,α-DIBUTYL
| | | | |
|---|---|---|---|
| 5-HO | H | H | 57:P7235b |

## DISUBSTITUTED TRYPTAMINES:

| RING | | N | N | CA CITATION |
|------|------|------|------|-------------|

**2-CARBON CHAIN**

1,2 ————————————————————————

| 1-Me | 2-Me | H | H | 91:58663e |
|------|------|------|------|-------------|
| 1-Me | 2-Me | — CCCCC — | | 52:P10202h |
| 1-Me | 2-Et | Me | Me | 69:86857u |
| 1-Me | 2-C=C | H | H | 117:7726j |
| 1-Me | 2-propynyl | propynyl | Me | 83:178702g |
| 1-Me | 2-propynyl | propynyl | Et | 86:P106380q |
| 1-Me | 2-propynyl | Bz | propynyl | 83:178702g |
| 1-Me | 2-EtO | H | H | 123:285838x |
| 1-Me | 2-MeCOO | H | H | 94:3948e |
| 1-Me | 2-NH$_2$ | H | H | 93:114247m |
| 1-Et | 2-Me | H | H | 68:104883k |
| 1-allyl | 2-Br | Et | Et | 80:P82649g |
| 1-cyclopentyl | 2-Me | H | H | 124:P233030d |
| 1-Bz | 2-Me | H | H | 69:27788z |
| 1-Bz | 2-Me | Me | H | 76:14237p |
| 1-Bz | 2-Me | Me | Me | 72:P31606t |
| 1-Bz | 2-Me | Et | Et | 66:115533f |
| 1-Bz | C=C | H | H | 117:7726j |
| 1-Bz | 2-allyl | Me | propynyl | 83:178702g |
| 1-Bz | 2-propynyl | Et | propynyl | 86:P106380q |
| 1-Bz | 2-EtO | H | H | 123:285838x |

1,4 ————————————————————————

| 1-Me | 4-HO | Me | Me | 61:P5613g phosphate, CMY |
|------|------|------|------|-------------|
| 1-Me | 4-HO | Et | Et | 61:P5613h |
| 1-Me | 4-MeO | Me | Me | 65:8860g |
| 1-Me | 4-BzO | Me | Me | 61:P4319d |
| 1-Me | 4-BzO | Et | Et | 63:P2959a |
| 1-Me | 4-BzO | — CCCCC — | | 61:P5613g |
| 1-Et | 4-HO | Me | Me | 61:P4319e |
| 1-Et | 4-BzO | Me | Me | 61:P4319d |
| 1-allyl | 4-HO | Me | Me | 62:9402a |
| 1-allyl | 4-I | Me | Me | 122:31265g |
| 1-iPr | 4-HO | Me | Me | 72:130696d |
| 1-butyl | 4-BzO | H | H | 61:P4319e |

| | | | | |
|---|---|---|---|---|
| 1-Bz | 4-HO | Me | Me | 61:P4319d |
| 1-Bz | 4-MeO | Me | Me | 80:145952y |
| 1-Bz | 4-BzO | Me | Me | 54:18472b |
| 1-Bz | 4-I | Et | Et | 115:8498g |
| 1-MeCO | 4-BzO | Me | Me | 54:18472b |

1,5 —————————————————————

| | | | | |
|---|---|---|---|---|
| 1-Me | 5-Me | H | H | 101:P171091p |
| 1-Me | 5-t-Bu | H | H | 124:P343124v |
| 1-Me | 5-HO | H | H | — many — |
| 1-Me | 5-MeO | H | H | 50:5624b |
| 1-Me | 5-MeO | Me | H | 78:15961y |
| 1-Me | 5-MeO | Me | Me | 50:5623i |
| 1-Me | 5-BzO | H | H | 63:4822a |
| 1-Me | 5-BzO | Me | Me | 53:11342d |
| 1-Me | 5-Br | H | H | 101:P171091p |
| 1-Me | 5-NO$_2$ | H | H | 51:15516i |
| 1-Et | 5-HO | H | H | 67:1848c |
| 1-Et | 5-BzO | H | H | 67:1848c |
| 1-iPr | 5-Me | H | H | 119:152256b |
| 1-iPr | 5-Me | Me | H | 115:130758g |
| 1-iPr | 5-HO | Pr | Pr | 119:152256b |
| 1-iPr | 5-MeO | H | H | 119:217618t |
| 1-iPr | 5-Br | H | H | 119:63691x |
| 1-propynyl | 5-MeO | H | H | 64:2041f |
| 1-Bu | 5-HO | H | H | 67:1848c |
| 1-Bu | 5-BzO | H | H | 67:1848c |
| 1-cyclopentyl | 5-Me | H | H | 123:9837u |
| 1-Bz | 5-HO | H | H | 67:1848c |
| 1-Bz | 5-MeO | H | H | 50:5624b |
| 1-Bz | 5-MeO | Me | Me | 50:5624c |
| 1-Bz | 5-MeO | Et | Et | 54:21487c |
| 1-Bz | 5-MeO | — CCCCC — | | 57:9786h |
| 1-Bz | 5-BzO | Me | Me | 56:440i |
| 1-Bz | 5-MeS | H | H | 59:P578a |
| 1-Bz | 5-MeS | allyl | H | 56:P15468h |
| 1-MeCO | 5-MeO | H | H | 56:4711a |
| 1-MeCO | 5-MeO | Me | Me | 78:3422k |
| 1-MeCO | 5-BzO | H | H | 57:11655a |
| 1-CF$_3$CO | 5-Me | Me | Me | 88:117167t |
| 1-PrCO | 5-MeO | Me | Me | 89:99491h |

## 1,6 ——————————————————————

| | | | | |
|------|-------|----|----|-------------|
| 1-Me | 6-HO  | H  | H  | 83:79445u   |
| 1-Me | 6-MeO | H  | H  | — many —    |
| 1-Me | 6-MeO | Me | Me | 64:11697f   |
| 1-Me | 6-BzO | H  | H  | 86:189638d  |

## 1,7 ——————————————————————

| | | | | |
|------|------|---|---|----------|
| 1-Me | 7-Me | H | H | 45:7577a |

## 2,4 ——————————————————————

| | | | | |
|------|-------|---|---|-----------|
| 2-Me | 4-MeO | H | H | 68P29592j |

## 2,5 ——————————————————————

| | | | | |
|------|-------|-------------|-------------|-------------|
| 2-Me | 5-Me  | H           | H           | 62:10398e   |
| 2-Me | 5-Me  | Me          | H           | 62;10398e   |
| 2-Me | 5-Me  | Me          | Me          | 62:10398e   |
| 2-Me | 5-Me  | — CCCC —    |             | 62:10398e   |
| 2-Me | 5-HO  | H           | H           | — many —    |
| 2-Me | 5-HO  | Me          | Me          | 60:489e     |
| 2-Me | 5-HO  | Et          | Et          | 60:489g     |
| 2-Me | 5-HO  | — CCCCC —   |             | 60:489g     |
| 2-Me | 5-HO  | — CCOCC —   |             | 60:489g     |
| 2-Me | 5-MeO | H           | H           | 50:5624b    |
| 2-Me | 5-MeO | Me          | Me          | 50:5624c    |
| 2-Me | 5-MeO | Pr          | Pr          | 93:107063v  |
| 2-Me | 5-MeO | iPr         | iPr         | 87:P102164v |
| 2-Me | 5-MeO | Bu          | Bu          | 67:1850x    |
| 2-Me | 5-MeO | Bz          | Bz          | 50:5624b    |
| 2-Me | 5-BzO | H           | H           | 50:5624c    |
| 2-Me | 5-BzO | Me          | Me          | 60:489f     |
| 2-Me | 5-BzO | Et          | Et          | 60:489f     |
| 2-Me | 5-BzO | iPr         | H           | 51:P15588i  |
| 2-Me | 5-BzO | Bz          | Bz          | 50:P16870b  |
| 2-Me | 5-BzO | — CCCCC —   |             | 60:489f     |
| 2-Me | 5-BzO | — CCOCC —   |             | 60:489f     |
| 2-Me | 5-F   | H           | H           | 62:10398f   |
| 2-Me | 5-F   | Me          | H           | 62:10398e   |
| 2-Me | 5-F   | Me          | Me          | 62:10398e   |
| 2-Me | 5-F   | — CCCC —    |             | 62:10398e   |

| | | | | |
|---|---|---|---|---|
| 2-Me | 5-Cl | H | H | 62:10398e,f |
| 2-Me | 5-Cl | Me | H | 62:10398e,f |
| 2-Me | 5-Cl | Me | Me | 62:10398e,f |
| 2-Me | 5-Br | H | H | 62:10398e,f |
| 2-Me | 5-Br | Me | H | 62:10398e,f |
| 2-Me | 5-Br | Me | Me | 62:10398e,f |
| 2-Me | 5-Br | — CCCC — | | 62:10398e,f |
| 2-Me | 5-NO$_2$ | H | H | 48:4512h |
| 2-Me | 5-NH$_2$ | H | H | 48:4513b |
| 2-Me | 5-NH$_2$ | Bz | Bz | 47:10734a |
| 2-Me | 5-Me$_2$N | Me | Me | 48:9544e |
| 2-Et | 5-MeO | H | H | 124:P175864r |
| 2-iPr | 5-MeO | H | H | 120:77615h |
| 2-cyclohexyl | 5-MeO | H | H | 120:77615h |
| 2-BzO | 5-MeO | H | H | 112:35618r |
| 2-Br | 5-MeO | H | H | 120:77615h |
| 2-I | 5-MeO | H | H | 103:215112u |
| 2-HS | 5-HO | H | H | 86:16928v |

2,6 ——————————————————————————

| | | | | |
|---|---|---|---|---|
| 2-Me | 6-MeO | H | H | 63:13711d |

2,7 ——————————————————————————

| | | | | |
|---|---|---|---|---|
| 2-Me | 7-Me | H | H | 68:P29592j |
| 2-Me | 7-MeO | H | H | 69:27788z |

4,5 ——————————————————————————

| | | | | | |
|---|---|---|---|---|---|
| 4-Me | 5-Me | H | H | 94:139775r | |
| 4-Me | 5-HO | H | H | 103:98325c | |
| 4-Me | 5-PrO | H | H | 118:P254747j | |
| 4-Me | 5-PrO | Me | Me | 118:P254747j | |
| 4-HO | 5-MeO | Me | Me | 63:8297f | |
| 4-HO | 5-EtO | H | H | 113: 103208e | |
| 4-BzO | 5-MeO | H | H | 63:8297h | |
| 4-BzO | 5-MeO | Me | Me | 63:8297h | |
| 4-BzO | 5-MeO | Et | Et | 63:8297h | |
| — OCO — | | Me | Me | 97:56085b | 4,5-MDO-DMT |
| — OCO — | | iPr | iPr | 97:56085b | 4,5-MDO-DIPT |

| | | | | |
|---|---|---|---|---|
| 4-F | 5-Me | H | H | 121:P134097n |
| 4-Cl | 5-HO | H | H | 100:221284n |
| 4-Cl | 5-HO | Me | Me | 118:P254747j |
| 4-Cl | 5-MeO | H | H | 118:P254747j |
| 4-Cl | 5-MeO | Me | H | 118:P254747j |
| 4-Cl | 5-MeO | Me | Me | 118:P254747j |
| 4-Cl | 5-MeO | Pr | H | 118:P254747j |
| 4-Cl | 5-PrO | H | H | 118:P254747j |
| 4-Cl | 5-PrO | Me | H | 118:P254747j |
| 4-Cl | 5-PrO | Me | Me | 118:P254747j |
| 4-Cl | 5-PrO | Et | Me | 118:P254747j |
| 4-Cl | 5-iPrO | H | H | 118:P254747j |
| 4-Cl | 5-iPrO | Me | Me | 118:P254747j |
| 4-Cl | 5-BuO | Me | Me | 118:P254747j |
| 4-Cl | 5-c-propylmethoxy | Me | Me | 118:P254747j |
| 4-Cl | 5-t-Bu-methoxy | Me | Me | 118:P254747j |
| 4-Cl | 5-BzO | H | H | 118:P254747j |
| 4-Cl | 5-BzO | Me | Me | 118:P254747j |
| 4-Cl | 5-F | H | H | 113:55090m |
| 4-Cl | 5-Cl | H | H | 102:490w |
| 4-Cl | 5-Br | H | H | 113:55090m |
| 4-Br | 5-MeO | Me | Me | 118:P254747j |
| 4-Br | 5-PrO | H | H | 118:P254747j |
| 4-Br | 5-PrO | Me | Me | 118:P254747j |
| 4-I | 5-PrO | Me | Me | 118:P254747j |
| 4-$NH_2$ | 5-MeO | H | H | 109:37706e |
| 4-$NO_2$ | 5-MeO | H | H | 106:172034n |

4,6————————————————————————

| | | | | |
|---|---|---|---|---|
| 4-Me | 6-Me | H | H | 94:P139775r |
| 4-MeO | 6-MeO | H | H | 111:126747m |
| 4-HO | 6-MeO | Me | Me | 63:15381d |
| 4-MeO | 6-MeO | Me | Me | 63:15381d |
| 4-BzO | 6-MeO | H | H | 117:P191684t |
| 4-Cl | 6-MeO | H | H | 113:55090m |
| 4-Cl | 6-Cl | H | H | 61:P14738h |

4,7————————————————————————

| | | | | |
|---|---|---|---|---|
| 4-Me | 7-Me | H | H | 102:95490w |
| 4-MeO | 7-MeO | H | H | 56:11542b,c |

| 4-MeO | 7-MeO | Bz | Bz | 56:11542b | |
| 4-BzO | 7-BzO | H | H | 120:163883a | |
| 4-F | 7-Me | H | H | 55:7415c | |
| 4-Cl | 7-MeO | H | H | 55:P14481a | |
| 4-Cl | 7-Cl | H | H | 54:P24800i | |
| 4-Cl | 7-MeO | H | H | 52:18479e | |
| 4-Br | 7-MeO | Me | Me | 96:142621j | |
| 4-NO$_2$ | 7-Me | H | H | 102:95490 | |
| 4-NO$_2$ | 7-MeO | H | H | 102:95491x | |

5,6————————————————————————————————

| 5-Me | 6-Me | H | H | 94:P139775r | |
| 5-HO | 6-F | H | H | 86:139739s | |
| 5-HO | 6-Me | H | H | 103:135762r | |
| 5-HO | 6-MeO | H | H | — many — | |
| 5-MeO | 6-Me | Me | Me | 93:197541 | |
| 5-MeO | 6-HO | H | H | 85:72575u | |
| 5-MeO | 6-HO | Me | Me | 73:75482s | |
| 5-MeO | 6-MeO | H | H | — many — | |
| 5-MeO | 6-MeO | Me | Me | 50:4901c | 5,6-MeO-DMT |
| 5-MeO | 6-MeO | Et | Et | 65:3871c | 5,6-MeO-DET |
| 5-MeO | 6-MeO | iPr | Me | 113:155f | 5,6-MeO-DIPT |
| 5-MeO | 6-MeO | cyclopropyl | H | 94:15482y | |
| 5-MeO | 6-MeO | Bu | Bu | 65:3871c | 5,6-MeO-DBT |
| 5-MeO | 6-MeO | Bz | cyclopropyl | 94:15482y | |
| 5-MeO | 6-MeO | Bz | Bz | 52:P3866h | |
| 5-MeO | 6-MeO | — CCCC — | | 65:3871c | 5,6-MeO-pyr-T |
| 5-MeO | 6-MeO | — CCCCC — | | 65:3871c | 5,6-MeO-pip-T |
| 5-MeO | 6-MeO | — CCOCC — | | 65:3871c | 5,6-MeO-mor-T |
| 5-MeO | 6-BzO | H | H | 63:16904f | |
| 5-MeO | 6-BzO | Me | H | 63:8297f | |
| 5-MeO | 6-BzO | Me | Me | 63:8297e | |
| 5-MeO | 6-BzO | Et | Et | 63:8297f | |
| 5-MeO | 6-F | H | H | 90:48848t | |
| 5-MeO | 6-Cl | H | H | 64:P15890g | |
| 5-MeO | 6-Br | H | H | 112:198874k | |
| 5-MeO | 6-Br | OH | H | 113:97885e | |
| — OCO — | | H | H | 96:135318n | |
| — OCO — | | Me | Me | 100:6370a | 5,6-MDO-DMT |
| — OCO — | | iPr | Me | 100:6370a | 5,6-MDO-MIPT |
| — OCO — | | iPr | iPr | 100:6370a | 5,6-MDO-DIPT |

| | | | | | |
|---|---|---|---|---|---|
| — OCO — | | cyclopropyl | H | 100:6370a | |
| — OCO — | | cyclopropyl | Me | 100:6370a | |
| — OCO — | | cyclopropylmethyl | Me | 100:6370a | |
| — OCO — | | cyclobutyl | Me | 100:6370a | |
| — OCO — | | cyclopentyl | Me | 100:6370a | |
| — OCO — | | Bz | Me | 100:6370a | |
| — OCO — | | Bz | cyclopropyl | 100:6370a | |
| — OCO — | | — CCCC — | | 100:6370a | 5,6-MDO-pyr-T |
| — OCO — | | — CCCCC — | | 100:6370a | 5,6-MDO-pip-T |
| — OCO — | | — CCOCC — | | 100:6370a | 5,6-MDO-mor-T |
| 5-BzO | 6-MeO | H | H | 64:5032h | |
| 5-BzO | 6-BzO | H | H | 58:13889f | |
| 5-Cl | 6-MeO | H | H | 52:18479e | |
| 5-Cl | 6-Cl | H | H | 102:95490w | |
| 5-Br | 6-Br | H | H | 78:121636f | |
| 5-Br | 6-Br | Me | H | 78:121636f | |
| 5-Br | 6-Br | Me | Me | 92:177683a | |

5,7————————————————————

| | | | | |
|---|---|---|---|---|
| 5-Me | 7-Me | H | H | 62:P603d |
| 5-Me | 7-Me | Me | Me | 93:197541b |
| 5-Me | 7-Cl | H | H | 64:9814bf |
| 5-Me | 7-Cl | Me | H | 70:37597w |
| 5-Me | 7-Cl | Me | Me | 70:37597w |
| 5-Me | 7-Cl | Et | Et | 70:37597w |
| 5-Me | 7-Cl | — CCCCC — | | 70:37597w |
| 5-Me | 7-Cl | — CCOCC — | | 70:37597w |
| 5-Me | 7-Br | H | H | 70:37597w |
| 5-Me | 7-Br | Me | H | 70:37597w |
| 5-Me | 7-Br | Me | Me | 70:37597w |
| 5-Me | 7-Br | Et | Et | 70:37597w |
| 5-Me | 7-Br | — CCCCC — | | 70:37597w |
| 5-Me | 7-Br | — CCOCC — | | 70:37597w |
| 5-Me | 7-NH$_2$ | H | H | 62:7717a |
| 5-Me | 7-NO$_2$ | H | H | 102:95490w |
| 5-cyclohexyl | 7-Cl | H | H | 124:P333120b |
| 5-HO | 7-Me | H | H | 64:5032f |
| 5-HO | 7-MeO | H | H | 93:89392v |
| 5-HO | 7-Cl | H | H | 79:126219c |
| 5-HO | 7-I | H | H | 121:271853v |
| 5-MeO | 7-Me | H | H | 62:P2803a |

| | | | | |
|---|---|---|---|---|
| 5-MeO | 7-Me | Me | Me | 86:5256y |
| 5-MeO | 7-MeO | H | H | 83:243v |
| 5-MeO | 7-MeO | Me | H | 85:87116u |
| 5-MeO | 7-MeO | Me | Me | 85:87116u |
| 5-MeO | 7-MeO | Et | H | 85:87116u |
| 5-MeO | 7-MeO | Et | Et | 85:87116u |
| 5-MeO | 7-MeO | Bz | Bz | 72:P12564m |
| 5-MeO | 7-Cl | H | H | 63:198192c |
| 5-MeO | 7-NH$_2$ | H | H | 62:7717a |
| 5-MeO | 7-NO$_2$ | H | H | 102:95490w |
| 5-BzO | 7-Me | H | H | 64:5032f |
| 5-BzO | 7-BzO | H | H | 79:126219c |
| 5-BzO | 7-BzO | Me | H | 79:126219c |
| 5-BzO | 7-BzO | Me | Me | 79:126219c |
| 5-BzO | 7-BzO | Et | H | 79:126219c |
| 5-BzO | 7-BzO | Et | Et | 79:126219c |
| 5-BzO | 7-Cl | H | H | 79:126219c |
| 5-F | 7-F | H | H | 122:P31501f |
| 5-Cl | 7-Me | H | H | 70:37597w |
| 5-Cl | 7-Me | Me | H | 70:37597w |
| 5-Cl | 7-Me | Me | Me | 70:37597w |
| 5-Cl | 7-Me | Et | Et | 74:111851a |
| 5-Cl | 7-Me | — CCCCC — | | 70:37597w |
| 5-Cl | 7-Me | — CCOCC — | | 70:37597w |
| 5-Cl | 7-MeO | H | H | 61:P10730b |
| 5-Cl | 7-Cl | H | H | 102:95490w |
| 5-Br | 7-Me | H | H | 70:37597w |
| 5-Br | 7-Me | Me | Me | 70:37597w |
| 5-Br | 7-Me | — CCCCC — | | 70:37597w |
| 5-Br | 7-Me | — CCOCC — | | 70:37597w |
| 5-NH$_2$ | 7-Me | H | H | 62:7717a |
| 5-NO$_2$ | 7-Me | H | H | 102:95491x |

6,7 —————————————————————————————————————

| | | | | |
|---|---|---|---|---|
| 6-Me | 7-Me | H | H | 122:P31501f |
| 6-Me | 7-Cl | H | H | 122:P31501f |
| 6-Me | 7-Br | H | H | 122:P31501f |
| 6-MeO | 7-MeO | cyclopropyl | H | 94:15482y |
| 6-MeO | 7-MeO | Bz | Me | 119:49715b |
| 6-MeO | 7-MeO | Bz | cyclopropyl | 94:15482y |
| 6-MeO | 7-Cl | H | H | 52:18479e |

| | | | | |
|---|---|---|---|---|
| 6-BzO | 7-MeO | Me | Me | 63:8297f |
| 6-BzO | 7-MeO | Et | Et | 63:8297f |
| 6-BzO | 7-BzO | H | H | 79:12619c |
| 6-BzO | 7-BzO | Me | H | 120:54765t |
| 6-Cl | 7-MeO | H | H | 52:18479e |
| 6-Cl | 7-Cl | H | H | 56:P2429b |
| 6-Br | 7-Me | H | H | 124:P333120b |

## 3-CARBON CHAIN

### α-METHYL

| | | | | |
|---|---|---|---|---|
| 1-Me | 4-HO | H | H | 62:P14634d |
| 1-Me | 5-HO | H | H | 57:P7235b |
| 1-Me | 5-MeO | H | H | 54:9880f |
| 1-Me | 5-MeO | Me | H | 117:233776g |
| 1-Me | 5-MeO | propynyl | H | 117:233776g |
| 1-Me | 5-MeO | propynyl | Me | 117:233776g |
| 1-Me | 5-MeO | C=C=CC- | H | 117:233776g |
| 1-Me | 5-MeO | C=C=CC- | Me | 117:233776g |
| 1-Me | 5-MeO | CC≡CC- | H | 117:233776g |
| 1-Me | 5-MeO | CC≡CC- | Me | 117:233776g |
| 1-Me | 4-BzO | H | H | 61:P4319f |
| 1-Me | 5-BzO | H | H | 55:8382e |
| 1-Pr | 5-MeO | H | H | 113:224121e |
| 1-Bz | 5-MeO | H | H | 57:9787a |
| 2-Me | 5-MeO | H | H | 69:P19021d |
| 2-Me | 5-MeO | Et | H | 65:P691c |
| 4-Me | 7-Me | H | H | 57:P16564g |
| 5-MeO | 6-Cl | H | H | 90:48848t |
| 5-MeO | 7-MeO | H | H | 72:P12564m |
| 5-Cl | 7-Cl | H | H | 66:74683j |
| 5-Cl | 7-Cl | Me | H | 64:5032f |
| 6-Cl | 7-Cl | H | H | 64:5032f |

### β-METHYL

| | | | | |
|---|---|---|---|---|
| 1-Me | 5-MeO | H | H | 117:233776g |
| 1-Me | 5-MeO | Me | H | 117:233776g |
| 1-Me | 5-MeO | propynyl | Me | 117:233776g |
| 1-Me | 5-MeO | C=C=CC | Me | 117:233776g |
| 1-Bz | 5-MeO | H | H | 54:21487c |
| 5-MeO | 6-Cl | H | H | 110:P75310z |
| 5-BzO | 7-BzO | H | H | 79:126219c |

## 4- CARBON CHAIN

### α,α-DIMETHYL

| | | | | |
|---|---|---|---|---|
| 2-Me | 5-Me | H | H | 98:P125870p |
| 2-Me | 5-MeO | H | H | 123:P285773x |
| 5-Me | 6-Me | H | H | 110:23668c |

### α-ETHYL

| | | | | |
|---|---|---|---|---|
| 1-Me | 2-Me | H | H | 61:633a |
| 2-Me | 7-Me | H | H | 61:P8279h |
| 4-OH | 7-HO | H | H | 72:P66809p |

### β-ETHYL

| | | | | |
|---|---|---|---|---|
| 1-Me | 2-Me | H | H | 74:40779v |
| 2-Me | 7-Me | H | H | 66:P55383v |
| 4-MeO | 6-MeO | H | H | 74:40779v |
| 5-MeO | 6-MeO | H | H | 101:P151824b |
| 5-MeO | 7-MeO | H | H | 72:P12564 |

### β,β-DIMETHYL

| | | | | |
|---|---|---|---|---|
| 1-Bz | 5-MeO | H | H | 54:21487c |
| 1-Bz | 6-MeO | H | H | 57:9788h |

## 5-CARBON CHAIN

### α-ISOPROPYL

| | | | | |
|---|---|---|---|---|
| 1-Me | 5-MeO | H | H | 54:9881b |

### α-METHYL-α-ETHYL

| | | | | |
|---|---|---|---|---|
| 1-Me | 5-MeO | H | H | 81:P3767p |

### β-METHYL-α-ETHYL

| | | | | |
|---|---|---|---|---|
| 2-Me | 5-MeO | H | H | 65:P691d |

## 6-CARBON CHAIN

### α-BUTYL

| | | | | |
|---|---|---|---|---|
| 1-Bu | 5-HO | H | H | 57:P7235b |

### α-tert-BUTYL

| | | | | |
|---|---|---|---|---|
| 1-Me | 5-MeO | H | H | 54:9881c |

α-METHYL-α-PROPYL
1-Bu       5-HO       H          H          57:P7235b

## 8-CARBON CHAIN

α,α-DIPROPYL
1-Pr       5-HO       H          H          57:P7235b

## TRISUBSITUTED (AND HIGHER) TRYPTAMINES:

| RING | | | N | N | CA CITATION |
|------|------|------|------|------|-------------|
| **2-CARBON CHAIN** | | | | | |
| 1-Me | 2-Me | 4-MeO | H | H | 93:114792k |
| | | | | | |
| 1-Me | 2-Me | 5-MeO | H | H | 50:5624c |
| 1-Bz | 2-Me | 5-HO | H | H | 66:54024a |
| 1-Bz | 2-Me | 5-MeO | H | H | 50:5624c |
| 1-Bz | 2-Me | 5-MeO | Me | Me | 53:P22018f |
| 1-Bz | 2-Me | 5-MeO | Et | H | 56:P15486g |
| 1-Bz | 2-Me | 5-MeO | Et | Et | 64:P19564c |
| 1-Bz | 2-Me | 5-MeO | Pr | H | 56:P15486g |
| 1-Bz | 2-Me | 5-MeO | iPr | H | 56:P15486g |
| 1-Bz | 2-Me | 5-MeO | allyl | allyl | 56:P15486i |
| 1-Bz | 2-Me | 5-MeO | Bu | H | 56:P15486g |
| 1-Bz | 2-Me | 5-MeO | tBu | H | 56:P15486g |
| 1-Bz | 2-Me | 5-MeO | Bz | Bz | 55:2611a |
| 1-Bz | 2-Me | 5-MeO | — CCCC — | | 56:P15486h |
| 1-Bz | 2-Me | 5-MeO | — CCCCC — | | 56:P15486h |
| 1-Bz | 2-Me | 5-NH$_2$CCO | H | H | 54:16652i |
| 1-Bz | 2-Me | 5-BzO | H | H | 54:16652i |
| 1-Bz | 2-Me | 5-MeS | H | H | 57:P13726c |
| 1-Br | 2-Me | 5-HO | H | H | 56:12232b |
| 1-NH$_2$ | 2-Me | 5-HO | H | H | 74:P77652z |
| 1-MeCO | 2-Ph | 5-Cl | H | H | 61:16040f |
| | | | | | |
| 1-Me | 2-Me | 6-MeO | H | H | 88:7165h |
| | | | | | |
| 1-Me | 4-HO | 5-EtO | H | H | 113:P217782t |
| 1-allyl | 4-I | 5-Me | Me | Me | 122:31265g |
| 1-allyl | 4-I | 5-MeO | Me | Me | 122:31265g |
| 1-allyl | 4-I | 5-diallylamino | H | H | 122:31265g |

| | | | | | |
|---|---|---|---|---|---|
| 1-Me | 4-Me | 6-Me | H | H | 94:P139775r |

| | | | | | |
|---|---|---|---|---|---|
| 1-Bz | 5-MeO | 6-MeO | H | H | 54:21487b |
| 1-Bz | 5-MeO | 6-MeO | Me | Me | 54:21487c |

| | | | | | |
|---|---|---|---|---|---|
| 2-Me | 4-Me | 5-MeO | Me | Me | 80:10259g |
| 2-Me | 4-Me | 5-MeO | Pr | Pr | 77:P151921s |
| 2-Me | 4-Me | 5-MeO | allyl | Et | 77:P15191s |
| 2-Me | 4-Me | 5-MeO | allyl | allyl | 77:P151921s |
| 2-Me | 4-Me | 5-MeO | methallyl | H | 77:P151921s |
| 2-Me | 4-CF$_3$ | 5-MeO | Me | Me | 78:147723g |
| 2-Me | 4-CF$_3$ | 5-MeO | — CCCC — | | 71:P49764g |
| 2-Me | 4-HO | 5-MeO | H | H | 113:P217782t |
| 2-Me | 4-HO | 5-EtO | H | H | 113:P217782t |

| | | | | | |
|---|---|---|---|---|---|
| 2-Me | 4-MeO | 7-Br | H | H | 70:96527w |

| | | | | | |
|---|---|---|---|---|---|
| 2-Me | 5-HO | 6-Me | H | H | 79:132894k |
| 2-Me | 5-MeO | 6-Me | H | H | 79:132894k |
| 2-Me | 5-MeO | 6-Me | Me | H | 79:132894k |
| 2-Me | 5-MeO | 6-Me | Me | Me | 72:P66809p |
| 2-Me | 5-MeO | 6-Me | Et | Et | 77:P151921s |
| 2-Me | 5-MeO | 6-Me | methallyl | H | 77:P151921s |
| 2-Me | 5-EtO | 6-Me | Me | Me | 77:P151921s |
| 2-Br | 5-MeO | 6-Br | H | H | 121:P9157f |
| 2-NH$_2$ | 5-MeO | 6-MeO | Me | Me | 50:4901c |

| | | | | | |
|---|---|---|---|---|---|
| 2-Me | 5-HO | 7-Me | H | H | 79:132894k |
| 2-Me | 5-HO | 7-Me | Me | Me | 79:132894k |
| 2-Me | 5-MeO | 7-Me | H | H | 79:132294k |
| 2-Me | 5-MeO | 7-Me | Me | H | 79:132894k |
| 2-Me | 5-MeO | 7-Me | Me | Me | 77:P151921s |

| | | | | | |
|---|---|---|---|---|---|
| 2-Me | 5-MeO | 7-Me | Et | Et | 77:P151921s |
| 2-Me | 5-MeO | 7-Me | $CF_3CH_2$- | H | 77:P151921s |
| 2-Me | 5-MeO | 7-Me | CCSCC- | H | 77:P151921s |
| 2-Me | 5-MeO | 7-Me | Pr | Pr | 77:P151921s |
| 2-Me | 5-MeO | 7-Me | iPr | H | 77:P151921s |
| 2-Me | 5-MeO | 7-Me | iPr | Me | 77:P151921s |
| 2-Me | 5-MeO | 7-Me | allyl | H | 77:P151921s |
| 2-Me | 5-MeO | 7-Me | allyl | Et | 79:132894k |
| 2-Me | 5-MeO | 7-Me | allyl | allyl | 77:P151921s |
| 2-Me | 5-MeO | 7-Me | nBu | H | 79:132894k |
| 2-Me | 5-MeO | 7-Me | methallyl | H | 77:P151921s |
| 2-Me | 5-MeO | 7-Me | cyclohexyl | H | 79:132894k |
| 2-Me | 5-MeO | 7-Me | Bz | Me | 77:P151921s |
| 2-Me | 5-MeO | 7-Me | — CCCCC — | | 72:P66809p |
| | | | | | |
| 4-Me | 5-MeO | 6-Me | H | H | 94:P139775r |
| 4-MeO | 5-MeO | 6-MeO | H | H | 52:18479f |
| 4-MeO | 5-MeO | 6-MeO | Me | Me | 59:3864e |
| 4-F | 5-HO | 6-F | H | H | 109:20611x |
| 4-F | 5-MeO | 6-F | H | H | 86:139739s |
| 4-F | 5-BzO | 6-BzO | H | H | 113:59812w |
| | | | | | |
| 4-Me | 5-Me | 7-Me | H | H | 94:P139775 |
| 4-F | 5-BzO | 7-BzO | H | H | 114:101520x |
| | | | | | |
| 4-MeO | 6-MeO | 7-MeO | Bz | Bz | 122:187848k |
| | | | | | |
| 5-Me | 6-Me | 7-Me | Me | Me | 55:8385f |
| 5-MeO | 6-MeO | 7-MeO | H | H | 55:8384e |
| 5-MeO | 6-MeO | 7-MeO | Me | Me | 60:15815g |
| 5-MeO | 6-Cl | 7-Cl | H | H | 106:P4768m |
| 5-BzO | 6-BzO | 7-F | H | H | 113:59812w |
| 5-BzO | 6-F | 7-BzO | H | H | 114:101520x |

## 3- CARBON CHAIN

### α-METHYL

| | | | | | |
|---|---|---|---|---|---|
| 1-Bz | 2-Me | 5-MeO | H | H | 56:P15486i |
| 1-Et | 5-MeO | 7-I | H | H | 121:271853v |

### β-METHYL

| | | | | | |
|---|---|---|---|---|---|
| 1-Bz | 2-Me | 5-MeO | H | H | 57:9786f |
| 1-Bz | 2-Me | 5-MeO | Me | Me | 57:9786g |
| 1-Bz | 2-Me | 5-MeO | Et | Et | 57:9786h |
| 5-MeO | 6-Cl | 7-Cl | H | H | 110:P75310z |

## 4- CARBON CHAIN

### β,β-DIMETHYL

| | | | | | |
|---|---|---|---|---|---|
| 1-Bz | 2-Me | 5-MeO | H | H | 57:14403b |

### TETRASUBSTITUTED

| | | | | | |
|---|---|---|---|---|---|
| 2-Me | 4-Cl | 5-OH | 7-Cl | H | H | 79:132894 k |
| 2-Me | 5-MeO | 6-Cl | 7-Cl | H | H | 106:P4768m |
| 4-Me | 5-Me | 6-Me | 7-Me | H | H | 79:19057b |
| 4-F | 5-F | 6-F | 7-F | H | H | 100:85536k |

## 3- CARBON CHAIN

### α-METHYL

| | | | | | |
|---|---|---|---|---|---|
| 4-Me | 5-Me | 6-Me | 7-Me | H | H | 79:19057b |

## RELOCATION OF THE 2-AMINOETHYL GROUP FROM THE INDOLE 3 POSITION:

| RING | | | N | N | CA CITATION |
|------|---|---|---|---|-------------|

## AT THE 1-POSITION

### 2-CARBON CHAIN

| RING | | | N | N | CA CITATION |
|------|---|---|-----|-----|-------------|
| H | | | H | H | — many — |
| H | | | Me | H | 119:P95332x |
| H | | | Me | Me | 79:53128k |
| H | | | Et | Et | 49:6225f |
| H | | | — CCCC — | | 43:4257e |
| 2-Me | | | Et | Et | 47:9317f |
| 3-Me | | | H | H | 55:14427g |
| 4-Me | | | H | H | 110:R185342u |
| 4-Me | | | Me | Me | 100:22986m |
| 4-BzO | | | Me | Me | 54:18473b |
| 5-Me | | | H | H | 110:R185342u |
| 5-Me | | | Me | Me | 100:22986m |
| 5-MeO | | | H | H | 110:R185342u |
| 5-MeO | | | Me | Me | 100:22986m |
| 5-BzO | | | Me | Me | 54:492g |
| 5-F | | | H | H | 123:P285766x |
| 5-Cl | | | H | H | 123:P285766x |
| 5-Cl | | | Me | Me | 112:35616p |
| 6-Me | | | Me | Me | 100:22986m |
| 6-MeO | | | H | H | 110:R185342u |
| 6-MeO | | | Me | Me | 100:22986m |
| 6-NH$_2$ | | | Me | Me | 124:P232466p |
| 6-NO$_2$ | | | Me | Me | 124:P232466p |
| 7-Me | | | H | H | 110:R185342u |
| 7-Me | | | Me | Me | 100:22986m |
| 2 Me | 4-Cl | | Et | Et | 52:P17289a |
| 2 Me | 6-Cl | | Et | Et | 52:P17289a |
| 3-MeO | 4-Me | | H | H | 123:P285766x |
| 3-MeO | 5-F | | H | H | 123:P285766x |
| 4-Cl | 5-F | | H | H | 123:P285766x |
| 5-F | 6-Cl | | H | H | 123:P285766x |
| 2-Me | 3-Me | 5-MeO | Me | Me | 70:68209a |
| 3-MeO | 4-Cl | 5-F | H | H | 123:P285766x |

## 3-CARBON CHAIN

### α-METHYL

| | | | | | Ref |
|---|---|---|---|---|---|
| H | | | Me | Me | 48:692g |
| 4-Me | | | H | H | 123:P285766x |
| 5-Me | | | H | H | 123:P285766x |
| 5-F | | | H | H | 123:P285766x |
| 5-Cl | | | H | H | 123:P285766x |
| 5-Br | | | H | H | 123:P285766x |
| 6-Me | | | H | H | 123:P285766x |
| 6-F | | | H | H | 123:P285766x |
| 2-Me | 5-Cl | | H | H | 123:P285766x |
| 2-Et | 5-F | | H | H | 123:P285766x |
| 3-MeO | 4-Me | | H | H | 123:P285766x |
| 3-Me | 5-F | | H | H | 123:P285766x |
| 4-iPr | 5-F | | H | H | 123:P285766x |
| 4-CF$_3$ | 5-F | | H | H | 123:P285766x |
| 4-Cl | 5-F | | H | H | 123:P285766x |
| 5-CF$_3$ | 6-F | | H | H | 123:P285766x |
| 5-F | 6-iPr | | H | H | 123:P285766x |
| 5-F | 6-CF$_3$ | | H | H | 123:P285766x |
| 5-F | 6-F | | H | H | 123:P285766x |
| 5-F | 6-Cl | | H | H | 123:P285766x |
| 5-Cl | 6-F | | H | H | 123:P285766x |
| 6-F | 7-Cl | | H | H | 123:P285766x |
| 3-Et | 4-Cl | 5-F | H | H | 123:P285766x |
| 3-MeO | 4-Me | 5-F | H | H | 123:P285766x |
| 3-Me | 5-F | 6-Cl | H | H | 123:P285766x |
| 3-Et | 5-F | 6-Cl | H | H | 123:P285766x |

### β-METHYL

| | | | | | Ref |
|---|---|---|---|---|---|
| 2-Me | 3-Bz | | Me | Me | 60:P8000d |
| 2-Me | 5-F | | Me | Me | 105:P78832d |

### α-ETHYL

| | | | | Ref |
|---|---|---|---|---|
| 5-F | | H | H | 123:P285766x |

## AT THE 2-POSITION

## 2-CARBON CHAIN

| | | | Ref |
|---|---|---|---|
| H | | H | H | — many — |
| H | | Me | H | 71:124102v |

| | | | | |
|---|---|---|---|---|
| H | | Me | Me | 51:4551e |
| H | | Et | Et | 71:124102v |
| H | | — CCCC — | | 71:124102v |
| H | | — CCCCC — | | 71:124102v |
| H | | — CCOCC — | | 71:124102v |
| 1-Me | | H | H | 83:178873p |
| 1-Me | | Me | Me | 55:4473f |
| 1-Me | | iPr | H | 74:141438p |
| 1-Me | | Bz | H | 84:43754a |
| 1-Et | | H | H | 78:111172 |
| 3-Me | | H | H | 65:10574e |
| 3-Me | | Me | Me | 86:37493q |
| 3-Me | | Et | H | 74:76387e |
| 3-Me | | Bz | H | 74:76387e |
| 3-Et | | H | H | 123:143832s |
| 3-EtSMe- | | Me | Me | 84:P90000m |
| 3-iPr | | H | H | 123:143832s |
| 4-BzO | | Me | Me | 54:18473b |
| 4-Cl | | H | H | 81:105166j |
| 5-Me | | H | H | 83:28044e |
| 5-HO | | H | H | 92:110767n |
| 5-HO | | Me | Me | 80:26452a |
| 5-MeO | | H | H | 59:4251g |
| 5-EtO | | H | H | 74:53406w |
| 5-BzO | | H | H | 52:3765b |
| 5-BzO | | Et | Et | 54:492g |
| 5-Cl | | H | H | 92:110767n |
| 5-Br | | H | H | 81:105166j |
| 5-$NH_2$ | | H | H | 47:10734a |
| 6-BzO | | Et | H | 64:17522d |
| 6-Cl | | H | H | 81:105166j |
| 7-MeO | | H | H | 74:53406w |
| 7-EtO | | H | H | 74:53406w |
| 7-Cl | | H | H | 81:105166j |
| 7-Br | | H | H | 81:105166j |
| 1-Me | 3-Me | Me | H | 84:43754a |
| 1-Me | 3-Me | Me | Me | 62:10398g |
| 1-Me | 3-Me | — CCCCC — | | 62:1-398h |
| 1-Me | 3-EtSMe- | Me | Me | 84:P90000m |
| 1-Bz | 3-Me | H | H | 74:76387e |
| 1-Bz | 3-Me | Me | H | 74:76387e |
| 1-Bz | 3-Me | Me | Me | 62:10398h |
| 1-Me | 5-MeO | H | H | 123:339610n |

| | | | | | |
|---|---|---|---|---|---|
| 1-Me | 5-MeO | | Me | H | 123:339610n |
| 1-Me | 5-MeO | | propynyl | Me | 123:339610n |
| 1-Me | 5-MeO | | C=C=CC- | Me | 123:339610n |
| 1-Me | 5-MeO | | CC≡CC- | Me | 123:339610n |
| 3-Me | 5-Me | | Me | Me | 86:37493q |
| 3-Me | 5-MeO | | H | H | 74:53406w |
| 3-Me | 5-MeO | | Me | H | 116:151710w |
| 3-Me | 5-MeO | | Me | Me | — many — |
| 3-Me | 5-MeO | | Et | Me | 116:151710w |
| 3-Me | 5-EtO | | H | H | 74:53406w |
| 3-Me | 5-Cl | | Me | H | 85:56573m |
| 3-Et | 5-Me | | Me | Me | 95:203680f |
| EtOMe- | 5-Me | | Me | Me | 95:203680f |
| 3-Bz | 5-Me | | Me | Me | 95:205680f |
| 3-Me | 7-MeO | | H | H | 74:53406w |
| 4-Me | 7-Me | | H | H | 85:21176g |
| 5-MeO | 6-Me | | Me | Me | 87:145577z |
| 5-Me | 7-Me | | H | H | 85:21176g |
| 5-Me | 7-Cl | | H | H | 81:105166j |
| 5-Me | 7-Br | | H | H | 81:105166j |
| 5-Cl | 7-Me | | H | H | 81:105166j |
| 1-Me | 3-Me | 5-Cl | H | H | 78:P13635h |

## 3-CARBON CHAIN

### α-METHYL

| | | | |
|---|---|---|---|
| H | | H | H | 64:5621g |
| H | | Me | H | 95:54631m |
| 3-Me | | H | H | 115:P71637s |
| 4-Me | | H | H | 95:54631m |
| 4-Me | | Me | H | 95:54631m |
| 4-Cl | | H | H | 81:105166j |
| 5-MeO | | H | H | 74:53406w |
| 5-MeO | | Me | H | 95:54631m |
| 5-EtO | | H | H | 74:53406w |
| 5-Cl | | H | H | — many— |
| 5-Cl | | Me | H | 95:54631m |
| 5-Br | | H | H | 81:105166j |
| 6-Me | | H | H | 95:54631m |
| 6-Me | | Me | H | 95:54631m |
| 6-MeO | | H | H | 95:54631m |
| 6-MeO | | Me | H | 95:54631m |
| 6-Cl | | Me | H | 95:54631m |

| | | | | |
|---|---|---|---|---|
| 7-Me | | H | H | 95:54631m |
| 7-MeO | | H | H | 82:38457k |
| 7-Cl | | H | H | 81:105166j |
| 7-Br | | H | H | 81:105166j |
| 1-Me | 5-MeO | H | H | 123:252s |
| 1-Me | 5-MeO | Me | H | 123:252s |
| 1-Me | 5-MeO | propynyl | H | 123:252s |
| 1-Me | 5-MeO | propynyl | Me | 123:252s |
| 1-Me | 5-MeO | C=C=CC- | H | 123:252s |
| 1-Me | 5-MeO | C=C=CC- | Me | 123:252s |
| 1-Me | 5-MeO | CC≡CC- | H | 123:252s |
| 1-Me | 5-MeO | CC≡CC- | Me | 123:252s |
| 3-Me | 5-MeO | H | H | 74:53406w |
| 3-Me | 5-EtO | H | H | 74:53406w |
| 3-Me | 7-MeO | H | H | 74:53406w |
| 5-Me | 7-Cl | H | H | 81:105166j |
| 5-Me | 7-Br | H | H | 81:105166j |
| 5-Cl | 7-Me | H | H | 81:105166j |
| 5-Cl | 7-Cl | H | H | 95:54631m |

### β-METHYL

| | | | | |
|---|---|---|---|---|
| 5-Me | | Me | Me | 96:28265w |
| 1-Me | 5-MeO | H | H | 123:252s |
| 1-Me | 5-MeO | Me | H | 123:252s |
| 1-Me | 5-MeO | propynyl | Me | 123:252s |
| 1-Me | 5-MeO | C=C=CC- | Me | 123:252s |
| 3-Me | 5-Cl | Me | H | 74:76387e |

## 4-CARBON CHAIN

### α,α-DIMETHYL

| | | | |
|---|---|---|---|
| H | H | H | — many — |
| 1-Me | H | H | 79:126361t |

### β,β-DIMETHYL

| | | | |
|---|---|---|---|
| H | H | H | 115:P71637s |

## 5-CARBON CHAIN

### α-ISOPROPYL

| | | | |
|---|---|---|---|
| H | H | H | 66:45281w |
| 5-Me | H | H | 68:114347c |

## AT THE 4-POSITION

### 2-CARBON CHAIN

| | | | | |
|---|---|---|---|---|
| H | | H | H | — many — |
| H | | Me | H | 60:P11989c |
| H | | Me | Me | 60:P11989d |
| H | | Et | Et | 98:53604e |
| H | | Pr | H | 115:158886w |
| H | | Pr | Me | 115:158886w |
| H | | Pr | Pr | — many — |
| H | | Pr | allyl | 115:158886w |
| H | | Bu | Pr | 115:158886w |
| H | | Bu | Bu | 115:158886w |
| 5-Et | | H | H | 96:46343z |
| 5-HO | | H | H | 69:77048d |
| 5-HO | | Pr | Pr | 117:184656g |
| 5-MeO | | H | H | 70:57568r |
| 5-MeO | | Me | Me | 80:47100z |
| 5-MeO | | Pr | Pr | 117:184656g |
| 5-BzO | | Pr | Pr | 117:184656g |
| 5-Cl | | H | H | 112:55570x |
| 5-Cl | | Me | H | 112:55570x |
| 6-HO | | Me | Me | 107:126474d |
| 6-HO | | Pr | Pr | 100:85539p |
| 6-Br | | H | H | 106:P156272h |
| 7-MeO | | Pr | Pr | 98:179154b |
| 7-BzO | | H | H | 106:P156272h |
| 1-Me | 5-HO | Pr | Pr | 117:184656g |
| 1-Me | 5-MeO | Pr | Pr | 117:184656g |
| 1-Me | 5-BzO | Pr | Pr | 117:184656g |
| 5-MeO | 7-MeO | H | H | 84:P31033b |
| 1-Me 2-Me 7-MeO | | Et | H | 110:75859k |
| 1-Me 2-Me 5-HO 7-MeO | Me | | H | 110:75859k |

### 3-CARBON CHAIN

#### α-METHYL

| | | | | |
|---|---|---|---|---|
| H | | H | H | 60:P11989c |
| H | | Me | H | 60:P11989c |
| 5-HO | | H | H | 69:77048d |
| 3-Me | 5-HO | H | H | 69:77048d |

## 4-CARBON CHAIN

### α-ETHYL
| | | | |
|---|---|---|---|
| H | H | H | 60:P11989c |

## AT THE 5-POSITION

## 2-CARBON CHAIN

| | | | |
|---|---|---|---|
| H | H | H | 70:28749v |
| 1-Me | H | H | 93:149357z |
| 1-Et | H | H | 93:149357z |
| 6-HO | Pr | Pr | 121:57263j |
| 7-MeO | Pr | Pr | 120:77149j |

## 3-CARBON CHAIN

### α-METHYL
| | | | |
|---|---|---|---|
| H | H | H | 60:P11989d |
| 3-Me | H | H | 69:P43799j |

## AT THE 6-POSITION

## 2-CARBON CHAIN

| | | | |
|---|---|---|---|
| H | H | H | 60:P11989d |
| H | Pr | Pr | 111:173948d |

### α-METHYL
| | | | |
|---|---|---|---|
| H | H | H | 60:P11989b |
| H | Me | H | 60:P11989c |
| H | Me | Me | 60:P11989d |
| H | Et | H | 60:P11989d |
| H | Bz | H | 69:P43800c |
| H | Bz | Me | 69:P43800c |
| 1-Me | H | H | 70:28749v |
| 2-Me | H | H | 69:P43799j |
| 4-Me | H | H | 69:P43799j |

### α-ETHYL
| | | | |
|---|---|---|---|
| H | H | H | 60:P11989c |

## AT THE 7-POSITION

### 2-CARBON CHAIN

| H | | H | H | 70:28749v |
| 4-MeO  6-MeO | | H | H | 71:91200v |

### 3-CARBON CHAIN

α-METHYL

| H | | H | H | 72:130697e |

α,α-DIMETHYL

| 6-HO | | H | H | 69:77048d |

# APPENDIX I: LONG INDEX TO BOOK II

This is a chemical index of the specific compounds mentioned in Book 2, The Chemistry Continues. Multiple entries are a result of naming each material from the point of view of its skeleton (as a tryptamine, or indole, or carboline, for example) or from the substituents that are present. Rather than employing the current Chemical Abstracts priority rules for alphabetization, all substituents will be placed in unsophisticated alphabetical order. Identifying location markers (numbers and Greek letters) are ignored. Atoms that locate a group (N, O, S) are also ignored, but if they are part of the structure (F, Cl, Br, or I) then they are respected. Branching indicators (n, i, s, t, and c for cyclo) are ignored except for isopropyl. All taxinomic binomials are excluded.

---

Abrin   see under 5-HO-DMT #19
Abrine   see under 5-HO-DMT #19
Acetamide, N-[2-(5-methoxyindol-3-yl)ethyl]   see Melatonin #35
3-(2-Acetamidoethyl)-5-methoxyindole   see Melatonin #35
Acetaminophen   see under Melatonin #35
5-Acetoxy-N,N-dimethyltryptamine   see under 5-HO-DMT #19
4-Acetoxy-N-methyl-N-isopropyltryptamine   see under 4-HO-MIPT #22
1-Acetyl-N,N-diethyllysergamide   see under LSD #26
O-Acetyl-N,N-dimethylserotonin   see under 5-HO-DMT #19
1-Acetyl-LSD   see under LSD #26
1-Acetyllysergide   see under LSD #26
N-Acetyl-5-methoxytryptamine   see Melatonin #35
N-Acetyl-O-methylserotonin   see Melatonin #35
Acid   see LSD #26
4-AcO-MIPT   see under 4-HO-MIPT #22
Adrenoglomerulotropin   see 6-MeO-THH #44

Brom-LSD   see under LSD #26

Bromlysergide   see under LSD #26

2-Bromo-N,N-diethyllysergamide   see under LSD #26

2-Bromo-N,N-diethyl-1-methyllysergamide   see under LSD #26

2-Bromo-LSD   see under LSD  #26

2-Bromolysergide   see under LSD  #26

Bufotenidine   see under 5-HO-DMT #19

Bufotenine   see under 5-HO-DMT #19

Bufotenine ethyl ether   see under 5-HO-DMT #19

Bufotenine methyl ether   see 5-MeO-DMT #38

Bufothionine   see under 5-HO-DMT #19

Bufoviridine   see under 5-HO-DMT #19

BU-LAD   see under PRO-LAD #51

Butane, 2-amino-1-(3-indolyl)   see $\alpha$-ET #11

Butane, 2-amino-1-(5-methoxy-3-indolyl)   see under $\alpha$-ET #11

3-[2-(Butylamino)ethyl]indole   see under NET #49

3-[2-(i-Butylamino)ethyl]indole   see under NET #49

3-[2-(s-Butylamino)ethyl]indole   see under NET #49

3-[2-(t-Butylamino)ethyl]indole   see under NET #49

6-Butyl-9,10-didehydro-N,N-diethylergoline-8$\beta$-carboxamide   see under PRO-LAD#5

N-Butyl-4-hydroxy-N-methyltryptamine   see under 4-HO-MPT #23

N-i-Butyl-4-hydroxy-N-methyltryptamine   see under 4-HO-MPT #23

N-s-Butyl-4-hydroxy-N-methyltryptamine   see under 4-HO-MPT #23

N-t-Butyl-4-hydroxy-N-methyltryptamine   see under 4-HO-MPT #23

3-[2-(Butylisopropylamino)ethyl]indole   see under EIPT #10

N-Butyl-N-isopropyltryptamine   see under EIPT #10

3-[2-(Butylmethylamino)ethyl]indole   see under MBT #27

3-[2-(i-Butylmethylamino)ethyl]-4-indolol   see under 4-HO-MPT #23

3-[2-(s-Butylmethylamino)ethyl]-4-indolol   see under 4-HO-MPT #23

3-[2-(t-Butylmethylamino)ethyl]-4-indolol   see under 4-HO-MPT #23

N-s-Butyl-N-methyltryptamine   see under MBT #27

N-Butyl nor-LSD   see under PRO-LAD #51

N-Butylnorlysergic acid, N,N-diethylamide   see under PRO-LAD #51

N-Butyltryptamine   see under NET #49

N-i-Butyltryptamine   see under NET #49

N-s-Butyltryptamine   see under NET #49

N-t-Butyltryptamine   see under NET #49

O-Butyryl-N,N-dimethylserotonin   see under 5-HO-DMT #19

O-i-Butyryl-N,N-dimethylserotonin   see under 5-HO-DMT #19

5-Butyryloxy-N,N-dimethyltryptamine   see under 5-HO-DMT #19

5-i-Butyryloxy-N,N-dimethyltryptamine   see under 5-HO-DMT #19

N-t-Butyltryptamine   see under MIPT #47

4-Hydroxy-α-methyltryptamine  see under α-MT #48
5-Hydroxy-α-methyltryptamine  see under α-MT #48
4-Hydroxy-N-methyl-N-c-pentyltryptamine  see under 4-HO-MIPT #22
1-Hydroxymethyl-LSD  see under LSD #26
1-Hydroxymethyllysergide  see under LSD #26
N-[α-(Hydroxymethyl)ethyl]-lysergamide  see under LSD #26
N-[α-(Hydroxymethyl)propyl]lysergamide  see under LSD #26
4-Hydroxy-N-methyl-N-propyltryptamine  see under 4-HO-MPT #23
6-Hydroxy-1-methyltetrahydro-β-carboline  see under 6-MeO-THH #44
7-Hydroxy-1-methyl-1,2,3,4-tetrahydro-β-carboline  see under 6-MeO-THH #44
2-Hydroxy-N-methyltryptamine  see under DMT #6
4-Hydroxy-N-methyltryptamine  see under 4-HO-DMT #18
N-Hydroxy-N-methyltryptamine  see under DMT #6
5-Hydroxy-α-methyltryptamine  see under α-MT #48
5-Hydroxy-N-methyltryptamine  see under 5-HO-DMT #19
6-Hydroxy-9-methyltryptoline  see under 6-MeO-THH #44
"4-Hydroxymorpholinyltryptamine"  see under 4-HO-pyr-T #24
4-Hydroxy-3-[2-(1-morpholinyl)ethyl]indole  see under 4-HO-pyr-T #24
4-Hydroxy-N,N-pentamethylenetryptamine  see under 4-HO-pyr-T #24
4-Hydroxy-3-[2-(1-piperidinyl)ethyl]indole  see under 4-HO-pyr-T #24
"4-Hydroxypiperidinyltryptamine"  see under 4-HO-pyr-T #24
4-Hydroxy-3-[2-(1-pyrrolidinyl)ethyl]indole  see under 4-HO-pyr-T #24
"4-Hydroxypyrrolidinyltryptamine"  see 4-HO-pyr-T #24
6-Hydroxy-1,2,3,4-tetrahydro-β-carboline  see under 6-MeO-THH #44
6-Hydroxytetrahydroharman  see under 6-MeO-THH #44
4-Hydroxy-N,N-tetramethylenetryptamine  see 4-HO-pyr-T #24
4-Hydroxy-1,N,N-trimethyltryptamine  see under 4-HO-DMT #18
5-Hydroxy-N,N,N-trimethyltryptammonium salt  see under 5-HO-DMT #19
4-Hydroxytryptamine  see under 4-HO-DMT #18
5-Hydroxytryptamine  see under Melatonin #35
6-Hydroxytryptamine  see under Melatonin #35
5-Hydroxytryptoline  see under 6-MeO-THH #44
**Ibogaine #25  Page 487**
Indapex  see 5-MeO-TMT #45
Indole, 3-(2-acetamidoethyl)-5-methoxy  see Melatonin #35
Indole-3-acetic acid  see under T #53
Indole, 3-(2-aminobutyl)  see α-ET #11
Indole, 3-(2-aminobutyl)-5-methoxy  see under α-ET #11
Indole, 3-(2-aminoethyl)  see T #53
Indole, 3-(2-aminoethyl)-4-methoxy  see under 4-MeO-MIPT #39
Indole, 3-(2-aminoethyl)-5-methoxy  see under 5-MeO-DMT #38
Indole, 3-(2-aminoethyl)-6-methoxy  see under 5-MeO-MIPT #40
Indole, 3-(2-aminoethyl)-7-methoxy  see under 5-MeO-MIPT #40

Indole, 3-[2-(dimethylamino)ethyl]  see DMT #6
Indole, 3-[2-(dimethylamino)ethyl]-4-methoxy  see under 4-MeO-MIPT #39
Indole, 3-[2-(dimethylamino)ethyl]-5-methoxy  see 5-MeO-DMT #38
Indole, 3-[2-(dimethylamino)ethyl]-6-methoxy  see under 4-MeO-MIPT #39
Indole, 3-[2-(dimethylamino)ethyl]-7-methoxy  see under 4-MeO-MIPT #39
Indole, 3-[2-(dimethylamino)ethyl]-5-methoxy-2-methyl  see 5-MeO-TMT #45
Indole, 3-[2-(dimethylamino)ethyl]-5-methoxy-6-methyl  see under 5,6-MeO-MIPT #41
Indole, 3-[2-(dimethylamino)ethyl]-2-methyl  see 2-Me-DMT #34
Indole, 3-[2-(dimethylamino)ethyl]-4,5-methylenedioxy  see 4,5-MDO-DMT #30
Indole, 3-[2-(dimethylamino)ethyl]-5,6-methylenedioxy  see 5,6-MDO-DMT #31
Indole, 3-[2-(dimethylamino)ethyl]-4-methylthio  see under 5-MeS-DMT #46
Indole, 3-[2-(dimethylamino)ethyl]-5-methylthio  see 5-MeS-DMT #46
Indole, 3-[2-(dimethylamino)ethyl]-6-methylthio  see under 5-MeS-DMT #46
Indole, 3-(dimethylamino)methyl  see under DMT #6
Indole, 3-[2-(dimethylamino)propyl]  see under α,N-DMT #8
Indole, 3-[3-(dimethylamino)propyl]  see DMT #6
Indole, 3-[2-(dipropylamino)ethyl]  see DPT #9
Indole, 3-[2-(dipropylamino)ethyl]-5-methoxy  see 5-MeO-DET #36
Indole, 3-[2-(dipropylamino)ethyl]-1-propyl  see under DPT #9
Indole, 3-ethanol  see under T #53
Indole, 3-[2-(ethylamino)ethyl]  see NET #49
Indole, 3-[2-(ethylamino)propyl]  see under α,N-DMT #8
Indole, 3-[2-(ethylisopropylamino)ethyl]  see EIPT #10
Indole, 3-[2-(ethylmethylamino)ethyl]  see under MIPT #47
Indole, 3-(2-heptofluorobutyroytlamidoethyl)-5-methoxy  see under Melatonin #35
Indole, 3-(2-hexanoylamidoethyl)-5-methoxy  see under Melatonin #35
Indole, 3-[2-(hexylamino)ethyl]  see under NET #49
Indole, 3-(2-hydroxyethyl)  see under Melatonin #35
Indole, 3-[2-(isopropylamine)ethyl]-7-methoxy  see under 5-MeO-MIPT #40
Indole, 3-[2-(isopropylamino)ethyl]  see under NET #49
Indole, 3-[2-(isopropylamino)ethyl]-7-methoxy  see under 5-MeO-MIPT #40
Indole, 3-[2-(isopropylamino)propyl]  see under α,N-DMT #8
Indole, 3-[2-(isopropylmethylamino)ethyl]  see MIPT #47
Indole, 3-[2-(isopropylmethylamino)ethyl]-4-methoxy  see 4-MeO-MIPT #39
Indole, 3-[2-(isopropylmethylamino)ethyl]-5-methoxy  see 5-MeO-MIPT #40
Indole, 3-[2-(isopropylmethylamino)ethyl]-6-methoxy  see under 5-MeO-MIPT #40
Indole, 3-[2-(isopropylmethylamino)ethyl]-7-methoxy  see under 5-MeO-MIPT #40
Indole, 3-[2-(isopropylmethylamino)ethyl]-4,5-methylenedioxy  see under 4,5-MDO-DIP'
                                                                                    #2
Indole, 3-[2-(isopropylmethylamino)ethyl]-5,6-methylenedioxy  see 5,6-MDO-MIPT #32
Indole, 3-[2-(isopropylmethylamino)ethyl]-5-methylthio  see under 5-MeS-DMT #46
Indole, 3-[2-(isopropylpropylamino)ethyl]  see under EIPT #10

O-Methylnordehydrobufotonine   see under 5-MeO-DMT #38
O-Methyl-N-octanoylserotonin   see under Melatonin #35
N-Methyl-4-phenylpyridinium salt   see under Harmine #14
N-Methyl-4-phenyl-1,2,3,6-tetrahydropyridine   see under Harmine #14
1-Methylpinoline   see 6-MeO-THH #44
3-[2-(Methylpropylamino)ethyl]indole   see under MIPT #47
3-[2-(Methylpropylamino)ethyl]indol-4-ol   see 4-HO-MPT #23
N-Methyl-N-propyltryptamine   see under MIPT #47
1-Methylpsilocin   see under 4-HO-DMT #18
1-Methyl-9H-pyrid-[3,4-b]-indole   see under 6-MeO-THH #44
α-Methylserotonin   see under α-MT #48
N-Methylserotonin   see under 5-HO-DMT #19
1-Methyl-1,2,3,4-tetrahydro-β-carboline   see under 6-MeO-THH #44
2-Methyl-1,2,3,4-tetrahydro-β-carboline   see under 6-MeO-THH #44
1-Methyl-1,2,3,4-tetrahydro-β-carboline, 3-carboxylic acid  see under 6-MeO-THH #44
1-Methyltetrahydropinoline   see 6-MeO-THH #44
2-Methyltryptamine   see under T #53
α-Methyltryptamine   see α-MT #48
N-Methyltryptamine   see NMT #50
Methyltryptoline, 5-hydroxy   see under 6-MeO-THH #44
Methysergide   see under LSD #26
Mexamine   see under 5-MeO-DMT #38 and under Melatonin #35
α-M-5-HT    see under α-MT #48
MIL   see under LSD #26
**MIPT  #47  Page 562**
α-MIPT   see under α,N-DMT #8
α,N-MIPT   see under α,N-DMT #8
MLD-41   see under LSD #26
MLA-74   see under LSD #26
Monase   see α-ET #11
Monomethyltryptamine   see NMT #50
Morpholine, 4-[2-(5,6-dimethoxyindol-3-yl)ethyl]   see under 5,6-MeO-MIPT #41
Morpholine, 4-[2-[3-(4-hydroxy)indolyl]ethyl]]   see under 4-HO-pyr-T #24
Morpholine, 4-[2-(3-indolyl)ethyl]   see under pyr-T #52
Morpholine, 4-[2-(5-methoxyindol-3-yl)ethyl]   see under 5-MeO-pyr-T #43
Morpholine, 4-[2-(5,6-methylenedioxyindol-3-yl)ethyl]   see under 5,6-MDO-DIPT #29
"Morpholinyl-5,6-methyledioxytryptamine"   see under 5,6-MDO-DIPT #29
"Morpholinyl-5,6-dimethoxytryptamine"   see under 5,6-MeO-MIPT #41
3-[2-(4-Morpholinyl)ethyl]indole   see under pyr-T #52
3-[2-(4-Morpholinyl)ethyl]indol-4-ol   see under 4-HO-pyr-T #24
"Morpholinyl-5-methoxyltryptamine"   see under 5-MeO-pyr-T #43
"Morpholinyltryptamine"   see under pyr-T #52